Effective Instruction

Effective Instruction

A Handbook of Evidence-Based Strategies

Myles I. Friedman,
Diane H. Harwell, and
Katherine C. Schnepel

THE INSTITUTE FOR EVIDENCE-BASED
DECISION-MAKING IN EDUCATION, INC.

Library of Congress Control Number: 2006924260
ISBN: 0-9666588-4-1

First published in 2006

The Institute for Evidence-Based Decision-Making in Education, Inc.
A South Carolina non-profit corporation
P.O. Box 122, Columbia, SC 29202

Printed in the United States of America

The paper used in this book complies with the
Permanent Paper Standard issued by the National
Information Standards Organization (Z39.48–1984).

10   9   8   7   6   5   4   3   2   1

Educational administration, school buildings,
counseling, equipment, busing, and other factors
may be essential to schooling, but
INSTRUCTION
has the greatest and most direct impact
on learning.

Contents

Acknowledgments

We are most grateful to Drs. Lorin Anderson, Patricia Burns, Jacqueline Jacobs, Lee Johnson, William Johnston, James Kulik, Lawrence Lezotte, Dondra Maney, Anne Reynolds, Arthur Stellar, Robert Stevens, Kenneth Sutton, Carol Tomlinson, and Hersh Waxman and Mrs. Lucinda Saylor for critiquing and improving the first draft of the handbook. Also, we wish to acknowledge Dr. Jacqueline Jacobs for writing "Standards for Evaluating Curricula." We also want to thank Gabriela Pitariu and Shelli Foster for the many hours they spent searching for research pertaining to instructional strategies that increase student academic achievement. Further, thanks go to Gabriela Pitariu, Shelli Foster, Sheima Sumer, Carrie Caudell, Joe Foster, and Dr. Gidget Leonard for assisting with typing references. We appreciate the guidance of Drs. Marvin Efron, Charles Hatch, and John King in the development of the book and the work of John Donohue in the preparation of the manuscript.

Special thanks for their support, patience, devotion, and assistance with many tasks are extended to our spouses—Betty Friedman, Bob Harwell, and Ed Schnepel.

Acknowledgements

User's Guide

Effective Instruction: A Handbook of Evidence-Based Strategies is unique in many ways and, if used appropriately, can have a very beneficial effect on education. In this guide the reader is acquainted with the handbook and how to use it to greatest advantage.

PURPOSE OF THE HANDBOOK

The purpose of the handbook is to present effective instructional strategies that can be incorporated into most instructional programs being planned or presently being used in schools and other educational settings and to provide evidence of the effectiveness of the instructional strategies in enhancing learning. Evidence is described in plain English. Technical data such as statistical tables and footnotes are presented in a separate chapter for those who are interested and prepared to interpret them. All too often, instructional strategies are adopted without evidence of their effectiveness being considered. Pressure for change tends to accelerate the number of unproven instructional innovations that are adopted. Too many instructional decisions are based on political agendas, special interest group pressures, the biases of educational executives, and commercial sales pitches, ignoring available evidence. The handbook makes it possible to consider instructional strategies that work and to understand the evidence that demonstrates their effectiveness in enhancing learning.

THE IMPORTANCE OF THE HANDBOOK

A handbook that describes effective instructional strategies and shows educators how to use them is sorely needed. First, educators need to focus their efforts on improving instruction because all educational institutions are established to instill desired learning in students, and instruction is the means of producing desired learning. Other educational factors such as buildings, administration, facilities, and busing are supportive of instruction but less central. The preeminence of instruction in generating desired learning was demonstrated by the compelling seminal research of John Carroll (1963) and Benjamin Bloom (1968) over an extended period of time. (Also see Block and Anderson, 1975). They found that all but the most psychologically handicapped students are able to achieve all the learning objectives required through high school. The difference among students is the amount of instruction they may need to achieve the objectives. The No Child Left Behind Act was enacted by the federal government, and other accountability legislation was enacted in most of the states because schools are failing to instill desired learning in a sufficient number of students. Far too many high school graduates are entering the job market illiterate or undereducated, unqualified for entry-level positions. To meet the demands of accountability legislation, educators need to learn more about effective instruction and concentrate on applying it in their schools.

Second, educators need to focus more on adopting and adapting particular instructional strategies that have been proven to work than on adopting entire instructional programs and texts. Sales promotions of publishers and manufacturers of instructional texts and programs urge educators to buy their extensive programs and textbook series, which tend to structure and dominate education in America. Yet there is little if any research evidence that these mega-instructional programs in total are effective in producing desired learning. Rather, when comprehensive programs that do have a desirable effect are analyzed, they have common instructional strategies. It appears that it is the instructional strategies that are responsible for their effectiveness rather than the programs as a whole. The evidence indicates that particular instructional strategies enhance learning and that those instructional programs that enhance learning incorporate them. Teachers who are taught to apply comprehensive lock-step instructional programs may have little time or latitude to deal with individual differences and provide the one-to-one tutoring that many of their students may need. In contrast, teachers can be taught to apply the instructional strategies shown by research to increase academic achievement with assurance that their students will achieve class learning objectives. Without further instructional confinement, teachers will have latitude to enrich the curriculum and attend to the personal needs and aspirations of students.

The effective instructional strategies described in the handbook can be incorporated into most instructional programs presently in use or planned to be used without undue inconvenience. The evidence that supports their adoption should be reviewed, and their adoption should be seriously considered. Neither present instructional objectives nor the subject matter students are to learn needs to be changed.

WHO BENEFITS FROM THE HANDBOOK

The handbook is written for practitioners and decision-makers rather than researchers. Instructional planners, teachers, and trainers of instructional planners and teachers will benefit directly from the handbook. Instructional planners can incorporate the strategies in the instructional programs they are presently designing and introduce them into existing instructional programs that are under their supervision; teachers can incorporate them in their lesson plans and apply them during teaching to guide their interactions with students; and trainers of instructional planners and teachers can teach them in both preservice and in-service training. Unfortunately, teachers and instructional planners are frequently persuaded, if not coerced, to adopt instructional programs and ploys that are in vogue without being provided with evidence of their effectiveness. The pressure to improve instruction through innovation results in the introduction of one fad after another. *It is time to base instructional decisions on evidence.*

The handbook will also be of value to educational administrators and school board members who want to become more familiar with effective instructional strategies. Since the primary goal of education is to enhance learning and since instruction has a direct and primary effect on learning, administrators and school board members need to know more about effective instruction in general.

The ultimate beneficiaries of the handbook are the students themselves, who learn more because of the strategies, and the societies that sponsor education and benefit from more learned, competent citizens. In essence, the evidence provided in the handbook enables educators to make more informed, cogent instructional decisions that will result in increased student achievement.

FEATURES AND FOCUS OF THE HANDBOOK

Effective Rather Than Efficient Strategies

The focus of the handbook is solely on the *effectiveness of instruction* in generating desired learning rather than on the efficiency of instruction. To be considered an effective strategy, the findings of at least 50 research studies must support its effectiveness in improving academic achievement. The primary aim is to identify instructional strategies that work. After desired learning has been produced, efficiency factors such as time and money can become the focus of inquiry. What good is it to use efficient instructional strategies that don't work? It is not uncommon in research reports to find instructional strategies recommended because they are more efficient, without considering the effectiveness of the strategies. Effective instruction, not efficient instruction, produces desired learning. Even if effective instruction is costly at first, its efficiency may be improved over time. Almost all strategies are more costly when they are first introduced and become more efficient to administer with experience over time.

Generalizable Strategies

The primary concern is with instructional strategies that are more generalizable.

Instructional strategies are more valuable when they can be applied across more academic disciplines, types of students, and educational settings such as military, industrial, higher education, elementary, and secondary institutions as well as home schooling. Instructional strategies that have been shown to work only in a very limited situation are simply not as useful and cannot be recommended as general practice.

Profiting from Technology

Advances in technology are rapidly increasing instructional alternatives. It is important to evaluate the alternatives so that instruction can profit from technology that works. For instance, research confirms the effectiveness of computerized instruction in increasing academic achievement. See Chapter 20.

It is equally important to evaluate the side effects of a technology before adopting it. Precautions need to be taken to avoid potentially deleterious side effects. For example, if students spend too much time being taught by computer, then classroom discussion, student-teacher rapport, teacher demonstrations, and/or teacher effectiveness may be compromised.

For the Practitioner

Many, if not most, research reports are written using symbols that are understood by academicians with a sophisticated knowledge of research. As a result, many practitioners are not able to benefit from the research findings; so, researchers and practitioners tend to go their separate ways and valuable research findings all too seldom benefit practice. The handbook is written for practitioners in plain English so they may derive maximum benefit from the research findings. Research findings in a professional field are of little value if they are not translated into effective practice. Statistical findings that confirm the efficacy of strategies are in Part IV for those interested in perusing them.

Teaching Rather Than Teachers

The focus is on teaching rather than teachers because research has failed to establish that teacher characteristics have a direct impact on student achievement. Teacher personality characteristics do not appear to affect student achievement directly (Getzels & Jackson, 1963); nor does teacher knowledge (Shulman, 1986). It appears that teacher characteristics have the most significant impact on student achievement as they affect teaching. Teaching has a more direct impact on achievement. Similarly, the physical classroom environment does not appear to have a direct impact on student achievement (Loughlin, 1992). However, it may have an indirect impact as it affects teaching. Therefore, the physical instructional environment will be a concern only as it affects teaching. Chapter 25 discusses the development of teaching proficiency.

Evidence-Based Decision-Making

Many decisions made in education are not evidence-based decisions, and this may be a primary cause of educational failures. As indicated, educational decisions are often made because of the bias of administrators or special interest group pressures, a convincing sales pitch, or political agendas. Businesses and industries that do not base their decisions on evidence go bankrupt. Educational institutions that do not base their decisions on evidence continue on and on despite their failures. The decision to recommend the instructional strategies in the handbook is based solely on scientific evidence, which is presented for the reader's consideration.

Twenty-one effective instructional strategies are described in the handbook. From 68 to over 600 research studies are cited to support the effectiveness of each strategy in increasing student achievement in a number of content areas across a variety of student populations. Many of the strategies are familiar to educators and can be readily taught in preservice and in-service teacher education. It is no longer necessary or tenable to rely on expert opinion to make instructional decisions. The handbook makes it feasible to select instructional strategies based on research findings with confidence that they are effective in increasing student achievement.

Now the mandates of the No Child Left Behind Act and state accountability legislation to use instructional methods shown by research to be effective can be satisfied with confidence. Educators can choose to incorporate any or all of the 21 effective instructional strategies in their instruction knowing that there is an abundance of evidence they can present to support their choice. As Dr. Arthur Stellar, Superintendent of Taunton, Massachusetts, public schools (A. Stellar, personal communication, October 29, 2005) states, "Educators who are striving to reach the challenges of No Child Left Behind will discover many of the answers to their questions within *Effective Instruction*." (Dr. Stellar was formerly CEO of High/Scope Educational Research Foundation and President of ASCD.)

THE PRESENTATION FORMAT

The following format will be used in presenting each instructional strategy.

Description of Each Instructional Strategy

Title of the Strategy

Introduction. An orientation to the strategy.

Student Beneficiaries. Types of students who have benefited from the strategy and their ages or grade levels are described.

Learning Achieved. The learning or academic achievement enhanced by the instructional strategies in the content areas covered are described.

Instructional Tactics. Tactics used in different studies to apply the strategy are integrated and summarized.

Cautions and Comments. Constraints in applying the strategy are discussed, and comments are made to clarify the presentation further.

Discretion was required in distinguishing among strategies. Lines of demarcation among strategies were not always obvious. Moreover, different researchers tended to define different strategies in different ways. These differences needed to be reconciled in order to derive a parsimonious number of strategies that overlapped as little as possible. Every effort was made to allow evidence rather than personal opinion or logic to influence decision-making. However, in the handbook, the statistical findings supporting the use of particular tactics are presented in a separate section, Part IV, so that readers may determine the implications of the evidence for themselves.

Generalizations. A generalization is provided highlighting the efficacy of the strategy in increasing academic achievement.

Descriptions of Supporting Research

Studies are described that provide evidence supporting the use of the strategy. The following format is used to describe the research.

Author(s) of the research.

Students included in the research.

Learning achieved in the research.

Instructional Tactics used in the research. Occasionally, purely research procedures are included under instructional tactics to clarify how instructional tactics were employed in the study.

Findings of the research. Technical findings, such as statistical data, are presented in Part IV of the handbook.

Research integrating groups of studies will be presented first. Then individual studies will be presented.

Extensive references for each effective instructional strategy are located in Part V of the handbook by chapter. The references provide access to additional detail and corroboration. Extensive references are provided because the handbook is intended to serve as a reference book as well as a handbook. When research integrating groups of studies is reported, the individual studies included in the group are cued by symbols so that they can be easily identified in the references.

Instructional tactics are presented in outline form. First, a summary outline of tactics is presented for each strategy. Afterward, the tactics used in each study from which the summary is derived are outlined and occasionally include research procedures to clarify how the instructional tactics were employed in the study. This enables instructional planners and teachers to use the outlines as guides in creating their own instructional plans, adapted to their own students and educational setting. Although the strategies are generalizable, their effectiveness can be improved if they are adapted to the particular students and education milieu where they are being applied by instructional planners and teachers familiar with the characteristics of the students and milieu.

Effective instructional strategies are presented in Part I of the handbook.

PROMISING INSTRUCTIONAL STRATEGY

In this section, an instructional strategy that bears watching is discussed. There is some evidence to suggest that the instructional strategy may be effective, but there is not sufficient evidence to warrant its adoption as a generalization at this time. Additional research is needed to determine its effectiveness and should be encouraged and supported. If proven effective, the strategy has the potential to enhance instruction in the future. Readers might wish to pilot test the strategy to assess its effectiveness in their locale for their purposes.

QUESTIONABLE INSTRUCTIONAL STRATEGIES

In addition to effective instructional strategies and a promising instructional strategy, there are questionable strategies. There is evidence indicating that the questionable strategies are not effective in enhancing learning and/or can have deleterious side effects. Some of these questionable strategies are in common use. In this section, questionable strategies are reviewed and evidence is presented to caution against their use.

Promising and questionable strategies are presented in Part II of the handbook.

INSTRUCTIONAL AIDS

Part III of the handbook focuses on practices that support classroom instruction and learning even though their impact might be indirect. For example, Chapter 24, "Controlling Classroom Disruptions," presents a strategy shown by research to reduce classroom disruptions. And, of course, classroom disruptions interfere with teaching and learning. Curriculum, evaluation, teacher education, and other factors that indirectly influence classroom instruction are also dealt with in Part III.

STATISTICAL FINDINGS

After all of the strategies have been presented, statistical findings that support conclusions pertaining to effective instructional strategies described are presented in Part IV. Statistical findings are cross-referenced with the particular strategies to which they pertain so that they can be readily accessed.

REFERENCE PRESENTATIONS

There are three presentations of references in the handbook: (1) the Index of Researchers, which includes all of the authors cited in the handbook, along with the page numbers indicating where each author is cited; (2) the references at the end of each chapter that pertain to the authors cited in that chapter; and (3) the reference lists for each chapter of effective instructional strategies in Part V of the handbook, even references not cited in the chapters. Part V reduces the amount of library searching required to locate primary sources of research included in the various meta-analyses and logical syntheses cited in the handbook.

SUGGESTIONS FOR USING THE HANDBOOK

The handbook is a resource and a reference book, and there are many ways in which the information in the handbook can be accessed and utilized, depending on your purpose at a particular time. Hence, there is no standard or right way to use the handbook. However, there is an inherent logic in the way the handbook is organized to enable you to glean information about strategies to the degree or depth required at the time. Consider the following suggestions for using the handbook.

Considering Instructional Strategies for Adoption

There are 21 effective strategies that can be advantageously incorporated into your present instructional program or an instructional program you may be planning. You are probably aware of many of them to a greater or lesser extent. You can become more familiar with all 21 effective instructional strategies by reading the Introduction to each of them found at the beginning of the first 21 chapters. Very little reading is required to acquaint yourself with the entire repertoire of effective instructional strategies in the handbook.

You can learn more about an instructional strategy you might wish to adopt by reading a very few pages further at the beginning of a chapter. You will learn about (1) students who have benefited from the strategy under the heading "Student Beneficiaries," (2) the subject areas in which the strategy was used effectively under the heading "Learning Achieved," (3) tactics that are used to implement the strategy in brief summary form under the heading "Instructional Tactics," and (4) limitations and nuances that should be considered when employing the strategy, which are discussed under the heading "Cautions and Comments." All of the above are presented in approximately two to four pages at the beginning of each chapter.

Should you wish to probe further into the implementation of an instructional strategy, you can continue on in a chapter and read about the various studies conducted to demonstrate the effectiveness of the instructional strategy. Those studies are summarized in easy-to-understand language, devoid of statistics.

Should you wish to learn more about a particular effective instructional strategy, a detailed reference list for each chapter is provided in Part V. The reference list includes all of the studies that could be found pertaining to an instructional strategy.

Those interested in inspecting the statistical evidence that supports the effectiveness of an instructional strategy can find the evidence in Part IV. The page number where statistical evidence can be found for each effective strategy is given in the Table of Contents. An effort was made to make the statistical tables clear and understandable.

In considering the 21 instructional strategies for adoption, it is well to understand that they are not totally independent of each other. There is some overlap among them, and they are used for different purposes. For example, some strategies facilitate rapid recall; others facilitate rather slow, methodical deliberation. Some pertain to the presentation of information to students; others pertain to knowledge and skills that are to be taught to students. Many of the strategies can be used advantageously in combination. For instance, strategies in chapters 4, 5, and 6 pertain to the effective allocation and utilization of time. These strategies can be combined with many other strategies that deal with instructional issues other than time.

Keep in mind that the effective instructional strategies described in the handbook were derived inductively from research findings. They were not conceptualized as discrete parts of a logical system of instructional strategies. The research evidence shows that each of the strategies works. It is up to educators to determine how the strategies might best be utilized for their purposes in their educational setting.

Considering Questionable Instructional Strategies

You can quickly identify questionable instructional strategies by reading their names listed under Chapter 23 in the Table of Contents. Reading the introductions to them in Chapter 23 will further acquaint you with the questionable strategies.

If you are presently using or planning to use any of the questionable strategies, you should read the entire description of the strategies and the evidence that challenges their use. You should then reconsider using them. Not all of the questionable strategies described are ineffective under all conditions for all purposes. You need to reconsider using them for your purpose.

Considering the Promising Instructional Strategy

The promising strategy described in the handbook is included because it is distinct from and complementary to the 21 effective instructional strategies reviewed in the first 21 chapters. Although there is evidence indicating that it is effective, the evidence is insufficient. Its effectiveness needs to be tested further before considering it for adoption. You might want to read about "Enlisting the Control Motive" in Chapter 22 if you are interested in pilot testing a strategy to enlist student motivation to enhance learning.

Following the preceding suggestions enables you to avail yourself of most of the benefits that can be gleaned from the book. Should you need to clarify the meaning of key terms used in the book as you consider the suggestions, consult the glossary presented later in the User's Guide. Also presented later in the User's Guide is "Guidelines for Making Instructional Decisions." A simple rendition of the instruction process is derived, within which major instructional decision-making points are identified. The presentation of the instructional process provides a context for relating instructional strategies to the instructional process and for defining key terms that are used consistently in discussions of the different strategies. You might find the renditions useful and clarifying if you have not already subscribed to one of the many versions of instruction that have been promulgated over the years. However, remember that the effective instructional strategies in the handbook are empirically derived and validated and can be understood in the context of any presentation of the instructional process that is congruent with scientific evidence. You will need to determine the extent to which the version in the handbook is helpful to you.

Identifying major decision-making points within our rendition of the instructional process provides a basis for specifying guidelines for instructional decision-making. The guidelines enable you to consider and utilize the 21 effective instructional strategies described in the handbook to make evidence-based instructional decisions. The strategies need to be considered in instructional decision-making if they are to benefit instructional practice and, therefore, student learning.

Next, instructional failures are systematically reviewed in the context of the decision-making process, highlighting possible breakdowns in the process that can result from inept decision-making. Finally, instructional planning is discussed because it precedes and enables instruction.

Keep in mind that this is a resource and reference book designed to help you make more effective instructional decisions however you may decide to tap and utilize its resources.

To recap, the 21 effective instructional strategies described in the handbook are generalizable in that they are generalizable (1) across many research studies; that is, a compelling number of research studies support the effectiveness of each strategy in enhancing learning; (2) across many content areas; that is, they have been effectively applied in a variety of academic disciplines; and (3) across students of varying ages in various educational settings. For these reasons, teachers, teacher educators, instructional planners, and educational administrators should consider incorporating them in instructional programs presently being used or being planned for use. When adapted to local conditions, they may well increase student achievement although all of them may not be suitable for a particular educational setting. The presentation of each effective instructional strategy includes a description of the number of research studies that support the effectiveness of the strategy, the content areas in which the strategy was shown to be effective, and the types of students that have benefited from each strategy. This information enables teachers, instructional planners, teacher educators, and administrators to ascertain the suitability of a particular strategy for their purposes in their educational setting.

Although the effective instructional strategies to be described can be expected to enhance student achievement under many educational conditions, they should not be regarded as a panacea. The generalizations derived for each strategy have not been proven to be as invariant as the universal laws found in physical sciences such as physics; for example, Boyle's Law and Charles' Law. Such laws may be more than we can expect to achieve in education, at least at this time. Nevertheless, the effective strategies described are generalizable, and the extent of their generalizability is discussed. They can be expected to enhance student achievement in a variety of circumstances, as specified. There is little doubt that teachers, teacher educators, instructional planners, and educational administrators can make more informed and effective instructional decisions if they take the strategies into account in their decision-making.

FLEXIBILITY IN PRESCRIBING INSTRUCTION

Effective decision-making requires some freedom to choose from among alternatives. Educators, like other professionals, need flexibility in practicing their profession. To succeed, they must be able to adjust their prescriptions and actions to meet the needs of different students and different instructional conditions. "One size fits all" does not work. Individual differences among students' readiness to learn are too pronounced. Therefore, educators must be leery of models of instruction and teacher education programs that prescribe a set way of teaching. Teachers, like doctors, must have an array of strategies and tools they know how to use to meet the various needs of the people they serve.

The 21 effective instructional strategies and the aids described in the handbook are resources educators must learn how to use. They must also learn when to use them. Then they must be allowed to apply them to provide for individual differences to maximize the achievement of their students. The success of educators is inextricably tied to the achievement of their students. Educators are more successful when more of their students achieve learning objectives.

Holding educators accountable for their students' achievement of learning objectives may be defensible. Holding them accountable for conforming to a lockstep instructional program is not.

DELIMITATIONS OF THE HANDBOOK

No attempt was made in the handbook to cover all the complexities of instruction or everything that should be taught in teacher education programs. It is advocated that discretion be used in the ways the 21 effective instructional strategies and instructional aids are used in instruction. It is also suggested that consideration be given to the discontinuation of the questionable instructional strategies described, keeping in mind that a given strategy may have merit under certain conditions.

Scientific research is not considered to be a panacea for instruction. Teachers might be able to employ all 21 effective instructional strategies and other practices shown by research to work but still fail. Other factors beyond the teacher's control at the time may contribute to failure; for example, lack of student readiness, inaccurate testing instruments, mandated inferior teaching aids, too little time allowed for instruction, unreachable learning objectives, and so on.

Nevertheless, the utilization of instructional strategies and other practices scientifically proven to increase academic achievement can be expected to work most of the time. Teaching, or some facets of teaching, may be considered an art. Still, artists benefit from scientifically proven technology. The computer can enhance the graphic arts and music as well as instruction. Teachers should not be deprived of using instructional practices confirmed by research to be effective. Any theory conceived to explain academic achievement is obliged to consider scientifically proven factors. Any teacher education program designed to increase academic achievement is obliged to include practices scientifically proven to work. The fact that there are exceptions to every scientifically confirmed generalization does not nullify the usefulness of the generalization.

In addition to teaching subject matter, teachers often choose or are required by administrators to teach students skills they can use to improve learning. Examples of such skills include study skills, ways to read and understand textbooks, reading comprehension techniques such as SQ3R, developing and using graphic organizers, and ways to generate questions. Such skills are aids for student learning.

GUIDELINES FOR MAKING INSTRUCTIONAL DECISIONS

In this section, a simple conceptualization of the instructional process is presented to facilitate decision-making. First, functions of instruction are related. Then, instructional failures are analyzed. Finally, instructional planning is described to clarify functions that precede and enable instruction. The conceptualization was used to derive accurate internally consistent definitions of key functions and their relationships and to provide an orienting frame of reference for decision-making. There are so many terms associated with instruction and so many complicated renditions of the instructional process that it is easy to become confused.

Functions of Instruction

The following presentation is intended to provide only guidelines for decision-making to help educators improve instruction in their schools.

INSTRUCTION

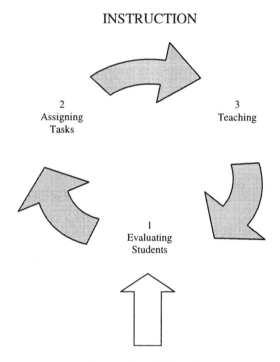

Instructional Planning

As the cycle shows, instruction for the purpose of achieving a learning objective begins after instructional planning has been completed. First, students are evaluated to determine their readiness to perform tasks leading to the achievement of the learning objective. Second, they are assigned progressive or corrective tasks based on the evaluation. Third, teaching ensues. The cycle is repeated over and over until the learning objective being pursued is achieved.

Here are key definitions and elaborations to clarify instruction.

Learning objectives are defined as tasks students are required to learn to perform by means of instruction. Tasks are defined as student/subject matter interactions formulated to enable students to achieve learning of objectives. Learning objectives are organized into hierarchies. Learning objective hierarchies are defined as sequences of tasks designed so that student mastery of each preceding task in a sequence provides students with the readiness capabilities they need to perform the next more advanced task in the sequence. Two kinds of tasks may be assigned to students: progressive tasks and corrective tasks. A progressive task is the next more advanced task in a sequence. Corrective tasks are assigned to students who inadequately perform a progressive task to enable them to master the progressive task on a subsequent attempt. Teaching is defined as guiding and facilitating student task performance in order to achieve a learning objective. Teachers guide and facilitate student performance of both progressive and corrective tasks as need be to achieve learning objectives. Instructional evaluation is the comparison of student task performance with criteria of competent performance for the purpose of assessing student achievement of learning objectives and inadequacies in performance. Evaluation should reveal student progress and diagnose causes of failure to progress that need to be corrected so that progress can be made.

Instructional Failures

Instructional failures occur because of faulty instruction, which may in turn be attributable indirectly to failures in instructional planning. Since the primary purpose of instruction is to achieve learning objectives, the ultimate failure of instruction is failure to achieve a learning objective being pursued. Failure to achieve a learning objective manifests itself in the learning process during the evaluation phase when student ability to perform assigned tasks is evaluated. Failures during each of the three phases of instruction (evaluating students, assigning tasks, and teaching) can contribute to the failure to achieve a learning objective as follows.

Failure in Evaluating Students

Failure in evaluating students may be due to inadequacies in the procedures used (1) to assess student task performance, (2) to compare student task performance to criteria of competent task performance, and/or (3) to diagnose student insufficiencies in task performance. Incorrectly assessing and comparing student task performance to criteria of competent performance would result in the incorrect assignment of a progressive or corrective task to a student. Incorrectly diagnosing student failure to perform a task would result in an incorrect corrective task being assigned to a student.

Failure in Assigning Tasks to Students

If evaluation procedures are accurate, failure to assign students to perform tasks that are appropriate for their readiness capabilities may be responsible for students not achieving the learning objective being pursued.

Failure in Teaching

Both evaluation and task assignment may be accurate, and students may fail to achieve the learning objective because teaching is ineffective. That is, student performance of assigned tasks may not be adequately guided and facilitated.

Instructional Planning

Instructional planning needs to be discussed because it precedes and enables instruction. If mistakes in instructional planning are not caught and compensated for during instruction, the efficacy of instruction can be seriously compromised.

Instructional planning entails (1) establishing learning objectives, (2) planning assignments, (3) planning teaching, and (4) planning evaluations. Aspects of planning occur at three levels: (1) the policy level, (2) the curriculum level, and (3) the teaching level. Not all planning functions are addressed at each of the three levels. Books have been written about each of the three levels. They are being discussed here briefly to clarify instruction.

The Policy Level

At the policy level, policymakers such as legislatures and school boards proceed as follows:

- *Establishing learning objectives.* Policymakers establish learning objectives by specifying attributes desirable for students to possess upon completing school in order to enter and be successful in post-secondary education or training, to raise a family, and to contribute to the community and workforce successfully.

- *Planning assignments.* Responsibility for achieving the learning objectives is assigned to the school system the policymakers oversee.

- *Planning evaluations.* Arrangements are made for student achievement of the learning objectives to be evaluated. The purpose is to hold educators accountable for achieving the learning objectives. In addition, in some states, policy makers also review instructional materials for alignment with standards and for appropriateness.

The Curriculum Level

At the curriculum level, curriculum development specialists proceed as follows.

- *Establishing learning objectives.* Learning objectives established by the policy group are transposed into terminal tasks students are to be able to perform competently upon completing school.

Next, a hierarchy of enabling learning objectives is derived to facilitate achievement of each terminal learning objective. (As indicated, achievement of each prior task in a hierarchical sequence is to provide students the readiness capability needed to perform the next more advanced task in the sequence.)

- *Planning assignments.* Segments of learning objective sequences are assigned to be achieved at particular grade levels. Teachers are assigned to achieve grade level objectives. Students are assigned to teachers to form classes.

- *Planning teaching.* Teaching aids such as textbooks are prescribed to facilitate student achievement of learning objectives.

- *Planning evaluations.* Evaluations are designed to assess student achievement of grade-level objectives and inadequacies in their performance. Such evaluations are used to place, promote, and graduate students.

The Teaching Level

Teachers engage in instructional planning at the teaching level as follows.

- *Establishing learning objectives.* Teachers sequence class learning objectives that lead progressively to the achievement of each grade-level objective (so that attainment of a prior objective in a sequence provides students with the readiness capabilities they need to achieve the next more advanced objective in the sequence).

- *Planning teaching.* Each learning objective established by a teacher becomes a progressive task students are required to master. Teachers must also plan corrective tasks for students who inadequately perform progressive tasks. A number of corrective tasks are planned to help students achieve each progressive task. In addition, teachers plan methods of guiding and facilitating student achievement of each task planned.

- *Planning assignments.* Teachers plan to use test results to assign progressive tasks to students who perform competently and corrective tasks to remediate diagnosed inadequacies. Teachers also plan to use test results to assign grades to students. For instance, a plan for aggregating test scores to derive grades is devised. Test results also can be used to assign students for further diagnosis of underlying causes of failure to learn such as poor hearing.

Notice that tasks are the basic element used to lend simplicity and consistency to our descriptions of instruction and instructional planning. Competent performance of specified tasks is the learning objective pursued. Students are assigned tasks to achieve objectives. Teaching entails guiding and facilitating student task performance. Then, task performance is assessed to evaluate student competency.

GLOSSARY

The definitions in the following glossary are relevant to instruction and pertain to instructional contexts and settings. Some of the terms defined in the glossary are key terms in the "Guidelines for Making Instructional Decisions"; others are key terms in the strategies that are presented. A couple of terms relate to types of research used in the handbook. The terms may well have other definitions in other contexts and disciplines and in dictionaries of the English language.

ability grouping   The grouping of students according to their ability level for the purpose of instruction.

contiguity   The proximity of to-be-associated events in space and time.

control motive   The penchant to improve the control of outcomes.

corrective tasks   See **remedial tasks**.

decision-making   Selecting a course of action.

evaluation   See **instructional evaluation**.

expectations   See **instructional expectations**.

field-dependent/field-independent cognitive style   The tendency to perceive events as either (1) independent of their surrounding field or (2) dependent upon their surrounding field.

instruction   A process in which educators evaluate students, assign tasks to students based on the evaluations, and teach students to perform assigned tasks in order to achieve a learning objective.

instructional conditions   Assignment conditions that can affect students' task performance such as class size, disruptions, equipment, time allowed for task performance, and safety.

instructional cycle   The cyclical execution of the acts of evaluating → assigning tasks → teaching in order to achieve a learning objective. It may be necessary to repeat the cycle a number of times to achieve a learning objective.

instructional evaluation   The comparison of the performance of an instructional task with criteria of competent performance and the diagnosis of insufficiencies in task performance.

instructional expectations   (1) Objectives students are assigned to achieve, (2) procedures to be followed to achieve the objectives, and (3) criteria specifying successful achievement of the objectives.

instructional planning The process of (1) deriving learning objectives, (2) planning instructional tasks, (3) planning evaluations, (4) planning task assignments, and (5) planning teaching.

instructional strategies Procedures used to enhance the achievement of learning objectives.

instructional units Units of instruction consisting of a sequence of evaluation, task assignment, and teaching tactics leading progressively to the achievement of a unit learning objective. A number of unit objectives are achieved as a means of achieving a policy objective.

learning objectives Terminal tasks students are to learn to perform by means of instruction.

learning time Time allotted to students for performing assigned tasks.

logical synthesis of instructional research Logically inferring from the results of a number of studies the effect of an instructional strategy on academic achievement.

meta-analysis of instructional research A statistical method for pooling the results of a number of studies to estimate the effect of an instructional strategy on academic achievement.

objectives See **learning objectives** and **policy objectives**.

planning See **instructional planning**.

policy objectives Desired student outcomes to be achieved by educators. Policy objectives for educators to achieve are established by policymakers such as school boards.

predictive ability The ability to forecast outcomes from antecedent conditions.

progressive tasks A continuum of tasks leading progressively from entry-level tasks appropriate for students with specified readiness characteristics to the achievement of a learning objective.

readiness Student knowledge, skills, and disposition necessary to perform a task.

reinforcement The attempt to increase the probability that a desired assigned task will be performed by providing for the satisfaction of a motive when the desired task is performed.

remedial tasks Tasks formulated to remediate students' failure to perform a task adequately.

remediation The correction of inadequate task performance.

reminders Memory joggers or mnemonics designed and used to facilitate and improve recall of to-be-learned information or skills.

repetition   The repeated presentation to students of to-be-learned material and/or student repetition of to-be-learned skills.

strategies   See **instructional strategies**.

student/teacher ratio   The proportion of teachers to students the teachers are assigned to teach.

students   People being taught.

subject matter   The content to be learned by students.

subject matter unifiers   Presentations of the parts/whole relationships in subject matter students are assigned to learn to enhance their learning of the subject matter.

task planning   The formulating and organizing of progressive tasks and remedial tasks to achieve a learning objective based on student readiness characteristics.

tasks   Student/subject matter interactions formulated to enable students to achieve learning objectives.

teaching   Guiding and facilitating student task performance in order to achieve a learning objective.

teaching time   The proportion of learning time spent guiding and facilitating student performance of assigned tasks.

teamwork   Cooperation among people to achieve a common objective.

time on task   The amount of time students spend focused on the performance of assigned tasks.

transfer of learning   The application of prior learning to enable the performance of new tasks.

unifiers   See **subject matter unifiers**.

REFERENCE LIST

Block, J. H., & Anderson, L. S. (1975). *Mastery learning in classroom instruction.* New York: Macmillan.

Bloom, B. S. (1968). Learning for mastery. *Evaluation Comments, 1*(2), 1–12.

Carroll, J. (1963). A model of school learning. *Teachers College Record, 64,* 723–733.

Getzels, J. W., & Jackson, P. W. (1963). The teacher's personality and characteristics. In N. L. Gage (Ed.), *Handbook of research on teaching* (pp. 506–582). Chicago: Rand McNally.

Loughlin, C. E. (1992). Classroom physical environments. In M. C. Alkin (Ed.), *Encyclopedia of educational research* (Vol. 1, 6th ed., pp. 161–164). New York: Macmillan.

Shulman, L. S. (1986). Paradigms and research programs in the study of teaching: A contemporary perspective. In M. C. Wittrock (Ed.), *Handbook of research on teaching* (3rd ed., pp. 1–36). New York: Macmillan.

I

Effective Instructional Strategies

All of the 21 instructional strategies described in Part I are shown by research to increase academic achievement in a number of subject areas across a variety of student populations. In short, they can be effectively applied in many classroom settings as well as in tutoring individual students. The limitations of strategies are clearly noted. From 68 to over 600 research studies are cited to support the effectiveness of each strategy. The effects of more than one strategy may be tested in a study. A study is cited as supportive of the strategy being reviewed in a chapter because the strategy is applied in the study and the findings show that academic achievement is increased. The strategies can be incorporated individually or in combination in most existing instructional programs or programs being planned with little or no extra burden or expense. Many of them are in common use.

A list of tactics specified to ensure the correct application of a strategy is provided. The tactics operationally define each strategy and serve to reduce any ambiguity in executing a strategy. Each tactic specifies behaviors and activities that are performed in applying a strategy, making it easy to teach the strategies in any preservice or in-service teacher education program.

Many of the 21 effective strategies may be familiar to you. Some are taught in existing teacher preparation programs. Others are advocated by experts. Still others have been described by researchers and theorists you may have studied. We have attempted to distill and simplify the strategies and present them in plain English devoid of abstract jargon. It is not our intention to take credit for them but rather to summarize them and to make them as useful as possible to the practicing educator.

The following format is used to present each strategy.

Introduction. Context is provided to facilitate the understanding of each strategy.

Student Beneficiaries. The student populations used in the supportive research studies cited are summarized.

Learning Achieved. The content areas in the supportive research studies cited are summarized.

Instructional Tactics. A list of tactics performed to execute each strategy is specified.

Cautions and Comments. Limitations and implications of each strategy are noted.

Generalization. The broad applicability of each strategy to the improvement of academic achievement is highlighted in one brief statement.

Supportive Research. The number of studies that support the effectiveness of each strategy in raising student achievement is specified, and both groups of supportive studies and noteworthy individual studies are summarized.

Reference List. All supportive studies are referenced.

There are numerous ways in which the 21 strategies presented in Part I might be subdivided. We decided to avoid subdividing the strategies in the Table of Contents. We did not want to impose our perceptions on the readers and chance biasing their interpretations. With this caveat, here are some sub groupings that occurred to us, should they be of interest. You probably can conceive of others.

Phases of the instructional process. The following instructional strategies might be viewed as phases of the instructional process. They are listed in the order they are often performed.

1. Taking readiness into account
2. Defining instructional expectations
3. Providing instructional evaluation
4. Providing corrective instruction

Time management

5. Keeping students on task
6. Maximizing teaching time
7. Providing ample learning time

Memory enhancers to facilitate the retention and recall of information

8. Utilizing reminders
9. Utilizing unifiers

10. Providing contiguity

11. Utilizing repetition effectively

Learning to deliberate to make choices

12. Providing transfer of learning instruction

13. Providing decision-making instruction

14. Providing prediction and problem-solving instruction

These three strategies should probably be taught in the sequence shown. Transfer of learning is an important part of decision-making. Relevant known facts are applied to make sound decisions. Decision-making is an important part of problem solving. It is necessary to make sound decisions in order to solve problems.

1

Taking Student Readiness into Account

INTRODUCTION

Readiness is defined as student knowledge, skills, and dispositions necessary to perform a task. For students to achieve learning objectives, readiness characteristics of the students must be taken into account while planning instruction. In planning tasks, entry-level tasks should be designed for students with particular readiness capabilities, and succeeding tasks in a sequence leading to the achievement of the learning objective should be designed so that mastery of preceding tasks in the sequence provides students with the readiness capabilities necessary to perform subsequent tasks. Readiness characteristics of students must enable students to perform the assigned tasks. In addition, readiness characteristics must be taken into account when teaching. Teaching should continue until students have mastered the performance of an assigned task and are ready to perform the next task in a sequence. Finally, in the evaluation process, evaluation instruments must be designed to indicate the readiness level of students so the appropriate task assignments can be made.

STUDENT BENEFICIARIES

The evidence indicates that taking into consideration student readiness when planning, teaching, assigning, and evaluating performance of tasks enhances the academic achievement of students in preschool, kindergarten, elementary, secondary, college, and adult learning classrooms. Moreover, academic achievement was improved in a wide range of content areas. No evidence could be found to suggest that student readiness should not be stressed in all subject areas for all types of students.

LEARNING ACHIEVED

Achievement in the content areas of mathematics, history, physics, writing, foreign languages, English, language arts, reading, social sciences, sciences, social studies, business, and occupational areas is enhanced when student readiness is taken into consideration in the planning, teaching, assigning, and evaluating performance of tasks. In studies reviewed, student readiness was positively related to student achievement.

INSTRUCTIONAL TACTICS

The evidence well supports the need to consider student readiness when planning, teaching, assigning, and evaluating performance of tasks. The following tactics are derived from studies that demonstrate the benefits of considering student readiness when planning, teaching, assigning, and evaluating performance of tasks. Discretion has been used to interpret and reduce overlap in tactics used in different studies and to elaborate tactics.

Tactics employed are:

Planning: Tasks leading to the achievement of a learning objective should be sequenced so that earlier tasks in the sequence provide students with the skills and knowledge they need to perform subsequent tasks. The number of tasks planned in a sequence should be based on the difficulty level of the learning objective to be achieved. A greater number of tasks should be planned to achieve a more difficult learning objective.

Evaluation: Accurately evaluating the students' current knowledge and skills should be a basis for assigning tasks to students.

Assigning Tasks: In assigning tasks, the knowledge and skills of the students must be sufficient to meet the demands of the tasks.

Teaching: A mastery level of performance should be attained for each task so that students who learn to perform a task are ready to perform the next task in the sequence.

Elaboration of the above summary of tactics can be obtained from reading the studies that are to follow. To be most effective, the instructional tactics need to be integrated into the particular instructional program being planned or presently being used.

CAUTIONS AND COMMENTS

The preeminence of readiness in determining student success in achieving learning objectives cannot be overemphasized. Students who do not have the knowledge and skills necessary to perform the tasks that enable the achievement of a learning objective are not likely to achieve the objective, even if other effective strategies are employed in teaching the students.

GENERALIZATION: ON STUDENT READINESS

Achievement of learning objectives is enhanced when students possess the readiness capabilities necessary to achieve the learning objectives.

Supportive Research on Student Readiness
Total number of supportive studies covered: 352+

Groups of Studies

Author: Anderson (1994): Synthesis of seven meta-analyses

Students: Kindergarten, elementary, secondary, college, and other adult students

Learning: Achievement

Instructional Tactics: The following tactics associated with readiness and Mastery Learning are also presented in Bloom (1985), Block (1980), and others. Other tactics associated with Mastery Learning are applicable to other generalizations and are covered in the appropriate chapters.

- Accurately diagnose the students' current level of knowledge in relation to that required for the material to be learned.
- Divide the material to be learned into units with each unit providing prerequisite skills for subsequent units.
- Determine a mastery level the student must achieve prior to moving on to the next unit.

Findings: Positive achievement gains associated with Mastery Learning were seen in 64–93 percent of the studies reviewed in the seven meta-analyses.

Individual studies analyzed by these meta-analyses are identified in the reference list in Part V by the following symbols:

Kulik et al. (1990a) *

Kulik et al. (1990b) #

Slavin (1990) @

Guskey & Pigott (1988) $

Guskey & Gates (1986) &

Block & Burns (1976) +

It was not possible to determine the individual studies for which readiness was an instructional tactic for the Willett (1983) analysis.

Author: Rosenshine et al. (1996)

Students: Upper elementary (grade 3 and up), junior high, secondary, and college

Learning: Reading comprehension across subject matters, mathematics, physics, and writing

Instructional Tactics:

- Anticipate potential difficulties students may have with the subject matter or tasks.
- Regulate the difficulty of the material based on student readiness. The following are examples from studies cited in Rosenshine et al. (1996).

Palincsar (1987) had teachers model to students how to generate questions first from a single sentence. Then the students practiced the skill. Next, the teacher modeled asking questions after students' reading of a paragraph. Again, there was student practice on generating questions. Last, the teacher modeled generating questions after reading an entire passage. Once more the students practiced the skill.

Studies by Andre and Anderson (1979) and Dreher and Gambrell (1985) show that teachers begin student comprehension with a single paragraph, then move to a double paragraph, and finally to a 450-word passage.

In a study by Wong and Jones (1982), the researchers regulated the difficulty of the task by decreasing the prompts given to students. First, students worked with a paragraph using procedural prompts. When they mastered the single paragraph with prompts, they were given a longer passage with prompts. Upon mastery of that level, students were given a passage to comprehend without prompts.

Other instructional tactics are employed in these studies that are applicable to other generalizations and will be presented in the appropriate chapters.

Findings: Use of the above tactics was found to enhance reading comprehension.

Individual studies analyzed by this meta-analysis are identified in the reference list in Part V by the symbol =.

Author: Education Commission of the States (1999)

Students: Elementary (K–6)

Learning: Language arts, reading, and mathematics

Instructional Tactics:

- Students are taught a sequence of skills and/or knowledge with each new level built upon the previous one.
- Students are then taught a new concept based on the previously learned skills or knowledge.

Other instructional tactics are employed in these studies that are applicable to other generalizations and will be presented in the appropriate chapters.

Findings: Use of the above tactics was found to enhance academic achievement.

Individual studies and groups of studies in this logical synthesis are identified with the symbol ! in the reference list in Part V. Statistical data are not included in this synthesis of studies.

Author: Ehri et al. (2001)

Students: Preschool, kindergarten, and elementary

Learning: Phonemic awareness

Instructional Tactics:

- Provide instruction one phoneme at a time.
- Teach the letter of the alphabet following the introduction of the phoneme.
- Provide practice with manipulatives such as letters.
- Teach the application of the phoneme skill to reading and to spelling.
- Assess learning in a variety of ways. Example: Show a written word; then ask which of two spoken choices match the written word; for example, "Does this say cat or hat?"

Other instructional tactics are employed in these studies that are applicable to other generalizations and will be presented in the appropriate chapters.

Findings: Use of the above tactics was found to enhance achievement in phoneme awareness and to enhance achievement in reading and in spelling.

Studies in this meta-analysis are designated in the reference list in Part V with the symbol).

❖   ❖   ❖

Author: Swanson (2001)

Students: Adolescents with learning disabilities

Learning: Higher order processing (problem solving)

Instructional Tactics:

• Present new material based on the previous lesson.

Other instructional tactics are employed in these studies that are applicable to other generalizations and will be presented in the appropriate chapters.

Findings: Use of the above tactic led to higher levels of achievement by students with learning disabilities in problem solving as measured by standardized tests in reading and in mathematics.

Studies associated with this meta-analysis are in the reference list in Part V and are identified by the symbol /.

❖   ❖   ❖

Author: Rosenshine & Stevens (1986)

Students: Elementary and secondary

Learning: Mathematics, English, science, history, and reading achievement

Instructional Tactics:

• Begin a lesson with a short review of previous, prerequisite learning.
• Teach skills in a step-by-step manner, with skills learned in one step being applicable to the learning of skills in a subsequent step or subsequent steps.

Other instructional tactics are employed in these studies that are applicable to other generalizations and will be presented in the appropriate chapters.

Findings: These tactics were found to be related to greater achievement.

Groups of studies reviewed in this logical synthesis of research did not provide statistical evidence. However, many of the individual studies included in the logical synthesis of research do contain statistical evidence. In the event that a reader wishes to view this evidence, an extensive listing of the individual studies reviewed

is provided in the reference list in Part V (the studies are identified by the symbol %).

Author: Carlton & Winsler (1999)

Students: Kindergarten

Learning: Achievement

Instructional Tactics:

- Modulate tasks at appropriately challenging levels.
- Monitor and regulate the amount of adult assistance.
- Withdraw assistance as task competence increases.
- Use verbal problem-solving strategies to assist students with the task; for example, use leading questions.

Findings: The tactics listed above were found to enhance student achievement.

It was not possible to determine the individual studies for which readiness was an instructional tactic in this logical synthesis of research, and no statistics were provided.

Author: Martens & Witt (2004)

Students: Ages 6–12

Learning: Academic achievement in elementary subjects

Instructional Tactics:

- Determine the level at which students are functioning in the specific content area.
- Provide instruction at students' functioning level.

Other instructional tactics from this review are applicable to other generalizations and are presented in the appropriate chapters of this book.

Findings: Use of the tactics listed above was found to be effective in improving student achievement across content areas.

This logical synthesis of research does not provide statistical data. The studies, some of which are meta-analyses, are designated with the symbol + in the references in Part V.

Author: Karweit (1993)

Students: Preschool and kindergarten

Learning: Achievement

Instructional Tactics:

- Diagnose student readiness by administering readiness tests and analyzing the resulting data for instructional purposes.
- Formulate detailed objectives based on the data.
- Provide additional time for corrective instruction and/or enrichment activities.
- Assess learning styles and modalities of students.
- Individualize instruction based on assessment of readiness and of learning traits.
- Plan sequential lessons and sequence of skills within a lesson.
- Apply a task analysis for each learning activity.
- Provide practice in increasingly more difficult skills.

Other instructional tactics from this review are applicable to other generalizations and are presented in the appropriate chapters of this book.

Findings: Use of the above tactics was found across this review of research studies to be effective in enhancing achievement of kindergarten children.

It was not possible to determine the individual studies for which readiness was an instructional tactic in this review of research on preschool and kindergarten readiness.

Individual Studies

Author: Obando & Hymel (1991)

Students: Grade 9

Learning: Spanish language achievement

Instructional Tactics:

- Accurately diagnose the students' current level of knowledge in relation to that required for the material to be learned.
- Divide the material to be learned into units with each unit providing prerequisite skills for subsequent units.
- Determine a mastery level the student must achieve prior to moving on to the next unit.

Other instructional tactics are employed in this study that are applicable to other generalizations and will be presented in the appropriate chapters.

Findings: Achievement was significantly higher for students who benefited from these tactics.

REFERENCE LIST

Anderson, S. A. (1994). *Synthesis of research on mastery learning* (Information Analysis). (ERIC Document Reproduction Service No. ED 382 567)

Block, J. H. (1980). Success rate. In C. Denham & A. Liberman (Eds.), *Time to learn* (pp. 95–106). Washington, DC: U.S. Government Printing Office.

Block, J. H., & Burns, R. B. (1976). Mastery Learning. In L. Schulman (Ed.), *Review of research in education* (Vol. 4, pp. 3–49). Itasca, IL: F. E. Peacock.

Bloom, B. S. (1985). Learning for mastery. In C. W. Fisher & D. C. Berliner (Eds.), *Perspectives on instructional time.* White Plains, NY: Longman.

Carlton, M. P., & Winsler, A. (1999). School readiness: The need for a paradigm shift. *The School Psychology Review, 28*(3), 338–352.

Education Commission of the States. (1999). *Direct instruction.* Denver, CO: Education Commission of the States.

Ehri, L. C., Nunes, S. R., Willows, D. M., Schuster, B. V., Yaghoub-Zadeh, Z., & Shanahan, T. (2001). Phonemic awareness instruction helps children learn to read: Evidence from the National Reading Panel's meta-analysis. *Reading Research Quarterly, 36*(3), 250–287.

Guskey, T. R., & Gates, S. L. (1986). Synthesis of research on the effects of mastery learning in elementary and secondary classrooms. *Educational Leadership, 33*(8), 73–80.

Guskey, T. R., & Pigott, T. D. (1988). Research on group-based mastery learning programs: A meta-analysis. *Journal of Educational Research, 81*(4), 197–216.

Karweit, N. (1993). Effective preschool and kindergarten programs for students at risk. In B. Spodek (Ed.), *Handbook of research on the education of young children* (pp. 385–411). New York: Macmillan.

Kulik, C., Kulik, J., & Bangert-Drowns, R. (1990a). Effectiveness of mastery learning programs: A meta-analysis. *Review of Educational Research, 60*(2), 265–269.

Kulik, J., Kulik, C., & Bangert-Drowns, R. (1990b). Is there better evidence on mastery learning? A response to Slavin. *Review of Educational Research, 60*(2), 303–307.

Martens, B. K., & Witt, J. C. (2004). Competence, persistence, and success: The positive psychology of behavioral skill instruction. *Psychology in the Schools, 41*(1), 19–30.

Obando, L. T., & Hymel, G. M. (1991, March). *The effect of mastery learning instruction on the entry-level Spanish proficiency of secondary school students.* Paper presented at the annual meeting to the American Educational Research Association, New Orleans. (ERIC Document Reproduction Service No. ED 359 253)

Rosenshine, B., Meister, C., & Chapman, S. (1996). Teaching students to generate questions: A review of the intervention studies. *Review of Educational Research, 66*(2), 181–221.

Rosenshine, B., & Stevens, R. (1986). Teaching functions. In M. C. Wittrock (Ed.), *Handbook of research on teaching* (3rd ed., pp. 376–391). New York: Macmillan.

Slavin, R. E. (1990). Mastery learning re-considered. *Review of Educational Research, 60*(2), 300–302.

Swanson, H. L. (2001). Research on interventions for adolescents with learning disabilities: A meta-analysis of outcomes related to higher-order processing. *The Elementary School Journal, 101*(13), 331–349.

Willett, J., Yamashita, J., & Anderson, R. (1983). A meta-analysis of instructional systems applied in science teaching. *Journal of Research in Science Teaching, 20*(5), 405–417.

2

Defining Instructional Expectations

INTRODUCTION

In order for students to accomplish a learning objective, it is necessary that they know prior to instruction (1) what the learning objective is, (2) what procedures are necessary to perform the tasks required to achieve the learning objective, and (3) what the criteria are for successful accomplishment of the learning objective. In the absence of this knowledge, the student may not be able to process the available information to determine what is relevant and what is not, may not be able to determine the appropriate procedures needed to accomplish the learning objective, and may have difficulty in determining when they have successfully achieved the objective. They may flounder, become frustrated, and perform poorly.

STUDENT BENEFICIARIES

The evidence indicates that defining instructional expectations enhances the academic achievement of students in kindergarten, elementary, secondary, college, and other adult classrooms. No evidence could be found to suggest that defining instructional expectations should not be stressed for all types of students.

LEARNING ACHIEVED

Achievement in the content areas of reading, English, mathematics, history, language arts, social sciences, sciences, and social studies is enhanced when instructional expectations are defined prior to instruction. In studies reviewed, defining instructional expectations was positively related to student achievement. Moreover, academic achievement was improved in a wide range of content areas.

INSTRUCTIONAL TACTICS

The evidence well supports the need to define instructional expectations prior to instruction and student performance of tasks. The following tactics are derived from studies that demonstrate the benefits of defining instructional expectations. Discretion has been used to interpret and reduce overlap in tactics used in different studies and to elaborate tactics.

Tactics employed are:

- The learning objective must be defined. This is necessary for the student to understand the learning objective. In essence, defining the learning objective assists the student in processing the available information. For instance, if the learning objective is adding fractions, "the learner must be able to identify 2/5 as a fraction and .4 as not a fraction" (Gagné, 1962a).

- How the student is to achieve the learning objective must be defined. Students need to know what procedures they are to employ in achieving the learning objectives. In the foregoing example by Gagné (1962a), if the students do not know that the learning objective is to add fractions, they may take the easier route and add decimals. The students may need to know that they are to convert decimals to fractions and then add. In the absence of instructions on how and what they are to do in order to accomplish the learning objective, they may quite simply not know what to do.

- Performance criteria must be defined. The student needs to know what the criteria are for achieving mastery of the learning objective. For example, if the task is adding fractions and if the students are to express the answer as a fraction, it may be necessary for the learner to identify 15¾ as an adequate answer and 15.75 as an inadequate one. Additionally, if letter grades are used, the student needs to know what task performance level is required to achieve that grade.

CAUTIONS AND COMMENTS

Defining instructional expectations may be seen as orienting the student to the learning goals and the means of achieving them. Although the examples used under "Instructional Tactics" to orient the student are seen as one way of accomplishing the orientation of the student, there are other means and examples available in the 358+ reference list citations. Should one wish to view other specific examples, it is recommended that readers review some of the many studies cited in the reference list in Part V.

GENERALIZATION: ON DEFINING INSTRUCTIONAL EXPECTATIONS

Student achievement of learning objectives is enhanced when prior to instruction, (1) learning objectives are defined for students, (2) procedures to be used in the performance of tasks to achieve the objectives are identified, and (3) student outcomes designating achievement of the objectives are defined.

Supportive Research on Defining Instructional Expectations
Total number of supportive studies covered: 358+

Groups of Studies

Author: Anderson (1994): Synthesis of seven meta-analyses

Students: Kindergarten, elementary, secondary, college, and other adult students

Learning: Mathematics, history, language arts, social sciences, sciences, and social studies achievement

Instructional Tactics: The following tactics associated with defining instructional expectations and Mastery Learning are also presented in Bloom (1985), Block (1980), and others. Other tactics associated with learning for mastery are applicable to other generalizations and are covered in the appropriate chapters.

Prior to instruction, students are oriented as to:

- Procedures to be used
- What they are expected to learn
- To what level they are expected to learn

Findings: Positive achievement gains associated with Mastery Learning were seen in 64–93 percent of the studies reviewed in the seven meta-analyses.

Individual studies analyzed by these meta-analyses are identified in the reference list in Part V by the following symbols:

Kulik et al. (1990a) *
Kulik et al. (1990b) #
Slavin (1990) @
Guskey & Pigott (1988) $
Guskey & Gates (1986) &
Block & Burns (1976) +

It was not possible to determine the individual studies for which defining instructional expectations was an instructional tactic for the Willett et al. (1983) analysis.

Author: Wise (1996)

Students: Middle and secondary

Learning: Science—all content areas

Instructional Tactics:

- Alert students to the purpose of the instruction.
- Provide objectives at the beginning, middle, or closing of a lesson.
- Use advance organizers to alert students.

Other instructional tactics from this review are applicable to other generalizations and are presented in the appropriate chapters of this book.

Findings: Use of the above focusing tactics was found to be effective in science achievement.

Individual studies in this meta-analysis were not identified by the author.

Author: Swanson (2001)

Students: Adolescents with learning disabilities

Learning: Higher order processing (problem solving) skills in reading and mathematics

Instructional Tactics:

- Direct students to look over material prior to instruction.
- Direct students to focus on particular information.
- Provide students with prior information about a task.
- State the objectives of instruction.

Other instructional tactics from this review are applicable to other generalizations and are presented in the appropriate chapters of this book.

Findings: Use of the above tactics led to higher levels of achievement by students with learning disabilities in problem solving as measured by standardized tests in reading and in mathematics.

Studies associated with this meta-analysis are identified by the symbol ^ in the reference list in Part V.

Author: Rosenshine & Stevens (1986)

Students: Elementary and secondary

Learning: Mathematics, English, science, history, and reading achievement

Instructional Tactics:

* Begin a lesson with a short statement of goals and objectives.
* Demonstrate what is to be learned, giving explicit step-by-step directions.

Other instructional tactics are employed in these studies that are applicable to other generalizations and are presented in the appropriate chapters.

Findings: The above tactics were found to be related to enhanced student achievement.

Groups of studies reviewed in this logical synthesis of research did not provide statistical evidence. However, many of the individual studies included in the logical synthesis of research do contain statistical evidence. In the event that a reader wishes to view this evidence, an extensive listing of the individual studies reviewed is provided in the reference list in Part V, and the studies are identified by the symbol %.

REFERENCE LIST

Anderson, S. A. (1994). *Synthesis of research on mastery learning* (Information Analysis). (ERIC Document Reproduction Service No. ED 382 567)

Block, J. H. (1980). Success rate. In C. Denham & A. Lieberman (Eds.), *Time to learn* (pp. 95–106). Washington, DC: U.S. Government Printing Office.

Block, J. H., & Burns, R. B. (1976). Mastery learning. In L. Schulman (Ed.), *Review of research in education* (Vol. 4, pp. 3–49). Itasca, IL: F. E. Peacock.

Bloom, B. S. (1985). Learning for mastery. In C. W. Fisher & D. C. Berliner (Eds.), *Perspectives on instructional time*. White Plains, NY: Longman.

Gagné, R. M. (1962a). The acquisition of knowledge. *Psychological Review, 69*(4), 355–365.

Guskey, T. R., & Gates, S. L. (1986). Synthesis of research on the effects of mastery learning in elementary and secondary classrooms. *Educational Leadership, 33*(8), 73–80.

Guskey, T. R., & Pigott, T. D. (1988). Research on group-based mastery learning programs: A meta-analysis. *Journal of Educational Research, 81*(4), 197–216.

Kulik, C., Kulik, J., & Bangert-Drowns, R. (1990a). Effectiveness of mastery learning programs: A meta-analysis. *Review of Educational Research, 60* (2), 265–269.

Kulik, J., Kulik, C., & Bangert-Drowns, R. (1990b). Is there better evidence on mastery learning? A response to Slavin. *Review of Educational Research, 60*(2), 303–307.

Rosenshine, B., & Stevens, R. (1986). Teaching functions. In M. C. Wittrock (Ed.), *Handbook of research on teaching* (3rd ed., pp. 376–391). New York: Macmillan.

Slavin, R. E. (1990). Mastery learning re-considered. *Review of Educational Research, 60*(2), 300–302.

Swanson, H. L. (2001). Research on interventions for adolescents with learning disabilities: A meta-analysis of outcomes related to higher-order processing. *The Elementary School Journal, 101*(13), 331–349.

Willett, J., Yamashita, J., & Anderson, R. (1983). A meta-analysis of instructional systems applied in science teaching. *Journal of Research in Science Teaching, 20*(5), 405–417.

Wise, K. C. (1996). Strategies for teaching science: What works? *The Clearing House, 69*(6), 337–338.

3

Providing Instructional Evaluation

INTRODUCTION

In the present context, evaluation is defined as assessing student task performance for the purpose of (1) certifying student competence in performing the tasks being evaluated and (2) diagnosing causes of inadequacy. Corrective instruction is the correction of inadequate task performance. Evaluation and corrective instruction tend to be closely linked in the research studies reviewed. Corrective instruction is based on evaluation and, when indicated, is to be prescribed and initiated immediately following evaluation. When evaluations are conducted, students are to be given immediate feedback on the competence of their task performance, and new tasks are assigned to students based on evaluation results. Students whose task performance is judged to be competent are assigned more advanced tasks. Students who have not as yet achieved competence are provided corrective instruction to correct inadequacies diagnosed during evaluation. This could be seen as a diagnostic and prescriptive cycle or loop, with feedback occurring between or linking the two. Evaluations serve as diagnostic tools for determining competent or inadequate task performance. In the case of inadequacy, the evaluations should provide for the diagnosis of the cause as well as the inadequacy itself. Once the inadequacy and causes are identified, appropriate corrective instruction tasks leading to competence can be prescribed. In the case of competence, the prescription is for the student to exit the current cycle and move on to more complex tasks and a new evaluation-feedback-corrective instruction cycle.

Far too many evaluation procedures provide for the assessment of competency without providing for the diagnosis of causes of inadequate task performance. This neglect prevents the correction of inadequate task performance. In such cases, feedback of evaluation results can convey to students only that their performance is competent or inadequate. When students are told that evaluation results indicate that their task performance is inadequate, they must suffer the insult. There is no cogent basis for correcting their inadequacy. Instruction is ineffective and student achievement of learning objectives is severely impaired when evaluation procedures do not diagnose the causes of students' inadequate task performance.

Since most students do not often achieve competent task performance without identifying and correcting inadequacies along the way, effective corrective instruction, as well as diagnostic procedures, must be provided for beforehand. When evaluation results indicate the need for corrective instruction, corrective action must be taken without delay so that students do not wallow in their failure and become discouraged. Excessive failure to learn is frustrating and can generate perceptions of helplessness and dissuade students from trying to learn.

STUDENT BENEFICIARIES

The evidence indicates that the academic achievement of students in kindergarten, elementary, junior high, secondary, college, and adult learning classrooms is enhanced when student performance of assigned tasks is evaluated, corrective instruction on the performance is provided, and incorrect performance is corrected. Moreover, academic achievement was improved in a wide range of content areas.

LEARNING ACHIEVED

Achievement in the content areas of mathematics, history, foreign languages, English, language arts, reading, social sciences, sciences, social studies, physics, biology, writing, management information, business, and occupational areas is enhanced when student performance of tasks is evaluated and the results of that evaluation are used to determine the next instructional assignments. In studies reviewed, instruction incorporating effective evaluation was positively associated with enhanced student achievement.

INSTRUCTIONAL TACTICS

The following tactics are derived from studies that demonstrate their benefit on student achievement. Discretion has been used in interpreting, elaborating, and reducing overlap in tactics used in different studies.

Tactics employed are:

- Establish criteria of adequate performance of assigned tasks.
- Utilize observation procedures to assess student performance of assigned tasks employing testing instruments as needed.
- Compare student performance on assigned tasks to criteria of adequate performance.
- Diagnose and rate student performance and record the findings, including student inadequacies.

- Determine students' next instructional assignment based on the findings.
- Report inadequacies and ratings of student performance.

Elaborations of the above summary of tactics can be obtained from reading the studies that follow. To be most effective, the instructional tactics need to be integrated into the particular instructional program being planned or presently being used.

CAUTIONS AND COMMENTS

The importance of student success in achieving learning objectives cannot be overemphasized. Students who consistently fail in their attempts to achieve the learning objectives eventually tire of trying to learn. They become frustrated and feel helpless, at times even angry. Eventually they may become "dropouts" and burdens on society. It is important that evaluation instruments provide diagnostic information that can be used as the basis for prescribing effective instructional assignments and corrective instruction.

GENERALIZATION: ON INSTRUCTIONAL EVALUATION

Achievement of learning objectives is enhanced when: (1) evaluation procedures are determined when task sequences are planned; (2) student task performance is frequently evaluated; (3) feedback on evaluation is given to students without delay; and (4) evaluation results are used to determine appropriate corrective instruction which occurs immediately after the performance is evaluated.

Supportive Research on Instructional Evaluation
Total number of supportive studies covered: 292+

Groups of Studies

Author: Kulik & Kulik (1987)

Students: Elementary, secondary, and college

Learning: Achievement in mathematics, science, and social studies

Instructional Tactics:

- Students work on unit material and repeat unit quizzes until they demonstrate mastery or receive special tutorial assistance before moving on to new material.
- A mastery level is set for each quiz and/or unit test.
- Students can retake quizzes from one time to an unlimited number of times.
- Students who fail to reach the mastery level on a quiz are provided remedial support, usually individual tutoring.

- Either a single form of a quiz for repeated testing on a unit or different quiz forms for repeated testing are employed.

- Students are allowed adequate time for learning to reach mastery.

Other instructional tactics from this review are applicable to other generalizations and are presented in the appropriate chapters of this book.

Findings: Use of the above tactics about mastery testing was found to enhance achievement.

The individual studies in this meta-analysis are listed in the references in Part V with the symbol =.

Author: Anderson (1994): Synthesis of seven meta-analyses

Students: Kindergarten, elementary, secondary, college, and other adult students

Learning: Achievement

Instructional Tactics: The following tactics, associated with readiness and Mastery Learning, are also presented in Bloom (1985), Block (1980), and others. Other tactics associated with Mastery Learning are applicable to other generalizations and are covered in the appropriate chapters.

- Subject matter should be divided into small units of learning in order to enhance the possibilities for student success, and student learning should be tested at the end of each unit.

- Alternative instructional materials, procedures, or correctives are developed for each item on a test that is designed to reteach the material tested in ways different from the original instruction.

- Students are provided feedback on their errors after each test.

- Based on the results of the test, the needs of each student are diagnosed and the appropriate pre-developed alternative learning materials, procedures, or correctives are assigned to be accomplished either inside or outside of the class.

Findings: Positive achievement gains associated with Mastery Learning were seen in 64–93 percent of the studies reviewed in the seven meta-analyses.

Individual studies analyzed by these meta-analyses are included in the reference list in Part V and are identified by the following symbols:

Kulik et al. (1990a) *

Kulik et al. (1990b) #

Slavin (1990) @

Guskey & Pigott (1988) $

Guskey & Gates (1986) &

Block & Burns (1976) +

It was not possible to determine the individual studies for which readiness was an instructional tactic of the Willett et al. (1983) analysis.

Author: Rosenshine et al. (1996)

Students: Upper elementary (grade 3 and up), junior high, secondary, and college

Learning: Reading comprehension across subject matters, mathematics, physics, and writing

Instructional Tactics:

- Scaffolds (temporary support) such as a model of the completed task and a checklist for students are planned and provided for students to use in completing the task to assist them in the acquisition of subject matter.
- Procedural prompts are provided to help students with specific procedures or suggestions to complete the task. Examples of procedural prompts are signal words, generic question stems and generic questions, the main idea of a paragraph, question types, and story grammar categories. These procedural prompts are followed by some or all of the following instructional tactics:

  —Provide models of appropriate responses.

  —Model by thinking through a problem out loud in order for the students to hear a method to solve problems.

  —Anticipate and plan for potential difficulties.

  —Regulate the difficulty of the material.

  —Provide a cue card.

  —Guide student practice.

  —Provide feedback and corrections during practice.

  —Provide and teach a checklist for student use.

  —Assess student mastery of the subject matter.

- Reciprocal questioning technique is used with no prompts:

  —First a question is generated which the students answer.

—The generated question serves as a model for the students in generating their own questions.

—The students then generate a question which the teacher answers.

—Extensive student practice of question generation is provided.

—Students may practice individually or in pairs, both with guidance.

—Students' ability to ask questions throughout the lesson is assessed.

—The students are asked to summarize the passage at the completion of the reading.

—The students' ability to ask questions is assessed at the end of the learning unit along with their comprehension of the subject matter.

Other instructional tactics are employed in these studies that are applicable to other generalizations and will be presented in the appropriate chapters.

Findings: Use of the above tactics was found to enhance achievement in reading comprehension.

Individual studies analyzed by this meta-analysis are identified in the reference list in Part V by the symbol ^.

❖   ❖   ❖

Author: Rosenshine & Stevens (1986)

Students: Elementary and secondary

Learning: Mathematics, English, science, history, and reading achievement

Instructional Tactics:

- A large number of questions relevant to the to-be-learned material are prepared.

- During instruction and student practice, students are asked a large number of questions to check for their understanding of the subject matter.

- Frequent tests are given.

- Correct responses to questions are acknowledged as correct.

- Correct responses should be provided to the student if an incorrect response is determined to be a careless error on the part of the student.

- When a student's incorrect response is due to a lack of knowledge or understanding, one of two options are pursued as deemed most appropriate: (1) provide students with prompts or hints to lead them to the correct answer or (2) reteach the material to the students who do not understand.

- Provide students with praise for correct responses and encouragement for incorrect responses.

Other instructional tactics are employed in these studies that are applicable to other generalizations and will be presented in the appropriate chapters.

Findings: Use of these tactics was found to be related to greater levels of student achievement.

Groups of studies reviewed in this logical synthesis of research did not provide statistical evidence. However, many of the individual studies included in the logical synthesis of research do contain statistical evidence. In the event that a reader wishes to view this evidence, an extensive listing of the individual studies reviewed is provided in the reference list in Part V. The studies are identified by the symbol %.

Author: Brophy & Good (1986)

Students: Elementary and secondary

Learning: Reading, mathematics, English, and biology achievement

Instructional Tactics:

- Ask questions that focus on academic content in ordered turns to ensure that all students have an opportunity to respond.
- Acknowledge correct responses.
- Ensure that the correct response is revealed when incorrect responses are made. Provide the correct response or continue questioning until the correct response emerges as discretion indicates.
- Provide additional instruction or opportunity for practice as deemed appropriate.
- Provide encouragement and reinforce correct responses.

Other instructional tactics are employed in these studies that are applicable to other generalizations and will be presented in the appropriate chapters.

Findings: Use of the preceding instructional tactics was found to be related positively to student achievement.

Individual studies in this research synthesis are included in the reference list in Part V and are identified by the symbol !.

Author: Education Commission of the States (1999)

Students: Elementary (K–6)

Learning: Language arts, reading, and mathematics

Instructional Tactics:

- Students are frequently assessed for mastery of subject matter content.
- Students are frequently assessed for need for corrective instruction.

Other instructional tactics are employed in these studies that are applicable to other generalizations and will be presented in the appropriate chapters.

Findings: Use of the above tactics was found to enhance academic achievement.

Individual studies and groups of studies in this logical synthesis are identified with the symbol > in the reference list in Part V. Statistical data are not included in this synthesis of studies.

❖ ❖ ❖

Author: Baker et al. (2002)

Students: Elementary and secondary (low-achieving)

Learning: Mathematics achievement

Instructional Tactics:

- Students are provided instruction based on state standards.
- Students are administered weekly tests, using a computer, with items reflecting state standards on which instruction has been based.

Other instructional tactics are employed in these studies that are applicable to other generalizations and will be presented in the appropriate chapters.

Findings: Use of the above tactics was found to have a positive effect on math achievement.

Groups of studies reviewed in this logical synthesis of research did not always provide statistical evidence. Individual studies from this logical synthesis related to contextualized mathematics instruction are marked in the end of chapter references with the symbol /.

Author: Martens & Witt (2004)—40 studies

Students: Ages 6–12

Learning: Academic achievement in elementary subjects

Instructional Tactics:

- Provide students with errorless learning opportunities—a gradual movement one small increment at a time from an easy task to a more difficult task.
- Use formative evaluation of content, continuous progress monitoring.
- Determine students' knowledge and provide instruction from that point in small increments.
- Check regularly for students' understanding of the subject matter.
- Assess learning regularly in a formal way such as tests.
- Guide students through a number of practice opportunities with assistance or "learning trials."
- Model or show students how to perform a skill.
- Provide enough help that students can perform the skill themselves with prompting.
- Correct student errors or reinforce correct responses.
- Withdraw or "fade" the assistance or prompts gradually.

Other instructional tactics are employed in these studies that are applicable to other generalizations and will be presented in the appropriate chapters.

Findings: Use of the tactics listed above was found to be effective in improving student achievement across content areas.

This research synthesis does not provide statistical data. The studies, some of which are meta-analyses, are designated with the symbol < in the references in Part V.

Individual Studies

Author: Obando & Hymel (1991)

Students: Grade 9

Learning: Spanish language achievement

Instructional Tactics:

- Administer diagnostic formative trial tests to the students.
- Provide students feedback on their performance on the formative tests.

- Provide corrective instruction in the form of additional assignments and tutoring sessions when necessary based on the results of the tests.

Other instructional tactics are employed in this study that are applicable to other generalizations and will be presented in the appropriate chapters.

Findings: Achievement was significantly higher for students who benefited from these tactics on unit exams and the National Spanish Examination as compared to students who did not.

Author: Montazemi & Wang (1995)

Students: Undergraduate

Learning: Achievement in management information systems

Instructional Tactics:

- Students are provided instruction using a computer program which has a pre-specified sequence of learning-lessons.
- Students are required to complete at the mastery level all learning-lessons within a section.
- Student mastery of learning-lessons is assessed as follows:
  —Students receive a set of questions to test their knowledge of the learning-lesson in a section.
  —An incorrect response leads the student to a related learning-lesson.
  —Students can spend as much time as they feel needed to learn the content of a learning-lesson.
  —Upon exiting a learning-lesson, a student is presented a randomly selected question of either multiple-choice or true-false format about the content of that learning-lesson.
  —Students who answer an item incorrectly are given feedback and the content of the learning-lesson is displayed on the screen again. Feedback does not include the correct answer.
  —Students can again exit the learning-lesson and receive another randomly generated question to answer.
  —Repetition of this process occurs until the question related to the learning-lesson is answered correctly.
- Students must master all sections (learning-lessons) of a chapter before going to the next chapter.
- Students are assessed at the end of each chapter.
  —Students are given several questions which test mastery of all sections in the chapter.

—Students receive simple feedback for correct answers.

—Students receive the correct answer for an incorrect response.

- Students are administered weekly lab-tests in a micro-lab setting consisting of 50 questions derived from a set of pre-scheduled chapters. Students are given the correct answer for any incorrect response.

- Students are administered a final exam covering all twenty chapters of the textbook.

Other instructional tactics are employed in these studies that are applicable to other generalizations and will be presented in the appropriate chapters.

Findings: Use of the above tactics related to mastery testing was found to have a positive effect on achievement.

Author: Aviles (1998)

Students: Undergraduate

Learning: Achievement in social work

Instructional Tactics:

- Provide clear learning expectations.

- Prepare a table of specifications.

- Provide formative evaluations in the form of quizzes.

- Allow students to self-score quizzes immediately.

- Provide corrective instruction based on errors on quizzes.

- Provide summative evaluation in the form of a graded criterion-referenced exam.

- Provide feedback.

- Provide corrective instruction by re-teaching content, through new materials or with other methods.

- Provide students the opportunity to take a parallel form of the exam to improve their grades.

Other instructional tactics are employed in these studies that are applicable to other generalizations and will be presented in the appropriate chapters.

Findings: Use of the above tactics was found to improve students' achievement in introductory social work courses.

Author: Ross (2004)

Students: Grade 3

Learning: Achievement in reading and writing

Instructional Tactics:

- Have the student sit or stand beside the adult to read a text both can see.

- Code each word read (running record).

- Report the percentage of words correctly read; the self-correction ratio (the ratio of errors and self-corrections divided by the number of self-corrections); and the categories of errors made (meaning, visual, or structure).

- Prompt the student to retell the story after reading it.

- Ask the student questions about the story's meaning.

- Repeat the formative evaluation (running record) until the student has responded correctly to the questions about meaning and has read with 90–94 percent accuracy.

- Determine subsequent instruction for the student based on the level of the passage read and the types of errors the student made.

Findings: Use of the above tactics related to formative evaluation using a running record was found to have a positive effect on student achievement in reading and writing.

REFERENCE LIST

Anderson, S. A. (1994). *Synthesis of research on mastery learning* (Information Analysis). (ERIC Document Reproduction Service No. ED 382 567)

Aviles, C. B. (1998). *A contrast of mastery learning and non-mastery learning instruction in an undergraduate social work course*. Paper presented at the annual meeting of the Council on Social Work Education, Orlando, FL.

Baker, S., Gersten, R., & Lee, D-S. (2002). A synthesis of empirical research on teaching mathematics to low-achieving students. *The Elementary School Journal, 103*(1), 51–92.

Block, J. H. (1980). Success rate. In C. Denham & A. Lieberman (Eds.), *Time to learn* (pp. 95–106). Washington, DC: U.S. Government Printing Office.

Block, J. H., & Burns, R. B. (1976). Mastery learning. In L. Schulman (Ed.), *Review of research in education* (Vol. 4, pp. 3–49). Itasca, IL: F. E. Peacock.

Bloom, B. S. (1985). Learning for mastery. In C. W. Fisher & D. C. Berliner (Eds.), *Perspectives on instructional time*. White Plains, NY: Longman.

Brophy, J., & Good, T. (1986). Teacher behavior and student achievement. In M. C. Wittrock (Ed.), *Handbook of research on teaching* (3rd ed., pp. 328–375). New York: Macmillan.

Education Commission of the States. (1999). *Direct instruction*. Denver, CO: Education Commission of the States.

Guskey, T. R., & Gates, S. L. (1986). Synthesis of research on the effects of mastery learning in elementary and secondary classrooms. *Educational Leadership, 33*(8), 73–80.

Guskey, T. R., & Pigott, T. D. (1988). Research on group-based mastery learning programs: A meta-analysis. *Journal of Educational Research, 81*(4), 197–216.

Kulik, C., Kulik, J., & Bangert-Drowns, R. (1990a). Effectiveness of mastery learning programs: A meta-analysis. *Review of Educational Research, 60*(2), 265–269.

Kulik, J., Kulik, C., & Bangert-Drowns, R. (1990b). Is there better evidence on mastery learning? A response to Slavin. *Review of Educational Research, 60*(2), 303–307.

Kulik, L. C., & Kulik, J. A. (1987). Mastery testing and student learning: A meta-analysis. *Journal of Educational Technology Systems, 15*(3), 325–345.

Martens, B. K., & Witt, J. C. (2004). Competence, persistence, and success: The positive psychology of behavioral skill instruction. *Psychology in the Schools, 41*(1), 19–30.

Montazemi, A. R., & Wang, F. (1995). An empirical investigation of CBI in support of mastery learning. *Journal of Educational Computing Research, 13*(2), 185–205.

Obando, L. T., & Hymel, G. M. (1991, March). *The effect of mastery learning instruction on the entry-level Spanish proficiency of secondary school students.* Paper presented at the annual meeting to the American Educational Research Association, New Orleans. (ERIC Document Reproduction Service No. ED 359 253)

Rosenshine, B., Meister, C., & Chapman, S. (1996). Teaching students to generate questions: A review of the intervention studies. *Review of Educational Research, 66*(2), 181–221.

Rosenshine, B., & Stevens, R. (1986). Teaching functions. In M. C. Wittrock (Ed.), *Handbook of research on teaching* (3rd ed., pp. 376–391). New York: Macmillan.

Ross, J. A. (2004). Effects of running records assessment on early literacy achievement. *The Journal of Educational Research, 97*(4), 186–194.

Slavin, R. E. (1990). Mastery learning re-considered. *Review of Educational Research, 60*(2), 300–302.

Willett, J., Yamashita, J., & Anderson, R. (1983). A meta-analysis of instructional systems applied in science teaching. *Journal of Research in Science Teaching, 20*(5), 405–417.

4

Providing Corrective Instruction

INTRODUCTION

The importance of promptly correcting student inadequacies in performing assigned tasks cannot be overemphasized. Providing sufficient corrective instruction to prevent student failure may be the greatest challenge to education. The research shows that dropouts fall farther and farther behind before dropping out of school. Moreover, while in school, far more students than need be fail to achieve learning objectives. Academic achievement can be increased substantially by giving students as much corrective tutoring as they may need to succeed. The most effective corrective instruction is provided by one-to-one tutoring (see Chapter 14 for more on one-to-one tutoring) and is based on the accurate evaluation of student performance.

STUDENT BENEFICIARIES

The evidence indicates that the academic achievement of students in preschool, kindergarten, elementary, junior high, secondary, college, and adult learning classrooms is enhanced when feedback on correctness of performance is provided and corrective instruction is given for incorrect performance. Moreover, academic achievement was improved in a wide range of content areas. Academic achievement is enhanced for the subpopulation of students with special needs at the elementary and secondary levels. No evidence could be found to suggest that corrective instruction should not be utilized in all subject areas for all types of students.

LEARNING ACHIEVED

Achievement in the content areas of mathematics, history, chemistry, biology, foreign languages, English, language arts, reading, social sciences, psychology, education, sciences, social studies, physics, writing, and ROTC is enhanced when feedback on the correctness of performance is provided, corrective instruction is given for incorrect performance, and the student is afforded the opportunity to correct his errors. In studies reviewed, instruction incorporating effective corrective instruction tactics was associated positively with enhanced student achievement.

INSTRUCTIONAL TACTICS

The following tactics are derived from studies that demonstrate their benefit on student achievement. Discretion has been used in interpreting, elaborating, and reducing overlap in tactics used in different studies.

- Corrective tasks to remediate inadequate student task performance are planned beforehand.
- Students are made aware of their strengths, and their inadequacies are clarified.
- Students are assured that they (1) have the ability to perform the tasks that have been difficult for them and (2) will be given all the help they need to succeed.
- The benefits of succeeding are emphasized, and students are encouraged to keep trying.
- Students are guided in the performance of the assigned corrective task.

CAUTIONS AND COMMENTS

The importance of corrective instruction on student success in achieving learning objectives cannot be overemphasized. Students who are not given feedback about their incorrect performance are unaware of how to improve. Students who receive the feedback about their incorrect performance but are not given corrective instruction become frustrated that they do not know how to correct their failures and be successful. This continuous cycle of frustration and failure leads students to give up on learning. It is important to remember that the evaluation of student performance serves as a basis for prescribing corrective instruction. The two are closely linked in the research studies reviewed. Subpopulations positively affected by corrective instruction include racial/ethnic groups and students with special needs.

GENERALIZATION: ON CORRECTIVE INSTRUCTION

Achievement of learning objectives is enhanced when appropriate corrective instruction is provided: (1) corrective tasks are formulated when task sequences are planned; (2) feedback on incorrect performance is based on frequent evaluation of student work; (3) feedback on evaluation is given to students without delay; and (4) incorrect performance is immediately corrected.

Supportive Research on Corrective Instruction
Total number of studies covered: 504+

Groups of Studies

Author: Kulik & Kulik (1988)

Students: Kindergarten, elementary, secondary, and college

Learning: Chemistry, psychology, physics, science, mathematics, ROTC, and reading

Instructional Tactics:

• Provide immediate feedback on responses to test items.

Findings: Use of the above tactic was found to enhance student achievement.

Studies in this meta-analysis are indicated in the reference list in Part V by the symbol ~.

Author: Bangert-Drowns et al. (1991)

Students: Elementary, junior high, high school, and college

Learning: Math, science, social science/education, and language arts/reading

Instructional Tactics: Performance tasks come in a variety of formats as indicated below. In each type of performance task, the student is given feedback on the adequacies and inadequacies of the performance. Feedback leads to a new or corrective task performance.

• Students are presented a series of small frames that constitute a continuous text. After responding to a frame, the student receives feedback and then moves to the next frame.

• Students are provided blocks of text followed by questions. After responding to the questions, students receive feedback and then continue to another block of text if there is another one.

• Students receive classroom instruction and are then tested on the content. Students receive item specific performance feedback on their test performance. After a period of time, the students are asked to respond to a criterion measure that covers the same content.

• Students receive instruction via computer, sometimes along with programmed instruction or text comprehension programs. Computer-assisted instruction includes drill-and-practice and tutorials.

• Students are provided a variety of feedback types: supplying right/wrong feedback, telling wrong answer so student must continue responding until correct answer is given, giving an explanation of correct response, and providing the correct answer.

Other instructional tactics are employed in these studies that are applicable to other generalizations and will be presented in the appropriate chapters.

Findings: Use of the above tactics was found to produce very large achievement gains. However, those tactics that do not allow pre-search (peeking ahead) tend to produce more gain than those which allow pre-search. Feedback in programmed instruction and computer-based instruction is less effective than feedback in conventional testing situations and in text comprehension. In addition, supplying right/wrong feedback is not as effective as the other types of feedback. Immediate feedback is recommended for conventional educational purposes, as in instruction followed by testing followed by feedback. Further, the amount of information in feedback is not as important as the correct answer in feedback. Ample evidence indicates that students use feedback to check the correctness of their answers, thus leading to error correction.

Individual studies analyzed by this meta-analysis are identified in the reference list in Part V by the symbol ^.

Author: Anderson (1994): Synthesis of seven meta-analyses

Students: Kindergarten, elementary, secondary, college, and other adult students

Learning: Achievement

Instructional Tactics: The following tactics associated with readiness and Mastery Learning are also presented in Bloom (1985), Block (1980), and others. Other tactics associated with Mastery Learning are applicable to other generalizations and are covered in the appropriate chapters.

- Subject matter should be divided into small units of learning in order to enhance the possibilities for student success, and student learning should be tested at the end of each unit.

- Alternative instructional materials, procedures, or correctives are developed by the teacher for each item on a test that is designed to reteach the tested material in ways different from the original instruction.

- Feedback is provided to the students on their errors after each test.

- The developed alternative learning materials, procedures, or correctives are provided and are to be accomplished either inside or outside of the class as appropriate for each student.

Findings: Positive achievement gains associated with Mastery Learning were seen in 64–93 percent of the studies reviewed in the seven meta-analyses.

Individual studies analyzed by these meta-analyses are identified in the reference list in Part V by the following symbols:

Kulik et al. (1990a) *
Kulik et al. (1990b) #
Slavin (1990) @
Guskey & Pigott (1988) $
Guskey & Gates (1986) &
Block & Burns (1976) +

It was not possible to determine the individual studies for which corrective instruction was an instructional tactic for Willett et al. (1983) analysis.

Author: Rosenshine et al. (1996)

Students: Upper elementary (grade 3 and up), junior high, secondary, and college

Learning: Reading comprehension across subject matters, mathematics, physics, and writing

Instructional Tactics:

- Provide feedback and corrections during the dialogues with students.
- Provide feedback and corrections during guided practice.
- Give feedback in the form of hints, questions, and suggestions.
- Guide students in generating their questions tied to the passage, in meeting in small groups, in asking each other questions, and in comparing their generated questions within the group.
- Provide additional instruction, based on assessment results, when necessary for mastery.

Other instructional tactics are employed in these studies that are applicable to other generalizations and will be presented in the appropriate chapters.

Findings: Use of the above tactics was found to enhance reading comprehension.

Individual studies analyzed by this meta-analysis are identified in the reference list in Part V by the symbol <.

❖   ❖   ❖

Author: Gersten & Baker (2001)

Students: Learning disabled

Learning: Expressive writing

Instructional Tactics:

- Students are given a writing task.
- Students are provided feedback related to overall quality of writing, missing elements, and strengths.
- Adults and students have a common language with which to discuss the writing.
- The adult and student participate in an interactive dialogue which provides the student with corrective instruction as the student considers the problems in the written work.
- Students engage in interactive dialogue with peers using an organizational framework for the discussion of the writing, especially in the revision process.

Other instructional tactics are employed in these studies that are applicable to other generalizations and will be presented in the appropriate chapters.

Findings: Use of the above tactics was found to enhance achievement related to writing.

Studies associated with this meta-analysis are identified by the symbol > in the reference list in Part V.

❖   ❖   ❖

Author: Swanson (2001)

Students: Adolescents with learning disabilities

Learning: Higher order processing (problem solving)

Instructional Tactics:

- Provide students with daily feedback.

Other instructional tactics are employed in these studies that are applicable to other generalizations and will be presented in the appropriate chapters.

Findings: Use of the above tactic led to higher levels of achievement by students with learning disabilities in problem solving as measured by standardized tests in reading and in mathematics.

Studies associated with this meta-analysis are identified by the symbol / in the reference list in Part V.

❖ ❖ ❖

Author: Gersten et al. (2001)

Students: School-age children

Learning: Achievement in reading

Instructional Tactics:

• Provide students with extensive teacher feedback during the students' use of a structured learning strategy in reading.

Other instructional tactics are employed in these studies that are applicable to other generalizations and will be presented in the appropriate chapters.

Findings: Use of the above tactic was found to be effective for students with learning disabilities.

Studies from the meta-analyses related to narrative texts are marked in the end of chapter references with the symbol =.

❖ ❖ ❖

Author: Kroesbergen & Van Luit (2003)

Students: Elementary with special education needs

Learning: Mathematics

Instructional Tactics:

• Provide training (corrective instruction) to students in the basic math skill until a set criterion is reached.

Findings: Use of the mastery learning tactic listed above was found to be effective in students' achievement of basic math skills.

Studies cited in this meta-analysis are designated with the symbol \ in the references in Part V.

Author: Therrien (2004)

Students: Preschool and elementary

Learning: Reading fluency

Instructional Tactics: When students are reading the same passage multiple times:

• Correct students' mispronunciations as they occur.

• Correct students' mispronunciations when students request assistance.

When students are reading a new passage after having read other passages multiple times:

• Correct mispronunciations or omissions while students are reading.

• Correct mispronunciations or omissions after students finish reading.

• Allow other students to intervene by correcting mispronunciations or omissions.

• Provide the students with the correct pronunciations.

• Prompt students to sound out the word or reread the word.

Other instructional tactics are employed in these studies that are applicable to other generalizations and will be presented in the appropriate chapters.

Findings: Use of the above tactics was found to be effective in students' achievement of reading fluency. When students are reading a new passage, teacher interventions were even more effective in producing reading fluency than were student interventions.

Studies included in this meta-analysis are marked with the symbol ? in the references in Part V.

Author: Rosenshine & Stevens (1986)

Students: Elementary and secondary

Learning: Mathematics, English, science, history, and reading achievement

Instructional Tactics:

• Prepare a large number of questions relevant to the to-be-learned material.

• Ask a large number of questions to check for student understanding during instruction and student practice.

• Give frequent tests.

• Acknowledge correct responses to questions as correct.

- Provide the correct response to the student if an incorrect response is determined to be a careless error on the part of the student.

- Pursue one of two options as deemed most appropriate when a student's incorrect response is due to a lack of knowledge or understanding: (1) provide students with prompts or hints to lead them to the correct answer or (2) reteach the material to the students who do not understand.

- Provide praise for correct responses and encouragement for incorrect responses.

Other instructional tactics are employed in these studies that are applicable to other generalizations and will be presented in the appropriate chapters.

Findings: Use of these tactics was found to be related to greater levels of student achievement.

Groups of studies reviewed in this logical synthesis of research did not provide statistical evidence. However, many of the individual studies included in the logical synthesis of research do contain statistical evidence. In the event that a reader wishes to view this evidence, an extensive listing of the individual studies reviewed is provided in the reference list in Part V. The studies are identified by the symbol %.

Author: Brophy & Good (1986)

Students: Elementary and secondary

Learning: Reading, mathematics, English, and biology achievement

Instructional Tactics:

- Ask questions that focus on academic content in ordered turns to ensure that all students have an opportunity to respond.

- Acknowledge correct responses.

- When incorrect responses are made, ensure that the correct response is revealed. Provide the correct response or continue questioning until the correct response emerges as discretion indicates.

- Provide additional instruction or opportunity for practice as deemed appropriate.

- Provide encouragement and reinforce correct responses.

Other instructional tactics are employed in these studies that are applicable to other generalizations and will be presented in the appropriate chapters.

Findings: Use of the preceding instructional tactics was found to be related positively to student achievement.

Individual studies included in this research synthesis are identified by the symbol ! in the reference list in Part V.

Author: Heubusch & Lloyd (1998)

Students: Preschool, elementary, junior high, and secondary

Learning: Reading—decoding and comprehension—achievement

Instructional Tactics:

- Base correction techniques on the reading goals for the lesson.
- Provide corrective instruction immediately.
- Provide corrective instruction that is direct and clear to the student.
- Require an active and correct response from students.
- Interrupt the reading process to provide corrective instruction.

Findings: Use of the above tactics was found to enhance achievement in oral reading.

Studies in this research synthesis did not provide statistical evidence. Individual studies included in this research synthesis are identified by the symbol } in the reference list in Part V.

Author: Baker et al. (2002)

Students: Elementary and secondary (low-achieving)

Learning: Mathematics achievement

Instructional Tactics:

- Review with students copies of the individual student's performance graphs created by software following weekly tests taken on the computer and based on math standards which have been taught in class.
- Determine the corrective instruction and new instruction needed based on the whole class summary report of performance on the specific standards.
- Group students for corrective instruction based on the test results.
- Use computer-generated lists of lessons with individual students based on their needs.
- Use computer-generated lists of suggestions for employing the tactic of

peer tutoring as a means of corrective instruction. Peer tutoring is designed to assist students with practice of and reinforcement for the concepts and skills which are causing the most difficulty.

Other instructional tactics are employed in these studies that are applicable to other generalizations and will be presented in the appropriate chapters.

Findings: Use of the above tactics was found to have a positive effect on math achievement.

Groups of studies reviewed in this logical synthesis of research did not always provide statistical evidence. Individual studies from this logical synthesis are marked in the references in Part V with the symbol {.

Individual Studies

Author: Obando & Hymel (1991)

Students: Grade 9

Learning: Spanish language achievement

Instructional Tactics:

- Diagnostic formative trial tests are administered to the students.
- Students are provided feedback on their performance on the formative tests.
- Learning correctives are provided in the form of additional assignments and tutoring sessions when necessary.

Other instructional tactics are employed in this study that are applicable to other generalizations and will be presented in the appropriate chapters.

Findings: Achievement was significantly higher for students who benefited from these tactics on unit exams and the National Spanish Examination as compared to students who did not.

❖　❖　❖

Author: Mevarech & Kramarski (1997)

Students: Middle level—seventh graders

Learning: Mathematics

Instructional Tactics:

- Students are given a formative assessment at the end of each unit of mathematics content.

- Students must reach 80 percent mastery on the assessment.

- Students are provided corrective instruction or enrichment activities to complete.

- Students work in homogeneous groups during the corrective-enrichment sessions.

- Students are provided time to make corrections to their learning and are given an alternative form of the assessment.

Other instructional tactics are employed in these studies that are applicable to other generalizations and will be presented in the appropriate chapters.

Findings: Use of the above tactics was found to enhance student achievement in mathematics.

REFERENCE LIST

Anderson, S. A. (1994). *Synthesis of research on mastery learning* (Information Analysis). (ERIC Document Reproduction Service No. ED 382 567)

Baker, S., Gersten, R., & Lee, D-S. (2002). A synthesis of empirical research on teaching mathematics to low-achieving students. *The Elementary School Journal, 103*(1), 51–92.

Bangert-Drowns, R. L., Kulik, C-L. C., Kulik, J. A., & Morgan, M. T. (1991). The instructional effect of feedback in test-like events. *Review of Educational Research, 61*(2), 213–238.

Block, J. H. (1980). Success rate. In C. Denham & A. Lieberman (Eds.), *Time to learn* (pp. 95–106). Washington, DC: U.S. Government Printing Office.

Block, J. H., & Burns, R. B. (1976). Mastery learning. In L. Schulman (Ed.), *Review of research in education* (Vol. 4, pp. 3–49). Itasca, IL: F. E. Peacock.

Bloom, B. S. (1985). Learning for mastery. In C. W. Fisher & D. C. Berliner (Eds.), *Perspectives on instructional time*. White Plains, NY: Longman.

Brophy, J., & Good, T. (1986). Teacher behavior and student achievement. In M. C. Wittrock (Ed.), *Handbook of research on teaching* (3rd ed., pp. 328–375). New York: Macmillan.

Gersten, R., & Baker, S. (2001). Teaching expressive writing to students with learning disabilities: A meta-analysis. *The Elementary School Journal, 101*(3), 251–273.

Gersten, R., Fuchs, L. S., Williams, J. P., & Baker, S. (2001). Teaching reading comprehension strategies to students with learning disabilities: A review of research. *Review of Educational Research, 71*(2), 279–320.

Guskey, T. R., & Gates, S. L. (1986). Synthesis of research on the effects of mastery learning in elementary and secondary classrooms. *Educational Leadership, 33*(8), 73–80.

Guskey, T. R., & Pigott, T. D. (1988). Research on group-based mastery learning programs: A meta-analysis. *Journal of Educational Research, 81*(4), 197–216.

Heubusch, J. D., & Lloyd, J. W. (1998). Corrective feedback in oral reading. *Journal of Behavioral Education, 8*(1), 63–79.

Kroesbergen, E. H., & Van Luit, J.E.H. (2003). Mathematics interventions for children with special educational needs: A meta-analysis. *Remedial and Special Education, 24*(2), 97–114.

Kulik, C., Kulik, J., & Bangert-Drowns, R. (1990a). Effectiveness of mastery learning programs: A meta-analysis. *Review of Educational Research, 60*(2), 265-269.

Kulik, J., Kulik, C., & Bangert-Drowns, R. (1990b). Is there better evidence on mastery learning? A response to Slavin. *Review of Educational Research, 60*(2), 303–307.

Kulik, J. A., & Kulik, C. C. (1988). Timing of feedback and verbal learning. *Review of Educational Research, 58*(1), 79–97.

Mevarech, Z. R., & Kramarski, B. (1997). IMPROVE: A multidimensional method for teaching mathematics in heterogeneous classrooms. *American Educational Research Journal, 34*(2), 365–394.

Obando, L. T., & Hymel, G. M. (1991, March). *The effect of mastery learning instruction on the entry-level Spanish proficiency of secondary school students.* Paper presented at the annual meeting to the American Educational Research Association, New Orleans. (ERIC Document Reproduction Service No. ED 359 253)

Rosenshine, B., Meister, C., & Chapman, S. (1996). Teaching students to generate questions: A review of the intervention studies. *Review of Educational Research, 66*(2), 181–221.

Rosenshine, B., & Stevens, R. (1986). Teaching functions. In M. C. Wittrock (Ed.), *Handbook of research on teaching* (3rd ed., pp. 376–391). New York: Macmillan.

Slavin, R. E. (1990). Mastery learning re-considered. *Review of Educational Research, 60*(2), 300–302.

Swanson, H. L. (2001). Research on interventions for adolescents with learning disabilities: A meta-analysis of outcomes related to higher-order processing. *The Elementary School Journal, 101*(13), 331–349.

Therrien, W. J. (2004). Fluency and comprehension gains as a result of repeated reading: A meta-analysis. *Remedial and Special Education, 25*(4), 252–261.

Willett, J., Yamashita, J., & Anderson, R. (1983). A meta-analysis of instructional systems applied in science teaching. *Journal of Research in Science Teaching, 20*(5), 405–417.

5

Keeping Students on Task

INTRODUCTION

The evidence shows quite conclusively that the more time students spend focused on the performance of assigned tasks that enable achievement of learning objectives without distractions, the more likely it is they will achieve the learning objectives. Although students' bodily presence may be mandated and coerced, students control what they attend to and learn and will not continue to focus on the performance of assigned tasks if they do not want to do so. Instructional planners and teachers must make every effort to ensure that students are ready to perform assigned tasks, that their interest in performing assigned tasks is stimulated, that the learning environment is conducive to performing assigned tasks, and that they are given every opportunity to succeed in performing assigned tasks. Students who do not attend to assigned learning tasks fail to learn and may eventually become student dropouts. Student time focused on assigned tasks is fundamental.

STUDENT BENEFICIARIES

The evidence indicates that students spending more time focused on performance of assigned tasks that enable achievement of learning objectives have greater success achieving the objectives in elementary and secondary classrooms. No evidence could be found to suggest that students' spending more time focused on performance of assigned tasks should not be advocated in all subject areas for all types of students, including students in military, community, business, and adult education settings.

LEARNING ACHIEVED

Students' spending more time on task has been shown to lead to greater achievement in mathematics, reading, English, language arts, sciences, social studies, and biology. It may be reasonable to expect that achievement may be enhanced in other content areas as well. In studies reviewed, student achievement was shown to be positively related to time on task.

INSTRUCTIONAL TACTICS

The benefits of students focusing more time on performance of assigned tasks that enable achievement of the learning objectives are well supported by the evidence. However, there is a need for instructional planners and teachers to know the particular tactics that can be used to ensure that students are focusing more time on performance of assigned tasks. The following tactics are derived from the studies that demonstrate the benefits of students focusing more time on performance of assigned tasks. Discretion has been used to interpret and reduce overlap in tactics used in different studies and to elaborate tactics.

Tactics that ensure that students spend more time focused on performance of assigned tasks that enable achievement of the learning objectives are:

- Assign only learning tasks that are relevant to achievement of the learning objective.
- Assign only learning tasks that students possess the readiness capabilities to perform. If this is not adhered to, students will be unable to perform assigned tasks, time will be wasted, and students may be dissuaded from learning.
- Make sure that instruction is well planned and organized.
- Spend more time on demonstration and guided practice (as opposed to independent student practice).
- Make sure the students are ready to work alone before assigning independent learning tasks.
- Make sure that independent learning tasks are directly relevant to prior demonstration and guided practice.
- Assign independent learning tasks to follow the guided practice activities immediately.
- Provide detailed instructions on how to perform learning tasks.
- Use question-and-answer instruction to ensure that students understand instructions for performance of assigned tasks.
- Supervise independent activity.
- Minimize disruptions, distractions, and interruptions.

Elaborations of the above summary of tactics can be obtained from reading the studies that are to follow. To be most effective, the instructional tactics need to be integrated into the particular instructional program being planned or presently being used.

CAUTIONS AND COMMENTS

Tactics not mentioned above apparently affect the time students stay focused on assigned tasks. For instance, the relationship between motivation and behavior has, in general, been established. The hypothesis needs to be tested asserting that students' interest in performing an assigned task is directly related to the amount of time they spend attending to the task and attempting to master the performance of it. Meanwhile, based on general research, it might be a good idea to take students' interests into account when assigning tasks and to make an effort to stimulate their interest in assigned tasks.

Threats to personal safety often prevent students from focusing on the performance of assigned tasks. In schools where violence is commonplace, students are frequently preoccupied with self-protection, which precludes their attending to assigned tasks. Although providing for student safety is not an instructional function, threats of bodily harm can make effective instruction difficult if not impossible. Student safety is prerequisite to effective instruction.

GENERALIZATION: ON KEEPING STUDENTS ON TASK

Achievement of learning objectives is enhanced when students spend more time attending to tasks formulated to enable them to achieve the learning objectives.

Supportive Research on Keeping Students on Task
Total number of supportive studies covered: 95

Groups of Studies

Author: Brophy & Good (1986)

Students: Elementary and secondary

Learning: Reading, mathematics, English, and biology achievement

Instructional Tactics:

- Assign learning tasks that are relevant to achievement of the learning objective.

- Formulate learning tasks in accordance with the diagnosis of the students' readiness characteristics.

- Control the formulation and assignment of tasks (as opposed to students' being left to their own devices).

- Spend more time on demonstration and guided practice (as opposed to independent student practice).

- Make sure the students are ready to work alone before assigning independent learning tasks.
- Assign independent learning tasks to follow immediately the guided practice activities.
- Supervise independent activities.

Other instructional tactics are employed in these studies that are applicable to other generalizations and will be presented in the appropriate chapters.

Findings: Use of the above instructional tactics was found to:

- Lead to greater student engagement time in the performance of tasks they are assigned.
- Lead to greater achievement than for students who did not have the benefit of the above instructional tactics.

The following are more specific findings associated with the use of the above instructional tactics:

- Teacher control of student behavior was shown to be related positively to student achievement and student engaged time.
- Supervision of seatwork was positively related to student achievement.
- Students' being expected to manage their learning on their own is negatively related to student achievement.
- Achievement gains were maximized when students consistently completed their work with few interruptions due to confusion or the need for help (achieved by selection of appropriate tasks and explaining thoroughly prior to assigning students to independent work).
- High rates of questioning of nonvolunteers leading to incorrect or no response was found to be associated negatively with achievement.
- Student engaged time was higher in classes where teachers were well organized. Student engaged time and teachers' being well organized were found to be related positively to student achievement.
- The teacher's ability to predict the difficulty students will have with particular items and the appropriateness of tasks they assign to students was found to be associated positively with student achievement.
- Amount of time spent working without supervision was found to be associated with low achievement gains.
- The percentage of assigned problems attempted by students was found to be related to achievement.

- Selection of appropriate goals and objectives was found to be associated positively with student achievement.
- Poor classroom management was found to be related negatively to student achievement.
- Achievement gain was found to be related to classroom management techniques that maximize task engagement and minimize interruptions.
- The number of student-relevant responses to teacher questions was found to be associated with student achievement.

Individual studies included in this research synthesis are identified by the symbol * in the reference list in Part V.

Author: Rosenshine & Stevens (1986)

Students: Elementary and secondary

Learning: Mathematics and reading achievement

Instructional Tactics:

- Spend more time in demonstrations and guided practice.
- Make sure that students are ready to work alone.
- Plan the seatwork activity to follow directly the guided practice.
- Ensure the seatwork activities are directly relevant to the demonstration and guided practice activities.

Other instructional tactics are employed in these studies that are applicable to other generalizations and will be presented in the appropriate chapters.

Findings: Use of the above instructional tactics was found to be related positively to student achievement.

Individual studies included in this research synthesis are identified by the symbol # in the reference list in Part V.

Author: Martens & Witt (2004)

Students: Ages 6–12

Learning: Academic achievement in elementary subjects

Instructional Tactics:

- Assign students tasks at their functioning level.

- Ensure students work at their mastery level rather than their frustrational level.
- Assign tasks with appropriate difficulty level, which can be defined as the ratio of knowns to unknowns in a task, assuring that the number of "knowns" increases.
- Intersperse, among more difficult problems, easy problems that students can complete quickly.
- Design lessons that incorporate peer tutoring.

Other instructional tactics from this review are applicable to other generalizations and are presented in the appropriate chapters of this book.

Findings: Use of the tactics listed above was found to be related positively to student achievement across content areas and to lead to greater engagement time by students on assigned tasks.

This research synthesis does not provide statistical data. The studies, some of which are meta-analyses, are designated with the symbol % in the references in Part V.

REFERENCE LIST

Brophy, J., & Good, T. (1986). Teacher behavior and student achievement. In M. C. Wittrock (Ed.), *Handbook of research on teaching* (3rd ed., pp. 328–375). New York: Macmillan.

Martens, B. K., & Witt, J. C. (2004). Competence, persistence, and success: The positive psychology of behavioral skill instruction. *Psychology in the Schools, 41*(1), 19–30.

Rosenshine, B., & Stevens, R. (1986). Teaching functions. In M. C. Wittrock (Ed.), *Handbook of research on teaching* (3rd ed., pp. 376–391). New York: Macmillan.

6

Maximizing Teaching Time

INTRODUCTION

The more guidance and facilitation students receive, the more likely they are to achieve the learning objectives. It is beneficial for students to receive guidance before performing tasks they are assigned to perform and for students to be given guidance while attempting to perform tasks they have been assigned to perform. When students receive more guidance and facilitation, they are more likely to perform assigned tasks correctly and to achieve the learning objective. Leaving them to their own devices in the performance of learning tasks may lead to incorrect or diminished performance as a result of lack of understanding or the temptation to engage in off-task behavior.

Achievement of learning objectives over time requires that teaching continually facilitates task performance and keeps students focused on tasks that enable the achievement of the learning objectives. Time spent on or dealing with activities such as administrative interruptions, socializing with students, returning papers or other assignments, moving students from place to place, music, arts and crafts, dance, and student disruptions directs time away from pursuit of the learning objectives. Such distractions are to be avoided if the learning objectives are to be achieved.

STUDENT BENEFICIARIES

The evidence indicates that the amount of time spent engaged in teaching activities enhances the academic achievement of students in elementary and secondary classrooms in the subject areas of English, reading, and mathematics. No evidence could be found to suggest that maximizing teaching time should not be stressed in all subject areas for all types of students including students in college, military, community, business, and adult education settings.

LEARNING ACHIEVED

Achievement in the content areas of English, reading, and mathematics is enhanced when more teaching time is devoted to the pursuit of intended learning objectives. It may be reasonable to expect that achievement may be enhanced in other content areas as well. In studies reviewed, student achievement was shown to be positively related to the amount of teaching time devoted to the pursuit of the learning objectives.

INSTRUCTIONAL TACTICS

The benefits of increasing the amount of time teachers engage in teaching activities is well supported by the evidence. There is a need for instructional planners and teachers to know the particular tactics that can be used to maximize teaching time. The following tactics are derived from the studies that demonstrate the benefits of increasing teaching time. Discretion has been used to interpret and reduce overlap in tactics used in different studies and to elaborate tactics.

Academic achievement is enhanced when teachers:

- Operate their classroom as a learning environment and spend most of their time on teacher-directed academic activities. In addition to providing the information necessary for students to accomplish tasks they are assigned to perform, the teacher should monitor students as they perform their assigned tasks.

- Minimize or avoid assigning students to independent activities such as silent reading, written assignments, and other independent task performance. Students are more likely to daydream, doodle, or socialize with other students during independent activities than if they are guided by the teacher during the task performance.

- Avoid assigning students to "busy work" or other activities designed to "kill time."

- Devote time available to teaching and not to getting organized. Be well prepared and plan daily activities productively. Use available teacher planning time wisely to this end.

- Avoid nonacademic student activities such as group sharing of personal issues, socializing, arts and crafts, music, and dance during the teaching of academic subjects. Such activities reduce the amount of time available to teach the academic subjects. Increasing the amount of time students are engaged in these activities has been shown to be negatively associated with student academic achievement. Although important, nonacademic activities should be scheduled in nonacademic settings and should not reduce the time needed for academic instruction.

- Except in the case of emergency, administrative intrusions into scheduled teaching time, whether in person or over a public address system, should be restricted to normally scheduled break times.

Elaborations of the above summary of tactics can be obtained from reading the studies that are to follow. To be most effective, the instructional tactics need to be integrated into the particular instructional program being planned or presently in use.

CAUTIONS AND COMMENTS

Although increasing the time a teacher teaches is related to greater student achievement, the benefits may be low or nonexistent for an ineffective teacher. Increasing teaching time and emphasis on the effectiveness of teaching during teaching time may be necessary to ensure greater student achievement. Information on what constitutes effective teaching is the subject of many other chapters in this handbook.

GENERALIZATION: ON MAXIMIZING TEACHING TIME

Achievement of learning objectives is enhanced when more teaching time is devoted to students to guiding students and facilitating their performance of academic tasks they are assigned to perform (rather than students performing tasks on their own, teachers dealing with outside intrusions, or students being assigned to nonacademic tasks).

Supportive Research on Maximizing Teaching Time
Total number of supportive studies covered: 68

Groups of Studies

Author: Brophy & Good (1986)

Students: Elementary and secondary

Learning: English, reading, and mathematics achievement

Instructional Tactics:

- Operate classroom as a learning environment and spend most of time on teacher-directed academic activities.
- Avoid or minimize nonacademic student activities such as group sharing, socializing, arts and crafts, music, and dance.
- Minimize outside intrusions.
- Devote time to teaching and not to getting organized. Be well prepared and plan daily activities proactively.

- Minimize or avoid assigning students to independent activities such as silent reading and written assignments during time that could be used for teaching.

Other instructional tactics are employed in these studies that are applicable to other generalizations and will be presented in the appropriate chapters.

Findings: Students who spent most of their time being taught by their teachers and less of their time engaged in games, group sharing, or socializing experienced greater gains in achievement. Time spent in nonacademic activities such as dance, music, arts and crafts, and storytelling was found to be negatively related to achievement. Teachers' getting organized rather than teaching was found to be negatively related to achievement. Students' working independently on activities such as silent reading and written assignments is negatively associated with student achievement.

Individual studies included in this logical synthesis of research are identified by the symbol * in the reference list in Part V.

Author: Anderson (1995)

Students: Elementary and secondary

Learning: Achievement

Instructional Tactics:

- Minimize time spent taking attendance, disciplining students, cleaning up and putting away, and moving from activity to activity.
- Maximize the amount of time spent actively teaching in relation to the amount of time available for teaching.

Other instructional tactics are employed in these studies that are applicable to other generalizations and will be presented in the appropriate chapters.

Findings: Teaching time is positively related to student achievement. In one study, the difference between allocated time for teaching and teaching time was 25 percent for high-achieving schools and 50 percent for low-achieving schools.

Individual studies included in this logical synthesis of research are identified by the symbol # in the reference list in Part V.

Individual Studies

Author: Mevarech & Kramarski (2003)

Students: Eighth graders

Learning: Algebra

Instructional Tactics:

- Students were placed in heterogeneous classes which met for 50 minutes for algebra instruction.
- The teacher introduced the new material during the first 10 minutes of class.
- Students were assigned to heterogeneous groups during which the students worked cooperatively solving problems for 30 minutes.
- The teacher worked as part of one group for about 10 to 15 minutes and provided help to other small groups upon request during the remaining group time.
- The teacher pulled the groups together to review the new concepts, to solve any problems giving most groups a problem, and to respond to students' questions during the last 10 minutes of class time.

Findings: Use of the above tactics related to use of teaching time was found to enhance academic achievement in mathematics.

Author: Blatchford et al. (2003)

Students: Primary (British reception year, year 1, and year 2)

Learning: Literacy and mathematics

Instructional Tactics:

- Minimize time spent on management and other non-teaching activities such as collecting dinner money and taking the register as a result of reduction in class size.
- Maximize time for more teaching activities such as working with the whole class, working one-on-one with a student, or working with a small group.

Findings: Use of the above tactics led to academic achievement in literacy and mathematics. The smaller the class, the more teaching overall took place. Children in small classes interacted more frequently with their teachers. Also, in small classes each child had more of the teacher's personal attention whether in a one-on-one situation, in a small group setting, or even in a whole class learning environment. In large classes, children interacted more with each other and less with the teacher and the content. Further, in large classes, the teacher spent more time on procedural talk.

Author: Smith et al. (2003)

Students: Primary

Learning: Achievement in reading, language arts, and mathematics

Instructional Tactics:

• Spend more time teaching.

• Provide students with more individual attention.

• Spend less time on classroom management and paperwork.

• Spend more time on hands-on, individualized activities.

• Spend less time disciplining students.

Findings: Teaching time is positively related to student achievement. In this study, the increase in teaching time is due to reduction in class size to 15:1. Findings support that fewer students means more teacher attention for each student; more teacher attention translates into fewer students falling behind; and more teaching time means students get more personal help with their work.

REFERENCE LIST

Anderson, L. W. (1995). Time, allocated, and instructional. In L. W. Anderson (Ed.), *International encyclopedia of teaching and teacher education* (2nd ed., pp. 204–207). Oxford: Pergamon Press.

Blatchford, P., Bassett, P., Goldstein, H., & Martin, C. (2003). Are class size differences related to pupils' educational progress and classroom processes? Findings from the Institute of Education Class Size Study of Children Aged 5–7 Years. *British Educational Research Journal, 29,* 709–730.

Brophy, J., & Good, T. (1986). Teacher behavior and student achievement. In M. C. Wittrock (Ed.), *Handbook of research on teaching* (3rd ed., pp. 328–375). New York: Macmillan.

Mevarech, Z. R., & Kramarski, B. (2003). The effects of metacognitive training versus worked-out examples on students' mathematical reasoning. *British Journal of Educational Psychology, 73,* 449–471.

Smith, P., Molnar, A., & Zahorik, J. (2003). Class-size reduction: A fresh look at the data. *Educational Leadership, 61*(1), 72–74.

7

Providing Ample Learning Time

INTRODUCTION

Students must be allowed the time necessary to perform correctly the tasks they are assigned if they are to achieve the desired level of performance. Students need time to contemplate their performance beforehand, to test the behaviors they hypothesize will result in correct performance, to evaluate the results of their performance, and to make refinements if need be. Students need time for trial and error. Excessively restricting the amount of time allowed for the performance of assigned tasks may lead to unnecessary student failure. Additionally, instructional planners and teachers, not students, are responsible for determining what is adequate time for the purpose of achieving the desired level of performance on tasks they are assigned to perform.

STUDENT BENEFICIARIES

The evidence indicates that allowing ample time to perform tasks correctly enhances the academic achievement of students in early childhood, preschool, kindergarten, elementary, middle, secondary, college, and adult learning classrooms. Moreover, academic achievement was improved in a wide range of content areas. No evidence could be found to suggest that allowing ample time for task performance should not be a priority in all subject areas for all types of students.

LEARNING ACHIEVED

Achievement in the content areas of mathematics, history, foreign languages, English, language arts, word recognition, spelling, writing, vocabulary, literature, reading, social sciences, sciences, social studies, nursing, management, business, and occupational areas is enhanced when ample time is allocated for the performance of tasks. In studies reviewed, allowing ample time for the performance of tasks was positively related to student achievement.

INSTRUCTIONAL TACTICS

The evidence well supports the need to allow students ample time for the performance of tasks. The following tactics are derived from studies that demonstrate the need to allow students ample time for the performance of tasks. Discretion has been used to interpret and reduce overlap in tactics used in different studies and to elaborate tactics.

Tactics employed are:

- Sufficient time should be allocated to permit students to perform assigned tasks correctly on an initial attempt.
- In the event a student does not perform a task correctly during the original allocated time, the student should be allowed additional time to perform the task correctly.
- Ample time for students to achieve the learning objectives needs to be planned for all assigned tasks such as in-class learning activities, homework, library projects, and laboratory activities.

Elaborations of the above summary of tactics can be obtained from reading the studies that are to follow. To be most effective, the instructional tactics need to be integrated into the particular instructional program being planned or presently being used.

CAUTIONS AND COMMENTS

Allocation of time for performance of assigned tasks should be based on the instructional planner's or the teacher's assessment of the ability of most of the students, not all of the students. Additional time should be afforded those students who cannot master an assigned task during the time most of the students could be expected to perform a task. Allocation of too much time in an attempt to accommodate all students may unnecessarily slow the progress of other students.

Although some research suggests a positive relationship between achievement and homework, insufficient research has been conducted, either in this country or internationally, to support this conclusively.

GENERALIZATION: ON AMPLE LEARNING TIME

Achievement of learning objectives is enhanced when students are given ample time to perform assigned tasks.

Supportive Research on Ample Learning Time
Total number of supportive studies covered: 456+

Groups of Studies

Author: Anderson (1985)

Students: Elementary and secondary

Learning: Achievement

Instructional Tactics:

- In the event a student does not perform a task correctly during the original allocated time, the student will be allowed additional time to perform the task correctly.
- Additional time may be either inside or outside the classroom, depending on the teacher's assessment.

Other instructional tactics are employed in these studies that are applicable to other generalizations and will be presented in the appropriate chapters.

Findings: The preceding instructional tactics were found to be associated with greater achievement. Additionally, it has been found that these tactics result in as high as 80 percent of the students mastering a learning task for which only 20 percent of the students achieve a level of mastery in a more traditional time allocation. Allocation of additional time to perform assigned tasks was *not* found to be related to an increase in off-task behavior.

Groups of studies reviewed in this logical synthesis of research did not provide statistical evidence. However, many of the individual studies included in the logical synthesis of research do contain statistical evidence. In the event that a reader wishes to view this evidence, an extensive listing of the individual studies reviewed is provided in the reference list in Part V. The studies are identified by the symbol %.

Author: Marliave & Filby (1985)

Students: Elementary and secondary

Learning: Reading and mathematics achievement

Instructional Tactics:

- The pace should be appropriate to the student and the subject matter.
- Students who do not perform a task correctly the first time are allowed additional time to perform the task correctly.

Other instructional tactics are employed in these studies that are applicable to other generalizations and will be presented in the appropriate chapters.

Findings: The preceding instructional tactics were found to be related to greater student achievement.

Groups of studies reviewed in this logical synthesis of research did not provide statistical evidence. However, many of the individual studies included in the logical synthesis of research do contain statistical evidence. In the event that a reader wishes to view this evidence, an extensive listing of the individual studies reviewed is provided in the reference list in Part V. The studies are identified by the symbol !.

Author: Kulik & Kulik (1987)

Students: Elementary, secondary, and college

Learning: Achievement in mathematics, science, and social studies

Instructional Tactics:

- Students work on unit material and repeat unit quizzes until they demonstrate mastery (Keller's model) or receive special tutorial assistance before moving on to new material (Bloom's model).
- A mastery level for each quiz and/or unit test is set.
- Students can retake quizzes from one to an unlimited number of times.
- Students who fail to reach the mastery level on a quiz are provided remedial support, usually individual tutoring.
- Students are allowed adequate time for learning in order to reach mastery.

Other instructional tactics from this review are applicable to other generalizations and are presented in the appropriate chapters of this book.

Findings: Use of the above tactics about mastery testing was found to enhance achievement.

The individual studies in this meta-analysis are listed in the references in Part V with the symbol =.

Author: Anderson (1994)

Students: Kindergarten, elementary, secondary, college, and other adult students

Learning: Achievement

Instructional Tactics: The following tactic associated with ample learning time and mastery learning is also presented in Bloom (1985), Block (1980), and others. Other tactics associated with Mastery Learning are applicable to other generalizations and are covered in the appropriate chapters.

- In the event a student does not perform a task correctly during the original allocated time, the student will be allowed additional time to perform the task correctly.

Findings: Positive achievement gains associated with Mastery Learning were seen in 90 percent of the studies reviewed in the seven meta-analyses.

Individual studies analyzed by these meta-analyses are identified in the reference list in Part V by the following symbols:

Kulik et al. (1990a) *

Kulik et al. (1990b) #

Slavin (1990) @

Guskey & Pigott (1988) $

Guskey & Gates (1986) &

Block & Burns (1976) +

It was not possible to determine the individual studies for which ample learning time was an instructional tactic for the Willett et al. (1983) analysis.

❖ ❖ ❖

Author: Swanson (2000)

Students: Learning disabled

Learning: Achievement in word recognition, reading comprehension, spelling memory/recall, mathematics, writing, vocabulary

Instructional Tactics:

- Provide student additional time to practice and to do repeated practice.

Other instructional tactics from this review are applicable to other generalizations and are presented in the appropriate chapters of this book.

Findings: Use of the above tactics was found to enhance achievement.

In this chapter, the author did not specifically identify the individual studies included in the meta-analysis.

Author: Bangert-Drowns et al. (2004)

Students: Elementary, middle, secondary, and college

Learning: Achievement (mathematics, science, social studies, literature, nursing, management, and natural resources

Instructional Tactics:

• Provide in-class time for a learning activity to be completed.

Findings: Use of this tactic was found to have a positive effect on academic achievement. Specifically, achievement in the content areas was enhanced when in-class time was allowed for writing assignments.

Studies in this meta-analysis are designated with the symbol ^ in the reference list in Part V.

Author: Martens & Witt (2004)

Students: Ages 6–12

Learning: Academic achievement in elementary subjects

Instructional Tactics:

• Provide frequent time for practice opportunities.
• Determine rates of practice.
  —Use choral responding during adult-led instruction.
  —Determine explicit timing during independent practice (seatwork).
• Help students set goals for homework completion; for example, complete 5 items in 10 minutes.

Other instructional tactics from this review are applicable to other generalizations and are presented in the appropriate chapters of this book.

Findings: Use of the tactics listed above was found to be effective in improving student achievement across content areas.

This research synthesis does not provide statistical data. The studies, some of which are meta-analyses, are designated with the symbol < in the references in Part V.

Author: Stallings & Stipek (1986)

Students: Early childhood and elementary

Learning: Achievement

Instructional Tactics:

• In the mastery learning approach, the amount of learning is a function of the amount of time spent in learning to the amount of time needed to learn the subject matter. Students are given additional time to reach the mastery level.

Findings: Additional time on learning leads to improved achievement. Sometimes the additional amount of time is from 10 percent to 50 percent.

The individual studies are not specified by the author; however, statistical data are included.

Author: Karweit (1993)

Students: Preschool and kindergarten

Learning: Achievement

Instructional Tactics:

• Increase the instructional time from half day to full day.

Findings: Use of the above tactics was found across this review of research studies to be effective in increasing achievement of disadvantaged kindergarten children.

It was not possible to determine the individual studies for which providing ample learning time was an instructional tactic in this synthesis of research.

Individual Studies

Author: Clark et al. (1983)

Students: College

Learning: Education

Instructional Tactics:

• Objectives are clearly specified.
• Diagnostic and formative evaluation is regular.
• Feedback is given following the evaluations.
• Corrective activities are keyed to the evaluations.
• Students not attaining 90 percent mastery completed the corrective work outside of class.

Findings: Use of the above tactics was found to enhance achievement. In addition, absences decreased in number, thus time in class was also a favorable factor.

Author: Gettinger (1984)

Students: Grades 4 and 5

Learning: Reading and spelling achievement

Instructional Tactics:

- One group of students was told to work on a task until each had achieved 100 percent accuracy.
- A second group of students was told the goal was to achieve 100 percent accuracy, and members were allowed to determine the time they needed to work on the task on their own.

Findings: The group of students that worked on the learning tasks until they achieved 100 percent accuracy scored an average 12.49 points higher on a spelling retention test and 12.80 points higher on a reading test than the group that was allowed to determine how much time they should spend on the assigned tasks.

❖   ❖   ❖

Author: Montazemi & Wang (1995)

Students: Undergraduate

Learning: Achievement in management information systems

Instructional Tactics:

- Students are provided instruction using a computer program which has a prespecified sequence of learning-lessons.
- Students are required to complete all learning-lessons within a section at the mastery level.
- Student mastery of learning-lessons is assessed when the student exits the learning-lesson.
- Students can spend as much time as they feel needed to learn the content of a learning-lesson.
- Students must master all sections (learning-lessons) of a chapter before going to the next chapter.

Other instructional tactics from this review are applicable to other generalizations and are presented in the appropriate chapters of this book.

Findings: Use of the above tactics was found to have a positive effect on achievement.

❖ ❖ ❖

Author: Aviles (1998)

Students: Undergraduate

Learning: Achievement in social work

Instructional Tactics:

- Provide clear learning expectations.
- Provide summative evaluation in the form of a graded criterion-referenced exam.
- Provide additional learning time in the form of feedback and corrective instruction.
- Provide students the opportunity to take another form of the exam for mastery.

Other instructional tactics from this review are applicable to other generalizations and are presented in the appropriate chapters of this book.

Findings: Use of the above tactics was found to improve students' achievement in introductory social work courses.

❖ ❖ ❖

Author: Krank & Moon (2001)

Students: College

Learning: Social sciences

Instructional Tactics:

- Students in one group worked to a mastery level, thus additional time was allowed for students to perform the task correctly.

Findings: Use of the above tactic was found to enhance achievement in the social sciences. Positive gains in achievement were associated with mastery learning combined with cooperative learning.

REFERENCE LIST

Anderson, L. W. (1985). Time and learning. In C. W. Fisher & D. C. Berliner (Eds.), *Perspectives on instructional time* (pp. 157–168). White Plains, NY: Longman.

Anderson, S. A. (1994). *Synthesis of research on mastery learning* (Information Analysis). (ERIC Document Reproduction Service No. ED 382 567)

Aviles, C. B. (1998). *A contrast of mastery learning and non-mastery learning instruction in an undergraduate social work course.* Paper presented at the annual meeting of the Council on Social Work Education, Orlando, FL.

Bangert-Drowns, R. L., Hurley, M. M., & Wilkinson, B. (2004). The effects of school-based writing-to-learn interventions on academic achievement: A meta-analysis. *Review of Educational Research, 74*(1), 29–58.

Block, J. H. (1980). Success rate. In C. Denham & A. Liberman (Eds.), *Time to learn* (pp. 95–106). Washington, DC: U.S. Government Printing Office.

Block, J. H., & Burns, R. B. (1976). Mastery learning. In L. Schulman (Ed.), *Review of research in education* (Vol. 4, pp. 3–49). Itasca, IL: F. E. Peacock.

Bloom, B. S. (1985). Learning for mastery. In C. W. Fisher & D. C. Berliner (Eds.), *Perspectives on instructional time.* White Plains, NY: Longman.

Clark, C. R., Guskey, T. R., & Benninga, J. S. (1983). The effectiveness of mastery learning strategies in undergraduate education courses. *Journal of Educational Research, 76*(4), 210–214.

Gettinger, M. (1984). Achievement as a function of time spent and learning and time needed for learning. *American Educational Research Journal, 21*(3), 617–628.

Guskey, T. R., & Gates, S. L. (1986). Synthesis of research on the effects of mastery learning in elementary and secondary classrooms. *Educational Leadership, 33*(8), 73–80.

Guskey, T. R., & Pigott, T. D. (1988). Research on group-based mastery learning programs: A meta-analysis. *Journal of Educational Research, 81*(4), 197–216.

Karweit, N. (1993). Effective preschool and kindergarten programs for students at risk. In B. Spodek (Ed.), *Handbook of research on the education of young children* (pp. 385–411). New York: Macmillan.

Krank, H. M., & Moon, C. E. Can a combined master/cooperative learning environment positively impact undergraduate academic and affective outcomes? *Journal of College Reading and Learning, 31*(2), 195–208.

Kulik, C., Kulik, J., & Bangert-Drowns, R. (1990a). Effectiveness of mastery learning programs: A meta-analysis. *Review of Educational Research, 60*(2), 265–269.

Kulik, C-L. C., & Kulik, J. A. (1987). Mastery testing and student learning: A meta-analysis. *Journal of Educational Technology Systems, 15*(3), 325–345.

Kulik, J., Kulik, C., & Bangert-Drowns, R. (1990b). Is there better evidence on mastery learning? A response to Slavin. *Review of Educational Research, 60*(2), 303–307.

Marliave, R., & Filby, N. N. (1985). Success rate: A measure of task appropriateness. In C. W. Fisher & D. C. Berliner (Eds.), *Perspectives on instructional time* (pp. 217–235). White Plains, NY: Longman.

Martens, B. K., & Witt, J. C. (2004). Competence, persistence, and success: The positive psychology of behavioral skill instruction. *Psychology in the Schools, 41*(1), 19–30.

Montazemi, A. R., & Wang, F. (1995). An empirical investigation of CBI in support of mastery learning. *Journal of Educational Computing Research, 13*(2), 185–205.

Slavin, R. E. (1990). Mastery learning re-considered. *Review of Educational Research, 60*(2), 300–302.

Stallings, J. A., & Stipek, D. (1986). Research on early childhood and elementary school teaching programs. In M. C. Wittrock (Ed.), *Handbook of research on teaching* (3rd ed.). New York: Macmillan.

Swanson, H. L. (2000). What instruction works for students with learning disabilities? Summarizing the results from a meta-analysis of intervention studies. In R. M. Gersten,

E. P. Schiller, & S. Vaughn (Eds.), *Contemporary special education research: Syntheses of the knowledge base on critical instructional issues* (pp. 1–30). Mahwah, NJ: Erlbaum.

Willett, J., Yamashita, J., & Anderson, R. (1983). A meta-analysis of instructional systems applied in science teaching. *Journal of Research in Science Teaching, 20*(5), 405–417.

8

Providing Transfer of Learning Instruction

INTRODUCTION

In our context, transfer of learning is defined as the application of prior learning to enable the performance of new tasks. That people transfer learning is an established fact, manifested in research findings as well as everyday experience. If people did not transfer what they learned to solve new problems that confront them, learning would be useless and adaptation and success in society would be virtually impossible.

The challenge to education is to facilitate the transfer of learning that is necessary for the achievement of learning objectives. Any sequence of tasks students are to perform to achieve a learning objective must be formulated so that the performance of earlier tasks in the sequence enables the performance of subsequent tasks. In essence, this ensures the readiness conditions that facilitate transfer. Under these conditions, to move progressively through the sequence of tasks to the achievement of the learning objective, students are able to transfer what they have learned from performing earlier tasks to complete the subsequent tasks in the sequence successfully.

It is a major responsibility of instruction to facilitate the transfer of learning needed to progress from one assigned task in a sequence to the next. Instruction must be planned and executed so that students acquire the learning they need to transfer in order to perform the next task in the sequence successfully. In addition, students need to be given instruction on how to determine the relevance of prior learning to the performance of the new tasks they are assigned to perform. In other words, students need to be taught the knowledge and skills they need to transfer in order to perform the new tasks they are assigned to perform. They also need to be taught how to determine the relevance of the knowledge and skills they have learned to the performance of new tasks. In general, it might be said that the more a task successfully performed in the past has in common with a newly assigned task, the more likely it is that the procedures used to perform the old task can be used to perform the newly assigned task successfully.

STUDENT BENEFICIARIES

The evidence indicates that transfer of learning instruction enhances the academic achievement of students in preschool, kindergarten, elementary, middle, junior high, secondary, college, and vocational classrooms. Additionally, transfer of learning instruction has been shown to enhance achievement in business and industry training situations. No evidence could be found to suggest that transfer of learning instruction should not be stressed in all subject areas for all types of students including students in military, community, and adult education settings.

LEARNING ACHIEVED

Achievement and transfer of learning in the content areas of reading, mathematics, science, social studies, the social sciences, algebra, physics, writing, vocabulary, related arts, literature, and vocational education are enhanced when transfer of learning instruction tactics are incorporated into the instruction. It may be reasonable to expect that achievement and transfer may be enhanced in other content areas as well. In studies reviewed, student achievement and transfer were shown to be enhanced when transfer of learning instruction was incorporated into the instruction.

INSTRUCTIONAL TACTICS

The following tactics are derived from the studies that demonstrate the benefits of transfer of learning instruction. Discretion has been used to interpret and reduce overlap in tactics used in different studies and to elaborate tactics.

- Ensure that students possess the readiness characteristics necessary to perform assigned tasks. Students cannot transfer skills they do not possess.
- Teach students to assess the extent to which they are able to perform assigned tasks.
- Teach procedures for performing tasks and the conditions for applying the procedures, relevant to the students' lives.
- Have students determine how procedures they are learning might be applied to perform tasks in the future.
- Teach students to detect correspondence between tasks and procedures.
- Show students how procedures used to perform one task can be used to perform analogous tasks, but not different tasks.

- Teach students to select a procedure to perform an assigned task that has been used successfully to perform analogous tasks.

- Give students practice selecting procedures to perform assigned tasks that have been used successfully to perform analogous tasks. Have students defend their selections based on analogy, then have them test the effectiveness of the procedure they have selected and evaluate the result.

CAUTIONS AND COMMENTS

Since learning is useful to the extent it can be transferred, educators need to maximize students' ability to transfer the learning they acquire to perform the tasks that confront them. Students' ability to transfer learning can be developed far beyond their native capacity to transfer learning automatically; for example, automatically greeting an acquaintance by name. Students can be taught *deliberately* how to transfer learning to perform current tasks. The method of instruction has been supplied under "Instructional Tactics." The *deliberate* transfer of learning stored in memory and repositories is an important part of systematic decision-making and problem solving.

GENERALIZATION: ON TRANSFER OF LEARNING INSTRUCTION

Achievement of learning objectives is enhanced when students are taught beforehand the knowledge and skills needed to perform assigned tasks and how to determine when learned knowledge and skills can be used to perform assigned tasks.

Supportive Research on Transfer of Learning Instruction
Total number of supportive studies covered: 244

Groups of Studies

Author: Rosenshine et al. (1996)

Students: Upper elementary (grade 3 and up), junior high, secondary, and college

Learning: Reading comprehension across subjects, mathematics, physics, and writing

Instructional Tactics:

- Model skills for students to use in reading a passage.

- Provide students with procedural prompts to guide their reading.

- Provide a passage for students to read.

- Give students feedback and provide corrective instruction as they read.

- Assess students on transfer of learning skills by assigning them a new passage to read followed by discussion in pairs using the procedural prompts.

Other instructional tactics are employed in these studies that are applicable to other generalizations and will be presented in the appropriate chapters.

Findings: Use of the above tactics was found to enhance transfer of skills leading to reading comprehension.

Individual studies analyzed by this meta-analysis are identified in the reference list in Part V by the symbol %.

Author: Fukkink & de Glopper (1998)

Students: Upper elementary and secondary

Learning: Vocabulary from context

Instructional Tactics:

- Teach students rules for learning the meaning of words in context—clue, cloze, and strategy.
- Provide explanation of clue and cloze procedures and provide explanation and modeling of strategy procedures.
- Provide practice in the use of the rules.
- Encourage students to use the rules when deciding on word meaning in a passage.
- Provide new material for students to apply the rules for learning the meaning of words in context.

Other instructional tactics from this review are applicable to other generalizations and are presented in the appropriate chapters of this book.

Findings: Use of the above tactics was found to be effective in achievement of word meaning comprehension in new material.

Studies in this meta-analysis are in the reference list in Part V and are marked with the symbol @.

Author: Gersten & Baker (2001)

Students: Learning disabled

Learning: Expressive writing

Instructional Tactics:

- Teach students transcription skills (spelling, grammar, and punctuation) and provide corrective instruction on those skills.
- Provide students with opportunities to use transcription skills within the writing process.
- Provide students daily writing instruction that includes time devoted to the transcription skills and the writing process. Students increase their automaticity with transcription skills which enable them to focus more on the planning, composing, and revising of the expressive writing.
- Provide students with opportunities to reflect on the relationship between the writing process and the written product.
- Require a new writing assignment to assess students' ability to transfer the previous learning of transcription skills and writing process skills.

Other instructional tactics from this review are applicable to other generalizations and are presented in the appropriate chapters of this book.

Findings: Use of the above tactics was found to enhance the transfer of learning related to writing achievement.

Studies associated with this meta-analysis are identified by the symbol + in the reference list in Part V.

❖   ❖   ❖

Author: Misko (1995)

Students: College, vocational school, and business and industry training

Learning: Achievement and transfer of learning

Instructional Tactics: The following instructional tactics that teach students how to achieve transfer of previous learning to current learning or problem-solving situations were derived by the author from studies reviewed:

- Teach facts, strategies, and relevant application of strategies together, prompting students to use previously acquired knowledge to solve current problems.
- Focus initially on the facts; then, once the student has acquired the facts, focus on the underlying principles.
- Alert students to take note of how information, facts, and principles currently being learned can be analogous to other contexts.

- Teach students to manipulate information presented to them by redefining the problem, transforming the problem into components that can be dealt with better, and looking for patterns and comparisons.

- Teach students to group items into smaller groups, rather than leaving them in one large group. When successful, the students are then asked to describe what they have done. This should be followed by a reminder that the strategy can be used for new tasks in the future.

- Teach students to use analogies by modeling and giving students ample time to practice using analogies to answer questions.

- Allow students time to practice looking for analogies and providing their reasons for their selection.

- Provide students relevant hands-on analogous tasks with which to practice.

Specific examples of the above tactics were not provided by the author. Many of the individual studies reviewed in this synthesis of research do provide specific information.

> *Findings*: Use of the above tactics was found to enhance learning and transfer of prior learning to new learning situations within and beyond the classroom.

Groups of studies reviewed in this logical synthesis of research did not provide statistical evidence. However, many of the individual studies included in the logical synthesis of research do contain statistical evidence. In the event that a reader wishes to view this evidence, an extensive listing of the individual studies reviewed is provided in the reference list in Part V. The studies are identified by the symbol *.

Author: Prawat (1989)

Students: Elementary, secondary, and college

Learning: Reading, mathematics, science, vocabulary, literature, and social studies achievement and transfer

Instructional Tactics: The following instructional tactics that facilitate knowledge acquisition and utilization were derived by the author from studies reviewed for this synthesis of research. The author divides these tactics into those associated with organization and those associated with student awareness.

Organization

- Develop comparisons between various ways of representing concepts and procedures through the use of concrete materials of various sorts.

- Use and teach students to use analogies to foster connections between objects and events in the real world and their symbolic connections.
- Teach in a way that makes explicit how important elements of the knowledge base, such as mathematics concepts and procedures, can be compared to one another.

Awareness

- Teach students to be aware of what they know and do not know.
- Provide students with information on other contexts in which known concepts or procedures may be used.
- Teach strategies in the context of analogous real situations.

Findings: Utilization of the above tactics was reported to enhance achievement and transfer.

Groups of studies reviewed in this logical synthesis of research did not provide statistical evidence. However, many of the individual studies included in the logical synthesis of research do contain statistical evidence. In the event that a reader wishes to view this evidence, an extensive listing of the individual studies reviewed is provided in the reference list in Part V. The studies are identified by the symbol #.

Author: Barley et al. (2002)

Students: Kindergarten, elementary, middle, and secondary at-risk students

Learning: Academic achievement (reading, writing and oral language, and mathematics)

Instructional Tactics:

- Self-questioning procedures and cognitive skills are modeled.
  - —Self-questioning procedures might include planning/preparation, idea generation, and self-regulation.
  - —Cognitive skills might include the "how to's" to accomplish tasks such as summarizing, identifying main ideas, using visual imagery, mapping elements/concepts of texts, verbalization of ideas/details, and note taking.
- Modeling is followed by explicit explanation of the procedures and skills.
- Materials are varied and include texts and problems that are meaningful and/or relevant to students.
- Time is arranged for instructional conversations about the use of procedures and skills.
- Time is provided for cooperative group work during which students have

opportunities to share ideas, provide feedback to each other, reflect on the process as well as the content, and explore multiple solutions.

• The above learning strategies are applied to novel content.

Other instructional tactics from this review are applicable to other generalizations and are presented in the appropriate chapters of this book.

Findings: Use of the above tactics led to improved academic achievement of at-risk students in reading, writing and oral language, and mathematics.

Studies in this synthesis directly related to decision-making instruction are designated with the symbol $ in the reference list in Part V.

Individual Studies

Author: Marzolf & DeLoach (1994)

Experiment 1

Students: 2½-year-old preschoolers

Learning: Transfer of learning to similar and dissimilar tasks

Instructional Tactics:

• Children in the experimental group were exposed to the easier similar task before being exposed to the more difficult dissimilar task. Children in the control group were exposed to the more difficult dissimilar task on two subsequent trials.

• The similar task involved the child's watching the researcher hide a small plastic toy dog (3 cm) in some location within a small model of a room. The researcher then hid a slightly larger plastic toy dog (7 cm) in a location within a slightly larger room (2:1 scale) corresponding to the location in which the smaller toy dog was hidden in the smaller room. The appearance and location of the furnishings, appearance of the room, and appearance of the toy dog were the same except for the size difference. The child was told that the larger toy dog was hiding in the same place in the larger room that the smaller toy dog was hiding in for the smaller room. The child was then instructed to try to find the larger toy dog in the larger room.

• For the dissimilar task, the same small model of a room and 3 cm plastic toy dog were used to show the child where the toy dog was hiding. For this task, the larger room was much larger (16:1) than the smaller room. The larger toy dog was a 15 cm stuffed toy dog. Otherwise, the room and location and appearance of the furniture were the same as for the smaller room. After showing the child where the smaller toy dog was hiding in the smaller room, the researcher hid the larger toy dog in the larger room in a location that corresponded to the location of the smaller toy dog in the smaller room. The child was then instructed to try to find the larger toy dog in the larger room.

- The children for both groups were shown the toy dogs for each task prior to performing the actual tasks.

Findings: The experimental group performed better on the similar task than the control group did performing the dissimilar task on the first trial without the prior exposure to the similar task. The experimental group was correct 67 percent of the time on its first try, and the control group was correct 27 percent of the time on its first try. When comparing the experimental group performance on the dissimilar task following performing the similar task to the control group's performance on its first trial on the dissimilar difficult task, without prior benefit of performing the similar or dissimilar tasks, the experimental group was correct 65 percent of the time on its first try as compared to the control group's being correct 27 percent of the time on its first try. On the comparison of the experimental group's performance on the dissimilar task after completing the similar task to the control group's second trial on the dissimilar task, the experimental group was correct 65 percent of the time on its first try as compared to the control group's being correct 35 percent of the time on its first try.

Experiment 2

Students: Three-year-old preschool children

Learning: Transfer of learning to similar and dissimilar tasks

Instructional Tactics:

- Children in the experimental group were exposed to an easier similar task before being exposed to a more difficult dissimilar task. Children in the control group were exposed to the more difficult dissimilar task on two subsequent trials. The strategies used in this experiment were similar to those used in experiment 1 with the exceptions that follow.

- The similar task involved the child's watching the researcher hide a small toy dog in some location within a small model of a room. The researcher then hid a larger toy dog in a location within a larger room corresponding to the location where the smaller toy dog was hidden in the smaller room. The appearance and location of the furnishings, appearance of the room, and the appearance of the toy dog were the same except for the size difference. The child was told that the larger toy dog was hiding in the same place in the larger room that the smaller toy dog was hiding in the smaller room. The child was then instructed to find the larger toy dog in the larger room.

- For the dissimilar task, the same small model of a room and small toy dog were used to show the child where the toy dog was hiding. For this task, the larger room's appearance and location of the furniture were the same as for the smaller room. However, for this task the colors of the furniture in the two rooms differed. After showing the child where the smaller toy dog was hiding in the smaller room, the researcher hid the larger toy dog in the larger room in a location that corresponded to the location where the smaller toy dog was in the smaller room. The child was then instructed to try to find the larger toy dog in the larger room.

Findings: The experimental group performed better on the similar task than the control group did performing the dissimilar task on the first trial without the prior exposure to the similar task. The experimental group was correct 88 percent of the time on its first try and the control group was correct 30 percent of the time on its first try. When comparing the experimental group's performance on the dissimilar task following performing the similar task to the control group's performance on its first trial on the dissimilar difficult task, without prior benefit of performing the similar or dissimilar tasks, the experimental group was correct 88 percent of the time on its first try as compared to the control group's being correct 30 percent of the time on its first try. On the comparison of the experimental group's performance on the dissimilar task after completing the similar task to the control group's second trial on the dissimilar task, the experimental group was correct 88 percent of the time on its first try as compared to the control group's being correct 65 percent of the time on its first try.

Author: Farrell (1988)

Experiment 1

Students: Eighth grade

Learning: Science transfer of learning

Instructional Tactics:

- The students were informed that they would be trying a new way to study science.

- All students were pretested on their knowledge of physical science principles associated with the balance beam, inclined plane, and hydraulic lift.

- The students were then randomly assigned to groups to study instructional material associated with the balance beam, inclined plane, or hydraulic lift. Each group studied only one topic area.

- Each group was further divided into two groups. One group received traditional science text material to study, and the other group received the traditional text material to study plus additional study on setting up and calculating proportions associated with the topic they were studying.

- Following the study periods, each student was posttested on all three topic areas. The tests required the student to fill in a missing distance or weight number associated with a condition for the balance beam, inclined plane, or hydraulic lift.

Findings: Students' score for the content area they individually studied were dropped from their posttest. Only scores associated with the content areas they had not studied were analyzed. Students receiving additional instruction in proportions scored on average 67.3 percent on the posttest as compared to 34.8 percent for students who had received only the traditional instruction.

Experiment 2

Students: Eighth grade students in a different school than those for experiment 1

Learning: Science achievement and transfer for learning

Instructional Tactics: The same as for experiment 1

Findings: Students' scores for the content area they individually studied were dropped from their posttest. Only scores associated with the content areas they had not studied were analyzed. Students receiving additional instruction in proportions scored on average 72.4 percent on the posttest as compared to 50.4 percent for students who had received only the traditional instruction.

Author: Gott et al. (1995)

Students: U.S. Air Force apprentice and master technicians

Learning: Avionics achievement and transfer of learning

Instructional Tactics:

- An experimental group received instruction, coaching, tutoring, and post-session feedback in its development of electronics equipment trouble-shooting skills via a computer instructional program. "The learning activity is centered in a computer simulated work environment" (p. 2).

- The work environment consisted of computer graphic displays, simulated controls, and icons for diagnostic meter probes.

- The activities involved hands-on practice solving problems in defective avionics equipment associated with the job for which the student was being trained.

- The student could request assistance from the computer coach/tutor at any time during the practice session.

- Assistance available was computer critique of the student's most recent action, information on what an expert would have done in this situation, and frequent hyper-graphic displays of equipment diagrams with textual definitions associated with the problem on which the student was working.

- Reasons behind procedural and strategic steps were made explicit.

- A standard trouble-shooting goal structure was used in coaching for all scenarios.

- General terminology was used rather than problem-specific terminology to allow for broader application.

- The student received reflective follow up from the computer in the form of a record and critique of the student's solution to the problem and provided a side-by-side expert solution to the problem with an accompanying cost-benefit reasoning for the expert solution.

- The reflective follow up emphasized general troubleshooting principles.

The control group received a "more traditional academic classroom" (p. 6) form of instruction. The instruction received by both groups related to human-controlled manual test stations. The transfer test tested the students' ability to transfer their acquired knowledge to a novel automated computer controlled system, which included technical data for programming information and the programming language.

Findings: Of the experimental group, 70.6 percent achieved the correct solution to the novel transfer test as compared to 63.6 percent for the control group. The experimental group committed 9 violations of the logical troubleshooting sequence as compared to 21 for the control group. The control group swapped 50 components without testing as compared to 3 for the experimental group.

Author: Mevarech & Kramarski (1997)

Students: Middle level—seventh graders

Learning: Mathematics

Instructional Tactics:

- Students are taught mathematics problem-solving strategies.

- Students are placed in heterogeneous groups of four and are given a mathematics problem.

- Students are also given prompt cards containing structured self-questioning strategies.

- Each student in the small group, in turn, tries to solve the problem and explain the reasons for the solution by using the self-questioning questions on the prompt card.

- Each student puts the problem in his own words using previously learned mathematical language.

- Through discussion with others in the group, the student determines the differences and similarities in this problem and problems solved in the past.

- The students determine which previously learned problem-solving strategies would be beneficial in solving the current problem; they determine why a particular strategy is appropriate; and they determine how to use the strategy to solve the problem.

- The students use the diversity of their own prior strategy and content knowledge to help solve new problems.

Other instructional tactics from this review are applicable to other generalizations and are presented in the appropriate chapters of this book.

Findings: Use of the above tactics was found to improve student achievement and to enhance structured self-questioning skills.

Author: Mevarech & Kramarski (2003)

Students: Eighth graders

Learning: Algebra

Instructional Tactics:

- Students were placed in heterogeneous classes for algebra instruction.

- Students were trained to use a structured self-questioning approach to solving problems.

   —Structured questions associated with the IMPROVE (acronym for *I*ntroducing new concepts, *M*etacognitive questioning, *P*racticing, *R*eviewing, *O*btaining mastery on cognitive processes, *V*erification, and *E*nrichment) program include the following types: comprehension, connection, strategic, and reflection.

   —Comprehension example—"What is the problem all about?"

   —Connection example—"How is the problem different from and/or similar to problems that have already been solved?"

   —Strategy example—"What strategies are appropriate for solving the problem and why are they appropriate?"

   —Reflection example—"Does this solution make any sense?" and "Why am I stuck?"

- Students were given a mathematics pretest.
- Students were then taught new algebra concepts using the cooperative learning structure.
- Students were given a booklet with content embedded within higher order thinking activities and with the four kinds of structured questions printed in the booklet for student use.
- The teacher introduced the new concept using a question-answer technique and modeled the structured self-questioning techniques to resolve the algebraic problems.
- Students were assigned to heterogeneous groups of one low, two middle, and one high achieving students based on their pretest performance.
- Students were given four algebra word problems of varying difficulty to solve, but the problem was of the same type as the teacher had modeled.
- Students were told to use the structured self-questions to solve the problems.
- Students formulated and answered structured self-questions while working on the problem.
- Each student read aloud a problem and attempted to solve the problem by using the structured self-questioning procedure.
- Students discussed the problem (participated in mathematical discourse) until group consensus on a response was reached.
- Students asked for teacher assistance only when they failed to reach group consensus on the answer.
- Students were expected to answer the structured self-questions orally and to write their answers.
- This process was repeated with new content.

Other instructional tactics from this review are applicable to other generalizations and are presented in the appropriate chapters of this book.

Findings: Use of the above tactics was found to enhance academic achievement in mathematics.

Author: Alfassi (2004)

Experiment I

Students: Secondary—ninth graders

Learning: Reading comprehension in language arts

Instructional Tactics:

- Students were explicitly taught reading comprehension strategies—questioning, summarizing, clarifying, and predicting.
- Teachers also modeled the strategies being taught.
- Students worked in small groups on an assigned content area text, taking turns leading discussion of the text while practicing the four comprehension strategies.
- Students provided feedback to each other related to strategy and content.
- Students were told that the reading comprehension strategies would apply to other content area texts and that they should use the strategies when reading silently or studying for a test.

Other instructional tactics from this review are applicable to other generalizations and are presented in the appropriate chapters of this book.

Findings: Use of the above tactics was found to increase reading comprehension.

Experiment II

Students: Secondary—tenth graders

Learning: Reading comprehension in social studies, science, related arts, and mathematics

Instructional Tactics:

- Students were given a pretest: four reading assessment passages.
- Teachers taught explicitly the four comprehension strategies—questioning, summarizing, clarifying, and predicting.
- Teachers modeled the strategies.
- Students were provided, during 20-day sessions, the interventions used in Experiment I.
- Students were given novel reading assessment passages to read along with questions to answer. Students used the four comprehension strategies.
- At the end of the year, students were again given four new reading assessment passages to read for comprehension using the four strategies and to answer questions about the content.

Other instructional tactics from this review are applicable to other generalizations and are presented in the appropriate chapters of this book.

Findings: Use of the above tactics was found to increase reading comprehension in responding to implicit questions in the areas of social studies, science, related arts, and mathematics.

REFERENCE LIST

Alfassi, M. (2004). Reading to learn: Effects of combined strategy instruction on high school students. *The Journal of Educational Research, 97*(4), 171–184.

Barley, Z., Lauer, P. A., Arens, S. A., Apthorp, H. S., Englert, K. S., Snow, D., & Akiba, M. (2002). *Helping at-risk students meet standards: A synthesis of evidence-based classroom practices*. Aurora, CO: Mid-continent Research for Education and Learning.

Farrell, E. (1988). How teaching proportionally affects transfer of learning: Science and math teachers need each other. *School Science and Mathematics, 88*(8), 688–695.

Fukkink, R. G., & de Glopper, K. (1998). Effects of instruction in deriving word meaning from context: A meta-analysis. *Review of Educational Research, 68*(4), 450–469.

Gersten, R., & Baker, S. (2001). Teaching expressive writing to students with learning disabilities: A meta-analysis. *The Elementary School Journal, 101*(3), 251–273.

Gott, S. P., et al. (1995, February). *Tutoring for transfer of technical competence*. Report from Armstrong Lab, Brooks AFB, TX. (ERIC Document Reproduction Service No. ED 382 817)

Marzolf, D. P., & DeLoach, J. S. (1994). Transfer in young children's understanding of spatial representations. *Child Development, 65*, 1–15.

Mevarech, Z. R., & Kramarski, B. (1997). IMPROVE: A multidimensional method for teaching mathematics in heterogeneous classrooms. *American Educational Research Journal, 34*(2), 365–394.

Mevarech, Z. R., & Kramarski, B. (2003). The effects of metacognitive training versus worked-out examples on students' mathematical reasoning. *British Journal of Educational Psychology, 73*, 449–471.

Misko, J. (1995). *Transfer: Using learning in new contexts*. Leabrook, Australia: National Centre for Vocational Education Research. (ERIC Document Reproduction Service No. ED 383 895)

Prawat, R. S. (1989). Promoting access to knowledge, strategy, and disposition in students: A research synthesis. *Review of Educational Research, 59*(1), 1–41.

Rosenshine, B., Meister, C., & Chapman, S. (1996). Teaching students to generate questions: A review of the intervention studies. *Review of Educational Research, 66*(2), 181–221.

9

Providing Decision-Making Instruction

INTRODUCTION

Some of the procedures people use to perform familiar, routine tasks are selected automatically and performed as habits; for example, procedures for brushing one's teeth, bathing, and getting dressed in the morning. Other procedures used primarily to perform less familiar, novel, and complex tasks are selected by means of reflective, deliberative decision-making; for instance, planning a vacation to a foreign country, developing a household budget for the first time, and learning a new subject in school. Whenever people do not know for certain how to proceed to perform a task, they revert to deliberate decision-making, which requires the relatively slow consideration of relevant factors and alternatives as a basis for deciding on a procedure to perform the task.

Assigned tasks are (1) to be based on student readiness capabilities and (2) to present students with new challenges so they can extend their learning. Quite often students do not know for certain what procedures to use to accomplish the tasks they are assigned. They need to employ deliberative decision-making tactics to derive a procedure. Research shows that when students are taught how to use decision-making tactics, their academic achievement is enhanced. In this chapter, effective decision-making instruction is described.

STUDENT BENEFICIARIES

The evidence indicates that decision-making instruction enhances the academic achievement of students in kindergarten, elementary, middle, secondary, college, and adult learning situations. No evidence could be found to suggest that decision-making instruction should not be stressed in all subject areas for all types of students including students in military, business and industry, and community education settings.

LEARNING ACHIEVED

Achievement in the content areas of reading, mathematics, science, social studies, language arts, literature, writing, oral language, and algebra is enhanced when decision-making instructional tactics are incorporated into the instruction. It may be reasonable to expect that achievement may be enhanced in other content areas as well. In studies reviewed, student achievement was shown to be enhanced when decision-making instruction was incorporated into the instruction.

INSTRUCTIONAL TACTICS

Instruction should be provided to help students to:

- Clarify task assignments. Ask, "What outcome am I to achieve? Are there any constraints such as time limits?" Ask for clarification of instruction if need be.

- Analyze the assigned task and instructions for clues that suggest the correct procedure to use. Ask, "What am I required to do to accomplish the assigned task?"

- Consider procedures that have been used to accomplish similar tasks. Ask, "Do I know of procedures that have been used to accomplish similar tasks? How can I find out about other procedures?" Students should be assisted in learning about additional procedures.

- Consider the relative merits of alternative procedures you know about or have found out about for accomplishing assigned tasks. Ask, "Which procedure is most likely to accomplish the assigned task? Do I have the ability and resources to execute the procedure?"

- Tentatively select a procedure for accomplishing the assigned task that can be predicted to succeed and is feasible to execute.

- Reevaluate the tentatively selected procedure and attempt to defend that it is feasible to execute and likely to accomplish the assigned task. Ask, "Am I overlooking any relevant factors or contingencies?"

- Decide on a procedure to test. Ask, "Why do I think the procedure will work?"

Students should be informed that the most considered procedure selected might fail. They can learn from their failure and select a procedure that is likely to succeed on an ensuing attempt.

Students need to be given the opportunity and time to practice decision-making, and teachers should model the correct decision-making behavior for the students.

CAUTIONS AND COMMENTS

It would make little sense to try to teach students to employ decision-making tactics if they do not possess the readiness characteristics necessary to achieve the learning objectives to begin with. Attempts to do so will merely result in frustrated students.

The reviews of studies and the individual studies included in these reviews utilize terms such as metacognition, metamemory, self-monitoring, self-regulation, and other jargon instead of the term decision-making.

GENERALIZATION: ON DECISION-MAKING INSTRUCTION

Achievement of learning objectives is enhanced when students are shown how to use decision-making tactics to consider and select procedures to perform assigned tasks.

Supportive Research on Decision-Making Instruction
Total number of supportive studies covered: 202

Groups of Studies

Additional instructional tactics are employed in the studies cited in the following reviews of research that are applicable to other generalizations and are presented in the appropriate chapters.

Author: Kucan & Beck (1997)

Students: Elementary and secondary

Learning: Reading comprehension

Instructional Tactics:

- *The teacher models a comprehension monitoring and hypothesis formation strategy.*
  - —The following example was derived from Collins & Smith (1982) and cited and elaborated on by Kucan & Beck (1997): "The basic idea of the modeling stage is that the teacher reads a story or other text aloud, making comments while reading. . . . As the text is being read, the teacher interrupts maybe once or twice a paragraph to make comments about . . . different aspects of the comprehension process . . . such as generating hypotheses, citing evidence to support or refute a hypothesis, expressing confusion, or making critical comments about text content" (p. 279).
- *The teacher elicits and guides student participation in the strategy activities.*

—The following example was derived from a Kucan & Beck (1997) description of tactics used in studies conducted by Brown & Palincsar (1989): "A teacher supports a small group of students in developing more sophisticated ways of interacting with the text by engaging them in a dialogue about the text that includes a consistent format of asking questions, identifying sections in the text that require clarification, summarizing the text, and making predictions about it" (p. 281).

• *The students are left to utilize the strategies taught on their own while they read.*

—In a study conducted by Miller (1985), students employed the following strategies while reading on their own: "Students were taught the use of a set of statements such as: 'First, I am going to decide if this story has any problems.' . . . Second, as I read I will ask myself, 'Is there anything wrong with the story?'" (p. 282).

—In a study conducted by Schunk & Rice (1985), students were taught the following strategy to answer questions about text they were assigned to read: Students were taught to verbalize statements such as "What do I have to do? (1) Read the question, (2) Read the story, and (3) Look for key words" (p. 283).

Findings: Use of the above tactics was found to lead to enhanced reading comprehension.

Groups of studies reviewed in this logical synthesis of research did not provide statistical evidence. However, many of the individual studies included in the logical synthesis of research do contain statistical evidence. In the event that a reader wishes to view this evidence, an extensive listing of the individual studies reviewed is provided in the reference list in Part V. The studies are identified by the symbol @.

Author: Dole et al. (1991)

Students: Elementary and secondary

Learning: Reading comprehension

Instructional Tactics:

• Students receive instructions to promote student-generated questions.
   —In an example from Singer & Donlan (1982), "Students were taught to generate story-specific questions from a list of general questions. . . . 'Who are the main characters in the story? What does the leading character initiate?' to create their own more specific questions about the particular story they were reading" (p. 246).

Findings: Use of the above tactic was found to lead to enhanced reading comprehension.

Groups of studies reviewed in this logical synthesis of research did not provide statistical evidence. However, many of the individual studies included in the logical synthesis of research do contain statistical evidence. In the event that a reader wishes to view this evidence, an extensive listing of the individual studies reviewed is provided in the reference list in Part V. The studies are identified by the symbol $.

Author: Rosenshine & Meister (1994)

Students: Elementary and secondary

Learning: Reading comprehension

Instructional Tactics:

- The student receives instruction on *comprehension-fostering* strategies and practices the strategies such as (1) question generation, (2) summarization, (3) prediction, and (4) clarification.
- The strategies are modeled.
- Students are initially guided in their use of newly learned strategies.
- Students are encouraged to initiate discussion and to react to other students' statements by (1) suggesting other questions, (2) elaborating on a summary, and (3) commenting on another's predictions.

Findings: Use of the above tactics led to enhanced reading comprehension.

Specific examples of the above tactics were not provided by the author. Many of the individual studies reviewed in this synthesis of research do provide specific information. These studies appear in the reference list in Part V. These studies are identified by the symbol !.

Author: Salomon & Perkins (1989)

Students: Elementary, secondary, and adults

Learning: Mathematics, science, and reading achievement

Instructional Tactics:

- Teach students not to jump to conclusions based on their first impulse as to what their correct decision should be.

- Teach students to examine provided information for task-relevant clues or underlying meanings that may help them in determining the correct course of action to take.

- Teach students to question whether or not something they have learned in some other content area, or related prior learning, might assist them in making the correct decision as to the correct procedure to apply to the current learning task.

  —The following example is provided: "A student pondering a physics problem . . . might ask, 'Do I know anything from calculus that might address this?'"

- Teach students to question their understanding and their decisions on how to proceed.

- Allow students time to practice decision-making tactics.

Findings: Use of the above tactics was found to enhance achievement.

Other than the one example cited, specific examples of the above tactics and statistical evidence were not provided by the author. Many of the individual studies reviewed in this synthesis of research do provide specific information. These studies appear in the reference list in Part V and are identified by the symbol *.

Author: Prawat (1989)

Students: Elementary, secondary, and college

Learning: Mathematics, science, reading, literature, and social studies

Instructional Tactics:

- Teach students to examine how important concepts and procedures previously learned might be applied to a current assigned task.

- Teach students to analyze problems in terms of initial goals, available resources, problem limitations, and anticipated outcomes as an aid to deciding on procedures to employ.

- Require students to explain, elaborate, or defend a course of action they have decided on to others.

- Provide students with information on how known concepts or procedures applicable to one content area may be used in other content areas.

Findings: Use of the above tactics was found to enhance achievement.

Specific examples of the above tactics and statistical evidence were not provided by the author. Many of the individual studies reviewed in this synthesis of research do provide specific information. These studies appear in the reference list in Part V and are identified by the symbol #.

❖ ❖ ❖

Author: Rosenshine et al. (1996)

Students: Elementary, secondary, and college

Learning: Reading comprehension

Instructional Tactics: The following instructional tactics, reported as procedural prompts, were identified by the authors in their review of the research.

• *Signal Words*: Students are provided with a list of words for starting questions such as "who, what, where, when, why, and how." Students are then taught how to use these words to generate questions about the to-be-learned material.

• *Generic question stems and generic questions*: Students are provided with a list of generic questions or stems of generic questions to aid them in the formulation of their own questions. The following examples are from studies as cited by Rosenshine et al. (1996).

—King (1989, 1990, and 1992) used the following generic question stems: "How are . . . and . . . alike?" "What is the main idea of . . .?" "What are the strengths and weaknesses of . . .?" "How does . . . affect . . .?" "How does . . . tie in with what we have learned before?" "What is a new example of . . .?" "What conclusions can you draw about . . .?" and "Why is it important that . . .?"

—Weiner (1978) provided students with the following list of generic questions: "How does this passage or chapter relate to what I already know about the topic?" " What is the main idea of this passage or chapter?" "What are five important ideas that the author develops that relate to the main idea?" "How does the author put the ideas in order?" "What are the key vocabulary words? Do I know what they all mean?" and "What special things does the passage make me think about?"

• *Main Idea*: Students are taught to identify the main idea of a paragraph and to use the main idea to formulate questions.

—Dreher & Gambrell (1985) suggested the following to students: (1) identify the main idea for each paragraph; (2) form questions which ask for new examples of the main idea; (3) if it is difficult to ask for a new instance, then write a question about a concept in the paragraph in a paraphrased form.

—Nolte & Singer (1985) taught students to identify four elements of a story and to use the elements to generate questions. The four elements of a story they used are (1) setting, (2) main character, (3) characters' goal, and (4) obstacles. Students were taught that possible questions for the character element might be: "Who is the leading character?" "What action does the character initiate?" and "What do you learn about the character from this action?"

Findings: Use of the above tactics was found to enhance reading comprehension.

Additional examples of the above tactics may be provided by the authors of the individual studies reviewed in this synthesis of research. These studies appear in the reference list in Part V and are identified by the symbol &.

Author: Barley et al. (2002)

Students: Kindergarten, elementary, middle, and secondary at-risk students

Learning: Academic achievement (reading, writing and oral language, and mathematics)

Instructional Tactics:

- Self-questioning procedures and cognitive skills are modeled.
  - —Self-questioning procedures might include planning/preparation, idea generation, and self-regulation.
  - —Cognitive skills might include the "how to's" to accomplish tasks such as summarizing, identifying main ideas, using visual imagery, mapping elements/concepts of texts, verbalization of ideas/details, and note taking.
- Modeling might be followed by explicit explanation of the procedures and skills.
- Materials are varied and include texts and problems that are meaningful and/or relevant to students.
- Time is arranged for instructional conversations about the use of procedures and skills.
- Time is provided for peer-guided and independent practice.
- Time is provided for cooperative group work during which students have opportunities to share ideas, provide feedback to each other, reflect on the process as well as the content, and explore multiple solutions.

Other instructional tactics from this review are applicable to other generalizations and are presented in the appropriate chapters of this book.

Findings: Use of the above tactics led to improved academic achievement of at-risk students in reading, writing and oral language, and mathematics.

Studies in this synthesis directly related to decision-making instruction are designated with the symbol + in the reference list in Part V.

Individual Studies

Author: Mevarech & Kramarski (1997)

Students: Middle level—seventh graders

Learning: Mathematics

Instructional Tactics:

- Students are given a mathematics word problem.
- Students are also given prompt cards to hold which contain structured self-questioning procedures used to get to a goal.
- Students use the prompt cards during practice and lesson discussion settings to prompt their discussion.
- Each student in the small group, in turn, tries to solve the problem and explain the reasons for the solution by using the questions on the prompt card.
- Students provide each other feedback by asking questions.
- The cards contain three questions:
  —A comprehension question: What is in the problem?
  —A connection question: What are the differences between the problem being worked on and previous problems worked on?
  —A strategic question: What is the procedure/tactic/principle appropriate for solving the problem?
  —Students are taught that the prompt questions are designed to help them think about the problem before solving it, to focus on differences and similarities of previous problems, and to think about the tasks along with a rationale that are appropriate for solving the problem.
- The student reads the question aloud, describes in his own words the concept, and leads discussion about the meaning of the concept or the ways the problem concept can be classified. The student works through this process orally—thinking aloud.
- Through discussion with others in the group, the student determines the differences and similarities in this problem and problems solved in the past. Students correct each others' errors through discussion and adhering to the prompt card concept.
- The students determine which previously learned procedures would be beneficial in solving the current problem, they determine why that procedure is appropriate, and they determine how to use the procedure to solve the problem.

- The students use the diversity of their own prior knowledge to self-regulate their learning.

Other instructional tactics from this review are applicable to other generalizations and are presented in the appropriate chapters of this book.

Findings: Use of the above tactics related to decision-making instruction was found to improve student achievement and to enhance decision-making skills.

Author: Mevarech & Kramarski (2003)

Students: Eighth graders

Learning: Algebra

Instructional Tactics:

- Students were trained to use a structured self-questioning procedure to solve problems.

  —Structured questions associated with the IMPROVE (acronym for *I*ntroducing new concepts, *M*etacognitive questioning, *P*racticing, *R*eviewing, *O*btaining mastery on cognitive processes, *V*erification, and *E*nrichment) program include the following types: comprehension, connection, strategic, and reflection.
  —Comprehension example: "What is the problem all about?"
  —Connection example: "How is the problem different from and/or similar to problems that have already been solved?"
  —Strategic example: "What procedures are appropriate for solving the problem and why are they appropriate?"
  —Reflection example: "Does this solution make any sense?" and "Why am I stuck?"

- The new concept was introduced using a question-answer technique and modeling the structured self-questioning procedures to resolve the algebraic problems.

- Students within cooperative groups were given algebra word problems to solve.

- Students formulated and answered structured questions while working on the problem.

- Students discussed the problem (participated in mathematical discourse) until consensus on a response was reached.

- Students asked for assistance only when they failed to reach consensus on the answer.

- Students were expected to answer the structured self-question procedure questions orally and to write the answers.

Other instructional tactics from this review are applicable to other generalizations and are presented in the appropriate chapters of this book.

Findings: Use of the above tactics was found to enhance academic achievement.

❖ ❖ ❖

Author: Alfassi (2004)

Students: Secondary—ninth graders

Learning: Reading comprehension in language arts

Instructional Tactics:

Experiment I

- Teachers taught and modeled the reading comprehension strategies below:
  - —*Generating questions*: The teacher explained that during reading of a passage, the reader should ask himself questions to assure understanding and that the best questions to ask are those the teacher would ask on a test such as main facts and key terms. The teacher modeled ways to generate questions and illustrated this by continuously verbalizing her thought processes about the facts and terms, thus sharing her reasoning about the generation of questions.
  - —*Summarizing*: The teacher used the same oral reasoning process to illustrate the finding of main ideas and supporting ideas in a passage. She demonstrated how to summarize in one or two sentences. Further, she modeled the generation of main idea questions.
  - —*Clarifying*: The teacher, upon hearing words unfamiliar to students or passages they found difficult to understand, modeled ways to understand the words within the context of the passage. Again, the teacher orally modeled inferential and clarifying questions to enable understanding of the passage.
  - —*Predicting*: The teacher orally shared possible predictions for the next paragraph in a passage, then the teacher orally constructed predicting questions which often were based on prior knowledge.
  - —Throughout the modeling and oral thought processing, the teacher differentiated among factual knowledge questions, inferred questions, and prior knowledge questions.
- Time was provided for guided practice during which students used the structured self-questioning procedures.

- Cues and scaffolding were provided during the guided practice.
- Scaffolding was diminished over time.
- Students worked in small groups on an assigned content area text taking turns leading discussion of the text while practicing the four comprehension techniques.
- Students provided feedback to each other using the techniques modeled orally by the teachers.
- Students were told that the reading comprehension techniques would apply to other content area texts and that they should use the techniques when reading silently or studying for a test.
- Students were given a new set of four reading assessment passages on which they were to apply the techniques they learned.

Other instructional tactics from this review are applicable to other generalizations and are presented in the appropriate chapters of this book.

Findings: Use of the above tactics was found to increase reading comprehension.

REFERENCE LIST

Alfassi, M. (2004). Reading to learn: Effects of combined strategy instruction on high school students. *The Journal of Educational Research, 97*(4), 171–184.

Barley, Z., Lauer, P. A., Arens, S. A., Apthrop, H. S., Englert, K. S., Snow, D., & Akiba, M. (2002). *Helping at-risk students meet standards: A synthesis of evidence-based classroom practices.* Aurora, CO: Mid-continent Research for Education and Learning.

Brown, A. L., & Palincsar, A. S. (1989). Guided, cooperative learning, and individual knowledge acquisition. In L. B. Resnick (Ed.), *Knowing, learning, and instruction: Essays in honor of Robert Glaser* (pp. 393–451). Hillsdale, NJ: Erlbaum.

Collins, R., & Smith, E. E. (1982). Teaching the process of reading comprehension. In D. K. Detterman & R. J. Sternberg (Eds.), *How and how much can intelligence be increased?* (pp. 173–185). Norwood, NJ: Ablex.

Dole, J. A., Duffy, G. G., Roehler, L. R., & Pearson, P. D. (1991). Moving from the old to the new: Research on reading comprehension instruction. *Review of Educational Research, 61*(2), 239–264.

Dreher, M. J., & Gambrell, L. B. (1985). Teaching children to use a self questioning strategy for studying expository text. *Reading Improvement, 22*, 2–7.

King, A. (1989). Effects of self-questioning training on college students' comprehension of lectures. *Contemporary Educational Psychology, 14*, 366–381.

King, A. (1990). Improving lecture comprehension: Effects of a metacognitive strategy. *Applied Educational Psychology, 5*, 331–346.

King, A. (1992). Comparison of self questioning, summarizing, and notetaking-review as strategies for learning from lectures. *American Educational Research Journal, 29*, 303–325.

Kucan, L., & Beck, I. L. (1997). Thinking aloud and reading comprehension research: Inquiry, instruction, and social interaction. *Review of Educational Research, 67*(3), 271–299.

Mevarech, Z. R., & Kramarski, B. (1997). IMPROVE: A multidimensional method for teaching mathematics in heterogeneous classrooms. *American Educational Research Journal, 34*(2), 365–394.

Mevarech, Z. R., & Kramarski, B. (2003). The effects of metacognitive training versus worked-out examples on students' mathematical reasoning. *British Journal of Educational Psychology, 73*, 449–471.

Miller, G. E. (1985). The effects of general and specific-instruction training on children's comprehension monitoring performance during reading. *Reading Research Quarterly, 20*(5), 616–628.

Nolte, R. Y., & Singer, H. (1985). Active comprehension: Teaching a process of reading comprehension and its effects on reading achievement. *The Reading Teacher, 39*, 24–31.

Prawat, R. S. (1989). Promotion access to knowledge, strategy, and disposition in students: A research synthesis. *Review of Educational Research, 59*(1), 1–41.

Rosenshine, B., & Meister, C. (1994). Reciprocal teaching: A review of the research. *Review of Educational Research, 64*(4), 479–530.

Rosenshine, B., Meister, C., & Chapman, S. (1996). Teaching students to generate questions: A review of intervention studies. *Review of Educational Research, 66*(2), 181–221.

Saloman, G., & Perkins, D. N. (1989). Rocky roads to transfer: Rethinking mechanisms of a neglected phenomenon. *Educational Psychologist, 24*(2), 113–142.

Schunk, D. H., & Rice, J. M. (1985). Verbalization of comprehension strategies: Effects on children's achievement outcomes. *Human Learning, 4*(1), 1–10.

Singer, H., & Dolan, D. (1982). Active comprehension: Problem solving schema with question generation for comprehension of complex short stories. *Reading Research Quarterly, 17*, 166–186.

Weiner, C. J. (1978). *The effect of training in questioning and student question-generation on reading achievement.* Paper presented at the annual meeting of the American Educational Research Association, Toronto.

$\boxed{10}$

Providing Prediction and Problem-Solving Instruction

INTRODUCTION

Predictive ability is defined as the ability to forecast accurately outcomes from antecedent conditions. To appreciate the value of predictive ability in improving academic achievement and achieving other goals, whatever they may be, it is helpful to understand that predictive ability has many applications. Predictive ability not only involves ability to predict that something will happen again because it has a history of happening in a particular pattern but also involves being able to predict what might happen in the future that has never happened before and being able to predict ways of making it happen or preventing it from happening.

Predictive ability is largely responsible for discovery and invention as well as academic and everyday achievements. Sports coaches must be able to predict strategies that will win games, or they will be replaced. Students must be able to predict that study and test-taking skills will yield higher grades, or they will fail in school. Businessmen must be able to predict how to realize a profit, or they will go under. To avoid accidents, drivers must be able to predict how to avoid cars and other obstacles.

In addition to its general contribution to problem solving of any kind, there is evidence that predictive ability enhances academic achievement and that students' predictive ability can be improved through instruction. Research corroborates the relationship of predictive ability to academic achievement. Several studies indicate that good readers are good predictors (Benz & Rosemier, 1966; Greeno & Noreen, 1974; Henderson & Long, 1968; Freeman, 1982; Zinar, 1990). In a more general context, Dykes (1997) demonstrated that predictive ability contributes substantially to academic success in high school. In many cases predictive ability proves to be a better predictor of success in general and learning in particular than does I.Q. (Friedman, 1974; Dykes, 1997).

A number of studies show that instruction designed to enhance predictive ability improves academic achievement (Denner & McGinley, 1990; Walker & Mohr, 1985;

Hunt & Joseph, 1990; Reutzel & Fawson, 1991; Chia, 1995; Hurst & Milkent, 1994; Nolan, 1991; Friedman & Maddock, 1980).

STUDENT BENEFICIARIES

Research shows that predictive and problem solving ability is related to academic achievement in higher education, college, high school, middle school, and elementary school. Predictive and problem solving ability has also been shown to be related to achievement in the military and in industry.

LEARNING ACHIEVED

Instruction that enhances predictive and problem solving ability has been related to increased academic achievement in the areas of reading, basic sciences, clinical sciences, and language arts as well as the content areas covered by the Comprehensive Test of Basic Skills and the National Board of Medical Examiners.

INSTRUCTIONAL TACTICS

Instructional tactics involve teaching the prediction cycle as an effective means of problem solving in all academic areas as well as daily living.

First, students are given an overview of the prediction cycle so that they can see the parts/whole relationships and how the functions in the cycle are coordinated to solve problems.

Problem solving begins when motivation is aroused and presses for satisfaction. Motivation activates the activities in the prediction cycle, which consists of four stages. Stage 1, Diagnosing Problems, and Stage 2, Predicting Solutions, involve making predictions. Stage 3, Implementing Solutions, and Stage 4, Assessing Achievement, involve testing predictions as shown in the diagram of the prediction cycle on the next page. A brief overview and example of the process follows.

PROVIDING AN OVERVIEW OF THE PREDICTION CYCLE

Motivation

People are motivated to satisfy their desires without knowing initially what to do about them. For example, a student is worried about failing science and is motivated to do something about the situation.

Making Predictions

The student needs to predict a way to alleviate this worry. To proceed, the student (1) diagnoses the problem as a basis for (2) predicting a solution.

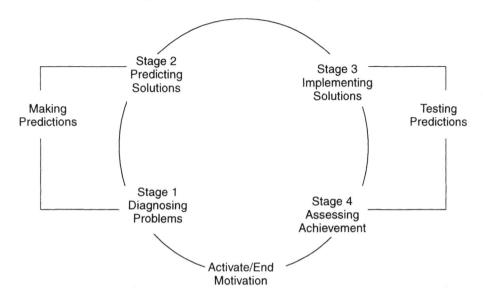

Stage 1, Diagnosing Problems

Defining the Problem. To satisfy desires it is advantageous to define them as problems. A problem can be defined as a discrepancy between an existing state and a desired state. To continue with our example, the existing state is: The student is earning a grade of "F" in science. The desired state is: The student wants to earn a "B" in science by the end of the school term.

Once the problem is defined, the solution becomes clear: to progress from a grade of "F" to a grade of "B." To complete the diagnosis, factors that need to be controlled to achieve a solution are determined.

Factors to Be Controlled. Factors that need to be controlled are those factors that must be attended to or manipulated to generate progress from the existing state to the desired state.

For example, the student must identify the particular tasks that must be performed competently to raise the science grade to a "B." A conference with the teacher might reveal the following factors to be controlled.

- Earn a "B" on the science project.
- Improve performance on weekly quizzes.
- Earn a "B" on the final exam.

Constraints. In addition to defining the problem and identifying factors to be controlled, constraints are identified so that realistic limitations can be dealt with. Continuing with the example, one constraint would be earning a "B" by the end of the school term.

Stage 2, Predicting Solutions

Once factors to be controlled and constraints are identified to solve the problem, an attempt is made to predict a solution by (1) identifying means of controlling the factors, providing for the constraints, and (2) prescribing procedures to apply the means.

Means of Controlling the Factors.

- Means of controlling the factors are identified through recall and research, if need be.
- Common elements of previous science projects that won awards are identified, and a similar science project is selected.
- Engage a tutor to improve the student's understanding of science and to teach test-taking skills.
- Increase study time.

Prescribing Procedures. A procedure is prescribed to coordinate the means of controlling the factors providing for constraints. For instance a procedure is derived to implement the science project, engage a tutor and schedule tutoring lessons, and increase study time in time to raise the student's grade to a "B" within this school term.

Testing Predictions

After the problem is diagnosed at Stage 1 and a solution is predicted in Stage 2, it is necessary to test the prediction that the proposed solution will solve the problem. This entails implementing the solution and then assessing the outcome.

Stage 3, Implementing Solutions

To implement solutions, the prescribed procedure is executed according to specifications. For example, the procedure prescribed for completing the science project, being tutored, and increasing study time are implemented exactly as planned.

Stage 4, Assessing Achievement

After implementing the solution, observations are made of the outcome. Then the outcome is compared to the desired state to see the extent to which the desired state has been achieved. If it is achieved, the implemented solution would be considered to be effective. Side effects are also observed, as well as efficiency factors, such as costs of implementing the solution. For instance, at the end of the school term the student notes the grade on his report card to see if he has earned the final grade of "B" as desired. He also determines the final cost of the tutoring he received, as well as side effects. Improved study tactics taught by his tutor might have improved his grades in other courses.

This completes the initial execution of the prediction cycle.

Motivation

After the completion of each prediction cycle, motivation is revisited and reappraised. If the desired state is achieved, the problem might be considered solved, and there might not be any motivation to continue. In this case, attention would be turned to other problems which people are motivated to solve. This would constitute the end of this problem-solving mission. For example, the student might earn a final grade of "B" and turn his attention elsewhere to solve other disturbing problems he is motivated to solve. On the other hand, the desired state might be achieved and there might be motivation to recycle to increase efficiency; for example, to reduce the time and money that was required to implement the solution the first time; or recycling might be initiated to remove an undesirable side effect. To recycle, people move to Stage 1 again to diagnose the problem anew and then proceed through the remaining stages to complete the prediction cycle another time.

If the desired state is not achieved, there might be motivation to recycle to try again to solve the problem. Many problems are not solved on the first attempt. Rather, they are solved by successive approximation, when one cycle after another is executed until the problem is solved. Each time the cycle is completed, something new can be learned that makes it more likely that a solution will be achieved on a subsequent attempt. In contrast, there may be no motivation to continue to try to solve the problem. The pursuit might be abandoned because there is no longer any interest in solving the problem or resources are insufficient to continue pursuing a solution.

For whatever reason motivation is sufficient to recycle, the motivation activates the recycling and the four stages of the cycle are repeated in order.

Demonstrating the Relevance of the Prediction Cycle

Once an overview of the prediction cycle is presented to students and they understand the parts/whole relationships of the cycle, the relevance of the cycle to solving problems in all subject areas and daily living are demonstrated for the students. This can be achieved by showing students how the prediction cycle can be applied to solve problems in science, math, language arts, and social studies as well as in their daily lives.

Detailing Each Stage of the Prediction Cycle

After students understand how the cycle can be used to solve any kind of problem, it is necessary to teach them how to perform each stage of the cycle in detail. It takes more than a general understanding of the cycle to be able to apply it. Students must become proficient in performing each stage of the cycle. Following are some of the nuances and details students need to learn.

Stage 1, Diagnosing Problems

Defining Problems. Students are taught the advantages of defining a problem as a discrepancy between an existing state and a desired state, rather than just specifying a desired state as a goal or objective. Defining an existing state as a starting point as well as a desired state facilitates predicting solutions at Stage 2 and assessing achievement at Stage 4. It is advantageous to know both the existing state or starting point and the desired state when planning a solution, rather than knowing only the desired state since the solution must produce progress from the existing to the desired state. It is also advantageous to know both the existing state and the desired state when constructing an observation instrument to detect progress from the existing to the desired state, rather than just knowing the desired state.

Factors to Be Controlled. Many factors that need to be controlled to generate progress from the existing to the desired state are causal agents. Students need to learn about cause-effect relationships so that they can understand that causal agents may need to be identified when the effect being pursued is a specified desired state.

Constraints. Students are taught that desired states cannot be pursued without considering constraints. It is often necessary to avoid harmful side effects when solving problems, and it is often necessary to attempt to solve problems with limited resources.

After students understand in detail how problems are diagnosed, they are assigned to diagnose problems in various subject areas and in their daily lives until they become competent.

Stage 2, Predicting Solutions

To become competent at predicting solutions, students must be able to identify means of controlling the factors that were identified in Stage 1 and prescribe procedures for solving the problem.

Means of Controlling the Factors. Students must be taught how to conduct research to identify means of controlling factors they are interested in controlling. They need to be taught how to access and locate information in libraries and computer data banks. Sophistication can be developed gradually over time.

Prescribing Procedures. Initially students should be taught to find appropriate procedures by searching libraries and data banks. Later they can be taught methods of deriving procedures when standard operating procedures are not available.

Many methods for planning procedures are available; for instance, Project Evaluation and Review Technique (PERT) as well as various methods of deriving computer and other programs. Students are also taught that a predicted solution might be to do nothing but wait. Such is the case when it is predicted that the problem will dissipate with the passage of time.

Students' ability to predict solutions is tested in the various content areas and daily living and remediated as needed until the students become proficient.

Stage 3, Implementing Solutions

Students are taught that unless predicted solutions are implemented as prescribed according to specifications, the effectiveness of the solution in solving the problem cannot be tested. Every effort must be made to detect and correct deviations from predicted solution specifications. When predicted solutions are complicated, training is often necessary to ensure that the solution is implemented as prescribed. During training, performance is monitored and corrected until it can be certified as proficient. Monitoring devices such as video and audio recorders can be used to monitor and analyze performance.

Once students understand how to implement solutions, their ability to implement solutions to problems in science, math, language arts, social studies, and daily living is tested and remediated as needed until they become proficient. Initially, assignments should not require knowledge of monitoring devices or how to estimate the resources needed to implement solutions. Students should eventually learn how to estimate the resources needed to implement solutions.

Stage 4, Assessing Achievement

Students are taught how to make observations of existing states, both quantitative observations by means of measurement and qualitative observations. They should eventually become familiar with the various kinds of instruments that can be used to make observations and how to assess their accuracy (validity, reliability, and objectivity). Students are also taught how to compare existing states with desired states to determine any discrepancies that might be present. Eventually, students should be taught to determine the probability that a derived discrepancy is a chance factor and to determine the importance of a discrepancy (effect size). This requires knowledge of statistics. Students should also eventually learn how to assess side effects and efficiency factors such as costs.

When students understand how to assess achievement, their ability to assess achievement in science, math, language arts, social studies, and daily living is tested and remediated until students become proficient. Initially, students should not need to know how to use sophisticated instruments to make observations, statistics, or ways to assess side effects or efficiency factors.

Developing Student Proficiency in Applying the Prediction Cycle

After students have been presented an overview of how the prediction cycle is applied and have become proficient in administering the four stages individually, they are taught how to coordinate the stages in applying the entire cycle. Students' ability to apply the cycle to identify and solve problems in science, math, language arts, social studies, and daily living is then tested and remediated as needed until they become proficient.

Student proficiency includes estimating achievement, side effects, and available resources after each cycle is completed as a basis for deciding whether to recycle or not. Ultimately, it is the authorized decision-maker(s) who use the estimates to decide whether or not to recycle. The decision depends on their motivation after they are fully informed. Initial applications of the cycle should be kept simple, not requiring students to estimate side effects and available resources or to use sophisticated observation instruments or statistics to estimate achievement.

CAUTIONS AND COMMENTS

An advantage of teaching students to use the prediction cycle proficiently is that they can use it from then on to solve almost all problems they need to solve that require extended effort. Predictive ability instruction can be incorporated into most existing courses or can be taught independently in a course designed for the purpose. It is applicable whenever systematic problem solving is required. Although tactics in the to-be-cited supportive research vary from those in the prediction cycle, they all teach students how to generate and test hypotheses to solve problems. Some of the to-be-cited studies use the term "problem-based learning" for generating and testing hypotheses.

GENERALIZATION: ON PREDICTION AND PROBLEM-SOLVING INSTRUCTION

Achievement of learning objectives is enhanced when students are taught how to use the prediction cycle to solve problems.

Supportive Research on Prediction and Problem Solving
Total number of supportive studies covered: 72

Groups of Studies

Author: Kalaian et al. (1991)

Students: Medical students

Learning: Achievement in basic science and clinical science

Instructional Tactics:

• Teach the learning process to students and continue to emphasize the process.

• Give students a pretest on science content.

- Develop problem based learning materials.
- Place students in small groups.
- Engage students in the analysis of clinically relevant problems.
- Train and use tutors.
- Use problem based learning process consistently.
- Assess students using the standardized assessment of the National Board of Medical Examiners, Parts I, II, and III.

Findings: Use of the above tactics was found to enhance achievement particularly in clinical science.

Studies in this meta-analysis are included in the six entries marked with the symbol * in the reference list in Part V.

Author: Dochy et al. (2003)

Students: Tertiary: higher education, college, high school

Learning: Achievement across a variety of disciplines

Instructional Tactics:

- Emphasize student-centered learning.
- Assign students to small groups with a tutor.
- Train the tutor as a facilitator or guide to the small group.
- Provide authentic problems to the students prior to any student preparation or study.
- Prepare the problems to serve as a tool to achieve the knowledge and the problem-solving skills essential to solve the problem.
- Provide environment for students to acquire new information through self-directed learning.
- Provide assessments that require students to apply their knowledge to both commonly occurring and important problem-solving situations.

Findings: Use of the above tactics was found to enhance achievement of skills used to apply knowledge. Further, the positive effect of problem-based learning on application of knowledge (skills) by students tends to be immediate and lasting.

Studies in this meta-analysis are marked with the symbol # in the reference list in Part V.

Individual Studies

Author: Dykes (1997)

Students: High school seniors

Learning: Grade point ratio

Findings: In general, predictive ability was related to academic achievement. High school seniors who had high scores on a predictive ability test also had higher GPRs. Predictive ability was a better predictor of high school success than an I.Q. test.

Author: Friedman & Maddock (1980)

Students: Fifth, sixth, seventh, and eighth grade students in rural, urban, and suburban public schools

Learning: Performance on the Comprehensive Test of Basic Skills (CTBS)

Instructional Tactics: An earlier version of the prediction cycle was taught to students as prescribed earlier under instructional tactics.

Findings: Students who received predictive ability instruction scored higher on the average on the CTBS than students who did not receive predictive ability instruction.

REFERENCE LIST

Benz, D., & Rosemier, R. (1966). Concurrent validity of the Gates level of comprehension test and the Bond, Clymer, Hoyt reading diagnostic tests. *Educational and Psychological Measurement, 26,* 1057–1062.

Chia, T. (1995). *Learning difficulty in applying notion of vector in physics among "A" level students in Singapore.* (ERIC Document Reproduction Service No. ED 389 528)

Denner, P. R., & McGinley, W. J. (1990). *Effects of prediction combined with storytelling versus listing predictions as prereading activities on subsequent story comprehension.* Paper presented at the annual meeting of the National Reading Conference, Miami.

Dochy, F., Segers, M., Van den Bossche, P., & Gijbels, D. (2003). Effects of problem-based learning: A meta-analysis. *Learning and Instruction, 13*(5), 533–568.

Dykes, S. (1997). *A test of proposition, of prediction theory.* Doctoral dissertation, University of South Carolina.

Freeman, R. H. (1982). *Improving comprehension of stories using predictive strategies.* Paper presented at the annual meeting of the International Reading Association, Chicago.

Friedman, M. I. (1974). *Predictive ability tests: Verbal and nonverbal forms.* Columbia, SC: M. I. Friedman.

Friedman, M. I., & Maddock, M. (1980). *Predictive ability instruction.* Research report published for participating school districts in South Carolina.

Greeno, J., & Noreen, D. (1974). Time to read semantically related sentences. *Memory and Cognition, 2*(1A), 117–120.

Henderson, E., & Long, B. (1968). Correlation of reading readiness and children of varying backgrounds. *The Reading Teacher, 22,* 40–44.

Hunt, J., & Joseph, D. (1990). Using prediction to improve reading comprehension of low-achieving readers. *Journal of Clinical Reading, Research and Programs, 3*(2), 14–17.

Hurst, R., & Milkent, M. (1994). *Facilitating successful predictive reasoning in biology through application of skill theory.* Paper presented at the annual meeting of the National Association for Research in Science Teaching, Anaheim, CA, March 19–26. (ERIC Document Reproduction Service No. ED 368 582)

Kalaian, H. A., Mullan, P. B., & Kasim, R. M. (1999). What can studies of Problem-Based Learning tell us? Synthesizing and modeling PBL effects on National Board of Medical Examination Performance: Hierarchical liner modeling meta-analytic approach. *Advances in Health Sciences Education, 4,* 209–221.

Nolan, T. (1991). Self-questioning and prediction: Combining metacognitive strategies. *Journal of Reading, 35*(2), 77–101.

Reutzel, D., & Fawson, P. (1991). Literature webbing predictable books: A prediction strategy that helps below-average, first-grade children. *Reading Research and Instruction, 30*(4), 20–30.

Walker, B. J., & Mohr, T. (1985). *The effects of ongoing self-directed questioning on silent comprehension.* Paper presented at the annual meeting of the Reading Research Conference, Seattle, WA.

Walker, K., & Bates, R. (1985). *The effects of ongoing self-directed questioning on silent comprehension.* Paper presented at the annual meeting of the Reading Research Conference, St. Petersburg, FL.

Zinar, S. (1990). Fifth-graders' recall of proposition content and causal relationships from expository prose. *Journal of Reading Behavior, 22,* 2.

11

Providing Contiguity

INTRODUCTION

When the relationship between events is being demonstrated to students, the events must appear sufficiently close together in time and space for their relationship to be perceived. For instance, students' understanding of the relationship between planting a bulb and the blooming of a flower can be facilitated by using time-lapse photography to shorten the time between the two events. It is also easier for a student to associate correction and remediation activities with their incorrect responses if remediation is provided sooner, rather than later, after the incorrect response. When young children misbehave, it is more likely that they will associate any corrective action with their misbehavior if the corrective action is taken soon after the misbehavior occurs.

STUDENT BENEFICIARIES

The evidence indicates that making events contiguous when teaching, assigning, evaluating and remediating performance of tasks enhances the academic achievement of students in preschool, kindergarten, elementary, junior high, secondary, college, and adult learning classrooms. Moreover, academic achievement was improved in a wide range of content areas and with learning disabled students. No evidence could be found to suggest that contiguity should not be stressed in all subject areas for all types of students.

LEARNING ACHIEVED

Achievement in the content areas of mathematics, history, foreign languages, English, language arts, spelling, writing, word recognition, vocabulary, reading, social sciences, science, social studies, business, and occupational areas is enhanced when events are made contiguous in the teaching, assigning, evaluating, and remediating of performance tasks. In studies reviewed, contiguity was positively related to student achievement.

INSTRUCTIONAL TACTICS

The evidence supports the need to make events contiguous when teaching, assigning, evaluating, and remediating performance of tasks. The following tactics are derived from studies that demonstrate the benefits of contiguity when teaching, assigning, evaluating, and remediating performance of tasks. Discretion has been used to interpret and reduce overlap in tactics used in different studies and to elaborate tactics.

Tactics employed are:

- *Instructional Planning*: The tasks students are to perform to achieve the learning objective should be broken down into small increments so that they will be performed as close together as possible.

- *Teaching*: To-be-associated events should be presented to students as close together as possible. This applies to the connection of to-be-associated subject matter to consequences that are to be associated with student behavior. Teaching devices that can be used to promote contiguity among to-be-associated events include: (1) focusing attention on and highlighting relationships; for example, focusing students' attention on a constellation in the sky, say the Big Dipper, and pointing out the configuration of stars in it; (2) condensing time; for example, using time-lapse photography to show the relationship between a newborn and an adult animal; (3) condensing space; for example, drawing a map to show the relationship among places that are far away from one another.

- *During the Instructional Process*: Student task performance should follow instruction as soon as possible; evaluation of student task performance should occur during or immediately after student task performance; feedback to students on the correctness of their task performance should occur immediately or very soon after evaluation; and remediation should occur immediately following feedback.

CAUTIONS AND COMMENTS

Much of the supportive research to be cited highlights the importance of contiguity during the instructional process as described above. For the most part this research was conducted in the classroom setting in the late 1900s. However, contiguity has long been known to be a condition of associative learning dating back to the 1800s. It was the cornerstone of Edwin R. Guthrie's (1886–1959) theory of contiguous conditioning. In addition, the Gestalt psychologists' "Law of Proximity" emphasizes the importance of contiguity in perception. Many other learning theorists have recognized the importance of contiguity, and a sizable amount of research has accumulated over the years attesting to its validity. The book *Theories of Learning*, by Bower and Hilgard (Prentice-Hall, 1981), provides additional information on contiguity.

GENERALIZATION: ON CONTIGUITY

Achievement of learning objectives is enhanced when events students are to associate are presented to them close together in time and space.

Supportive Research on Contiguity
Total number of supportive studies covered: 496+

Groups of Studies

Author: Rosenshine & Stevens (1986)

Students: Elementary and secondary

Learning: Mathematics, science, reading, history, and English achievement

Instructional Tactics:

- Divide to-be-learned material into smaller segments, with each succeeding segment being related to the previous segment, and following the preceding segment as closely as possible.
- Incorporate in each segment, student instruction, student practice of assigned tasks, and evaluation of student performance of assigned tasks.
- Follow instruction immediately with student practice.
- Follow student practice immediately with evaluation of student practice, either written or verbal.
- Give feedback on evaluations and corrections immediately following evaluation and correction.

Other instructional tactics from this review are applicable to other generalizations and are presented in the appropriate chapters of this book.

Findings: Use of the above tactics was found to be associated with higher student achievement. Teaching to-be-learned material in its entirety as one lesson, discontinuity in the form of allowing too much time to pass between instruction and student practice, not evaluating student task performance during or immediately after student practice, and delays in or lack of feedback and corrections were found to be associated with lower student achievement.

Groups of studies reviewed in this logical synthesis of research did not provide statistical evidence. However, many of the individual studies included the logical synthesis of research do contain statistical evidence. In the event that a reader wishes to view this evidence, an extensive listing of the individual studies reviewed is provided in the reference list in Part V (the studies are identified by the symbol %).

Author: Bangert-Drowns et al. (1991)

Students: Elementary, junior high, high school, and college

Learning: Mathematics, science, social science/education, and language arts/reading

Instructional Tactics:

- Students are presented a series of small frames that constituted a continuous text. After responding to a frame, the student receives feedback and then moves to the next frame.
- Students are provided blocks of text followed by questions. After responding to the questions, students receive feedback and then continue to another block of text if there is another one.
- Students receive classroom instruction and are then tested on the content.
- Students receive item-specific performance feedback on their test performance.
- Students are asked to respond to a criterion measure that covers the same content.

Other instructional tactics from this review are applicable to other generalizations and are presented in the appropriate chapters of this book.

Findings: Use of the above tactics was found to produce very large achievement gains. Immediate feedback is recommended for conventional educational purposes as in instruction followed by testing followed by feedback.

Individual studies analyzed by this meta-analysis are identified in the reference list in Part V by the symbol ^.

Author: Anderson (1994)

Students: Kindergarten, elementary, secondary, college, and other adult students

Learning: Achievement

Instructional Tactics: The following tactics associated with readiness and Mastery Learning are also presented in Bloom (1985), Block (1980), and others. Other tactics associated with Mastery Learning are applicable to other generalizations and are covered in the appropriate chapters.

- To-be-learned knowledge and skills are divided into smaller units, with each succeeding unit being related to the previous unit and following the preceding unit as closely as possible.
- Student task performance occurs immediately or as closely as possible following instruction on needed knowledge and skills.
- Evaluation of student task performance occurs as soon as possible following task performance.
- Ideally, feedback to students and corrections should immediately follow evaluation of their task performance.

Findings: Use of the above tactics was found to be related to enhanced student achievement.

Individual studies analyzed by these meta-analyses are identified in the reference list in Part V by the following symbols:

Kulik et al. (1990a) *

Kulik et al. (1990b) #

Slavin (1990) @

Guskey & Pigott (1988) $

Guskey & Gates (1986) &

Block & Burns (1976) +

It was not possible to determine the individual studies for which contiguity was an instructional tactic for the Willett et al. (1983) analysis.

Author: Swanson (2000)

Students: Learning disabled

Learning: Achievement in word recognition, reading comprehension, spelling memory/recall, mathematics, writing, and vocabulary

Instructional Tactics:

- Break tasks into small units.
- Sequence short activities.

- Use step-by-step instruction and prompts.
- Give daily evaluation of skills.
- Provide student practice and repeated practice.
- Provide daily feedback and/or weekly review.
- Provide segmentation of targeted skills and then guide students to synthesize parts to whole.

Other instructional tactics from this review are applicable to other generalizations and are presented in the appropriate chapters of this book.

Findings: Use of the above tactics was found to contribute significantly to achievement.

In this chapter, the author did not specifically identify the individual studies included in the meta-analysis.

Author: Gersten & Baker (2001)

Students: Learning disabled

Learning: Expressive writing

Instructional Tactics:

- Provide instruction in transcription skills (spelling, grammar, and punctuation).
- Provide students opportunity to practice transcription skills.
- Provide corrective instruction when needed.
- Provide opportunities to use transcription skills within the writing process.
- Provide students daily writing instruction that contains time devoted to the transcription skills and the writing process.

Other instructional tactics from this review are applicable to other generalizations and are presented in the appropriate chapters of this book.

Findings: Use of the above tactics was found to enhance writing achievement. Students were found to increase their automaticity with transcription skills which enabled them to focus more on the planning, composing, and revising of the expressive writing.

Studies associated with this meta-analysis are identified by the symbol ! in the reference list in Part V.

Author: Ehri et al. (2001)

Students: Preschool, kindergarten, and elementary

Learning: Phonemic awareness

Instructional Tactics:

- Provide instruction one phoneme at a time.
- Provide practice with manipulatives such as letters, mirrors, and markers for identifying phonemes—sound to sight.
- Provide the letter of the alphabet following the introduction of the phoneme.
- Teach the application of the phoneme skill to reading and to spelling.
- Assess learning in a variety of ways; for example, show a written word; then ask which of two spoken choices match the written word; for example, "Does this say cat or hat?"
- Continue instruction with the next phoneme.

Other instructional tactics from this review are applicable to other generalizations and are presented in the appropriate chapters of this book.

Findings: Use of the above tactics was found to enhance achievement.

Studies in this meta-analysis are designated in the reference list in Part V with the symbol =.

❖   ❖   ❖

Author: Martens & Witt (2004)

Students: Ages 6–12

Learning: Academic achievement in elementary subjects

Instructional Tactics:

- Provide students with errorless learning—gradual movement one small increment at a time from an easy task to a more difficult task.
- Use formative evaluation of content—continuous monitoring of progress.
- Determine students' knowledge and provide instruction from that point in small increments.
- Check regularly for students' understanding of the subject matter.
- Assess learning regularly in a formal way such as through tests.
- Guide students through a number of practice opportunities with assistance or "learning trials."

- Model or show students how to perform a skill.
- Correct student errors or reinforce correct responses.
- Assess student learning.

Other instructional tactics from this review are applicable to other generalizations and are presented in the appropriate chapters of this book.

Findings: Use of the tactics listed above was found to be effective in improving student achievement across content areas.

This research synthesis does not provide statistical data. The studies, some of which are meta-analyses, are designated with the symbol < in the reference list in Part V.

REFERENCE LIST

Anderson, S. A. (1994). *Synthesis of research on mastery learning* (Information Analysis). (ERIC Document Reproduction Service No. ED 382 567)

Bangert-Drowns, R. L., Kulik, C-L. C., Kulik, J. A., & Morgan, M. T. (1991). The instructional effect of feedback in test-like events. *Review of Educational Research, 61*(2), 213–238.

Block, J. H. (1980). Success rate. In C. Denham & A. Lieberman (Eds.), *Time to learn* (pp. 95–106). Washington, DC: U.S. Government Printing Office.

Block, J. H., & Burns, R. B. (1976). Mastery learning. In L. Schulman (Ed.), *Review of research in education* (Vol. 4, pp. 3–49). Itasca, IL: F. E. Peacock.

Bloom, B. S. (1985). Learning for mastery. In C. W. Fisher & D. C. Berliner (Eds.), *Perspectives on instructional time*. White Plains, NY: Longman.

Bowers, G., & Hilgard, E. (1981). *Theories of learning*. Englewood Cliffs, NJ: Prentice Hall.

Ehri, L. C., Nunes, S. R., Willows, D. M., Schuster, B. V., Yaghoub-Zadeh, Z., & Shanahan, T. (2001). Phonemic awareness instruction helps children learn to read: Evidence from the National Reading Panel's meta-analysis. *Reading Research Quarterly, 36*(3), 250–287.

Gersten, R., & Baker, S. (2001). Teaching expressive writing to students with learning disabilities: A meta-analysis. *The Elementary School Journal, 101*(3), 251–273.

Guskey, T. R., & Gates, S. L. (1986). Synthesis of research on the effects of mastery learning in elementary and secondary classrooms. *Educational Leadership, 33*(8), 73–80.

Guskey, T. R., & Pigott, T. D. (1988). Research on group-based mastery learning programs: A meta-analysis. *Journal of Educational Research, 81*(4), 197–216.

Kulik, C., Kulik, J., & Bangert-Drowns, R. (1990a). Effectiveness of mastery learning programs: A meta-analysis. *Review of Educational Research, 60*(2), 265–269.

Kulik, J., Kulik, C., & Bangert-Drowns, R. (1990b). Is there better evidence on mastery learning? A response to Slavin. *Review of Educational Research, 60*(2), 303–307.

Martens, B. K., & Witt, J. C. (2004). Competence, persistence, and success: The positive psychology of behavioral skill instruction. *Psychology in the Schools, 41*(1), 19–30.

Rosenshine, B., & Stevens, R. (1986). Teaching functions. In M. C. Wittrock (Ed.), *Handbook of research on teaching* (3rd ed., pp. 376–391). New York: Macmillan.

Slavin, R. E. (1990). Mastery learning re-considered. *Review Educational of Research, 60*(2), 300–302.

Swanson, H. L. (2000). What instruction works for students with learning disabilities? Summarizing the results from a meta-analysis of intervention studies. In R. M. Gersten & E. P. Schiller (Eds.), *Contemporary special education research: Synthesis of the knowledge base on critical instructional issues* (pp. 1–30). Mahwah, NJ: Lawrence Erlbaum Associates.

Willett, J., Yamashita, J., & Anderson, R. (1983). A meta-analysis of instructional systems applied in science teaching. *Journal of Research in Science Teaching, 20*(5), 405–417.

12

Utilizing Repetition Effectively

INTRODUCTION

Most people are at least vaguely familiar with the benefits of repetition to learning. They have heard that "practice makes perfect" and have memorized a poem or a part in a play by repeating the lines. Further, they may have mastered typing, playing a musical instrument, or playing a sport such as tennis by practicing the skills. The challenge is to apply the benefits of repetition in instruction to improve learning.

Two modes of repetition enhance learning:

1. The repeated presentation of to-be-learned information to students enhances their learning of the information; for example, the repeated presentation of names, numbers, or instructions enhances learning of that information.

2. Students' repetition of assigned tasks or students' practice of a task enhances their learning of the tasks; for instance, learning of tasks such as handwriting and multiplication tables is enhanced when students repeatedly practice their handwriting or multiplication tables.

The importance and application of these modes of repetition to learning will become clearer as we proceed through the chapter.

STUDENT BENEFICIARIES

Student achievement over a wide range of content areas in elementary classrooms, secondary classrooms, college classrooms, and military training situations will be enhanced by repetition in instruction and tasks students are assigned to perform. Students in adult, community, and business education and training settings may also experience the beneficial achievement effects of repetition. Another population which may benefit from repetition of instruction and of tasks is students with learning disabilities.

LEARNING ACHIEVED

Achievement in the content areas of mathematics, science, English, history, foreign languages, and reading is enhanced by instructional strategies which provide for repetition in instruction and in tasks students are assigned to perform. It may be reasonable to expect that achievement may be enhanced in other content areas as well. In studies reviewed, student achievement was shown to be enhanced by repetition.

INSTRUCTIONAL TACTICS

The studies to be presented indicate that repetition will enhance learning if the following tactics are employed.

- To-be-learned information is repeatedly presented to students.
- To-be-learned tasks are repeated or practiced by students.
- Repetition is frequent. In general, frequent repetition enhances learning more than infrequent repetition.
- Repetitions are varied in order to avoid boredom. Presentations of the same information can be varied with respect to the media used; for example, oral, written, and pictorial presentation of the same information can be made. Also, examples, applications, and demonstrations can vary from one presentation to the next, and repeated performance of the same task can be varied. For instance, in learning to write, students might write in different contexts such as an informal essay, a newspaper article, or a letter.
- Repeatedly testing students on to-be-learned information enhances their learning of the information.

The following format for incorporating repetition in instruction in order to achieve learning objectives was inferred from the studies to be presented shortly.

Instructional Period 1
- Present the to-be-learned information
- Assign homework on the information
- Quiz the students on the information

Instructional Period 2
- Review the to-be-learned information presented during Period 1

- Present new to-be-learned information
- Assign homework on the new information
- Quiz students on the information presented in Periods 1 and 2

Instructional Period 3

- Review the to-be-learned information presented during Periods 1 and 2
- Present new to-be-learned information
- Assign homework on the new information
- Quiz students on the information presented during Periods 1, 2, and 3

And so on. Progress is made in this way to take advantage of the benefits of repetition in teaching and testing while progressing toward the achievement of the learning objective being pursued. Progress must be planned in addition to repetition to avoid boredom. The format is intended to be only one illustration of the appropriate use of repetition in instruction.

Elaborations of the above summary of tactics can be obtained from reading the studies that are to follow. To be most effective, the instructional tactics need to be integrated into the particular instructional program being planned or presently being used.

CAUTIONS AND COMMENTS

Research indicates that too much repetition may interfere with learning of to-be-learned material and recall of previously learned material (Rosenshine, 1986, and others). Once a student has mastered the material, additional repetition and elaboration may result in the student's becoming bored.

GENERALIZATION: ON REPETITION

Achievement of learning objectives is enhanced when there is repetition in instruction and in tasks students are assigned to perform.

Supportive Research on Repetition
Total number of supportive studies covered: 183

Groups of Studies

Author: Kulik et al. (1984)

Students: Elementary, secondary, and postsecondary students

Learning: Achievement

Instructional Tactics: Practice on identical and parallel tests prior to taking the criterion test.

Findings: The review of parallel forms and identical forms of criterion measures found that there was a significant relationship between performance on a criterion measure and the number of practice tests taken. It was found that as the number of the practice tests taken increased, the size of the effect on the criterion measure increased. The effect for taking seven practice tests of the identical form was 4.5 times that for taking one practice test of the identical form. The effect for taking seven practice tests of a parallel form was 3.2 times that for taking one practice test of the parallel form. Findings indicate the effect for practice on identical forms of the criterion measure was 1.8 times the effect found for practice on parallel forms of the criterion measure when the number of practice tests was one. When the number of practice tests increased to seven, the effect for practice on identical forms was 2.5 times the effect for practice on parallel forms of the criterion measure.

Studies associated with this meta-analysis are identified by the symbol * in the reference list in Part V.

Author: Swanson & Sachse-Lee (2000)

Students: Children and adults with average intelligence but having problems in a particular academic, social, and/or related behavior domain

Learning: Across a variety of instructional domains

Instructional Tactics:

• Use drill-repetition-practice-review.

• Distribute review and practice over specified time.

• Use redundant materials or text.

• Provide repeated practice.

• Provide sequenced reviews in the form of daily feedback and/or weekly reviews.

Findings: The measure of achievement in each of the 85 single-subject-design intervention studies was based on baseline and treatment differences. One of the instructional components was drill/repetition and practice/review which is defined as statements in the treatment description related to mastery criteria, distributed review and practice, redundant materials or text, repeated practice, sequenced reviews, daily feedback, and/or weekly reviews. Findings concluded that instructional components related to drill-repetition-practice-review, segmentation, small interactive groups, and the implementation of cues to use strategies contributed significant variance (15 percent) to estimates of effect size.

Studies associated with this meta-analysis are identified by the symbol & in the reference list in Part V.

Author: Therrien (2004)

Students: Ages 5–18

Learning: Reading fluency and comprehension

Instructional Tactics:

- Repeated reading of material with achievement based on the differences between pretest and posttest scores.

Other instructional tactics from this review are applicable to other generalizations and are presented in the appropriate chapters of this book.

Findings: Repeated reading improves the reading fluency and comprehension of both nondisabled students and learning disabled students. Results were separated into nontransfer measures (the ability to read fluently or comprehend a passage after reading it multiple times) and transfer measures (ability to read fluently or comprehend new passages after having previously reread other reading material). Nontransfer measures include interventions of cued reading, corrective feedback, and performance criteria. Transfer measures include interventions conducted by an adult or peer, modeling, corrective feedback, comprehension component, and charting. Repeated reading has the potential to improve overall reading fluency and comprehension abilities in both nontransfer and transfer measures. Whether for fluency or comprehension achievement, repeated reading should occur with an adult since effect sizes were 3 times larger when the intervention was conducted by an adult than when the intervention was conducted by a peer. Further, students should be told if they are reading for fluency only, comprehension only, or a combination of fluency and comprehension. They should also be told the number of times to repeat the reading although four of the 18 studies found that gains in comprehension were not significant after the fourth reading. Findings recommend that corrective feedback be used with the rereading which means that students reread until a given performance criterion is reached. When a performance criterion was used, the studies found that the mean fluency effect size increase was more than four times larger than that obtained by interventions using a fixed number of readings.

Studies associated with this meta-analysis are identified by the symbol + in the reference list in Part V.

Author: Rosenshine (1986)

Students: Elementary, secondary, and postsecondary

Learning: Mathematics, science, reading, and English achievement

Instructional Tactics:

- Review daily with the students relevant previous learning.
- Review homework daily with the students.
- Review prerequisite skills and knowledge for the lesson with the students.
- Provide for frequent practice by the students of newly acquired knowledge and skills.
- Review with the students every Monday the work of the previous week.
- Review with the students every fourth Monday the work of the previous month.
- Assess students' learning with frequent quizzes (provide students with review and practice for exams that evaluate achievement of the learning objectives pursued).

Other instructional tactics from this review are applicable to other generalizations and are presented in the appropriate chapters of this book.

Findings: For all studies reviewed, teachers of classes with high achievement levels for the students provided practice and review. An important finding was that it is the frequency of practice and review that enhances student achievement.

Studies associated with this logical synthesis are identified by the symbol # in the reference list in Part V.

Author: Chard et al. (2002)

Students: Elementary students with learning disabilities

Learning: Reading fluency

Instructional Tactics:

- Provide repeated reading.
  —Assign a passage for repeated reading
  —Assign a specific number of repetitions
  —Assign silent and oral repeated reading
  —May assign repeated reading with overlapping words
  —May assign the student to the same passage to multiple audiences

—May require the repeated reading be with an adult model
—May allow repeated reading modeled by a more proficient peer
—May provide modeling by audiotape or computer for the repeated reading
—May use feedback with the repeated reading
—May use a fixed rate or set individual improvement criterion for the repeated reading

- Provide drill and practice.
- Provide word practice.

Findings: The synthesis of studies findings suggests that repeated reading for LD students leads to greater fluency—rate, accuracy, and comprehension. Teacher modeling of repeated reading seems to be more effective than repeated reading with no model. Even taped or computer modeled reading has more effect than having no model. Repeated reading with a peer has yielded equivocal results. Repeated reading with someone not one's age seems to produce moderate effect. Gradually adding difficulty to text and offering corrections also tend to produce greater fluency. There is little evidence to support silent reading as a way to boost fluency.

Studies associated with this logical synthesis are identified by the symbol ^ in the reference list in Part V.

Individual Studies

Author: Ausubel & Youseff (1965)

Students: College

Learning: Endocrinology recall

Instructional Tactics: During a 25-minute first session, the experimental group read and studied a passage on the endocrinology of pubescence, and the control group read an unrelated passage. During a second 25-minute session two days later, both groups read and studied the endocrinology passage utilized in session one. Both groups of students were administered a multiple-choice test of the content of the endocrinology passage two days after session two.

Findings: The average test score for the group that read the endocrinology passage twice was 19 percent higher than the average test score for the group that read the endocrinology passage once.

❖　❖　❖

Author: Peterson et al. (1935)

Students: College

Learning: History achievement and retention

Instructional Tactics: All students studied an historical passage on monasticism in Western Europe, followed by an immediate recall test. Four control groups received no additional study or review of the original content studied prior to being tested at two-, three-, six-, or 18-week intervals following instruction. Four experimental groups received one review of the original content studied prior to testing at two-, three-, six-, or 18-week intervals. Two experimental groups received two reviews of the original content studied prior to testing at six- or 18-week intervals.

Findings: Retention for the one-review groups as compared to the no-review groups was 47 percent higher at two and three weeks, 28 percent higher at six weeks, and 18 percent higher at 18 weeks. Retention for the two-review groups as compared to the no-review groups was 75 percent at six weeks and 57 percent at 18 weeks. Ratios of retention scores to immediate recall scores, expressed as percentages, indicate that for the no-review groups, at two and three weeks performance on retention was about 60 percent of that on the day of immediate recall testing. Although not reported, observation of given graphs seems to indicate that performance for all four no-review groups on retention was between 50 percent and 60 percent of that on the day of immediate recall testing. The one-review groups are reported to have "had almost as much as they had on the day of learning" (p. 67). Review of the provided graphs, under Statistical Evidence on Repetition, indicates that the one-review groups' ratio of retention to immediate recall ranged from about 90 percent at week 2 to 70 percent at week 18, with gradual declines over the four testing intervals. The two-review groups' ratios were slightly over 100 percent at six weeks and about 90 percent at 18 weeks.

Author: Nelson (1977)

Students: College

Learning: Word recall

Instructional Tactics:

Experiment 1: Twenty unrelated words (concrete nouns) were randomly divided into five blocks of four words. The words were ordered randomly within each block, and the blocks were then ordered randomly to form the first list of words. The process was repeated to form a second list of words. The two word lists contained the same words in a different order.

Students were visually presented the words individually from either one or both word lists. Following presentation of the word list(s) the students were given a sheet of paper with 20 lines on it. Students were allowed three minutes to write down as many of the 20 words they could recall from list(s) of words they had seen.

Experiment 2: Twelve words were selected from the list of words used in experiment 1. The twelve words were formed into word lists in the following formats:

1. No repetition (i.e., "A, B, C, . . . K, L, M") (p. 156).
2. Back-to-back repetition (i.e., "A, A, B, B, . . . K, K, L, L") (p. 156).
3. Two-spaced repetitions with four words being repeated at an interval of every seventh word, four words repeated at an interval of every eleventh word, and four words being repeated at an interval of every fifteenth word. The word list was constructed in two blocks, with each block containing two words for each of the three interval appearances (i.e., "A, B, C, D, E, F, G, H, I, J, K, L, E(7), F(7), C(11), D(11), A(15), B(15), K(7), L(7), I(11), J(11), G(15), H(15))") (p. 156).

Students were assigned in equal numbers to three groups, with each group being assigned to view one of the preceding arrangements of words. Students in each group viewed their respective word lists individually. Each group saw the words for their respective list presented in a continuous fashion, with the student being allowed to view the word for five seconds. Following the word list presentations, the students were given a piece of paper. They were allowed three minutes to write down as many of the twelve words they had viewed as they could recall.

Experiment 3: A procedure similar to that for Experiment 1 was used to form two lists of 30 words. The two lists contained the same words ordered differently in each list. Students were visually presented the words individually from either one or both word lists.

Findings:

Experiment 1: Findings indicated that the groups that saw the same word twice (both word lists) recalled significantly more words than did the groups that saw the words only once (one word list). The average percentages of words recalled for the two groups that saw the same words twice (both word lists) were 7 percent to 10 percent higher than average percentages of words recalled by the two groups that saw the words once (one word list).

Experiment 2: Students in the two-repetitions conditions recalled a significantly higher percentage of words than the students in the one repetition condition. The average percentage of words recalled for students who viewed words in the back-to-back two-repetition word list was 16 percent higher than the average percentage of words recalled for students who saw each word only once. The average percentage of words recalled for students who viewed the spaced-repetition word lists was 24 percent higher than the average percentage of words recalled for students who saw each word only once.

Experiment 3: Findings indicate that recall was significantly higher for students seeing each word twice as compared to the level of recall for students seeing each word only once.

❖　❖　❖

Author: Petros & Hoving (1980)

Students: Second grade

Learning: Prose main idea retention

Instructional Tactics:

1. One group of students listened to the same stories a second time one week after hearing the stories the first time.

2. One week after hearing the stories for the first time, the teacher led a review session for students in another group. The teacher used leading questions and prompts to elicit verbal responses from the students on the main ideas of the stories (i.e., "What kind of boy did the story say [name] was? Tell me as much as you can remember about what [name] did in the story. Can you tell me anything more about the story?") (p. 37). Students were allowed to respond to questions until they indicated that they could not recall any more information about the story.

3. Another group of students reviewed the stories by listening to audio tapes of the teacher-led review session, which included the teacher's questions/ prompts and the students' responses.

4. Another group of students heard the stories once and received no review.

5. One group of students was required to write down as many of the story main idea units as they could recall immediately after hearing the stories once.

All students were tested on recall of story main idea units two weeks after hearing the stories the first time.

Findings: The average percentages of main idea units recalled of all types of review were higher than the average percentage of main idea units recalled by students who heard the stories only once and had no additional review. The average percentage of main idea units recalled by the group that heard the same stories twice was 19 percent higher than the average percentage of main idea units recalled by the group that heard the stories once with no subsequent review. The average percentage of main idea units recalled by the group that was required to recall as many idea units as they could immediately after hearing the stories was 10 percent higher than the average percentage of main idea units recalled by the group that heard the stories once with no subsequent review. The average percentage of main idea units recalled by the group that reviewed the stories in a teacher-led session was 8 percent higher than the average percentage of main idea units recalled by the group that heard the stories once with no subsequent review. The average percentage of main idea units recalled by the group that heard the audiotape of the teacher-led review session was 7 percent higher than the average percentage of main idea units recalled by the group that heard the stories once with no subsequent review.

Author: Watkins & Kerkar (1985)

Students: College

Learning: Word recall

Instructional Tactics:

Experiment 1: Word lists were created containing 20 bisyllabic words. Ten words appeared only once on the list and five words appeared twice. Students viewed the 20 words individually on cards held up by the experimenter. The students were allowed to view each word for a two-second time period. Following presentation of all of the words, students were then allowed one minute to write down as many words as they could recall.

Experiment 2: A list of 24 nouns paired with 24 different adjectives was used for this study. Twelve nouns appeared only once and six nouns appeared twice. Students were presented the individual pairs of words on a television screen. The students saw each pair of words for 2.5 seconds. Following the presentation of all of the word pairs, the students were allowed one minute to recall as many of the nouns as they could remember.

Experiment 3: The procedure was the same as for Experiment 2, except that names of famous people were used.

Findings:

Experiment 1: Students recalled 28 percent more twice-presented words than once-presented words.

Experiment 2: Students recalled 25 percent more twice-presented nouns than once-presented nouns.

Experiment 3: Students recalled 25 percent more twice-repeated names than once-repeated names.

Author: Hines et al. (1985)

Students: College

Learning: Mathematics achievement

Instructional Tactics: The tactics employed in this study are as reported in Cruickshank et al. (1979, pp. 28–30). The tactics used in this study are reported under the heading "Clarity of Communication." Others are not relevant to the strategies presented in this handbook.

- Repeat and stress directions and different points.
- Provide practice.
- Repeat questions and explanations if students do not understand.
- Use verbal repetition.

Findings: Instructional tactics associated with repetition were found to be positively and significantly related to learner achievement.

Author: Péladeau et al. (2003)

Students: College students enrolled in introductory quantitative methods classes

Learning: Academic performance of all students and long-term retention and attitudes toward the course, the subject matter, and computerized practice were measured on a sub sample of students about six months after the course ended.

Instructional Tactics:

- A control group of students received no mastery level or special instructions for the computerized practice of units of study.
- The mastery group students were given a unit of study to practice using the computer until they reached a stable level of 85 percent mastery. Then that unit was removed from the student's practice load.
- One overlearning group also was given a unit of study to practice until a stable level of 85 percent mastery was reached. This group, however, had to continue practicing the mastered unit twice a week for up to five weeks during which time the students were instructed to focus on the maintenance of their learning or increase their accuracy levels.
- The other overlearning group had to reach the initial mastery criterion but then had to practice the mastered material twice a week for five consecutive weeks. Further, these students were asked to focus on increasing their correct response rate.

Findings: In terms of academic achievement, the greatest difference observed between the non-mastery condition and the other three groups was directly related to group failure rate in the course. Usually one third of the students who finished the course failed to make a passing grade. The results of the treatment were more satisfactory with an overall failure rate of only 20 percent; and, except for one person, all the failure belonged to the non-mastery group which then had a 41 percent failure rate. Interestingly, the instructor whose students in the non-mastery group participated the least in the computerized practice had the highest failure rates. Results for those who engaged in overlearning were slightly-to-moderately better than for those who merely reached the mastery criterion. In terms of retention, the overlearning groups outperformed the mastery group in recall and transfer, and all three mastery groups outperformed the non-mastery group in recall and transfer.

REFERENCE LIST

Ausubel, D. P., & Youseff, M. (1965). The effect of space repetition on meaningful retention. *The Journal of General Psychology, 73*, 147–150.

Chard, D. J., Vaughn, S., & Tyler, B. J. (2002). A synthesis of research on effective interventions for building reading fluency with elementary students with learning disabilities. *Journal of Learning Disabilities, 35*(5), 21–60.

Hines, C. V., Cruickshank, D. R., & Kennedy, J. J. (1985). Teacher clarity and its relationship to student achievement and satisfaction. *American Educational Research Journal, 22*(1), 87–99.

Kulik, J. A., Kulik, C. C., & Bangert, R. L. (1984). Effects of practice on aptitude and achievement scores. *American Educational Research Journal, 21*(2), 434–447.

Nelson, T. O. (1977). Repetition and depth of processing. *Journal of Verbal Learning and Verbal Behavior, 16*, 151–171.

Péladeau, N., Forget, J., & Gagné, F. (2003). Effect of paced and unpaced practice on skill application and retention: How much is enough? *American Educational Research Journal, 40*(3), 769–801.

Peterson, H. A., Ellis, M., Toohill, N., & Kloess, P. (1935). Some measurements of the effects of reviews. *The Journal of Educational Psychology, 26*(2), 65–72.

Petros, T., & Hoving, K. (1980). The effects of review and young children's memory for prose. *Journal of Experimental Child Psychology, 30*, 33–43.

Rosenshine, B. V. (1986). Synthesis of research on explicit teaching. *Educational Leadership, 43*(7), 60–69.

Swanson, L., & Sachse-Lee, C. (2000). A meta-analysis of single-subject-design intervention research for students with LD. *Journal of Learning Disabilities, 33*(2), 114–136.

Therrien, W. J. (2004). Fluency and comprehension gains as a result of repeated reading: A meta-analysis. *Remedial and Special Education, 25*(4), 252–261.

Watkins, M. J., & Kerkar, S. P. (1985). Recall of twice-presented item without recall of either presentation: Generic memory for events. *Journal of Memory and Language, 24*, 666–678.

13

Utilizing Unifiers

INTRODUCTION

Most people are aware that subject matter tends to be presented in an organized manner. They know that books provide a table of contents; that calendars and clocks organize time into related segments; and that symphonies are organized into movements. What many people may not know is that subject matter, whatever form it may take, is easier to understand and manage when inherent relationships are conveyed. A large number of research studies have attempted to determine how to convey subject matter relationships best. The results of the research have important implications for instruction.

Research shows that highlighting parts/whole relationships in the subject matter students are assigned to learn appreciably enhances their learning of the subject matter. In general, this revelation indicates that parts/whole relationships in subject matter need to be highlighted during instructional planning and to be conveyed to students during teaching. Specifics are explained in the remainder of the chapter.

STUDENT BENEFICIARIES

The evidence indicates that incorporating the use of unifying schemes in the teaching of subject matter enhances the academic achievement of students in pre-school, elementary, middle, junior high, secondary, college, and adult learning classrooms as well as disabled students. Moreover, academic achievement was improved in a wide range of content areas. No evidence could be found to suggest that the use of unifiers should not be stressed in all subject areas for all types of students.

LEARNING ACHIEVED

Achievement in the content areas of mathematics, history, reading, social sciences, sciences, social studies, physics, writing, vocabulary, hotel/business management, health, English, linguistics, algebra, and communication is enhanced when subject matter unifiers are used. In studies reviewed, the use of subject matter unifiers led to enhanced student achievement. The evidence indicates that the use of unifiers may elevate student achievement by as much as five times that for students in learning situations where unifiers were not used.

INSTRUCTIONAL TACTICS

- Either the teacher or instructional planner provides a unifying scheme that highlights the parts to whole relationships within the subject matter. The evidence indicates this may be accomplished prior to, during, or after instruction. The evidence is not conclusive on which is best.

- Students are taught to construct their own unifying scheme either during or after instruction. The evidence does not seem to support students' constructing their own unifying scheme prior to instruction.

Unifying schemes employed to highlight relationships in the subject matter in the studies reviewed by the research syntheses incorporated into this chapter were (1) textual summaries, (2) hierarchical tree diagrams, (3) pictorial representations, and (4) subject matter outlines.

The following examples were derived from individual studies incorporated into the research syntheses. Each individual example may be seen as taking the form of one or more of the previously mentioned formats.

Bower et al. (1969)

Students were presented four conceptual hierarchies for minerals presented in the form of a vertical tree diagram.

Level

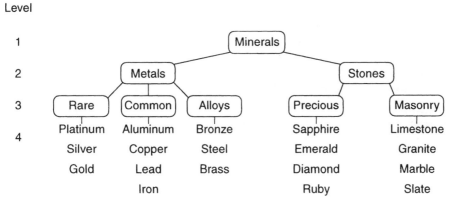

Hawk (1986)

The following unifying schemes are hand-drawn unifiers used to highlight the relationships in chapters to be taught in a sixth- and seventh-grade life sciences course.

UNIT I – The Living World
Chap. 3 "The Variety of Life"

classify	Linnaeus	binomial system

Need for system of classification:
1- same organisms had different names in different languages.
2- common names were misleading.

Method of Classification

KINGDOM
PHYLUM
CLASS
ORDER
FAMILY
GENUS
SPECIES

Binomial System

EXAMPLES

Common Name	Genus	Species
1- lion	Felis	leo
2- tiger	Felis	tigris
3- house cat	Felis	catus

MAJOR CLASSIFICATION

Nonliving   Living

Animal Kingdom   Plant Kingdom   Protist Kingdom

--- CHARACTISTICS USED IN CLASSIFICATION ---

Animals
* blood temperature
* type of support system
* adaptation for body functions
* body covering
* shape of body
* type of body openings
* no. of body sections

* no. of apendages
* types of reproduction
* method of birth
* nourishment of young

Plants
* cellular structure
* reproduction
* leaf structure
* roots, stems, leaves

Protists
* Algae
* Fungi
* Protozoans
* bacteria
* viruses

© N. McLeod

154

III. Protoplasm

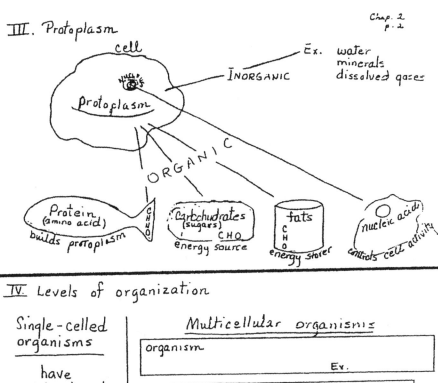

cell

protoplasm

INORGANIC — Ex. water, minerals, dissolved gases

ORGANIC

Protein (amino acid) — builds protoplasm — C H N O

Carbohydrates (sugars) — CHO — energy source

fats — C H O — energy storer

nucleic acid — controls cell activity

IV. Levels of organization

Single-celled organisms	Multicellular organisms
have Specialized parts to perform necessary life functions	

Levels pp. 81, 86

organism   Ex.

System   Ex

Organ   Ex.

tissue   Ex

specialized cell   Ex.

© N. McLeod

155

Robinson & Schraw (1994)

The following unifying schemes were used to highlight the relationships in a fictional text on types of fish. One unifier is a matrix presentation of the relationships within the subject matter, and the other unifier employed is an outline of the relationships within the subject matter.

Matrix

Depth:	200 ft		400 ft		600 ft	
Fish:	Hat	Lup	Arch	Bone	Tin	Scale
Social group:	Solitary	Small	Solitary	School	Small	School
Color:	Black	Brown	Blue	Orange	Yellow	White
Size:	30 cm		45 cm		70 cm	
Diet:	Shrimp		Krill		Prawn	

Outline

Depth	Fish	Characteristics
200 ft	Hat	Social Group—Solitary Color—Black Size—30 cm Diet—Shrimp
	Lup	Social Group—Small Color—Brown Size—30 cm Diet—Shrimp
400 ft	Arch	Social Group—Solitary Color—Blue Size—45 cm Diet—Krill
	Bone	Social Group—School Color—Orange Size—45 cm Diet—Krill
600 ft	Tin	Social Group—Small Color—Yellow Size—70 cm Diet—Prawn
	Scale	Social Group—School Color—White Size—70 cm Diet—Prawn

Simmons et al. (1988)

The following is a graphical unifying scheme highlighting the relationships in an experimental passage on the *Building Blocks of Matter.*

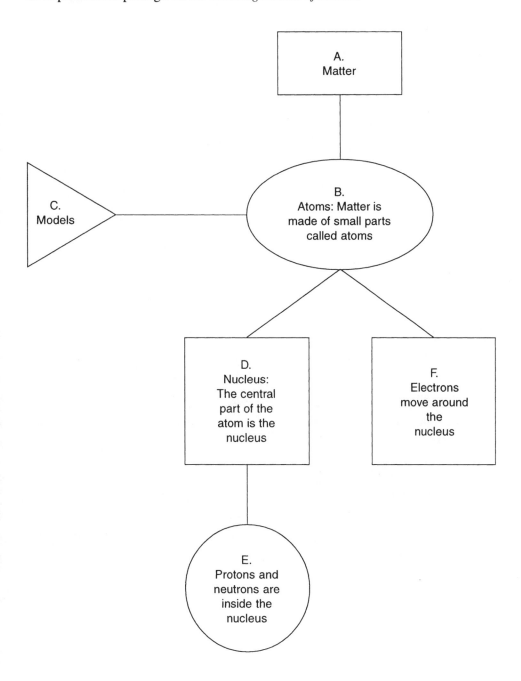

Denner (1986)

The following unifying scheme was used to highlight the relationships within a story passage that describes a locksmith named Horace, who has a mania for old rare books. Once a year he steals jewels to pay for the books. This time, however, he is caught by a pretty young lady who tricks him into opening a safe. Horace is later arrested for jewel robbery and ends up as the assistant prison librarian because no one believes his story about the young lady.

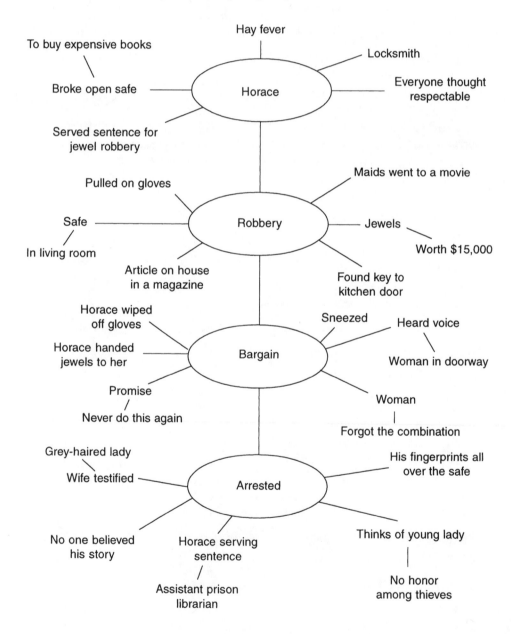

Gilles (1984)

The following textual summary was given to students prior to instruction on peripheral circulatory disorders. The unifying scheme outlines the metabolic consequences of cellular ischemia; possible cardiac, vascular, and humoral causes for ischemia; and proposed principles of ischemia relief.

> Ischemia is inadequate perfusion of tissues with blood of sufficient quantity or quality to meet cellular needs for oxygen and nutrients. Ischemia can result from cardiac pump failure, vascular obstruction, decreased blood volume, or increased blood viscosity. Ischemia impairs cellular metabolism because needed oxygen, nutrients, and hormones fail to reach the cell and toxic wastes are retained in tissues.
>
> When adequate oxygen is available, the cell breaks down each molecule of glucose to CO_2 and H_2O, and forms 38 molecules of high energy ATP. When oxygen is lacking, each molecule of glucose breaks down only to pyruvate, and only two molecules of ATP are formed. Thus, ischemic tissues are deprived of energy because available glucose yields only part of its energy. Further, the pyruvate resulting from anaerobic glycolysis is converted to lactic acid, which lowers tissue pH and impairs cellular metabolism.
>
> General ischemia and ischemia of highly active tissues (brain, liver, kidney, myocardium) often result from cardiac pump failure. Thus, lowered blood pressure following myocardial infarction may cause stroke, hepatic necrosis, renal tubular necrosis, or a second myocardial infarction. Localized ischemia usually results from vascular obstruction or changes in blood volume or viscosity. In arteriosclerosis, subintimal plaques roughen arterial linings and rupture platelets, initiating clot formation and blocking blood flow. Impaired venous blood flow may result from external pressure, varicosities, or phlebothrombosis. In these conditions increased venous pressure is referred backward to capillaries, causing edema formation. Tissue edema compresses capillaries, arterioles, and arteries, producing ischemia. Increased blood viscosity in polycythemia, increased platelet stickiness in disseminated malignancy, and red cell distortion in sickle cell disease may all cause intravascular clotting and tissue ischemia.
>
> Ischemia can be alleviated either by decreasing cellular needs for oxygen and nutrients or by improving arterial blood flow through positioning, removal of external pressure, or use of anticoagulants.

Selinger (1995)

The following are directions given to students to assist them in developing parts/ whole summaries of the relationships within subject matter.

1. Read the entire article to get a general impression of what it is about.

2. Write a thesis statement for the entire article on planning paper. (This may be more than one sentence if necessary.)

3. Underneath your thesis statement write sentence for each topic heading describing what that section is telling the reader. This should be the most general statement you can make about the section. Leave about ten lines between each statement.

4. Look at each section and write down major points that describe in more detail the statements you made in step 3. Write this in the space you left under each statement. You may underline parts of the text if that helps. Remember that often a major point will be the topic sentence of a paragraph, but you cannot rely on this. It may be necessary to write several sentences to describe your major point adequately.

CAUTIONS AND COMMENTS

Research has shown that highlighting the parts/whole relationships within the subject matter enhances student learning. Many textbooks used in instruction continue to do an inadequate job of highlighting parts/whole relationships within the subject matter. It is not unusual for a teacher to have to move from one part of a text to another in order to present the subject matter units in an organized manner. Additionally, organization within the individual units is often inadequate in the highlighting of the relationships within the subject matter and may often contain irrelevant information in the form of pictures or diagrams intended merely to make the text more attractive. As a result, there is a need for instructional planners to consider incorporating the use of unifying schemes into instruction in order to assist students in the identification of the important parts/whole relationships within the subject matter they are to learn. Authors and publishers of texts need to be more cognizant of the importance of highlighting the parts/whole relationships within the subject matter when designing and organizing textbooks. Additionally, the evidence is of sufficient strength to suggest that authors and publishers consider incorporating unifying schemes into each unit of a textbook. Research indicates that graphic organizers are helpful to teachers in planning for content delivery.

GENERALIZATION: ON UNIFIERS

Achievement of learning objectives is enhanced when a scheme is used to highlight parts/whole relationships in the subject matter students are assigned to learn.

Supportive Research on Unifiers
Total number of supportive studies covered: 370+

Groups of Studies

Author: Rosenshine et al. (1996)

Students: Upper elementary (grade 3 and up), junior high, secondary, and college

Learning: Reading comprehension across subject matters, mathematics, physics, and writing

Instructional Tactics:

- Provide students with story grammar categories to guide their reading.
- Teach students a summarizing strategy (Wong et al., 1984).
  —Students practice the strategy until they reach 90 percent accuracy over three days.
  —Students are given the following self-questioning prompt:
    - What's the most important sentence in this paragraph? Let me underline it.
    - Let me summarize the paragraph. To summarize I rewrite the main idea sentence and add important details.
    - Let me review my summary statements for the whole subsection.
    - Do my summary statements link up with one another?
  —Students write summaries of passages using the prompt until mastery is achieved.
- Give students a self-evaluation checklist to guide their comprehension process after four instructional sessions (Davey & McBride, 1986).
  —How well did I identify important information?
  —How well did I link information together?
  —How well could I answer my questions?
  —Did my "think questions" use different language from the text?
  —Did I use good signal words?

Other instructional tactics from this review are applicable to other generalizations and are presented in the appropriate chapters of this book.

Findings: Use of the above tactics was found to enhance reading comprehension.

Individual studies analyzed by this meta-analysis are identified in the reference list in Part V by the symbol *.

Author: Wise (1996)

Students: Middle and secondary

Learning: Science—all content areas

Instructional Tactics:

- Ask students to work or practice with physical objects.
- Provide students the opportunity to operate apparatus, develop skills, or draw or construct something.
- Modify instructional materials; for example, rewrite or annotate text passages.
- Provide tape recorded directions.
- Provide simplified laboratory apparatus for students to use.

Other instructional tactics from this review are applicable to other generalizations and are presented in the appropriate chapters of this book.

Findings: Use of the above focusing tactics was found to be effective in science achievement.

Individual studies in this meta-analysis were not identified by the author.

Author: Hattie et al. (1996)

Students: Primary, elementary, junior high, secondary, college, and adults

Learning: Achievement

Instructional Tactics:

- Provide students with advance organizers about the material.
- Provide students with summaries of material.
- Teach students to construct graphic organizers.
- Teach students summarizing techniques.

Findings: Use of the above tactics was found to enhance academic achievement.

Individual studies are designated with the symbol = in the reference list in Part V.

Author: Guzzetti (2000)

Students: Elementary, secondary, and adult

Learning: Counter-intuitive science concepts

Instructional Tactics:

- Provide students with highlighted text arguing against (refutational) a concept.
- Provide refutational text guided by an adult using a web to guide the discussion.

Findings: Use of the above tactics led to increased achievement in students' understanding of science concepts. Discussions that require students to support their opinions of a science concept from refutational (arguing against the concept) texts are most likely to ensure long-term change in the students' achievement of the science concept.

The studies analyzed by this meta-analysis are identified in the reference list in Part V by the symbol +.

Author: Gersten & Baker (2001)

Students: Learning disabled

Learning: Expressive writing

Instructional Tactics:

- Students are provided explicit step-by-step instruction in writing with those steps supported by a "think sheet," a prompt card, or a mnemonic. The "think sheet" helps students plan their writing through a series of sequential and structured prompts.
- Students are guided in the writing process with a plan of action, a "procedural facilitator," which gives the students a permanent visual reminder of the content and structure of the writing task and provides a common language with which to discuss the writing task.

Other instructional tactics from this review are applicable to other generalizations and are presented in the appropriate chapters of this book.

Findings: Use of the above tactics led to higher levels of achievement in expressive writing.

Studies associated with this meta-analysis are identified by the symbol @ in the reference list in Part V.

Author: Griffin & Tulbert (1995)

Students: Elementary, middle, secondary, community college, and postsecondary; students with learning disabilities

Learning: Vocabulary relationships; content-area reading (science, social studies, hotel/business management)

Instructional Tactics:

- Students are given constructed graphic organizers in advance of the learning unit.
- Students are given constructed graphic organizers during the learning unit.
- Students are given constructed graphic organizers following the learning unit.
- Students receive training in the construction and the use of graphic organizers.
- Students construct graphic organizers in conjunction with the learning unit.
- Students are given teacher-constructed graphic organizers and construct their own graphic organizers.

Findings: Use of the above instructional tactics was found to have a positive effect on student achievement. Providing the students with training in the development and use of graphic organizers was found to enhance achievement on the given learning units. Also, graphic postorganizers tended to have a greater effect on student achievement of the learning units than did graphic advance organizers or graphic organizers used during the learning unit.

Studies associated with this logical synthesis are identified by the symbol # in the reference list in Part V.

Author: Yan & Jitendra (1999)

Students: Elementary, secondary, and postsecondary; learning disabled, mixed disabilities, and at-risk

Learning: Achievement in mathematical word problems

Instructional Tactics:

- Students are provided pictorial (diagramming) representation approaches.
- Students are provided concrete (manipulatives) representation approaches.
- Students are provided mapping (schema-based) representation approaches.

Other instructional tactics from this review are applicable to other generalizations and are presented in the appropriate chapters of this book.

Findings: Use of the representation tactics listed above was found to be effective in facilitating word-problem-solving achievement.

The studies in this logical synthesis are marked with the symbol & in the reference list in Part V.

❖   ❖   ❖

Author: Gersten et al. (2001)

Students: School-age children with learning disabilities

Learning: Achievement reading

Instructional Tactics:

- Provide students with a structure for reading narratives such as story-grammar elements including questions and story maps.
- Model the use of the story-grammar elements for the students.

Other instructional tactics from this review are applicable to other generalizations and are presented in the appropriate chapters of this book.

Findings: Use of the above tactics was found to be effective in increasing student achievement in reading comprehension of narrative writing.

❖   ❖   ❖

Author: Gersten et al. (2001)

Students: School-age children with learning disabilities

Learning: Recall

Instructional Tactics:

- Give students a graphic organizer.
- Teach students the reminder—POSSE.

  P—predicting ideas
  O—organizing predicted ideas and background knowledge based on text structure
  S—searching for the text structure
  S—summarizing the main ideas
  E—evaluating comprehension

- Model the strategies for the students using the graphic organizer.
- Encourage dialogue by the students supporting the use of the strategies.

Other instructional tactics from this review are applicable to other generalizations and are presented in the appropriate chapters of this book.

Findings: Use of the above tactics related to reminders was found to be effective in improving achievement in recall for students with learning disabilities and without learning disabilities.

Groups of studies reviewed in this logical synthesis of research did not provide statistical evidence. Individual studies from this logical synthesis related to narrative texts are marked in the reference list in Part V with the symbol %.

Author: Baker et al. (2002)

Students: Elementary and secondary (low-achieving)

Learning: Mathematics achievement

Instructional Tactics:

• Provide students with visual representations of math problems.

• Provide examples of physical manipulatives used to solve math problems.

• Guide students in developing their own visual representations by using pie chart diagrams and wood block rectangles, squares, or cubes.

Other instructional tactics from this review are applicable to other generalizations and are presented in the appropriate chapters of this book.

Findings: Use of the above tactics was found to have a positive effect on math achievement.

Groups of studies reviewed in this logical synthesis of research did not always provide statistical evidence. Individual studies from this logical synthesis related to contextualized mathematics instruction are marked in the reference list in Part V with the symbol $.

Author: Horton et al. (1993)

Students: Elementary, secondary, and college

Learning: Science achievement

Instructional Tactics:

• Preparation of concept maps for important concepts within the subject matter: these were prepared by the teachers, the students, or both.

• The concept maps produced the greatest achievement when they were prepared in class.

Findings: Use of the above tactics was found to enhance science achievement.

Author: Fisher (1997)

Students: Preschool, elementary, secondary, college, adult

Learning: Mathematics, reading, science, social studies, social science, and history

Instructional Tactics:

- Students were provided with conceptual hierarchies in the form of tree diagrams highlighting relationships within the subject matter.

- Students were provided with partially completed conceptual hierarchies in the form of tree diagrams which they were required to complete.

- Students were taught how to construct their own conceptual hierarchies in the form of tree diagrams.

- Students were provided textual summaries that highlighted relationships within the subject matter.

- Students were provided outlines that highlighted the relationships within the subject matter.

- Students were provided a pictorial representation that highlighted the relationships within the subject matter.

Findings: Use of the above instructional tactics led to higher levels of student achievement as compared to students for whom the above tactics were not used. Achievement was enhanced regardless of whether the unifying scheme was presented prior to, during, or after instruction.

Individual Studies

Author: Bower et al. (1969)

Students: High school and college

Learning: Vocabulary recall

Instructional Tactics:

Experiment I

- Students were assigned to instructional conditions defined as either a random or blocked condition.

- The blocked condition (organized) consisted of exposure to four word lists presented in hierarchies organized in vertical trees displaying category and subcategory relationships.

- The random condition (unorganized) consisted of the same word lists being scrambled and assigned in an unorganized fashion to four vertical trees.

Experiment II

- Students were assigned to instructional conditions defined as either a random or blocked condition.

- The blocked condition (organized) consisted of exposure to four word lists presented in hierarchies organized in vertical trees displaying category and subcategory relationships.

- The random condition (unorganized) consisted of the same word lists being scrambled and assigned in an unorganized fashion to four vertical trees.

Experiment III

- Students were assigned to either a rest control (control), irrelevant interpolation (unorganized), or relevant interpolation (organized) condition.

- Initially all three groups were exposed to two trials of word list 1, organized into association level hierarchies.

- While the Irrelevant and Relevant groups studied a second word list, the rest control group then read "Peanuts" cartoons.

- For the Relevant group, the words were presented in a tree form relevant for classifying level four words learned in word list 1.

- The list for the Irrelevant group was also presented in tree form but was not relevant for classifying words from word list 1.

- The three groups were then re-tested on word list 1.

Experiment IV

- Words were listed in an organized way across an associative hierarchy and levels in a manner displaying the parts-to-whole relationship and a condition in which words were scattered randomly throughout an associative hierarchy and its levels.

- The words were presented in the form of trees in written material for both groups.

- Following a study period, both groups then recalled as many words as they could by writing them on a blank sheet of paper.

Findings: In experiments I, II, and IV, the groups exposed to a unifying scheme recalled significantly more words than the groups not employing a unifying scheme. There was no significant difference between groups for experiment III.

Author: Tompkins (1991)

Students: High school

Learning: History achievement

Instructional Tactics:

• Students were instructed on the application of a partially completed graphic organizer, displaying the parts/whole relationships, for textual material to be learned.

Findings: Students using a partially completed graphic organizer recalled significantly more information than students who did not use a graphic organizer.

Author: Alvermann (1982)

Students: Grade 10

Learning: Health science achievement

Instructional Tactics:

• The teacher constructs a graphic organizer showing the main idea units reflecting either a comparison/contrast or cause/effect relationship and showing empty boxes for subordinate idea units.

• Students are taught how to use a compare and contrast procedure to identify important information in the text. For example, students might be taught how remembering the color, shape, texture, or taste of one fruit might help them identify and recall the same characteristics of a different fruit.

• Students are taught how to search for information in the text to fill in the empty boxes mentally using the compare and contrast procedure they have been taught.

Findings: Students using the graphic organizer exhibited higher levels of recall than did students not using a graphic organizer.

Author: Selinger (1995)

Students: College

Learning: English achievement

Instructional Tactics:

• Students were taught how to use a hierarchical top-down approach (identifying main ideas followed by subordinate ideas) to summarize textual information they were to learn.

Findings: Students who were taught to summarize text in a hierarchical fashion scored significantly higher on a written posttest than students who were in a control group not using the procedure.

❖   ❖   ❖

Author: Dean & Kulhavy (1981)

Students: College

Learning: Text recall

Instructional Tactics:

Experiments I and II

- Students were assigned to read a passage about a mythical African tribe. The passage contained information on the topography of the area, economics, government, and tribal ritual practices.
- Students in the experimental conditions were instructed to construct a map of the territory and events described in the passage after they had read the passage.

Findings: Students who constructed maps of the territories and events scored significantly higher on multiple choice, constructed response, and recall of main idea units tests than did students who did not construct maps.

❖   ❖   ❖

Author: Corkill et al. (1988)

Experiment I

Students: College

Learning: Science recall

Instructional Tactics:

- Students were assigned either to a concrete organizer, abstract organizer, or control condition.
- The concrete organizer was written in terms which may be seen as highlighting relationships in the subject matter specific to an instructional passage on astronomical models.
- The abstract organizers described the use of scientific models in terms not associated with the instructional passage.
- A control group simply read the passage on astronomy.

Findings: Students who employed the concrete organizer scored significantly higher on recall of main idea units than those in the abstract organizer or control conditions. There was no significant difference between the control and abstract organizer conditions.

Experiment II

Students: College

Learning: Linguistics recall

Instructional Tactics:

- Students were assigned either to a concrete organizer, abstract organizer, or control condition.
- The concrete organizer was written in terms which may be seen as highlighting relationships in the subject matter specific to an instructional passage on language usage.
- The abstract organizers described the use of scientific models in terms not associated with the instructional passage.
- A control group simply read the passage on language usage.

Findings: Students who employed the concrete organizer scored significantly higher on recall of main idea units than those in the abstract organizer or control conditions. There was no significant difference between the control and abstract organizer conditions.

Author: Witzel et al. (2003)

Students: Sixth and seventh grade students including but not limited to those who are learning disabled and at risk of failing

Learning: Achievement in algebra

Instructional Tactics:

- Provide explicit instruction: modeling, guided-practice, and independent-practice strategies.
- Provide students with sequential steps to solve algebra problems that are concrete, abstract, and representational.
  - Provide manipulatives for students to use.
  - Allow students to manipulate objects to solve concrete problems.
  - Model a pictorial representation that closely represents the concrete objects.
  - Guide students in drawing steps to solve the representational problem.
  - Model an abstract problem using Arabic symbols (typically used in textbooks and on standardized tests).

—Have students write in Arabic symbols each step to solve the abstract problem.

Other instructional tactics from this review are applicable to other generalizations and are presented in the appropriate chapters of this book.

Findings: Use of the above tactics related to concrete, representational, and abstract problem solving was found to effect achievement in algebra positively.

❖   ❖   ❖

Author: Titsworth & Kiewra (2004)

Students: Undergraduate

Learning: Basic communication

Instructional Tactics: This individual study focused on using cues during lectures. Tactics include:

- Provide students with a brief advance organizer preceding the lecture which organizes the content to be presented. This may be written or spoken.
- Provide oral cues which signal a topic or subtopic name.
- Provide oral cues which signal the sequence of points in the lecture content.
- Provide students with a matrix showing major topics across the top as column headings and subtopics down the left side of the page as row labels, leaving room for notes within the cells of the matrix.
- Provide students with a linear major topic outline on which to enter notes beneath each topic or subtopic.
- Write important ideas on the board or present them on a transparency or PowerPoint slides.

Other instructional tactics from this review are applicable to other generalizations and are presented in the appropriate chapters of this book.

Findings: Use of the above tactics, both in organizational structure of the lecture and in details of the lecture, was found to be tied positively to achievement. Cues, written and spoken, were found to have profound effects on notetaking and recall. The positive effect of cues on notetaking supported the earlier research that the quantity and detail of notetaking, without cues during lecture, led to achievement in content matter. Thus, cues during lecture are an added value to notetaking.

REFERENCE LIST

Alvermann, D. E. (1982). Restructuring text facilitates written recall of main ideas. *Journal of Reading, 25*(8), 754–758.

Baker, S., Gersten, R., & Lee, D-S. (2002). A synthesis of empirical research on teaching mathematics to low-achieving students. *The Elementary School Journal, 103*(1), 51–92.

Bower, G. H., Clark, M. C., Lesgold, A. M., & Winzenz, D. (1969). Hierarchical retrieval schemes in recall of categorized word lists. *Journal of Verbal Learning and Verbal Behavior, 8,* 323–343.

Corkill, A. J., Bruning, R. H., & Glover, J. A. (1988). Advance organizers: Concrete versus abstract. *Journal of Educational Research, 82*(2), 76–81.

Corkill, A. J., Bruning, R. H., Glover, J. A., & Krug, D. (1988). Advance organizers: Retrieval context hypothesis. *Journal of Educational Psychology, 80*(3), 304–311.

Davey, B., & McBride, S. (1986). Effects of question-generation on reading comprehension. *Journal of Educational Psychology, 78,* 256–262.

Dean, R. S., & Kulhavy, R. W. (1981). Influence of spatial organization in prose learning. *Journal of Educational Psychology, 73*(1), 57–64.

Denner, P. R. (1986, June). *Comparison of the effects of episodic organizers and traditional notetaking on story recall.* Paper submitted to the Faculty Research Committee of Idaho State University. (ERIC Document Reproduction Service No. ED 270 731)

Fisher, S. (1997). *Subject matter unifiers: Synthesis of a body of research.* Unpublished manuscript. Columbia: University of South Carolina.

Gersten, R., & Baker, S. (2001). Teaching expressive writing to students with learning disabilities: A meta-analysis. *The Elementary School Journal, 101*(3), 251–273.

Gersten, R., Fuchs, L. S., Williams, J. P., & Baker, S. (2001). Teaching reading comprehension strategies to students with learning disabilities: A review of research. *Review of Educational Research, 71*(2), 279–320.

Gillies, D. A. (1984). Effect of advance organizers on learning medical surgical nursing content by baccalaureate nursing students. *Research in Nursing and Health, 7,* 173–180.

Griffin, C. C., & Tulbert, B. L. (1995). The effect of graphic organizers on students' comprehension and recall of expository text: A review of the research and implications for practice. *Reading & Writing Quarterly: Overcoming Learning Difficulties, 11,* 73–89.

Guzzetti, B. J. (2000). Learning counter-intuitive science concepts: What have we learned from over a decade of research? *Reading & Writing Quarterly, 16,* 89–96.

Hattie, J., Biggs, J., & Purdie, N. (1996). Effects of learning skills interventions on student learning: A meta-analysis. *Review of Educational Research, 66*(2), 99–136.

Hawk, P. P. (1986). Using graphic organizers to increase achievement in middle school life science. *Science Education, 70*(1), 81–87.

Horton, P. B., McConney, A. A., Gallo, M., Woods, A. L., Senn, G. J., & Hamil, D. (1993). An investigation of the effects of concept mapping as an instructional tool. *Science Education, 77*(1), 95–111.

Robinson, D. H., & Schraw, G. (1994). Computational efficiency through visual argument: Do graphic organizers communicate relations and text too effectively? *Contemporary Educational Psychology, 19,* 399–415.

Rosenshine, B., Meister, C., & Chapman, S. (1996). Teaching students to generate questions: A review of the intervention studies. *Review of Educational Research, 66*(2), 181–221.

Selinger, B. M. (1995). Summarizing text: Developmental students demonstrate a successful method. *Journal of Developmental Education, 19*(2), 14–19.

Simmons, D. C., Griffin, C. C., & Kameenui, E. J. (1988). Effects of teacher-constructed pre- and post-graphic organizer instruction on sixth-grade science students' comprehension and recall. *Journal of Educational Research, 82*(1), 15–21.

Titsworth, B. S., & Kiewra, K. A. (2004). Spoken organizational lecture cues and student notetaking as facilitators of student learning. *Contemporary Educational Psychology, 29*(4), 447–461.

Tompkins, R. S. (1991, April). *The use of a spatial learning strategy to enhance reading comprehension of secondary subject area text.* Paper presented at the annual Indiana Reading Conference, Indianapolis, IN.

Wise, K. C. (1996). Strategies for teaching science: What works? *The Clearing House, 69*(6), 337–338.

Witzel, B. S., Mercer, C. D., & Miller, M. D. (2003). Teaching algebra to students with learning difficulties: An investigation of an explicit instruction model. *Learning Disabilities Research & Practice, 18*(2), 121–131.

Wong, B.Y.L., & Wilson, M. (1984). Investigating awareness of and teaching passage organization in learning disabled children. *Journal of Learning Disabilities, 17*(8), 477–482.

Yan, P. X., & Jitendra, A. K. (1999). The effects of instruction in solving mathematical word problems for students with learning problems: A meta-analysis. *Journal of Special Education, 32*(4), 207–238.

14

Providing One-to-One Tutoring

INTRODUCTION

The seminal research of Benjamin Bloom (1981) and his disciples Anania (1981) and Burke (1983) show how much more effective one-to-one tutoring is than regular classroom instruction in increasing academic achievement.

- The academic achievement of tutored students is about two standard deviations above students taught in conventional classrooms. Put another way, the average tutored student outperforms 98 percent of students taught in conventional classrooms.
- Tutored students do not require nearly as much corrective instruction as students taught in conventional classrooms.
- About 90 percent of tutored students attain a level of achievement attained by only the highest 20 percent of students taught in conventional classrooms.

Wasik and Slavin (2000) cite convincing research showing the effectiveness of one-to-one tutoring in preventing and remediating inadequacies of at-risk students in the early grades as well as of students with disabilities. There is little doubt that one-to-one tutoring is more effective than classroom instruction in producing academic achievement and in preventing and remediating inadequacies in student achievement. One-to-one tutoring can be used as a supplement to classroom instruction to reduce appreciably the number of students who fail in school.

Tutoring can occur in a number of ways. Teachers may be the tutors. Other adults such as teaching assistants, volunteers, and college students may serve as tutors. In some circumstances, even qualified peers can be tutors.

STUDENT BENEFICIARIES

The evidence indicates that students at all levels of schooling benefit from one-to-one tutoring—preschool, kindergarten, elementary, middle, secondary, and adult students. Further, achievement is especially enhanced by one-to-one tutoring at the kindergarten and primary levels. Evidence also indicates that one-to-one tutoring is a valuable instructional strategy for students with learning disabilities. Use of one-to-one tutoring in reading is perhaps the most pervasive; however, this strategy is used across many content areas and learning strategies such as problem solving. Evidence supports that the strategy is beneficial in all content areas at the high school level. No evidence could be found to suggest that one-to-one tutoring should not be stressed in all subject areas for all types of students.

LEARNING ACHIEVED

Achievement in the content areas of reading, reading comprehension, reading fluency, mathematics, higher order processing (problem solving), and language arts and all content areas at the high school level is enhanced when students are given one-to-one tutoring. In studies reviewed, student achievement was shown to be enhanced when one-to-one tutoring was incorporated into the instruction even for very brief periods of time.

INSTRUCTIONAL TACTICS

The following tactics are derived from studies that demonstrate the benefit of one-to-one tutoring.

- Tutors are given tutoring instruction (at the least, tutoring instructions are provided; and, at most, training and certification are required).
- Tutoring aids are made available for tutoring sessions; for example, textbooks, workbooks, and students' prior test and assignment results.
- The student attends tutoring sessions until the learning objective is achieved or evaluations indicate the need for reassignment.

CAUTIONS AND COMMENTS

The importance of one-to-one tutoring in reading in the early grades can not be emphasized too much. Evidence supports the benefits of this tutoring for establishing a strong foundation for future academic success for all students including those with learning disabilities, from low socioeconomic backgrounds, and across races and ethnicities. See Chapter 27 for suggestions on implementing preventive tutoring programs.

GENERALIZATION: ON ONE-TO-ONE TUTORING

Achievement of learning objectives is enhanced when students are provided one-to-one tutoring as needed.

Supportive Research on One-to-One Tutoring
Total number of supportive studies covered: 500+

Groups of Studies

Author: Cohen et al. (1982)

Students: Elementary and secondary

Learning: Achievement (mathematics)

Instructional Tactics:

- Structure a tutoring program which allows each student to be both the tutor and the tutee.
- Limit the sessions to 0 to 18 weeks; then form new pairs.
- Focus the content and materials for the tutoring program on lower-level skills.
- Develop and administer a test on the content material.

Findings: Use of the above tactics led to improved achievement in mathematics. In addition, the tutors also benefited from the tutoring session.

It was not possible to determine the individual studies involved in this meta-analysis about tutoring.

❖ ❖ ❖

Author: Swanson & Hoskyn (1998)

Students: Children and adults with learning disabilities

Learning: Achievement

Instructional Tactics: The meta-analysis included an overlap of strategy instruction and direct instruction.
- Provide one-to-one instruction.
- Plan for time for dialogues between teacher and a student.

Other instructional tactics from this review are applicable to other generalizations and are presented in the appropriate chapters of this book.

Findings: Use of a combination of the above tactics led to enhanced achievement in multiple content areas.

Specific studies in this meta-analysis are marked with the symbol * in the reference list in Part V.

Author: Elbaum et al. (1999)

Students: Elementary—students with disabilities

Learning: Reading achievement

Instructional Tactics:

- Students are placed in peer-tutoring pairs.
- Students act as reciprocal tutor-tutees.

Findings: Use of the above tactic with disabled students was found to lead to improved student achievement in decoding and reading comprehension skills.

Studies used in this meta-analysis are marked with the symbol & in the reference list in Part V.

Author: Elbaum et al. (2000)

Students: Elementary

Learning: Achievement in reading

Instructional Tactics: In this meta-analysis, a number of reading programs were used with the tutors adhering to the criteria of the programs.

- Students receive one-to-one tutoring from an adult (teacher, college student, paraprofessionals, and volunteers) on a regular basis, usually several times a week over a number of weeks and months, from 20 to 60 minutes each session.
- Tutors use materials from the specific reading program being used in the school.

Findings: Use of the above tactics was found to enhance academic achievement in reading skills.

Studies in this meta-analysis are marked in the reference list in Part V with the symbol #.

Author: Swanson (2001)

Students: Adolescents with learning disabilities

Learning: Higher-order processing (problem solving)

Instructional Tactics:

- Provide activities related to independent practice.
- Provide tutoring.
- Provide instruction that is individually paced.
- Provide instruction that is individually tailored.

Other instructional tactics from this review are applicable to other generalizations and are presented in the appropriate chapters of this book.

Findings: Use of the above tactics led to higher levels of achievement by students with learning disabilities in problem solving as measured by standardized tests in reading and in mathematics.

Studies associated with this meta-analysis are identified by the symbol % in the reference list in Part V.

❖ ❖ ❖

Author: Therrien (2004)

Students: Preschool and elementary

Learning: Reading fluency and comprehension

Instructional Tactics: When students are reading a new passage after having read other passages multiple times:

- Intervene to provide one-to-one tutoring.

Other instructional tactics from this review are applicable to other generalizations and are presented in the appropriate chapters of this book.

Findings: Use of the above tactic was found to be highly effective in students' achievement of reading fluency and comprehension.

Studies included in this meta-analysis are marked with the symbol ! in the reference list in Part V.

❖ ❖ ❖

Author: Education Commission of the States (1999)

Students: Elementary (K–6)

Learning: Language arts, reading, and mathematics

Instructional Tactics:

- Students are provided one-on-one tutoring by a teacher or a paraprofessional.

Other instructional tactics from this review are applicable to other generalizations and are presented in the appropriate chapters of this book.

Findings: Use of the above tactic was found to enhance academic achievement.

Individual studies and groups of studies in this logical synthesis are identified with the symbol + in the reference list in Part V. Statistical data are not included in this synthesis of studies.

Author: Baker et al. (2002)

Students: Elementary and secondary (low-achieving)

Learning: Mathematics achievement

Instructional Tactics:

- Students work in pairs determined by assessment results.
- Students work on content determined by assessment results.
- Students receive training in tutoring techniques and use prompt cards to guide their tutoring. They also are taught some teaching strategies to use as they tutor.
- Students share in the roles of tutor and tutee.
- Students may tutor only on computational skills.
- Students are provided a step-by-step process to use in approaching each type of problem.
- Students may construct explanations of their own.
- Student tutors are encouraged to use visuals and manipulatives.

Other instructional tactics from this review are applicable to other generalizations and are presented in the appropriate chapters of this book.

Findings: Use of the above tactics was found to have a positive effect on math achievement.

Groups of studies reviewed in this logical synthesis of research did not always provide statistical evidence. Individual studies from this logical synthesis are marked in the reference list in Part V with the symbol =.

Author: Barley et al. (2002)

Students: Kindergarten, elementary, middle, and secondary at-risk students

Learning: Academic achievement (reading at all grade levels and all content areas at high school level)

Instructional Tactics:

- Students are identified either through test scores or teacher judgment.
- Students are provided one-to-one tutoring by a professional including licensed teachers and trained specialists.
- Students are provided one-to-one tutoring by adult volunteers including college students, senior citizens, and other adults.
- Students are provided one-to-one tutoring by other students who are significantly older than the tutees or more advanced in the skill levels than the tutees.
- Tutors are provided some training.
- Materials, instructional space, and scheduling are made available to the tutors.
- Tutoring sessions are monitored and adapted as needed.
- Teachers diagnose needs and offer prescriptions for the tutors to follow.

The following instructional strategies are associated with the Classwide Peer Tutoring (CWPT) method:

- Students work in pairs for approximately 30 minutes each day or for two to five days of the week during time typically spent on workbook assignments or other self-directed activities.
- Materials are prepared for the students to use: scripted tutor and tutee interactions that include task presentation, question asking, error correction, point earning, feedback, and positive reinforcement.
- The students are trained to be both a tutor and a tutee.
- Students, initially, are assigned to pairs; the students rotate roles; their work is monitored. Students remain in the same paired situation for one week.

The following tactics are associated with the Peer-Assisted Learning Strategies (PALS) which used CWPT as a foundation:

- In addition to the tactics in CWPT, the material is content specific (reading or math).
- Students may not always engage in reciprocal tutoring; thus one student only tutors, and the other only receives the tutoring.

- Sometimes a mini-lesson on the content is delivered for the low achievers prior to the peer tutoring session.

The following tactics are associated with the Reciprocal Peer Tutoring (RPT) in mathematics:

- Although many of the tactics of RPT are the same as those of CWPT and PALS, its focus is on mathematics content.
- The pairs are randomly assigned, rather than based on pretest or teacher judgment.
- The pair of students alternate between a teacher role and a student role.
- The peer teacher prompts and praises the peer student.
- The peer teacher seeks help from the adult, if needed.
- The pair of students is involved in goal setting, thus establishing interdependence.
- The students are allowed to select their rewards from a menu of choices which enhances learner control.

Other instructional tactics from this review are applicable to other generalizations and are presented in the appropriate chapters of this book.

Findings: Use of the above tactics was found to lead to improved academic achievement of at-risk students.

Studies in this synthesis directly related to decision-making instruction are designated with the symbol ^ in the reference list in Part V.

Individual Studies

Author: Bryant et al. (1995)

Students: Elementary (grades 1–8)—low-achieving

Learning: Achievement in reading

Instructional Tactics:
- Students are given a pretest.
- Teachers use the Help One Student to Succeed (HOSTS) program.
- Appropriate materials are secured and listed in a data base for the one-on-one mentoring session.
- Teachers prepare mentor-friendly education packets individually designed for each child.

- Mentors (volunteer community person) receive training to work with the students.
- The student visits the HOSTS center to work with a mentor for 30 minutes each day Monday through Thursday.
- Teachers assess student progress and develop a new packet on Fridays for the next one-to-one mentoring session.
- The mentor, using the prepared lesson plan and materials, guides the student through the lesson.
- The mentor, at the end of the session, records what the student has learned to enable the teacher to prepare for the next session.
- Students work with their mentors on reading while the other classmates are working on reading in class.
- Students remain in the HOSTS program until they reach the appropriate reading level.
- Students are given a posttest. (California Achievement Test)

Findings: Use of the above tactics led to increased student achievement. While the federal program, Chapter 1, requires 1 NCE as a measure of success, the students in this study made gains ranging from +3.41 to +11.52 NCEs.

Author: Fuchs et al. (1997)

Students: Elementary—low achievers with disabilities, low achievers without disabilities, and average achievers

Learning: Achievement in reading

Instructional Tactics:

- Students are given a pretest.
- Reading materials are determined.
- Students are put in pairs by ranking them on the reading performance measured by the pretest, splitting the ranked list in half, and pairing the top two from each list and continuing that pairing down to the bottom two students.
- Pairs remain together for four weeks; then new pairings are made.
- Students assume the roles of both tutor and tutee.
- Students engage in three strategic reading activities, replacing the typical adult-directed instruction, which include
  —Partner reading with retell
  —Paragraph summary
  —Prediction relay

- Students are trained to correct word recognition error and to encourage the reader to reread for accuracy.

- Students serving as tutors prompt their tutees during the retelling time with questions such as "What did you learn first?" and "What did you learn next?"

- During paragraph summary to assist the tutees in identifying topics and main ideas, tutors use cue cards with questions such as "Who or what was the paragraph about?" and "Tell me the most important thing you learned from reading or listening to the paragraph."

- Student readers make a prediction about what will be learned on the next page, then read aloud the page, confirm the prediction, summarize the just read page, make a new prediction, and continue the cycle.

- Tutors and the adult award points; students maintain points on a score card.

- Students are given a posttest.

Findings: Use of the above tactics was found to increase achievement in reading.

❖   ❖   ❖

Author: Trout et al. (2003)

Students: Kindergarten—at risk of emotional disturbance

Learning: Achievement in reading

Instructional Tactics:

- Students are provided a half-hour, one-on-one tutoring session daily over a seven-month period.

- Students participate in their regular classroom instruction.

- Trained graduate students provide the tutoring.

Findings: Use of the above tactics was found to enhance achievement in reading. The students receiving the one-on-one tutoring in addition to their regular classroom instruction performed better in letter sounds and blends than the students in a matched at-risk group not receiving the treatment and the students in the norm-referencing group. The treatment group outperformed the matched group in high-frequency sight words and performed almost as well as the norm-referencing group.

REFERENCE LIST

Anania, J. (1981). *The effects of quality of instruction on the cognitive and affective learning of students.* Unpublished doctoral dissertation, University of Chicago.

Baker, S., Gersten, R., & Lee, D-S. (2002). A synthesis of empirical research on teaching mathematics to low-achieving students. *The Elementary School Journal, 103*(1), 51–92.

Barley, Z., Lauer, P. A., Arens, S. A., Apthorp, H. S., Englert, K. S., Snow, D., & Akiba, M. (2002). *Helping at-risk students meet standards: A synthesis of evidence-based classroom practices.* Aurora, CO: Mid-continent Research for Education and Learning.

Bloom, B. S. (1984, May). The search for methods of group instruction as effective as one-to-one tutoring. *Educational Leadership*, 4–17.

Bryant, H. D., Edwards, J. P., & LeFiles, D. C. (1995, Fall). Early intervention and one-to-one mentoring help students succeed. *ERS Spectrum*, 3–6.

Burke, A. J. (1983). *Students' potential for learning contrasted under tutorial and group approaches to instruction.* Unpublished doctoral dissertation, University of Chicago.

Cohen, P. A., Kulik, J. A., & Kulik, C-L. C. (1982). Educational outcomes of tutoring: A meta-analysis of findings. *American Educational Research Journal, 19*(2), 237–248.

Education Commission of the States. (1999). *Direct instruction.* Denver, CO: Education Commission of the States.

Elbaum, B., Vaughn, S., Hughes, M., & Moody, S. W. (1999). Grouping practices and reading outcomes for students with disabilities. *Exceptional Children, 65*(3), 399–416.

Elbaum, B., Vaughn, S., Hughes, M. T., & Moody, S. W. (2000). How effective are one-to-one tutoring programs in reading for elementary students at risk for reading failure? A meta-analysis of the intervention research. *Journal of Educational Psychology, 92*(4), 605–619.

Fuchs, D., Fuchs, L. S., Mathes, P. G., & Simmons, D. C. (1997). Peer-assisted learning strategies: Making classrooms more responsive to diversity. *American Educational Research Journal, 34*(1), 174–206.

Swanson, H. L. (2001). Research on interventions for adolescents with learning disabilities: A meta-analysis of outcomes related to higher-order processing. *The Elementary School Journal, 101*(13), 331–349.

Swanson, H. L., & Hoskyn, M. (1998). Experimental intervention research on students with learning disabilities: A meta-analysis of treatment outcomes. *Review of Educational Research, 68*(3), 277–321.

Therrien, W. J. (2004). Fluency and comprehension gains as a result of repeated reading: A meta-analysis. *Remedial and Special Education, 25*(4), 252–261.

Trout, A. L., Epstein, M. H., Mikelson, W. T., Nelson, J. R., & Lewis, L. M. (2003). Effects of a reading intervention for kindergarten students at risk for emotional disturbance and reading deficits. *Behavioral Disorders, 28*, 313–326.

Wasik, B. A., & Slavin, R. E. (2000). *Preventing early reading failure with one-to-one tutoring: A review of five programs.* Baltimore, MD: Johns Hopkins University, Center for Research on Effective Schooling for Disadvantaged Students.

15

Utilizing Reminders

INTRODUCTION

The use of reminders to recall things is an established everyday practice. People use a number of strategies to remember things. A "string tied around one's finger" might be used to remind someone to do something. A word such as "money" or "bank" written on a piece of paper might be used to remind someone of the need to go to the bank and make a deposit or withdrawal. The phrase "post office" might remind someone he needs stamps or needs to mail a letter or package. Many people use appointment books or daily planners to remind them of important upcoming events. This list could go on.

In education there is a continuing need for students to recall words and factual information that must be committed to memory. In order to engage in problem solving or to write an essay, the student must be able to remember and recall factual information. Although there is currently an emphasis on assessing students' higher order thinking skills and a supposed de-emphasis on memorization of facts and concepts, much of testing, at all levels of education regardless of the format, continues to be closed-book recall of names, dates, places, things, events, definitions, and concepts. Moreover, students take notes to remind themselves of information they need to pass a test. The use of reminders would seem to be a viable tool when properly used in the appropriate situation to facilitate students' remembering.

STUDENT BENEFICIARIES

The evidence indicates that teaching students how to use reminders enhances achievement in elementary, junior high, secondary, college, military and adult education settings. Moreover, achievement is enhanced in a wide range of content areas. No evidence could be found to suggest that teaching students to use reminders should not be stressed for all types of students in all subject matter areas that require the recall of factual information. However, there is evidence to suggest that more complex reminder tactics may not be beneficial for students in the lower elementary grades.

LEARNING ACHIEVED

Achievement in the content areas of mathematics, reading, English, foreign languages, physical science, life science, spelling, vocabulary, science, social studies, art, physics, writing, and algebra is enhanced when students are taught to use reminders.

INSTRUCTIONAL TACTICS

Reminders have been found to be useful in three types of learning situations requiring variation in the instructional tactics for each situation. They are (1) when to-be-learned material consists of a short list or small group of interrelated objects or concepts; (2) when a larger number of concepts are to be recalled, and (3) when the focus of instruction is English, foreign language vocabulary instruction, science taxonomies, or other more complex learning situations. There are instructional tactics generic to all three situations as well as instructional tactics specific to each situation.

GENERAL INSTRUCTIONAL TACTICS

- Provide instruction on commonly used effective reminders and how to use them; for example, acronyms, mental images, rhyming, note taking, and so forth.
- Provide students instruction on how to formulate and use reminders appropriate to the particular learning situation. (In some situations, such as when students' readiness characteristics are inadequate or the material to be learned is complex, it may be beneficial for the teacher to formulate the reminders to be used rather than leave the students to their own devices.)
- Allow students ample time to practice using the reminder tactics they have been taught.
- Monitor the students' practice. When students are found to be having difficulty employing the instructional tactics, provide guidance as necessary.

Instructional tactics for short lists or small groups of interrelated objects or concepts:

- A question is asked which necessitates recall.

- A keyword is produced by the student or provided by the teacher which directs an association to the to-be-learned material.
- The answer is given by the student.

Example from Bellezza (1996):

1. The question might be "What are the names of the Great Lakes?"
2. An appropriate keyword might be "HOMES."
3. The correct answer—Huron, Ontario, Michigan, Erie, Superior.

Instructional tactics to be used when a larger number of concepts are to be recalled:

- The question is asked requiring an answer consisting of multiple responses such as the reasons for why something happened or a long list of items.
- Rhyming keywords are then produced by the student or provided by the teacher for each of the required responses.
- The student then is to create a mental image of the relationship between the keyword and the required answers.
- The answer is given by the student.

Example from Morrison and Levin (1987):

- For this example the student is asked to provide eight possible reasons for the extinction of the dinosaurs.
- The student uses keywords that rhyme with the number associated with each reason (e.g., 1 is bun, 2 is shoe, 3 is tree, and so on).
- The student then forms a mental image that will remind the student of the correct answer (e.g., for reason number three the keyword is tree, for which the student might form a mental image of a Christmas tree with an exploding star on the tree which will remind the student that exploding stars might be an explanation for the extinction of the dinosaurs).
- The student provides the answer.

Instructional tactics to be used when the focus of instruction is English, foreign language vocabulary instruction, science taxonomies, or other more complex learning situations:

- The teacher asks the question.
- The to-be-learned word is presented to the student, along with a keyword that rhymes with the to-be-learned word.

- The student then uses the sound of the to-be-learned word to recall the rhymed keyword.

- The student then forms a mental image that includes the meaning of the keyword and the meaning of the to-be-learned word.

- The student provides the answer.

Examples from Bellezza (1996):

1. Example for the Spanish word *carta*:

Question: What does the word *carta* mean? The student might use the key-word *cart* and form a mental picture of a large postal letter being pushed in a grocery cart. Later, when the word *carta* is seen or heard, the image of a postal letter being pushed in a cart should be elicited. This image would re-mind the student that the word *carta* means letter.

2. Example for a complex learning situation:

Students are asked to recall the five types of vertebrates:

A drawing of a farm is provided with a sign over the entrance reading FARM-B, which represents fish, amphibian, reptile, mammal, bird. Five piles of *dirt* are pictured on the farm with *dirt* being the keyword for *vert*-ebrates. On one pile of dirt there is a picture of a fish, on the second a frog wearing a bib, on the third an alligator and tiles, on the fourth a camel, and on the fifth a bird. These images help the student recall the five types of vertebrates: fish, am-*phib*-ian, rep-*tiles*, mammal, and bird.

CAUTIONS AND COMMENTS

Reminders supposedly enhance higher mental functions such as comprehension and problem solving, but this may happen because reminders cue recall of informa-tion needed immediately to perform higher mental functions. Many assigned tasks allow students time to look up information they need; for example, library research. Many other assigned tasks require the immediate recall of information; for ex-ample, answering questions on a multiple-choice test in the time allotted.

Reviews of studies cited in the "Supportive Research" section of this chapter use the terminology "mnemonics," mnemotechnics," and other jargon rather than the term "reminders." Reviews of studies also use the educational jargon "meta-cognitive" rather than "a structured self-questioning procedure used to reach a goal" or decision-making.

GENERALIZATION: ON REMINDERS

Achievement of learning objectives is enhanced when reminders are used to cue the recall of information needed to perform assigned tasks.

Supportive Research on Utilizing Reminders
Total number of supportive studies covered: 173

Groups of Studies

Author: Rosenshine et al. (1996)

Students: Upper elementary (grade 3 and up), junior high, secondary, and college

Learning: Reading comprehension across subject matters, mathematics, physics, and writing

Instructional Tactics:

- Give students procedural prompts (hints, cues, and suggestions) to assist in reading and listening comprehension mastery. Those prompts are signal words, generic question stems and generic questions, the main idea of a passage, question types, and story grammar categories.

  —Signal words for starting questions might be *who, what, where, when, why,* and *how*.

  —An example of a generic question is "How does the author put the ideas in order?" A generic question stem is "How are ____ and ____ alike?"

  —Using a booklet, students are directed to (1) identify the main idea of each paragraph, (2) form questions which ask for new examples of the main idea, and (3) write a question about a concept in the paragraph in a paraphrased form.

  —Question types include factual (a question whose answer can be found in a single sentence), inferential (a question that requires integrating two or more sentences of text), and background based (a question whose answer cannot be found in the text but requires students to use a schema or background knowledge). Students used this cue to generate questions and to identify questions they were asked.

  —A story grammar with four elements: setting, main character, character's goal, and obstacles might be used. These elements cued students to generate questions to comprehend passages.

- Teach students specific rules to determine a good question from a non question and a good question from a poor question. For example, a good question begins with a question word or a good question asks about important details of the passage.

- Provide students with cue cards listing, for example, signal words, steps in a process, or generic questions to guide their understanding of a passage.

- Provide students with charts listing, for example, elements or steps to follow in reading a passage.

- Give students cue cards following their reading of a passage which list specific questions or question stems to assist them in understanding the passage.

Other instructional tactics from this review are applicable to other generalizations and are presented in the appropriate chapters of this book.

Findings: Use of the above tactics was found to enhance reading comprehension.

Individual studies analyzed by this meta-analysis are identified in the reference list in Part V by the symbol +.

Author: Fukkink & de Glopper (1998)

Students: Upper elementary and secondary

Learning: Vocabulary from context

Instructional Tactics:

- Teach students rules for learning the meaning of words in context—clue, cloze, and strategy.
- Provide explanation of clue procedures.

 —Find a definition in the dictionary
 —Find a synonym
 —Find an antonym or think of a contrast
 —Think of an experience that is similar
 —Provide an illustration

- Provide explanation of cloze procedures.

 —Supply the missing key words in a passage
 —Select from two alternatives for a specific blank

- Provide explanation and modeling of strategy procedures.

 —Consider a rule such as "When there's a hard word in a sentence, look for other words in the story that tell you more about the word"
 —"Look at morphemes within a word" and "look around at the flow of events and mood in the part of the story in which the word appeared"
 —Use the acronym SCAR: substitute, check the fit, accept the substitution, or rethink
 —Use the acronym SCANR:
   - Substitute a word or expression for the unknown word
   - Check the context for clues that support the idea
   - Ask if substitution fits all context clues
   - Need a new idea?

- Revise the idea to fit the context
—Use the brake, track, and zoom-in tactics
    - Brake: stop to learn the word
    - Track: make a substitution sentence; ask Wh- questions (where, why, who, etc.); find a synonym or a definition; check whether this synonym or definition fits the context
    - Zoom-in: focus on the word and check whether this yields information that confirms the word meaning derived so far
- Provide practice in the use of the rules.
- Encourage students to use the rules when deciding on word meaning in a passage.

Other instructional tactics from this review are applicable to other generalizations and are presented in the appropriate chapters of this book.

Findings: Use of the above tactics was found to be effective in achievement of word meaning comprehension.

Studies in this meta-analysis are in the reference list in Part V and are marked with the symbol %.

❖   ❖   ❖

Author: Gersten & Baker (2001)

Students: Learning disabled

Learning: Expressive writing

Instructional Tactics:

- Students are provided, during the corrective instruction time, a text structure to remind them of the essential elements to be included in their writing.
    —An example of a text structure for guiding expressive writing includes the following elements: introduction of the topic; inclusion of a sequence of steps; inclusion of key organization words such as first, second, and third; and adherence to an organizational technique acceptable for the particular type of writing.
    —Another example of text structure is the story grammar which includes the following elements: main character, locale, time, starter event, goal, action, ending, and reaction.

Other instructional tactics from this review are applicable to other generalizations and are presented in the appropriate chapters of this book.

Findings: Use of the above tactics was found to enhance writing achievement.

Studies associated with this meta-analysis are identified by the symbol = in the reference list in Part V.

Author: Bellezza (1996)

Students: Elementary, secondary, college, and adult education

Learning: English, foreign language, physical science, life science, spelling, and mathematics recall

Instructional Tactics:

• The student connects the word to be learned with a keyword and creates a mental image connecting the keyword to the meaning of the word to be learned.

• In the future, when the student sees or hears the word to be learned, he should think of the keyword assigned to it and the mental image associated with it.

• For more complex situations, it may be better for the student to be provided the keyword(s) and imagery.

Findings: These instructional tactics, when used, "have been shown to, at least, double the amount of information retained by regular students."

Individual studies included in this research synthesis are identified by the symbol * in the reference list in Part V.

Author: Levin (1993)

Students: "Students of all ages" (grade levels are not provided by the author)

Learning: English, science, social studies, and mathematics achievement and retention

Instructional Tactics:

• Provide students instruction in how to use memory strategies that enhance recall of to-be-learned information.

• Have the students recode unfamiliar information into familiar terms such as:

—*Keyword*: the word "accolade" could be recoded by the student to be "kool-aid," with the student forming a mental picture of a group of people raising their glasses of kool-aid in a toast to someone being honored.

—*Pegword*: the student transforms the numbers one to ten into rhyming words such as 1 is bun, 2 is shoe, . . . , and 10 is a hen. The students are then to relate the pegwords to to-be-learned information such as the top ten reasons for . . .

Combinations of these and other methods of enhancing students' recall of to-be-learned information may be used.

• Allow students time to practice the newly learned strategies.

The focus of this review was to provide a "report card" for memory-enhancing strategies and not to provide a complete list of instructional tactics on how to employ them. For a more complete list of instructional tactics and information on how they were or should be employed, refer to the studies identified by the symbol # in the reference list in Part V. Additionally, Joel Levin, as well as many of the other authors included in the reference list, has published additional literature on instructional tactics associated with reminders.

Findings: The above tactics have been found to enhance students' recall and retention of difficult-to-remember factual information, unfamiliar names and terminology, and previously learned information. The tactics have been found to enhance recall and integration of previously learned information for the purposes of problem solving. The tactics have been successfully used to convey hierarchical relationships among concept families and to teach arithmetic operations.

Complex methods such as those which combine the above-named tactics with other tactics have led to inconsistent findings, especially for younger children.

Individual studies included in this research synthesis are identified by the symbol # in the reference list in Part V.

Author: Carney et al. (1993)

Students: "Ranging from young children to college age adults and the elderly"

Learning: English, foreign vocabulary, reading, social studies, mathematics, and art recall

Instructional Tactics:

• Recode or change an unfamiliar word into a more familiar word, termed a keyword.

• Relate the keyword in some meaningful way to the information to be learned in the form of a mental picture.

- The keyword and the mental picture are put together to recall the new word and the meaning of the new word.

Findings: Use of the preceding tactics has been found to enhance recall of to-be-learned information, recall of information to be used in novel problem-solving situations, and complex hierarchical concept classifications.

Individual studies included in this research synthesis are identified by the symbol $ in the reference list in Part V.

Author: Levin (1988)

Students: Elementary, secondary, college, and adult education

Learning: Recall and retention of information to be learned

Instructional Tactics:

- Provided elaborations (reminders) should be meaningful to the learner.
- Elaborations should integrate the stimulus and response terms; for instance, the telephone (stimulus) is next to the glass (response).
- Elaborations should provide logical connections.

Example for sentences about different people:

(a) The thirsty woman climbed the hill . . .

(b) The embarrassed woman put on the hat . . .

Students are asked to study these in order to answer questions of the following kind:

(a) Who climbed the hill?

(b) Who put on the hat?

Logically appropriate elaborations complete the original sentences:

(a) . . . to look for the oasis.

(b) . . . when her wig blew off.

- Elaborations should prompt active information processing on the part of the learner. The student should have to think about the elaboration in relation to what is to be learned.
- With inefficient learners, it is better for the teacher to provide the elaboration than it is to have the students generate their own.

Findings: Research evidence supports the use of the preceding tactics for enhancing recall of material to be learned.

Individual studies included in this research synthesis are identified by the symbol @ in the reference list in Part V.

❖ ❖ ❖

Author: Griffith (1979)

Students: College and military personnel

Learning: Numeric, word, information, and concept recall

Instructional Tactics: Reminders-only tactics for which empirical evidence was provided are included below.

1. *Numeric Pegword*: "To use this technique the student must first memorize rhyme pegwords for the digits 1–10. For example, 1 is bun, 2 is shoe, 3 is a tree, 4 is a door, 5 is a hive, 6 is a stick, 7 is heaven, 8 is gate, 9 is wine, and 10 is hen" (p. 5). It should be noted that the technique is not limited to 10 numbers. It could be 20, 50, 100, and so on. These could then be used to learn the following list of words by forming a visual image linked to the rhyme pegword.

   1—helicopter   1—a helicopter wrapped in a bun
   2—rifle   2—a rifle stuck in a shoe
   3—jeep   3—a jeep up in a tree
   4—desk   4—a desk blocking a door

2. *Alphabet Pegwords*: The following pegwords might be developed based on the alphabet:

   A—Ape
   B—Bum
   C—Cat
   D—Dog

3. *Linking (Story)*: Each recalled item is used as a retrieval cue for succeeding items to be recalled: "for example, the task of learning the following chain of command: President, Secretary of Defense, Secretary of the Army, Chief of Staff, FORSCOM Commander, Corps Commander, Division Commander, Brigade Commander, Battalion Commander, Company Commander. One could link these elements as follows: the first image could be of the President talking to a secretary who is acting defensively and who has a big 'D' on her sweater (Secretary of Defense); this secretary could, in turn, be pictured speaking to another secretary who is wearing an army uniform (Secretary of the Army); then one could imagine this secretary talking to an Indian Chief holding a staff (Chief of Staff) . . ." (p. 8).

4. *Substitute Word or Keyword*: A substitute word or keyword is developed based on the sound of the vocabulary word to be learned:

Example: "the Spanish word for horse, Caballo (Pronounced cab' eye o) . . . first a substitute word or phrase (a cab eyeing an "o") or a keyword (eye) would be developed based on the sound of the target word. Next, an image would be generated linking the meaning of the target word to the substitute phrase (a cab eyeing the (o) mark on a horse, or keyword (a cyclopean horse))" (p. 12).

5. *Reminder for Pictorial Symbols*: The Navy uses the following for learning Navy signal flags:

The flag for "B" (Bravo) is red and shaped as follows:

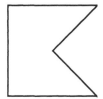

The reminder is that the red flag is a Bullfighter's cape and the crowd is yelling BRAVO for him; or the flag for "E" (Echo) has a blue top and a red bottom and is shaped as follows:

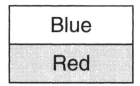

Here the reminder is "Blue Sky—Red Earth" (pp. 16–17).

Findings: Twenty experimental studies involving a control group were reviewed. Two studies indicated no significant differences. One study reviewed indicated no difference for longer-term delayed recall between using mnemonic strategies and not using a mnemonic strategy but found a significant difference in favor of mnemonics on immediate and shorter-term delayed recall. One study found no significant difference on immediate recall but found a significant difference in favor of the mnemonic group on delayed recall. Eighteen studies reported a significant difference in favor of the use of a mnemonic strategy, with the difference in recall for using a mnemonic strategy as high as four times the level of recall for not using a mnemonic strategy.

Individual studies included in this research synthesis are identified by the symbol & in the reference list in Part V.

Author: Gersten et al. (2001)

Students: School-age children

Learning: Achievement in recall of novel expository passages read aloud to students

Instructional Tactics:

- Give students a graphic organizer.
- Teach students the reminder—POSSE.

  P—predicting ideas
  O—organizing predicted ideas and background knowledge based on text structure
  S—searching for the text structure
  S—summarizing the main ideas
  E—evaluating comprehension

- Model the strategies for the students using the graphic organizer.
- Encourage dialogue by the students supporting the use of the strategies.

Other instructional tactics from this review are applicable to other generalizations and are presented in the appropriate chapters of this book.

Findings: Use of the above tactics related to reminders was found to be effective in improving achievement in recall for students with learning disabilities and without learning disabilities.

Studies from this logical synthesis related to expository texts are marked with the symbol ! in the reference list in Part V.

Individual Studies

Author: Mevarech & Kramarski (2003)

Students: Eighth graders

Learning: Algebra

Instructional Tactics:

- Students were trained to use a structured self-questioning procedure for solving problems.

  —Structured questions associated with the IMPROVE program (acronym for *I*ntroducing new concepts, *M*etacognitive questioning, *P*racticing, *Re*viewing, *O*btaining mastery on cognitive processes, *V*erification, and *En*richment) include the following types: comprehension, connection, strategic, and reflection.

—Comprehension example: "What is the problem all about?"
—Connection example: "How is the problem different from and/or similar to problems that have already been solved?"
—Strategic example: "What strategies are appropriate for solving the problem and why are they appropriate?"
—Reflection example: "Does this solution make any sense?" and "Why am I stuck?"

- Students were given a booklet with content embedded within decision-making activities and with the four kinds of structured questions printed in the booklet for their use in solving algebra problems.

Other instructional tactics from this review are applicable to other generalizations and are presented in the appropriate chapters of this book.

Findings: Use of the above tactics was found to enhance academic achievement in mathematics immediately and over time.

REFERENCE LIST

Bellezza, F. S. (1996). A mnemonic based on arranging words on visual patterns. *Journal of Educational Psychology, 78,* 217–224.

Carney, R. N., Levin, M. E., & Levin, J. R. (1993). Mnemonic strategies: Instructional techniques worth remembering. *Teaching Exceptional Children, 25*(4), 24–30.

Fukkink, R. G., & de Glopper, K. (1998). Effects of instruction in deriving word meaning from context: A meta-analysis. *Review of Educational Research, 68*(4), 450–469.

Gersten, R., & Baker, S. (2001). Teaching expressive writing to students with learning disabilities: A meta-analysis. *The Elementary School Journal, 101*(3), 251–273.

Gersten, R., Fuchs, L. S., Williams, J. P., & Baker, S. (2001). Teaching reading comprehension strategies to students with learning disabilities: A review of research. *Review of Educational Research, 71*(2), 279–320.

Griffith, D. (1979). *A review of the literature on memory enhancement: The potential and relevance of mnemotechnics for military training* (Technical Report No. 436). Fort Hood, TX: U.S. Army Research Unit for the Behavioral and Social Sciences.

Levin, J. (1988). Elaboration-based learning strategies: Powerful theory = powerful application. *Contemporary Educational Psychology, 13,* 191–205.

Levin, J. (1993). Mnemonic strategies and classroom learning: A twenty year report card. *The Elementary School Journal, 94*(2), 235–244.

Mevarech, Z. R., & Kramarski, B. (2003). The effects of metacognitive training versus worked-out examples on students' mathematical reasoning. *British Journal of Educational Psychology, 73,* 449–471.

Morrison, C. R., & Levin, J. (1987). Degree of mnemonic support and students' acquisition of science facts. *Educational Communication and Technology Journal, 35,* 67–74.

Rosenshine, B., Meister, C., & Chapman, S. (1996). Teaching students to generate questions: A review of the intervention studies. *Review of Educational Research, 66*(2), 181–221.

16

Utilizing Teamwork

INTRODUCTION

Instructing students on teamwork and having students work on task performance in teams can increase both group and individual achievement. To be successful in the modern world, students must be able to work as team members to achieve team goals and objectives. In the world of work, they will have to know how to perform as team members in problem solving, determination of goals and objectives, and getting along with co-workers if the organization they work for is to be successful and if they are to remain employed. If they are to have successful families as adults, they will have to be able to work as teams with their partners in determining their goals and objectives, appropriately dividing the labors, being able to resolve conflicts rationally, and sharing in their successes and failures. To be productive members of their social communities, they will have to be able to function as team members within the community if they are to address any problems confronting the community. Additionally, participation in team sports and games requires one to participate as a team member. Teamwork can be successful when the group goal is to enhance the achievement of individual members and/or the group.

As the statistical evidence shows, group teaching does not produce the highest individual student academic achievement effects. One-on-one teacher tutoring continues to produce the highest levels of student achievement, as much as two times more than group teaching. The primary benefit of group instruction is that it is the only way to teach teamwork. Since teamwork is essential to success in civilized societies, the teaching of teamwork needs to be emphasized to a much greater extent than it is now.

STUDENT BENEFICIARIES

The evidence indicates that teaching students to function as team members enhances the achievement of individual and group goals in elementary, middle, secondary, and college classrooms. Moreover, group achievement was improved in a wide range of content areas. No evidence could be found to suggest that the teaching of teamwork should not be stressed when the achievement of group goals is being pursued.

LEARNING ACHIEVED

Achievement in the content areas of mathematics, history, foreign languages, English, language arts, literature, psychology, physical education, American history, reading, word recognition, spelling, writing, vocabulary, social sciences, sciences, social studies, ESL, geography, drafting, biology, chemistry, algebra, and precalculus is enhanced when student teamwork is taught.

INSTRUCTIONAL TACTICS

- Students' readiness capabilities should be diagnosed on the basis of their prior performance and/or pretesting, and only those with the potential to succeed as team members should begin the instructional program.
- Students should be assigned to work in four- to five-member teams.
- Before starting a learning program, team-building exercises should be conducted to allow team members a chance to get to know one another and build rapport. This might take the form of the individuals in the teams interviewing one another to get to know their names, interests, common interests, and background. The importance of group goals and rewards that can be obtained should be stressed at this time.
- Initial presentation of the knowledge and skills to be learned should be made to the entire group, then individual team members should receive the instruction they need to perform their function.
- The group presentation should be followed by team practice, where the entire group works together on tasks assigned. "Brainstorming" within the team and mutual assistance within the team should be encouraged for solving problems.
- Students should be provided assistance any time they need help.
- Evaluation should be conducted of both team and individual performance, with appropriate feedback and opportunity for remediation. Individuals are held accountable for their performance.
- Teams are recognized for progress toward their goals.

Elaborations of the above summary of tactics can be obtained from reading the studies that follow. To be most effective, the instructional tactics need to be integrated into the particular instructional program being planned or presently being used.

CAUTIONS AND COMMENTS

The studies reviewed had many different purposes. The focus of some of the studies was not on group achievement. However, group achievement was assessed in all studies reported, enabling us to conclude that the teaching of teamwork enhances group achievement. Other benefits of group instruction indicated by research studies include individual achievement, integration of people from diverse cultures, and attitudinal changes.

Since teamwork is so important for success in society, more studies need to be conducted that focus directly on the effect of teamwork instruction.

GENERALIZATION: ON TEAMWORK

Achievement of learning objectives is enhanced when students are taught to perform complementary tasks as a team in pursuit of the objectives.

Supportive Research on Utilizing Teamwork
Total number of supportive studies covered: 383+

Groups of Studies

Author: Swanson (2000)

Students: School-aged children—learning disabled

Learning: Achievement in word recognition, reading comprehension, spelling memory/recall, mathematics, writing, vocabulary

Instructional Tactics:

• Assign students to small groups.

• Provide instruction to the small groups.

• Allow students to work with group members on the assigned task.

• Join a group and interact with the group members, providing assistance as needed.

Other instructional tactics are employed in these studies that are applicable to other generalizations and will be presented in the appropriate chapters.

Findings: Use of the above tactics was found to contribute significantly to achievement.

In this chapter, the author did not specifically identify the individual studies included in the meta-analysis.

Author: Slavin (1995) (A "best evidence synthesis" of cooperative learning methods)

Students: Grades 1–12

Learning: Reading, mathematics, sciences, social studies, spelling, language arts, literature, geography, writing, history, and drafting achievement

Instructional Tactics: The following tactics are associated with the "Learning Together" method:

- Students are assigned to work in four-to-five member groups of mixed composition.
- Each student must learn the names of the other members of the group.
- Each student in the team interviews another team member in a manner that results in all team members being interviewed, and students present the information they have obtained during their interview to the entire team.
- Each team is to decide on team name, log, or mural.
- The entire group works together on tasks assigned.
- "Brainstorming" within the group is encouraged in problem-solving situations.
- Each team is graded on its task performance.
- Evaluation of each team member's individual mastery of the material to be learned is conducted.

The following instructional tactics are associated with the "Student Teams–Achievement Divisions" (STAD) method:

- Compute a base score for each student in the class based on prior performance.
- Students are assigned to work in four- to five-member groups of mixed composition in terms of academic performance, sex, and race or ethnicity.
- Before starting the learning program, team-building exercises are conducted to allow team members a chance to get to know one another.
- Learning material is initially presented in a class by teacher or audiovisual presentation.
- The classroom presentation is followed by team practice.
- All team members are responsible for making sure their teammates have learned the material.
- All team members must participate until all teammates have mastered the material to be learned.
- Team members are required to ask questions of their teammates before asking the teacher.

- After one or two class presentations and one or two team practice sessions, students are administered a quiz. This quiz is to be an individual assessment of what the students have learned as individuals.

- Improvement points are calculated for individual students based on their quiz score in relation to their initial base score. These points are than totaled for the team members of each team and divided by the number of team members to come up with a team improvement score.

- Teams are recognized for their degree of improvement.

- The individual base score for determining improvement is recomputed after each quiz.

- Individual grades are to be based on their actual test (quiz) performance.

The following instructional tactics are associated with the "Teams-Games-Tournaments" (TGT) method:

- Instructional tactics are the same as for the STAD method except that quizzes and the individual improvement score system are replaced by academic tournaments, in which a team member of one team competes with a team member of another team of equal ability based on prior performance. The "games" for the tournament consist of content-relevant questions.

The following instructional tactics are associated with the "Team Assisted-Individualization" (TAI) (mathematics) method:

- Students are pretested at the beginning of the program to determine their placement level.

- Students are assigned to four- to five-member heterogeneous teams.

- Each day the teacher works for 10 to 15 minutes with each of two or three small teaching groups of students who are at the same point in the curriculum.

- Students are given a guide page reviewing the concepts introduced by the teacher in the teaching group.

- Students from the teaching groups are given several skill-practice pages consisting of 16 practice problems broken down into blocks of four problems, with each skill-practice representing a subskill that leads to mastery of the entire skill, two formative tests, and a unit test.

- Students return to their teams, where they are instructed to read their guide pages and ask teammates or the teacher for help when needed.

- Students are formed into pairs or triads for the purpose of checking.

- Each student works on the first block of four problems. When students finish, they have a teammate check the problems against a provided answer sheet. If they fail to get all four correct, they must proceed to the next four practice problems for that subskill page and continue to do so until they get four problems correct. If the student gets all four correct, he is allowed to proceed to the first four practice problems for the next subskill practice page.

- Once a student has successfully proceeded through all of the subskill practice pages, he takes a 10-question formative test that is graded by a teammate. If the student gets at least eight questions correct, the teammate signs the test certifying it, and the student is allowed to take the unit test. If the student does not get at least eight questions correct, the teacher is called in to diagnose the problem and assign additional practice.

- At the end of each week, team recognition is given based on the number of units each team has completed and the accuracy on unit tests.

Instructional tactics associated with the "Cooperative Integrated Reading and Composition" method are the same as for the "Team Assisted-Individualization" method except that they are tailored to reading.

The following instructional tactics are associated with the "Group Investigation" method:

- The teacher presents a broad problem or issue to the entire class.
- Students meet in groups to determine the subtopics to be investigated.
- Once the subtopics are determined, the students form groups according to the subtopic in which they are interested.
- The students in each group plan what and how they will study.
- Each group plans the division of labor.
- Students within the groups gather information, analyze data, and reach conclusions with each group member contributing to the group effort.
- Students exchange, discuss, clarify, and synthesize ideas.
- Group members plan what they will report and how they will present their findings to the whole class.
- Teachers and students collaborate in evaluating student learning.

The following instructional tactics are associated with "Jigsaw II" and "Jigsaw" methods:

- Team assignment is the same as for other methods, where the teacher makes the assignments.
- Each student in a team is given individual topics and reads assigned material.

- Students from the different teams who were assigned the same topic meet and discuss the topic.
- The students then return to their team and teach the topic to their fellow team members.
- Students take individual quizzes covering all topics.
- Team scores are computed for the purpose of giving team recognition.

Findings: In general, group achievement was higher for teamwork instruction as compared to more traditional methods.

Individual studies included in this "best evidence synthesis" are identified by the symbol * in the reference list in Part V.

Author: Sharan (1980)

Students: Grades 1–12

Learning: English, mathematics, language arts, reading, and social studies achievement

Instructional Tactics: Instructional tactics are listed following the name of the cooperative learning method reviewed.

Jigsaw Method

- The material to be learned is divided into as many parts as there are group members.
- Each student initially learns only one part of the total material and is responsible for teaching that part to his groupmates.
- Each group member is responsible for learning all of the curriculum.

TGT Method

- The students are formed into four- or five-member teams that reflect a cross-section of the class ability levels, sexes, and racial/ethnic groups.
- The teams prepare their members through peer tutoring for learning-game tournaments.
- For the academic tournaments, a team member of one team competes with a team member of another team of equal ability based on prior performance. The "games" for the tournament consist of content-relevant questions.

STAD Method

- Team given instructions to work together.
- Team reward with an individual task.

A broader and clearer description of instructional tactics associated with this method is available in the Slavin (1995) synthesis.

Group Investigation Method

- Students select specific subtopics within a general problem area presented by the teacher.
- Students and the teacher cooperatively plan specific learning procedures, tasks, and goals.
- Students carry out the plan they have formulated.
- Students analyze and evaluate information.
- Students plan how the information obtained will be summarized for display or presentation.
- Teachers and students collaborate in evaluating student learning.

Findings: Across all team-learning methods, group achievement was superior as compared to traditional classrooms. In the review of TGT and STAD studies, peer-tutoring was found not to produce a positive effect on achievement.

Individual studies included in this research synthesis are identified by the symbol # in the reference list in Part V.

Author: Johnson et al. (1981)

Students: Elementary, secondary, and college

Learning: Language arts, reading, mathematics, science, social studies, psychology, and physical education achievement

Instructional Tactics:

- Group cooperation.
- Group cooperation with intergroup competition.
- Interpersonal competition.
- Individualistic efforts.

Findings:

1. There is no difference in achievement for group cooperation without intergroup competition as compared to group cooperation with intergroup competition.
2. Group cooperation promotes higher achievement than does individual competition.
3. Group cooperation with intergroup competition promotes higher achievement than does interpersonal competition.

4. Group cooperation without intergroup competition promotes higher achievement than does individualistic effort.

5. Group cooperation with intergroup competition promotes higher achievement than does individualistic effort.

6. There was no difference on achievement between individual competition and individualistic effort.

Individual studies included in this meta-analysis are identified by the symbol @ in the reference list in Part V.

Author: Slavin (1997)

Students: Elementary, middle, and secondary

Learning: Achievement in language arts, mathematics, social studies, ESL, reading, science, spelling, geography

Instructional Tactics:

• Place students in cooperative groups.

• Provide the groups with a goal; members in a group work together to achieve the group's goal.

• Provide incentives for the group's reaching its goal.

• Require individual accountability within the group.

Findings: Use of the above tactics was found to enhance students' academic achievement across a variety of content areas.

The identified studies reviewed are marked by the symbol $ in the reference list in Part V.

Author: Newmann & Thompson (1987) (A "best evidence synthesis" of cooperative learning)

Students: Secondary—grades 7–12

Learning: Achievement in mathematics, social studies, language arts, geography, science, physical education, biology, chemistry, and American history

Instructional Tactics: The following tactics are associated with the Student Teams–Achievement Divisions (STAD) method:

• The teacher presents a lesson.

• Students are assigned to teams of four to five members.

- Students are given worksheets and help each other master the content on the worksheets.
- Each student takes a quiz on the material.
- Individual student scores, based on the degree of individual improvement over previous score, contribute to a team score.
- Teams with high scores are recognized in a weekly class newsletter.

The following tactics are associated with the Teams-Games-Tournaments (TGT) method:

- The teacher presents a lesson.
- Students are assigned to teams of four to five members.
- Students are given worksheets and help each other learn the material.
- Students compete with classmates from other teams having similar achievement levels.
- Students earn points for their own team based on their relative success against competitors from the other teams.
- Teams with high scores are recognized publicly.

The following tactics are associated with the Jigsaw (JIG) method:

- Students are assigned to groups of five to six members.
- Each group is given unique information about the topic that is being studied by the whole group.
- Students read the material.
- Students then meet in "expert groups" with their counterparts from other teams to discuss and master the information.
- Students then return to their teams to teach the material to their teammates.
- Students are given tests to complete individually.
- Team scores are publicized in a class newsletter.

The following tactics are associated with the Learning Together (LT) method:

- Students are placed in small groups on assignments to produce a single group product.
- Students are taught positive group processing and dynamics skills in order to work together.
- Students ask for adult help only after seeking help from group members.
- Students earn rewards on a combination of their individual work and that of their group. There is no competition within or among groups.
- Teachers reward with praise, grades, tokens, and privileges.

The following tactics are associated with the Group Investigation (GI) method:

- Teachers determine the material topic and assign students to small groups.
- Each group of students takes on a different task or project related to the topic, deciding what information is necessary, how to organize the information, and how to present the new learning as a group to their classmates.
- Students must assume considerable responsibility for directing their own learning.

Findings: Use of the above tactics was found to enhance achievement. Students in grades 8 and 9 have the highest success rate. Cooperative grouping is used more rarely in grades 10–12; however, for those students who did participate, outcomes were lower than the outcomes for the students in grades 7, 8, and 9 who participated.

Studies are included in the reference list in Part V and are marked with the symbol +.

Individual Studies

Author: Mevarech & Kramarski (1997)

Students: Middle level—seventh graders

Learning: Mathematics

Instructional Tactics:

- Students are given a pretest on initial unit of mathematics content.
- Students are placed in groups of four based on the pretest results: one high, two middle, and one low achieving.
- New material is presented to the whole class using a question-answer technique.
- Three structured questions are used:
  —What's the problem?
  —What are the differences/similarities between . . . and . . .?
  —What strategies/tactics/principles are appropriate for solving the problem?
- Reasons for the answers are modeled orally by the adult.
- The adult, again orally, thinks through how to check the accuracy of the answer and what plan to use if the answer is incorrect.
- The adult presents to the whole group keeping the diversity of the class in mind by selecting problems of varying difficulty, providing explanations based on highly diverse preexisting knowledge and levels of thinking, and

using the structured questions in more complex ways such as using several strategies to solve a problem.

- Students work in their heterogeneous groups by:
  —Talking about the problem
  —Explaining the problem to each other
  —Comparing it to what is already known
  —Approaching it from different perspectives
  —Balancing the perspectives against each other
  —Proceeding with the solution based on what seems to be the best option.
  —Writing the group answer along with the rationale and a sample of their responses to the structured questions
  —Asking for help if the group cannot solve the problem

- The groups are reconvened as a whole class to review the main ideas of the problem and its solution.

- The focus is on any common problems observed during the group discussions.

- The adult becomes part of each team at least once a week and functions as a group member, modeling the process of answering the structured questions.

Other instructional tactics are employed in these studies that are applicable to other generalizations and will be presented in the appropriate chapters.

Findings: Use of the above tactics was found to enhance student achievement in mathematics.

❖ ❖ ❖

Author: Henderson & Landesman (2001)

Students: Middle—students of Mexican descent

Learning: Mathematics achievement

Instructional Tactics:

- Organize content around themes. Select themes that relate to students' present experiences and their concerns about what the future might hold for them.

- Assign students to groups to work together to resolve a problem related to the theme.

- Engage students in instructional conversations.

Findings: Use of the above tactics led to higher achievement on mathematical concepts and applications.

Author: Lampe et al. (2001)

Students: Elementary—fourth grade Hispanic students

Learning: Achievement in social studies

Instructional Tactics:

- Structure heterogeneous cooperative groups.
- Incorporate basic elements of cooperative learning: positive interdependence, face-to-face interaction, individual accountability, social skill development, and group processing.
- Specify academic objectives.
- Assign roles within groups.
- Describe procedures for the learning activity.
- Use a variety of cooperative-learning group methods such as Jigsaw II and Group Investigation.
- Facilitate and monitor student group learning.
- Evaluate student learning.

Findings: Use of the above tactics was found to enhance Hispanic students' achievement in social studies.

❖   ❖   ❖

Author: Whicker et al. (2001)

Students: Secondary—eleventh and twelfth grades

Learning: Achievement in precalculus

Instructional Tactics:

- Provide students instruction in how to work in small groups.
- Teach the lesson.
- Assign students to groups.
- Provide time for group work.
  —Students work for two days on teacher-developed worksheets.
  —Students explain answers to each other.
  —Students ask each other, rather than the adult, clarifying questions.
  —Students must meet mastery requirement of 100 percent before the task is completed.
- Administer tests and award points based on how much the individual student's score exceeded the individual's base score.
- Compute team scores by adding all points earned by group members and dividing the sum by the number of members in the group who took the test.

- Recognize team performance.

Findings: Use of the above tactics was found to promote mathematics achievement in the secondary grades.

Author: Mevarech & Kramarski (2003)

Students: Eighth graders

Learning: Algebra

Instructional Tactics:

- Students are given a mathematics pretest.
- Students are then taught new algebra concepts using cooperative learning structure which they have been using since the beginning of seventh grade.
- The new concept is introduced using a question-answer technique, and the structured self-questioning technique is modeled to assist the students in resolving the algebraic problems.
- Students are assigned to heterogeneous groups of one low, two middle, and one high achieving students based on their pretest performance.
- The groups are given four algebra word problems of varying difficulty to solve. These are similar to the type of problem the teacher had presented.
- Students discuss the problem (participated in mathematical discourse) within the group using the structured self-questioning technique until group consensus on a response is reached.
- Students ask for adult assistance only when they fail to reach group consensus on the answer.
- Students in the groups are also expected to answer the structured self-questioning questions orally and to write the answers.
- The groups are reconvened as a whole class to review the new concepts, to solve any problems giving most groups a problem, and receive answers to their questions.
- Immediately after the unit of study, students are administered a posttest, the results of which can be used to make new group assignments.

Other instructional tactics are employed in these studies that are applicable to other generalizations and will be presented in the appropriate chapters.

Findings: Use of the above tactics was found to enhance academic achievement in mathematics immediately and over time.

REFERENCE LIST

Henderson, R. W., & Landesman, E. M. (2001). Effects of thematically integrated mathematics instruction on students of Mexican descent. *The Journal of Educational Research, 88*(5), 290–300.

Johnson, D. W., Muruyama, G., Johnson, R., Nelson, D., & Skon, L. (1981). Effects of cooperative, competitive, and individualistic goal structures on achievement: A meta-analysis. *Psychological Bulletin, 89*(1), 47–62.

Lampe, J. R., Booze, G. E., & Tallent-Runnels, M. (2001). Effects of cooperative learning among Hispanic students in elementary social studies. *The Journal of Educational Research, 89*(3), 187–191.

Mevarech, Z. R., & Kramarski, B. (1997). IMPROVE: A multidimensional method for teaching mathematics in heterogeneous classrooms. *American Educational Research Journal, 34*(2), 365–394.

Mevarech, Z. R., & Kramarski, B. (2003). The effects of metacognitive training versus worked-out examples on students' mathematical reasoning. *British Journal of Educational Psychology, 73*, 449–471.

Newmann, F. M., & Thompson, J. A. (1987). *Effects of cooperative learning on achievement in secondary schools: A summary of research*. Unpublished manuscript, University of Wisconsin–Madison, School of Education, partially funded by National Center on Effective Secondary Schools.

Sharan, S. (1980). Cooperative learning in small groups: Recent methods and effects on achievement, attitudes, and ethnic relations. *Review of Educational Research, 50*(2), 241–271.

Slavin, R. E. (1977). *Student learning team techniques: Narrowing the achievement gap between the races* (Report No. 228). Baltimore, MD: Johns Hopkins University, Center for Social Organization of Schools.

Slavin, R. E. (1995). *Cooperative learning* (2nd ed.). Boston: Allyn and Bacon.

Swanson, H. L. (2000). What instruction works for students with learning disabilities? Summarizing the results from a meta-analysis of intervention studies. In R. M. Gersten, E. P. Schiller, & S. Vaughn (Eds.), *Contemporary special education research: Syntheses of the knowledge base on critical instructional issues* (pp. 1–30). Mahwah, NJ: Erlbaum.

Whicker, K. M., Bol, L., & Nunnery, J. A. (2001). Cooperative Learning in the secondary mathematics classroom. *The Journal of Educational Research, 91*(1), 42–48.

17

Reducing Student/Teacher Ratio Below 21 to 1

INTRODUCTION

Most educators are familiar with different classroom configurations that are dictated by the particular teaching method used. For example, the discussion method is best applied when discussants are in a circle facing each other, and the lecture method is best applied when all students are facing the lecturer. Most educators also are aware that lecture classes can be larger than discussion classes. What many educators may not be fully cognizant of is how class size in general affects student achievement. Generally speaking, larger student-to-teacher ratios are associated with lower student achievement. As class size increases from a ratio of 1:1 to a ratio of 21:1, there is a steady decrease in student achievement. In classes above the ratio of 21:1, academic achievement continues to decrease; however, the degree of the decrease is not as great as that occurring from a ratio of 1:1 to a ratio of 21:1. There appear to be several reasons for this. In larger classes, teachers may need to spend more time on classroom management and less time on teaching. When tasks are formulated to be performed by larger numbers of students at the same time, it is less likely that the readiness capabilities of individual students can be accommodated. In addition, there is more opportunity for off-task behavior, resulting in diminished student focus and performance. However, more is known about the effect of student-to-teacher ratio on achievement than these generalities.

STUDENT BENEFICIARIES

The evidence indicates that reducing the student-to-teacher ratio enhances the academic achievement of students in kindergarten, primary, elementary, middle, secondary, and college classrooms. No evidence could be found to suggest that lower student-to-teacher ratios should not be stressed in all subject areas for all types of students including students in college, military, community, business, and adult education settings.

LEARNING ACHIEVED

Achievement of learning objectives in the content areas of reading, mathematics, language, psychology, physical sciences, social studies, physical education, composition, art, vocabulary, language arts, and history is enhanced when there are smaller student-to-teacher ratios. It may be reasonable to expect that achievement may be enhanced in other content areas as well. In studies reviewed, student achievement was shown to be positively related to student-to-teacher ratio.

INSTRUCTIONAL TACTICS

- To maximize student achievement, conduct one-to-one tutoring. Bloom (1984) has shown that one-to-one tutoring results in as much as twice the achievement when compared to larger student-to-teacher ratios. Group instruction achieves superior results only when teamwork is being taught for the purpose of enhancing group achievement. See the teamwork instructional tactics in Chapter 16. The only other justification for group instruction is the saving of money and time.

- In group instruction, keep student-to-teacher ratios below 21:1 and as low as possible. The smaller the group size below 21:1, the higher the academic achievement will be, with 1:1 producing the highest achievement.

- When conducting group instruction, assess and diagnose student performance often and provide remediation for inadequate performance on an individual basis. Presentations and instructions may be given to the group as a whole, but diagnosis and remediation of inadequate student performance must be done on an individual basis. See corrective instruction tactics in Chapter 4.

- Although discussed under the heading "Instructional Tactics," decisions pertaining to student/teacher ratio are not an integral part of the instructional process (according to our definition of instruction and other definitions of which we are aware). Most often administrators have more to do with establishing student/teacher ratios, working within policy constraints, than do teachers. Teacher influence is often limited to suggestions and complaints. In the final analysis, it is important to recognize that teachers' failure to achieve the learning objectives they are held responsible for achieving may be due to excessively large classes they are assigned to teach.

CAUTIONS AND COMMENTS

Reducing the student-to-teacher ratio may not enhance student achievement by itself. In addition, the use of other effective instructional tactics, such as those associated with student readiness, remediation, teaching time, and so forth, is required to ensure that higher levels of student achievement are realized. However, it may be that reducing the student-to-teacher ratio may allow the teacher more opportunity to employ other instructional tactics related to higher levels of student achievement. Additionally, the effect of reducing the student-to-teacher ratio will not be the same for classes which primarily involve lecture as opposed to classes with a great deal of student discussion or participation.

Research has demonstrated that up to the student/teacher ratio of 21:1 there is clear association between increased student/teacher ratio and decreased student achievement. This is not intended to imply linearity. Beyond the student/teacher ratio of 21:1, research has not been able consistently to show an association between higher student/teacher ratio and lower student achievement, which may be indicative of the law of diminishing returns or a curvilinear relationship.

A lower student/teacher ratio is needed in the early grades. Students at this level have more difficulty staying on task since they are easily distracted. Further, students at this early grade level still need help taking care of their personal needs.

GENERALIZATION: ON REDUCING STUDENT/TEACHER RATIO

Achievement of learning objectives is enhanced when there is a lower student-to-teacher ratio in teaching situations.

Supportive Research on Student/Teacher Ratio
Total number of supportive studies covered: 193

Groups of Studies

Author: Glass et al. (1982)

Students: Elementary, secondary, and college

Learning: Reading, mathematics, language, psychology, physical sciences, social studies, physical education, and history achievement

Instructional Tactics:

• Reduction of the student-to-teacher ratio.

Findings: For 98 percent of the comparisons of student-to-teacher ratios of 2:1 and 28:1, the smaller student/teacher ratio had higher levels of achievement regardless of grade level or content area. For 69 percent of the comparisons of student-to-teacher ratios of 18:1 and 28:1, the smaller student-to-teacher ratio had higher levels of achievement regardless of grade level or content area. For about 50 percent of the comparisons of student-to-teacher ratios over 30:1 and over 60:1, the smaller student-to-teacher ratio had higher levels of achievement. For fourteen experimental studies student-to-teacher ratios of 1:1, 2:1, 3:1, and 5:1 had the highest levels of achievement. The student-to-teacher ratio of 1:1 has the largest positive effect on achievement even when compared to a student-to-teacher ratio of 2:1. When the smaller student-to-teacher ratio was 14:1, 15:1, or 16:1, the effect on achievement was much smaller though positive as compared to the smaller student-to-teacher ratios identified above.

Studies analyzed in this meta-analysis are identified by the symbol * in the reference list in Part V.

❖   ❖   ❖

Author: Biddle & Berliner (2002)

Students: Elementary, middle, and secondary

Learning: Academic achievement, predominantly in reading and mathematics but also in other content areas

Instructional Tactics:

• Reduction in class size to 20 or fewer students in the early grades.

Findings: Generally speaking, small classes in the early grades lead to substantial gains for students and those gains are greater the longer students are in smaller classes. When the class size is below 20, the extra gains are larger. Students who are in smaller classes in the early grades tend to continue making or retaining their gains in standard-sized classes in upper, middle, and high school grades.

This logical synthesis included individual studies and meta-analyses; they are listed in the reference list in Part V and are marked with the symbol %.

❖   ❖   ❖

Author: Word et al. (1990)

Students: Elementary

Learning: Reading, mathematics, composition, art, and vocabulary achievement

Instructional Tactics:

• Reduction of the student-to-teacher ratio.

Findings: Smaller student-to-teacher ratios led to higher levels of achievement for students in those classes when compared to students in classes with larger student-to-teacher ratios. Student-to-teacher ratios of less than 20:1 led to more dramatic increases in student achievement.

Studies reviewed with this logical synthesis are identified by the symbol # in the reference list in Part V.

Author: McGivern et al. (1989)

Students: Second grade

Learning: Reading and mathematics achievement

Instructional Tactics:

- Reduction of the student-to-teacher ratio to an average of 19.1 as compared to an average of 26.4 for regular classes.

Findings: Overall, achievement was higher for the smaller student-to-teacher ratio across 24 comparisons. However, the findings were not consistent in favor of the lower student-to-teacher ratio of 19.1:1. Nine of the 24 comparisons indicated higher levels of achievement for the larger student-to-teacher ratio.

Author: Achilles (2005)

Students: Primary, elementary, middle, and secondary

Learning: Academic achievement

Instructional Tactics:

- Reduce class size to below 20 to 1, preferably 15 to 1.
- Introduce early intervention of small class size, either in kindergarten or pre-kindergarten.
- Ensure that the student spends all day, every day in the small class.
- Maintain the small class for at least three years, preferably four.
- Use random assignment in early grades to facilitate peer tutoring, problem-solving groups, and student-to-student cooperation.
- Employ a cohort model for several years.

Findings: Use of the above tactics was found to enhance academic achievement. Further, the achievement gains were found to be maintained through middle and secondary grades.

All the studies in this review of research were not specifically named. References used by the author are listed in the reference list in Part V and are marked with the symbol &.

Individual Studies

Author: Mosteller (1995)

Students: Kindergarten through third grade

Learning: Reading and mathematics achievement

Instructional Tactics:

- Student-to-teacher ratios were reduced to 13–17:1 from 22–26:1.
- Classes with a student-to-teacher ratio of 22–26:1 either had an added teacher's aide or no teacher's aide.

Findings: Over the four-year period of the project, reading and mathematics achievement scores were higher for the students in classes with a student-to-teacher ratio of 13–17:1. Percentile ranks for average reading and mathematics scores based on national norms were higher for students in classes with a student-to-teacher ratio of 13–17:1. The addition of a teacher's aide to classes with the larger student-to-teacher ratio had no significant effect on student reading or mathematics achievement.

Author: Blatchford et al. (2003)

Students: Primary (British reception year, year 1, and year 2)

Learning: Literacy and mathematics

Instructional Tactics:

- Randomly chosen reception year classes were selected for the study from schools varying in class size categories: large (30+:1), large medium (26-29:1), small medium (20–25:1), and small (19 and below:1).
- Within-class grouping often occurred with group size typically being four to six children; however, in larger classes, the groups were sometimes as large as 7–10 children or even 11+ children.

Findings: Within each class, students were split into three ability groups (bottom 25 percent, middle 50 percent, and top 25 percent) based on their pre-Reception year literacy scores. An increase in attainment occurred for each of the three groups but there was a much larger effect for pupils with lower baseline attainment. When the class size was reduced from 30 to 20 pupils, there was an increase in attainment for all groups but, again, more for the lower attainers in literacy. In mathematics, a reduction in class size from 30 to 20 pupils resulted in an increase in attainment.

Author: Smith et al. (2003)

Students: Primary

Learning: Achievement in reading, language arts, and mathematics

Instructional Tactics:

• Reduction in class size to 15:1 in grades 1, 2, and 3.

Findings: Results from 1996 to 2001 cohorts of students in grades 1, 2, and 3 indicated a positive achievement gain in reading, language arts, and mathematics on subtests of the CTBS. First graders scored significantly higher than did the comparison group on the subtests, showing a 25–30 percent higher level of academic achievement than that of their counterparts in larger classes. In addition, they maintained that gain through third grade which was the last year of the program of 15:1 class size. By the end of third grade, the students in the 15:1 classes were achieving at a level of one-third to one-half a year ahead of students in the larger third grade classes. The students at the end of first grade, in addition, outperformed the comparison group in reading and math in terms of the expected gain for a year's work.

Author: NICHD Early Child Care Research Network (2004)

Students: First grade

Learning: Literacy skill achievement

Instructional Tactics:

• Reduction of first grade class size from 22–27:1 to 15–17:1.

Findings: There was a significant drop in achievement scores (WJ-R Achievement) at the class size of 21. In follow-up comparisons, children in classrooms above class size 21 had lower composite achievement scores than those in classes with fewer than 21 children. Across all class sizes, as teacher reported class size increased, scores (WJ-R Word Attack) decreased. For the observed child-adult ratio, a significant drop occurred at a ratio of 22:1. Follow-up comparisons indicated that children in classrooms with ratios lower than 22:1 performed significantly better than did children in classrooms with ratios higher than 22:1.

REFERENCE LIST

Achilles, C. M. (2005). Class size and learning. In L. W. Hughes (Ed.), *Current issues in school leadership* (pp. 105–124). Mahwah, NJ: Erlbaum.

Biddle, B. J., & Berliner, D. C. (2002). Small class size and its effects. *Educational Leadership, 59*(5), 12–23.

Blatchford, P., Bassett, P., Goldstein, H., & Martin, C. (2003). Are class size differences related to pupils' educational progress and classroom processes? Findings from the Institute of Education Class Size Study of Children Aged 5–7 Years. *British Educational Research Journal, 29*(5), 709–730.

Bloom, B. (1984). The 2 sigma problem: The search for methods of group instruction as effective as one-to-one tutoring. *Journal of Educational Research, 13*, 4–16.

Glass, G. V., Cahen, L. S., Smith, M. L., & Filby, N. N. (1982). *School class size: Research and policy*. Beverly Hills, CA: Sage Publications.

McGivern, J., Gilman, D., & Tillitski, C. (1989). A meta-analysis of the relation between class size and achievement. *The Elementary School Journal, 90*(1), 47–56.

Mosteller, F. (1995). The Tennessee study of class size in the early school grades. *The Future of Children, 5*(2), 113–127.

NICHD Early Child Care Research Network. (2004). Does class size in first grade relate to children's academic and social performance or observed classroom processes? *Developmental Psychology, 40*(5), 651–664.

Smith, P., Molnar, A., & Zahorik, J. (2003). Class-size reduction: A fresh look at the data. *Educational Leadership, 61*(1), 72–74

Word, E. R., et al. (1990). *The State of Tennessee's Student/Teacher Achievement Ratio (STAR) Project: Technical Report*. Review of Literature (pp. 199–205). Nashville: Tennessee State University, Center of Excellence for Research in Basic Skills.

18

Clarifying Communication

INTRODUCTION

An essential aspect of instruction is the clear communication of information to students to facilitate their understanding of (1) the learning objectives they are assigned to pursue, (2) the tasks they are assigned to perform to enhance their achievement of the learning objectives, and (3) the means of evaluating their performance. Although educators may appreciate the importance of clear communication in conversation and in professions such as "newscaster" and "trial lawyer," the following explicates the relevance of clear communication to instruction, elements of clear communication, and tactics for achieving clear communication. Clarity of communication has a distinct application to instruction and learning.

STUDENT BENEFICIARIES

The evidence indicates that clarity of communication enhances the academic achievement of students in elementary, secondary, and college classrooms. Moreover, clarity of communication improves academic achievement in a wide range of content areas. No evidence could be found to suggest that clarity of communication should not be stressed in all subject areas for all types of students including students in military, community, business, and adult education settings.

LEARNING ACHIEVED

Achievement in the content areas of mathematics, reading, science, social studies, psychology, communication, and the social sciences is enhanced when clear communication tactics are incorporated in instruction. It may be reasonable to expect that achievement may be enhanced in other content areas as well. In studies reviewed, student achievement was shown to be related positively to clarity of communication during instruction. Some studies indicated that students exposed to clear communication during instruction achieved at a rate one and one-half to three times higher than students exposed to instruction which lacked clarity.

INSTRUCTIONAL TACTICS

The benefits of clear communication to students are well supported by the evidence. However, there is a need for instructional planners and teachers to know the particular tactics that can be used to ensure clear communication. The following tactics are derived from the studies that demonstrate the benefits of clear communication. Discretion has been used to interpret and reduce overlap in tactics used in different studies and to elaborate tactics.

Tactics that ensure clear communication are:

- Providing examples and illustrations of concepts being taught.
- When speaking, avoiding the use of "er," "um," "uh," "ah," "you know," and other halts in the flow of speech.
- Avoiding irrelevant interjections of subject matter and relevant interjections at inappropriate times.
- Being precise in statement, including sufficient detail in presentations to avoid vagueness.
- Using transitional terms such as "next," "the last item is," "this concludes," "tomorrow we will," "these were the four causes of . . . 1, 2, 3, 4," "first we will . . . ," "second we will . . . ," and "third we will . . ."
- Providing explanations to clarify cause-effect relations. This is necessary in answering the question "Why?"
- Describing the tasks students are to perform, explaining and demonstrating how to perform tasks, and defining performance standards.
- Showing the relevancy of concepts being taught to students' lives.
- Using multiple and diverse approaches to clarify a concept: for instance, using a number of different illustrations or using media that involve a number of senses such as sight and hearing.
- Providing for question-and-answer instruction. Questioning students and correcting their answers, as well as answering student-initiated questions, sharpens their understanding and corrects misconceptions. Question-and-answer instruction may be incorporated in textbooks and in lesson plans, or teachers can encourage students to ask questions at any time.
- Using simple language. Rarely used and excessively complex terminology is to be avoided.

Elaboration of the above summary of tactics can be obtained from reading the studies that follow. To be most effective, the instructional tactics need to be integrated into the particular instructional program being planned or presently being used.

CAUTIONS AND COMMENTS

The second tactic, "avoiding halts in speech," pertains to speaking. Most of the other tactics pertain to any mode of communication; for example, "using simple language." Some tactics pertain most particularly to instruction; for instance, "describing the task students are to perform," "explaining and demonstrating how to perform tasks," and "defining performance standards," as well as "providing question-and-answer instruction." Question-and-answer instruction has been shown to be especially effective in enhancing achievement. (See Chapter 19.)

GENERALIZATION: ON CLARIFYING COMMUNICATION

Achievement of learning objectives is enhanced when information on learning objectives, tasks, and evaluations is clearly communicated to students over time.

Supportive Research on Clarifying Communication
Total number of supportive studies covered: 125+

Groups of Studies

Author: Land (1985)

Students: Elementary, high school, and college

Learning: Social studies, science, mathematics, and psychology achievement

Instructional Tactics: Some of the tactics used in studies summarized by Land (1985) to enhance learning involved avoiding low-clarity instructional communication. Tactics having a negative effect on student achievement include vagueness terms, mazes, "uhs," specification of selected content, extra content, and signals of transition and discontinuity. Vagueness terms are words or phrases which lack clarity or may indicate a lack of assurance on the part of the teacher. Mazes relate to the teacher's speaking correctly, avoiding false starts or halts in speech, redundantly stated words, tangles of words, and "uhs," "ahs," and "ums." Specification of selected content includes descriptions, explanations, and providing specific details. Clear transition is the presence of such transitional terms as "now" and "the last item was." Discontinuity is defined as interruptions of the flow of the lesson, with irrelevant interjections of subject matter and relevant interjections at inappropriate times.

The following are examples of clear and unclear instruction as provided by Land (1979):

Clear: "A concept is a word or phrase (but not a complete statement) or symbol that refers to a group of one or more objects, qualities, actions, or things possessing common characteristics. Here are three examples of concepts. Bacteria is an example because it is a word that refers to a group of common organisms. Parts of speech is an example because it is a phrase that refers to a group of things with common characteristics. HCI is an example because it is a symbol" (p. 797).

Unclear: "A concept is a word or phrase, phrase (but not, uh, a complete statement) or symbol that refers to a group of some objects, qualities, actions, or things possessing common characteristics. Bacteria. Parts of speech. HCI. Concepts can be classified as concrete versus abstract and as conjunctive, disjunctive, and relational" (p. 797).

The following are examples of clear instruction and unclear instruction for a geometry lesson as provided by Smith and Cotten (1980):

No vagueness, no discontinuity (Clear): "The first theorem involves two chords intersecting at one point in a circle. Look at figure 1. AB intersects CD at point E. Look at figure 2. The length of line segment AE is 4 units. The length of line segment EB is 3 units. The length of line segment ED is 6 units. The length of line segment EC is 2 units. Notice that $4 \times 3 = 2 \times 6$. Look at figure 7. The third theorem means that $AE \times AD = AF \times GA$. The length of the secant AE is 8 units. The length of the external segment is 3 units. The length of the secant AF is 6 units. We can determine the length of the external segment GA" (p. 672).

Vagueness, no discontinuity: "The first theorem sort of involves a couple of chords intersecting at one point in a circle. I guess we probably should look at figure 1. AB intersects CD at point E, you see. Look at figure 2. The length of line segment AE is 4 units. The length of line segment EB is 3 units. The length of line segment ED is 6 units, you see. The length of line segment EC, you know, is 2 units. You might notice that $4 \times 3 = 2 \times 6$. Look at figure 7 a few seconds. The third theorem ordinarily means that $AE \times AD = AF \times GA$. The length of the secant AE is 8 units. The length of the external segment is 3 units. The length of the secant AF is 6 units, as you know. Chances are we can determine the length of the external segment GA" (p. 672).

Discontinuity, no vagueness: "The first theorem involves two chords intersecting at one point in a circle. Look at figure 1. Did you know that the word geometry is derived from the Greek words for earth and measure? AB intersects CD at point E. Look at figure 2. It is shaped somewhat like a baseball diamond. The length of line segment AE is 4 units. The length of line segment EB is 3 units. The length of line segment ED is 6 units. The length of the line segment EC is 2 units. From your work with areas, you will recall that area is represented in terms of square units. Notice that $4 \times 3 = 2 \times 6$. Look at figure 7. Although the word geometry is a noun, the word geometrize is a verb. The third theorem means that $AE \times AD = AF \times GA$. The length of the secant AE is 8 units. The length of the external segment is 3 units. If you square 3 and subtract 1, the result is 8. This is a coincidence, but it is interesting. The length of the secant AF is 6 units. We can determine the length of the external segment GA. Try to remember that the second theorem involved tangents" (p. 672).

The vagueness and discontinuity lesson contained all of the vagueness terms and instances of discontinuity present in the previous examples.

Findings: In eight of the 10 studies involving multiple variables associated with teacher clarity of communication, students exposed to clear teacher behaviors performed significantly higher on achievement tests than did students exposed to unclear teacher behaviors. In five experimental studies on the effects of vagueness terms on student achievement, students exposed to instruction containing many vagueness terms performed at a significantly lower level than did students not exposed to instruction containing vagueness terms. The same findings were found in three of the five correlational studies reviewed.

Individual studies reviewed in this logical synthesis of research are identified by the symbol # in the reference list in Part V.

Author: Brophy & Good (1986)

Students: Elementary and secondary

Learning: Reading and mathematics achievement

Instructional Tactics: The following tactics were derived from the review of studies:

- Give clear and detailed instructions.
- Ask many clear and relevant academic questions and check for student understanding.
- Ask questions one at a time, be clear, and present them at an appropriate level of difficulty so that students can understand them.
- Wait for answers to questions.
- Explain answers when necessary.
- Encourage student questions.
- Answer all student questions.
- Use examples and illustrations to clarify concepts.

- Show analogies between new material and events and those with which students are already familiar.

- Present material in a systematic and structured manner.

- Avoid vague words and phrases such as "all of this," "somewhere," "not many," "not very," "almost," "pretty much," "anyway," "of course," "excuse me," "not sure," "some," "a few," "sorts," "factors," "may," "could be," "sometimes," "often," "some things," "usually," "probably," and "as you know."

- Avoid using "um," "uh," and "ah."

- Avoid interjecting irrelevant content.

Other instructional tactics are employed in these studies that are applicable to other generalizations and will be presented in the appropriate chapters.

Findings: Use of the above tactics was related to enhanced achievement across the relevant studies included in these reviews.

Groups of studies reviewed in this logical synthesis of research did not provide statistical evidence. However, many of the individual studies included in the logical synthesis of research do contain statistical evidence. In the event that a reader wishes to view this evidence, an extensive listing of the individual studies reviewed is provided in the reference list in Part V. The studies are identified by the symbol *.

Individual Studies

Author: Hines et al. (1985)

Students: College

Learning: Mathematics achievement

Instructional Tactics: The Hines et al. (1982) study summarized by Land (1985) and the Hines et al. (1985) study used the following teaching clarity behaviors reported in Cruickshank et al. (1979).

- Communicate so the students can understand.

- Explain the work to be done and how to do it.

- Repeat questions and explanations if students do not understand.

- Ask students before they start work if they know what to do and how to do it.

- Give explanations that the students understand.

- Provide for student understanding.

- Demonstrate a high degree of verbal fluency.

Findings: Teacher clarity was found to be related positively and significantly to learner achievement.

Author: Chesebro (1999)

Students: College

Learning: Factual and conceptual recall

Instructional Tactics: The author's review of the research related to teacher clarity provides a number of variables related to clear teaching. They include "instructor expressiveness (Perry, Abrami, & Leventhal, 1979), instructor enthusiasm (Solomon, 1966), instructor immediacy (Mehrabian, 1981), lesson vagueness (Land, 1979), discontinuity (Smith & Cotten, 1980), mazes (Land, 1979), explicit teaching (Rosenshine, 1987; Rosenshine & Stevens, 1986), advance organizers (Ausubel, 1963; Mayer, 1979), notetaking facilitation (Kiewra, 1985), and message organization (Feldman, 1989; Kallison, 1986; Murray, 1991)" (Chesebro, 1999, p. 3). A process definition for teacher clarity includes three components: nonverbal messages, verbal messages, and structure.

First, *nonverbal messages* would include immediacy, expressiveness, and enthusiasm. These all relate to teacher behaviors in the classroom and include eye contact, vocal variety, smiling, energy, and "presence." These can be restated as physical and psychological closeness of the teacher to the students. These immediacy traits are foundational for the other components of teacher clarity.

Second, *verbal messages* include vagueness, fluency, and mazes. Vagueness is words that create uncertainty and approximation. Fluency would not include the "uhs," etc., in verbal messages. Mazes are the unintended pauses, false starts, redundant words, and confusion of words.

Some clear verbal messages teachers use as tactics, as stated by students, include:

- "explains things simply"
- "gives explanations we understand"
- "tries to find out if we don't understand and repeats things"
- "asks if we know what to do and how to do it"
- "repeats things when we don't understand"
- "explains something and then works an example" (Cruickshank & Kennedy, 1986, p. 58)

Some nonverbal behavioral tactics used by teachers, considered by students, include:

- "teaches at a pace appropriate to the topic and students"
- "stays with the topic until we understand" (Cruickshank & Kennedy, 1986, p. 58)

Third, the *structure* component includes discontinuity, effective transitions, explicit teaching, advance organizers, and organization. Just the use of organization would encompass tactics such as providing a preliminary overview of the lesson, making an outline visible to students, and using a PowerPoint presentation to guide students' notetaking. Using transitions prepare students for what is to follow and provide a step-by-step procedure for learning. Probably the most practiced tactic is explicit teaching (Rosenshine, 1987; Rosenshine & Stevens, 1986). Explicit teaching tactics are:

- Begin a lesson with a short statement of goals.
- Begin a lesson with a short review of previous, prerequisite learning.
- Present new material in small steps, with student practice after each step.
- Give clear and detailed instructions and explanations.
- Provide a high level of active practice for all students.
- Ask many questions, check for student understanding, and obtain responses from all students.
- Guide students during initial practice.
- Provide systematic feedback and corrections.
- Provide explicit instruction and practice for seatwork exercises and, when necessary, monitor students during seatwork.
- Continue practice until students are independent and confident. (Rosenshine, 1987)

A synthesis of the research indicates that a clear teacher employs the following tactics:

- Presents structured learning experiences, complete with reviews, previews, and internal summaries.
- Stays on task at an appropriate pace.
- Speaks fluently.
- Provides examples.
- Checks for students' understanding while presenting information.

Findings: The review of research indicates that immediacy behaviors play a significant role in the retention of content (Kelley & Gorham, 1988; Perry & Penner, 1990). Other studies found that the verbal messages, having vagueness, disfluency, and mazes, have a negative effect on student achievement

(Smith, 1977); however, clear teaching is linked to increased student achievement (Alexander, Frankiewicz & Williams, 1979; Hines, Cruickshank, & Kennedy, 1985; Smith & Cotten, 1980; Smith & Land, 1981).

The author's individual study was based on the profile of the clear teacher in the review of research studies; therefore, the instructional tactics are similar:

- Use previews, reviews, summaries, and visible outlines, such as on Power-Point.
- Stay "on task."
- Explain information with concise and relevant examples.
- Pace instruction appropriately.

Findings: Use of the above tactics of clear teaching leads to greater recall of content matter.

Studies included in the summary of research above are in the reference list in Part V and are designated by the symbol @.

Author: Titsworth & Kiewra (2004)

Students: Undergraduate

Learning: Basic communication

Instructional Tactics: This individual study focused on using cues during lectures. Tactics include:

- Provide students with a brief advance organizer preceding the lecture which organizes the content to be presented. This may be written or spoken.
- Provide oral cues which signal a topic or subtopic name.
- Provide oral cues which signal the sequence of points in the lecture content.
- Provide students with a matrix showing major topics across the top as column headings and subtopics down the left side of the page as row labels, leaving room for notes within the cells of the matrix.
- Provide students with a linear major topic outline on which to enter notes beneath each topic or subtopic.
- Write important ideas on the board or present them on a transparency or PowerPoint slides.

Other instructional tactics are employed in these studies that are applicable to other generalizations and will be presented in the appropriate chapters.

Findings: Use of the above tactics, both in organizational structure of the lecture and in details of the lecture, was found to be tied positively to achievement. Cues, written and spoken, were found to have profound effects on notetaking and recall. The positive effect of cues on notetaking made the earlier research that the quantity and detail of notetaking, without cues during lecture, led to achievement of subject matter. Thus, cues during lecture are an added value to notetaking.

REFERENCE LIST

Alexander, L., Frankiewicz, R., & Williams, R. (1979). Facilitation of learning and retention of oral instruction using advance and post organizers. *Journal of Educational Psychology, 71*, 701–707.

Ausubel, D. (1963). *The psychology of meaningful verbal learning*. New York: Grune and Stratton.

Brophy, J., & Good, T. (1986). Teacher behavior and student achievement. In M. C. Wittrock (Ed.), *Handbook of research on teaching* (3rd ed., pp. 328–375). New York: Macmillan.

Chesebro, J. L. (1999). *The effects of teacher clarity and immediacy on student learning, apprehension, and affect*. Unpublished doctoral dissertation, University of West Virginia.

Cruickshank, D., & Kennedy, J. (1986). Teacher clarity. *Teaching & Teacher Education, 2*(1), 43–67.

Cruickshank, D. R., Kennedy, J. J., Bush, A., & Myers, B. (1979). Clear teaching: What is it? *British Journal of Teacher Education, 5*(1), 27–32.

Feldman, K. (1989). The association between student ratings of specific instructional dimensions and student achievement: Refining and extending the synthesis of data from multisection validity studies. *Research in Higher Education, 30*, 583–645.

Hines, C. V., Cruickshank, D. R., & Kennedy, J. J. (1982). *Measures of teacher clarity and their relationships to student achievement and satisfaction*. Paper presented at the annual meeting of the American Educational Research Association, New York.

Hines, C. V., Cruickshank, D. R., & Kennedy, J. J. (1985). Teacher clarity and its relationship to student achievement and satisfaction. *American Educational Research Journal, 22*(1), 87–99.

Kallison, J., Jr. (1986). Effects of lesson organization on achievement. *American Educational Research Journal, 23*, 337–347.

Kelley, D., & Gorham, J. (1988). Effects of immediacy on recall of information. *Communication Education, 37*, 198–207.

Kiewra, K. (1985). Providing the instructor's notes: An effective addition to student notetaking. *Educational Psychologist, 20*, 33–39.

Land, M. L. (1979). Low-inference variables of teacher clarity effects on student concept learning. *Journal of Educational Psychology, 71*(6), 795–799.

Land, M. L. (1985). Vagueness and clarity in the classroom. In T. Husen & T. Postlethwaite (Eds.), *The International Encyclopedia of Education Research and Studies* (Vol. 9, pp. 5405–5410). Oxford: Pergamon Press.

Mayer, R. (1979). Twenty years of research on advance organizers: Assimilation theory is still the best predictor of results. *Instructional Science, 8*, 133–167.

Mehrabian, A. (1981). *Silent messages: Implicit communication of emotions and attitudes* (2nd ed.). Belmont, CA: Wadsworth.

Murray, H. (1991). Effective teaching behaviors in the college classroom. In J. Smart (Ed.), *Higher education: Handbook of theory and research* (Vol. 7). New York: Agathon Press.

Perry, R., Abrami, P., & Leventhal, L. (1979). Educational seduction: The effect of instructor expressiveness and lecture content on student ratings and achievement. *Journal of Educational Psychology, 71*, 109–116.

Perry, R., & Penner, K. (1990). Enhancing academic achievement in college students through attributional retraining and instruction. *Journal of Educational Psychology, 82*, 262–271.

Rosenshine, B. (1987). Explicit teaching. In D. C. Berliner & B. V. Rosenshine (Eds.), *Talks to teachers* (pp. 75–92). New York: Random House.

Rosenshine, B., & Stevens, R. (1986). Teaching functions. In M. C. Wittrock (Ed.), *Handbook of research on teaching* (3rd ed., pp. 376–391). New York: Macmillan.

Smith, D. (1977). College classroom interactions and critical thinking. *Journal of Educational Psychology, 69*, 180–190.

Smith, L. (1977). Aspects of teacher discourse in student achievement in mathematics. *Journal for Research in Mathematics Education, 8*, 195–204.

Smith, L., & Land, M. (1981). Low-inference verbal behaviors related to teacher clarity. *Journal of Classroom Interaction, 17*, 37–42.

Smith, L. R., & Cotten, M. L. (1980). Effect of lesson vagueness and discontinuity on student achievement and attitudes. *Journal of Educational Psychology, 72*(5), 670–675.

Solomon, D. (1966). Teacher behavior dimensions, course characteristics, and student evaluations of teachers. *American Educational Research Journal, 3*, 35–47.

Titsworth, B. S., & Kiewra, K. A. (2004). Spoken organizational lecture cues and student notetaking as facilitators of student learning. *Contemporary Educational Psychology, 29*(4), 447–461.

19

Utilizing Question and Answer Instruction

INTRODUCTION

Questions have been used as an instructional device at least as far back as ancient Greece when the Socratic method was used to guide students to desired insights. Socrates and just about every teacher since have employed a questioning strategy in their instruction with little objective proof that it increases the achievement of their students. Despite its logical appeal, questions and answer instruction has been practiced more as an art than a science. However, times have changed. As classroom research on question and answer instruction increased, objective evidence supporting the effectiveness of one strategy became more and more compelling.

There is now a sizable amount of evidence showing that routinely incorporating question and answer instruction into lesson plans and systematically applying it during class sessions increases academic achievement. During question and answer sessions, instruction varies depending on student responses to the planned questions. Correct answers are acknowledged as correct and incorrect answers are acknowledged as incorrect. Reteaching is engaged to remediate incorrect answers at the teacher's discretion. Slight misconceptions are corrected and explained immediately. Extended reteaching may be required to remediate serious misunderstandings. The strategy is effective across a number of student populations in teaching a variety of subjects.

Other questioning strategies may also work. However, they have not been sufficiently tested as yet.

STUDENT BENEFICIARIES

The evidence indicates that question and answer instruction enhances achievement in elementary, secondary, and adult education settings. Utilizing question and answer instruction has been found to aid those with learning disabilities. Moreover, achievement is enhanced in multiple content areas. Utilizing question and answer instruction has been beneficial to students in solving problems and using higher level thought processes. Further, question and answer instruction benefits students with special needs. No evidence could be found to suggest that utilizing question and answer instruction should not be stressed for all types of students in all subject matter areas and levels of thought processes.

LEARNING ACHIEVED

Achievement in the content areas of mathematics, reading, English, science, history, biology, and higher order processing (problem solving) is enhanced when question and answer instruction is utilized.

INSTRUCTIONAL TACTICS

- Include questions to ask in each lesson plan to improve understanding of each concept to be taught.
- Ask the questions when the lesson is being taught.
- Solicit answers to each question immediately after it is asked.
- If an answer is incorrect, acknowledge it and reteach the concept.
- If the answer is satisfactory, acknowledge it and proceed to the next question until all questions have been asked.

CAUTIONS AND COMMENTS

It is important to remember that the question and answer strategy must be planned carefully to increase students' academic achievement, as noted previously in the "Instructional Tactics." Questions serve different purposes. Some questions are asked by the teacher to solidify students' learning. Others are to create interest in the subject matter being taught. Further, other questions allow students to ponder the answer for further insight. When students ask questions simply to be talking or ask questions unrelated to the content being taught, the instructional process is interrupted. Such disruptions cause all students to lose concentration on the instructional objective.

GENERALIZATION: ON QUESTION AND ANSWER INSTRUCTION

Achievement of learning objectives is enhanced when question and answer sessions are planned and included in lessons to clarify the concepts being taught.

Supportive Research on Utilizing Question and Answer Instruction
Total number of supportive studies covered: 246

Groups of Studies

Author: Swanson & Hoskyn (1998)

Students: Children and adults with learning disabilities

Learning: Achievement in multiple subject matter areas

Instructional Tactics: The synthesis included an overlap of strategy instruction and direct instruction.

• Prepare and ask students questions.

• Engage students in dialogue to hear their responses to questions.

Other instructional tactics are employed in these studies that are applicable to other generalizations and will be presented in the appropriate chapters.

Findings: Use of a combination of the above tactics led to enhanced achievement in multiple content areas.

Specific studies in this meta-analysis are marked with the symbol * in the reference list in Part V.

Author: Swanson (2001)

Students: Adolescents with learning disabilities

Learning: Higher-order processing (problem solving) in reading and mathematics

Instructional Tactics:

• Engage students in dialogue through questions and answers.

• Ask students questions to prove their understanding of the learning objectives.

Other instructional tactics are employed in these studies that are applicable to other generalizations and will be presented in the appropriate chapters.

Findings: Use of the above tactics was found to lead to higher levels of achievement by students with learning disabilities in problem solving as measured by standardized tests in reading and in mathematics.

Studies associated with this meta-analysis are identified by the symbol # in the reference list in Part V.

Author: Rosenshine & Stevens (1986)

Students: Elementary and secondary

Learning: Mathematics, English, science, history, and reading achievement

Instructional Tactics:

- A large number of questions relevant to the to-be-learned material are prepared.
- During instruction and student practice, students are asked a large number of questions to check for their understanding of the subject matter.
- Correct responses to questions are acknowledged as correct.
- Correct responses should be provided to the student if an incorrect response is determined to be a careless error on the part of the student.
- When a student's incorrect response is due to a lack of knowledge or understanding, one of two options are pursued as deemed most appropriate: (1) provide students with prompts or hints to lead them to the correct answer or (2) reteach the material to the students who do not understand.
- Students are given praise for providing correct responses and encouragement when they provide incorrect responses.

Other instructional tactics are employed in these studies that are applicable to other generalizations and will be presented in the appropriate chapters.

Findings: Use of these tactics was found to be related to greater levels of student achievement.

Groups of studies reviewed in this logical synthesis of research did not provide statistical evidence. However, many of the individual studies included in the logical synthesis of research do contain statistical evidence. In the event that a reader wishes to view this evidence, an extensive listing of the individual studies reviewed is provided in the reference list in Part V. The studies are identified by the symbol %.

Author: Brophy & Good (1986)

Students: Elementary and secondary

Learning: Reading, mathematics, English, and biology achievement

Instructional Tactics:

- Ask many clear and relevant academic questions and check for student understanding.

- Ask questions one at a time, be clear, and present them at an appropriate level of difficulty so that students can understand them.

- Provide time for students to consider the correct response before calling on a student to respond.

- Acknowledge correct responses.

- Ensure that the correct response is revealed when incorrect responses are made. Provide the correct response or continue questioning until the correct response emerges as discretion indicates.

- Provide encouragement and reinforce correct responses.

Other instructional tactics are employed in these studies that are applicable to other generalizations and will be presented in the appropriate chapters.

Findings: Use of the preceding instructional tactics was found to be related positively to student achievement.

Individual studies in this research synthesis are included in the reference list in Part V and are identified by the symbol !.

REFERENCE LIST

Brophy, J., & Good, T. (1986). Teacher behavior and student achievement. In M. C. Wittrock (Ed.), *Handbook of research on teaching* (3rd ed., pp. 328–375). New York: Macmillan.

Rosenshine, B., & Stevens, R. (1986). Teaching functions. In M. C. Wittrock (Ed.), *Handbook of research on teaching* (3rd ed., pp. 376–391). New York: Macmillan.

Swanson, H. L. (2001). Research on interventions for adolescents with learning disabilities: A meta-analysis of outcomes related to higher-order processing. *The Elementary School Journal, 101*(13), 331–349.

Swanson, H. L., & Hoskyn, M. (1998). Experimental intervention research on students with learning disabilities: A meta-analysis of treatment outcomes. *Review of Educational Research, 68*(3), 277–321.

20

Utilizing Computerized Instruction

INTRODUCTION

In this technology age, students have grown up with television, video games, computers, and other technological devices. They have become strong audio and video learners rather than only verbal learners. Thus, logging on to a computer and following an instructional program is second nature to most of them. Also, following a computerized instructional program seems enjoyable to most students because they equate it with games and the Internet and things that they like. Most children are computer literate even if they don't have a computer at home; and if they are not computer literate, they learn the mechanics of operating the computer very quickly. Just the act of using the computer seems to be motivation to follow the instructional program and to learn the content. Computerized instruction is non-judgmental and gives frequent and immediate feedback. It can often be individualized and gives the student a feeling of autonomy thus contributing to the control motive. It provides a multi-sensory learning environment through images, sounds, and words.

STUDENT BENEFICIARIES

The evidence indicates that utilizing computerized instruction enhances the academic achievement of students in kindergarten, primary, elementary, middle, secondary, and college classrooms as well as for learning disabled, mixed disabilities, and at-risk students. No evidence could be found to suggest that computerized instruction should not be used for all types of students.

LEARNING ACHIEVED

Achievement in the content areas of reading, mathematics, and language arts, and, in fact, over all content areas is enhanced when computerized instruction is used. In studies reviewed, using computerized instruction was positively related to student achievement in a wide range of content areas.

INSTRUCTIONAL TACTICS

1. Prescribe a computerized instructional program to achieve a learning objective based on evaluation of students' readiness.
2. Teach students how to use the program.
3. Assign students to the entry task in the program appropriate for their readiness.
4. Allow students to operate the computer to learn the task.
5. Evaluate students' learning of the task.
6. Assign the next task based on the evaluation.
7. Repeat steps 4, 5, and 6 until the learning objective is achieved or another instructional program is prescribed.

CAUTIONS AND COMMENTS

Caution must be used in not allowing the computerized programs to replace the teacher or even to minimize the role of the teacher in the classroom. The teacher must take an active part in first prescribing the programs based on evaluation of students' readiness, then teaching the students how to use the program, and finally evaluating the students' learning of the task.

GENERALIZATION: ON COMPUTERIZED INSTRUCTION

Achievement of learning objectives is enhanced when computerized instruction is used as an instructional strategy.

Supportive Research on Utilizing Computerized Instruction
Total number of supportive studies covered: 202

Groups of Studies

Author: Azevedo & Bernard (1995)

Students: Primary, secondary, and college

Learning: Achievement

Instructional Tactics:

- Gather diagnostic data on content achievement.
- Provide students with computer-based instruction.
- Select computer-based instruction with feedback mechanism in a variety of feedback topologies such as right-wrong statements, elaborate corrective statements, and adaptive which adjusts to individualized needs of students.

- Administer an immediate posttest or administer a delayed posttest.

Findings: Use of the above tactics was found to enhance achievement. Greater gains in achievement occurred with immediate testing than with delayed testing although there were gains with both.

Studies in this meta-analysis are marked with the symbol % in the reference list in Part V.

❖　❖　❖

Author: Yan & Jitendra (1999)

Students: Elementary, secondary, and postsecondary; learning disabled, mixed disabilities, and at-risk

Learning: Achievement in mathematical word problems

Instructional Tactics:

- Students were provided tutorials via computer programs.
- Students were provided interactive videodisc programs via computer.

Other instructional tactics are employed in these studies that are applicable to other generalizations and will be presented in the appropriate chapters.

Findings: Use of computer intervention approaches was found to be especially effective when empirically validated strategies and curriculum design principles were included. Specifically, the use of videodisc programs resulted in significantly higher scores than the use of basal mathematics textbooks.

The studies in this logical synthesis are marked with the symbol * in the reference list in Part V.

❖　❖　❖

Author: Christmann & Badgett (2003)

Students: Elementary

Learning: Academic achievement over all subject areas

Instructional Tactics:

- Gather baseline achievement data.
- Provide students with traditional methods of instruction.
- Supplement instruction by using computer-assisted instruction.
- Give students a post-achievement assessment.

Findings: Use of the above tactics was found to enhance academic achievement for the average student in comparison to students receiving no supplemental computer-assisted instruction.

Studies in this meta-analysis are identified with the symbol # in the reference list at the end of the chapter.

Author: Barley et al. (2002)

Students: Kindergarten, elementary, middle, and secondary at-risk students

Learning: Academic achievement (literacy and mathematics)

Instructional Tactics:

• The computer is used to provide students with pre and post assessments.

• The computer is used to present instructional material.

• The computer is used to monitor the progress of learning.

• The computer is used to select additional teaching materials in view of a learners' immediate level of performance.

• Students work alone with the computer program during regular school time.

• The teacher's role is either as a facilitator of instruction or a software trouble shooter.

Some researchers suggest that the following characteristics of computer-assisted instruction (CAI) contribute to the academic achievement of at-risk students:

CAI

• is non-judgmental and is motivational.

• gives frequent and immediate feedback, thus offering opportunities for corrective instruction.

• can individualize learning through designs to meet students' needs.

• allows more student autonomy, thus providing for the control motive.

• provides a multi-sensory learning environment through images, sounds, and symbols, thus making the learning more meaningful to the student.

Findings: Use of the above tactics led to improved academic achievement of at-risk students in literacy and mathematics.

Twenty-one studies in this synthesis, part of a meta-analysis of 118 studies and directly related to computer-assisted instruction, are designated with the symbol @ in the reference list in Part V.

REFERENCE LIST

Azevedo, R., & Bernard, R. N. (1995). *The effects of computer-presented feedback on learning from computer-based instruction: A meta-analysis.* Paper presented at the annual meeting of the American Educational Research Association, San Francisco. (ERIC Document Reproduction Service No. ED 385235)

Barley, Z., Lauer, P. A., Arens, S. A., Apthrop, H. S., Englert, K. S., Snow, D., & Akiba, M. (2002). *Helping at-risk students meet standards: A synthesis of evidence-based classroom practices.* Aurora, CO: Mid-continent Research for Education and Learning.

Christmann, E. P., & Badgett, J. L. (2003). A meta-analytic comparison of the effects of computer-assisted instruction on elementary students' academic achievement. *Information Technology in Childhood Education Annual, 1,* 91–104.

Yan, P. X., & Jitendra, A. K. (1999). The effects of instruction in solving mathematical word problems for students with learning problems: A meta-analysis. *Journal of Special Education, 32*(4), 207–238.

21

Utilizing Demonstrations

INTRODUCTION

When learning something new such as how to play a game or make a dress or build a cabinet, it is beneficial to be given step-by-step instructions and to be told or shown the end result of implementing the instructions; for example, being told what winning the game means, seeing the picture of the dress on the front of the pattern package, or seeing a picture of the cabinet. These instructions may be verbal; however, some people learn even better by actually seeing those steps in action. It is helpful to be shown the game board and all the pieces for the game and read the directions. A person would want to read the pattern guide pages in order to gather the cloth, thread, and notions if the goal is to make the dress. Further, a person would gather the appropriate materials to build the cabinet and would read and follow the blueprints in order to begin the actual building of the cabinet. Although a person could do any of the above projects alone, it is much easier to have assistance from someone else who can guide the person in the process and correct errors along the way. A person trying to attain any of these goals would want to be able to ask procedural questions of someone who is more accomplished or has had more experience. The same is true of students and their learning.

Students should be told what procedures will be necessary for them to achieve the learning objective. If special materials are needed, the students must be told about them or given them. Next, students need to be shown how to execute the procedures which will lead to the achievement of the learning objective. Demonstrations may be given as oral step-by-step instructions, as diagrams to explain the procedures, or as pictures in a sequence which can be followed to reach the expected outcome. These alone are not enough. It is most helpful for the students to have guidance and support as they follow the procedures. As errors are made, they should be corrected immediately in order to ensure success and avoid failures and frustration. Students need to feel free to ask questions and anticipate clear, helpful responses. Demonstrations are most helpful in understanding and employing procedures.

STUDENT BENEFICIARIES

The evidence indicates that the academic achievement of students in kindergarten, elementary, middle, junior high, secondary, college, and adult learning classes is enhanced when demonstrations are provided. Moreover, academic achievement was improved in a wide range of content areas. Further, utilizing demonstrations enhanced achievement for at-risk students and for children and adults with learning disabilities. No evidence could be found to suggest that demonstrations should not be utilized in all subject areas for all types of students.

LEARNING ACHIEVED

Achievement in the content areas of reading, mathematics, sciences, social studies, language arts, writing, physics, algebra, and business communication is enhanced when demonstrations are provided. In studies reviewed, instruction utilizing demonstrations was associated positively with enhanced student achievement.

INSTRUCTIONAL TACTICS

- Orientation: Tell students about the procedure to be demonstrated, the end result sought, resources needed to execute it, behaviors performed in executing the procedure.
- Show students how the procedure is executed via personal performance, diagrams, or picture sequences.
- Guide students through the execution of the procedures, correcting their errors along the way.
- Answer students' questions about the procedure.

CAUTIONS AND COMMENTS

It is most important to remember that demonstrations are provided for step-by-step procedures in order to complete a task. Often in the studies reviewed, the term "modeling" is used for "demonstrating."

GENERALIZATION: ON DEMONSTRATIONS

Achievement of learning objectives is enhanced when students are demonstrated the sequential steps needed to perform assigned tasks.

Supportive Research on Utilizing Demonstrations
Total number of supportive studies covered: 578

Groups of Studies

Author: Ross (1988)

Students: Elementary, middle, secondary, college, and adult

Learning: Academic achievement in science

Instructional Tactics:

• Provide demonstrations of step-by-step operations for experiments.

• Provide manipulatives for student use in applying the steps.

• Require students to imitate the demonstration in the way they put together their own experiments.

Findings: Use of the above tactics was found to enhance academic achievement.

The individual studies in this meta-analysis are indicated with the symbol * in the reference list in Part V.

Author: Wise (1996)

Students: Middle and secondary

Learning: Sciences

Instructional Tactics:

• Ask students to work or practice with physical objects.

• Provide students the opportunity to operate apparatus, develop skills, or draw or construct something.

• Modify instructional materials; for example, rewrite or annotate text passages.

• Provide tape recorded instructions for completing the task.

• Provide simplified laboratory apparatus for students to use.

Findings: Use of the above tactics was found to be effective in science achievement.

Individual studies in this meta-analysis were not identified by the author.

Author: Rosenshine et al. (1996)

Students: Upper elementary (grade 3 and up), junior high, secondary, and college

Learning: Reading comprehension across subject matters, mathematics, physics, and writing

Instructional Tactics:

• Procedural prompts are provided to help students with specific procedures or suggestions to complete the task. These procedural prompts are followed by some or all of the following instructional tactics:

—Provide models of appropriate responses.
—Demonstrate sequential problem-solving skills by thinking through a problem out loud in order for the students to hear a method to solve problems.
—Guide student practice.
—Provide feedback and corrections during practice.

Other instructional tactics are employed in these studies that are applicable to other generalizations and will be presented in the appropriate chapters.

Findings: Use of the above tactics was found to enhance achievement in reading comprehension.

Individual studies analyzed by this meta-analysis are identified in the reference list in Part V by the symbol #.

❖ ❖ ❖

Author: Swanson & Hoskyn (1998)

Students: Children and adults with learning disabilities

Learning: Achievement

Instructional Tactics: The synthesis included an overlap of strategy instruction and content instruction.

• Break tasks into small steps.

• Provide pictorial or diagrammatic presentations.

• Provide elaborate explanations.

• Demonstrate the steps in the procedure.

• Give reminders to students to use specific strategies or procedures.

• Provide step-by-step prompts or instructions for multiple processes.

Other instructional tactics are employed in these studies that are applicable to other generalizations and will be presented in the appropriate chapters.

Findings: Use of the above tactics led to enhanced achievement.

Specific studies in this meta-analysis are marked with the symbol & in the reference list in Part V.

❖   ❖   ❖

Author: Barley et al. (2002)

Students: Kindergarten, elementary, middle, and secondary at-risk students

Learning: Academic achievement (mathematics, science, social studies, and language arts)

Instructional Tactics:

• Model successful thinking and problem solving strategies in a sequential manner.

• Follow modeling with explicit explanation of the procedures and skills.

• Answer students' questions about the use of procedures and skills.

Other instructional tactics are employed in these studies that are applicable to other generalizations and will be presented in the appropriate chapters.

Findings: Use of the above tactics led to improved academic achievement of at-risk students.

Studies in this synthesis directly related to demonstrations are designated with the symbol @ in the reference list in Part V.

❖   ❖   ❖

Author: Martens & Witt (2004)

Students: Ages 6–12

Learning: Academic achievement in elementary subjects

Instructional Tactics:

• Show students how to perform a skill step by step.

Other instructional tactics are employed in these studies that are applicable to other generalizations and will be presented in the appropriate chapters.

Findings: Use of the tactic listed above was found to be related positively to student achievement.

This research synthesis does not provide statistical data. The studies, some of which are meta-analyses, are designated with the symbol + in the reference list in Part V.

Individual Studies

Author: Smeltzer & Watson (1985)

Students: University

Learning: Academic achievement in business communication

Instructional Tactics:

- Provide students a series of videos demonstrating appropriate listening skills.

Findings: Use of the above tactic was found to increase academic achievement in listening skills.

❖ ❖ ❖

Author: Butler et al. (2003)

Students: Ages 11–15—with math disabilities

Learning: Mathematics

Instructional Tactics: In this study, the following tactics were used in the ten scripted lessons:

- The study compared two groups of students by using two instructional sequences: concrete-representational-abstract (CRA) and representational-abstract (RA). The only difference between the two treatment groups in terms of the instructional tactics listed below was that the CRA group used concrete manipulatives during the first three of ten lessons and the RA group used only representational drawings.
- The teacher tied the current lesson to previous learning, told the students the learning objective for the lesson, and provided a reason the students should learn the skill.
- The teacher demonstrated the skill to be used while describing the steps out loud. Then the teacher and students solved two problems working collaboratively using question and answer instruction.
- The teacher assigned the students to solve three problems, first giving prompts and cues but decreasing assistance as the students gained skill.
- The teacher then assigned students seven problems on a learning sheet to solve independently using the skills they had learned; the teacher provided no assistance.
- The students were expected to achieve a daily score of 80 percent or better on the learning sheet. The teacher met with each student individually to

discuss the daily work and give corrective feedback. Students not meeting the daily criterion were directed to rework the problems under the teacher's guidance. During corrective instruction, the CRA students were allowed to use concrete manipulative devices while the RA group used pictorial representations only.

- The teacher provided the students with prepared cue cards and printed notes to use if they forgot the steps in the process or became confused.

Findings: Use of the above tactics was found to improve mathematics achievement on fractions for both groups based on a pretest-posttest measure. The CRA group scored higher on all measures of the posttest than did the RA group.

Author: Witzel et al. (2003)

Students: Sixth and seventh grade students including but not limited to those who are learning disabled and at risk of failing

Learning: Achievement in algebra

Instructional Tactics:

- Provide explicit instruction: modeling, guided-practice, and independent-practice strategies.
- Provide students with sequential steps to solve algebra problems that are concrete, abstract, and representational.
  —Provide manipulatives for students to use.
  —Allow students to manipulate objects to solve concrete problems.
  —Model a pictorial representation that closely represents the concrete objects.
  —Guide students in drawing steps to solve the representational problem.
  —Model an abstract problem using Arabic symbols (typically used in textbooks and on standardized tests).
  —Have students write in Arabic symbols each step to solve the abstract problem.

Other instructional tactics are employed in these studies that are applicable to other generalizations and will be presented in the appropriate chapters.

Findings: Use of the above tactics related to concrete, representational and abstract problem solving was found to effect achievement in algebra positively.

Author: Alfassi (2004)

Students: Secondary—ninth graders

Learning: Reading comprehension in language arts

Instructional Tactics: Experiment I

- Teachers taught and modeled the reading comprehension strategies below:
  - —*Generating questions*: The teacher explained that during reading of a passage, the reader should ask himself questions to assure understanding and that the best questions to ask are those the teacher would ask on a test such as main facts and key terms. The teacher modeled ways to generate questions and illustrated this by continuously verbalizing her thought processes about the facts and terms, thus sharing her reasoning about the generation of questions.
  - —*Summarizing*: The teacher used the same oral reasoning process to illustrate the finding of main ideas and supporting ideas in a passage. She demonstrated how to summarize in one or two sentences. Further, she modeled the generation of main idea questions.
  - —*Clarifying*: The teacher, upon hearing words unfamiliar to students or passages they found difficult to understand, modeled ways to understand the words within the context of the passage. Again, the teacher orally modeled inferential and clarifying questions to enable understanding of the passage.
  - —*Predicting*: The teacher orally shared possible predictions for the next paragraph in a passage; then the teacher orally constructed predicting questions which often were based on prior knowledge.
  - —Throughout the modeling and oral thought processing, the teacher differentiated among factual knowledge questions, inferred questions, and prior knowledge questions.
- Time was provided for guided practice during which students used the structured self-questioning procedures.
- Cues and scaffolding were provided during the guided practice; scaffolding was diminished over time.
- Students provided feedback to each other using the techniques modeled orally by the teachers.

Other instructional tactics are employed in these studies that are applicable to other generalizations and will be presented in the appropriate chapters.

Findings: Use of the above tactics was found to increase reading comprehension.

REFERENCE LIST

Alfassi, M. (2004). Reading to learn: Effects of combined strategy instruction on high school students. *The Journal of Educational Research, 97*(4), 171–184.

Barley, Z., Lauer, P. A., Arens, S. A., Apthorp, H. S., Englert, K. S., Snow, D., & Akiba, M. (2002). *Helping at-risk students meet standards: A synthesis of evidence-based classroom practices.* Aurora, CO: Mid-continent Research for Education and Learning.

Butler, F. M., Miller, S. P., Crehan, K., Babbitt, B., & Pierce, T. (2003). Fraction instruction for students with mathematics disabilities: Comparing two teaching sequences. *Learning Disabilities Research & Practice, 18*(2), 99–111.

Martens, B. K., & Witt, J. C. (2004). Competence, persistence, and success: The positive psychology of behavioral skill instruction. *Psychology in the Schools, 41*(1), 19–30.

Rosenshine, B., Meister, C., & Chapman, S. (1996). Teaching students to generate questions: A review of the intervention studies. *Review of Educational Research, 66*(2), 181–221.

Ross, J. A. (1988). Controlling variables: A meta-analysis of training studies. *Review of Educational Research, 58*(4), 405–437.

Smeltzer, L. R., & Watson, K. W. (1985). A test of instructional strategies for listening improvement in a simulated business setting. *The Journal of Business Communication, 22*(4), 33–42.

Swanson, H. L., & Hoskyn, M. (1998). Experimental intervention research on students with learning disabilities: A meta-analysis of treatment outcomes. *Review of Educational Research, 68*(3), 277–321.

Wise, K. C. (1996). Strategies for teaching science: What works? *The Clearing House, 69*(6), 337–338.

Witzel, B. S., Mercer, C. D., & Miller, M. D. (2003). Teaching algebra to students with learning difficulties: An investigation of an explicit instruction model. *Learning Disabilities Research & Practice, 18*(2), 121–131.

II

Instructional Alerts

The tactics of 21 effective instructional strategies have been succinctly and simply described in Part I. From 68 to over 600 research studies have been presented to confirm the effectiveness of each strategy. The strategies can be accommodated in almost any instructional program existing or being planned. They can be taught in any preservice or in-service teacher education program. An Instructor's Manual is available for guidance. So, teaching the 21 strategies can be managed without much difficulty in a relatively short time with the expectation that academic achievement will increase as a result, provided the teacher education program is not stuffed with too much additional content that is not directly related to improving academic achievement.

Typically, more content is added to teacher preparation programs than is eliminated over time. Much of the added material does not pertain to the teacher behaviors and activities necessary to maximize academic achievement. In addition, teachers are assigned to perform many duties other than teaching and are responsible for many things other than student achievement. Much of the content teachers are taught and assignments teachers are given detract from and conflict with their primary responsibility—ensuring students achieve learning objectives. The best prospect for increasing academic achievement is to ensure that teachers learn and apply the 21 effective instructional strategies without compromise.

To maximize student achievement, not only is it necessary to eliminate irrelevant content from teacher education and irrelevant teacher assignments, but also it is necessary to be able to detect and eliminate instructional strategies that do not work. Many instructional strategies shown by research not to increase academic achievement are still commonly used in our schools.

In Part II, "Instructional Alerts," questionable instructional strategies in common practice are exposed. In addition to being a waste of time, they interfere with effective instruction and can have serious side effects. Part II also includes one promising instructional strategy that may be worth considering and pilot testing locally. It is worth considering because there is some evidence that it can be used to motivate students to achieve learning objectives. To improve academic achievement continually, it is necessary to identify strategies for adoption that are shown by research to work and to cull out the questionable strategies that have accumulated over the years.

22

Promising Instructional Strategy

In this chapter, a promising instructional strategy is described. There is some research support for this strategy but not nearly the support that there is for those instructional strategies labeled effective. In some cases there may be substantial research support for promising instructional strategies in related fields but less support with regard to instructional effectiveness.

The instructional strategy listed as promising should not be adopted without further research to support its effectiveness. However, it is quite appropriate for particular educational institutions to pilot test a promising strategy on their students. Then, if it proves to be effective, its adoption might be considered. It would take, however, many additional studies across many educational settings to establish the generalizability of a promising strategy. Nevertheless, with further validation, a promising strategy could prove to have a significant effect on student achievement.

The promising strategy is not presented in as much detail as effective strategies, but ample references are provided for greater detail as well as for statistical findings.

Enlisting the Control Motive

INTRODUCTION

Motivation determines what people will pursue and what they will try to avoid. Since in free societies it is generally illegal to coerce people to do one's bidding against their will, there is great interest in inducing people to do willingly what one wants them to do. As a result, huge sums of money are spent on motivational research. Businesses and industries want to know how to entice people to buy their goods and services and how to encourage employees to be more productive. Welfare agencies want to determine how to get people on welfare to want to work.

Charities want to know how to entice people to donate more money. Crime prevention agencies would like to know how to get convicts to choose to obey the law. Parents want to know how to induce their children to cooperate without undue coercion. Educational institutions would like to find ways to enlist students' interest in pursuing the learning objectives they are assigned to achieve.

Students control what they will attend to, focus on, and try to learn. Consequently, an effort must be made to enlist their motivation to learn the knowledge and skills they are assigned to learn. Instruction would be so much easier and more successful if educators were able to induce students to learn eagerly what they are assigned to learn.

The challenge is to identify a motive that can be enlisted to induce students to achieve assigned learning objectives. Such a motive would need to meet certain conditions: (1) it must be a motive that can be enlisted to enhance the pursuit of learning objectives in educational settings without harmful side effects and (2) it must be a stable, prevalent motive inherent in most students most of the time so that it can be reliably enlisted and worked with in group instruction.

Sex is an example of a prevalent motive that cannot be satisfied in a school setting to induce students to achieve learning objectives without deleterious side effects. People are asked to restrain their sexual urges in the workplace and in schools because, as you know, the unbridled expression and satisfaction of the sex motive can be disruptive to achieving both work and learning objectives. Moreover, the open public expression of the sex motive is most often illegal. Hunger is another motive that is not enlisted and satisfied during work and instruction. In free, modern societies, people are generally not starving, and it is illegal to starve them. Eating can interfere with work and learning. There are times and places set aside for eating, and other times and places set aside for work and formal education.

Other motives are transient. They are not sufficiently prevalent to be reliable. They are here one minute and gone the next. For example, anger is frequently fleeting. A parent may be angry with his child one minute and be forgiving the next. Avarice, too, is often fleeting. A child may want a toy and be satisfied when given the toy. If not, the child might be distracted or soon become interested in some other attraction. In addition, bribing children to complete assignments by offering a gift can have adverse side effects. They learn to expect rewards for doing assignments instead of doing assignments because the learning that accrues is inherently beneficial.

Although knowledge of human motivation is still quite primitive, one motive has been emerging that seems to meet instructional requirements—the *control motive*. It appears to be reliably present and can be worked with to induce students to pursue instructional objectives without deleterious side effects. For our purposes, the control motive is defined as *the penchant to improve the control of outcomes.*

Unlike many other motives, satisfying the control motive is compatible with the pursuit of fundamental instructional objectives. Education is the primary means for developing productive citizens, and the development of control is essential to productive citizenship. To be productive, people must be able to exercise sufficient control to take care of themselves and to work successfully. People who are unable to exercise sufficient control become social wards.

Moreover, achieving most instructional objectives requires the control of outcomes. Writing a composition requires control of one's handwriting and descriptive ability. In science, control is exercised in laboratory experiments. In math, control is needed to execute the appropriate formula to solve problems. Additionally, the acquisition of knowledge requires control: finding facts requires control, memorizing facts requires control, and so does recalling facts (see the chapter on reminders). Now that the compatibility of satisfying the control motive and pursuing learning objectives has been discussed, we need to demonstrate the presence of the control motive as a force that reliably directs people's behavior.

There is mounting evidence that when people improve their control they derive personal satisfaction. Moreover, when they perceive that they can control the achievement of an outcome they will pursue it; and when they do not perceive that they can control the achievement of an outcome, their interest in pursuing the outcome diminishes, and they may not try.

A great deal of evidence demonstrating the importance of the control motive has been amassed in the field of health. People who perceive that they have control over outcomes in their life fare much better health wise (O'Leary, 1985). Nursing home studies show that inducing perceptions of control in older patients improves their well-being, including a reduction in both disease and mortality rate (Langer & Rodin, 1976; Schultz & Hoyer, 1976; Langer et al., 1979; Banzinger & Roush, 1983). So people who perceive that they have control over their life enjoy better health. When people who have lost control are made to perceive that they are more in control, their health improves. Furthermore, people who perceive that they are more in control take better care of themselves. They take greater responsibility for their health needs (Wallston et al., 1976), they learn more about their illnesses (Toner & Manuck, 1979), and they are more likely to benefit from health education programs (Walker & Bates, 1992). They also are less withdrawn, have a more active social life, and feel better about their life and environment (Lemke & Moos, 1981; Moos, 1981; Moos & Ingra, 1980; Hickson, Housely, & Boyle, 1988). The evidence becomes more compelling as research accumulates.

Evidence demonstrating the relationship between the control motive and academic achievement is not yet compelling, but it is mounting. People who perceive that they can control outcomes obtain higher scores on measures of academic achievement and also process information more efficiently than people who do not (Lefcourt, 1973, 1982). Additional research shows that people who perceive that they can control outcomes perform better in problem solving situations (Wolk & DuCette, 1974). Stipek and Weisz (1981) also provide evidence indicating that perceived control of outcomes is related to academic achievement. Gordon (1977) shows that perceived control is related to higher self-esteem as well as a greater academic achievement.

The above evidence makes working with the control motive to enhance educational achievement worth considering, as well as indicating the need for further research on the relationship.

STUDENT BENEFICIARIES

From a societal and educational perspective, enlisting the control motive to facilitate the achievement of learning objectives students are assigned to achieve will benefit all students. The students will be learning the knowledge and skills educational establishments deem necessary to equip them to succeed and to make social contributions.

To enlist the control motive, it is necessary to design instruction to satisfy the control motive as well as to achieve other learning objectives. Under these conditions, students should get more satisfaction from pursuing and achieving learning objectives.

LEARNING ACHIEVED

In addition to achieving the learning objectives they are assigned to achieve, students would be increasing their ability to control outcomes. As indicated, in large measure society benefits from citizens who can control outcomes. Citizens who cannot control outcomes become burdens to society.

INSTRUCTIONAL TACTICS

Three types of instructional tactics need to be employed:

1. Students need to be taught about control. Since people often have difficulty understanding and coping with their own motivation, it is important to clarify for them the control motive and how it affects behavior.

2. Students need to be taught how to improve their control.

3. The control motive should be enlisted to enhance achievement of learning objectives.

4. Instruction must be designed to engender perceptions of control in students.

CLARIFYING MOTIVATION TO CONTROL

As soon as they are old enough to understand, it can be explained to students that while we tend to be acutely aware of our intense motives such as hunger and sex urges, other motives are important not because of their intensity but because of their prevalence. Those motives are prompting our behavior a great deal of the time. A most prevalent motive is our motivation to improve our control. Most of the time we are attempting to improve our control of something—be it controlling our weight, our mood, our cholesterol level, or other people or getting food, a car, or money. Unlike many very intense motives, we are not always aware of our motivation to control. When eating delicious food to satisfy our hunger, we are aware of the delightful taste of the food; we are much less aware of our desire to control the acquisition of food, that is, getting the food to our mouths and providing for our future meals.

The important thing to realize is that whatever we may want at the time, be it food, companionship, or a car, we want to control its acquisition. If we are able to control its acquisition, we can make certain that it is available when we want it again in the future. We are interested in controlling all sources of satisfaction. Although the particular things we want change from time to time, we spend most of our waking hours trying to control something. That is why our motivation to control is so prevalent.

We not only want to control to get things, but also we find improving our control satisfying in itself. We feel good about ourselves when we are a "take control" person – in control of our lives. We feel more competent, more capable. Every time we set a goal and control its achievement we are satisfied with ourselves.

To succeed in improving our control, it is necessary to understand the nature of control. *By control, we mean influencing things or people, including oneself, to bring about desired outcomes.*

For one thing, we are intensely interested in controlling our environment so we can get from it the things we want when we want them. Physical objects we usually control by physically manipulating them—we turn on a stove, ride a bicycle, and close a door through physical manipulation.

People themselves are sometimes controlled by physical manipulation. For example, parents physically manipulate infants to diaper and feed them. Criminals are sometimes controlled by physical manipulation; they are handcuffed and forced into jail. However, when we are dealing with people who can understand what we say, we usually attempt to control them by talking to them. When people are dealing with subordinates, they often give them orders. In the army, drill sergeants give marching orders to their troops. Parents give orders to their children when they tell them to finish their food or go to bed. Teachers give orders when they give homework assignments or tell their class to be quiet.

On the other hand, when we are dealing with people who are under no obligation to take orders from us, we control them by asking and persuading them to do what we want them to do. If we want to make a date with someone, we ask the person for a date. If a person has something we want, we ask the person for it; for example, we may ask to borrow a pencil from a friend or ask a teacher to answer a question.

Quite often we need to work with others to control an outcome. Then, cooperation is required. Such is the case when we join a team—members of a sports team must cooperate to win games, and members of work teams must cooperate to manufacture products. If the team we join is to be successful in controlling desired out-comes, team members must place cooperation above conflicting personal prefer-ences.

It is important to realize that self-control is a prerequisite to environmental con-trol. If we want to drive a car, we must control our actions to start the car, shift the gears, and steer the car. If we want to make friends, we must do and say things that are appealing to other people. The bottom line is that if we can't control ourselves, we can't control anything else.

Self-control can have personal as well as environmental benefits. It is required when we want to diet to lose weight, or when we want to exercise to build strength, or when we want to rest to recuperate when we are weary.

It is through education that people learn to control outcomes. Learning to speak enables children to ask adults to help them control things they cannot control them-selves; learning hygiene and how to obtain medical assistance enables people to control their health; learning how to drive enables people to control a car; and learning an occupation enables people to get and hold a job. People can learn to control some primitive outcomes by themselves such as crawling, but it is through education that people learn how to control the outcomes primarily responsible for achieving personal aspirations, whatever they may be, and succeeding in society.

TEACHING STUDENTS HOW TO CONTROL OUTCOMES

Students' motivation to control is elicited. To capture students' interest, they are informed that they are about to be taught a technique that will help them control the achievement of any outcome they may want to achieve. Learning the technique will help them get what they want, whatever that may be.

Students are taught to behave purposefully. Students are informed that the tech-nique they are about to learn is how to behave purposefully. Purposeful behavior has four defining characteristics. Purposeful behavior is (1) directed toward an outcome rather than aimless, (2) based on learning rather than instincts, (3) based on prediction rather than hindsight or ideas of the moment, and (4) selected rather than predetermined or imposed. Students are informed that the technique involves first selecting an outcome they want to pursue at the time and then selecting a behavior to achieve the outcome as follows.

SELECTING AN OUTCOME TO ACHIEVE

The first step in behaving purposefully is to select an outcome to pursue at the time—be it obtaining money, a bicycle, a pet, or a car or taking a vacation. Al-though people may want to achieve many outcomes, to be successful they need to establish their preferences and plan to pursue one outcome at a time. Otherwise, they might become confused and ineffectual.

SELECTING A BEHAVIOR PREDICTED TO ACHIEVE THE OUTCOME

A behavior is selected because it is predicted to achieve the outcome. It must be made clear to students that they frequently and routinely predict the outcomes of their behavior. When turning the page of a novel they predict the story will continue on the next page. They predict that washing will make them and other things clean, that drinking will quench their thirst, that dating a particular person will be satisfying, that dieting and exercise will result in weight loss, and that following a particular route will lead them to school. Because particular behaviors have frequently achieved particular outcomes in the past, they have learned to predict with confidence that the behaviors will achieve the outcomes in the future. When their learning does not enable confident predictions, they can consult libraries and data banks to find out whether cumulative learning recorded over the years enables them to make confident predictions. In addition, they can learn statistics to estimate probability in order to make more accurate predictions.

Students must be made aware that when they behave purposefully to control outcomes, they are taking an active part in shaping their own destiny through foresight and preparation, rather than reacting to things that are imposed upon them. When they behave purposefully, they are more apt to make things turn out as they choose.

ENLISTING THE CONTROL MOTIVE TO FACILITATE ACHIEVEMENT OF LEARNING OBJECTIVES

Most important, the control motive should be enlisted during instruction to achieve the learning objective being pursued. In order to enlist motivation to control, students would need to be shown how pursuing an assigned learning objective can improve their control of outcomes. In general, this can be accomplished by translating assigned tasks designed to achieve a learning objective into behavior → outcome units. The performance of all tasks requires students to execute behaviors to achieve specified outcomes. Breaking down assigned tasks into behavior → outcome units during instruction not only conveys to students how their behavior can control outcomes, it simplifies the teaching of task performance. The task of performing long division can be broken down into component behavior → outcome units, and so can shopping, developing a household budget, driving a car, writing a composition, and so on. The performance of almost all tasks can be taught in behavior → outcome units. Even if students are not especially interested in achieving a particular assigned learning objective, they are interested in improving their control. Hence, if they can see that they are learning behaviors to control outcomes, thereby improving their control, the achievement of the assigned learning objective will be more attractive to them.

Motivation to control can be enlisted when teaching in any subject area, provided students are shown how the to-be-learned subject matter can improve their control of outcomes. It has been said that making instruction relevant to students' lives increases their enthusiasm for learning. By eliciting the control motive in teaching subject matter, the subject matter is not only made relevant to students' lives, it is made useful and important to them because they are being shown how to improve their control of outcomes.

Following are examples of how motivation to control can be enlisted while teaching in a subject area. When teaching social studies, students can be shown how voting (behavior) elects candidates for office (outcome), how writing to a congressman (behavior) can initiate the enactment of a law (outcome), and how breaking the law (behavior) can result in being arrested (outcome). In teaching language arts, students can be shown how learning to write (behavior) enables them to send a message to people with whom they are not in face-to-face contact (outcome) and how reading books (behavior) can bring them enjoyment (outcome). When teaching science, students can be shown that conducting a lab experiment (behavior) increases their ability to manipulate physical matter (outcome) and how studying the scientific method (behavior) enables them to make discoveries (outcome). In math, students can be shown how learning arithmetic (behavior) enables them to check the change they receive when shopping (outcome) and how learning to measure (behavior) enables them to follow recipes when cooking (outcome).

ENGENDERING PERCEPTIONS OF CONTROL IN STUDENTS

When students are assigned tasks to perform, it is most important that they perceive that they can control the achievement of the tasks. If they do not, they may well not try at all or they may make a feeble effort to perform the tasks. It is incumbent upon instructional planners and teachers to engender in students the perception that they can control the achievement of assigned tasks so that they will persist in attempting to perform the tasks.

One factor that contributes to students' perceiving that they can perform assigned tasks is that they have often performed them successfully in the past. This gives them confidence that they will succeed in the future. Instructional planners and teachers can inspire confidence in students by ensuring student success. This can be accomplished by making certain (1) that students have the readiness ability to perform assigned tasks, (2) that earlier tasks in a task sequence enable the performance of subsequent tasks, and (3) that task sequences are designed in small graded steps or increments.

Second, in providing students feedback on their task performance, they are given a clear understanding of their strengths and weaknesses, they are commended on their efforts and achievements as appropriate, and they are told that they have the ability to perform the next assigned tasks if they make a concerted effort, and they will be given the assistance they need to succeed. These assurances must not be in vain or when students fail they will rightfully blame and mistrust the instructional system and refuse to cooperate.

The above explanation of how purposeful behavior is used to improve control explains in part why the instructional tactics prescribed in the chapter on decision-making enhance student achievement.

CAUTIONS AND COMMENTS

The foregoing description of the control motive and its use in achieving assigned tasks is only an introduction. A more complete presentation is made in *Taking Control: Vitalizing Education* (Friedman, 1993). Moreover, to be most effective the instructional tactics described need to be adapted to the particular instructional program in use or being planned. Although the control motive has been enlisted to achieve goals in other fields, more research needs to be done on its use in education. Meanwhile, its application in education should be restricted to pilot testing.

Enlisting the control motive to achieve learning objectives requires that behavior → outcome relationships be emphasized in instruction. In this way students will be learning how to plan their behavior to control outcomes, thereby improving their control. As a result they will be motivated to achieve the learning objectives. This instructional emphasis mandates against the teaching of isolated facts so prevalent in many curricula. Facts should be incorporated in the teaching of behavior or procedures to guide behaviors to achieve particular outcomes.

Teaching facts in isolation does not satisfy the control motive because students cannot see the relationship between the facts and the improvement of their control. However, it is often the case that facts can be taught as components of a procedure used to control the achievement of a particular kind of outcome. For example, scientific method can be taught as a procedure for increasing knowledge. The components of scientific method can be taught as parts of the procedure. Then students can be guided in the execution of scientific method to enable them to see for themselves that it works. When they do, they will see that their ability to control outcomes has been improved, and they will be gratified.

REFERENCE LIST

Bacon, D. R., & Anderson, E. S. (2004). Assessing and enhancing the basic writing skills of marketing students. *Business Communication Quarterly, 67*(4), 443–454.

Banzinger, G., & Roush, S. (1983). Nursing home for the birds: A control relevant intervention test with bird feeders. *Gerontologist, 23*(5), 527–531.

Eshel, Y., & Kohavi, R. (2003). Perceived classroom control, self-regulated learning strategies, and academic achievement. *Educational Psychology, 23*(3), 249–260.

Friedman, M. I. (1993). *Taking control: Vitalizing education.* Westport, CT: Praeger.

Gordon, D. (1977). Children's beliefs in internal-external and self-esteem as related to academic achievement. *Journal of Personality Assessment, 41*(4), 333–336.

Henderson, R. W., & Landesman, E. M. (2001). Effects of thematically integrated mathematics instruction on students of Mexican descent. *The Journal of Educational Research, 88*(5), 290–300.

Hickson, J., Housely, W. F., & Boyle, C. (1988). The relationship of locus of control to life satisfaction and death anxiety in older persons. *International Journal of Aging and Human Development, 26*(3), 191–199.

Langer, E., & Rodin, J. (1976). The effects of choice and enhanced personal responsibility for the aged: A field experiment in an institutional setting. *Journal of Personality and Social Psychology, 34*(2), 191–198.

Langer, E., Rodin, J., Beck, P., Weinman, C., & Spitzer, L. (1979). Environmental determinants of memory improvement in late adulthood. *Journal of Personality and Social Psychology, 37*, 2003–2013.

Lefcourt, H. M. (1973). The function of the illusions of control and freedom. *American Psychologist, 28*, 417–425.

Lefcourt, H. M. (1982). *Locus of control: Current trends in theory and research.* Hillsdale, NJ: Erlbaum.

Lemke, S., & Moos, R. (1981). The suprapersonal environments of sheltered care settings. *Journal of Gerontology, 36*(2), 233–243.

Moos, R. (1981). Environmental choice and control in community care settings for older people. *Journal of Applied Social Psychology, 11*(1), 23–43.

Moos, R., & Ingra, A. (1980). Detriments of the social environments of sheltered care settings. *Journal of Health and Social Behavior, 21*, 88–98.

O'Leary, A. (1985). Self-efficacy and health. *Journal of Behavior Research and Therapy, 23*, 437–451.

Rawsthorne, L. J., & Elliot, A. J. (1999). Achievement goals and intrinsic motivation: A meta-analytic review. *Personality and Social Psychology Review, 3*(4), 326–344.

Schultz, N. R., Jr., & Hoyer, W. J. (1976). Feedback effects on spatial egocentrism in old age. *Journal of Gerontology, 31*(1), 72–75.

Stipek, D. J., & Weisz, J. R. (1981). Perceived personal control and academic achievement. *Review of Educational Research, 51*(1), 101–137.

Toner, J., & Manuck, S. B. (1979). Health locus of control and health related information seeking at hypertension screening. *Journal of Social Science and Medicine (Medical Psychology and Medical Sociology), 13A*(6), 823–825.

Walker, K., & Bates, R. (1992). Health locus and self-efficacy beliefs in a healthy elderly sample. *American Journal of Health Promotion, 6*(4), 302–309.

Wallston, B., Wallston, K., Kaplan, G., & Maides, S. (1976). Development and validation of the health locus of control scale. *Journal of Consulting and Clinical Psychology, 44*(4), 580–585.

Wolk, S., & DuCette, J. (1974). Intentional performance and incidental learning as a function of personality and task dimensions. *Journal of Personality and Social Psychology, 29*, 90–101.

23

Questionable Instructional Strategies

There are many instructional strategies that are not supported by research evidence. Some are in common use, and there are still advocates of the strategies who are promoting wider adoption. Moreover, teachers are being taught to adopt them and to use them. They are being taught in both pre-service and in-service teacher training, and familiarity with one or more of them is sometimes a prerequisite for teacher certification.

The purpose of this chapter is to review the research evidence on these questionable instructional strategies and to discuss their limitations, being careful not to "throw the baby out with the bath water." Although the evidence does not support the generalizability of the strategies discussed in this chapter, in some cases the evidence supports the effectiveness of a strategy for particular purposes. You need to evaluate the use of a strategy for your purpose. One of the strategies reviewed is widely used to assess the effectiveness of instruction. Because this strategy, portfolio testing, is not an instructional strategy but an evaluation strategy, the format of the "Portfolio Testing" section is not the same as that for the other strategies in this chapter.

Matching Student–Teacher Field-Dependent/ Field-Independent Cognitive Styles

INTRODUCTION

Witkin et al. (1977) identify field-dependence-independence as representing one dimension of cognitive style. They define this dimension as being

> the extent to which the person perceives part of a field as discrete from the surrounding field as a whole, rather than embedded in the field; or the extent to which the organization of the prevailing field determines the perception of its components; or, to put it in everyday terminology, the extent to which the

person perceives analytically. Because at one extreme of the performance range perception is strongly dominated by the prevailing field, that mode of perceptions was designated "field dependent." At the other extreme, where the person experiences items as more or less separate from surrounding fields, the designation "field independent" was used. (p. 7)

Witkin et al. indicate that intelligence and ability to learn are unrelated to cognitive style. There are teachers and educators who feel matching student–teacher cognitive styles is important to enhancing student achievement. However, research has failed to demonstrate the efficacy of matching student–teacher field-dependent/ field-independent cognitive styles for the enhancing of student achievement. There is a need to evaluate the effectiveness of matching student–teacher cognitive styles for the purposes of enhancing student learning. More research needs to be conducted to determine if cognitive styles can improve students' academic achievement.

STUDENT BENEFICIARIES

There is no evidence to support the use of matching student–teacher cognitive styles at any age or grade level. The limited amount of research that has been conducted has found no difference in student achievement between matching and mismatching student–teacher cognitive styles for the grades K–college. Matching student–teacher cognitive styles cannot be regarded as a generalization that is applicable to students at any level of instruction. To be applicable as a generalization, evidence would need to support the use of matching student–teacher cognitive styles to most students.

LEARNING ACHIEVED

No evidence was found to indicate that matching student–teacher cognitive styles enhances student achievement in any content area. Matching student–teacher cognitive styles should be seen as having no content area generalizability.

INSTRUCTIONAL TACTICS

Matching student–teacher cognitive styles employs the following instructional tactics regardless of grade level or content area:

- Identify students and teachers as either field-independent or field-dependent in cognitive style.
- Match field-independent students with field-independent teachers.
- Match field-dependent students with field-dependent teachers.

CAUTIONS AND COMMENTS

There is no empirical evidence to support the use of matching student–teacher cognitive styles. It is recognized that the existing body of research is very small and limited. One needs to question whether these instructional tactics may have long-term negative effects on student achievement. Witkin et al. (1977) suggest, "the possibilities that have been listed reflect the complexity of the relation between cognitive style match-mismatch and student achievement, and they provide a strong note of caution against deciding about the desirability of matching before a great deal more is known as to the consequences of matching for student learning" (p. 37). If the matching of student–teacher cognitive styles is to be considered further by teachers and educators, a great deal more research needs to be done. However, before one considers pursuing the matching of student–teacher cognitive styles further, one may wish to look at some of the practical aspects and first weigh the costs against any potential benefits. The only means found for identifying field-independent and field-dependent cognitive styles was the *Embedded Figures Test*. Witkin et al. (1977) indicate that an individual's cognitive style can change over time. Students and teachers would have to be tested and retested to maintain the homogeneity of the groups. Would it be wise to change teachers prior to the end of a term? What is to be done if there are not enough teachers of one cognitive style to match with the number of groups of students of the same cognitive style? Would one hire matching teachers and replace mismatched teachers?

REFERENCE LIST

Garlinger, D. K., & Frank, B. M. (1986). Teacher–student cognitive style and academic achievement: A review and mini-meta-analysis. *Journal of Classroom Instruction, 21*(2), 2–8.

Sipe, T. A., & Curlette, W. L. (1997). A meta-analysis of factors relating to educational achievement. *International Journal of Educational Research, 25*(7), 591–698.

Witkin, H. A., Moore, C. A., Goodenough, D. R., & Cox, P. W. (1977). Field-dependent and field-independent cognitive styles and their educational implications. *Review of Educational Research, 47*(1), 1–64.

Ability Grouping Students

INRODUCTION

The grouping of students according to ability level for the purpose of instruction is a tactic that has been in use, to varying degrees, throughout much of this century. Ability grouping of students has been tried in many forms for many years. In general, the evidence does not support its use. The body of research on teacher-expectancy offers one explanation for the failure of ability grouping. Reviews of this body of research have shown that teachers teach to their perception of the level of ability of the student, with the result being the level of achievement that would be expected for that ability level (Dusek, 1975; Cooper, 1979; Jamieson et al., 1987; Hamachek, 1995). Studies have been conducted which have demonstrated that when teachers are led to believe that high-ability students are of low ability, the resulting student achievement is consistent with that of low-ability students and, vice versa, when low-ability students were identified as high-ability (Dusek, 1975). Ability grouping of students for the purposes of enhancing student learning continues to be a common practice at most levels of education. However, decades of research have failed to provide evidence in support of the continued use of ability grouping. There is a need to curtail its use as a means of enhancing student learning.

STUDENT BENEFICIARIES

An insufficient number of studies have been conducted on ability grouping of students prior to grade 4 and subsequent to grade 9 to warrant any conclusions with regard to efficacy of ability grouping for students in the early elementary grades and high school. Research over the past 60-70 years has failed to support the use of ability grouping across all ability groups and grade levels. Research conducted during the past twenty years has shown that, overall, there is in essence no enhancement of achievement by ability grouping of students, with notable exceptions. Research has indicated moderate to strong effects on the enhancement of achievement for gifted and talented pull-out programs that accelerate and enrich the curriculum. Research also shows that student achievement in math and science can be enhanced in cross-grade and within-class grouping programs when curricula are adjusted to group skills (Kulik, 2004).

In view of the evidence that has been accumulated over the past 60-70 years, ability grouping cannot be regarded as a generalization that is applicable to most students. To be applicable to most students, ability grouping would have to enhance learning consistently in students at all grade levels and at all ability levels.

LEARNING ACHIEVED

Studies of ability grouping have involved almost all curriculum areas. There is very weak meta-analytic evidence for limited generalizability of ability grouping for the enhancement of learning in the content areas of reading (cross-grade ability grouping) and mathematics (within-grade ability grouping). However, across most curriculum areas there is no evidence that ability grouping enhances student learning. Ability grouping is not generalizable across content areas.

INSTRUCTIONAL TACTICS

The following are ability grouping instructional tactics most often studied by researchers.

- Students are grouped according to ability, and instruction is provided in separate classrooms for each ability group. Instruction may be for one, multiple, or all subjects. In high school this most often takes the form of academic, general, and vocational tracks. In middle school this frequently occurs in the form of advanced, basic, and remedial tracks (Kulik & Kulik, 1992; Slavin, 1990).

- Students from several grade levels are grouped together, regardless of their grade level, according to their level of academic achievement in a particular subject matter area. This tactic is used most often in elementary reading and is often referred to as the Joplin Plan (Kulik & Kulik, 1992; Slavin, 1987).

- Students within a single classroom are formed into groups based on ability, and the teacher provides instruction appropriate to each group's level of ability. This tactic has been used primarily for elementary school mathematics (Kulik & Kulik, 1992).

- High-ability students are placed in groups separate from other students and instructed using an enhanced curriculum.

In recent years, a number of initiatives, Tech Prep and School to Work being examples, have been implemented to reduce ability grouping or tracking at the high school level. Although they should be seen as important steps in the right direction and their intention was to prepare all students for some form of post-secondary education, they most often have simply led to high school academic and vocational tracks, with the former group being seen as prepared for college and the latter prepared to go to work upon completion of high school. All students must be prepared for some form of post-secondary education if they are to be productive members of society.

CAUTIONS AND COMMENTS

There is only evidence on the effectiveness of ability grouping for gifted and talented pull-out programs, with curricular enhancement for students in grades 4–9. Ability grouping is not effective for most students. There is insufficient empirical evidence to support ability grouping of any kind for grades 1–3 and for high school. Seventy years of controversy should not be ignored. The evidence indicates that ability grouping is ineffective, with one exception being middle school gifted and talented programs that provide enriched curriculum for the students.

REFERENCE LIST

Barley, Z., Lauer, P. A., Arens, S. A., Apthorp, H. S., Englert, K. S., Snow, D., & Akiba, M. (2002). *Helping at-risk students meet standards: A synthesis of evidence-based classroom practices.* Aurora, CO: Mid-continent Research for Education and Learning.

Chi, M.T.H., & Bassok, M. (1989). Learning from examples via self-explanations. In L. B. Resnik (Ed.), *Knowing, learning and instruction: Essays in honour of R. Glaser* (pp. 251–283). Hillsdale, NJ: Erlbaum.

Cooper, H. M. (1979). Pygmalion grows up: A model for teacher expectation communication and performance influence. *Review of Educational Research, 49*(3), 389–410

Dusek, J. B. (1975). Do teachers bias children's learning? *Review of Educational Research, 45*(4), 661–684.

Hamachek, D. (1995). Expectations revisited: Implications for teachers and counselors and questions for self-assessment. *Journal of Humanistic Education and Development, 34*(2), 65–74.

Jamieson, D. W., Lydon, J. E., Stewart, G., & Zanna, M. P. (1987). Pygmalion revisited: New evidence for student expectancy in the classroom. *Journal of Educational Psychology, 79*(4), 461–466.

Kulik, J. A. (2004). Grouping, tracking, and de-tracking: Conclusions from experimental, correlational, and ethnographic research. In H. J. Walberg, A. J. Reynolds, & M. C. Wang (Eds.), *Can unlike students learn together? Grade retention, tracking, and grouping*. Greenwich, CT: Information Age Publishers.

Kulik, J. A., & Kulik, C. C. (1992). Meta-analytic findings on grouping programs. *Gifted Child Quarterly, 36*(2), 73–77.

Lindle, J. C. (1994). *Review of the literature on tracking and ability grouping* (second draft). Washington, DC: ERIC.

Mevarech, Z. R. (1999). Effects of metacognitive training embedded in cooperative settings on mathematical problem solving. *Journal of Educational Research, 92*(4), 195–205.

Mevarech, Z. R., & Kramarski, B. (1997). IMPROVE: A multidimensional method for teaching mathematics in heterogeneous classrooms. *American Educational Research Journal, 34*(2), 365–394.

Mevarech, Z. R., & Kramarski, B. (2003). The effects of metacognitive training versus worked-out examples on students' mathematical reasoning. *British Journal of Educational Psychology, 73*, 449–471.

Sipe, T. A., & Curlette, W. L. (1997). A meta-analysis of factors relating to educational achievement. *International Journal of Educational Research, 25*(7), 591–698.

Slavin, R. E. (1987). Ability grouping and student achievement in elementary schools: A best-evidence synthesis. *Review of Educational Research, 57*(3), 293–336.

Slavin, R. E. (1990). Achievement effects of ability grouping in secondary schools: A best evidence synthesis. *Review of Educational Research, 60*(3), 471–499.

Yager, S., Johnson, D. W., & Johnson, R. T. (1985). Oral discussion, group-to-individual transfer, and achievement in cooperative learning groups. *Journal of Educational Psychology, 77*(1), 60–66.

Providing Whole Language Instruction

INTRODUCTION

Whole language approaches to language instruction are characterized as indirect and unsystematic. They explicitly avoid the use of skill sequences in the organization of instruction. Individual word recognition and sound-symbol relationships are not taught unless they are in the context of the whole text. It is difficult to formulate a specific example, or definition, as the proponents consider whole language instruction to be philosophy rather than a specific method of instruction. Pre-service and in-service teacher education programs today continue to emphasize the whole language approach to language instruction. However, research has failed to support the continued use of whole language approaches.

STUDENT BENEFICIARIES

There is a weak support for the use of whole language instruction in the beginning stages (kindergarten in most regions of the United States) of language arts instruction. As the students move beyond beginning stages, the direction of the evidence shifts in favor of traditional approaches to instruction. Research has fairly consistently found no difference between whole language and traditional forms of language arts instruction for student achievement in grades K–6. Therefore, whole language cannot be regarded as a generalization that is applicable to most students. To be applicable to most students, whole language instruction would need consistently to enhance learning in most students – not just students in kindergarten or in first grade in regions where this is the beginning of formal instruction. Even for this category of students, the evidence is weak at best.

LEARNING ACHIEVED

Whole language instruction is intended to enhance student learning in the language arts of reading, writing, speaking, and listening. There is weak evidence in support of whole language instruction for initial reading and writing instruction as well as for word recognition. In terms of reading comprehension, the evidence shifts in favor of traditional forms of instruction. No evidence was found to support the use of whole language instruction to teach writing mechanics such as sentence construction, punctuation, or spelling. In essence, whole language instruction should be seen as having limited generalizability to only beginning language instruction. However, the evidence supporting beginning language instruction should be seen as sufficiently weak to raise serious questions as to any generalizability. Proponents of whole language, in their preoccupation with the whole, would seem to have neglected the important relationships the parts have to the whole.

INSTRUCTIONAL TACTICS

Proponents' insistence that whole language instruction is a philosophy rather than a method of instruction makes it difficult to arrive at a list of employed instructional tactics. However, the following derived tactics appear to be utilized by many, if not most, whole language approaches to language arts instruction.

- Skill sequences are not used to organize instruction.
- Children move from oral to written language using words for which they know the meaning.
- Individual words and sound-symbol relationships are taught only if they are needed to understand the whole lesson and not in isolation.
- Children are encouraged to use invented spelling.
- The interrelationships among and the interdependence of reading, writing, speaking, and listening are stressed.

CAUTIONS AND COMMENTS

The empirical evidence does not support the continued use of whole language instruction for the teaching of language. The evidence associated with limited student and content area (beginning language arts instruction) generalizability is at best weak. Evidence in support of generalizability beyond students in beginning language instruction is nonexistent. Although whole language instruction stresses the importance of the parts/whole relationships of reading, writing, speaking, and listening to the overall whole of communication, it neglects the important parts/whole relationships within each of these areas of communication. Does not a competent writer understand fundamental relationships among the component acts of writing? Does not problem solving in any area require that students be able to see the relationship between specific tactics necessary to the solution of a problem? Could not whole language deprive students of a thorough understanding of individual communication skills and impair their performance on verbal standardized achievement tests?

REFERENCE LIST

Carnine, D. (1992). Expanding the notion of teachers' rights: Access to tools that work. *Journal of Applied Behavior Analysis, 25*, 13–19.

Jeynes, W. H., & Littell, S. W. (2000). A meta-analysis of studies examining the effect of whole language instruction on the literacy of low-SES students. *The Elementary School Journal, 101*(1), 21–36.

Martens, B. K., & Witt, J. C. (2004). Competence, persistence, and success: The positive psychology of behavioral skill instruction. *Psychology in the Schools, 41*(1), 19–30.

Sipe, T. A., & Curlette, W. L. (1997). A meta-analysis of factors relating to educational achievement. *International Journal of Educational Research, 25*(7), 591–698.

Stahl, S. A., & Kuhn, M. R. (1995). Does whole language or instruction matched to learning styles help children learn to read? *School Psychology Review, 24*, 393–404.

Stahl, S. A., & Miller, P. D. (1989). Whole language and language experience approaches for beginning reading: A quantitative research synthesis. *Review of Educational Research, 59*(1), 87–116.

Providing Reinforcements

INTRODUCTION

The term *reinforcement* emanates from conditioning psychology. In this context, reinforcement entails repeatedly rewarding behavior that a trainer/conditioner considers desirable to condition a subject to perform the behavior automatically. For example, a dog trainer repeatedly gives a dog food the dog likes for sitting when the trainer gives the command to sit until the dog sits habitually on command. Reinforcement may be the most widely researched psychological phenomenon of all. Moreover, conditioning psychologists have advocated that reinforcement be used in instruction for a long time. Many teachers have been taught in pre-service and in-service training to adopt and use reinforcement in their teaching. However, all psychological principles derived primarily from research on lower animals are not advantageously applied to human instruction and learning. There is a need to revisit and reevaluate the effectiveness of reinforcement on classroom instruction.

STUDENT BENEFICIARIES

Reinforcement appears to work with less mentally competent people. When used in the classroom, it was not, in general, an effective means of producing academic achievement. It was effective primarily with young children and mentally retarded youth. This is a conclusion that the well-respected educational researchers Brophy and Good (1986) drew after considering the available research. The present authors came to the same conclusion based on their independent review of the research. Thus it should not be regarded as a generalization that is applicable to most human students. To be applicable to most students, reinforcement would, in addition, need to enhance academic achievement consistently in students who are not mentally retarded or very young. The majority of students are not mentally retarded or very young.

Since reinforcement has been used to shape behavior for such a long time and is advocated by so many, it is helpful to understand the limitations of its generalizability. The remainder of the discussion on reinforcement is devoted to clarifying its meanings and applications and explaining its limited generalizability.

Fundamental laws of reinforcement were derived by psychologists, ranging over time from Pavlov to Skinner, who did research using food to shape the behavior of captive starved lower animals. Such laws are as applicable to shaping the behavior of lower animals today as they ever were. Also the laws appear to be applicable to mentally retarded and young children as well. This may be because reinforcement is more effective in shaping the behavior of less mentally competent animals and humans than in shaping the behavior of more mentally competent humans. More mentally competent humans are not as likely to respond as automatons to prompts.

They are more capable of using their knowledge and are more likely to use it to deliberate alternatives before acting. More mentally competent humans are not as habit bound and are not as prone to be conditioned to react in a particular way to a particular prompt or stimulus.

Another reason laws of reinforcement have limited generalizability is because the captive lower animals used in traditional reinforcement research are placed in highly confining environments, which severely restrict their movements and choice. The environments are contrived to ensure that the desired behavior will occur so that it can be reinforced and habituated. For example, rats are conditioned to receive a food pellet by pressing a bar which has been placed in a small box with nothing obtruding but the bar in it. Because the rats are starved, they are active and will press the bar in a very short time. Such restrictiveness imposed upon human learners would be illegal in free countries that provide for free choice. Laws of reinforcement derived from such contrived, restrictive environments not only are not generalizable to human behavior but also have not been proven to be generalizable to the behavior of rats in their natural environment.

In addition, laws of reinforcement derived from rewarding starved lower animals with food are not generalizable to human learning environments in free countries because it is illegal for educators to starve human learners. In preparation for conditioning, rats are starved by depriving them of food (1) for a certain amount of time or (2) until they lose a certain amount of weight.

Moreover, the laws of reinforcement are derived from conditioning individual animals one at a time, not from conditioning groups of animals. Thus the laws are not generalizable to the group instruction of lower animals or human students. It is not only unwarranted, but impractical as well, for teachers to administer reinforcement to a class of students. The teacher would be required to reward every student in the class for the performance of every desirable behavior. Punishment is not allowed; so, the teacher must await the performance of every desirable behavior from all students, say 20, and promptly reward them without being able to punish misbehavior. This is a recipe for chaos, as many classroom teachers who have been trained and required to administer reinforcement in their classrooms report.

In conclusion, "laws of reinforcement" are generalizable to the conditioning of single captive starved lower animals and mentally retarded and very young human students, but not beyond. Therefore, they do not qualify as generalizations of the human instruction when the objective is academic achievement.

LEARNING ACHIEVED

Most of the learning produced by reinforcement is the learning of automatic behavior or habits. Although reinforcement evidently can be used to condition habits in young and mentally retarded students, only a small percentage of the learning objectives pursued in school pertain to the conditioning of habits. Such learning objectives would include the automatic recognition of words, numbers, letters of the alphabet, and significant others by name. In addition, while students may be expected to be able to recite the multiplication tables automatically as well as recite the Pledge of Allegiance to the United States flag and sing "The Star-Spangled Banner," such learning pertains primarily to the indoctrination of young children into society. More advanced learning such as problem solving requires students to deliberate options as the basis for choosing a solution. Young children's automatic responses are often impulsive and impair deriving tenable solutions. They are often told not to act impulsively but rather to think before they act.

The teaching of automatic behavior is much more in keeping with totalitarian governments where people are to obey commands without questioning them and in communist states where individual penchants are to be sacrificed for the common good. In the United States, where students have the freedom to pursue happiness as they choose and are encouraged to think for themselves, conditioning students to perform as robots is frowned upon and is illegal when it deprives them of their legal rights to free choice.

Moreover, education pertains to more than performing desired behaviors habitually. It pertains to the acquisition of knowledge, knowledge people can apply as they deem appropriate and desirable. Conditioners are concerned primarily with the shaping of behavior, not with the acquisition of knowledge.

INSTRUCTIONAL TACTICS

The basic instructional tactic in (operant) conditioning is to repeatedly administer rewards to subjects for performing desirable behaviors until the behaviors are performed automatically or "stamped in" while neither rewarding nor punishing other behaviors. The challenge is to identify rewards that are broadly applicable across students. So far the only reward found to be unambiguously generalizable is food, but only to hungry subjects. Subjects satiated with food are indifferent to it. Subjects glutted with food find food repugnant at the time.

Now porpoises and whales, which are taught to perform tricks for paying audiences, are conditioned to perform tricks using food as a reward. But those animals are captive, and their intake of food is controlled by their keepers and trainers. Consequently, they can be kept sufficiently hungry to ensure that food serves as a reward.

On the other hand, in free countries where, as indicated earlier, starving people is illegal, it is difficult to find a reinforcing agent or reward that all people are interested in most of the time. Food is rewarding when it satisfies the internal motive hunger. Most people in the United States are not hungry most of the time. And motives other than hunger cease to be motives for the time being when they are satisfied. It has been difficult to find a reward that satisfies most people's motives most of the time.

The would-be rewards that have been tried on students have not been nearly as successful as the food used to condition hungry lower animals. Oral forms of reinforcement, such as words of praise and encouragement as well as indulgent attention for desired behavior, have achieved mixed, inconsistent results on humans. On reflection, it can be understood that attention and praise in general are not rewarding. Praise from a white teacher to a black student or from a female teacher to a male teenager in the company of his buddies may not be rewarding. Moreover, repeated praise is often regarded as insincere.

To ensure that students will be motivated to receive offerings, tokens are offered as rewards for desired behavior. The tokens can be cashed in for one of a number of options of the students' choice. Tokens seem to work best when students can choose from among a wide variety of attractive options so that students are more certain to find an option they consider rewarding. The rationale is akin to the "Green Stamp" promotion that allowed customers to choose merchandise from a vast array of options in a catalog. This is hardly feasible in a school setting.

It might be more effective to offer money to students as a reward for desired behavior. Money is certain to be more rewarding to students than tokens; students can trade the money for a much greater variety of treats and merchandise. However, many consider giving money to students for achieving learning objectives to be bribery, more so than giving tokens. Other professionals feel that learning is intrinsically rewarding because it empowers students and that offering extrinsic rewards like candy, praise, or attention for achieving learning objectives is diverting and subverting to the learning process and to schooling.

It is exceedingly important not to confuse reinforcement and feedback, which is described in the generalization on corrective instruction. Some professionals contend that feedback provides, or at least should provide, reinforcement if done appropriately. They believe that it is reinforcing for students to find out that their response is correct and that encouraging students to proceed with their next assigned task, whether they succeeded or failed in performing their last task, is also reinforcing. This blunts and perverts the important distinction between the functions of feedback and reinforcement. The purpose of reinforcing a behavior is to increase the probability that it becomes a habit. To be reinforcing the offering given or said to a student must satisfy an internal motive, as food satisfies the hunger motive. However, as indicated, the verbal endorsement of a behavior cannot be relied upon to satisfy students' motives; so, it is doubtful that telling students anything will reliably act as reinforcement.

The purpose of feedback is quite different from reinforcement. The purpose of feedback is to impart to students one of two things: (1) their behavior is correct and they are ready to attempt to perform the next more advanced task or (2) their behavior is incorrect and they need to perform corrective tasks until they master the behavior. In both cases the underlying purpose is to advance the knowledge and skills of students.

In short, the function of reinforcement is to induce habits. The function of feedback is to enable students continually to advance their capabilities.

One reason reinforcement and feedback become intermingled, if not confused, is because the difference in the ability of humans and lower animals is not fully appreciated and taken into account. Humans are more intelligent than infrahumans and capable of understanding more sophisticated linguistic communication. Consequently, when people perform correctly, they can be informed through language that they have performed correctly and are ready for the next challenge, and when they perform incorrectly, they can be informed of their incorrect behavior. In addition, and most significantly, they can be informed of the desired behavior and shown how to perform it.

In contrast, reinforcement of a correct behavior of a porpoise encourages the porpoise to repeat the behavior to be reinforced again. This may be said, in a sense, to inform a porpoise that it has performed correctly. In addition, punishment of a porpoise for incorrect or undesirable behavior will tend to dissuade the porpoise from repeating the behavior. However, in contrast to humans, and most important, conditioners cannot communicate clearly to a porpoise what the correct behavior is and how to perform the correct behavior. This explains in part why conditioners use reward in conditioning animals, but not punishment. Reward communicates to them that their behavior is desirable. Punishment communicates that their behavior is undesirable but does not indicate the desired behavior. Moreover, continuous punishment can be harmful and can cause the animal to flee or attack.

Humans and lower animals are quite different, and their difference needs to be taken into account for instruction to be successful. Punishment that is painful and harmful should not be used on humans. It can injure them and cause them to be hostile and rebellious. There is evidence indicating that continued intense corporal punishment has long-term deleterious effects on youth. In teaching youth, it is necessary to keep in mind that the aim is to discourage undesirable behavior and to encourage and instill desirable behavior by means of corrective instruction. Undesirable behavior needs to be discouraged rather than punished. This often can be accomplished by telling the youth that his behavior is undesirable and explaining why and then immediately telling him what the desirable behavior is and showing him how to execute it. This is the essence of corrective instruction, which has been shown previously to be a most valuable instructional strategy for humans. Discouragement, not punishment, is used because the aim is to dissuade undesirable behavior, not to inflict pain and perhaps incite youth to rebel and spitefully increase the undesirable behavior. Most important, the performance of undesirable behavior is the signal to the sophisticated teacher to initiate the corrective instruction process. When discouragement is used, students must immediately be encouraged to perform corrective tasks with assurance that the corrective tasks will enable them to succeed.

It is also important not to confuse reinforcement (such as food), used to condition captive lower creatures to do what the conditioners desire, with the sophisticated tactics used by free humans to influence other people to do what they desire.

For instance, doing favors for others influences them to return favors, and complimenting others tends to be ingratiating and influences them to do one's bidding, while insulting others tends to alienate them. However, compliments are not equivalent to reinforcements such as food, nor are insults equivalent to punishments such as intense electric shock. In the final analysis, efforts to persuade free people to do one's bidding and to discourage them from doing what one dislikes will succeed only if they want to comply or they are obligated to comply.

In instruction, it is more productive to refer to task performance as either correct or incorrect rather than as behavior that the teacher desires or does not desire. This places the emphasis where it belongs, on performing tasks correctly in order to achieve a learning objective rather than on pleasing the teacher, even though the two may often be congruent. In addition, the emphasis should be on encouraging students to try to perform the next assigned task correctly in order to achieve the learning objective. When completing a task, students who perform it correctly may be complimented on their success and encouraged to meet the next challenge. Students who perform the task incorrectly cannot be complimented on their achievement. This would be encouraging students to fail. When they strive to succeed but fail, they can be complimented on their effort and be encouraged to undertake corrective tasks with assurances that they will succeed. This presupposes that the teacher has had success in the past when using the corrective tasks. It would also be helpful if the teacher showed students how achieving the learning objective benefits and empowers them.

CAUTIONS AND COMMENTS

In conclusion, research results confirm conclusively that reinforcing captive, starved, individual lower animals repeatedly with food for performing behavior the conditioner deems desirable will condition the animals to perform the desired behavior. However, these reinforcement conditions do not have sufficient generalizability to be applicable to the education of most children and adults when the goal is academic achievement. Moreover, the conditions have virtually no generalizability to the educational environments of humans living in free modern nations such as England, Switzerland, and the United States, to name a few. Other so-called reinforcements such as toys, praise, attention, candy, and tokens have not been consistently effective on human students when used as reinforcing agents to achieve learning objectives. Moreover, bribing students to achieve learning objectives might dissuade them from learning for personal advantage and empowerment. Students who are bribed to learn come to expect rewards for doing what others want them to do. Even though reinforcement can be used to entice some students to comply overtly with the teachers' instruction (Martens & Witt, 2004), it cannot be expected to increase academic achievement and can have undesirable side effects.

REFERENCE LIST

Brophy, J., & Good, T. L. (1986). Teacher behavior and student achievement. In M. C. Wittrock (Ed.), *Handbook of research on teaching* (3rd ed., pp. 328–375). New York: Macmillan.

Martens, B. K., & Witt, J. C. (2004). Competence, persistence, and success: The positive psychology of behavioral skill instruction. *Psychology in the Schools, 41*(1), 19–30.

Portfolio Testing

All tests need to be valid, reliable, and objective. However, as multiple testing fads come and go, some stray from validity, reliability, and objectivity requirements (e.g., portfolio testing). Feuer and Fulton (1993) defined portfolios as "collections of a student's work assembled over time" (p. 478). According to Airasian (1996), their purpose is "to collect a series of pupil performances or products that show the pupil's accomplishments or improvement over time" (p. 162). Portfolios have been used for a long time for evaluation in fields such as art, music, photography, journalism, commercial art, and modeling (Winograd & Gaskins, 1992). Presently the use of portfolios has extended beyond creative activities. Now they are used in academic areas such as reading, math, and science to document and evaluate student achievement and have been recognized as an evaluation tool in many states including Vermont, Kentucky, California, and Pennsylvania.

A portfolio might include classroom assignments, work developed especially for the portfolio, a list of books that have been read, tests, checklists, journal entries, completed projects, response logs, artwork, and so on (Polin, 1991). Completed projects may be group as well as individual projects. A wide variety of work may be included in portfolios, depending on what students as well as teachers may want to include. Teachers also have been urged to allow students to establish their own performance standards (Tierney, Carter, & Desai, 1991; Winograd & Gaskins, 1992). Although teachers may be responsible for the evaluation of portfolios, many contend that the evaluation process should be broadened to include evaluations by the students themselves, their classmates, their parents, and other family members (Adams, 1991; Arter & Spandel, 1992; Salend, 1998; Tierney et al., 1991; Winograd & Gaskins, 1992).

So, it is quite possible that portfolio performance standards, the work included in portfolios, and evaluations of the work may not be directly related to required class learning objectives. What are equally troubling from a testing perspective are the questionable validity, reliability, and objectivity of many portfolio assessment formats. The reliance on the subjective judgments and evaluations of portfolio entries by students, their teachers, classmates, parents, and other family members casts doubt on the objectivity of portfolio assessment, and the inclusion in the portfolio of students' work that may not be relevant to the required class learning objectives casts suspicion on the validity of portfolio assessment. The inclusion of such a diverse variety of student work makes it difficult to establish the reliability of portfolio testing. In short, portfolio assessment as it is frequently practiced does not conform to validity, reliability, and objectivity requirements.

Without specific criteria to guide the evaluation of multiple and complex samples of students' work, portfolio assessment is prone to subjective scoring. Dwyer (1993) indicates that testing reforms encourage subjective evaluations. Reform efforts allow "increasing tolerance for subjective judgment—even intuition—over precise decision rules and logical operations" (p. 269). Oosterhof (1994) also challenges the objectivity of portfolio assessment. In evaluating writing portfolios in Vermont, the average correlations among the scores of different raters ranged from .33 to .43 (Koretz, 1993, p. 2). McLoughlin and Lewis (2001) challenge the validity of portfolio assessment: "Validity is another concern, particularly the predictive validity of portfolio assessment in relation to future success in school and adult pursuits" (p. 156).

Furthermore, it can be a monumental and practically insurmountable task to aggregate the scores of the various student entries in a portfolio to derive a grade. For instance, suppose a teacher wants to assign a grade to a student based on the sixteen items in the student's portfolio prepared for a zoology course. The portfolio contains one videotape of a student's class presentation on cats, two papers about snakes, and six journal entries on the student's reactions to evolution. Scores are derived for each item on a scale from 1 to 6, 6 being the highest rating. How does the teacher combine the scores to assign a grade? Different aggregation procedures will yield different summary evaluations, which might result in the assignment of different grades.

To complicate further assigning grades to students, samples of group projects are frequently allowed to be included in students' portfolios. Report cards are generally issued to individual students, not groups of students. In order for report card grades to be valid they must be derived from the performance of individual students. It is difficult, if not impossible, to determine individual performance from a group project. It is important to recognize that although groups are taught in school, individual students are supposed to learn and do learn most subject matter that is taught.

Herman and Winters (1994) say that many portfolio advocates, arguing against the measurement experts who, they believe, have long defined assessment practice and used it to drive curriculum and instruction, do not seem to give much importance to technical characteristics. Herman and Winters state "a dearth of empirical research exists. In fact, of 89 entries on portfolio assessment topics found in the literature over the past ten years, only seven articles either report technical data or employ accepted research methods. Instead, most articles explain the rationale for portfolio assessment; present ideas and models for how portfolios should be constituted and used; or share details of how portfolios have been implemented in a particular class, school, or district, or state. Relatively absent is attention to technical quality, to serious indicators of impact, or to rigorous testing of assumptions" (p. 48).

Salvia and Ysseldyke (2001) state that the "absence of theory and empirical research to guide practice in portfolio assessment stands in stark contrast to the situation for other approaches to classroom assessment (for example, curriculum-based assessment)" (p. 246). Also, Salvia and Ysseldyke state, "Currently there appears to be more conviction than empirical support for the use of portfolios. Even given the most optimistic interpretation of the validity of portfolio assessment, we believe that the current literature provides an insufficient basis for an acceptance of portfolio assessment on any basis other than experimental" (p. 259).

So many educators have made so many different recommendations for conducting portfolio assessment that it is difficult to determine exactly what portfolio assessment is and what it is not. There is no reason why a portfolio assessment format cannot be derived that is not subject to the criticisms that have been levied against it. There is certainly nothing wrong with assembling samples of students' work as a basis for assigning grades to students. Still, in order to defend any multiple-testing technique, attention must be paid to validity, reliability, and objectivity requirements for each testing instrument used and to the aggregation of test scores to assign grades to students.

REFERENCE LIST

Adams, M. (1991). Writing portfolios: A powerful assessment and conversation tool. *Writing Teacher*, 12–15.

Airasian, P. W. (1996). *Assessment in the classroom.* New York: McGraw-Hill.

Arter, J., & Spandel, V. (1992). Using portfolios of student work in instruction and assessment. *Educational Measurement: Issues and Practice, 11*(1), 36–44.

Dwyer, C. A. (1993). Innovation and reform: Examples from teacher assessment. In R. Bennett & W. Ward (Eds.), *Construction versus choice in cognitive measurement: Issues in constructed response, performance testing, and portfolio assessment* (pp. 265–289). Hillsdale, NJ: Erlbaum.

Feuer, M. J., & Fulton, K. (1993). The many faces of performance assessment. *Phi Delta Kappan, 74*, 478.

Herman, J. L., & Winters, L. (1994). Portfolio research: A slim collection. *Educational Leadership, 52*(2), 48–55.

Koretz, D. (1993). New report on Vermont portfolio project documents challenges. *National Council on Measurement in Education Quarterly Newsletter, 1*(4), 1–2.

McLoughlin, J. A., & Lewis, R. B. (2001). *Assessing students with special needs.* Upper Saddle River, NJ: Merrill/Prentice Hall.

Oosterhof, A. (1994). *Classroom applications of educational measurement* (2nd ed.). New York: Merrill/Macmillan.

Polin, L. (1991, January/February). Writing technology, teacher education: K–12 and college portfolio assessment. *The Writing Notebook*, 25–28.

Salend, S. (1998). Using portfolios to assess student performance. *Teaching Exceptional Children, 31*(2), 36–43.

Salvia, J., & Ysseldyke, J. E. (2001). *Assessment* (8th ed.). Boston: Houghton Mifflin.

Tierney, R., Carter, M., & Desai, L. (1991). *Portfolio assessment in reading and writing classrooms*. New York: Christopher-Gorelon.

Winograd, P., & Gaskins, R. (1992). Improving the assessment of literacy: The power of portfolios. *Pennsylvania Reporter, 23*(2), 1–6.

III

Instructional Aids

In Parts I and II, the sole focus is on the direct effect of strategies on academic achievement. Chapter 23, "Questionable Instructional Strategies," describes commonly used strategies that are not shown by research to increase academic achievement. All of the other strategies in Parts I and II are shown by research to increase academic achievement. In Part III, "Instructional Aids," the focus is on practices that support instruction and learning even though their impact on academic achievement may be indirect or tangential.

Chapter 24, "Controlling Classroom Disruptions," describes a strategy shown by research to reduce classroom disruptions. The strategy indirectly impacts academic achievement because disruptions interfere with instruction and learning. Chapter 25, "Developing Teaching Proficiency," deals with the indirect impact of teacher education on the academic achievement of students. Teachers who are taught the 21 effective instructional strategies described in Part I are more likely to increase the academic achievement of their students. Chapter 26, "Preschool Instruction," describes the application of effective instructional strategies to the unique needs of preschool students. Chapter 27, "Developing Preventive Tutoring Programs," shows how preventive tutoring can be introduced and provided as part of a school's program, taking advantage of the powerful effect of one-to-one tutoring on academic achievement. Chapter 28, "Remedial Tutoring Programs," describes instruction programs that increase academic achievement when regular classroom instruction fails to work for students with pronounced learning difficulties. Chapter 29, "Instructional Testing and Evaluation," shows educators how to improve their instructional prescriptions through diagnostic evaluation of student inadequacies. Chapter 30, "Standards for Evaluating Curricula," describes standards derived by national professional organizations that can be used to evaluate the curricular offerings in local schools. Chapter 31, "Signs of Common Disabilities," helps educators determine when to refer failing students for in-depth evaluations.

Although it seems reasonable to concede that libraries contribute to academic achievement, it is difficult to find sufficient scientific evidence to prove that they do. Libraries were not included as an effective instructional strategy in Part I of the handbook because the criterion was not met. Fifty or more studies were not found establishing that libraries increase academic achievement. A handful of states (e.g., Colorado, Alaska, Pennsylvania, Texas, Massachusetts, Oregon, Iowa, California, and North Carolina) studies have been conducted since 1993 which have been successful in establishing a strong connection between student achievement and library media programs along with library/information skills (Neuman, 2003). During The White House Conference on School Libraries (June 2002), "experts and panelists offered stories of the power of school libraries to make a difference in student achievement" and the proceedings document contains "resources for capitalizing on the school library's potential to positively affect student achievement" (abstract). According to Neuman, school library media research during the next few years should be heavily focused on determining the direct influence of the library on student learning. Despite the inconclusive evidence that libraries raise academic achievement, they need to be acknowledged as instructional aids. Books have been written about the many and varied services libraries can and do provide, more information than can be described in a chapter on instructional aids.

All of the following chapters are of benefit to educators and help them in their dedication to improve student achievement.

REFERENCE LIST

Institute of Museum and Library Services. (2002). *The White House Conference on school libraries proceedings.* Retrieved on May 16, 2005, from http://www.imls.gov/pubs/whitehouse0602/whitehouse.htm

Neuman, D. (2003). Research in school library media for the next decade: Polishing the diamond. *Library Trends, 51*(4), 503–524.

24

Controlling Classroom Disruptions

Teaching is difficult. Teaching in the midst of classroom disruption is impossible. Even if teachers persist in their efforts to teach when disruptions are occurring, students will be distracted and unable to attend to the teacher's presentation. Some background noise from traffic or heating and air conditioning apparatus can be adjusted to and filtered out without disrupting the teaching-learning process, but blatant classroom disruptions will inevitably preclude learning and must be prevented. Some blatant disruptions can be easily prevented. For example, a simple administrative regulation can prevent messages from blaring into the classroom over loudspeakers during class. On the other hand, preventing student behavior from disrupting the class is more difficult to manage and depends on teacher know-how. It takes skill to manage student outbursts, infringements on classmates, acting out, and unruly and attention-seeking behavior. However, student disruptions can be managed by establishing and enforcing student rules of conduct. Moreover, research shows how to establish and enforce rules of conduct. Student disruptions vary in intrusiveness and the harm they can do, ranging from passive disruptions such as tardiness and failure to be seated promptly to aggressive disruptions such as verbal harangues and violence toward the teacher or another student—all of which must be dealt with. Teachers who are successful in controlling disruptive behavior differ from unsuccessful teachers in the way they introduce classroom rules and provide consequences for violations and in their consistency in invoking consequences when rules violations occur.

TACTICS

The following are tactics for establishing and enforcing student rules of conduct that research shows to be effective. The tactics have been inferred from 50 studies (of the total 152 studies reviewed which support the reduction of classroom disruptions). Students in the studies range from grades 1 to 12. Grade level and ability level of students must be taken into account when determining how to teach rules to students.

- Rules of conduct and consequences for violating them need to be established, clarified, and justified during the first meeting with students, before academic instruction begins.
- Rules need to be few in number (about five) and of sufficient brevity and clarity to be memorized by the students involved.
- Students' knowledge of rules and the consequences for violating them must be ensured as soon as possible.
- Consequences for violations of rules need to be given promptly and briefly with as little disruption to instruction as possible.
- Prompts need to be used to maintain order and prevent rules violations. Prompts may be (1) nonverbal such as direct eye contact, gestures, or proximity to disruptive students or (2) verbal, ranging from simple prompts such as "shh," "stop," or "no" to more assertive desist commands such as "return to your seat" or "keep your hands to yourself."

CAUTIONS AND COMMENTS

Student rules of conduct established for a classroom do not exist in isolation. They must be compatible with the rules and laws of the social milieu in which the classroom exists. School and school district regulations as well as city, county, state, and federal laws must be taken into account when establishing rules for a class. If students are old enough, they should be informed of the importance of rules and laws for civilized intercourse among people. In addition, the relationship between class rules and the regulations and laws of governing social institutions might be discussed briefly. When establishing classroom rules, it is important to keep in mind that there is no evidence that student participation in the process is of any advantage in reducing classroom disruptions. The crucial factor is that class rules of conduct be established and enforced as specified. However, no system of rules can consistently control students' inappropriate and disruptive behavior if instruction is not proficient or is inadequately matched to students' needs and abilities. It is also important to make the rationale for the rules clear to students (for example, to enhance learning and to promote safety).

In addition to establishing and enforcing student rules of conduct, teachers need to discriminate between rules and procedures. Students must be told that procedures are the ways to get things done in the classroom. Using procedures for getting things done creates an orderly and positive classroom learning environment with fewer possibilities for disruptions. Examples of classroom procedures include turning in papers, sharpening pencils, lining up to leave and enter the classroom, being excused to go to the bathroom, ways to get the teacher's attention or assistance, and ways to be recognized in order to respond to questions or ask questions. Having procedures for these and other activities helps control classroom disruptions. Once teachers have determined procedures for ways to get things done in the classroom, they must teach the students the procedures as needed. Moreover, procedures will need to be practiced until the students have learned the procedures. It is likely that if a procedure is not used for a period of time, it will need to be taught again before its next use. Just as with the rules of conduct, procedures must be promptly and consistently enforced if they are to benefit in maintaining an orderly and positive classroom learning environment.

Research studies have been conducted to determine which consequences tend to reduce disruptive behaviors. We don't recommend any specific consequences because many of them are based on the policies of particular institutions. If you are interested in reading about some consequences with a research base, see the studies in the meta-analysis (Stage & Quiroz, 1997) which are designated with an * in the reference list at the end of this chapter.

REFERENCE LIST

References marked with an * are the studies in the meta-analysis conducted by Stage and Quiroz (1997).

*Amerikaner, M., & Summerlin, M. L. (1982). Group counseling with learning disabled children: Effects of social skills and relaxation training on self-concept and classroom behavior. *Journal of Learning Disabilities, 15*, 340–343.

*Ayllon, T., Garber, S., & Pisor, K. (1975). The elimination of discipline problems through a combined school-home motivational system. *Behavior Therapy, 6*, 616–626.

*Ayllon, T., & Roberts, M. D. (1974). Eliminating discipline problems by strengthening academic performance. *Journal of Applied Behavior Analysis, 7*, 71–76.

Ball, S. J. (1980). Initial encounters in the classroom and the process of establishment. In P. Woods (Ed.), *Pupil strategies: Exploration in the sociology of the school* (pp. 143–161). London: Croom Helm.

*Barrish, H. H., Saunders, M., & Wolf, M. M. (1969). Good behavior game: Effects of individual contingencies for group consequences on disruptive behavior in a classroom. *Journal of Applied Behavior Analysis, 2*, 119–124.

*Bellafiore, L. A., & Salend, S. J. (1983). Modifying inappropriate behaviors through a peer-confrontation system. *Behavioral Disorders, 8*, 274–279.

*Birkimer, J. C., & Brown, J. H. (1979). The effects of student self-control on the reduction of children's problem behaviors. *Behavioral Disorders, 4*, 131–136.

*Bloomquist, M. L., August, G. J., & Ostrander, R. (1991). Effects of a school-based cognitive-behavioral intervention for ADHD children. *Journal of Abnormal Child Psychology, 19*, 591–605.

Blumenfeld, P. C., Hamilton, V. L., Wessels, K., & Falkner, D. (1979). Teaching responsibility to first graders. *Theory into Practice, 18*(3), 174–180.

*Bolstad, O. D., & Johnson, S. M. (1972). Self-regulations in the modification of disruptive classroom behavior. *Journal of Applied Behavior Analysis, 5*(4), 443–454.

*Bornstein, R. H., Hamilton, S. B., & Quevillon, R. R. (1977). Behavior modification by long distance: Demonstration of functional control over disruptive behavior in a rural classroom setting. *Behavior Modification, 1*, 369–380.

Bremme, F., & Erickson, F. (1977). Relationships among verbal and non-verbal classroom behaviors. *Theory into Practice, 5*, 153–161.

*Broden, M., Hall, R. V., & Mitts, B. (1971). The effect of self-recording on the classroom behavior of two eighth-grade students. *Journal of Applied Behavior Analysis, 4*, 191–199.

Brooks, D. M., & Wagenhauser, B. (1980). Completion time as a non-verbal component of teacher attitude. *Elementary School Journal, 81*(1), 24–27.

*Broussard, C. D., & Northup, J. (1995). An approach to functional assessment and analysis of disruptive behavior in regular education classrooms. *School Psychology Quarterly, 10*, 151–164.

*Brown, D., Reschly, D., & Sabers, D. (1974). Using group contingencies with punishment and positive reinforcement to modify aggressive behaviors in a Head Start classroom. *The Psychological Record, 24*, 491–496.

Carter, K., & Doyle, W. (1982, March). *Variations in academic tasks in high- and average-ability classes.* Paper presented at the annual meeting of the American Educational Research Association, New York.

Cartledge, G., & Milburn, J. (1978). The case for teaching social skills in the classroom: A review. *Review of Educational Research, 48*, 133–156.

Cazden, D. B. (1981). Social contexts of learning to read. In J. T. Guthrie (Ed.), *Comprehension and teaching: Research reviews* (pp. 118–139). Newark, DE: International Reading Association.

*Christie, D. J., Hiss, M., & Lozanoff, B. (1984). Modification of inattentive classroom behavior: Hyperactive children's use of self-recording with teacher guidance. *Behavior Modification, 8*, 391–406.

*Clarke, S., Dunlap, G., Foster-Johnson, L., Childs, K. E., Wilson, D., White, R., & Vera, A. (1995). Improving the conduct of students with behavioral disorders by incorporating student interests into curricular activities. *Behavioral Disorders, 20*, 221–237.

*Coleman, R. G. (1973). A procedure for fading from experimenter-school-based to parent-home-based control of classroom behavior. *Journal of School Psychology, 11*, 71–79.

*Colozzi, G. A., Coleman-Kennedy, M., Fay, R., Hurley, W., Magliozzi, M., Schackle, K., & Walsh, P. (1986, September). Data-based integration of a student with moderate special needs. *Education and Training of the Mentally Retarded*, 192–199.

Cone, R. (1978, March). *Teacher decisions in managing student behavior.* Paper presented at the annual meeting of the American Educational Research Association, Toronto.

*Cowen, E. L., Orgel, A. R., Gesten, E. L., & Wilson, A. B. (1979). The evaluation of an intervention program for young schoolchildren with acting-out problems. *Journal of Abnormal Child Psychology, 7*, 381–396.

*Darveaux, D. X. (1984). The good behavior game plus merit: Controlling disruptive behavior and improving student motivation. *School Psychology Review, 13*, 510–514.

*Davis, R. A. (1979). The impact of self-modeling on problem behaviors in school-age children. *School Psychology Digest, 8*, 128–132.

*Deitz, S. M. (1977). An analysis of programming DRL schedules in educational settings. *Behavioral Research & Therapy, 15*, 103–111.

*Deitz, S. M., & Repp, A. C. (1973). Decreasing classroom misbehavior through the use of DRL schedules and reinforcement. *Journal of Applied Behavior Analysis, 6*, 457–463.

*Deitz, S. M., Slack, D. J., Schwarzmueller, E. B., Wilander, A. P., Weatherly, T. J., & Hilliard, G. (1978). Reducing inappropriate behavior in special classrooms by reinforcing average interresponse times: Interval DRL. *Behavior Therapy, 9*, 37–46.

*Dougherty, E. H., & Dougherty, A. (1977). The daily report card: A simplified and flexible package for classroom behavior management. *Psychology in the Schools, 14*, 191–195.

Doyle, W. (1979). Making managerial decisions in classrooms. In D. L. Duke (Ed.), *Classroom management* (78th yearbook of the National Society for the Study of Education, Part 2) (pp. 42–74). Chicago: University of Chicago Press.

Doyle, W. (1984). How order is achieved in classrooms: An interim report. *Journal of Curriculum Studies, 16*(3), 259–277.

*Drabman, R. S., & Lahey, B. B. (1974). Feedback in classroom behavior modification: Effects on the target and her classmates. *Journal of Applied Behavior Analysis, 7*, 591–598.

*Drege, R., & Beare, R. L. (1991). The effect of a token reinforcement system with a time-out backup consequence on the classroom behavior of E/BD students. *British Columbia Journal of Special Education, 15*, 39–46.

*Dunlap, G., Clarke, S., Jackson, M., Wright, S., Ramos, E., & Brinson, S. (1995). Self-monitoring of classroom behaviors with students exhibiting emotional and behavioral challenges. *School Psychology Quarterly, 10*, 165–177.

*Dunlap, G., DePerczel, M., Clarke, S., Wilson, D., Wright, S., White, R., & Gomez, A. (1994). Choice making to promote adaptive behavior for students with emotional and behavioral challenges. *Journal of Applied Behavior Analysis, 27*, 505–518.

*Dunlap, G., Kem-Dunlap, L., Clarke, S., & Robbins, E. R. (1991). Functional assessment, curricular revision, and severe behavior problems. *Journal of Applied Behavior Analysis, 24*, 387–397.

Eder, D. (1982). The impact of management and turn-allocation activities on student performance. *Discourse Processes, 5*, 147–159.

*Eleftherios, C. P., Shoudt, J. T., & Strang, H. R. (1972). The game machine: A technological approach to classroom control. *Journal of School Psychology, 10*, 55–60.

Emmer, E., Evertson, C., & Anderson, L. (1980). Effective classroom management at the beginning of the school year. *Elementary School Journal, 80*(5), 219–230.

Emmer, E. T., Sanford, J. P., Clements, B. S., & Martin, J. (1982). *Improving classroom management and organization in junior high schools: An experimental investigation* (R & D Center Rep. No. 6153). Austin: University of Texas, R & D Center for Teacher Education.

Emmer, E. T., Sanford, J. P., Evertson, C. M., Clements, B. S., & Martin, J. (1981). *The classroom management improvement study: An experiment in elementary school classrooms* (R & D Center Rep. No. 6050). Austin: University of Texas, R & D Center for Teacher Education.

*Epstein, M. H., Repp, A. C., & Cullinan, D. (1978). Decreasing "obscene" language of behaviorally disordered children through the use of a DRL schedule. *Psychology in the Schools, 15*, 419–423.

*Epstein, R., & Goss, C. M. (1978). Case study: A self-control procedure for the maintenance of nondisruptive behavior in an elementary school child. *Behavior Therapy, 9*, 109–117.

Erickson, F., & Mohatt, G. (1982). Cultural organization of participation structures in two classrooms of Indian students. In G. Spindler (Ed.), *Doing the ethnography of schooling* (pp. 132–174). New York: Holt, Rinehart, & Winston.

*Evans, W. H., Evans, S. S., Schmid, R. E., & Pennypacker, H. S. (1985, November). The effects of exercise on selected classroom behaviors of behaviorally disordered adolescents. *Behavioral Disorders*, 42–51.

Evertson, C. M. (1982). Differences in instructional activities in higher and lower achieving junior high English and math classes. *Elementary School Journal, 82*(4), 329–350.

Evertson, C. M. (1985). Training teachers in classroom management: An experimental study in secondary school classrooms. *Journal of Educational Research, 79*(1), 51–58.

Evertson, C. M. (1987). Managing classrooms: A framework for teachers. In D. C. Berliner & B. V. Rosenshine (Eds.), *Talks to teachers* (pp. 54–74). New York: Random House.

Evertson, C. M. (1989). Improving elementary classroom management: A school-based training program for beginning the year. *Journal of Educational Research, 83*(2), 82–90.

Evertson, C. M. (1995). *Classroom organization and management program*. Revalidation Submission to the Program Effectiveness Panel, U.S. Department of Education.

Evertson, C. M., & Emmer, E. T. (1982). Effective management at the beginning of the school year in junior high classes. *Journal of Educational Psychology, 74*, 485–498.

Filcheck, H. A., McNeil, C. B., Greco, L. A., & Bernard, R. S. (2004). Using a whole-class token economy and coaching of teacher skills in a preschool classroom to manage disruptive behavior. *Psychology in the Schools, 41*(3), 351–361.

Florio, S., & Shultz, J. (1979). Social competence at home and at school. *Theory into Practice, 18*, 234–243.

Gettinger, M. (1988). Methods of proactive classroom management. *School Psychology Review, 17*, 227–242.

Gordon, T. (1974). *Teacher effectiveness training*. New York: Peter H. Wyden.

*Gottfredson, D. C., Gottfredson, G. D., & Hybl, L. G. (1993). Managing adolescent behavior: A multiyear, multischool study. *American Educational Research Journal, 30*, 179–215.

*Grandy, G. S., Madsen, C. H., Jr., & De Mersseman, L. M. (1973). The effects of individual and interdependent contingencies on inappropriate classroom behavior. *Psychology in Schools, 10*, 488–493.

*Grieger, T., Kauffman, J. M., & Grieger, R. M. (1976). Effects of peer reporting on cooperative play and aggression of kindergarten children. *Journal of School Psychology, 14*, 307–312.

Griffin, P., & Mehan, H. (1979). Sense and ritual in classroom discourse. In F. Coulman (Ed.), *Conversational routine: Explorations in standardized communication situations and prepatterned speech*. The Hague: Mouton.

*Guevremont, D. C., & Foster, S. L. (1993). Impact of social problem-solving training on aggressive boys: Skill acquisition, behavior change, and generalization. *Journal of Abnormal Child Psychology, 21*, 13–27.

Gump, P. V. (1967). *The classroom behavior setting: Its nature and relations to student behavior*. Washington, DC: U.S. Office of Education, Bureau of Research.

*Hall, R. V., Fox, R., Willard, D., Goldsmith, L., Emerson, M., Owen, M., Davis, E., & Porcia, E. (1971). The teacher as observer and experimenter in the modification of disputing and talking-out behaviors. *Journal of Applied Behavior Analysis, 4*, 141–149.

*Hall, R. V., Lund, D., & Jackson, D. (1968). Effects of teacher attention on study behavior. *Journal of Applied Behavior Analysis, 1*, 1–12.

Hargreaves, D. H., Hester, S. K., & Mellor, F. J. (1975). *Deviance in classrooms.* London: Routledge & Kegan Paul.

Humphrey, F. M. (1979). *"Shh!": A sociolinguistic study of teachers' turn-taking sanctions in primary school lessons.* Unpublished doctoral dissertation, Georgetown University, Washington, DC.

*Iwata, B. A., & Bailey, J. S. (1974). Reward versus cost token systems: An analysis of the effects on students and teacher. *Journal of Applied Behavior Analysis, 7,* 567–576.

Johnson, M., & Brooks, H. (1979). Conceptualizing classroom management. In D. L. Duke (Ed.), *Classroom management* (78th yearbook of the National Society for the Study of Education, Part 2) (pp. 1–41). Chicago: University of Chicago Press.

Johnson, T., Stoner, G., & Green, S. (1996). Demonstrating the experimenting society model with classwide behavior management interventions. *Research into Practice, 25,* 199–214.

Jones, V. F., & Jones, L. S. (1981). *Responsible classroom discipline.* Boston: Allyn & Bacon.

*Kent, R. N., & O'Leary, K. D. (1976). A controlled evaluation of behavior modification with conduct problem children. *Journal of Consulting and Clinical Psychology, 44,* 586–596.

*Knapczyk, D. R. (1988). Reducing aggressive behaviors in special and regular class settings by training alternative social responses. *Behavioral Disorders, 14,* 27–39.

Kounin, J., & Gump, P. (1958). The ripple effect in discipline. *Elementary School Journal, 59,* 158–162.

Kounin, J. S. (1970). *Discipline and group management in classrooms.* New York: Holt, Rinehart, & Winston.

*Kubany, E. S., Weiss, L. E., & Sloggett, B. B. (1971). The good behavior clock: A reinforcement/time out procedure for reducing disruptive classroom behavior. *Journal of Behavioral Therapy & Experimental Psychiatry, 2,* 173–179.

LeCompte, M. D. (1980). The civilizing of children: How young children learn to become students. In A. A. VanFleet (Ed.), *Anthology of education: Methods and applications* (pp. 105–127). Norman: University of Oklahoma Press.

*Lobitz, W. C. (1974). A simple stimulus cue for controlling disruptive classroom behavior. *Journal of Abnormal Child Psychology, 2,* 143–152.

*Lochman, J. E. (1992). Cognitive-behavioral intervention with aggressive boys: Three-year follow-up and preventive effects. *Journal of Consulting and Clinical Psychology, 60,* 426–432.

*Lochman, J. E., Burch, P. R., Curry, J. E., & Lampron, L. B. (1984). Treatment and generalization effects of cognitive-behavioral and goal-setting interventions with aggressive boys. *Journal of Consulting and Clinical Psychology, 52,* 915–916.

*Lochman, J. E., Lampron, L. B., Burch, P. R., & Curry, J. E. (1985). Client characteristics associated with behavior change for treated and untreated aggressive boys. *Journal of Abnormal Child Psychology, 13,* 527–538.

*Lovitt, T. C., Lovitt, A. O., Eaton, M. D., & Kirkwood, M. (1973). The deceleration of inappropriate comments by a natural consequence. *Journal of School Psychology, 11,* 148–154.

*Luiselli, J. K., Pollow, R. S., Colozzi, G. A., & Teitelbaum, M. (1981). Application of differential reinforcement to control disruptive behaviours of mentally retarded students during remedial instruction. *Journal of Mental Deficiency Research, 25,* 265–273.

*Madsen, C. H., Jr., Becker, W. C., & Thomas, D. R. (1968). Rules, praise, and ignoring: Elements of elementary and classroom control. *Journal of Applied Behavior Analysis, 1*, 139–150.

*Maglio, C. L., & McLaughlin, T. E. (1981). Effects of a token reinforcement system and teacher attention in reducing inappropriate verbalizations with a junior high school student. *Corrective & Social Psychiatry & Journal of Behavior Technology, Methods & Therapy, 27*, 149–155.

*Marandola, P., & Imber, S. C. (1979). Glasser's classroom meeting: A humanistic approach to behavior change with preadolescent inner-city learning disabled children. *Journal of Learning Disabilities, 12*, 30–34.

*Marholin, D., II, & Steinman, W. M. (1977). Stimulus control in the classroom as a function of the behavior reinforced. *Journal of Applied Behavior Analysis, 10*, 465–478.

*McAllister, L. W., Stachowiak, J. G., Baer, D. M., & Conderman, L. (1969). The application of operant conditioning techniques in a secondary school classroom. *Journal of Applied Behavior Analysis, 2*, 277–285.

*McCain, A. P., & Kelley, M. L. (1994). Improving classroom performance in underachieving preadolescents: The additive effects of response cost to a school-home note system. *Child & Family Behavior Therapy, 16*, 27–41.

McDermott, R. P. (1976). *Kids make sense: An ethnographic account of the interactional management of success and failure in one first grade classroom.* Unpublished doctoral dissertation, Stanford University, Stanford, CA.

McGinnis, C., Frederick, B., & Edwards, R. (1995). Enhancing classroom management through proactive rules and procedures. *Psychology in the Schools, 32*, 220–224.

McKee, W. T., & Witt, J. C. (1990). Effective teaching: A review of instructional and environmental variables. In T. B. Guitkin & C. R. Reynolds (Eds.), *The handbook of school psychology* (2nd ed., pp. 821–846). New York: Wiley.

*McLaughlin, T., & Malaby, J. (1972). Reducing and measuring inappropriate verbalizations in a token classroom. *Journal of Applied Behavior Analysis, 5*, 329–333.

Metz, M. (1978). *Classrooms and corridors.* Berkeley: University of California Press.

*Middleton, M. B., & Cartledge, G. (1995). The effects of social skills instruction and parental involvement on the aggressive behavior of African-American males. *Behavior Modification, 19*, 192–210.

Moskowitz, G., & Hayman, J. (1975). Success strategies of inner-city teachers: A year-long study. *Journal of Educational Research, 69*, 283–289.

*Nay, W. R., Schulman, J. A., Bailey, K. G., & Huntsinger, G. M. (1976). Territory and classroom management: An exploratory case study. *Behavior Therapy, 7*, 240–246.

Neef, N. A., & Lutz, M. N. (2001). Assessment of variables affecting choice and application to classroom interventions. *School Psychology Quarterly, 16*(3), 239–252.

*Nelson, G., & Carson, P. (1988). Evaluation of a social problem-solving skills program for third- and fourth-grade students. *American Journal of Community Psychology, 16*, 79–99.

*O'Leary, K. D., & Becker, W. C. (1967, May). Behavior modification of an adjustment class: A token reinforcement program. *Exceptional Children*, 637–642.

*O'Leary, K. D., & Becker, W. C. (1968–1969). The effects of the intensity of a teacher's reprimands on children's behavior. *Journal of School Psychology, 7*, 811.

O'Leary, K. D., Becker, W. C., Evans, M. B., & Saudargas, T. (1969). A token reinforcement program in a public school: A replication and systematic analysis. *Journal of Applied Behavior Analysis, 2*, 3–13.

*O'Leary, K. D., Drabman, R. S., & Kass, R. E. (1973). Maintenance of appropriate behavior in a token program. *Journal of Abnormal Child Psychology, 1,* 127–138.

*Olexa, D. E., & Forman, S. G. (1984). Effects of social problem-solving training on classroom behavior of urban disadvantaged students. *Journal of School Psychology, 22,* 165–175.

Paine, S. C., Radicchi, J., Rosellini, L. C., & Darch, C. B. (1983). *Structuring your classroom for academic success.* Champaign, IL: Research Press.

Phillips, S. U. (1972). Participation structures and communicative competence: Warm Springs children in community and classrooms. In C. B. Cazden, V. F. Johns, & D. Hymes (Eds.), *Function of language in the classroom* (pp. 370–394). New York: Teachers College Press, Columbia University.

Pittman, S. I. (1985). A cognitive ethnography and quantification of a first grade teacher's selection routines for classroom management. *Elementary School Journal, 85,* 541–557.

*Prinz, R. J., Blechman, E. A., & Dumas, J. E. (1994). An evaluation of peer coping-skills training for childhood aggression. *Journal of Clinical Child Psychology, 23,* 193–203.

*Ramp, E., Ulrich, R., & Dulaney, S. (1971). Delayed timeout as a procedure for reducing disruptive classroom behavior: A case study. *Journal of Applied Behavior Analysis, 4,* 235–239.

*Repp, A. C., & Karsh, K. G. (1994). Hypothesis-based interventions for tantrum behaviors of persons with developmental disabilities in school settings. *Journal of Applied Behavior Analysis, 27,* 21–31.

Rhode, G., Jenson, R. J., & Reavis, H. K. (1993). *The tough kid book: Practical classroom management strategies.* Longmont, CO: Sopris West.

*Rollins, H. A., McCandless, B. R., Thompson, M., & Brassell, W. R. (1974). Project success environment: An extended application of contingency management in inner-city schools. *Journal of Educational Psychology, 66,* 167–178.

Rosenburg, M. S. (1986). Maximizing the effectiveness of structured classroom management programs: Implementing rule-review procedures with disruptive and distractible students. *Behavioral Disorders, 11,* 239–248.

*Safer, D. J., Heaton, R. C., & Parker, E. C. (1981). A behavioral program for disruptive junior high school students: Results and follow-up. *Journal of Abnormal Child Psychology, 9,* 483–494.

*Salend, S. J., & Allen, E. M. (1985). Comparative effects of externally managed and self-managed response-cost systems on inappropriate classroom behavior. *Journal of School Psychology, 23,* 59–67.

*Salend, S. J., & Gordon, B. D. (1987, February). A group-oriented timeout ribbon procedure. *Behavioral Disorders,* 131–137.

*Salend, S. J., & Henry, K. (1981). Response cost in mainstreamed settings. *Journal of School Psychology, 19,* 242–249.

*Salend, S. J., Jantzen, N. R., & Giek, K. (1992). Using a peer confrontation system in a group setting. *Behavioral Disorders, 17,* 211–218.

*Salend, S. J., & Lamb, E. A. (1986). Effectiveness of a group-managed interdependent contingency system. *Learning Disability Quarterly, 9,* 268–273.

*Salend, S. J., Whitaker, C. R., & Reeder, E. (1992). Group evaluation: A collaborative peer-mediated behavior management system. *Exceptional Children, 59,* 203–209.

*Sandler, A. G., Arnold, L. B., Gable, R. A., & Strain, P. S. (1987, February). Effects of peer pressure on disruptive behavior of behaviorally disordered classmates. *Behavioral Disorders*, 104–111.

Sanford, J. P., Emmer, E. T., & Clements, B. S. (1983). Improving classroom management. *Educational Leadership, 40*, 56–60.

*Schilling, D., & Cuvo, A. J. (1983, February). The effects of a contingency-based lottery on the behavior of a special education class. *Education and Training of the Mentally Retarded*, 52–58.

Shultz, J., & Florio, S. (1979). Stop and freeze: The negotiation of social and physical space in a kindergarten/first grade classroom. *Anthropology and Education Quarterly, 10*, 166–181.

Sieber, R. T. (1976). *Schooling in the bureaucratic classroom: Socialization and social reproduction in Chestnut Heights*. Unpublished doctoral dissertation, New York University.

*Simmons, J. T., & Wasik, B. H. (1973). Use of small group contingencies and special activity times to manage behavior in a first-grade classroom. *Journal of School Psychology, 11*, 228–238.

*Smith, D. J., Young, K. R., West, R. P., & Rhode, G. (1988). Reducing the disruptive behavior of junior high school students: A classroom self-management procedure. *Behavioral Disorders, 13*, 231–239.

Smith, L. M., & Geoffrey, W. (1968). *The complexities of an urban classroom*. New York: Holt, Rinehart, & Winston.

*Smith, S. W., Siegel, E. M., O'Connor, A. M., & Thomas, S. B. (1994). Effects of cognitive-behavioral training on angry behavior and aggression of three elementary-aged students. *Behavioral Disorders, 19*, 126–135.

*Solomon, R., & Tyne, T. E. (1979). A comparison of individual and group contingency systems in a first grade class. *Psychology in the Schools, 16*, 193–200.

*Solomon, R. W., & Wahler, R. G. (1973). Peer reinforcement control of classroom problem behavior. *Journal of Applied Behavior Analysis, 6*, 49–56.

Stage, S. C., & Quiroz, D. R. (1997). A meta-analysis of interventions to decrease disruptive classroom behavior in public education. *School Psychology Review, 26*(3), 333–369.

*Stainback, W., Stainback, S., Etscheidt, S., & Doud, J. (1986, Fall). A nonintrusive intervention for acting-out behavior. *Teaching Exceptional Children*, 38–41.

*Stem, G. W., Fowler, S. A., & Kohler, E. W. (1988). A comparison of two intervention roles: Peer monitor and point earner. *Journal of Applied Behavior Analysis, 21*, 103–109.

*Strayhorn, J. M., & Weidman, C. S. (1991). Follow-up one year after parent-child interaction training: Effects on behavior of preschool children. *Journal of the American Academy of Child and Adolescent Psychiatry, 30*, 138–143.

*Sugai, G., & Rowe, P. (1984, February). The effect of self-recording on out-of-seat behavior of an EMR student. *Education and Training of the Mentally Retarded*, 23–28.

*Taylor, V. L., Cornwell, D. D., & Riley, M. T. (1984). Home-based contingency management programs that teachers can use. *Psychology in the Schools, 21*, 368–374.

Thomas, A., & Grimes, J. (Eds.). (1990). *Best practices in school psychology—II*. Washington, DC: National Association of School Psychologists.

*Umbreit, J. (1995). Functional assessment and intervention in a regular classroom setting for the disruptive behavior of a student with attention deficit hyperactivity disorder. *Behavioral Disorders, 20*, 267–278.

*Van Houten, R. V., & Nau, P. A. (1980). A comparison of the effects of fixed and variable ratio schedules of reinforcement on the behavior of deaf children. *Journal of Applied Behavior Analysis, 13*, 13–21.

*Van Houten, R. V., Nau, P. A., MacKenzie-Keating, S. E., Sameoto, D., & Colavecchia, B. (1982). An analysis of some variables influencing the effectiveness of reprimands. *Journal of Applied Behavior Analysis, 15*, 65–83.

Wallat, C., & Green, J. L. (1979). Social rules and communicative contexts in kindergarten. *Theory into Practice, 18*(4), 275–284.

*Weissberg, R. P., Gesten, E. L., Carnrike, C. L., Toro, P. A., Rapkin, B. D., Davidson, E., & Cowen, E. L. (1981). Social problem-solving skills training: A competence-building intervention with second- to fourth-grade children. *American Journal of Community Psychology, 9*, 411–423.

Wheldall, K., & Lam, Y. Y. (1987). Rows versus Tables. II. The effects of two classroom seating arrangements on classroom disruption rate, on-task behaviour and teacher behaviour in three special school classes. *Educational Psychology, 7*(4), 303–312.

*Whitman, T. L., Scibak, J. W., Butler, K. M., Richter, R., & Johnson, M. R. (1982). Improving classroom behavior in mentally retarded children through correspondence training. *Journal of Applied Behavior Analysis, 15*, 545–564.

*Wilson, C. W., & Hopkins, B. L. (1973). The effects of contingent music on the intensity of noise in junior high home economics classes. *Journal of Applied Behavior Analysis, 6*, 269–275.

*Wilson, S. H., & Williams, R. L. (1973). The effects of group contingencies on first graders' academic and social behaviors. *Journal of School Psychology, 11*, 110–117.

*Winer-Elkin, J. I., Weissberg, R. R., & Cowen, E. L. (1988). Evaluation of a planned short-term intervention for school children with focal adjustment problems. *Journal of Clinical Child Psychology, 17*, 106–115.

*Witt, J. C., Hannafin, M. J., & Martens, B. K. (1983). Home-based reinforcement: Behavioral covariation between academic performance and inappropriate behavior. *Journal of School Psychology, 21*, 337–348.

*Wolf, M. M., Hanley, E. L., King, L. A., Lachowicz, J., & Giles, D. K. (1970, October). The timer game: A variable interval contingency for the management of out-of-seat behavior. *Exceptional Children*, 67–73.

*Workman, E. A., & Dickinson, D. J. (1979). The use of covert positive reinforcement in the treatment of a hyperactive child: An empirical case study. *Journal of School Psychology, 17*, 67–73.

*Workman, E. A., Kindall, L. M., & Williams, R. L. (1980). The consultative merits of praise-ignore versus praise-reprimand instruction. *Journal of School Psychology, 18*, 373–381.

*Yell, M. L. (1988). The effects of jogging on the rates of selected target behaviors of behaviorally disordered students. *Behavioral Disorders, 13*, 273–279.

Yinger, R. J. (1977). *A study of teacher planning: Description and theory development using ethnographic and information processing methods.* Unpublished doctoral dissertation, Michigan State University, East Lansing.

25

Developing Teaching Proficiency

To increase student achievement, it is necessary to improve teacher pre-service and in-service education in developing teaching proficiency.

To become more proficient, teachers must be taught how to use teaching strategies that have been proven to increase student achievement, to construct more accurate achievement tests to assess their students' achievement, and to evaluate test results.

Teaching can certainly be improved if teachers and prospective teachers are taught to utilize the 21 strategies previously discussed. Explicit tactics for applying each strategy have been detailed previously.

Being able to apply proven instructional strategies is necessary to proficient teaching but not sufficient. In addition, teachers must be able to assess their students' progress in learning the lessons they teach and to diagnose learning inadequacies as a basis for prescribing corrective instruction. Students seldom master skills they are taught on their first attempt. Teachers must be able to identify inadequacies from the mistakes students make on class tests and assignments so that they can reteach lessons with which students are having difficulty. Effective corrective instruction depends on the accurate diagnosis of student difficulties. Teachers also need to be taught how to score and aggregate scores on class tests and assignments to assign grades and how to interpret results of standardized tests commonly used in education. Standardized tests can help teachers and administrators assess student performance and compare their students to students in other venues who took the tests.

Unfortunately, most teacher education programs do not provide sufficient instruction in achievement testing. Teachers have not been prepared and certified to construct accurate achievement tests to assess student learning of the lessons they teach, nor have they been adequately taught how to interpret the results of standardized tests their students routinely take. Teacher-made tests do not need to be inferior to standardized tests. They can be superior in assessing achievement of classroom objectives. Standardized achievement tests are constructed to assess what is commonly taught across the United States and may not accurately measure the curriculum taught in particular classes and schools. With the appropriate instruction, teachers can learn how to construct and defend their achievement tests and test results with confidence to students, parents, and grievance committees and in court, if need be.

TEACHING EVALUATION

The focus needs to be on teaching evaluation instead of teacher evaluation. There has been a sizeable amount of research on teacher traits, for example, knowledge and personality. There is no evidence proving that teacher traits are linked directly with an increase in academic achievement. On the other hand, all of the effective teaching strategies discussed earlier have been shown to increase student achievement. These strategies can be learned and their execution evaluated and perfected.

The key to student success is perfecting teaching based on observations and evaluations of teaching performance. Teaching cannot be evaluated using paper and pencil tests, oral exams, interviews, or peer or student opinion. Teaching can only be evaluated through observation of teachers or teachers-in-training in the act of teaching students and comparing their teaching against criteria of effective teaching proven to optimize student achievement. Teaching evaluation might take place in a classroom or a tutoring session, either actual or simulated. Evaluators might be present or behind a one-way mirror; or a videotape of an earlier session might be used.

Since research shows that teaching techniques rather than teacher traits are responsible for increasing academic achievement, it is folly to focus on teacher evaluation. Teachers with odd traits can be very proficient at teaching. Moreover, it is all too easy to neglect teaching evaluation in favor of teacher evaluation. More teachers may have been dismissed because of bizarre or sub moral behavior than because of poor teaching. Finally, most personal traits may not be alterable through teacher education.

Although hardly anyone enjoys being evaluated, teaching evaluation tends to be less personally threatening and more productive than teacher evaluation. The emphasis is on routinely improving the teaching skills of all teachers, not on a personal makeover. Screening of applicants for teaching can ensure that the vast majority who are hired do not have problems that impair teaching, for instance, a serious speech impediment.

Proficient teaching requires the development of skills proven to increase student achievement. Yet their development is often neglected. Knowledge about teaching and schooling is also important and usually easier to teach and assess than teaching skills. However, we cannot allow knowledge to be taught instead of the skills necessary for proficient teaching. It is also counterproductive to teach pet teaching methods of instructors instead of methods proven to raise academic achievement.

Since more topics and courses tend to be added to teacher education programs than eliminated, priorities must be established.

An Instructor's Manual is available to assist in developing teaching proficiency. The Instructor's Manual contains suggestions for teaching the effective teaching strategies and evaluating student learning of the strategies. It includes (1) guidelines for developing a course outline, (2) test items for evaluating student learning of the strategies, and (3) specifications for students to use in order to develop a plan for applying the strategies to achieve a simple learning objective, as well as criteria for scoring the student's plan.

See our Web site, www.edieinstitute.net, for more information.

26

Preschool Instruction

Early childhood programs tend to be wide in scope and variable. They may provide community support and services and include parenting education, health care, and babysitting for young children. Preschoolers are taught self-control, self-help skills including eating, toileting, dressing and hygiene, motor skills, and how to relate to peers and adults. The research on effects of these programs shows convincingly that fewer children in them are later retained in grade, assigned to special education programs, or have behavior problems. More show immediate gains in academic achievement, if and when academic subjects are taught. (See Barnett, 1995 and Burchinal, 1999 for an introduction to the research.)

The research also shows that preschoolers are capable of learning fundamentals of all academic subjects: math, science, language, social studies—even problem solving. We cannot afford to waste the opportunity to give our children an academic head start. More time needs to be spent introducing preschoolers to rudimentary academics, especially math and language. Preschool teachers need to be academically literate and know how to use effective instructional strategies to improve all of their teaching.

Effective Preschool Instructional Strategies

The following is a review of the effective instructional strategies discussed in previous chapters and their application to preschool instruction. The review is written with the presumption that the reader understands the effective instructional strategies described earlier in the book.

REDUCING STUDENT/TEACHER RATIO

There should be as few preschool students per teacher as feasible for the following reasons. The research shows that the lower the student/teacher ratio is below

21, the higher the academic achievement tends to be. Preschool children require more personal attention and care than older children require. The smaller the class size the more likely they are to receive personal attention and care they need.

The most important inference that can be made from the preschool research is that students be given as much one-on-one tutoring as they may need to achieve a learning objective. Although preschool class sizes varied and teachers presented information to the class as a whole, students were given as much one-on-one tutoring as they needed to master each task assignment. Of course, the amount of one-on-one tutoring required to master performance of a task varies from student to student. The following studies illustrate how student/teacher ratio can be reduced in effective instruction: Carnine (1977); Lawton and Fowell (1978); Rickel and Fields (1983).

DEFINING INSTRUCTIONAL EXPECTATIONS

Defining instructional expectations for students turns out to be at least as important in preschool instruction as it is in more advanced grades, with some modifications needed in preschool. In general, the research shows that academic achievement increases when prior to instruction students are told (1) what the learning objective is, (2) what procedures are necessary to perform the tasks required to achieve the learning objective, and (3) what the criteria are for successful achievement of the learning objective. Although these specifications are appropriate for older students, they are too stringent, complex, and overwhelming for preschool instruction. Instead of defining the educational objectives in detail for preschoolers, they can be told in simple language what they are about to be taught. Instead of specifying in detail the procedures they are to employ to achieve the objective, they can be told in simple language beforehand what they are going to do to learn it. As feasible, the teacher should model or demonstrate the behavior the preschoolers will be performing. Finally, preschoolers are too young to comprehend fully criteria of successful performance and to take the responsibility for conforming themselves to the criteria. Instead, the teacher should know the criteria for successful performance of assigned tasks and guide and facilitate preschoolers to conform to the criteria, most often by successive approximation and practice.

Instructional expectations are defined for each task students are assigned to perform, and all task assignments are based on student readiness. The following studies illustrate how defining instructional expectations can be used in effective preschool instruction: Carnine (1977); Lawton and Fowell (1978); Perlmutter and Meyers (1975); Stipek et al. (1995); Toyama, Lee, and Muto (1997); Wolff (1972).

TAKING STUDENT READINESS INTO ACCOUNT

Student readiness is taken into account at three different times:

1. *Instructional Planning.* Task sequences must be constructed for students with particular readiness or entry-level characteristics. Since preschoolers cannot be expected to have prior academic experience, the entry-level task of a sequence must be based on maturational readiness more than academic readiness. To be ready for instruction of any kind, preschoolers must be sufficiently mature to take simple directions from a teacher and to perform according to the directions. This assumes, of course, that the preschoolers have been weaned sufficiently from their parents or guardians to relate to the teacher and have sufficient attention spans and coordination to perform the simple tasks in a sequence designed for them.

2. *Placement.* Students are placed in task sequences being considered for them when their readiness characteristics match the entry-level tasks of the sequences. If academic task sequences designed for preschoolers are to require only maturational readiness, academic readiness is not an issue. Adjustments might need to be made when an initial placement reveals that students already have learned to perform the assigned tasks from home schooling. Typically, at the preschool level, placements are made initially at the lowest level of an academic sequence and adjusted afterwards, if need be. In contrast, at more advanced grade levels, student placements are based on test results and other academic data in the student's file, making placement more complex.

3. *Task Assignment* (after placement). After preschoolers are assigned to tasks and their performance is evaluated, there is a basis for determining their readiness for the next task assignment. In general, if their task performance is adequate, students are ready to be assigned to the next more advanced task in the sequence. If students' task performance is inadequate, they are assigned corrective tasks until their inadequacies have been remediated and they are ready to advance. The Lawton and Fowell study (1978) illustrates how readiness can be taken into account in effective preschool instruction.

PROVIDING EFFECTIVE INSTRUCTIONAL EVALUATION

Instructional evaluation was defined as the comparison of a student's performance of instructional tasks with standards of adequate performance and the diagnosis of inadequacies in task performance. In higher grades, evaluation is often conducted after teaching, using an evaluation instrument constructed for the purpose of determining the extent to which the lessons previously taught have been learned. Standards of adequate performance on the instruments are often determined as cutoff scores. In formal test development the validity, reliability, and objectivity of the testing instruments need to be established. In preschool, evaluation is quite different. Most often evaluation of preschoolers' task performance is conducted during teaching as the teacher guides and facilitates the students' performance of the assigned tasks and evaluates the students' performance attempts. Evaluation is most often conducted by the teacher's direct observation of the students' attempts. As teachers watch and listen to students' performance, they evaluate student progress and diagnose students' inadequacies as a basis for adjusting their teaching to maximize the students' opportunity to succeed. The following studies illustrate how effective evaluation can be provided in successful preschool instruction: Carnine (1977); Lawton and Fowell (1978); Stipek et al. (1995).

PROVIDING CORRECTIVE INSTRUCTION

At higher grade levels, corrective instruction is prescribed based on students' performance on testing instruments. In grading testing instruments, teachers make note of students' inadequacies and prescribe for corrective instruction accordingly. However, corrective instruction is not administered until after the teachers provide feedback to the students to acquaint them with their inadequacies and to explain the plans for corrective instruction.

In contrast, at the preschool level, evaluation, feedback, and corrective instruction tend to occur one after the other during the teaching process. The teacher sees an inadequacy in the students' performance, tells the students their performance is incorrect, informs them of the correct performance or models it, and guides the students to the correct performance. On occasion corrective instruction may be separated from evaluation on the preschool level. Teachers may detect an incorrect performance and not know how to provide corrective instruction at the moment. They may need time to seek advice on how to conceive of a prescription to correct the inadequacy. The following studies illustrate how effective corrective instruction can be provided in successful preschool instruction: Carnine (1977); Lawton and Fowell (1978); Stipek et al. (1995). At the preschool level, corrective instruction is almost always one-on-one.

Defining instructional expectations, taking student readiness into account, providing effective evaluation, and providing corrective instruction represent components of the teaching process that teachers need to coordinate. The following instructional strategies represent other techniques teachers can apply to improve academic achievement.

PROVIDING AMPLE TEACHING TIME

It is generally the case that academic achievement is enhanced when teachers spend more time preparing students to perform assigned tasks, guide and facilitate their performance, and monitor their attempts in order to detect and correct inadequacies in their performance, rather than assigning students to independent activities.

Preschoolers require more teacher guidance than older students. Older students are more self-reliant and have acquired study skills that enable them to learn on their own. Preschoolers need teacher guidance almost all of the time. Furthermore, they require more one-on-one teacher guidance. Older students can be taught as a class more effectively than preschoolers can. About the only things that can be done to teach preschoolers as a class is defining simple instructional expectations and modeling or demonstrating behavior required to perform the assigned tasks. Most other teaching needs to be conducted one-on-one.

The following studies illustrate how ample teaching time can be provided in effective preschool instruction: Hong (1996); Toyama et al. (1997).

KEEPING STUDENTS ON TASK

It has been proven rather conclusively that academic achievement is increased when students stay focused on assigned tasks that enable the achievement of the learning objectives being pursued. This generalization is as valid for preschoolers as it is for older students. The problem in teaching preschoolers is that it is much more difficult to keep preschoolers focused on assigned tasks; they are more easily distracted by activities around them and by their personal needs and urges at the moment. It is probably the case that designing task sequences in small graded increments helps to keep preschoolers on task. It is also probably the case that it is easier to keep preschoolers focused on the task at hand when teaching them to play fun games than when teaching them fundamentals of academic subjects such as math and language. The study by Stipek et al. (1995) illustrates how students can be kept on task in effective preschool instruction.

UTILIZING REPETITION EFFECTIVELY

In general, the repetition of to-be-learned information and behavior enhances the learning of the information and behavior. Most educators seem to know that repetition facilitates learning and attempt to use it. However, many educators are not proficient at incorporating repetition in their teaching. Teachers need to be able to (1) incorporate repetition in the presentation of to-be-learned information, (2) plan for students to repeat or practice to-be-learned behavior, and (3) combine repeated presentation and student practice in their lessons. Quite often, repeated presentation and student practice are planned for and used separately. For example, a teacher may plan a lecture with the main points summarized at the end without being concerned with student practice at the time. Student practice might be considered later when students are required, in homework assignments, to write compositions incorporating the to-be-learned information.

Consider another example in which practice is planned without considering the repeated presentation of information at the time. A teacher models or demonstrates the correct behavior for using a microscope and then has the students practice the behavior to perfect it. In considering this example, it is important to realize that the repeated presentation of information could have been incorporated in the teacher's plan. For instance, before modeling the correct behavior for using a microscope, the teacher might have distributed a handout that describes the correct procedure before showing a sequence of pictures depicting the correct use of a microscope.

The purpose of the above example is to show that although repeated presentation and student practice can be and are used separately, they can often be used advantageously in combination. Teachers need to know how to plan for and use repeated presentation and student practice in combination and to be well enough informed about the use of repetition to use enlightened discretion when planning instruction.

Now in preschool education, repetition of teacher demonstrations and student practice are often used in combination. In teaching phonics, for example, teachers first demonstrate the correct pronunciation of letters and words a few times before requiring students to mimic their pronunciation over and over until the students' pronunciation is accurate. Repeated demonstration and student practice are frequently used together when it is desirable for students to learn habits. Such is the case when students are required, when seeing a letter or word, to pronounce it correctly, automatically. Reciting the multiplication tables automatically is another example of the learning of a habit.

Much of preschool academic education requires the use of both repeated presentation and student practice. However, the excessive teaching of habits through drill or practice can be detrimental to effective development. Students need to acquire and use knowledge as well as habits. Human capacity extends far beyond the limits of habitual behavior. Students begin to acquire knowledge in preschool and continue as they progress through school, and they are taught to use their knowledge to consider alternative behaviors before acting. As they become more proficient at deliberating alternatives, they are taught to think before they act rather than responding habitually to the impulse of the moment. So much of early learning is the learning of habits because fundamentals of language and math must be learned as habits. In addition, early learning begins to plant seeds of knowledge to be used to deliberate alternatives as a basis for making decisions. This brings us to a very important application of repeated presentation and student practice in combination.

Repetition needs to be used to teach know-how as well as behavior. To explain, first, repetition in presentation is used to teach students to conceptualize procedures for executing desired behavior. This may be done by describing the to-be-conceptualized procedure in words. Then a graphic presentation of the procedure can be provided for the students in one form or another. Once students have conceptualized the procedure accurately, they can begin practicing its execution and continue until they execute the procedure smoothly with little or no error.

Conceptualizing a procedure accurately before attempting to execute it enables students to guide their own behavior and monitor, detect, and correct their own mistakes. When students are trained like lower animals to execute a behavior without being taught to conceptualize the correct execution of the behavior first, they cannot guide their own behavior or detect and correct their own mistakes. Trainees in the armed services were once taught to assemble and disassemble guns by seeing and copying demonstrations. It has since been found to be more effective prior to demonstration to show soldiers diagrams of the guns' assembly and to explain the relationship among each gun's parts, its form, and its function. Golfers and batters in baseball are frequently taught to visualize the correct swing as they attempt to execute it.

Although preschool children are too young to be able to conceptualize complex procedures, they can be taught to conceptualize simple behaviors before attempting to execute them. They can be told how to play a simple game before seeing a demonstration or attempting to play it. In one study, stories were used to help preschoolers conceptualize solutions to problems they were asked to solve. Preschoolers were able to transfer the solution described in a story to solve the problem confronting them (Rickel and Fields, 1983). Preschoolers can and do learn to conceptualize simple procedures to guide their behavior, even when the procedures are conveyed in words rather than pictures, providing they understand the meaning of the words.

Utilizing repetition in teaching is most important at the preschool level. As explained, many math and language fundamentals need to be learned as habits, and repetition is vital in the teaching of habits. Furthermore, preschool teachers need to become proficient at applying repetition (1) in the presentation of information, (2) in assigning and guiding student practice, and (3) in utilizing repetition in presentations and student practice in combination. The following studies illustrate how repetition can be utilized effectively in successful preschool instruction: Carnine (1977); Hong (1996); Lawton and Fowell (1978); Stipek et al. (1995); Rickel and Fields (1983); Toyama et al. (1997); Wolff (1972).

PROVIDING CONTIGUITY

It has generally been established that for associations to be learned, the events to be associated must be perceived sufficiently close together in space and time. This applies to the association of occurrences in the students' environment, the association of teacher or teaching behaviors, and the association of the students' behavior with resulting consequences. For preschoolers, to-be-associated events must be arranged closer in space and time than for older students. Preschoolers cannot abstract and extrapolate as well as older children; they learn best through concrete experiences in the here and now. They cannot make associations when to-be-associated events occur too far apart in either space or time; it is best to present to-be-associated events together in their immediate perceptual field. The following studies illustrate how contiguity can be provided in effective preschool instruction: Carnine (1977); Hong (1996); Lawton and Fowell (1978); Perlmutter and Meyers (1975); Rickel and Fields (1983); Stipek et al. (1995). Successful preschool instruction must provide contiguity of to-be-associated events. Although at times contiguity may be provided inadvertently, effective teachers need to provide it purposefully.

PROVIDING SUBJECT MATTER UNIFIERS

Academic achievement is increased when parts/whole relationships in the subject matter being taught are conveyed and displayed to students. This generalization is as true in preschool instruction as it is at other grade levels. In the previous discussion of providing contiguity, it was pointed out that to-be-associated events must be presented close together in time and space. However, the examples given of providing contiguity require learning simple relationships between two events. Contiguity must be ensured when providing subject matter unifiers. But most often in providing subject matter unifiers, the relationships being taught are more complex. Students are being taught a pattern of relationships. For example, graphic subject matter unifiers, perhaps in the form of pictures, are used to teach the complex parts/whole relations of human body parts.

Although subject matter unifiers convey more complex relationships, they are as useful in teaching preschoolers as they are in teaching older children. A simple one-dimensional drawing displaying the parts/whole relations of major human body parts can be used to teach preschoolers about the human body. Simple maps are also used by preschool teachers to display relationships among geographical locations. In the study by Lawton and Fowell (1978), pictures on flannel boards, posters, and bulletin boards were used to convey relationships among main ideas of stories and procedural relationships for accomplishing assigned tasks. Subject matter unifiers have many uses in effective preschool instruction.

CLARIFYING COMMUNICATION

Every educator knows that clarity of communication is essential for effective teaching. Clear communication is more difficult when teaching preschoolers because of their very limited knowledge of language and low tolerance of ambiguity. A special effort needs to be made by teachers to speak distinctly, to use simple words and transitional terms, and to avoid vagueness and irrelevant interjections. These practices apply to all forms of effective communication.

Effective instructional communication has its own special requirements. Question-and-answer instruction is used to clarify communication, and so are many of the effective instructional strategies previously discussed. Communication is clarified when instructional expectations are defined and repetition, contiguity, subject matter unifiers, corrective instruction, and ample teaching time are provided.

Five instructional strategies shown to be effective in increasing academic achievement above the preschool level were not confirmed to be effective at the preschool level: (1) providing transfer of learning instruction, (2) providing decision-making instruction, (3) utilizing reminders, (4) providing teamwork instruction, and (5) providing ample learning time. These strategies warrant discussion.

In transfer of learning instruction, students are taught how to enhance their effectiveness in transferring learning to perform tasks they need or want to perform. Obviously preschoolers are not ready to master this challenge. They are too young to understand the concept of transfer of learning, and it will be a while before they are ready to learn how to facilitate transfer of learning on their own. However, they are not too young to transfer learning to perform an assigned task when the learning prescribes procedures for performing similar tasks. Although the ability to transfer learning becomes more proficient with learning and maturation over time, some ability to transfer learning appears to be innate, and this endowment is essential to adaptation. Without being able to transfer learning to perform new tasks, learning would be useless.

Rickel and Fields (1983) take advantage of preschoolers' ability to transfer learning. First, they gave preschoolers a simple problem to solve. Then they exposed the preschoolers to a story, quite similar to the situation confronting them, which describes how to solve the problem. Preschoolers were able to transfer the solution depicted in the story to solve their immediate problem.

It is obvious that decision-making instruction is too advanced for preschoolers. Decision-making instruction is more advanced than transfer of learning instruction because decision-making know-how presupposes and incorporates transfer of learning know-how.

Utilizing reminders is an interesting instructional strategy. It is evident that preschoolers are too young to be taught how to create their own reminders, but it appears that certain kinds of reminders can be and are used to help preschoolers commit things to memory. Although no research could be found validating the effective use of reminders at the preschool level, there is abundant research confirming the effective use of reminders by teachers in higher grade levels (for example, the use by teachers of the acronym HOMES to help students remember the names of the Great Lakes). Preschool teachers can be observed using reminders to help preschoolers remember such things as the letters of the alphabet. For instance, teachers have preschoolers sing little ditties as they recite the alphabet to help them remember the letters. Research should be conducted to test the hypothesis that preschool teachers can effectively use simple reminders to help preschoolers remember such rudiments as words, letters, and numbers.

Providing teamwork instruction is another curious instructional strategy. Middle school and older students can be taught how to work together to maximize achievement of group goals, an asset they can use in most walks of life. Although preschoolers are not yet able to work together with the competency required to maximize achievement, they can be and are taught underlying fundamentals. They are taught the basics of cooperation while having fun playing simple group games.

Finally, providing ample learning time does not seem to be as much of an issue at the preschool level as it is at higher grade levels. At higher grade levels, teachers need to provide ample time to complete extended seatwork, homework, and project and term paper assignments, something a preschooler will need to accomplish a few years hence. Providing ample learning time is an issue at all levels during spontaneous teaching when students are asked to perform a task. Under these conditions, teachers must make certain they give students ample time to perform the assigned task, perhaps with some teacher guidance and cueing, as necessary, to help them succeed. Spontaneous teaching occurs, for example, during question-and-answer instruction. A major difference between preschoolers and older students is that preschoolers typically have a shorter attention span and should only be required to perform tasks that they can perform immediately or in a short span of time. In addition, they need more teacher guidance.

The following instructional strategy is not one of the instructional strategies shown to be generally effective above the preschool level. However, it was shown to be effective at the preschool level.

PROVIDING SENSORY CONTACT

Although providing sensory contact is not an effective instructional strategy that is generalizable above the preschool level, it appears to be very important in the instruction of young children. This is because, in general, over the years learning proceeds from the concrete to the abstract, and learning the characteristics of concrete objects in the early years occurs through sensory contact with the objects. Thus, when preschool learning involves concrete objects, as it most often does, sensory contact with the objects needs to be provided. It is also the case that when preschoolers are being taught basic abstractions such as categories, they need to be able to distinguish examples from nonexamples of the categories. This requires that they have sensory contact with the examples and the nonexamples.

Rather than become involved in arguments that favor one type of sensory exposure over another, it is more advantageous to point out that whenever students are assigned to learn about concrete objects, whatever age they may be, sensory contact with the objects is advantageous, the more senses involved the better. For example, in using repetition to learn about a peach, it is advised that students be given the opportunity to see, taste, feel, and smell a peach and to hear the sound made when a peach is being eaten.

Wolff (1972) used sensory contact successfully when teaching preschoolers to associate one toy with another. Preschoolers who had sensory contact with the toys were better able to associate paired toys. Toyama et al. (1997) showed that sensory contact with animals improved preschoolers' knowledge of biology and their predictive ability.

PROVIDING ONE-TO-ONE TUTORING

This instructional strategy is presented last because not only is it effective on its own, but also it is related to the success of many other strategies. Research shows that students who are tutored one-to-one achieve two standard deviations higher than students taught in regular classrooms. One-to-one tutoring is of special importance to preschoolers who need so much more personal attention and care than older students.

There are interesting and symbiotic relations between one-to-one tutoring and other instructional strategies. Certainly, Defining Instructional Expectations, Clarifying Communication, Taking Readiness into Account, Providing Effective Evaluation, Providing Corrective Instruction, Keeping Students on Task, and Providing Ample Teaching Time are facilitated when teachers can observe, prompt, and react to student cues face-to-face, one-to-one. It also may be the case that student achievement increases as student/teacher ratio is decreased below 21:1 because one-to-one tutoring can be and probably is provided. Each of the exemplary preschool studies (Carnine, 1977; Lawton and Fowell, 1978; Rickel and Fields, 1983; Stipek et al., 1995; Hong, 1996; Toyama et al., 1997; Wolff, 1972) cited the student/teacher ratio as well below 15:1.

REFERENCE LIST

Barnett, W. S. (1995). Long-term effects of early childhood programs on cognitive and school outcomes. *The Future of Children, 5*(3), 25–36.

Burchinal, M. R. (1999). Child care experiences and developmental outcomes. *The Annals of the American Academy of Political and Social Science, 563*(2), 73.

Carnine, D. W. (1977). Phonics versus Look-Say: Transfer to new words. *The Reading Teacher, 30*, 636–639.

Hong, H. (1996). Effects of mathematics learning through children's literature on math achievement and dispositional outcomes. *Early Childhood Research Quarterly, 11*, 477–494.

Lawton, J. T., & Fowell, N. (1978). Effects of advance organizers on preschool children's learning of mathematics concepts. *Journal of Experimental Education, 14*(1), 25–43.

Perlmutter, M., & Meyers, N. A. (1975). Young children's coding and storage of visual and verbal material. *Child Development, 46*, 271–272.

Rickel, A. U., & Fields, R. B. (1983). Storybook models and achievement behavior of preschool children. *Psychology in the Schools, 20*, 105–112.

Stipek, D., Feiler, R., Daniels, D., & Milburns, S. (1995). Effects of different instructional approaches on young children's achievement and motivation. *Child Development, 66*(1), 209–223.

Toyama, N., Lee, Y. M., & Muto, T. (1997). Japanese preschoolers' understanding of biological concepts related to procedures for animal care. *Early Childhood Research Quarterly, 12*, 347–360.

Wolff, P. (1972). The role of stimulus-correlated activity in children's recognition of nonsense forms. *Journal of Experimental Child Psychology, 14*, 427–441.

27

Developing Preventive Tutoring Programs

Preventive tutoring should not be confused with the remedial tutoring received by disabled students in special education. Remedial tutoring is primarily for students who have already failed in a regular classroom setting. There are well-established special education programs for disabled students. What's missing is preventive tutoring to keep students from failing; many failing students might otherwise eventually need special education. The focus of preventive tutoring is on reteaching specific topics with which students are having difficulty. Here is an encapsulation of core tactics.

1. Teachers identify topics students fail to grasp from their performance on class assignments or tests and tutor them on the topics as time permits.
2. Teachers request a tutor who is qualified to teach the topics.
3. Teachers meet with tutors to share information on the mistakes students make on class assignments and tests (without violating privacy rights) as well as on the textbooks and other materials used to teach the topics in class.
4. Tutors receive texts and other teaching aids they can use to tutor the topics and guidance they may request during tutoring.
5. Tutors provide tutoring to correct students' misconceptions until students' performance on class tests and assignments is adequate.

This simplistic rendition highlights essentials of preventive tutoring without addressing administrative details that must be considered, and, of course, the devil is in the details. Let's consider some administrative details.

PROGRAM CONSIDERATIONS

It is evident that schools are obligated to provide more preventive tutoring. For one thing, tutoring is prescribed in the No Child Left Behind Act. Following are suggestions for developing a preventive tutoring program. Suggestions are offered rather than prescriptions because local laws and fiscal constraints as well as preferences must and can be taken into account in developing a preventive tutoring program over time.

Administrators are not starting from scratch. They can take advantage of the many resources already available in their school. Every teacher is well qualified to offer preventive tutoring if relieved of other assignments to spend more time on instruction. Special education teachers and resource rooms are invaluable resources for tutoring as local law permits. Special education teachers are well qualified to diagnose academic inadequacies, provide sophisticated tutoring, and train other tutors. Many resource room materials used to tutor disabled students can be used in preventive tutoring as well. In addition, there are many programs used in private enterprises that can be adapted to preventive tutoring. Sylvan, Kaplan, and others make a profit tutoring students failing in school when their parents can afford the cost. Some of these enterprises guarantee student success. Some sell their tutoring programs and provide guidance for tutors; for example, the Lindamood-Bell Clinical Instruction Program, Reading Recovery, and the Kumon Math and Reading Program. Many of these programs focus on the fundamentals of reading and math (see Chapter 28).

Part-time volunteers can provide most of the out-of-class preventive tutoring at no cost to the school. Parents, retirees, peers, and employees in the community often volunteer to do part-time tutoring. A sufficient number needs to be recruited to cover the subjects taught in the school and to meet the demand. Some tutors may need to be hired; for example, teachers seeking extra pay.

All tutors need to be well founded in the subjects they are engaged to teach. They can begin tutoring after a brief orientation and advisement. Guidance should be available during tutoring assignments and short workshops can be held to improve the teaching skills of tutors.

Parental tutoring is convenient and every effective. Just helping their child with homework can go a long way toward preventing failure. There usually is no stigma attached to being helped by a parent. Parents can offer a variety of enrichment opportunities to stimulate their child's interest, such as magazine subscriptions and visits to museums. Parents can identify misconceptions in the tests and assignments their child brings home, and they have access to the teacher for clarification and advice. Involving parents directly in the instruction of their children is enormously productive.

Peer tutoring has proven to be very effective. Although older students usually tutor younger ones, same-age tutoring can also be effective. In fact, one reason heterogeneous groupings work better than ability grouping may be that more advanced students pitch in to help their peers.

Many tutors are now offering their services over the telephone and Internet. One problem with this relatively new phenomenon is that it can be hard to check a tutor's qualifications. They may not be competent or able to diagnose accurately the root cause of a problem.

The best tutoring is one-on-one and face-to-face where the tutor can monitor nonverbal communication and watch the students perform their assignments. Through personal observation, a tutor can prompt and direct desired performance, correct mistakes, and provide encouragement as the students go along. Computers can serve as an aid to tutors and be used to supplement assignments, but they are no substitute for live preventive tutoring.

Comfortable, quiet, well-lit space devoid of interruptions and distractions is a requirement for tutoring. Some students fail to learn in classrooms because they have difficulty concentrating in a busy classroom environment. A resource room might be spacious enough to accommodate preventive tutoring as well as special education tutoring.

A tutoring director is needed to manage a tutoring program. Directors' responsibilities include coordinating tutors and classroom teachers, recruiting and training tutors, testing tutees to diagnose academic deficits, identifying students who may need special education services, providing space for tutoring, and supplying instructional materials. Special education teachers with management skills are well qualified to direct a tutoring program.

Tutoring programs can be developed grade level by grade level, progressing from the primary grades where illiteracy is born to the higher grades.

MASTERY CENTERS

Once students referred by their teachers for preventive tutoring are being successfully tutored, the tutoring services can be extended as desired. For instance, other students can be encouraged to volunteer for preventive tutoring when they are having difficulty with classroom topics. Marginal students earning "D" grades in a subject know when they are in need of help. Allowing voluntary access to preventive tutoring can further reduce the failure rate. Furthermore, it reduces the stigma of being tutored. If all students have free access to tutoring and take advantage of it, being tutored in school is less embarrassing.

Eventually, as an ideal, it might be best for students if schools had mastery centers instead of resource rooms. Mastery centers have an open-door policy. All students who come to a mastery center to learn are given personal attention, even if they are doing well in school and are simply pursuing their interests. Curiosity and ambition are too valuable to waste. It may be that the best way to serve the needs of talented and gifted students is through individualized guidance. After all, classroom instruction, by its very nature, imposes conformity—at least conformity to class rules and requirements. Innovation needs to be nurtured; American industry thrives on innovation. Students would clamor to take advantage of a mastery center that helps any student learn any subject he or she may need or want to learn.

28

Remedial Tutoring Programs

Remedial tutoring programs are designed for students with learning difficulties who need more than the instruction provided by their classroom teachers. With the classroom instruction given them, they have failed to achieve class learning objectives. Most often these students have deficits in fundamentals of reading, spelling, writing, and/or math and need supplemental help.

Remedial tutoring is clinical in nature. It follows a diagnosis/treatment format. Diagnostic procedures are administered first to identify problems. Then treatment procedures are prescribed based on the diagnosis, specifically to remedy the problems that were diagnosed. Many achievement tests, including standardized achievement tests, are inadequate in diagnosing the particular cause(s) of student failure to learn. They indicate level of performance but do not sufficiently indicate causes of inadequate performance. If we do not know what students have failed, we have no basis for remediating their failure. Diagnostic achievement tests are available as are diagnostic tests for other underlying causes such as inadequate vision or hearing.

The following are remedial tutoring program options designed for students with learning difficulties. Although there is considerable variation among them, they all tend to be structured and intense. The review of tutoring programs is intended to be representative, not exhaustive. A number of free enterprise companies make a profit using one-to-one tutoring to remediate students who fail in school. At least one of them guarantees success.

The Orton-Gillingham Instructional Program

Introduction: The Orton-Gillingham (O-G) approach to language instruction is designed to be structured, sequential, and cumulative, yet flexible. Emphasis is on cognition and multisensory exposure of students to language elements. It is utilized for teaching individuals and groups.

Grade Levels Covered: Primary grades through adults

Subject Areas Covered: Reading, writing, and spelling

Instructional Tactics: Teaching sessions are action oriented and utilize multi-sensory training. Auditory, visual, and kinetic exposure reinforces one another. This aids students having difficulties with a specific sensory modality. Students learn to read and spell simultaneously, which differs from traditional phonics instruction. In addition, students study the history of language and study the rules that govern its structure.

The Tutor: The Orton-Gillingham Instructional Program is implemented systematically. Students begin by reading and writing sounds in isolation. Then they blend the sounds into syllables and words. They continue to learn elements of language, the composition of language, and the comprehension of language in a structured, sequential, and cumulative manner. As students learn new material, they continue to review old material until it is mastered. Tutoring is diagnostic-prescriptive in nature. The tutor assesses student performance and prescribes instruction accordingly.

Strict control is maintained over tutor training. O-G tutors must have at least a bachelor's degree, 45 hours of course work in the O-G curriculum, and 100 hours of supervised practicum teaching. Additional requirements must be met to achieve a more advanced level of qualification.

Additional Sources to Consult: More information can be obtained from the Language Tutoring Center, 3229 Debbie Drive, Hendersonville, NC 28739. Required teaching materials can be obtained from Educators' Publishing Service, 1-800-225-5750.

The Wilson Reading System

Introduction: First published in 1988, the Wilson Reading System provided a step-by-step method for teachers working with students who require direct, multisensory, structured language teaching. In 1989, the Wilsons began to provide training to educators in its use. By 1991, their focus had shifted from tutoring to training teachers and distributing Wilson Reading System materials through the Wilson Language Training Corporation.

Grade Levels Covered: Elementary grades through adulthood

Subject Areas Covered: Reading and spelling

Instructional Tactics: The Wilson Reading System teaches students the structure of words through a carefully sequenced, 12-step program that helps them master decoding and spelling in English. Unlike other programs that overwhelm the student with rules, the Wilson Reading System allows the student to learn in small graded increments by using language. Emphasis is on multi-sensory exposure to language. The system is appropriate for students with and without learning difficulties. Students use readers, workbooks, and group sets provided in the Wilson materials.

The Tutor: Tutors need to be trained for two weeks in the appropriate use of the Wilson Reading System. They are to follow the Wilson instructional system faithfully and use the materials supplied by Wilson. Materials provided for teachers include manuals, rules notebooks, test forms, sound cards, and word cards. Tutor training videos are available but are not intended to replace prescribed training by the Wilson staff. Wilson provides everything needed to utilize its system, for both tutors and students.

The following is a list of the materials provided in the Deluxe Set.

Instructor Materials

- Instructor's Manual
- Dictation Book (Steps 1–6)
- Dictation Book (Steps 7–12)
- Rules Notebook
- WADE: Wilson Assessment of Decoding and Encoding
- Sound Cards in Plastic Box
- Word Cards
- Syllable Cards (Steps 3–6)
- Syllable Cards (Steps 7–12)
- Group Sound Cards (Steps 1–6)
- Group Sound Cards (Steps 7–12)

Student and Additional Materials

- Student Readers 1–12 in Slipcase
- Student Workbooks 1–12, Either A or B Level or Both A and B Level

Additional Sources to Consult: This program is available nationwide. However, teacher training is limited, depending on location. Contact Wilson Language Training, 175 West Main Street, Milbury, MA 01527-1441. Phone: 508-865-5699.

TEACH

Introduction: TEACH is a tutoring program developed by Silver and Hagin (1990) in the Learning Disorders Unit of the New York University Medical Center. The purpose of the program is to diagnose deficits in the component skills of reading and to remediate these specific skills. Emphasis is on diagnosing and treating perceptual weaknesses.

Instructional Levels Covered: First and second grades

Subject Area Covered: Reading

Instructional Tactics: TEACH focuses on teaching four skills needed in reading: (1) pre-reading skills, which include the visual discrimination of letters, recognition of symbols in their correct orientation, the ability to organize symbols in groups, and auditory skills; (2) word attack skills, which involve the use of phonics to decipher words, and the identification of whole words using visual cues, such as letter combinations; (3) comprehension, which involves having a rich vocabulary, being able to select the right meaning of a word, and making inferences; and (4) study skills, which are the tools for acquiring information. However, the actual instructional program focuses more on matching, copying, recognizing, and recalling letters and words than on other reading skills. Students come to tutoring for 30 minutes three to five times a week. Student weaknesses are first diagnosed by an assessment technique called SEARCH, and instructional treatments are prescribed and used accordingly to remediate deficits.

The Tutor: Tutors are certified teachers. The tutor's job is to remediate particular reading difficulties that have been diagnosed by SEARCH, using TEACH instructional techniques. Tutors are given instruction on the appropriate use of the TEACH instructional program. However, nothing explicit could be found on the length of tutor training or the training routine.

Additional Sources to Consult: For more information, contact the Prevention of Disabilities Program, Learning Disorders Unit, the New York University Medical School. See also the following references (listed at the end of this chapter): Arnold et al. (1977); Hagin, Silver, and Beecher (1978); Silver and Hagin (1990).

Programmed Tutorial Reading

Introduction: Doug Ellison of Indiana University developed the instructional program initially for reading with expectations of expanding it to other subject areas. Emphasis is on sight reading, word analysis, phonics, and comprehension. Students learn the components of reading and how to synthesize them systematically.

Grade Levels Covered: Tutoring begins in the first grade and has been extended beyond.

Subject Area Covered: Reading

Instructional Tactics: Students are selected for tutoring because of their poor performance on standardized reading tests. The program is highly structured. Students learn in small, sequential steps and are reinforced for correct responses. Subsequent assignments depend on students' prior responses.

The Tutor: Tutors do not need to be certified teachers. Many are paid paraprofessionals, volunteers, or parents. Tutors are trained to follow the tutorial program explicitly as prescribed. The tight structure of the program does not leave much room for tutor discretion. Specifics could not be found on the length of tutor training or the training routine.

Additional Sources to Consult: For more information, contact Douglas Ellison at Indiana University. See also the following references: Ellison, Harris, and Barber (1968); McCleary (1971).

The Wallach Tutoring Program

Introduction: The Wallachs contend that reading is a skill that can be broken down into components. Students should first be taught to master the components, and then they should be taught how to integrate the components until they can read proficiently. Students must first become proficient in the recognition and manipulation of sounds and then acquire proficiency in using the alphabetic code and in blending. Finally, they need to be taught to apply those skills in reading printed material.

Grade Level Covered: First grade

Subject Area Covered: Reading

Instructional Tactics: Students are selected for tutoring who score low on standardized reading tests. They are tutored 30 minutes a day for a year. Students are taught in stages. For the first 10 weeks, students are taught to recognize initial phonemes in words that are read to them, to recognize letters, and to associate letters with phonemes. In the second stage, students spend two to three weeks learning to sound out and blend words. For the remainder of the year, students apply their skills as they learn to read beginning reading materials.

The Tutor: Paraprofessionals have been used in the Wallach Program. No detailed specifications were given for required tutor qualifications or for a tutor training regimen. Although there is some latitude for tutor discretion, the prescribed format and stages are to be followed.

Additional Sources to Consult: The following references provide additional information on the Wallach Program: Dorval, Wallach, and Wallach (1978); Wallach and Wallach (1976).

Reading Recovery

Introduction: The Reading Recovery program, developed by Marie Clay (1985) in New Zealand, appears to be fairly noncontroversial in the world of reading instruction, which can be divided into advocates of intensive phonics instruction and advocates of the whole language approach. The program places emphasis on the development of phonics skills as well as the use of contextual information to assist reading. It is designed for students having trouble learning to read. These students have already had one year of formal instruction. The program is intended to be a short-term, one-on-one tutorial program, supplemental to other reading instruction in the classroom setting.

Grade Level Covered: First grade

Subject Areas Covered: Reading and writing

Instructional Tactics: The Reading Recovery program is administered during half-hour sessions for 12 to 16 weeks. During their daily half-hour sessions, children read many small books. Some of these books are written in a style resembling oral language, while other books use language which the child can readily anticipate. Children also read slightly more difficult texts that they have not previously read. At this point the teacher provides the student detailed support. Children also compose and read their own stories. Reading skills are taught as students read and write, occasionally aided by the use of magnetic letters.

The Tutor: Tutor training is an essential part of this program, with a year's training being required. The tutors learn to observe, analyze, and interpret the reading and writing behaviors of students and design and implement an individualized program for each student. They keep a detailed, running record analyzing the students' performance, moment to moment.

During the first year of training, in addition to teaching a class and tutoring four students, the tutors attend weekly seminars during which they receive training in observational, diagnostic, and assessment techniques. The tutors also participate in weekly "behind the glass" demonstration lessons where they observe, critique, and discuss actual tutoring sessions with their trainers. Follow-up training continues after the first year. The tutors are certified teachers.

Additional Sources to Consult: "Reading Recovery" is a registered trademark of The Ohio State University, with development of most of the authorized materials by Marie Clay. However, most of the Reading Recovery programs in the United States differ to a degree as to how they are developed, implemented, and assessed. For additional information, contact: G. S. Pinnell, C. A. Lyons, D. E. DeFord, A. S. Bryk, or M. Seltzer at The Ohio State University. Relevant references include: Clay (1979); Huck and Pinnell (1986); Lyons et al. (1989); Pinnell et al. (1986).

Success for All Language Tutoring

Introduction: There are several components of the Success for All program, including language arts, mathematics, social studies, science, and a beginning language tutoring program. The beginning language tutoring program will be described here.

The Success for All tutoring program is based on the premise that students need to learn to read in meaningful contexts and at the same time be given a systematic presentation of word attack skills. There is a certain regularity to language, and direct presentation of phonics is viewed as a helpful strategy which children can use to decipher words. Children also need to build a strong sight vocabulary that will help in identifying words that are not decodable. Along with the systematic presentation of phonics, children engage in reading meaningful connected text. The program has been utilized in public schools to teach disadvantaged students.

Grade Levels Covered: First and second grades

Subject Areas Covered: Beginning reading and writing

Instructional Tactics: There are four components to the Success for All tutoring program. First, children learn to read by reading meaningful text. Reading skills are not acquired by children learning isolated, unconnected information about print. Second, phonics needs to be taught systematically as a strategy for deciphering the reading code. Children engage in reading stories that are meaningful and interesting, yet have a phonetically controlled vocabulary. Third, children need to be taught the relationship between reading words and comprehending what they read. The emphasis on comprehension is directly related to the fourth component, the emphasis on children's need to be taught strategies to help them become successful readers.

In Success for All, the tutoring model is completely integrated with the classroom reading program. The tutor's most important responsibility is to make sure that the student is making adequate progress on the specific skills and concepts being taught in the reading class. Students receive tutoring as long as they need it. Although most students receive tutoring for part of a year, some receive it all year and then continue to be tutored into the next grade. Students are initially selected for tutoring on the basis of individually administered, informal reading inventories given in September. After that, students are assessed every eight weeks to determine their progress through the reading curriculum. Students receive tutoring for 20 minutes each day. A typical tutoring session begins with the student reading out loud a familiar story that he or she has read before in tutoring and in the reading class. This is followed by a one-minute drill of letter sounds to give the student the opportunity to practice the letter sounds taught in class. The major portion of the tutoring session is spent on reading aloud "shared stories" that correspond to the beginning reading lessons. The shared stories are interesting, predictable stories that have phonemically controlled vocabulary in large type and other elements of the story in small type. The teacher reads aloud the small type sections to provide a context for the large type portions read by the students. The tutor works with the student to sound out the phonetically regular words, asks comprehension questions about the whole story, and has the students reread passages out loud to gain fluency. Writing activities are incorporated into the reading activities.

The Tutor: The tutors are certified teachers who also teach a reading class in the school. They are fully aware of what the reading program is. In many cases, tutors work with students who are also in their reading class. When scheduling does not allow this, the student's reading teacher fills out a tutor/ teacher communication form that indicates what lesson the student is working on in class and the teacher's assessment of the specific problems the student is having with that lesson. The tutor uses this information to plan the tutoring session. This communication ensures coordination between the classroom instruction and tutoring.

The tutors receive two days of training to learn to teach the Success for All beginning reading program, and then they receive four additional days of training on assessment and on tutoring itself. Tutors are observed weekly by the program facilitator and given direct feedback on the sessions. Tutors are trained to teach explicitly self-questioning (metacognitive) strategies to help students monitor their own comprehension. For example, a tutor will teach a student to stop at the end of each page and ask, "Did I understand what I just read?" The students learn to check their own comprehension and to go back and reread what they did not understand.

Additional Sources to Consult: For more information, contact the Success for All Foundation, 200 W. Towsontown Blvd., Baltimore, MD 21286. Phone: 1-800-548-4998. Relevant references include Madden et al. (1991); Slavin et al. (1992).

Lindamood-Bell Clinical Instruction Program

Introduction: Lindamood-Bell reports that instruction is "based on an individual's learning needs and embodies an interactive, balanced approach. Through Socratic questioning, clinicians teach students to integrate sensory information to help them become self-correcting and independent in all tasks." The program is available nationally.

Grade Levels Covered: Five-year-olds through adults

Subject Areas Covered: Reading, spelling, math

Instructional Tactics: Instruction can occur in one of two ways: (1) Regular—one hour a day for four to six months or (2) Intensive—four hours a day for four to six weeks. Follow-up treatment ranges from one consultation per week to daily sessions.

The following programs are utilized in the instruction:

- Phonemic Awareness for Reading, Spelling & Speech (Lindamood Phoneme Sequencing Program)

- Concept Imagery for Comprehension & Thinking (Visualizing and Verbalizing Program)

- Symbol Imagery for Sight Words, Phonemic Awareness & Spelling (Seeing Stars Program)

- Visual-Motor Skills (Drawing with Language Program)

- Math Computation & Reasoning (On Cloud Nine Math Program)

The Tutor: The tutor is called a clinician. His/her role is to follow the program precisely. Intensive training is available through workshops, conferences, and internships. On-site consulting is offered.

Additional Sources to Consult: For more information, contact Lindamood-Bell Programs, 1-800-233-1819.

Laubach Literacy Program

Introduction: Laubach Literacy International is a nonprofit educational corporation founded by Dr. Frank C. Laubach. Its purpose is to enable adults and older youths to acquire the skills they need to solve the problems encountered in daily life.

Grade Levels Covered: Teenagers and adults

Subject Areas Covered: Listening, speaking, reading, writing, and math

Instructional Tactics: The Laubach instructional programs are highly structured. Teaching, student evaluation, and remediation of student errors occur sequentially. Reporting and illustrative materials are used to augment initial presentations and demonstrations. Diplomas are given to students when they reach levels of mastery.

The Tutor: No defined credentials are required to teach using the Laubach method. However, to use the method, teachers need to follow the instructor's manuals and use the prescribed materials systematically. The following are the materials used to teach beginning literacy at their Level 1.

There are four levels that approximate the first through fourth grade reading levels in the public school system. (This is only an approximate comparison.)

Materials available for Level 1 are:

For the Students:

- Skill Book 1—Text-workbook in reading and writing
- In the Valley—Reader that is utilized after Skill Book 1 is well started
- Checkups for Skill Book 1—Evaluation of student's mastery of skills taught in Skill Book 1
- Diploma for Skill Book 1

For the Tutor:

- Teacher's Manual for Skill Book 1 (Contains guides for teaching the skills in students' Skill Book 1)
- English as a Second Language (ESOL) Teacher's Manual for Skill Book 1 (Contains guide for evaluating achievement of skills in students' Skill Book 1)
- ESOL Illustrations supporting ESOL Teacher's Manual for Skill Book 1 Levels 2, 3, and 4

Similar style workbooks, readers, evaluations, and diplomas are available for all levels.

Supplementary Materials:

For the Students:

- Focus on Phonics 1—Sounds and names for letters
- More Stories 1—Controlled reader with three extra stories for each lesson
- Crossword Puzzles for Skill Books 1 and 2

For the Teacher:

- Focus on Phonics 1—Teacher's Edition
- Various wall charts, audiotapes, videotapes, and photocopy masters are available at the Center
- Similar style supplementary materials are available at all levels

The materials listed above are utilized within a typical Laubach lesson, which includes the introduction of new phonic sounds, practice drilling the phonic sound, practice reading the story, and writing the new sounds.

Listed below are the typical parts of a Laubach lesson:

- Language experience activity (optional)
- Introduction and review of a new letter from a keyword and key picture

- Review of keywords and new words in a story
- Story read by learners with help from a tutor as needed
- Questions asked about the story
- Other activities for teaching reading and writing as appropriate
- Review of letters from previous lessons
- New letters and words written to reinforce reading, letter formation, and spelling
- Creative writing

This program is available nationally at no cost.

Additional Sources to Consult: For more information, contact Laubach Literacy, 1320 Jamesville Avenue, Box 131, Syracuse, NY 13210.

The Orton-Gillingham Program and the Wilson Reading System are multisensory instructional programs designed to teach language fundamentals to students who have a deficit in a particular sensory modality such as students with dyslexia. The Orton-Gillingham Program teaches reading, writing, and spelling; the Wilson system teaches reading and spelling. The TEACH program appears to be designed to teach students with perceptual/neurological deficits to read. The Programmed Tutorial Reading technique and the Wallach Tutoring Program also focus on the teaching of reading. In both programs, students learn component reading skills before synthesizing them in reading print. The Reading Recovery and Success for All programs have both been adopted by public schools and teach writing as well as reading. Success for All tutoring is designed to be integrated with classroom instruction; Reading Recovery is not. In both programs, students engage in reading before they have completed mastery of component reading skills. The Lindamood-Bell and Laubach Literacy programs teach math as well as language skills. The Laubach Literacy Program is designed for teenagers and adults.

In addition to programs, there are learning centers that provide corrective tutoring. Students with learning difficulties attend the centers on a regularly scheduled basis. The centers provide their own unique environment. The centers charge a fee and usually cater to students across a wider range of grade levels; the fees charged by these centers can be sizable. Many families cannot afford the investment.

So, available one-on-one tutoring methods are quite varied in the grade levels served, subject areas covered, and their approaches. Still, all of the tutoring techniques are designed to remediate students with learning difficulties. They are all highly structured and prescriptive. Tutors are required to follow the prescribed methods using prescribed materials, and little latitude is allowed for teacher innovation. All of the programs deal with reading problems, recognizing how important reading is to independent and lifelong learning as well as learning in all content areas. Tutoring programs are available to treat beginning reading problems in students of all ages. Many programs are designed for beginning readers in the primary grades to nip reading problems in the bud and enable students to read as early as possible. Once students begin to read, the need to read is so prevalent that they are bound to practice and improve their reading skills and scope. Some of the programs focus entirely on reading; some extend to the teaching of other language skills such as speaking, writing, and spelling. The second most popular tutoring programs are those designed to remedy problems in the learning of math. Some more academically oriented tutoring methods are designed to remediate student inadequacies by reteaching in new ways assignments students failed to master during classroom instruction. Other more clinical programs are designed to diagnose and treat underlying causes when academic reteaching is insufficient in overcoming learning difficulties.

REFERENCE LIST

Arnold, L. E., Barnebey, N., McManus, J., Smeltzer, D. J., Conrad, A., & Descranges, L. (1977). Prevention of specific perceptual remediation for vulnerable first-graders. *Archives of General Psychiatry, 34*, 1279–1294.

Clay, M. M. (1979). *Reading: The patterning of reading difficulties.* Exeter, NH: Heinemann.

Dorval, B., Wallach, L., & Wallach, M. A. (1978). Field evaluation of a tutorial reading program emphasizing phoneme identification skills. *The Reading Teacher, 31*, 748–790.

Ellison, D. G., Harris, P., & Barber, L. (1968). A field test of programmed and directed tutoring. *Reading Research Quarterly, 3*, 307–367.

Hagin, R. A., Silver, A. A., & Beecher, R. (1978). Scanning, diagnosis, and intervention in the prevention of learning disabilities: II. TEACH: Learning tasks for the prevention of learning disabilities. *Journal of Learning Disabilities, 11*(7), 54–57.

Huck, C. S., & Pinnell, G. S. (1986). *The Reading Recovery Project in Columbus, Ohio. Pilot Year, 1984–1985.* Columbus, OH: Ohio State University.

Lyons, C., Pinnell, G. S., Deford, D., McCarrier, A., & Schnug, J. (1989). *The Reading Recovery Project in Columbus, Ohio. Year 3: 1988–1989.* Columbus, OH: Ohio State University.

Madden, N. A., Slavin, R. E., Karweit, N. L., Dolan, L. J., Wasik, B. A., Shaw, A., Leighton, M., & Mainzer, K. L. (1991, April). *Success for All third-year results.* Paper presented at the annual convention of the American Educational Research Association, Chicago.

McCleary, E. (1971). Report of results of Tutorial Reading Project. *The Reading Teacher, 24*, 556–559.

Pinnell, G. S., Short, A. G., Lyons, C. A., & Yolng, P. (1986). *The Reading Recovery Project in Columbus, Ohio. Year 1: 1985–1986.* Columbus, OH: Ohio State University.

Silver, A. A., & Hagin, R. A. (1990). *Disorders of learning in childhood.* New York: John Wiley & Sons.

Slavin, R. E., Madden, N. A., Karweit, N. L., Dolan, L., & Wasik, B. A. (1992). *Success for All: A relentless approach to prevention and early intervention in elementary schools.* Arlington, VA: Educational Research Service.

Wallach, M. A., & Wallach, L. (1976). *Teaching all children to read.* Chicago: University of Chicago Press.

29

Instructional Testing and Evaluation

Once students are placed in instructional programs, instruction begins. After instruction prescribed to achieve learning objectives is completed, instructional prescription testing is done as a basis for prescribing subsequent instruction. Test results are used to make one of two decisions: (1) students have achieved the learning objective and are ready to pursue the next, more advanced learning objective in the program or (2) students have not yet achieved the learning objective and need corrective instruction to be ready to advance. In other words, students have learning deficiencies in need of remediation.

To be useful in making instructional prescription decisions, instructional prescription tests must indicate achievement of learning objectives so that students who achieve them can be advanced and students with deficiencies that need to be remediated can achieve the learning objectives. The more an instructional prescription test reveals about student deficiencies, the more useful it is in prescribing remedial instruction. The least an instructional prescription test must be able to do is indicate the degree of deficiency of the characteristic or skill being assessed. This tends to indicate the amount of corrective instruction needed for students to achieve the learning objective. Students with greater deficiencies need more corrective instruction over time to achieve the objective. Plans can be made to reteach the skills students failed to master using various instructional techniques shown by research to be effective. Instructional prescription tests can be more effective to the extent that they reveal deficiencies in subskills that contribute to the performance of the primary skill being taught. For example, if the skill being taught is solving basic arithmetic story problems, students might exhibit a deficiency in choosing the appropriate procedure (addition, subtraction, multiplication, or division) or the deficiency might be in calculation. An instructional prescription test that not only reveals the degree of deficiency in solving arithmetic story problems but also reveals whether the deficiency results from choosing the correct arithmetic procedures, executing the calculations correctly, or both is useful in prescribing corrective instruction because it indicates subskill deficiencies that must be remediated to increase student overall performance on an arithmetic story problem test.

The accountability testing movement was initiated largely because students with learning deficiencies were being promoted and graduated despite their inability to contribute to their own or society's best interests. Although accountability testing legislation may be successful in preventing social promotion and graduation, it does not address students' failure to achieve learning objectives. These students must receive remedial instruction so that they can earn promotion. In order for remedial instruction to be effective, it must be prescribed to correct particular learning deficiencies that caused the students to fail. This requires that instructional prescription tests reveal student academic deficiencies.

After instructional programs have been taught lesson by lesson, it is necessary to certify the achievement of the students in the program by administering achievement certification tests. Achievement certification tests summarize students' learning of the various lessons taught in one or more instructional programs. In that sense, achievement certification tests are comprehensive tests covering all of the knowledge and skills taught in the lessons of one or more instructional programs. Student performance on achievement certification tests is used to assign grades to students, promote them, or graduate them. Grade assignment decisions are made before promotion decisions, and promotion decisions are presumably based on assigned grades. Promotion decisions are made before graduation decisions, and graduations typically are conferred as a result of progressive promotions.

Ideally, achievement certification tests are given after instructional programs are completed to assess the learning generated by the programs. And, ideally, the instructional programs provide all students with the instruction they need to pass the tests. However, this is seldom the case. There is no guarantee that the tests will not be given before teachers complete instructional programs. Time constraints are imposed. Grades are due at pre-set time intervals. Promotions occur at set times, as do graduations. This makes it possible for students to be given achievement certification tests before they complete the instructional programs the tests were designed to assess. Although teachers may have completed instructional programs before corresponding achievement certification tests are given, there is no assurance that all students received all of the instruction they need to pass the tests. It is not only possible but also probable that many students who fail achievement certification tests might have passed the tests if they had been given the extra instruction they needed during a grading period. So, time constraints and the amount of instruction teachers are able to provide during a grading period can affect students' performance on achievement certification tests. Too often achievement certification testing is considered separately from the instruction needed to pass the tests.

It takes more than achievement results to make justifiable decisions that impact people's lives. Justifiable decisions are most often derived from a comparison of achievement results and established criteria of desirable achievement—a process we call evaluation. In education, student achievement is compared to establishing learning objectives to determine grades, promotion, and graduation. Accurate evaluations depend upon accurate comparisons of student achievement with learning objectives and the accurate reporting of the discrepancy between the two. Inaccurate evaluation decisions occur because of (1) inaccurate assessment of student achievement, (2) use of unauthorized learning objectives, (3) inaccurate comparison of achievement and objectives, and/or (4) inaccurate reporting of the discrepancy between student achievement and learning objectives.

Grade inflation and unjustified promotion and graduation were a result of pressure not to fail students. The practice of unwarranted promotion became known as "social promotion." Accountability legislation was enacted because too many students were promoted and graduated without achieving learning objectives, resulting in a flood of illiterate and undereducated students entering the job market. Objective accountability testing resulted in a great many students who would have been promoted routinely to be retained in grade. Teachers and administrators who previously received acceptable evaluations also suffered because of accountability legislation. However they may have been evaluated in the past, accountability legislation imposes severe penalties on them when their students did not meet accountability standards. At present, students, parents, teachers, and administrators are all stunned by the consequences of accountability legislation and testing.

Social promotion can be curbed without states engaging in testing overkill and entering the test construction business. Accurate, comprehensive, nationally standardized achievement certification tests are available from reputable test publishers. They can be administered in as little as six hours and scored by the publishers.

30

Standards for Evaluating Criteria

The literature in curriculum and instruction has been unnecessarily complex, often confusing. Few clear-cut prescriptions for practice have been identified. To simplify and clarify issues somewhat, instruction can be distinguished as pertaining to *how* students are taught and curriculum to *what* they are taught. The 21 effective instructional strategies we have identified in this book go a long way toward simplifying and clarifying *how* students should be taught. Each of them has been shown to increase academic achievement significantly in the various subjects taught in school. They can be incorporated into almost any existing instructional program or program being planned. If the 21 effective instructional strategies are used, students can learn almost any curriculum one may want to teach them.

So, the choice of what curriculum to teach students can be based on what it is *desirable* to teach students or on value judgment. It follows that curriculum evaluation is conducted by comparing the desired curriculum content with the actual content. Instructional evaluation is conducted by comparing learning objectives with actual student achievement. It is necessary to conduct ongoing evaluation of both curriculum and instruction.

The following standards represent what specialists in particular subject areas deem desirable to teach. Both instructional and curriculum evaluation needs to be used to evaluate the achievement of these standards.

Curriculum Standards for English Language Arts

Derivation of Criteria: The National Council of Teachers of English and the International Reading Association, through an intensive four-year project published in 1996, developed the standards for English language arts. Thousands of educators were involved in writing, reviewing, and revising the many drafts of the document, along with researchers, parents, policymakers, and others across the country who jointly developed the criteria for the standards. The English Language Arts Standards Project was a field-based process that was open and inclusive.

Criteria: The 12 standards for English language arts should be viewed as interrelated and be considered as a whole. The standards assume that literacy begins before children start school, and these standards should be used to encourage the development of instruction and curricula that make use of the literacy abilities children bring to school. The standards are defined in the following section.

English Language Arts Standards

Standard and Explanation

1. Students read a wide range of print and non-print texts to build an understanding of texts, of themselves, and of the cultures of the United States and the world; to acquire new information; to respond to the needs and demands of society and the workplace; and for personal fulfillment. Among these texts are fiction and nonfiction, classic and contemporary works.

2. Students read a wide range of literature from many periods in many genres to build an understanding of the many dimensions (e.g., philosophical, ethical, aesthetic) of human experience.

3. Students apply a wide range of strategies to comprehend, interpret, evaluate, and appreciate texts. They draw on their prior experience, their interactions with other readers and writers, their knowledge of word meaning and of other texts, their word identification strategies, and their understanding of textual features (e.g., sound-letter correspondence, sentence structure, context graphics).

4. Students adjust their use of spoken, written, and visual language (e.g., conventions, style, vocabulary) to communicate effectively with a variety of audiences and for different purposes.

5. Students employ a wide range of strategies as they write and use different writing process elements appropriately to communicate with different audiences for a variety of purposes.

6. Students apply knowledge of language structure, language conventions (e.g., spelling and punctuation), media techniques, figurative language, and genres to create, critique, and discuss print and non-print texts.

7. Students conduct research on issues and interests by generating ideas and questions and by posing problems. They gather, evaluate, and synthesize data from a variety of sources (e.g., print and non-print texts, artifacts, people) to communicate their discoveries in ways that suit their purpose and audience.

8. Students use a variety of technological and information resources (e.g., libraries, data bases, computer networks, video) to gather and synthesize information and to create and communicate knowledge.

9. Students develop an understanding of and respect for diversity in language use, patterns, and dialects across cultures, ethnic groups, geographic regions, and social roles.

10. Students whose first language is not English make use of their first language to develop competency in the English language arts and to develop understanding of content across the curriculum.

11. Students participate as knowledgeable, reflective, creative, and critical members of a variety of literacy communities.

12. Students use spoken, written, and visual language to accomplish their own purposes (e.g., for learning, enjoyment, persuasion, and the exchange of information).

Sources: http://www.ncte.org/standards/standards.shtml or http://www.ira.org/advocacy/elastandards/.

Cautions and Comments: The standards, while extensive, are broad in their descriptions and may complicate the ability to assess student performance and program success. Prior to conducting the evaluation, it will be incumbent upon the evaluator to clarify the purpose of the evaluation and the aspect(s) of any or all standards to be evaluated. Given the developers' caution that the standards are not intended to be distinct and separable, the ability to create any program evaluation in English language arts will require great care and discussion.

Publishers: The National Council of Teachers of English, 1111 West Kenyon Road, Urbana, IL 61801-1096; Phone: 800-369-6283; Fax: 217-328-9645; Web site: http://www.ncte.org.

The International Reading Association, 800 Barksdale Road, P.O. Box 8139, Newark, DE 19714-8139; Phone: 802-731-1600; Fax: 302-731-1057; Web site: http://www.ira.org.

Curriculum Standards for English as a Second Language

Derivation of Criteria: Several groups have contributed to the development of standards for English as a Second Language (ESL) programs, including Teachers of English to Speaker of Other Languages (TESOL), teachers representing individual states, and members of the National Association for Bilingual Education (NABE). Content area standards were examined as part of the process. The standards were released for review and comment in 1996 from educators with experience in linguistically and culturally diverse student learning. TESOL published the final standards in 1997.

Criteria: The ESL standards were written for English Language Learners (ELL) with three goals and three standards within each goal. The standards are as follows:

National Standards for ESL

Goal	*Standards*
To use English to communicate in social settings.	Students will use English to participate in social interactions.
	Students will interact in, through, and with spoken and written English for personal expression and enjoyment.
	Students will use learning strategies to extend their communicative competence.
To use English to achieve academically in all content areas.	Students will use English to interact in the classroom.
	Students will use English to obtain, process, construct, and provide subject matter information in spoken and written form.
	Students will use appropriate learning strategies to construct and apply academic knowledge.
To use English in socially and culturally appropriate ways.	Students will use appropriate language variety, register, and genre according to audience, purpose, and setting.
	Students will use nonverbal communication appropriate to audience, purpose, and setting.
	Students will use appropriate learning strategies to extend their sociolinguistic and sociocultural competence.

Source: http://www.cal.org/ericcll/digest/0013eslstandards.html.

Cautions and Comments: The standards for ESL learning are intended to state what students should know and be able to do as a result of ESL instruction. Any evaluation of ESL programs will have to ensure attention to the time frame in which students have had to learn English as well as the quality of the instruction received. Acquisition of a second language can be influenced by many factors including age at introduction, opportunities for successful practice, and cultural factors related to acquiring a new language. The evaluator will want to include considerations for these and, possibly, other factors in program evaluation. Some forms of evaluation may be difficult (e.g., surveys) unless they are administered in the individual's native language. This may be particularly true when surveying parents.

Publisher: Teachers of English as a Second Language, 700 South Washington Street, Suite 200, Alexandria, VA 22314; Phone: 703-836-0774; Fax: 703-836-7864; Web site: http://www.tesol.org.

Curriculum Standards for Information Literacy

Derivation of Criteria: The American Association of School Libraries (AASL), a division of the American Library Association (ALA), published standards in 1998 that provide information literacy standards for student learning.

Criteria: The nine standards for information literacy are divided into three areas. The standards follow.

National Information Literacy Standards

Information Literacy	*Independent Learning*	*Social Responsibility*
The student who is information literate:	The student who is an independent learner is information literate and:	The student who contributes positively to the learning community and to society is information literate and:
accesses information efficiently and effectively.	pursues information related to personal interests.	recognizes the importance of information to a democratic society.
evaluates information critically and competently.	appreciates literature and other creative expressions of information.	practices ethical behavior in regard to information and information technology.
uses information accurately and creatively.	strives for excellence in information seeking and knowledge generation.	participates effectively in groups to pursue and generate information.

Source: http://www.ala.org/aasla.

Cautions and Comments: The information literacy standards of the AASL provide a framework for the development of library media programs, which can be developed in a school or for a district. The standards are broad and do not provide specific criteria for addressing them. However, the AASL provides support through its web site, conferences, and publications to assist library media specialists in the development and evaluation of programs. In addition to the national standards, evaluators will need to consider specific curriculum goals that have been established at the local or state level in evaluating the effectiveness of a given program in meeting these standards.

Publisher: AASL/YALSA, 50 East Huron, Chicago, IL 60611; Phone: 800-545-2433; AASL direct dial: 312-280-4386; Fax: 312-664-7459; Web site: http://www.ala.org/aasl/.

Curriculum Standards for Mathematics

Derivation of Criteria: The National Council of Teachers of Mathematics (NCTM) has released four major works related to standards in mathematics. In 1989, *Curriculum and Evaluation Standards for School Mathematics* was released, followed by *Professional Teaching Standards for School Mathematics* in 1991 and *Assessment Standards for School Mathematics* in 1995. The most recent publication, *Principles and Standards for School Mathematics* (2000), was designed to offer common language, examples, and recommendations to engage productive dialogue about mathematics education. These standards and principles were developed by groups of teachers and university faculty who are members of the NCTM and were revised based on an extensive open review process by others in the field.

Criteria: The principles and standards serve two different purposes. The principles address issues that influence the development of curriculum frameworks and materials and the planning of lessons, the design of assessment, the assignment of teachers and students to classes, instructional decisions, and staff development.

The standards provide an update to the standards from 1989 to meet students' and society's needs in the twenty-first century. They are created to cover the range of education from pre-kindergarten through twelfth grade. The NCTM provides extensive resources to address the standards on its web site. The principles and standards are presented in the following figures.

NCTM Principles for School Mathematics

Principle	*Explanation*
Equity	Equity is a core element which demands that reasonable and appropriate accommodations are made to promote access and attainment for all students.
Curriculum	Mathematical ideas are linked to and build on one another so that students' understanding and knowledge deepens and their ability to apply mathematics expands.
Teaching	Effective teaching in mathematics requires understanding what students know and need to learn and then challenging and supporting them to learn it well.
Learning	Learning requires the alliance of factual knowledge, procedural proficiency, and conceptual understanding.

Principle	*Explanation*
Assessment	Assessment should enhance students' learning.
Technology	Technology allows students to focus on decision-making, reflection, reasoning, and problem solving.

NCTM Standards for Mathematics

Standard	*Explanation*
Number and operations	The mathematics program should enable all students to understand numbers, understand meanings of operations, and compute fluently.
Algebra	The mathematics program should enable all students to understand patterns, represent and analyze mathematical situations and structures using algebraic symbols, use mathematical models to represent and understand quantitative relationships, and analyze change in various contexts.
Geometry	The mathematics program should enable all students to learn about geometric shapes and structures and to analyze their characteristics and relationships.
Measurement	The mathematics program should enable all students to understand measurable attributes and apply appropriate techniques, tools, and formulas to determine measurements.
Data analysis and probability	The mathematics program should enable all students to formulate questions, select and use appropriate statistical methods, develop and evaluate inferences and predictions based on data, and understand and apply basic concepts of probability.
Problem solving	The mathematics program should enable all students to build new mathematical knowledge, solve problems, apply and adapt a variety of appropriate strategies, and monitor and reflect on the process of problem solving.
Reasoning and proof	The mathematics program should enable all students to recognize reasoning and proof as fundamental aspects of mathematics, make and investigate mathematical conjectures, develop and evaluate mathematical arguments and proofs, and select and use various types of reasoning and methods of proofs.
Communication	The mathematics program should enable all students to organize and consolidate mathematical thinking through communication, communicate their mathematical think-

Standard	*Explanation*
	ing coherently and clearly, analyze and evaluate the mathematical thinking and strategies of others, and use the language of mathematics to express mathematical ideas precisely.
Connections	The mathematics program should enable all students to recognize and use connections among mathematical ideas, understand how mathematical ideas interconnect, and recognize and apply mathematics in contexts outside mathematics.
Representation	The mathematics program should enable all students to create and use representations to organize, record, and communicate mathematical ideas; select, apply, and translate among mathematical representations; and use representations to model and interpret physical, social, and mathematical phenomena.

Source: http://www.nctm.org.

Cautions and Comments: There are two aspects of the NCTM *Principles and Standards for School Mathematics* which have implications for program evaluation. First, the six principles serve to address the concern of the members of the organization that mathematics is more than any specific curriculum and that there is recognition that different districts and states may have different reasons for developing specific curricula. These principles can provide a framework for assessing the mathematics program in general in a given school or district. Second, the 10 standards provide a common foundation of mathematics to be learned by all students with consideration for the six principles.

Evaluation procedures used will depend on the purpose of the evaluation and the information desired. For example, a committee of teachers, administrators, and parents might be used to determine if the district curriculum and instructional program in mathematics adheres to the six principles set forth by the NCTM. A note of caution requires that consideration be given to the objectivity needed to analyze critically one's own program. Another example might be a more quantitative analysis of student test scores on standardized tests to evaluate current student achievement toward the standards. Yet another example might be a curriculum matching task conducted by teachers and administrators to ensure that lesson plans and instruction are aligned with the district curriculum and state and national standards as set forth by the NCTM.

Publisher: National Council of Teachers of Mathematics (NCTM), 1906 Association Drive, Reston, VA 20191-1502; Phone: 703-620-9840; Fax: 703-476-2970; Web site: http://www.nctm.org.

Curriculum Standards for Physical Education

Derivation of Criteria: In 1995, the National Association for Sport and Physical Education (NASPE) developed standards for physical education following the development (in 1986) of five major focus areas that define what a physically educated person can do. The standards are supported by sample performance benchmarks to describe developmentally appropriate behaviors.

Criteria : The standards are based on five major focus areas defined to specify that a physically educated person (1) has learned skills necessary to perform a variety of physical activities, (2) is physically fit, (3) participates regularly in physical activity, (4) knows the implications of and the benefits from involvement in physical activities, and (5) values physical activity and its contribution to a healthful lifestyle. The content standards are as follows:

National Physical Education Standards

- Demonstrates competency in many movement forms and proficiency in a few movement forms.
- Applies involvement concepts and principles to the learning and development of motor skills.
- Exhibits a physically active lifestyle.
- Achieves and maintains a health-enhancing level of physical fitness.
- Demonstrates responsible personal and social behavior in physical activity settings.
- Demonstrates understanding and respect for differences among people in physical activity settings.
- Understands that physical activity provides opportunities for enjoyment, challenge, self-expression, and social interaction.

Source: http://www.ed.gov/databases/eric_digests/ed406361.html.

Cautions and Comments: The physical education standards provide a framework for the development of curriculum. The NASPE provides curricular recommendations and sample benchmarks for the implementation of developmentally appropriate activities. Evaluation of programs in physical education will likely be highly performance based, and curricula should be measured against the framework provided in the standards.

Publisher: The American Alliance for Health, Physical Education, Recreation & Dance, 1900 Association Drive, Reston, VA 20192-1598; Phone: 800-213-7193; Web site: http://www.aahperd.org/naspe/template.cfm.

Curriculum Standards for Adapted Physical Education

Derivation of Criteria: The first definitive national standards in adapted physical education define what any professional needs to know to teach students with disabilities. The standards were developed through a committee process where a professional in the field headed each standard. The standards were developed through the *National Consortium for Physical Education and Recreation for Individuals with Disabilities* (NCPERID).

Criteria:

National Adapted Physical Education Standards

1. Human Development
2. Motor Behavior
3. Exercise Science
4. Measurement and Evaluation
5. History and Philosophy
6. Unique Attributes of Learners
7. Curriculum Theory and Development
8. Assessment
9. Instructional Design and Planning
10. Teaching
11. Consultation and Staff Development
12. Student and Program Evaluation
13. Continuing Education
14. Ethics
15. Communication

Source: http://www.twu.edu/o/apens/natstnd.html.

Cautions and Comments: The adapted physical education standards provide a framework for the development of curriculum for teaching individuals with disabilities. The NCPERID provides information on major components of the standard, subcomponents, adapted physical education content, and applications of content knowledge for assessing individuals with disabilities in adapted physical education. Evaluation of programs in adapted physical education will likely be highly performance based, and curricula should be measured against the framework provided in the standards.

Publisher: The National Consortium for Physical Education and Recreation for Individuals with Disabilities (NCPERID); Phone 813-974-3443; Fax: 813-974-4979; Web site: http://www.twu.edu/o/apens/ncperid.htm.

Curriculum Standards for Science

Derivation of Criteria: The Governing Board of the National Research Council (NRC) approved the National Science Education Standards in 1996. The NRC members are drawn from the councils of the National Academy of Sciences, the National Academy of Engineering, and the Institute of Medicine. The NRC reports that the committee responsible for the report of the standards was chosen for their specific competences and with regard for balance. The National Science Teachers Association (NSTA) supports the use of the standards to guide a vision of science education in schools and suggests that the standards provide a framework to make decisions about how well an educational system supports and is progressing toward a scientifically literate society.

Criteria: The standards for science teaching are grounded in five assumptions: (1) changes are needed throughout the entire system, (2) teaching greatly influences what students learn, (3) teachers' perceptions of science as an enterprise and a subject to be taught and learned affects their actions, (4) individual and social processes actively contribute to constructing student understanding, and (5) teachers' actions deeply influence their understanding and relationships with students. The standards focus on qualities most associated with science teaching and the vision of science education described in the following.

The National Science Education Standards

- *Science Teaching Standards*: Define what teachers of science should know and be able to do.

- *Professional Development Standards*: Present a vision for the development of professional knowledge and skills among teachers.

- *Assessment Standards*: Provide criteria against which to judge the quality of assessment practices.

- *Science Content Standards*: Outline what students should know, understand, and be able to do in the natural sciences over the course of K–12 education.

- *Science Education Program Standards*: Describe the conditions necessary for quality school programs.

- *Science Education System Standards*: Provide criteria for judging the performance of the overall science education system.

Source: http://www.nsta.org/159&id=24.

Cautions and Comments: The standards are organized in six general areas and cover the range of teaching, content, assessment, professional development, and program standards. Each of the areas is extensively described and supporting documentation is provided. The NSTA is working through various groups to ensure the implementation of the standards and encourages evaluation of them. Depending on the purpose of the evaluation, the specific criteria and descriptions would have to be examined and decisions made regarding which aspects should be included in the evaluation.

Publisher: The National Academies, 2101 Constitution Avenue NW, Washington, DC 20418; Phone: 202-334-2000; Web site: http://www.national academies.org/nrc/governing.html.

Curriculum Standards for Social Studies

Derivation of Criteria: The Curriculum Standards for Social Studies were developed by a Task Force of the National Council for the Social Studies (NCSS) and approved by the NCSS Board of Directors in April 1994.

Criteria: According to the NCSS, the social studies standards provide an irreducible minimum of what is essential in social studies. The standards are established as 10 thematic curriculum standards, and the NCSS provides student performance expectations and instructional guidelines. The standards (presented below) were intended to provide criteria for making decisions about why to teach social studies, what to teach, how to teach well to all students, and how to assess what students can apply of what they have learned. The 10 thematic curriculum standards and accompanying sets of student performance expectations constitute an irreducible minimum of what is essential in social studies.

NCSS Social Studies Standards

- *Culture*: Social studies programs should include experiences that provide for the study of culture and cultural diversity.
- *Time, continuity, and change*: Social studies programs should include experiences that provide for the study of the ways human beings view themselves in and over time.
- *People, places, and environments*: Social studies programs should include experiences that provide for the study of people, places, and environments.
- *Individual development and identity*: Social studies programs should include experiences that provide for the study of individual development and identity.
- *Individuals, groups, and institutions*: Social studies programs should include experiences that provide for the study of interactions among individuals, groups, and institutions.
- *Power, authority, and governance*: Social studies programs should include experiences that provide for the study of how people create and change structures of power, authority, and governance.

- *Production, distribution, and consumption*: Social studies programs should include experiences that provide for the study of how people organize for the production, distribution, and consumption of goods and services.

- *Science, technology, and society*: Social studies programs should include experiences that provide for the study of relationships among science, technology, and society.

- *Global connections*: Social studies programs should include experiences that provide for the study of global connections and interdependence.

- *Civic ideals and practices*: Social studies programs should include experiences that provide for the study of the ideals, principles, and practices of citizenship in a democratic republic.

Source: http://www.ncss.org/standards.

Caution and Comments: The Curriculum Standards for Social Studies provide a broad framework from which curriculum developers can create specific curricula for schools, districts, and states. While they can be used to assess programs in social studies, the evaluation would need to include the curriculum which has been designed based on the standards.

Publisher: National Council for the Social Studies, 8555 Sixteenth Street, Suite 500, Silver Spring, MD 20910; Phone: 301-588-1800; Fax: 301-588-2049; Web site: http://www.ncss.org.

Content Standards for Special Education

Derivation of Criteria: The Council for Exceptional Children (CEC) has identified 10 standards that are designed to be used across all programs that train teachers for serving students with disabilities. These standards have been approved by the National Council for Accreditation of Teacher Education and were used in 2002 for program approval.

Criteria: The three areas for evaluation of special education programs are: Field Experience and Clinical Practice Standards, Assessment System Standards, and Special Education Content Standards. The standards are presented in the figure that follows. Extensive narrative is provided with each of the standards through the CEC.

National Standards for Special Education Program Evaluation

Field Experiences and Clinical Practice Standard	*Assessment System Standards*	*Content Standards*
	Assessments address components of each content standard	Foundations

Field Experiences and Clinical Practice Standard	*Assessment System Standards*	*Content Standards*
	Assessments are relevant and consistent with each content standard	Development characteristics of learners
	Assessments are planned, refined, and implemented by key stakeholders	Individual learning differences
	Multiple measures both internal and external) are used and are systematic and ongoing across components of the program	Instructional strategies
	The assessment system is clearly delineated and communicated to candidates	Learning environments and social interactions
	Assessments are credible and rigorous	Language
	The assessment system includes critical decision points	Instructional planning
	The assessment data are regularly and systematically compiled, analyzed, and summarized	Assessment
	The assessment data are used for program improvement	Professional and ethical practice; Collaboration

Source: http://www.cec.sped.org.

Cautions and Comments: The purpose of these standards is to address the preparation of teachers for positions in special education. The unique nature of this field of education requires that there be attention to the specific needs that are evidenced by the disability being addressed. These are addressed in the narrative provided by the CEC. While the standards are, for the most part, used by faculty in college and university teacher preparation programs, they serve to inform school administrators of expectations established for the preparation that future employees in this field should demonstrate.

Publisher: Council for Exceptional Children, 1110 North Glebe Road, Suite 300, Arlington, VA 22201; Voice phone: 703-620-3660; TTY: 703-264-9446; Fax: 703-264-9494; Web site: http://www.cecsped.org.

These standards give a structure to be used by states and school districts to construct the curricula they consider desirable to teach in these content areas. Exactly what is contained in those curricula is, again, a value judgment and may differ according to what parents, teachers, and administrators in a particular state or district desire. If the twenty-one effective instructional strategies identified in this book are used, any curriculum can be taught effectively. Whatever the curriculum, evaluation of it is conducted by comparing the curriculum constructed by the state and district to the actual content being taught.

31

Signs of Common Disabilities

Teachers are in an excellent position to identify and refer students with learning difficulties to parents, school professionals, or outside clinicians for further evaluation and treatment they may need to succeed in school. However, many teachers have not been sufficiently prepared to recognize signs of common disabilities that underlie the learning difficulties students in their classes may have. This makes them ambivalent about engaging in referral assessment. They recognize the importance of identifying and treating underlying causes of student failure to learn and want to help. On the other hand, they are keenly aware of their limitations in diagnosing and treating impediments to learning that require the expertise of clinical specialists. Until educators learn to conduct the simple screening needed to make referrals, we cannot expect matters to improve. How much they need to learn to make referrals is debatable. It is the purpose of this chapter to introduce educators to observable signs of common underlying causes of failure to learn: impaired vision, impaired hearing, problem behavior, perceptual-motor impairment, and inadequate adaptive behavior. Referral assessment is reviewed in greater detail in the *Educators' Handbook on Effective Testing* (see Nickerson, 2003).

VISION IMPAIRMENT REFERRALS

Much of learning occurs through the visual system, and unresolved visual problems can impact a student's ability to respond fully to educational instruction. It has been shown that students with learning problems have a higher incidence of vision disorders than children who do not have learning problems (Birnbaum, 1993; Hoffman, 1980; Optometric Extension Program Foundation, 1998).

The visual system involves both eyesight and vision. Eyesight is the ability to see, whereas vision is the ability to interpret and understand information that comes through the eyes. Schools typically screen for problems with students' eyesight with tools such as the Snellen Eye Chart. However, eye professionals caution that children assessed to have perfect (20/20) eyesight may still have vision problems that could interfere with learning. In fact, many children with vision problems that affect learning actually have above-average visual acuity (Optometric Extension Program Foundation, 1998).

There are several types of vision, which will be briefly described below. Although educators need not be overly concerned about detecting distinctions between the various types of sight and vision, it is important to have some knowledge of the types of vision, in addition to the common signs and symptoms that may indicate a referral for more extensive vision assessment.

The first type of vision is ocular motility, or eye movement skills. These skills include the speed and control of visual inspection that are involved in tasks such as scanning instructional materials. A second type of vision is binocularity, or eye teaming skills. This involves the two eyes working together, which is a skill that is acquired by children in the preschool years. Eye-hand coordination skills specifically refer to the integration of the eye and hand as paired learning tools and are involved in tasks such as drawing and copying. Visual form perception is how people relate experiences to the pictures and words seen on printed pages. Refractive status refers to nearsightedness and farsightedness and is the type of vision with which educators may be most familiar (Optometric Extension Program Foundation, 1985).

The following descriptions of observable manifestations for each of these types of vision were compiled from guidelines by Green (2000), Jose (1983), and the Optometric Extension Program Foundation (1985). Problems with eye movement skills would most likely be observed when the student is reading or completing worksheets. Signs to look for include slow, clumsy, or jumpy eye movements; shortened attention to visually demanding materials; movement of the head back and forth when reading; using the finger to underscore words when reading; and increased fatigue and/or restlessness when involved in these activities.

Signs suggesting a problem with binocularity include general clumsiness, squinting or blinking, and little interest in visually demanding tasks, with a strong preference for listening activities. A student with this problem may report double vision, which he or she may try to adapt to by resting his or her head while writing, sitting in an awkward position when reading, or covering one eye when reading or writing.

Children with eye-hand coordination problems may produce paperwork that shows a lack of coordination and illegibility. These children may be unable to stay within the lines when coloring or be slow to copy information off the board. In addition, they may appear to be clumsy in sports and other activities.

Students with problems in visual form perception are regarded as careless about details. They often confuse similarities by reversing letter forms and letter sequences in words. Other signs to look for include difficulty recognizing the same word in the next sentence or page or apparent lack of skill in drawing.

Lastly, the most obvious sign of problems with nearsightedness or farsightedness is avoidance of specific tasks. For example, a child may avoid nearsighted tasks (e.g., desk activity and workbooks) or tasks that require seeing from a distance (e.g., copying from a chalkboard).

Useful information about a child's possible vision problems can be obtained by listening to the child read. Birnbaum (1993) outlines reading habits that may indicate vision problems, as compared to those that may suggest learning difficulties. For example, students with inadequate visual form perception may have poor sight recognition and show a tendency to read in a slow, laborious fashion. They may also have difficulty recognizing familiar words and confuse words that look alike. In contrast, students with poor phonic skills may recognize familiar words but be unable to decode unfamiliar or multisyllabic words.

HEARING IMPAIRMENT REFERRALS

Like vision, hearing is closely tied to learning. Undetected hearing loss in children can lead to delayed speech and language development and can contribute to academic as well as social and emotional problems (Gersten, 1997). Hearing problems fall under the broader area of communication disorders including speech, language, and hearing disorders. Schools tend to screen for hearing problems with a portable screening audiometer. Hearing screenings are usually conducted by trained professionals in the schools such as speech and language therapists or school nurses.

Related to hearing is central auditory processing, which is described as what an individual does with what he or she hears. These problems are not as easily detected by hearing screenings and may require more extensive evaluations by professionals such as speech and language pathologists. Because of the importance of hearing and auditory processing to learning, educators need to be aware of signs of these problems and to refer children who may need more extensive testing.

Educators should be aware of observable signs that may indicate a problem with hearing or auditory processing. The following signs are adapted from Katz and Masters (2000) and Sanger (1986). First, children with hearing problems and auditory processing problems may exhibit behavioral signs, such as daydreaming, distractibility, irritability or frustration. When one considers the vast amount of information in school that is presented verbally and required to be heard and understood through the auditory system, it is no surprise that children with difficulties in this area may become easily frustrated or exhibit behaviors often seen as incompatible with learning.

Second, individuals with hearing or auditory processing problems may appear to ignore a person who is speaking to them or respond by saying "what?" or "huh?" or ask for the statement to be repeated. Their understanding may be enhanced when their attention is gained, through making eye contact or being in one-to-one situations. A rule of thumb offered by Adler (1988) is that any third grader who presents with poor selective attention and problems with retaining information should be referred to a speech and language clinician. Prior to this point distractibility is common, but third grade is generally the time when these problems decrease markedly for the typical child.

Third, children with these difficulties may have delayed responses or give inappropriate responses to questions asked. They may misunderstand what is being said and have trouble following multi-step tasks. Another possible manifestation of auditory processing problems is that these children may be slower at learning routines and may prefer to watch other children before doing things on their own.

Fourth, lack of interest in reading may be indicative of auditory processing problems. Children with these difficulties are often better at sight reading than in using phonics. These students may appear to lack motivation or be fatigued by the end of the lesson.

PERCEPTUAL-MOTOR REFERRALS

Perceptual-motor skills typically involve an individual's ability to perceive information, usually through the visual system and to respond to it with motor skills. For example, tasks involving copying symbols and taking notes involve perceptual-motor skills. Perceptual-motor skills are typically assessed for three purposes: (1) screening large groups of children, (2) assessing students with learning difficulties to determine if perceptual-motor deficits are interfering with learning, and (3) diagnosing brain injury (Salvia & Ysseldyke, 2001).

Direct systematic observation of perceptual-motor skills in the natural environment is the most useful way to assess these potential difficulties for children (Salvia & Ysseldyke, 2001; Witt et al., 1998). Because they involve visual perception and motor control, tasks such as writing and copying are good examples of these skills. Several indicators to look for in students' writing include (1) spacing between letters and words, (2) letter size, (3) alignment (proportion of parts of letters in relation to the different parts of the line), (4) quality of lines (consistency of pressure), (5) slant of letters, (6) formation of upper- and lower-case letters, and (7) style such as cursive versus print. The teacher may notice that a child has large spaces between some letters and small spaces between others, or the child may switch between cursive writing and printing. As with any assessment, educators should consider typical performance depending on the child's age and the expectations in the classroom. For example, it is common for young children to reverse letters when first learning to write, and children whose teachers expect them to print should not be penalized for not having neat cursive writing.

In addition to the perceptual-motor difficulties mentioned above that focus specifically on fine motor skills, motor proficiency also involves gross motor skills. Gross motor behavior involves using the arms and legs for movement and coordination and includes such skills as walking, running, and climbing. Impairments in gross motor skills may indicate developmental delays, such as mental retardation.

Basic gross motor skills, such as walking and running, are typically assessed in young children such as those in day care or preschool. Those who fail to meet developmental milestones, such as walking by 18 months, should be referred for further evaluation. Other more complex gross motor skills, such as catching, kicking, and weaving in and out of cones, can be assessed for older children. Possible indicators of gross motor impairment that may be noted by educators include taking extra time in moving from one place to another, clumsiness or poor coordination, and lack of strength compared to children of the same gender, age, and physical build.

ADAPTIVE BEHAVIOR REFERRALS

Adaptive behavior is defined as "the performance of the daily activities required for personal and social sufficiency" (Harrison, 1985, p. 6). Inherent in the definition, and important for assessment, is the degree to which the individual functions independently. Adaptive behavior is largely influenced by cultural norms and age-related expectations (Horn & Fuchs, 1987). Traditionally, adaptive behavior is assessed by having a trained professional such as a psychologist, interview or gather information from people who know the child best such as the parent and/or teacher. Therefore, teachers are critical to the reliable assessment of adaptive behavior.

Adaptive behavior is most often assessed when trying to determine if a person has mental retardation. Although many people think of mental retardation as being an intellectual deficiency, a diagnosis of mental retardation can only be made if there are also deficits in adaptive behavior. Adaptive difficulties for individuals with mental retardation are most evident in practical intelligence (i.e., the ability to maintain oneself as an independent person in the activities of daily living) and social intelligence, or the ability to conduct oneself appropriately in social situations (American Association on Mental Retardation, 1992).

The American Association on Mental Retardation (AAMR, 1992) has identified 10 areas of adaptive skills that are central to successful life functioning. These areas are communication, self-care, home living, social skills, community use, self-direction, health and safety, functional academics, leisure, and work. Communication skills are those that involve comprehending and expressing both verbal and nonverbal information. Self-care skills are involved in toileting, eating, dressing, and grooming oneself. Home living skills are those needed to function in a household, such as housekeeping and cooking. Social skills refer to the skills needed to interact with other individuals, such as recognizing emotions, sharing, and making choices. Community use skills involve using community resources such as purchasing goods from stores and using public restrooms. Self-direction skills are those related to following a schedule, completing tasks, and resolving problems. Health and safety skills are related to maintaining one's health by eating, using basic first aid, and looking both ways before crossing the street. Functional academic skills are those skills that have a direct application to one's life, such as reading and using practical math concepts. Leisure skills are those activities that the individual engages in during free time, and includes skills such as choosing interests, playing socially with others, and behaving appropriately in recreational settings. Finally, work skills are those skills related to holding a job in the community such as completing tasks, managing money, and interacting with coworkers.

Educators are in an excellent position to observe children's adaptive skills and compare them to the skills of same-aged peers. This is particularly important since adaptive behavior is so closely tied to the expectations of behavior for a certain age group. Teachers can use various observation techniques to assess the adaptive skills of students in the 10 areas outlined by the AAMR (1992).

One way to observe and record adaptive skills is through narrative recording. In this method, a teacher makes an anecdotal record of a student's behavior that does not meet the standards expected for his or her age. For example, a kindergarten teacher may be concerned about a child who does not seem to have average communication skills for this age (e.g., able to listen to a story, look at other children when talking, follow verbal instructions to end a task, and answer questions with relevant, complete sentences). She may decide to observe the child during free time every day for a week and keep a narrative of the child's communication. The narrative could read something like this:

> When free time was announced, Johnny continues to sit in his chair while the other students went to the pay centers in the room. After about a minute, he stood up and walked over to the puppet center and picked up a puppet. When his classmate asked him what his puppet's name was, Johnny did not make eye contact and put the puppet on the floor. He wandered over to the art center, and when the teaching assistant asked him if he would like to color and held out a crayon, he took it. After watching another student draw on the paper, Johnny drew a line down the center of the page and made several scribble marks. When the teaching assistant guided the students in writing their names on the paper, Johnny appeared confused and wrote only the first letter of his name, and then looked at the assistant for help.

In this example, the teacher provided useful information about the child's receptive, expressive, and written communication that suggests the child may be functioning at a level lower than his peers. Another method of recording observational data is event recording, or frequency recording. In this method of observation, a behavior could be identified (e.g., asks for help on a lesson). Each time the behavior occurs, the teacher could simply make a hash mark on a piece of paper within a specified time period. The teacher might record how many times a child asks for help within a 30-minute lesson and compare this number to the amount of time an "average" child asks for help, to provide information about how that child functions compared to other children in the class.

One final method of recording observational data that may be useful in the assessment of adaptive skills is duration recording. In this method, the amount of time it takes an individual to perform a task or engage in a behavior is recorded. For example, a teacher may notice that a child seems particularly slow in putting on his or her coat and mittens before going outside. The teacher may actually decide to time how long this takes from the time when she gives the instruction to put coats and mittens on to when the child puts on his coat and mittens and goes to the door. Data that document teachers' observations may be very helpful when making a referral for concerns over a child's adaptive behavior.

PROBLEM BEHAVIOR REFERRALS

Problem behavior is a general term that can include a wide range of behaviors that interfere with a child's learning and development. The large majority of the time, the classroom teacher is the first person to recognize a child's emotional and behavioral difficulties and to initiate a referral.

A commonly accepted and well-researched way to categorize problem behaviors is to divide them into internalizing and externalizing behaviors. Internalizing refers to a class of behavior problems that are directed inwardly and often involve deficits in behaviors such as lack of social skills, withdrawal, and isolation. If these problems are severe enough and interfere with the child's functioning, they may indicate depression or anxiety. Externalizing behaviors, which are often those referred in schools, are those that are directed outwardly and often involve behavior excesses that tend to be disruptive such as physical aggression, hyperactivity, and defiance or noncompliance (Walker et al., 1990).

The first step when observing behavior is to choose a target behavior and create a specific observable definition of it. For example, if a teacher is concerned about a child's being socially isolated, the target behavior may include solitary activity. This may be defined as the time the child spends alone, with a distance of five or more feet between him and the other children, engaging in activities such as reading or playing a game alone. This could be compared to group activity, which would involve the child's interacting with at least one other child by talking, playing a game, or participating in a group activity.

The next stop in observing behavior is to select the type of observational recording method that will be used. As mentioned above in the discussion of adaptive behavior, there are several methods of observation that can be used such as narrative recording, event (or frequency) recording, and duration recording. A final type of recording that may be useful for the educator is interval recording. In this type of recording, the observer selects a segment of time (e.g., 20 minutes) and breaks it into several intervals (e.g., four five-minute intervals or 10 two-minute intervals). At the end of each interval, the observer decides whether or not the behavior occurred during that interval of time.

Externalizing behaviors also lend themselves well to observation, especially since the behaviors are outwardly directed. These problems are the ones that are usually recognized in schools since educators tend to find these behavior problems disturbing and disruptive (Mooney & Algozzine, 1978; Safran & Safran, 1984). Observable manifestations of these difficulties may include calling out or being out of seat, being verbally aggressive (e.g., teasing, swearing, threatening), destroying property, being off task or easily distracted, and refusing to follow directions.

The above review enables educators to understand better five disabilities commonly responsible for student failure to learn and to observe manifestations of them. Records of educators' observations help them decide whether to refer students for an in-depth clinical evaluation and helps clinicians derive an accurate diagnosis. In addition to learning observational techniques for recognizing disability, educators can learn to use informal testing procedures and published tests that require no specialized training to administer and interpret. See "Referral Testing and Decision-Making" in the *Educators' Handbook on Effective Testing* (Nickerson, 2003) for a more comprehensive description of referral assessment tools and recommendations. It would reduce the frustration of teachers and many failing students in their classes if the teachers were prepared to recognize signs and symptoms of common disabilities as a basis for making informed referrals.

REFERENCE LIST

Adler, S. (1988). An introduction to communicative behavior. In S. Adler (Ed.), *Oral communication problems in children and adolescents* (pp. 3–7). Philadelphia: Grune and Stratton.

American Association on Mental Retardation. (1992). *Mental retardation: Definition, classification, and system of supports* (9th ed.). Washington, DC: Author.

Birnbaum, M. H. (1993). Vision disorders frequently interfere with reading and learning: They should be diagnosed and treated. *Journal of Behavioral Optometry, 4*(3), 66–71.

Gersten, C. R. (1997). Detecting potential hearing problems in young children. *Healthy Child Care America, 1*(3), 3–4.

Green, N. S. (2000). The vision connection to learning charts [online]. Available: http://www.kidcite.net/vision_connect.htm.

Harrison, P. L. (1985). *Vineland Adaptive Behavior Rating Scales: Classroom edition manual.* Circle Pines, MN: American Guidance Service.

Hoffman, L. G. (1980). Incidence of vision difficulties in children with learning disabilities. *Journal of the American Optometric Association, 51*(5), 447–451.

Horn, E., & Fuchs, D. (1987). Using adaptive behavior in assessment and intervention: An overview. *The Journal of Special Education, 21*(1), 11–26.

Jose, R. T. (1983). Minimum assessment sequence: The optometrist's viewpoint. In R. T. Jose (Ed.), *Understanding low vision* (pp. 75–83). New York: American Foundation for the Blind.

Katz, J., & Masters, M. B. (2000, October). *Central auditory processing: A coherent approach.* Workshop presented at the United Cerebral Palsy of Philadelphia and Vicinity, Philadelphia, PA.

Mooney, C., & Algozzine, B. (1978). A comparison of the disturbingness of behavior related to learning disabilities and emotional disturbance. *Journal of Abnormal Child Psychology, 6*(3), 401–406.

Nickerson, A. B. (2003). Referral testing and decision-making. In M. I. Friedman, C. W. Hatch, J. E. Jacobs, A. C. Lau-Dickinson, A. B. Nickerson, & K. C. Schnepel, *Educators' handbook on effective testing* (pp. 647–772). Columbia, SC: Institute for Evidence-Based Decision-Making in Education.

Optometric Extension Program Foundation. (1985). Educator's guide to classroom vision problems [online]. Available: http://www.healthy.net/oep/educate.htm.

Optometric Extension Program Foundation. (1998). *When a bright child has trouble reading*. Santa Ana, CA: Author.

Safran, S. P., & Safran, J. S. (1984). Elementary teachers' tolerance of problem behaviors. *Elementary School Journal, 85*(2), 237–243.

Salvia, J., & Ysseldyke, J. E. (2001). *Assessment* (8th ed.). Boston: Houghton Mifflin.

Sanger, D. D. (1986). *Observational profile of classroom communication*. Lincoln: University of Nebraska.

Walker, H. M., Severson, H. H., Todis, B. J., Block-Pedego, A. E., Williams, G. J., Haring, N. G., & Barckley, M. (1990). Systematic screening for behavior disorders (SSBD): Further validation, replication, and normative data. *Remedial and Special Education, 11*(2), 32–46.

Witt, J. C., Elliott, S. M., Daly, E. J., Gresham, F. M., & Kramer, J. J. (1998). *Assessment of at-risk and special needs children* (2nd ed.). Boston: McGraw-Hill.

IV

Statistical Findings by Chapter for Effective Instructional Strategies

INTRODUCTION

This chapter presents the statistical findings used as evidence in support of the instructional tactics associated with each generalization, or chapters 1–21, presented in this handbook. The findings were derived from reviews of groups of research studies and, in some cases, individual studies. The criteria used to include groups of studies and individual studies were (1) that student achievement must be the dependent or outcome variable and (2) that the strategies used must be ones to be used by teachers, not skills that they teach students to use (i.e., study skills). A total of 50 individual studies, representing a combination of reviews of groups of studies and individual studies, was considered the minimum necessary to be considered sufficient research evidence in support of a generalization. There are from 68 to over 600 studies supporting the generalizations.

TYPES OF STUDIES

Reviews of research studies took two forms, one being the logical synthesis of research in which experts in the field look at the results of many individual research studies that pertain to a particular instructional strategy to determine the effect the strategy has on student achievement. To arrive at their conclusions, they look for patterns in the findings across the many studies. The second form of review of research is that of the meta-analysis. Here researchers calculate statistical measures of the effect instructional strategies have on achievement across many studies. It should be noted that quite often both types of review tend to arrive at the same conclusions with respect to the efficacy of instructional strategies on student achievement.

The statistical findings presented, whether from individual studies or meta-analysis of studies, were derived basically from two types of research studies: correlational and group comparison. Correlational studies are used to determine the percentage of variation in students' achievement scores for which an instructional strategy accounts and whether that variation is associated meaningfully with student achievement. Quite typically, many instructional strategies are correlated with a large group of students' achievement scores to determine how much the individual tactics are associated with that particular group of students' achievement. It should be noted that this group of students can represent more than one group of students being analyzed in combination. Group comparison studies are designed to compare the achievement scores of two or more groups of students to determine if differences in instructional strategies employed are likely to generate any meaningful difference in student achievement. They usually compare a group or groups of students being taught using some new instructional strategy to a group of control students being taught using a traditional strategy.

STATISTICAL PROCEDURES

Correlational studies employ basically two types of procedures: simple correlational procedures such as Pearson's r and multiple correlation procedures such as factor analysis, multiple regression, and path analysis. Simple correlational procedures correlate student achievement scores for students who were taught using a new instructional strategy with student achievement scores for students not taught using the new instructional strategy. The result produces a measure of the degree to which new instructional strategies are associated with an effect on student achievement. Multiple correlational procedures correlate multiple instructional strategies with a group or groups of students' achievement scores to measure the degree to which the individual strategies are associated with the students' achievement scores and the degree to which two or more strategies might share in the effect on student achievement scores.

Group comparison studies employ procedures designed to determine the likelihood that any differences measured in student achievement for two or more groups of students are meaningful. In the case of more than two groups of students, the procedures most often used were analysis of variance (ANOVA) and analysis of covariance (ANCOVA). Both procedures provide the researcher information on the likelihood that differences exist in the level of student achievement between the groups of students. Additionally, ANCOVA attempts to control for differences between the groups in such things as student ability and prior achievement. For both procedures, when it was determined that there were likely meaningful differences among the groups, the groups were then analyzed in pairs to determine which group(s) were likely to be meaningfully different from the others in terms of effects on student achievement. The appropriate procedures used most often were t-test, Tukey, and Scheffé pairwise comparison procedures.

Meta-analyses employ statistical procedures to transform the findings of many correlational and group comparison studies into an estimated measure of the effect innovative instructional strategies, in relation to traditional instructional strategies, have on student achievement. Statistical procedures are available to transform any type of statistic into a standardized estimated measure of the effect an instructional strategy has on student achievement. Basically, a group of related research studies is located and estimated measures of the effect on student achievement are calculated for each individual study. The calculated measures are then pooled to arrive at a single measure of estimated effect on student achievement across all of the studies. For the purposes of this handbook, a criterion of 0.5 was used in determining whether the evidence was sufficient to support a generalization. Cohen (1988) identifies an effect size of 0.2 as small, 0.5 as medium, and 0.8 as large, with 0.5 being an important finding in social science research. The following basic descriptions of the most commonly utilized procedures for calculating standardized measures of effect size in meta-analyses were derived from Rosenthal (1994). The most common procedure is the Glass's Δ, where the difference in the mean scores for two groups is divided by the control groups standard deviation. Variations sometimes employed are Cohen's d and Hedges's g, which are similar to Glass's Δ except that they pool the standard deviations for the two groups. Significance tests such as the t-test can be mathematically transformed into Glass's Δ, Hedges's g, or Cohen's d. Cohen's q utilizes the difference between Fisher Zr transformations of correlations of two groups' scores to arrive at a standardized estimate of effect size. Probit d utilizes the difference in standard normal transformed proportions for two groups. Further information on these and additional procedures may be found in Rosenthal (1994), Hedges & Olkin (1985), and Glass et al. (1981).

CAUTIONS AND COMMENTS

Much of the evidence used in support of the generalizations presented in this handbook was derived from reviews of research. Some reviewed correlational studies, some reviewed group comparison studies, and some reviewed a combination thereof. Many researchers consider the findings of group comparison studies to be superior to correlational studies in demonstrating the effects of an independent variable on a dependent variable. However, this position often overlooks the importance of replication of findings across many studies. When a finding keeps recurring across many correlational studies, it should be seen as being important and as evidence in support of the primary relationship between an instructional strategy and learning. Some researchers feel that much of the "experimental research" conducted in education is likewise limited in terms of the strength of the evidence produced because true experiments are seldom possible in natural school settings. As a result, researchers have arrived at the concept of meta-analysis. Although meta-analyses can include correlational studies, they most often are limited to experimental or group comparison-type studies. This review procedure produces a standardized statistical measure of effect across many studies; in essence, a measure of the degree of replication of findings.

REFERENCE LIST

Glass, G. V., McGaw, B., & Smith, M. L. (1981). *Meta-analysis in social research.* Newbury Park, CA: Sage.

Hedges, L. V., & Olkin, I. (1985). *Statistical methods for meta-analysis.* Boston: Academic Press.

Rosenthal, R. (1994). Parametric measures of effect size. In H. Cooper & L. V. Hedges (Eds.), *The handbook of research* (pp. 231–244). New York: Russell Sage.

Statistical Evidence on Taking Student Readiness into Account

GENERALIZATION TESTED: ON STUDENT READINESS—CHAPTER 1

Achievement of learning objectives is enhanced when students possess the readiness capabilities necessary to achieve the learning objectives.

Total number of studies covered: 352+

Table 1.1
Anderson (1994)
Synthesis of Mastery Learning (Meta-analysis) Achievement Outcomes
Number of studies included: 7

Study	Percent Positive	Total N	ES	Grade Level
Kulik et al. (1990a)	93.2%	NR	.52	K–College
Slavin (1990)	NR	NR	.27	K–12
Kulik et al. (1990b)	63.6%	NR	.40	K–12
Guskey & Pigott (1988)	89.1%	11,532	.41 Psych.	K–12
			.50 Science	
			.53 Soc. Stud.	
			.60 Lang. Arts	
			.70 Math	
			.94 Elementary	
			.48 High School	
			.41 College	
Willett et al. (1983)	NR		.64	K–12
Guskey & Gates (1985)	92.2%	8,074	.65–.94	K–College
Block & Burns (1976)	89.0%	2,767	.83	K–College

N = number of students; ES = effect size.

Individual studies analyzed by these meta-analyses are identified in the reference list in Part V by the following symbols:

Kulik et al. (1990a) *
Kulik et al. (1990b) #
Slavin (1990) @
Guskey & Pigott (1988) $
Guskey & Gates (1985) &
Block & Burns (1976) +

It was not possible to determine the individual studies for which readiness was an instructional tactic for the Willett et al. (1983) analysis.

Table 1.2
Rosenshine et al. (1996)
Teaching Students to Generate Questions: A Review of the Intervention Studies
Number of studies included: 26

| | **Overall Median Effect Sizes by Type of Prompt** | | | | | |
| | **Standardized Test** | | | **Experimenter-Developed Test** | | |
Prompt	**Reciprocal Teaching (n = 6)**	**Regular Instruction (n = 7)**	**Combined (n = 13)**	**Reciprocal Teaching (n = 12)**	**Regular Instruction (n = 19)**	**Combined (n = 19)**
Signal words	0.34 (4)	0.46 (2)	0.36 (6)	0.88 (5)	0.67 (2)	0.85 (7)
Generic questions/ Stems					1.12 (4)	1.12 (4)
Main idea		0.70 (1)	0.70 (1)	1.24 (1)	0.13 (4)	0.25 (5)
Question type	0.02 (2)	0.00 (1)	0.00 (3)	3.37 (1)		3.37 (1)
Story grammar					1.08 (2)	1.08 (2)
No facilitator		0.14 (3)	0.14 (3)			

N = number of studies.

Education Commission of the States (1999)
Direct Instruction
Number of studies included: 10

Groups of studies reviewed in this logical synthesis of research did not provide statistical evidence. However, many of the individual studies included in the logical synthesis of research do contain statistical evidence. In the event that a reader wishes to view this evidence, an extensive listing of the individual studies reviewed is provided in the reference list in Part V (the studies are identified by the symbol !).

Ehri et al. (2001)
Phonemic Awareness Instruction Helps Children Learn to Read:
Evidence from the National Reading Panel's Meta-analysis
Number of studies included: 52

The effect size statistic measures how much the mean of the PA-instructed group exceeded the mean of the control group in standard deviation units. An effect size of 1 indicates that the treatment group mean was one standard deviation higher than the control group mean, revealing a strong effect of instruction. An effect size of 0 indicates that treatment and control group means were identical, showing that instruction had no effect. All of the effect sizes involving PA and reading outcomes were statistically greater than zero ($p < .05$). This indicates that instruction was uniformly effective in teaching PA and in facilitating transfer to reading across all levels of the moderator variables that were considered.

The overall effect size of PA instruction on the acquisition of PA was large, $d = 0.86$, based on 72 comparisons. The overall effect size on reading was moderate, $d = 0.53$, based on 90 comparisons. These findings lead us to conclude with much confidence that phonemic awareness instruction is more effective that alternative forms of instruction or no instruction in helping children acquire phonemic awareness and in facilitating transfer of PA skills to reading and spelling.

Swanson (2001)
Research on Interventions for Adolescents with Learning Disabilities:
A Meta-analysis of Outcomes Related to Higher-Order Processing
Number of studies included: 58

Fifty-eight studies included measures of higher-order skills. The average ES across studies was .82 (SD = .66). Instructional components reported in studies were:

1. Advanced organizers
2. Attributions
3. Control difficulty
4. Elaboration
5. Extended practice
6. Large-group learning
7. New skills
8. One-to-one instruction
9. Peer modeling
10. Questioning
11. Reinforcement
12. Sequencing
13. Skill modeling
14. Small-group instruction
15. Strategy cues
16. Supplemental instruction
17. Task reduction
18. Technology

When a factor referred to as "organization/extended practice"—which was the combination of (a) advanced organizers, (b) new content/skills, and (c) extended practice—was entered into the regression model first, followed by age and method, it was significant at $p < .001$. This "organization/extended practice" factor was the only combination factor, which contributed significant variance to effect size.

Rosenshine & Stevens (1986)

Groups of studies reviewed in this logical synthesis of research did not provide statistical evidence. However, many of the individual studies included in the logical synthesis of research do contain statistical evidence. In the event that a reader wishes to view this evidence, an extensive listing of the individual studies reviewed is provided in the reference list in Part V (the studies are identified by the symbol %).

Table 1.3
Carlton & Winsler (1999)
School Readiness: The Need for a Paradigm Shift

Measure	Correlation to Future Achievement	
Gesell Screening Rest	.23	Achievement Test Scores
Gesell School Readiness	.11	Achievement Test Scores
Test-Kindergarten	.23–.64	School Placement
Metropolitan Readiness Tests	.58	Reading Achievement Scores
	.55	Math Achievement Scores
Brigance K–11 Screen	.56	Teacher Referrals
Denver II	.23	Psychological Assessment
Brigance K–1 Screen	.63	Achievement Test Scores
DIAL-R	.53	Special Ed Placement

Martens & Witt (2004)
Competence, Persistence, and Success: The Positive Psychology of Behavioral Skill Instruction
Number of studies included: 40

Groups of studies reviewed in this logical synthesis of research did not provide statistical evidence. However, many of the individual studies included in the logical synthesis of research do contain statistical evidence. In the event that a reader wishes to view this evidence, an extensive listing of the individual studies reviewed is provided in the reference list in Part V (the studies are identified by the symbol ?).

Table 1.4
Karweit (1993)
Effective Preschool and Kindergarten Programs for Students at Risk
Number of studies included: 20

Programs Evaluated with Random Assignment or Matched Control Group Design

Name	Developer	Grade	Content	Instructional Strategy	Evaluation Design	Measures	Effects
Alpha Phonics	So. San Francisco U.S.D.	K	Rdg. Readiness	Readiness phonics program focusing on sequential learning, immediate correction, feedback & game-like presentation for about 1 hr./day.	Post ANOVA treatment sch. & remaining 12 in district. Stated that IQ & background of T & C equivalent. All students there for K–3.	Metropolitan ach. readiness ach. G1 ach. G2 ach. G3	.89 1.14 .90 1.07
Astra Math	So. San Francisco U.S.D.	K	Math Readiness	Comprehensive, structured, and sequenced curriculum with 22 self-contained units. Uses multisensory approach, Behavior modification, and high-interest materials.	Pre-post random assignment to treatment—control 3 classes each.	CTBS fall–spring	.45<1> (adj) .30 (not adj)
MECCA	Trumbull Public Schools (CT)	K	Development & implementation of early identification procedures & prescriptive educational programs for children entering K with specific potential handicaps	Pre-post random assignment to treatment and control.	JANSKY Metropol. Monroe .67 .88	.57 .96
TALK	Rockford, IL school system	K–3	Language	Lang. specialist in class instruction in listening skills for 4 wk ½ hour for 6 mos than classroom tchr continues lessons.	Pre-post ANCOVA on treatment and matched control. Original study—(75–6); replication—(76–77).	PPVT WISC PPVT (K)	75 .25 / 76 .42 / 75 .38 / 76 .46 / 75 .26 (K) / 76 .74 / 75 .38 (K) / 76 .55

Program	Location	Grade	Subject	Description	Design	Test	Result
Every Student Every Day	St. Mary Parish	K–4 K–6	Math and reading	Daily diagnosis, evaluation, and prescription, computer scoring for coordination. Pullout design using 40 min. each day.	Pre-post design; changing percentile; fall to spring. 7 52 (76) 7 59 (77) 7 32 (82) 2 40 (83)	TOBE (preschool & K)	+
Baptist Hill K	Baptist Hill K, Greenville, AL	K	Reading and math	Full-day K, learning centers, diagnose individual learning needs on continuous basis with appropriate learning activities.	Pre-post design; fall to spring.		TOBE
Early Prevention of School Failure	Peotone District, IL	4-, 5-, 6-year-olds		Early identification of developmental needs and learning styles of 4-, 5-, and 6-yr-olds. Screening, planning and pull-out; 20–30 minute instruction in different modalities at learning centers	Improvement per month on different scales—no comparison data either w/a control group or pre-implementation.	getting data	+
First Level Math	PRIMAK Educational Foundation	K or 1	Math	Sequential curriculum and management system that is diagnostic/prescriptive. Instructional groups formed on basis of pretests. Instruction in 3–4 groups for about 20–30 minutes.	Pre-post design; fall to spring.	CIRCUS	+ not possible to compute
New Adventure in Learning	Moore Elem. School, Tallahassee, FL	K		Individually determined instruction with positive behavior management.	Pre-post; nat'l norm comparison using expected growth.	PPVT—mean improvmt 1.67/ math. Gilmore oral reading test—10% on grade level at pre, 57% at post.	no current data

Table 1.4 (continued)

Name	Developer	Grade	Content	Instructional Strategy	Evaluation Design	Measures	Effects	
							#1	#2
MARC	Walkulla City and Crawford-ville, FL	K–1	Reading	Continuous progress using multisensory activities and systematic instruction. Diagnostic and record-keeping instrument, skill sheets provided.	Post ANOVA on treatment and matched local control at end of K and end of 1st. Pre ANOVA to ensure equivalence.	SESAT (II) letters	1.12	.55
						word rdg.	.88	na
						sent rdg.	.25	na
						BOEHM	ns	
						KUHLMAN	ns	
						ANDERSON	ns	
						SESAT (I)		
INSRUCT	Lincoln Public Schools	K–3	Reading	Individual placement & progress through multi-unit model.	ANCOVA comparisons of treatment and comparable schools chosen on similar SES, school organization, and number of compensatory students.	Metropolitan word know.	.35**	
						reading	.25*	
						spelling	<2>	
							ns	
PLAY	Bristol, VA	K–1 and ¾ years	Motor/cognitive	Diagnostic/prescriptive direct instruction in perceptual/motor skills; monthly home reinforcement and activities.	ANOVA on treatment and control. Control were eligibles (score below cut off) not enrolled because positions filled.	BOEHM 75–76	1.77	
						76–77	.23	
						77–78	1.33	
CLIMB	Middlesex, NJ	K–12	Reading and math	Diagnostic/prescription approach in acquisition of reading and math skills, providing a management design for coordinating & integrating classroom & support personnel.	Spring-to-spring achievement compared to nat'l norms and compensatory growth.	CTBS	+	
STAMM	Lakewood, CO	K–8	Math	Continuous progress math with management system.	Pre-post implementation scores for district and adoption site.	CAT	+	
Education Assessment & Inst. for the Educationally Deprived	Kenosha, WI	K–10	Language	Extended day K 2–3 hrs in afternoon, additional time for remedial instruction.	Pre-post design.	PPVT	+	

Program	Location	Grade	Focus	Description	Design/Comparison	Test	Result
Strategies in Early Childhood Education	Waupun, WI	preK and K	Screening	Developmental and screening model. Self instructional, individually paced, learning centers, developmentally sequenced materials.	Ad hoc comparison of treatment children with another group. No evidence of prior comparability.		
Right to read	Glassboro, NJ	K–3	Reading	Diagnostic, prescriptive, individual progress model. Upgraded.	No control; 325 children; pre-post.	CRI Classroom Reading Inventory	Avg. gain 1.52 yr.
Project Catch Up	Newport Mesa, CA	K–6	Reading and math	Remedial instruction in reading & math to underachieving students using diagnoses, prescription. Positive contacts with family.	Mean gain by grade on CTBS from fall to spring. No data on K.	CTBS fall–spring	
Amphitheater School District KIP	Tucson, AZ	K		Parent involvement; once a week training of parents in game or activity that gives practice in basic skills with followup practice with students who need practice in that skill and monitoring of student progress.	Comparison to comparable school on percent scoring above 30 percentile 1 year after.	CAT	66% vs. 38%
VIP	Spokane, WA	K	Develop skills	Develop friendly, feeling parents and school, provide training for parents in how to help children at home, to send home games that reinforce skills learned at school.	Santa Clara Inventory gain of 2.32 mo. in developmental age/ month; no control group.	Santa Clara Inventory (note problem with fall–spring)	

Pretest effect size = −.15 was added to posttest effect size .30 to arrive at the adjusted effect size. Effect sizes were computed by determining the t value to generate p < .01 and .05 respectively.

Table 1.5
Obando & Hymel (1991)
The Effect of Mastery Learning Instruction on the Entry-Level Spanish
Proficiency of Secondary School Students

	N	Mean	SD	Adjusted Mean
Test #1				
Experimental	22	79.23	8.94	29.30
Control	19	72.53	8.52	72.43
Test #2				
Experimental	22	81.14	7.38	82.45
Control	19	75.57	7.54	74.06
Nat'l Spanish Exam				
Experimental	22	35.41	4.34	35.05
Control	19	30.47	4.95	30.73

N = number of students; SD = standard deviation.

Table 1.6
Obando & Hymel (1991)
The Effect of Mastery Learning Instruction on the Entry-Level Spanish
Proficiency of Secondary School Students

Source	SS	df	MS	F	p
Test #1					
Main Effect	350.64	1	350.64	4.35	< .05
Covariates	192.72	3	64.24		
Error	2903.03	36	80.64		
Total	3448.39	40	86.16		
Test #2					
Main Effect	522.36	1	522.36	9.27	< .05
Covariates	22.70	3	7.57		
Error	1934.78	36	53.74		
Total	2480.10	40	62.00		
National Spanish Exam					
Main Effect	296.67	1	296.67	13.88	< .05
Covariates	20.31	3	6.77		
Error	796.41	36	21.37		
Total	1086.39	40	27.16		

SS = sums of squares; df = degrees of freedom; MS = mean square.

Statistical Evidence on Defining Instructional Expectations

GENERALIZATION TESTED: ON DEFINING INSTRUCTIONAL EXPECTATIONS—CHAPTER 2

Student achievement of learning objectives is enhanced when prior to instruction, (1) learning objectives are defined for students, (2) procedures to be used in the performance of tasks to achieve the objectives are identified, and (3) student outcomes designating achievement of the objectives are defined.

Total number of studies covered: 358+

Table 2.1
Anderson (1994)
Synthesis of Mastery Learning (Meta-analysis) Achievement Outcomes
Number of studies included: 7

Study	Percent Positive	Total N	ES	Grade Level
Kulik et al. (1990a)	93.2%	NR	.52	K–College
Slavin (1990)	NR	NR	.27	K–12
Kulik et al. (1990b)	63.6%	NR	.40	K–12
Guskey & Pigott (1988)	89.1%	11,532	.41 Psych.	K–12
			.50 Science	
			.53 Soc. Stud.	
			.60 Lang. Arts	
			.70 Math	
			.94 Elementary	
			.48 High School	
			.41 College	
Willett et al. (1983)	NR		.64	K–12
Guskey & Gates (1985)	92.2%	8,074	.65–.94	K–College
Block & Burns (1976)	89.0%	2,767	.83	K–College

N = number of students; ES = effect size.

Individual studies analyzed by these meta-analyses are identified in the reference list by the following symbols:

Kulik et al. (1990a) *
Kulik et al. (1990b) #
Slavin (1990) @
Guskey & Pigott (1988) $

Guskey & Gates (1985) &
Block & Burns (1976) +

It was not possible to determine the individual studies for which readiness was an instructional tactic for the Willett et al. (1983) analysis.

Wise (1996)
Strategies for Teaching Science: What Works?
Number of studies included: 140

Average effect size is .32 for all the alternative science teaching strategies considered in this analysis.

Focusing strategies involve times when teachers do something to alert students to the intent of the instruction. The effect size for focusing strategies is +.57.

Swanson (2001)
Research on Interventions for Adolescents with Learning Disabilities:
A Meta-analysis of Outcomes Related to Higher-Order Processing
Number of studies included: 58

Fifty-eight studies included measures of higher-order skills. The average ES across studies was .82 (SD = .66). Instructional components reported in studies were:

1. Advanced organizers
2. Attributions
3. Control difficulty
4. Elaboration
5. Extended practice
6. Large-group learning
7. New skills
8. One-to-one instruction
9. Peer modeling
10. Questioning
11. Reinforcement
12. Sequencing
13. Skill modeling
14. Small-group instruction
15. Strategy cues
16. Supplemental instruction
17. Task reduction
18. Technology

When a factor referred to as "organization/extended practice"—which was the combination of (a) advanced organizers, (b) new content/skills, and (c) extended practice—was entered into the regression model first, followed by age and method, it was significant at $p < .001$. This "organization/extended practice" factor was the only combination factor, which contributed significant variance to effect size.

Rosenshine & Stevens (1986)

Groups of studies reviewed in this logical synthesis of research did not provide statistical evidence. However, many of the individual studies included in the logical synthesis of research do contain statistical evidence. In the event that a reader wishes to view this evidence, an extensive listing of the individual studies reviewed

is provided in the reference list in Part V (the studies are identified by the symbol %).

Statistical Evidence on Providing Instructional Evaluation

GENERALIZATION TESTED: ON INSTRUCTIONAL EVALUATION—CHAPTER 3

Achievement of learning objectives is enhanced when (1) evaluation procedures are determined when task sequences are planned; (2) student task performance is frequently evaluated; (3) feedback on evaluation is given to students without delay; and (4) evaluation results are used to determine appropriate corrective instruction which occurs immediately after the performance is evaluated.

Total number of studies covered: 292+

Table 3.1
Kulik & Kulik (1987)
Mastery Testing and Student Learning: A Meta-analysis
Number of studies included: 49

Class Level	Course Content	Duration in Weeks	Mastery Level	Effect Size
3 and 4th n = 1	Psychology n = 15	1 wk n = 2	80 n = 13	−0.42
4th and 5th n = 1	Math n = 11	2 wk n = 5	70 n = 1	to 1.46
7th n = 6	Science n = 9	3 wk n = 1	75 n = 2	
8th n = 3	Math & Science n = 1	4 wk n = 4	85 n = 2	
9th n = 3	Biology n = 2	5 wk n = 5	90 n = 11	
7th–9th n = 2	Social studies n = 3	6 wk n = 2	93 n = 1	
10th n = 2	Physics n = 1	7 wk n = 2	95 n = 1	
Senior hi n = 1	Chemistry n = 1	8 wk n = 3	100 n =15	
College n = 30	Engineering n = 1	10 wk n = 3		
	Education n = 1	11 wk n = 2		
	Sailing n = 1	12 wk n = 3		
	Statistics n = 1	13 wk n = 1		
	9 courses n = 1	15 wk n = 2		
	Geography n = 1	16 wk n = 4		
		17 wk n = 1		
		18 wk n = 2		
		26 wk n = 1		
		32 wk n = 2		

n = number of studies.

Table 3.2
Anderson (1994)
Synthesis of Mastery Learning (Meta-analysis) Achievement Outcomes
Number of studies included: 7

Study	Percent Positive	Total N	ES	Grade Level
Kulik et al. (1990a)	93.2%	NR	.52	K–College
Slavin (1990)	NR	NR	.27	K–12
Kulik et al. (1990b)	63.6%	NR	.40	K–12
Guskey & Pigott (1988)	89.1%	11,532	.41 Psych.	K–12
			.50 Science	
			.53 Soc. Stud.	
			.60 Lang. Arts	
			.70 Math	
			.94 Elementary	
			.48 High School	
			.41 College	
Willett et al. (1983)	NR		.64	K–12
Guskey & Gates (1985)	92.2%	8,074	.65–.94	K–College
Block & Burns (1976)	89.0%	2,767	.83	K–College

N = number of students; ES = effect size.

Individual studies analyzed by these meta-analyses are identified in the reference list by the following symbols:

Kulik et al. (1990a) *
Kulik et al. (1990b) #
Slavin (1990) @
Guskey & Pigott (1988) $
Guskey & Gates (1985) &
Block & Burns (1976) +

It was not possible to determine the individual studies for which readiness was an instructional tactic for the Willett et al. (1983) analysis.

Table 3.3
Rosenshine et al. (1996)
Teaching Students to Generate Questions: A Review of the Intervention Studies
Number of studies included: 26

	Overall Median Effect Sizes by Type of Prompt					
	Standardized Test			Experimenter-Developed Test		
Prompt	**Reciprocal Teaching** $(n = 6)$	**Regular Instruction** $(n = 7)$	**Combined** $(n = 13)$	**Reciprocal Teaching** $(n = 12)$	**Regular Instruction** $(n = 19)$	**Combined** $(n = 19)$
Signal words	0.34 (4)	0.46 (2)	0.36 (6)	0.88 (5)	0.67 (2)	0.85 (7)
Generic questions/ Stems					1.12 (4)	1.12 (4)
Main idea		0.70 (1)	0.70 (1)	1.24 (1)	0.13 (4)	0.25 (5)
Question type	0.02 (2)	0.00 (1)	0.00 (3)	3.37 (1)		3.37 (1)
Story grammar					1.08 (2)	1.08 (2)
No facilitator		0.14 (3)	0.14 (3)			

N = number of studies.

Rosenshine & Stevens (1986)

Groups of studies reviewed in this logical synthesis of research did not provide statistical evidence. However, many of the individual studies included in the logical synthesis of research do contain statistical evidence. In the event that a reader wishes to view this evidence, an extensive listing of the individual studies reviewed is provided in the reference list in Part V (the studies are identified by the symbol %).

Brophy & Good (1986)

Groups of studies reviewed in these logical syntheses of research did not provide statistical evidence. However, many of the individual studies included in these logical syntheses of research do contain statistical evidence. In the event that a reader wishes to view this evidence, an extensive listing of the individual studies reviewed is provided in the reference list in Part V. Studies associated with Brophy & Good (1986) are identified by the symbol !.

Education Commission of the States (1999)
Direct Instruction
Number of studies included: 10

Groups of studies reviewed in this logical synthesis of research did not provide statistical evidence. However, many of the individual studies included in the logical synthesis of research do contain statistical evidence. In the event that a reader wishes to view this evidence, an extensive listing of the individual studies reviewed is provided in the reference list in Part V (the studies are identified by the symbol !).

Baker et al. (2002)
A Synthesis of Empirical Research on Teaching Mathematics to
Low-Achieving Students
Number of studies included: 17

Groups of studies reviewed in this logical synthesis of research did not provide statistical evidence. However, many of the individual studies included in the logical synthesis of research do contain statistical evidence. In the event that a reader wishes to view this evidence, an extensive listing of the individual studies reviewed is provided in the reference list in Part V (the studies are identified by the symbol /).

Martens & Witt (2004)
Competence, Persistence, and Success: The Positive Psychology
of Behavioral Skill Instruction
Number of studies included: 40

Groups of studies reviewed in this logical synthesis of research did not provide statistical evidence. However, many of the individual studies included in the logical synthesis of research do contain statistical evidence. In the event that a reader wishes to view this evidence, an extensive listing of the individual studies reviewed is provided in the reference list in Part V (the studies are identified by the symbol <).

Table 3.4
Obando & Hymel (1991)
The Effect of Mastery Learning Instruction on the Entry-Level Spanish
Proficiency of Secondary School Students

	N	Mean	SD	Adjusted Mean
Test #1				
Experimental	22	79.23	8.94	29.30
Control	19	72.53	8.52	72.43
Test #2				
Experimental	22	81.14	7.38	82.45
Control	19	75.57	7.54	74.06
Nat'l Spanish Exam				
Experimental	22	35.41	4.34	35.05
Control	19	30.47	4.95	30.73

N = number of students; SD = standard deviation.

Table 3.5
Obando & Hymel (1991)
The Effect of Mastery Learning Instruction on the Entry-Level Spanish
Proficiency of Secondary School Students

Source	SS	df	MS	F	p
Test #1					
Main Effect	350.64	1	350.64	4.35	< .05
Covariates	192.72	3	64.24		
Error	2903.03	36	80.64		
Total	3448.39	40	86.16		
Test #2					
Main Effect	522.36	1	522.36	9.27	< .05
Covariates	22.70	3	7.57		
Error	1934.78	36	53.74		
Total	2480.10	40	62.00		
National Spanish Exam					
Main Effect	296.67	1	296.67	13.88	< .05
Covariates	20.31	3	6.77		
Error	796.41	36	21.37		
Total	1086.39	40	27.16		

SS = sums of squares; df = degrees of freedom; MS = mean square.

Table 3.6
Montazemi & Wang (1995)
An Empirical Investigation of CBI in Support of Mastery Learning

	MANOVA Test of Variation of Performance in Tutorial-Tests across Twenty Chapters				
Source of Variation	**SS**	**df**	**MS**	**F**	**Sig. of F**
Between-Subjects Effect					
Within cells	41.27	330	0.14		
Regression	0.01	1	0.01	0.04	0.837
Constant	416.93	1	416.93	2878.90	0.000
Two types of students	4.10	1	4.10	28.28	0.000
Within-subjects Effect					
Within cells	108.22	5434	0.02		
Chapter	17.30	19	0.91	45.73	0.000
Two student type by chapter	1.37	19	0.07	3.61	0.000
	B	**Beta**	**Std. Err.**	**t-value**	**Sig. of t**
Covariates					
Computer anxiety	0.000	0.01218	0.000	0.205	0.837
Computer efficacy	0.000	0.04661	0.001	0.788	0.433

Mauchly Sphericity Test W = 0.0068.
Chi-Square Approx. = 1394.8969 with 189 df.
Significance = 0.000.

Table 3.7
Montazemi & Wang (1995)
An Empirical Investigation of CBI in Support of Mastery Learning

MANOVA Test of Variation of Performance in Nine Lab-tests					
Source of Variation	**SS**	**df**	**MS**	**F**	**Sig. of t**
Between-Subjects Effect					
Within cells	14.27	330	0.04		
Regression	0.13	1	0.13	3.03	0.082
Constant	279.02	1	279.02	6450.87	0.000
Two student types	2.80	1	2.80	64.08	0.000
Within-subjects Effect					
Within cells	21.77	2648	0.01		
Lab-test	13.29	8	1.66	202.08	0.000
Two student types by Lab-test	0.96	8	0.12	14.63	0.000
	B	**Beta**	**Std. Err.**	**t-value**	**Sig. of t**
Covariates					
Computer Anxiety	−0.000	−0.030	0.000	−0.553	0.581
Computer Efficacy	−0.001	−0.044	0.001	−0.798	0.426

Mauchly Sphericity Test W = 0.35437.
Chi-Square Approx. = 340.40106 with 35 df.

Table 3.8

Aviles (1998)

A Contrast of Mastery Learning and Non-Mastery Learning Instruction in an Undergraduate Social Work Course

Mean Exam Scores before Make-up Exams

	Mastery		Non-Mastery		Diff.
	M	SD	M	SD	
Exam 1	81.12	10.44	82.10	11.50	0.98
Exam 2	84.44	10.01	83.90	10.80	0.54
Exam 3	75.09	10.85	79.00	11.70	3.91

Mean Make-up Exam Scores and Corresponding Exam Scores

	Make-up Exams Taken	Original Exam Score	Make-up Exam Score	Change
Exam 1	29	M 74.40	90.80	+16.10**
		SD 10.00	7.30	
Exam 2	22	M 77.10	82.10	+5.00**
Exam 3	27	M 66.00	83.00	+17.00**
Total	n = 79			

Notes: * p < .01; ** p < .0001.

Mean Exam Scores after Make-up Exam Score Replacement

	Mastery		Non-Mastery		Diff.
	M	SD	M	SD	
Exam 1	88.00	7.90	82.10	11.50	5.90*
Exam 2	86.40	7.90	83.90	10.80	2.50
Exam 3	81.70	7.80	79.00	11.70	2.70

Note: * p < .05.

Mean Retention Scores: Exam One and Retention Test

	Mastery		Non-Mastery		Diff.
	M	SD	M	SD	
Exam 1R**	18.85	3.59	19.39	3.93	0.54
Retention***	13.29	2.77	12.73	4.15	0.56
Difference	5.56	3.04	6.75	3.48	1.19*

Notes: * p < .05, two-tailed. Max score possible = 26.00; ** 1R = scores the 26 items generated on exam one; *** Retention = scores the same 26 items generated on exam three.

Table 3.9
Ross (2004)
Effects of Running Records Assessment on Early Literacy Achievement

Effects of Condition Assignment on Grade 3 Reading and Writing, Controlling for Prior Achievement and Collective Teacher Efficacy: Univariate Effects

Source	Subject	Significance Test	Partial $\eta2$
Corrected model	Reading	$F(3,69) = 14.222$, $p < .001$	.382
	Writing	$F(3,69) = 16.009$, $p < .001$	.410
Intercept	Reading	$F(1,72) = 2.490$, $p = .119$	.035
	Writing	$F(1,72) = 1.168$, $p = .284$	.017
Collective teacher efficacy	Reading	$F(1,72) = 5.598$, $p = .021$	.075
	Writing	$F(1,72) = 6.398$, $p = .014$	.085
Writing 2001	Reading	$F(1,72) = 20.786$, $p < .001$	.232
	Writing	$F(1,72) = 26.915$, $p < .001$	.281
Experimental condition	Reading	$F(1,72) = 7.163$, $p = .009$	.092
	Writing	$F(1,72) = 4.314$, $p = .041$	.057

Statistical Evidence on Providing Corrective Instruction

GENERALIZATION TESTED: ON CORRECTIVE INSTRUCTION—CHAPTER 4

Achievement of learning objectives is enhanced when appropriate corrective instruction is provided: (1) corrective tasks are formulated when task sequences are planned; (2) feedback on incorrect performance is based on frequent evaluation of student work; (3) feedback on evaluation is given to students without delay; and (4) incorrect performance is immediately corrected.

Total number of studies covered: 504+

Table 4.1
Kulik & Kulik (1988)
Timing of Feedback and Verbal Learning
Number of studies included: 53

Means and Standard Errors for 27 List-Learning Studies

Study feature	N	Effect size M	SE
Timing of delayed feedback*			
After item	20	0.55	0.18
After test	7	−0.24	0.19
Stimulus reexposure*			
Yes	17	0.09	0.14
No	10	0.76	0.31
Duration of treatment			
1 day	24	0.40	0.16
2 to 7 days	3	−0.11	0.18
Class level			
Precollege	9	0.32	0.20
College	18	0.35	0.21
Year of publication			
Before 1966	15	0.42	0.24
1966 and later	12	0.24	0.17
Source of publication			
Unpublished	3	0.24	0.24
Published	24	0.35	0.15

Note: * $p < .05$.

Table 4.2
Kulik & Kulik (1988)
Timing of Feedback and Verbal Learning

	Delayed Feedback to Test—Stimulus Present	Delayed Feedback to Item Stimulus Present	Stimulus Absent
M	−0.24	0.33	0.76
SE	0.18	0.15	0.31
N	7	10	10

A one-way analysis of variance showed a difference in result from the three study stypes $F(2,24) = 4.07$. $p < .03$.

Table 4.3
Bangert-Drowns et al. (1991)
The Instructional Effect of Feedback in Test-like Events
Number of studies included: 40

Histogram showing the distribution of 58 effect sizes from research on feedback effects.

Table 4.4
Anderson (1994)
Synthesis of Mastery Learning (Meta-analysis) Achievement Outcomes
Number of studies included: 7

Study	Percent Positive	Total N	ES	Grade Level
Kulik et al. (1990a)	93.2%	NR	.52	K–College
Slavin (1990)	NR	NR	.27	K–12
Kulik et al. (1990b)	63.6%	NR	.40	K–12
Guskey & Pigott (1988)	89.1%	11,532	.41 Psych.	K–12
			.50 Science	
			.53 Soc. Stud.	
			.60 Lang. Arts	
			.70 Math	
			.94 Elementary	
			.48 High School	
			.41 College	

(continued)

Table 4.4 (continued)

Study	Percent Positive	Total N	ES	Grade Level
Willett et al. (1983)	NR		.64	K–12
Guskey & Gates (1985)	92.2%	8,074	.65–.94	K–College
Block & Burns (1976)	89.0%	2,767	.83	K–College

N = number of students; ES = effect size.

Individual studies analyzed by these meta-analyses are identified in the reference list by the following symbols:

Kulik et al. (1990a) *
Kulik et al. (1990b) #
Slavin (1990) @
Guskey & Pigott (1988) $
Guskey & Gates (1985) &
Block & Burns (1976) +

It was not possible to determine the individual studies for which readiness was an instructional tactic for the Willett et al. (1983) analysis.

Table 4.5
Rosenshine et al. (1996)
Teaching Students to Generate Questions: A Review of the Intervention Studies
Number of studies included: 26

	Overall Median Effect Sizes by Type of Prompt					
	Standardized Test			Experimenter-Developed Test		
Prompt	Reciprocal Teaching (*n* = 6)	Regular Instruction (*n* = 7)	Combined (*n* = 13)	Reciprocal Teaching (*n* = 12)	Regular Instruction (*n* = 19)	Combined (*n* = 19)
Signal words	0.34 (4)	0.46 (2)	0.36 (6)	0.88 (5)	0.67 (2)	0.85 (7)
Generic questions/ Stems					1.12 (4)	1.12 (4)
Main idea		0.70 (1)	0.70 (1)	1.24 (1)	0.13 (4)	0.25 (5)
Question type	0.02 (2)	0.00 (1)	0.00 (3)	3.37 (1)		3.37 (1)
Story grammar					1.08 (2)	1.08 (2)
No facilitator		0.14 (3)	0.14 (3)			

Note: *n* = number of studies. Number in parentheses refers to the number of studies used to compute an effect size.

Gersten & Baker (2001)
Teaching Expressive Writing to Students with Learning Disabilities:
A Meta-analysis
Number of studies included: 13

Summed across all 13 studies, the mean effect size on the aggregate writing measure was 0.81. The 95 percent confidence interval was 0.65–0.97, providing clear evidence that the writing interventions had a significant positive effect on the quality of students' writing. Positive effect sizes were found in each of the 13 studies, ranging in magnitude from 0.30 to 1.73.

Swanson (2001)
Research on Interventions for Adolescents with Learning Disabilities:
A Meta-analysis of Outcomes Related to Higher-Order Processing
Number of studies included: 58

The average ES across studies was .82 (SD = .66). Instructional components reported in studies were:

1. Advanced organizers
2. Attributions
3. Control difficulty
4. Elaboration
5. Extended practice
6. Large-group learning
7. New skills/content
8. One-to-one instruction
9. Peer modeling
10. Questioning
11. Reinforcement
12. Sequencing
13. Skill modeling
14. Small-group instruction
15. Strategy cues
16. Supplemental instruction
17. Task reduction
18. Technology

Gersten et al. (2001)
Teaching Reading Comprehension Strategies to Students with
Learning Disabilities: A Review of Research
Total number of studies included: 27

Groups of studies reviewed in this logical synthesis of research did not provide statistical evidence. However, many of the individual studies included in the logical synthesis of research do contain statistical evidence. In the event that a reader wishes to view this evidence, an extensive listing of the individual studies reviewed is provided in the reference list in Part V (the studies are identified by the symbol =).

Table 4.6
Kroesbergen & Van Luit (2003)
Mathematics Interventions for Children with Special Educational Needs:
A Meta-analysis
Number of studies included: 58

Effects of Nominal Variables Included in the Study

Variable	N	Sample Size	Effect Size M	SD	ES
Design					
baseline	21	155	2.27	0.79	2.16
experimental	40	2,254	0.68	0.73	0.62
Control condition					
no intervention	30	701	1.87	1.01	1.51
intervention	31	1,808	0.54	0.59	0.51
Special needs					
low performing	23	1,608	0.83	0.78	0.74
learning disabilities	23	416	1.65	1.11	1.36
mild mental retardation	8	192	1.01	1.27	0.80
mixed groups	7	293	1.09	1.12	0.73
Content					
preparatory	13	664	0.92	0.72	0.92
basic facts	17	521	0.84	0.86	0.63
Method					
direct instruction	35	1,671	1.13	0.94	0.91
self-instruction	16	372	1.77	1.12	1.45
mediated/assisted	10	466	0.52	0.97	0.34
Medium					
teacher	49	1,635	1.32	1.07	1.05
computer	12	872	0.64	0.79	0.51
Peer tutoring					
no	51	1,954	1.24	1.10	0.96
yes	10	555	0.92	0.76	0.87
Realistic math					
no	47	1.709	1.33	1.07	1.04
yes	14	800	0.71	0.88	0.70

N = no. of studies, M = mean, SD = standard deviation, ES = effect size.

Table 4.7
Therrien (2004)
Fluency and Comprehension Gains as a Result of Repeated Reading:
A Meta-analysis
Number of studies included: 18

	Nontransfer Intervention Component Analysis							
	Cue Type			**Corrective Feedback**		**No. of Times Passage Read**		
Dependent Variable	**Fluency**	**Comp.**	**Fluency & Comp.**	**Yes**	**No**	**2**	**3**	**4**
Fluency *n*	0.72	.081	0.94	0.68	0.88	0.57	0.85	0.95
	2	8	3	3	13	2	10	3
Comp. *n*	0.66	0.75	0.67	–	–	–	0.66	0.71
	2	6	3	–	–	–	10	2

Note: *n* indicates number of effect sizes. Dash indicates effect size not calculated or available.

Rosenshine & Stevens (1986)

Groups of studies reviewed in this logical synthesis of research did not provide statistical evidence. However, many of the individual studies included in the logical synthesis of research do contain statistical evidence. In the event that a reader wishes to view this evidence, an extensive listing of the individual studies reviewed is provided in the reference list in Part V (the studies are identified by the symbol %).

Brophy & Good (1986)
Teacher Behavior and Student Achievement

Groups of studies reviewed in these logical syntheses of research did not provide statistical evidence. However, many of the individual studies included in these logical syntheses of research do contain statistical evidence. In the event that a reader wishes to view this evidence, an extensive listing of the individual studies reviewed is provided in the reference list in Part V. Studies associated with Brophy & Good (1986) are identified by the symbol !.

Table 4.8
Heubusch & Lloyd (1998)
Corrective Feedback in Oral Reading
Number of studies included: 24

Features of Oral Reading Corrective Feedback Studies

Authors	Participants	Conditions	Word Recognition Effects	Comprehension Effects
Barbetta, Heron, & Heward (1993)	6 students with learning disabilities aged 8–9	Active student response vs. no student response	Active student response superior to no student response on all tests for majority of students	N/A
Barbetta, Heward, & Bradley (1993)	5 students with developmental disabilities	Word supply vs. phonetic emphasis	Word supply superior to phonetic emphasis	N/A
Barbetta, Heward, Bradley, & Miller (1994)	4 students with developmental disabilities aged 7–9	Word supply using immediate vs. delayed error correction	Immediate error correction superior to delayed error correction on all tests	N/A
Cardine (1980)	9 beginning readers	Word supply vs. phonetic emphasis	Phonetic emphasis superior to word supply during training and on transfer tests	N/A
Espin & Deno (1989)	8 students with learning disabilities	Word supply vs. phonetic emphasis	Word supply superior to phonetic emphasis prompt immediate and maintenance tests	N/A
Fleisher & Jenkins (1983)	21 students with learning disabilities	Word supply vs. comprehension emphasis vs. comprehension and word emphasis	Word emphasis superior to comprehension on new words in isolation; comprehension plus word emphasis superior to comprehension on new words in isolation	No differences between the groups
Jenkins & Larson (1979)	5 junior high boys with learning disabilities aged 13–14	Word supply vs. no correction vs. sentence repeat vs. end of page review vs. word meaning vs. drill	Word drill superior to no correction, sentence repeat, end of page review, word meaning on isolated and context measures. Word supply superior to no correction.	N/A
Jenkins, Larson, & Fleisher (1983)	17 students with learning disabilities	Word supply vs. drill	Drill superior to word supply on word recognition in isolation and context.	Drill superior to word supply on maze comprehension and comprehension questions

(continued)

Table 4.8 (continued)

Features of Oral Reading Corrective Feedback Studies

Authors	Participants	Conditions	Word Recognition Effects	Comprehension Effects
Meyer (1982)	58 students in special education	Word supply vs. phonetic analysis	No significant differences.	N/A
O'Shea, Munson, & O'Shea (1984)	5 students with learning disabilities aged 7–11	Word supply vs. word drill vs. phase drill	Word drill and phase drill superior in isolation tasks; phase drill superior in context tasks.	N/A
Pany, McCoy, & Peters (1981)	34 remedial readers	Corrective feedback vs. no correction	Correction similar to no correction	Correction similar to no correction
Perkins (1988)	48 students with learning disabilities	General feedback vs. no feedback; word supply vs. phonetic emphasis	General feedback superior to no feedback; corrective feedback superior to general feedback on posttest & maint.	N/A
Rose, McEntire, & Dowdy (1982)	5 students with learning disabilities aged 8–11	Word supply vs. phonetic emphasis	Word supply superior to phonetic emphasis for 3 learners.	N/A
Rosenberg (1986)	4 students with learning disabilities aged 12–14	Word supply vs. drill vs. phonetic drill rehearsal	Drill equal to drill rehearsal on accuracy; Drill superior to drill rehearsal on reading fluency.	N/A
Singh & Singh (1986)	4 students with mental retardation aged 11–17	Positive practice vs. drill	Positive practice superior to drill on immediate tests; both facilitated retention	N/A
Singh (1990)	3 students with mental retardation aged 13–15	Word supply vs. sentence repeat	Sentence repeat superior for all students	N/A
Spaai, Ellermann, & Reitsma (1991) Experiment 1	60 beginning readers aged 6–7	Word supply vs. phonetic emphasis using microcomputer	No significant differences between groups on accuracy or time.	N/A
Spaai, Ellermann, & Reitsma (1991) Experiment 2	66 beginning readers aged 6	Whole word vs. phonetic emphasis using microcomputer	Whole word superior to phonic analysis on posttest.	N/A

Table 4.9
Baker et al. (2002)
A Synthesis of Empirical Research on Teaching Mathematics to Low-Achieving Students
Number of studies included: 15

Summary of Aggregate Effect Sizes for Four Categories of Studies Reviewed

Category	No. of Comparisons	N	Effect Size		95% Confidence Interval	
			Average	Weighted	Lower	Upper
Providing data or recommendations to teachers and students:						
Providing student with data/information*	5	200	.71	.57	.27	.87
Providing instructional recommendations to teachers	1	20	.51	.51	-.36	1.40
Peer-assisted learning*	6	302	.62	.66	.43	.89
Explicit teacher-led and contextualized teacher-facilitated approaches:						
Explicit instruction	4	485	.65	.56	.40	.77
Teacher-facilitated instruction and practice	4	203	.04	.01	-.26	.29
Concrete feedback to parents	2	81	.43	.43	-.02	.87

*Effect size is significantly greater than zero.

Table 4.10
Obando & Hymel (1991)
Mean and Adjusted Mean Criterion Scores—Simple Statistics

	N	Mean	SD	Adjusted Mean
Test #1				
Experimental	22	79.23	8.94	29.30
Control	19	72.53	8.52	72.43
Test #2				
Experimental	22	81.14	7.38	82.45
Control	19	75.57	7.54	74.06
Nat'l Spanish Exam				
Experimental	22	35.41	4.34	35.05
Control	19	30.47	4.95	30.73

N = number of students; SD = standard deviation.

Table 4.11
Obando & Hymel (1991)
ANCOVA

Source	SS	df	MS	F	p
Test #1					
Main Effect	350.64	1	350.64	4.35	< .05
Covariates	192.72	3	64.24		
Error	2903.03	36	80.64		
Total	3448.39	40	86.16		
Test #2					
Main Effect	522.36	1	522.36	9.27	< .05
Covariates	22.70	3	7.57		
Error	1934.78	36	53.74		
Total	2480.10	40	62.00		
National Spanish Exam					
Main Effect	296.67	1	296.67	13.88	< .05
Covariates	20.31	3	6.77		
Error	796.41	36	21.37		
Total	1086.39	40	27.16		

SS = sums of squares; df = degrees of freedom; MS = mean square.

Table 4.12
Mevarech & Kramarski (1997)
IMPROVE: A Multidimensional Method for Teaching Mathematics in
Heterogeneous Classrooms
Number of studies included: 2

Mean Scores and Standard Deviations (in Terms of Percent Correct) on Algebra by Treatment

| Treatment | IMPROVE | | | CONTROL | | |
Ability	Low	Middle	High	Low	Middle	High
Pretest						
M	50.71	76.20	92.19	52.32	74.52	90.39
S	13.29	5.59	4.33	10.40	5.65	4.35
Algebra (Overall)						
M	55.90	73.94	86.58	52.65	63.72	71.77
S	20.95	21.09	16.60	30.08	18.88	22.30
Numerals						
M	68.57	80.88	90.30	63.21	75.09	77.95
S	20.24	17.16	13.72	28.35	15.38	19.76
Substitution						
M	55.00	71.04	83.91	49.62	62.50	70.38
S	21.96	25.78	20.27	34.17	25.28	27.37
Expressions						
M	53.18	71.92	87.06	51.58	57.84	73.30
S	28.11	30.84	19.26	29.20	25.73	28.76
Word Problems						
M	46.32	70.44	84.57	45.45	57.15	66.20
S	27.92	24.84	20.47	34.97	22.64	27.87

Table 4.13
Mevarech & Kramarski (1997)
IMPROVE: A Multidimensional Method for Teaching Mathematics in
Heterogeneous Classrooms

Mean Scores and Standard Deviations (in Terms of Percent Correct) by Time, Treatment, and Ability on Introduction-to-Algebra and Mathematics Reasoning

| Treatment | IMPROVE | | | CONTROL | | |
Ability	Low	Middle	High	Low	Middle	High
Pretest						
M	37.76	66.46	86.33	40.20	66.89	86.85
S	8.17	6.63	6.48	9.87	7.93	5.42

(continued)

Table 4.13 (continued)

Treatment	IMPROVE			CONTROL		
Ability	Low	Middle	High	Low	Middle	High
Introduction-to-Algebra						
M	48.28	79.52	88.20	45.97	67.24	82.27
S	16.31	10.06	8.55	21.03	18.97	13.05
Mathematical Reasoning						
M	41.37	64.00	74.74	32.60	50.98	67.47
S	14.41	16.38	12.98	20.68	17.79	15.34

Statistical Evidence on Keeping Students on Task

GENERALIZATION TESTED: ON KEEPING STUDENTS ON TASK—CHAPTER 5

Achievement of learning objectives is enhanced when students spend more time attending to tasks formulated to enable them to achieve the learning objectives.

Total number of studies covered: 95

Brophy & Good (1986)

Groups of studies reviewed in these logical syntheses of research did not provide statistical evidence. However, many of the individual studies included in these logical syntheses of research do contain statistical evidence. In the event that a reader wishes to view this evidence, an extensive listing of the individual studies reviewed is provided in the reference list in Part V. Studies associated with Brophy & Good (1986) are identified by the symbol *.

Rosenshine & Stevens (1986)

Groups of studies reviewed in this logical synthesis of research did not provide statistical evidence. However, many of the individual studies included in the logical synthesis of research do contain statistical evidence. In the event that a reader wishes to view this evidence, an extensive listing of the individual studies reviewed is provided in the reference list in Part V (the studies are identified by the symbol #).

Martens & Witt (2004)
Competence, Persistence, and Success: The Positive Psychology of
Behavioral Skill Instruction
Number of studies included: 40

Groups of studies reviewed in this logical synthesis of research did not provide statistical evidence. However, many of the individual studies included in the logical synthesis of research do contain statistical evidence. In the event that a reader wishes to view this evidence, an extensive listing of the individual studies reviewed is provided in the reference list in Part V (the studies are identified by the symbol %).

Statistical Evidence on Maximizing Teaching Time

GENERALIZATION TESTED: ON MAXIMIZING TEACHING TIME—CHAPTER 6

Achievement of learning objectives is enhanced when more teaching time is devoted to students to guide and facilitate their performance of academic tasks they are assigned to perform (rather than students performing tasks on their own, teachers dealing with outside intrusions, or students being assigned to nonacademic tasks).

Total number of studies covered: 68

Brophy & Good (1986); Anderson (1995)

Groups of studies reviewed in these logical syntheses of research did not provide statistical evidence. However, many of the individual studies included in these logical syntheses of research do contain statistical evidence. In the event that a reader wishes to view this evidence, an extensive listing of the individual studies reviewed is provided in the reference list in Part V. Studies associated with Brophy & Good (1986) are identified by the symbol * and studies associated with Anderson (1995) are identified by the symbol #.

Table 6.1
Mevarech & Kramarski (2003)
The Effects of Metacognitive Training versus Worked-Out Examples on Students'
Mathematical Reasoning

Analysis of the pretest scores indicated that neither the treatment main effect, $F(1,118) < 1.00$, $p > .05$, nor the interaction between the treatment and prior knowledge, $F(1,118) < 1.00$, $p > .05$, were significant. Only the prior knowledge main effect was significant, $F(1,118) = 181.05$, $p > .001$. Thus, no significant differences between MT and WE students were found on the pretest scores for lower achievers (M = 66.19 and 64.48; SD = 17.06 and 12.89 for WE and MT, respectively) or higher achievers (M = 92.88 and 92.43; SD = 4.50 and 4.34 for WE and MT, respectively).

Table 6.1 (continued)

Mean Scores and Standard Deviations on the Pretest and Post-test Measures by Treatment and Level of Prior Knowledge

	Worked-Out Examples		Metacognitive Training	
	Lower Ach. N = 27	Higher Ach. N = 25	Lower Ach. N = 35	Higher Ach. N = 35
Pretest				
M	66.19	92.88	64.48	92.43
SD	(17.06)	(4.50)	(12.89)	(4.34)
Immediate Post-test (Total Score)				
M	58.88	85.56	69.91	87.11
SD	(21.53)	(11.50)	(19.36)	(14.69)
Verbal Explanations				
M	5.20	7.12	7.60	9.85
SD	(4.20)	(4.90)	(4.04)	(4.70)
Algebraic Representations				
M	6.00	5.24	8.31	8.54
SD	(4.50)	(5.09)	(4.14)	(4.92)
Algebraic Solution				
M	5.29	6.16	8.03	9.60
SD	(5.12)	(5.69)	(4.63)	(5.40)

The two-way ANOVA of the immediate post-test scores indicated, however, significant main effects for the treatment (MS = 1190.11; $F(1,118) = 3.98$, p < .05) and prior knowledge (MS = 14381.38; $F(1,118) = 48.08$, p < .001), but the interaction between the treatment and prior knowledge was not significant (MS = 660.48; $F(1,118) = 2.21$, p > .05). The MT students significantly outperformed the WE students (M = 78.54 and 72.72; SD = 19.14 and 21.89 for the MT and WE groups, respectively. In particular lower achievers benefited from the MT method, but their gains did not come at the expense of higher achievers (ESs for the lower and higher achiever groups, respectively, were .51 and .14 favouring the MT group).

To gain further insight on students' mathematical reasoning, we analyzed students' written mathematical responses by focusing on three criteria: students' verbal explanations of their mathematical reasoning, algebraic representations of verbal situations, and algebraic solutions. The table above presents also the mean scores and standard deviations on the three criteria by treatment and level of prior knowledge. ANOVA indicated significant main effects for their treatment, $F(1,118) = 9.89$, 10.84, and 10.51, for students' verbal explanations of their mathematical reasoning, algebraic representations of verbal situations, and algebraic solutions, respectively; all p values < .05, but none of the interactions between the treatment and prior knowledge was significant; all $F(1,118)$ values < 1.00, all p values > .05. Within the lower achiever group, the MT students significantly outperformed the WE students on verbal explanations of mathematical reasoning, algebraic representations, and algebraic solutions (*ES*s for the three criteria, respectively, were .57, .51, and .54 standard deviations). Also within the higher achiever group, MT students significantly outperformed the WE students on all three criteria (respective ESs = .56, .65, and .60 standard deviations).

Table 6.2
Blatchford et al. (2003)
Are Class Size Differences Related to Pupils' Educational Progress and Classroom Processes?

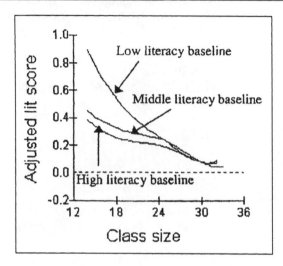

Relationship between reception year class size and literacy progress (adjusted for school entry scores).

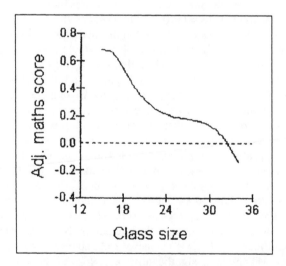

Relationship between class size and mathematics attainment in reception (adjusted for school entry scores).

Table 6.2 (continued)

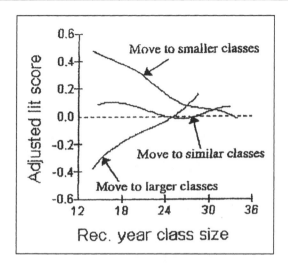

Relationship between reception class size and literacy progress in year 1.

Table 6.3
Smith et al. (2003)
Class-Size Reduction: A Fresh Look at the Data

In this analysis average growth curves (AGC)—a means of charting and predicting the average expected performance of a test's norm group over time—were used to measure Wisconsin's SAGE (Student Achievement Guarantee in Education) program's effect on the achievement of the cohort of SAGE students entering first grade in 1997–1998.

AGC for Reading Subscore

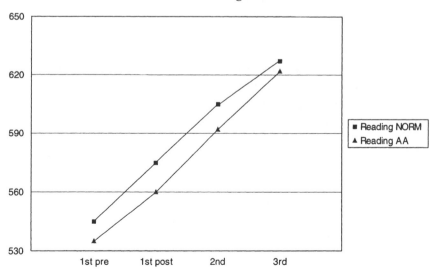

Table 6.3 (continued)

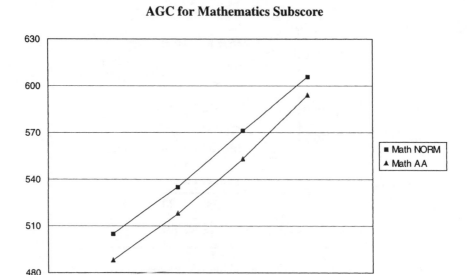

AGC for Mathematics Subscore

Legend: ■ Math NORM, ▲ Math AA

Statistical Evidence on Providing Ample Learning Time

GENERALIZATION: ON AMPLE LEARNING TIME—CHAPTER 7

Achievement of learning objectives is enhanced when students are given ample time to perform assigned tasks.

Total number of studies covered: 456+

Anderson (1985)

Groups of studies reviewed in this logical synthesis of research did not provide statistical evidence. However, many of the individual studies included in the logical synthesis of research do contain statistical evidence. In the event that a reader wishes to view this evidence, an extensive listing of the individual studies reviewed is provided in the reference list in Part V (the studies are identified by the symbol %).

Marliave & Filby (1985)

Groups of studies reviewed in this logical synthesis of research did not provide statistical evidence. However, many of the individual studies included in the logical synthesis of research do contain statistical evidence. In the event that a reader wishes to view this evidence, an extensive listing of the individual studies reviewed

is provided in the reference list in Part V (the studies are identified by the symbol !).

Table 7.1
Kulik & Kulik (1987)
Mastery Testing and Student Learning: A Meta-analysis
Number of studies included: 49

Class Level	Course Content	Duration in Weeks	Mastery Level	Effect Size
3 and 4th n = 1	Psychology n = 15	1 wk n = 2	80 n = 13	–0.42
4th and 5th n = 1	Math n = 11	2 wk n = 5	70 n = 1	to 1.46
7th n = 6	Science n = 9	3 wk n = 1	75 n = 2	
8th n = 3	Math & Science n = 1	4 wk n = 4	85 n = 2	
9th n = 3	Biology n = 2	5 wk n = 5	90 n = 11	
7th–9th n = 2	Social studies n = 3	6 wk n = 2	93 n = 1	
10th n = 2	Physics n = 1	7 wk n = 2	95 n = 1	
Senior hi n = 1	Chemistry n = 1	8 wk n = 3	100 n =15	
College n = 30	Engineering n = 1	10 wk n = 3		
	Education n = 1	11 wk n = 2		
	Sailing n = 1	12 wk n = 3		
	Statistics n = 1	13 wk n = 1		
	9 courses n = 1	15 wk n = 2		
	Geography n = 1	16 wk n = 4		
		17 wk n = 1		
		18 wk n = 2		
		26 wk n = 1		
		32 wk n = 2		

n = number of studies.

Table 7.2
Anderson (1994)
Synthesis of Mastery Learning (Meta-analysis) Achievement Outcomes
Number of studies included: 7

Study	Percent Positive	Total N	ES	Grade Level
Kulik et al. (1990a)	93.2%	NR	.52	K–College
Slavin (1990)	NR	NR	.27	K–12
Kulik et al. (1990b)	63.6%	NR	.40	K–12
Guskey & Pigott (1988)	89.1%	11,532	.41 Psych.	K–12
			.50 Science	
			.53 Soc. Stud.	
			.60 Lang. Arts	
			.70 Math	
			.94 Elementary	
			.48 High School	
			.41 College	
Willett et al. (1983)	NR		.64	K–12
Guskey & Gates (1985)	92.2%	8,074	.65–.94	K–College
Block & Burns (1976)	89.0%	2,767	.83	K–College

N = number of students; ES = effect size.

Individual studies analyzed by these meta-analyses are identified in the reference list by the following symbols:

Kulik et al. (1990a) *
Kulik et al. (1990b) #
Slavin (1990) @
Guskey & Pigott (1988) $
Guskey & Gates (1985) &
Block & Burns (1976) +

It was not possible to determine the individual studies for which readiness was an instructional tactic for the Willett et al. (1983) analysis.

Table 7.3

Swanson (2000)

What Instruction Works for Students with Learning Disabilities? Summarizing the Results from a Meta-analysis of Intervention Studies

Number of studies included: 180

Weighted Mean Effect Sizes for Group Design Studies as a Function of Dependent Measure Category

				LD Treatment versus LD Control					
			Effect Size of Unweighted	Effect Size of Weighted	95% Confidence Interval for Weighted Effects Lower	Upper	Standard Error	Homogeneity (Q)	
		N	K						
1.	*Cognitive Processing*	41	115	.87 (.64)	.54	.48	.61	.03	311.67**
1a.	Metacognitive	9	27	.98	.80	.66	.94	.07	83.91**
1b.	Attribution	7	17	.79	.62	.44	.79	.08	31.99*
1c.	Other Processes	25	71	.65	.46	.38	.53	.03	176.07**
2.	*Word Recognition*	54	159	.71 (.56)	.57	.52	.62	.02	431.45**
2a.	Standardized	23	79	.79	.62	.54	.69	.04	205.61**
2b.	Experimental	35	80	.72	.53	.48	.60	.03	223.07**
3.	*Reading Comprehension*	58	176	.82 (.60)	.72	.68	.77	.02	565.95**
3a.	Standardized	16	38	.45	.45	.36	.54	.05	33.87
3b.	Experimental	44	138	.84	.81	.75	.86	.02	489.54**
4.	*Spelling*	24	54	.54 (.53)	.44	.37	.52	.04	100.44**
4a.	Standardized	8	20	.61	.45	.34	.57	.06	34.45
4b.	Experimental	18	34	.48	.44	.33	.54	.05	65.94**
5.	*Memory/Recall*	12	33	.81 (.46)	.56	.43	.70	.06	42.72

(continued)

Table 7.3 (continued)

	N	K	Effect Size of Unweighted	Effect Size of Weighted	95% Confidence Interval for Weighted Effects Lower	Upper	Standard Error	Homogeneity (Q)
6. *Mathematics*	28	71	.58 (.45)	.40	.33	.46	.04	128.28**
6a. Standardized	9	22	.41	.33	.23	.46	.05	25.72
6b. Experimental	21	49	.59	.42	.34	.51	.04	101.43**
7. *Writing*	19	67	.84 (.60)	.63	.54	.72	.05	157.45**
7a. Standardized	3	7	.37	.36	.14	.58	.11	5.01
7b. Experimental	16	60	.80	.68	.59	.78	.04	145.27**
8. *Vocabulary*	11	20	.79 (.44)	.78	.66	.89	.05	38.58**
9. *Attitude/Self-Concept*	25	86	.68 (.69)	.39	.33	.45	.03	210.65**
10. *Intelligence*	9	32	.58 (.59)	.41	.30	.52	.06	54.37**
11. *General Reading*	15	31	.60 (.50)	.52	.41	.65	.06	55.15*
12. *Phonics/Orthographic Skills*	29	175	.70 (.36)	.64	.60	.69	.02	453.70**
12a. Standardized Phonics	8	60	.72	.67	.62	.73	.03	275.87**
12b. Experimental Phonics	21	78	.76	.60	.52	.67	.04	175.22**
13. *Global Achievement* (grades, total achievement)	10	21	.91 (.76)	.45	.31	.58	.07	56.64**
14. *Creativity*	3	11	.84 (.49)	.70	.52	.87	.09	33.61**
15. *Social Skills*	13	36	.46 (.22)	.41	.30	.51	.05	28.46
16. *Perceptual Processes*	10	37	.74 (.65)	.26	.17	.35	.04	46.64
17. *Language*	9	52	.54 (.48)	.36	.28	.44	.04	75.53**

Notes: numbers in parentheses = standard deviation; * p < .01; ** p < .001.

Table 7.4
Bangert-Drowns et al. (2004)
**The Effects of School-Based Writing-to-Learn Interventions on Academic
Achievement: A Meta-analysis**
Number of studies included: 46

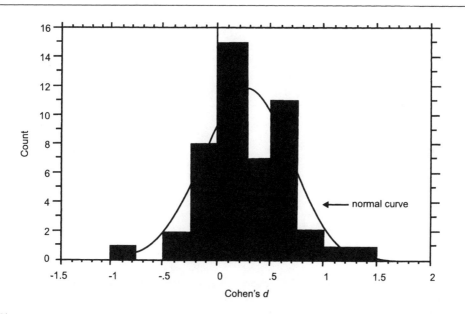

Histogram comparing the frequency distribution of 48 unweighted achievement effect sizes
to the normal distribution.

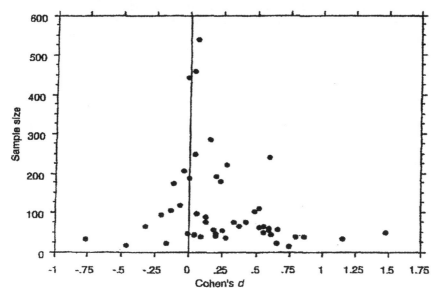

Scatterplot of the distribution of unweighted achievement effect sizes by total sample sizes
of 48 treatment comparisons.

Table 7.5
Stallings & Stipeck (1986)
Research on Early Childhood and Elementary School Teaching Programs
Number of studies included: 17

	Summary of Mastery Learning Research										
	Achievement						Retention				
	Level of Learning				Variability of Learning		Level of Learning				Variability of Learning	
LFM Studies	(>)	(>)	(<)	(<)	(≤)	(>)	(>)	(>)	(<)	(<)	(≤)	(>)
Anderson (1976a)	3	8	4	3	17	1	3	2	0	0	5	0
Burrows & Okey (1975)	1	0	0	0	1	0	1	0	0	0	1	0
Kim et al. (1974)	2	0	0	0	0	2						
Lee et al. (1971)	4	0	0	0	3	1						
Okey (1974)	1	4	0	0	3	2						
Okey (1975)	7	7	0	0	9	5						
LFM Total	18	19	4	3	33	11	4	2	0	0	6	0

Note: From "Mastery Learning" by J. Block and R. Burns, 1976, *Review of Research in Education*, p. 32. Copyright 1976 by James Block and Robert Burns. Abbreviated version reprinted by permission.

* The symbols in the heading indicate the following:
Level of Learning:
   (>) Scores of mastery group statistically greater than scores of nonmastery group (p < .05).
   (>) Scores of mastery group greater, but not statistically greater, than scores of nonmastery group.
   (<) Scores of mastery group less than, but not statistically less than, scores of nonmastery group.
   (<) Scores of mastery group statistically less than scores of nonmastery group (p < .05).
Variability of Learning:
   (≤) Mastery group achievement variance less than or equal to nonmastery achievement variance.
   (>) Mastery group achievement variance greater than nonmastery achievement variance.

Table 7.6
Clark et al. (1983)
The Effectiveness of Mastery Learning Strategies in Undergraduate Education Courses

Summary of Multivariate Multiple Regression Analysis

Source of Variation	df	Multivariate F-Statistic	Univariate F-Statistics		
			Final Test	Grade	Absences
Sex	1	3 82	6 33**	5 16**	0 29
Self-concept (SC) eliminating sex	1	3 35*	5 28**	4 44*	0 74
Affect (AFF) eliminating sex & SC	1	61	1 17	1 47	4 47**
Treatment eliminating sex, SC & AFF	1	4 87**	5 28**	0 07	3 49*
Residual	192	Mean Squares	16 54	59	12.97

$* p < .05; ** p < .01.$

Table 7.7
Clark et al. (1983)
The Effectiveness of Mastery Learning Strategies in Undergraduate Education Courses

Intercorrelations among Student Variables by Treatment Group

Variables	Pretest	Sex	Self-concept	Affect	Final test	Grade	Absences
Pretest		− 154	077	− .067	099	163	168
Sex	057			.448**	− 036	− 060	130
Self-concept	247*	.286**	*Mastery*	333*	084	144	324*
Affect	079	.267*	648** *Control*		− 247	− 335*	144
Final test	356**	.289**	338**	020		682**	− .340*
Grade	088	.287**	302**	065	.772*		− .349*
Absences	− 229	.253*	058	279*	− .188	− 207	

$* p < .05; ** p < .01.$

Table 7.8
Karweit (1993)
Effective Preschool and Kindergarten Programs for Students at Risk
Number of studies included: 20

Programs Evaluated with Random Assignment or Matched Control Group Design

Name	Developer	Grade	Content	Instructional Strategy	Evaluation Design	Measures	Effects
Alpha Phonics	So. San Francisco U.S.D.	K	Rdg. Readiness	Readiness phonics program focusing on sequential learning, immediate correction, feedback & game-like presentation for about 1 hr/day.	Post ANOVA treatment sch. & remaining 12 in district. Stated that IQ & background of T & C equivalent. All students there for K–3.	Metropolitan ach. readiness ach. G1 ach. G2 ach. G3	.89 1.14 .90 1.07
Astra Math	So. San Francisco U.S.D.	K	Math Readiness	Comprehensive, structured, and sequenced curriculum with 22 self-contained units. Uses multisensory approach, Behavior modification, and high-interest materials.	Pre-post random assignment to treatment—control 3 classes each.	CTBS fall-spring	.45<1> (adj) .30 (not adj)
MECCA	Trumbull Public Schools (CT)	K	Development & implementation of early identification procedures & prescriptive educational programs for children entering K with specific potential handicaps	Pre-post random assignment to treatment and control.	JANSKY Metropol. Monroe	.67 .88	.57 .96
TALK	Rockford, IL school system	K–3	Language	Lang. specialist in class instruction in listening skills for 4 wk ½ hour for 6 mos than classroom tchr continues lessons.	Pre-post ANCOVA on treatment and matched control. Original study—(75–6); replication—(76–77).	PPVT WISC PPVT (K)	75 .25 76 .42 75 .38 76 .46 75 .26 (K) 76 .74 75 .38 (K) 76 .55

Program	Site	Grade	Subject	Description	Evaluation Design	Instrument	Results
Every Student Every Day	St. Mary Parish	K–4 K–6	Math and reading	Daily diagnosis, evaluation, and prescription, computer scoring for coordination. Pullout design using 40 min. each day.	Pre-post design; changing percentile; fall to spring. 7 52 (76) 7 59 (77) 7 32 (82) 2 40 (83)	TOBE (preschool & K)	+
Baptist Hill K	Baptist Hill K, Greenville, AL	K	Reading and math	Full-day K, learning centers, diagnose individual learning needs on continuous basis with appropriate learning activities.	Pre-post design; fall to spring.	TOBE	
Early Prevention of School Failure	Peotone District, IL	4-, 5-, 6-year-olds		Early identification of developmental needs and learning styles of 4-, 5-, and 6-yr-olds. Screening, planning and pull-out; 20–30 minute instruction in different modalities at learning centers	Improvement per month on different scales—no comparison data either w/a control group or pre-implementation.	getting data	+
First Level Math	PRIMAK Educational Foundation	K or 1	Math	Sequential curriculum and management system that is diagnostic/prescriptive. Instructional groups formed on basis of pretests. Instruction in 3–4 groups for about 20–30 minutes.	Pre-post design; fall to spring.	CIRCUS	+ not possible to compute
New Adventure in Learning	Moore Elem. School, Tallahassee, FL	K		Individually determined instruction with positive behavior management.	Pre-post; nat'l norm comparison using expected growth.	PPVT—mean improvmt 1.67/ math. Gilmore oral reading test—10% on grade level at pre, 57% at post.	no current data

Table 7.8 (continued)

Name	Developer	Grade	Content	Instructional Strategy	Evaluation Design	Measures	Effects	
							#1	#2
MARC	Walkulla City and Crawford-ville, FL	K–1	Reading	Continuous progress using multisensory activities and systematic instruction. Diagnostic and record-keeping instrument, skill sheets provided.	Post ANOVA on treatment and matched local control at end of K and end of 1st. Pre ANOVA to ensure equivalence.	SESAT (II) letters word rdg. sent rdg.	1.12 .88 .25	.55 na na
						BOEHM KUHLMAN ANDERSON SESAT (I)	ns ns ns	
INSRUJCT	Lincoln Public Schools	K–3	Reading	Individual placement & progress through multi-unit model.	ANCOVA comparisons of treatment and comparable schools chosen on similar SES, school organization, and number of compensatory students.	Metropolitan word know. reading spelling	.35** .25* <2> ns	
PLAY	Bristol, VA	K–1 and ¾ years	Motor/cognitive	Diagnostic/prescriptive direct instruction in perceptual/motor skills; monthly home reinforcement and activities.	ANOVA on treatment and control. Control were eligibles (score below cut off) not enrolled because positions filled.	BOEHM 75–76 76–77 77–78	1.77 .23 1.33	
CLIMB	Middlesex, NJ	K–12	Reading and math	Diagnostic/prescription approach in acquisition of reading and math skills, providing a management design for coordinating & integrating classroom & support personnel.	Spring-to-spring achievement compared to nat'l norms and compensatory growth.	CTBS	+	
STAMM	Lakewood, CO	K–8	Math	Continuous progress math with management system.	Pre-post implementation scores for district and adoption site.	CAT	+	
Education Assessment & Inst. for the Educationally Deprived	Kenosha, WI	K–10	Language	Extended day K 2–3 hrs in afternoon, additional time for remedial instruction.	Pre-post design.	PPVT	+	

Program	Location	Grade	Focus	Description	Evaluation	Measure	Results
Strategies in Early Childhood Education	Waupun, WI	preK and K	Screening	Developmental and screening model. Self instructional, individually paced, learning centers, developmentally sequenced materials.	Ad hoc comparison of treatment children with another group. No evidence of prior comparability.		
Right to read	Glassboro, NJ	K–3	Reading	Diagnostic, prescriptive, individual progress model. Upgraded.	No control; 325 children; pre-post.	CRI Classroom Reading Inventory	Avg. gain 1.52 yr.
Project Catch Up	Newport Mesa, CA	K–6	Reading and math	Remedial instruction in reading & math to underachieving students using diagnoses, prescription. Positive contacts with family.	Mean gain by grade on CTBS from fall to spring. No data on K.	CTBS fall–spring	
Amphitheater School District KIP	Tucson, AZ	K		Parent involvement; once a week training of parents in game or activity that gives practice in basic skills with followup practice with students who need practice in that skill and monitoring of student progress.	Comparison to comparable school on percent scoring above 30 percentile 1 year after.	CAT	66% vs. 38%
VIP	Spokane, WA	K	Develop skills	Develop friendly, feeling parents and school, provide training for parents in how to help children at home, to send home games that reinforce skills learned at school.	Santa Clara Inventory gain of 2.32 mo. in developmental age/ month; no control group.	Santa Clara Inventory (note problem with fall–spring)	

Pretest effect size = −.15 was added to posttest effect size .30 to arrive at the adjusted effect size. Effect sizes were computed by determining the t value to generate p < .01 and .05 respectively.

Table 7.9
Gettinger (1984)
Means and Standard Deviations for Retention

Variable	Reading Task		Spelling Task	
	M	SD	M	SD
Time Spent Learning	80.08	18.38	72.39	18.29
Time Needed to Learn	92.99	12.49	84.88	17.88

M = mean score; SD = standard deviation.

Table 7.10
Montazemi & Wang (1995)
An Empirical Investigation of CBI in Support of Mastery Learning

MANOVA Test of Variation of Performance in Nine Lab-tests

Source of Variation	SS	df	MS	F	Sig. of t
Between-Subjects Effect					
Within cells	14.27	330	0.04		
Regression	0.13	1	0.13	3.03	0.082
Constant	279.02	1	279.02	6450.87	0.000
Two student types	2.80	1	2.80	64.08	0.000
Within-subjects Effect					
Within cells	21.77	2648	0.01		
Lab-test	13.29	8	1.66	202.08	0.000
Two student types by Lab-test	0.96	8	0.12	14.63	0.000

	B	Beta	Std. Err.	t-value	Sig. of t
Covariates					
Computer Anxiety	–0.000	–0.030	0.000	–0.553	0.581
Computer Efficacy	–0.001	–0.044	0.001	–0.798	0.426

Mauchly Sphericity Test W = 0.35437.
Chi-Square Approx. = 340.40106 with 35 df.

Table 7.11
Montazemi & Wang (1995)
An Empirical Investigation of CBI in Support of Mastery Learning

MANOVA Test of Variation of Performance in Tutorial-Tests
across Twenty Chapters

Source of Variation	SS	df	MS	F	Sig. of F
Between-Subjects Effect					
Within cells	41.27	330	0.14		
Regression	0.01	1	0.01	0.04	0.837
Constant	416.93	1	416.93	2878.90	0.000
Two types of students	4.10	1	4.10	28.28	0.000
Within-subjects Effect					
Within cells	108.22	5434	0.02		
Chapter	17.30	19	0.91	45.73	0.000
Two student type by chapter	1.37	19	0.07	3.61	0.000

	B	Beta	Std. Err.	t-value	Sig. of t
Covariates					
Computer anxiety	0.000	0.01218	0.000	0.205	0.837
Computer efficacy	0.000	0.04661	0.001	0.788	0.433

Mauchly Sphericity Test W = 0.0068.
Chi-Square Approx. = 1394.8969 with 189 df.
Significance = 0.000.

Table 7.12
Aviles (1998)
A Contrast of Mastery Learning and Non-Mastery Learning Instruction in an Undergraduate Social Work Course

Mean Exam Scores before Make-up Exams

	Mastery		Non-Mastery		Diff.
	M	SD	M	SD	
Exam 1	81.12	10.44	82.10	11.50	0.98
Exam 2	84.44	10.01	83.90	10.80	0.54
Exam 3	75.09	10.85	79.00	11.70	3.91

Mean Make-up Exam Scores and Corresponding Exam Scores

	Make-up Exams Taken	Original Exam Score	Make-up Exam Score	Change
Exam 1	29	M 74.40	90.80	+16.10**
		SD 10.00	7.30	
Exam 2	22	M 77.10	82.10	+5.00**
Exam 3	27	M 66.00	83.00	+17.00**
Total	n = 79			

Notes: * p < .01; ** p < .0001.

Mean Exam Scores after Make-up Exam Score Replacement

	Mastery		Non-Mastery		Diff.
	M	SD	M	SD	
Exam 1	88.00	7.90	82.10	11.50	5.90*
Exam 2	86.40	7.90	83.90	10.80	2.50
Exam 3	81.70	7.80	79.00	11.70	2.70

Note: * p < .05.

Mean Retention Scores: Exam One and Retention Test

	Mastery		Non-Mastery		Diff.
	M	SD	M	SD	
Exam 1R**	18.85	3.59	19.39	3.93	0.54
Retention***	13.29	2.77	12.73	4.15	0.56
Difference	5.56	3.04	6.75	3.48	1.19*

Notes: * p < .05, two-tailed. Max score possible = 26.00; ** 1R = scores the 26 items generated on exam one; *** Retention = scores the same 26 items generated on exam three.

Table 7.13
Krank & Moon (2001)
Can a Combined Mastery/Cooperative Learning Environment Positively Impact Undergraduate Academic and Affective Outcomes?

Summary Statistics for All Measures by Cooperative Learning (CL), Mastery Learning (ML), and Combined Cooperative/Mastery Learning (CL/ML)

Treatment Condition

Measure	Cooperative Learning		Mastery Learning	
SDQII (b)	**M**	**SD**	**M**	**SD**
Pretest	89.68	10.30	89.47	13.32
Posttest	90.24	6.56	89.75	13.75
Final Exam (c)	24.87	6.64	25.56	6.45
n	38		36	

Measure	Combined ML/CL	
SQDII (b)	**M**	**SD**
Pretest	83.97	10.14
Posttest	87.53	10.68
Final Exam (c)	29.53	5.79
n	30	

(b) Student Description Questionnaire III. Higher scores indicate more positive academic self-concepts.
(c) Scores on the final exam were the number correct. The maximum more positive score was 40.

Statistical Evidence on Providing Transfer of Learning Instruction

GENERALIZATION TESTED: ON TRANSFER OF LEARNING INSTRUCTION—CHAPTER 8

Achievement of learning objectives is enhanced when students are taught beforehand the knowledge and skills needed to perform assigned tasks and how to determine when learned knowledge and skills can be used to perform assigned tasks.

Total number of studies covered: 244

Table 8.1
Rosenshine et al. (1996)
Teaching Students to Generate Questions: A Review of the Intervention Studies
Number of studies included: 26

Prompt	Overall Median Effect Sizes by Type of Prompt					
	Standardized Test			Experimenter-Developed Test		
	Reciprocal Teaching (*n* = 6)	Regular Instruction (*n* = 7)	Combined (*n* = 13)	Reciprocal Teaching (*n* = 12)	Regular Instruction (*n* = 19)	Combined (*n* = 19)
Signal words	0.34 (4)	0.46 (2)	0.36 (6)	0.88 (5)	0.67 (2)	0.85 (7)
Generic questions/ Stems					1.12 (4)	1.12 (4)
Main idea		0.70 (1)	0.70 (1)	1.24 (1)	0.13 (4)	0.25 (5)
Question type	0.02 (2)	0.00 (1)	0.00 (3)	3.37 (1)		3.37 (1)
Story grammar					1.08 (2)	1.08 (2)
No facilitator		0.14 (3)	0.14 (3)			

Note: *n* = number of studies. Number in parentheses refers to the number of studies used to compute an effect size.

Table 8.2

Fukkink & de Glopper (1998)

Effects of Instruction in Deriving Word Meaning from Context: A Meta-analysis

Number of studies included: 22

Summary of Features and Effect Sizes of the Studies Included in the Meta-analysis

Study	$N_e + N_c$	PPD	A	Mean	Test	α	Pre	Age	CS	Dur.	Type	d	se
Guarino (1960): Syracuse study	85 + 82	1	NR	NA	MC	.83	.34	15	28.3	360	clue	.60	.16
Guarino (1960): Michigan study	153 + 148	1	NR	NA	MC	.79	.02	15	25.5	495	clue	.32	.12
Cox (1974): Cloze 1-group	25 + 22	0	R	NA	MC	.84	-.06	9	25	720	cloze	-.12	.29
Cox (1974): Cloze 2-group	24 + 22	0	R	NA	MC	.84	-.07	9	24	720	cloze	.21	.30
Bissell (1982): Cloze	30 + 28	1	R	NA	MC	.38	.00	18.5	23.5	238	cloze	.00	.26
Bissell (1982): Forced Cloze	29 + 28	1	R	NA	MC	.38	.00	18.5	23.5	238	cloze	.23	.27
Sampson et al. (1982)	46 + 46	1	R	A	C	.85	—	8	7	662	cloze	.73	.22
Carnine et al. (1984): rule	12 + 12	0	R	NA	MC	.55	.00	10	1	90	strategy	.82	.43
Carnine et al (1984): practice	12 + 12	0	R	NA	MC	.55	.00	10	1	90	practice	.73	.42
Schwartz & Raphael (1985): Exp. I	8 + 8	0	R	NA	def	.55	.00	9	8	160	definition	5.45	1.19
Schwartz & Raphael (1985): practice	14 + 28	1	R	NA	def	.61	-.04	10	14	160	practice	.35	.11
Schwartz & Raphael (1985): training	14 + 28	1	R	NA	def	.61	.59	10	14	160	definition	1.22	.12
Herman & Weaver (1988)	14 + 16	0	NR	NA	def	.13	.15	13	14	325	strategy	.57	.37
Kranzer (1988): textbook context	19 + 19	0	NR	NA	def	.66	.24	13	23	155	strategy	.50	.33
Kranzer (1988): enriched context	21 + 19	0	NR	NA	def	.66	.01	13	23	155	strategy	-.40	.32
Kranzer (1988): definition + context	21 + 19	0	NR	NA	def	.66	.20	13	23	155	strategy	.43	.32
Jenkins et al. (1989): low	22 + 22	0	NR	NA	def	.61	.00	10	23	135	strategy	.03	.30
Jenkins et al. (1989): medium	22 + 22	0	NR	NA	def	.61	.00	10	23	165	strategy	.48	.31
Jenkins et al. (1989): high	22 + 22	0	NR	NA	def	.61	.00	10	23	300	strategy	.71	.31
Buikema & Graves (1993)	19 + 19	0	NR	NA	MC	.61	.28	12.5	19	250	clue	.80	.34
De Glopper et al. (1997)	29 + 30	1	R	A	def	.78	—	11	8	480	strategy	.15	.26
Tomesen & Aarnoutse (1998)	16 + 15	0	NR	NA	def	.84	-.21	9	4	450	cloze	1.53	.41

Note: $N_e + N_c$ = size of the experimental group + size of the control group; PPD: 1 = pretest posttest design, 0 = other design; Assignment: R = random, NR = not random; Means: A = means are adjusted by covariance analysis; NA = means are not adjusted; Test: MC = multiple choice, c = cloze test, def = definition task; α = Cronbach's alpha of the posttest (estimated values in italics); Pre: difference in the pretest in standard deviation units between experimental and control group (estimated values in italics); Age = average age of students; CS = class size; Dur.: duration of the instruction in minutes; Type: type of instruction; d = effect size d; se = standard error of the effect size.

Gersten & Baker (2001)
Teaching Expressive Writing to Students with Learning Disabilities:
A Meta-analysis
Number of studies included: 13

Summed across all 13 studies, the mean effect size on the aggregate writing measure was 0.81. The 95 percent confidence interval was 0.65–0.97, providing clear evidence that the writing interventions had a significant positive effect on the quality of students' writing. Positive effect sizes were found in each of the 13 studies, ranging in magnitude from 0.30 to 1.73.

Ehri et al. (2001)
Phonemic Awareness Instruction Helps Children Learn to Read:
Evidence from the National Reading Panel's Meta-analysis
Number of studies included: 52

The effect size statistic measures how much the mean of the PA-instructed group exceeded the mean of the control group in standard deviation units. An effect size of 1 indicates that the treatment group mean was one standard deviation higher than the control group mean, revealing a strong effect of instruction. An effect size of 0 indicates that treatment and control group means were identical, showing that instruction had no effect. All of the effect sizes involving PA and reading outcomes were statistically greater than zero ($p < .05$). This indicates that instruction was uniformly effective in teaching PA and in facilitating transfer to reading across all levels of the moderator variables that were considered.

The overall effect size of PA instruction on the acquisition of PA was large, $d = 0.86$, based on 72 comparisons. The overall effect size on reading was moderate, $d = 0.53$, based on 90 comparisons. These findings lead us to conclude with much confidence that phonemic awareness instruction is more effective than alternative forms of instruction or no instruction in helping children acquire phonemic awareness and in facilitating transfer of PA skills to reading and spelling.

Misko (1995)
Transfer: Using Learning in New Contexts

Groups of studies reviewed in this logical synthesis of research did not provide statistical evidence. However, many of the individual studies included in the logical synthesis of research do contain statistical evidence. In the event that a reader wishes to view this evidence, an extensive listing of the individual studies reviewed is provided in the reference list in Part V. The studies are identified by the symbol *.

Prawat (1989)
Promoting Access to Knowledge, Strategy, and Disposition in
Students: A Research Synthesis

Groups of studies reviewed in this logical synthesis of research did not provide statistical evidence. However, many of the individual studies included in the logical synthesis of research do contain statistical evidence. In the event that a reader wishes to view this evidence, an extensive listing of the individual studies reviewed is provided in the reference list in Part V. The studies are identified by the symbol #.

Table 8.3
Barley et al. (2002)
Helping At-Risk Students Meet Standards: A Synthesis of Evidence-Based
Classroom Practices
Number of studies included: 118

Summary of Research Synthesis

Strategy	Type	Number of High-Quality Studies	Selected Implementation Considerations[a]	Synthesis Results on Positive Effects of Strategy on Student Achievement
General Instruction	Approach	4	Balance of direct instruction and authentic learning	Inconclusive
Cognitively Oriented Instruction	Approach	4	Student practice Student interaction Teacher modeling	Preliminary
Grouping Structures	Intervention	4	Heterogeneous groups Teacher training Student instructions	Preliminary
Tutoring	Intervention	5	Tutor training Program monitoring	Preliminary
Peer Tutoring	Intervention	13	Structured tasks Teacher monitoring Participant training	Preliminary
Computer-Assisted Instruction	Intervention	10	Subject matter	Conclusive

[a] Other implementation issues are described in the individual chapters on each strategy.

Statistical Findings by Chapter

Table 8.4
Marzolf & DeLoach (1994)
Transfer in Young Children's Understanding of Spatial Representations

	Mean Number of Errorless Retrievals			
	Retrieval 1		Retrieval 2	
	Mean	**Std Dev**	**Mean**	**Std Dev**
Experiment 1				
Transfer Group				
Day 1	2.67	1.23	3.50	.67
Day 2	2.58	1.31	3.08	.67
Control Group				
Day 1	1.08	.90	2.92	1.00
Day 2	1.42	1.00	3.08	.79
Experiment 2				
Transfer Group				
Day 1	3.50	.71	3.50	.53
Day 2	3.50	.97	3.80	.42
Control Group				
Day 1	1.20	.79	3.30	.95
Day 2	2.60	1.08	3.80	.42

Table 8.5
Farrell (1988)
How Teaching Proportionality Affects Transfer of Learning: Science and Math Teachers Need Each Other

	Transfer Test and Pretest Scores				
Instruction Method	**Percent Correct**	**Mean**	**Standard Deviation**	**z**	**p**
Experiment 1					
Transfer Test					
Proportional	67.3	10.77	4.45	5.68	< .001
Standard	34.8	5.58	4.54		
Pretest					
Proportional	31.5	7.55	4.52	1.17	.121
Standard	26.4	6.34	5.57		

(continued)

Table 8.5 (continued)

Instruction Method	Percent Correct	Mean	Standard Deviation	z	p
Experiment 2					
Transfer Test					
Proportional	72.4	11.58	4.33	3.39	< .001
Standard	50.4	8.07	4.76		
Pretest					
Proportional	47.4	11.36	5.98	1.87	.031
Standard	37.2	8.93	5.21		

Table 8.6
Gott et al. (1995)
Tutoring for Transfer of Technical Competence

Sherlock 2 Posttest Measures of Troubleshooting Proficiency				
Group	**N**	**Test**	**Mean**	**Std Dev**
Novices		VTT3		
Control	23		59	37
Experimental	18		95	5
Masters	13		85	12
Novices		VTT4		
Control	23		58	37
Experimental	18		91	7
Masters	13		86	11
Novices		NIT		
Control	23		75	14
Experimental	18		87	12
Masters	13		86	11

Table 8.7
Gott et al. (1995)
Tutoring for Transfer of Technical Competence

Frankenstation Posttest Measures of Transfer			
Novices		VTT	
Control	21	55	31
Experimental	17	82	23
Masters	12	91	22
Novices		NIT	
Control	21	72	4
Experimental	17	80	10
Masters	12	88	12

Table 8.8
Gott et al. (1995)
Tutoring for Transfer of Technical Competence

	Effect Size for Postest Measures						
	Control			**Experimental**			**Effect**
Measure	**N**	**M**	**SD**	**N**	**M**	**SD**	**Size**
Sherlock VTT3	23	59	37	18	95	5	1.27
Sherlock VTT4	23	58	37	18	91	7	1.17
Sherlock NIT	23	75	14	18	87	12	.87
Frankenstation VTT	21	55	31	17	82	23	.96
Frankenstation NIT	21	72	11	17	80	10	.76

N = number of students; M = mean score; SD = standard deviation.

Table 8.9
Gott et al. (1995)
Tutoring for Transfer of Technical Competence

	Frequency of Component Swapping Without Complete Testing	
Group	**Swaps After No Testing**	**Swaps After Partial Testing**
Controls	50	12
Experimentals	3	13
Masters	8	15

Table 8.10
Gott et al. (1995)
Tutoring for Transfer of Technical Competence

Frequency and Quality of Self-Test Use		
Group	**Self-Test Use**	**Frequency of Inefficient Use**
Controls	16	11
Experimentals	12	4
Masters	14	2

Table 8.11
Gott et al. (1995)
Tutoring for Transfer of Technical Competence

Number of Violations in Logical Sequence of Troubleshooting	
Group	**Number of Violations**
Controls	21
Experimentals	9
Masters	20

Table 8.12
Gott et al. (1995)
Tutoring for Transfer of Technical Competence

Percentage of Solutions to Frankenstation VTT by Group	
Group	**Percentage Achieving Solution**
Controls	63.6
Experimentals	70.6
Masters	83.3

Table 8.13
Mevarech & Kramarski (1997)
IMPROVE: A Multidimensional Method for Teaching Mathematics in Heterogeneous Classrooms
Number of studies included: 2

Mean Scores and Standard Deviations (in Terms of Percent Correct) by Time, Treatment, and Ability on Introduction-to-Algebra and Mathematics Reasoning

| Treatment | IMPROVE | | | CONTROL | | |
Ability	Low	Middle	High	Low	Middle	High
Pretest						
M	37.76	66.46	86.33	40.20	66.89	86.85
S	8.17	6.63	6.48	9.87	7.93	5.42
Introduction-to-Algebra						
M	48.28	79.52	88.20	45.97	67.24	82.27
S	16.31	10.06	8.55	21.03	18.97	13.05
Mathematical Reasoning						
M	41.37	64.00	74.74	32.60	50.98	67.47
S	14.41	16.38	12.98	20.68	17.79	15.34

Table 8.14
Mevarech & Kramarski (1997)
IMPROVE: A Multidimensional Method for Teaching Mathematics in Heterogeneous Classrooms

Mean Scores and Standard Deviations (in Terms of Percent Correct) on Algebra by Treatment

| Treatment | IMPROVE | | | CONTROL | | |
Ability	Low	Middle	High	Low	Middle	High
Pretest						
M	50.71	76.20	92.19	52.32	74.52	90.39
S	13.29	5.59	4.33	10.40	5.65	4.35
Algebra (Overall)						
M	55.90	73.94	86.58	52.65	63.72	71.77
S	20.95	21.09	16.60	30.08	18.88	22.30
Numerals						
M	68.57	80.88	90.30	63.21	75.09	77.95
S	20.24	17.16	13.72	28.35	15.38	19.76
Substitution						
M	55.00	71.04	83.91	49.62	62.50	70.38
S	21.96	25.78	20.27	34.17	25.28	27.37

(continued)

Table 8.14 (continued)

Treatment	IMPROVE			CONTROL		
Ability	Low	Middle	High	Low	Middle	High
Expressions						
M	53.18	71.92	87.06	51.58	57.84	73.30
S	28.11	30.84	19.26	29.20	25.73	28.76
Word Problems						
M	46.32	70.44	84.57	45.45	57.15	66.20
S	27.92	24.84	20.47	34.97	22.64	27.87

Table 8.15

Mevarech & Kramarski (2003)

The Effects of Metacognitive Training versus Worked-Out Examples on Students' Mathematical Reasoning

Mean Scores and Standard Deviations of Students' Behaviours in Small Groups by Task and Treatment

	Task A		Task B	
	WE 3 teams	MT 5 teams	WE 3 yeams	MT 5 teams
Overall Number of Statements				
M	7.66	5.40	17.33	32.20
SD	(3.51)	(1.50)	(15.30)	(15.71)
Cognitive Statements				
M	4.66	4.80	6.01	10.81
SD	(2.08)	(1.32)	(3.00)	(5.82)
Metacognitive Statements				
M	3.00	.60	11.33	21.40
SD	(1.73)	(1.36)	(12.30)	(11.21)
Quality of Cognitive Discourse				
M	2.66	2.40	2.33	3.20
SD	(.57)	(1.45)	(.57)	(1.50)
Quality of Metacognitive Discourse				
M	2.30	.80	2.33	3.40
SD	(1.52)	(.86)	(1.52)	(1.90)
Level of Cooperative Behaviour				
M	3.00	2.30	3.01	3.62
SD	(0.00)	(1.13)	(1.73)	(.70)

Table 8.16
Mevarech & Kramarski (2003)
The Effects of Metacognitive Training versus Worked-Out Examples on Students'
Mathematical Reasoning

		Mean Scores and Standard Deviations on the Immediate and Delayed Post-test by Treatment	
		WE	MT
		$N = 52$	$N = 70$
Immediate Post-test			
Total	M	72.22	78.554
	SD	(21.89)	(19.14)
Verbal Explanations	M	6.16	8.73
	SD	(4.61)	(4.50)
Algebraic Representations	M	5.62	8.43
	SD	(4.76)	(4.51)
Algebraic Solution	M	572	8.81
	SD	(5.36)	(5.06)
Delayed Post-test			
Total	M	68.51	76.01
	SD	(28.67)	(23.23)
Verbal Explanations	M	10.03	11.77
	SD	(4.37)	(4.30)
Algebraic Representations	M	6.47	6.83
	SD	(2.16)	(2.58)
Algebraic Solution	M	9.73	10.20
	SD	4.10	2.15

Table 8.17
Mevarech & Kramarski (2003)
The Effects of Metacognitive Training versus Worked-Out Examples on Students'
Mathematical Reasoning

Mean Scores and Standard Deviations on the Pretest and Post-test Measures
by Treatment and Level of Prior Knowledge

	Worked-Out Examples		Metacognitive Training	
	Lower Ach.	Higher Ach.	Lower Ach.	Higher Ach.
	N = 27	N = 25	N = 35	N = 35
Pretest				
M	66.19	92.88	64.48	92.43
SD	(17.06)	(4.50)	(12.89)	(4.34)
Immediate Post-test (Total Score)				
M	58.88	85.56	69.91	87.17
SD	(21.53)	(11.50)	(19.36)	(14.69)
Verbal Explanations				
M	5.20	7.12	7.60	9.85
SD	(4.20)	(4.90)	(4.04)	(4.70)
Algebraic Representations				
M	6.00	5.24	8.31	8.54
SD	(4.50)	(5.09)	(4.14)	(4.92)
Algebraic Solution				
M	5.29	6.16	8.03	9.60
SD	(5.12)	(5.69)	(4.63)	(5.40)

Table 8.18
Alfassi (2004)
Reading to Learn: Effects of Combined Strategy Instruction on High School Students
Number of studies included: 2

Means, Standard Deviations, and Univariate ANCOVA Tests
of the Different Reading Measures Over Phases of Intervention

Phase	Experimental		Control		$F(1, 45)$
	M	SD	M	SD	
	Reading assessment[a]				
Pretesting	73	22.8	68	27.0	4.57*
Posttesting	80	19.9	71	25.8	

(continued)

Table 8.18 (continued)

Phase	M	SD	M	SD	F(1, 45)
		Standardized reading measure			
Pretesting	57.83	19.17	52.70	20.30	4.77*
Posttesting	61.72	18.84	50.50	22.47	

Note: ANCOVA = analysis of covariance.

[a] The values represent mean percentages of correctly answered questions on the reading assessment passages.

* $p < .05$.

Table 8.19
Alfassi (2004)
Reading to Learn: Effects of Combined Strategy Instruction on High School Students

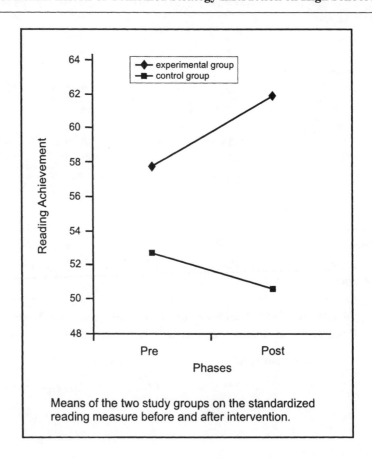

Means of the two study groups on the standardized reading measure before and after intervention.

Table 8.20
Alfassi (2004)
Reading to Learn: Effects of Combined Strategy Instruction on High School Students

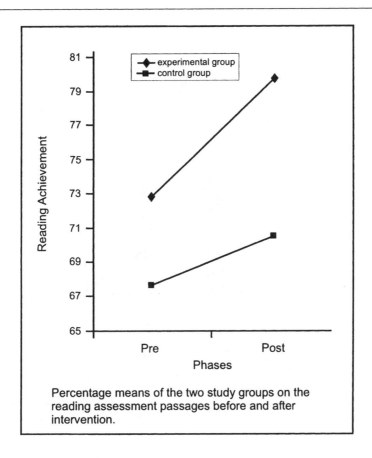

Percentage means of the two study groups on the reading assessment passages before and after intervention.

Statistical Evidence on Providing Decision-Making Instruction

GENERALIZATION: ON DECISION-MAKING INSTRUCTION—CHAPTER 9

Achievement of learning objectives is enhanced when students are shown how to use decision-making tactics to consider and select procedures to perform assigned tasks.

Total number of studies covered: 202

Table 9.1
Bangert-Drowns et al. (2004)
The Effects of School-Based Writing-to-Learn Interventions on Academic
Achievement: A Meta-analysis
Number of studies included: 46

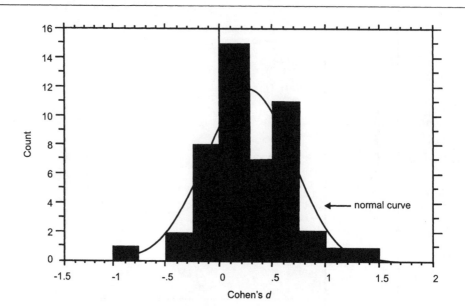

Histogram comparing the frequency distribution of 48 unweighted achievement effect sizes to the normal distribution.

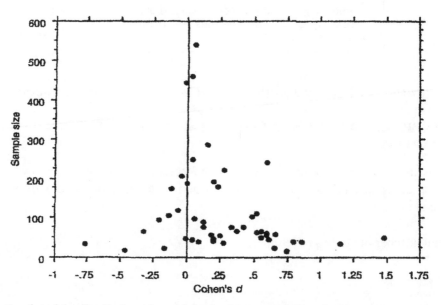

Scatterplot of the distribution of unweighted achievement effect sizes by total sample sizes of 48 treatment comparisons.

Kucan & Beck (1997)

Groups of studies reviewed in this logical synthesis of research did not provide statistical evidence. However, many of the individual studies included in the logical synthesis of research do contain statistical evidence. In the event that a reader wishes to view this evidence, an extensive listing of the individual studies reviewed is provided in the reference list in Part V (the studies are identified by the symbol @).

Dole et al. (1991)

Groups of studies reviewed in this logical synthesis of research did not provide statistical evidence. However, many of the individual studies included in the logical synthesis of research do contain statistical evidence. In the event that a reader wishes to view this evidence, an extensive listing of the individual studies reviewed is provided in the reference list in Part V (the studies are identified by the symbol $).

Table 9.2
Rosenshine & Meister (1994) Meta-analysis
Effect Sizes Based on Quality of Study

	Standardized Test	Short-Answer Test	Summarization Test	Experimenter Developed Test
All studies	.32	1.00	.85	.88
High quality	.31	1.00	.77	.86
Middle quality	.36	1.06	1.10	.87
Low quality	−.12			

Salomon & Perkins (1989)

Groups of studies reviewed in this logical synthesis of research did not provide statistical evidence. However, many of the individual studies included in the logical synthesis of research do contain statistical evidence. In the event that a reader wishes to view this evidence, an extensive listing of the individual studies reviewed is provided in the reference list in Part V (the studies are identified by the symbol *).

Prawat (1989)

Groups of studies reviewed in this logical synthesis of research did not provide statistical evidence. However, many of the individual studies included in the logical synthesis of research do contain statistical evidence. In the event that a reader wishes to view this evidence, an extensive listing of the individual studies reviewed is provided in the reference list in Part V (the studies are identified by the symbol #).

Table 9.3
Rosenshine et al. (1996) Meta-analysis
Overall Effect Sizes by Type of Test

| | Instructional Approach | | |
| | Reciprocal Teaching | Regular Instruction | Combined |
Type of test	(n = 9)	(n = 17)	(n = 26)
Standardized	0.34 (6)	0.35 (7)	0.36 (13)
Exp. short answer	1.00 (5)	0.88 (11)	0.87 (16)
Summary	0.85 (3)	0.81 (2)	0.85 (5)

Number in parentheses refers to the number of studies used to compute the effect size.

Table 9.4
Barley et al. (2002)
Helping At-Risk Students Meet Standards: A Synthesis of Evidence-Based Classroom Practices
Number of studies included: 118

| | Summary of Research Synthesis | | | |
Strategy	Type	Number of High-Quality Studies	Selected Implementation Considerations[a]	Synthesis Results on Positive Effects of Strategy on Student Achievement
General Instruction	Approach	4	Balance of direct instruction and authentic learning	Inconclusive
Cognitively Oriented Instruction	Approach	4	Student practice Student interaction Teacher modeling	Preliminary
Grouping Structures	Intervention	4	Heterogeneous groups Teacher training Student instructions	Preliminary
Tutoring	Intervention	5	Tutor training Program monitoring	Preliminary
Peer Tutoring	Intervention	13	Structured tasks Teacher monitoring Participant training	Preliminary
Computer-Assisted Instruction	Intervention	10	Subject matter	Conclusive

[a] Other implementation issues are described in the individual chapters on each strategy.

Table 9.5
Mevarech & Kramarski (1997)
IMPROVE: A Multidimensional Method for Teaching Mathematics in
Heterogeneous Classrooms
Number of studies included: 2

Mean Scores and Standard Deviations (in Terms of Percent Correct)
on Algebra by Treatment

Treatment	IMPROVE			CONTROL		
Ability	Low	Middle	High	Low	Middle	High
Pretest						
M	50.71	76.20	92.19	52.32	74.52	90.39
S	13.29	5.59	4.33	10.40	5.65	4.35
Algebra (Overall)						
M	55.90	73.94	86.58	52.65	63.72	71.77
S	20.95	21.09	16.60	30.08	18.88	22.30
Numerals						
M	68.57	80.88	90.30	63.21	75.09	77.95
S	20.24	17.16	13.72	28.35	15.38	19.76
Substitution						
M	55.00	71.04	83.91	49.62	62.50	70.38
S	21.96	25.78	20.27	34.17	25.28	27.37
Expressions						
M	53.18	71.92	87.06	51.58	57.84	73.30
S	28.11	30.84	19.26	29.20	25.73	28.76
Word Problems						
M	46.32	70.44	84.57	45.45	57.15	66.20
S	27.92	24.84	20.47	34.97	22.64	27.87

Table 9.6
Mevarech & Kramarski (1997)
IMPROVE: A Multidimensional Method for Teaching Mathematics in
Heterogeneous Classrooms

Mean Scores and Standard Deviations (in Terms of Percent Correct) by Time,
Treatment, and Ability on Introduction-to-Algebra and Mathematics Reasoning

Treatment	IMPROVE			CONTROL		
Ability	Low	Middle	High	Low	Middle	High
Pretest						
M	37.76	66.46	86.33	40.20	66.89	86.85
S	8.17	6.63	6.48	9.87	7.93	5.42

(continued)

Table 9.6 (continued)

Treatment	IMPROVE			CONTROL		
Ability	Low	Middle	High	Low	Middle	High
Introduction-to-Algebra						
M	48.28	79.52	88.20	45.97	67.24	82.27
S	16.31	10.06	8.55	21.03	18.97	13.05
Mathematical Reasoning						
M	41.37	64.00	74.74	32.60	50.98	67.47
S	14.41	16.38	12.98	20.68	17.79	15.34

Table 9.7
Mevarech & Kramarski (2003)
The Effects of Metacognitive Training versus Worked-Out Examples on Students' Mathematical Reasoning

Analysis of the pretest scores indicated that neither the treatment main effect, $F(1,118) < 1.00$, p > .05, nor the interaction between the treatment and prior knowledge, $F(1,118) < 1.00$, p > .05, were significant. Only the prior knowledge main effect was significant, $F(1,118) = 181.05$, p > .001. Thus, no significant differences between MT and WE students were found on the pretest scores for lower achievers (M = 66.19 and 64.48; SD = 17.06 and 12.89 for WE and MT, respectively) or higher achievers (M = 92.88 and 92.43; SD = 4.50 and 4.34 for WE and MT, respectively).

The two-way ANOVA of the immediate post-test scores indicated, however, significant main effects for the treatment (MS = 1190.11; $F(1,118) = 3.98$, p < .05) and prior knowledge (MS = 14381.38; $F(1,118) = 48.08$, p < .001), but the interaction between the treatment and prior knowledge was not significant (MS = 660.48; $F(1,118) = 2.21$, p > .05). The MT students significantly outperformed the WE students (M = 78.54 and 72.72; SD = 19.14 and 21.89 for the MT and WE groups, respectively. In particular lower achievers benefited from the MT method, but their gains did not come at the expense of higher achievers (ESs for the lower and higher achiever groups, respectively, were .51 and .14 favouring the MT group).

To gain further insight on students' mathematical reasoning, we analyzed students' written mathematical responses by focusing on three criteria: students' verbal explanations of their mathematical reasoning, algebraic representations of verbal situations, and algebraic solutions. The table above presents also the mean scores and standard deviations on the three criteria by treatment and level of prior knowledge. ANOVA indicated significant main effects for their treatment, $F(1,118) = 9.89$, 10.84, and 10.51, for students' verbal explanations of their mathematical reasoning, algebraic representations of verbal situations, and algebraic solutions, respectively; all *p* values < .05, but none of the interactions between the treatment and prior knowledge was significant; all $F(1,118)$ values < 1.00, all p values > .05. Within the lower achiever group, the MT students significantly outperformed the WE students on verbal explanations of mathematical reasoning, algebraic representations, and algebraic solutions (*ESs* for the three criteria, respectively, were .57, .51, and .54 standard deviations). Also within the higher achiever group, MT students significantly outperformed the WE students on all three criteria (respective ESs = .56, .65, and .60 standard deviations).

Table 9.7 (continued)

Mean Scores and Standard Deviations on the Pretest and Post-test Measures by Treatment and Level of Prior Knowledge

	Worked-Out Examples		Metacognitive Training	
	Lower Ach. N = 27	Higher Ach. N = 25	Lower Ach. N = 35	Higher Ach. N = 35
Pretest				
M	66.19	92.88	64.48	92.43
SD	(17.06)	(4.50)	(12.89)	(4.34)
Immediate Post-test (Total Score)				
M	58.88	85.56	69.91	87.17
SD	(21.53)	(11.50)	(19.36)	(14.69)
Verbal Explanations				
M	5.20	7.12	7.60	9.85
SD	(4.20)	(4.90)	(4.04)	(4.70)
Algebraic Representations				
M	6.00	5.24	8.31	8.54
SD	(4.50)	(5.09)	(4.14)	(4.92)
Algebraic Solution				
M	5.29	6.16	8.03	9.60
SD	(5.12)	(5.69)	(4.63)	(5.40)

Table 9.8
Mevarech & Kramarski (2003)
The Effects of Metacognitive Training versus Worked-Out Examples on Students' Mathematical Reasoning

Mean Scores and Standard Deviations of Students' Behaviours in Small Groups by Task and Treatment

	Task A		Task B	
	WE 3 teams	MT 5 teams	WE 3 yeams	MT 5 teams
Overall Number of Statements				
M	7.66	5.40	17.33	32.20
SD	(3.51)	(1.50)	(15.30)	(15.71)
Cognitive Statements				
M	4.66	4.80	6.01	10.81
SD	(2.08)	(1.32)	(3.00)	(5.82)
Metacognitive Statements				
M	3.00	.60	11.33	21.40
SD	(1.73)	(1.36)	(12.30)	(11.21)

(continued)

Table 9.8 (continued)

	WE 3 teams	MT 5 teams	WE 3 yeams	MT 5 teams
Quality of Cognitive Discourse				
M	2.66	2.40	2.33	3.20
SD	(.57)	(1.45)	(.57)	(1.50)
Quality of Metacognitive Discourse				
M	2.30	.80	2.33	3.40
SD	(1.52)	(.86)	(1.52)	(1.90)
Level of Cooperative Behaviour				
M	3.00	2.30	3.01	3.62
SD	(0.00)	(1.13)	(1.73)	(.70)

Table 9.9
Mevarech & Kramarski (2003)
**The Effects of Metacognitive Training versus Worked-Out Examples on Students'
Mathematical Reasoning**

**Mean Scores and Standard Deviations on the Pretest and Post-test Measures
by Treatment and Level of Prior Knowledge**

	Worked-Out Examples		Metacognitive Training	
	Lower Ach. N = 27	Higher Ach. N = 25	Lower Ach. N = 35	Higher Ach. N = 35
Pretest				
M	66.19	92.88	64.48	92.43
SD	(17.06)	(4.50)	(12.89)	(4.34)
Immediate Post-test (Total Score)				
M	58.88	85.56	69.91	87.17
SD	(21.53)	(11.50)	(19.36)	(14.69)
Verbal Explanations				
M	5.20	7.12	7.60	9.85
SD	(4.20)	(4.90)	(4.04)	(4.70)
Algebraic Representations				
M	6.00	5.24	8.31	8.54
SD	(4.50)	(5.09)	(4.14)	(4.92)
Algebraic Solution				
M	5.29	6.16	8.03	9.60
SD	(5.12)	(5.69)	(4.63)	(5.40)

Table 9.10
Mevarech & Kramarski (2003)
The Effects of Metacognitive Training versus Worked-Out Examples on Students'
Mathematical Reasoning

		Mean Scores and Standard Deviations on the Immediate and Delayed Post-test by Treatment	
		WE	**MT**
		N = 52	*N* = 70
Immediate Post-test			
Total	M	72.22	78.554
	SD	(21.89)	(19.14)
Verbal Explanations	M	6.16	8.73
	SD	(4.61)	(4.50)
Algebraic Representations	M	5.62	8.43
	SD	(4.76)	(4.51)
Algebraic Solution	M	572	8.81
	SD	(5.36)	(5.06)
Delayed Post-test			
Total	M	68.51	76.01
	SD	(28.67)	(23.23)
Verbal Explanations	M	10.03	11.77
	SD	(4.37)	(4.30)
Algebraic Representations	M	6.47	6.83
	SD	(2.16)	(2.58)
Algebraic Solution	M	9.73	10.20
	SD	4.10	2.15

Table 9.11
Alfassi (2004)
Reading to Learn: Effects of Combined Strategy Instruction on High School Students
Number of studies included: 2

Means, Standard Deviations, and Univariate ANCOVA Tests
of the Different Reading Measures Over Phases of Intervention

Phase	Experimental		Control		$F(1, 45)$
	M	SD	M	SD	
Reading assessment[a]					
Pretesting	73	22.8	68	27.0	4.57*
Posttesting	80	19.9	71	25.8	
Standardized reading measure					
Pretesting	57.83	19.17	52.70	20.30	4.77*
Posttesting	61.72	18.84	50.50	22.47	

Note: ANCOVA = analysis of covariance.

[a] The values represent mean percentages of correctly answered questions on the reading assessment passages.

* $p < .05$.

Table 9.12
Alfassi (2004)
Reading to Learn: Effects of Combined Strategy Instruction on High School Students

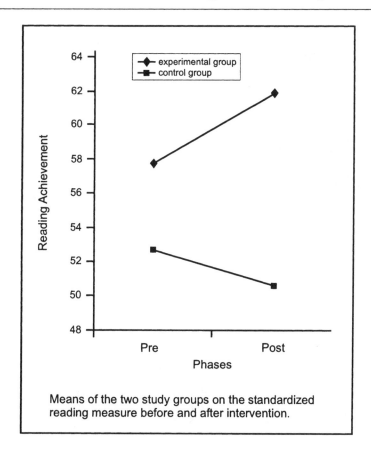

Means of the two study groups on the standardized reading measure before and after intervention.

Table 9.13
Alfassi (2004)
Reading to Learn: Effects of Combined Strategy Instruction on High School Students

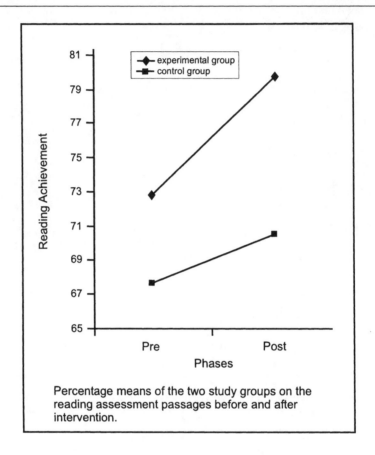

Percentage means of the two study groups on the reading assessment passages before and after intervention.

Statistical Evidence on Providing Prediction and Problem-Solving Instruction

GENERALIZATION TESTED: ON PREDICTION AND PROBLEM-SOLVING INSTRUCTION—CHAPTER 10

Achievement of learning objectives is enhanced when students are provided instruction in the use of the prediction cycle to solve problems.

Total number of studies covered: 72

Table 10.1

Kalaian et al. (1991)

What Can Studies of Problem-Based Learning Tell Us? Synthesizing and Modeling PBL Effects on National Board of Medical Examination Performance: Hierarchical Linear Modeling Meta-analytic Approach

Number of studies included: 31

Primary Studies Evaluating Impact of PBL on NBME I Performance[1]								
Study Source and Publication Year	**Cohort Year**	**Study Design**	**Years of PBL Experience**	**PBL *n***	**Tradi-tional *n***	**Effect Size (?)**	**Variance of Effect Size**
Morgan, 1977	1973	0	1.0	15	82	0.104	0.079
	1974	0	2.0	15	76	0.218	0.080
	1975	0	3.0	16	81	−0.010	0.075
Jones, 1984	1977–1978	0	6.5	63	138	1.600	0.029
Kaufman, 1989	1983	0	4.0	20	53	−0.594	0.071
	1984	0	5.0	20	53	−0.910	0.075
	1985	0	6.0	20	53	−0.396	0.070
	1986	0	7.0	20	53	−0.247	0.069
	1987	0	8.0	20	53	−0.336	0.070
	1988	0	9.0	20	53	−0.139	0.069
	1989	0	10.0	20	53	−0.425	0.070
	1990	0	11.0	20	53	−1.019	0.076
Goodman, 1991	1984	1	1.0	15	100	−0.343	0.071
	1985	1	2.0	15	100	−1.642	0.088
	1986	1	3.0	15	100	0.000	0.077
	1987	1	4.0	15	100	0.365	0.077
	1988	1	5.0	15	100	0.107	0.077
Bridgham, 1991	1982–1983	0	10.5	64	131	0.013	0.023
	1984–1985	0	11.5	103	91	0.028	0.021
	1986–1988	0	14.0	95	212	0.007	0.015
	1989–1990	0	15.5	58	130	0.035	0.025
Richards, 1993	1993	1	1.0	18	62	0.010	0.072

[1] The table above displays cohorts as they are represented in the publication source. Richards and Kaufman report cohorts of graduating classes; Goodman, Jones, and Morgan, entering class cohorts; and Bridgham, cohorts defined by year of first administration of NBME I. As Goodman and Kaufman report only the aggravated number of participants across study years, the average is reported as the estimated for individual cohorts. Richards study reports NBME results only of students who also returned a survey about their study habits; this survey elicited the participation of 81% of traditional students, and 78% of the PBL students. Bridgham also made available the following numerical table for the data represented in graph form in his published work:

(continued)

Table 10.1 (continued)

Cohort	PBL Students			Traditional Students		
	NBME I	n	Std. Dev.	NBME I	n	Std. Dev.
1982–1983	49.8	64	11.1	48.2	131	10.8
1983–1984	53.0	103	8.7	50.2	91	11.3
1984–1985	50.2	95	9.2	49.5	212	10.3
1985–1986	51.9	58	9.0	49.2	130	8.7

Study design: 0 = no randomization in assigning students to PBL and traditional programs; 1 = randomization in assigning students to PBL and traditional programs.

Years of PBL Experience: calculated by subtracting the year in which the PBL program was implemented from the year in which the reported NBME results occurred.

Table 10.2

Kalaian et al. (1991)

What Can Studies of Problem-Based Learning Tell Us? Synthesizing and Modeling PBL Effects on National Board of Medical Examination Performance: Hierarchical Linear Modeling Meta-analytic Approach

Primary Studies Evaluating Impact of PBL on NBME I Performance[1]

Study Source and Publication Year	Cohort Year	Study Design	Years of PBL Experience	PBL n	Tradi- tional n	Effect Size (?)	Variance of Effect Size
Kaufman, 1989	1983	0	5	20	53	–0.049	0.069
	1984	0	6	20	53	–0.099	0.069
	1985	0	7	20	53	0.445	0.070
	1986	0	8	20	53	0.445	0.070
	1987	0	9	20	53	0.297	0.069
	1988	0	10	20	53	0.396	0.070
Goodman, 1991	1984	1	2	15	100	0.000	0.077
	1985	1	3	15	100	–0.060	0.077
	1986	1	4	15	100	0.060	0.077

[1] The table above displays Cohort years as they are represented in the publication source. Kaufman reports cohorts of graduating classes; Goodman, entering class cohorts. As Goodman and Kaufman report only the aggravted number of participants across study years, the average is reported as the estimated for individual cohorts.

Study design: 0 = no randomization in assigning students to PBL and traditional programs; 1 = randomization in assigning students to PBL and traditional programs.

Years of PBL Experience: calculated by subtracting the year in which the PBL program was implemented from the year in which the reported NBME results occurred.

(continued)

Table 10.2 (continued)

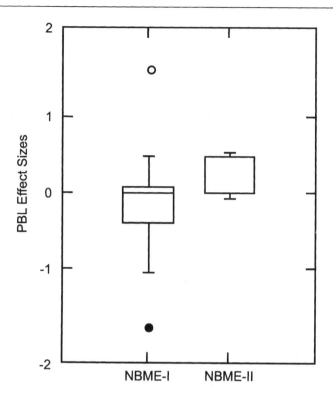

National Board Medical Examination (NBME)

In this box plot depiction of NBME effect sizes, the presence of two outliers is identified. O represents the study by Jones et al. (1984), which found a positive effect of 1.60; ● denotes the second outlier, representing the 1985 cohort in the Goodman et al., 1991 study, which reported a negative effect size of comparable magnitude (-1.64).

Box Plot of PBL Effect Sizes for NBME I and NBME II.

Table 10.3
Kalaian et al. (1991)
What Can Studies of Problem-Based Learning Tell Us? Synthesizing and Modeling PBL Effects on National Board of Medical Examination Performance: Hierarchical Linear Modeling Meta-analytic Approach

Unconditional and Conditional HLM Results for the Meta-analysis of the PBL Effects on NBME

Effect: Fixed Parameter	Estimate	Std. Error	t	p	Effect: Random r^2	df	$\chi2$	p
		Outcome: NBME I Model: Unconditional						
Average PBL effect, $\gamma0$	−0.15	0.07	−2.11	0.05	0.05	19	37.01	0.01
		Outcome: NBME II Model: Unconditional						
Average PBL effect, $\gamma0$	0.16	0.09	1.83	0.10	0.00004	8	6.09	> 0.50
		Outcome: NBME I Model: Conditional						
Intercept, $\gamma0$	4.53	1.82	2.49	0.02	0.02	16	23.55	0.10
Study design, $\gamma1$	0.82	0.26	3.12	0.01				
Publication year, $\gamma2$	−0.06	0.02	−2.69	0.02				
PBL experience, $\gamma3$	0.07	0.02	2.74	0.02				

Table 10.4
Dochy et al. (2003)
Effects of Problem-Based Learning: A Meta-analysis
Number of studies included: 43

Main Effects of PBL

Outcome	Sign.+[c]	Sign. −[c]	Studies N[d]	Average ES Unweighted	Average ES Weighted (CI 95%)	Qt
Knowledge	7	15	18	−0.776	−0.223 (+/−0.058)	1379.6 (p = 0.0)
Skills	14	0	17	+0.658	+0.460 (+/−0.058)	57.1 (p = 0.0)

Table 10.5
Dykes (1997)
A Test of Proposition, of Prediction Theory

Direct and Indirect Effects of Predictive Ability on Achievement from Path Analysis

Independent Variable	Direct Effect on Achievement	Indirect Effect on Achievement
Predictive Ability	.31	.13
IQ	.20	.20
Self-Confidence	.09	.13
Attendance	.12	.05

n = 88 students.

Table 10.6
Dykes (1997)
A Test of Proposition, of Prediction Theory

Correlation Analysis for Cases Used in Path Analysis

Variable	Predictive Ability	IQ	Self-Confidence	Attendance
Predictive Ability				
IQ	.5135 (p = .000)			
Self-Confidence	.2195 (p = .040)	.2410 (p = .024)		
Attendance	.0359 (p = .740)	.1433 (p = .183)	.1502 (p = .162)	
Achievement	.4350 (p = .000)	.3974 (p = .000)	.2234 (p = .036)	.1705 (p = .112)

n = 88.

Statistical Evidence on Providing Contiguity

GENERALIZATION TESTED: ON CONTIGUITY—CHAPTER 11

Achievement of learning objectives is enhanced when events students are to associate are presented to them close together in time and space.

Total number of studies covered: 496+

Rosenshine & Stevens (1986)

Groups of studies reviewed in this logical synthesis of research did not provide statistical evidence. However, many of the individual studies included in the logical synthesis of research do contain statistical evidence. In the event that a reader wishes to view this evidence, an extensive listing of the individual studies reviewed is provided in the reference list in Part V (the studies are identified by the symbol %).

Table 11.1
Bangert-Drowns et al. (1991)
The Instructional Effect of Feedback in Test-like Events
Number of studies included: 40

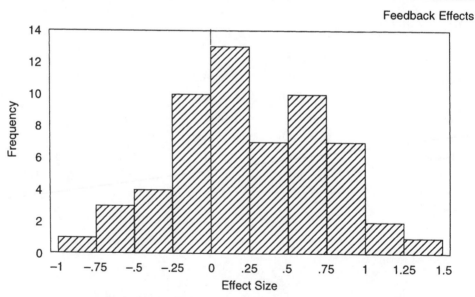

Histogram showing the distribution of 58 effect sizes from research on feedback effects.

Table 11.2
Anderson (1994)
Synthesis of Mastery Learning (Meta-analysis) Achievement Outcomes
Number of studies included: 7

Study	Percent Positive	Total N	ES	Grade Level
Kulik et al. (1990a)	93.2%	NR	.52	K–College
Slavin (1990)	NR	NR	.27	K–12
Kulik et al. (1990b)	63.6%	NR	.40	K–12
Guskey & Pigott (1988)	89.1%	11,532	.41 Psych.	K–12
			.50 Science	
			.53 Soc. Stud.	
			.60 Lang. Arts	
			.70 Math	
			.94 Elementary	
			.48 High School	
			.41 College	
Willett et al. (1983)	NR		.64	K–12
Guskey & Gates (1985)	92.2%	8,074	.65–.94	K–College
Block & Burns (1976)	89.0%	2,767	.83	K–College

N = number of students; ES = effect size.

Individual studies analyzed by these meta-analyses are identified in the reference list by the following symbols:

Kulik et al. (1990a) *
Kulik et al. (1990b) #
Slavin (1990) @
Guskey & Pigott (1988) $
Guskey & Gates (1985) &
Block & Burns (1976) +

It was not possible to determine the individual studies for which readiness was an instructional tactic for the Willett et al. (1983) analysis.

Table 11.3

Swanson (2000)

What Instruction Works for Students with Learning Disabilities? Summarizing the Results from a Meta-analysis of Intervention Studies

Number of studies included: 180

Weighted Mean Effect Sizes for Group Design Studies as a Function of Dependent Measure Category

LD Treatment versus LD Control

	N	K	Effect Size of Unweighted	Effect Size of Weighted	95% Confidence Interval for Weighted Effects Lower	Upper	Standard Error	Homogeneity (Q)
1. *Cognitive Processing*	41	115	.87 (.64)	.54	.48	.61	.03	311.67**
1a. Metacognitive	9	27	.98	.80	.66	.94	.07	83.91**
1b. Attribution	7	17	.79	.62	.44	.79	.08	31.99*
1c. Other Processes	25	71	.65	.46	.38	.53	.03	176.07**
2. *Word Recognition*	54	159	.71 (.56)	.57	.52	.62	.02	431.45**
2a. Standardized	23	79	.79	.62	.54	.69	.04	205.61**
2b. Experimental	35	80	.72	.53	.48	.60	.03	223.07**
3. *Reading Comprehension*	58	176	.82 (.60)	.72	.68	.77	.02	565.95**
3a. Standardized	16	38	.45	.45	.36	.54	.05	33.87
3b. Experimental	44	138	.84	.81	.75	.86	.02	489.54**
4. *Spelling*	24	54	.54 (.53)	.44	.37	.52	.04	100.44**
4a. Standardized	8	20	.61	.45	.34	.57	.06	34.45
4b. Experimental	18	34	.48	.44	.33	.54	.05	65.94**
5. *Memory/Recall*	12	33	.81 (.46)	.56	.43	.70	.06	42.72

6.	*Mathematics*	28	71	.58 (.45)	.40	.33	.46	.04	128.28**
6a.	Standardized	9	22	.41	.33	.23	.46	.05	25.72
6b.	Experimental	21	49	.59	.42	.34	.51	.04	101.43**
7.	*Writing*	19	67	.84 (.60)	.63	.54	.72	.05	157.45**
7a.	Standardized	3	7	.37	.36	.14	.58	.11	5.01
7b.	Experimental	16	60	.80	.68	.59	.78	.04	145.27**
8.	Vocabulary	11	20	.79 (.44)	.78	.66	.89	.05	38.58**
9.	*Attitude/Self-Concept*	25	86	.68 (.69)	.39	.33	.45	.03	210.65**
10.	*Intelligence*	9	32	.58 (.59)	.41	.30	.52	.06	54.37**
11.	*General Reading*	15	31	.60 (.50)	.52	.41	.65	.06	55.15*
12.	*Phonics/Orthographic Skills*	29	175	.70 (.36)	.64	.60	.69	.02	453.70**
12a.	Standardized Phonics	8	60	.72	.67	.62	.73	.03	275.87**
12b.	Experimental Phonics	21	78	.76	.60	.52	.67	.04	175.22**
13.	*Global Achievement*								
	(grades, total achievement)	10	21	.91 (.76)	.45	.31	.58	.07	56.64**
14.	*Creativity*	3	11	.84 (.49)	.70	.52	.87	.09	33.61**
15.	*Social Skills*	13	36	.46 (.22)	.41	.30	.51	.05	28.46
16.	*Perceptual Processes*	10	37	.74 (.65)	.26	.17	.35	.04	46.64
17.	*Language*	9	52	.54 (.48)	.36	.28	.44	.04	75.53*

Notes: numbers in parentheses = standard deviation; * p < .01; ** p < .001.

Gersten & Baker (2001)
Teaching Expressive Writing to Students with Learning Disabilities:
A Meta-analysis
Number of studies included: 13

Summed across all 13 studies, the mean effect size on the aggregate writing measure was 0.81. The 95 percent confidence interval was 0.65–0.97, providing clear evidence that the writing interventions had a significant positive effect on the quality of students' writing. The weighted and unweighted effect sizes were 0.81 and 0.99, suggesting that the studies with larger sample sizes resulted in somewhat smaller effects. Positive effect sizes were found in each of the 13 studies, ranging in magnitude from 0.30 (MacArthur et al., 1995) to 1.73 (Wong et al., 1996).

Ehri et al. (2001)
Phonemic Awareness Instruction Helps Children Learn to Read:
Evidence from the National Reading Panel's Meta-analysis
Number of studies included: 52

The effect size statistic measures how much the mean of the PA-instructed group exceeded the mean of the control group in standard deviation units. An effect size of 1 indicates that the treatment group mean was one standard deviation higher than the control group mean, revealing a strong effect of instruction. An effect size of 0 indicates that treatment and control group means were identical, showing that instruction had no effect. All of the effect sizes involving PA and reading outcomes were statistically greater than zero ($p < .05$). This indicates that instruction was uniformly effective in teaching PA and in facilitating transfer to reading across all levels of the moderator variables that were considered.

The overall effect size of PA instruction on the acquisition of PA was large, $d = 0.86$, based on 72 comparisons. The overall effect size on reading was moderate, $d = 0.53$, based on 90 comparisons. These findings lead us to conclude with much confidence that phonemic awareness instruction is more effective that alternative forms of instruction or no instruction in helping children acquire phonemic awareness and in facilitating transfer of PA skills to reading and spelling.

Martens & Witt (2004)
Competence, Persistence, and Success: The Positive Psychology of
Behavioral Skill Instruction
Number of studies included: 40

Groups of studies reviewed in this logical synthesis of research did not provide statistical evidence. However, many of the individual studies included in the logical synthesis of research do contain statistical evidence. In the event that a reader wishes to view this evidence, an extensive listing of the individual studies reviewed

is provided in the reference list in Part V (the studies are identified by the symbol <).

Statistical Evidence on Utilizing Repetition Effectively

GENERALIZATION TESTED: ON REPETITION—CHAPTER 12

Achievement of learning objectives is enhanced when there is repetition in instruction and in tasks students are assigned to perform.

Total number of studies covered: 183

Table 12.1
Kulik et al. (1984)
Effects of Practice on Aptitude and Achievement Test Scores

Means and Standard Errors of Effect Sizes for Different Numbers of Practice Tests

Number of Practice Tests	Identical Tests			Parallel Tests		
	Number of Studies	Effect Size M	SE	Number of Studies	Effect Size M	SE
1	19	.42	.08	21	.23	.04
2	6	.70	.30	5	.32	.04
3	5	.96	.37	4	.35	.07
4	3	1.35	.60	3	.47	.18
5	3	1.42	.59	2	.52	.16
6	2	1.94	.79	1	.73	
7	2	1.89	.86	1	.74	

M = mean effect size; SE = standard error.

Studies associated with this meta-analysis are identified by the symbol * in the reference list in Part V.

Table 12.2

Swanson & Sachse-Lee (2000)

A Meta-analysis of Single-Subject-Design Intervention Research for Students with LD

Number of studies included: 87

Dependent Measures and Domains (N = 85)	Sample Size	Number of Studies	Unadjusted Effect Size	Adjusted Effect Size[a]	SD	SE	Low[b]	High	Q
				Single-Subject-Design Studies					
1. Cognitive processes	77	12	1.46	.87	.34	.06	.74	1.01	9.00
2. Word recognition	108	20	1.26	.82	.43	.06	.69	.96	20.29
3. Reading comprehension	69	11	1.36	.95	.45	.08	.78	1.13	13.86
4. Spelling	67	8	1.16	.77	.62	.07	.62	.93	25.41
5. Mathematics	195	14	1.31	.91	.61	.03	.83	.49	73.18
6. Writing	122	14	1.36	.82	.63	.05	.72	.92	48.30
7. General reading	3	2	1.78	.90	.09	.49	.06	1.87	.01
8. Word skills	10	4	1.42	.87	.22	.44	.03	1.75	.44
9. Global achievement	76	7	1.06	1.07	.38	.05	.95	1.19	10.89
10. Social skills	13	2	1.51	.85	.23	.29	.27	1.43	.63
11. Perceptual/motor (handwriting)	14	6	1.22	.58	.62	.20	.18	.98	4.68
12. Language	1	1	1.80	1.13	—	—	—	—	—
13. Other	37	5	1.17	.79	.52	.10	.59	.99	9.85

Note: From *Interventions for Students with Learning Disabilities: A Meta-Analysis of Treatment Outcomes*, by H. L. Swanson, with M. Hoskyn and C. Lee, 1999. New York: Guilford. Copyright 1999 by Guilford. Adapted with permission. [a] Adjust for correlation between last three baseline and last three treatment observations. [b] 95% confidence interval.

Table 12.3
Therrien (2004)
Fluency and Comprehension Gains as a Result of Repeated Reading:
A Meta-analysis
Number of studies included: 18

	Nontransfer Intervention Component Analysis							
	Cue Type			Corrective Feedback		No. of Times Passage Read		
Dependent Variable	Fluency	Comp.	Fluency & Comp.	Yes	No	2	3	4
Fluency *n*	0.72	.081	0.94	0.68	0.88	0.57	0.85	0.95
	2	8	3	3	13	2	10	3
Comp. *n*	0.66	0.75	0.67	–	–	–	0.66	0.71
	2	6	3	–	–	–	10	2

Note: *n* indicates number of effect sizes. Dash indicates effect size not calculated or available.

Rosenshine (1986)

Groups of studies reviewed in this logical synthesis of research did not provide statistical evidence. However, many of the individual studies included in the logical synthesis of research do contain statistical evidence. In the event that a reader wishes to view this evidence, an extensive listing of the individual studies reviewed is provided in the reference list in Part V (the studies are identified by the symbol #).

Chard et al. (2002)

Groups of studies reviewed in this logical synthesis of research did not provide statistical evidence. However, Many of the individual studies included in the logical synthesis of research do contain statistical evidence. In the event that a reader wishes to view this evidence, an extensive listing of the individual studies reviewed is provided in the reference list in Part V (the studies are identified by the symbol ^).

Table 12.4
Ausubel & Youseff (1965)
The Effect of Spaced Repetition on Meaningful Retention

Retention Test Scores of Experimental and Control Groups on Learning Passage

Group	Treatment	Mean	SD
Experimental	Repetition	24.25	5.79
Control	No Repetition	19.65	5.26

Calculated effect size = .88; SD = standard deviation.
An unspecified test for difference of the means was reported significant at the .001 level.

Table 12.5
Peterson et al. (1935)
Some Measurements of the Effects of Reviews

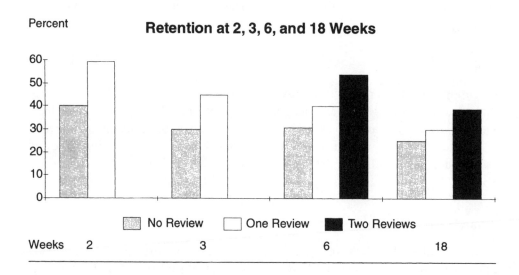

Percent

Retention at 2, 3, 6, and 18 Weeks

No Review   One Review   Two Reviews

Weeks   2   3   6   18

Table 12.6
Peterson et al. (1935)
Some Measurements of the Effects of Reviews

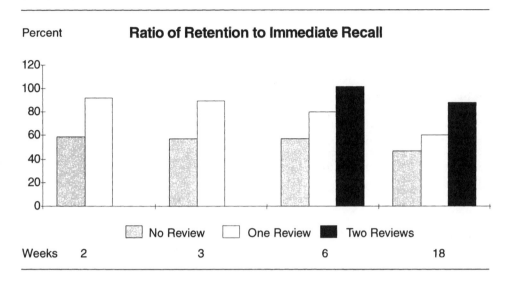

Table 12.7
Nelson (1977)
Repetition and Depth of Processing

Experiment 1: Mean Percentage of Correct Responses for Each Condition

Condition			
1 Repetition **@ 4 seconds**	**1 Repetition** **@ 8 seconds**	**2 Repetitions** **(Same)** **@ 4 seconds**	**2 Repetitions** **(Different)** **@ 4 seconds**
25	23	33	32

Table 12.8
Nelson (1977)
Repetition and Depth of Processing

Three Planned Orthogonal Comparisons (constructed from data presented in results)

Comparison	F	p
The two two-repetition groups to the two one-repetition groups	30.42	< .005
One repetition @ 4 seconds to one repetition @ 8 seconds	< 1.00	> .10
(Same) two-repetition groups to (different) two-repetition group	< 1.00	> .10

Table 12.9
Nelson (1977)
Repetition and Depth of Processing

Experiment 2: Mean Percentage of Correct Responses for Each Condition

One Repetition	Two Repetitions				
	Massed	**Spaced**			
		Lag 7	**Lag 11**	**Lag 15**	**Ave.**
24	40	46	47	50	48

Lag = number of seconds between presentations.

Table 12.10
Nelson (1977)
Repetition and Depth of Processing

Experiment 2: Scheffé Post-Hoc Comparisons (p values not given)
(created from data reported in results)

Comparison	F
Two back-to-back repetitions to one repetition	8.05*
Two spaced repetitions to one repetition	17.85*
Two back-to-back repetitions to two spaced repetitions	1.92**
Comparison of spaced intervals	< 1.00**

---

* Reported as significant; ** Reported as not significant.

Experiment 3: Repetition and Depth of Processing

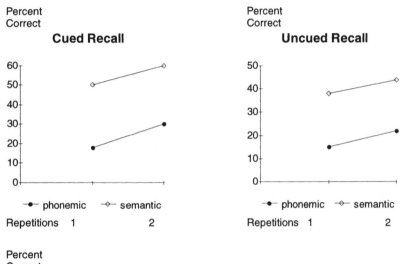

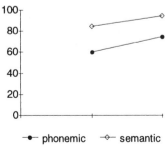

Table 12.11
Nelson (1977)
Repetition and Depth of Processing

Experiment 3: ANOVA Statistics (Tables created from statistics presented in results)

Uncued

Variable	df	F	(p values not given)
Repetition	1, 92	11.83	
Processing	1, 92	129.56	
Repetition × Processing	not given	< 1.00	

Cued

Variable	df	F	(p values not given)
Repetition	1, 92	10.13	
Processing	1, 92	108.81	
Repetition × Processing	not given	< 1.00	

Recognition

Variable	df	F	(p values not given)
Repetition	1, 92	23.96	
Processing	1, 92	87.95	
Repetition × Processing	1, 92	23.96	

---

*Analysis of simple effects indicated two repetitions produced a larger effect for both the semantic and phonemic conditions.

Table 12.12
Petros & Hoving (1980)
The Effects of Review on Young Children's Memory for Prose

Mean Proportion of Idea Units Correctly Recalled

Importance Level	Delayed Recall				
	Group 1	Group 2	Group 3	Group 4	Group 5
High	.455	.366	.374	.264	.387
Medium	.347	.268	.243	.175	.237
Low	.327	.196	.170	.138	.263
Total	.376	.276	.262	.192	.296

Table 12.13
Watkins & Kerkar (1985)
Recall of Twice-Presented Item without Recall of Either Presentation: Generic Memory for Events

| | | Percentage of Items Recalled | | |
| | | | Twice-Presented Items | |
Experiment	Items	Observed	Predicted*	Superadditivity
1	17.67	45.89	31.81	14.08**
2	17.22	43.89	31.11	12.78**
3	26.67	56.08	45.46	10.62**

*Calculated by an equation intended to correct for the probability of guessing an item correctly; ** $p < .001$.

Table 12.14
Hines et al. (1985)
Teacher Clarity and Its Relationship to Student Achievement and Satisfaction

Relationships between Measures of Teacher Behaviors and Student Outcomes

Level of Measurement	Measurement Source	Canonical Analysis Correlation	Regression Analysis Achievement
Low-inference	observers	.75	.72*
	students	.95**	.69*
	teachers	.67*	.53
Intermediate-inference	observers	.70**	.67**
			Zero-Order Correlation
High-inference	observers	.65**	.63**
	students	.73**	.53**
	teachers	.45*	.34*

*$p < .05$; **$p < .01$.

Table 12.15
Péladeau et al. (2003)
Effect of Paced and Unpaced Practice on Skills Application and Retention: How Much Is Enough?

Differences between Experimental Conditions on Pooled Periodic Exams and Final Exams, in *SD* Units (95% Confidence Intervals)

Academic Performance	Non-Mastery	Mastery	High Accuracy
Mastery			
Unadjusted effect size	0.56 (0.34, 0.78) $p = .000$		
Adjusted effect size	0.31 (0.09, 0.53) $p = .006$		
High accuracy			
Unadjusted effect size	0.83 (0.50, 1.09) $p = .000$	0.57 (0.25, 0.91) $p = .000$	
Adjusted effect size	0.43 (0.19, 0.67) $p = .000$		
Fluency			
Unadjusted effect size	0.57 (0.33, 0.83) $p = .000$	0.42 (0.05, 0.76) $p = .025$	−0.03 (−0.49, 0.39) $p = .878$
Adjusted effect size	0.16 (−0.08, 0.40) $p = .201$		

Note: Effect sizes in this table result from a meta-analytic synthesis of effect sizes computed on twelve control exams. Confidence intervals are given in parentheses.

Statistical Evidence on Utilizing Unifiers

GENERALIZATION: ON UNIFIERS—CHAPTER 13

Achievement of learning objectives is enhanced when a scheme is used to highlight parts/whole relationships in the subject matter students are assigned to learn.

Total number of studies covered: 370+

Table 13.1
Rosenshine et al. (1996)
Teaching Students to Generate Questions: A Review of the Intervention Studies

Overall Effect Sizes by Type of Test

Instructional Approach

Prompt	Reciprocal Teaching (*n* = 9)	Regular Instruction (*n* = 17)	Combined (*n* = 26)
Standardized	0.34 (6)	0.35 (7)	0.36 (13)
Exp. short answer	1.00 (5)	0.88 (11)	0.87 (16)
Summary	0.85 (3)	0.81 (2)	0.85 (5)

Note: *n* = number of studies. Number in parentheses refers to the number of studies used to compute an effect size.

Overall Median Effect Sizes by Type of Prompt

	Standardized Test			Experimenter-Developed Test		
Prompt	Reciprocal Teaching (*n* = 6)	Regular Instruction (*n* = 7)	Combined (*n* = 13)	Reciprocal Teaching (*n* = 12)	Regular Instruction (*n* = 19)	Combined (*n* = 19)
Signal words	0.34 (4)	0.46 (2)	0.36 (6)	0.88 (5)	0.67 (2)	0.85 (7)
Generic questions/ Stems					1.12 (4)	1.12 (4)
Main idea		0.70 (1)	0.70 (1)	1.24 (1)	0.13 (4)	0.25 (5)
Question type	0.02 (2)	0.00 (1)	0.00 (3)	3.37 (1)		3.37 (1)
Story grammar					1.08 (2)	1.08 (2)
No facilitator		0.14 (3)	0.14 (3)			

Note: *n* = number of studies. Number in parentheses refers to the number of studies used to compute an effect size.

Wise (1996)
Strategies for Teaching Science: What Works?
Number of studies included: 140

Focusing strategies involve times when teachers do something to alert students to the intent of the instruction. The effect size for focusing strategies is +.57 from twenty-eight student achievement measures.

Table 13.2
Hattie et al. (1996)
Effects of Learning Skills Interventions on Student Learning: A Meta-analysis
Number of studies included: 51

Hattie, Biggs, and Purdie

−0.9	86
−0.8	10
−0.7	2
−0.6	7
−0.5	774
−0.4	88
−0.3	8732211
−0.2	96422
−0.1	988776654443320
−0.0	9999877764443331
0.0	011111222334455567777779
0.1	00111222223333444555556777889
0.2	11123455577777778999
0.3	000011122334445555566678999
0.4	1333445667788889
0.5	0001233566667889
0.6	0112445
0.7	0235667779
0.8	01122589
0.9	114445667
1.0	012444557
1.1	0111136799
1.2	12479
1.3	
1.4	009
1.5	0378
1.6	4666788
1.7	4
1.8	25678
1.9	
2.0	45
2.1	6
2.2	35
2.3	
2.4	6

Table 13.3
Hattie et al. (1996)
Effects of Learning Skills Interventions on Student Learning: A Meta-analysis

Summary of Relationships to Achievement

	No. of Studies	Overall Effect Size
School	4,310	0.25
Physical attributes	1,850	−0.05
Finances	658	0.12
Aims & policy	542	0.24
Parent involvement	339	0.46
Class environment	921	0.56
Social	1,124	0.39
Mass media	274	−0.12
Peer	122	0.38
Home	728	0.67
Instructor	5,009	0.44
Style	1,075	0.42
Inservice education	3,912	0.49
Background	22	0.60
Instruction	5,710	0.47
Quantity	80	0.84
Quality	22	1.00
Methods	5,608	0.36
Mathematics	1,713	0.32
Science	1,562	0.36
Reading	2,333	0.50
Others	60	0.28
Pupil	2,249	0.47
Physical	905	0.21
Affective	355	0.24
Disposition to learn	93	0.61
Cognitive	896	1.04
Methods of instruction	21,382	0.29
Team teaching	41	0.06
Individualization	630	0.14
Audio-visual aids	6,060	0.16
Programmed instruction	220	0.18
Ability grouping	3,385	0.18
Learning hierarchies	24	0.19
Calculators	231	0.24

(continued)

Table 13.3 (continued)

	No. of Studies	Overall Effect Size
Instructional media	4,421	0.30
Testing	1,817	0.30
Computer-assisted instruction	566	0.31
Simulation & games	111	0.34
Questioning	134	0.41
Homework	110	0.43
Tutoring	125	0.50
Mastery learning	104	0.50
Bilingual programs	285	0.51
Goals	2,703	0.52
Acceleration	162	0.72
Direct instruction	253	0.82
Learning strategies	783	0.61
Behavioral objectives	111	0.12
Advance organizers	387	0.37
Remediation/feedback	146	0.65
Reinforcement	139	1.13
Grand total/mean	40,567	0.40

Guzzetti (2000)
Learning Counter-intuitive Science Concepts: What Have We Learned from over a Decade of Research?
Number of studies included: 70

Groups of studies reviewed in this logical synthesis of research did not provide statistical evidence. However, many of the individual studies included in the logical synthesis of research do contain statistical evidence. In the event that a reader wishes to view this evidence, an extensive listing of the individual studies reviewed is provided in the reference list in Part V (the studies are identified by the symbol +).

Gersten & Baker (2001)
Teaching Expressive Writing to Students with Learning Disabilities: A Meta-analysis
Number of studies included: 13

Summed across all 13 studies, the mean effect size on the aggregate writing measure was 0.81. The 95 percent confidence interval was 0.65–0.97, providing clear evidence that the writing interventions had a significant positive effect on the quality of students' writing. Positive effect sizes were found in each of the 13 studies, ranging in magnitude from 0.30 to 1.73.

Griffin & Tulbert (1995)
The Effect of Graphic Organizers on Students' Comprehension and Recall of Expository Text: A Review of the Research and Implications for Practice

Groups of studies reviewed in this logical synthesis of research did not provide statistical evidence. However, many of the individual studies included in the logical synthesis of research do contain statistical evidence. In the event that a reader wishes to view this evidence, an extensive listing of the individual studies reviewed is provided in the reference list in Part V (the studies are identified by the symbol #).

Table 13.4
Yan & Jitendra (1999)
The Effects of Instruction in Solving Mathematical Word Problems for Students with Learning Problems: A Meta-analysis

Variable and Class	[Q.sub.B]	k	d+
Summary of Effect Sizes before Outliers Were Removed			
Sample characteristics			
Grade/age	8.34		
Elementary		12	+1.00
Secondary		16	+0.73
Postsecondary		7	+1.20
IQ	19.47(*)		
< 85		3	+1.87
> 85		17	+0.45
Label	74.10(*)		
LD		25	+0.68
Mixed		2	+1.96
At-risk		8	+2.22
Instructional features			
Intervention approach	87.83(*)		
Representation		8	+1.05
Strategy		16	+1.01
CAI		6	+2.46
Other		5	+0.00
Setting	1.07		
Pull-out		11	+0.84
Classroom		23	+0.97
Length of treatment	18.05(*)		
Short		18	+1.10

(continued)

Table 13.4 (continued)

Variable and Class	[Q.sub.B]	k	d+
Intermediate		14	+0.62
Long		3	+1.25
Instructional arrangement	38.26(*)		
Individual		5	+2.18
Group		30	+0.78
Inst. implemented	48.45(*)		
Teacher		9	+0.50
Researcher		22	+0.95
Both		4	+2.58
Word problem task	5.56		
One-step problems		20	+0.96
Multistep problems		3	+0.38
Mixed problems		12	+0.89
Student directed	0.36		
Low		27	+0.87
High		8	+0.95
Methodological features			
Publication bias	12.72(*)		
Published		24	+0.74
Unpublished		11	+1.21
Group assignment	76.72(*)		
Random		21	+1.15
Matched		4	+2.58
Intact		9	+0.31

Note: k = number of effect sizes; d+ = effect size corrected for sample size. Significance of d+ was assessed by the z distribution, and nonsignificant Q reflects homogeneity within category. [Q.sub.B] = homoegeneity between-class effect.

(*) $p < .01$.

Table 13.5
Yan & Jitendra (1999)
The Effects of Instruction in Solving Mathematical Word Problems for Students with Learning Problems: A Meta-analysis

Variable and Class	95% CI		
	Lower	Upper	[O.sub.W]
Sample characteristics			
Grade/age			
Elementary	+0.80	+1.20	66.05(*)
Secondary	+0.56	+0.90	165.28(*)
Postsecondary	+0.88	+1.51	27.15(*)
IQ			
< 85	+1.26	+2.49	2.43
> 85	+0.30	+0.60	63.12(*)
Label			
LD	+0.55	+0.81	53.55(*)
Mixed	+1.18	+2.74	1.06
At-risk	+1.88	+2.56	51.61(*)
Instructional features			
Intervention approach			
Representation	+0.79	+1.31	37.24(*)
Strategy	+0.85	+1.18	78.53(*)
CAI	+1.97	+2.94	41.19(*)
Other	−0.26	+0.26	5.72
Setting			
Pull-out	+0.66	+1.06	37.24(*)
Classroom	+0.81	+1.14	225.50(*)
Length of treatment			
Short	+0.92	+1.29	101.09(*)
Intermediate	+0.44	+0.79	110.56(*)
Long	+0.87	+1.63	37.12(*)
Instructional arrangement			
Individual	+1.76	+2.61	9.00
Group	+0.66	+0.91	219.56(*)
Inst. implemented			
Teacher	+0.28	+0.72	70.91(*)
Researcher	+0.80	+1.10	100.14(*)
Both	+2.02	+3.13	47.32(*)
Word problem task			
One-step problems	+0.80	+1.13	173.48(*)

(continued)

Table 13.5 (continued)

Variable and Class	Lower	Upper	[Q.sub.W]
Multistep problems	−0.08	+0.83	0.94
Mixed problems	+0.71	+1.08	67.17(*)
Student directed			
Low	+0.73	+1.01	219.61(*)
High	+0.73	+1.18	46.85(*)
Methodological features			
Publication bias			
Published	+0.60	+0.89	188.92(*)
Unpublished	+1.00	+1.42	65.17(*)
Group assignment			
Random	+0.99	+1.31	92.41(*)
Matched	+2.02	+3.13	47.32(*)
Intact	+0.11	+0.52	47.35

Note: CI = confidence interval. [Q.sub.W] = homoegeneity within each class.
(*) p < .01.

Gersten et al. (2001)
Teaching Reading Comprehension Strategies to Students with
Learning Disabilities: A Review of Research
Number of studies included: 27

Groups of studies reviewed in this logical synthesis of research did not provide statistical evidence. However, many of the individual studies included in the logical synthesis of research do contain statistical evidence. In the event that a reader wishes to view this evidence, an extensive listing of the individual studies reviewed is provided in the reference list in Part V (the studies are identified by the symbol %).

Baker et al. (2002)
A Synthesis of Empirical Research on Teaching Mathematics to
Low-Achieving Students
Number of studies included: 17

Groups of studies reviewed in this logical synthesis of research did not provide statistical evidence. However, many of the individual studies included in the logical synthesis of research do contain statistical evidence. In the event that a reader wishes to view this evidence, an extensive listing of the individual studies reviewed is provided in the reference list in Part V (the studies are identified by the symbol $).

Table 13.6
Horton et al. (1993)
An Investigation of the Effects of Concept Mapping as an Instructional Tool

	n	Median	Mean	SE
		Achievement Effect Sizes		
Grade Level				
Elementary	2	0.84	0.84	0.14
Middle	2	0.27	0.27	0.12
High School	9	0.11	0.31	0.23
College	5	0.52	0.63	0.27
Overall	18		0.46	0.14

n = number of studies; SE = standard error.

Table 13.7
Fisher (1997)
Subject Matter Unifiers: Synthesis of a Body of Research

Variable	N	Mean	St Dev	Min	Q1	Median	Q3	Max
			Effect Size Descriptive Statistics					
Combined	48	0.51	0.44	−0.49	0.29	0.46	0.72	1.71
Immediate Recall	31	0.57	0.35	−0.12	0.32	0.54	0.76	1.46
Delayed Recall	17	0.40	0.56	−0.49	0.10	0.32	0.58	1.71

N = number of studies; St Dev = standard deviation; Min = minimum; Q1= first quartile; Q3 = third quartile; Max = maximum.

Table 13.8
Bower et al. (1969)
Hierarchical Retrieval Schemes in Recall of Categorized Word Lists

	Experiment I: Average Words Recalled over Four Trials			
	Trials			
	1	**2**	**3**	**4**
Words Presented	112	112	112	112
Words Recalled				
Blocked	73.0	106.1	112	112
Random	20.6	38.9	52.8	70.1

(continued)

Table 13.8 (continued)

	Trials			
	1	**2**	**3**	**4**
Recall of Level Four Words				
Words Presented	73.5	73.5	73.5	73.5
Words Recalled				
Blocked	44.6	69.6	73.5	73.5
Random	13.2	22.8	35.2	44.8

Table 13.9
Bower et al. (1969)
Hierarchical Retrieval Schemes in Recall of Categorized Word Lists

Experiment II: Percentage of Words Recalled

	Trial	
Condition	**T1**	**T2**
Blocked		
LL	.61	.89
LN	.65	—
NL	—	.88
Random		
LL	.21	.43
LN	.29	—
NL	—	.39

Table 13.10
Bower et al. (1969)
Hierarchical Retrieval Schemes in Recall of Categorized Word Lists

**Experiment III: Proportion of Clusters Recalled and Mean Words
per Recalled Cluster on Trial 2 and Final Recall Trial**

	Proportion of Clusters		Words per Cluster (of 4)	
Group	**Trial 2**	**Final**	**Trial 2**	**Final**
Relevant	.84	.98	3.52	3.58
Irrelevant	.89	.99	3.20	3.35
Rest Control	.86	.98	3.40	3.42

Bower et al. (1969)
Experiment IV

Tables not provided. Blocked condition reported as exceeding the random condition on recall with all p's < .01.

Table 13.11
Selinger (1995)
Summarizing Text: Developmental Students Demonstrate a Successful Method

	Summary of Writing Posttest Scores				
	n	**Low Score**	**High Score**	**Mean Score**	**SD**
Control	28	12	82	49.29	19
Treatment	30	53	90	74.10	9

F 1, 55 = 37.25, p < .001.

Table 13.12
Dean & Kulhavy (1981)
Influence of Spatial Organization in Prose Learning

	Experiment I: Means and Standard Deviations	
	Treatment Group	
Dependent Measure	**Map Construction**	**No Construction**
Multiple Choice		
M	21.50	17.15
SD	4.27	3.77
Constructed Response		
M	20.55	14.95
SD	4.61	5.29
Idea Units		
M	25.50	19.40
SD	7.00	4.07

Table 13.13
Dean & Kulhavy (1981)
Influence of Spatial Organization in Prose Learning

Experiment II: Means and Standard Deviations

Dependent Measure		Map Construction	No Construction	Provided Map
		Treatment Group		
Multiple Choice				
	M	27.25	17.83	19.15
	SD	4.13	4.69	4.25
Constructed Response				
	M	24.35	14.81	16.40
	SD	4.54	5.01	4.99
Idea Units				
	M	28.10	16.44	18.13
	SD	6.91	4.54	4.91

Table 13.14
Witzel et al. (2003)
Teaching Algebra to Students with Learning Difficulties: An Investigation of an Explicit Instruction Model

Mean and Standard Deviations for Each Test within Each Instructional Group

	N	Maximum	M	SD
		Descriptive Statistics		
PRETEST CRA	34	2	0.12	0.41
PRETEST Abstract	34	2	0.06	0.34
POST CRA	34	23	7.32	5.48
POST Abstract	34	17	3.06	4.37
FOLLOW CRA	34	22	6.68	6.32
FOLLOW Abstract	34	21	3.71	5.21

Note: Total possible score is 27 for each mesaure.

Follow-up analyses on group means indicated that the students who received CRA instruction over the four-week intervention outperformed matched students who received traditional instruction during the same time period with the same teacher. Although there was no significant difference between the pretest scores ($t(33) = 0.63$, $p = 0.27$) of the two groups, there were significant differences at posttest and follow-up. On the posttest the group receiving CRA instruction ($M = 7.32$; $SD = 5.48$) outperformed the group who received abstract instruction ($M = 3.03$; $SD = 4.39$), $t(33) = 6.52$, $p < 0.01$. The group who received CRA instruction ($M = 6.68$; $SD = 6.32$) also outperformed the abstract group ($M = 3.71$; $SD = 5.21$) on the three-week follow-up test ($t(33) = 3.28$, $p < 0.01$).

Statistical Evidence on Providing One-to-One Tutoring

GENERALIZATION TESTED: ON ONE-TO-ONE TUTORING—CHAPTER 14

Achievement of learning objectives is enhanced when students are provided one-to-one tutoring as needed.

Total number of studies covered: 500+

Table 14.1
Cohen et al. (1982)
Educational Outcomes of Tutoring: A Meta-analysis of Findings
Number of studies included: 65

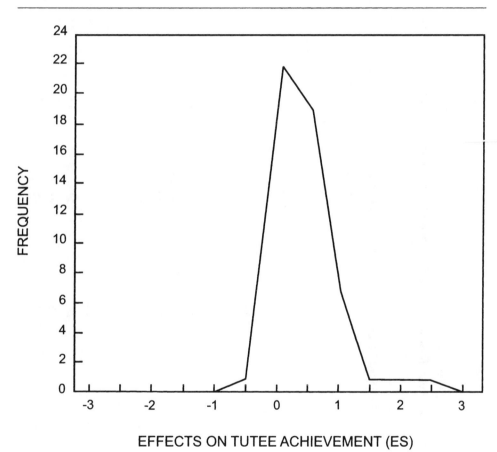

EFFECTS ON TUTEE ACHIEVEMENT (ES)

Distribution showing the effects of tutoring on tutee achievement in 52 studies.

Table 14.2

Swanson & Hoskyn (1998)

Experimental Intervention Research on Students with Learning Disabilities: A Meta-analysis of Treatment Outcomes

Number of studies included: 180

Weighted Mean Effect Sizes for Group Design Studies as a Function of Dependent Measure Category

LD Treatment versus LD Control

		N	K	Effect Size of Unweighted	Effect Size of Weighted	95% Confidence Interval for Weighted Effects Lower	Upper	Standard Error	Homogeneity (Q)
1.	Cognitive Processing	41	115	.87 (.64)	.54	.48	.61		311.67**
1a.	Metacognitive	9	27	.98	.80	.66	.94	.07	83.91**
1b.	Attribution	7	17	.79	.62	.44	.79	.08	31.99*
1c.	Other Processes	25	71	.65	.46	.38	.53	.03	176.07**
2.	Word Recognition	54	159	.71 (.56)	.57	.52	.62	.02	431.45**
2a.	Standardized	23	79	.79	.62	.54	.69	.04	205.61**
2b.	Experimental	35	80	.72	.53	.48	.60	.03	223.07**
3.	Reading Comprehension	58	176	.82 (.60)	.72	.68	.77	.02	565.95**
3a.	Standardized	16	38	.45	.45	.36	.54	.05	33.87
3b.	Experimental	44	138	.84	.81	.75	.86	.02	489.54**
4.	Spelling	24	54	.54 (.53)	.44	.37	.52	.04	100.44**
4a.	Standardized	8	20	.61	.45	.34	.57	.06	34.45
4b.	Experimental	18	34	.48	.44	.33	.54	.05	65.94**
5.	Memory/Recall	12	33	.81 (.46)	.56	.43	.70	.06	42.72

6.	Mathematics	28	71	.58 (.45)	.40	.33	.46	.04	128.28**
6a.	Standardized	9	22	.41	.33	.23	.46	.05	25.72
6b.	Experimental	21	49	.59	.42	.34	.51	.04	101.43**
7.	Writing	19	67	.84 (.60)	.63	.54	.72	.05	157.45**
7a.	Standardized	3	7	.37	.36	.14	.58	.11	5.01
7b.	Experimental	16	60	.80	.68	.59	.78	.04	145.27**
8.	Vocabulary	11	20	.79 (.44)	.78	.66	.89	.05	38.58***
9.	Attitude/Self-Concept	25	86	.68 (.69)	.39	.33	.45	.03	210.65**
10.	Intelligence	9	32	.58 (.59)	.41	.30	.52	.06	54.37***
11.	General Reading	15	31	.60 (.50)	.52	.41	.65	.06	55.15*
12.	Phonics/Orthographic	29	175	.70 (.36)	.64	.60	.69	.02	453.70**
12a.	Standardized Phonics	8	60	.72	.67	.62	.73	.03	275.87**
12b.	Experimental Phonics	21	78	.76	.60	.52	.67	.04	175.22**
13.	Global Achievement (grades, total achievement)	10	21	.91 (.76)	.45	.31	.58	.07	56.64**
14.	Creativity	3	11	.84 (.49)	.70	.52	.87	.09	33.61
15.	Social Skills	13	36	.46 (.22)	.41	.30	.51	.05	28.46
16.	Perceptual Processes	10	37	.74 (.65)	.26	.17	.35	.04	46.64
17.	Language	9	52	.54 (.48)	.36	.28	.44	.04	75.53*

Notes: numbers in parentheses = standard deviation; * p < .01; ** p < .001.

Table 14.3
Elbaum et al. (1999)
Grouping Practices and Reading Outcomes for Students with Disabilities
Number of studies included: 20

Analysis by Treatment and Assessment Variables				
Variable	**[Q.sub.B]**	**k**	**[Delta]**	**[Delta]+**
Length of Intervention	.82	18	.28	.32(a)
"Short"		10	.21	.24
"Long"		8	.36	.40(a)
Focus of Instruction	7.05(*)	28	.41	.43(a)
General Reading		11	.51	.62(a)
Comprehension		4	.58	.57(a)
Word Recognition		13	.27	.19
Type of Outcome Measure	34.40(*)	70	.36	.40(a)
Reading Comprehension		21	.43	.41(a)
Oral Reading of Words		16	.25	.27(a)
Oral Reading of Passages		11	.14	.09
General Reading		7	.57	.59(a)
Decoding		7	.88	1.02(a)
Spelling		4	.04	.05
Composition/Writing		3	.17	.35
Language Mechanics		1	.14	.14

Variable	**95% C. I.**		**[Q.Sub.W]**
Length of Intervention	.14,	.50	33.88(*)
"Short"	−.01,	.49	17.90(*)
"Long"	.27,	.53	15.16(*)
Focus of Instruction	.28,	.58	48.15(*)
General Reading	.39,	.85	16.62
Comprehension	.18,	.96	7.43
Word Recognition	−.11,	.49	17.05
Type of Outcome Measure	.30,	.49	179.58(*)
Reading Comprehension	.25,	.57	55.34(*)
Oral Reading of Words	.03,	.51	28.74(*)
Oral Reading of Passages	.14,	.32	15.00
General Reading	.33,	.85	27.02(*)
Decoding	.62,	1.42	16.72(*)
Spelling	−.72,	.62	0.06(*)
Composition/Writing	−.29,	.99	2.30
Language Mechanics	−.82,	1.10	0.00

(a) 95% confidence interval does not include 0.
(*) $p < .05$.

Table 14.4

Elbaum et al. (2000)

How Effective Are One-to-One Tutoring Programs in Reading for Elementary Students at Risk for Reading Failure? A Meta-analysis of the Intervention Research

Number of studies included: 31

Summary Information on Interventions Included in the Meta-analysis by Sample

Study	Grade Level	Intervention Sample Size	Instructor	Focus of Instruction	n of within-sample ES	Mean within-sample ES
Arnold et al. (1977)	1	23	No information	V-P skills	2	0.00
Butler (1991)	4–6	20	College students	Mixed	4	0.75
Center, Wheldall, Freeman, Outhred, and McNaught (1995)[a]	1	22	Teachers	Mixed	4	1.08
Chapman, Tunmer, and Prochnow: Sample 1 (1998)[a]	1	26	Teachers	Mixed	8	−0.43
Chapman, Tunmer, and Prochnow: Sample 2 (1998)[a]	1	6	Teachers	Mixed	8	−1.32
Compton (1992)[a]	1	80[b]	College students	Mixed	1	1.83
Dorval, Wallach, and Wallach (1978)	1	20	Paraprofessionals	PA–phonics	1	0.68
Graves: Sample 1 (1986)	4–6	8	Teachers	Comprehension	2	1.85
Graves: Sample 2 (1986)	4–6	8	Teachers	Comprehension	2	3.34
Hagin, Silver, and Beecher (1978)	Range	63	Teachers	Mixed	3	0.49
Hedrick (1996)	1	80[b]	Teachers	Mixed	1	−0.01
Iversen and Tunmer: Sample 1 (1993)[a]	1	32	Teachers	Mixed	6	2.46
Iversen and Tunmer: Sample 2 (1993)[a]	1	32	Teachers	Mixed	6	2.53
Juel (1996)	2–3	6	College students	Mixed	1	3.15
Knapp and Winsor (1998)	2–3	8	Teachers	Underspecified	2	0.71
Lafave (1995)[a]	1	23	Teachers	Mixed	6	0.36
Mantzicopoulos, Morrison, Stone, and Setrakian: Sample 1 (1992)	1	59	Teachers	V-P skills	6	0.05
Mantzicopoulos, Morrison, Stone, and Setrakian: Sample 2 (1992)	1	52	Teachers	PA–phonics	6	0.09
McCarthy, Newby, and Recht (1995)	1	19	Teachers	Mixed	15	0.68
McGrady (1994)	4–6	35	No information	Mixed	1	−0.37

(continued)

Table 14.4 (continued)

Study	Grade Level	Intervention Sample Size	Instructor	Focus of Instruction	n of within-sample ES	Mean within-sample ES
Morris, Shaw, and Perney (1990)	2–3	30	Volunteers	Mixed	6	0.52
Nielson (1991)	2–3	14	Volunteers	Mixed	1	0.38
Pinnell: Sample 1 (1988)[a]	1	80[b]	Teachers	Mixed	9	0.65
Pinnell: Sample 2 (1988)[a]	1	37	Teachers	Mixed	9	0.58
Pinnell, Lyons, DeFord, Bryk, and Seltzer: Sample 1 (1994)[a]	1	31	Teachers	Mixed	4	0.74
Pinnell, Lyons, DeFord, Bryk, and Seltzer: Sample 2 (1994)[a]	1	38	Teachers	Mixed	4	0.13
Pinnell, Lyons, DeFord, Bryk, and Seltzer: Sample 3 (1994)[a]	1	3	Teachers	Mixed	4	-0.05
Ramaswami: Sample 1 (1994)[a]	1	12	Teachers	Mixed	5	2.17
Ramaswami: Sample 2 (1994)[a]	1	5	Teachers	Mixed	5	1.20
Ramaswami: Sample 3 (1994)[a]	1	19	Teachers	Mixed	6	0.35
Ramaswami: Sample 4 (1994)[a]	1	13	Teachers	Mixed	6	-0.37
Ramsey: Sample 1 (1991)	2–3	18	Volunteers	Underspecified	1	0.00
Ramsey: Sample 2 (1991)	4–6	59	Volunteers	Underspecified	1	-0.25
Saginaw Public Schools (1992)[a]	1	35	Teachers	Mixed	6	0.92
Torgeson et al.: Sample 1 (1998)	2–3	33	Teachers	PA-phonics	8	0.68
Torgeson et al.: Sample 2 (1998)	2–3	36	Teachers	Mixed	8	0.16
Torgeson et al.: Sample 3 (1998)	2–3	37	Teachers	Underspecified	8	0.05
Vadasy, Jenkins, Antil, Wayne, and O'Connor: Sample 1 (1997)	1	6	Volunteers	Mixed	11	0.85
Vadasy, Jenkins, Antil, Wayne, and O'Connor: Sample 2 (1997)	1	14	Volunteers	Mixed	11	0.06
Vadasy, Jenkins, and Pool (1998)	1	23	Volunteers	Mixed	9	0.98
Wallach and Wallach (1976)	1	36	Volunteers	PA-phonics	6	0.67
Weeks (1992)[a]	1	20	Teachers	Mixed	3	-0.35

Note: ES = unweighted effect size; V-P = visual-perceptual skills; PA-phonics = phonemic awareness–phonics.
[a] Reading Recovery intervention. [b] Winsorized sample size.

Table 14.5

Swanson (2001)

Research on Interventions for Adolescents with Learning Disabilities: A Meta-analysis of Outcomes Related to Higher-Order Processing

Instructional Components Reported in Studies as a Function of Percentage, Correlations with Effect Size, and Regression Analysis

	(N = .58)	r	[chi square]	Beta	SE
Methods composite		−.23	.84	−.05	.04
Chronological age		−.03	.08	−.001	.04
Instructional components:					
1. Advanced organizers	29.3	.11	.01	.04	.18
2. Attributions	1.7	.02	.02	−.03	.75
3. Control difficulty	37.9	.02	.74	.02	.19
4. Elaboration	8.6	.16	6.58	.57	.44
5. Extended practice	31.0	.34(*)	13.05(*)	.68	.22
6. Large-group learning	51.7	−.16	3.49	−.46	.20
7. New skills/content	37.9	.12	.15	−.17	.21
8. One-to-one instruction	70.7	.32	3.04	.47	.21
9. Peer modeling	6.9	−.14	.64	.11	.43
10. Questioning	17.2	−0.9	2.57	.63	.30
11. Reinforcement	3.4	.09	1.96	−.21	.48
12. Sequencing	53.4	−.01	1.22	−.24	.24
13. Skill modeling	34.5	.11	2.40	.09	.21
14. Small-group instruction	15.5	.07	.01	−.23	.28
15. Strategy cues	22.4	−.11	3.51	−.48	.29
16. Supplemental instruction	5.2	−.08	1.66	.49	.64
17. Task reduction	50.0	.10	1.59	.37	.24
18. Technology	41.4	−.11	2.24	−.24	.18

Note: [R.sup.2] = .46, [chi square] (20, N = 58) = 57.34, p < .01; adjusted [R.sup.2] = .21, intercept = .79, SE = .70.

(*) p < .001.

Table 14.6
Therrien (2004)
Fluency and Comprehension Gains as a Result of Repeated Reading:
A Meta-analysis
Number of studies included: 18

	Nontransfer Intervention Component Analysis							
	Cue Type			**Corrective Feedback**		**No. of Times Passage Read**		
Dependent Variable	**Fluency**	**Comp.**	**Fluency & Comp.**	**Yes**	**No**	**2**	**3**	**4**
Fluency *n*	0.72	.081	0.94	0.68	0.88	0.57	0.85	0.95
	2	8	3	3	13	2	10	3
Comp. *n*	0.66	0.75	0.67	–	–	–	0.66	0.71
	2	6	3	–	–	–	10	2

Note: *n* indicates number of effect sizes. Dash indicates effect size not calculated or available.

Education Commission of the States (1999)
Direct Instruction
Number of studies included: 10

Groups of studies reviewed in this logical synthesis of research did not provide statistical evidence. However, many of the individual studies included in the logical synthesis of research do contain statistical evidence. In the event that a reader wishes to view this evidence, an extensive listing of the individual studies reviewed is provided in the reference list in Part V (the studies are identified by the symbol +).

Baker et al. (2002)
A Synthesis of Empirical Research on Teaching Mathematics to
Low-Achieving Students
Number of studies included: 17

Groups of studies reviewed in this logical synthesis of research did not provide statistical evidence. However, many of the individual studies included in the logical synthesis of research do contain statistical evidence. In the event that a reader wishes to view this evidence, an extensive listing of the individual studies reviewed is provided in the reference list in Part V (the studies are identified by the symbol =).

Table 14.7
Barley et al. (2002)
Helping At-Risk Students Meet Standards: A Synthesis of Evidence-Based Classroom Practices
Number of studies included: 118

		Summary of Research Synthesis		
Strategy	**Type**	**Number of High-Quality Studies**	**Selected Implementation Considerations**[a]	**Synthesis Results on Positive Effects of Strategy on Student Achievement**
General Instruction	Approach	4	Balance of direct instruction and authentic learning	Inconclusive
Cognitively Oriented Instruction	Approach	4	Student practice Student interaction Teacher modeling	Preliminary
Grouping Structures	Intervention	4	Heterogeneous groups Teacher training Student instructions	Preliminary
Tutoring	Intervention	5	Tutor training Program monitoring	Preliminary
Peer Tutoring	Intervention	13	Structured tasks Teacher monitoring Participant training	Preliminary
Computer-Assisted Instruction	Intervention	10	Subject matter	Conclusive

[a] Other implementation issues are described in the individual chapters on each strategy.

Table 14.8
Bryant et al. (1995)
The HOSTS Program: Early Intervention and One-to-One Mentoring Help Students Succeed

Edgecomb County, North Carolina, Schools HOSTS Reading Program Results, 1994–95

Schools utilizing HOSTS for 7 months:
  Average gains from pre- to post-program, CAT reading scores by school
    Pattillo—grade 3   44 students   +5.53 NCEs
    Princeville—grades 1 & 2   44 students   +12.14 NCEs
    Stocks—grades 1 & 2   40 students   +10.06 NCEs

(continued)

Table 14.8 (continued)

Average gains from pre- to post-program, End of Grade Tests by school
Phillips—grades 4–8   46 students   +1.78 NCEs

Schools utilizing HOSTS for 4.5 months:
Average gains from pre- to post-program, CAT reading scores by school
Bullcuk—grades 1 & 2   36 students   +11.52 NCEs
W. Edgecombe—grade 3   20 students   +3.41 NCEs

Systemwide Results:
Total served: 230 students
Average gain: +7.41 NCEs

Table 14.9
Trout et al. (2003)
Effects of a Reading Intervention for Kindergarten Students at Risk for Emotional Disturbance and Reading Deficits

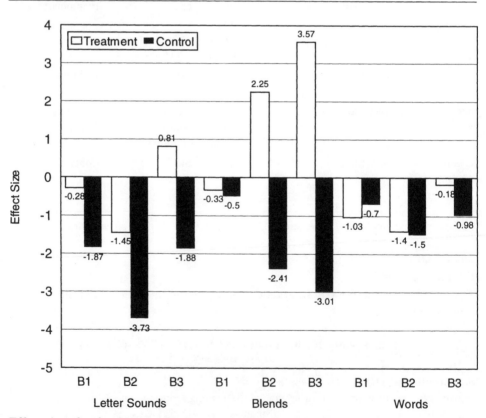

Effect sizes for the three reading measures of students in the treatment and control-risk groups compared to their norm-referenced peers.

Table 14.10

Fuchs et al. (1997)

Peer-Assisted Learning Strategies: Making Classrooms More Responsive to Diversity

Reading Achievement by Treatment, CRAB Score, Student Type, and Trial

| | PALS | | | | | | No PALS | | | | | | ES | | |
| | WC | | QC | | MC | | WC | | QC | | MC | | WC | QC | MC |
Student type/trial	M	(SD)	M	(SD)	M	(SD)	M	(SD)	M	(SD)	M	(SD)			
Learning disabled															
Pre	203.15	(123.86)	3.78	(2.29)	8.90	(5.71)	202.20	(132.80)	3.73	(2.22)	8.60	(6.13)			
Post	254.23	(117.99)	5.68	(2.28)	11.30	(5.72)	230.88	(116.78)	4.15	(2.55)	8.60	(5.35)			
Growth	51.08	(29.60)	1.90	(1.24)	2.40	(4.54)	28.68	(28.91)	.43	(1.60)	.00	(5.55)	.20	.68	.42
Low performing															
Pre	243.50	(109.37)	3.40	(2.20)	9.05	(5.50)	187.98	(113.05)	3.38	(2.10)	7.70	(4.92)			
Post	290.75	(95.67)	5.30	(2.21)	12.90	(5.30)	228.33	(119.78)	4.45	(1.99)	10.30	(5.43)			
Growth	56.25	(36.82)	1.90	(1.88)	3.85	(2.87)	40.35	(28.38)	1.08	(1.35)	2.60	(2.98)	.14	.40	.23
Average achieving															
Pre	291.58	(104.46)	5.75	(2.18)	10.75	(5.76)	310.98	(110.65)	5.95	(2.13)	13.95	(4.95)			
Post	351.08	(116.94)	6.95	(1.87)	14.60	(5.21)	348.35	(106.29)	6.95	(1.78)	14.55	(4.55)			
Growth	59.50	(47.32)	1.20	(1.77)	3.85	(4.00)	37.38	(45.25)	1.00	(1.42)	.60	(4.39)	.20	.10	.66
Across student type															
Pre	243.08	(100.99)	4.31	(1.92)	9.57	(5.04)	233.72	(101.68)	4.35	(1.73)	10.08	(4.57)			
Post	298.68	(98.71)	5.98	(1.79)	12.93	(4.50)	269.18	(96.07)	5.18	(1.66)	11.15	(3.88)			
Growth	55.61	(27.25)	1.67	(1.29)	3.37	(2.05)	35.47	(24.24)	.83	(1.05)	1.07	(2.68)	.22	.55	.56

Note: On the Comprehensive Reading Assessment Battery (CRAB), WC is average number of words correct read in 3 min. across two passages; QC is average number of questions correct (out of 10) across two passages; MC is number of correct maze replacements in 2 min. ES = effect size.

Statistical Evidence on Utilizing Reminders

GENERALIZATION TESTED: ON REMINDERS—CHAPTER 15

Achievement of learning objectives is enhanced when reminders are used to cue the recall of information needed to perform assigned tasks.

Total number of studies covered: 173

Table 15.1
Rosenshine et al. (1996)
Teaching Students to Generate Questions: A Review of the Intervention Studies
Number of studies included: 26

| | Overall Median Effect Sizes by Type of Prompt | | | | | |
| | Standardized Test | | | Experimenter-Developed Test | | |
Prompt	**Reciprocal Teaching** ($n = 6$)	**Regular Instruction** ($n = 7$)	**Combined** ($n = 13$)	**Reciprocal Teaching** ($n = 12$)	**Regular Instruction** ($n = 19$)	**Combined** ($n = 19$)
Signal words	0.34 (4)	0.46 (2)	0.36 (6)	0.88 (5)	0.67 (2)	0.85 (7)
Generic questions/ Stems					1.12 (4)	1.12 (4)
Main idea		0.70 (1)	0.70 (1)	1.24 (1)	0.13 (4)	0.25 (5)
Question type	0.02 (2)	0.00 (1)	0.00 (3)	3.37 (1)		3.37 (1)
Story grammar					1.08 (2)	1.08 (2)
No facilitator		0.14 (3)	0.14 (3)			

Note: n = number of studies. Number in parentheses refers to the number of studies used to compute an effect size.

Table 15.2

Fukkink & de Glopper (1998)

Effects of Instruction in Deriving Word Meaning from Context: A Meta-analysis

Number of studies included: 22

Summary of Features and Effect Sizes of the Studies Included in the Meta-analysis

Study	$N_e + N_c$	PPD	A	Mean	Test	α	Pre	Age	CS	Dur.	Type	d	se
Guarino (1960): Syracuse study	85 + 82	1	NR	NA	MC	.83	.34	15	28.3	360	clue	.60	.16
Guarino (1960): Michigan study	153 + 148	1	NR	NA	MC	.79	.02	15	25.5	495	clue	.32	.12
Cox (1974): Cloze 1-group	25 + 22	0	R	NA	MC	.84	-.06	9	25	720	cloze	-.12	.29
Cox (1974): Cloze 2-group	24 + 22	0	R	NA	MC	.84	-.07	9	24	720	cloze	.21	.30
Bissell (1982): Cloze	30 + 28	1	R	NA	MC	.38	.00	18.5	23.5	238	cloze	.00	.26
Bissell (1982): Forced Cloze	29 + 28	1	R	NA	MC	.38	.00	18.5	23.5	238	cloze	.23	.27
Sampson et al. (1982)	46 + 46	1	R	A	C	.85	—	8	7	662	cloze	.73	.22
Carnine et al. (1984): rule	12 + 12	0	R	NA	MC	.55	.00	10	1	90	strategy	.82	.43
Carnine et al (1984): practice	12 + 12	0	R	NA	MC	.55	.00	10	1	90	practice	.73	.42
Schwartz & Raphael (1985): Exp. I	8 + 8	0	R	NA	def	.55	.00	9	8	160	definition	5.45	1.19
Schwartz & Raphael (1985): practice	14 + 28	1	R	NA	def	.61	-.04	10	14	160	practice	.35	.11
Schwartz & Raphael (1985): training	14 + 28	1	R	NA	def	.61	.59	10	14	160	definition	1.22	.12
Herman & Weaver (1988)	14 + 16	0	NR	NA	def	.13	.15	13	14	325	strategy	.57	.37
Kranzer (1988): textbook context	19 + 19	0	NR	NA	def	.66	.24	13	23	155	strategy	.50	.33
Kranzer (1988): enriched context	21 + 19	0	NR	NA	def	.66	.01	13	23	155	strategy	-.40	.32
Kranzer (1988): definition + context	21 + 19	0	NR	NA	def	.66	.20	13	23	155	strategy	.43	.32
Jenkins et al. (1989): low	22 + 22	0	NR	NA	def	.61	.00	10	23	135	strategy	.03	.30
Jenkins et al. (1989): medium	22 + 22	0	NR	NA	def	.61	.00	10	23	165	strategy	.48	.31
Jenkins et al. (1989): high	22 + 22	0	NR	NA	def	.61	.00	10	23	300	strategy	.71	.31
Buikema & Graves (1993)	19 + 19	1	NR	NA	MC	.61	.28	12.5	19	250	clue	.80	.34
De Glopper et al. (1997)	29 + 30	1	R	A	def	.78	—	11	8	480	strategy	.15	.26
Tomesen & Aarnoutse (1998)	16 + 15	0	NR	NA	def	.84	-.21	9	4	450	cloze	1.53	.41

Note: $N_e + N_c$ = size of the experimental group + size of the control group; PPD: 1 = pretest posttest design, 0 = other design; Assignment: R = random, NR = not random; Means: A = means are adjusted by covariance analysis; NA = means are not adjusted; Test: MC = multiple choice, c = cloze test, def = definition task; α = Cronbach's alpha of the posttest (estimated values in italics); Pre: difference in the pretest in standard deviation units between experimental and control group (estimated values in italics); Age = average age of students; CS = class size; Dur.: duration of the instruction in minutes; Type: type of instruction; d = effect size d; se = standard error of the effect size.

Gersten & Baker (2001)
Teaching Expressive Writing to Students with Learning Disabilities:
A Meta-analysis
Total number of studies included: 13

Summed across all 13 studies the mean effect size on the aggregate writing measure was 0.81. The weighted and unweighted effect sizes were 0.81 and 0.99, suggesting that the studies with larger sample sizes resulted in somewhat smaller effects. Positive effect sizes were found in each of the 13 studies, ranging in magnitude from 0.30 (MacArthur et al., 1995) to 1.73 (Wong et al., 1996).

Belleza (1996); Levin (1993); Carney et al. (1993); Levin (1988)

Groups of studies reviewed in these logical syntheses of research did not provide statistical evidence. However, many of the individual studies included in these logical syntheses of research do contain statistical evidence. In the event that a reader wishes to view this evidence, an extensive listing of the individual studies reviewed is provided in the reference list in Part V. Studies reviewed by Belleza (1996) are identified by the symbol *; studies reviewed by Levin (1993) are identified by the symbol #; studies reviewed by Carney et al. (1993) are identified by the symbol $; and studies reviewed by Levin (1988) are identified by the symbol @.

Table 15.3
Griffith (1979)
A Review of the Literature on Memory Enhancement: The Potential and Relevance of Mnemotechnics for Military Training

Table of Studies Reviewed (created from the text); Significant Findings
$p < .05$ Although Students Not Given for Most Studies (Griffith states most
studies used college students)

Author	Mnemotechnic	Students	Findings
Croninger (1971) (1971)	Method of Loci	College	Recall superior to a control group at 1 week and 5 weeks.
Robertson et al. (1976)	Method of Loci	Senior citizens	Higher pretest-posttest recall than a control group.
Four other Method of Loci studies reviewed that were criticized for lack of control group			
Smith & Nobel (1965)	Pegword	not given	No significant difference during learning phase. Significantly enhanced recall at 24 hours as compared to a control group.

(continued)

Table 15.3 (continued)

Author	Mnemotechnic	Students	Findings
Senter & Hauser (1968)	Hook (pegword)	not given	Effective for recall at two association levels as compared to control subjects.
Berla et al. (1969)	Pegword	not given	The word list was learned significantly faster by students in the experimental condition.
Perensky & Senter (1969)	Pegword	not given	Two pegword conditions performed significantly better on immediate recall and 24-hour delayed recall.
Bugelski et al. (1968)	Pegword	not given	No significant enhancement at a 2-second rate. Significant enhancement at 4- and 8-second rates as compared to a rhyme control and standard control groups.
Bugelski (1968)	Pegword	not given	On final recall the mnemonic group recalled 63% and the control group recalled 22%.
Keppel & Zavortink (1969)	Pegword	not given	Partially replicated the findings of Bugelski (1968).
Griffith & Atkinson (1978)	Pegword	Military	Individuals with GT scores over 110 experienced significantly enhanced recall. Findings were not significant for lower GT levels.
Bower & Reitman (1972)	Compared two means of employing pegwords—no significant difference.		
Pavio (1968)			
Departo & Baker (1974)	Addressed pegword concreteness.		
Wortman & Sparling (1974)			
Wood (1967)	Linking	not given	Recall for the linking group was superior to that of a control group.

(continued)

Table 15.3 (continued)

Author	Mnemotechnic	Students	Findings
Bugelski (1974)	Linking	College, Grade 8	Serial recall was superior for linking groups as compared to control groups.
Bower & Clark (1969)	Linking	not given	No difference on immediate recall. On final recall the experimental group outperformed the control group by a factor close to 4.
Murray (1974)	Linking	not given	Significant difference in favor of the experimental group for the end of session test and for day 7 retention test. No significant difference for day 14 and day 28 retention tests.
Gamst & Freund (1978)	Linking	not given	No significant findings for 2 experiments.
Ott et al. (1973)	Keyword	not given	Experimental group performed significantly better than controls on learning and retention tests. No significant difference on delayed retention.
Raugh & Atkinson (1974, 1975)	Keyword	not given	*Experiment 1*: Experimental group final test score 88% correct as compared to 28% correct for the control group. *Experiment 2*: Final test score was 59% correct for the experimental group and 30% correct for the control group.
Atkinson & Raugh (1975)	Keyword	not given	Average percentage correct on a comprehension test was 72% for the keyword group and 46% for the control group. On a delayed comprehension test, recall was 43% for the keyword group and 28% for the control group.

(continued)

Table 15.3 (continued)

Author	Mnemotechnic	Students	Findings
Willerman (1977)	Keyword	College	No significant findings.
Griffith & Atkinson (1978)	Pictorial	not given	No significant findings.

Table 15.4
Mevarech & Kramarski (2003)
The Effects of Metacognitive Training versus Worked-Out Examples on Students' Mathematical Reasoning

Mean Scores and Standard Deviations on the Pretest and Post-test
Measures by Treatment and Level of Prior Knowledge

	Worked-Out Examples		Metacognitive Training	
	Lower Ach. N = 27	Higher Ach. N = 25	Lower Ach. N = 35	Higher Ach. N = 35
Pretest				
M	66.19	92.88	64.48	92.43
SD	(17.06)	(4.50)	(12.89)	(4.34)
Immediate Post-test (Total Score)				
M	58.88	85.56	69.91	87.17
SD	(21.53)	(11.50)	(19.36)	(14.69)
Verbal Explanations				
M	5.20	7.12	7.60	9.85
SD	(4.20)	(4.90)	(4.04)	(4.70)
Algebraic Representations				
M	6.00	5.24	8.31	8.54
SD	(4.50)	(5.09)	(4.14)	(4.92)
Algebraic Solution				
M	5.29	6.16	8.03	9.60
SD	(5.12)	(5.69)	(4.63)	(5.40)

Analysis of the pretest scores indicated that neither the treatment main effect, $F(1,118) < 1.00$, $p > .05$, nor the interaction between the treatment and prior knowledge, $F(1,118) < 1.00$, $p > .05$, were significant. Only the prior knowledge main effect was significant, $F(1,118) = 181.05$, $p > .001$. Thus, no significant differences between MT and WE students were found on the pretest scores for lower achievers (M = 66.19 and 64.48; SD = 17.06 and 12.89 for WE and MT, respectively) or higher achievers (M = 92.88 and 92.43; SD = 4.50 and 4.34 for WE and MT, respectively).

The two-way ANOVA of the immediate post-test scores indicated, however, significant main effects for the treatment (MS = 1190.11; $F(1,118) = 3.98$, $p < .05$) and prior knowledge (MS = 14381.38; $F(1,118) = 48.08$, $p < .001$), but the interaction between the treatment and prior knowledge was not significant (MS = 660.48; $F(1,118) = 2.21$, $p > .05$). The MT

(continued)

Table 15.4 (continued)

---

students significantly outperformed the WE students (M = 78.54 and 72.72; SD = 19.14 and 21.89 for the MT and WE groups, respectively. In particular lower achievers benefited from the MT method, but their gains did not come at the expense of higher achievers (ESs for the lower and higher achiever groups, respectively, were .51 and .14 favouring the MT group).

To gain further insight on students' mathematical reasoning, we analyzed students' written mathematical responses by focusing on three criteria: students' verbal explanations of their mathematical reasoning, algebraic representations of verbal situations, and algebraic solutions. The table above presents also the mean scores and standard deviations on the three criteria by treatment and level of prior knowledge. ANOVA indicated significant main effects for their treatment, $F(1,118) = 9.89$, 10.84, and 10.51, for students' verbal explanations of their mathematical reasoning, algebraic representations of verbal situations, and algebraic solutions, respectively; all p values < .05, but none of the interactions between the treatment and prior knowledge was significant; all $F(1,118)$ values < 1.00, all p values > .05. Within the lower achiever group, the MT students significantly outperformed the WE students on verbal explanations of mathematical reasoning, algebraic representations, and algebraic solutions (*ES*s for the three criteria, respectively, were .57, .51, and .54 standard deviations). Also within the higher achiever group, MT students significantly outperformed the WE students on all three criteria (respective ESs = .56, .65, and .60 standard deviations).

Table 15.5
Mevarech & Kramarski (2003)
The Effects of Metacognitive Training versus Worked-Out Examples on Students'
Mathematical Reasoning

Mean Scores and Standard Deviations of Students' Behaviours in Small Groups by Task and Treatment

	Task A		Task B	
	WE 3 teams	MT 5 teams	WE 3 yeams	MT 5 teams
Overall Number of Statements				
M	7.66	5.40	17.33	32.20
SD	(3.51)	(1.50)	(15.30)	(15.71)
Cognitive Statements				
M	4.66	4.80	6.01	10.81
SD	(2.08)	(1.32)	(3.00)	(5.82)
Metacognitive Statements				
M	3.00	.60	11.33	21.40
SD	(1.73)	(1.36)	(12.30)	(11.21)
Quality of Cognitive Discourse				
M	2.66	2.40	2.33	3.20
SD	(.57)	(1.45)	(.57)	(1.50)

(continued)

Table 15.5 (continued)

	WE 3 teams	MT 5 teams	WE 3 yeams	MT 5 teams
Quality of Metacognitive Discourse				
M	2.30	.80	2.33	3.40
SD	(1.52)	(.86)	(1.52)	(1.90)
Level of Cooperative Behaviour				
M	3.00	2.30	3.01	3.62
SD	(0.00)	(1.13)	(1.73)	(.70)

Table 15.6
Mevarech & Kramarski (2003)
The Effects of Metacognitive Training versus Worked-Out Examples on Students' Mathematical Reasoning

Mean Scores and Standard Deviations on the Immediate and Delayed Post-test by Treatment

		WE $N = 52$	MT $N = 70$
Immediate Post-test			
Total	M	72.22	78.554
	SD	(21.89)	(19.14)
Verbal Explanations	M	6.16	8.73
	SD	(4.61)	(4.50)
Algebraic Representations	M	5.62	8.43
	SD	(4.76)	(4.51)
Algebraic Solution	M	572	8.81
	SD	(5.36)	(5.06)
Delayed Post-test			
Total	M	68.51	76.01
	SD	(28.67)	(23.23)
Verbal Explanations	M	10.03	11.77
	SD	(4.37)	(4.30)
Algebraic Representations	M	6.47	6.83
	SD	(2.16)	(2.58)
Algebraic Solution	M	9.73	10.20
	SD	4.10	2.15

Table 15.7
Mevarech & Kramarski (2003)
The Effects of Metacognitive Training versus Worked-Out Examples on Students'
Mathematical Reasoning

Mean Scores and Standard Deviations on the Pretest and Post-test Measures
by Treatment and Level of Prior Knowledge

	Worked-Out Examples		Metacognitive Training	
	Lower Ach.	Higher Ach.	Lower Ach.	Higher Ach.
	N = 27	N = 25	N = 35	N = 35
Pretest				
M	66.19	92.88	64.48	92.43
SD	(17.06)	(4.50)	(12.89)	(4.34)
Immediate Post-test (Total Score)				
M	58.88	85.56	69.91	87.17
SD	(21.53)	(11.50)	(19.36)	(14.69)
Verbal Explanations				
M	5.20	7.12	7.60	9.85
SD	(4.20)	(4.90)	(4.04)	(4.70)
Algebraic Representations				
M	6.00	5.24	8.31	8.54
SD	(4.50)	(5.09)	(4.14)	(4.92)
Algebraic Solution				
M	5.29	6.16	8.03	9.60
SD	(5.12)	(5.69)	(4.63)	(5.40)

Statistical Evidence on Utilizing Teamwork

GENERALIZATION TESTED: ON TEAMWORK—CHAPTER 16

Achievement of the learning objective group achievement is enhanced when students are taught to perform complementary tasks as a team in pursuit of the objectives.

Total number of studies covered: 383+

Table 16.1

Swanson (2000)

What Instruction Works for Students with Learning Disabilities? Summarizing the Results from a Meta-analysis of Intervention Studies

Number of studies included: 180

Weighted Mean Effect Sizes for Group Design Studies as a Function of Dependent Measure Category

LD Treatment versus LD Control

	N	K	Effect Size of Unweighted	Effect Size of Weighted	95% Confidence Interval for Weighted Effects Lower	Upper	Standard Error	Homogeneity (Q)
1. *Cognitive Processing*	41	115	.87 (.64)	.54	.48	.61	.03	311.67**
1a. Metacognitive	9	27	.98	.80	.66	.94	.07	83.91**
1b. Attribution	7	17	.79	.62	.44	.79	.08	31.99*
1c. Other Processes	25	71	.65	.46	.38	.53	.03	176.07**
2. *Word Recognition*	54	159	.71 (.56)	.57	.52	.62	.02	431.45**
2a. Standardized	23	79	.79	.62	.54	.69	.04	205.61**
2b. Experimental	35	80	.72	.53	.48	.60	.03	223.07**
3. *Reading Comprehension*	58	176	.82 (.60)	.72	.68	.77	.02	565.95**
3a. Standardized	16	38	.45	.45	.36	.54	.05	33.87
3b. Experimental	44	138	.84	.81	.75	.86	.02	489.54**
4. *Spelling*	24	54	.54 (.53)	.44	.37	.52	.04	100.44**
4a. Standardized	8	20	.61	.45	.34	.57	.06	34.45
4b. Experimental	18	34	.48	.44	.33	.54	.05	65.94**
5. *Memory/Recall*	12	33	.81 (.46)	.56	.43	.70	.06	42.72

(continued)

Table 16.1 (continued)

	N	K	Effect Size of Unweighted	Effect Size of Weighted	95% Confidence Interval for Weighted Effects		Standard Error	Homogeneity (Q)
					Lower	Upper		
6. *Mathematics*	28	71	.58 (.45)	.40	.33	.46	.04	128.28**
6a. Standardized	9	22	.41	.33	.23	.46	.05	25.72
6b. Experimental	21	49	.59	.42	.34	.51	.04	101.43**
7. *Writing*	19	67	.84 (.60)	.63	.54	.72	.05	157.45**
7a. Standardized	3	7	.37	.36	.14	.58	.11	5.01
7b. Experimental	16	60	.80	.68	.59	.78	.04	145.27**
8. *Vocabulary*	11	20	.79 (.44)	.78	.66	.89	.05	38.58**
9. *Attitude/Self-Concept*	25	86	.68 (.69)	.39	.33	.45	.03	210.65**
10. *Intelligence*	9	32	.58 (.59)	.41	.30	.52	.06	54.37**
11. *General Reading*	15	31	.60 (.50)	.52	.41	.65	.06	55.15*
12. *Phonics/Orthographic Skills*	29	175	.70 (.36)	.64	.60	.69	.02	453.70**
12a. Standardized Phonics	8	60	.72	.67	.62	.73	.03	275.87**
12b. Experimental Phonics	21	78	.76	.60	.52	.67	.04	175.22**
13. *Global Achievement* (grades, total achievement)	10	21	.91 (.76)	.45	.31	.58	.07	56.64**
14. *Creativity*	3	11	.84 (.49)	.70	.52	.87	.09	33.61**
15. *Social Skills*	13	36	.46 (.22)	.41	.30	.51	.05	28.46
16. *Perceptual Processes*	10	37	.74 (.65)	.26	.17	.35	.04	46.64
17. *Language*	9	52	.54 (.48)	.36	.28	.44	.04	75.53**

Notes: numbers in parentheses = standard deviation; * p < .01; ** p < .001.

Table 16.2
Slavin (1995)
Cooperative Learning

Effect Sizes by Cooperative Methods

Method	Mean ES	Mean ES Standardized Tests	Percentage of Studies		
			Significantly Positive	No Difference	Significantly Negative
All Studies	.26		64	31	5
STAD	.32	.21	69	31	0
TGT	.38	.40	75	25	0
CIRC	.29	.23	100	0	0
TAI	.15	.15	100	0	0
Learning Together	.04		42	42	17
Jigsaw	.12		31	46	23
Group Investigation	.06		50	50	0
Structured Dyads	.86		100	0	0
Other	.10		29	71	0
Group Goals and Individual Accountability	.32		78	22	0
Group Goals Only	.07		22	56	22
Individual Accountability (Task specialization)	.07		35	47	18
No Group Goals or Individual Accountability	.16		56	44	0

ES = effect size.

Individual studies included in this "best evidence synthesis" are identified by the symbol *
  in the reference list in Part V.

Sharan (1980)

Groups of studies reviewed in this logical synthesis of research did not provide statistical evidence. However, many of the individual studies included in this logical synthesis of research do contain statistical evidence. In the event that a reader wishes to view this evidence, an extensive listing of the individual studies reviewed is provided in the reference list in Part V (the studies are identified by the symbol #).

Table 16.3
Johnson et al. (1981)
Effects of Cooperative, Competitive, and Individualistic Goal Structures on Achievement: A Meta-analysis

	Method								
	Voting			Effect Size			z score		
Condition	N	ND	P	M	SD	N	z	N	Fail-safe n
Cooperative vs group competitive	3	6	4	.00	.63	9	.16	13	
Cooperative vs competitive	8	36	65	.78	.99	70	16.00	84	7,859
Group competitive vs competitive	3	22	19	.37	.78	16	6.39	31	430
Cooperative vs individualistic	6	42	108	.78	.91	104	24.01	132	27,998
Group competitive vs individualistic	1	10	20	.50	.37	20	11.37	29	1,356
Competitive vs individualistic	12	38	9	.03	1.02	48	4.82	50	380

Voting: N = negative; ND = no difference; P = positive. *Effect size*: M = mean; SD = standard deviation; N = number of studies. z score: N = number of studies; fail safe n = number of students required.

Individual studies included in this meta-analysis are identified by the symbol @ in the reference list in Part V.

Table 16.4
Slavin (1997)
When Does Cooperative Learning Increase Student Achievement?
Number of studies included: 46

Major Reports	N	Grade Level	Duration (Weeks)	Level of Random Assignment	Location	Subject Area	Achievement Effects
		Group study with group reward for learning					
Student Teams–Achievement Divisions (STAD)							
Slavin, 1978b	205	7	10	Class	Rural town East	Language arts	0
Slavin, Note 6	62	7	10	Class	Urban East	Language arts	+
Slavin, 1980b	424	4	12	Class	Rural East	Language arts	+
Slavin, 1979	424	7–8	12	Class	Urban east	Language arts	0
Slavin & Oickle, 1981	230	6–8	12	Class	Rural east	Language arts	
Black students							+
White students							0
Madden & Slavin, in press	175	3–6	6	Class	Urban East	Mathematics	+
Allen & VanSickle, Note 7	51	9	6	Class	Rural South	Geography	+
Slavin & Karweit, Note 8	569	9	30	Teacher	Urban East	Mathematics	+
Huber, Bogatzki, & Winter, Note 2	170	7	3	Class	Urban Germany	Mathematics	+
Sharan, in press	436	7	16	Teacher	Urban Israel	English as a second language	+
Teams-Games-Tournament (TGT)							
Edwards, DeVries & Snyder, 1972	96	7	9	Class	Urban East	Mathematics	+
Edwards & DeVries, Note 9	117	7	4	Student	Urban East	Mathematics	0
Edwards & DeVries, Note 10	128	7	12	Student	Urban East	Mathematics	+
Hulten & DeVries, Note 11	299	7	10	Class	Urban East	Social studies	0
						Mathematics	+

(continued)

Table 16.4 (continued)

Major Reports	N	Grade Level	Duration (Weeks)	Level of Random Assignment	Location	Subject Area	Achievement Effects
DeVries, Edwards, & Wells, Note 12	191	10–12	12	Class	Suburban South	Social studies	(+)
DeVries & Mescon, Note 13	60	3	6	Student	Suburban East	Language arts	+
DeVries, Mescon, & Shackman, Note 14	53	3	6	Student	Suburban East	Language arts	+
DeVries, Mescon, & Shackman, Note 15	53	3	5	Student	Suburban East	Reading	+
DeVries, Lucasse, & Shackman, Note 16	1742	7–8	10	Teacher	Suburban Midwest	Language arts	+
Combined student team learning program (STAD + TGT + Jigsaw II)							
Slavin & Karweit, 1981	559	4–5	16	Nonrandom (matched)	Rural East		
Language arts (STAD)							
Mathematics (TGT)							
Social studies (Jigsaw II)							
Reading (STAD, Jigsaw II)							
Team Assisted Individualization (TAI)							
Slavin, Leavey, & Madden, in press							
Experiment 1	506	3–5	8	School	Suburban East	Mathematics	+
Experiment 2	320	4–6	10	Nonrandom (matched)	Suburban East	Mathematics	+
Slavin, Leavey, & Madden, Note 4	1317	3–5	24	Nonrandom (matched)	Suburban East	Mathematics	+
Other							
Humphreys, Johnson, & Johnson, 1982 (Learning Together with Group Reward for Learning)	44	9	6	Student	Suburban Midwest	Science	+
Hamblin, Hathaway, & Wodarski, 1971							
Experiment 1	34	4	3	Nonrandom: Latin square	Urban Midwest	Spelling, mathematics, reading	+

Experiment 2	60	5	3	Nonrandom: Latin square	Urban Midwest	Mathematics	+
Lew & Bryant, Note 1	27	4	9	Nonrandom: ABABAB design	Suburban East	Spelling	+

Group study with reward for group product

Learning Together							
Johnson, Johnson, Johnson, & Anderson, 1976	30	5	4	Student	Urban Midwest	Language arts	0
Johnson, Johnson, & Scott, 1978	30	5-6	10	Student	Suburban Midwest	Mathematics	–
Robertson, 1982	166	2-3	6	Class	Suburban East	Mathematics	0
Other							
Wheeler & Ryan, 1973	88	5-6	4	Student	Suburban Midwest	Social studies	0
Peterson & Janicki, 1979	100	4-6	2	Student	Rural Midwest	Mathematics	0

Group study with individual reward

Peterson, Janicki, & Swing, 1981	93	4-5	2	Student	Rural Midwest	Mathematics	0
Webb & Kinderski, in press	107	7-8	3	Nonrandom (matched)	Urban California	Mathematics	0
Starr & Schoerman, 1974	48	7	3	Class	Suburban Midwest	Life science	0
Huber, Bogatzki, & Winter, Note 2	204	7	3	Class	Urban Germany	Mathematics	0

Task specialization with group reward for learning

Jigsaw II							
Ziegler, 1981	146	6	8	Class	Urban Canada	Social studies	+

Task specialization with group reward for group product

Group investigation							
Sharan, Hertz-Lazarowitz, & Ackerman, 1980	217	2-6	3	Nonrandom (matched)	Urban Israel	Social studies	
						Grades 2, 4, 6	+
						Grades 3, 5	0

(continued)

Table 16.4 (continued)

Major Reports	N	Grade Level	Duration (Weeks)	Level of Random Assignment	Location	Subject Area	Achievement Effects
Hertz-Lazarowitz, Sapir, & Sharan, Note 5	67	8	5	Nonrandom (matched)	Urban Israel	Arabic language and culture	0
Sharan, in press	467	7	18	Teacher	Urban Israel	English as a second language	+
Other							
Wheeler, Note 3	88	5–6	2	Student	Rural town South	Social studies	+
Task specialization with individual reward							
Jigsaw							
Lucker, Rosenfield, Sikes, & Aronson, 1976	303	5–6	2	Nonrandom (matched)	Urban Southwest	Social studies	
Black and Hispanic students							+
Anglo-American students							0
Baird, Lazarowitz, Hertz-Lazarowitz, & Jenkins, in press							
Experiment 1	113	10–12	6	Nonrandom (matched)	Rural town West	Biology	0
Experiment 2	83	10–12	3	Class	Rural town West	Geology	0
Experiment 3	69	10–12	2	Class	Rural town West	Genetics	–
Gonzales, Note 17	182	3–4	20	Nonrandom (matched)	Rural California (bilingual classes)	Social studies	0

Note: Geographical designations refer to areas of the United States. 0 indicates no differences; + indicates a statistically significant ($p < .05$) positive achievement affect; (+) indicates a marginally significant ($p < .10$) positive effect; – indicates that a control group significantly exceeded an experimental group in achievement. Adapted from *Cooperative Learning* by R. E. Slavin. New York: Longman, 1983. Copyright 1983 by Longman. Reprinted by permission.

Newmann & Thompson (1987)
Effects of Cooperative Learning on Achievement in Secondary Schools:
A Summary of Research
Number of studies included: 27

Twenty-seven reports of high-quality studies were reviewed, involving 37 comparisons of cooperative versus control methods. Twenty-five (68%) of these comparisons favored a cooperative learning method at the .05 level of significance.

Table 16.5
Mevarech & Kramarski (1997)
IMPROVE: A Multidimensional Method for Teaching Mathematics in Heterogeneous Classrooms
Number of studies included: 2

Mean Scores and Standard Deviations (in Terms of Percent Correct) on Algebra by Treatment						
Treatment	**IMPROVE**			**CONTROL**		
Ability	**Low**	**Middle**	**High**	**Low**	**Middle**	**High**
Pretest						
M	50.71	76.20	92.19	52.32	74.52	90.39
S	13.29	5.59	4.33	10.40	5.65	4.35
Algebra (Overall)						
M	55.90	73.94	86.58	52.65	63.72	71.77
S	20.95	21.09	16.60	30.08	18.88	22.30
Numerals						
M	68.57	80.88	90.30	63.21	75.09	77.95
S	20.24	17.16	13.72	28.35	15.38	19.76
Substitution						
M	55.00	71.04	83.91	49.62	62.50	70.38
S	21.96	25.78	20.27	34.17	25.28	27.37
Expressions						
M	53.18	71.92	87.06	51.58	57.84	73.30
S	28.11	30.84	19.26	29.20	25.73	28.76
Word Problems						
M	46.32	70.44	84.57	45.45	57.15	66.20
S	27.92	24.84	20.47	34.97	22.64	27.87

Table 16.6
Mevarech & Kramarski (1997)
IMPROVE: A Multidimensional Method for Teaching Mathematics in Heterogeneous Classrooms

Mean Scores and Standard Deviations (in Terms of Percent Correct) by Time, Treatment, and Ability on Introduction-to-Algebra and Mathematics Reasoning

Treatment	IMPROVE			CONTROL		
Ability	Low	Middle	High	Low	Middle	High
Pretest						
M	37.76	66.46	86.33	40.20	66.89	86.85
S	8.17	6.63	6.48	9.87	7.93	5.42
Introduction-to-Algebra						
M	48.28	79.52	88.20	45.97	67.24	82.27
S	16.31	10.06	8.55	21.03	18.97	13.05
Mathematical Reasoning						
M	41.37	64.00	74.74	32.60	50.98	67.47
S	14.41	16.38	12.98	20.68	17.79	15.34

Table 16.7
Henderson & Landesman (2001)
Effects of Thematically Integrated Mathematics Instruction on Students of Mexican Descent

Multivariate test statistics
  Wilks's lambda = 0.910
  $F(2, 168) = 8.274, p = .001$

Univariate F Tests	SS	df	MS	F	p
Computation	.807	1	.807	.795	.374
Error	171.476	169	1.015		
Concepts	11.202	1	11.202	12.511	.001
Error	151.319	169	.895		

Table 16.8
Whicker et al. (2001)
Cooperative Learning in the Secondary Mathematics Classroom

Test	M	Adj. M	SD
Descriptive Statistics on the Pretest and Three Chapter Tests for the Cooperative Learning and Comparison Groups			
Cooperative (n = 15)			
Pretest	86.93		6.48
Chapter test			
1	42.53	42.71	7.53
2	41.53	41.54	5.78
3	40.00	40.08	5.93
Comparison (n = 16)			
Pretest	88.00		4.41
Chapter test			
1	42.19	42.01	4.25
2	36.69	39.68	5.41
3	35.94	35.86	5.27

Table 16.9
Whicker et al. (2001)
Cooperative Learning in the Secondary Mathematics Classroom

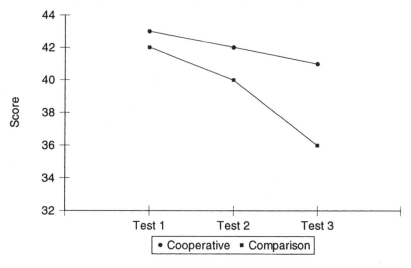

Adjusted Mean Achievement Scores for the Cooperative Learning and
Comparison Groups across the Three Prealgebra Chapter Tests

Table 16.10
Mevarech & Kramarski (2003)
The Effects of Metacognitive Training versus Worked-Out Examples on Students'
Mathematical Reasoning

	Worked-Out Examples		Metacognitive Training	
	Lower Ach. N = 27	Higher Ach. N = 25	Lower Ach. N = 35	Higher Ach. N = 35
Pretest				
M	66.19	92.88	64.48	92.43
SD	(17.06)	(4.50)	(12.89)	(4.34)
Immediate Post-test (Total Score)				
M	58.88	85.56	69.91	87.17
SD	(21.53)	(11.50)	(19.36)	(14.69)
Verbal Explanations				
M	5.20	7.12	7.60	9.85
SD	(4.20)	(4.90)	(4.04)	(4.70)
Algebraic Representations				
M	6.00	5.24	8.31	8.54
SD	(4.50)	(5.09)	(4.14)	(4.92)
Algebraic Solution				
M	5.29	6.16	8.03	9.60
SD	(5.12)	(5.69)	(4.63)	(5.40)

Mean Scores and Standard Deviations on the Pretest and Post-test Measures by Treatment and Level of Prior Knowledge

Analysis of the pretest scores indicated that neither the treatment main effect, $F(1,118) <$ 1.00, p > .05, nor the interaction between the treatment and prior knowledge, $F(1,118) <$ 1.00, p > .05, were significant. Only the prior knowledge main effect was significant, $F(1,118)$ = 181.05, p > .001. Thus, no significant differences between MT and WE students were found on the pretest scores for lower achievers (M = 66.19 and 64.48; SD = 17.06 and 12.89 for WE and MT, respectively) or higher achievers (M = 92.88 and 92.43; SD = 4.50 and 4.34 for WE and MT, respectively).

The two-way ANOVA of the immediate post-test scores indicated, however, significant main effects for the treatment (MS = 1190.11; $F(1,118)$ = 3.98, p < .05) and prior knowledge (MS = 14381.38; $F(1,118)$ = 48.08, p < .001), but the interaction between the treatment and prior knowledge was not significant (MS = 660.48; $F(1,118)$ = 2.21, p > .05). The MT students significantly outperformed the WE students (M = 78.54 and 72.72; SD = 19.14 and 21.89 for the MT and WE groups, respectively. In particular lower achievers benefited from the MT method, but their gains did not come at the expense of higher achievers (ESs for the lower and higher achiever groups, respectively, were .51 and .14 favouring the MT group).

To gain further insight on students' mathematical reasoning, we analyzed students' written mathematical responses by focusing on three criteria: students' verbal explanations of their mathematical reasoning, algebraic representations of verbal situations, and algebraic solutions. The table above presents also the mean scores and standard deviations on the three criteria by treatment and level of prior knowledge. ANOVA indicated significant main effects for

(continued)

Table 16.10 (continued)

their treatment, $F(1,118) = 9.89$, 10.84, and 10.51, for students' verbal explanations of their mathematical reasoning, algebraic representations of verbal situations, and algebraic solutions, respectively; all p values < .05, but none of the interactions between the treatment and prior knowledge was significant; all $F(1,118)$ values < 1.00, all p values > .05. Within the lower achiever group, the MT students significantly outperformed the WE students on verbal explanations of mathematical reasoning, algebraic representations, and algebraic solutions (*ESs* for the three criteria, respectively, were .57, .51, and .54 standard deviations). Also within the higher achiever group, MT students significantly outperformed the WE students on all three criteria (respective ESs = .56, .65, and .60 standard deviations).

Table 16.11
Mevarech & Kramarski (2003)
The Effects of Metacognitive Training versus Worked-Out Examples on Students' Mathematical Reasoning

Mean Scores and Standard Deviations of Students' Behaviours in Small Groups by Task and Treatment

	Task A		Task B	
	WE 3 teams	MT 5 teams	WE 3 yeams	MT 5 teams
Overall Number of Statements				
M	7.66	5.40	17.33	32.20
SD	(3.51)	(1.50)	(15.30)	(15.71)
Cognitive Statements				
M	4.66	4.80	6.01	10.81
SD	(2.08)	(1.32)	(3.00)	(5.82)
Metacognitive Statements				
M	3.00	.60	11.33	21.40
SD	(1.73)	(1.36)	(12.30)	(11.21)
Quality of Cognitive Discourse				
M	2.66	2.40	2.33	3.20
SD	(.57)	(1.45)	(.57)	(1.50)
Quality of Metacognitive Discourse				
M	2.30	.80	2.33	3.40
SD	(1.52)	(.86)	(1.52)	(1.90)
Level of Cooperative Behaviour				
M	3.00	2.30	3.01	3.62
SD	(0.00)	(1.13)	(1.73)	(.70)

Table 16.12
Mevarech & Kramarski (2003)
The Effects of Metacognitive Training versus Worked-Out Examples on Students'
Mathematical Reasoning

		Mean Scores and Standard Deviations on the Immediate and Delayed Post-test by Treatment	
		WE	**MT**
		N = 52	*N* = 70
Immediate Post-test			
Total	M	72.22	78.554
	SD	(21.89)	(19.14)
Verbal Explanations	M	6.16	8.73
	SD	(4.61)	(4.50)
Algebraic Representations	M	5.62	8.43
	SD	(4.76)	(4.51)
Algebraic Solution	M	572	8.81
	SD	(5.36)	(5.06)
Delayed Post-test			
Total	M	68.51	76.01
	SD	(28.67)	(23.23)
Verbal Explanations	M	10.03	11.77
	SD	(4.37)	(4.30)
Algebraic Representations	M	6.47	6.83
	SD	(2.16)	(2.58)
Algebraic Solution	M	9.73	10.20
	SD	4.10	2.15

Table 16.13
Mevarech & Kramarski (2003)
The Effects of Metacognitive Training versus Worked-Out Examples on Students'
Mathematical Reasoning

Mean Scores and Standard Deviations on the Pretest and Post-test Measures
by Treatment and Level of Prior Knowledge

	Worked-Out Examples		Metacognitive Training	
	Lower Ach.	Higher Ach.	Lower Ach.	Higher Ach.
	N = 27	N = 25	N = 35	N = 35
Pretest				
M	66.19	92.88	64.48	92.43
SD	(17.06)	(4.50)	(12.89)	(4.34)
Immediate Post-test (Total Score)				
M	58.88	85.56	69.91	87.17
SD	(21.53)	(11.50)	(19.36)	(14.69)
Verbal Explanations				
M	5.20	7.12	7.60	9.85
SD	(4.20)	(4.90)	(4.04)	(4.70)
Algebraic Representations				
M	6.00	5.24	8.31	8.54
SD	(4.50)	(5.09)	(4.14)	(4.92)
Algebraic Solution				
M	5.29	6.16	8.03	9.60
SD	(5.12)	(5.69)	(4.63)	(5.40)

Statistical Evidence on Reducing Student/Teacher Ratio Below 21 to 1

GENERALIZATION TESTED: ON REDUCING STUDENT/ TEACHER RATIO—CHAPTER 17

Achievement of learning objectives is enhanced when the student-to-teacher ratio is reduced below 21 to 1 in teaching situations.

Total number of studies covered: 193

Table 17.1
Glass et al. (1982)
School Class Size: Research and Policy

Data on the Relationship of Class Size and Achievement from Studies Using Random Assignment of Pupils

Study Number	Size of Larger Class	Size of Smaller Class	loge(L/S)	Effect Size
1	25	1	3.22	.32
2	3	1	1.10	.22
2	25	1	3.22	1.52
2	25	3	2.12	1.22
3	35	17	.72	−.29
4	112	28	1.39	−.03
5	2	1	.69	.36
5	5	1	1.61	.52
5	23	1	3.14	.83
5	5	2	.92	.22
5	23	2	2.44	.57
5	23	5	1.53	.31
6	30	15	.69	.17
7	23	16	.36	.05
7	30	16	.63	.04
7	37	16	.84	.08
7	30	23	.27	.04
7	37	23	.48	.04
7	37	30	.21	0.00
8	28	20	.33	.15
9	50	26	.65	.29
10	32	1	3.46	.65
11	37	15	.90	.40
11	60	15	1.38	1.25
11	60	37	.48	.65
12	8	1	2.08	.30
13	45	15	1.10	.07
14	14	1	2.64	.72
14	30	1	3.40	.78
14	30	14	.76	.17
		Average:	1.42	.38

Table 17.2
Biddle & Berliner (2002)
What Does the Evidence Say about the Effects of Reducing Class Size?
Number of studies included: 24+

Average Months of Grade-Equivalent Advantage in Achievement Scores for Students Who Experienced One or More Years of Small Classes

Legend for Chart:
A—Grade When Test Administered
B—Months of Advantage Reading Scores
C—Months of Advantage Mathematics Scores
D—Months of Advantage Science Scores
E—Months of Advantage Social Studies Scores

A	B	C	D	E
4	3.9	2.4	3.1	4.6
6	3.0	3.1	1.0	5.1
8	4.1	3.4	4.3	4.8

Percentage of Students Who Took the ACT or SAT College Entrance Exam by Early-Grade Class Type

Legend for Chart:
B—Percent Taking ACT or SAT Small Classes
C—Percent Taking ACT or SAT Regular Classes

A	B	C
All students	43.7	40.0
White students	46.3	45.0
African American	40.2	31.7

Word et al. (1990)

Groups of studies reviewed in this logical synthesis of research did not provide statistical evidence. However, many of the individual studies included in this logical synthesis of research do contain statistical evidence. In the event that a reader wishes to view this evidence, an extensive listing of the individual studies reviewed is provided in the reference list in Part V (the studies are identified by the symbol #).

Table 17.3
McGivern et al. (1989)
A Meta-analysis of the Relation between Class Size and Achievement

		colspan="9" align="center"	**Estimate of Effect Sizes—PRIMETIME**

Test	School/ Subject	**Control** X	s	n	**PRIMETIME** X	s	n	**Pooled** SD	**Effect** Size
1:	School System A								
ITBS	Reading	46.07	15.02	27	67.96	13.41	24	14.29	1.53
	Math	32.46	19.86	26	76.43	19.30	23	19.60	2.24
	Composite	44.25	13.62	25	70.70	16.68	23	15.16	1.74
2:	School System B								
SAT	Reading	50.97	20.24	54	47.66	20.50	47	20.36	−.16
	Math	56.99	22.68	54	52.20	23.24	47	22.94	−.21
3:	School System C								
ITBS	Reading	54.50	23.10	164	68.90	25.10	145	24.22	.59
	Math	63.10	24.10	164	66.40	24.40	145	24.40	.14
	Composite	63.20	21.90	164	71.40	22.80	145	22.47	.36
4:	School System D								
ITBS	Reading	52.78	21.09	131	54.29	18.89	131	20.02	.07
	Math	53.36	19.64	131	58.71	17.13	131	18.43	.29
	Composite	54.35	20.48	131	57.04	18.33	131	19.43	.14
5:	School System E School E1:								
ITBS	Reading	102.80	11.65	56	96.73	10.06	44	10.98	−.55
CAT	Composite	99.80	15.24	55	101.26	14.76	74	14.97	.10
6:	School E2:								
CAT	Composite	102.47	11.59	58	96.50	10.24	44	11.03	−.54
7:	School E3:								
CAT	Composite	99.06	12.28	49	98.32	13.84	57	13.14	−.74
8:	School System F School F1:								
ITBS	Reading	60.8	2.90	81	62.3	6.10	84	4.80	.31
	Math	63.9	4.00	81	69.8	2.40	84	3.28	.52
	Composite	64.4	2.00	81	67.2	4.70	84	3.44	.29
9:	School F2:								
ITBS	Reading	60.8	4.30	69	58.6	3.00	63	3.74	−.59
	Math	63.9	4.80	69	59.9	8.00	63	6.52	−.61
	Composite	64.4	4.30	69	61.9	5.10	63	4.70	−.53

(continued)

Table 17.3 (continued)

| Test | School/ | Control | | | PRIMETIME | | | Pooled Effect | |
	Subject	X	s	n	X	s	n	SD	Size
10:	School F3:								
ITBS	Reading	52.2	2.80	96	57.4	4.10	96	3.51	1.48
	Math	50.2	4.80	96	55.2	5.50	96	5.16	.97
	Composite	52.5	5.00	96	59.0	5.00	96	5.00	1.30

ITBS = Iowa Tests of Basic Skills; SAT = Stanford Achievement Test; CAT = Cognitive Abilities Test; X = mean score; s = standard deviation; n = number of classes; SD = standard deviation.

Achilles (2005)
Class Size and Learning
Number of studies included: 4

Groups of studies reviewed in this logical synthesis of research did not provide statistical evidence. However, many of the individual studies included in this logical synthesis of research do contain statistical evidence. In the event that a reader wishes to view this evidence, an extensive listing of the individual studies reviewed is provided in the reference list in Part V (the studies are identified by the symbol &).

Table 17.4
Mosteller (1995)
The Tennessee Study of Class Size in the Early School Grades

| | Estimates of Mean Effect Sizes, 1985–1989 | | | |
	SAT Reading	BSF Reading	SAT Math	BSF Math
Comparision of class size 13–17:1 to 22–25:1	.23	.21	.27	.13
Comparison of class size 22–25:1 with an aide to class size 22–25:1 without an aide	.14	.08	.10	.05

(continued)

Table 17.4 (continued)

Percentile Ranks of Average Scores Based on National Test Norms

	Percentile			
Grade Level	**K**	**1**	**2**	**3**
Total Reading SAT				
Small Classes	59	64	61	62
Regular without an aide	53	53	52	55
Regular with an aide	54	58	54	54
Total Math SAT				
Small Classes	66	59	76	76
Regular without an aide	61	48	68	69
Regular with an aide	61	51	69	68

SAT = Stanford Achivement Test.
Percentile ranks are based on Stanford's multilevel norms.

Table 17.5
Blatchford et al. (2003)
Are Class Size Differences Related to Pupils' Educational Progress and Classroom Processes? Findings from the Institute of Education Class Size Study of Children Aged 5–7 Years

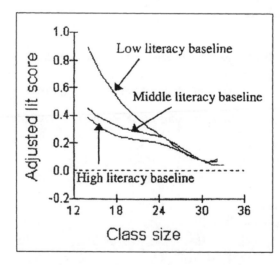

Relationship between reception year class size and literacy progress (adjusted for school entry scores).

Table 17.5 (continued)

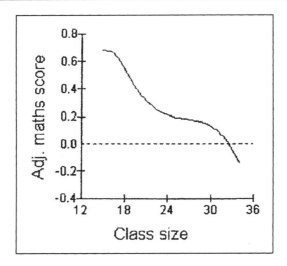

Relationship between class size and mathematics attainment in reception (adjusted for school entry scores).

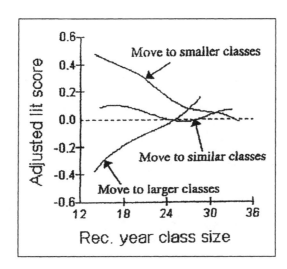

Relationship between reception class size and literacy progress in year 1.

Smith et al. (2003)
Class-Size Reduction: A Fresh Look at the Data

To gauge how much of an effect SAGE has had on student achievement, the academic performance of students in 30 schools from the 21 school districts that initially participated in the program were tracked from 1996 to 2001. The academic performance of SAGE students was compared to that of a comparable group of students in larger classes from 17 non-SAGE schools in the same district.

Overall, SAGE first graders scored significantly higher than did the comparison group on the reading, language arts, and mathematics subtest of the CTBS. At the end of first grade, SAGE students' test results showed a 25–30 percent higher level of academic achievement than those of their counterparts in larger classes, and they maintained that gain through third grade—the last year of the program. By the end of third grade, SAGE students were achieving at a level one-third to one-half a year ahead of students in larger classes.

Table 17.6
NICHD Early Child Care Research Network (2004)
Does Class Size in First Grade Relate to Children's Academic and Social Performance or Observed Classroom Processes?

Adjusted Associations between Class Size and Child Outcomes

Outcome	Teacher-reported class size						Observed child–teacher ratio					
	Standard Regression β	Discontinuous piecewise (spline) regression					Standard Regression β	Discontinuous piecewise (spline) regression				
		β	Δ in Intercept at:	Intercept Effect	Δ in Slope at:	Slope Effect		β	Δ in Intercept at:	Intercept Effect	Δ in Slope at:	Slope Effect
Cognitive outcomes												
WJ-R Achievement	−0.01	0.06	21	−0.10*			−0.03	−0.05			35:1	0.07*
WJ-R Letter-Word	−0.02	−0.06					−0.02	−0.04				
WJ-R Word Attack	−0.04	−0.10*					−0.03	0.03	22:1	−0.11*		
Social outcomes												
TRF Externalizing	0.02	−0.22*			21	0.26*	−0.00	0.00				
SSRS Total	−0.02	2.08**			17	−2.10*	−0.07	−0.07				
Teacher–child conflict	0.03	0.03					0.03	0.03				
Teacher–child closeness	−0.04	0.20*	22	−0.15*			−0.06	−0.06				
			28	−0.19**								

Note: WJ-R = Woodcock–Johnson Psychoeducational Battery—Revised; TRF = Child Behavior Checklist, Teacher Report Form; SSRS = Social Skills Rating Scale.
* $p < .05$. ** $p < .01$.

Statistical Evidence on Clarifying Communication

GENERALIZATION TESTED: ON CLARIFYING COMMUNICATION—CHAPTER 18

Achievement of learning objectives is enhanced when information on learning objectives, tasks, and evaluations is clearly communicated to students over time.

Total number of studies covered: 125+

Table 18.1
Land (1985)
Vagueness and Clarity in the Classroom

Vagueness Terms and Student Achievement

Experimental Studies

Study	Significance	Content	Grade Level	N
Smith & Edmond 1978	0.05	Mathematics	College	204 students
Land & Smith 1979a	0.05	Mathematics	College	50 students
Land & Smith 1979b	0.07	Mathematics	College	160 students
Smith & Cotton 1980	0.001	Mathematics	Elementary	100 students
Smith & Bramblett 1981	0.05	Biology	High school	48 students

Table 18.2
Land (1985)
Vagueness and Clarity in the Classroom

Correlational Studies

Study	Significance	Content	Grade Level	N
Hiller et al. 1969	0.01 to 0.001	Social Studies	High school	32 teachers 672 students
Smith 1977	0.05	Mathematics	High school	20 teachers 455 students
Dunkin 1978	ns	Social Studies	Elementary	29 teachers 827 students
Dunkin & Doenau 1980	0.05	Social Studies	Elementary	28 teachers 723 students
Dunkin & Doenau 1980	ns	Social Studies	Elementary	26 teachers 741 students

Table 18.3
Land (1985)
Vagueness and Clarity in the Classroom

	Correlational Studies: Clusters of Low-Inference Clarity Variables and Student Achievement				
Study	**Variables**	**Significance**	**Content**	**Grade Level**	**N**
Hiller et al. 1969	Teacher verbal fluency: (average sentence length, comma proportions, utterances of "uh")	0.01	Social Studies	High school	32 classes
		0.05	Social Studies	High school	23 classes
Clark et al. 1979	Teacher structuring: (Reviewing main ideas and facts, stating objectives,	ns	Science	Elementary	408
Dunkin 1978	outining lesson content signaling transitions, indicating important points, summarizing)	0.05	Social studies	Elementary	827
Denham & Land 1981	Clarity: (verbal mazes, vagueness terms, emphasis,	0.001	Psychology	College	129
Land 1979	transitions, additional	0.01	Psychology	College	78
Land 1980	unexplained content)	0.02	Psychology	College	77
Land & Smith 1981	Clarity: (verbal mazes, vagueness	ns	Social Studies	College	80
Land 1981	terms)	0.05	Mathematics	College	84
Hines et al. 1982	29 Clarity variables	0.03	Mathematics	College	32

Brophy & Good (1986)

Groups of studies reviewed in this logical synthesis of research did not provide statistical evidence. However, many of the individual studies included in the logical synthesis of research do contain statistical evidence. In the event that a reader wishes to view this evidence, an extensive listing of the individual studies reviewed is provided in the reference list in Part V (the studies are identified by the symbol *).

Table 18.4
Hines et al. (1985)
Teacher Clarity and Its Relationship to Student Achievement and Satisfaction

Relationships between Measures of Teacher Behaviors and Student Outcomes

Level of Measurement	Measurement Source	Canonical Analysis Correlation	Regression Analysis Achievement
Low-inference	observers	.75	.72*
	students	.95**	.69*
	teachers	.67*	.53
Intermediate-inference	observers	.70**	.67**
			Zero-Order Correlation
High-inference	observers	.65**	.63**
	students	.73**	.53**
	teachers	.45*	.34*

*p < .05; **p < .01.

Table 18.5
Chesebro (1999)
The Effects of Teacher Clarity and Immediacy on Student Learning,
Apprehension, and Affect
Number of studies included: 20+

Means and Standard Deviations

Immediacy	Clarity	n	Low-Level Learning	
			Mean	SD
High	High	46	4.58	1.75
High	Low	56	1.23	1.79
Low	High	49	4.81	1.81
Low	Low	39	1.00	1.27
Immediacy	**Clarity**	**n**	**High-Level Learning**	
			Mean	SD
High	High	46	3.67	1.44
High	Low	56	2.76	1.22
Low	High	49	3.75	1.33
Low	Low	39	2.82	1.27

Table 18.6
Chesebro (1999)
The Effects of Teacher Clarity and Immediacy on Student Learning,
Apprehension, and Affect

ANOVA Results

Low-Level Learning		IV	DF	F Value	Variance
		Immediacy	3, 189	0.00	–
	*	Clarity	3, 189	207.34	52%
		Immediacy × Clarity	3, 189	.86	–
High-Level Learning		**IV**	**DF**	**F Value**	**Variance**
		Immediacy	3, 189	.12	–
	*	Clarity	3, 189	22.79	11%
		Immediacy × Clarity	3, 189	.01	–

* = significant at the $p < .001$ level.

Table 18.7
Titsworth & Kiewra (2004)
Spoken Organizational Lecture Cues and Student Note Taking as Facilitators of Student Learning

	Percentage of Information Recalled on the Organization and Detail Tests					
	Achievement Tests					
	Organization Test ($M = 7.50$, $SD = 8.32$			Detail Test ($M = 5.97$, $SD = 3.57$)		
	Notes	No Notes	Overall	Notes	No Notes	Overall
With organizational cues	64%	41%	55%	49%	24%	39%
M	15.44	9.92	13.23	9.78	4.75	7.77
SD	8.69	6.73	8.31	3.02	1.82	3.59
Without organizational cues	10%	5%	7%	20%	22%	21%
M	2.40	1.13	1.77	4.00	4.33	4.17
SD	2.38	1.13	1.94	2.80	2.32	2.53
Overall	30%	21%		48%	23%	
M	7.15	5.04		9.52	4.52	
SD	4.10	6.30		9.28	2.08	

Table 18.8
Titsworth & Kiewra (2004)
Spoken Organizational Lecture Cues and Student Note Taking as Facilitators of Student Learning

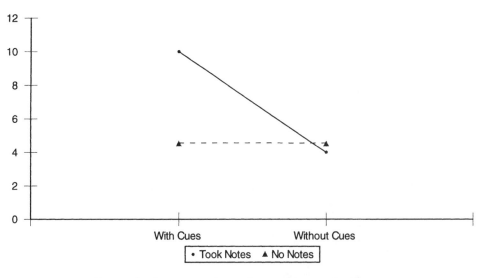

Interaction between cuing and notetaking on detail test.

Correlation Coefficients for Notetaking Measures and Test Scores

	Test Scores	
	Organization Test	**Detail Test**
Notetaking measures		
Organizational points	0.66	0.76
Details	0.61	0.70

Statistical Evidence on Utilizing Question and Answer Instruction

GENERALIZATION TESTED: ON QUESTION AND ANSWER INSTRUCTION—CHAPTER 19

Achievement of learning objectives is enhanced when question and answer sessions are planned and included in lessons to clarify the concepts being taught.

Total number of studies covered: 246

Table 19.1

Swanson & Hoskyn (1998)

Experimental Intervention Research on Students with Learning Disabilities: A Meta-analysis of Treatment Outcomes

Number of studies included: 180

Weighted Mean Effect Sizes for Group Design Studies as a Function of Dependent Measure Category

LD Treatment versus LD Control

	N	K	Effect Size of Unweighted	Effect Size of Weighted	95% Confidence Interval for Weighted Effects		Standard Error	Homogeneity (Q)
					Lower	Upper		
1. Cognitive Processing	41	115	.87 (.64)	.54	.48	.61		311.67**
1a. Metacognitive	9	27	.98	.80	.66	.94	.07	83.91**
1b. Attribution	7	17	.79	.62	.44	.79	.08	31.99*
1c. Other Processes	25	71	.65	.46	.38	.53	.03	176.07**
2. Word Recognition	54	159	.71 (.56)	.57	.52	.62	.02	431.45**
2a. Standardized	23	79	.79	.62	.54	.69	.04	205.61**
2b. Experimental	35	80	.72	.53	.48	.60	.03	223.07**
3. Reading Comprehension	58	176	.82 (.60)	.72	.68	.77	.02	565.95**
3a. Standardized	16	38	.45	.45	.36	.54	.05	33.87
3b. Experimental	44	138	.84	.81	.75	.86	.02	489.54**
4. Spelling	24	54	.54 (.53)	.44	.37	.52	.04	100.44**
4a. Standardized	8	20	.61	.45	.34	.57	.06	34.45
4b. Experimental	18	34	.48	.44	.33	.54	.05	65.94**
5. Memory/Recall	12	33	.81 (.46)	.56	.43	.70	.06	42.72

6.	Mathematics	28	71	.58 (.45)	.40	.33	.46	.04	128.28**
6a.	Standardized	9	22	.41	.33	.23	.46	.05	25.72
6b.	Experimental	21	49	.59	.42	.34	.51	.04	101.43**
7.	Writing	19	67	.84 (.60)	.63	.54	.72	.05	157.45**
7a.	Standardized	3	7	.37	.36	.14	.58	.11	5.01
7b.	Experimental	16	60	.80	.68	.59	.78	.04	145.27**
8.	Vocabulary	11	20	.79 (.44)	.78	.66	.89	.05	38.58***
9.	Attitude/Self-Concept	25	86	.68 (.69)	.39	.33	.45	.03	210.65**
10.	Intelligence	9	32	.58 (.59)	.41	.30	.52	.06	54.37**
11.	General Reading	15	31	.60 (.50)	.52	.41	.65	.06	55.15*
12.	Phonics/Orthographic	29	175	.70 (.36)	.64	.60	.69	.02	453.70**
12a.	Standardized Phonics	8	60	.72	.67	.62	.73	.03	275.87***
12b.	Experimental Phonics	21	78	.76	.60	.52	.67	.04	175.22**
13.	Global Achievement (grades, total achievement)	10	21	.91 (.76)	.45	.31	.58	.07	56.64**
14.	Creativity	3	11	.84 (.49)	.70	.52	.87	.09	33.61
15.	Social Skills	13	36	.46 (.22)	.41	.30	.51	.05	28.46
16.	Perceptual Processes	10	37	.74 (.65)	.26	.17	.35	.04	46.64
17.	Language	9	52	.54 (.48)	.36	.28	.44	.04	75.53*

Notes: numbers in parentheses = standard deviation; * p < .01; ** p < .001.

Swanson (2001)
Research on Interventions for Adolescents with Learning Disabilities:
A Meta-analysis of Outcomes Related to Higher-Order Processing
Number of studies included: 58

Fifty-eight studies included measures of higher-order skills. The average ES across studies was .82 (SD = .66). Instructional components reported in studies were:

1. Advanced organizers
2. Attributions
3. Control difficulty
4. Elaboration
5. Extended practice
6. Large-group learning
7. New skills
8. One-to-one instruction
9. Peer modeling
10. Questioning
11. Reinforcement
12. Sequencing
13. Skill modeling
14. Small-group instruction
15. Strategy cues
16. Supplemental instruction
17. Task reduction
18. Technology

When a factor referred to as "organization/extended practice"—which was the combination of (a) advanced organizers, (b) new content/skills, and (c) extended practice—was entered into the regression model first, followed by age and method, it was significant at p < .001. This "organization/extended practice" factor was the only combination factor, which contributed significant variance to effect size.

Rosenshine & Stevens (1986)

Groups of studies reviewed in this logical synthesis of research did not provide statistical evidence. However, many of the individual studies included in the logical synthesis of research do contain statistical evidence. In the event that a reader wishes to view this evidence, an extensive listing of the individual studies reviewed is provided in the reference list in Part V (the studies are identified by the symbol %).

Brophy & Good (1986)
Teacher Education and Student Achievement

Groups of studies reviewed in these logical syntheses of research did not provide statistical evidence. However, many of the individual studies included in these logical syntheses of research do contain statistical evidence. In the event that a reader wishes to view this evidence, an extensive listing of the individual studies reviewed is provided in the reference list in Part V. Studies associated with Brophy & Good (1986) are identified by the symbol !.

Statistical Evidence on Utilizing Computerized Instruction

GENERALIZATION TESTED: ON COMPUTERIZED INSTRUCTION—CHAPTER 20

Achievement of learning objectives is enhanced when computerized instruction is used as an instructional strategy.

Total number of studies covered: 202

Table 20.1
Azevedo & Bernard (1995)
The Effects of Computer-Presented Feedback on Learning from Computer-Based Instruction: A Meta-analysis
Number of studies included: 22

Effect Sizes Extracted from Studies Involving Immediate Posttest Administration

Authors	CBE Typology	N	n^e	n^c	d
Anderson et al., 1971, Study 1	Linear CAI	168			0.03
Hines et al., 1988	Branching CAI	221			0.07
Bumgamer, 1984	Branching CAI	41			0.12
Hodes, 1985	Branching CAI	41	21	20	0.14
Gaynor, 1981	Linear CAI	92			0.15
Arnone et al., 1992	CDIV	52	25	27	0.18
Gaynor, 1981	Linear CAI	92			0.20
Gaynor, 1981	Linear CAI	92			0.22
Schloss et al., 1988	Linear CAI	25	7	18	0.31
Gilman, 1969b	Linear CAI	75			0.38
Schloss et al., 1988	Linear CAI	25	7	18	0.40
Elliot, 1986	Linear CAI	42	20	22	0.42
Anderson et al., 1972	Linear CAI	48	24	24	0.43
Armour-Thomas et al., 1987	Linear CAI	45	22	23	0.45
Armour-Thomas et al., 1987	Linear CAI	46	23	23	0.46
Gilman, 1969a	Linear CAI	75			0.46
Armour-Thomas et al., 1987	Linear CAI	44	21	23	0.54
Elliot, 1986	Linear CAI	42	20	22	0.55
Schloss et al., 1988	Linear CAI	25	7	18	0.57
Tennyson et al., 1980	MAIS	139			0.69
Chanond, 1988	Linear CAI	120			0.77
Clariana et al., 1991	Branching CAI	100			0.80
Tennyson, 1981, Study 2	MAIS	47			0.90

(continued)

Table 20.1 (continued)

Authors	CBE Typology	N	n^e	n^c	d
Roper, 1977	Linear CAI	36			0.92
Tennyson, 1980	MAIS	46	23	23	0.93
Schaffer et al., 1986	CDIV	98			0.99
Tennyson, 1981, Study 2	MAIS	47			1.00
Tennyson, 1981, Study 2	MAIS	47			1.36
Schloss et al., 1988	Linear CAI	25	7	18	1.37
Johansen et al., 1983	MAIS	32	16	16	1.48
Tennyson, 1981, Study 1	MAIS	63			1.63
Tennyson, 1980	MAIS	46	23	23	1.81
Johansen et al., 1983	MAIS	32	16	16	1.94
Johansen et al., 1983	MAIS	32	16	16	2.12

Note: N = total sample size; n^e = experimental group sample size; n^c = control group sample size. Unweighted ES = .73, Weighted ES = .80, *SD* =57.

Table 20.2
Azevedo & Bernard (1995)
The Effects of Computer-Presented Feedback on Learning from Computer-Based Instruction: A Meta-analysis

Effect Sizes Extracted from Studies Involving Delayed Posttest Administration

Authors	CBE Typology	N	n^e	n^c	d
Gaynor, 1981	Linear CAI	92			0.15
Gaynor, 1981	Linear CAI	92			0.18
Gaynor, 1981	Linear CAI	92			0.22
Chanond, 1988	Linear CAI	103			0.26
Armour-Thomas et al., 1987	Linear CAI	45	22	23	0.28
Armour-Thomas et al., 1987	Linear CAI	46	23	23	0.30
Armour-Thomas et al., 1987	Linear CAI	44	21	23	0.42
Clariana et al., 1991	Branching CAI	100			0.60
Anderson et al., 1971, Study 2	Linear CAI	50	24	26	0.62

Note: N = total sample size; n^e = experimental group sample size; n^c = control group sample size. Unweighted ES = .34, Weighted ES = .35, *SD* =17.

Yan & Jitendra (1999)
The Effects of Instruction in Solving Mathematical Word Problems for Students with Learning Problems: A Meta-analysis
Number of studies included: 25

All intervention approaches, with the exception of the "other" approach, yielded moderate to large mean effect sizes (range = .74 to 1.80). The largest effect size was obtained from the samples coded as CAI (computer assisted instruction) intervention.

Table 20.3
Christmann & Badgett (2003)
A Meta-analytic Comparison of the Effects of Computer-Assisted Instruction on Elementary Students' Academic Achievement

Author, Date, Sample Size, and Effect Size of Each Study			
Author(s)	**Date**	***n***	***ES***
Borton	1988	98	0.553
Borton	1988	98	0.650
Childers	1989	114	0.945
Collis et al.	1990	91	0.111
Collis et al.	1990	91	0.025
Collis et al.	1990	91	−0.031
Collis et al.	1990	91	0.094
Ferrell	1986	91	0.488
Fraser	1991	484	0.144
Fraser	1991	357	−0.109
Gilman et al.	1988	57	0.274
Gilman et al.	1988	57	0.117
Haines	1988	134	0.292
Haines	1988	134	0.396
Hawley et al.	1986	41	0.477
Hawley et al.	1986	38	0.315
Hess et al.	1987	164	0.516
Hesser	1988	66	0.358
Hesser	1988	66	0.667
Hirsch	1986	38	0.497
Hoffman	1984	24	−0.411
Hoffman	1984	20	0.022
Hoffman	1984	31	−0.253
Hoffman	1984	21	−0.371
Hopkins	1989	27	−0.554
Larter	1987	60	0.493

(continued)

Table 20.3 (continued)

Author(s)	Date	*n*	*ES*
Larter	1987	60	−0.539
Larter	1987	60	0.025
Leahy	1991	548	0.171
Little	1987	47	−1.063
Liu et al.	1998	21	0.274
Liu et al.	1998	21	0.447
MacArthur et al.	1990	44	0.406
MacGregor	1988	48	0.572
MacGregor	1988	48	1.008
MacGregor	1988	48	0.993
Manuel	1987	28	−0.073
Mason	1984	49	0.884
McClurg et al.	1989	33	0.650
McClurg et al.	1989	28	0.355
McCollister et al.	1986	53	0.604
McCormack	1985	72	0.619
Meyer	1986	49	−0.357
Meyer	1986	46	0.395
Miller et al.	1995	289	0.269
Miller et al.	1995	289	0.347
Miller et al.	1995	289	0.402
Orabuchi	1992	122	0.187
Phillips et al.	1992	336	0.353
Powell-Rahlfs	1984	30	0.545
Powell-Rahlfs	1984	30	−0.159
Sexton	1989	80	0.601
Shanoski	1986	32	0.066
Shutrump	1993	930	0.100
Suppes et al.	1969	114	0.678
Suppes et al.	1969	79	1.193
Suppes et al.	1969	78	1.064
Suppes et al.	1969	133	0.459
Suppes et al.	1969	217	0.468
Suppes et al.	1969	435	0.498
Uhde	1988	94	0.222
Underwood et al.	1996	39	0.400
Ward	1986	51	1.103
Watkins	1986	82	0.436
Watkins et al.	1985	103	0.363
Westbrook	1987	80	0.932
Westbrook	1987	80	0.948
Westbrook	1987	80	0.689

Table 20.4
Barley et al. (2002)
Helping At-Risk Students Meet Standards: A Synthesis of Evidence-Based Classroom Practices
Number of studies included: 118

		Summary of Research Synthesis		
Strategy	**Type**	**Number of High-Quality Studies**	**Selected Implementation Considerations[a]**	**Synthesis Results on Positive Effects of Strategy on Student Achievement**
General Instruction	Approach	4	Balance of direct instruction and authentic learning	Inconclusive
Cognitively Oriented Instruction	Approach	4	Student practice Student interaction Teacher modeling	Preliminary
Grouping Structures	Intervention	4	Heterogeneous groups Teacher training Student instructions	Preliminary
Tutoring	Intervention	5	Tutor training Program monitoring	Preliminary
Peer Tutoring	Intervention	13	Structured tasks Teacher monitoring Participant training	Preliminary
Computer-Assisted Instruction	Intervention	10	Subject matter	Conclusive

[a] Other implementation issues are described in the individual chapters on each strategy.

Statistical Evidence on Utilizing Demonstrations

GENERALIZATION TESTED: ON DEMONSTRATIONS— CHAPTER 21

Achievement of learning objectives is enhanced when students are demonstrated the sequential steps needed to perform assigned tasks.

Total number of studies covered: 578

Table 21.1

Ross (1988)

Controlling Variables: A Meta-analysis of Training Studies

| | | | | | Controlling Variables Training Studies | Post | Retention |
	Study	Treatment Sample	Treatment	Control	Outcome Measure	ES	ES
	Armstrong, 1983	38 grade 9	LCIS	Neo-Herbartian (similar to treatment)	Lawson, 1978	.14	.44
	Bluhm, 1979	20 college	Instructor modeling	No treatment	Application of process skills	1.56	—
	Bowyer, Chen, & Thier, 1978	20 grade 6	Free choice experimenting	No treatment	Design and explain an experiment	.46	—
	Bowyer & Linn, 1978	312 grade 6	SCIS exploration	Traditional	Recognize uncontrolled experiment	.31	—
	Bredderman, 1973	27 grade 5–8	(a) Reinforcement (b) Cognitive conflict	No treatment	Design experiment (Piagetian interview)	(a) .21 (b) .29	— —
	Case, 1974	28 grade 1–3, grade 5–6	Neo-Piagetian performance model	No treatment	Design experiment (Piagetian interview)	.95	—
	Case, 1977, Study 5	20 grade 2	Neo-Piagetian performance model	No treatment	Design experiment (Piagetian interview)	.48	—
	Case & Fry, 1973	15 low SES 14-year-olds	Designing experiments to rule out counter-explorations	No treatment	Designing and diagnosing controlled experiments	2.91	—
	Crow, 1987	23 college	Instruction in principles of logic	No treatment	Tobin & Capie, 1982	.55	—
	Danner & Day, 1977 Study 2	20 17-year-olds	Successive prompts leading to controlled variable modeling	No treatment	Design experiment (Piagetian interview)	.77	—
	de Ribaupierre, 1975	34 grade 7–10	Performance-feedback-practice	No treatment	Design and experiment (Piagetian & analogous tasks)	.03	—

Study	Sample	Treatment	Control	Measure		
Denson, 1986	45 college	Investigative Lab Program	Verification Lab (traditional)	Dillashaw & Okey, 1980	.14	—
Doty, 1985	67 grade 9	Energy: A Sequel to IPS	Traditional	Dillashaw & Okey, 1980	-.14	—
Howe & Mierzwa, 1977	41 grade 8	Concept clarification strategy	Traditional	Karplus, 1975	1.16	—
Jaus, 1975	31 college	ISPS self-instruction	No treatment	Experimenting test	2.62	—
Klausmier & Sipple, 1980	120 grade 5	SAPA enriched with concepts	SAPA without concept enrichment	Distinguishing instances and noninstances of CV		
				(i) Trained task	1.11	—
				(ii) Novel task	1.67	—
Kuhn & Angelev, 1976	15 grade 4–5	(a) Twice per week practice	No treatment	Design pendulum	(a) 1.50	1.72
	14 grade 4–5	(b) Once per week practice	No treatment	Experiment (Piagetian)	(b) 1.14	1.39
	13 grade 4–5	(c) Once per week practice with demonstration	No treatment	Experiment (Piagetian)	(c) 1.50	1.59
	13 grade 4–5	(d) Once per two week practice	No treatment	Experiment (Piagetian)	(d) .75	.58
Lawson, Blake, & Nordland, 1975	33 14–17-year-olds	SCIS exploration	No treatment	Design experiment (Piagetian)		
				(i) Trained task	.72	—
				(ii) Novel task	.00	—
Lawson & Wollman, 1976	32 grade 5–7	Procedure for fair tests developed interactively	No treatment	Design experiment (Piagetian)		
				(i) Trained task	1.84	—
				(ii) Novel task	1.39	—
Leising, 1986	41 grade 9	Variety of analogous puzzles with feedback	No puzzles (similar to treatment)	Dillashaw & Okey, 1980	.17	—
Leonard, 1976	114 grade 9	Increased student discretion in BSCS unit	BSCS with low student discretion	Science Process Inventory	.12	—
Lewis, 1986	22 grade 10	Concrete activities	Traditional	(i) Dillashaw & Okey, 1980	.04	.36
				(ii) Tobin & Capie, 1982	1.21	1.82

(continued)

Table 21.1 (continued)

Study	Treatment Sample	Treatment	Control	Outcome Measure	Post ES	Retention ES
Linn, 1978, Study 2	20 grade 6	(a) Lecture—demonstration	Practice alone (similar to treatment)	(i) Controlling (ii) Screen	(a) 1.03 .79	— —
	20 grade 6	(b) Lecture—demonstration with practice	Practice alone	(i) Controlling (ii) Screen	(b) .32 .04	— —
Linn, 1980a	20 grade 6	(a) Lecture—demonstration	Free choice experimenting (similar to treatment)	(i) Criticize experiment (ii) Design experiment	(a) .34 .54	— —
	19 grade 6	(b) Lecture—demonstration with free choice experimenting	Free choice experimenting alone	(i) Criticize experiment (ii) Design experiment	(b) .57 .90	— —
Linn, 1980b, Study 2	20 grade 7	(a) Lecture—demonstration	Exposure to experimenting (similar to treatment)	(i) Criticize experiment (ii) Design experiment	(a) .41 -.07	— —
	19 grade 7	(b) Lecture—demonstration with exposure	Exposure alone	(i) Criticize experiment (ii) Design experiment	(b) .20 -.10	— —
Linn, 1980b, Study 3	20 grade 7	(a) Lecture—demonstration with remedial tutoring	Exposure to experimenting (similar to treatment)	(i) Criticize experiment (ii) Design experiment	(a) .34 .19	— —
	20 grade 7	(b) Lecture—demonstration with remedial tutoring and exposure	Exposure alone	(i) Criticize experiment (ii) Design experiment	(b) .15 -.16	— —
Linn, Chen, & Thier, 1976	52 grade 5	(a) SCIS exploration cycle	Traditional	(i) Criticize experiment (ii) Design experiment	(a) .99 .28	— —
	52 grade 5	(b) SCIS exploration with free choice experimenting	Traditional	(i) Criticize experiment (ii) Design experiment	(b) .72 .66	— —
Linn, Chen, & Thier, 1977	65 grade 5–6	(a) Individual free choice	No treatment	Design and criticize experiment	(a) .11	—

Study	n grade	Treatment	Control	Measure	Effect size	
	37 grade 5–6	(b) Paired free choice experimenting	No treatment	Design and criticize experiment	(b) .47	—
Linn & Thier, 1975	1,170 grade 5	SCIS exploration cycle	Traditional	Interpret experiment Renner, 1979	1.31	—
Mazzei, Fogli-Muciaccia, & Picciarelli, 1986	18 grade 9	Piagetian mini lab	No treatment	Renner, 1979	.92	—
McKinnon & Renner, 1971	69 college	Inquiry cycle	Traditional	Design experiment (Piagetian)	.26	—
O'Sullivan, 1985	624 grade 10	Students as lab assistants in project of professional scientist	No treatment	Dillashaw & Okey, 1980	-.27	—
Padilla, Okey, & Garrard, 1984	168 grade 6–8	(a) Experimenting model with practice	No treatment	(i) Dillashaw & Okey, 1980	(a) .28	—
				(ii) Tobin & Capie, 1982	.11	—
	85 grade 6–8	(b) Experimenting model alone	No treatment	(i) Dillashaw & Okey, 1980	(b) –.08	—
				(ii) Tobin & Capie, 1982	-.06	—
Pendarvis, 1986	344 grade 6–9	SCIS exploration cycle	No treatment	Dillashaw & Okey, 1980	.44	—
Peterson, 1977	26 grade 11–12	(a) Science inquiry training	Traditional	Fluidity of ideas in designing an experiment	(a) 1.55	—
	17 grade 11–12	(b) Verbal instruction without explicit inquiry skill attention	Traditional	Fluidity of ideas in designing an experiment	(b) .39	—
Purser & Renner, 1983	68 grade 9–10	SCIS exploration cycle	Traditional	Renner, 1979	.87	—
Rivers & Vockell, 1987, Study 2	91 grade 9–10	Guided computer simulation	Traditional	Dillashaw & Okey, 1980	.35	—
Ross, 1986	82 grade 5	Elaborative rules for a CV experiment	Traditional	Design an experiment	3.83	—
Ross, 1988a, Study 2	85 grade 4	(a) Cooperative learning groups	Traditional	Design an experiment	(a) 2.09	.73
		(b) Whole class strategy	Traditional	Design an experiment	(b) 3.08	1.65

(continued)

525

Table 21.1 (continued)

Study	Treatment Sample	Treatment	Control	Outcome Measure	Post ES	Retention ES
Ross, forthcoming	189 grade 5	Explicit rules for a CV experiment	Traditional	Design an experiment (i) Variables not identified	.72	—
				(ii) Variables identified	.80	—
Ross & Maynes, 1983a	237 grade 7–8	Implicit rules for a CV experiment	Traditional	Design an experiment	.42	—
Ross & Maynes, 1983b	136 grade 6	Implicit rules for a CV experiment	Traditional	Design an experiment (i) Multiple choice	.28	—
				(ii) Open ended	.24	.81
Rowell & Dawson, 1984	46 grade 8	General solution procedure	No treatment	Design and criticize experiments	.72	—
Rowell & Dawson, 1985	20 grade 8	General solution procedure	No treatment	Design and criticize experiments	.68	—
Saunders & Shepardson, 1984	57 grade 6	SCIS exploration cycle	Traditional	Lawson, 1978	.61	—
Scardamalia, 1977	65 ages 8–12 to adult	Neo-Piagetian performance model	No treatment	Design experiment (Piagetian and analogous tasks)	1.17	—
Schneider & Renner, 1980	23 grade 9	SCIS exploration cycle	Traditional	Renner, 1979	.27	.35
Shaw, 1983	46 grade 6	SAPA units	Traditional	Identification of CV in experimental situation	.58	—
Sheehan, 1970	30 grade 7	(a) Performing experiments	No treatment	Identification of CV	(a) .02	—
	30 grade 7	(b) Performing experiments with explanations provided	No treatment	Identification of CV	(b) .10	—
Siegler, Liebert, & Liebert, 1973	12 grade 5	(a) Conceptual framework and analogue	No treatment	Design experiment (Piagetian)	(a) .97	—

Study	Sample	Treatment	Control	Test		
	6 grade 5	(b) Analogue method	No treatment	Design experiment (Piagetian)	(b) 1.33	—
	6 grade 5	(c) Conceptual framework	No treatment	Design experiment (Piagetian)	(c) .88	—
Sneider, Kurlich, Pulos, & Friedman, 1984, Study 2	22 9–12-year-olds	Modeling procedure for controlled experiment	No treatment	Design and criticize experiment (i) Group test	.06	—
				(ii) Individual test	.85	—
Stallings & Snyder, 1977	178 grade 7	ISCS	Traditional	Complex inquiry skill problems	.02	—
Stone & Day, 1978	32 grade 5–7	Explicit rule	No treatment	Design and criticize experiment	.19	—
Strawitz, 1984a	38 grade 6	Procedure for fair tests	Very similar	Design experiment (i) Trained task	1.83	—
				(ii) Novel task	.80	—
Strawitz, 1984b	21 grade 6	(a) Procedure for fair tests	No treatment	Design experiment (i) Trained task	—	2.13
				(ii) Novel task	—	1.07
	22 grade 6	(b) Open ended practice	No treatment	Design experiment (i) Trained task	—	.49
				(ii) Novel task	—	.46
Strawitz, 1987	38 college females	Programmed instruction	Direct teaching (similar to treatment)	Dillashaw & Okey, 1980	.42	—
Strawitz & Malone, 1987	14 college	Self-instructional materials	Direct teaching (similar to treatment)	Dillashaw & Okey, 1980	.96	—
Thomas & Grouws, 1984	14 college	(a) Structured interaction on analogous game	No treatment	4 items from Renner, 1979	(a) 1.81	—
	13 college	(b) Neutral interaction on analogous game	No treatment	4 items from Renner, 1979	(b) .71	—

(continued)

Table 21.1 (continued)

Study	Treatment Sample	Treatment	Control	Outcome Measure	Post ES	Retention ES
Tobin, 1980	156 grade 6–8	Extended wait time and higher quality questioning	Basic procedure with traditional questioning	Items from Tobin & Capie, 1982	.46	.36
Tomlinson-Keasey, 1972	72 female grade 6, college, and adult	Cognitive conflict	No treatment	Design experiment (Piagetian)	—	1.14
Vockell & Rivers, 1984 Study 1	14 grade 9–10	Unguided computer simulation	No treatment	Dillashaw & Okey, 1980	.32	—
Vockell & Rivers, 1984 Study 3	90 grade 9–10	(a) Guided computer simulation	No treatment	Dillashaw & Okey, 1980	(a) –.07	—
	104 grade 9–10	(b) Unguided computer simulation	No treatment	Dillashaw & Okey, 1980	(b) –.18	—
Walkosz & Yeany, 1984	127 college	Training in integrated process skills	Recording data from lab activities	Dillashaw & Okey, 1980	.57	—
Wilson, 1987	26 college	Modeling principles of formal thought	No treatment	Formal operation test	.88	.00
Wollman & Chen, 1982	56 grade 5	Social interaction	Practice alone (similar to treatment)	Design experiment (Piagetian)	.94	.70

Note: LCIS = Learning Cycle Instructional Strategy; SCIS = Science Curriculum Improvement Study; IPS = Introductory Physical Science; ISPS = Integrated Science Processes Skills; SAPA = Science: A Process Approach; BSCS = Biological Sciences Curriculum Study; ISCS = Intermediate Science Curriculum Study.

Wise (1996)
Strategies for Teaching Science: What Works?
Number of studies included: 140

Focusing strategies involve times when teachers do something to alert students to the intent of the instruction. The effect size for focusing strategies is +.57 from twenty-eight student achievement measures.

Table 21.2
Rosenshine et al. (1996)
Teaching Students to Generate Questions: A Review of the Intervention Studies
Number of studies included: 26

	Overall Median Effect Sizes by Type of Prompt					
	Standardized Test			**Experimenter-Developed Test**		
Prompt	**Reciprocal Teaching** (*n* = 6)	**Regular Instruction** (*n* = 7)	**Combined** (*n* = 13)	**Reciprocal Teaching** (*n* = 12)	**Regular Instruction** (*n* = 19)	**Combined** (*n* = 19)
Signal words	0.34 (4)	0.46 (2)	0.36 (6)	0.88 (5)	0.67 (2)	0.85 (7)
Generic questions/ Stems					1.12 (4)	1.12 (4)
Main idea		0.70 (1)	0.70 (1)	1.24 (1)	0.13 (4)	0.25 (5)
Question type	0.02 (2)	0.00 (1)	0.00 (3)	3.37 (1)		3.37 (1)
Story grammar					1.08 (2)	1.08 (2)
No facilitator		0.14 (3)	0.14 (3)			

Note: *n* = number of studies. Number in parentheses refers to the number of studies used to compute an effect size.

Table 21.3

Swanson & Hoskyn (1998)

Experimental Intervention Research on Students with Learning Disabilities: A Meta-analysis of Treatment Outcomes

Number of studies included: 180

Weighted Mean Effect Sizes for Group Design Studies as a Function of Dependent Measure Category

LD Treatment versus LD Control

	N	K	Effect Size of Unweighted	Effect Size of Weighted	95% Confidence Interval for Weighted Effects Lower	Upper	Standard Error	Homogeneity (Q)
1. Cognitive Processing	41	115	.87 (.64)	.54	.48	.61		311.67**
1a. Metacognitive	9	27	.98	.80	.66	.94	.07	83.91**
1b. Attribution	7	17	.79	.62	.44	.79	.08	31.99*
1c. Other Processes	25	71	.65	.46	.38	.53	.03	176.07**
2. Word Recognition	54	159	.71 (.56)	.57	.52	.62	.02	431.45**
2a. Standardized	23	79	.79	.62	.54	.69	.04	205.61**
2b. Experimental	35	80	.72	.53	.48	.60	.03	223.07**
3. Reading Comprehension	58	176	.82 (.60)	.72	.68	.77	.02	565.95**
3a. Standardized	16	38	.45	.45	.36	.54	.05	33.87
3b. Experimental	44	138	.84	.81	.75	.86	.02	489.54**
4. Spelling	24	54	.54 (.53)	.44	.37	.52	.04	100.44**
4a. Standardized	8	20	.61	.45	.34	.57	.06	34.45
4b. Experimental	18	34	.48	.44	.33	.54	.05	65.94**
5. Memory/Recall	12	33	.81 (.46)	.56	.43	.70	.06	42.72

#								
6.	Mathematics	28	71	.58 (.45)	.40	.33	.46	.04	128.28**
6a.	Standardized	9	22	.41	.33	.23	.46	.05	25.72
6b.	Experimental	21	49	.59	.42	.34	.51	.04	101.43**
7.	Writing	19	67	.84 (.60)	.63	.54	.72	.05	157.45***
7a.	Standardized	3	7	.37	.36	.14	.58	.11	5.01
7b.	Experimental	16	60	.80	.68	.59	.78	.04	145.27**
8.	Vocabulary	11	20	.79 (.44)	.78	.66	.89	.05	38.58***
9.	Attitude/Self-Concept	25	86	.68 (.69)	.39	.33	.45	.03	210.65**
10.	Intelligence	9	32	.58 (.59)	.41	.30	.52	.06	54.37**
11.	General Reading	15	31	.60 (.50)	.52	.41	.65	.06	55.15*
12.	Phonics/Orthographic	29	175	.70 (.36)	.64	.60	.69	.02	453.70**
12a.	Standardized Phonics	8	60	.72	.67	.62	.73	.03	275.87***
12b.	Experimental Phonics	21	78	.76	.60	.52	.67	.04	175.22**
13.	Global Achievement (grades, total achievement)	10	21	.91 (.76)	.45	.31	.58	.07	56.64**
14.	Creativity	3	11	.84 (.49)	.70	.52	.87	.09	33.61
15.	Social Skills	13	36	.46 (.22)	.41	.30	.51	.05	28.46
16.	Perceptual Processes	10	37	.74 (.65)	.26	.17	.35	.04	46.64
17.	Language	9	52	.54 (.48)	.36	.28	.44	.04	75.53*

Notes: numbers in parentheses = standard deviation; * $p < .01$; ** $p < .001$.

Table 21.4
Barley et al. (2002)
Helping At-Risk Students Meet Standards: A Synthesis of Evidence-Based Classroom Practices
Number of studies included: 118

		Summary of Research Synthesis		
Strategy	**Type**	**Number of High-Quality Studies**	**Selected Implementation Considerations[a]**	**Synthesis Results on Positive Effects of Strategy on Student Achievement**
General Instruction	Approach	4	Balance of direct instruction and authentic learning	Inconclusive
Cognitively Oriented Instruction	Approach	4	Student practice Student interaction Teacher modeling	Preliminary
Grouping Structures	Intervention	4	Heterogeneous groups Teacher training Student instructions	Preliminary
Tutoring	Intervention	5	Tutor training Program monitoring	Preliminary
Peer Tutoring	Intervention	13	Structured tasks Teacher monitoring Participant training	Preliminary
Computer-Assisted Instruction	Intervention	10	Subject matter	Conclusive

[a] Other implementation issues are described in the individual chapters on each strategy.

Martens & Witt (2004)
Competence, Persistence, and Success: The Positive Psychology of Behavioral Skill Instruction
Number of studies included: 40

Groups of studies reviewed in this logical synthesis of research did not provide statistical evidence. However, many of the individual studies included in the logical synthesis of research do contain statistical evidence. In the event that a reader wishes to view this evidence, an extensive listing of the individual studies reviewed is provided in the reference list in Part V (the studies are identified by the symbol +).

Table 21.5
Smeltzer & Watson (1985)
A Test of Instructional Strategies for Listening Improvement in a Simulated Business Setting

Analysis of Variance Summary Comparison of Four Treatment Groups on the Number of Questions Asked

Source	DF	SS	MS	F Value
Between Groups	3	63.21	21.07	8.11*
Within Groups	95	350.55	3.69	
Total	99	413.76		

* Significant at the .01 level.

Table 21.6
Smeltzer & Watson (1985)
A Test of Instructional Strategies for Listening Improvement in a Simulated Business Setting

Mean Number of Questions Asked by the Four Groups

Group	Mean Number of Questions Asked
Control Group	1.36
Lecture	1.87
Video Role Model	2.97
Lecture plus Video Role Model	3.18

Table 21.7
Smeltzer & Watson (1985)
A Test of Instructional Strategies for Listening Improvement in a Simulated Business Setting

Percentage of Students in Each Group Who Took Notes

Group	Percentage Who Did Take Notes
Control Group	79*
Lecture	91
Video Role Model	85
Lecture plus Video Role Model	87

* The control group is significantly different from the other three groups.

Table 21.8
Smeltzer & Watson (1985)
A Test of Instructional Strategies for Listening Improvement in a Simulated Business Setting

Group	N	Poor	Percent	Good	Percent	Excellent	Percent
			Quality of Students' Summaries				
Control Group	19	5	26	8	43	6	31
Lecture	31	3	9	12	36	16	55
Video Role Model	27	3	11	13	48	11	41
Lecture plus Video Role Model	22	1	4	12	55	9	41

Table 21.9
Butler et al. (2003)
Fraction Instruction for Students with Mathematics Disabilities: Comparing Two Teaching Sequences

Measure	Mean	SD	Mean	SD	t-value	Cohen's d
			Pretest-Posttest Comparison for Treatment Groups			
CRA (n = 26)						
Attitude	20.81	5.15	23.42	2.30	2.768*	1.11
Area Fractions	88.42	24.36	97.81	3.66	1.912	0.08
Quantity Fractions	30.54	23.83	77.31	20.63	7.267*	2.91
Abstract Fractions	16.08	22.46	79.46	21.54	11.963*	4.79
Improper Fractions	15.31	22.44	70.96	18.69	10.252*	4.10
Word Problems	6.69	19.37	69.12	30.68	9.382*	3.75
RA (n = 24)						
Attitude	21.92	4.14	24.21	3.28	2.277*	0.95
Area Fractions	80.46	35.84	97.33	3.75	2.264*	0.94
Quantity Fractions	28.42	17.20	55.33	21.95	6.682*	2.79
Abstract Fractions	8.21	9.56	70.54	32.59	9.219*	3.87
Improper Fractions	18.79	19.05	63.42	28.14	8.387*	3.50
Word Problems	3.46	9.52	63.42	37.30	7.679*	3.20

Note: The values represent mean percentages of correct responses.

* Significant differences are starred ($p < 0.05$).

Table 21.10
Witzel et al. (2003)
Teaching Algebra to Students with Learning Difficulties: An Investigation of an Explicit Instruction Model

Mean and Standard Deviations for Each Test within Each Instructional Group

Descriptive Statistics

	N	Maximum	M	SD
PRETEST CRA	34	2	0.12	0.41
PRETEST Abstract	34	2	0.06	0.34
POST CRA	34	23	7.32	5.48
POST Abstract	34	17	3.06	4.37
FOLLOW CRA	34	22	6.68	6.32
FOLLOW Abstract	34	21	3.71	5.21

Note: Total possible score is 27 for each mesaure.

Follow-up analyses on group means indicated that the students who received CRA instruction over the four-week intervention outperformed matched students who received traditional instruction during the same time period with the same teacher. Although there was no significant difference between the pretest scores ($t(33) = 0.63$, $p = 0.27$) of the two groups, there were significant differences at posttest and follow-up. On the posttest the group receiving CRA instruction ($M = 7.32$; $SD = 5.48$) outperformed the group who received abstract instruction ($M = 3.03$; $SD = 4.39$), $t(33) = 6.52$, $p < 0.01$. The group who received CRA instruction ($M = 6.68$; $SD = 6.32$) also outperformed the abstract group ($M = 3.71$; $SD = 5.21$) on the three-week follow-up test ($t(33) = 3.28$, $p < 0.01$).

Table 21.11
Alfassi (2004)
Reading to Learn: Effects of Combined Strategy Instruction on High School Students
Number of studies included: 2

**Means, Standard Deviations, and Univariate ANCOVA Tests
of the Different Reading Measures Over Phases of Intervention**

	Experimental		Control		
Phase	*M*	*SD*	*M*	*SD*	$F(1, 45)$
		Reading assessment[a]			
Pretesting	73	22.8	68	27.0	4.57*
Posttesting	80	19.9	71	25.8	

(continued)

Table 21.11 (continued)

Phase	M	SD	M	SD	F(1, 45)
		Standardized reading measure			
Pretesting	57.83	19.17	52.70	20.30	4.77*
Posttesting	61.72	18.84	50.50	22.47	

Note: ANCOVA = analysis of covariance.

[a] The values represent mean percentages of correctly answered questions on the reading assessment passages.

* $p < .05$.

Table 21.12
Alfassi (2004)
Reading to Learn: Effects of Combined Strategy Instruction on High School Students

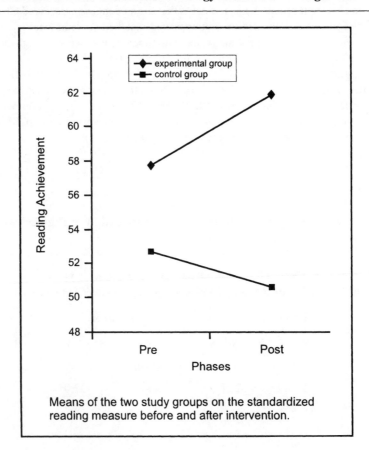

Means of the two study groups on the standardized reading measure before and after intervention.

Table 21.13
Alfassi (2004)
Reading to Learn: Effects of Combined Strategy Instruction on High School Students

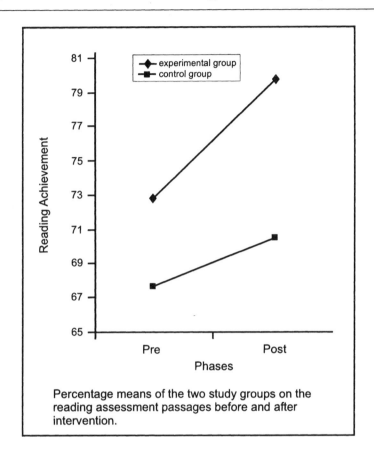

Percentage means of the two study groups on the reading assessment passages before and after intervention.

V

Detailed References by Chapter for Effective Instructional Strategies

In Part I, meta-analyses, logical syntheses, and individual supportive studies were described for each effective instructional strategy. References were provided at the end of each chapter accordingly. In Part V, references are provided for all supportive studies that could be found. References to individual supportive studies that were used in meta-analyses and logical syntheses have been added to provide access to primary sources. Individual studies are important to include because they report in detail the data and findings upon which initial conclusions are based, as well as the procedures applied to derive the findings. Meta-analyses and logical syntheses do not. Comprehensive references are provided to support all 21 effective instructional strategies. From 68 to over 600 research studies support the effectiveness of each effective strategy. Educators who choose to incorporate one or more effective instructional strategies in their teaching have an abundance of research to support their choice.

Part V has 21 sections, one for each of the effective instructional strategies. Following is the key to understanding the symbols used to identify the references in Part V. In chapters 1–21, following the findings of each meta-analysis and logical synthesis for which individual studies were able to be identified, a statement indicates the symbol used to designate the individual studies in the reference lists in Part V. Because some individual studies were included in more than one meta-analysis or logical synthesis for a particular effective instructional strategy, a reference may be preceded by one or more symbols. Symbols are unique to each chapter. Any references in Part V not preceded by a symbol are cited in the chapter; such citations also include the meta-analyses, logical syntheses, and individual studies listed in the "Supportive Research" section of each chapter.

REFERENCES FOR TAKING STUDENT READINESS
INTO ACCOUNT

*+Abraham, F. J., & Newton, J. M. (1974). *The interview technique as a personalized system of instruction for economics: The Oregon experience.* Paper presented at the National Conference on Personalized Instruction in Higher Education, Washington, DC.

!Adams, G., & Engelmann, S. (1996). *Research on Direct Instruction: 20 years beyond DISTAR.* Seattle, WA: Educational Achievement Systems.

!American Federation of Teachers. (1998). *Building on the best. Learning from what works: Seven promising reading and English language arts programs.* Washington, DC: American Federation of Teachers.

$Anania, J. (1981). *The effects of quality of instruction on the cognitive and affective learning of students.* Unpublished doctoral dissertation, University of Chicago.

%Anderson, L. M., & Brophy, J. E., (1982). *Principles of small group instruction* (Occasional paper no. 32). East Lansing: Michigan State University, Institute for Research on Teaching.

%Anderson, L. M., Evertson, C. M., & Brophy, J. E. (1979). An experimental study of effective teaching in first-grade reading groups. *The Elementary School Journal, 79,* 193–222.

+Anderson, L. W. (1973). *Time and school learning.* Unpublished doctoral dissertation, University of Chicago.

*$Anderson, L. W. (1975a). Student involvement in learning and school achievement. *California Journal of Educational Research, 26,* 53–62.

*$Anderson, L. W. (1975b). *Time to criterion: An experimental study.* Paper presented at the annual meeting of the American Educational Research Association, Washington, DC. (ERIC Document Reproduction Service No. ED 108 006)

*$&+Anderson, L. W. (1976). An empirical investigation of individual differences in time to learn. *Journal of Educational Psychology, 68,* 226–233.

*#@$&Anderson, L. W., Scott, C., & Hutlock, N. (1976, April). *The effects of a mastery learning program on selected cognitive, affective, and ecological variables in grades 1 through 6.* Paper presented at the annual meeting of the American Educational Research Association, San Francisco.

+Anderson, O. T., & Artman, R. A. (1972). A self-paced independent study, introductory physics sequence—description and evaluation. *American Journal of Physics, 40,* 1737–1742.

Anderson, S. A. (1994). *Synthesis of research on mastery learning* (Information Analysis). (ERIC Document Reproduction Service No. ED 382 567)

=Andre, M.C.A., & Anderson, T. H. (1979). The development and evaluation of a self-questioning study technique. *Reading Research Quarterly, 14,* 605–623.

*$&%Arlin, M., & Webster, J. (1983). Time costs of mastery learning. *Journal of Educational Psychology, 75,* 187–195.

*Austin, S. M., & Gilbert, K .E. (1973). Student performance in a Keller-Plan course in introductory electricity and magnetism. *American Journal of Physics, 41,* 12–18.

*Badia, P., Stutts, C., & Harsh, J. (1978). Do methods of instruction and measures of different abilities and study habits interact? In J. G. Sherman, R. S. Ruskin, & R. M. Lazar (Eds.), *Personalized instruction in education today* (pp. 113–128). San Francisco: San Francisco Press.

?Baer, D. M., Blount, R. L., Detrich, R., & Stokes, T. F. (1987). Using intermittent rein-forcement to program maintenance of verbal/nonverbal correspondence. *Journal of Applied Behavior Analysis, 20,* 179–184.

)Ball, E., & Blachman, B. (1991). Does phoneme awareness training in kindergarten make a difference in early word recognition and developmental spelling? *Reading Research Quarterly, 26,* 49–66.

?Ballinger, C. (1993). *Annual report to the association on the status of year-round educa-tion.* (ERIC Document Reproduction Service No. ED 024 990).

)Barker, T., & Torgesen, J. (1995). An evaluation of computer-assisted instruction in phono-logical awareness with below average readers. *Journal of Educational Computing Research, 19,* 89–103.

%Becker, W. C. (1977). Teaching reading and language to the disadvantaged—What we have learned from field research. *Harvard Educational Review, 47,* 518–543.

*Benson, J. S., & Yeany, R. H. (1980, April). *Generalizability of diagnostic-prescriptive teaching strategies across student locus of control and multiple instructional units.* Paper presented at the annual meeting of the American Educational Research Asso-ciation, Boston. (ERIC Reproduction Service No. 187 534)

)Bentin, S., & Leshem, H. (1993). On the interaction between phonological awareness and reading acquisition: It's a two-way street. *Annals of Dyslexia, 43,* 125–148.

?Berkowitz, M. J., & Martens, B. K. (2001). Assessing teachers' and students' preferences for school-based reinforcement: Agreement across methods and different effort re-quirements. *Journal of Developmental and Physical Disabilities, 13,* 373–387.

*&Billings, D. B. (1974). PSI versus the lecture course in the principles of economics: A quasi-controlled experiment. In R. S. Ruskin & S. F. Bono (Eds.), *Personalized in-struction in higher education* (pp. 30–37). Washington, DC: Center for Personalized Instruction.

*$)Blachman, B., Ball, E., Black, R., & Tangel, D. (1994). Kindergarten teachers develop phoneme awareness in low-income, inner-city classrooms: Does it make a difference? *Reading and Writing: An Interdisciplinary Journal, 6,* 1–18.

*$Blackburn, K. T., & Nelson, D. (1985, April). *Differences between a group using a tradi-tional format with mastery learning and a group using an traditional format only in developmental mathematics courses at the university level: Implications for teacher education programs.* Paper presented at the annual meeting of the American Educa-tional Research Association, Chicago. (ERIC Reproduction Service No. ED 258 948)

=Blaha, B. A. (1979). *The effects of answering self-generated questions on reading.* Un-published doctoral dissertation, Boston University School of Education.

*Blasingame, J. W. (1975). Student attitude and performance in a personalized system of instruction course in business administration—Correlates of performance with per-sonality traits. *Dissertation Abstracts International, 36,* 3840. (University Microfilms No. 75-2834)

$&+Block, J. H. (1972). Student learning and the setting of mastery performance standards. *Educational Horizons, 50,* 183–191.

+Block, J. H. (1973). *Mastery performance standards and student learning.* Unpublished study, University of California, Santa Barbara.

Block, J. H. (1980). Success rate. In C. Denham & A. Liberman (Eds.), *Time to learn* (pp. 95–106). Washington, DC: U.S. Government Printing Office.

Block, J. H., & Burns, R. B. (1976). Mastery Learning. In L. Schulman (Ed.), *Review of research in education* (Vol. 4, pp. 3–49). Itasca, IL: F. E. Peacock.

!Block, J. H., Everson, S. T., & Guskey, T. R. (1995). *School improvement programs: A handbook for educational leaders*. New York: Scholastic.

$+Block, J. H., & Tierney, M. (1974). An exploration of two correction procedures used in mastery learning approaches to instruction. *Journal of Educational Psychology, 66*, 962–967.

Bloom, B. S. (1985). Learning for mastery. In C. W. Fisher & D. C. Berliner (Eds.), *Perspectives on instructional time*. White Plains, NY: Longman.

&+Born, D. G., & Davis, M. L. (1974). Amount and distribution of study in a personalized instruction course and in a lecture course. *Journal of Applied Behavior Analysis, 7*, 365–375.

&+Born, D. G., Gledhill, S. M., & Davis, M. L. (1972). Examination performance in lecture-discussion and personalized instruction courses. *Journal of Applied Behavior Analysis, 5*, 33–43.

/Bos, C. S., & Anders, P. L. (1990). Effects of interactive vocabulary instruction on the vocabulary learning and reading comprehension of junior high learning-disabled students. *Learning Disability Quarterly, 13*, 31–42.

/Bos, C. S., & Anders, P. L. (1992). Using interactive teaching and learning strategies to promote text comprehension and content learning for students with learning disabilities. *International Journal of Disability, Development and Education, 39*, 225–238.

)Bradley, L., & Bryant, P. (1983). Categorizing sounds and learning to read: A causal connection. *Nature, 301*, 419–421.

)Bradley, L., & Bryant, P. (1985). *Rhyme and reason in reading and spelling*. Ann Arbor: University of Michigan Press. (This is a more complete report of Bradley & Bryant, 1983).

=Brady, P. L. (1990). *Improving the reading comprehension of middle school students through reciprocal teaching and semantic mapping strategies*. Unpublished doctoral dissertation, University of Alaska.

)Brady, S., Fowler, A., Stone, B., & Winbury, N. (1994). Training phonological awareness: A study with inner-city kindergarten children. *Annals of Dyslexia, 44*, 26–59.

&+Breland, N. S., & Smith, M. P. (1974). A comparison of PSI and traditional methods of instruction for teaching introduction to psychology. In R. S. Ruskin & S. F. Bono (Eds.), *Personalized instruction in higher education* (pp. 21–25). Washington, DC: Center for Personalized Instruction.

)Brennan, F., & Ireson, J. (1997). Training phonological awareness: A study to evaluate the effects of a program of metalinguistic games in kindergarten. *Reading and Writing: An Interdisciplinary Journal, 9*, 241–263.

/Brigham, F. J., Scruggs, T. E., & Mastropieri, M. A. (1992). Teacher enthusiasm in learning disabilities classrooms: Effects on learning and behavior. *Learning Disabilities Research & Practice, 7*, 68–73.

/Brown, R. T., & Alford, N. (1984). Ameliorating attentional deficits and concomitant academic deficiencies in learning disabled children through cognitive training. *Journal of Learning Disabilities, 17*, 20–26.

$&Bryant, N. D., Fayne, H. R., & Gettinger, M. (1982). Applying the mastery model to sight word instruction for disabled readers. *Journal of Experimental Education, 50*, 116–121.

/Bulgren, J., Schumaker, J. B., & Deshler, D. D. (1988). Effectiveness of a concept teaching routine in enhancing the performance of LD students in secondary-level mainstream classes. *Learning Disability Quarterly, 11*(1), 317.

$Burke, A. (1983). *Students' potential for learning contrasted under tutorial and group approaches to instruction.* Unpublished doctoral dissertation, University of Chicago.

$&+Burrows, C. K., & Okey, J. R. (1975, March–April). *The effects of a mastery learning strategy on achievement.* Paper presented at the annual meeting of the American Educational Research Association, Washington, DC.

)Bus, A. (1986). Preparatory reading instruction in kindergarten: Some comparative research into methods of auditory and auditory-visual training of phonemic analysis and blending. *Perceptual and Motor Skills, 62,* 11–24.

)Byrne, B., & Fielding-Barnsley, R. (1991). Evaluation of a program to teach phonemic awareness to young children. *Journal of Educational Psychology, 83,* 451–455.

)Byrne, B., & Fielding-Barnsley, R. (1993). Evaluation of a program to teach phonemic awareness to young children: A 1-year follow-up. *Journal of Educational Psychology, 85,* 104–111. (This is a first follow-up to Byrne & Fielding-Barnsley, 1991).

)Byrne, B., & Fielding-Barnsley, R. (1995). Evaluation of a program to teach phonemic awareness to young children: A 2- and 3-year follow-up and a new preschool trial. *Journal of Educational Psychology, 87,* 488–503. (This is a second follow-up to Byrnes & Fielding-Barnsley, 1991).

*#$&Cabezon, E. (1984). *The effects of marked changes in student achievement pattern on the students, their teachers, and their parents: The Chilean case.* Unpublished doctoral dissertation, University of Chicago.

Carlton, M. P., & Winsler, A. (1999). School readiness: The need for a paradigm shift. *The School Psychology Review, 28*(3), 338–352.

?Carnine, D. (1992). Expanding the notion of teachers' rights: Access to tools that work. *Journal of Applied Behavior Analysis, 24,* 13–19.

?Carr, E. G., & Durand, V. M. (1985). Reducing behavior problems through functional communication training. *Journal of Behavior Analysis, 18,* 111–126.

)Castle, J., Riach, J., & Nicholson, T. (1994). Getting off to a better start in reading and spelling: The effects of phonemic awareness instruction within a whole language program. *Journal of Educational Psychology, 86,* 350–359.

/Chan, L.K.S. (1991). Promoting strategy generalization through self-instructional training in students with reading disabilities. *Journal of Learning Disabilities, 24,* 427–433.

/Chan, L.K.S., & Cole, P. G. (1986). The effects of comprehension-monitoring training on the reading competence of learning disabled and regular class students. *Remedial and Special Education, 7,* 33–40.

/Chan, L.K.S., Cole, P. G., & Morris, J. N. (1990). Effects of instruction in the use of a visual-imagery strategy on the reading-comprehension competence of disabled and average readers. *Learning Disability Quarterly, 13,* 2–11.

/Chase, C. H., Schmitt, R. L., Russell, G., & Tallal, P. (1984). A new chemotherapeutic investigation: Piracetam effects on dyslexia. *Annals of Dyslexia, 34,* 29–43.

$Chiappetta, E. L., & McBride, J. W. (1980). Exploring the effects of general remediation on ninth-graders' achievement of the mole concept. *Science Education, 64,* 609–614.

*$Clark, C. P., Guskey, T. P., & Benninga, J. S. (1983). The effectiveness of mastery learning strategies in undergraduate education courses. *Journal of Educational Research, 76,* 210–214.

*Clark, S. G. (1975). An innovation for introductory sociology: Personalized system of instruction. In J. M. Johnston (Ed.), *Behavior research and technology in higher education* (pp. 117–124). Springfield, IL: Charles C. Thomas.

=Cohen, R. (1983). Students generate questions as an aid to reading comprehension. *Reading Teacher, 36*, 770–775.

*+Coldeway, D. O., Santowski, M., O'Brien, R., & Lagowski, V. (1975). Comparison of small group contingency management with the personalized system of instruction and the lecture system. In J. M. Johnston (Ed.), *Research and technology in college and university teaching* (pp. 215–224). Gainesville: University of Florida.

*+Cole, C., Martin, S., & Vincent, J. (1975). A comparison of two teaching formats at the college level. In J. M. Johnston (Ed.), *Behavior research and technology in higher education* (pp. 61–74). Springfield, IL: Charles C. Thomas.

/Collins, M., & Carnine, D. (1988). Evaluating the field test revision process by comparing two versions of a reasoning skills CAI program. *Journal of Learning Disabilities, 21*, 375–379.

*Condo, P. (1974, April). *The analysis and evaluation of a self-paced course in calculus.* Paper presented at the National Conference on Personalized Instruction in Higher Education, Washington, DC.

?Cooper, B., Nye, B., Charlton, K., Lindsay, J., & Greathouse, S. (1996). The effects of summer vacation on achievement test scores: A narrative and meta-analytic review. *Review of Educational Research, 66*, 227–268.

*+Cooper, J. L., & Greiner, J. M. (1971). Contingency management in an introductory psychology course produces better retention. *Psychological Record, 21*, 391–400.

*Corey, J. R., & McMichael, J. S. (1974). Retention in a PSI introductory psychology course. In J. G. Sherman (Ed.), *PSI germinal papers* (pp. 17–19). Washington, DC: Center for Personalized Instruction.

+Corey, J. R., McMichael, J. S., & Tremont, P. J. (1970, April). *Long-term effects of personalized instruction in an introductory psychology course.* Paper presented at the meeting of the Eastern Psychology Association, Atlantic City.

*Cote, J. D. (1976). Biology by PSI in a community college. In B. A. Green Jr. (Ed.), *Personalized instruction and higher education.* Washington, DC: Center for Personalized Instruction.

*Cross, M. Z., & Semb, G. (1976). An analysis of the effects of personalized instruction on students at different initial performance levels in an introductory college nutrition course. *Journal of Personalized Instruction, 1*, 47–50.

)Cunningham, A. (1990). Explicit versus implicit instruction in phonemic awareness. *Journal of Experimental Child Psychology, 50*, 429–444.

?Daly, E. J., Lentz, F. E., & Boyer, J. (1996). The instructional hierarchy: A conceptual model for understanding the effective components of reading interventions. *School Psychology Quarterly, 11*, 369–386.

?Daly, E. J., Martens, B. K., Hamler, K., Dool, E. J., & Eckert, T. L. (1999). A brief experimental analysis for identifying instructional components needed to improve oral reading fluency. *Journal of Applied Behavior Analysis, 32*, 83–94.

/Darch, C., & Eaves, R. C. (1986). Visual displays to increase comprehension of high school learning-disabled students. *Journal of Special Education, 20*, 309–318.

/Darch, C., & Gersten, R. (1986). Direction-setting activities in reading comprehension: A comparison of two approaches. *Learning Disability Quarterly, 9*, 235–243.

=Davey, B., & McBride, S. (1986). Effects of question-generation on reading comprehension. *Journal of Educational Psychology, 78*, 256–262.

)Davidson, M., & Jenkins, J. (1994). Effects of phonemic processes on word reading and spelling. *Journal of Educational Research, 87*, 148–157.

/De La Paz, S. (1995). *An analysis of the effects of dictation and planning instruction on the writing of students with learning disabilities.* Unpublished doctoral dissertation, University of Maryland, College Park.

*Decker, D. F. (1976). *Teaching to achieve learning mastery by using retesting techniques.* Doctoral dissertation, Nova University. (ERIC Document Reproduction Service No. ED 133 002)

)Defior, S., & Tudela, P. (1994). Effect of phonological training on reading and writing acquisition. *Reading and Writing: An Interdisciplinary Journal, 6*, 299–320.

$Denton, W. L., Ory, J. C., Glassnap, D. R., & Poggio, J. P. (1976). *Grade expectations within a mastery learning strategy.* Paper presented at the annual meeting of the American Educational Research Association, San Francisco. (ERIC Document Reproduction Service No. ED 126 105)

=Dermody, M. (1988, February). *Metacognitive strategies for development of reading comprehension for younger children.* Paper presented at the annual meeting of the American Association of Colleges for Teacher Education, New Orleans, LA.

*$Dillashaw, F. G., & Okey, J. R. (1983). Effects of a modified mastery learning strategy on achievement, attitudes, and on-task behavior of high school chemistry students. *Journal of Research and Science Teaching, 20*, 203–211.

/Dixon, M. E. (1984). *Questioning strategy instruction participation and reading comprehension of learning disabled students.* (Doctoral dissertation, University of Arizona, 1983). *Dissertation Abstracts International, 44*(11-A), 3349.

=Dreher, M. J., & Gambrell, L. B. (1985). Teaching children to use a self-questioning strategy for studying expository text. *Reading Improvement, 22*, 2–7.

$Duby, P. B. (1981). *Attributions and attribution change: Effects of a mastery learning instructional approach.* Paper presented at the annual meeting of the American Educational Research Association, Los Angeles. (ERIC Document Reproduction Service No. ED 200 640)

?DuPaul, G. J., & Henningson, P. N. (1993). Peer tutoring effects on the classroom performance of children with Attention Deficit Hyperactivity Disorder. *School Psychology Review, 22*, 134–143.

Education Commission of the States. (1999). *Direct instruction.* Denver, CO: Education Commission of the States.

)Ehri, L., & Wilce, L. (1987a). Does learning to spell help beginners learn to read words? *Reading Research Quarterly, 22*, 48–65.

Ehri, L. C., Nunes, S. R., Willows, D. M., Schuster, B. V., Yaghoub-Zadeh, Z., & Shanahan, T. (2001). Phonemic awareness instruction helps children learn to read: Evidence from the National Reading Panel's meta-analysis. *Reading Research Quarterly, 36*(3), 250–287.

?Eisenberger, R., & Cameron, J. (1996). Detrimental effects of reward: Reality or myth? *American Psychologist, 51*, 1153–1166.

!Ellis, A. K., & Fouts, J. T. (1997). *Research on educational innovations* (2nd ed.). New York: Eye on Education.

%Emmer, E. T., Evertson, C., Sanford, J., & Clements, B. (1982). Improving classroom management: *An experimental study in junior high school classrooms.* Austin: Research and Development Center for Teacher Education, University of Texas.

?Erchul, W. P., & Martens, B. K. (2002). *School consultation: Conceptual and empirical bases of practice* (2nd ed.). New York: Plenum.

%Evertson, C. M., Emmer, E. T., Sanford, J. P., & Clements, B. S. (1983). Improving classroom management: An experiment and elementary classrooms. *Elementary School Journal, 84*, 173–188.

*#&Fagan, J. S. (1976). Mastery learning: The relationship of mastery procedures and aptitude to the achievement and retention of transportation-environment concepts by seventh-grade students. *Dissertation Abstracts International, 36*, 5981. (University Microfilms No. 76-6402)

)Farmer, A., Nixon, M., & White, R. (1976). Sound blending and learning to read: An experimental investigation. *British Journal of Educational Psychology, 46*, 155–163.

/Farmer, M. E., Klein, R., & Bryson, S. E. (1992). Computer-assisted reading: Effects of whole word feedback on fluency and comprehension in readers with severe disabilities. *Remedial and Special Education, 13*, 50–60.

*Fehlen, J. E. (1976). Mastery learning techniques in the traditional classroom setting. *School Science and Mathematics, 76*, 241–245.

*Fernald, P. S., & DuNann, D. H. (1975). Effects of individualized instruction upon low- and high-achieving students' study behavior and students' evaluation of mastery. *Journal of Experimental Education, 43*, 27–34.

/Fiedorowicz, C.A.M. (1986). Training of component reading skills. *Annals of Dyslexia, 36*, 318–334.

/Fiedorowicz, C.A.M., & Trites, R. L. (1987). *An evaluation of the effectiveness of computer-assisted component reading subskills training.* Toronto: Queen's Printer.

$&+Fiel, R. L., & Okey, J. R. (1974). Effects of formative evaluation and remediation on mastery of intellectual skill. *Journal of Educational Research, 68*, 253–255.

%Fisher, C. W., Berliner, D. C., Filby, N. N., Marliave, R., Cahen, L. S., & Dishaw, M. M. (1980). Teaching behaviors, academic learning time, and student achievement: An overview. In C. Denham & A. Lieberman (Eds.), *Time to learn* (pp. 7–32). Washington DC: U.S. Government Printing Office.

%Fitzpatrick, K. A. (1981). *An investigation of secondary classroom material strategies for increasing student academic engaged time.* Doctoral dissertation, University of Illinois at Urbana–Champaign.

%Fitzpatrick, K. A. (1982). *The effect of a secondary classroom management training program on teacher and student behavior.* Paper presented at the annual meeting of the American Educational Research Association, New York.

/Foster, K. (1983). *The influence of computer-assisted instruction and workbook on the learning of multiplication facts by learning disabled and normal students.* Doctoral dissertation, Florida State University. *Dissertation Abstracts International, 42*(9-A), 3953.

)Fox, B., & Routh, D. (1976). Phonemic analysis and synthesis as word-attack skills. *Journal of Educational Psychology, 68*, 70–74.

)Fox, B., & Routh, D. (1984). Phonemic analysis and synthesis as word-attack skills. Revisited. *Journal of Educational Psychology, 76*, 1059–1064.

?Fuchs, L. S., & Fuchs, D. (1986). Effects of systematic formative evaluation on student achievement: A meta-analysis. *Exceptional Children, 53*, 199–208.

/Gajria, M., & Salvia, J. (1992). The effects of summarization instruction on text comprehension of students with learning disabilities. *Exceptional Children, 58*, 508–516.

!Gersten, R., & Keating. T. (1987). Long-term benefits from Direct Instruction. *Educational Leadership, 44*, 28–31.

!Gersten, R., Keating, T., & Becker, W. (1988). The continued impact of the Direct Instruction model: Longitudinal studies of follow through students. *Education and Treatment of Children, 11*(4), 318–327.

?Gickling, E. E., & Armstrong, D. L. (1978). Levels of instructional difficulty as related to on-task behavior, task completion, and comprehension. *Journal of Learning Disabilities, 11*, 32–39.

+Glassnap, B. R., Poggio, J. P., & Ory, J. C. (1975, March–April). *Cognitive and affective consequences of mastery and non-mastery instructional strategies.* Paper presented at the annual meeting of the American Educational Research Association, Washington, DC.

*Goldwater, B. C., & Acker, L. E. (1975). Instructor-paced, mass-testing for mastery performance in an introductory psychology course. *Teaching of Psychology, 2*, 152–155.

%Good, T. L., & Grouws, D. A. (1979). The Missouri mathematics effectiveness project. *Journal of Educational Psychology, 71*, 355–362.

/Graham, S., & Harris, K. R. (1989). Components analysis of cognitive strategy instruction: Effects on learning disabled students' compositions and self-efficacy. *Journal of Educational Psychology, 81*, 353–361.

/Graves, A. W. (1986). Effects of direct instruction and metacomprehension training on finding main ideas. *Learning Disabilities Research, 1*, 90–100.

*Gregory, I., Smeltzer, D. J., Knopp, W., & Gardner, M. (1976). *Teaching of psychiatry by PSI: Impact on National Board Examinations Scores.* Unpublished manuscript, Ohio State University, Columbus.

/Griffin, C. C., Simmons, D. C., & Kameenui, E. J. (1991). Investigating the effectiveness of graphic organizer instruction on the comprehension and recall of science content by students with learning disabilities. *Reading, Writing and Learning Disabilities, 7*, 355–376.

)Gross, J., & Garnett, J. (1994). Preventing reading difficulties: Rhyme and alliteration in the real world. *Educational Psychology in Practice, 9*, 235–240.

*$&Guskey, T. R. (1982). The effects of staff development on teachers' perceptions about effective teaching. *Journal of Educational Research, 76*, 378–381.

*$&Guskey, T. R. (1984). The influence of changes in instructional effectiveness upon the affective characteristics of teachers. *American Educational Research Journal, 21*, 245–259.

$Guskey, T. R. (1985). The effects of staff development on teachers' perceptions about effective teaching. *Journal of Educational Research, 79*, 378–381.

*$Guskey, T. R., Benninga, J. S., & Clark, C. B. (1984). Mastery learning and students' attributions at the college level. *Research and Higher Education, 20*, 491–498.

Guskey, T. R., & Gates, S. L. (1986). Synthesis of research on the effects of mastery learning in elementary and secondary classrooms. *Educational Leadership, 43*(8), 73–80.

*$Guskey, T. R., & Monsaas, J. A. (1979). Mastery learning: A model for academic success in urban junior colleges. *Research and Higher Education, 11*, 263–274.

Guskey, T. R., & Pigott, T. D. (1988). Research on group-based mastery learning programs: A meta-analysis. *Journal of Educational Research, 81*(4), 197–216.

/Guyer, B. P., & Sabatino, D. (1989). The effectiveness of a multisensory alphabetic phonetic approach with college students who are learning disabled. *Journal of Learning Disabilities, 22*, 430–434.

)Haddock, M. (1976). Effects of an auditory and an auditory-visual method of blending instruction on the ability of prereaders to decode synthetic words. *Journal of Educational Psychology, 68*, 825–831.

*Hardin, L. D. (1977). A study of the influence of a physics personalized system of instruction versus lecture on cognitive reason, achievement, attitudes and critical thinking. *Dissertation Abstracts International, 38*, 4711A–4712 A. (University Microfilms No. 77-30826)

?Haring, N. G., Lovitt, T. C., Eaton, M. D., & Hansen, C. L. (1978). *The fourth R: Research in the classroom.* Columbus, OH: Merrill.

)Hatcher, P., Hulme, C., & Ellis, A. (1994). Ameliorating early reading failure by integrating the teaching of reading and phonological skills: The phonological linkage hypothesis. *Child Development, 66*, 41–57.

*Hecht, L. W. (1980, April). *Stalking mastery learning in its natural habitat.* Paper presented at the annual meeting of the American Educational Research Association, Boston.

*Heffley, P. D. (1974). The implementation of the personalized system of instruction in the freshman chemistry course at Censius College. In R. S. Ruskin & S. F. Bono (Eds.), *Personalized instruction in higher education* (pp. 140–145). Washington, DC: Center for Personalized Instruction.

=Helfeldt, J. P., & Lalik, R. (1976). Reciprocal student-teacher questioning. *Reading Teacher, 33*, 283–287.

*Herring, B.G. (1975, December). *Cataloguing and classification.* Austin: University of Texas.

*Herring, B. G. (1977). *The written PSI study guide in a non-PSI course.* Austin: University of Texas.

*Herrmann, T. (1984, August). *TELIDON as an enhancer of student interest and performance.* Paper presented at the annual meeting of the American Psychological Association, Toronto. (ERIC Document Reproduction Service No. ED 251 004)

*Hindman, C. D. (1974). Evaluation of three programming techniques in introductory psychology courses. In R. S. Ruskin & S. F. Bono (Eds.), *Personalized instruction in higher education* (pp. 38–42). Washington, DC: Center for Personalized Instruction.

)Hohn, W., & Ehri, L. (1983). Do alphabet letters help prereaders acquire phonemic segmentation skill? *Journal of Educational Psychology, 75*, 752–762.

/Hollingsworth, M., & Woodward, J. (1993). Integrated learning: Explicit strategies and their role in problem-solving instruction for students with learning disabilities. *Exceptional Children, 59*, 444–455.

*Honeycutt, J. K. (1974, April). *The effect of computer managed instruction on content learning of undergraduate students.* Paper presented at the annual meeting of the American Educational Research Association, Chicago. (ERIC Document Reproduction Service No. ED 089 682)

?Horner, R. H., Day, H. M., Sprague, J. R., O'Brien, M., & Heathfield, L. T. (1991). Interspersed requests: A nonaversive procedure for reducing aggression and self-injury during instruction. *Journal of Applied Behavior Analysis, 24*, 265–278.

)Hurford, D., Johnston, M., Nepote, P., et al. (1994). Early identification and remediation of phonological-processing deficits in first-grade children at risk for reading disabilities. *Journal of Learning Disabilities, 27*, 647–659.

/Hutchinson, N. L. (1993). Effects of cognitive strategy instruction on algebra problem solving of adolescents with learning disabilities. *Learning Disability Quarterly, 16*, 6–18.

/Hutchinson, N. L., Freeman, J. G., Downey, K. H., & Kilbreath, L. (1992). Development and evaluation of an instructional module to promote career maturity for youth with learning disabilities. *Canadian Journal of Counseling, 26*, 290–299.

*Hymel, G. M. (1974). *An investigation of John B. Carrol's model of school learning as a theoretical basis for the organizational structuring of schools* (Final Report, NIE Project No. 3-1359). University of New Orleans, New Orleans, LA.

*Hymel, G. M., & Matthews, G. (1980). Effects of a mastery approach on social studies achievement and unit evaluation. *Southern Journal of Educational Research, 14,* 191–204.

)Iversen, S., & Tunmer, W. (1993). Phonological processing skills and the Reading Recovery Program. *Journal of Educational Psychology, 85,* 112–126.

*Jackman, L. E. (1982). Evaluation of a modified Keller method in a biochemistry laboratory course. *Journal of Chemical Education, 59,* 225–227.

*Jacko, E. J. (1974). Lecture instruction versus a personalized system of instruction: Effects on individuals with differing achievement anxiety and academic achievement. *Dissertation Abstracts International, 35,* 3521. (University Microfilms No. AAD 74-27211)

/Johnson, L., Graham, S., & Harris, K. R. (in press). *The effects of goal setting and self-instructions on learning a reading comprehension strategy: A study with students with learning disabilities.* Unpublished manuscript.

?Johnson, M. D., & Fawcett, S. B. (1994). Courteous service: Its assessment and modification in a human service organization. *Journal of Applied Behavior Analysis, 27,* 145–152.

+Johnston, J. M., & Pennypacker, H. S. (1971). A behavioral approach to college teaching. *American Psychologist, 26,* 219–244.

*#@$&Jones, B. F., Monsaas, J. A., & Katims, M. (1979, April). *Improving reading comprehension: Embedding diverse learning strategies within a mastery learning instructional framework.* Paper presented at the annual meeting of the American Educational Research Association, San Francisco. (ERIC Document Reproduction Service No. ED 170 698)

$+Jones, E. L., Gordon, H. A., & Stectman, G. L. (1975). *Mastery learning: A strategy for academic success in a community college.* Los Angeles: ERIC Clearinghouse for Junior Colleges. (ERIC Document Reproduction Service No. 115 315)

+Jones, F. G. (1974). *The effects of mastery and aptitude on learning, retention, and time.* Unpublished doctoral dissertation, University of Georgia.

/Jones, K. M., Torgesen, J. K., & Sexton, M. A. (1987). Using computer-guided practice to increase decoding fluency in learning disabled children: A study using the Hint and Hunt I program. *Journal of Learning Disabilities, 20,* 122–128.

/Kane, B. J., & Alley, G.R. (1980). A peer-tutored, instructional management program in computational mathematics for incarcerated learning-disabled juvenile delinquents. *Journal of Learning Disabilities, 13,* 148–151.

+Karlin, B. M. (1972). *The Keller method of instruction compared to the traditional method of instruction in a Lafayette College history course.* Unpublished paper, Lafayette College, Lafayette, PA.

Karweit, N. (1993). Effective preschool and kindergarten programs for students at risk. In B. Spodek (Ed.), *Handbook of Research on the Education of Young Children* (pp. 385–411). New York: Macmillan.

*#@Katims, M., Smith, J. K., Steele, C., & Wick, J. W. (1977, April). *The Chicago mastery learning reading program: An interim evaluation.* Paper presented at the annual meeting of the American Educational Research Association, New York. (ERIC Document Reproduction Service No. ED 137 737)

/)Kennedy, K. M., & Backman, J. (1993). Effectiveness of the Lindamood Auditory Discrimination In-Depth Program with students with learning disabilities. *Learning Disabilities Research & Practice, 8,* 253–259.

*$@Kersh, M. E. (1970). *A strategy of mastery learning in fifth grade arithmetic.* Unpublished doctoral dissertation, University of Chicago.

/Kershner, J. R., Cummings, R. L., Clarke, K. A., Hadfield, A. J., & Kershner, B. A. (1990). Two-year evaluation of the Tomatis Listening Training Program with learning disabled children. *Learning Disability Quarterly, 13,* 43–53.

+Kim, Y., Cho, G., Park, J., & Park, M. (1974). *An application of a new instructional model* (Research Report No. 8). Seoul, Korea: Korean Educational Development Institute.

=King, A. (1989). Effects of self-questioning training on college students' comprehension of lectures. *Contemporary Educational Psychology, 14,* 366–381.

=King, A. (1990). Improving Lecture Comprehension: Effects of a metacognitive strategy. *Applied Educational Psychology, 5,* 331–346.

=King, A. (1992). Comparison of self-questioning, summarizing, and notetaking-review as strategies for learning from lectures. *American Educational Research Journal, 29,* 303–325.

/Klingner, J. K., & Vaughn, S. (1996). Reciprocal teaching of reading comprehension strategies for students with learning disabilities who use English as a second language. *Elementary School Journal, 96,* 275–293.

*Knight, J. M., Williams J. D., & Jardon, M. L. (1975). The effects of contingency avoidance on programmed student achievement. *Research in Higher Education, 3,* 11–17.

)Korkman, M., & Peltomaa, A. (1993). Preventative treatment of dyslexia by a preschool training program for children with language impairments. *Journal of Clinical Child Psychology, 22,* 277–287.

)Kozminsky, L., & Kozminsky, E. (1995). The effects of early phonological awareness training on reading success. *Learning and Instruction, 5,* 187–201.

!Kuder, J. (1990). Effectiveness of the DISTAR Reading Program for children with learning disabilities. *Journal of Learning Disabilities, 23*(1), 69–71.

*Kulik, C., & Kulik, J. (1976). PSI and the mastery model. In B. A. Green, Jr. (Ed.), *Personalized instruction in higher education* (pp. 155–159). Washington, DC: Center for Personalized Instruction.

Kulik, C., Kulik, J., & Bangert-Drowns, R. (1990a). Effectiveness of mastery learning programs: A meta-analysis. *Review of Educational Research, 60*(2), 265–269.

Kulik, J., Kulik, C., & Bangert-Drowns, R. (1990b). Is there better evidence on mastery learning? A response to Slavin. *Review of Educational Research, 60*(2), 303–307.

+Kulik, J. A., Kulik, C., & Carmichael, K. (1974). The Keller Plan in science teaching. *Science, 183,* 379–383.

=Labercane, G., & Battle, J. (1987). Cognitive processing strategies, self-esteem, and reading comprehension of learning disabled students. *Journal of Special Education, 11,* 167–185.

+Lee, Y. D., Kim, C. S., Kim, H., Park B. Y., Yoo, H. K., Chang, S. M., & Kim, S. C. (1971). *Interaction improvement studies of the Mastery Learning Project* (Final Report on the Mastery Learning Project, April–November 1971). Seoul, Korea: Educational Research Center, Seoul National University.

/Leong, C. K., Simmons, D. R., & Izatt-Gambell, M. A. (1990). The effect of systematic training in elaboration on word meaning and prose comprehension in poor readers. *Annals of Dyslexia, 40,* 192–215.

*Leppman, P. K., & Herrmann, T. F. (1981, August). *PSI—What are the critical elements?* Paper presented at the annual meeting of the American Psychological Association, Los Angeles. (ERIC Document Reproduction Service No. ED 214 502)

/Lerner, C. H. (1978). *The comparative effectiveness of a language experience approach and a basal-type approach to remedial reading instruction for severely disabled readers in a senior high school.* Doctoral dissertation, Temple University. *Dissertation Abstracts International, 39*(2-A), 779–780.

\$+Levin, T. (1975). *The effect of content prerequisites and process-oriented experiences on application ability in a learning of probability.* Unpublished doctoral dissertation, University of Chicago.

*Lewis, E. W. (1984). The effects of a mastery learning strategy and an interactive computerized quiz strategy on student achievement and attitude in college trigonometry. *Dissertation Abstracts International, 45,* 2430A. (University Microfilms No. DA84-24 589)

*Leyton, F. S. (1983). *The extent to which group instruction supplemented by mastery of initial cognitive prerequisites approximates the learning effectiveness of one-to-one tutorial methods.* Unpublished doctoral dissertation, University of Chicago.

)Lie, A. (1991). Effects of a training program for stimulating skills in word analysis in first-grade children. *Reading Research Quarterly, 26,* 234–250.

*Locksley, N. (1977). The Personalized System of Instruction (PSI) in a university mathematics class. *Dissertation Abstracts International, 37,* 4194. (University Microfilms No. ADD 76-28194)

=Lonberger, R. B. (1988). *The effects of training in a self-generated learning strategy on the prose processing abilities of fourth and sixth graders.* Unpublished doctoral dissertation, State University of New York at Buffalo.

#@Long, J. C., Okey, J. R., & Yeany, R. H. (1978). The effects of diagnosis with teacher on student directed remediation on science achievement and attitudes. *Journal of Research in Science Teaching, 15,* 505–511.

/Losh, M. A. (1991). *The effect of the strategies intervention model on the academic achievement of junior high learning-disabled students.* Doctoral dissertation, University of Nebraska. *Dissertation Abstracts International, 52*(3-A), 880.

)Lovett, M., Barron, R., Forbes, J., et al. (1994). Computer speech-based training of literacy skills in neurologically impaired children: A controlled evaluation. *Brain and Language, 47,* 117–154.

?Lovitt, T. C., & Esveldt, K. A. (1970). The relative effects on math performance of single- versus multiple-ratio schedules: A case study. *Journal of Applied Behavior Analysis, 3,* 261–270.

*Lu, M. C. (1976). The retention of material learned by PSI in a mathematics course. In B. A. Green, Jr. (Ed.), *Personalized instruction in higher education* (pp. 151–154). Washington, DC: Center for Personalized Instruction.

*Lu, P. H. (1976). Teaching human growth and development by The Personalized System for Instruction. *Teaching of Psychology, 3,* 127–128.

*Lubkin, J. L. (1974). Engineering statistics: A Keller Plan course with novel problems and novel features. In R. S. Ruskin & S. F. Bono (Eds.), *Personalized instruction in higher education* (pp. 153–161). Washington, DC: Center for Personalized Instruction.

*#@Lueckmeyer, C. L., & Chiappetta, W. L. (1981). An investigation into the effects of a

modified mastery learning strategy on achievement in a high school human physiology unit. *Journal of Research in Science Teaching, 18*, 269–273.

)Lundberg, I., Frost, J., & Petersen, O. (1988). Effects of an extensive program for stimulating phonological awareness in preschool children. *Reading Research Quarterly, 23*, 263–284.

=Lysynchuk, L., Pressley, M., & Vye, G. (1990). Reciprocal instruction improves reading comprehension performance in poor grade school comprehenders. *Elementary School Journal, 40*, 471–484.

/MacArthur, C. A., Schwartz, S. S., & Graham, S. (1991). Effects of a reciprocal peer revision strategy in special education classrooms. *Learning Disabilities Research, 6*(4), 201–210.

=MacGregor, S. K. (1988). Use of self-questioning with a computer-mediated text system and measures of reading performance. *Journal of Reading Behavior, 20*, 131–148.

*Malec, M. A. (1975). PSI: A brief report and reply to Francis. *Teaching Sociology, 2*, 212–217.

=Manzo, A. V. (1969). *Improving reading comprehension through reciprocal teaching.* Unpublished doctoral dissertation, Syracuse University.

?Martens, B. K., Ardoin, S. P., Hilt, A., Lannie, A. L., Panahon, C. J., & Wolfe, L. (2002). Sensitivity of children's behavior to probabilistic reward: Effects of a decreasing-ratio lottery system on math performance. *Journal of Applied Behavior Analysis, 35*, 403–406.

?Martens, B. K., & Daly, E. J. (1999). Discovering the alphabetic principle: A lost opportunity for educational reform. *Journal of Behavioral Education, 9*, 33–41.

?Martens, B. K., Hilt, A. M., Needham, L. R., Sutterer, J. R., Panahon, C. J., & Lannie, A. L. (2003). Carryover effects of free reinforcement on children's work completion. *Behavior Modification, 27*, 560–577.

Martens, B. K., & Witt, J. C. (2004). Competence, persistence, and success: The positive psychology of behavioral skill instruction. *Psychology in the Schools, 41*(1), 19–30.

*Martin, R. R., & Srikameswaran, K. (1974). Correlation between frequent testing and student performance. *Journal of Chemical Education, 51*, 485–486.

$Matthews, G. S. (1982). *Effects of a mastery learning strategy on the cognitive knowledge and unit evaluation of students in high school social studies.* Unpublished doctoral dissertation, University of Southern Mississippi.

/McCollum, P. S., & Anderson, R. P. (1974). Group counseling with reading-disabled children. *Journal of Counseling Psychology, 21*(2), 150–155.

?McCurdy, M., Skinner, C. H., Grantham, K., Watson, T. S., & Hindman, P. M. (2001). Increasing on-task behavior in an elementary student during mathematics seatwork by interspersing additional brief problems. *School Psychology Review, 30*, 23–32.

?McDowell, C., & Keenan, M. (2001). Developing fluency and endurance in a child diagnosed with attention deficit hyperactivity disorder. *Journal of Applied Behavior Analysis, 34*, 345–348.

*McFarland, B. (1976). An individualized course in elementary composition for the marginal student. In B. A. Green, Jr. (Ed.), *Personalized instruction in higher education* (pp. 45–52). Washington, DC: Center for Personalized Instruction.

?McGinnis, J. C., Friman, P. C., & Carlyon, W. D. (1999). The effect of token rewards on "intrinsic" motivation for doing math. *Journal of Applied Behavior Analysis, 32*, 375–379.

)McGuinness, D., McGuinness, C., & Donohue, J. (1995). Phonological training and the alphabet principle: Evidence for reciprocal causality. *Reading Research Quarterly, 30*, 830–852.

*+McMichael, J., & Corey, J. R. (1969). Contingency management in an introductory psychology course produces better learning. *Journal of Applied Behavior Analysis, 2*, 79–83.

*#@Mevarech, Z. R. (1980). *The role of teaching-learning strategies and feedback-corrective procedures in developing higher cognitive achievement.* Unpublished doctoral dissertation, University of Chicago.

$&Mevarech, Z. R. (1981, April). *Attaining mastery on higher cognitive achievement.* Paper presented at the annual meeting of the American Educational Research Association, Los Angeles.

*Mevarech, Z. R. (1985). The effects of cooperative mastery learning strategies on mathematical achievement. *Journal of Educational Research, 78*, 372–377.

*#@Mevarech, Z. R. (1986). The role of feedback corrective procedures in developing mathematics achievement and self-concept in desegregated classrooms. *Studies in Educational Evaluation, 12*, 197–203.

*Mevarech, Z. R., & Werner, S. (1985). Are mastery learning strategies beneficial for developing problem solving skills? *Higher Education, 14*, 425–432.

/Meyer, L. A. (1982). The relative effects of word-analysis and word supply correction procedures with poor readers during word-attack training. *Reading Research Quarterly, 17*(4), 544–555.

!Meyer, L. A. (1984). Long-term academic effects of the Direct Instruction Project Follow Through. *Elementary School Journal, 84*, 380–394.

*Meyers, R. R. (1976). The effects of mastery and aptitude on achievement and attitude in an introductory college geography course. *Dissertation Abstracts International, 36*, 5874. (University Microfilms No. 76-6436)

?Miller, D. L., & Kelley, M. L. (1994). The use of goal setting and contingency contracting for improving children's homework performance. *Journal of Applied Behavior Analysis, 27*, 73–84.

/Montague, M., Applegate, B., & Marquard, K. (1993). Cognitive strategy instruction and mathematical problem-solving performance of students with learning disabilities. *Learning Disabilities Research & Practice, 8*(4), 223–232.

/Morgan, A. V. (1991). *A study of the effects of attribution retraining and cognitive self-instruction upon the academic and attentional skills, cognitive-behavioral trends of elementary-age children served in self-contained learning disability programs.* Doctoral dissertation, College of William and Mary, 1990. *Dissertation Abstracts International, 51*(8-B), 4035.

*+Morris, C., & Kimbrill, G. (1972). Performance and attitudinal effects of the Keller method in an introductory psychology course. *Psychological Record, 22*, 523–530.

)Murray, B. (1998). Gaining alphabetic insight: Is phoneme manipulation skill or identity knowledge causal? *Journal of Educational Psychology, 90*, 461–475.

*Nation, J. R., Knight, J. M., Lamberth, J., & Dyck, D. (1974). Programmed student achievement: A test of the avoidance hypothesis. *Journal of Experimental Education, 42*, 57–61.

*Nation, J. R., Massad, P., & Wilkerson, P. (1977). Student performance in introductory psychology following termination of the programmed achievement contingency at mid-semester. *Teaching of Psychology, 4*, 116–119.

*Nation, J. R., & Roop, S. S. (1975). A comparison of two mastery approaches to teaching introductory psychology. *Teaching of Psychology, 2*, 108–111.

*+Nazzaro, J. R., Todorov, J. C., & Nazzaro, J. N. (1972). Student ability and individualized instruction. *Journal of College Science Teaching, 2*, 29–30.

?Neef, N. A., & Lutz, M. N. (2001). Assessment of variables affecting choice and application to classroom interventions. *School Psychology Quarterly, 16*, 239–252.

?Neef, N. A., Shade, D., & Miller, M. S. (1994). Assessing influential dimensions of reinforcers on choice in students with serious emotional disturbance. *Journal of Applied Behavior Analysis, 27*, 575–583.

=Nolte, R. Y., & Singer, H. (1985). Active comprehension: Teaching a process of reading comprehension and its effects on reading achievement. *The Reading Teacher, 39*, 24–31.

*Nord, S. B. (1975). Comparative achievement and attitude in individualized and class instructional settings. *Dissertation Abstracts International, 35*, 529A. (University Microfilms No. 75-02314)

$Nordin, A. B. (1979). *The effects of different qualities of instruction on selected cognitive, affective, and time variables.* Unpublished doctoral dissertation, University of Chicago.

?Northup, J., George, T., Jones, K., Broussard, C., & Vollmer, T. R. (1996). A comparison of reinforcer assessment methods: The utility of verbal and pictorial choice procedures. *Journal of Applied Behavior Analysis, 29*, 201–212.

Obando, L. T., & Hymel, G. M. (1991, March). *The effect of mastery learning instruction on the entry-level Spanish proficiency of secondary school students.* Paper presented at the annual meeting to the American Educational Research Association, New Orleans. (ERIC Document Reproduction Service No. ED 359 253)

/O'Connor, P. D., Stuck, G. B., & Wyne, M. D. (1979). Effects of a short-term intervention resource-room program on task orientation and achievement. *Journal of Special Education, 13*(4), 375–385.

)O'Connor, R., & Jenkins, J. (1995). Improving the generalization of sound/symbol knowledge: Teaching spelling to kindergarten children with disabilities. *The Journal of Special Education, 29*, 255–275.

)O'Connor, R., Jenkins, J., & Slocum, T. (1995). Transfer among phonological tasks in kindergarten: Essential instructional content. *Journal of Educational Psychology, 87*, 202–217.

)O'Connor, R., Notari-Syverson, A., & Vadasy, P. (1996). Ladders to literacy: The effects of teacher-led phonological activities for kindergarten children with and without disabilities. *Exceptional Children, 63*, 117–130.

)O'Connor, R., Notari-Syverson, A., & Vadasy, P. (1998). First-grade effects of teacher-led phonological activities for kindergarten children with mild disabilities: A follow-up study. *Learning Disabilities Research & Practice, 13*, 43–52.

$+Okey, J. R. (1974). Altering teacher and pupil behavior with mastery teaching. *Social Science and Mathematics, 74*, 530–535.

+Okey, J. R. (1975). *Development of mastery teaching materials* (Final Evaluation Report, USOE G-74-2990). Bloomington: Indiana University.

$&Okey, J. R. (1977). The consequences of training teachers to use a mastery learning strategy. *Journal of Teacher Education, 28*(5), 57–62.

/Olofsson, A. (1992). Synthetic speech and computer-aided reading for reading-disabled children. *Reading and Writing, 4*(2), 165–178.

)Olofsson, A., & Lundberg, I. (1983). Can phonemic awareness be trained in kindergarten? *Scandinavian Journal of Psychology, 24*, 35–44.

)Olofsson, A., & Lundberg, I. (1985). Evaluation of long term effects of phonemic awareness training in kindergarten: Illustrations of some methodological problems in evaluation research. *Scandinavian Journal of Psychology, 26*, 21–34.

/Olsen, J. L., Wong, B.Y.L., & Marx, R. W. (1983). Linguistic and metacognitive aspects of normally achieving and learning disabled children's communication process. *Learning Disability Quarterly, 6*(3), 289–304.

*$Omelich, C. L., & Covington, M. V. (1981). *Do the learning benefits of behavioral instruction outweigh the psychological costs?* Paper presented at the annual meeting of the Western Psychological Association, Los Angeles.

=Palincsar, A. S. (1987, April). *Collaborating for collaborative learning of text comprehension.* Paper presented at the annual meeting of the American Educational Research Association, Washington, DC.

=Palincsar, A. S., & Brown, A. L. (1984). Reciprocal teaching of comprehension-fostering and comprehension-monitoring activities. *Cognition and Instruction, 2*, 117–175.

*Pascarela, E. T. (1977, April). *Aptitude-treatment interaction in a college calculus course taught in personalized system of instruction and conventional formats.* Paper presented at the annual meeting of the American Educational Research Association, New York. (ERIC Document Reproduction Service No. ED 137 137)

?Patterson, G. R., Reid, J. B., & Dishion, T. J. (1992). *Antisocial boys.* Eugene, OR: Castalia Publishing.

*Peluso, A., & Baranchik, A. J. (1977). Self-paced mathematics instruction: A statistical comparison with traditional teaching. *The American Mathematical Monthly, 84*, 124–129.

*+Phillippas, M. A., & Sommerfeldt, R. W. (1972). Keller vs. lecture method in general physics instruction. *American Journal of Physics, 40*, 1800.

+Poggio, J. P. (1976, April). *Long-term cognitive retention resulting from the mastery learning paradigm.* Paper presented at the annual meeting of the American Educational Research Association, San Francisco.

*Pollack, N. F., & Roeder, P. W. (1975). Individualized instruction in an introductory government course. *Teaching Political Science, 8*, 18–36.

/Prior, M., Frye, S., & Fletcher, C. (1987). Remediation for subgroups of retarded readers using a modified oral spelling procedure. *Developmental Medicine and Child Neurology, 29*, 64–71.

%Reid, E. R. (1978–1982). *The Reader Newsletter.* Salt Lake City: Exemplary Center for Reading Instruction.

/Reilly, J. P. (1991). *Effects of a cognitive-behavioral program designed to increase the reading comprehension skills of learning-disabled students.* Doctoral dissertation, College of William and Mary. *Dissertation Abstracts International, 52*(3-A), 865.

)Reitsma, P., & Wesseling, R. (1998). Effects of computer-assisted training of blending skills in kindergartners. *Scientific Studies of Reading, 2*, 301–320.

/Reynolds, C. J. (1986). *The effects of instruction in cognitive revision strategies on the writing skills of secondary learning disabled students.* Doctoral dissertation, Ohio State University, 1985. *Dissertation Abstracts International, 46*(9-A), 2662.

?Rhymer, K. N., Henington, C., Skinner, C. H., & Looby, E. J. (1999). The effects of explicit timing on mathematics performance in Caucasian and African American second-grade students. *School Psychology Quarterly, 14*, 397–407.

=Ritchie, P. (1985). The effects of instruction in main idea and question generation. *Reading Canada Lecture, 3*, 139–146.

*+Rosati, P. A. (1975). A comparison of the personalized system of instruction with the lecture method in teaching elementary dynamics. In J. M. Johnston (Ed.), *Behavior research and technology in higher education.* Springfield, IL: Charles C. Thomas.

Rosenshine, B., Meister, C., & Chapman, S. (1996). Teaching students to generate questions: A review of the intervention studies. *Review of Educational Research, 66*(2), 181–221.

Rosenshine, B., & Stevens, R. (1986). Teaching functions. In M. C. Wittrock (Ed.), *Handbook of research on teaching* (3rd ed., pp. 376–391). New York: Macmillan.

+Roth, C. H., Jr. (1973). Continuing effectiveness on personalized self-paced instruction in digital systems engineering. *Engineering Education, 63*(6), 447–450.

*Roth, C. H., Jr. (1975, December). *Electrical engineering laboratory I* (One of a series of reports on the projects titled Expansion of Keller Plan Instruction in Engineering and Selected Other Disciplines). Austin: University of Texas.

/Rudel, R. G., & Helfgott, E. (1984). Effect of piracetam on verbal memory of dyslexic boys. *American Academy of Child Psychiatry, 23*, 695–699.

)Sanchez, E., & Rueda, M. (1991). Segmental awareness and dyslexia: Is it possible to lean to segment well and yet continue to read and write poorly? *Reading and Writing: An Interdisciplinary Journal, 3*, 11–18.

*Saunders-Harris, R. L., & Yeany, R. H. (1981). Diagnosis, remediation, and locus of control: Effects of the immediate and retained achievement and attitude. *Journal of Experimental Education, 49*, 220–224.

*Schielack, V. P., Jr. (1983). A personalized system of instruction versus a conventional method in a mathematics course for elementary education majors. *Dissertation Abstracts International, 43*, 2267. (University Microfilms No. 82-27717)

*Schimpfhauser, F., Horrocks, L., Richardson, K., Alben, J., Schumm, D., & Sprecher, H. (1974). The personalized system of instruction as an adaptable alternative within the traditional structure of medical basic sciences. In R. S. Ruskin & S. F. Bono (Eds.), *Personalized instruction in higher education* (pp. 61–69). Washington, DC: Center for Personalized Instruction.

)Schneider, W., Kuspert, P., Roth, E., et al. (1997). Short- and long-term effects of training phonological awareness in kindergarten: Evidence from two German studies. *Journal of Experimental Child Psychology, 66*, 311–340.

/Schunk, D. H. (1985). Participation in goal-setting: Effects on self-efficacy and skills of learning-disabled children. *Journal of Special Education, 19*, 305–317.

/Schunk, D. H., & Cox, P. D. (1986). Strategy training and attributional feedback with learning-disabled students. *Journal of Educational Psychology, 78*, 201–209.

*Schwartz, P. L. (1981). Retention of knowledge in clinical biochemistry and the effect of the Keller Plan. *Journal of Medical Education, 56*, 778–781.

*Sharples, D. K., Smith, D. J., & Strasler, G. M. (1976). *Individually-paced learning in civil engineering technology: An approach to mastery.* Columbia: South Carolina State Board for Technical and Comprehensive Education. (ERIC Document Reproduction Service No. ED 131 870)

*$Sheldon, M. S., & Miller, E. D. (1973). *Behavioral objectives and mastery learning applied to two areas of junior college instruction.* Los Angeles: University of California at Los Angeles. (ERIC Document Reproduction Service No. ED 082 730)

*Sheppard, W. C., & MacDermott, H. G. (1970). Design and evaluation of a programmed course in introductory psychology. *Journal of Applied Behavior Analysis, 3*, 5–11.

?Shinn, M. R. (1989). *Curriculum-based measurement: Assessing special children.* New York: Guilford.

=Short, E. J., & Ryan, E. B. (1984). Metacognitive differences between skilled and less-skilled readers: Remediating deficits through story grammar and attribution training. *Journal of Educational Psychology, 76*, 225–235.

*Siegfried, J. J., & Strand, S. H. (1976). An evaluation of the Vanderbilt JCEE experimental PSI course in elementary economics. *The Journal of Economic Education, 8*, 9–26.

*+Silberman, R., & Parker, B. (1974). Student attitudes and the Keller Plan. *Journal of Chemical Education, 51*, 393.

?Simonton, D. K. (2000). Creativity: Cognitive, personal, developmental, and social aspects. *American Psychologist, 55*, 151–158.

=Simpson, P. S. (1989). *The effects of direct training in active comprehension on reading achievement, self-concepts, and reading attitudes of at-risk sixth grade students.* Unpublished doctoral dissertation, Texas Tech University.

?Skinner, C. H. (2002). An empirical analysis of interspersal research: Evidence, implications, and applications of the discrete task completion hypothesis. *Journal of School Psychology, 40*, 347–368.

?Skinner, C. H., Fletcher, P. A., & Henington, C. (1996). Increasing learning trial rates by increasing student response rates: A summary of research. *School Psychology Quarterly, 11*, 313–325.

Slavin, R. E. (1990). Mastery learning re-considered. *Review of Educational Research, 60*(2), 300–302.

*#@$&Slavin, R. E., & Karweit, N. L. (1984). Mastery learning and student teams: A factor role experiment in urban general mathematics classes. *American Educational Research Journal, 21*, 725–736.

*Smiernow, G. A., & Lawley, A. (1980). Decentralized sequence instruction (DSI) at Drexel. *Engineering Education, 70*, 423–426.

*Smith, J. E. (1976). A comparison of the traditional method and a personalized system of instruction in college mathematics. *Dissertation Abstracts International, 37*, 904. (University Microfilms No. AAD 76-18370)

/Smith, M. A. (1989). *The efficacy of mnemonics for teaching recognition of letter clusters to reading disabled students.* Doctoral dissertation, University of Oregon. *Dissertation Abstracts International, 50*(5-A), 1259–1260.

=Smith, N. J. (1977). *The effects of training teachers to teach students at different reading ability levels to formulate three types of questions on reading comprehension and question generation ability.* Unpublished doctoral dissertation, University of Georgia.

/Snider, V. E. (1989). Reading comprehension performance of adolescents with learning disabilities. *Learning Disability Quarterly, 12*(2), 87–96.

)Solity, J. (1996). Phonological awareness: Learning disabilities revisited? *Educational & Child Psychology, 13*, 103–113.

*Spector, L. C. (1976). The effectiveness of personalized instruction system of instruction in economics. *Journal of Personalized Instruction, I*, 118–122.

*Spevack, H. M. (1976). A comparison of the personalized system of instruction with the lecture recitation system for nonscience oriented chemistry students at an open enrollment community college. *Dissertation Abstracts International, 36,* 4385A–4386A. (University Microfilms No. 76-01757)

?Stahl, S. A., & Kuhn, M. R. (1995). Does whole language or instruction matched to learning styles help children learn to read? *School Psychology Review, 24,* 393–404.

*Steele, W. F. (1974). *Mathematics 101 at Heileberg College—PSI vs. tradition.* Paper presented at the National Conference on Personalized Instruction in Higher Education, Washington, DC.

*Stout, L. J. (1978). A comparison of four different pacing strategies of personalized system of instruction and a traditional lecture format. *Dissertation Abstracts International, 38,* 6205. (University Microfilms No. AAD 78-08600)

*$Strasler, G. M. (1979, April). *The process of transfer and learning for mastery setting.* Paper presented at the annual meeting of the American Educational Research Association, San Francisco. (ERIC Document Reproduction Service No. ED 174 642)

/Sullivan, J. (1972). The effects of Kephart's perceptual motor training on a reading clinic sample. *Journal of Learning Disabilities, 5,* 545–551.

*$&Swanson, D. H., & Denton, J. J. (1976). Learning for Mastery versus Personalized System of Instruction: A comparison of remediation strategies for secondary school chemistry students. *Journal of Research in Science Teaching, 14,* 515–524.

Swanson, H. L. (2001). Research on interventions for adolescents with learning disabilities: A meta-analysis of outcomes related to higher-order processing. *The Elementary School Journal, 101*(13), 331–349.

)Tangel, D., & Blachman, B. (1992). Effect of phoneme awareness instruction on kindergarten children's invented spelling. *Journal of Reading Behavior, 24,* 233–261.

=Taylor, B. M., & Frye, B.J. (1992). Comprehension strategy instruction in the intermediate grades. *Reading Research and Instruction, 92,* 39–48.

*Taylor, V. (1977, April). *Individualized calculus for the "life-long" learner: A two semester comparison of attitudes and effectiveness.* Paper presented at the Fourth National Conference of the Center for Personalized Instruction, San Francisco.

$Tenenbaum, G. (1982). *A method of group instruction which is as effective as one-to-one tutorial instruction.* Unpublished doctoral dissertation, University of Chicago.

!Texas Center for Educational Research. (1997). *Reading programs for students in the lower elementary grades: What does the research say?* Austin, TX: TCER.

*&Thompson, S. B. (1980). Do individualized mastery and traditional instructional systems yield different course effects in college calculus? *American Educational Research Journal, 17,* 361–375.

*Tietenberg, T. H. (1975). Teaching intermediate microeconomics using the personalized system of instruction. In J. M. Johnston (Ed.), *Behavior research and technology in higher education* (pp. 75–89). Springfield, IL: Charles C. Thomas.

*Toepher, C., Shaw, D., & Moniot, D. (1972). *The effect of item exposure in a contingency management system.* Paper presented at the annual meeting of the American Psychological Association, Honolulu, HI.

/Tollefson, N., Tracy, D. B., Johnsen, E. P., Farmer, A. W., & Buenning, M. (1984). Goal setting and personal responsibility training for LD adolescents. *Psychology in the Schools, 21,* 224–233.

)Torgesen, J., Morgan, S., & Davis, C. (1992). Effects of two types of phonological awareness training on word learning in kindergarten children. *Journal of Educational Psychology, 84,* 364–370.

/Trapani, C., & Gettinger, M. (1989). Effects of social skills training and cross-age tutoring on academic achievement and social behaviors of boys with learning disabilities. *Journal of Research and Development in Education, 23*, 1–9.

)Treiman, R., & Baron, J. (1983). Phonemic-analysis training helps children benefit from spelling sound rules. *Memory and Cognition, 11*, 382–389.

)Uhry, J., & Shepherd, M. (1993). Segmentation/spelling instruction as part of a first-grade reading program: Effects on several measures of reading. *Reading Research Quarterly, 28*, 218–233.

)Vadasy, P., Jenkins, J., Antil, L., et al. (1997a). Community-based early reading intervention for at-risk first graders. *Learning Disabilities Research & Practice, 12*, 29–39.

)Vadasy, P., Jenkins, J., Antil, L., et al. (1997b). The effectiveness of one-to-one tutoring by community tutors for at-risk beginning readers. *Learning Disability Quarterly, 20*, 126–139.

*Van Verth, J. E., & Dinan, F. J. (1974). A Keller Plan course in organic chemistry. In R. S. Ruskin & S. F. Bono (Eds.), *Personalized instruction in higher education* (pp. 162–168). Washington, DC: Center for Personalized Instruction.

*Vandenbroucke, A. C., Jr. (1974, April). *Evaluation of the use of a personalized system of instruction in general chemistry.* Paper presented at the National Conference on Personalized Instruction in Higher Education, Washington, DC.

)Vellutino, F., & Scanlon, D. (1987). Phonological coding, phonological awareness, and reading ability: Evidence from a longitudinal and experimental study. *Merrill-Palmer Quarterly, 33*, 321–363.

?Vollmer, T. R., Ringdahl, J. E., Roane, H. S., & Marcus, B. (1997). Negative side effects of noncontingent reinforcement. *Journal of Applied Behavior Analysis, 30*, 161–164.

*Walsh, R. G., Sr. (1977). The Keller Plan in college introductory physical geology: A comparison with the conventional teaching method. *Dissertation Abstracts International, 37*, 4257. (University Microfilms No. AAD 76-30292)

)Warrick, N., Rubin, H., & Rowe-Walsh, S. (1993). Phoneme awareness in language-delayed children: Comparative studies and intervention. *Annals of Dyslexia, 43*, 153–173.

?Weeks, M., & Gaylord-Ross, R. (1981). Task difficulty and aberrant behavior in severely handicapped students. *Journal of Applied Behavior Analysis, 14*, 19–36.

=Weiner, C. J. (1978, March). *The effect of training in questioning and student question-generation on reading achievement.* Paper presented at the annual meeting of the American Educational Research Association, Toronto. (ERIC Document Reproduction Service No. ED 158 223)

)Weiner, S. (1994). Effects of phonemic awareness training on low- and middle-achieving first graders' phonemic awareness and reading ability. *Journal of Reading Behavior, 26*, 277–300.

$&+Wentling, T. L. (1973). Mastery versus nonmastery instruction with varying test item feedback treatments. *Journal of Educational Psychology, 65*, 50–58.

/White, C. V., Pascarella, E. T., & Pflaum, S. W. (1981). Effects of training in sentence construction on the comprehension of learning-disabled children. *Journal of Educational Psychology, 71*, 697–704.

*White, M. E. (1974). Different equations by PSI. In R. S. Ruskin & S. F. Bono (Eds.), *Personalized instruction in higher education* (pp. 169–171). Washington, DC: Center for Personalized Instruction.

!White, W.A.T. (1988). A meta-analysis of the effects of Direct Instruction in special education. *Education and Treatment of Children, 11*(4), 364–374.

Willett, J., Yamashita, J., & Anderson, R. (1983). A meta-analysis of instructional systems applied in science teaching. *Journal of Research in Science Teaching, 20*(5), 405–417.

)Williams, J. (1980). Teaching decoding with an emphasis on phoneme analysis and phoneme blending. *Journal of Educational Psychology, 72*, 1–15.

/Williams, J. P., Brown, L. G., Silverstein, A. K., & deCani, J. S. (1994). An instructional program in comprehension of narrative themes for adolescents with learning disabilities. *Learning Disability Quarterly, 17*, 205–221.

=Williamson, R. A. (1989). *The effect of reciprocal teaching on student performance gains in third grade basal reading instruction.* Unpublished doctoral dissertation, Texas A&M University.

)Wilson, J., & Frederickson, N. (1995). Phonological awareness training: An evaluation. *Educational & Child Psychology, 12*, 68–79.

$Wire, D. R. (1979). *Mastery learning program at Durham College: Report on progress toward the first year, September 1, 1978–August 31, 1979.* Durham, NC. (ERIC Document Reproduction Service No. ED 187 387)

)Wise, B., Ring, J., & Olson, R. (1999). Training phonological awareness with and without explicit attention to articulation. *Journal of Experimental Child Psychology, 72*, 271–304.

)Wise, B., Ring, J., & Olson, R. (2000). Individual differences in benefits from computer-assisted remedial reading. *Journal of Experimental Child Psychology, 77*, 197–235.

?Witt, J. C., & Elliott, S. N. (1982). The response cost lottery: A time efficient and effective classroom intervention. *Journal of School Psychology, 20*, 155–161.

*Witters, D. R., & Kent, G. W. (1972). Teaching without lecturing—evidence in the case for individualized instruction. *The Psychological Record, 22*, 169–175.

?Wolery, M., Bailey, D. B., & Sugai, G. M. (1988). *Effective teaching: Principles and procedures of applied behavior analysis with exceptional students.* Boston: Allyn & Bacon.

/Wong, B.Y.L., Butler, D. L., Ficzere, S. A., & Kuperis, S. (1996). Teaching low achievers and students with learning disabilities to plan, write, and revise opinion essays. *Journal of Learning Disabilities, 29*, 197–212.

/Wong, B.Y.L., Butler, D. L., Ficzere, S. A., Kuperis, S., Corden, M., & Zelmer, J. (1994). Teaching problem learners revision skills and sensitivity to audience through two instructional modes: Student-teacher versus student-student interactive dialogues. *Learning Disabilities Research & Practice, 9*, 78–90.

=/Wong, B.Y.L., & Jones, W. (1982). Increasing metacomprehension in learning disabled and normally achieving students through self-questioning training. *Learning Disability Quarterly, 5*, 228–239.

$Wortham, S. C. (1980). *Mastery learning in secondary schools: A first-year report.* San Antonio, TX. (ERIC Document Reproduction Service No. ED 194 453)

*Yeany, R. H., Dost, R. J., & Matthew, R. W. (1980). The effects of diagnostic-prescriptive instruction and locus of control on the achievement and attitudes of university students. *Journal of Research in Science Teaching, 17*, 537–545.

$Yildren, G. (1977). *The effects of level of cognitive achievement on selected learning criteria under mastery learning and normal classroom instruction.* Unpublished doctoral dissertation, University of Chicago.

REFERENCES FOR DEFINING INSTRUCTIONAL EXPECTATIONS

*+Abraham, F. J., & Newton, J. M. (1974). *The interview technique as a personalized system of instruction for economics: The Oregon experience.* Paper presented at the National Conference on Personalized Instruction in Higher Education, Washington, DC.

$Anania, J. (1981). *The effects of quality instruction on the cognitive and affective learning of students.* Unpublished doctoral dissertation, University of Chicago.

%Anderson, L. M., Evertson, C. M., & Brophy, J. E. (1979). An experimental study of effective teaching in first-grade reading groups. *The Elementary School Journal, 79,* 193–222.

%Anderson, L. M., Evertson, C. M., & Brophy, J. E. (1982). *Principles of small group instruction* (Occasional paper no. 32). East Lansing: Michigan State University, Institute for Research on Teaching.

+Anderson, L. W. (1973). *Time and school learning.* Unpublished doctoral dissertation, University of Chicago.

*$&Anderson, L. W. (1975a). Student involvement in learning and school achievement. *California Journal of Education Research, 26,* 53–62.

$&Anderson L. W. (1975b). *Time to criterion: An experimental study.* Paper presented at the annual meeting of the American Education Research Association, Washington, DC. (ERIC Document Reproduction Service No. ED 108 006)

*$&Anderson L. W. (1976). An empirical investigation of individual differences in time to learn. *Journal of Educational Psychology, 68,* 226–233.

*#@$&Anderson L. W., Scott, C., & Hutlock, N. (1976, April). *The effects of the mastery learning program on selected cognitive, affective, and ecological variables in grades 1 through 6.* Paper presented at the annual meeting of the American Education Research Association, San Francisco.

+Anderson, O. T., & Artman, R. A. (1972). A self-paced independent study, introductory physics sequence—description and evaluation. *American Journal of Physics, 40,* 1737–1742.

Anderson, S. A. (1994). *Synthesis of research on mastery learning* (Information Analysis). (ERIC Document Reproduction Service No. ED 382 567)

*$&%Arlin, M., & Webster, J. (1983). Time costs of mastery learning. *Journal of Educational Psychology, 75,* 187–195.

*Austin, S. M., & Gilbert, K. E. (1973). Student performance in a Keller-Plan course in introductory electricity and magnetism. *American Journal of Physics, 41,* 12–18.

*Badia, P., Stutts, C., & Harsh, J. (1978). Do a methods of instruction and measures of different abilities and study habits interact? In J. G. Sherman, R. S. Ruskin, & R. M. Lazar (Eds.), *Personalized instruction and education today* (pp. 113–128). San Francisco: San Francisco Press.

%Becker, W. C. (1977). Teaching reading and language to the disadvantage—What we have learned from field research. *Harvard Educational Review, 47,* 518–543.

*Benson, J. S., & Yeany, R. H. (1980, April). *Generalizability of diagnostic-prescriptive teaching strategies across student locus of control of multiple instructional units.* Paper presented at the annual meeting of the American Educational Research Association, Boston. (ERIC Document Reproduction Service No. 187 534)

*+Billings, D. B. (1974). PSI versus the lecture course in the principles of economics: A quasi-controlled experiment. In R. S. Ruskin & S. F. Bono (Eds.), *Personalized in-*

struction in higher education (pp. 30–37). Washington, DC: Center for Personalized Instruction.

*\$Blackburn, K. T., & Nelson, D. (1985, April). *Differences between a group using a traditional format with mastery learning and a group using traditional format only in developmental mathematics courses at the university level: Implications for teacher education programs.* Paper presented at the annual meeting of the American Educational Research Association, Chicago. (ERIC Document Reproduction Service No. ED 258 948)

*Blasingame, J. W. (1975). Student attitude and performance in a personalized system of instruction course in business administration—Correlates of performance with personality traits. *Dissertation Abstracts International, 36,* 3840. (University Microfilms No. 75-2834)

\$&+Block, J. H. (1972). Student learning and the setting of mastery performance standards. *Educational Horizons, 50,* 183–191.

+Block, J. H. (1973). *Mastery performance standards and student learning.* Unpublished study, University of California, Santa Barbara.

Block, J. H. (1980). Success rate. In C. Denham & A. Lieberman (Eds.), *Time to learn* (pp. 95–106). Washington, DC: U.S. Government Printing Office.

Block, J. H., & Burns, R. B. (1976). Mastery Learning. In L. Schulman (Ed.), *Review of research in education* (Vol. 4, pp. 3–49). Itasca, IL: F. E. Peacock.

\$+Block, J. H., & Tierney, M. (1974). An exploration of two correction procedures used in mastery learning approaches to instruction. *Journal of Educational Psychology, 66,* 962–967.

Bloom, B. S. (1985). Learning for mastery. In C. W. Fisher & D. C. Berliner (Eds.), *Perspectives on instructional time.* White Plains, NY: Longman.

*+Born, D. G., & Davis, M. L. (1974). Amount and distribution of study in a personalized instruction course and in a lecture course. *Journal of Applied Behavior Analysis, 7,* 365–375.

*+Born, D. G., Gledhill, S. M., & Davis, M. L. (1972). Examination performance in lecture-discussion and personalized instruction courses. *Journal of Applied Behavior Analysis, 5,* 33–43.

^Bos, C. S., & Anders, P. L. (1990). Effects of interactive vocabulary instruction on the vocabulary learning and reading comprehension of junior high learning-disabled students. *Learning Disability Quarterly, 13,* 31–42.

^Bos, C. S., & Anders, P. L. (1992). Using interactive teaching and learning strategies to promote text comprehension and content learning for students with learning disabilities. *International Journal of Disability, Development and Education, 39,* 225–238.

*+Breland, N. S., & Smith, M. P. (1974). A comparison of PSI and traditional methods of instruction for teaching introduction to psychology. In R. S. Ruskin & S. F. Bono (Eds.), *Personalized instruction in higher education* (pp. 21–25). Washington, DC: Center for Personalized Instruction.

^Brigham, F. J., Scruggs, T. E., & Mastropieri, M. A. (1992). Teacher enthusiasm in learning disabilities classrooms: Effects on learning and behavior. *Learning Disabilities Research & Practice, 7,* 68–73.

^Brown, R. T., & Alford, N. (1984). Ameliorating attentional deficits and concomitant academic deficiencies in learning disabled children through cognitive training. *Journal of Learning Disabilities, 17,* 20–26.

*$Bryant, N. D., Fayne, H. R., & Gettinger, M. (1982). Applying the mastery model to sight word for disabled readers. *Journal of Experimental Education, 50,* 116–121.

^Bulgren, J., Schumaker, J. B., & Deshler, D. D. (1988). Effectiveness of a concept teaching routine in enhancing the performance of LD students in secondary-level mainstream classes. *Learning Disability Quarterly, 11*(1), 317.

$Burke, A. (1983). *Students' potential for learning contrasted under tutorial and group approaches to instruction.* Unpublished doctoral dissertation, University of Chicago.

$&+Burrows, C. K., & Okey, J. R. (1975, March–April). *The effects of a mastery learning strategy on achievement.* Paper presented at the annual meeting of the American Educational Research Association, Washington, DC.

*#@$Cabezon, E. (1984). *The effects of marked changes in student achievement pattern on the students, their teachers, and their parents: The Chilean case.* Unpublished doctoral dissertation, University of Chicago.

^Chan, L.K.S. (1991). Promoting strategy generalization through self-instructional training in students with reading disabilities. *Journal of Learning Disabilities, 24,* 427–433.

^Chan, L.K.S., & Cole, P. G. (1986). The effects of comprehension-monitoring training on the reading competence of learning disabled and regular class students. *Remedial and Special Education, 7,* 33–40.

^Chan, L.K.S., Cole, P. G., & Morris, J. N. (1990). Effects of instruction in the use of a visual-imagery strategy on the reading-comprehension competence of disabled and average readers. *Learning Disability Quarterly, 13,* 2–11.

^Chase, C. H., Schmitt, R. L., Russell, G., & Tallal, P. (1984). A new chemotherapeutic investigation: Piracetam effects on dyslexia. *Annals of Dyslexia, 34,* 29–43.

$Chiappetta, E. L., & McBride, J. W. (1980). Exploring the effects of general remediation on ninth-graders' achievement of the mole concept. *Science Education, 64,* 609–614.

*$Clark, C. P., Guskey, T. P., & Benninga, J. S. (1983). The effectiveness of mastery learning strategies in undergraduate education courses. *Journal of Educational Research, 76,* 210–214.

*Clark, S. G. (1975). An innovation for introductory sociology: Personalized system of instruction. In J. M. Johnston (Ed.), *Behavior research and technology in higher education* (pp. 117–124). Springfield, IL: Charles C. Thomas.

*+Coldeway, D. O., Santowski, M., O'Brien, R., & Lagowski, V. (1975). Comparison of small group contingency management with the personalized system of instruction and the lecture system. In J. M. Johnston (Ed.), *Research and technology in college and university teaching* (pp. 215–224). Gainesville: University of Florida.

*+Cole, C., Martin, S., & Vincent, J. (1975). A comparison of two teaching formats at the college level. In J. M. Johnston (Ed.), *Behavior research and technology in higher education* (pp. 61–74). Springfield, IL: Charles C. Thomas.

^Collins, M., & Carnine, D. (1988). Evaluating the field test revision process by comparing two versions of a reasoning skills CAI program. *Journal of Learning Disabilities, 21,* 375–379.

*Condo, P. (1974, April). *The analysis and evaluation of a self-paced course in calculus.* Paper presented at the National Conference on Personalized Instruction in Higher Education, Washington, DC.

*+Cooper, J. L., & Greiner, J. M. (1971). Contingency management in an introductory psychology course produces better retention. *Psychological Record, 21,* 391–400.

*Corey, J. R., & McMichael, J. S. (1974). Retention in a PSI introductory psychology course.

In J. G. Sherman (Ed.), *PSI germinal papers* (pp. 17–19). Washington, DC: Center for Personalized Instruction.

+Corey, J. R., McMichael, J. S., & Tremont, P. J. (1970, April). *Long-term effects of personalized instruction in an introductory psychology course.* Paper presented at the meeting of the Eastern Psychology Association, Atlantic City.

*Cote, J. D. (1976). Biology by PSI in a community college. In B. A. Green, Jr. (Ed.), *Personalized instruction in higher education.* Washington, DC: Center for Personalized Instruction.

*Cross, M. Z., & Semb, G. (1976). An analysis of the effects of personalized instruction on students at different initial performance levels in an introductory college nutrition course. *Journal of Personalized Instruction, 1*, 47–50.

^Darch, C., & Eaves, R. C. (1986). Visual displays to increase comprehension of high school learning-disabled students. *Journal of Special Education, 20*, 309–318.

^Darch, C., & Gersten, R. (1986). Direction-setting activities in reading comprehension: A comparison of two approaches. *Learning Disability Quarterly, 9*, 235–243.

^De La Paz, S. (1995). *An analysis of the effects of dictation and planning instruction on the writing of students with learning disabilities.* Unpublished doctoral dissertation, University of Maryland, College Park.

*Decker, D. F. (1976). *Teaching to achieve learning mastery by using retesting techniques.* Doctoral dissertation, Nova University. (ERIC Document Reproduction Service No. ED 133 002)

*$Dillashaw, F. G., & Okey, J. R. (1983). Effects of a modified mastery learning strategy on achievement, attitudes, and on-task behavior of high school chemistry students. *Journal of Research and Science Teaching, 20*, 203–211.

^Dixon, M. E. (1984). *Questioning strategy instruction participation and reading comprehension of learning disabled students.* Doctoral dissertation, University of Arizona, 1983. *Dissertation Abstracts International, 44*(11-A), 3349.

$Duby, P. B. (1981). *Attributions and attribution change: Effects of the mastery learning instructional approach.* Paper presented at the annual meeting of the American Educational Research Association, Los Angeles. (ERIC Document Reproduction Service No. ED 200 640)

%Emmer, E. T., Evertson, C., Sanford, J., & Clements, B. (1982). *Improving instruction management: An experimental study in junior high classrooms.* Austin: Research and Development Center for Teacher Education, University of Texas.

*#@Fagan, J. S. (1976). Mastery learning: The relationship of mastery procedures and aptitude to the achievement and retention of transportation-environment concepts by seventh-grade students. *Dissertation Abstracts International, 36*, 5981. (University Microfilms No. 76-6402)

^Farmer, M. E., Klein, R., & Bryson, S. E. (1992). Computer-assisted reading: Effects of whole word feedback on fluency and comprehension in readers with severe disabilities. *Remedial and Special Education, 13*, 50–60.

*Fehlen, J. E. (1976). Mastery learning techniques in a traditional classroom setting. *School Science and Mathematics, 76*, 241–245.

*Fernald, P. S., & DuNann, D. H. (1975). Effects of individualized instruction upon low- and high-achieving students' study behavior in students' evaluation of mastery. *Journal of Experimental Education, 43*, 27–34.

^Fiedorowicz, C.A.M. (1986). Training of component reading skills. *Annals of Dyslexia, 36*, 318–334.

^Fiedorowicz, C.A.M., & Trites, R. L. (1987). *An evaluation of the effectiveness of computer-assisted component reading subskills training.* Toronto: Queen's Printer.

$&+Fiel, R. L., & Okey, J. R. (1974). The effects of formative evaluation and remediation on mastery of intellectual skill. *Journal of Educational Research, 68*, 253–255.

%Fisher, C. W., Berliner, D. C., Filby, N. N., Marliave, R., Cahen, L. S., & Dishaw, M. M. (1980). Teaching behaviors, academic learning time, and student achievement: An overview. In C. Denham & A. Lieberman (Eds.), *Time to learn* (pp. 7–32). Washington, DC: U.S. Government Printing Office.

%Fitzpatrick, K. A. (1981). *An investigation of secondary classroom material strategies for increasing student academic engaged time.* Doctoral dissertation, University of Illinois at Urbana–Champaign.

%Fitzpatrick, K. A. (1982). *The effect of a secondary classroom management training program on teacher and student behavior.* Paper presented at the annual meeting of the American Educational Research Association, New York.

$&Fitzpatrick, K. A. (1985, April). *Group-based mastery learning: A Robin Hood approach to instruction?* Paper presented at the annual meeting of the American Educational Research Association, Chicago.

^Foster, K. (1983). *The influence of computer-assisted instruction and workbook on the learning of multiplication facts by learning disabled and normal students.* Doctoral dissertation, Florida State University. *Dissertation Abstracts International, 42*(9-A), 3953.

Gagné, R. M. (1962a). The acquisition of knowledge. *Psychological Review, 69*(4), 355–365.

Gagné, R. M. (1962b). Military training and principles of learning. *American Psychologist, 17*, 83–91.

^Gajria, M., & Salvia, J. (1992). The effects of summarization instruction on text comprehension of students with learning disabilities. *Exceptional Children, 58*, 508–516.

+Glassnap, D. R., Poggio, J. P., & Ory, J. C. (1975, March–April). *Cognitive and affective consequences of mastery and non-mastery instructional strategies.* Paper presented at the annual meeting of the American Educational Research Association, Washington, DC.

*Goldwater, B. C., & Acker, L. E. (1975). Instructor-paced, mass-testing for mastery performance in an introductory psychology course. *Teaching of Psychology, 2*, 152–155.

%Good, T. L., & Grouws, D. A. (1979). The Missouri mathematics effectiveness project. *Journal of Educational Psychology, 71*, 355–362.

^Graham, S., & Harris, K. R. (1989). Components analysis of cognitive strategy instruction: Effects on learning disabled students' compositions and self-efficacy. *Journal of Educational Psychology, 81*, 353–361.

^Graves, A. W. (1986). Effects of direct instruction and metacomprehension training on finding main ideas. *Learning Disabilities Research, 1*, 90–100.

*Gregory, I., Smeltzer, D. J., Knopp, W., & Gardner, M. (1976). *Teaching of psychiatry by PSI: Impact on National Board Examination scores.* Unpublished manuscript, Ohio State University, Columbus.

^Griffin, C. C., Simmons, D. C., & Kameenui, E. J. (1991). Investigating the effectiveness of graphic organizer instruction on the comprehension and recall of science content by students with learning disabilities. *Reading, Writing and Learning Disabilities, 7*, 355–376.

*$&Guskey, T. R. (1982). The effects of staff development on teachers' perceptions about effective teaching. *Journal of Educational Research, 76*, 378–381.

*$&Guskey, T. R. (1984). The influence of changes in instructional effectiveness upon the affective characteristics of teachers. *American Educational Research Journal, 21*, 245–259.

$Guskey, T. R. (1985). The effects of staff development on teachers' perceptions about effective teaching. *Journal of Educational Research, 79*, 378–381.

*$Guskey, T. R., Benninga, J. S., & Clark, C. B. (1984). Mastery learning and students' attributions at the college level. *Research and Higher Education, 20*, 491–498.

Guskey, T. R., & Gates, S. L. (1986). Synthesis of research on the effects of mastery learning in elementary and secondary classrooms. *Educational Leadership, 43*(8), 73–80.

*$Guskey, T. R., & Monsaas, J. A. (1979). Mastery learning: A model for academic success in urban junior colleges. *Research and Higher Education, 11*, 263–274.

Guskey, T. R., & Pigott, T. D. (1988). Research on group-based mastery learning programs: A meta-analysis. *Journal of Educational Research, 81*(4), 197–216.

^Guyer, B. P., & Sabatino, D. (1989). The effectiveness of a multisensory alphabetic phonetic approach with college students who are learning disabled. *Journal of Learning Disabilities, 22*, 430–434.

*Hardin, L. D. (1977). A study of the influence of a physics personalized system of instruction versus lecture on cognitive reason, achievement, attitudes and critical thinking. *Dissertation Abstracts International, 38*, 4711A–4712A. (University Microfilms No. 77-30826)

*Hecht, L. W. (1980, April). *Stalking mastery learning in its natural habitat.* Paper presented at the annual meeting of the American Educational Research Association, Boston.

*Heffley, P. D. (1974). The implementation of the personalized system of instruction in the freshman chemistry course at Censius College. In R. S. Ruskin & S. F. Bono (Eds.), *Personalized instruction in higher education* (pp. 140–145). Washington, DC: Center for Personalized Instruction.

*Herring, B. G. (1975, December). *Cataloguing and classification.* Austin: University of Texas.

*Herring, B. G. (1977). *The written PSI study guide in a non-PSI course.* Austin: University of Texas.

*Herrmann, T. (1984, August). *TELIDON as an enhancer of student interest and performance.* Paper presented at the annual meeting of the American Psychological Association, Toronto. (ERIC Document Reproduction Service No. ED 251 004)

*Hindman, C. D. (1974). Evaluation of three programming techniques in introductory psychology courses. In R. S. Ruskin & S. F. Bono (Eds.), *Personalized instruction in higher education* (pp. 38–42). Washington, DC: Center for Personalized Instruction.

^Hollingsworth, M., & Woodward, J. (1993). Integrated learning: Explicit strategies and their role in problem-solving instruction for students with learning disabilities. *Exceptional Children, 59*, 444–455.

*Honeycutt, J. K. (1974, April). *The effect of computer managed instruction on content learning of undergraduate students.* Paper presented at the annual meeting of the American Educational Research Association, Chicago. (ERIC Document Reproduction Service No. ED 089 682)

^Hutchinson, N. L. (1993). Effects of cognitive strategy instruction on algebra problem solving of adolescents with learning disabilities. *Learning Disability Quarterly, 16,* 6–18.

^Hutchinson, N. L., Freeman, J. G., Downey, K. H., & Kilbreath, L. (1992). Development and evaluation of an instructional module to promote career maturity for youth with learning disabilities. *Canadian Journal of Counseling, 26,* 290–299.

*Hymel, G. M. (1974). *An investigation of John B. Carrol's model of school learning as a theoretical basis for the organizational structuring of schools* (Final Report, NIE Project No. 3-1359). University of New Orleans, New Orleans, LA.

*Hymel, G. M., & Matthews, G. (1980). Effects of a mastery approach on social studies achievement and unit evaluation. *Southern Journal of Educational Research, 14,* 191–204.

*Jackman, L. E. (1982). Evaluation of a modified Keller method in a biochemistry laboratory course. *Journal of Chemical Education, 59,* 225–227.

*Jacko, E. J. (1974). Lecture instruction versus a personalized system of instruction: Effects on individuals with differing achievement anxiety and academic achievement. *Dissertation Abstracts International, 35,* 3521. (University Microfilms No. AAD 74-27211)

^Johnson, L., Graham, S., & Harris, K. R. (in press). *The effects of goal setting and self-instructions on learning a reading comprehension strategy: A study with students with learning disabilities.* Unpublished manuscript.

+Johnston, J. M., & Pennypacker, H. S. (1971). A behavioral approach to college teaching. *American Psychologist, 26,* 219–244.

*#@$&Jones, B. F., Monsaas, J. A., & Katims, M. (1979, April). *Improving reading comprehension: Embedding diverse learning strategies within a mastery learning instructional framework.* Paper presented at the annual meeting of the American Educational Research Association, San Francisco. (ERIC Document Reproduction Service No. ED 170 698)

$+Jones, E. L., Gordon, H. A., & Stectman, G. L. (1975). *Mastery learning: A strategy for academic success in a community college.* Los Angeles: ERIC Clearinghouse for Junior Colleges. ERIC Document Reproduction Service No. 115 315)

+Jones, F. G. (1974). *The effects of mastery and aptitude on learning, retention, and time.* Unpublished doctoral dissertation, University of Georgia.

^Jones, K. M., Torgesen, J. K., & Sexton, M. A. (1987). Using computer-guided practice to increase decoding fluency in learning disabled children: A study using the Hint and Hunt I program. *Journal of Learning Disabilities, 20,* 122–128.

^Kane, B. J., & Alley, G. R. (1980). A peer-tutored, instructional management program in computational mathematics for incarcerated learning-disabled juvenile delinquents. *Journal of Learning Disabilities, 13,* 148–151.

+Karlin, B. M. (1972). *The Keller method of instruction compared to the traditional method of instruction in a Lafayette College history course.* Unpublished paper, Lafayette College, Lafayette, PA.

*#@Katims, M., Smith, J. K., Steele, C., & Wick, J. W. (1977, April). *The Chicago mastery learning reading program: An interim evaluation.* Paper presented at the annual meeting of the American Educational Research Association, New York. (ERIC Document Reproduction Service No. ED 137 737)

^Kennedy, K. M., & Backman, J. (1993). Effectiveness of the Lindamood Auditory Discrimination In-Depth Program with students with learning disabilities. *Learning Disabilities Research & Practice, 8,* 253–259.

*#@Kersh, M. E. (1970). *A strategy of mastery learning in fifth grade arithmetic.* Unpublished doctoral dissertation, University of Chicago.

^Kershner, J. R., Cummings, R. L., Clarke, K. A., Hadfield, A. J., & Kershner, B. A. (1990). Two-year evaluation of the Tomatis Listening Training Program with learning disabled children. *Learning Disability Quarterly, 13,* 43–53.

+Kim, Y., Cho, G., Park, J., & Park, M. (1974). *An application of a new instructional model* (Research Report No. 8). Seoul, Korea: Korean Educational Development Institute.

^Klingner, J. K., & Vaughn, S. (1996). Reciprocal teaching of reading comprehension strategies for students with learning disabilities who use English as a second language. *Elementary School Journal, 96,* 275–293.

*Knight, J. M., Williams J. D., & Jardon, M. L. (1975). The effects of contingency avoidance on programmed student achievement. *Research in Higher Education, 3,* 11–17.

*Kulik, C., & Kulik, J. (1976). PSI and the mastery model. In B. A. Green, Jr. (Ed.), *Personalized instruction in higher education* (pp. 155–159). Washington, DC: Center for Personalized Instruction.

Kulik, C., Kulik, J., & Bangert-Drowns, R. (1990a). Effectiveness of mastery learning programs: A meta-analysis. *Review of Educational Research, 60*(2), 265–269.

Kulik, J., Kulik, C., & Bangert-Drowns, R. (1990b). Is there better evidence on mastery learning? A response to Slavin. *Review of Educational Research, 60*(2), 303–307.

+Kulik, J. A., Kulik, C., & Carmichael, K. (1974). The Keller Plan in science teaching. *Science, 183,* 379–383.

+Lee, Y. D., Kim, C. S., Kim, H., Park B. Y., Yoo, H. K., Chang, S. M., & Kim, S. C. (1971). *Interaction improvement studies of the Mastery Learning Project* (Final Report on the Mastery Learning Project, April–November 1971). Seoul, Korea: Educational Research Center, Seoul National University.

^Leong, C. K., Simmons, D. R., & Izatt-Gambell, M. A. (1990). The effect of systematic training in elaboration on word meaning and prose comprehension in poor readers. *Annals of Dyslexia, 40,* 192–215.

*Leppman, P. K., & Herrmann, T. F. (1981, August). *PSI—What are the critical elements?* Paper presented at the annual meeting of the American Psychological Association, Los Angeles. (ERIC Document Reproduction Service No. ED 214 502)

^Lerner, C. H. (1978). *The comparative effectiveness of a language experience approach and a basal-type approach to remedial reading instruction for severely disabled readers in a senior high school.* Doctoral dissertation, Temple University. *Dissertation Abstracts International, 39*(2-A), 779–780.

$+Levin, T. (1975). *The effect of content prerequisites and process-oriented experiences on application ability in a learning of probability.* Unpublished doctoral dissertation, University of Chicago.

*Lewis, E. W. (1984). The effects of a mastery learning strategy and an interactive computerized quiz strategy on student achievement and attitude in college trigonometry. *Dissertation Abstracts International, 45,* 2430A. (University Microfilms No. DA84-24 589)

*Leyton, F. S. (1983). *The extent to which group instruction supplemented by mastery of initial cognitive prerequisites approximates the learning effectiveness of one-to-one tutorial methods.* Unpublished doctoral dissertation, University of Chicago.

*Locksley, N. (1977). The Personalized System of Instruction (PSI) in a university mathematics class. *Dissertation Abstracts International, 37*, 4194. (University Microfilms No. ADD 76-28194)

#@Long, J. C., Okey, J. R., & Yeany, R. H. (1978). The effects of diagnosis with teacher on student directed remediation on science achievement and attitudes. *Journal of Research in Science Teaching, 15*, 505–511.

^Losh, M. A. (1991). *The effect of the strategies intervention model on the academic achievement of junior high learning-disabled students.* Doctoral dissertation, University of Nebraska. *Dissertation Abstracts International, 52*(3-A), 880.

*Lu, M. C. (1976). The retention of material learned by PSI in a mathematics course. In B. A. Green, Jr. (Ed.), *Personalized instruction in higher education* (pp. 151–154). Washington, DC: Center for Personalized Instruction.

*Lu, P. H. (1976). Teaching human growth and development by The Personalized System for Instruction. *Teaching of Psychology, 3*, 127–128.

*Lubkin, J. L. (1974). Engineering statistics: A Keller Plan course with novel problems and novel features. In R. S. Ruskin & S. F. Bono (Eds.), *Personalized instruction in higher education* (pp. 153–161). Washington, DC: Center for Personalized Instruction.

*#@Lueckmeyer, C. L., & Chiappetta, W. L. (1981). An investigation into the effects of a modified mastery learning strategy on achievement in a high school human physiology unit. *Journal of Research in Science Teaching, 18*, 269–273.

^MacArthur, C. A., Schwartz, S. S., & Graham, S. (1991). Effects of a reciprocal peer revision strategy in special education classrooms. *Learning Disabilities Research, 6*(4), 201–210.

*Malec, M. A. (1975). PSI: A brief report and reply to Francis. *Teaching Sociology, 2*, 212–217.

*Martin, R. R., & Srikameswaran, K. (1974). Correlation between frequent testing and student performance. *Journal of Chemical Education, 51*, 485–486.

$Matthews, G. S. (1982). *Effects of a mastery learning strategy on the cognitive knowledge and unit evaluation of students in high school social studies.* Unpublished doctoral dissertation, University of Southern Mississippi.

^McCollum, P. S., & Anderson, R. P. (1974). Group counseling with reading-disabled children. *Journal of Counseling Psychology, 21*(2), 150–155.

*McFarland, B. (1976). An individualized course in elementary composition for the marginal student. In B. A. Green, Jr. (Ed.), *Personalized instruction in higher education* (pp. 45–52). Washington, DC: Center for Personalized Instruction.

*+McMichael, J., & Corey, J. R. (1969). Contingency management in an introductory psychology course produces better learning. *Journal of Applied Behavior Analysis, 2*, 79–83.

*#@Mevarech, Z. R. (1980). *The role of teaching-learning strategies and feedback-corrective procedures in developing higher cognitive achievement.* Unpublished doctoral dissertation, University of Chicago.

$&Mevarech, Z. R. (1981, April). *Attaining mastery on higher cognitive achievement.* Paper presented at the annual meeting of the American Educational Research Association, Los Angeles.

*Mevarech, Z. R. (1985). The effects of cooperative mastery learning strategies on mathematical achievement. *Journal of Educational Research, 78*, 372–377.

*#@Mevarech, Z. R. (1986). The role of feedback corrective procedures in developing

mathematics achievement and self-concept in desegregated classrooms. *Studies in Educational Evaluation, 12,* 197–203.

*Mevarech, Z. R., & Werner, S. (1985). Are mastery learning strategies beneficial for developing problem solving skills? *Higher Education, 14,* 425–432.

^Meyer, L. A. (1982). The relative effects of word-analysis and word supply correction procedures with poor readers during word-attack training. *Reading Research Quarterly, 17*(4), 544–555.

*Meyers, R. R. (1976). The effects of mastery and aptitude on achievement and attitude in an introductory college geography course. *Dissertation Abstracts International, 36,* 5874. (University Microfilms No. 76-6436)

^Montague, M., Applegate, B., & Marquard, K. (1993). Cognitive strategy instruction and mathematical problem-solving performance of students with learning disabilities. *Learning Disabilities Research & Practice, 8*(4), 223–232.

^Morgan, A. V. (1991). *A study of the effects of attribution retraining and cognitive self-instruction upon the academic and attentional skills, cognitive-behavioral trends of elementary-age children served in self-contained learning disability programs.* Doctoral dissertation, College of William and Mary, 1990. *Dissertation Abstracts International, 51*(8-B), 4035.

*+Morris, C., & Kimbrill, G. (1972). Performance and attitudinal effects of the Keller method in an introductory psychology course. *Psychological Record, 22,* 523–530.

*Nation, J. R., Knight, J. M, Lamberth, J., & Dyck, D. (1974). Programmed student achievement: A test of the avoidance hypothesis. *Journal of Experimental Education, 42,* 57–61.

*Nation, J. R., Massad, P., & Wilkerson, P. (1977). Student performance in introductory psychology following termination of the programmed achievement contingency at mid-semester. *Teaching of Psychology, 4,* 116–119.

*Nation, J. R., & Roop, S. S. (1975). A comparison of two mastery approaches to teaching introductory psychology. *Teaching of Psychology, 2,* 108–111.

*+Nazzaro, J. R., Todorov, J. C., & Nazzaro, J. N. (1972). Student ability and individualized instruction. *Journal of College Science Teaching, 2,* 29–30.

*Nord, S. B. (1975). Comparative achievement and attitude in individualized and class instructional settings. *Dissertation Abstracts International, 35,* 529A. (University Microfilms No. 75-02314)

$Nordin, A. B. (1979). *The effects of different qualities of instruction on selected cognitive, affective, and time variables.* Unpublished doctoral dissertation, University of Chicago.

Obando, L. T., & Hymel, G. M. (1991, March). *The effect of mastery learning instruction on the entry-level Spanish proficiency of secondary school students.* Paper presented at the annual meeting to the American Educational Research Association, New Orleans. (ERIC Document Reproduction Service No. ED 359 253)

^O'Connor, P. D., Stuck, G. B., & Wyne, M. D. (1979). Effects of a short-term intervention resource-room program on task orientation and achievement. *Journal of Special Education, 13*(4), 375–385.

*$+Okey, J. R. (1974). Altering teacher and pupil behavior with mastery teaching. *Social Science and Mathematics, 74,* 530–535.

+Okey, J. R. (1975). *Development of mastery teaching materials* (Final Evaluation Report, USOE G-74-2990). Bloomington: Indiana University.

$&Okey, J. R. (1977). The consequences of training teachers to use a mastery learning strategy. *Journal of Teacher Education, 28*(5), 57–62.

^Olofsson, A. (1992). Synthetic speech and computer-aided reading for reading-disabled children. *Reading and Writing, 4*(2), 165–178.

^Olsen, J. L., Wong, B.Y.L., & Marx, R. W. (1983). Linguistic and metacognitive aspects of normally achieving and learning disabled children's communication process. *Learning Disability Quarterly, 6*(3), 289–304.

*$Omelich, C. L., & Covington, M. V. (1981). *Do the learning benefits of behavioral instruction outweigh the psychological costs?* Paper presented at the annual meeting of the Western Psychological Association, Los Angeles.

*Pascarela, E. T. (1977, April). *Aptitude-treatment interaction in a college calculus course taught in personalized system of instruction and conventional formats.* Paper presented at the annual meeting of the American Educational Research Association, New York. (ERIC Document Reproduction Service No. ED 137 137)

*Peluso, A., & Baranchik, A. J. (1977). Self-paced mathematics instruction: A statistical comparison with traditional teaching. *The American Mathematical Monthly, 84*, 124–129.

*+Phillippas, M. A., & Sommerfeldt, R. W. (1972). Keller vs. lecture method in general physics instruction. *American Journal of Physics, 40*, 1800.

+Poggio, J. P. (1976, April). *Long-term cognitive retention resulting from the mastery learning paradigm.* Paper presented at the annual meeting of the American Educational Research Association, San Francisco.

*Pollack, N. F., & Roeder, P. W. (1975). Individualized instruction in an introductory government course. *Teaching Political Science, 8*, 18–36.

^Prior, M., Frye, S., & Fletcher, C. (1987). Remediation for subgroups of retarded readers using a modified oral spelling procedure. *Developmental Medicine and Child Neurology, 29*, 64–71.

%Reid, E. R. (1978–1982). *The Reader Newsletter.* Salt Lake City: Exemplary Center for Reading Instruction.

^Reilly, J. P. (1991). *Effects of a cognitive-behavioral program designed to increase the reading comprehension skills of learning-disabled students.* Doctoral dissertation, College of William and Mary. *Dissertation Abstracts International, 52*(3-A), 865.

^Reynolds, C. J. (1986). *The effects of instruction in cognitive revision strategies on the writing skills of secondary learning disabled students.* Doctoral dissertation, Ohio State University, 1985. *Dissertation Abstracts International, 46*(9-A), 2662.

*+Rosati, P. A. (1975). A comparison of the personalized system of instruction with the lecture method in teaching elementary dynamics. In J. M. Johnston (Ed.), *Behavior research and technology in higher education.* Springfield, IL: Charles C. Thomas.

Rosenshine, B., & Stevens, R. (1986). Teaching functions. In M. C. Wittrock (Ed.), *Handbook of research on teaching* (3rd ed., pp. 376–391). New York: Macmillan.

*Roth, C. H., Jr. (1973). Continuing effectiveness on personalized self-paced instruction in digital systems engineering. *Engineering Education, 63*(6), 447–450.

*Roth, C. H., Jr. (1975, December). *Electrical engineering laboratory I* (One of a series of reports on the projects titled Expansion of Keller Plan Instruction in Engineering and Selected Other Disciplines). Austin: University of Texas.

^Rudel, R. G., & Helfgott, E. (1984). Effect of piracetam on verbal memory of dyslexic boys. *American Academy of Child Psychiatry, 23*, 695–699.

*Saunders-Harris, R. L., & Yeany, R. H. (1981). Diagnosis, remediation, and locus of control: Effects of the immediate and retained achievement and attitude. *Journal of Experimental Education, 49*, 220–224.

*Schielack, V. P., Jr. (1983). A personalized system of instruction versus a conventional method in a mathematics course for elementary education majors. *Dissertation Abstracts International, 43*, 2267. (University Microfilms No. 82-27717)

*Schimpfhauser, F., Horrocks, L., Richardson, K., Alben, J., Schumm, D., & Sprecher, H. (1974). The personalized system of instruction as an adaptable alternative within the traditional structure of medical basic sciences. In R. S. Ruskin & S. F. Bono (Eds.), *Personalized instruction in higher education* (pp. 61–69). Washington, DC: Center for Personalized Instruction.

^Schunk, D. H. (1985). Participation in goal-setting: Effects on self-efficacy and skills of learning-disabled children. *Journal of Special Education, 19*, 305–317.

^Schunk, D. H., & Cox, P. D. (1986). Strategy training and attributional feedback with learning-disabled students. *Journal of Educational Psychology, 78*, 201–209.

*Schwartz, P. L. (1981). Retention of knowledge in clinical biochemistry and the effect of the Keller Plan. *Journal of Medical Education, 56*, 778–781.

*Sharples, D. K., Smith, D. J., & Strasler, G. M. (1976). *Individually-paced learning in civil engineering technology: An approach to mastery.* Columbia: South Carolina State Board for Technical and Comprehensive Education. (ERIC Document Reproduction Service No. ED 131 870)

*$Sheldon, M. S., & Miller, E. D. (1973). *Behavioral objectives and mastery learning applied to two areas of junior college instruction.* Los Angeles: University of California at Los Angeles. (ERIC Document Reproduction Service No. ED 082 730)

*Sheppard, W. C., & MacDermott, H. G. (1970). Design and evaluation of a programmed course in introductory psychology. *Journal of Applied Behavior Analysis, 3*, 5–11.

*Siegfried, J. J., & Strand, S. H. (1976). An evaluation of the Vanderbilt JCEE experimental PSI course in elementary economics. *The Journal of Economic Education, 8*, 9–26.

*+Silberman, R., & Parker, B. (1974). Student attitudes and the Keller Plan. *Journal of Chemical Education, 51*, 393.

Slavin, R. E. (1990). Mastery learning re-considered. *Review of Educational Research, 60*(2), 300–302.

*#@$&Slavin, R. E., & Karweit, N. L. (1984). Mastery learning and student teams: A factor role experiment in urban general mathematics classes. *American Educational Research Journal, 21*, 725–736.

*Smiernow, G. A., & Lawley, A. (1980). Decentralized sequence instruction (DSI) at Drexel. *Engineering Education, 70*, 423–426.

*Smith, J. E. (1976). A comparison of the traditional method and a personalized system of instruction in college mathematics. *Dissertation Abstracts International, 37*, 904. (University Microfilms No. AAD 76-18370)

^Smith, M. A. (1989). *The efficacy of mnemonics for teaching recognition of letter clusters to reading disabled students.* Doctoral dissertation, University of Oregon. *Dissertation Abstracts International, 50*(5-A), 1259–1260.

^Snider, V. E. (1989). Reading comprehension performance of adolescents with learning disabilities. *Learning Disability Quarterly, 12*(2), 87–96.

*Spector, L. C. (1976). The effectiveness of personalized instruction system of instruction in economics. *Journal of Personalized Instruction, I*, 118–122.

*Spevack, H. M. (1976). A comparison of the personalized system of instruction with the lecture recitation system for nonscience oriented chemistry students at an open enrollment community college. *Dissertation Abstracts International, 36*, 4385A–4386A. (University Microfilms No. 76-01757)

*Steele, W. F. (1974). *Mathematics 101 at Heileberg College—PSI vs. tradition.* Paper presented at the National Conference on Personalized Instruction in Higher Education, Washington, DC.

*Stout, L. J. (1978). A comparison of four different pacing strategies of personalized system of instruction and a traditional lecture format. *Dissertation Abstracts International, 38,* 6205. (University Microfilms No. AAD 78-08600)

*$Strasler, G. M. (1979, April). *The process of transfer and learning for mastery setting.* Paper presented at the annual meeting of the American Educational Research Association, San Francisco. (ERIC Document Reproduction Service No. ED 174 642)

^Sullivan, J. (1972). The effects of Kephart's perceptual motor training on a reading clinic sample. *Journal of Learning Disabilities, 5,* 545–551.

*$&Swanson, D. H., & Denton J. J. (1976). Learning for Mastery versus Personalized System of Instruction: A comparison of remediation strategies for secondary school chemistry students. *Journal of Research in Science Teaching, 14,* 515–524.

Swanson, H. L. (2001). Research on interventions for adolescents with learning disabilities: A meta-analysis of outcomes related to higher-order processing. *The Elementary School Journal, 101*(13), 331–349.

*Taylor, V. (1977, April). *Individualized calculus for the "life-long" learner: A two semester comparison of attitudes and effectiveness.* Paper presented at the Fourth National Conference of the Center for Personalized Instruction, San Francisco.

$Tenenbaum, G. (1982). *A method of group instruction which is as effective as one-to-one tutorial instruction.* Unpublished doctoral dissertation, University of Chicago.

*&Thompson, S. B. (1980). Do individualized mastery and traditional instructional systems yield different course effects in college calculus? *American Educational Research Journal, 17,* 361–375.

*Tietenberg, T. H. (1975). Teaching intermediate microeconomics using the personalized system of instruction. In J. M. Johnston (Ed.), *Behavior research and technology in higher education* (pp. 75–89). Springfield, IL: Charles C. Thomas.

*Toepher, C., Shaw, D., & Moniot, D. (1972). *The effect of item exposure in a contingency management system.* Paper presented at the annual meeting of the American Psychological Association, Honolulu, HI.

^Tollefson, N., Tracy, D. B., Johnsen, E. P., Farmer, A. W., & Buenning, M. (1984). Goal setting and personal responsibility training for LD adolescents. *Psychology in the Schools, 21,* 224–233.

^Trapani, C., & Gettinger, M. (1989). Effects of social skills training and cross-age tutoring on academic achievement and social behaviors of boys with learning disabilities. *Journal of Research and Development in Education, 23,* 1–9.

*Van Verth, J. E., & Dinan, F. J. (1974). A Keller Plan course in organic chemistry. In R. S. Ruskin & S. F. Bono (Eds.), *Personalized instruction in higher education* (pp. 162–168). Washington, DC: Center for Personalized Instruction.

*Vandenbroucke, A. C., Jr. (1974, April). *Evaluation of the use of a personalized system of instruction in general chemistry.* Paper presented at the National Conference on Personalized Instruction in Higher Education, Washington, DC.

*Walsh, R. G., Sr. (1977). The Keller Plan in college introductory physical geology: A comparison with the conventional teaching method. *Dissertation Abstracts International, 37,* 4257. (University Microfilms No. AAD 76-30292)

$&+Wentling, T. L. (1973). Mastery versus nonmastery instruction with varying test item feedback treatments. *Journal of Educational Psychology, 65,* 50–58.

^White, C. V., Pascarella, E. T., & Pflaum, S. W. (1981). Effects of training in sentence construction on the comprehension of learning-disabled children. *Journal of Educational Psychology, 71*, 697–704.

*White, M. E. (1974). Different equations by PSI. In R. S. Ruskin & S. F. Bono (Eds.), *Personalized instruction in higher education* (pp. 169–171). Washington, DC: Center for Personalized Instruction.

Willett, J., Yamashita, J., & Anderson, R. (1983). A meta-analysis of instructional systems applied in science teaching. *Journal of Research in Science Teaching, 20*(5), 405–417.

^Williams, J. P., Brown, L. G., Silverstein, A. K., & deCani, J. S. (1994). An instructional program in comprehension of narrative themes for adolescents with learning disabilities. *Learning Disability Quarterly, 17*, 205–221.

$Wire, D. R. (1979). *Mastery learning program at Durham College: Report on progress toward the first year, September 1, 1978–August 31, 1979*. Durham, NC. (ERIC Document Reproduction Service No. ED 187 387)

Wise, K. C. (1996). Strategies for teaching science: What works? *The Clearing House, 69*(6), 337–338.

*Witters, D. R., & Kent, G. W. (1972). Teaching without lecturing—evidence in the case for individualized instruction. *The Psychological Record, 22*, 169–175.

^Wong, B.Y.L., Butler, D. L., Ficzere, S. A., & Kuperis, S. (1996). Teaching low achievers and students with learning disabilities to plan, write, and revise opinion essays. *Journal of Learning Disabilities, 29*, 197–212.

^Wong, B.Y.L., Butler, D. L., Ficzere, S. A., Kuperis, S., Corden, M., & Zelmer, J. (1994). Teaching problem learners revision skills and sensitivity to audience through two instructional modes: Student-teacher versus student-student interactive dialogues. *Learning Disabilities Research & Practice, 9*, 78–90.

^$Wong, B.Y.L., & Jones, W. (1982). Increasing metacomprehension in learning disabled and normally achieving students through self-questioning training. *Learning Disability Quarterly, 5*, 228–240.

Wortham, S. C. (1980). *Mastery learning in secondary schools: A first-year report*. San Antonio, TX. (ERIC Document Reproduction Service No. ED 194 453)

*Yeany, R. H., Dost, R. J., & Matthew, R. W. (1980). The effects of diagnostic- prescriptive instruction and locus of control on the achievement and attitudes of university students. *Journal of Research in Science Teaching, 17*, 537–545.

$Yildren, G. (1977). *The effects of level of cognitive achievement on selected learning criteria under mastery learning and normal classroom instruction*. Unpublished doctoral dissertation, University of Chicago.

REFERENCES FOR PROVIDING INSTRUCTIONAL EVALUATION

*+Abraham, F. J., & Newton, J. M. (1974). *The interview technique as a personalized system of instruction for economics: The Oregon experience*. Paper presented at the National Conference on Personalized Instruction in Higher Education, Washington, DC.

!Acland, H. (1976). Stability of teacher effectiveness: A replication. *Journal of Educational Research, 69*, 289–292.

>Adams, G., & Engelmann, S. (1996). *Research on Direct Instruction: 20 years beyond DISTAR*. Seattle, WA: Educational Achievement Systems.

>American Federation of Teachers. (1998). *Building on the best. Learning from what works: Seven promising reading and English language arts programs*. Washington, DC: American Federation of Teachers.

$Anania, J. (1981). *The effects of quality instruction on the cognitive and affective learning of students*. Unpublished doctoral dissertation, University of Chicago.

!%Anderson, L. M., Evertson, C. M., & Brophy, J. E. (1979). An experimental study of effective teaching in first-grade reading groups. *The Elementary School Journal, 79*, 193–222.

!%Anderson, L. M., Evertson, C. M., & Brophy, J. E. (1982). *Principles of small group instruction* (Occasional paper no. 32). East Lansing: Michigan State University, Institute for Research on Teaching.

+Anderson, L. W. (1973). *Time and school learning*. Unpublished doctoral dissertation, University of Chicago.

*$&Anderson, L. W. (1975a). Student involvement in learning and school achievement. *California Journal of Education Research, 26*, 53–62.

$&Anderson L. W. (1975b). *Time to criterion: An experimental study*. Paper presented at the annual meeting of the American Education Research Association, Washington, DC. (ERIC Document Reproduction Service No. ED 108 006)

*$&+Anderson L. W. (1976). An empirical investigation of individual differences in time to learn. *Journal of Educational Psychology, 68*, 226–233.

*#@$&Anderson L. W., Scott, C., & Hutlock, N. (1976, April). *The effects of the mastery learning program on selected cognitive, affective, and ecological variables in grades 1 through 6*. Paper presented at the annual meeting of the American Education Research Association, San Francisco.

+Anderson, O. T., & Artman, R. A. (1972). A self-paced independent study, introductory physics sequence—description and evaluation. *American Journal of Physics, 40*, 1737–1742.

Anderson, S. A. (1994). *Synthesis of research on mastery learning* (Information Analysis). (ERIC Document Reproduction Service No. ED 382 567)

!Arehart, J. (1979). Student opportunity to learn related to student achievement of objectives in a probability unit. *Journal of Educational Research, 72*, 253–269.

*$&%=Arlin, M., & Webster, J. (1983). Time cost of mastery learning. *Journal of Educational Psychology, 75*, 187–195.

*Austin, S. M., & Gilbert, K. E. (1973). Student performance in the Keller-Plan course in introductory electricity and magnetism. *American Journal of Physics, 41*, 12–18.

Aviles, C. B. (1998). *A contrast of mastery learning and non-mastery learning instruction in an undergraduate social work course*. Paper presented at the annual meeting of the Council on Social Work Education, Orlando, FL.

*Badia, P., Stutts, C., & Harsh, J. (1978). Do methods of instruction and measures of different abilities and study habits interact? In J. G. Sherman, R. S. Ruskin, & R. M. Lazar (Eds.), *Personalized instruction and education today* (pp. 113–128). San Francisco: San Francisco Press.

<Baer, D. M., Blount, R. L., Detrich, R., & Stokes, T. F. (1987). Using intermittent reinforcement to program maintenance of verbal/nonverbal correspondence. *Journal of Applied Behavior Analysis, 20*, 179–184.

Baker, S., Gersten, R., & Lee, D-S. (2002). A synthesis of empirical research on teaching mathematics to low-achieving students. *The Elementary School Journal, 103*(1), 51–92.

<Ballinger, C. (1993). *Annual report to the association on the status of year-round education*. (ERIC Document Reproduction Service No. ED 024 990).

%Becker, W. C. (1977). Teaching reading and language to the disadvantage—What we have learned from field research. *Harvard Educational Review, 47*, 518–543.

*=Benson, J. S., & Yeany, R. H. (1980, April). *Generalizability of Diagnostic-prescriptive Teaching Strategies Across Student Locus of Control and Multiple Instructional Units*. Paper presented at the annual meeting of the American Educational Research Association, Boston. (ERIC Document Reproduction Service No. ED 187 534)

<Berkowitz, M. J., & Martens, B. K. (2001). Assessing teachers' and students' preferences for school-based reinforcement: Agreement across methods and different effort requirements. *Journal of Developmental and Physical Disabilities, 13*, 373–387.

!Berliner, D., Fisher, C., Filby, N., & Marliave, R. (1978). *Executive summary of Beginning Teacher Evaluation Study*. San Francisco: Far West Laboratory.

*=Billings, D. B. (1974). PSI versus the lecture course in the principles of economics: A quasi-controlled experiment. In R. S. Ruskin & S. F. Bono (Eds.), *Personalized instruction in higher education* (pp. 30–37). Washington, DC: Center for Personalized Instruction.

*$=Blackburn, K. T., & Nelson, D. (1985, April). *Differences between a group using a traditional format with mastery learning and a group using traditional format only in developmental mathematics courses at the university level: Implications for teacher education programs*. Paper presented at the annual meeting of the American Educational Research Association, Chicago. (ERIC Document Reproduction Service No. ED 258 948)

^Blaha, B. A. (1979). *The effects of answering self-generated questions on reading*. Unpublished doctoral dissertation, Boston University School of Education.

*Blasingame, J. W. (1975). Student attitude performance in a personalized system of instruction course in business administration—Correlates of performance with personality traits. *Dissertation Abstracts International, 36*, 3840. (University Microfilms No. 75-2834)

$&+=Block, J. H. (1972). Student learning and the setting of mastery performance standards. *Educational Horizons, 50*, 183–191.

+Block, J. H. (1973). *Mastery performance standards and student learning*. Unpublished study, University of California, Santa Barbara.

Block, J. H. (1980). Success rate. In C. Denham & A. Lieberman (Eds.), *Time to learn* (pp. 95–106). Washington, DC: U.S. Government Printing Office.

Block, J. H., & Burns, R. B. (1976). Mastery Learning. In L. Schulman (Ed.), *Review of research in education* (Vol. 4, pp. 3–49). Itasca, IL: F. E. Peacock.

>Block, J. H., Everson, S. T., & Guskey, T. R. (1995). *School improvement programs: A handbook for educational leaders*. New York: Scholastic.

$+Block, J. H., & Tierney, M. (1974). An exploration of two correction procedures used in mastery learning approaches to instruction. *Journal of Educational Psychology, 66*, 962–967.

Bloom, B. S. (1985). Learning for mastery. In C. W. Fisher & D. C. Berliner (Eds.), *Perspectives on instructional time*. White Plains, NY: Longman.

*+Born, D. G., & Davis, M. L. (1974). Amount and distribution of study in a personalized instruction course and in a lecture course. *Journal of Applied Behavior Analysis, 7*, 365–375.

*+Born, D. G., Gledhill, S. M., & Davis, M. L. (1972). Examination performance in lecture-discussion and personalized instruction courses. *Journal of Applied Behavior Analysis, 5*, 33–43.

=Bostow, D. E., & O'Connor, R. J. (1973). A comparison of two college classroom testing procedures: Required remediation versus no remediation. *Journal of Applied Behavior Analysis, 6*, 599–607.

^Brady, P. L. (1990). *Improving the reading comprehension of middle school students through reciprocal teaching and semantic mapping strategies.* Unpublished doctoral dissertation, University of Alaska.

*+Breland, N. S., & Smith, M. P. (1974). A comparison of PSI and traditional methods of instruction for teaching introduction to psychology. In R. S. Ruskin & S. F. Bono (Eds.), *Personalized instruction in higher education* (pp. 21–25). Washington, DC: Center for Personalized Instruction.

!Brophy, J. (1973). Stability of teacher effectiveness. *American Educational Research Journal, 10*, 245–252.

!Brophy, J., & Evertson, C. (1974a). *Process-product correlations in a Texas Teacher Effectiveness Study: Final report* (Research Report 74-4). Austin: Research and Development Center for Teacher Education, University of Texas. (ERIC Document Reproduction Service No. ED 091 094)

!Brophy, J., & Evertson, C. (1974b). *The Texas Teacher Effectiveness Project: Presentation of non-linear relationships and summary discussion* (Research Report 74-6). Austin: Research and Development Center for Teacher Education, University of Texas. (ERIC Document Reproduction Service No. ED 099 345)

%!Brophy, J., & Evertson, C. (1976). *Learning from teaching: A developmental perspective.* Boston: Allyn and Bacon.

Brophy, J., & Good, T. (1986). Teacher behavior and student achievement. In M. C. Wittrock (Ed.), *Handbook of research on teaching* (3rd ed., pp. 328–375). New York: Macmillan.

*$Bryant, N. D., Fayne, H. R., & Gettinger, M. (1982). Applying the mastery model to sight word for disabled readers. *Journal of Experimental Education, 50*, 116–121.

$Burke, A. (1983). *Students' potential for learning contrasted under tutorial and group approaches to instruction.* Unpublished doctoral dissertation, University of Chicago.

$&+=Burrows, C. K., & Okey, J. R. (1975, March–April). *The effects of a mastery learning strategy on achievement.* Paper presented at the annual meeting of the American Educational Research Association, Washington, DC.

*#@$Cabezon, E. (1984). *The effects of marked changes in student achievement pattern on the students, their teachers, and their parents: The Chilean case.* Unpublished doctoral dissertation, University of Chicago.

=Caldwell, E. C., Bissonnette, K., Klishis, M. J., Ripley, M., Farudi, P. P., Hochstetter, G. T., & Radiker, J. E. (1978). Mastery: The essential essential in PSI. *Teaching of Psychology, 5*, 59–65.

<Carnine, D. (1992). Expanding the notion of teachers' rights: Access to tools that work. *Journal of Applied Behavior Analysis, 24*, 13–19.

<Carr, E. G., & Durand, V. M. (1985). Reducing behavior problems through functional communication training. *Journal of Behavior Analysis, 18*, 111–126.

$=Chiappetta, E. L., & McBride, J. W. (1980). Exploring the effects of general remediation on ninth-graders' achievement of the mole concept. *Science Education, 64*, 609–614.

/Clairiana, R. B., & Smith, L. J. (1989). *Progress reports improve students' course completion rate and achievement in math computer-assisted instruction.* (ERIC Document Reproduction Service No. ED 317 170)

*$=Clark, C. P., Guskey, T. P., & Benninga, J. S. (1983). The effectiveness of mastery learning strategies in undergraduate education courses. *Journal of Educational Research, 76,* 210–214.

*Clark, S. G. (1975). An innovation for introductory sociology: Personalized system of instruction. In J. M. Johnston (Ed.), *Behavior research and technology in higher education* (pp. 117–124). Springfield, IL: Charles C. Thomas.

^Cohen, R. (1983). Students generate questions as an aid to reading comprehension. *Reading Teacher, 36,* 770–775.

!Coker, H., Medley, D., & Soar, R. (1980). How valid are expert opinions about effective teaching? *Phi Delta Kappan, 62,* 131–134, 149.

*+Coldeway, D. O., Santowski, M., O'Brien, R., & Lagowski, V. (1975). Comparison of small group contingency management with the personalized system of instruction and the lecture system. In J. M. Johnston (Ed.), *Research and technology in college and university teaching* (pp. 215–224). Gainesville: University of Florida.

*+Cole, C., Martin, S., & Vincent, J. (1975). A comparison of two teaching formats at the college level. In J. M. Johnston (Ed.), *Behavior research and technology in higher education* (pp. 61–74). Springfield, IL: Charles C. Thomas.

*Condo, P. (1974, April). *The analysis and evaluation of a self-paced course in calculus.* Paper presented at the National Conference on Personalized Instruction in Higher Education, Washington, DC.

<Cooper, B., Nye, B., Charlton, K., Lindsay, J., & Greathouse, S. (1996). The effects of summer vacation on achievement test scores: A narrative and meta-analytic review. *Review of Educational Research, 66,* 227–268.

*+Cooper, J. L., & Greiner, J. M. (1971). Contingency management in an introductory psychology course produces better retention. *Psychological Record, 21,* 391–400.

*Corey, J. R., & McMichael, J. S. (1974). Retention in a PSI introductory psychology course. In J. G. Sherman (Ed.), *PSI germinal papers* (pp. 17–19). Washington, DC: Center for Personalized Instruction.

+Corey, J. R., McMichael, J. S., & Tremont, P. J. (1970, April). *Long-term effects of personalized instruction in an introductory psychology course.* Paper presented at the meeting of the Eastern Psychology Association, Atlantic City.

*Cote, J. D. (1976). Biology by PSI in a community college. In B. A. Green, Jr. (Ed.), *Personalized instruction in higher education.* Washington, DC: Center for Personalized Instruction.

!Crawford, J. (1983). A study of instructional processes in Title I classes: 1981–82. *Journal of Research and Evaluation of the Oklahoma City Public Schools, 13*(1).

*Cross, M. Z., & Semb, G. (1976). An analysis of the effects of personalized instruction on students at different initial performance levels in an introductory college nutrition course. *Journal of Personalized Instruction, 1,* 47–50.

<Daly, E. J., Lentz, F. E., & Boyer, J. (1996). The instructional hierarchy: A conceptual model for understanding the effective components of reading interventions. *School Psychology Quarterly, 11,* 369–386.

<Daly, E. J., Martens, B. K., Hamler, K., Dool, E. J., & Eckert, T. L. (1999). A brief experimental analysis for identifying instructional components needed to improve oral reading fluency. *Journal of Applied Behavior Analysis, 32,* 83–94.

^Davey, B., & McBride, S. (1986). Effects of question-generation on reading comprehension. *Journal of Educational Psychology, 78,* 256–262.

*=Decker, D. F. (1976). *Teaching to achieve learning mastery by using retesting techniques.* Doctoral dissertation, Nova University. (ERIC Document Reproduction Service No. ED 133 002)

$Denton, W. L., Ory, J. C., Glassnap, D. R., & Poggio, J. P. (1976). *Grade expectations within a master learning strategy.* Paper presented at the annual meeting of the American Educational Research Association, San Francisco. (ERIC Document Reproduction Service No. ED 126 105)

^Dermody, M. (1988, February). *Metacognitive strategies for development of reading comprehension for younger children.* Paper presented at the annual meeting of the American Association of Colleges for Teacher Education. New Orleans, LA.

*$=Dillashaw, F. G., & Okey, J. R. (1983). Effects of a modified mastery learning strategy on achievement, attitudes, and on-task behavior of high school chemistry students. *Journal of Research in Science Teaching, 20,* 203–211.

^Dreher, M. J., & Gambrell, L.B. (1985). Teaching children to use a self-questioning strategy for studying expository text. *Reading Improvement, 22,* 2–7.

$Duby, P. B. (1981). *Attributions and attribution change: Effects of the mastery learning instructional approach.* Paper presented at the annual meeting of the American Educational Research Association, Los Angeles. (ERIC Document Reproduction Service No. ED 200 640)

=Dulkelberger, G. E., & Heikkinen, H. (1984). The influence of repeatable testing on retention in mastery learning. *School Science and Mathematics, 84,* 590–597.

!Dunkin, M. J. (1978). Student characteristics, classroom processes, and student achievement. *Journal of Educational Psychology, 70,* 998–1009.

<DuPaul, G. J., & Henningson, P. N. (1993). Peer tutoring effects on the classroom performance of children with Attention Deficit Hyperactivity Disorder. *School Psychology Review, 22,* 134–143.

=Dustin, D. S., & Johnson, S. L. (1974). *Some effects of a test criterion.* Unpublished manuscript, State University of New York, Plattsburgh.

!Ebmier, H., & Good, T. (1979). The effects of instructing teachers about good teaching on mathematics achievement of fourth-grade students. *American Educational Research Journal, 16,* 1–16.

Education Commission of the States. (1999). *Direct instruction.* Denver, CO: Education Commission of the States.

<Eisenberger, R., & Cameron, J. (1996). Detrimental effects of reward: Reality or myth? *American Psychologist, 51,* 1153–1166.

>Ellis, A. K., & Fouts, J. T. (1997). *Research on educational innovations* (2nd ed.). New York: Eye on Education.

!Emmer, E., Evertson, C., & Anderson, L. (1980). Effective classroom management at the beginning of the school year. *Elementary School Journal, 80,* 219–231.

!Emmer, E., Evertson, C., & Brophy, J. (1979). Stability of teacher effects in junior high school classrooms. *American Educational Research Journal, 16,* 71–75.

!%Emmer, E. T., Evertson, C., Sanford, J., & Clements, B. (1982). *Improving instruction management: An experimental study in junior high classrooms.* Austin: Research and Development Center for Teacher Education, University of Texas.

<Erchul, W. P., & Martens, B. K. (2002). *School consultation: Conceptual and empirical bases of practice* (2nd ed.). New York: Plenum.

%Evertson, C. (1982). Differences in instructional activities in higher and lower achieving junior high English and mathematics classrooms. *Elementary School Journal, 82*, 329–351.

!%Evertson, C., Anderson, C., Anderson, L., & Brophy, J. (1980). Relationships between classroom behaviors and student outcomes in junior high mathematics and English classes. *American Educational Research Journal, 17*, 43–60.

!Evertson, C., Anderson, L., & Brophy, J. (1978). *Texas Junior High School Study—Final report of process-outcome relationship* (Report No. 4061). Austin: Research and Development Center for Teacher Education, University of Texas.

!Evertson, C., & Brophy, J. (1973). High-inference behavioral ratings as correlates of teacher effectiveness. *JSAS Catalog of Selected Documents in Psychology, 3*, 97.

!Evertson, C., & Brophy, J. (1974). *Texas Teacher Effectiveness Project: Questionnaire and interview data* (Research Report No. 74-5). Austin: Research and Development Center for Teacher Education, University of Texas.

!%Evertson, C., Emmer, E., & Brophy, J., (1980). Predictors of effective teaching in junior high mathematics classrooms. *Journal for Research in Mathematics Education, 11*, 167–178.

%Evertson, C. M., Emmer, E. T., Sanford, J. P., & Clements, B. S. (1983). Improving classroom management: An experiment in elementary classrooms. *Elementary School Journal, 84*, 174–188.

*#@=Fagan, J. S. (1976). Mastery learning: The relationship of mastery procedures and aptitude to the achievement and retention of transportation—Environmental concepts by seventh grade students. *Dissertation Abstracts International, 36*, 5981. (University Microfilms No. 76-6402)

*=Fehlen, J. E. (1976). Mastery learning techniques in the traditional classroom setting. *School Science and Mathematics, 76*(3), 241–245.

=Fernald, P. S., Chiseri, M. J., Lawson, D. W., Scroggs, G. F., & Riddell, J. C. (1975). Systematic manipulation of student pacing, the perfection requirement, and contact with a teaching assistant in an introductory psychology course. *Teaching of Psychology, 2*, 147–151.

*Fernald, P. S., & DuNann, D. H. (1975). Effects of individualized instruction upon low- and high-achieving students' study behavior in students' evaluation of mastery. *Journal of Experimental Education, 43*, 27–34.

$&+=Fiel, R. L., & Okey, J. R. (1974). The effects of formative evaluation and remediation on mastery of intellectual skill. *Journal of Educational Research, 68*, 253–255.

!%Fisher, C. W., Berliner, D. C., Filby, N. N., Marliave, R., Cahen, L. S., & Dishaw, M. M. (1980). Teaching behaviors, academic learning time, and student achievement: An overview. In C. Denham & A. Lieberman (Eds.), *Time to learn* (pp. 7–32). Washington, DC: U.S. Government Printing Office.

!%Fitzpatrick, K. A. (1981). *An investigation of secondary classroom material strategies for increasing student academic engaged time*. Doctoral dissertation, University of Illinois at Urbana–Champaign.

!%Fitzpatrick, K. A. (1982). *The effect of a secondary classroom management training program on teacher and student behavior*. Paper presented at the annual meeting of the American Educational Research Association, New York.

$&Fitzpatrick, K. A. (1985, April). *Group-based mastery learning: A Robin Hood approach to instruction?* Paper presented at the annual meeting of the American Educational Research Association, Chicago.

<Fuchs, L. S., & Fuchs, D. (1986). Effects of systematic formative evaluation on student achievement: A meta-analysis. *Exceptional Children, 53*, 199–208.

/Fuchs, L. S., Fuchs, D., Hamlett, C. L., Phillips, N. B., & Bentz, J. (1994). Classwide curriculum-based measurement: Helping general educators meet the challenge of student diversity. *Exceptional Children, 60*, 518–537.

/Fuchs, L. S., Fuchs, D., Karns, K., Hamlett, C. L., Katzaroff, M., & Dutka, S. (1997). Effects of task-focused goals on low-achieving students with and without learning disabilities. *American Educational Research Journal, 34*, 513–543.

>Gersten, R., & Keating, T. (1987). Long-term benefits from Direct Instruction. *Educational Leadership, 44*, 28–31.

>Gersten, R., Keating, T., & Becker, W. (1988). The continued impact of the Direct Instruction model: Longitudinal studies of follow through students. *Education and Treatment of Children, 11*(4), 318–327.

<Gickling, E. E., & Armstrong, D. L. (1978). Levels of instructional difficulty as related to on-task behavior, task completion, and comprehension. *Journal of Learning Disabilities, 11*, 32–39.

+Glassnap, D. R., Poggio, J. P., & Ory, J. C. (1975, March–April). *Cognitive and affective consequences of mastery and non-mastery instructional strategies.* Paper presented at the annual meeting of the American Educational Research Association, Washington, DC.

*=Goldwater, B. C., & Acker, L. E. (1975). Instructor-paced, mass-testing for mastery performance in an introductory psychology course. *Teaching of Psychology, 2*, 152–155.

!Good, T., Ebmeier, H., & Beckerman, T. (1978). Teaching mathematics in high and low SES classrooms: An empirical comparison. *Journal of Teacher Education, 29*, 85–90.

!Good, T., Grouws, D., & Beckerman, T. (1978). Curriculum pacing: Some empirical data in mathematics. *Journal of Curriculum Studies, 10*, 75–81.

!%Good, T., Grouws, D., & Ebmeier, M. (1983). *Active mathematics teaching.* New York: Longman.

!%Good, T. L., & Grouws, D. A. (1977). Teaching effects: A process-product study in fourth-grade mathematics classrooms. *Journal of Teacher Education, 28*(3), 49–54.

!Good, T. L., & Grouws, D. A. (1979a). *Experimental Study of Mathematics Instruction in Elementary Schools* (Final Report, National Institute of Education Grant No. NIE-G-79-0103). Columbia: University of Missouri, Center for the Study of Social Behavior.

!Good, T. L., & Grouws, D. A. (1979b). The Missouri mathematics effectiveness project. *Journal of Educational Psychology, 71*, 355–362.

!Good, T. L., & Grouws, D. A. (1981). *Experimental research in secondary mathematics* (Final Report, National Institute of Education Grant No. NIE-G-79-0103). Columbia: University of Missouri, Center for the Study of Social Behavior.

*Gregory, I., Smeltzer, D. J., Knopp, W., & Gardner, M. (1976). *Teaching of psychiatry by PSI: Impact on National Board Examination scores.* Unpublished manuscript, Ohio State University, Columbus.

*$&Guskey, T. R. (1982). The effects of staff development on teachers' perceptions about effective teaching. *Journal of Educational Research, 76*, 378–381.

*$&Guskey, T. R. (1984). The influence of changes in instructional effectiveness upon the affective characteristics of teachers. *American Educational Research Journal, 21*, 245–259.

$Guskey, T. R. (1985). The effects of staff development on teachers' perceptions about effective teaching. *Journal of Educational Research, 79*, 378–381.

*$=Guskey, T. R., Benninga, J. S., & Clark, C. B. (1984). Mastery learning and students' attributions at the college level. *Research in Higher Education, 20*, 491–498.

Guskey, T. R., & Gates, S. L. (1986). Synthesis of research on the effects of mastery learning in elementary and secondary classrooms. *Educational Leadership, 43*(8), 73–80.

*$=Guskey, T. R., & Monsaas, J. A. (1979). Mastery learning: A model for academic success in urban junior colleges. *Research in Higher Education, 11*, 263–274.

Guskey, T. R., & Pigott, T. D. (1988). Research on group-based mastery learning programs: A meta-analysis. *Journal of Educational Research, 81*(4), 197–216.

*Hardin, L. D. (1977). A study of the influence of a physics personalized system of instruction versus lecture on cognitive reason, achievement, attitudes and critical thinking. *Dissertation Abstracts International, 38*, 4711A–4712 A. (University Microfilms No. 77-30826)

<Haring, N. G., Lovitt, T. C., Eaton, M. D., & Hansen, C. L. (1978). *The fourth R: Research in the classroom.* Columbus, OH: Merrill.

*Hecht, L. W. (1980, April). *Stalking mastery learning in its natural habitat.* Paper presented at the annual meeting of the American Educational Research Association, Boston.

*Heffley, P. D. (1974). The implementation of the personalized system of instruction in the freshman chemistry course at Censius College. In R. S. Ruskin & S. F. Bono (Eds.), *Personalized instruction in higher education* (pp. 140–145). Washington, DC: Center for Personalized Instruction.

*^Helfeldt, J. P., & Lalik, R. (1976). Reciprocal student-teacher questioning. *Reading Teacher, 33*, 283–287.

*Herring, B. G. (1975, December). *Cataloguing and classification.* Austin: University of Texas.

*Herring, B. G. (1977). The written PSI study guide in a non-PSI course. Austin: University of Texas.

*Herrmann, T. (1984, August). *TELIDON as an enhancer of student interest and performance.* Paper presented at the annual meeting of the American Psychological Association, Toronto. (ERIC Document Reproduction Service No. ED 251 004)

*Hindman, C. D. (1974). Evaluation of three programming techniques in introductory psychology courses. In R. S. Ruskin & S. F. Bono (Eds.), *Personalized instruction in higher education* (pp. 38–42). Washington, DC: Center for Personalized Instruction.

*=Honeycutt, J. K. (1974, April). *The effect of computer managed instruction on content learning of undergraduate students.* Paper presented at the annual meeting of the American Educational Research Association, Chicago. (ERIC Document Reproduction Service No. ED 089 682)

<Horner, R. H., Day, H. M., Sprague, J. R., O'Brien, M., & Heathfield, L. T. (1991). Interspersed requests: A nonaversive procedure for reducing aggression and self-injury during instruction. *Journal of Applied Behavior Analysis, 24*, 265–278.

!Hughes, D. (1973). An experimental investigation of the effect of pupil responding and teacher reacting on pupil achievement. *American Educational Research Journal, 10*, 21–37.

=Hutchcraft, F. R., & Kruger, B. S. (1977, April). *An empirical validation of the unit perfection requirement in personalized systems of instruction methodology.* Paper presented at the Fourth National Conference on Personalized Instruction in Higher Education, San Francisco.

*Hymel, G. M. (1974). *An investigation of John B. Carrol's model of school learning as a theoretical basis for the organizational structuring of schools* (Final Report, NIE Project No. 3-1359). University of New Orleans, New Orleans, LA.

=Hymel, G. M., & Gaines, W. G. (1977, April). *An investigation of John B. Carroll's Model of School Learning as a basis for facilitating individualized instruction by way of school organizational patterning.* Paper presented at the annual meeting of the American Educational Research Association, New York. (ERIC Document Reproduction Service No. ED 136 414)

*=Hymel, G. M., & Matthews, G. (1980). Effects of a mastery approach on social studies achievement and unit evaluation. *Southern Journal of Educational Research, 14*, 191–204.

*Jackman, L. E. (1982). Evaluation of a modified Keller method in a biochemistry laboratory course. *Journal of Chemical Education, 59*, 225–227.

*Jacko, E. J. (1974). Lecture instruction versus a personalized system of instruction: Effects on individuals with differing achievement anxiety and academic achievement. *Dissertation Abstracts International, 35*, 3521. (University Microfilms No. AAD 74-27211)

<Johnson, M. D., & Fawcett, S. B. (1994). Courteous service: Its assessment and modification in a human service organization. *Journal of Applied Behavior Analysis, 27*, 145–152.

+Johnston, J. M., & Pennypacker, H. S. (1971). A behavioral approach to college teaching. *American Psychologist, 26*, 219–244.

*#@$&Jones, B. F., Monsaas, J. A., & Katims, M. (1979, April). *Improving reading comprehension: Embedding diverse learning strategies within a mastery learning instructional framework.* Paper presented at the annual meeting of the American Educational Research Association, San Francisco. (ERIC Document Reproduction Service No. ED 170 698)

$+Jones, E. L., Gordon, H. A., & Stectman, G. L. (1975). *Mastery learning: A strategy for academic success in a community college.* Los Angeles: ERIC Clearinghouse for Junior Colleges. (ERIC Document Reproduction Service No. 115 315)

+=Jones, F. G. (1975). The effects of mastery and aptitude on learning, retention, and time. Doctoral dissertation, University of Georgia, 1974. *Dissertation Abstracts International, 35*, 6537.

+Karlin, B. M. (1972). *The Keller method of instruction compared to the traditional method of instruction in a Lafayette College history course.* Unpublished paper, Lafayette College, Lafayette, PA.

*#@Katims, M., Smith, J. K., Steele, C., & Wick, J. W. (1977, April). *The Chicago mastery learning reading program: An interim evaluation.* Paper presented at the annual meeting of the American Educational Research Association, New York. (ERIC Document Reproduction Service No. ED 137 737)

*#@Kersh, M. E. (1970). *A strategy of mastery learning in fifth grade arithmetic.* Unpublished doctoral dissertation, University of Chicago.

+Kim, Y., Cho, G., Park, J., & Park, M. (1974). *An application of a new instructional model* (Research Report No. 8). Seoul, Korea: Korean Educational Development Institute.

^King, A. (1989). Effects of self-questioning training on college students' comprehension of lectures. *Contemporary Educational Psychology, 14*, 366–381.

^King, A. (1990). Improving lecture comprehension: Effects of a metacognitive strategy. *Applied Educational Psychology, 5*, 331–346.

^King, A. (1992). Comparison of self-questioning, summarizing, and notetaking-review as strategies for learning from lectures. *American Educational Research Journal, 29*, 303–325.

*=Knight, J. M., Williams, J. D., & Jardon, M. L. (1975). The effects of contingency avoidance on programmed student achievement. *Research in Higher Education, 3*, 11–17.

=Komaridis, G. V. (1971). The effects of four testing systems on schedules of study, test performance, and retention of materials. *Dissertation Abstracts International, 32*, 790A. (University Microfilms No. 71-19,498)

!Kounin, J. (1970). *Discipline and group management in classrooms.* New York: Holt, Rinehart, & Winston.

>Kuder, J. (1990). Effectiveness of the DISTAR Reading Program for children with learning disabilities. *Journal of Learning Disabilities, 23*(1), 69–71.

*Kulik, C., & Kulik, J. (1976). PSI and the mastery model. In B. A. Green, Jr. (Ed.), *Personalized instruction in higher education* (pp. 155–159). Washington, DC: Center for Personalized Instruction.

Kulik, C., Kulik, J., & Bangert-Drowns, R. (1990a). Effectiveness of mastery learning programs: A meta-analysis. *Review of Educational Research, 60*(2), 265–269.

Kulik, J., Kulik, C., & Bangert-Drowns, R. (1990b). Is there better evidence on mastery learning? A response to Slavin. *Review of Educational Research, 60*(2), 303–307.

+Kulik, J. A., Kulik, C., & Carmichael, K. (1974). The Keller Plan in science teaching. *Science, 183*, 379–383.

=Kulik, J. A., Kulik, L. C., & Hertzler, E. C. (1977). Modular college teaching with and without required remediation. *Journal of Personalized Instruction, 2*, 70–75.

Kulik, L. C., & Kulik, J. A. (1987). Mastery testing and student learning: A meta-analysis. *Journal of Educational Technology Systems, 15*(3), 325–345.

^Labercane, G., & Battle, J. (1987). Cognitive processing strategies, self-esteem, and reading comprehension of learning disabled students. *Journal of Special Education, 11*, 167–185.

!Larrivee, B., & Algina, J. (1983, April). *Identification of teaching behaviors which predict success from mainstream students.* Paper presented at the annual meeting of the American Educational Research Association. Montreal. (ERIC Document Reproduction Service No. ED 232 362)

=Lawler, R. M. (1971). An investigation of selected instructional strategies in an undergraduate computer-managed instruction course. *Dissertation Abstracts International, 32*, 1190A–1191A. (University Microfilms No. 71-24, 610)

+Lee, Y. D., Kim, C. S., Kim, H., Park B. Y., Yoo, H. K., Chang, S. M., & Kim, S. C. (1971). *Interaction improvement studies of the Mastery Learning Project* (Final Report on the Mastery Learning Project, April–November 1971). Seoul, Korea: Educational Research Center, Seoul National University.

*=Leppmann, P. K., & Herrmann, T. F. (1981, August). *PSI—What are the critical elements?* Paper presented at the annual meeting of the American Psychological Association, Los Angeles. (ERIC Document Reproduction Service No. ED 214 502)

$+Levin, T. (1975). *The effect of content prerequisites and process-oriented experiences on application ability in a learning of probability.* Unpublished doctoral dissertation, University of Chicago.

*=Lewis, E. W. (1984). The effects of mastery learning strategy and an interactive computerized quiz strategy on student achievement and attitude in college trigonometry. *Dissertation Abstracts International, 45,* 2430A. (University Microfilms No. 8424589)

*Leyton, F. S. (1983). *The extent to which group instruction supplemented by mastery of initial cognitive prerequisites approximates the learning effectiveness of one-to-one tutorial methods.* Unpublished doctoral dissertation, University of Chicago.

*Locksley, N. (1977). The Personalized System of Instruction (PSI) in a university mathematics class. *Dissertation Abstracts International, 37,* 4194. (University Microfilms No. ADD 76-28194)

^Lonberger, R. B. (1988). *The effects of training in a self-generated learning strategy on the prose processing abilities of fourth and sixth graders.* Unpublished doctoral dissertation, State University of New York at Buffalo.

#@=Long, J. C., Okey, J. R., & Yeany, R. H. (1978). The effects of diagnosis with teacher or student directed remediation on science achievement and attitudes. *Journal of Research in Science Teaching, 15,* 505–511.

<Lovitt, T. C., & Esveldt, K. A. (1970). The relative effects on math performance of single-versus multiple-ratio schedules: A case study. *Journal of Applied Behavior Analysis, 3,* 261–270.

*Lu, M. C. (1976). The retention of material learned by PSI in a mathematics course. In B. A. Green, Jr. (Ed.), *Personalized instruction in higher education* (pp. 151–154). Washington, DC: Center for Personalized Instruction.

*Lu, P. H. (1976). Teaching human growth and development by The Personalized System for Instruction. *Teaching of Psychology, 3,* 127–128.

*Lubkin, J. L. (1974). Engineering statistics: A Keller Plan course with novel problems and novel features. In R. S. Ruskin & S. F. Bono (Eds.), *Personalized instruction in higher education* (pp. 153–161). Washington, DC: Center for Personalized Instruction.

*#@=Lueckmeyer, C. L., & Chiappetta, W. L. (1981). An investigation into the effects of a modified mastery learning strategy on achievement in a high school human physiology unit. *Journal of Research in Science Teaching, 18,* 269–273.

^Lysynchuk, L., Pressley, M., & Vye, G. (1990). Reciprocal instruction improves reading comprehension performance in poor grade school comprehenders. *Elementary School Journal, 40,* 471–484.

^MacGregor, S. K. (1988). Use of self-questioning with a computer-mediated text system and measures of reading performance. *Journal of Reading Behavior, 20,* 131–148.

*Malec, M. A. (1975). PSI: A brief report and reply to Francis. *Teaching Sociology, 2,* 212–217.

^Manzo, A. V. (1969). *Improving reading comprehension through reciprocal teaching.* Unpublished doctoral dissertation, Syracuse University.

<Martens, B. K., Ardoin, S. P., Hilt, A. Lannie, A. L., Panahon, C. J., & Wolfe, L. (2002). Sensitivity of children's behavior to probabilistic reward: Effects of a decreasing-ratio lottery system on math performance. *Journal of Applied Behavior Analysis, 35,* 403–406.

<Martens, B. K., & Daly, E. J. (1999). Discovering the alphabetic principle: A lost opportunity for educational reform. *Journal of Behavioral Education, 9,* 33–41.

<Martens, B. K., Hilt, A. M., Needham, L. R. Sutterer, J. R., Panahon, C. J., & Lannie, A. L. (2003). Carryover effects of free reinforcement on children's work completion. *Behavior Modification, 27,* 560–577.

Martens, B. K., & Witt, J. C. (2004). Competence, persistence, and success: The positive psychology of behavioral skill instruction. *Psychology in the Schools, 41*(1), 19–30.

*=Martin, R. R., & Srikameswaran, K. (1974). Correlation between frequent testing and student performance. *Journal of Chemical Education, 51*, 485–486.

$Matthews, G. S. (1982). *Effects of a mastery learning strategy on the cognitive knowledge and unit evaluation of students in high school social studies.* Unpublished doctoral dissertation, University of Southern Mississippi.

!McConnell, J. (1977). *Relationship between selected teacher behaviors and attitudes/ achievement of algebra classes.* Paper presented at the annual meeting of the American Educational Research Association. New York. (ERIC Document Reproduction Service No. ED 141 118)

<McCurdy, M., Skinner, C. H., Grantham, K., Watson, T. S., & Hindman, P. M. (2001). Increasing on-task behavior in an elementary student during mathematics seatwork by interspersing additional brief problems. *School Psychology Review, 30*, 23–32.

!McDonald, F. (1976). Report on Phase II of the Beginning Teacher Evaluation Study. *Journal of Teacher Education, 27*(1), 39–42.

!McDonald, F. (1977). Research on teaching: Report on Phase II of the Beginning Teacher Evaluation Study. In G. Borich & K. Fenton (Eds.), *The appraisal of teaching: Concepts and process.* Reading, MA: Addison-Wesley.

!McDonald, F., & Elias, P. (1976). *Executive Summary Report: Beginning Teacher Evaluation Study, Phase II.* Princeton, NJ: Educational Testing Service.

<McDowell, C., & Keenan, M. (2001). Developing fluency and endurance in a child diagnosed with attention deficit hyperactivity disorder. *Journal of Applied Behavior Analysis, 34*, 345–348.

*McFarland, B. (1976). An individualized course in elementary composition for the marginal student. In B. A. Green, Jr. (Ed.), *Personalized instruction in higher education* (pp. 45–52). Washington, DC: Center for Personalized Instruction.

<McGinnis, J. C., Friman, P. C., & Carlyon, W. D. (1999). The effect of token rewards on "intrinsic" motivation for doing math. *Journal of Applied Behavior Analysis, 32*, 375–379.

*+McMichael, J., & Corey, J. R. (1969). Contingency management in an introductory psychology course produces better learning. *Journal of Applied Behavior Analysis, 2*, 79–83.

*#@Mevarech, Z. R. (1980). *The role of teaching-learning strategies and feedback-corrective procedures in developing higher cognitive achievement.* Unpublished doctoral dissertation, University of Chicago.

$&Mevarech, Z. R. (1981, April). *Attaining mastery on higher cognitive achievement.* Paper presented at the annual meeting of the American Educational Research Association, Los Angeles.

*Mevarech, Z. R. (1985). The effects of cooperative mastery learning strategies on mathematical achievement. *Journal of Educational Research, 78*, 372–377.

*#@Mevarech, Z. R. (1986). The role of feedback corrective procedures in developing mathematics achievement and self-concept in desegregated classrooms. *Studies in Educational Evaluation, 12*, 197–203.

*Mevarech, Z. R., & Werner, S. (1985). Are mastery learning strategies beneficial for developing problem solving skills? *Higher Education, 14*, 425–432.

>Meyer, L. A. (1984). Long-term academic effects of the Direct Instruction Project Follow Through. *Elementary School Journal, 84*, 380–394.

*=Meyers, R. R. (1976). The effects of mastery and aptitude on achievement and attitude in an introductory college geography course. *Dissertation Abstracts International, 36,* 5874. (University Microfilms No. 76-6436)

=Meznarich, R. A. (1978). The personalized system of instruction with and without repeated testing to mastery. *Dissertation Abstracts International, 39,* 2103A. (University Microfilms No. 7817198)

<Miller, D. L., & Kelley, M. L. (1994). The use of goal setting and contingency contracting for improving children's homework performance. *Journal of Applied Behavior Analysis, 27,* 73–84.

Montazemi, A. R., & Wang, F. (1995). An empirical investigation of CBI in support of mastery learning. *Journal of Educational Computing Research, 13*(2), 185–205.

*+Morris, C., & Kimbrill, G. (1972). Performance and attitudinal effects of the Keller method in an introductory psychology course. *Psychological Record, 22,* 523–530.

*=Nation, J. R., Knight, J. M, Lamberth, J., & Dyck, D. (1974). Programmed student achievement: A test of the avoidance hypothesis. *Journal of Experimental Education, 42,* 57–61.

*=Nation, J. R., Massad, P., & Wilkerson, P. (1977). Student performance in introductory psychology following termination of the programmed achievement contingency at mid-semester. *Teaching of Psychology, 4,* 116–119.

*=Nation, J. R., & Roop, S. S. (1975). A comparison of two mastery approaches to teaching introductory psychology. *Teaching of Psychology, 2,* 108–111.

*+Nazzaro, J. R., Todorov, J. C., & Nazzaro, J. N. (1972). Student ability and individualized instruction. *Journal of College Science Teaching, 2,* 29–30.

<Neef, N. A., & Lutz, M. N. (2001). Assessment of variables affecting choice and application to classroom interventions. *School Psychology Quarterly, 16,* 239–252.

<Neef, N. A., Shade, D., & Miller, M. S. (1994). Assessing influential dimensions of reinforcers on choice in students with serious emotional disturbance. *Journal of Applied Behavior Analysis, 27,* 575–583.

^Nolte, R. Y., & Singer, H. (1985). Active comprehension: Teaching a process of reading comprehension and its effects on reading achievement. *The Reading Teacher, 39,* 24–31.

*Nord, S. B. (1975). Comparative achievement and attitude in individualized and class instructional settings. *Dissertation Abstracts International, 35,* 529A. (University Microfilms No. 75-02314)

$Nordin, A. B. (1979). *The effects of different qualities of instruction on selected cognitive, affective, and time variables.* Unpublished doctoral dissertation, University of Chicago.

<Northup, J., George, T., Jones, K., Broussard, C., & Vollmer, T. R. (1996). A comparison of reinforcer assessment methods: The utility of verbal and pictorial choice procedures. *Journal of Applied Behavior Analysis, 29,* 201–212.

!Nuthall, G., & Church, J. (1973). Experimental studies of teaching behavior. In G. Chanan (Ed.), *Towards a science of teaching.* London: National Foundation for Educational Research.

Obando, L. T., & Hymel, G. M. (1991, March). *The effect of mastery learning instruction on the entry-level Spanish proficiency of secondary school students.* Paper presented at the annual meeting of the American Educational Research Association, New Orleans. (ERIC Document Reproduction Service No. ED 359 253)

*$+=Okey, J. R. (1974). Altering teacher and pupil behavior with mastery teaching. *School Science and Mathematics, 74,* 530–535.

+Okey, J. R. (1975). *Development of mastery teaching materials* (Final Evaluation Report, USOE G-74-2990). Bloomington: Indiana University.

$&Okey, J. R. (1977). The consequences of training teachers to use a mastery learning strategy. *Journal of Teacher Education, 28*(5), 57–62.

=Okey, J. R., Brown, J. L., & Field, R. L. (1972). Diagnostic evaluation methods in individualized instruction. *Science Education, 56,* 207–212.

*$Omelich, C. L., & Covington, M. V. (1981). *Do the learning benefits of behavioral instruction outweigh the psychological costs?* Paper presented at the annual meeting of the Western Psychological Association, Los Angeles.

^Palincsar, A. S. (1987, April). *Collaborating for collaborative learning of text comprehension.* Paper presented at the annual meeting of the American Educational Research Association, Washington, DC.

^Palincsar, A. S., & Brown, A. L. (1984). Reciprocal teaching of comprehension-fostering and comprehension-monitoring activities. *Cognition and Instruction, 2,* 117–175.

*Pascarela, E. T. (1977, April). *Aptitude-treatment interaction in a college calculus course taught in personalized system of instruction and conventional formats.* Paper presented at the annual meeting of the American Educational Research Association, New York. (ERIC Document Reproduction Service No. ED 137 137)

<Patterson, G. R., Reid, J. B., & Dishion, T. J. (1992). *Antisocial boys.* Eugene, OR: Castalia Publishing.

*Peluso, A., & Baranchik, A. J. (1977). Self-paced mathematics instruction: A statistical comparison with traditional teaching. *The American Mathematical Monthly, 84,* 124–129.

*+Phillippas, M. A., & Sommerfeldt, R. W. (1972). Keller vs. lecture method in general physics instruction. *American Journal of Physics, 40,* 1800.

+Poggio, J. P. (1976, April). *Long-term cognitive retention resulting from the mastery learning paradigm.* Paper presented at the annual meeting of the American Educational Research Association, San Francisco.

*Pollack, N. F., & Roeder, P. W. (1975). Individualized instruction in an introductory government course. *Teaching Political Science, 8,* 18–36.

!%Reid, E. R. (1978–1982). *The Reader Newsletter.* Salt Lake City: Exemplary Center for Reading Instruction.

<Rhymer, K. N., Henington, C., Skinner, C. H., & Looby, E. J. (1999). The effects of explicit timing on mathematics performance in Caucasian and African American second-grade students. *School Psychology Quarterly, 14,* 397–407.

^Ritchie, P. (1985). The effects of instruction in main idea and question generation. *Reading Canada Lecture, 3,* 139–146.

*+Rosati, P. A. (1975). A comparison of the personalized system of instruction with the lecture method in teaching elementary dynamics. In J. M. Johnston (Ed.), *Behavior research and technology in higher education.* Springfield, IL: Charles C. Thomas.

Rosenshine, B., Meister, C., & Chapman, S. (1996). Teaching students to generate questions: A review of the intervention studies. *Review of Educational Research, 66*(2), 181–221.

Rosenshine, B., & Stevens, R. (1986). Teaching functions. In M. C. Wittrock (Ed.), *Handbook of research on teaching* (3rd ed., pp. 376–391). New York: Macmillan.

Ross, J. A. (2004). Effects of running records assessment on early literacy achievement. *The Journal of Educational Research, 97*(4), 186–194.

+Roth, C. H., Jr. (1973). Continuing effectiveness on personalized self-paced instruction in digital systems engineering. *Engineering Education, 63*(6), 447–450.

*Roth, C. H., Jr. (1975, December). *Electrical engineering laboratory I* (One of a series of reports on the projects titled Expansion of Keller Plan Instruction in Engineering and Selected Other Disciplines). Austin: University of Texas.

*=Saunders-Harris, R. L., & Yeany, R. H. (1981). Diagnosis, remediation, and locus of control: Effects of the immediate and retained achievement and attitude. *Journal of Experimental Education, 49*, 220–224.

*Schielack, V. P., Jr. (1983). A personalized system of instruction versus a conventional method in a mathematics course for elementary education majors. *Dissertation Abstracts International, 43*, 2267. (University Microfilms No. 82-27717)

*Schimpfhauser, F., Horrocks, L., Richardson, K., Alben, J., Schumm, D., & Sprecher, H. (1974). The personalized system of instruction as an adaptable alternative within the traditional structure of medical basic sciences. In R. S. Ruskin & S. F. Bono (Eds.), *Personalized instruction in higher education* (pp. 61–69). Washington, DC: Center for Personalized Instruction.

!Schuck, R. (1981). The impact of set induction on student achievement and retention. *Journal of Educational Research, 74*, 227–232.

/Schunk, D. H. (1982). *Efficacy and skill development through social comparison and goal setting.* (ERIC Document Reproduction Service No. ED 222 279)

*Schwartz, P. L. (1981). Retention of knowledge in clinical biochemistry and the effect of the Keller Plan. *Journal of Medical Education, 56*, 778–781.

=Semb, G. (1974). The effects of mastery criteria and assignment length on college-student test performance. *Journal of Applied Behavior Analysis, 7*, 61–69.

*Sharples, D. K., Smith, D. J., & Strasler, G. M. (1976). *Individually-paced learning in civil engineering technology: An approach to mastery.* Columbia: South Carolina State Board for Technical and Comprehensive Education. (ERIC Document Reproduction Service No. ED 131 870)

*$=Sheldon, M. S., & Miller, E. D. (1973). *Behavioral objectives and mastery learning applied to two areas of junior college instruction.* Los Angeles: University of California at Los Angeles. (ERIC Document Reproduction Service No. ED 082 730)

*Sheppard, W. C., & MacDermott, H. G. (1970). Design and evaluation of a programmed course in introductory psychology. *Journal of Applied Behavior Analysis, 3*, 5–11.

<Shinn, M. R. (1989). *Curriculum-based measurement: Assessing special children.* New York: Guilford.

^Short, E. J., & Ryan, E. B. (1984). Metacognitive differences between skilled and less-skilled readers: Remediating deficits through story grammar and attribution training. *Journal of Educational Psychology, 76*, 225–235.

*Siegfried, J. J., & Strand, S. H. (1976). An evaluation of the Vanderbilt JCEE experimental PSI course in elementary economics. *The Journal of Economic Education, 8*, 9–26.

*+Silberman, R., & Parker, B. (1974). Student attitudes and the Keller Plan. *Journal of Chemical Education, 51*, 393.

<Simonton, D. K. (2000). Creativity: Cognitive, personal, developmental, and social aspects. *American Psychologist, 55*, 151–158.

^Simpson, P. S. (1989). *The effects of direct training in active comprehension on reading achievement, self-concepts, and reading attitudes of at-risk sixth grade students.* Unpublished doctoral dissertation, Texas Tech University.

<Skinner, C. H. (2002). An empirical analysis of interspersal research: Evidence, implications, and applications of the discrete task completion hypothesis. *Journal of School Psychology, 40*, 347–368.

<Skinner, C. H., Fletcher, P. A., & Henington, C. (1996). Increasing learning trial rates by increasing student response rates: A summary of research. *School Psychology Quarterly, 11*, 313–325.

Slavin, R. E. (1990). Mastery learning re-considered. *Review of Educational Research, 60*(2), 300–302.

*#@$&Slavin, R. E., & Karweit, N. L. (1984). Mastery learning and student teams: A factorial experiment in urban general mathematics classes. *American Educational Research Journal, 21*, 725–736.

*Smiernow, G. A., & Lawley, A. (1980). Decentralized sequence instruction (DSI) at Drexel. *Engineering Education, 70*, 423–426.

*Smith, J. E. (1976). A comparison of the traditional method and a personalized system of instruction in college mathematics. *Dissertation Abstracts International, 37*, 904. (University Microfilms No. AAD 76-18370)

^Smith, N. J. (1977). *The effects of training teachers to teach students at different reading ability levels to formulate three types of questions on reading comprehension and question generation ability.* Unpublished doctoral dissertation, University of Georgia.

!Soar, R. S. (1966). *An integrative approach to classroom learning* (Report for NIMH Projects No. 5-R11 MH 01096 and R-11 MH 02045). Philadelphia: Temple University. (ERIC Document Reproduction Service No. ED 033 749)

!Soar, R. S. (1968). Optimal teacher-pupil interaction for pupil growth. *Educational Leadership, 26*, 275–280.

!Soar, R. S. (1973). *Follow-Through classroom process measurement and pupil growth (1970–1971) final report.* Gainesville: College of Education, University of Florida.

!Soar, R. S. (1977). An integration of findings from four studies of teacher effectiveness. In G. Borich & K. Fenton (Eds.), *The appraisal of teaching: Concepts and process.* Reading, MA: Addison-Wesley.

!Soar, R. S., & Soar, R. M. (1972). An empirical analysis of selected Follow Through Programs: An appraisal of a process approach to evaluation. In G. Borich & K. Fenton (Eds.).*The appraisal of teaching: Concepts and process.* Reading, MA: Addison-Wesley.

!Soar, R. S., & Soar, R. M. (1973). *Classroom behavior, pupil characteristics, and pupil growth for the school year and the summer.* Gainesville: University of Florida, Institute for Development of Human Resources.

!Soar, R. S., & Soar, R. M. (1978). *Setting variables, classroom interaction, and multiple pupil outcomes* (Final Report, Project No. 6-0432, Grant No. NIE-G-76-0100). Washington, DC: National Institute of Education.

!Soar, R. S., & Soar, R. M. (1979). Emotional climate and management. In P. Peterson & H. Walberg (Eds.), *Research on teaching: Concepts, findings, and implications.* Berkeley, CA: McCutchan.

!Solomon, D., & Kendall, A. (1979). *Children in classrooms: An investigation person-environment interaction.* New York: Praeger.

*Spector, L. C. (1976). The effectiveness of personalized instruction system of instruction in economics. *Journal of Personalized Instruction, I*, 118–122.

*Spevack, H. M. (1976). A comparison of the personalized system of instruction with the lecture recitation system for nonscience oriented chemistry students at an open enrollment community college. *Dissertation Abstracts International, 36*, 4385A–4386A. (University Microfilms No. 76-01757)

<Stahl, S. A., & Kuhn, M. R. (1995). Does whole language or instruction matched to learning styles help children learn to read? *School Psychology Review, 24*, 393–404.

!Stallings, J. (1980). Allocated academic learning time revisited, or beyond time on task. *Educational Researcher, 8*(11), 11–16.

!%Stallings, J., Corey, R., Fairweather, J., & Needles, M. (1977). *Early Childhood Education classroom evaluation.* Menlo Park, CA: SRI International.

!%Stallings, J., Needles, M., & Staybrook, N. (1979). *The teaching of basic reading skills in secondary schools, Phase II and Phase III.* Menlo Park, CA: SRI International.

!%Stallings, J. A., & Kaskowitz, D. (1974). *Follow-Through Classroom Observation.* Menlo Park, CA: SRI International.

*Steele, W. F. (1974). *Mathematics 101 at Heileberg College—PSI vs. tradition.* Paper presented at the National Conference on Personalized Instruction in Higher Education, Washington, DC.

*Stout, L. J. (1978). A comparison of four different pacing strategies of personalized system of instruction and a traditional lecture format. *Dissertation Abstracts International, 38*, 6205. (University Microfilms No. AAD 78-08600)

*$Strasler, G. M. (1979, April). *The process of transfer and learning for mastery setting.* Paper presented at the annual meeting of the American Educational Research Association, San Francisco. (ERIC Document Reproduction Service No. ED 174 642)

*$&Swanson, D. H., & Denton, J. J. (1976). Learning for Mastery versus Personalized System of Instruction: A comparison of remediation strategies for secondary school chemistry students. *Journal of Research in Science Teaching, 14*, 515–524.

^Taylor, B. M., & Frye, B. J. (1992). Comprehension strategy instruction in the intermediate grades. *Reading Research and Instruction, 92*, 39–48.

*Taylor, V. (1977, April). *Individualized calculus for the "life-long" learner: A two semester comparison of attitudes and effectiveness.* Paper presented at the Fourth National Conference of the Center for Personalized Instruction, San Francisco.

$Tenenbaum, G. (1982). *A method of group instruction which is as effective as one-to-one tutorial instruction.* Unpublished doctoral dissertation, University of Chicago.

>Texas Center for Educational Research. (1997). *Reading programs for students in the lower elementary grades: What does the research say?* Austin, TX: TCER.

*&Thompson, S. B. (1980). Do individualized mastery and traditional instructional systems yield different course effects in college calculus? *American Educational Research Journal, 17*, 361–375.

*Tietenberg, T. H. (1975). Teaching intermediate microeconomics using the personalized system of instruction. In J. M. Johnston (Ed.), *Behavior research and technology in higher education* (pp. 75–89). Springfield, IL: Charles C. Thomas.

!Tobin, K., & Caple, W. (1982). Relationships between classroom process variables and middle-school science achievement. *Journal of Educational Psychology, 74*, 441–454.

*Toepher, C., Shaw, D., & Moniot, D. (1972). *The effect of item exposure in a contingency management system.* Paper presented at the annual meeting of the American Psychological Association, Honolulu, HI.

*Van Verth, J. E., & Dinan, F. J. (1974). A Keller Plan course in organic chemistry. In R. S. Ruskin & S. F. Bono (Eds.), *Personalized instruction in higher education* (pp. 162–168). Washington, DC: Center for Personalized Instruction.

*Vandenbroucke, A. C., Jr. (1974, April). *Evaluation of the use of a personalized system of instruction in general chemistry.* Paper presented at the National Conference on Personalized Instruction in Higher Education, Washington, DC.

<Vollmer, T. R., Ringdahl, J. E., Roane, H. S., & Marcus, B. (1997). Negative side effects of noncontingent reinforcement. *Journal of Applied Behavior Analysis, 30*, 161–164.

*Walsh, R. G., Sr. (1977). The Keller Plan in college introductory physical geology: A comparison with the conventional teaching method. *Dissertation Abstracts International, 37*, 4257. (University Microfilms No. AAD 76-30292)

<Weeks, M., & Gaylord-Ross, R. (1981). Task difficulty and aberrant behavior in severely handicapped students. *Journal of Applied Behavior Analysis, 14*, 19–36.

^Weiner, C. J. (1978, March). *The effect of training in questioning and student question-generation on reading achievement.* Paper presented at the annual meeting of the American Educational Research Association, Toronto. (ERIC Document Reproduction Service No. ED 158 223)

$&+=Wentling, T. L. (1973). Mastery versus nonmastery instruction with varying test item feedback treatments. *Journal of Educational Psychology, 65*, 50–58.

*White, M. E. (1974). Different equations by PSI. In R. S. Ruskin & S. F. Bono (Eds.), *Personalized instruction in higher education* (pp. 169–171). Washington, DC: Center for Personalized Instruction.

>White, W.A.T. (1988). A meta-analysis of the effects of Direct Instruction in special education. *Education and Treatment of Children, 11*(4), 364–374.

Willett, J., Yamashita, J., & Anderson, R. (1983). A meta-analysis of instructional systems applied in science teaching. *Journal of Research in Science Teaching, 20*(5), 405–417.

^Williamson, R. A. (1989). *The effect of reciprocal teaching on student performance gains in third grade basal reading instruction.* Unpublished doctoral dissertation, Texas A&M University.

$Wire, D. R. (1979). *Mastery learning program at Durham College: Report on progress toward the first year, September 1, 1978–August 31, 1979.* Durham, NC. (ERIC Document Reproduction Service No. ED 187 387)

<Witt, J. C., & Elliott, S. N. (1982). The response cost lottery: A time efficient and effective classroom intervention. *Journal of School Psychology, 20*, 155–161.

*Witters, D. R., & Kent, G. W. (1972). Teaching without lecturing—evidence in the case for individualized instruction. *The Psychological Record, 22*, 169–175.

<Wolery, M., Bailey, D. B., & Sugai, G. M. (1988). *Effective teaching: Principles and procedures of applied behavior analysis with exceptional students.* Boston: Allyn & Bacon.

^Wong, B.Y.L., & Jones, W. (1982). Increasing metacomprehension in learning disabled and normally achieving students through self-questioning training. *Learning Disability Quarterly, 5*, 228–239.

$Wortham, S. C. (1980). *Mastery learning in secondary schools: A first-year report.* San Antonio, TX. (ERIC Document Reproduction Service No. ED 194 453)

*=Yeany, R. H., Dost, R. J., & Matthew, R. W. (1980). The effects of diagnostic-prescriptive instruction and locus of control on the achievement and attitudes of university students. *Journal of Research in Science Teaching, 17*, 537–545.

$Yildren, G. (1977). *The effects of level of cognitive achievement on selected learning criteria under mastery learning and normal classroom instruction.* Unpublished doctoral dissertation, University of Chicago.

REFERENCES FOR PROVIDING CORRECTIVE INSTRUCTION

*+Abraham, F. J., & Newton, J. M. (1974). *The interview technique as a personalized system of instruction for economics: The Oregon experience*. Paper presented at the National Conference on Personalized Instruction in Higher Education, Washington, DC.

!Acland, H. (1976). Stability of teacher effectiveness: A replication. *Journal of Educational Research, 69*, 289–292.

\Ainsworth, S., Wood, D., & O'Malley, C. (1998). There is more than one way to solve a problem: Evaluating a learning environment that supports the development of children's multiplication skills. *Learning and Instruction, 8*, 141–157.

^Anane, F. (1987). The delay-retention phenomena: The effect of differential instructions on the learning and remembering of prose text material. *Dissertation Abstracts International, 48*, 2831A. (University Microfilms No. 871-28, 257).

$Anania, J. (1981). *The effects of quality instruction on the cognitive and affective learning of students*. Unpublished doctoral dissertation, University of Chicago.

!%Anderson, L. M., Evertson, C. M., & Brophy, J. E. (1979). An experimental study of effective teaching in first-grade reading groups. *The Elementary School Journal, 79*, 193–222.

!%Anderson, L. M., Evertson, C. M., & Brophy, J. E. (1982). *Principles of small group instruction* (Occasional paper no. 32). East Lansing: Michigan State University, Institute for Research on Teaching.

$&Anderson, L. W. (1975a). Student involvement in learning and school achievement. *California Journal of Education Research, 26*, 53–62.

&Anderson L. W. (1975b). *Time to criterion: An experimental study*. Paper presented at the annual meeting of the American Education Research Association, Washington, DC (ERIC Document Reproduction Service No. ED 108 006)

$&+Anderson L. W. (1976). An empirical investigation of individual differences in time to learn. *Journal of Educational Psychology, 68*, 226–233.

#@$&Anderson L. W., Scott, C., & Hutlock, N. (1976, April). *The effects of the mastery learning program on selected cognitive, affective, and ecological variables in grades 1 through 6*. Paper presented at the annual meeting of the American Education Research Association, San Francisco.

+Anderson, O. T., & Artman, R. A. (1972). A self-paced independent study, introductory physics sequence—description and evaluation. *American Journal of Physics, 40*, 1737–1742.

^Anderson, R., Kulhavy, R., & Andre, T. (1971). Feedback procedures in programmed instruction. *Journal of Educational Psychology, 62*, 148–156.

^Anderson, R., Kulhavy, R., & Andre, T. (1972). Conditions under which feedback facilitates learning from programmed lessons. *Journal of Educational Psychology, 63*, 186–188.

Anderson, S. A. (1994). *Synthesis of research on mastery learning* (Information Analysis). (ERIC Document Reproduction Service No. ED 382 567)

~Angell, G. W. (1949). The effect of immediate knowledge of quiz results on final examination scores in freshman chemistry. *Journal of Educational Research, 42*, 391–394.

!Arehart, J. (1979). Student opportunity to learn related to student achievement of objectives in a probability unit. *Journal of Educational Research, 72*, 253–269.

*$&%Arlin, M., & Webster, J. (1983). Time costs of mastery learning. *Journal of Educational Psychology, 75*, 187–195.

^Arnett, P. (1985). Effects of feedback placement and completeness within Gagne's model for computer assisted instruction lesson development on concept and rule learning. *Dissertation Abstracts International, 46,* 2537A. (University Microfilms No. 85-24, 309).

^Aumiller, L. (1963). The effects of knowledge of results on learning to spell new words by third and fifth grade pupils. *Dissertation Abstracts International, 24,* 5187. (University Microfilms No. 64-5336).

*Austin, S. M., & Gilbert, K. E. (1973). Student performance in a Keller-Plan course in introductory electricity and magnetism. *American Journal of Physics, 41,* 12–18.

*Badia, P., Stutts, C., & Harsh, J. (1978). Do methods of instruction and measures of different abilities and study habits interact? In J. G. Sherman, R. S. Ruskin, & R. M. Lazar (Eds.), *Personalized instruction and education today* (pp. 113–128). San Francisco: San Francisco Press.

!}Baker, J. D. (1992). Correcting the oral reading errors of a beginning reader. *Journal of Behavioral Education, 4,* 337–343.

Baker, S., Gersten, R., & Lee, D-S. (2002). A synthesis of empirical research on teaching mathematics to low-achieving students. *The Elementary School Journal, 103*(1), 51–92.

~Baller, W. W. (1970). Effects of temporal position of knowledge of results and difficulty level of material on acquisition and retention. *Dissertation Abstracts International, 30,* 3772A. (University Microfilms No. 70-02955).

Bangert-Drowns, R. L., Kulik, C-L. C., Kulik, J. A., & Morgan, M. T. (1991). The instructional effect of feedback in test-like events. *Review of Educational Research, 61*(2), 213–238.

}Barbetta, P. M., Heron, T. E., & Heward, W. L. (1993). Effects of active student response during error correction on the acquisition, maintenance, and generalization of sight words by students with developmental disabilities. *Journal of Applied Behavior Analysis, 26,* 111–119.

}Barbetta, P. M., Heward, W. L., & Bradley, D. M. (1993). Relative effects of whole-word and phonetic-prompt error correction on the acquisition and maintenance of sight words by students with developmental disabilities. *Journal of Applied Behavior Analysis, 26,* 99–110.

}Barbetta, P. M., Heward, W. L., Bradley, D. M., & Miller, A. D. (1994). Effects of immediate and delayed error correction on the acquisition and maintenance of sight words by students with developmental disabilities. *Journal of Applied Behavior Analysis, 27,* 177–178.

~Battig, W. F., & Brackett, H. R. (1961). Comparison of anticipation and recall methods in paired-associate learning. *Psychological Reports, 9,* 59–65.

~Becker, W. C. (1977). Teaching reading and language to the disadvantage—What we have learned from field research. *Harvard Educational Review, 47,* 518–543.

\Beirne-Smith, M. (1991). Peer tutoring in arithmetic for children with learning disabilities. *Exceptional Children, 57,* 330–337.

*Benson, J. S., & Yeany, R. H. (1980, April). *Generalizability of diagnostic-prescriptive teaching strategies across student locus of control of multiple instructional units.* Paper presented at the annual meeting of the American Educational Research Association, Boston. (ERIC Document Reproduction Service No. 187 534)

!Berliner, D., Fisher, C., Filby, N., & Marliave, R. (1978). *Executive summary of Beginning Teacher Evaluation Study.* San Francisco: Far West Laboratory.

*+Billings, D. B. (1974). PSI versus the lecture course in the principles of economics: A quasi-controlled experiment. In R. S. Ruskin & S. F. Bono (Eds.), *Personalized instruction in higher education* (pp. 30–37). Washington, DC: Center for Personalized Instruction.

*$Blackburn, K. T., & Nelson, D. (1985, April). *Differences between a group using a traditional format with mastery learning and a group using traditional format only in developmental mathematics courses at the university level: Implications for teacher education programs.* Paper presented at the annual meeting of the American Educational Research Association, Chicago. (ERIC Document Reproduction Service No. ED 258 948)

<Blaha, B. A. (1979). *The effects of answering self-generated questions on reading.* Unpublished doctoral dissertation, Boston University School of Education.

~Blaker, K. E. (1966). The effects of delayed knowledge of results on learning and retention for differing age levels of school age children. *Dissertation Abstracts International, 26,* 5858A. (University Microfilms No. 66-01067)

*Blasingame, J. W. (1975). Student attitude performance in a personalized system of instruction course in business administration—Correlates of performance with personality traits. *Dissertation Abstracts International, 36,* 3840. (University Microfilms No. 75-2834)

$&+Block, J. H. (1972). Student learning and the setting of mastery performance standards. *Educational Horizons, 50,* 183–191.

+Block, J. H. (1973). *Mastery performance standards and student learning.* Unpublished study, University of California, Santa Barbara.

Block, J. H. (1980). Success rate. In C. Denham & A. Lieberman (Eds.), *Time to learn* (pp. 95–106). Washington, DC: U.S. Government Printing Office.

Block, J. H., & Burns, R. B. (1976). Mastery Learning. In L. Schulman (Ed.), *Review of research in education* (Vol. 4, pp. 3–49). Itasca, IL: F. E. Peacock.

$+Block, J. H., & Tierney, M. (1974). An exploration of two correction procedures used in mastery learning approaches to instruction. *Journal of Educational Psychology, 66,* 962–967.

Bloom, B. S. (1985). Learning for mastery. In C. W. Fisher & D. C. Berliner (Eds.), *Perspectives on instructional time.* White Plains, NY: Longman.

~Boersma, F. J. (1966). Effects of delay of information feedback and length of postfeedback interval on linear programming. *Journal of Educational Psychology, 57,* 140–145.

*+Born, D. G., & Davis, M. L. (1974). Amount and distribution of study in a personalized instruction course and in a lecture course. *Journal of Applied Behavior Analysis, 7,* 365–375.

*+Born, D. G., Gledhill, S. M., & Davis, M. L. (1972). Examination performance in lecture-discussion and personalized instruction courses. *Journal of Applied Behavior Analysis, 5,* 33–43.

/Bos, C. S., & Anders, P. L. (1990). Effects of interactive vocabulary instruction on the vocabulary learning and reading comprehension of junior high learning-disabled students. *Learning Disability Quarterly, 13,* 31–42.

/Bos, C. S., & Anders, P. L. (1992). Using interactive teaching and learning strategies to promote text comprehension and content learning for students with learning disabilities. *International Journal of Disability, Development and Education, 39,* 225–238.

~Bourne, L. E., Jr. (1957). Effect of information feedback and task complexity on the identification of concepts. *Journal of Experimental Psychology, 54,* 201–207.

~Brackbill, Y., Bravos, A., & Starr, R. H. (1962). Delay improved retention on a difficult task. *Journal of Comparative and Physiological Psychology, 55*(6), 947–952.

~Brackbill, Y., Isaacs, R. B., & Smelkinson, N. (1962). Delay of reinforcement and the retention of unfamiliar, meaningless material. *Psychological Reports, 11*, 553–554.

~Brackbill, Y., & Kappy, M. S. (1962). Delay of reinforcement and retention. *Journal of Comparative and Physiological Psychology, 55*(1), 14–18.

<Brady, P. L. (1990). *Improving the reading comprehension of middle school students through reciprocal teaching and semantic mapping strategies.* Unpublished doctoral dissertation, University of Alaska.

*+Breland, N. S., & Smith, M. P. (1974). A comparison of PSI and traditional methods of instruction for teaching introduction to psychology. In R. S. Ruskin & S. F. Bono (Eds.), *Personalized instruction in higher education* (pp. 21–25). Washington, DC: Center for Personalized Instruction.

/Brigham, F. J., Scruggs, T. E., & Mastropieri, M. A. (1992). Teacher enthusiasm in learning disabilities classrooms: Effects on learning and behavior. *Learning Disabilities Research & Practice, 7*, 68–73.

!Brophy, J. (1973). Stability of teacher effectiveness. *American Educational Research Journal, 10*, 245–252.

!Brophy, J., & Evertson, C. (1974a). *Process-product correlations in a Texas Teacher Effectiveness Study: Final report* (Research Report 74-4). Austin: Research and Development Center for Teacher Education, University of Texas. (ERIC Document Reproduction Service No. ED 091 094)

!Brophy, J., & Evertson, C. (1974b). *The Texas Teacher Effectiveness Project: Presentation of non-linear relationships and summary discussion* (Research Report 74-6). Austin: Research and Development Center for Teacher Education, University of Texas. (ERIC Document Reproduction Service No. ED 099 345)

!%Brophy, J., & Evertson, C. (1976). *Learning from teaching: A developmental perspective.* Boston: Allyn and Bacon.

Brophy, J., & Good, T. (1986). Teacher behavior and student achievement. In M. C. Wittrock (Ed.), *Handbook of research on teaching* (3rd ed., pp. 328–375). New York: Macmillan.

^Brown, R. S. (1964). An experimental study of knowledge of results in complex human learning. *Dissertation Abstracts International, 24*, 2356. (University Microfilms No. 64-696).

/Brown, R. T., & Alford, N. (1984). Ameliorating attentional deficits and concomitant academic deficiencies in learning disabled children through cognitive training. *Journal of Learning Disabilities, 17*, 20–26.

?Bryant, D. P., Vaughn, S., Linan-Thompson, S., Ugel, N., Hamff, A., & Hougen, M. (2000). Reading outcomes for students with and without reading disabilities in general education middle-school content area classes. *Learning Disability Quarterly, 23*, 238–252.

*$Bryant, N. D., Fayne, H. R., & Gettinger, M. (1982). Applying the mastery model to sight word for disabled readers. *Journal of Experimental Education, 50*, 116–121.

/Bulgren, J., Schumaker, J. B., & Deshler, D. D. (1988). Effectiveness of a concept teaching routine in enhancing the performance of LD students in secondary-level mainstream classes. *Learning Disability Quarterly, 11*(1), 317.

$Burke, A. (1983). *Students' potential for learning contrasted under tutorial and group approaches to instruction.* Unpublished doctoral dissertation, University of Chicago.

$&+Burrows, C. K., & Okey, J. R. (1975, March–April). *The effects of a mastery learning strategy on achievement.* Paper presented at the annual meeting of the American Educational Research Association, Washington, DC.

*#@Cabezon, E. (1984). *The effects of marked changes in student achievement pattern on the students, their teachers, and their parents: The Chilean case.* Unpublished doctoral dissertation, University of Chicago.

^Carels, E. J. (1975). The effects of false feedback, sex, and personality on learning, retention, and the Zeigarnik effect in programmed instruction. *Dissertation Abstracts International, 36,* 2094A. (University Microfilms No. 75-22, 345)

}Carnine, D. (1980). Phonic vs. whole word correction procedures following phonic instruction. *Education and Treatment of Children, 3,* 323–330.

=Carnine, D., & Kinder, B. (1985). Teaching low-performing students to apply generative and schema strategies to narrative and expository material. *Remedial and Special Education, 6,* 20–30.

\Case, L. P., Harries, K. R., & Graham, S. (1992). Improving the mathematical problem-solving skills of students with learning disabilities: Self-regulated strategy development. *The Journal of Special Education, 26,* 1–19.

\Cassel, J., & Reid, R. (1996). Use of a self-regulated strategy intervention to improve word problem-solving skills of students with mild disabilities. *Journal of Behavioral Education, 6,* 153–172.

=Chan, L., & Cole, P. (1986). The effects of comprehension monitoring training on the reading competence of learning disabled and regular class students. *Remedial and Special Education, 7,* 33–40.

=Chan, L., Cole, P., & Barfett, S. (1987). Comprehension monitoring: Detection and identification of text inconsistencies by learning disabled and normal students. *Learning Disability Quarterly, 10,* 114–124.

/Chan, L.K.S. (1991). Promoting strategy generalization through self-instructional training in students with reading disabilities. *Journal of Learning Disabilities, 24,* 427–433.

/Chan, L.K.S., & Cole, P. G. (1986). The effects of comprehension-monitoring training on the reading competence of learning disabled and regular class students. *Remedial and Special Education, 7,* 33–40.

/Chan, L.K.S., Cole, P. G., & Morris, J. N. (1990). Effects of instruction in the use of a visual-imagery strategy on the reading-comprehension competence of disabled and average readers. *Learning Disability Quarterly, 13,* 2–11.

^Chanond, K. (1988, January). *The effects of feedback, correctness of response, and response confidence on learner's retention in computer-assisted instruction.* Paper presented at the annual meeting of the Association for Educational Communications and Technology, New Orleans. (ERIC Document Reproduction Service No. ED 295 632)

/Chase, C. H., Schmitt, R. L., Russell, G., & Tallal, P. (1984). A new chemotherapeutic investigation: Piracetam effects on dyslexia. *Annals of Dyslexia, 34,* 29–43.

$Chiappetta, E. L., & McBride, J. W. (1980). Exploring the effects of general remediation on ninth-graders' achievement of the mole concept. *Science Education, 64,* 609–614.

{Clairiana, R. B., & Smith, L. J. (1989). *Progress reports improve students' course completion rate and achievement in math computer-assisted instruction.* (ERIC Document Reproduction Service No. ED 317 170)

*$Clark, C. P., Guskey, T. P., & Benninga, J. S. (1983). The effectiveness of mastery learning strategies in undergraduate education courses. *Journal of Educational Research, 76,* 210–214.

*Clark, S. G. (1975). An innovation for introductory sociology: Personalized system of instruction. In J. M. Johnston (Ed.), *Behavior research and technology in higher education* (pp. 117–124). Springfield, IL: Charles C. Thomas.

^~Clodfelder, D. L. (1968). The quiz, knowledge of results, and individual differences in achievement orientation. *Dissertation Abstracts International, 29*, 2217. (University Microfilms No. 68-17181)

~Cofer, C. N., Diamond, F., Olsen, R. A., Stein, J. S., & Walker, H. (1967). Comparison of anticipation and recall methods in paired-associate learning. *Journal of Experimental Psychology, 75*, 545–558.

<Cohen, R. (1983). Students generate questions as an aid to reading comprehension. *Reading Teacher, 36*, 770–775.

!Coker, H., Medley, D., & Soar, R. (1980). How valid are expert opinions about effective teaching? *Phi Delta Kappan, 62*, 131–134, 149.

*+Coldeway, D. O., Santowski, M., O'Brien, R., & Lagowski, V. (1975). Comparison of small group contingency management with the personalized system of instruction and the lecture system. In J. M. Johnston (Ed.), *Research and technology in college and university teaching* (pp. 215–224). Gainesville: University of Florida.

*+Cole, C., Martin, S., & Vincent, J. (1975). A comparison of two teaching formats at the college level. In J. M. Johnston (Ed.), *Behavior research and technology in higher education* (pp. 61–74). Springfield, IL: Charles C. Thomas.

/Collins, M., & Carnine, D. (1988). Evaluating the field test revision process by comparing two versions of a reasoning skills CAI program. *Journal of Learning Disabilities, 21*, 375–379.

*Condo, P. (1974, April). *The analysis and evaluation of a self-paced course in calculus.* Paper presented at the National Conference on Personalized Instruction in Higher Education, Washington, DC.

*+Cooper, J. L., & Greiner, J. M. (1971). Contingency management in an introductory psychology course produces better retention. *Psychological Record, 21*, 391–400.

*Corey, J. R., & McMichael, J. S. (1974). Retention in a PSI introductory psychology course. In J. G. Sherman (Ed.), *PSI germinal papers* (pp. 17–19). Washington, DC: Center for Personalized Instruction.

+Corey, J. R., McMichael, J. S., & Tremont, P. J. (1970, April). *Long-term effects of personalized instruction in an introductory psychology course.* Paper presented at the meeting of the Eastern Psychology Association, Atlantic City.

*Cote, J. D. (1976). Biology by PSI in a community college. In B. A. Green, Jr. (Ed.), *Personalized instruction in higher education.* Washington, DC: Center for Personalized Instruction.

!Crawford, J. (1983). A study of instructional processes in Title I classes: 1981–82. *Journal of Research and Evaluation of the Oklahoma City Public Schools, 13*(1).

*Cross, M. Z., & Semb, G. (1976). An analysis of the effects of personalized instruction on students at different initial performance levels in an introductory college nutrition course. *Journal of Personalized Instruction, 1*, 47–50.

/Darch, C., & Eaves, R. C. (1986). Visual displays to increase comprehension of high school learning-disabled students. *Journal of Special Education, 20*, 309–318.

/Darch, C., & Gersten, R. (1986). Direction-setting activities in reading comprehension: A comparison of two approaches. *Learning Disability Quarterly, 9*, 235–243.

<Davey, B., & McBride, S. (1986). Effects of question-generation on reading comprehension. *Journal of Educational Psychology, 78*, 256–262.

>/De La Paz, S. (1995). *An analysis of the effects of dictation and planning instruction on the writing of students with learning disabilities.* Unpublished doctoral dissertation, University of Maryland, College Park.

*Decker, D. F. (1976) *Teaching to achieve learning mastery by using retesting techniques.* Doctoral dissertation, Nova University. (ERIC Document Reproduction Service No. ED133 002)

$Denton, W. L., Ory, J. C., Glassnap, D. R., & Poggio, J. P. (1976). *Grade expectations within a mastery learning strategy.* Paper presented at the annual meeting of the American Educational Research Association, San Francisco. (ERIC Document Reproduction Service No. ED 126 105)

<Dermody, M. (1988, February). *Metacognitive strategies for development of reading comprehension for younger children.* Paper presented at the annual meeting of the American Association of Colleges for Teacher Education. New Orleans, LA.

*$Dillashaw, F. G., & Okey, J. R. (1983). Effects of a modified mastery learning strategy on achievement, attitudes, and on-task behavior of high school chemistry students. *Journal of Research and Science Teaching, 20*, 203–211.

/Dixon, M. E. (1984). *Questioning strategy instruction participation and reading comprehension of learning disabled students.* Doctoral dissertation, University of Arizona, 1983. *Dissertation Abstracts International, 44*(11-A), 3349.

?Downhower, S. L. (1987). Effects of repeated reading on second-grade transitional readers' fluency and comprehension. *Reading Research Quarterly, 22*, 389–406 (see Note 9).

<Dreher, M. J., & Gambrell, L.B. (1985). Teaching children to use a self-questioning strategy for studying expository text. *Reading Improvement, 22*, 2–7.

$Duby, P. B. (1981). *Attributions and attribution change: Effects of the mastery learning instructional approach.* Paper presented at the annual meeting of the American Educational Research Association, Los Angeles. (ERIC Document Reproduction Service No. ED 200 640)

!Dunkin, M. J. (1978). Student characteristics, classroom processes, and student achievement. *Journal of Educational Psychology, 70*, 998–1009.

\Dunlap, L. K., & Dunlap, G. (1989). A self-monitoring package for teaching substraction with regrouping to students with learning disabilities. *Journal of Applied Behavior Analysis, 22*, 309–314.

!Ebmier, H., & Good, T. (1979). The effects of instructing teachers about good teaching on mathematics achievement of fourth-grade students. *American Educational Research Journal, 16*, 1–16.

^Elliot, B. A. (1986). An investigation of the effects of computer feedback and interspersed questions on the text comprehension of poor readers. *Dissertation Abstracts International, 47*, 2971A. (University Microfilms No. 86-27, 446).

!Emmer, E., Evertson, C., & Anderson, L. (1980). Effective classroom management at the beginning of the school year. *Elementary School Journal, 80*, 219–231.

!Emmer, E., Evertson, C., & Brophy, J. (1979). Stability of teacher effects in junior high school classrooms. *American Educational Research Journal, 16*, 71–75.

!%Emmer, E. T., Evertson, C., Sanford, J., & Clements, B. (1982). *Improving instruction management: An experimental study in junior high classrooms.* Austin: Research and Development Center for Teacher Education, University of Texas.

>Englert, C. S., Garmon, A., Mariage, T., Rozendal, M., Tarrant, K., & Urba, J. (1995). The early literacy project: Connecting across the literacy curriculum. *Learning Disability Quarterly, 18*, 253–275.

\>Englert, C. S., Raphael, T. E., Anderson, L. M., Anthony, H. M., & Stevens, D. D. (1991). Making writing strategies and self-talk visible: Cognitive strategy instruction in regular and special education classrooms. *American Educational Research Journal, 28,* 337–372.

~English, R. A., & Kinzer, J. R. (1966). The effect of immediate and delayed feedback on retention of subject matter. *Psychology in the Schools, 3,* 143–147.

}Espin, C. A., & Deno, S. L. (1989). The effects of modeling and prompting feedback strategies on sight word reading of students labeled learning disabled. *Education and Treatment of Children, 12,* 219–231.

%Evertson, C. (1982). Differences in instructional activities in higher and lower achieving junior high English and mathematics classrooms. *Elementary School Journal, 82,* 329–351.

!%Evertson, C., Anderson, C., Anderson, L., & Brophy, J. (1980). Relationships between classroom behaviors and student outcomes in junior high mathematics and English classes. *American Educational Research Journal, 17,* 43–60.

!Evertson, C., Anderson, L., & Brophy, J. (1978). *Texas Junior High School Study—Final report of process-outcome relationship* (Report No. 4061). Austin: Research and Development Center for Teacher Education, University of Texas.

!Evertson, C., & Brophy, J. (1973). High-inference behavioral ratings as correlates of teacher effectiveness. *JSAS Catalog of Selected Documents in Psychology, 3,* 97.

!Evertson, C., & Brophy, J. (1974). *Texas Teacher Effectiveness Project: Questionnaire and interview data* (Research Report No. 74-5). Austin: Research and Development Center for Teacher Education, University of Texas.

!%Evertson, C., Emmer, E., & Brophy, J., (1980). Predictors of effective teaching in junior high mathematics classrooms. *Journal for Research in Mathematics Education, 11,* 167–178.

%Evertson, C. M., Emmer, E. T., Sanford, J. P., & Clements, B. S. (1983). Improving classroom management: An experiment in elementary classrooms. *Elementary School Journal, 84,* 173–188.

*#@Fagan, J. S. (1976). Mastery learning: The relationship of mastery procedures and aptitude to the achievement and retention of transportation-environment concepts by seventh-grade students. *Dissertation Abstracts International, 36,* 5981. (University Microfilms No. 76-6402)

\Fantuzzo, J. W., Davis, G. Y., & Ginsburg, M. D. (1995). Effects of parent involvement in isolation or in combination with peer tutoring on student self-concept and mathematical achievement. *Journal of Educational Psychology, 87,* 272–281.

\Fantuzzo, J. W., King, J. A., & Heller, L. R. (1992). Effects of reciprocal peer tutoring on mathematics and school adjustment: A component analysis. *Journal of Educational Psychology, 84,* 331–339.

/Farmer, M. E., Klein, R., & Bryson, S. E. (1992). Computer-assisted reading: Effects of whole word feedback on fluency and comprehension in readers with severe disabilities. *Remedial and Special Education, 13,* 50–60.

^Farragher, P., & Szabo, M. (1986). Learning environmental science from text aided by a diagnostic and prescriptive instructional strategy. *Journal of Research in Science Teaching, 23,* 557–569.

?Faulkner, H. J., & Levy, B. A. (1999). Fluent and nonfluent forms of transfer in reading: Words and their message. *Psychonomic Bulletin and Review, 6,* 111–116.

*Fehlen, J. E. (1976). Mastery learning techniques in a traditional classroom setting. *School Science and Mathematics, 76*, 241–245.

^Feldhusen, J., & Birt, A. (1962). A study of nine methods of presentation of programmed learning material. *The Journal of Educational Research, 5*, 461–466.

*Fernald, P. S., & DuNann, D. H. (1975). Effects of individualized instruction upon low- and high-achieving students' study behavior in students' evaluation of mastery. *Journal of Experimental Education, 43*, 27–34.

/Fiedorowicz, C.A.M. (1986). Training of component reading skills. *Annals of Dyslexia, 36*, 318–334.

/Fiedorowicz, C.A.M., & Trites, R. L. (1987). *An evaluation of the effectiveness of computer-assisted component reading subskills training.* Toronto: Queen's Printer.

$&+Fiel, R. L., & Okey, J. R. (1974). The effects of formative evaluation and remediation on mastery of intellectual skill. *Journal of Educational Research, 68*, 253–255.

!%Fisher, C. W., Berliner, D. C., Filby, N. N., Marliave, R., Cahen, L. S., & Dishaw, M. M. (1980). Teaching behaviors, academic learning time, and student achievement: An overview. In C. Denham & A. Lieberman (Eds.), *Time to learn* (pp. 7–32). Washington, DC: U.S.Government Printing Office.

!%Fitzpatrick, K. A. (1981). *An investigation of secondary classroom material strategies for increasing student academic engaged time.* Doctoral dissertation, University of Illinois at Urbana–Champaign.

!%Fitzpatrick, K. A. (1982). *The effect of a secondary classroom management training program on teacher and student behavior.* Paper presented at the annual meeting of the American Educational Research Association, New York.

$&Fitzpatrick, K. A. (1985, April). *Group-based mastery learning: A Robin Hood approach to instruction?* Paper presented at the annual meeting of the American Educational Research Association, Chicago.

}Fleisher, L. S., & Jenkins, J. R. (1983). The effect of word- and comprehension-emphasis instruction on reading performance. *Learning Disability Quarterly, 6*, 146–154.

>Fortner, V. L. (1986). Generalization of creative productive-thinking training to LD students' written expression. *Learning Disability Quarterly, 9*(4), 274–284.

/Foster, K. (1983). *The influence of computer-assisted instruction and workbook on the learning of multiplication facts by learning disabled and normal students.* Doctoral dissertation, Florida State University. *Dissertation Abstracts International, 42*(9-A), 3953.

~Frederick, F. J. (1965). Effects of delay of knowledge of results and past knowledge of results delay on observational paired-associate learning. *Dissertation Abstracts International, 26*, 5911. (University Microfilms No. 65-14038)

=Fuchs, D., Fuchs, L, Mathes, P., & Simmons, D. (1997). Peer-assisted learning strategies: Making classrooms more responsive to diversity. *American Educational Research Journal, 34*, 174–206.

=Fuchs, L., & Fuchs, D. (1994). Academic assessment and instrumentation. In S. Vaughn & C. Bos (Eds.), *Research issues in learning disabilities: Theory, methodology, assessment, and ethics* (pp. 233–245). New York: Springer-Verlag.

{Fuchs, L. S., Fuchs, D., Hamlett, C. L., Phillips, N. B., & Bentz, J. (1994). Classwide curriculum-based measurement: Helping general educators meet the challenge of student diversity. *Exceptional Children, 60*, 518–537.

{\Fuchs, L. S., Fuchs, D., Karns, K., Hamlett, C. L., Katzaroff, M., & Dutka, S. (1997).

Effects of task-focused goals on low-achieving students with and without learning disabilities. *American Educational Research Journal, 34,* 513–543.

/Gajria, M., & Salvia, J. (1992). The effects of summarization instruction on text comprehension of students with learning disabilities. *Exceptional Children, 58,* 508–516.

Gersten, R., & Baker, S. (2001). Teaching expressive writing to students with learning disabilities: A meta-analysis. *The Elementary School Journal, 101*(3), 251–273.

Gersten, R., Fuchs, L. S., Williams, J. P., & Baker, S. (2001). Teaching reading comprehension strategies to students with learning disabilities: A review of research. *Review of Educational Research, 71*(2), 279–320.

^Gherfal, I. R. (1982). The application of principles of reinforcement to the teaching of English as a second language in a developing country: an experiment with Libyan male preparatory school students from culturally diverse rural and urban communities. *Dissertation Abstracts International, 43,* 147A. (University Microfilms No. 82-13, 750)

\Ginsburg-Block, M., & Fantuzzo, J. (1997). Reciprocal peer tutoring: An analysis of "teacher" and "student" interaction as a function of training and experience. *School Psychology Quarterly, 12,* 134–149.

\Ginsburg-Block, M., & Fantuzzo, J. (1998). An evaluation of the relative effectiveness of NCTM standards-based interventions for low-achieving urban elementary students. *Journal of Educational Psychology, 90,* 560–569.

+Glassnap, D. R., Poggio, J. P., & Ory, J. C. (1975, March–April). *Cognitive and affective consequences of mastery and non-mastery instructional strategies.* Paper presented at the annual meeting of the American Educational Research Association, Washington, DC.

*Goldwater, B. C., & Acker, L. E. (1975). Instructor-paced, mass-testing for mastery performance in an introductory psychology course. *Teaching of Psychology, 2,* 152–155.

*Good, T., Ebmeier, H., & Beckerman, T. (1978). Teaching mathematics in high and low SES classrooms: An empirical comparison. *Journal of Teacher Education, 29,* 85–90.

*Good, T., Grouws, D., & Beckerman, T. (1978). Curriculum pacing: Some empirical data in mathematics. *Journal of Curriculum Studies, 10,* 75–81.

!%Good, T., Grouws, D., & Ebmeier, M. (1983). *Active mathematics teaching.* New York: Longman.

!%Good, T. L., & Grouws, D. A. (1977). Teaching effects: A process-product study in fourth-grade mathematics classrooms. *Journal of Teacher Education, 28*(3), 49–54.

!Good, T. L., & Grouws, D. A. (1979a). *Experimental Study of Mathematics Instruction in Elementary Schools* (Final Report, National Institute of Education Grant No. NIE-G-79-0103). Columbia: University of Missouri, Center for the Study of Social Behavior.

!%Good, T. L., & Grouws, D. A. (1979b). The Missouri mathematics effectiveness project. *Journal of Educational Psychology, 71,* 355–362.

!Good, T. L., & Grouws, D. A. (1981). *Experimental research in secondary mathematics* (Final Report, National Institute of Education Grant No. NIE-G-79-0103). Columbia: University of Missouri, Center for the Study of Social Behavior.

/Graham, S., & Harris, K. R. (1989). Components analysis of cognitive strategy instruction: Effects on learning disabled students' compositions and self-efficacy. *Journal of Educational Psychology, 81,* 353–361.

/Graves, A. W. (1986). Effects of direct instruction and metacomprehension training on finding main ideas. *Learning Disabilities Research, 1,* 90–100.

\Greene, G. (1999). Mnemonic multiplication fact instruction for students with learning disabilities. *Learning Disabilities Research & Practice, 10,* 180–195.

*Gregory, I., Smeltzer, D. J., Knopp, W., & Gardner, M. (1976). *Teaching of psychiatry by PSI: Impact on National Board Examination scores.* Unpublished manuscript, Ohio State University, Columbus.

/Griffin, C. C., Simmons, D. C., & Kameenui, E. J. (1991). Investigating the effectiveness of graphic organizer instruction on the comprehension and recall of science content by students with learning disabilities. *Reading, Writing and Learning Disabilities, 7,* 355–376.

=Gurney, D., Gersten, R., Dimino, J., & Carnine, D. (1990). Story grammar: Effective literature instruction for high school students with learning disabilities. *Journal of Learning Disabilities, 23,* 335–348.

*$&Guskey, T. R. (1982). The effects of staff development on teachers' perceptions about effective teaching. *Journal of Educational Research, 76,* 378–381.

*$&Guskey, T. R. (1984). The influence of changes in instructional effectiveness upon the affective characteristics of teachers. *American Educational Research Journal, 21,* 245–259.

$Guskey, T. R. (1985). The effects of staff development on teachers' perceptions about effective teaching. *Journal of Educational Research, 79,* 378–381.

*$Guskey, T. R., Benninga, J. S., & Clark, C. B. (1984). Mastery learning and students' attributions at the college level. *Research and Higher Education, 20,* 491–498.

Guskey, T. R., & Gates, S. L. (1986). Synthesis of research on the effects of mastery learning in elementary and secondary classrooms. *Educational Leadership, 43*(8), 73–80.

*$Guskey, T. R., & Monsaas, J. A. (1979). Mastery learning: A model for academic success in urban junior colleges. *Research and Higher Education, 11,* 263–274.

Guskey, T. R., & Pigott, T. D. (1988). Research on group-based mastery learning programs: A meta-analysis. *Journal of Educational Research, 81*(4), 197–216.

/Guyer, B. P., & Sabatino, D. (1989). The effectiveness of a multisensory alphabetic phonetic approach with college students who are learning disabled. *Journal of Learning Disabilities, 22,* 430–434.

*Hardin, L. D. (1977). A study of the influence of a physics personalized system of instruction versus lecture on cognitive reason, achievement, attitudes and critical thinking. *Dissertation Abstracts International, 38,* 4711A–4712A. (University Microfilms No. 77-30826)

\Harris, C. A., Miller, S. P., & Mercer, C. D. (1995). Teaching initial multiplication skills to students with disabilities in general education classrooms. *Learning Disabilities Research & Practice, 10,* 180–195.

\Hasselbring, T. S., & Moore, P. R. (1996). Developing mathematical literacy through the use of contextualized learning environments. *Journal of Computing in Childhood Education, 7,* 199–222.

^Heald, H. (1970). The effects of immediate knowledge of results and correction of errors and test anxiety upon test performance. *Dissertation Abstracts International, 31,* 1621A. (University Microfilms No. 70-17, 724).

*Hecht, L. W. (1980, April). *Stalking mastery learning in its natural habitat.* Paper presented at the annual meeting of the American Educational Research Association, Boston.

*Heffley, P. D. (1974). The implementation of the personalized system of instruction in the freshman chemistry course at Censius College. In R. S. Ruskin & S. F. Bono (Eds.), *Personalized instruction in higher education* (pp. 140–145). Washington, DC: Center for Personalized Instruction.

<Helfeldt, J. P., & Lalik, R. (1976). Reciprocal student-teacher questioning. *Reading Teacher, 33*, 283–287.

\Heller, L. R., & Fatuzzo, J. W. (1993). Reciprocal peer tutoring and parent partnership: Does parent involvement make a difference? *School Psychology Review, 22*, 517–534.

?Herman, P. A. (1985). The effects of repeated readings on reading rate, speech pauses, and word recognition accuracy. *Reading Research Quarterly, 20*, 553–565.

*Herring, B. G. (1975, December). *Cataloguing and classification*. Austin: University of Texas.

*Herring, B. G. (1977). *The written PSI study guide in a non-PSI course*. Austin: University of Texas.

*Herrmann, T. (1984, August). *TELIDON as an enhancer of student interest and performance*. Paper presented at the annual meeting of the American Psychological Association, Toronto. (ERIC Document Reproduction Service No. ED 251 004)

Heubusch, J. D., & Lloyd, J. W. (1998). Corrective feedback in oral reading. *Journal of Behavioral Education, 8*(1), 63–79.

*Hindman, C. D. (1974). Evaluation of three programming techniques in introductory psychology courses. In R. S. Ruskin & S. F. Bono (Eds.), *Personalized instruction in higher education* (pp. 38–42). Washington, DC: Center for Personalized Instruction.

^Hirsch, R. S. (1952). *The effects of knowledge of test results on learning meaningful material*. University Park: Pennsylvania State University. (ERIC Document Reproduction Service No. ED 002 435)

\Ho, C. S., & Cheng, F. S. (1997). Training in place-value concepts improves children's addition skills. *Contemporary Educational Psychology, 22*, 495–506.

^Hoffman, B. S. (1974). An examination of knowledge of results and step size in programmed instruction at high and low cognitive levels of objectives. *Dissertation Abstracts International, 35*, 6006A. (University Microfilms No. 75-01, 707)

/Hollingsworth, M., & Woodward, J. (1993). Integrated learning: Explicit strategies and their role in problem-solving instruction for students with learning disabilities. *Exceptional Children, 59*, 444–455.

?Homan, S. P., Klesius, J. P., & Hite, C. (1993). Effects of repeated readings and nonrepetitive strategies on students' fluency and comprehension. *Journal of Educational Research, 87*, 94–99.

*Honeycutt, J. K. (1974, April). *The effect of computer managed instruction on content learning of undergraduate students*. Paper presented at the annual meeting of the American Educational Research Association, Chicago. (ERIC Document Reproduction Service No. ED 089 682)

^Hough, J., & Revsin, B. (1963). Programmed instruction at the college level: A study of several factors influencing learning. *Phi Delta Kappan, 44*, 286–291.

!Hughes, D. (1973). An experimental investigation of the effect of pupil responding and teacher reacting on pupil achievement. *American Educational Research Journal, 10*, 21–37.

/Hutchinson, N. L. (1993). Effects of cognitive strategy instruction on algebra problem solving of adolescents with learning disabilities. *Learning Disability Quarterly, 16*, 6–18.

/Hutchinson, N. L., Freeman, J. G., Downey, K. H., & Kilbreath, L. (1992). Development and evaluation of an instructional module to promote career maturity for youth with learning disabilities. *Canadian Journal of Counseling, 26*, 290–299.

^Hyman, C., & Tobias, S. (1981, October). *Feedback and prior achievement.* Paper presented at the annual meeting of the Northeastern Educational Research Association, Ellenville, NY. (ERIC Document Reproduction Service No. 206 ED 206 739)

^Hymel, G., & Mathews, G. (1980, April). *A mastery approach to teaching U.S. history: The impact on cognitive achievement and unit evaluation.* Paper presented at the annual meeting of the American Educational Research Association, Boston. (ERIC Document Reproduction Service No. ED 184 929)

*Hymel, G. M. (1974). *An investigation of John B. Carrol's model of school learning as a theoretical basis for the organizational structuring of schools* (Final Report, NIE Project No. 3-1359). University of New Orleans, New Orleans, LA.

*Hymel, G. M., & Matthews, G. (1980). Effects of a mastery approach on social studies achievement and unit evaluation. *Southern Journal of Educational Research, 14*, 191–204.

=Idol, L. (1987). Group story mapping: A comprehension strategy for both skilled and unskilled reading. *Journal of Learning Disabilities, 20*, 196–205.

=Idol, L., & Croll, V. (1987). Story-mapping training as a means of improving reading comprehension. *Learning Disability Quarterly, 10*, 214–229.

>Jaben, T. H. (1983). The effects of creativity training on learning disabled students' creative written expression. *Journal of Learning Disabilities, 16*(5), 264–265.

>Jaben, T. H. (1987). Effects of training on learning disabled students' creative written expression. *Psychological Reports, 60*, 23–26.

*Jackman, L. E. (1982). Evaluation of a modified Keller method in a biochemistry laboratory course. *Journal of Chemical Education, 59*, 225–227.

*Jacko, E. J. (1974). Lecture instruction versus a personalized system of instruction: Effects on individuals with differing achievement anxiety and academic achievement. *Dissertation Abstracts International, 35*, 3521. (University Microfilms No. AAD 74-27211)

^Jacobs, P., & Kulkarni, S. (1966). A test of some assumptions underlying programmed instruction. *Psychological Reports, 18*, 103–110.

\Jaspers, M., & Van Lieshout, E. (1994). A CAI program for instructing text analysis and modeling of word problems to educable mentally retarded children. *Instructional Science, 22*, 115–136.

}Jenkins, J. R., & Larson, K. (1979). Evaluating error-correction procedures for oral reading. *Journal of Special Education, 13*, 145–146.

}Jenkins, J. R., Larson, K., & Fleisher, L. (1983). Effects of error correction on word recognition and reading comprehension. *Learning Disability Quarterly, 6*, 139–145.

\Jitendra, A., Griffin, C., McGoey, K., Gardill, M., Bhat, P., & Riley, T. (1998). Effects of mathematical word problem solving by students at risk or with mild disabilities. *Journal of Education Research, 91*, 345–355.

\Jitendra, A., & Hoff, K. (1996). The effects of schema-based instruction on the mathematical word-problem-solving performance of students with learning disabilities. *Journal of Learning Disabilities, 29*, 422–431.

+/Johnson, L., Graham, S., & Harris, K.R. (in press). *The effects of goal setting and self-instructions on learning a reading comprehension strategy: A study with students with learning disabilities.* Unpublished manuscript.

+Johnston, J. M., & Pennypacker, H. S. (1971). A behavioral approach to college teaching. *American Psychologist, 26*, 219–244.

*#@$&Jones, B. F., Monsaas, J. A., & Katims, M. (1979, April). *Improving reading comprehension: Embedding diverse learning strategies within a mastery learning instructional framework.* Paper presented at the annual meeting of the American Educational Research Association, San Francisco. (ERIC Document Reproduction Service No. ED 170 698)

$+Jones, E. L., Gordon, H. A., & Stectman, G. L. (1975). *Mastery learning: A strategy for academic success in a community college.* Los Angeles: ERIC Clearinghouse for Junior Colleges. (ERIC Document Reproduction Service No. 115 315)

+Jones, F. G. (1974). *The effects of mastery and aptitude on learning, retention, and time.* Unpublished doctoral dissertation, University of Georgia.

/Jones, K. M., Torgesen, J. K., & Sexton, M. A. (1987). Using computer-guided practice to increase decoding fluency in learning disabled children: A study using the Hint and Hunt I program. *Journal of Learning Disabilities, 20*, 122–128.

~Jones, R. E., & Bourne, L. Z., Jr. (1964). Delay of informative feedback in verbal learning. *Canadian Journal of Psychology, 18*, 266–280.

/Kane, B. J., & Alley, G. R. (1980). A peer-tutored, instructional management program in computational mathematics for incarcerated learning-disabled juvenile delinquents. *Journal of Learning Disabilities, 13*, 148–151.

+Karlin, B. M. (1972). *The Keller method of instruction compared to the traditional method of instruction in a Lafayette College history course.* Unpublished paper, Lafayette College, Lafayette, PA.

^Karraker, R. (1967). Knowledge of results and incorrect recall of plausible multiple-choice alternatives. *Journal of Educational Psychology, 58*, 11–14.

*#@Katims, M., Smith, J. K., Steele, C., & Wick, J. W. (1977, April). *The Chicago mastery learning reading program: An interim evaluation.* Paper presented at the annual meeting of the American Educational Research Association, New York. (ERIC Document Reproduction Service No. ED 137 737)

/Kennedy, K. M., & Backman, J. (1993). Effectiveness of the Lindamood Auditory Discrimination In-Depth Program with students with learning disabilities. *Learning Disabilities Research & Practice, 8*, 253–259.

\Keogh, D., Whitman, T., & Maxwell, S. (1988). Self-instruction versus external instruction: individual differences and training effectiveness. *Cognitive Therapy and Research, 12*, 591–610.

*#@Kersh, M. E. (1970). *A strategy of mastery learning in fifth grade arithmetic.* Unpublished doctoral dissertation, University of Chicago.

/Kershner, J. R., Cummings, R. L., Clarke, K. A., Hadfield, A. J., & Kershner, B. A. (1990). Two-year evaluation of the Tomatis Listening Training Program with learning disabled children. *Learning Disability Quarterly, 13*, 43–53.

+Kim, Y., Cho, G., Park, J., & Park, M. (1974). *An application of a new instructional model* (Research Report No. 8). Seoul, Korea: Korean Educational Development Institute.

<King, A. (1989). Effects of self-questioning training on college students' comprehension of lectures. *Contemporary Educational Psychology, 14*, 366–381.

<King, A. (1990). Improving Lecture Comprehension: Effects of a metacognitive strategy. *Applied Educational Psychology, 5*, 331–346.

<King, A. (1992). Comparison of self-questioning, summarizing, and notetaking-review as

strategies for learning from lectures. *American Educational Research Journal, 29,* 303–325.

/Klingner, J. K., & Vaughn, S. (1996). Reciprocal teaching of reading comprehension strategies for students with learning disabilities who use English as a second language. *Elementary School Journal, 96,* 275–293.

\Knapczyk, D. (1989). Generalization of student question asking from special class to regular class settings. *Journal of Applied Behavior Analysis, 22,* 77–83.

*Knight, J. M., Williams J. D., & Jardon, M. L. (1975). The effects of contingency avoidance on programmed student achievement. *Research in Higher Education, 3,* 11–17.

\Koscinski, S., & Gast, D. (1993). Computer-assisted instruction with constant time delay to teach multiplication facts to students with learning disabilities. *Learning Disabilities Research & Practice, 8,* 157–168.

*Kounin, J. (1970). *Discipline and group management in classrooms.* New York: Holt, Rinehart, & Winston.

Kroesbergen, E. H., & Van Luit, J.E.H. (2003). Mathematics interventions for children with special educational needs: A meta-analysis. *Remedial and Special Education, 24*(2), 97–114.

^Krumboltz, J., & Weisman, R. (1962). The effect of intermittent confirmation in programmed instruction. *Journal of Educational Psychology, 53,* 250–253.

^Kulhavy, R., Yekovich, F., & Dyer, J. (1976). Feedback and response confidence. *Journal of Educational Psychology, 68,* 522–528.

~Kulhavy, R. W., & Anderson, R. C. (1972). Delay-retention effect with multiple-choice tests. *Journal of Educational Psychology, 63,* 505–512.

*Kulik, C., & Kulik, J. (1976). PSI and the mastery model. In B. A. Green, Jr. (Ed.), *Personalized instruction in higher education* (pp. 155–159). Washington, DC: Center for Personalized Instruction.

Kulik, C., Kulik, J., & Bangert-Drowns, R. (1990a). Effectiveness of mastery learning programs: A meta-analysis. *Review of Educational Research, 60*(2), 265–269.

Kulik, J., Kulik, C., & Bangert-Drowns, R. (1990b). Is there better evidence on mastery learning? A response to Slavin. *Review of Educational Research, 60*(2), 303–307.

Kulik, J. A., & Kulik, C. C. (1988). Timing of feedback and verbal learning. *Review of Educational Research, 58*(1), 79–97.

*Kulik, J. A., Kulik, C., & Carmichael, K. (1974). The Keller Plan in science teaching. *Science, 183,* 379–383.

<Labercane, G., & Battle, J. (1987). Cognitive processing strategies, self-esteem, and reading comprehension of learning disabled students. *Journal of Special Education, 11,* 167–185.

~Landsman, H. J., & Turkewitz, M. (1962). Delay of knowledge of results and performance on a cognitive task. *Psychological Reports, 11,* 66.

!Larrivee, B., & Algina, J. (1983, April). *Identification of teaching behaviors which predict success from mainstream students.* Paper presented at the annual meeting of the American Educational Research Association. Montreal. (ERIC Document Reproduction Service No. ED 232 362)

+Lee, Y. D., Kim, C. S., Kim, H., Park B. Y., Yoo, H. K., Chang, S. M., & Kim, S. C. (1971). *Interaction improvement studies of the Mastery Learning Project* (Final Report on the Mastery Learning Project, April–November 1971). Seoul, Korea: Educational Research Center, Seoul National University.

~Leeds, R. D. (1970). The effects of immediate and delayed knowledge of results on immediate and delayed retention. *Dissertation Abstracts International, 31*, 3343A. (University Microfilms No. 70-17924)

/Leong, C. K., Simmons, D. R., & Izatt-Gambell, M. A. (1990). The effect of systematic training in elaboration on word meaning and prose comprehension in poor readers. *Annals of Dyslexia, 40*, 192–215.

*Leppman, P. K., & Herrmann, T. F. (1981, August). *PSI—What are the critical elements?* Paper presented at the annual meeting of the American Psychological Association, Los Angeles. (ERIC Document Reproduction Service No. ED 214 502)

/Lerner, C. H. (1978). *The comparative effectiveness of a language experience approach and a basal-type approach to remedial reading instruction for severely disabled readers in a senior high school.* Doctoral dissertation, Temple University. *Dissertation Abstracts International, 39*(2-A), 779–780.

$+Levin, T. (1975). *The effect of content prerequisites and process-oriented experiences on application ability in a learning of probability.* Unpublished doctoral dissertation, University of Chicago.

?Levy, B. A., Abello, B., & Lysynchuk, L. (1997). Transfer from word training to reading in context: Gains in reading fluency and comprehension. *Learning Disability Quarterly, 20*, 173–188.

*Lewis, E. W. (1984). The effects of a mastery learning strategy and an interactive computerized quiz strategy on student achievement and attitude in college trigonometry. *Dissertation Abstracts International, 45*, 2430A. (University Microfilms No. DA84-24 589)

*Leyton, F. S. (1983). *The extent to which group instruction supplemented by mastery of initial cognitive prerequisites approximates the learning effectiveness of one-to-one tutorial methods.* Unpublished doctoral dissertation, University of Chicago.

^Lhyle, K., & Kulhavy, R. (1987). Feedback processing and error correction. *Journal of Educational Psychology, 79*, 320–322.

\Lin, A., Podell, D., & Tournaki-Rein, N. (1994). CAI and the development of automaticity in mathematics skills in students with and without mild mental handicaps. *Computers in the Schools, 11*, 43–58.

*Locksley, N. (1977). The Personalized System of Instruction (PSI) in a university mathematics class. *Dissertation Abstracts International, 37*, 4194. (University Microfilms No. ADD 76-28194)

<Lonberger, R. B. (1988). *The effects of training in a self-generated learning strategy on the prose processing abilities of fourth and sixth graders.* Unpublished doctoral dissertation, State University of New York at Buffalo.

#@Long, J. C., Okey, J. R., & Yeany, R. H. (1978). The effects of diagnosis with teacher on student directed remediation on science achievement and attitudes. *Journal of Research in Science Teaching, 15*, 505–511.

/Losh, M. A. (1991). *The effect of the strategies intervention model on the academic achievement of junior high learning-disabled students.* Doctoral dissertation, University of Nebraska. *Dissertation Abstracts International, 52*(3-A), 880.

*Lu, M. C. (1976). The retention of material learned by PSI in a mathematics course. In B. A. Green, Jr. (Ed.), *Personalized instruction in higher education* (pp. 151–154). Washington, DC: Center for Personalized Instruction.

*Lu, P. H. (1976). Teaching human growth and development by The Personalized System for Instruction. *Teaching of Psychology, 3*, 127–128.

*Lubkin, J. L. (1974). Engineering statistics: A Keller Plan course with novel problems and novel features. In R. S. Ruskin & S. F. Bono (Eds.), *Personalized instruction in higher education* (pp. 153–161). Washington, DC: Center for Personalized Instruction.

^Lublin, S. (1965). Reinforcement schedules, scholastic aptitude, autonomy need, and achievement in a programmed course. *Journal of Educational Psychology, 56*, 295–302.

*#@Lueckmeyer, C. L., & Chiappetta, W. L. (1981). An investigation into the effects of a modified mastery learning strategy on achievement in a high school human physiology unit. *Journal of Research in Science Teaching, 18*, 269–273.

<Lysynchuk, L., Pressley, M., & Vye, G. (1990). Reciprocal instruction improves reading comprehension performance in poor grade school comprehenders. *Elementary School Journal, 40*, 471–484.

\Maag, J., Reid, R., & DiGangi, S. (1993). Differential effects of self-monitoring attention, accuracy, and productivity. *Journal of Applied Behavior Analysis, 26*, 329–344.

>MacArthur, C. A., Graham, S., Schwartz, S. S., & Schafer, W. D. (1995). Evaluation of a writing instruction model that integrated a process approach, strategy instruction, and word processing. *Learning Disability Quarterly, 18*, 278–291.

/>MacArthur, C. A., Schwartz, S. S., & Graham, S. (1991). Effects of reciprocal peer revision strategy in special education classrooms. *Learning Disabilities Research, 6*(4), 201–210.

<MacGregor, S. K. (1988). Use of self-questioning with a computer-mediated text system and measures of reading performance. *Journal of Reading Behavior, 20*, 131–148.

\Malabonga, V., Pasnak, R., Hendricks, C., Southard, M., & Lacey. S. (1995). Cognitive gains for kindergartners instructed in seriation and classification. *Child Study Journal, 25*, 79–96.

*Malec, M. A. (1975). PSI: A brief report and reply to Francis. *Teaching Sociology, 2*, 212–217.

<Manzo, A. V. (1969). *Improving reading comprehension through reciprocal teaching.* Unpublished doctoral dissertation, Syracuse University.

~Markowitz, W., & Renner, K. E. (1966). Feedback and delay-retention effect. *Journal of Experimental Psychology, 72*, 452–455.

\Marsh, L., & Cooke, N. (1996). The effects of using manipulatives in teaching math problem solving to students with learning disabilities. *Learning Disabilities Research & Practice, 11*, 58–65.

*Martin, R. R., & Srikameswaran, K. (1974). Correlation between frequent testing and student performance. *Journal of Chemical Education, 51*, 485–486.

?Mathes, P. G., & Fuchs, L. S. (1993). Peer-mediated reading instruction in special education resource rooms. *Learning Disabilities Research & Practice, 8*, 233–243.

$Matthews, G. S. (1982). *Effects of a mastery learning strategy on the cognitive knowledge and unit evaluation of students in high school social studies.* Unpublished doctoral dissertation, University of Southern Mississippi.

\Mattingly, J., & Bott, D. (1990). Teaching multiplication facts to students with learning problems. *Exceptional Children, 56*, 438–449.

/McCollum, P. S., & Anderson, R. P. (1974). Group counseling with reading-disabled children. *Journal of Counseling Psychology, 21*(2), 150–155.

!McConnell, J. (1977). *Relationship between selected teacher behaviors and attitudes/achievement of algebra classes.* Paper presented at the annual meeting of the American Educational Research Association. New York. (ERIC Document Reproduction Service No. ED 141 118)

!McDonald, F. (1976). Report on Phase II of the Beginning Teacher Evaluation Study. *Journal of Teacher Education, 27*(1), 39–42.

!McDonald, F. (1977). Research on teaching: Report on Phase II of the Beginning Teacher Evaluation Study. In G. Borich & K. Fenton (Eds.), *The appraisal of teaching: Concepts and process.* Reading, MA: Addison-Wesley.

!McDonald, F., & Elias, P. (1976). *Executive Summary Report: Beginning Teacher Evaluation Study, Phase II.* Princeton, NJ: Educational Testing Service.

*McFarland, B. (1976). An individualized course in elementary composition for the marginal student. In B. A. Green, Jr. (Ed.), *Personalized instruction in higher education* (pp. 45–52). Washington, DC: Center for Personalized Instruction.

*+McMichael, J., & Corey, J. R. (1969). Contingency management in an introductory psychology course produces better learning. *Journal of Applied Behavior Analysis, 2,* 79–83.

?Mercer, C. D., Campbell, K. U., Miller, M. D., Mercer, K. D., & Lane, H. B. (2000). Effects of a reading fluency intervention for middle schoolers with specific learning disabilities. *Learning Disabilities Research & Practice, 15,* 179–189.

\Mevarech, Z. (1985). Computer-assisted instructional methods: A factorial study within mathematics disadvantaged classrooms. *Journal of Experimental Education, 54,* 22–27.

\Mevarech, Z., & Rich, Y. (1985). Effects of computer-assisted mathematics instruction on disadvantaged pupils' cognitive and affective development. *Journal of Educational Research, 79,* 5–11.

#@Mevarech, Z. R. (1980). The role of teaching-learning strategies and feedback-corrective procedures in developing higher cognitive achievement.* Unpublished doctoral dissertation, University of Chicago.

$&Mevarech, Z. R. (1981, April). *Attaining mastery on higher cognitive achievement.* Paper presented at the annual meeting of the American Educational Research Association, Los Angeles.

*Mevarech, Z. R. (1985). The effects of cooperative mastery learning strategies on mathematical achievement. *Journal of Educational Research, 78,* 372–377.

*#@Mevarech, Z. R. (1986). The role of feedback corrective procedures in developing mathematics achievement and self-concept in desegregated classrooms. *Studies in Educational Evaluation, 12,* 197–203.

Mevarech, Z. R., & Kramarski, B. (1997). IMPROVE: A multidimensional method for teaching mathematics in heterogeneous classrooms. *American Educational Research Journal, 34*(2), 365–394.

*Mevarech, Z. R., & Werner, S. (1985). Are mastery learning strategies beneficial for developing problem solving skills? *Higher Education, 14,* 425–432.

\}Meyer, L. A. (1982). The relative effects of word-analysis and word-supply correction procedures with poor readers during word-attack training. *Reading Research Quarterly, 17*(4), 544–555.

*Meyers, R. R. (1976). The effects of mastery and aptitude on achievement and attitude in an introductory college geography course. *Dissertation Abstracts International, 36,* 5874. (University Microfilms No. 76-6436)

\Miller, S., & Mercer, C. (1993). Using data to learn concrete–semiconcrete–abstract instruction for students with math disabilities. *Learning Disabilities Research & Practice, 8,* 89–96.

~Monaghan, F. V. (1961). The effect of delay of knowledge of test results on learning in a natural science course. *Dissertation Abstracts International, 22,* 2723. (University Microfilms No. 61-06398)

/Montague, M., Applegate, B., & Marquard, K. (1993). Cognitive strategy instruction and mathematical problem-solving performance of students with learning disabilities. *Learning Disabilities Research & Practice, 8*(4), 223–232.

^Moore, J., & Smith, W. (1961). Knowledge of results in self-teaching spelling. *Psychological Reports, 9,* 717–726.

/Morgan, A. V. (1991). *A study of the effects of attribution retraining and cognitive self-instruction upon the academic and attentional skills, cognitive-behavioral trends of elementary-age children served in self-contained learning disability programs.* Doctoral dissertation, College of William and Mary, 1990. *Dissertation Abstracts International, 51*(8-B), 4035.

^Morgan, C., & Morgan, L. (1935). Effects and immediate awareness of success and failure upon objective examination scores. *Journal of Experimental Education, 4,* 63–66.

*+Morris, C., & Kimbrill, G. (1972). Performance and attitudinal effects of the Keller method in an introductory psychology course. *Psychological Record, 22,* 523–530.

\Naglieri, J., & Gottling, S. (1995). A study of planning and mathematics instruction for students with learning disabilities. *Psychological Reports, 76,* 1343–1354.

\Naglieri, J., & Gottling, S. (1997). Mathematics instruction and PASS cognitive processes: An intervention study. *Journal of Learning Disabilities, 30,* 513–520.

*Nation, J. R., Knight, J. M., Lamberth, J., & Dyck, D. (1974). Programmed student achievement: A test of the avoidance hypothesis. *Journal of Experimental Education, 42,* 57–61.

*Nation, J. R., Massad, P., & Wilkerson, P. (1977). Student performance in introductory psychology following termination of the programmed achievement contingency at mid-semester. *Teaching of Psychology, 4,* 116–119.

*Nation, J. R., & Roop, S. S. (1975). A comparison of two mastery approaches to teaching introductory psychology. *Teaching of Psychology, 2,* 108–111.

*+Nazzaro, J. R., Todorov, J. C., & Nazzaro, J. N. (1972). Student ability and individualized instruction. *Journal of College Science Teaching, 2,* 29–30.

=Newby, R., Caldwell, J., & Recht, D. (1989). Improving the reading comprehension of children with dysphonetic and dyseidetic dyslexia using story grammar. *Journal of Learning Disabilities, 22,* 373–380.

^~Newman, M. I., Williams, R. G., & Hiller, J. H. (1974). Delay of information feedback in an applied setting: Effects on initially learned and unlearned items. *Journal of Experimental Education, 42,* 55–59.

<Nolte, R. Y., & Singer, H. (1985). Active comprehension: Teaching a process of reading comprehension and its effects on reading achievement. *The Reading Teacher, 39,* 24–31.

*Nord, S. B. (1975). Comparative achievement and attitude in individualized and class instructional settings. *Dissertation Abstracts International, 35,* 529A. (University Microfilms No. 75-02314)

$Nordin, A. B. (1979). *The effects of different qualities of instruction on selected cognitive, affective, and time variables.* Unpublished doctoral dissertation, University of Chicago.

!Nuthall, G., & Church, J. (1973). Experimental studies of teaching behavior. In G. Chanan (Ed.), *Towards a science of teaching.* London: National Foundation for Educational Research.

Obando, L. T., & Hymel, G. M. (1991, March). *The effect of mastery learning instruction on the entry-level Spanish proficiency of secondary school students.* Paper presented at the annual meeting to the American Educational Research Association, New Orleans. (ERIC Document Reproduction Service No. ED 359 253)

/O'Connor, P. D., Stuck, G. B., & Wyne, M. D. (1979). Effects of a short-term intervention resource-room program on task orientation and achievement. *Journal of Special Education, 13*(4), 375–385.

*$+Okey, J. R. (1974). Altering teacher and pupil behavior with mastery teaching. *Social Science and Mathematics, 74*, 530–535.

+Okey, J. R. (1975). *Development of mastery teaching materials* (Final Evaluation Report, USOE G-74-2990). Bloomington: Indiana University.

$&Okey, J. R. (1977). The consequences of training teachers to use a mastery learning strategy. *Journal of Teacher Education, 28*(5), 57–62.

/Olofsson, A. (1992). Synthetic speech and computer-aided reading for reading-disabled children. *Reading and Writing, 4*(2), 165–178.

/Olsen, J. L., Wong, B.Y.L., & Marx, R. W. (1983). Linguistic and metacognitive aspects of normally achieving and learning disabled children's communication process. *Learning Disability Quarterly, 6*(3), 289–304.

^Olson, G. (1971). A multivariate examination of the effects of behavioral objectives, knowledge of results and the assignment of grades on the facilitation of classroom learning. *Dissertation Abstracts International, 32*, 6214A. (University Microfilms No. 72-13, 552)

*$Omelich, C. L., & Covington, M. V. (1981). *Do the learning benefits of behavioral instruction outweigh the psychological costs?* Paper presented at the annual meeting of the Western Psychological Association, Los Angeles.

}O'Shea, L. J., Munson, S. M., & O'Shea, D. J. (1984). Error correction in oral reading: Evaluating the effectiveness of three procedures. *Education and Treatment of Children, 7*, 203–214.

?O'Shea, L. J., Sindelar, P. T., & O'Shea, D. J. (1985). The effects of repeated reading and attentional cues on reading fluency and comprehension. *Journal of Reading Behavior, 17*, 129–141.

?O'Shea, L. J., Sindelar, P. T., & O'Shea, D. J. (1987). The effects of repeated reading and attentional cues on reading fluency and comprehension of learning disabled readers. *Learning Disabilities Research, 2*, 103–109.

~Paige, D. D. (1966). Learning while testing. *Journal of Educational Research, 59*, 276–277.

=Paivio, A. (1971). *Imagery and verbal processes.* New York: Holt, Rinehart & Winston.

<Palincsar, A. S. (1987, April). *Collaborating for collaborative learning of text comprehension.* Paper presented at the annual meeting of the American Educational Research Association, Washington, DC.

<Palincsar, A. S., & Brown, A. L. (1984). Reciprocal teaching of comprehension-fostering and comprehension-monitoring activities. *Cognition and Instruction, 2*, 117–175.

}Pany, D., & McCoy, K. M. (1988). Effects of corrective feedback on word accuracy and reading comprehension of readers with learning disabilities. *Journal of Learning Disabilities, 21*, 546–550.

}Pany, D., McCoy, K. M., & Peters, E. E. (1981). Effects of corrective feedback on comprehension skills of remedial students. *Journal of Reading Behavior, 13*, 131–143.

*Pascarela, E. T. (1977, April). *Aptitude-treatment interaction in a college calculus course taught in personalized system of instruction and conventional formats.* Paper presented at the annual meeting of the American Educational Research Association, New York. (ERIC Document Reproduction Service No. ED 137 137)

\Pasnak, R. (1987). Acceleration of cognitive development of kindergartners. *Psychology in the Schools, 24*, 358–363.

\Pasnak, R., Hansbarger, A., Dodson, S., Hart, J., & Blaha, J. (1996). Differential results of instruction of the preoperational/concrete operational transition. *Psychology in the Schools, 33*, 70–83.

\Pasnak, R., Holt, R., Campbell, J., & McCutcheon, L. (1991). Cognitive and achievement gains for kindergartners instructed in Piagetian operations. *Journal of Educational Research, 85*, 5–13.

\Pearce, M., & Norwich, B. (1986). A comparative evaluation of direct teaching and computer assisted methods to teach number estimation skills to children with moderate learning difficulties. *European Journal of Special Needs Education, 1*, 13–22.

^Peeck, A., Bosch, A., & Kreupling, W. (1985). Effects of informative feedback in relation to retention of initial responses. *Contemporary Educational Psychology, 10*, 303–313.

^Peeck, J., & Tillema, H. (1979). Learning from feedback: Comparison of two feedback procedures in a classroom setting. *Perceptual and Motor Skills, 48*, 351–354.

*Peluso, A., & Baranchik, A. J. (1977). Self-paced mathematics instruction: A statistical comparison with traditional teaching. *The American Mathematical Monthly, 84*, 124–129.

}Perkins, V. L. (1988). Feedback effects on oral reading errors of children with learning disabilities. *Journal of Learning Disabilities, 21*, 244–248.

\Perry, P., Pasnak, R., & Holt, R. (1992). Instruction on concrete operations for children who are mildly mentally retarded. *Education and Training in Mental Retardation, 27*, 273–281.

*+Phillippas, M. A., & Sommerfeldt, R. W. (1972). Keller vs. lecture method in general physics instruction. *American Journal of Physics, 40*, 1800.

~Phye, G., & Baller, W. (1970). Verbal retention as a function of the informativeness and delay of the informative feedback: A replication. *APA Experimental Publication System, 7*, MS-232-4.

\Pigott, H., Fantuzzo, J., & Clement, P. (1986). The effects of reciprocal peer tutoring and group contingencies on the academic performance of elementary school children. *Journal of Applied Behavior Analysis, 19*, 93–98.

\Podell, D., Tournak-Rein, N., & Lin, A. (1992). Automatization of mathematics skills via computer-assisted instruction among students with mild mental handicaps. *Education and Training in Mental Retardation, 27*, 200–206.

+Poggio, J. P. (1976, April). *Long-term cognitive retention resulting from the mastery learning paradigm.* Paper presented at the annual meeting of the American Educational Research Association, San Francisco.

*Pollack, N. F., & Roeder, P. W. (1975). Individualized instruction in an introductory government course. *Teaching Political Science, 8*, 18–36.

~Pressey, S. L. (1950). Development and appraisal of devices providing immediate automatic scoring of objective tests and concomitant self-instruction. *Journal of Psychology, 29*, 417–447.

/Prior, M., Frye, S., & Fletcher, C. (1987). Remediation for subgroups of retarded readers using a modified oral spelling procedure. *Developmental Medicine and Child Neurology, 29*, 64–71.

?Rasinski, T. (1990). Effects of repeated reading and listening-while-reading on reading fluency. *Journal of Educational Research, 83*, 147–150.

?Rasinski, T., Padak, N., Linek, W., & Sturtevant, E. (1994). Effects of fluency development on urban second-grade readers. *Journal of Educational Research, 87*, 158–165.

!%Reid, E. R. (1978–1982). *The Reader Newsletter*. Salt Lake City: Exemplary Center for Reading Instruction.

/Reilly, J. P. (1991). *Effects of a cognitive-behavioral program designed to increase the reading comprehension skills of learning-disabled students*. Doctoral dissertation, College of William and Mary. *Dissertation Abstracts International, 52*(3-A), 865.

>/Reynolds, C. J. (1986). *The effects of instruction in cognitive revision strategies on the writing skills of secondary learning disabled students* Doctoral dissertation, Ohio State University, 1985. *Dissertation Abstracts International, 46*(9-A), 2662.

^Ripple, R. (1963). Comparison of the effectiveness of a programmed text with three other methods of presentation. *Psychological Reports, 12*, 227–237.

<Ritchie, P. (1985). The effects of instruction in main idea and question generation. *Reading Canada Lecture, 3*, 139–146.

~Robin, A. L. (1978). The timing of feedback in personalized instruction. *Journal of Personalized Instruction, 3*, 81–88.

^Roper, W. (1977). Feedback in computer assisted instruction. *Programmed Learning and Educational Technology, 14*, 43–49.

*+Rosati, P. A. (1975). A comparison of the personalized system of instruction with the lecture method in teaching elementary dynamics. In J. M. Johnston (Ed.), *Behavior research and technology in higher education*. Springfield, IL: Charles C. Thomas.

}Rose, T. L., McEntire, E., & Dowdy, C. (1982). Effects of two error-correction procedures on oral reading. *Learning Disability Quarterly, 5*, 100–105.

}Rosenberg, M. S. (1986). Error-correction during oral reading: A comparison of three techniques. *Learning Disability Quarterly, 9*, 182–192.

Rosenshine, B., Meister, C., & Chapman, S. (1996). Teaching students to generate questions: A review of the intervention studies. *Review of Educational Research, 66*(2), 181–221.

Rosenshine, B., & Stevens, R. (1986). Teaching functions. In M. C. Wittrock (Ed.), *Handbook of research on teaching* (3rd ed., pp. 376–391). New York: Macmillan.

+Roth, C. H., Jr. (1973). Continuing effectiveness on personalized self-paced instruction in digital systems engineering. *Engineering Education, 63*(6), 447–450.

*Roth, C. H., Jr. (1975, December). *Electrical engineering laboratory I* (One of a series of reports on the projects titled Expansion of Keller Plan Instruction in Engineering and Selected Other Disciplines). Austin: University of Texas.

^Rothkopf, E. (1966). Learning from written instructive materials: An exploration of the control of inspection behavior by test-like events. *American Educational Research Journal, 3*, 241–249.

/Rudel, R. G., & Helfgott, E. (1984). Effect of piracetam on verbal memory of dyslexic boys. *American Academy of Child Psychiatry, 23*, 695–699.

~Saltzman, I. J. (1951). Delay of reward and human verbal learning. *Journal of Experimental Psychology, 41*, 437–439.

^Sassenrath, J., & Gaverick, C. (1965). Effects of differential feedback from examinations on retention and transfer. *Journal of Educational Psychology, 56*, 259–263.

~Sassenrath, J. M., & Yonge, G. D. (1968). Delayed information feedback, feedback cues, retention set, and delayed retention. *Journal of Educational Psychology, 59*, 69–73.

~Sassenrath, J. M., & Yonge, G. D. (1969). Effects of delayed information feedback and feedback cues in learning and retention. *Journal of Educational Psychology, 60*, 174–177.

*Saunders-Harris, R. L., & Yeany, R. H. (1981). Diagnosis, remediation, and locus of control: Effects of the immediate and retained achievement and attitude. *Journal of Experimental Education, 49*, 220–224.

~Saunderson, A. (1974). Effect of immediate knowledge of results on learning. *Australian Mathematics Teacher, 30*, 218–221.

>Sawyer, R. J., Graham, S., & Harris, K. R. (1992). Direct teaching, strategy instruction, and strategy instruction with explicit self-regulation: Effects on the composition skills and self-efficacy of students with learning disabilities. *Journal of Educational Psychology, 84*(3), 340–352.

~Sax, G. (1960). Concept acquisition as a function of differing schedules and delays of reinforcement. *Journal of Educational Psychology, 51*, 32–36.

*Schielack, V. P., Jr. (1983). A personalized system of instruction versus a conventional method in a mathematics course for elementary education majors. *Dissertation Abstracts International, 43*, 2267. (University Microfilms No. 82-27717)

*Schimpfhauser, F., Horrocks, L., Richardson, K., Alben, J., Schumm, D., & Sprecher, H. (1974). The personalized system of instruction as an adaptable alternative within the traditional structure of medical basic sciences. In R. S. Ruskin & S. F. Bono (Eds.), *Personalized instruction in higher education* (pp. 61–69). Washington, DC: Center for Personalized Instruction.

\Schopman, E., & Van Luit, J. (1996). Learning and transfer of preparatory arithmetic strategies among young children with a developmental lag. *Journal of Cognitive Education, 5*, 117–131.

!Schuck, R. (1981). The impact of set induction on student achievement and retention. *Journal of Educational Research, 74*, 227–232.

\Schunk, D., Hanson, A., & Cox, P. (1987). Peer-model attributes and children's achievement behaviors. *Journal of Educational Psychology, 79*, 54–61.

{ Schunk, D. H. (1982). *Efficacy and skill development through social comparison and goal setting.* (ERIC Document Reproduction Service No. ED 222 279)

/Schunk, D. H. (1985). Participation in goal-setting: Effects on self-efficacy and skills of learning-disabled children. *Journal of Special Education, 19*, 305–317.

/Schunk, D. H. & Cox, P. D. (1986). Strategy training and attributional feedback with learning-disabled students. *Journal of Educational Psychology, 78*, 201–209.

*Schwartz, P. L. (1981). Retention of knowledge in clinical biochemistry and the effect of the Keller Plan. *Journal of Medical Education, 56*, 778–781.

*Sharples, D. K., Smith, D. J., & Strasler, G. M. (1976). *Individually-paced learning in civil engineering technology: An approach to mastery.* Columbia: South Carolina State Board for Technical and Comprehensive Education. (ERIC Document Reproduction Service No. ED 131 870)

*$Sheldon, M. S., & Miller, E. D. (1973). *Behavioral objectives and mastery learning applied to two areas of junior college instruction.* Los Angeles: University of California at Los Angeles. (ERIC Document Reproduction Service No. ED 082 730)

*Sheppard, W. C., & MacDermott, H. G. (1970). Design and evaluation of a programmed course in introductory psychology. *Journal of Applied Behavior Analysis, 3*, 5–11.

\Shiah, R., Mastropieri, M., Scruggs, T., & Mushinski, B. (1995). The effects of computer-assisted instruction on the mathematical problem solving of students with learning disabilities. *Exceptionality, 5*, 131–161.

<Short, E. J., & Ryan, E. B. (1984). Metacognitive differences between skilled and less-skilled readers: Remediating deficits through story grammar and attribution training. *Journal of Educational Psychology, 76*, 225–235.

*Siegfried, J. J., & Strand, S. H. (1976). An evaluation of the Vanderbilt JCEE experimental PSI course in elementary economics. *The Journal of Economic Education, 8*, 9–26.

*+Silberman, R., & Parker, B. (1974). Student attitudes and the Keller Plan. *Journal of Chemical Education, 51*, 393.

?Simmons, D. C., Fuchs, D., Fuchs, L. S., Hodge, J. P., & Mathes, P. G. (1994). Importance of instructional complexity and role reciprocity to classwide peer tutoring. *Learning Disabilities Research & Practice, 9*, 203–212.

?Simmons, D. C., Fuchs, D., Fuchs, L. S., Mathes, P., & Hodge, J. P. (1995). Effects of explicit teaching and peer tutoring on the reading achievement of learning-disabled and low-performing students in regular classrooms. *The Elementary School Journal, 95*, 387–408.

<Simpson, P. S. (1989). *The effects of direct training in active comprehension on reading achievement, self-concepts, and reading attitudes of at-risk sixth grade students.* Unpublished doctoral dissertation, Texas Tech University.

?Sindelar, P. T., Monda, L. E., & O'Shea, L. J. (1990). Effects of repeated readings on instructional and mastery-level readers. *Journal of Educational Research, 83*, 220–226.

}Singh, J., & Singh, N. N. (1985). Comparison of word supply and word analysis error correction procedures on oral reading by mentally retarded children. *American Journal of Mental Deficiency, 90*, 64–70.

}Singh, J., & Singh, N. N. (1986). Increasing oral reading proficiency. *Behavior Modification, 10*, 115–130.

}Singh, J., & Singh, N. N. (1988). Increasing oral reading proficiency through overcorrection and phonic analysis. *American Journal on Mental Retardation, 93*, 312–319.

}Singh, N. N. (1990). Effects of two error-correction procedures on oral reading errors. *Behavior Modification, 14*, 188–199.

}Singh, N. N., Winton, A. S., & Singh, J. (1985). Effects of delayed versus immediate attention to oral reading errors on the reading proficiency of mentally retarded children. *Applied Research in Mental Retardation, 6*, 283–293.

\Skinner, C., Bamberg, H., Smith, E., & Powell, S. (1993). Cognitive cover, copy, and compare: Subvocal responding to increase rates of accurate division responding. *Remedial and Special Education, 14*(1), 49–56.

Slavin, R. E. (1990). Mastery learning re-considered. *Review of Educational Research, 60*(2), 300–302.

*#@$&Slavin, R. E., & Karweit, N. L. (1984). Mastery learning and student teams: A factor role experiment in urban general mathematics classes. *American Educational Research Journal, 21*, 725–736.

*Smiernow, G. A., & Lawley, A. (1980). Decentralized sequence instruction (DSI) at Drexel. *Engineering Education, 70*, 423–426.

*Smith, J. E. (1976). A comparison of the traditional method and a personalized system of instruction in college mathematics. *Dissertation Abstracts International, 37,* 904. (University Microfilms No. AAD 76-18370)

/Smith, M. A. (1989). *The efficacy of mnemonics for teaching recognition of letter clusters to reading disabled students.* Doctoral dissertation, University of Oregon. *Dissertation Abstracts International, 50*(5-A), 1259–1260.

<Smith, N. J. (1977). *The effects of training teachers to teach students at different reading ability levels to formulate three types of questions on reading comprehension and question generation ability.* Unpublished doctoral dissertation, University of Georgia.

/Snider, V. E. (1989). Reading comprehension performance of adolescents with learning disabilities. *Learning Disability Quarterly, 12*(2), 87–96.

!Soar, R. S. (1966). *An integrative approach to classroom learning* (Report for NIMH Projects No. 5-R11 MH 01096 and R-11 MH 02045). Philadelphia: Temple University. (ERIC Document Reproduction Service No. ED 033 749)

!Soar, R. S. (1968). Optimal teacher-pupil interaction for pupil growth. *Educational Leadership, 26,* 275–280.

!Soar, R. S. (1973). *Follow-Through classroom process measurement and pupil growth (1970–1971) final report.* Gainesville: College of Education, University of Florida.

!Soar, R. S. (1977). An integration of findings from four studies of teacher effectiveness. In G. Borich & K. Fenton (Eds.), *The appraisal of teaching: Concepts and process.* Reading, MA: Addison-Wesley.

!Soar, R. S., & Soar, R. M. (1972). An empirical analysis of selected Follow Through Programs: An appraisal of a process approach to evaluation. In G. Borich & K. Fenton (Eds.), *The appraisal of teaching: Concepts and process.* Reading, MA: Addison-Wesley.

!Soar, R. S., & Soar, R. M. (1973). *Classroom behavior, pupil characteristics, and pupil growth for the school year and the summer.* Gainesville: University of Florida, Institute for Development of Human Resources.

!Soar, R. S., & Soar, R. M. (1978). *Setting variables, classroom interaction, and multiple pupil outcomes* (Final Report, Project No. 6-0432, Grant No. NIE-G-76-0100). Washington, DC: National Institute of Education.

!Soar, R. S., & Soar, R. M. (1979). Emotional climate and management. In P. Peterson & H. Walberg (Eds.), *Research on teaching: Concepts, findings, and implications.* Berkeley, CA: McCutchan.

!Solomon, D., & Kendall, A. (1979). *Children in classrooms: An investigation person-environment interaction.* New York: Praeger.

}Spaai, G. W., Ellerman, H. H., & Reitsma, P. (1991). Effects of segmented and whole-word sound feedback on learning to read single words. *Journal of Education Research, 84,* 204–213.

*Spector, L. C. (1976). The effectiveness of personalized instruction system of instruction in economics. *Journal of Personalized Instruction, I,* 118–122.

*Spevack, H. M. (1976). A comparison of the personalized system of instruction with the lecture recitation system for nonscience oriented chemistry students at an open enrollment community college. *Dissertation Abstracts International, 36,* 4385A–4386A. (University Microfilms No. 76-01757)

!Stallings, J. (1980). Allocated academic learning time revisited, or beyond time on task. *Educational Researcher, 8*(11), 11–16.

!%Stallings, J., Corey, R., Fairweather, J., & Needles, M. (1977). *Early Childhood Education classroom evaluation.* Menlo Park, CA: SRI International.

!%Stallings, J., Needles, M., & Staybrook, N. (1979). *The teaching of basic reading skills in secondary schools, Phase II and Phase III.* Menlo Park, CA: SRI International.

!%Stallings, J. A., & Kaskowitz, D. (1974). *Follow-Through Classroom Observation.* Menlo Park, CA: SRI International.

*Steele, W. F. (1974). *Mathematics 101 at Heileberg College—PSI vs. tradition.* Paper presented at the National Conference on Personalized Instruction in Higher Education, Washington, DC.

\Stellingwerf, B., & Van Lieshout, E. (1999). Manipulatives and number sentences in computer-aided arithmetic word problem solving. *Instructional Science, 27*, 459–476.

?Stoddard, K., Valcante, G., Sindelar, P. T., O'Shea, L., & Algozzine, B. (1993). Increasing reading rate and comprehension: The effects of repeated readings, sentence segmentation, and intonation training. *Reading Research and Instruction, 32*, 53–65.

*Stout, L. J. (1978). A comparison of four different pacing strategies of personalized system of instruction and a traditional lecture format. *Dissertation Abstracts International, 38*, 6205. (University Microfilms No. AAD 78-08600)

*$Strasler, G. M. (1979, April). *The process of transfer and learning for mastery setting.* Paper presented at the annual meeting of the American Educational Research Association, San Francisco. (ERIC Document Reproduction Service No. ED 174 642)

~Sturges, P. T. (1969). Verbal retention as a function of the informativeness and delay of informative feedback. *Journal of Educational Psychology, 60*, 11–14.

~Sturges, P. T. (1972). Information delay and retention: Effect of information in feedback and tests. *Journal of Educational Psychology, 63*, 32–43.

~Sturges, P. T. (1978). Delay of informative feedback in computer-assisted testing. *Journal of Educational Psychology, 70*, 378–387.

~Sturges, P. T., Sarafino, E. P., & Donaldson, P. I. (1968). The delay-retention effect and informative feedback. *Journal of Experimental Psychology, 78*, 357–358.

\Sugai, G., & Smith, P. (1986). The equal additions method of subtraction taught with a modeling technique. *Remedial and Special Education, 7*(1), 40–48.

~Sullivan, H. J., Schutz, R. E., & Baker, R. L. (1971). Effects of systematic variations in reinforcement contingencies on learner performance. *American Educational Research Journal, 8*, 135–142.

/Sullivan, J. (1972). The effects of Kephart's perceptual motor training on a reading clinic sample. *Journal of Learning Disabilities, 5*, 545–551.

~Surber, J. R., & Anderson, R. C. (1975). Delay-retention effect in natural classroom settings. *Journal of Educational Psychology, 67*, 170–173.

*$&Swanson, D. H., & Denton J. J. (1976). Learning for Mastery versus Personalized System of Instruction: A comparison of remediation strategies for secondary school chemistry students. *Journal of Research in Science Teaching, 14*, 515–524.

\Swanson, H. (1985). Effects of cognitive-behavioral training on emotionally disturbed children's academic performance. *Cognitive Therapy and Research, 9*, 201–216.

Swanson, H. L. (2001). Research on interventions for adolescents with learning disabilities: A meta-analysis of outcomes related to higher-order processing. *The Elementary School Journal, 101*(13), 331–349.

~Tabachneck, A., & Hapkiewicz, W. (1986, April). *The effects of immediate and delayed feedback on the retention of factual rule learning.* Paper presented at the annual meeting of the American Educational Research Association, San Francisco.

^Tait, K., Hartley, J., & Anderson, R. (1973). Feedback procedures in computer-assisted arithmetic instruction. *British Journal of Educational Psychology, 43*, 161–171.

<Taylor, B. M., & Frye, B. J. (1992). Comprehension strategy instruction in the intermediate grades. *Reading Research and Instruction, 92*, 39–48.

*Taylor, V. (1977, April). *Individualized calculus for the "life-long" learner: A two semester comparison of attitudes and effectiveness.* Paper presented at the Fourth National Conference of the Center for Personalized Instruction, San Francisco.

$Tenenbaum, G. (1982). *A method of group instruction which is as effective as one-to-one tutorial instruction.* Unpublished doctoral dissertation, University of Chicago.

\Thackwray, D., Meyers, A., Schleser, R., & Cohen, R. (1985). Achieving generalization with general versus specific self-instructions: Effects on academically deficient children. *Cognitive Therapy and Research, 9*, 297–308.

Therrien, W. J. (2004). Fluency and comprehension gains as a result of repeated reading: A meta-analysis. *Remedial and Special Education, 25*(4), 252–261.

*&Thompson, S. B. (1980). Do individualized mastery and traditional instructional systems yield different course effects in college calculus? *American Educational Research Journal, 17*, 361–375.

*Tietenberg, T. H. (1975). Teaching intermediate microeconomics using the personalized system of instruction. In J. M. Johnston (Ed.), *Behavior research and technology in higher education* (pp. 75–89). Springfield, IL: Charles C. Thomas.

^Tobias, S. (1984, April). *Macroprocesses, individual differences, and instructional methods.* Paper presented at the annual meeting of the American Educational Research Association, New Orleans. (ERIC Document Reproduction Service No. ED 259 019)

!Tobin, K., & Caple, W. (1982). Relationships between classroom process variables and middle-school science achievement. *Journal of Educational Psychology, 74*, 441–454.

*Toepher, C., Shaw, D., & Moniot, D. (1972). *The effect of item exposure in a contingency management system.* Paper presented at the annual meeting of the American Psychological Association, Honolulu, HI.

/Tollefson, N., Tracy, D. B., Johnsen, E. P., Farmer, A. W., & Buenning, M. (1984). Goal setting and personal responsibility training for LD adolescents. *Psychology in the Schools, 21*, 224–233.

/Trapani, C., & Gettinger, M. (1989). Effects of social skills training and cross-age tutoring on academic achievement and social behaviors of boys with learning disabilities. *Journal of Research and Development in Education, 23*, 1–9.

^Tsao, P. (1977). The effects of error rate, knowledge of correct results and test anxiety in linear program. *Dissertation Abstracts International, 39*, 1426 A. (University Microfilms No. 78-15, 385)

\Van de Rijt, B., & Van Luit, J. (1998). Effectiveness of the Additional Early Mathematics program for teaching young children early mathematics. *Instructional Science, 26*, 337–358.

~Van Dyke, B. F., & Newton, J. M. (1972). Computer-assisted instruction: Performance and attitudes. *Journal of Educational Research, 65*(7), 291–293.

\Van Luit, J. (1987). Teaching impulsive children with arithmetic deficits in special education: A self-instructional training program. *European Journal of Special Needs Education, 2*, 237–246.

\Van Luit, J. (1994). The effectiveness of structural and realistic arithmetic curricula in children with special needs. *European Journal of Special Needs Education, 9*, 16–26.

\Van Luit, J., & Naglieri, J. (1999). Effectiveness of the MASTER strategy training program for teaching special children multiplication and division. *Journal of Learning Disabilities, 32*, 98–107.

\Van Luit, J., & Schopman, E. (2000). Improving early numeracy of young children with special educational needs. *Remedial and Special Education, 21*, 27–40.

\Van Luit, J., & Van der Aalsvoort, G. (1985). Learning subtraction in a special school: A self-instructional training strategy for educable mentally retarded children with arithmetic deficits. *Instructional Science, 14*, 179–189.

*Van Verth, J. E., & Dinan, F. J. (1974). A Keller Plan course in organic chemistry. In R. S. Ruskin & S. F. Bono (Eds.), *Personalized instruction in higher education* (pp. 162–168). Washington, DC: Center for Personalized Instruction.

*Vandenbroucke, A. C., Jr. (1974, April). *Evaluation of the use of a personalized system of instruction in general chemistry.* Paper presented at the National Conference on Personalized Instruction in Higher Education, Washington, DC.

?Vaughn, S., Chard, D. J., Bryant, D. P., Coleman, M., & Kouzekanani, K. (2000). Fluency and comprehension interventions for third-grade students. *Remedial and Special Education, 21*, 325–335.

\Waiss, S., & Pasnak, R. (1993). Instruction of young children on number conservation and unidimensional classification. *Bulletin of the Psychonomic Society, 31*, 205–208.

*Walsh, R. G., Sr. (1977). The Keller Plan in college introductory physical geology: A comparison with the conventional teaching method. *Dissertation Abstracts International, 37*, 4257. (University Microfilms No. AAD 76-30292)

<Weiner, C. J. (1978, March). *The effect of training in questioning and student question-generation on reading achievement.* Paper presented at the annual meeting of the American Educational Research Association, Toronto. (ERIC Document Reproduction Service No. ED 158 223).

>Welch, M. (1992). The PLEASE strategy: A meta-cognitive learning strategy for improving the paragraph writing of students with learning disabilities. *Learning Disability Quarterly, 15*(2), 119–128.

^Welsh, P., Antoinetti, J., & Thayer, P. (1965). An industrywide study of programmed instruction. *Journal of Applied Psychology, 49*, 61–73.

*$+Wentling, T. L. (1973). Mastery versus nonmastery instruction with varying test item feedback treatments. *Journal of Educational Psychology, 65*, 50–58.

/White, C. V., Pascarella, E. T., & Pflaum, S. W. (1981). Effects of training in sentence construction on the comprehension of learning-disabled children. *Journal of Educational Psychology, 71*, 697–704.

*White, M. E. (1974). Different equations by PSI. In R. S. Ruskin & S. F. Bono (Eds.), *Personalized instruction in higher education* (pp. 169–171). Washington, DC: Center for Personalized Instruction.

Willett, J., Yamashita, J., & Anderson, R. (1983). A meta-analysis of instructional systems applied in science teaching. *Journal of Research in Science Teaching, 20*(5), 405–417.

/=Williams, J. P., Brown, L. G., Silverstein, A. K., & deCani, J. S. (1994). An instructional program in comprehension of narrative themes for adolescents with learning disabilities. *Learning Disability Quarterly, 17*, 205–221.

<Williamson, R. A. (1989). *The effect of reciprocal teaching on student performance gains in third grade basal reading instruction.* Unpublished doctoral dissertation, Texas A&M University.

\Wilson, C., & Sindelar, P. (1991). Direct instruction in math word problems: Students with learning disabilities. *Exceptional Children, 57*, 512–519.

\Wilson, R., Majsterek, D., & Simmons, D. (1996). The effects of computer-assisted versus teacher-directed instruction on the multiplication performance of elementary students with learning disabilities. *Journal of Learning Disabilities, 29*, 382–390.

$Wire, D. R. (1979). *Mastery learning program at Durham College: Report on progress toward the first year, September 1, 1978–August 31, 1979.* Durham, NC. (ERIC Document Reproduction Service No. ED 187 387)

*Witters, D. R., & Kent, G. W. (1972). Teaching without lecturing—evidence in the case for individualized instruction. *The Psychological Record, 22*, 169–175.

/Wong, B.Y.L., Butler, D. L., Ficzere, S. A., & Kuperis, S. (1996). Teaching low achievers and students with learning disabilities to plan, write, and revise opinion essays. *Journal of Learning Disabilities, 29*, 197–212.

/Wong, B.Y.L., Butler, D. L., Ficzere, S. A., Kuperis, S., Corden, M., & Zelmer, J. (1994). Teaching problem learners revision skills and sensitivity to audience through two instructional modes: Student-teacher versus student-student interactive dialogues. *Learning Disabilities Research & Practice, 9*, 78–90.

/<Wong, B.Y.L., & Jones, W. (1982). Increasing metacomprehension in learning disabled and normally achieving students through self-questioning training. *Learning Disability Quarterly, 5*, 228–240.

\Wood, D., Frank, A., & Wacker, D. (1998). Teaching multiplication facts to students with learning disabilities. *Exceptional Children, 57*, 512–519.

\Wood, D., Rosenberg, M., & Carran, D. (1993). The effects of tape-recorded self-instruction cues on the mathematics performance of students with learning disabilities. *Journal of Learning Disabilities, 26*, 250–258.

\Woodward, J., & Baxter, J. (1997). The effects of an innovative approach to mathematics on academically low-achieving students in inclusive settings. *Exceptional Children, 63*, 373–388.

$Wortham, S. C. (1980). *Mastery learning in secondary schools: A first-year report.* San Antonio, TX. (ERIC Document Reproduction Service No. ED 194 453)

~Wright, J. H., & Gescheider, G. A. (1970). Role of immediate and delayed knowledge of results in paired-associate learning under the anticipation procedure. *Journal of Psychology: Interdisciplinary and Applied, 74*(2), 249–257.

~Wright, J. H., & Gescheider, G. A. (1970, November). Effects of stimulus similarity on paired-associate learning under immediate and delayed knowledge of results. *Journal of Psychology: Interdisciplinary and Applied, 76*(2), 181–186.

*Yeany, R. H., Dost, R. J., & Matthew, R. W. (1980). The effects of diagnostic-prescriptive instruction and locus of control on the achievement and attitudes of university students. *Journal of Research in Science Teaching, 17*, 537–545.

$Yildren, G. (1977). *The effects of level of cognitive achievement on selected learning criteria under mastery learning and normal classroom instruction.* Unpublished doctoral dissertation, University of Chicago.

?Young, A., Bowers, P. G., & MacKinnon, G. E. (1996). Effects of prosodic modeling and repeated reading on poor readers' fluency and comprehension. *Applied Psycholinguistics, 17*, 59–84.

REFERENCES FOR KEEPING STUDENTS ON TASK

*Acland, H. (1976). Stability of teacher effectiveness: A replication. *Journal of Educational Research, 69*, 289–292.

*#Anderson, L. M., Evertson, C. M., & Brophy, J. E. (1979). An experimental study of

effective teaching in first-grade reading groups. *The Elementary School Journal, 79,* 193–222.

*Arehart, J. (1979). Student opportunity to learn related to student achievement of objectives in a probability unit. *Journal of Educational Research, 72,* 253–269.

%Baer, D. M., Blount, R. L., Detrich, R., & Stokes, T. F. (1987). Using intermittent reinforcement to program maintenance of verbal/nonverbal correspondence. *Journal of Applied Behavior Analysis, 20,* 179–184.

%Ballinger, C. (1993). *Annual report to the association on the status of year-round education.* (ERIC Document Reproduction Service No. ED 024 990)

#Becker, W. C. (1977). Teaching reading and language to the disadvantaged—What we have learned from field research. *Harvard Educational Review, 47,* 518–543.

%Berkowitz, M. J., & Martens, B. K. (2001). Assessing teachers' and students' preferences for school-based reinforcement: Agreement across methods and different effort requirements. *Journal of Developmental and Physical Disabilities, 13,* 373–387.

*Berliner, D., Fisher, C., Filby, N., & Marliave, R. (1978). *Executive summary of Beginning Teacher Evaluation Study.* San Francisco: Far West Laboratory.

*Brophy, J. (1973). Stability of teacher effectiveness. *American Educational Research Journal, 10,* 245–252.

*Brophy, J., & Evertson, C. (1974a). *Process-product correlations in the Texas Teacher Effectiveness Study: Final report* (Research Report 74-4). Austin: Research and Development Center for Teacher Education, University of Texas. (ERIC Document Reproduction Service No. ED 091 094)

*Brophy, J., & Evertson, C. (1974b). *The Texas Teacher Effectiveness Project: Presentation of non-linear relationships and summary discussion* (Research Report 74-6). Austin: Research and Development Center for Teacher Education, University of Texas. (ERIC Document Reproduction Service No. ED 099 345)

*#Brophy, J., & Evertson, C. (1976). *Learning from teaching: A developmental perspective.* Boston: Allyn and Bacon.

Brophy, J., & Good, T. (1986). Teacher behavior and student achievement. In M. C. Wittrock (Ed.), *Handbook of research on teaching* (3rd ed., pp. 328–375). New York: Macmillan.

%Carnine, D. (1992). Expanding the notion of teachers' rights: Access to tools that work. *Journal of Applied Behavior Analysis, 24,* 13–19.

%Carr, E. G., & Durand, V. M. (1985). Reducing behavior problems through functional communication training. *Journal of Behavior Analysis, 18,* 111–126.

*Coker, H., Medley, D., & Soar, R. (1980). How valid are expert opinions about effective teaching? *Phi Delta Kappan, 62,* 131–134, 149.

%Cooper, B., Nye, B., Charlton, K., Lindsay, J., & Greathouse, S. (1996). The effects of summer vacation on achievement test scores: A narrative and meta-analytic review. *Review of Educational Research, 66,* 227–268.

*Crawford, J. (1983). A study of instructional processes in Title I classes: 1981–82. *Journal of Research and Evaluation of the Oklahoma City Public Schools, 13*(1).

%Daly, E. J., Lentz, F. E., & Boyer, J. (1996). The instructional hierarchy: A conceptual model for understanding the effective components of reading interventions. *School Psychology Quarterly, 11,* 369–386.

%Daly, E. J., Martens, B. K., Hamler, K., Dool, E. J., & Eckert, T. L. (1999). A brief experimental analysis for identifying instructional components needed to improve oral reading fluency. *Journal of Applied Behavior Analysis, 32,* 83–94.

*Dunkin, M. J. (1978). Student characteristics, classroom processes, and student achievement. *Journal of Educational Psychology, 70*, 998–1009.

%DuPaul, G. J., & Henningson, P. N. (1993). Peer tutoring effects on the classroom performance of children with Attention Deficit Hyperactivity Disorder. *School Psychology Review, 22*, 134–143.

*Ebmier, H., & Good, T. (1979). The effects of instructing teachers about good teaching on mathematics achievement of fourth grade students. *American Educational Research Journal, 16*, 1–16.

%Eisenberger, R., & Cameron, J. (1996). Detrimental effects of reward: Reality or myth? *American Psychologist, 51*, 1153–1166.

*Emmer, E., Evertson, C., & Anderson, L. (1980). Effective classroom management at the beginning of the school year. *Elementary School Journal, 80*, 219–231.

*Emmer, E., Evertson, C., & Brophy, J. (1979). Stability of teacher effects in junior high school classrooms. *American Educational Research Journal, 16*, 71–75.

#Emmer, E. T., Evertson, C., Sanford, J., & Clements, B. (1982). *Improving classroom management: An experimental study in junior high school classrooms.* Austin: Research and Development Center for Teacher Education, University of Texas.

%Erchul, W. P., & Martens, B. K. (2002). *School consultation: Conceptual and empirical bases of practice* (2nd ed.). New York: Plenum.

#Evertson, C. (1982). Differences in instructional activities in higher and lower achieving junior high English and mathematics classrooms. *Elementary School Journal, 82*, 329–351.

*#Evertson, C., Anderson, C., Anderson, L., & Brophy, J. (1980). Relationships between classroom behaviors and student outcomes in junior high mathematics and English classes. *American Educational Research Journal, 17*, 43–60.

*Evertson, C., Anderson, L., & Brophy, J. (1978). *Texas Junior High School Study: Final report of process-outcome relationship* (Report No. 4061). Austin: Research and Development Center for Teacher Education, University of Texas.

*Evertson, C., & Brophy, J. (1973). High-inference behavioral ratings as correlates of teacher effectiveness. *JSAS Catalog of Selected Documents in Psychology, 3*, 97.

*Evertson, C., & Brophy, J. (1974). *Texas Teacher Effectiveness Project: Questionnaire and interview data* (Research Report No. 74-5). Austin: Research and Development Center for Teacher Education, University of Texas.

*#Evertson, C., Emmer, E., & Brophy, J., (1980). Predictors of effective teaching in junior high mathematics classrooms. *Journal for Research in Mathematics Education, 11*, 167–178.

#Evertson, C. M., Emmer, E., Sandford, J. P., & Clements, B. S. (1983). Improving classroom management: An experiment in elementary classrooms. *Elementary School Journal, 84*, 173–188.

*#Fisher, C. W., Berliner, D. C., Filby, N. N., Marliave, R., Cahen, L. S., & Dishaw, M. M. (1980). Teaching behaviors, academic learning time, and student achievement: An overview. In C. Denham & A. Lieberman (Eds.), *Time to learn* (pp. 7–32). Washington, DC: U.S. Government Printing Office.

#Fitzpatrick, K. A. (1981). *An investigation of secondary classroom material strategies for increasing student academic engaged time.* Doctoral dissertation, University of Illinois at Urbana–Champaign.

#Fitzpatrick, K. A. (1982). *The effect of a secondary classroom management training pro-*

gram on teacher and student behavior. Paper presented at the annual meeting of the American Educational Research Association, New York.

%Fuchs, L. S., & Fuchs, D. (1986). Effects of systematic formative evaluation on student achievement: A meta-analysis. *Exceptional Children, 53,* 199–208.

%Gickling, E. E., & Armstrong, D. L. (1978). Levels of instructional difficulty as related to on-task behavior, task completion, and comprehension. *Journal of Learning Disabilities, 11,* 32–39.

*Good, T., Ebmeier, H., & Beckerman, T. (1978). Teaching mathematics in high and low SES classrooms: An empirical comparison. *Journal of Teacher Education, 29,* 85–90.

*Good, T., Grouws, D., & Beckerman, T. (1978). Curriculum pacing: Some empirical data in mathematics. *Journal of Curriculum Studies, 10,* 75–81.

*#Good, T., Grouws, D., & Ebmeier, M. (1983). *Active mathematics teaching.* New York: Longman.

*#Good, T. L., & Grouws, D. A. (1977). Teaching effects: A process-product study in fourth-grade mathematics classrooms. *Journal of Teacher Education, 28*(3), 49–54.

*Good, T. L., & Grouws, D. A. (1979a). *Experimental study of mathematics instruction in elementary schools* (Final Report, National Institute of Education Grant No. NIE-G-79-0103). Columbia: University of Missouri, Center for the Study of Social Behavior.

*#Good, T. L., & Grouws, D. A. (1979b). The Missouri mathematics effectiveness project. *Journal of Educational Psychology, 71,* 355–362.

*Good, T. L., & Grouws, D. A. (1981). *Experimental research in secondary mathematics* (Final Report, National Institute of Education Grant No. NIE-G-79-0103). Columbia: University of Missouri, Center for the Study of Social Behavior.

%Haring, N. G., Lovitt, T. C., Eaton, M. D., & Hansen, C. L. (1978). *The fourth R: Research in the classroom.* Columbus, OH: Merrill.

%Horner, R. H., Day, H. M., Sprague, J. R., O'Brien, M., & Heathfield, L. T. (1991). Interspersed requests: A nonaversive procedure for reducing aggression and self-injury during instruction. *Journal of Applied Behavior Analysis, 24,* 265–278.

*Hughes, D. (1973). An experimental investigation of the effect of pupil responding and teacher reacting on pupil achievement. *American Educational Research Journal, 10,* 21–37.

%Johnson, M. D., & Fawcett, S. B. (1994). Courteous service: Its assessment and modification in a human service organization. *Journal of Applied Behavior Analysis, 27,* 145–152.

*Kounin, J. (1970). *Discipline and group management in classrooms.* New York: Holt, Rinehart, & Winston.

*Larrivee, B., & Algina, J. (1983, April). *Identification of teaching behaviors which predict success for mainstream students.* Paper presented at the annual meeting of the American Educational Research Association. Montreal.

%Lovitt, T. C., & Esveldt, K. A. (1970). The relative effects on math performance of single- versus multiple-ratio schedules: A case study. *Journal of Applied Behavior Analysis, 3,* 261–270.

%Martens, B. K., Ardoin, S. P., Hilt, A. Lannie, A. L., Panahon, C. J., & Wolfe, L. (2002). Sensitivity of children's behavior to probabilistic reward: Effects of a decreasing-ratio lottery system on math performance. *Journal of Applied Behavior Analysis, 35,* 403–406.

%Martens, B. K., & Daly, E. J. (1999). Discovering the alphabetic principle: A lost opportunity for educational reform. *Journal of Behavioral Education, 9,* 33–41.

%Martens, B. K., Hilt, A. M., Needham, L. R., Sutterer, J. R., Panahon, C. J., & Lannie, A. L. (2003). Carryover effects of free reinforcement on children's work completion. *Behavior Modification, 27,* 560–577.

Martens, B. K., & Witt, J. C. (2004). Competence, persistence, and success: The positive psychology of behavioral skill instruction. *Psychology in the Schools, 41*(1), 19–30.

*McConnel, J. (1977). *Relationship between selected teacher behaviors and attitudes/ achievement of algebra classes.* Paper presented at the annual meeting of the American Educational Research Association, New York.

%McCurdy, M., Skinner, C. H., Grantham, K., Watson, T. S., & Hindman, P. M. (2001). Increasing on-task behavior in an elementary student during mathematics seatwork by interspersing additional brief problems. *School Psychology Review, 30,* 23–32.

*McDonald, F. (1976). Report on Phase II of the Beginning Teacher Evaluation Study. *Journal of Teacher Education, 27*(1), 39–42.

*McDonald, F. (1977). Research on teaching: Report on Phase II of the Beginning Teacher Evaluation Study. In G. Borich & K. Fenton (Eds.), *The appraisal of teaching: Concepts and process.* Reading, MA: Addison-Wesley.

*McDonald, F., & Elias, P. (1976). *Executive Summary Report: Beginning Teacher Evaluation Study, Phase II.* Princeton, NJ: Educational Testing Service.

%McDowell, C., & Keenan, M. (2001). Developing fluency and endurance in a child diagnosed with attention deficit hyperactivity disorder. *Journal of Applied Behavior Analysis, 34,* 345–348.

%McGinnis, J. C., Friman, P. C., & Carlyon, W. D. (1999). The effect of token rewards on "intrinsic" motivation for doing math. *Journal of Applied Behavior Analysis, 32,* 375–379.

%Miller, D. L., & Kelley, M. L. (1994). The use of goal setting and contingency contracting for improving children's homework performance. *Journal of Applied Behavior Analysis, 27,* 73–84.

%Neef, N. A., & Lutz, M. N. (2001). Assessment of variables affecting choice and application to classroom interventions. *School Psychology Quarterly, 16,* 239–252.

%Neef, N. A., Shade, D., & Miller, M. S. (1994). Assessing influential dimensions of reinforcers on choice in students with serious emotional disturbance. *Journal of Applied Behavior Analysis, 27,* 575–583.

%Northup, J., George, T., Jones, K., Broussard, C., & Vollmer, T. R. (1996). A comparison of reinforcer assessment methods: The utility of verbal and pictorial choice procedures. *Journal of Applied Behavior Analysis, 29,* 201–212.

*Nuthall, G., & Church, J. (1973). Experimental studies of teaching behavior. In G. Chanan (Ed.), *Towards a science of teaching.* London: National Foundation for Educational Research.

%Patterson, G. R., Reid, J. B., & Dishion, T. J. (1992). *Antisocial boys.* Eugene, OR: Castalia Publishing.

#Reid, E. R. (1978–1982). *The Reader Newsletter.* Salt Lake City: Exemplary Center for Reading Instruction.

%Rhymer, K. N., Henington, C., Skinner, C. H., & Looby, E. J. (1999). The effects of explicit timing on mathematics performance in Caucasian and African American second-grade students. *School Psychology Quarterly, 14,* 397–407.

Rosenshine, B., & Stevens, R. (1986). Teaching functions. In M. C. Wittrock (Ed.), *Handbook of research on teaching* (3rd ed., pp. 376–391). New York: Macmillan.

*Schuck, R. (1981). The impact of set induction on student achievement and retention. *Journal of Educational Research, 74,* 227–232.

%Shinn, M. R. (1989). *Curriculum-based measurement: Assessing special children.* New York: Guilford.

%Simonton, D. K. (2000). Creativity: Cognitive, personal, developmental, and social aspects. *American Psychologist, 55,* 151–158.

%Skinner, C. H. (2002). An empirical analysis of interspersal research: Evidence, implications, and applications of the discrete task completion hypothesis. *Journal of School Psychology, 40,* 347–368.

%Skinner, C. H., Fletcher, P. A., & Henington, C. (1996). Increasing learning trial rates by increasing student response rates: A summary of research. *School Psychology Quarterly, 11,* 313–325.

*Soar, R. S. (1966). *An integrative approach to classroom learning* (Report for NIMH Projects No. 5-R11 MH 01096 and R-11 MH 02045). Philadelphia: Temple University. (ERIC Document Reproduction Service No. ED 033 749)

*Soar, R. S. (1968). Optimum teacher-pupil interaction for pupil growth. *Educational Leadership, 26,* 275–280.

*Soar, R. S. (1973). *Follow-Through Classroom Process Measurement and Pupil Growth (1970–1971) Final Report.* Gainesville: College of Education, University of Florida.

*Soar, R. S. (1977). An integration of findings from four studies of teacher effectiveness. In G. Borich & K. Fenton (Eds.), *The appraisal of teaching: Concepts and process.* Reading, MA: Addison-Wesley.

*Soar, R. S., & Soar, R. M. (1972). An empirical analysis of selected Follow Through Programs: An appraisal of a process approach to evaluation. In G. Borich & K. Fenton (Eds.), *The appraisal of teaching: Concepts and process.* Reading, MA: Addison-Wesley.

*Soar, R. S., & Soar, R. M. (1973). *Classroom behavior, pupil characteristics, and pupil growth for the school year and the summer.* Gainesville: University of Florida, Institute for Development of Human Resources.

*Soar, R. S., & Soar, R. M. (1978). *Setting variables, classroom interaction, and multiple pupil outcomes* (Final Report, Project No. 6-0432, Grant No. NIE-G-76-0100). Washington, DC: National Institute of Education.

*Soar, R. S., & Soar, R. M. (1979). Emotional climate and management. In P. Peterson & H. Walberg (Eds.), *Research on teaching: Concepts, findings, and implications.* Berkeley, CA: McCutchan.

*Solomon, D., & Kendall, A. (1979). *Children in classrooms: An investigation person-environment interaction.* New York: Praeger.

%Stahl, S. A., & Kuhn, M. R. (1995). Does whole language or instruction matched to learning styles help children learn to read? *School Psychology Review, 24,* 393–404.

*Stallings, J. (1980). Allocated academic learning time revisited, or beyond time on task. *Educational Researcher, 8*(11), 11–16.

*#Stallings, J., Corey, R., Fairweather, J., & Needles, M. (1977). *Early Childhood Education classroom evaluation.* Menlo Park, CA: SRI International.

*#Stallings, J., Needles, M., & Staybrook, N. (1979). *The teaching of basic reading skills in secondary schools, Phase II and Phase III.* Menlo Park, CA: SRI International.

*#Stallings, J. A., & Kaskowitz, D. (1974). *Follow-Through Classroom Observation*. Menlo Park, CA: SRI International.

*Tobin, K., & Capie, W. (1982). Relationships between classroom process variables and middle-school science achievement. *Journal of Educational Psychology, 74,* 441–454.

%Vollmer, T. R., Ringdahl, J. E., Roane, H. S., & Marcus, B. (1997). Negative side effects of noncontingent reinforcement. *Journal of Applied Behavior Analysis, 30,* 161–164.

%Weeks, M., & Gaylord-Ross, R. (1981). Task difficulty and aberrant behavior in severely handicapped students. *Journal of Applied Behavior Analysis, 14,* 19–36.

%Witt, J. C., & Elliott, S. N. (1982). The response cost lottery: A time efficient and effective classroom intervention. *Journal of School Psychology, 20,* 155–161.

%Wolery, M., Bailey, D. B., & Sugai, G. M. (1988). *Effective teaching: Principles and procedures of applied behavior analysis with exceptional students*. Boston: Allyn & Bacon.

REFERENCES FOR MAXIMIZING TEACHING TIME

*Acland, H. (1976). Stability of teacher effectiveness: A replication. *Journal of Educational Research, 69,* 289–292.

*Anderson, L. M., Evertson, C. M., & Brophy, J. E. (1979). An experimental study of effective teaching in first-grade reading groups. *The Elementary School Journal, 79,* 193–222.

*Anderson, L. M., Evertson, C. M., & Brophy, J. E. (1982). *Principles of small group instruction* (Occasional paper no. 32). East Lansing: Michigan State University, Institute for Research on Teaching.

#Anderson, L. W. (1994). What time tells us. In L. W. Anderson & H. J. Walberg (Eds.), *Timepiece: Extending and enhancing learning time* (pp. 15–31). Reston, VA: National Association of Secondary School Principals.

Anderson, L. W. (1995). Time, allocated, and instructional. In L. W. Anderson (Ed.), *International encyclopedia of teaching and teacher education* (2nd ed., pp. 204–207). Oxford: Pergamon Press.

#Anderson, L. W., & Postlethwaite, T. N. (1989). What IEA studies say about teachers and teaching. In A. C. Purvis (Ed.), *International comparisons and educational reform*. Reston, VA: Association for Supervision and Curriculum Development.

#Anderson, L. W., Ryan, D. W., & Shapiro, B. J. (1989). *The IEA Classroom Environment Study*. Oxford: Pergamon Press.

*Arehart, J. (1979). Student opportunity to learn related to student achievement of objectives in a probability unit. *Journal of Educational Research, 72,* 253–269.

*Berliner, D., & Tikunoff, W. (1976). The California Beginning Teacher Evaluation Study: Overview of the ethnographic study. *Journal of Teacher Education, 27*(1), 24–30.

*Berliner, D., & Tikunoff, W. (1977). Ethnography in the classroom. In G. Borich & K. Fenton (Eds.), *The appraisal of teaching: Concepts and process*. Reading, MA: Addison-Wesley.

Blatchford, P., Bassett, P., Goldstein, H., & Martin, C. (2003). Are class size differences related to pupils' educational progress and classroom processes? Findings from the Institute of Education Class Size Study of Children Aged 5–7 Years. *British Educational Research Journal, 29,* 709–730.

*Borg, W. (1979). Teacher coverage of academic content and pupil achievement. *Journal of Educational Psychology, 71,* 635–645.

*Borg, W. (1980). Time and school learning. In C. Denham & A. Lieberman (Eds.), *Time to learn* (pp. 33–72). Washington, DC: National Institute of Education.

*Brophy, J. (1973). Stability of teacher effectiveness. *American Educational Research Journal, 10,* 245–252.

*Brophy, J. (1981). Teacher behavior and its effects. *Journal of Educational Psychology, 71,* 733–750.

*Brophy, J., & Evertson, C. (1974a). *Process-product correlations in a Texas Teacher Effectiveness Study: Final report* (Research Report 74-4). Austin: Research and Development Center for Teacher Education, University of Texas. (ERIC Document Reproduction Service No. ED 091 094)

*Brophy, J., & Evertson, C. (1974b). *The Texas Teacher Effectiveness Project: Presentation of non-linear relationships and summary discussion* (Research Report 74-6). Austin: Research and Development Center for Teacher Education, University of Texas. (ERIC Document Reproduction Service No. ED 099 345)

*Brophy, J., & Evertson, C. (1976). *Learning from teaching: A developmental perspective.* Boston: Allyn and Bacon.

Brophy, J., & Good, T. (1986). Teacher behavior and student achievement. In M. C. Wittrock (Ed.), *Handbook of research on teaching* (3rd ed., pp. 328–375). New York: Macmillan.

*Chang, S., & Rath, J. (1971). The schools' contribution to the cumulating deficit. *Journal of Educational Research, 64,* 272–276.

*Comber, L., & Keeves, J. (1973). *Science education in nineteen countries.* New York: Halsted Press.

*Cooley, W., & Leinhart, G. (1980). The Instructional Dimensions Study. *Educational Evaluation and Policy Analysis, 2,* 7–25.

*Crawford, J. (1983). A study of instructional processes in Title I classes: 1981–82. *Journal of Research and Evaluation of the Oklahoma City Public Schools, 13*(1).

*Dunkin, M. J. (1978). Student characteristics, classroom processes, and student achievement. *Journal of Educational Psychology, 70,* 998–1009.

#Durkin, D. (1978–1979). What classroom observations reveal about reading comprehension instruction. *Reading Research Quarterly, 14*(4), 481–533.

*Ebmier, H., & Good, T. (1979). The effects of instructing teachers about good teaching on mathematics achievement of fourth grade students. *American Educational Research Journal, 16,* 1–16.

*Emmer, E., Evertson, C., & Anderson, L. (1980). Effective classroom management at the beginning of the school year. *Elementary School Journal, 80,* 219–231.

*Emmer, E., Evertson, C., & Brophy, J. (1979). Stability of teacher effects in junior high school classrooms. *American Educational Research Journal, 16,* 71–75.

*Evertson, C., Anderson, C., Anderson, L., & Brophy, J. (1980). Relationships between classroom behaviors and student outcomes in junior high mathematics and English classes. *American Educational Research Journal, 17,* 43–60.

*Evertson, C., Anderson, L., & Brophy, J. (1978). *Texas Junior High School Study: Final report of process-outcome relationship* (Report No. 4061). Austin: Research and Development Center for Teacher Education, University of Texas.

*Evertson, C., & Emmer, E. (1982). Effective management at the beginning of the school year in junior high classes. *Journal of Educational Psychology, 74,* 485–498.

*Evertson, C., Emmer, E., & Brophy, J., (1980). Predictors of effective teaching in junior high mathematics classrooms. *Journal for Research in Mathematics Education, 11,* 167–178.

Fisher, C. W., & Berliner, D. C. (Eds.). (1985). *Perspectives on instructional time.* New York: Longman.

*Fisher, C. W., Berliner, D. C., Filby, N. N., Marliave, R., Cahen, L. S., & Dishaw, M. M. (1980). Teaching behaviors, academic learning time, and student achievement: An overview. In C. Denham & A. Lieberman (Eds.), *Time to learn* (pp. 7–32). Washington, DC: U.S. Government Printing Office.

#Fogleman, K. (1978). School attendance, attainment, and behavior. *British Journal of Educational Psychology, 48,* 148–158.

#Frederick, W. C. (1980). Instructional time. *Evaluation of Education, 4,* 117–118.

#Fuller, B. (1987). What factors raise achievement in the third world? *Review of Educational Research, 57,* 255–292.

*Gage, N., & Coladarci, T. (1980). *Replication of an experiment with a research-based inservice teacher education program.* Stanford, CA: Stanford University, Center for Educational Research, Program on Teaching Effectiveness.

*Good, T., Ebmeier, H., & Beckerman, T. (1978). Teaching mathematics in high and low SES classrooms: An empirical comparison. *Journal of Teacher Education, 29,* 85–90.

*Good, T., Grouws, D., & Beckerman, T. (1978). Curriculum pacing: Some empirical data in mathematics. *Journal of Curriculum Studies, 10,* 75–81.

*Good, T., Grouws, D., & Ebmeier, M. (1983). *Active mathematics teaching.* New York: Longman.

*Good, T. L., & Grouws, D. A. (1977). Teaching effects: A process-product study in fourth-grade mathematics classrooms. *Journal of Teacher Education, 28*(3), 49–54.

*Good, T. L., & Grouws, D. A. (1979a). *Experimental study of mathematics instruction in elementary schools* (Final Report, National Institute of Education Grant No. NIE-G-79-0103). Columbia: University of Missouri, Center for the Study of Social Behavior.

*Good, T. L., & Grouws, D. A. (1979b). The Missouri mathematics effectiveness project. *Journal of Educational Psychology, 71,* 355–362.

*Good, T. L., & Grouws, D. A. (1981). *Experimental research in secondary mathematics* (Final Report, National Institute of Education Grant No. NIE-G-79-0103). Columbia: University of Missouri, Center for the Study of Social Behavior.

*Harris, A., & Serwer, B. (1966). The CRAFT Project: Instructional time and reading research. *Reading Research Quarterly, 2,* 27–57.

*Husen, T. (Ed.). (1967). *International study of achievement in mathematics* (Vol. 1). New York: Wiley.

*Kounin, J. (1970). *Discipline and group management in classrooms.* New York: Holt, Rinehart, & Winston.

*Larrivee, B., & Algina, J. (1983, April). *Identification of teaching behaviors which predict success for mainstream students.* Paper presented at the annual meeting of the American Educational Research Association. Montreal.

#MacKay, A. (1979). *Project Quest: Teaching strategies and pupil achievement* (Research Report No. 79-1-3). Edmonton: University of Alberta, Centre for Research in Teaching, Faculty of Education.

*McConnel, J. (1977). *Relationship between selected teacher behaviors and attitudes/ achievement of algebra classes.* Paper presented at the annual meeting of the American Educational Research Association, New York.

*McDonald, F. (1976). Report on Phase II of the Beginning Teacher Evaluation Study. *Journal of Teacher Education, 27*(1), 39–42.

*McDonald, F. (1977). Research on teaching: Report on Phase II of the Beginning Teacher Evaluation Study. In G. Borich & K. Fenton (Eds.), *The appraisal of teaching: Concepts and process*. Reading, MA: Addison-Wesley.

*McDonald, F., & Elias, P. (1976). *Executive Summary Report: Beginning Teacher Evaluation Study, Phase II*. Princeton, NJ: Educational Testing Service.

Mevarech, Z. R., & Kramarski, B. (2003). The effects of metacognitive training versus worked-out examples on students' mathematical reasoning. *British Journal of Educational Psychology, 73*, 449–471.

*Nuthall, G., & Church, J. (1973). Experimental studies of teaching behavior. In G. Chanan (Ed.), *Towards a science of teaching*. London: National Foundation for Educational Research.

#Porter, A. (1989). A curriculum out of balance: The case of elementary school mathematics. *Educational Researcher, 18*(5), 9–15.

*Ramp, E., & Rhine, W. (1981). Behavior analysis model. In W. Rhine (Ed.), *Making schools more effective: New directions from Follow Through* (pp. 155–197). New York: Academic Press.

#Reynolds, A. J., & Walberg, H. J. (1991). A structural model of science achievement. *Journal of Educational Psychology, 83*(1), 97–107.

*Rosenshine, B. (1971). *Teaching behaviors and student achievement*. London: National Foundation for Educational Research.

#Sanford, J. P., & Evertson, C. M. (1983). Time use and activities in junior high classes. *Journal of Educational Research, 76*(3), 140–147.

*Smith, L. (1979). Task-oriented lessons and student achievement. *Journal of Educational Research, 73*, 16–19.

Smith, P., Molnar, A., & Zahorik, J. (2003). Class-size reduction: A fresh look at the data. *Educational Leadership, 61*(1), 72–74.

#Smythe, W. J. (1987). Time. In M. J. Dunkin (Ed.), *The international encyclopedia of teaching and teacher education*. Oxford: Pergamon Press.

*Stallings, J., Corey, R., Fairweather, J., & Needles, M. (1977). *Early Childhood Education classroom evaluation*. Menlo Park, CA: SRI International.

*Stallings, J., Needles, M., & Staybrook, N. (1979). *The teaching of basic reading skills in secondary schools, Phase II and Phase III*. Menlo Park, CA: SRI International.

*Stallings, J. A., & Kaskowitz, D. (1974). *Follow-Through Classroom Observation*. Menlo Park, CA: SRI International.

*Veldman, D., & Brophy, J. (1974). Measuring teacher effects on pupil achievement. *Journal of Educational Psychology, 66*, 319–324.

#Walberg, H. J., & Frederick, W. C. (1991). *Extending learning time*. Washington, DC: U.S. Department of Education, Office of Educational Research and Improvement.

#Welsh, W. W., Anderson, R. E., & Harris, L. J. (1982). The effects of schooling on mathematics achievement. *American Educational Research Journal, 19*, 145–153.

REFERENCES FOR PROVIDING AMPLE LEARNING TIME

*+Abraham, F. J., & Newton, J. M. (1974). *The interview technique as a personalized system of instruction for economics: The Oregon experience*. Paper presented at the National Conference on Personalized Instruction in Higher Education, Washington, DC.

$Anania, J. (1981). *The effects of quality of instruction on the cognitive and affective learning of students.* Unpublished doctoral dissertation, University of Chicago.

+Anderson, L. W. (1973). *Time and school learning.* Unpublished doctoral dissertation, University of Chicago.

$&Anderson, L. W. (1975a). Student involvement in learning and school achievement. *California Journal of Educational Research, 26,* 53–62.

*$&Anderson, L. W. (1975b). *Time to criterion: An experimental study.* Paper presented at the annual meeting of the American Educational Research Association, Washington, DC. (ERIC Document Reproduction Service No. ED 108 006)

*$&+Anderson, L. W. (1976). An empirical investigation of individual differences in time to learn. *Journal of Educational Psychology, 68,* 226–233.

Anderson, L. W. (1985). Time and learning. In C. W. Fisher & D. C. Berliner (Eds.), *Perspectives on instructional time* (pp. 157–168). White Plains, NY: Longman.

*#@$&Anderson, L. W., Scott, C., & Hutlock, N. (1976, April). *The effects of a mastery learning program on selected cognitive, affective, and ecological variables in grades 1 through 6.* Paper presented at the annual meeting of the American Educational Research Association, San Francisco.

+Anderson, O. T., & Artman, R. A. (1972). A self-paced independent study, introductory physics sequence—description and evaluation. *American Journal of Physics, 40,* 1737–1742.

Anderson, S. A. (1994). *Synthesis of research on mastery learning* (Information Analysis). (ERIC Document Reproduction Service No. ED 382 567)

=%Arlin, M., & Webster, J. (1983). Time cost of mastery learning. *Journal of Educational Psychology, 75,* 187–195.

*$&Arlin, M., & Westbury, I. (1976). The leveling effect of teacher pacing on science content mastery. *Journal of Research on Science Teaching, 13,* 213–219.

^Ashworth, T. (1992). Using writing-to-learn strategies in community college associate degree nursing programs. *Dissertation Abstracts International, 53*(03), 696A. (UMI No. 9223432).

*Austin, S. M., & Gilbert, K. E. (1973). Student performance in a Keller-Plan course in introductory electricity and magnetism. *American Journal of Physics, 41,* 12–18.

Aviles, C. B. (1998). A contrast of mastery learning and non-mastery learning instruction in an undergraduate social work course. Paper presented at the annual meeting of the Council on Social Work Education, Orlando, FL.

^Ayers, W. (1993). A study of the effectiveness of expressive writing as a learning enhancement in middle school science. *Dissertation Abstracts International, 54*(10), 3709A. (UMI No. 9408754)

*Badia, P., Stutts, C., & Harsh, J. (1978). Do methods of instruction and measures of different abilities and study habits interact? In J. G. Sherman, R. S. Ruskin, & R. M. Lazar (Eds.), *Personalized instruction in education today* (pp. 113–128). San Francisco: San Francisco Press.

<Baer, D. M., Blount, R. L., Detrich, R., & Stokes, T. F. (1987). Using intermittent reinforcement to program maintenance of verbal/nonverbal correspondence. *Journal of Applied Behavior Analysis, 20,* 179–184.

^Baisch, C. (1990). Writing methods used in the teaching of mathematics: An empirical study. *Masters Abstracts International, 29*(01), 17. (UMI No. 1341157)

^Baker, B. (1994). Analysis of the effect of in-class writing on the learning of function concepts in college algebra. *Dissertation Abstracts International, 55*(09), 2753A. (UMI No. 9503527)

<Ballinger, C. (1993). *Annual report to the association on the status of year-round education*. (ERIC Document Reproduction Service No. ED 024 990)

Bangert-Drowns, R. L., Hurley, M. M., & Wilkinson, B. (2004). The effects of school-based writing-to-learn interventions on academic achievement: A meta-analysis. *Review of Educational Research, 74*(1), 29–58.

!Barr, R. (1974). Instructional pace differences and their effect on reading acquisition. *Reading Research Quarterly, 9*, 526–554.

!Barr, R. (1975). How children are taught to read: Grouping and pacing. *School Review, 83*, 479–498.

^Bauman, M. (1992). The effect of teacher-directed and student-directed journal writing n fifth-grade student mathematics achievement. *Dissertation Abstracts International, 53*(06), 1830A. (UMI No. 9227116)

^Becker, R. (1996). Responses to teacher-directed and student-directed writing prompts and performance on the IEA survey of achievement in literature. *Dissertation Abstracts International, 57*(08), 3427A. (UMI No. 9701474)

^Bell, E. S., & Bell, R. N. (1985). Writing and mathematical problem solving: Arguments in favor of synthesis. *School Science and Mathematics, 85*(3), 210–221.

*=Benson, J. S., & Yeany, R. H. (1980, April). *Generalizability of diagnostic-prescriptive teaching strategies across student locus of control and multiple instructional units*. Paper presented at the annual meeting of the American Educational Research Association, Boston. (ERIC Document Reproduction Service No. 187 534)

<Berkowitz, M. J., & Martens, B. K. (2001). Assessing teachers' and students' preferences for school-based reinforcement: Agreement across methods and different effort requirements. *Journal of Developmental and Physical Disabilities, 13*, 373–387.

*+Billings, D. B. (1974). PSI versus the lecture course in the principles of economics: A quasi-controlled experiment. In R. S. Ruskin & S. F. Bono (Eds.), *Personalized instruction in higher education* (pp. 30–37). Washington, DC: Center for Personalized Instruction.

*$=Blackburn, K. T., & Nelson, D. (1985, April). *Differences between a group using a traditional format with mastery learning and a group using a traditional format only in developmental mathematics courses at the university level: Implications for teacher education programs*. Paper presented at the annual meeting of the American Educational Research Association, Chicago. (ERIC Document Reproduction Service No. ED 258 948)

*Blasingame, J. W. (1975). Student attitude and performance in a personalized system of instruction course in business administration—Correlates of performance with personality traits. *Dissertation Abstracts International, 36*, 3840. (University Microfilms No. 75-2834)

$&+=Block, J. H. (1972). Student learning and the setting of mastery performance standards. *Educational Horizons, 50*, 183–191.

+Block, J. H. (1973). *Mastery performance standards and student learning*. Unpublished study, University of California, Santa Barbara.

Block, J. H. (1980). Success rate. In C. Denham & A. Liberman (Eds.), *Time to learn* (pp. 95–106). Washington, DC: U.S. Government Printing Office.

Block, J. H., & Anderson, L. W. (1975). *Mastery learning in classroom instruction*. New York: Macmillan.

Block, J. H., & Burns, R. B. (1976). Mastery Learning. In L. Schulman (Ed.), *Review of research in education* (Vol. 4, pp. 3–49). Itasca, IL: F. E. Peacock.

$+Block, J. H., & Tierney, M. (1974). An exploration of two correction procedures used in mastery learning approaches to instruction. *Journal of Educational Psychology, 66,* 962–967.

Bloom, B. S. (1968). Learning for mastery. (UCLA-CSEIP) *Evaluation Comments, 1*(2), 1–12.

Bloom, B. S. (1985). Learning for mastery. In C. W. Fisher & D. C. Berliner (Eds.), *Perspectives on instructional time.* White Plains, NY: Longman.

*+Born, D. G., & Davis, M. L. (1974). Amount and distribution of study in a personalized instruction course and in a lecture course. *Journal of Applied Behavior Analysis, 7,* 365–375.

*+Born, D. G., Gledhill, S. M., & Davis, M. L. (1972). Examination performance in lecture-discussion and personalized instruction courses. *Journal of Applied Behavior Analysis, 5,* 33–43.

=Bostow, D. E., & O'Connor, R. J. (1973). A comparison of two college classroom testing procedures: Required remediation versus no remediation. *Journal of Applied Behavior Analysis, 6,* 599–607.

*+Breland, N. S., & Smith, M. P. (1974). A comparison of PSI and traditional methods of instruction for teaching introduction to psychology. In R. S. Ruskin & S. F. Bono (Eds.), *Personalized instruction in higher education* (pp. 21–25). Washington, DC: Center for Personalized Instruction.

^Brodney, S. (1994). The relationship between student achievement, student attitude, and student perception of teacher effectiveness and the use of journals as a learning tool in mathematics. *Dissertation Abstracts International, 54*(08), 2884A. (UMI No. 9402523)

*$Bryant, N. D., Payne, H. R., & Gettinger, M. (1982). Applying the mastery model to sight word instruction for disabled readers. *Journal of Experimental Education, 50,* 116–121.

$Burke, A. (1983). *Students' potential for learning contrasted under tutorial and group approaches to instruction.* Unpublished doctoral dissertation, University of Chicago.

$&+=Burrows, C. K., & Okey, J. R. (1975*). The effects of a mastery learning strategy on achievement.* Paper presented at the annual meeting of the American Educational Research Association, Washington, DC.

^Burton, G. (1986). Essay writing in college mathematics and its effect on achievement. *Dissertation Abstracts International, 47*(07), 2492A. (UMI No. 8623121)

*#@$Cabezon, E. (1984). *The effects of marked changes in student achievement pattern on the students, their teachers, and their parents: The Chilean case.* Unpublished doctoral dissertation, University of Chicago.

=Caldwell, E. C., Bissonnette, K., Klishis, M. J., Ripley, M., Farudi, P. P., Hochstetter, G. T., & Radiker, J. E. (1978). Mastery: The essential essential in PSI. *Teaching of Psychology, 5,* 59–65.

<Carnine, D. (1992). Expanding the notion of teachers' rights: Access to tools that work. *Journal of Applied Behavior Analysis, 24,* 13–19.

<Carr, E. G., & Durand, V. M. (1985). Reducing behavior problems through functional communication training. *Journal of Behavior Analysis, 18,* 111–126.

$=Chiappetta, E. L., & McBride, J. W. (1980). Exploring the effects of general remediation on ninth-graders' achievement of the mole concept. *Science Education, 64,* 609–614.

*$=Clark, C. P., Guskey, T. P., & Benninga, J. S. (1983). The effectiveness of mastery learning strategies in undergraduate education courses. *Journal of Educational Research, 76*, 210–214.

*Clark, S. G. (1975). An innovation for introductory sociology: Personalized system of instruction. In J. M. Johnston (Ed.), *Behavior research and technology in higher education* (pp. 117–124). Springfield, IL: Charles C. Thomas.

*+Coldeway, D. O., Santowski, M., O'Brien, R., & Lagowski, V. (1975). Comparison of small group contingency management with the personalized system of instruction and the lecture system. In J. M. Johnston (Ed.), *Research and technology in college and university teaching* (pp. 215–224). Gainesville: University of Florida.

*+Cole, C., Martin, S., & Vincent, J. (1975). A comparison of two teaching formats at the college level. In J. M. Johnston (Ed.), *Behavior research and technology in higher education* (pp. 61–74). Springfield, IL: Charles C. Thomas.

*Condo, P. (1974, April). *The analysis and evaluation of a self-paced course in calculus.* Paper presented at the National Conference on Personalized Instruction in Higher Education, Washington, DC.

<Cooper, B., Nye, B., Charlton, K., Lindsay, J., & Greathouse, S. (1996). The effects of summer vacation on achievement test scores: A narrative and meta-analytic review. *Review of Educational Research, 66*, 227–268.

*+Cooper, J. L., & Greiner, J. M. (1971). Contingency management in an introductory psychology course produces better retention. *Psychological Record, 21*, 391–400.

*Corey, J. R., & McMichael, J. S. (1974). Retention in a PSI introductory psychology course. In J. G. Sherman (Ed.), *PSI germinal papers* (pp. 17–19). Washington, DC: Center for Personalized Instruction.

+Corey, J. R., McMichael, J. S., & Tremont, P. J., (1970, April). *Long-term effects of personalized instruction in an introductory psychology course.* Paper presented at the meeting of the Eastern Psychology Association, Atlantic City.

*Cote, J. D. (1976). Biology by PSI in a community college. In B. A. Green Jr. (Ed.), *Personalized instruction and higher education.* Washington, DC: Center for Personalized Instruction.

*Cross, M. Z., & Semb, G. (1976). An analysis of the effects of personalized instruction on students at different initial performance levels in an introductory college nutrition course. *Journal of Personalized Instruction, 1*, 47–50.

<Daly, E. J., Lentz, F. E., & Boyer, J. (1996). The instructional hierarchy: A conceptual model for understanding the effective components of reading interventions. *School Psychology Quarterly, 11*, 369–386.

<Daly, E. J., Martens, B. K., Hamler, K., Dool, E. J., & Eckert, T. L. (1999). A brief experimental analysis for identifying instructional components needed to improve oral reading fluency. *Journal of Applied Behavior Analysis, 32*, 83–94.

^Davis, B. (1990). The effects of expressive writing on the social studies achievement, writing fluency, and learning retention of fourth-grade students. *Dissertation Abstracts International, 51*(09), 3003A. (UMI No. 9104761)

^Davis, J. (1996). An investigation of the relationship between writing-to-learn activities and learning outcomes for introductory statistics students. *Dissertation Abstracts International, 57*(06), 2399A. (UMI No. 9633645)

^Day, S. (1994). Learning in large sociology classes: Journals and attendance. *Teaching Sociology, 22*, 151–165.

*=Decker, D. F. (1976). *Teaching to achieve learning mastery by using retesting techniques.* Doctoral dissertation, Nova University. (ERIC Document Reproduction Service No. ED 133 002)

$Denton, W. L., Ory, J. C., Glassnap, D. R., & Poggio, J. P. (1976). *Grade expectations within a mastery learning strategy.* Paper presented at the annual meeting of the American Educational Research Association, San Francisco. (ERIC Document Reproduction Service No. ED 126 105)

*$=Dillashaw, F. G., & Okey, J. R. (1983). Effects of a modified mastery learning strategy on achievement, attitudes, and on-task behavior of high school chemistry students. *Journal of Research and Science Teaching, 20,* 203–211.

^DiPillo, M. (1994). A quantitative/qualitative analysis of student journal writing in middle-grade mathematics classes. *Dissertation Abstracts International, 55*(04), 0896A. (UMI No. 9425886)

$Duby, P. B. (1981). *Attributions and attribution change: Effects of a mastery learning instructional approach.* Paper presented at the annual meeting of the American Educational Research Association, Los Angeles. (ERIC Document Reproduction Service No. ED 200 640)

=Dulkelberger, G. E., & Heikkinen, H. (1984). The influence of repeatable testing on retention in mastery learning. *School Science and Mathematics, 84,* 590–597.

<DuPaul, G. J., & Henningson, P. N. (1993). Peer tutoring effects on the classroom performance of children with Attention Deficit Hyperactivity Disorder. *School Psychology Review, 22,* 134–143.

=Dustin, D. S., & Johnson, S. L. (1974). *Some Effects of a Test Criterion.* Unpublished manuscript, State University of New York, Plattsburgh.

<Eisenberger, R., & Cameron, J. (1996). Detrimental effects of reward: Reality or myth? *American Psychologist, 51,* 1153–1166.

<Erchul, W. P., & Martens, B. K. (2002). *School consultation: Conceptual and empirical bases of practice* (2nd ed.). New York: Plenum.

*#@=Fagan, J. S. (1976). Mastery learning: The relationship of mastery procedures and aptitude to the achievement and retention of transportation-environment concepts by seventh-grade students. *Dissertation Abstracts International, 36,* 5981. (University Microfilms No. 76-6402)

*=Fehlen, J. E. (1976). Mastery learning techniques in the traditional classroom setting. *School Science and Mathematics, 76*(3), 241–245.

=Fernald, P. S, Chiseri, M. J., Lawson, D. W., Scroggs, G. F., & Riddell, J. C. (1975). Systematic manipulation of student pacing, the perfection requirement, and contact with a teaching assistant in an introductory psychology course. *Teaching of Psychology, 2,* 147–151.

*Fernald, P. S., & DuNann, D. H. (1975). Effects of individualized instruction upon low- and high- achieving students' study behavior and students' evaluation of mastery. *Journal of Experimental Education, 43,* 27–34.

$&+=Fiel, R. L., & Okey, J. R. (1974). Effects of formative evaluation and remediation on mastery of intellectual skill. *Journal of Educational Research, 68,* 253–255.

%Fisher, C. W., Berliner, D.C., Filby, N. N., Marliave, R., Cahen, L. S., & Dishaw, M. M. (1980). Teaching behaviors, academic learning time, and student achievement: An overview. In C. Denham & A. Lieberman (Eds.), *Time to learn* (pp. 7–32). Washington, DC: U.S. Government Printing Office.

%Fitzpatrick, K. A. (1981). *An investigation of secondary classroom material strategies for increasing student academic engaged time.* Doctoral dissertation, University of Illinois at Urbana–Champaign.

%Fitzpatrick, K. A. (1982). *The effect of a secondary classroom management training program on teacher and student behavior.* Paper presented at the annual meeting of the American Educational Research Association, New York.

$&Fitzpatrick, K. A. (1985). *Group-based mastery learning: A Robin Hood approach to instruction?* Paper presented at the annual meeting of the American Educational Research Association, Chicago.

$&Frederick, W., & Walberg, H. (1979). *Learning as a function of time.* Paper presented at the annual meeting of the American Educational Research Association, San Francisco.

<Fuchs, L. S., & Fuchs, D. (1986). Effects of systematic formative evaluation on student achievement: A meta-analysis. *Exceptional Children, 53*, 199–208.

^Ganguli, A. (1989). Integrating writing in developmental mathematics. *College Teaching, 37*(4), 140–142.

Gettinger, M. (1984). Achievement as a function of time spent in learning and time needed for learning. *American Educational Research Journal, 21*(3), 617–628.

<Gickling, E. E., & Armstrong, D. L. (1978). Levels of instructional difficulty as related to on-task behavior, task completion, and comprehension. *Journal of Learning Disabilities, 11*, 32–39.

^Giovinazzo, A. (1996). Conceptual writing and its impact on performance in mathematical processes in college algebra. *Dissertation Abstracts International, 57*(12), 5089A. (UMI No. 9716790)

+Glassnap, B. R., Poggio, J. P., & Ory, J. C. (1975, March–April). *Cognitive and affective consequences of mastery and non-mastery instructional strategies.* Paper presented at the annual meeting of the American Educational Research Association, Washington, DC.

*=Goldwater, B. C., & Acker, L. E. (1975). Instructor-paced, mass-testing for mastery: Performance in an introductory psychology course. *Teaching of Psychology, 2*, 152–155.

!Good, T., Ebmeier, H., & Beckerman, T. (1978). Curriculum pacing: Some empirical data in mathematics. *Journal of Curriculum Studies, 10*, 75–81.

^Goss, M. (1998). Writing to learn: An experiment in calculus. *Dissertation Abstracts International, 59*(12), 4385A. (UMI No. 9916028)

^Greene, B., Johnson, L., Harris, W., & Flowers, J. (1990–1991). Revitalizing writing across the curriculum: Writing in the sciences. *Community Review, 11*(1–2), 46–75.

*Gregory, I., Smeltzer, D. J., Knopp, W., & Gardner, M. (1976). *Teaching of psychiatry by PSI: Impact on National Board Examinations Scores.* Unpublished manuscript, Ohio State University, Columbus.

^Guckin, A. (1992). The role of mathematics informal focussed writing in college mathematics instruction. *Dissertation Abstracts International, 53*(05), 1435A. (UMI No. 9226445)

*$&Guskey, T. R. (1982). The effects of staff development on teachers' perceptions about effective teaching. *Journal of Educational Research, 76*, 378–381.

*$&Guskey, T. R. (1984). The influence of changes in instructional effectiveness upon the affective characteristics of teachers. *American Educational Research Journal, 21*, 245–259.

$Guskey, T. R. (1985). The effects of staff development on teachers' perceptions about effective teaching. *Journal of Educational Research, 79,* 378–381.

*$=Guskey, T. R., Benninga, J. S., & Clark, C. B. (1984). Mastery learning and students' attributions at the college level. *Research in Higher Education, 20,* 491–498.

Guskey, T. R., & Gates, S. L. (1986). Synthesis of research on the effects of mastery learning in elementary and secondary classrooms. *Educational Leadership, 43*(8), 73–80.

*$=Guskey, T. R., & Monsaas, J. A. (1979). Mastery learning: A model for academic success in urban junior colleges. *Research and Higher Education, 11,* 263–274.

Guskey, T. R., & Pigott, T. D. (1988). Research on group-based mastery learning programs: A meta-analysis. *Journal of Educational Research, 81*(4), 197–216.

*Hardin, L. D. (1977). A study of the influence of a physics personalized system of instruction versus lecture on cognitive reason, achievement, attitudes and critical thinking. *Dissertation Abstracts International, 38,* 4711A–4712A. (University Microfilms No. 77-30826)

<Haring, N. G., Lovitt, T. C., Eaton, M. D., & Hansen, C. L. (1978). *The fourth R: Research in the classroom.* Columbus, OH: Merrill.

*Hecht, L. W. (1980, April). *Stalking mastery learning in its natural habitat.* Paper presented at the annual meeting of the American Educational Research Association, Boston.

*Heffley, P. D. (1974). The implementation of the personalized system of instruction in the freshman chemistry course at Censius College. In R. S. Ruskin & S. F. Bono (Eds.), *Personalized instruction in higher education* (pp. 140–145). Washington, DC: Center for Personalized Instruction.

*Herring, B. G. (1977). *The written PSI study guide in a non-PSI course.* Austin: University of Texas.

*Herring, B. G. (1975, December). *Cataloguing and classification.* Austin: University of Texas.

*Herrmann, T. (1984, August). *TELIDON as an enhancer of student interest and performance.* Paper presented at the annual meeting of the American Psychological Association, Toronto. (ERIC Document Reproduction Service No. ED 251 004)

*Hindman, C. D. (1974). Evaluation of three programming techniques in introductory psychology courses. In R. S. Ruskin & S. F. Bono (Eds.), *Personalized instruction in higher education* (pp. 38–42). Washington, DC: Center for Personalized Instruction.

*=Honeycutt, J. K. (1974, April). *The effect of computer managed instruction on content learning of undergraduate students.* Paper presented at the annual meeting of the American Educational Research Association, Chicago. (ERIC Document Reproduction Service No. ED 089 682)

<Horner, R. H., Day, H. M., Sprague, J. R., O'Brien, M., & Heathfield, L. T. (1991). Interspersed requests: A nonaversive procedure for reducing aggression and self-injury during instruction. *Journal of Applied Behavior Analysis, 24,* 265–278.

^Horton, P., Fronk, R., & Walton, R. (1985). The effect of writing assignments on achievement in college general chemistry. *Journal of Research in Science Teaching, 22*(6), 535–541.

=Hutchcraft, F. R., & Kruger, B. S. (1977, April). *An Empirical Validation of the Unit Perfection Requirement in Personalized Systems of Instruction Methodology.* Paper presented at the Fourth National Conference on Personalized Instruction in Higher Education, San Francisco.

*Hymel, G. M. (1974). *An investigation of John B. Carrol's model of school learning as a theoretical basis for the organizational structuring of schools* (Final Report, NIE Project No. 3-1359). University of New Orleans, New Orleans, LA.

=Hymel, G. M., & Gaines, W. G. (1977, April). *An Investigation of John B. Carroll's Model of School Learning as a Basis for Facilitating Individualized Instruction by Way of School Organizational Patterning.* Paper presented at the annual meeting of the American Educational Research Association, New York. (ERIC Document Reproduction Service No. ED 136 414).

*=Hymel, G. M., & Matthews, G. (1980). Effects of a mastery approach on social studies achievement and unit evaluation. *Southern Journal of Educational Research, 14,* 191–204.

^Hyser, C. (1992). Writing to learn: Specific applications in third-grade social studies. *Dissertation Abstracts International, 53*(06), 1828A. (UMI No. 9231040)

*Jackman, L. E. (1982). Evaluation of a modified Keller method in a biochemistry laboratory course. *Journal of Chemical Education, 59,* 225–227.

*Jacko, E. J. (1974). Lecture instruction versus a personalized system of instruction: Effects on individuals with differing achievement anxiety and academic achievement. *Dissertation Abstracts International, 35,* 3521. (University Microfilms No. AAD 74-27211)

^Johnson, L. (1991). Effects of essay writing on achievement in algebra. *Dissertation Abstracts International, 52*(03), 0833A. (UMI No. 9124202)

<Johnson, M. D., & Fawcett, S. B. (1994). Courteous service: Its assessment and modification in a human service organization. *Journal of Applied Behavior Analysis, 27,* 145–152.

^Johnson, V. (1998). An investigation of the effects of instructional strategies on conceptual understanding of young children in mathematics. *Dissertation Abstracts International, 59*(11), 4089A.

+Johnston, J. M., & Pennypacker, H. S. (1971). A behavioral approach to college teaching. *American Psychologist, 26,* 219–244.

*#@$&Jones, B. F., Monsaas, J. A., & Katims, M. (1979, April). *Improving reading comprehension: Embedding diverse learning strategies within a mastery learning instructional framework.* Paper presented at the annual meeting of the American Educational Research Association, San Francisco. (ERIC Document Reproduction Service No. ED 170 698)

$+Jones, E. L., Gordon, H. A., & Stectman, G. L. (1975). *Mastery learning: A strategy for academic success in a community college.* Los Angeles: ERIC Clearinghouse for Junior Colleges. (ERIC Document Reproduction Service No. 115 315)

+Jones, F. G. (1974). *The effects of mastery and aptitude on learning, retention, and time.* Unpublished doctoral dissertation, University of Georgia.

=Jones, F. G. (1975). The effects of mastery and aptitude on learning, retention, and time. *Dissertation Abstracts International, 35,* 6537. (University Microfilms No. 75-8126)

+Karlin, B. M. (1972). *The Keller method of instruction compared to the traditional method of instruction in a Lafayette College history course.* Unpublished paper, Lafayette College, Lafayette, PA.

Karweit, N. (1993). Effective preschool and kindergarten programs for students at risk. In B. Spodek (Ed.), *Handbook of research on the education of young children* (pp. 385–411). New York: Macmillan.

^Kasparek, R. (1993). Effects of integrated writing on attitude and algebra performance of high school students. *Dissertation Abstracts International, 54*(08), 2931A. (UMI No. 9402483)

*#@Katims, M., Smith, J. K., Steele, C., & Wick, J. W. (1977, April). *The Chicago mastery learning reading program: An interim evaluation.* Paper presented at the annual meeting of the American Educational Research Association, New York. (ERIC Document Reproduction Service No. ED 137 737)

*#@Kersh, M. E. (1970). *A strategy of mastery learning in fifth grade arithmetic.* Unpublished doctoral dissertation, University of Chicago.

+Kim, Y., Cho, G., Park, J., & Park, M. (1974). *An application of a new instructional model* (Research Report No. 8). Seoul, Korea: Korean Educational Development Institute.

*=Knight, J. M., Williams J. D., & Jardon, M. L. (1975). The effects of contingency avoidance on programmed student achievement. *Research in Higher Education, 3,* 11–17.

=Komaridis, G. V. (1971). The effects of four testing systems on schedules of study, test performance, and retention of materials. *Dissertation Abstracts International, 32,* 790A. (University Microfilms No. 71-19,498)

^Konopak, B., Martin, S., & Martin, M. (1990). Using a writing strategy to enhance sixth-grade students' comprehension of content material. *Journal of Reading Behavior, 22*(1), 19–37.

Krank, H. M., & Moon, C. E. Can a combined master/cooperative learning environment positively impact undergraduate academic and affective outcomes? *Journal of College Reading and Learning, 31*(2), 195–208.

*Kulik, C., & Kulik, J. (1976). PSI and the mastery model. In B. A. Green, Jr. (Ed.), *Personalized instruction in higher education* (pp. 155–159). Washington, DC: Center for Personalized Instruction.

Kulik, C., Kulik, J., & Bangert-Drowns, R. (1990a). Effectiveness of mastery learning programs: A meta-analysis. *Review of Educational Research, 60*(2), 265–269.

Kulik, C-L. C., & Kulik, J. A. (1987). Mastery testing and student learning: A meta-analysis. *Journal of Educational Technology Systems, 15*(3), 325–345.

Kulik, J., Kulik, C., & Bangert-Drowns, R. (1990b). Is there better evidence on mastery learning? A response to Slavin. *Review of Educational Research, 60*(2), 303–307.

+Kulik, J. A., Kulik, C., & Carmichael, K. (1974). The Keller Plan in science teaching. *Science, 183,* 379–383.

=Kulik, J. A, Kulik, L. C., & Hertzler, E. C. (1977). Modular college teaching with and without required remediation. *Journal of Personalized Instruction, 2,* 70–75.

^Langer, J., & Applebee, A. (1987). *How writing shapes thinking.* Urbana, IL: National Council of Teachers of English.

=Lawler, R. M. (1971). An investigation of selected instructional strategies in an undergraduate computer-managed instruction course. *Dissertation Abstracts International, 32,* 1190A–1191A. (University Microfilms No. 71-24, 610)

+Lee, Y. D., Kim, C. S., Kim, H., Park B. Y., Yoo, H. K., Chang, S. M., & Kim, S. C. (1971). *Interaction improvement studies of the Mastery Learning Project* (Final Report on the Mastery Learning Project, April–November 1971). Seoul, Korea: Educational Research Center, Seoul National University.

*=Leppman, P. K., & Herrmann, T. F. (1981, August). *PSI—What are the critical elements?* Paper presented at the annual meeting of the American Psychological Association, Los Angeles. (ERIC Document Reproduction Service No. ED 214 502)

$+Levin, T. (1975). *The effect of content prerequisites and process-oriented experiences on application ability in a learning of probability.* Unpublished doctoral dissertation, University of Chicago.

*=Lewis, E. W. (1984). The effects of mastery learning strategy and an interactive computerized quiz strategy on student achievement and attitude in college trigonometry. *Dissertation Abstracts International, 45,* 2430A. (University Microfilms No. 8424589)

*Leyton, F. S. (1983). *The extent to which group instruction supplemented by mastery of initial cognitive prerequisites approximates the learning effectiveness of one-to-one tutorial methods.* Unpublished doctoral dissertation, University of Chicago.

^Licata, K. (1993). Writing about mathematical relations in science: Effects of achievement. *Dissertation Abstracts International, 54*(06), 2109A. (UMI No. 9330090)

*Locksley, N. (1977). The Personalized System of Instruction (PSI) in a university mathematics class. *Dissertation Abstracts International, 37,* 4194. (University Microfilms No. ADD 76-28194)

^Lodholz, R. (1980). The effects of student composition of mathematical verbal problems on student problem solving performance. *Dissertation Abstracts International, 42*(08), 3483A. (UMI No. 8202649)

%Lomax, R., & Colley, W. (1979). *The student achievement–instructional time relationship.* Paper presented at the annual meeting of the American Educational Research Association, San Francisco.

#@=Long, J. C., Okey, J. R., & Yeany, R. H. (1978). The effects of diagnosis with teacher on student directed remediation on science achievement and attitudes. *Journal of Research in Science Teaching, 15,* 505–511.

<Lovitt, T. C., & Esveldt, K. A. (1970). The relative effects on math performance of single- versus multiple-ratio schedules: A case study. *Journal of Applied Behavior Analysis, 3,* 261–270.

*Lu, M. C. (1976). The retention of material learned by PSI in a mathematics course. In B. A. Green, Jr. (Ed.), *Personalized instruction in higher education* (pp. 151–154). Washington, DC: Center for Personalized Instruction.

*Lu, P. H. (1976). Teaching human growth and development by The Personalized System for Instruction. *Teaching of Psychology, 3,* 127–128.

*Lubkin, J. L. (1974). Engineering statistics: A Keller Plan course with novel problems and novel features. In R. S. Ruskin & S. F. Bono (Eds.), *Personalized instruction in higher education* (pp. 153–161). Washington, DC: Center for Personalized Instruction.

*#@=Lueckmeyer, C. L., & Chiappetta, W. L. (1981). An investigation into the effects of a modified mastery learning strategy on achievement in a high school human physiology unit. *Journal of Research in Science Teaching, 18,* 269–273.

^Madden, B. (1993). An investigation of the relationship between journal writing and mathematics achievement in fifth grade students in a rural unit school district. *Dissertation Abstracts International, 54*(02), 0451A. (UMI No. 9307322)

*Malec, M. A. (1975). PSI: A brief report and reply to Francis. *Teaching Sociology, 2,* 212–217.

Marliave, R., & Filby, N. N. (1985). Success rate: A measure of task appropriateness. In C. W. Fisher & D. C. Berliner (Eds.), *Perspectives on instructional time* (pp. 217–235). White Plains, NY: Longman.

<Martens, B. K., Ardoin, S. P., Hilt, A., Lannie, A. L., Panahon, C. J., & Wolfe, L. (2002). Sensitivity of children's behavior to probabilistic reward: Effects of a decreasing-ratio lottery system on math performance. *Journal of Applied Behavior Analysis, 35,* 403–406.

<Martens, B. K., & Daly, E. J. (1999). Discovering the alphabetic principle: A lost opportunity for educational reform. *Journal of Behavioral Education, 9*, 33–41.

<Martens, B. K., Hilt, A. M., Needham, L. R., Sutterer, J. R., Panahon, C. J., & Lannie, A. L. (2003). Carryover effects of free reinforcement on children's work completion. *Behavior Modification, 27*, 560–577.

Martens, B. K., & Witt, J. C. (2004). Competence, persistence, and success: The positive psychology of behavioral skill instruction. *Psychology in the Schools, 41*(1), 19–30.

*=Martin, R. R., & Srikameswaran, K. (1974). Correlation between frequent testing and student performance. *Journal of Chemical Education, 51*, 485–486.

$Matthews, G. S. (1982). *Effects of a mastery learning strategy on the cognitive knowledge and unit evaluation of students in high school social studies.* Unpublished doctoral dissertation, University of Southern Mississippi.

<McCurdy, M., Skinner, C. H., Grantham, K., Watson, T. S., & Hindman, P. M. (2001). Increasing on-task behavior in an elementary student during mathematics seatwork by interspersing additional brief problems. *School Psychology Review, 30*, 23–32.

<McDowell, C., & Keenan, M. (2001). Developing fluency and endurance in a child diagnosed with attention deficit hyperactivity disorder. *Journal of Applied Behavior Analysis, 34*, 345–348.

*McFarland, B. (1976). An individualized course in elementary composition for the marginal student. In B. A. Green, Jr. (Ed.), *Personalized instruction in higher education* (pp. 45–52). Washington, DC: Center for Personalized Instruction.

<McGinnis, J. C., Friman, P. C., & Carlyon, W. D. (1999). The effect of token rewards on "intrinsic" motivation for doing math. *Journal of Applied Behavior Analysis, 32*, 375–379.

*+McMichael, J., & Corey, J. R. (1969). Contingency management in an introductory psychology course produces better learning. *Journal of Applied Behavior Analysis, 2*, 79–83.

*#@Mevarech, Z. R. (1980). *The role of teaching-learning strategies and feedback-corrective procedures in developing higher cognitive achievement.* Unpublished doctoral dissertation, University of Chicago.

*&Mevarech, Z. R. (1981, April). *Attaining mastery on higher cognitive achievement.* Paper presented at the annual meeting of the American Educational Research Association, Los Angeles.

*Mevarech, Z. R. (1985). The effects of cooperative mastery learning strategies on mathematical achievement. *Journal of Educational Research, 78*, 372–377.

*#@Mevarech, Z. R. (1986). The role of feedback corrective procedures in developing mathematics achievement and self-concept in desegregated classrooms. *Studies in Educational Evaluation, 12*, 197–203.

*Mevarech, Z. R., & Werner, S. (1985). Are mastery learning strategies beneficial for developing problem solving skills? *Higher Education, 14*, 425–432.

*Meyers, R. R. (1976). The effects of mastery and aptitude on achievement and attitude in an introductory college geography course. *Dissertation Abstracts International, 36*, 5874. (University Microfilms No. 76-6436)

=Meznarich, R. A. (1978). The personalized system of instruction with and without repeated testing to mastery. *Dissertation Abstracts International, 39*, 2103A. (University Microfilms No. 7817198).

<Miller, D. L., & Kelley, M. L. (1994). The use of goal setting and contingency contracting

for improving children's homework performance. *Journal of Applied Behavior Analysis, 27*, 73–84.

^Millican, B. R. (1994). A model and study of the role of communication strategies in principles of management classes. *Dissertation Abstracts International, 55*(04), 0897A. (UMI No. 9424391)

Montazemi, A. R., & Wang, F. (1995). An empirical investigation of CBI in support of mastery learning. *Journal of Educational Computing Research, 13*(2), 185–205.

*+Morris, C., & Kimbrill, G. (1972). Performance and attitudinal effects of the Keller method in an introductory psychology course. *Psychological Record, 22*, 523–530.

^Moynihan, C. (1994). A model and study of the role of communication in the mathematics learning process. *Dissertation Abstracts International, 55*(06), 1462A. (UMI No. 9428784)

^Mulvaney, M. (1991). The effects of writing-across-the-curriculum strategies in principles of management classes. *Dissertation Abstracts International, 52*(12), 4209A. (UMI No. 9214640)

=Myers, R. R. (1976). The effect of mastery and aptitude on achievement and attitude in an introductory college geography course. *Dissertation Abstracts International, 37*, 5874. (University Microfilms No. 76-6436)

*=Nation, J. R., Knight, J. M., Lamberth, J., & Dyck, D. (1974). Programmed student achievement: A test of the avoidance hypothesis. *Journal of Experimental Education, 42*, 57–61.

*=Nation, J. R., Massad, P., & Wilkerson, P. (1977). Student performance in introductory psychology following termination of the programmed achievement contingency at mid-semester. *Teaching of Psychology, 4*, 116–119.

*=Nation, J. R., & Roop, S. S. (1975). A comparison of two mastery approaches to teaching introductory psychology. *Teaching of Psychology, 2*, 108–111.

*+Nazzaro, J. R., Todorov, J. C., & Nazzaro, J. N. (1972). Student ability and individualized instruction. *Journal of College Science Teaching, 2*, 29–30.

<Neef, N. A., & Lutz, M. N. (2001). Assessment of variables affecting choice and application to classroom interventions. *School Psychology Quarterly, 16*, 239–252.

<Neef, N. A., Shade, D., & Miller, M. S. (1994). Assessing influential dimensions of reinforcers on choice in students with serious emotional disturbance. *Journal of Applied Behavior Analysis, 27*, 575–583.

^Nieswandt, M. (1997, March). *Improving learning in chemistry classes through original writing about chemical facts*. Paper presented at the annual meeting of the American Educational Research Association, Chicago.

*Nord, S. B. (1975). Comparative achievement and attitude in individualized and class instructional settings. *Dissertation Abstracts International, 35*, 529A. (University Microfilms No. 75-02314)

$Nordin, A. B. (1979). *The effects of different qualities of instruction on selected cognitive, affective, and time variables*. Unpublished doctoral dissertation, University of Chicago.

<Northup, J., George, T., Jones, K., Broussard, C., & Vollmer, T. R. (1996). A comparison of reinforcer assessment methods: The utility of verbal and pictorial choice procedures. *Journal of Applied Behavior Analysis, 29*, 201–212.

*$+=Okey, J. R. (1974). Altering teacher and pupil behavior with mastery teaching. *Social Science and Mathematics, 74*, 530–535.

+Okey, J. R. (1975). *Development of mastery teaching materials* (Final Evaluation Report, USOE G-74-2990). Bloomington: Indiana University.

$&Okey, J. R. (1977). The consequences of training teachers to use a mastery learning strategy. *Journal of Teacher Education, 28*(5), 57–62.

=Okey, J. R., Brown, J. L., & Field, R. L. (1972). Diagnostic evaluation methods in individualized instruction. *Science Education, 56,* 207–212.

*$Omelich, C. L., & Covington, M. V. (1981). *Do the learning benefits of behavioral instruction outweigh the psychological costs?* Paper presented at the annual meeting of the Western Psychological Association, Los Angeles.

*Pascarella, E. T. (1977, April). *Aptitude-treatment interaction in a college calculus course taught in personalized system of instruction and conventional formats.* Paper presented at the annual meeting of the American Educational Research Association, New York. (ERIC Document Reproduction Service No. ED 137 137)

<Patterson, G. R., Reid, J. B., & Dishion, T. J. (1992). *Antisocial boys.* Eugene, OR: Castalia Publishing.

*Peluso, A., & Baranchik, A. J. (1977). Self-paced mathematics instruction: A statistical comparison with traditional teaching. *The American Mathematical Monthly, 84,* 124–129.

*+Phillippas, M. A., & Sommerfeldt, R. W. (1972). Keller vs. lecture method in general physics instruction. *American Journal of Physics, 40,* 1800.

+Poggio, J. P. (1976, April). *Long-term cognitive retention resulting from the mastery learning paradigm.* Paper presented at the annual meeting of the American Educational Research Association, San Francisco.

*Pollack, N. F., & Roeder, P. W. (1975). Individualized instruction in an introductory government course. *Teaching Political Science, 8,* 18–36.

^Radmacher, S. (1995). Summary writing: A tool to improve student comprehension and writing in psychology. *Teaching of Psychology, 22*(2), 113–115.

^Reaves, R. (1991). The effects of writing-to-learn activities on the content knowledge, retention of information, and attitudes toward writing of selected vocational agriculture education students. *Dissertation Abstracts International, 52*(05), 1614A. (UMI No. 9130824)

<Rhymer, K. N., Henington, C., Skinner, C. H., & Looby, E. J. (1999). The effects of explicit timing on mathematics performance in Caucasian and African American second-grade students. *School Psychology Quarterly, 14,* 397–407.

^Rivard, L. (1996). The effect of talk and writing, alone and combined, on learning in science: An exploratory study. *Dissertation Abstracts International, 57*(10), 4297A. (UMI No. NN13481)

^Rodgers, W. (1996). The effects of writing to learn on performance and attitude towards mathematics. *Dissertation Abstracts International, 57*(08), 3435A. (UMI No. 9701857)

*+Rosati, P. A. (1975). A comparison of the personalized system of instruction with the lecture method in teaching elementary dynamics. In J. M. Johnston (Ed.), *Behavior research and technology in higher education.* Springfield, IL: Charles C. Thomas.

^Ross, J., & Faucette, D. (1994). *College Algebra and Writing: A pilot project, Spring semester 1994: Final report for the Title III literacy across the curriculum team* (Report No. JC-950-468). Gilbert, AZ: Central Arizona College, Superstition Mountain Campus. (ERIC Document Reproduction Service No. ED 387166)

+Roth, C. H., Jr. (1973). Continuing effectiveness on personalized self-paced instruction in digital systems engineering. *Engineering Education, 63*(6), 447–450.

*Roth, C. H., Jr. (1975, December). *Electrical engineering laboratory I* (One of a series of reports on the projects titled Expansion of Keller Plan Instruction in Engineering and Selected Other Disciplines). Austin: University of Texas.

*=Saunders-Harris, R. L., & Yeany, R. H. (1981). Diagnosis, remediation, and locus of control: Effects of the immediate and retained achievement and attitude. *Journal of Experimental Education, 49*, 220–224.

*Schielack, V. P., Jr. (1983). A personalized system of instruction versus a conventional method in a mathematics course for elementary education majors. *Dissertation Abstracts International, 43*, 2267. (University Microfilms No. 82-27717)

*Schimpfhauser, F., Horrocks, L., Richardson, K., Alben, J., Schumm, D., & Sprecher, H. (1974). The personalized system of instruction as an adaptable alternative within the traditional structure of medical basic sciences. In R. S. Ruskin & S. F. Bono (Eds.), *Personalized instruction in higher education* (pp. 61–69). Washington, DC: Center for Personalized Instruction.

*Schwartz, P. L. (1981). Retention of knowledge in clinical biochemistry and the effect of the Keller Plan. *Journal of Medical Education, 56*, 778–781.

=Semb, G. (1974). The effects of mastery criteria and assignment length on college-student test performance. *Journal of Applied Behavior Analysis, 7*, 61–69.

^Sharp, J. (1987). Expressive summary writing to learn college biology. *Dissertation Abstracts International, 48*(03), 0586A. (UMI No. 8714454)

*Sharples, D. K., Smith, D. J., & Strasler, G. M. (1976). *Individually-paced learning in civil engineering technology: An approach to mastery.* Columbia: South Carolina State Board for Technical and Comprehensive Education. (ERIC Document Reproduction Service No. ED 131 870)

*$=Sheldon, M. S., & Miller, E. D. (1973). *Behavioral objectives and mastery learning applied to two areas of junior college instruction.* Los Angeles: University of California at Los Angeles. (ERIC Document Reproduction Service No. ED 082 730)

^Shepard, R. (1992). Using writing for conceptual development in mathematics instruction. *Dissertation Abstracts International, 53*(12), 4259A. (UMI No. 9310357)

*Sheppard, W. C., & MacDermott, H. G. (1970). Design and evaluation of a programmed course in introductory psychology. *Journal of Applied Behavior Analysis, 3*, 5–11.

<Shinn, M. R. (1989). *Curriculum-based measurement: Assessing special children.* New York: Guilford.

*Siegfried, J. J., & Strand, S. H. (1976). An evaluation of the Vanderbilt JCEE experimental PSI course in elementary economics. *The Journal of Economic Education, 8*, 9–26.

*+Silberman, R., & Parker, B. (1974). Student attitudes and the Keller Plan. *Journal of Chemical Education, 51*, 393.

<Simonton, D. K. (2000). Creativity: Cognitive, personal, developmental, and social aspects. *American Psychologist, 55*, 151–158.

<Skinner, C. H. (2002). An empirical analysis of interspersal research: Evidence, implications, and applications of the discrete task completion hypothesis. *Journal of School Psychology, 40*, 347–368.

<Skinner, C. H., Fletcher, P. A., & Henington, C. (1996). Increasing learning trial rates by increasing student response rates: A summary of research. *School Psychology Quarterly, 11*, 313–325.

Slavin, R. E. (1990). Mastery learning re-considered. *Review of Educational Research, 60*(2), 300–302.

*#@$&=Slavin, R. E., & Karweit, N. L. (1984). Mastery learning and student teams: A factor role experiment in urban general mathematics classes. *American Educational Research Journal, 21*, 725–736.

*Smiernow, G. A., & Lawley, A. (1980). Decentralized sequence instruction (DSI) at Drexel. *Engineering Education, 70*, 423–426.

*Smith, J. E. (1976). A comparison of the traditional method and a personalized system of instruction in college mathematics. *Dissertation Abstracts International, 37*, 904. (University Microfilms No. AAD 76-18370)

*Spector, L. C. (1976). The effectiveness of personalized instruction system of instruction in economics. *Journal of Personalized Instruction, 1*, 118–122.

*Spevack, H. M. (1976). A comparison of the personalized system of instruction with the lecture recitation system for nonscience oriented chemistry students at an open enrollment community college. *Dissertation Abstracts International, 36*, 4385A–4386A. (University Microfilms No. 76-01757)

<Stahl, S. A., & Kuhn, M. R. (1995). Does whole language or instruction matched to learning styles help children learn to read? *School Psychology Review, 24*, 393–404.

Stallings, J. A., & Stipek, D. (1986). Research on early childhood and elementary school teaching programs. In M. C. Wittrock (Ed.), *Handbook of research on teaching* (3rd ed.). New York: Macmillan.

*Steele, W. F. (1974). *Mathematics 101 at Heileberg College—PSI vs. tradition.* Paper presented at the National Conference on Personalized Instruction in Higher Education, Washington, DC.

^Stewart, C. (1992). Journal writing in mathematics classrooms: A practical inquiry. *Dissertation Abstracts International, 53*(12), 4242A. (UMI No. 9311458)

*Stout, L. J. (1978). A comparison of four different pacing strategies of personalized system of instruction and a traditional lecture format. *Dissertation Abstracts International, 38*, 6205. (University Microfilms No. AAD 78-08600)

*$=Strasler, G. M. (1979, April). *The process of transfer and learning for mastery setting.* Paper presented at the annual meeting of the American Educational Research Association, San Francisco. (ERIC Document Reproduction Service No. ED 174 642)

*$&Swanson, D. H., & Denton J. J. (1976). Learning for Mastery versus Personalized System of Instruction: A comparison of remediation strategies for secondary school chemistry students. *Journal of Research in Science Teaching, 14*, 515–524.

Swanson, H. L. (2000). What instruction works for students with learning disabilities? Summarizing the results from a meta-analysis of intervention studies. In R. M. Gersten, E. P. Schiller, & S. Vaughn (Eds.), *Contemporary special education research: Syntheses of the knowledge base on critical instructional issues* (pp. 1–30). Mahwah, NJ: Erlbaum.

*Taylor, V. (1977, April). *Individualized calculus for the "life-long" learner: A two semester comparison of attitudes and effectiveness.* Paper presented at the Fourth National Conference of the Center for Personalized Instruction, San Francisco.

$Tenenbaum, G. (1982). *A method of group instruction which is as effective as one-to-one tutorial instruction.* Unpublished doctoral dissertation, University of Chicago.

*&Thompson, S. B. (1980). Do individualized mastery and traditional instructional systems yield different course effects in college calculus? *American Educational Research Journal, 17*, 361–375.

*Tietenberg, T. H. (1975). Teaching intermediate microeconomics using the personalized system of instruction. In J. M. Johnston (Ed.), *Behavior research and technology in higher education* (pp. 75–89). Springfield, IL: Charles C. Thomas.

*Toepher, C., Shaw, D., & Moniot, D. (1972). *The effect of item exposure in a contingency* *management system.* Paper presented at the annual meeting of the American Psychological Association, Honolulu, HI.

^Ulrich, O. (1926). The effect of required themes on learning. *Journal of Educational Research, 14*(4), 294–303.

*Van Verth, J. E., & Dinan, F. J. (1974). A Keller Plan course in organic chemistry. In R. S. Ruskin & S. F. Bono (Eds.), *Personalized instruction in higher education* (pp. 162–168). Washington, DC: Center for Personalized Instruction.

*Vandenbroucke, A. C., Jr. (1974, April). *Evaluation of the use of a personalized system of instruction in general chemistry.* Paper presented at the National Conference on Personalized Instruction in Higher Education, Washington, DC.

<Vollmer, T. R., Ringdahl, J. E., Roane, H. S., & Marcus, B. (1997). Negative side effects of noncontingent reinforcement. *Journal of Applied Behavior Analysis, 30*, 161–164.

*Walsh, R. G., Sr. (1977). The Keller Plan in college introductory physical geology: A comparison with the conventional teaching method. *Dissertation Abstracts International, 37*, 4257. (University Microfilms No. AAD 76-30292)

<Weeks, M., & Gaylord-Ross, R. (1981). Task difficulty and aberrant behavior in severely handicapped students. *Journal of Applied Behavior Analysis, 14*, 19–36.

^Weiss, R. (1979, November). *Research on writing and learning: Some effects of learning-centered writing in five subject areas.* Paper presented at the annual meeting of the Conference on College Composition and Communication, Washington, DC. (ERIC Document Reproduction Service No. ED 189619)

^Wells, C. (1986). The relationship between journal writing and achievement in mathematical measurement and place value/regrouping among primary school children. *Dissertation Abstracts International, 47*(12), 4286A. (UMI No. 8703118)

*&+Wentling, T. L. (1973). Mastery versus nonmastery instruction with varying test item feedback treatments. *Journal of Educational Psychology, 65*, 50–58.

*White, M. E. (1974). Different equations by PSI. In R. S. Ruskin & S. F. Bono (Eds.), *Personalized instruction in higher education* (pp. 169–171). Washington, DC: Center for Personalized Instruction.

Willett, J., Yamashita, J., & Anderson, R. (1983). A meta-analysis of instructional systems applied in science teaching. *Journal of Research in Science Teaching, 20*(5), 405–417.

^Willey, L. (1988). The effects of selected writing-to-learn approaches on high school students' attitudes and achievement. *Dissertation Abstracts International, 49*(12), 3611A. (UMI No. 8905957)

$Wire, D. R. (1979). *Mastery learning program at Durham College: Report on progress toward the first year, September 1, 1978–August 31, 1979.* Durham, NC. (ERIC Document Reproduction Service No. ED 187 387)

<Witt, J. C., & Elliott, S. N. (1982). The response cost lottery: A time efficient and effective classroom intervention. *Journal of School Psychology, 20*, 155–161.

*Witters, D. R., & Kent, G. W. (1972). Teaching without lecturing—evidence in the case for individualized instruction. *The Psychological Record, 22*, 169–175.

<Wolery, M., Bailey, D. B., & Sugai, G. M. (1988). *Effective teaching: Principles and procedures of applied behavior analysis with exceptional students.* Boston: Allyn & Bacon.

$Wortham, S. C. (1980). *Mastery learning in secondary schools: A first-year report.* San Antonio, TX. (ERIC Document Reproduction Service No. ED 194 453)

*=Yeany, R. H., Dost, R. J., & Matthew, R. W. (1980). The effects of diagnostic-prescriptive

instruction and locus of control on the achievement and attitudes of university students. *Journal of Research in Science Teaching, 17*, 537–545.

$Yildren, G. (1977). *The effects of level of cognitive achievement on selected learning criteria under mastery learning and normal classroom instruction.* Unpublished doctoral dissertation, University of Chicago.

^Youngberg, S. (1989). The effect of writing assignments on student achievement in a college level elementary algebra class. *Dissertation Abstracts International, 50*(09), 2819A.

REFERENCES FOR PROVIDING TRANSFER OF LEARNING INSTRUCTION

Alfassi, M. (2004). Reading to learn: Effects of combined strategy instruction on high school students. *The Journal of Educational Research, 97*(4), 171–184.

Barley, Z., Lauer, P. A., Arens, S. A., Apthorp, H. S., Englert, K. S., Snow, D., & Akiba, M. (2002). *Helping at-risk students meet standards: A synthesis of evidence-based classroom practices.* Aurora, CO: Mid-continent Research for Education and Learning.

*#Bereiter, C., & Scardamalia, M. (1986). Educational relevance of the study of expertise. *Interchange, 17*(2), 10–19.

#Billett, S. (1994). Authenticity in workplace settings. In J. Stevenson (Ed.), *The development of vocational expertise.* Adelaide: NCVER.

@Bissell, L. (1982). *Training with forced-choice cloze tasks.* Ann Arbor: University of Michigan.

%Blaha, B. A. (1979). *The effects of answering self-generated questions on reading.* Unpublished doctoral dissertation, Boston University School of Education.

#Boldovici, J. A. (1997). Measuring transfer in military settings. In S. M. Cormier (Ed.), *Transfer of learning.* San Diego: Academic Press.

$Bottge, B. (1999). Effects of contextualized math instruction on problem solving of average and below-average achieving students. *The Journal of Special Education, 33*(2), 81–92.

%Brady, P. L. (1990). *Improving the reading comprehension of middle school students through reciprocal teaching and semantic mapping strategies.* Unpublished doctoral dissertation, University of Alaska.

#Bransford, J. D. (1979). *Human cognition: Learning, understanding, and remembering.* Belmont, CA: Wadsworth Publishing.

#Brown, A. L., & Kane, M. J. (1988). Preschool children can learn to transfer: Learning to learn and learning from example. *Cognitive Psychology, 20*, 493–523.

#Brown, A. L., & Palincsar, A. S. (1989). Guided, co-operative learning and individual knowledge acquisition. In L. B. Resnick (Ed.), *Knowing, learning, and instruction: Essays in honor of Robert Glaser* (pp. 393–451). Hillsdale, NJ: Erlbaum.

$Brown, D. (1995). *Assisting eighth-grade at-risk students in successfully reading their textbooks through support strategies.* Unpublished practicum report. Nova Southeastern University, Florida.

$Brown, R., Pressley, M., Van Meter, P., & Schuder, T. (1995). *A quasi-experimental validation of transactional strategies instruction with previously low-achieving, second-grade readers.* Reading Research Report No. 33. Universities of Georgia and Maryland, National Reading Research Center.

@Buikema, J., & Graves, M. (1993). Teaching students to use context clues to infer word meaning. *Journal of Reading, 36*(6), 450–457.

$Cardelle-Elawar, M. (1990). Effects of feedback tailored to bilingual students' mathematics needs on verbal problem solving. *The Elementary School Journal, 91*(2), 165–170.

@Carnine, D., Kameenui, E., & Coyle, G. (1984). Utilization of contextual information in determining the meaning of unfamiliar words. *Reading Research Quarterly, 19*(2), 188–204.

Catrambone, R. (1995). Aiding subgoal learning: Effects on transfer. *Journal of Educational Psychology, 87*(1), 5–17.

*Catrambone, R., & Holyoak, K. J. *The function of schemas in analogical problem solving.* Poster presented at the meeting of the American Psychological Association, Los Angeles.

*Charles, R. I., & Lester, F. K., Jr. (1984). An evaluation of a process-oriented instructional program in mathematical problem-solving in grades 5 and 7. *Journal of Research in Mathematical Education, 15,* 15–34.

#Chase, W. G. (1982). Spatial representations of taxi drivers. In *NATO conference on the acquisition of symbolic skills* (pp. 391–405). New York: Plenum.

#Chase, W. G., & Simon, H. A. (1973). Perception in chess. *Cognitive Psychology, 4,* 55–81.

#Chi, M.T.H. (1978). Knowledge structures and memory development. In R. S. Siegler (Ed.), *Children's thinking: What develops?* (pp. 73–96). Hillsdale, NJ: Erlbaum.

#Chi, M.T.H., & Bassok, M. (1989). Learning from examples of via self-explanations. In L. B. Resnick (Ed.), *Knowing, learning, and instruction: Essays in honor of Robert Glaser* (pp. 251–282). Hillsdale, NJ: Erlbaum.

*Chi, M.T.H., Feltovich, P., & Glaser, R. (1981). Categorization and representation of physics problems by experts and novices. *Cognitive Science, 5,* 121–152.

*Chi, M.T.H., Glaser, R., & Rees, E. (1981). *Expertise in problem solving* (Technical Report No. 5). Pittsburgh, PA: University of Pittsburgh, Learning Research and Development Center.

*Chi, M.T.H., & Koeske, R. D. (1983). Network representation of a child's dinosaur knowledge. *Developmental Psychology, 19,* 29–39.

*Clement, J. (1982, March). *Spontaneous analogies in problem solving: The progressive construction of mental models.* Paper presented at the annual meeting of the American Educational Research Association, New York.

%Cohen, R. (1983). Students generate questions as an aid to reading comprehension. *Reading Teacher, 36,* 770–775.

*Collins, A., Brown, J. S., & Newman, S. (1989). The new apprenticeship: Teaching students the craft of reading, writing, and mathematics. In L. B. Resnick (Ed.), *Knowing and learning* (pp. 283–305). Hillsdale, NJ: Erlbaum.

@Cox, J. (1974). A comparison of two instructional methods utilizing the cloze procedure and a more traditional method for improving reading. *Dissertation Abstracts International, 35*(10). (University Microfilms No. AAC75-9580)

@Daalen-Kapteijns, M., Schouten-van Parreren, C., & De Glopper, K. (1997). *The training of a word learning strategy: results in process and product* (Rep. No. 463). Amsterdam: SCO-Kohmstamm Institute.

*Dansereau, D. F. (1985). Learning strategy research. In J. W. Segal, S. F. Chipman, & R. Glaser (Eds.), *Thinking and learning skills: Vol. 1. Relating instruction to research* (pp. 209–239). Hillsdale, NJ: Erlbaum.

%Davey, B., & McBride, S. (1986). Effects of question-generation on reading comprehension. *Journal of Educational Psychology, 78,* 256–262.

#de Groot, A. D. (1965). *Thought and choice in chess.* The Hague, Netherlands: Mouton.

*de Jong, T., & Gerguson-Hessler, M.G.M. (1986). Cognitive structures of good and poor novice problem solvers in physics. *Journal of Educational Psychology, 78,* 279–288.

+De La Paz, S., & Graham, S. (1997). Effects of dictation and advanced planning instruction on the composing of students with writing and learning problems. *Journal of Educational Psychology, 89*(2), 203–222.

*DeCorte, E., & Verschaffel, L. (1981). Children's solution processes in elementary arithmetic problems. *Journal of Educational Psychology, 73,* 765–779.

$%Dermody, M. (1988, February). *Metacognitive strategies for development of reading comprehension for younger children.* Paper presented at the annual meeting of the American Association of Colleges for Teacher Education. New Orleans, LA.

$Dimino, J., Gersten, R., Carnine, D., & Blake, G. (1990). Story grammar: An approach for promoting at-risk secondary students' comprehension of literature. *The Elementary School Journal, 91*(1), 19–32.

%Dreher, M. J., & Gambrell, L. B. (1985). Teaching children to use a self-questioning strategy for studying expository text. *Reading Improvement, 22,* 2–7.

*Duncker, K. (1945). On problem-solving. *Psychological Monographs, 58*(Whole No. 270).

#Egan, D. E., & Schwartz, B. J. (1979). Checking recall of symbolic drawings. *Memory & Cognition, 7*(2), 149–158.

$Englert, C., Raphael, T. E., Anderson, L., Anthony, H., & Stevens, D. (1991). Making strategies and self-talk visible: Writing instruction in regular and special education classrooms. *American Educational Research Journal, 28*(2), 337–372.

+Englert, C. S., Garmon, A., Mariage, T., Rozendal, M., Tarrant, K., & Urba, J. (1995). The early literacy project: Connecting across the literacy curriculum. *Learning Disability Quarterly, 18,* 253–275.

+Englert, C. S., Raphael, T. E., Anderson, L. M., Anthony, H. M., & Stevens, D. D. (1991). Making writing strategies and self-talk visible: Cognitive strategy instruction in regular and special education classrooms. *American Educational Research Journal, 28,* 337–372.

Farrell, E. (1988). How teaching proportionally affects transfer of learning: Science and math teachers need each other. *School Science and Mathematics, 88*(8), 688–695.

+Fortner, V. L. (1986). Generalization of creative productive-thinking training to LD students' written expression. *Learning Disability Quarterly, 9*(4), 274–284.

Fukkink, R. G., & de Glopper, K. (1998). Effects of instruction in deriving word meaning from context: A meta-analysis. *Review of Educational Research, 68*(4), 450–469.

*Gentner, D. (1981). Generative analogies as mental models. In *Proceedings of the Third Annual Conference of the Cognitive Science Society* (pp. 97–100). Berkeley: University of California, Institute of Human Learning.

Gersten, R., & Baker, S. (2001). Teaching expressive writing to students with learning disabilities: A meta-analysis. *The Elementary School Journal, 101*(3), 251–273.

*Gick, M. L. (1986). Problem-solving strategies. *Educational Psychologist, 21,* 99–120.

*Gick., M. L., & Holyoak, K. J. (1980). Analogical problem solving. *Cognitive Psychology, 12,* 306–355.

*Gick., M. L., & Holyoak, K. J. (1983). Schema induction and analogical transfer. *Cognitive Psychology, 15,* 1–38.

#Gick., M. L., & Holyoak, K. J. (1987). The cognitive basis of knowledge transfer. In S. M. Cormier (Ed.), *Transfer of learning* (pp. 9–47). San Diego: Academic Press.

#Glaser, R., & Chi, M.T. H. (1988). Overview. In M. Chi, R. Glasser, & M. Farr (Eds.), *The nature of expertise*. Hillsdale, NJ: Erlbaum.

Gott, S. P., et al. (1995, February). *Tutoring for transfer of technical competence*. Report from Armstrong Lab, Brooks AFB, TX. (ERIC Document Reproduction Service No. ED 382 817)

*Gould, S. J. (1980). *The panda's thumb*. New York: Norton.

@Guarino, E. (1960). *An investigation of the effectiveness of instruction designed to improve the reader's skill in using context clues to derive word meaning*. Syracuse, NY: Syracuse University [dissertation, UMI].

$Guastello, E., Beasley, T., & Sinatra, R. (2000). Concept mapping effects on science content comprehension of low-achieving inner-city seventh graders. *Remedial and Special Education, 21*(6), 356–365.

*Hasselhorn, M., & Korkel, J. (1986). Metacognitive versus traditional reading instructions: The mediating role of domain-specific knowledge on children's text processing. *Human Learning, 5*, 75–90.

%Helfeldt, J. P., & Lalik, R. (1976). Reciprocal student-teacher questioning. *Reading Teacher, 33*, 283–287.

@Herman, P., & Weaver, C. (1988). *Contextual strategies for word meaning: Middle grade students look in and look around*. Paper presented at the National Reading Conference, Tucson, AZ.

*Hiebert, J. (1984). Children's mathematics learning: The struggle to link form and understanding. *Elementary School Journal, 84*, 497–513.

*Holyoak, K. J. (1985). The pragmatics of an analogical transfer. In G. Bower (Ed.), *The psychology of learning and motivation* (Vol. 19, pp. 59–87). New York: Academic Press.

+Jaben, T. H. (1983). The effects of creativity training on learning disabled students' creative written expression. *Journal of Learning Disabilities, 16*(5), 264–265.

+Jaben, T. H. (1987). Effects of training on learning disabled students' creative written expression. *Psychological Reports, 60*, 23–26.

$Jakupcak, J., Rushton, R., Jakupcak, M., & Lundt, J. (1996). Inclusive education. *The Science Teacher, 63*(5), 40–43.

*Janvier, C. (1987). Representations and understanding: The notion of function as an example. In C. Janvier (Ed.), *Problems of representation in the teaching and learning of mathematics* (pp. 67–71). Hillsdale, NJ: Erlbaum.

@Jenkins, J., Matlock, B., & Slocum, T. (1989). Two approaches to vocabulary instruction: The teaching of individual word meaning and practice in deriving word meaning from context. *Reading Research Quarterly, 24*(2), 215–235.

*Kaput, J. J. (1987). Representation systems and mathematics. In C. Janvier (Ed.), *Problems of representation in the teaching and learning of mathematics* (pp. 19–26). Hillsdale, NJ: Erlbaum.

$Ketter, J., & Pool, J. (2001). Exploring the impact of a high-stakes direct writing assessment in two high school classrooms. *Research in the Teaching of English, 35*, 344–393.

%King, A. (1989). Effects of self-questioning training on college students' comprehension of lectures. *Contemporary Educational Psychology, 14*, 366–381.

%King, A. (1990). Improving Lecture Comprehension: Effects of a metacognitive strategy. *Applied Educational Psychology, 5*, 331–346.

%King, A. (1992). Comparison of self-questioning, summarizing, and notetaking-review as strategies for learning from lectures. *American Educational Research Journal, 29*, 303–325.

@Kranzer, K. (1988). *A study of the effects of instruction on incidental word learning and on the ability to derive word meaning from context.* Newark: University of Delaware [dissertation, UMI].

%Labercane, G., & Battle, J. (1987). Cognitive processing strategies, self-esteem, and reading comprehension of learning disabled students. *Journal of Special Education, 11*, 167–185.

*Lampert, M. (1986). Knowing, doing, and teaching multiplication. *Cognition and Instruction, 3*, 305–342.

#Larkin, J. H. (1983). The role of problem representation in physics. In D. Getner & A. L. Stevens (Eds.), *Mental models* (pp. 75–98). Hillsdale, NJ: Erlbaum.

#Lesgold, A., & Lajoie, S. (1991). Complex problem solving in electronics. In R. J. Sternberg & P. A. Frensch (Eds.), *Complex problem solving: Principles and mechanisms* (pp. 287–316). Hillsdale, NJ: Erlbaum.

#Lesgold, A., Rubinson, H., Feltovich, P., Glaser, R., Klopfer, D., & Wang, Y. (1988). Expertise in a complex skill: Diagnosing x-ray pictures. In M. Chi, R. Glasser, & M. Farr (Eds.), *The nature of expertise.* Hillsdale, NJ: Erlbaum.

*Lesh, R., Behr, M., & Post, T. (1987). Rational numbers and proportions. In C. Janvier (Ed.), *Problems of representation in the teaching and learning of mathematics* (pp. 41–58). Hillsdale, NJ: Erlbaum.

*Lesh, R., Post, T., & Behr, M. (1987). Representations and translations among representations and mathematics learning and problem solving. In C. Janvier (Ed.), *Problems of representation in the teaching and learning of mathematics* (pp. 207–214). Hillsdale, NJ: Erlbaum.

*Lester, F. K. (1980). Research on mathematical problem solving. In R. J. Shumway (Ed.), *Research in mathematics education* (pp. 286–323). Reston, VA: National Council of Teachers of Mathematics.

%Lonberger, R. B. (1988). *The effects of training in a self-generated learning strategy on the prose processing abilities of fourth and sixth graders.* Unpublished doctoral dissertation, State University of New York at Buffalo.

%Lysynchuk, L., Pressley, M., & Vye, G. (1990). Reciprocal instruction improves reading comprehension performance in poor grade school comprehenders. *Elementary School Journal, 40*, 471–484.

+MacArthur, C. A., Graham, S., Schwartz, S. S., & Schafer, W. D. (1995). Evaluation of a writing instruction model that integrated a process approach, strategy instruction, and word processing. *Learning Disability Quarterly, 18*, 278–291.

+MacArthur, C. A., Schwartz, S. S., & Graham, S. (1991). Effects of reciprocal peer revision strategy in special education classrooms. *Learning Disabilities Research, 6*(4), 201–210.

%MacGregor, S. K. (1988). Use of self-questioning with a computer-mediated text system and measures of reading performance. *Journal of Reading Behavior, 20*, 131–148.

%Manzo, A. V. (1969). *Improving reading comprehension through reciprocal teaching.* Unpublished doctoral dissertation, Syracuse University.

Marzolf, D. P., & DeLoach, J. S. (1994). Transfer in young children's understanding of spatial representations. *Child Development, 65,* 1–15.

*#Mayer, R. E. (1975a). Different problem-solving competencies established in learning computer programming with and without meaningful models. *Journal of Educational Psychology, 67,* 725–734.

*Mayer, R. E. (1975b). Information processing variables in learning to solve problems. *Review of Educational Research, 45,* 525–541.

$McLain, K. (1991, November). *Effects of two comprehension monitoring strategies on the metacognitive awareness and reading achievement of third and fifth grade students.* Paper presented at the annual meeting of the National Reading Conference, Miami, FL.

Mevarech, Z. R., & Kramarski, B. (1997). IMPROVE: A multidimensional method for teaching mathematics in heterogeneous classrooms. *American Educational Research Journal, 34*(2), 365–394.

Mevarech, Z. R., & Kramarski, B. (2003). The effects of metacognitive training versus worked-out examples on students' mathematical reasoning. *British Journal of Educational Psychology, 73,* 449–471.

Misko, J. (1995). *Transfer: Using learning in new contexts.* Leabrook, Australia: National Centre for Vocational Education Research. (ERIC Document Reproduction Service No. ED 383 895)

*Nesher, P. (1986). Are mathematical understanding and algorithmic performance related? *For the Learning of Mathematics, 6,* 2–9.

*Nickerson, R. S. (1985). Understanding understanding. *American Journal of Education, 93,* 201–239.

%Nolte, R. Y., & Singer, H. (1985). Active comprehension: Teaching a process of reading comprehension and its effects on reading achievement. *The Reading Teacher, 39,* 24–31.

$O'Malley, J., Chamot, A., Stewner-Manzanares, G., Russo, R., & Kupper, L. (1985). Learning strategy applications with students of English as a second language. *TESOL Quarterly, 19*(3), 557–584.

*Paige, J. M., & Simon, H. A. (1966). Cognitive processes in solving algebra word problems. In B. Kleinmuntz (Ed.), *Problem solving: Research, method, and theory* (pp. 51–119). New York: Wiley.

%Palincsar, A. S. (1987, April). *Collaborating for collaborative learning of text comprehension.* Paper presented at the annual meeting of the American Educational Research Association, Washington, DC.

%Palincsar, A. S., & Brown, A. L. (1984). Reciprocal teaching of comprehension-fostering and comprehension-monitoring activities. *Cognition and Instruction, 2,* 117–175.

*Pea, R. D. (1987). Socializing the knowledge transfer problem. *International Journal of Educational Research, 11,* 639–663.

#Pea, R. D., & Kurland, D. M. (1984). On the cognitive effects of learning computer programming. *New Ideas Psychology, 2*(2), 137–168.

*Petrie, H. G. (1976). Do you see what I see? The epistemology of interdisciplinary inquiry. *Educational Researcher, 5*(2), 9–15.

#Polya, G. (1957). *How to solve it: A new aspect of mathematical method* (2nd ed.). Princeton, NJ: Princeton University Press.

*Porter, A. C., Floden, R. E., Freeman, D. J., Schmdit, W. H., & Schwille, J. R. (1986). *Content determinants* (Research Series No. 179). East Lansing: Michigan State University, Institute for Research on Teaching.

Prawat, R. S. (1989). Promoting access to knowledge, strategy, and disposition in students: A research synthesis. *Review of Educational Research, 59*(1), 1–41.

*Pressley, M., Goodchild, F., Fleet, J., Zejchowski, R., & Evans, E. D. (1989). The challenges of classroom strategy instruction. *Elementary School Journal, 89*, 301–342.

#Pressley, M., Symons, S., McDaniel, M., Snyder, B., & Turnure, J. (1988). Elaborative interrogation facilitates acquisition of confusing facts. *Journal of Educational Psychology, 80*(3), 268–278.

*Resnick, L. B. (1986). The development of mathematical intuition. In M. Perimutter (Ed.), *Perspectives on intellectual development: The Minnesota Symposia on Child Psychology* (Vol. 19, pp. 159–194). Hillsdale, NJ: Erlbaum.

#Resnick, L. B. (1987). Education and learning to think. In *Committee on Mathematics, Science and Technology Education.* Washington, DC: National Academy Press.

*Resnick L. B., & Omanson, S. F. (1987). Learning to understand arithmetic. In R. Glaser (Ed.), *Advances in instructional psychology* (pp. 41–95). Hillsdale, NJ: Erlbaum.

+Reynolds, C. J. (1986). *The effects of instruction in cognitive revision strategies on the writing skills of secondary learning disabled students* (Doctoral dissertation, Ohio State University, 1985). *Dissertation Abstracts International, 46*(9-A), 2662.

%Ritchie, P. (1985). The effects of instruction in main idea and question generation. *Reading Canada Lecture, 3*, 139–146.

Rosenshine, B., Meister, C., & Chapman, S. (1996). Teaching students to generate questions: A review of the intervention studies. *Review of Educational Research, 66*(2), 181–221.

@Sampson, M., Valmont, W., & Allen, R. (1982). The effects of instructional cloze on the comprehension, vocabulary, and divergent production of third-grade students. *Reading Research Quarterly, 17*(3), 389–399.

+Sawyer, R. J., Graham, S., & Harris, K. R. (1992). Direct teaching, strategy instruction, and strategy instruction with explicit self-regulation: Effects on the composition skills and self-efficacy of students with learning disabilities. *Journal of Educational Psychology, 84*(3), 340–352.

*Scardamalia, M., & Bereiter, C. (1984). Development of strategies and text processing. In H. Mandl, N. Stein, & T. Trabasso (Eds.), *Learning and comprehension of text* (pp. 379–406). Hillsdale, NJ: Erlbaum.

*Schoenfeld, A. (1986). On having and using geometric knowledge. In J. Heibert (Ed.), *Conceptual and procedural knowledge: The case of mathematics* (pp. 225–264). Hillsdale, NJ: Erlbaum.

*Schoenfeld, A. H. (1982). Measures of problem-solving performance and problem-solving instruction. *Journal for Research in Mathematics Education, 13*, 31–49.

%Short, E. J., & Ryan, E. B. (1984). Metacognitive differences between skilled and less-skilled readers: Remediating deficits through story grammar and attribution training. *Journal of Educational Psychology, 76*, 225–235.

*Simon, D. P., & Simon, H. A. (1978). Individual differences in solving physics problems. In R. S. Siegler (Ed.), *Children's thinking: What develops?* (pp. 325–348). Hillsdale, NJ: Erlbaum.

%Simpson, P. S. (1989). *The effects of direct training in active comprehension on reading achievement, self-concepts, and reading attitudes of at-risk sixth grade students.* Unpublished doctoral dissertation, Texas Tech University.

*Skemp, R. R. (1978). Relational understanding and instrumental understanding. *Arithmetic Teacher, 26*, 9–15.

%Smith, N. J. (1977). *The effects of training teachers to teach students at different reading ability levels to formulate three types of questions on reading comprehension and question generation ability.* Unpublished doctoral dissertation, University of Georgia.

$Spiegel, D., Jackson, F., Graham, M., & Ware, W. (1990, November). *The effects of four study strategies on main idea and detail comprehension of sixth grade students.* Paper presented at the annual meeting of the National Reading Conference, Miami, FL.

*Steinberg, R., Haymore, J., & Marks, R. (1985, April). *Teacher's knowledge and structuring content in mathematics.* Paper presented at the annual meeting of the American Educational Research Association, Chicago.

*Swing, S., Stoiber, K., & Peterson, P. L. (1988). Thinking skills versus learning time: Effects of alternative classroom-based interventions on students' mathematics problem-solving. *Cognition and Instruction, 5,* 123–121.

%Taylor, B. M., & Frye, B. J. (1992). Comprehension strategy instruction in the intermediate grades. *Reading Research and Instruction, 92,* 39–48.

@Tomesen, M., & Aarnoutse, C. (1998). Effecten van een instructieprogramma voor het afleiden van woordbetekenissen [Effects of a training program in deriving word meanings]. *Pedogogische Studien, 75,* 1–16.

*von Glaserfeld, E. (1987). Learning as a constructive activity. In C. Janvier (Ed.), *Problems of representation in the teaching and learning of mathematics* (pp. 3–17). Hillsdale, NJ: Erlbaum.

*Voss, J. F. (1987). Learning and transfer and subject-matter learning: A problem-solving model. *International Journal of Educational Research, 11,* 607–622.

$Waxman, H., de Felix, J., Martinez, A., Knight, S., & Padron, Y. (1994). Effects of implementing classroom instructional models on English language learners' cognitive and affective outcomes. *Bilingual Research Journal, 18*(3/4), 1–22.

%Weiner, C. J. (1978, March). *The effect of training in questioning and student question-generation on reading achievement.* Paper presented at the annual meeting of the American Educational Research Association, Toronto. (ERIC Document Reproduction Service No. ED 158 223)

*Weiss, I. (1978). *Report of the 1977 National Survey of Science, Mathematics, and Social Studies Education.* Research Triangle Park, NC: Research Triangle Institute, Center for Educational Research and Evaluation.

+Welch, M. (1992). The PLEASE strategy: A meta-cognitive learning strategy for improving the paragraph writing of students with learning disabilities. *Learning Disability Quarterly, 15*(2), 119–128.

%Williamson, R. A. (1989). *The effect of reciprocal teaching on student performance gains in third grade basal reading instruction.* Unpublished doctoral dissertation, Texas A&M University.

#Woloshyn, V. E., Pressley, M., & Schneider, W. (1992). Elaborative-interrogation and prior knowledge effects on learning of facts. *Journal of Educational Psychology, 82*(1), 115–124.

$Wong, B., Butler, D., Ficzere, S., & Kuperis, S. (1996). Teaching low achievers and students with learning disabilities to plan, write, and revise opinion essays. *Journal of Learning Disabilities, 29*(2), 197–212.

%Wong, B.Y.L., & Jones, W. (1982). Increasing metacomprehension in learning disabled and normally achieving students through self-questioning training. *Learning Disability Quarterly, 5,* 228–239.

#Wood, E., Pressley, M., & Winne, P. (1990). Elaborative interrogation effects on children's learning of factual content. *Journal of Educational Psychology, 82*, 741–748.

REFERENCES FOR PROVIDING DECISION-MAKING INSTRUCTION

Alfassi, M. (2004). Reading to learn: Effects of combined strategy instruction on high school students. *The Journal of Educational Research, 97*(4), 171–184.

@Anderson, V. A., & Roit, M. (1993). Planning and implementing collaborative strategy instruction for delayed readers in grades 6–10. *The Elementary School Journal, 94*(2), 121–137.

$!Andre, M.E.D.A., & Anderson, T. H. (1978–1979). The development and evaluation of a self-questioning study technique. *Reading Research Quarterly, 14*, 605–623.

$Baker, L., & Brown, A. L. (1984). Metacognitive skills and reading. In P. D. Pearson (Ed.), *Handbook of reading research* (pp. 353–394). New York: Longman.

*Bandura, A., & Cervone, M. (1986). Differential engagement of self-reactive influences in cognitive motivation. *Organizational Behavior and Human Decision Processes, 38*, 92–113.

Barley, Z., Lauer, P. A., Arens, S. A., Apthrop, H. S., Englert, K. S., Snow, D., & Akiba, M. (2002). *Helping at-risk students meet standards: A synthesis of evidence-based classroom practices.* Aurora, CO: Mid-continent Research for Education and Learning.

$Baumann, J. F. (1984). The effectiveness of a direct instruction paradigm for teaching main idea comprehension. *Reading Research Quarterly, 20*, 93–115.

$Baumann, J. F. (1986). The direct instruction of main idea comprehension ability. In J. F. Baumann (Ed.), *Teaching main idea comprehension* (pp. 133–178). Newark, DE: International Reading Association.

%Baumann, M. (1992). The effect of teacher-directed and student-directed journal writing in fifth-grade student mathematics achievement. *Dissertation Abstracts International, 53*(06), 1830A. (UMI No. 9227116)

@Beck, I. L., McKeown, M. G., Worthy, J., Sandora, C. A., & Kucan, L. (1996). Questioning the author: A year long classroom implementation to engage students with text. *The Elementary School Journal, 96*(4), 385–414.

@Bereiter, C., & Bird, M. (1985). Use of thinking aloud in identification and teaching of reading comprehension strategies. *Cognition and Instruction, 2*(2), 131–156.

&Blaha, B. A. (1979). *The effects of answering self-generated questions on reading.* Unpublished doctoral dissertation, Boston University School of Education.

+Bottge, B. (1999). Effects of contextualized math instruction on problem solving of average and below-average achieving students. *The Journal of Special Education, 33*(2), 81–92.

&!Brady, P. L. (1990). *Improving the reading comprehension of middle school students through reciprocal teaching and semantic mapping strategies.* Unpublished doctoral dissertation, University of Alaska.

#Bransford, J., Sherwood, R., Vye, N., & Reiser, J. (1986). Teaching thinking and problem solving. *American Psychologist, 41*, 1078–1089.

#Brown, A. L. (1985). *Teaching students to think as they read: Implications for curriculum reform* (Reading Rep. No. 58). Champaign: University of Illinois, Center for the Study of Reading.

*Brown, A. L., Bransford, J. D., Ferrara, R. A., & Campione, J. C. (1983). Learning, remembering, and understanding. In J. H. Flavell & E. M. Markman (Eds.), *Carmichael handbook of child psychology* (Vol. 3, pp. 515–529). New York: Wiley.

@Brown, A. L., & Campione, J. C. (1994). Guided discovery in a community of learners. In K. McGilly (Ed.), *Classroom lessons: Integrating cognitive theory and classroom practice* (pp. 229–270). Cambridge, MA: MIT Press.

*Brown, A. L., Campione, J. C., & Day, J. D. (1981). Learning to learn: On training students to learn from text. *Educational Researcher, 10,* 14–21.

@Brown, A. L., & Palincsar, A. S. (1982). Inducing strategic learning from text by means of informed, self-control training. *Topics in Learning and Learning Disabilities, 2*(1), 1–17.

$Brown, A. L., & Palincsar, A. S. (1985). *Reciprocal teaching of comprehension strategies: A natural history of one program for enhancing learning* (Tech. Rep. No. 334). Urbana: University of Illinois, Center for the Study of Reading.

@Brown, A. L., & Palincsar, A. S. (1989). Guided, cooperative learning, and individual knowledge acquisition. In L. B. Resnick (Ed.), *Knowing, learning, and instruction: Essays in honor of Robert Glaser* (pp. 393–451). Hillsdale, NJ: Erlbaum.

$Brown, A. L., Palincsar, A. S., & Armbruster, B. B. (1984). Instructing comprehension-fostering activities in interactive learning situations. In H. Mandl, N. L. Stein, & T. Trabasso (Eds.), *Learning in comprehension of text* (pp. 255–286). Hillsdale, NJ: Erlbaum.

+Brown, D. (1995). *Assisting eighth-grade at-risk students in successfully reading their textbooks through support strategies.* Unpublished practicum report, Nova Southeastern University, Florida.

+Brown, R., Pressley, M., Van Meter, P., & Schuder, T. (1995). *A quasi-experimental validation of transactional strategies instruction with previously low-achieving, second-grade readers.* Reading Research Report No. 33. Universities of Georgia and Maryland, National Reading Research Center.

+Cardelle-Elawar, M. (1990). Effects of feedback tailored to bilingual students' mathematics needs on verbal problem solving. *The Elementary School Journal, 91*(2), 165–170.

@Chi, M.T.H., de Leeuw, N., Chiu, M., & LaVancher, C. (1994). Eliciting self-explanations. *Cognitive Science, 18*(3), 439–477.

&!Cohen, R. (1983). Self-generated questions as an aid to reading comprehension. *The Reading Teacher, 36,* 770–775.

Collins, R., & Smith, E. E. (1982). Teaching the process of reading comprehension. In D. K. Detterman & R. J. Sternberg (Eds.), *How and how much can intelligence be increased?* (pp. 173–185). Norwood, NJ: Ablex.

$Craik, F.I.M., & Lockhart, R. S. (1972). Levels of processing: A framework for memory research. *Journal of Verbal Learning and Verbal Behavior, 11,* 671–684.

$Cunningham, J. W., & Moore, D. W. (1986). The confused world of main idea. In J. B. Bauman (Ed.), *Teaching main idea comprehension* (pp. 1–17). Newark, DE: International Reading Association.

&!Davey, B., & McBride, S. (1986). Effects of question-generation on reading comprehension. *Journal of Educational Psychology, 78,* 256–262.

&!Dermody, M. (1988, February). *Metacognitive strategies for development of reading comprehension for younger children.* Paper presented at the annual meeting of the American Association of Colleges for Teacher Education, New Orleans, LA.

+Dimino, J., Gersten, R., Carnine, D., & Blake, G. (1990). Story grammar: An approach for promoting at-risk secondary students' comprehension of literature. *The Elementary School Journal, 91*(1), 19–32.

Dole, J. A., Duffy, G. G., Roehler, L. R., & Pearson, P. D. (1991). Moving from the old to the new: Research on reading comprehension instruction. *Review of Educational Research, 61*(2), 239–264.

&Dreher, M. J., & Gambrell, L. B. (1985). Teaching children to use a self questioning strategy for studying expository text. *Reading Improvement, 22*, 2–7.

+Englert, C., Raphael, T. E., Anderson, L., Anthony, H., & Stevens, D. (1991). Making strategies and self-talk visible: Writing instruction in regular and special education classrooms. *American Educational Research Journal, 28*(2), 337–372.

!Fischer-Galbert, J. L. (1989). *An experimental study of reciprocal teaching of expository texts with third, fourth, and fifth-grade students enrolled in Chapter 1 Reading.* Unpublished doctoral dissertation, Ball State University, Muncie, IN.

+Guastello, E., Beasley, T., & Sinatra, R. (2000). Concept mapping effects on science content comprehension of low-achieving inner-city seventh graders. *Remedial and Special Education, 21*(6), 356–365.

#Hasselhorn, M., & Korkel, J. (1986). Metacognitive versus traditional reading instructions: The mediating role of domain-specific knowledge on children's text processing. *Human Learning, 5*, 75–90.

&Helfeldt, J. P., & Lalik, R. (1976). Reciprocal student-teacher questioning. *The Reading Teacher, 33*, 283–287.

Horton, P., Fronk, R., & Walton, R. (1985). The effect of writing assignments on achievement in college general chemistry. *Journal of Research in Science Teaching, 22*(6), 535–541.

+Jakupcak, J., Rushton, R., Jakupcak, M., & Lundt, J. (1996). Inclusive education. *The Science Teacher, 63*(5), 40–43.

!Jones, M. P. (1987). *Effects of reciprocal teaching method on third graders' decoding and comprehension abilities.* Unpublished doctoral dissertation, Texas A&M University.

*Kane, J. M., & Anderson, R. C. (1978). Death of processing and inference effects in the learning and remembering of sentences. *Journal of Educational Psychology, 70*, 626–635.

*Kerr, B. (1973). Processing demands during mental operations. *Memory & Cognition, 1*, 401–412.

+Ketter, J., & Pool, J. (2001). Exploring the impact of a high-stakes direct writing assessment in two high school classrooms. *Research in the Teaching of English, 35*, 344–393.

&King, A. (1989). Effects of self-questioning training on college students' comprehension of lectures. *Contemporary Educational Psychology, 14*, 366–381.

&King, A. (1990). Improving lecture comprehension: Effects of a metacognitive strategy. *Applied Educational Psychology, 5*, 331–346.

&King, A. (1992). Comparison of self questioning, summarizing, and notetaking-review as strategies for learning from lectures. *American Educational Research Journal, 29*, 303–325.

*Kintsch, W. (1977). *Memory and cognition.* New York: Wiley.

Kucan, L., & Beck, I. L. (1997). Thinking aloud and reading comprehension research: Inquiry, instruction, and social interaction. *Review of Educational Research, 67*(3), 271–299.

&!Labercane, G., & Battle, J. (1987). Cognitive processing strategies, self-esteem, and reading comprehension of learning disabled students. *Journal of Special Education, 11*, 167–185.

*Langer, D. J., & Imber, L. E. (1979). When practice makes perfect: The debilitating effects of overlearning. *Journal of Personality and Social Psychology, 37*, 2014–2024.

*Langer, E. J. (1985). Playing the middle against both ends: The influence of adult cognitive activity as a model for cognitive activity in childhood and old age. In S. R. Yussen (Ed.), *The development of reflection* (pp. 267–285). New York: Academic Press.

#Lawson, J. (1984). Being executive about metacognition. In J. R. Kirby (Ed.), *Cognitive strategies in educational performance* (pp. 89–109). New York: Academic Press.

!Levin, M. C. (1989). *An experimental investigation of reciprocal teaching and inform strategies for learning taught to learning-disabled intermediate school learners.* Unpublished doctoral dissertation, Teachers College, Columbia University.

&!Lonberger, R. B. (1988). *The effects of training in a self-generated learning strategy on the prose processing abilities of fourth and sixth graders.* Unpublished doctoral dissertation, State University of New York at Buffalo.

&!Lysybchuk, L., Pressley, M., & Vye, G. (1990). Reciprocal instruction improves reading comprehension performance in poor grade school comprehenders. *Elementary School Journal, 40*, 471–484.

&MacGregor, S. K. (1988). Use of self-questioning with a computer-mediated text system and measures of reading performance. *Journal of Reading Behavior, 20*, 131–148.

#&Manzo, A. V. (1969). *Improving reading comprehension through reciprocal teaching.* Unpublished doctoral dissertation, Syracuse University.

+McLain, K. (1991, November). *Effects of two comprehension monitoring strategies on the metacognitive awareness and reading achievement of third and fifth grade students.* Paper presented at the annual meeting of the National Reading Conference, Miami, FL.

Mevarech, Z. R., & Kramarski, B. (1997). IMPROVE: A multidimensional method for teaching mathematics in hetergoeneous classrooms. *American Educational Research Journal, 34*(2), 365–394.

Mevarech, Z. R., & Kramarski, B. (2003). The effects of metacognitive training versus worked-out examples on students' mathematical reasoning. *British Journal of Educational Psychology, 73*, 449–471.

@Miller, G. E. (1985). The effects of general and specific-instruction training on children's comprehension monitoring performance during reading. *Reading Research Quarterly, 20*(5), 616–628.

&Nolte, R. Y., & Singer, H. (1985). Active comprehension: Teaching a process of reading comprehension and its effects on reading achievement. *The Reading Teacher, 39*, 24–31.

+O'Malley, J., Chamot, A., Stewner-Manzanares, G., Russo, R., & Kupper, L. (1985). Learning strategy applications with students of English as a second language. *TESOL Quarterly, 19*(3), 557–584.

!Padron, Y. N. (1985). *Utilizing cognitive reading strategies to improve English reading comprehension of Spanish-speaking bilingual students.* Unpublished doctoral dissertation, University of Houston.

&!Palincsar, A. S. (1987, April). *Collaboration for collaborative learning of text comprehension.* Paper presented at the annual meeting of the American Educational Research Association, Washington, DC.

#&!Palincsar, A. S., & Brown, A. L. (1984). Reciprocal teaching of comprehension-fostering and comprehension-monitoring activities. *Cognition and Instruction, 2,* 117–175.

@Palincsar, A. S., & Brown, A. L. (1988). Teaching and practicing thinking skills to promote comprehension in the context of group problem solving. *Remedial and Special Education, 9*(1), 53–59.

@Palincsar, A. S., & Klenk, L. (1992). Fostering literacy learning in supportive contexts. *Journal of Learning Disabilities, 25*(4), 211–225, 229.

@Palincsar, A. S., & Klenk, L. (1993). Third invited response: Broader visions encompassing literacy, learners, and context. *Remedial and Special Education, 14*(4), 19–25.

*Pascual-Leone, J. (1984). Attention, dialectic, and mental effort: Toward an orgasmic theory of life stages. In M. L. Commons, F. A. Richards, & C. Armon (Eds.), *Beyond formal operations* (pp. 182–215). New York: Praeger.

#Petrie, H. G. (1976). Do you see what I see? The epistemology of interdisciplinary inquiry. *Educational Researcher, 5*(2), 9–15.

Prawat, R. S. (1989). Promotion access to knowledge, strategy, and disposition in students: A research synthesis. *Review of Educational Research, 59*(1), 1–41.

*Pressley, L. (1986). The relevance of the good strategy user to the teaching of mathematics. *Educational Psychologist, 21,* 139–162.

!Rich, R. Z. (1989). *The effects of training adult poor readers to use text comprehension strategies.* Unpublished doctoral dissertation, Teachers College, Columbia University.

!Risko, V. J., & Feldman, N. (1986). Teaching young remedial readers to generate questions as they read. *Reading Horizons, 27,* 54–64.

&Ritchie, P. (1985). The effects of instruction in main idea question generation. *Reading Canada Lecture, 3,* 139–146.

Rosenshine, B., & Meister, C. (1994). Reciprocal teaching: A review of the research. *Review of Educational Research, 64*(4), 479–530.

Rosenshine, B., Meister, C., & Chapman, S. (1996). Teaching students to generate questions: A review of intervention studies. *Review of Educational Research, 66*(2), 181–221.

!Rush, R. T., & Milburn, J. L. (1988, November). *The effects of reciprocal teaching on self-regulation of reading comprehension in a postsecondary technical school program.* Paper presented at the annual meeting of the National Reading Conference, Tucson, AZ.

Saloman, G., & Globerson, T. (1987). Skill is not enough: The role of mindfulness in learning and transfer. *International Journal of Research in Education, 11,* 623–638.

Saloman, G., & Perkins, D. N. (1989). Rocky roads to transfer: Rethinking mechanisms of a neglected phenomenon. *Educational Psychologist, 24*(2), 113–142.

@Schmit, M. C. (1988). The effects of an elaborated directed reading activity on the metacomprehension skills of third graders. In J. E. Readance & R. S. Baldwin (Eds.), *Dialogues in literacy research* (thirty-seventh yearbook of the National Reading Conference, pp. 167–181). Chicago: National Reading Conference.

@Schunk, D. H., & Rice, J. M. (1985). Verbalization of comprehension strategies: Effects on children's achievement outcomes. *Human Learning, 4*(1), 1–10

&Short, E. J., & Ryan, E. B. (1984). Metacognitive differences between skilled and less skilled readers: Remediating deficits through story grammar and attribution training. *Journal of Educational Psychology, 76,* 225–335.

!Shortland-Jones, B. (1986). *The development and testing of an instructional strategy for improving reading comprehension based on schema and metacognitive theories.* Unpublished doctoral dissertation, University of Oregon.

&Simpson, P. S. (1989). *The effects of direct training in active comprehension on reading achievement, self-concepts, and reading attitudes of at-risk sixth grade students.* Unpublished doctoral dissertation, Texas Tech University.

$Singer, H., & Dolan, D. (1982). Active comprehension: Problem solving schema with question generation for comprehension of complex short stories. *Reading Research Quarterly, 17,* 166–186.

&Smith, N. J. (1977). *The effects of training teachers to teach students at different reading ability levels to formulate three types of questions on reading comprehension and question generation ability.* Unpublished doctoral dissertation, University of Georgia.

+Spiegel, D., Jackson, F., Graham, M., & Ware, W. (1990, November). *The effects of four study strategies on main idea and detail comprehension of sixth grade students.* Paper presented at the annual meeting of the National Reading Conference, Miami, FL.

&!Taylor, B. M., & Frye, B. J. (1992). Comprehension strategy instruction in the intermediate grades. *Reading Research and Instruction, 92,* 39–48.

@Trabasso, T., & Magliano, J. P. (1996). How do children understand what they read and what can we do to help them? In M. Graves, P. van den Broek, & B. Taylor (Eds.), *The first R: Every child's right to read* (pp. 160–188). New York: Teachers College Press.

+Waxman, H., de Felix, J., Martinez, A., Knight, S., & Padron, Y. (1994). Effects of implementing classroom instructional models on English language learners' cognitive and affective outcomes. *Bilingual Research Journal, 18*(3/4), 1–22.

&Weiner, C. J. (1978). *The effect of training in questioning and student question-generation on reading achievement.* Paper presented at the annual meeting of the American Educational Research Association, Toronto.

$Williams, J. P. (1986a). Extracting information from text. In J. A. Niles & R. V. Lalik (Eds.), *Solving problems in literacy: Learners, teachers, and researchers* (thirty-fifth yearbook of the National Reading Conference, pp. 11–29). Rochester, NY: National Reading Conference.

$Williams, J. P. (1986b). Research and instructional development on main idea skills. In J. F. Bauman (Ed.), *Teaching main idea comprehension* (pp. 73–95). Newark, DE: International Reading Association.

&!Williamson, R. A. (1989). *The effects of reciprocal teaching on student performance gains in third grade basal reading instructions.* Unpublished doctoral dissertation, Texas A&M University.

$Winigrad, P. N., & Bridge, C. A. (1986). The comprehension of important information in written prose. In J. F. Bauman (Ed.), *Teaching main idea comprehension* (pp. 18–48). Newark, DE: International Reading Association.

+Wong, B., Butler, D., Ficzere, S., & Kuperis, S. (1996). Teaching low achievers and students with learning disabilities to plan, write, and revise opinion essays. *Journal of Learning Disabilities, 29*(2), 197–212.

&!Wong, B.Y.L., & Jones, W. (1982). Increasing metacomprehension in learning disabled and normally achieving students through self-questioning training. *Learning Disability Quarterly, 5,* 228–239.

REFERENCES FOR PROVIDING PREDICTION AND PROBLEM-SOLVING INSTRUCTION

#Aaron, S., Crocket, J., Morrish, D., et al. (1998). Assessment of exam performance after change to problem-based learning: Differential effects by question type. *Teaching and Learning in Medicine, 10*(2), 86–91.

#Albano, M., Cavallo, F., Hoogenboom, R., et al. (1996). An international comparison of knowledge levels of medical students: The Maastricht Progress Test. *Medical Education, 30,* 239–245.

#Antepohl, W., & Herzig, S. (1997). Problem-based learning supplementing in the course of basic pharmacology—results and perspectives from two medical schools. *Naunyn-Schmiedeberg's Archives of Pharmacology, 355,* R18.

#Antepohl, W., & Herzig, S. (1999). Problem-based learning versus lecture-based learning in a course of basic pharmacology: A controlled, randomized study. *Medical Education, 33*(2), 106–113.

#Baca, E., Mennin, S., Kaufman, A., & Moore-West, M. (1990). Comparison between a problem-based, community-oriented track and a traditional track within one medical school. In Z. M. Nooman, G. G. Schmidt, & E. Ezzat (Eds.), *Innovation in medical education: An evaluation of its present status* (pp. 9–26). New York: Springer.

#Barrows, H., & Tamblyn, R. (1976). An evaluation of problem-based learning in small groups utilizing a simulated patient. *Journal of Medical Education, 51,* 52–54.

Benz, D., & Rosemier, R. (1966). Concurrent validity of the Gates level of comprehension test and the Bond, Clymer, Hoyt reading diagnostic tests. *Educational and Psychological Measurement, 26,* 1057–1062.

#Bickley, H., Donner, R. S., Walker, A., & Tift, J. (1990). Pathology education in a problem-based medical curriculum. *Teaching and Learning in Medicine, 2*(1), 38–41.

#Block, S., & Moore, G. (1994). Project evaluation. In D. C. Tosteson, S. Adelstein, & S. Carver (Eds.), *New pathways to medical education: Learning to learn at Harvard Medical School.* Cambridge, MA: Harvard University Press.

#Boshuizen H., Schmidt, H., & Wassamer, A. (1993). Curriculum style and the integration of biomedical and clinical knowledge. In P. Bouhuys, H. Schmidt, & H. van Berkel (Eds.), *Problem-based learning as an educational strategy* (pp. 33–41). Maastricht: Network Publications.

*Bridgham, R., Solomon, D., & Haf, J. (1991). The effect of curriculum era on NBME Part 1 outcomes in a problem-based versus a traditional curriculum track. *Academic Medicine, 66*(Supplement), S82–S84.

Chia, T. (1995). *Learning difficulty in applying notion of vector in physics among "A" level students in Singapore.* (ERIC Document Reproduction Service No. ED 389 528)

Denner, P. R., & McGinley, W. J. (1990). *Effects of prediction combined with storytelling versus listing predictions as prereading activities on subsequent story comprehension.* Paper presented at the annual meeting of the National Reading Conference, Miami.

#Distlehorst, L., & Robbs, R. (1998). A comparison of problem-based learning and standard curriculum students: Three years of retrospective data. *Teaching and Learning in Medicine, 19*(3), 131–137.

Dochy, F., Segers, M., Van den Bossche, P., & Gijbels, D. (2003). Effects of problem-based learning: A meta-analysis. *Learning and Instruction, 13*(5), 533–568.

#Donner, R., & Bickley, H. (1990). Problem-based learning: An assessment of its feasibility and cost. *Human Pathology, 21*, 881–885.

#Doucet, M., Purdy, R., Kaufman, D., & Langille, D. (1998). Comparison of problem-based learning and lecture format in continuing medical education on headache diagnosis and management. *Medical Education, 32*(6), 590–596.

Dykes, S. (1997). *A test of proposition, of prediction theory.* Doctoral dissertation, University of South Carolina.

#Eisenstaedt, R., Barry, W., & Glanz, K. (1990). Probem-based learning: Cognitive retention and cohort traits of randomly selected participants and decliners. *Academic Medicine, 65*(9, September supplement), 11–12.

#Farquhar, L., Haf, J., & Kotabe, K. (1986). Effect of two preclinical curricula on NMBE part I examination performance. *Journal of Medical Education, 61*, 368–373.

#Finch, P. (1999). The effect of problem-based learning on the academic performance of students studying pediatric medicine in Ontario. *Medical Education, 33*(6), 411–417.

Freeman, R. H. (1982). *Improving comprehension of stories using predictive strategies.* Paper presented at the annual meeting of the International Reading Association, Chicago.

Friedman, M. I. (1974). *Predictive ability tests: Verbal and nonverbal forms.* Columbia, SC: M. I. Friedman.

Friedman, M. I., & Maddock, M. (1980). *Predictive ability instruction.* Research report published for participating school districts in South Carolina.

*#Goodman, L., Brueschke, E., Bone, R., Rose, W., Williams, E., & Paul, H. (1991). An experiment in medical education: A critical analysis using traditional criteria. *Journal of the American Medical Association, 265*, 2373–2376.

Greeno, J., & Noreen, D. (1974). Time to read semantically related sentences. *Memory and Cognition, 2*(1A), 117–120.

Henderson, E., & Long, B. (1968). Correlation of reading readiness and children of varying backgrounds. *The Reading Teacher, 22*, 40–44.

#Hmelo, C. (1998). Problem-based learning: Effects on the early acquisition of cognitive skill in medicine. *The Journal of the Learning Sciences, 7*, 173–236.

#Hmelo, C., Gotterer, G., & Bransford, J. (1997). A theory-driven approach to assessing the cognitive effects of PBL. *Instructional Science, 25*, 387–408.

Hunt, J., & Joseph, D. (1990). Using prediction to improve reading comprehension of low-achieving readers. *Journal of Clinical Reading, Research and Programs, 3*(2), 14–17.

Hurst, R., & Milkent, M. (1994). *Facilitating successful predictive reasoning in biology through application of skill theory.* Paper presented at the annual meeting of the National Association for Research in Science Teaching, Anaheim, CA, March 19–26. (ERIC Document Reproduction Service No. ED 368 582)

#Imbos, T., Drukker, J., van Mameren, H., & Verwijnen, M. (1984). The growth in knowledge of anatomy in a problem-based curriculum. In H. G. Schmidt & M. L. de Volder (Eds.), *Tutorials in problem-based learning: New direction in training for the health professions* (pp. 106–115). Assen, The Netherlands: Van Gorcum.

#Imbos, T., & Verwijnen, G. (1982). Voortgangstoetsing aan de medische faulteit Maastricht [Progress testing on the Faculty of Medicine of Maastricht]. In H. G. Schmidt (Ed.), *Probleemgestuurd Onderwijs: Bijdragen tot onderwijsresearchdagen 1981* (pp. 45–56). The Hague, The Netherlands: Stichting voor Onderzoek van het Onderwijs.

*#Jones, J., Bieber, L., Echt, R., Scheifley, V., & Ways, P. (1984). A problem-based curriculum: Ten years of experience. In H. G. Schmidt & M. L. de Volder (Eds.), *Tutorials in*

problem-based learning: New direction in training for the health professions (pp. 181–198). Assen, The Netherlands: Van Gorcum.

Kalaian, H. A., Mullan, P. B., & Kasim, R. M. (1999). What can studies of Problem-Based Learning tell us? Synthesizing and modeling PBL effects on National Board of Medical Examination Performance: Hierarchical liner modeling meta-analytic approach. *Advances in Health Sciences Education, 4*, 209–221.

*#Kaufman, A., Mennin, S., Waterman, R., Duban, S., Hansbarger, C., Silverblatt, H., Obenshain, S. S., Katrowitz, M., Becker, T., Samet, J., & Wiese, W. (1989). The Mexico experiment: Educational innovation and institutional change. *Academic Medicine, 64*, 285–294.

#Lewis, K. E., & Tamblyn, R. M. (1987). The problem-based learning approach in Baccalaureate nursing education: How effective is it? *Nursing Papers, 19*(2), 17–26.

#Martenson, D., Eriksson, H., & Ingelman-Sundberg, M. (1985). Medical chemistry: Evaluation of active and problem-oriented teaching methods. *Medical Education, 19*, 34–42.

#Mennin, S. P., Friedman, M., Skipper, B., Kalishman, S., & Snyder, J. (1993). Performances on the NMBE I, II, III by medical students in the problem-based learning and conventional tracks at the University of New Mexico, *Academic Medicine, 68*, 616–624.

#Moore, G. T., Blocks, S. D., Briggs-Style, C., & Mitchell, R. (1994). The influence of the New Pathway curriculum on Harvard medical students. *Academic Medicine, 69*, 983–989.

*#Morgan, H. R. (1977). A problem-oriented independent studies programme in basic medical sciences. *Medical Education, 11*, 394–398.

#Neufeld, V., & Sibley, J. (1989). Evaluation of heath sciences education programs: Program and student assessment at McMaster University. In H. G. Schmidt, M. Lipkinjr, M. W. Vries, & J. M. Greep (Eds.), *New directions for medical education: Problem-based learning and community-oriented medical education* (pp. 165–179). New York: Springer Verlag.

Nolan, T. (1991). Self-questioning and prediction: Combining metacognitive strategies. *Journal of Reading, 35*(2), 77–101.

#Patel, V. L., Groen, G. J., & Norman, G. R. (1991). Effects of conventional and problem-based medical curricula on problem-solving. *Academic Medicine, 66*, 380–389.

Reutzel, D., & Fawson, P. (1991). Literature webbing predictable books: A prediction strategy that helps below-average, first-grade children. *Reading Research and Instruction, 30*(4), 20–30.

*Richards, B., & Cariaga, L. (1993). A comparison between students in problem-based and traditional curricula at the same medical school: Preparing for the NBME Part 1. *Medical Education, 27*, 130–136.

#Richards, B. F., Ober, P., Cariaga-Lo, L., Camp, M. G., Philp, J., McFarlane, M., Rupp, R., & Zaccaro, D. J. (1996). Rating of students' performances in a third-year internal medicine clerkship: A comparison between problem-based and lecture-based curricula. *Academic Medicine, 71*(2), 187–189.

#Santos-Gomez, L., Kalishman, S., Rezler, A., Skipper, B., & Mennin, S. P. (1990). Residency performance of graduates from a problem-based and conventional curriculum. *Medical Education, 24*, 366–377.

#Saunders, N. A., Mcintosh, J., Mcpherson, J., & Engel, C. E. (1990). A comparison between University of Newcastle and University of Sydney final-year students: Knowledge and competence. In Z. H. Nooman, H. G. Schmidt, & E. S. Ezzat (Eds.), *Innovation in medical education: An evaluation of its present status* (pp. 50–54). New York: Springer.

#Schmidt, H. G., Machiels-Bongaerts, M., Herman, H, ten Cate, T. J., Venekamp, R., & Boshuizen, H.P.A. (1996). The development of diagnostic competence: Comparison of a problem-based, an integrated and a conventional medical curriculum. *Academic Medicine, 71,* 658–664.

#Schwartz, R. W., Burgett, J. E., Blue, A. V., Donnelly, M. B., & Sloan, D. A. (1997). Problem-based learning and performance-based testing: Effective alternatives for undergraduate surgical education and assessment of student performance. *Medical Teacher, 19,* 19–23.

#Son, B., & Van Sickle, R. L. (2000). Problem-solving instruction and students' acquisition, retention and structuring of economics knowledge. *Journal of Research and Development in Education, 33*(2), 95–105.

#Tans, R. W., Schmidt, H. G., Shade-Hoogeveen, B.E.J., & Gijselaers, W. H. (1986). Sturing van het onderwijsleerproces door middle van problem: Een veldexperiment [Guiding the learning process by means of problems: A field experiment]. *Tijdschrift voor Onderswijsresearch, 11,* 35–46.

#Van Hessen, P.A.W., & Verwijnen, G. M. (1990). Does problem-based learning provide other knowledge. In W. Bender, R. J. Hiemstra, A.J.J.A. Scherpbier, & R. P. Zwiestra (Eds.), *Teaching and assessing clinical competence* (pp. 446–451). Groningen: Boekwerk Publications.

#Verhoeven, B. H., Verwijnen, G. M., Scherpbier, A.J.J.A., Holdrinet, R.S.G., Oeseburg, B., Bulte, J. A., & Van Der Vleuten, C.P.M. (1998). An analysis of progress test results of PBL and non-PBL students. *Medical Teacher, 20*(4), 310–316.

#Verwijnen, M., Van Der Vleuten, C., & Imbros, T. (1990). A comparison of an innovative medical school with traditional schools: An analysis in the cognitive domain. In Z. H. Nooman, H. G. Schmidt, & E. S. Ezzat (Eds.), *Innovation in medical education: An evaluation of its present status* (pp. 41–49). New York: Springer.

Walker, B. J., & Mohr, T. (1985). *The effects of ongoing self-directed questioning on silent comprehension.* Paper presented at the annual meeting of the Reading Research Conference, Seattle, WA.

Walker, K., & Bates, R. (1985). *The effects of ongoing self-directed questioning on silent comprehension.* Paper presented at the annual meeting of the Reading Research Conference, St. Petersburg, FL.

Zinar, S. (1990). Fifth-graders' recall of proposition content and causal relationships from expository prose. *Journal of Reading Behavior, 22,* 2.

REFERENCES FOR PROVIDING CONTIGUITY

*+Abraham, F. J., & Newton, J. M. (1974). *The interview technique as a personalized system of instruction for economics: The Oregon experience.* Paper presented at the National Conference on Personalized Instruction in Higher Education, Washington, DC.

^Anane, F. (1987). The delay-retention phenomena: The effect of differential instructions on the learning and remembering of prose text material. *Dissertation Abstracts International, 48,* 2831A. (University Microfilms No. 87-28, 257)

$Anania, J. (1981). *The effects of quality of instruction on the cognitive and affective learning of students.* Unpublished doctoral dissertation, University of Chicago.

%Anderson, L. M., Evertson, C. M., & Brophy, J. E. (1979). An experimental study of effective teaching in first-grade reading groups. *The Elementary School Journal, 79,* 193–222.

%Anderson, L. M., Evertson, C. M., & Brophy, J. E. (1982). *Principles of small group instruction* (Occasional paper no. 32). East Lansing: Michigan State University, Institute for Research on Teaching.

+Anderson, L. W. (1973). *Time and school learning.* Unpublished doctoral dissertation, University of Chicago.

*$&Anderson, L. W. (1975a). Student involvement in learning and school achievement. *California Journal of Education Research, 26,* 53–62.

$&Anderson L. W. (1975b). *Time to criterion: An experimental study.* Paper presented at the annual meeting of the American Educational Research Association, Washington, DC. (ERIC Document Reproduction Service No. ED 108 006)

*$&+Anderson L. W. (1976). An empirical investigation of individual differences in time to learn. *Journal of Educational Psychology, 68,* 226–233.

*#@$&Anderson L. W., Scott, C., & Hutlock, N. (1976, April). *The effects of the mastery learning program on selected cognitive, affective, and ecological variables in grades 1 through 6.* Paper presented at the annual meeting of the American Educational Research Association, San Francisco.

+Anderson, O. T., & Artman, R. A. (1972). A self-paced independent study, introductory physics sequence—description and evaluation. *American Journal of Physics, 40,* 1737–1742.

^Anderson, R., Kulhavy, R., & Andre, T. (1971). Feedback procedures in programmed instruction. *Journal of Educational Psychology, 62,* 148–156.

^Anderson, R., Kulhavy, R., & Andre, T. (1972). Conditions under which feedback facilitates learning from programmed lessons. *Journal of Educational Psychology, 63,* 186–188.

Anderson, S. A. (1994). *Synthesis of research on mastery learning* (Information Analysis). (ERIC Document Reproduction Service No. ED 382 567)

*$&%Arlin, M., & Webster, J. (1983). Time costs of mastery learning. *Journal of Educational Psychology, 75,* 187–195.

^Arnett, P. (1985). Effects of feedback placement and completeness within Gagne's model for computer assisted instruction lesson development on concept and rule learning. *Dissertation Abstracts International, 46,* 2537A. (University Microfilms No. 85-24, 309)

^Aumiller, L. (1963). The effects of knowledge of results on learning to spell new words by third and fifth grade pupils. *Dissertation Abstracts International, 24,* 5187. (University Microfilms No. 64-5336)

*Austin, S. M., & Gilbert, K. E. (1973). Student performance in a Keller-Plan course in introductory electricity and magnetism. *American Journal of Physics, 41,* 12–18.

*Badia, P., Stutts, C., & Harsh, J. (1978). Do methods of instruction and measures of different abilities and study habits interact? In J. G. Sherman, R. S. Ruskin, & R. M. Lazar (Eds.), *Personalized instruction and education today* (pp. 113–128). San Francisco: San Francisco Press.

<Baer, D. M., Blount, R. L., Detrich, R., & Stokes, T. F. (1987). Using intermittent rein-

forcement to program maintenance of verbal/nonverbal correspondence. *Journal of Applied Behavior Analysis, 20*, 179–184.

=Ball, E., & Blachman, B. (1991). Does phoneme awareness training in kindergarten make a difference in early word recognition and developmental spelling? *Reading Research Quarterly, 26*, 49–66.

<Ballinger, C. (1993). *Annual report to the association on the status of year-round education.* (ERIC Document Reproduction Service No. ED 024 990)

Bangert-Drowns, R. L., Kulik, C-L. C., Kulik, J. A., & Morgan, M. T. (1991). The instructional effect of feedback in test-like events. *Review of Educational Research, 61*(2), 213–238.

=Barker, T., & Torgesen, J. (1995). An evaluation of computer-assisted instruction in phonological awareness with below average readers. *Journal of Educational Computing Research*, 19, 89–103.

%Becker, W. C. (1977). Teaching reading and language to the disadvantaged—What we have learned from field research. *Harvard Educational Review, 47*, 518–543.

*Benson, J. S., & Yeany, R. H. (1980, April). *Generalizability of diagnostic-prescriptive teaching strategies across student locus of control of multiple instructional units.* Paper presented at the annual meeting of the American Educational Research Association, Boston. (ERIC Document Reproduction Service No. 187 534)

=Bentin, S., & Leshem, H. (1993). On the interaction between phonological awareness and reading acquisition: It's a two-way street. *Annals of Dyslexia, 43*, 125–148.

<Berkowitz, M. J., & Martens, B. K. (2001). Assessing teachers' and students' preferences for school-based reinforcement: Agreement across methods and different effort requirements. *Journal of Developmental and Physical Disabilities, 13*, 373–387.

*+Billings, D. B. (1974). PSI versus the lecture course in the principles of economics: A quasi-controlled experiment. In R. S. Ruskin & S. F. Bono (Eds.), *Personalized instruction in higher education* (pp. 30–37). Washington, DC: Center for Personalized Instruction.

=Blachman, B., Ball, E., Black, R., & Tangel, D. (1994). Kindergarten teachers develop phoneme awareness in low-income, inner-city classrooms: Does it make a difference? *Reading and Writing: An Interdisciplinary Journal, 6*, 1–18.

*$Blackburn, K. T., & Nelson, D. (1985, April). *Differences between a group using a traditional format with mastery learning and a group using traditional format only in developmental mathematics courses at the university level: Implications for teacher education programs.* Paper presented at the annual meeting of the American Educational Research Association, Chicago. (ERIC Document Reproduction Service No. ED 258 948)

*Blasingame, J. W. (1975). Student attitude performance in a personalized system of instruction course in business administration—Correlates of performance with personality traits. *Dissertation Abstracts International, 36*, 3840. (University Microfilms No. 75-2834)

$&+Block, J. H. (1972). Student learning and the setting of mastery performance standards. *Educational Horizon, 50*, 183–191.

+Block, J. H. (1973). *Mastery performance standards and student learning.* Unpublished study, University of California, Santa Barbara.

Block, J. H. (1980). Success rate. In C. Denham & A. Lieberman (Eds.), *Time to learn* (pp. 95–106). Washington, DC: U.S. Government Printing Office.

Block, J. H., & Burns, R. B. (1976). Mastery Learning. In L. Schulman (Ed.), *Review of research in education* (Vol. 4, pp. 3–49). Itasca, IL: F. E. Peacock.

$+Block, J. H., & Tierney, M. (1974). An exploration of two correction procedures used in mastery learning approaches to instruction. *Journal of Educational Psychology, 66,* 962–967.

Bloom, B. S. (1985). Learning for mastery. In C. W. Fisher & D. C. Berliner (Eds.), *Perspectives on instructional time.* White Plains, NY: Longman.

&+Born, D. G., & Davis, M. L. (1974). Amount and distribution of study in a personalized instruction course and in a lecture course. *Journal of Applied Behavior Analysis, 7,* 365–375.

&+Born, D. G., Gledhill, S. M., & Davis, M. L. (1972). Examination performance in lecture-discussion and personalized instruction courses. *Journal of Applied Behavior Analysis, 5,* 33–43.

Bowers, G., & Hilgard, E. (1981). *Theories of learning.* Englewood Cliffs, NJ: Prentice Hall.

=Bradley, L., & Bryant, P. (1983). Categorizing sounds and learning to read: A causal connection. *Nature, 301,* 419–421.

=Bradley, L., & Bryant, P. (1985). *Rhyme and reason in reading and spelling.* Ann Arbor: University of Michigan Press. (This is a more complete report of Bradley & Bryant, 1983).

=Brady, S., Fowler, A., Stone, B., & Winbury, N. (1994). Training phonological awareness: A study with inner-city kindergarten children. *Annals of Dyslexia, 44,* 26–59.

&+Breland, N. S., & Smith, M. P. (1974). A comparison of PSI and traditional methods of instruction for teaching introduction to psychology. In R. S. Ruskin & S. F. Bono (Eds.), *Personalized instruction in higher education* (pp. 21–25). Washington, DC: Center for Personalized Instruction.

=Brennan, F., & Ireson, J. (1997). Training phonological awareness: A study to evaluate the effects of a program of metalinguistic games in kindergarten. *Reading and Writing: An Interdisciplinary Journal, 9,* 241–263.

%Brophy, J., & Evertson, C. (1976). *Learning from teaching: A developmental perspective.* Boston: Allyn and Bacon.

^Brown, R. (1964). An experimental study of knowledge of results in complex human learning. *Dissertation Abstracts International, 24,* 2356. (University Microfilms No. 64-696)

*$Bryant, N. D., Fayne, H. R, & Gettinger, M. (1982). Applying the mastery model to sight word for disabled readers. *Journal of Experimental Education, 50,* 116–121.

$Burke, A. (1983). *Students' potential for learning contrasted under tutorial and group approaches to instruction.* Unpublished doctoral dissertation, University of Chicago.

$&+Burrows, C. K., & Okey, J. R. (1975, March–April). *The effects of a mastery learning strategy on achievement.* Paper presented at the annual meeting of the American Educational Research Association, Washington, DC.

=Bus, A. (1986). Preparatory reading instruction in kindergarten: Some comparative research into methods of auditory and auditory-visual training of phonemic analysis and blending. *Perceptual and Motor Skills, 62,* 11–24.

=Byrne, B., & Fielding-Barnsley, R. (1991). Evaluation of a program to teach phonemic awareness to young children. *Journal of Educational Psychology, 83,* 451–455.

=Byrne, B., & Fielding-Barnsley, R. (1993). Evaluation of a program to teach phonemic awareness to young children. A 1-year follow-up. *Journal of Educational Psychology, 85*, 104–111. (This is a first follow-up to Byrne & Fielding-Barnsley, 1991.)

=Byrne, B., & Fielding-Barnsley, R. (1995). Evaluation of a program to teach phonemic awareness to young children: A 2- and 3-year follow-up and a new preschool trial. *Journal of Educational Psychology, 87*, 488–503. (This is a second follow-up to Byrnes & Fielding-Barnsley, 1991.)

*#@$Cabezon, E. (1984). *The effects of marked changes in student achievement pattern on the students, their teachers, and their parents: The Chilean case.* Unpublished doctoral dissertation, University of Chicago.

^Carels, E. J. (1975). The effects of false feedback, sex, and personality on learning, retention, and the Zeigarnik effect in programmed instruction. *Dissertation Abstracts International, 36*, 2094A. (University Microfilms No. 75-22, 345)

<Carnine, D. (1992). Expanding the notion of teachers' rights: Access to tools that work. *Journal of Applied Behavior Analysis, 24*, 13–19.

<Carr, E. G., & Durand, V. M. (1985). Reducing behavior problems through functional communication training. *Journal of Behavior Analysis, 18*, 111–126.

=Castle, J., Riach, J., & Nicholson, T. (1994). Getting off to a better start in reading and spelling: The effects of phonemic awareness instruction within a whole language program. *Journal of Educational Psychology, 86*, 350–359.

^Chanond, K. (1988, January). *The effects of feedback, correctness of response, and response confidence on learner's retention in computer-assisted instruction.* Paper presented at the annual meeting of the Association for Educational Communications and Technology, New Orleans. (ERIC Document Reproduction Service No. ED 295 632)

$Chiappetta, E. L., & McBride, J. W. (1980). Exploring the effects of general remediation on ninth-graders' achievement of the mole concept. *Science Education, 64*, 609–614.

*$Clark, C. P., Guskey, T. P., & Benninga, J. S. (1983). The effectiveness of mastery learning strategies in undergraduate education courses. *Journal of Educational Research, 76*, 210–214.

*Clark, S. G. (1975). An innovation for introductory sociology: Personalized system of instruction. In J. M. Johnston (Ed.), *Behavior research and technology in higher education* (pp. 117–124). Springfield, IL: Charles C. Thomas.

^Clodfelder, D. L. (1968). The quiz, knowledge of results, and individual differences in achievement orientation. *Dissertation Abstracts International, 29*, 2217. (University Microfilms No. 68-17181)

*!Coldeway, D. O., Santowski, M., O'Brien, R., & Lagowski, V. (1975). Comparison of small group contingency management with the personalized system of instruction and the lecture system. In J. M. Johnston (Ed.), *Research and technology in college and university teaching* (pp. 215–224). Gainesville: University of Florida.

*+Cole, C., Martin, S., & Vincent, J. (1975). A comparison of two teaching formats at the college level. In J. M. Johnston (Ed.), *Behavior research and technology in higher education* (pp. 61–74). Springfield, IL: Charles C. Thomas.

*Condo, P. (1974, April). *The analysis and evaluation of a self-paced course in calculus.* Paper presented at the National Conference on Personalized Instruction in Higher Education, Washington, DC.

*+<Cooper, B., Nye, B., Charlton, K., Lindsay, J., & Greathouse, S. (1996). The effects of summer vacation on achievement test scores: A narrative and meta-analytic review. *Review of Educational Research, 66*, 227–268.

*Corey, J. R., & McMichael, J. S. (1974). Retention in a PSI introductory psychology course. In J. G. Sherman (Ed.), *PSI germinal papers* (pp. 17–19). Washington, DC: Center for Personalized Instruction.

+Corey, J. R., McMichael, J. S., & Tremont, P. J. (1970, April). *Long-term effects of personalized instruction in an introductory psychology course.* Paper presented at the meeting of the Eastern Psychology Association, Atlantic City.

*Cote, J. D. (1976). Biology by PSI in a community college. In B. A. Green, Jr. (Ed.), *Personalized instruction in higher education.* Washington, DC: Center for Personalized Instruction.

*Cross, M. Z., & Semb, G. (1976). An analysis of the effects of personalized instruction on students at different initial performance levels in an introductory college nutrition course. *Journal of Personalized Instruction, 1*, 47–50.

=Cunningham, A. (1990). Explicit versus implicit instruction in phonemic awareness. *Journal of Experimental Child Psychology, 50*, 429–444.

<Daly, E. J., Lentz, F. E., & Boyer, J. (1996). The instructional hierarchy: A conceptual model for understanding the effective components of reading interventions. *School Psychology Quarterly, 11*, 369–386.

<Daly, E. J., Martens, B. K., Hamler, K., Dool, E. J., & Eckert, T. L. (1999). A brief experimental analysis for identifying instructional components needed to improve oral reading fluency. *Journal of Applied Behavior Analysis, 32*, 83–94.

=Davidson, M., & Jenkins, J. (1994). Effects of phonemic processes on word reading and spelling. *Journal of Educational Research, 87*, 148–157.

!De La Paz, S. (1995). *An analysis of the effects of dictation and planning instruction on the writing of students with learning disabilities.* Unpublished doctoral dissertation, University of Maryland, College Park.

!De La Paz, S., & Graham, S. (1997). Effects of dictation and advanced planning instruction on the composing of students with writing and learning problems. *Journal of Educational Psychology, 89*(2), 203–222.

*Decker, D. F. (1976). *Teaching to achieve learning mastery by using retesting techniques.* Doctoral dissertation, Nova University. (ERIC Document Reproduction Service No. ED 133 002)

=Defior, S., & Tudela, P. (1994). Effect of phonological training on reading and writing acquisition. *Reading and Writing: An Interdisciplinary Journal, 6*, 299–320.

$Denton, W. L., Ory, J. C., Glassnap, D. R., & Poggio, J. P. (1976). *Grade expectations within a mastery learning strategy.* Paper presented at the annual meeting of the American Educational Research Association, San Francisco. (ERIC Document Reproduction Service No. ED 126 105)

*$Dillashaw, F. G., & Okey, J. R. (1983). Effects of a modified mastery learning strategy on achievement, attitudes, and on-task behavior of high school chemistry students. *Journal of Research and Science Teaching, 20*, 203–211.

$Duby, P. B. (1981). *Attributions and attribution change: Effects of the mastery learning instructional approach.* Paper presented at the annual meeting of the American Educational Research Association, Los Angeles. (ERIC Document Reproduction Service No. ED 200 640)

<DuPaul, G. J., & Henningson, P. N. (1993). Peer tutoring effects on the classroom performance of children with Attention Deficit Hyperactivity Disorder. *School Psychology Review, 22*, 134–143.

=Ehri, L., & Wilce, L. (1987). Does learning to spell help beginners learn to read words? *Reading Research Quarterly, 22*, 48–65.

Ehri, L. C., Nunes, S. R., Willows, D. M., Schuster, B. V., Yaghoub-Zadeh, Z., & Shanahan, T. (2001). Phonemic awareness instruction helps children learn to read: Evidence from the National Reading Panel's meta-analysis. *Reading Research Quarterly, 36*(3), 250–287.

<Eisenberger, R., & Cameron, J. (1996). Detrimental effects of reward: Reality or myth? *American Psychologist, 51*, 1153–1166.

^Elliot, B. A. (1986). An investigation of the effects of computer feedback and interspersed questions on the text comprehension of poor readers. *Dissertation Abstracts International, 47*, 2971A. (University Microfilms No. 86-27, 446)

%Emmer, E. T., Evertson, C., Sanford, J., & Clements, B. (1982). *Improving instruction management: An experimental study in junior high classrooms*. Austin: Research and Development Center for Teacher Education, University of Texas.

!Englert, C. S., Garmon, A., Mariage, T., Rozendal, M., Tarrant, K., & Urba, J. (1995). The early literacy project: Connecting across the literacy curriculum. *Learning Disability Quarterly, 18*, 253–275.

!Englert, C. S., Raphael, T. E., Anderson, L. M., Anthony, H. M., & Stevens, D. D. (1991). Making writing strategies and self-talk visible: Cognitive strategy instruction in regular and special education classrooms. *American Educational Research Journal, 28*, 337–372.

<Erchul, W. P., & Martens, B. K. (2002). *School consultation: Conceptual and empirical bases of practice* (2nd ed.). New York: Plenum.

%Evertson, C. (1982). Differences in instructional activities in higher and lower achieving junior high English and mathematics classrooms. *Elementary School Journal, 82*, 329–351.

%Evertson, C., Anderson, C., Anderson, L. & Brophy, J. (1980). Relationships between classroom behaviors and student outcomes in junior high mathematics and English classes. *American Educational Research Journal, 17*, 43–60.

%Evertson, C., Emmer, E., & Brophy, J., (1980). Predictors of effective teaching in junior high mathematics classrooms. *Journal for Research in Mathematics Education, 11*, 167–178.

%Evertson, C. M., Emmer, E. T., Sanford, J. P., & Clements, B. S. (1983). Improving classroom management: An experiment in elementary classrooms. *Elementary School Journal, 84*, 173–188.

*#@Fagan, J. S. (1976). Mastery learning: The relationship of mastery procedures and aptitude to the achievement and retention of transportation-environment concepts by seventh-grade students. *Dissertation Abstracts International, 36*, 5981. (University Microfilms No. 76-6402)

=Farmer, A., Nixon, M., & White, R. (1976). Sound blending and learning to read: An experimental investigation. *British Journal of Educational Psychology, 46*, 155–163.

^Farragher, P., & Szabo, M. (1986). Learning environmental science from text aided by a diagnostic and prescriptive instructional strategy. *Journal of Research in Science Teaching, 23*, 557–569.

*Fehlen, J. E. (1976). Mastery learning techniques in a traditional classroom setting. *School Science and Mathematics, 76*, 241–245.

^Feldhusen, J., & Birt, A. (1962). A study of nine methods of presentation of programmed learning material. *The Journal of Educational Research, 5*, 461–466.

*Fernald, P. S., & DuNann, D. H. (1975). Effects of individualized instruction upon low- and high-achieving students' study behavior in students' evaluation of mastery. *Journal of Experimental Education, 43*, 27–34.

$&+Fiel, R. L., & Okey, J. R. (1974). The effects of formative evaluation and remediation on mastery of intellectual skill. *Journal of Educational Research, 68*, 253–255.

%Fisher, C. W., Berliner, D. C., Filby, N. N., Marliave, R., Cahen, L. S., & Dishaw, M. M. (1980). Teaching behaviors, academic learning time, and student achievement: An overview. In C. Denham & A. Lieberman (Eds.), *Time to learn* (pp. 7–32). Washington, DC: U.S. Government Printing Office.

%Fitzpatrick, K. A. (1981). *An investigation of secondary classroom material strategies for increasing student academic engaged time.* Doctoral dissertation, University of Illinois at Urbana–Champaign.

%Fitzpatrick, K. A. (1982). *The effect of a secondary classroom management training program on teacher and student behavior.* Paper presented at the annual meeting of the American Educational Research Association, New York.

$&Fitzpatrick, K. A. (1985, April). *Group-based mastery learning: A Robin Hood approach to instruction?* Paper presented at the annual meeting of the American Educational Research Association, Chicago.

!Fortner, V. L. (1986). Generalization of creative productive-thinking training to LD students' written expression. *Learning Disability Quarterly, 9*(4), 274–284.

=Fox, B., & Routh, D. (1976). Phonemic analysis and synthesis as word-attack skills. *Journal of Educational Psychology, 68*, 70–74.

=Fox, B., & Routh, D. (1984). Phonemic analysis and synthesis as word-attack skills. Revisited. *Journal of Educational Psychology, 76*, 1059–1064.

<Fuchs, L. S., & Fuchs, D. (1986). Effects of systematic formative evaluation on student achievement: A meta-analysis. *Exceptional Children, 53*, 199–208.

Gersten, R., & Baker, S. (2001). Teaching expressive writing to students with learning disabilities: A meta-analysis. *The Elementary School Journal, 101*(3), 251–273.

^Gherfal, I. R. (1982). The application of principles of reinforcement to the teaching of English as a second language in a developing country: An experiment with Libyan male preparatory school students from culturally diverse rural and urban communities. *Dissertation Abstracts International, 43*, 147A. (University Microfilms No. 82-13, 750)

<Gickling, E. E., & Armstrong, D. L. (1978). Levels of instructional difficulty as related to on-task behavior, task completion, and comprehension. *Journal of Learning Disabilities, 11*, 32–39.

+Glassnap, D. R., Poggio, J. P., & Ory, J. C. (1975, March–April). *Cognitive and affective consequences of mastery and non-mastery instructional strategies.* Paper presented at the annual meeting of the American Educational Research Association, Washington, DC.

*Goldwater, B. C., & Acker, L. E. (1975). Instructor-paced, mass-testing for mastery performance in an introductory psychology course. *Teaching of Psychology, 2*, 152–155.

%Good, T., Grouws, D., & Ebmier, M. (1983). *Active mathematics teaching.* New York: Longman.

%Good, T. L., & Grouws, D. A. (1977). Teaching effects: A process-product study in fourth-grade mathematics classrooms. *Journal of Teacher Education, 28*(3), 49–54.

%Good, T. L., & Grouws, D. A. (1979). The Missouri mathematics effectiveness project. *Journal of Educational Psychology, 71*, 355–362.

*Gregory, I., Smeltzer, D. J., Knopp, W., & Gardner, M. (1976). *Teaching of psychiatry by PSI: Impact on National Board Examination scores.* Unpublished manuscript, Ohio State University, Columbus.

=Gross, J., & Garnett, J. (1994). Preventing reading difficulties: Rhyme and alliteration in the real world. *Educational Psychology in Practice, 9,* 235–240.

*$&Guskey, T. R. (1982). The effects of staff development on teachers' perceptions about effective teaching. *Journal of Educational Research, 76,* 378–381.

*$&Guskey, T. R. (1984). The influence of changes in instructional effectiveness upon the affective characteristics of teachers. *American Educational Research Journal, 21,* 245–259.

$Guskey, T. R. (1985). The effects of staff development on teachers' perceptions about effective teaching. *Journal of Educational Research, 79,* 378–381.

*$Guskey, T. R., Benninga, J. S., & Clark, C. B. (1984). Mastery learning and students' attributions at the college level. *Research and Higher Education, 20,* 491–498.

Guskey, T. R., & Gates, S. L. (1986). Synthesis of research on the effects of mastery learning in elementary and secondary classrooms. *Educational Leadership, 43*(8), 73–80.

*$Guskey, T. R., & Monsaas, J. A. (1979). Mastery learning: A model for academic success in urban junior colleges. *Research and Higher Education, 11,* 263–274.

Guskey, T. R., & Pigott, T. D. (1988). Research on group-based mastery learning programs: A meta-analysis. *Journal of Educational Research, 81*(4), 197–216.

=Haddock, M. (1976). Effects of an auditory and an auditory-visual method of blending instruction on the ability of prereaders to decode synthetic words. *Journal of Educational Psychology, 68,* 825–831.

*Hardin, L. D. (1977). A study of the influence of a physics personalized system of instruction versus lecture on cognitive reason, achievement, attitudes and critical thinking. *Dissertation Abstracts International, 38,* 4711A–4712A. (University Microfilms No. 77-30826)

<Haring, N. G., Lovitt, T. C., Eaton, M. D., & Hansen, C. L. (1978). *The fourth R: Research in the classroom.* Columbus, OH: Merrill.

=Hatcher, P., Hulme, C., & Ellis, A. (1994). Ameliorating early reading failure by integrating the teaching of reading and phonological skills: The phonological linkage hypothesis. *Child Development, 66,* 41–57.

^Heald, H. (1970). The effects of immediate knowledge of results and correction of errors and test anxiety upon test performance. *Dissertation Abstracts International, 31,* 1621A. (University Microfilms No. 70-17, 724)

*Hecht, L. W. (1980, April). *Stalking mastery learning in its natural habitat.* Paper presented at the annual meeting of the American Educational Research Association, Boston.

*Heffley, P. D. (1974). The implementation of the personalized system of instruction in the freshman chemistry course at Censius College. In R. S. Ruskin & S. F. Bono (Eds.), *Personalized instruction in higher education* (pp. 140–145). Washington, DC: Center for Personalized Instruction.

*Herring, B.G. (1975, December). *Cataloguing and classification.* Austin: University of Texas.

*Herring, B. G. (1977). *The written PSI study guide in a non-PSI course.* Austin: University of Texas.

*Herrmann, T. (1984, August). *TELIDON as an enhancer of student interest and perfor-*

mance. Paper presented at the annual meeting of the American Psychological Association, Toronto. (ERIC Document Reproduction Service No. ED 251 004)

*Hindman, C. D. (1974). Evaluation of three programming techniques in introductory psychology courses. In R. S. Ruskin & S. F. Bono (Eds.), *Personalized instruction in higher education* (pp. 38–42). Washington, DC: Center for Personalized Instruction.

^Hirsch, R. S. (1952). *The effects of knowledge of test results on learning meaningful material.* University Park: Pennsylvania State University. (ERIC Document Reproduction Service No. ED 002 435)

^Hoffman, B. S. (1974). An examination of knowledge of results and step size in programmed instruction at high and low cognitive levels of objectives. *Dissertation Abstracts International, 35,* 6006A. (University Microfilms No. 75-01, 707)

=Hohn, W., & Ehri, L. (1983). Do alphabet letters help prereaders acquire phonemic segmentation skill? *Journal of Educational Psychology, 75,* 752–762.

*Honeycutt, J. K. (1974, April). *The effect of computer managed instruction on content learning of undergraduate students.* Paper presented at the annual meeting of the American Educational Research Association, Chicago. (ERIC Document Reproduction Service No. ED 089 682)

<Horner, R. H., Day, H. M., Sprague, J. R., O'Brien, M., & Heathfield, L. T. (1991). Interspersed requests: A nonaversive procedure for reducing aggression and self-injury during instruction. *Journal of Applied Behavior Analysis, 24,* 265–278.

^Hough, J., & Revsin, B. (1963). Programmed instruction at the college level: A study of several factors influencing learning. *Phi Delta Kappan, 44,* 286–291.

=Hurford, D., Johnston, M., Nepote, P., et al. (1994). Early identification and remediation of phonological-processing deficits in first-grade children at risk for reading disabilities. *Journal of Learning Disabilities, 27,* 647–659.

^Hyman, C., & Tobias, S. (1981, October). *Feedback and prior achievement.* Paper presented at the annual meeting of the Northeastern Educational Research Association, Ellenville, NY. (ERIC Document Reproduction Service No. ED 206 739)

*Hymel, G. M. (1974). *An investigation of John B. Carrol's model of school learning as a theoretical basis for the organizational structuring of schools* (Final Report, NIE Project No. 3-1359). University of New Orleans, New Orleans, LA.

*Hymel, G. M., & Matthews, G. (1980a). Effects of a mastery approach on social studies achievement and unit evaluation. *Southern Journal of Educational Research, 14,* 191–204.

^Hymel, G. M., & Mathews, G. (1980b, April). *A mastery approach to teaching U.S. history: The impact on cognitive achievement and unit evaluation.* Paper presented at the annual meeting of the American Educational Research Association, Boston. (ERIC Document Reproduction Service No. ED 184 929)

=Iversen, S., & Tunmer, W. (1993). Phonological processing skills and the Reading Recovery Program. *Journal of Educational Psychology, 85,* 112–126.

!Jaben, T. H. (1983). The effects of creativity training on learning disabled students' creative written expression. *Journal of Learning Disabilities, 16*(5), 264–265.

!Jaben, T. H. (1987). Effects of training on learning disabled students' creative written expression. *Psychological Reports, 60,* 23–26.

*Jackman, L. E. (1982). Evaluation of a modified Keller method in a biochemistry laboratory course. *Journal of Chemical Education, 59,* 225–227.

*Jacko, E. J. (1974). Lecture instruction versus a personalized system of instruction: Effects on individuals with differing achievement anxiety and academic achievement. *Dissertation Abstracts International, 35*, 3521. (University Microfilms No. AAD 74-27211)

^Jacobs, P., & Kulkarni, S. (1966). A test of some assumptions underlying programmed instruction. *Psychological Reports, 18*, 103–110.

<Johnson, M. D., & Fawcett, S. B. (1994). Courteous service: Its assessment and modification in a human service organization. *Journal of Applied Behavior Analysis, 27*, 145–152.

+Johnston, J. M., & Pennypacker, H. S. (1971). A behavioral approach to college teaching. *American Psychologist, 26*, 219–244.

*#@$&Jones, B. F., Monsaas, J. A., & Katims, M. (1979, April). *Improving reading comprehension: Embedding diverse learning strategies within a mastery learning instructional framework.* Paper presented at the annual meeting of the American Educational Research Association, San Francisco. (ERIC Document Reproduction Service No. ED 170 698)

$+Jones, E. L., Gordon, H. A., & Stectman, G. L. (1975). *Mastery learning: A strategy for academic success in a community college.* Los Angeles: ERIC Clearinghouse for Junior Colleges. (ERIC Document Reproduction Service No. 115 315)

+Jones, F. G. (1974). *The effects of mastery and aptitude on learning, retention, and time.* Unpublished doctoral dissertation, University of Georgia.

+Karlin, B. M. (1972). *The Keller method of instruction compared to the traditional method of instruction in a Lafayette College history course.* Unpublished paper, Lafayette College, Lafayette, PA.

^Karraker, R. (1967). Knowledge of results and incorrect recall of plausible multiple-choice alternatives. *Journal of Educational Psychology, 58*, 11–14.

*#@Katims, M., Smith, J. K., Steele, C., & Wick, J. W. (1977, April). *The Chicago mastery learning reading program: An interim evaluation.* Paper presented at the annual meeting of the American Educational Research Association, New York. (ERIC Document Reproduction Service No. ED 137 737)

=Kennedy, K., & Backman, J. (1993). Effectiveness of the Lindamood Auditory Discrimination in Depth program with students with learning disabilities. *Learning Disabilities Research & Practice, 8*, 253–259.

*#@Kersh, M. E. (1970). *A strategy of mastery learning in fifth grade arithmetic.* Unpublished doctoral dissertation, University of Chicago.

+Kim, Y., Cho, G., Park, J., & Park, M. (1974). *An application of a new instructional model* (Research Report No. 8). Seoul, Korea: Korean Educational Development Institute.

*Knight, J. M., Williams J. D., & Jardon, M. L. (1975). The effects of contingency avoidance on programmed student achievement. *Research in Higher Education, 3*, 11–17.

=Korkman, M., & Peltomaa, A. (1993). Preventative treatment of dyslexia by a preschool training program for children with language impairments. *Journal of Clinical Child Psychology, 22*, 277–287.

=Kozminsky, L., & Kozminsky, E. (1995). The effects of early phonological awareness training on reading success. *Learning and Instruction, 5*, 187–201.

^Krumboltz, J., & Weisman, R. (1962). The effect of intermittent confirmation in programmed instruction. *Journal of Educational Psychology, 53*, 250–253.

^Kulhavy, R., Yekovich, F., & Dyer, J. (1976). Feedback and response confidence. *Journal of Educational Psychology, 68*, 522–528.

*Kulik, C., & Kulik, J. (1976). PSI and the mastery model. In B. A. Green, Jr. (Ed.), *Person-*

alized instruction in higher education (pp. 155–159). Washington, DC: Center for Personalized Instruction.

Kulik, C., Kulik, J., & Bangert-Drowns, R. (1990a). Effectiveness of mastery learning programs: A meta-analysis. *Review of Educational Research, 60*(2), 265–269.

Kulik, J., Kulik, C., & Bangert-Drowns, R. (1990b). Is there better evidence on mastery learning? A response to Slavin. *Review of Educational Research, 60*(2), 303–307.

+Kulik, J. A., Kulik, C., & Carmichael, K. (1974). The Keller Plan in science teaching. *Science, 183*, 379–383.

+Lee, Y. D., Kim, C. S., Kim, H., Park B. Y., Yoo, H. K., Chang, S. M., & Kim, S. C. (1971). *Interaction improvement studies of the Mastery Learning Project* (Final Report on the Mastery Learning Project, April–November 1971). Seoul, Korea: Educational Research Center, Seoul National University.

*Leppman, P. K., & Herrmann, T. F. (1981, August). *PSI—What are the critical elements?* Paper presented at the annual meeting of the American Psychological Association, Los Angeles. (ERIC Document Reproduction Service No. ED 214 502)

$+Levin, T. (1975). *The effect of content prerequisites and process-oriented experiences on application ability in a learning of probability.* Unpublished doctoral dissertation, University of Chicago.

*Lewis, E. W. (1984). The effects of a mastery learning strategy and an interactive computerized quiz strategy on student achievement and attitude in college trigonometry. *Dissertation Abstracts International, 45*, 2430A. (University Microfilms No. DA84-24 589)

*Leyton, F. S. (1983). *The extent to which group instruction supplemented by mastery of initial cognitive prerequisites approximates the learning effectiveness of one-to-one tutorial methods.* Unpublished doctoral dissertation, University of Chicago.

^Lhyle, K., & Kulhavy, R. (1987). Feedback processing and error correction. *Journal of Educational Psychology, 79*, 320–322.

=Lie, A. (1991). Effects of a training program for stimulating skills in word analysis in first-grade children. *Reading Research Quarterly, 26*, 234–250.

*Locksley, N. (1977). The Personalized System of Instruction (PSI) in a university mathematics class. *Dissertation Abstracts International, 37*, 4194. (University Microfilms No. ADD 76-28194)

#@Long, J. C., Okey, J. R., & Yeany, R. H. (1978). The effects of diagnosis with teacher on student directed remediation on science achievement and attitudes. *Journal of Research in Science Teaching, 15*, 505–511.

=Lovett, M., Barron, R., Forbes, J., et al. (1994). Computer speech-based training of literacy skills in neurologically impaired children: A controlled evaluation. *Brain and Language, 47*, 117–154.

<Lovitt, T. C., & Esveldt, K. A. (1970). The relative effects on math performance of single- versus multiple-ratio schedules: A case study. *Journal of Applied Behavior Analysis, 3*, 261–270.

*Lu, M. C. (1976). The retention of material learned by PSI in a mathematics course. In B. A. Green, Jr. (Ed.), *Personalized instruction in higher education* (pp. 151–154). Washington, DC: Center for Personalized Instruction.

*Lu, P. H. (1976). Teaching human growth and development by The Personalized System for Instruction. *Teaching of Psychology, 3*, 127–128.

*Lubkin, J. L. (1974). Engineering statistics: A Keller Plan course with novel problems and novel features. In R. S. Ruskin & S. F. Bono (Eds.), *Personalized instruction in higher education* (pp. 153–161). Washington, DC: Center for Personalized Instruction.

^Lublin, S. (1965). Reinforcement schedules, scholastic aptitude, autonomy need, and achievement in a programmed course. *Journal of Educational Psychology, 56*, 295–302.

*#@Lueckmeyer, C. L., & Chiappetta, W. L. (1981). An investigation into the effects of a modified mastery learning strategy on achievement in a high school human physiology unit. *Journal of Research in Science Teaching, 18*, 269–273.

=Lundberg, I., Frost, J., & Petersen, O. (1988). Effects of an extensive program for stimulating phonological awareness in preschool children. *Reading Research Quarterly, 23*, 263–284.

!MacArthur, C. A., Graham, S., Schwartz, S. S., & Schafer, W. D. (1995). Evaluation of a writing instruction model that integrated a process approach, strategy instruction, and word processing. *Learning Disability Quarterly, 18*, 278–291.

!MacArthur, C. A., Schwartz, S. S., & Graham, S. (1991). Effects of reciprocal peer revision strategy in special education classrooms. *Learning Disabilities Research, 6*(4), 201–210.

*Malec, M. A. (1975). PSI: A brief report and reply to Francis. *Teaching Sociology, 2*, 212–217.

<Martens, B. K., Ardoin, S. P., Hilt, A., Lannie, A. L., Panahon, C. J., & Wolfe, L. (2002). Sensitivity of children's behavior to probabilistic reward: Effects of a decreasing-ratio lottery system on math performance. *Journal of Applied Behavior Analysis, 35*, 403–406.

<Martens, B. K., & Daly, E. J. (1999). Discovering the alphabetic principle: A lost opportunity for educational reform. *Journal of Behavioral Education, 9*, 33–41.

<Martens, B. K., Hilt, A. M., Needham, L. R., Sutterer, J. R., Panahon, C. J., & Lannie, A. L. (2003). Carryover effects of free reinforcement on children's work completion. *Behavior Modification, 27*, 560–577.

Martens, B. K., & Witt, J. C. (2004). Competence, persistence, and success: The positive psychology of behavioral skill instruction. *Psychology in the Schools, 41*(1), 19–30.

*Martin, R. R., & Srikameswarn, K. (1974). Correlation between frequent testing and student performance. *Journal of Chemical Education, 51*, 485–486.

$Matthews, G. S. (1982). *Effects of a mastery learning strategy on the cognitive knowledge and unit evaluation of students in high school social studies.* Unpublished doctoral dissertation, University of Southern Mississippi.

<McCurdy, M., Skinner, C. H., Grantham, K., Watson, T. S., & Hindman, P. M. (2001). Increasing on-task behavior in an elementary student during mathematics seatwork by interspersing additional brief problems. *School Psychology Review, 30*, 23–32.

<McDowell, C., & Keenan, M. (2001). Developing fluency and endurance in a child diagnosed with attention deficit hyperactivity disorder. *Journal of Applied Behavior Analysis, 34*, 345–348.

*McFarland, B. (1976). An individualized course in elementary composition for the marginal student. In B. A. Green, Jr. (Ed.), *Personalized instruction in higher education* (pp. 45–52). Washington, DC: Center for Personalized Instruction.

<McGinnis, J. C., Friman, P. C., & Carlyon, W. D. (1999). The effect of token rewards on "intrinsic" motivation for doing math. *Journal of Applied Behavior Analysis, 32*, 375–379.

=McGuinness, D., McGuinness, C., & Donohue, J. (1995). Phonological training and the alphabet principle: Evidence for reciprocal causality. *Reading Research Quarterly, 30*, 830–852.

*+McMichael, J., & Corey, J. R. (1969). Contingency management in an introductory psychology course produces better learning. *Journal of Applied Behavior Analysis, 2*, 79–83.

*#@Mevarech, Z. R. (1980). *The role of teaching-learning strategies and feedback-corrective procedures in developing higher cognitive achievement.* Unpublished doctoral dissertation, University of Chicago.

$&Mevarech, Z. R. (1981, April). *Attaining mastery on higher cognitive achievement.* Paper presented at the annual meeting of the American Educational Research Association, Los Angeles.

Mevarech, Z. R. (1985). The effects of cooperative mastery learning strategies on mathematical achievement. *Journal of Educational Research, 78*, 372–377.

*#@Mevarech, Z. R. (1986). The role of feedback corrective procedures in developing mathematics achievement and self-concept in desegregated classrooms. *Studies in Educational Evaluation, 12*, 197–203.

*Mevarech, Z. R., & Werner, S. (1985). Are mastery learning strategies beneficial for developing problem solving skills? *Higher Education, 14*, 425–432.

*Meyers, R. R. (1976). The effects of mastery and aptitude on achievement and attitude in an introductory college geography course. *Dissertation Abstracts International, 36*, 5874. (University Microfilms No. 76-6436)

<Miller, D. L., & Kelley, M. L. (1994). The use of goal setting and contingency contracting for improving children's homework performance. *Journal of Applied Behavior Analysis, 27*, 73–84.

^Moore, J., & Smith, W. (1961). Knowledge of results in self-teaching spelling. *Psychological Reports, 9*, 717–726.

^Morgan, C., & Morgan, L. (1935). Effects and immediate awareness of success and failure upon objective examination scores. *Journal of Experimental Education, 4*, 63–66.

*+Morris, C., & Kimbrill, G. (1972). Performance and attitudinal effects of the Keller method in an introductory psychology course. *Psychological Record, 22*, 523–530.

=Murray, B. (1998). Gaining alphabetic insight: Is phoneme manipulation skill or identity knowledge causal? *Journal of Educational Psychology, 90*, 461–475.

*Nation, J. R., Knight, J. M, Lamberth, J., & Dyck, D. (1974). Programmed student achievement: A test of the avoidance hypothesis. *Journal of Experimental Education, 42*, 57–61.

*Nation, J. R., Massad, P., & Wilkerson, P. (1977). Student performance in introductory psychology following termination of the programmed achievement contingency at mid-semester. *Teaching of Psychology, 4*, 116–119.

*Nation, J. R., & Roop, S. S. (1975). A comparison of two mastery approaches to teaching introductory psychology. *Teaching of Psychology, 2*, 108–111.

*+Nazzaro, J. R., Todorov, J. C., & Nazzaro, J. N. (1972). Student ability and individualized instruction. *Journal of College Science Teaching, 2*, 29–30.

<Neef, N. A., & Lutz, M. N. (2001). Assessment of variables affecting choice and application to classroom interventions. *School Psychology Quarterly, 16*, 239–252.

<Neef, N. A., Shade, D., & Miller, M. S. (1994). Assessing influential dimensions of reinforcers on choice in students with serious emotional disturbance. *Journal of Applied Behavior Analysis, 27*, 575–583.

^Newman, M. I., Williams, R. G., & Hiller, J. H. (1974). Delay of information feedback in an applied setting: Effects on initially learned and unlearned items. *Journal of Experimental Education, 42*, 55–59.

*Nord, S. B. (1975). Comparative achievement and attitude in individualized and class instructional settings. *Dissertation Abstracts International, 35*, 529A. (University Microfilms No. 75-02314)

$Nordin, A. B. (1979). *The effects of different qualities of instruction on selected cognitive, affective, and time variables.* Unpublished doctoral dissertation, University of Chicago.

<Northup, J., George, T., Jones, K., Broussard, C., & Vollmer, T. R. (1996). A comparison of reinforcer assessment methods: The utility of verbal and pictorial choice procedures. *Journal of Applied Behavior Analysis, 29*, 201–212.

=O'Connor, R., & Jenkins, J. (1995). Improving the generalization of sound/symbol knowledge: Teaching spelling to kindergarten children with disabilities. *The Journal of Special Education, 29*, 255–275.

=O'Connor, R., Jenkins, J., & Slocum, T. (1995). Transfer among phonological tasks in kindergarten: Essential instructional content. *Journal of Educational Psychology, 87*, 202–217.

=O'Connor, R., Notari-Syverson, A., & Vadasy, P. (1996). Ladders to literacy: The effects of teacher-led phonological activities for kindergarten children with and without disabilities. *Exceptional Children, 63*, 117–130.

=O'Connor, R., Notari-Syverson, A., & Vadasy, P. (1998). First-grade effects of teacher-led phonological activities for kindergarten children with mild disabilities: A follow-up study. *Learning Disabilities Research & Practice, 13*, 43–52. (This is a follow-up to O'Connor et al., 1996.)

*$+Okey, J. R. (1974). Altering teacher and pupil behavior with mastery teaching. *Social Science and Mathematics, 74*, 530–535.

+Okey, J. R. (1975). *Development of mastery teaching materials* (Final Evaluation Report, USOE G-74-2990). Bloomington: Indiana University.

$&Okey, J. R. (1977). The consequences of training teachers to use a mastery learning strategy. *Journal of Teacher Education, 28*(5), 57–62.

=Olofsson, A., & Lundberg, I. (1983). Can phonemic awareness be trained in kindergarten? *Scandinavian Journal of Psychology, 24*, 35–44.

=Olofsson, A., & Lundberg, I. (1985). Evaluation of long term effects of phonemic awareness training in kindergarten: Illustrations of some methodological problems in evaluation research. *Scandinavian Journal of Psychology, 26*, 21–34. (This is a follow-up to Olofsson & Lundberg, 1983).

^Olson, G. (1971). A multivariate examination of the effects of behavioral objectives, knowledge of results and the assignment of grades on the facilitation of classroom learning. *Dissertation Abstracts International, 32*, 6214A. (University Microfilms No. 72-13, 552)

*$Omelich, C. L., & Covington, M. V. (1981). *Do the learning benefits of behavioral instruction outweigh the psychological costs?* Paper presented at the annual meeting of the Western Psychological Association, Los Angeles.

*Pascarella, E. T. (1977, April). *Aptitude-treatment interaction in a college calculus course taught in personalized system of instruction and conventional formats.* Paper presented at the annual meeting of the American Educational Research Association, New York. (ERIC Document Reproduction Service No. ED 137 137)

<Patterson, G. R., Reid, J. B., & Dishion, T. J. (1992). *Antisocial boys*. Eugene, OR: Castalia Publishing.

^Peeck, A., Bosch, A., & Kreupling, W. (1985). Effects of informative feedback in relation to retention of initial responses. *Contemporary Educational Psychology, 10*, 303–313.

^Peeck, J., & Tillema, H. (1979). Learning from feedback: Comparison of two feedback procedures in a classroom setting. *Perceptual and Motor Skills, 48*, 351–354.

*Peluso, A., & Baranchik, A. J. (1977). Self-paced mathematics instruction: A statistical comparison with traditional teaching. *The American Mathematical Monthly, 84*, 124–129.

*+Phillippas, M. A., & Sommerfeldt, R. W. (1972). Keller vs. lecture method in general physics instruction. *American Journal of Physics, 40*, 1800.

+Poggio, J. P. (1976, April). *Long-term cognitive retention resulting from the mastery learning paradigm*. Paper presented at the annual meeting of the American Educational Research Association, San Francisco.

*Pollack, N. F., & Roeder, P. W. (1975). Individualized instruction in an introductory government course. *Teaching Political Science, 8*, 18–36.

=Reitsma, P., & Wesseling, R. (1998). Effects of computer-assisted training of blending skills in kindergartners. *Scientific Studies of Reading, 2*, 301–320.

!Reynolds, C. J. (1986). *The effects of instruction in cognitive revision strategies on the writing skills of secondary learning disabled students*. Doctoral dissertation, Ohio State University, 1985. *Dissertation Abstracts International, 46*(9-A), 2662.

<Rhymer, K. N., Henington, C., Skinner, C. H., & Looby, E. J. (1999). The effects of explicit timing on mathematics performance in Caucasian and African American second-grade students. *School Psychology Quarterly, 14*, 397–407.

^Ripple, R. (1963). Comparison of the effectiveness of a programmed text with three other methods of presentation. *Psychological Reports, 12*, 227–237.

^Roper, W. (1977). Feedback in computer assisted instruction. *Programmed Learning and Educational Technology, 14*, 43–49.

*+Rosati, P. A. (1975). A comparison of the personalized system of instruction with the lecture method in teaching elementary dynamics. In J. M. Johnston (Ed.), *Behavior research and technology in higher education*. Springfield, IL: Charles C. Thomas.

Rosenshine, B., & Stevens, R. (1986). Teaching functions. In M. C. Wittrock (Ed.), *Handbook of research on teaching* (3rd ed., pp. 376–391). New York: Macmillan.

+Roth, C. H., Jr. (1973). Continuing effectiveness on personalized self-paced instruction in digital systems engineering. *Engineering Education, 63*(6), 447–450.

*Roth, C. H., Jr. (1975, December). *Electrical engineering laboratory I* (One of a series of reports on the projects titled Expansion of Keller Plan Instruction in Engineering and Selected Other Disciplines). Austin: University of Texas.

^Rothkopf, E. (1966). Learning from written instructive materials: An exploration of the control of inspection behavior by test-like events. *American Educational Research Journal, 3*, 241–249.

=Sanchez, E., & Rueda, M. (1991). Segmental awareness and dyslexia: Is it possible to learn to segment well and yet continue to read and write poorly? *Reading and Writing: An Interdisciplinary Journal, 3*, 11–18.

^Sassenrath, J., & Gaverick, C. (1965). Effects of differential feedback from examinations on retention and transfer. *Journal of Educational Psychology, 56*, 259–263.

*Saunders-Harris, R. L., & Yeany, R. H. (1981). Diagnosis, remediation, and locus of control: Effects of the immediate and retained achievement and attitude. *Journal of Experimental Education, 49*, 220–224.

!Sawyer, R. J., Graham, S., & Harris, K. R. (1992). Direct teaching, strategy instruction, and strategy instruction with explicit self-regulation: Effects on the composition skills and self-efficacy of students with learning disabilities. *Journal of Educational Psychology, 84*(3), 340–352.

*Schielack, V. P., Jr. (1983). A personalized system of instruction versus a conventional method in a mathematics course for elementary education majors. *Dissertation Abstracts International, 43*, 2267. (University Microfilms No. 82-27717)

*Schimpfhauser, F., Horrocks, L., Richardson, K., Alben, J., Schumm, D., & Sprecher, H. (1974). The personalized system of instruction as an adaptable alternative within the traditional structure of medical basic sciences. In R. S. Ruskin & S. F. Bono (Eds.), *Personalized instruction in higher education* (pp. 61–69). Washington, DC: Center for Personalized Instruction.

=Schneider, W., Kuspert, P., Roth, E., et al. (1997). Short-and-long-term effects of training phonological awareness in kindergarten: Evidence from two German studies. *Journal of Experimental Child Psychology, 66*, 311–340.

*Schwartz, P. L. (1981). Retention of knowledge in clinical biochemistry and the effect of the Keller Plan. *Journal of Medical Education, 56*, 778–781.

*Sharples, D. K., Smith, D. J., & Strasler, G. M. (1976). *Individually-paced learning in civil engineering technology: An approach to mastery.* Columbia: South Carolina State Board for Technical and Comprehensive Education. (ERIC Document Reproduction Service No. ED 131 870)

*$Sheldon, M. S., & Miller, E. D. (1973). *Behavioral objectives and mastery learning applied to two areas of junior college instruction.* Los Angeles: University of California at Los Angeles. (ERIC Document Reproduction Service No. ED 082 730)

*Sheppard, W. C., & MacDermott, H. G. (1970). Design and evaluation of a programmed course in introductory psychology. *Journal of Applied Behavior Analysis, 3*, 5–11.

<Shinn, M. R. (1989). *Curriculum-based measurement: Assessing special children.* New York: Guilford.

*Siegfried, J. J., & Strand, S. H. (1976). An evaluation of the Vanderbilt JCEE experimental PSI course in elementary economics. *The Journal of Economic Education, 8*, 9–26.

*+Silberman, R., & Parker, B. (1974). Student attitudes and the Keller Plan. *Journal of Chemical Education, 51*, 393.

<Simonton, D. K. (2000). Creativity: Cognitive, personal, developmental, and social aspects. *American Psychologist, 55*, 151–158.

<Skinner, C. H. (2002). An empirical analysis of interspersal research: Evidence, implications, and applications of the discrete task completion hypothesis. *Journal of School Psychology, 40*, 347–368.

<Skinner, C. H., Fletcher, P. A., & Henington, C. (1996). Increasing learning trial rates by increasing student response rates: A summary of research. *School Psychology Quarterly, 11*, 313–325.

Slavin, R. E. (1990). Mastery learning re-considered. *Review of Educational Research, 60*(2), 300–302.

*#@$&Slavin, R. E., & Karweit, N. L. (1984). Mastery learning and student teams: A factor role experiment in urban general mathematics classes. *American Educational Research Journal, 21*, 725–736.

*Smiernow, G. A., & Lawley, A. (1980). Decentralized sequence instruction (DSI) at Drexel. *Engineering Education, 70*, 423–426.

*Smith, J. E. (1976). A comparison of the traditional method and a personalized system of instruction in college mathematics. *Dissertation Abstracts International, 37*, 904. (University Microfilms No. AAD 76-18370)

=Snider, V. E. (1989). Reading comprehension performance of adolescents with learning disabilities. *Learning Disability Quarterly, 12*(2), 87–96.

=Solity, J. (1996). Phonological awareness: Learning disabilities revisited? *Educational & Child Psychology, 13*, 103–113.

*Spector, L. C. (1976). The effectiveness of personalized instruction system of instruction in economics. *Journal of Personalized Instruction, I*, 118–122.

*Spevack, H. M. (1976). A comparison of the personalized system of instruction with the lecture recitation system for nonscience oriented chemistry students at an open enrollment community college. *Dissertation Abstracts International, 36*, 4385A–4386A. (University Microfilms No. 76-01757)

<Stahl, S. A., & Kuhn, M. R. (1995). Does whole language or instruction matched to learning styles help children learn to read? *School Psychology Review, 24*, 393–404.

*Stallings, J., Corey, R., Fairweather, J., & Needles, M. (1977). *Early Childhood Education classroom evaluation.* Menlo Park, CA: SRI International.

%Stallings, J., Needles, M., & Staybrook, N. (1979). *The teaching of basic reading skills in secondary schools, Phase II and Phase III.* Menlo Park, CA: SRI International.

%Stallings, J. A., & Kaskowitz, D. (1974). *Follow-Through Classroom Observation.* Menlo Park, CA: SRI International.

*Steele, W. F. (1974). *Mathematics 101 at Heileberg College—PSI vs. tradition.* Paper presented at the National Conference on Personalized Instruction in Higher Education, Washington, DC.

*Stout, L. J. (1978). A comparison of four different pacing strategies of personalized system of instruction and a traditional lecture format. *Dissertation Abstracts International, 38*, 6205. (University Microfilms No. AAD 78-08600)

*$Strasler, G. M. (1979, April). *The process of transfer and learning for mastery setting.* Paper presented at the annual meeting of the American Educational Research Association, San Francisco. (ERIC Document Reproduction Service No. ED 174 642)

*$&Swanson, D. H., & Denton, J. J. (1976). Learning for Mastery versus Personalized System of Instruction: A comparison of remediation strategies for secondary school chemistry students. *Journal of Research in Science Teaching, 14*, 515–524.

Swanson, H. L. (2000). What instruction works for students with learning disabilities? Summarizing the results from a meta-analysis of intervention studies. In R. M. Gersten & E. P. Schiller (Eds.), *Contemporary special education research: Synthesis of the knowledge base on critical instructional issues* (pp. 1–30). Mahwah, NJ: Lawrence Erlbaum Associates.

^Tait, K., Hartley, J., & Anderson, R. (1973). Feedback procedures in computer-assisted arithmetic instruction. *British Journal of Educational Psychology, 43*, 161–171.

=Tangel, D., & Blachman, B. (1992). Effect of phoneme awareness instruction on kindergarten children's invented spelling. *Journal of Reading Behavior, 24*, 233–261.

*Taylor, V. (1977, April). *Individualized calculus for the "life-long" learner: A two semester comparison of attitudes and effectiveness.* Paper presented at the Fourth National Conference of the Center for Personalized Instruction, San Francisco.

$Tenenbaum, G. (1982). *A method of group instruction which is as effective as one-to-one tutorial instruction.* Unpublished doctoral dissertation, University of Chicago.

*&Thompson, S. B. (1980). Do individualized mastery and traditional instructional systems yield different course effects in college calculus? *American Educational Research Journal, 17*, 361–375.

*Tietenberg, T. H. (1975). Teaching intermediate microeconomics using the personalized system of instruction. In J. M. Johnston (Ed.), *Behavior research and technology in higher education* (pp. 75–89). Springfield, IL: Charles C. Thomas.

%Tobias, S. (1982). When do instructional methods make a difference? *Educational Researcher, 11*, 4–10.

^Tobias, S. (1984, April). *Macroprocesses, individual differences, and instructional methods.* Paper presented at the annual meeting of the American Educational Research Association, New Orleans. (ERIC Document Reproduction Service No. ED 259 019)

*Toepher, C., Shaw, D., & Moniot, D. (1972). *The effect of item exposure in a contingency management system.* Paper presented at the annual meeting of the American Psychological Association, Honolulu, HI.

=Torgesen, J., Morgan, S., & Davis, C. (1992). Effects of two types of phonological awareness training on word learning in kindergarten children. *Journal of Educational Psychology, 84*, 364–370.

=Treiman, R., & Baron, J. (1983). Phonemic-analysis training helps children benefit from spelling sound rules. *Memory and Cognition, 11*, 382–389.

^Tsao, P. (1977). The effects of error rate, knowledge of correct results and test anxiety in linear program. *Dissertation Abstracts International, 39*, 1426 A. (University Microfilms No. 78–15, 385)

=Uhry, J., & Shepherd, M. (1993). Segmentation/spelling instruction as part of a first-grade reading program: Effects on several measures of reading. *Reading Research Quarterly, 28*, 218–233.

=Vadasy, P., Jenkins, J. Antil, L., et al. (1997a). Community-based early reading intervention for at-risk first graders. *Learning Disabilities Research & Practice, 12*, 29–39.

=Vadasy, P., Jenkins, J., Antil, L., et al. (1997b). The effectiveness of one-to-one tutoring by community tutors for at-risk beginning readers. *Learning Disability Quarterly, 20*, 126–139.

*Van Verth, J. E., & Dinan, F. J. (1974). A Keller Plan course in organic chemistry. In R. S. Ruskin & S. F. Bono (Eds.), *Personalized instruction in higher education* (pp. 162–168). Washington, DC: Center for Personalized Instruction.

*Vandenbroucke, A. C., Jr. (1974, April). *Evaluation of the use of a personalized system of instruction in general chemistry.* Paper presented at the National Conference on Personalized Instruction in Higher Education, Washington, DC.

=Vellutino, F., & Scanlon, D. (1987). Phonological coding, phonological awareness, and reading ability: Evidence from a longitudinal and experimental study. *Merril-Palmer Quarterly, 33*, 321–363.

<Vollmer, T. R., Ringdahl, J. E., Roane, H. S., & Marcus, B. (1997). Negative side effects of noncontingent reinforcement. *Journal of Applied Behavior Analysis, 30*, 161–164.

*Walsh, R. G., Sr. (1977). The Keller Plan in college introductory physical geology: A comparison with the conventional teaching method. *Dissertation Abstracts International, 37*, 4257. (University Microfilms No. AAD 76-30292)

=Warrick, N., Rubin, H., & Rowe-Walsh, S. (1993). Phoneme awareness in language-delayed children: Comparative studies and intervention. *Annals of Dyslexia, 43*, 153–173.

<Weeks, M., & Gaylord-Ross, R. (1981). Task difficulty and aberrant behavior in severely handicapped students. *Journal of Applied Behavior Analysis, 14*, 19–36.

=Weiner, S. (1994). Effects of phonemic awareness training on low- and middle-achieving first graders' phonemic awareness and reading ability. *Journal of Reading Behavior, 26*, 277–300.

!Welch, M. (1992). The PLEASE strategy: A meta-cognitive learning strategy for improving the paragraph writing of students with learning disabilities. *Learning Disability Quarterly, 15*(2), 119–128.

^Welsh, P., Antoinetti, J. & Thayer, P. (1965). An industrywide study of programmed instruction. *Journal of Applied Psychology, 49*, 61–73.

$&+Wentling, T. L. (1973). Mastery versus nonmastery instruction with varying test item feedback treatments. *Journal of Educational Psychology, 65*, 50–58.

*White, M. E. (1974). Different equations by PSI. In R. S. Ruskin & S. F. Bono (Eds.), *Personalized instruction in higher education* (pp. 169–171). Washington, DC: Center for Personalized Instruction.

Willett, J., Yamashita, J., & Anderson, R. (1983). A meta-analysis of instructional systems applied in science teaching. *Journal of Research in Science Teaching, 20*(5), 405–417.

=Williams, J. (1980). Teaching decoding with an emphasis on phoneme analysis and phoneme blending. *Journal of Educational Psychology, 72*, 1–15.

=Wilson, J., & Frederickson, N. (1995). Phonological awareness training: An evaluation. *Educational & Child Psychology, 12*, 68–79.

$Wire, D. R. (1979). *Mastery learning program at Durham College: Report on progress toward the first year, September 1, 1978–August 31, 1979.* Durham, NC. (ERIC Document Reproduction Service No. ED 187 387)

=Wise, B., Ring, J., & Olson, R. (1999). Training phonological awareness with and without explicit attention to articulation. *Journal of Experimental Child Psychology, 72*, 271–304.

=Wise, B., Ring, J., & Olson, R. (2000). Individual differences in benefits from computer-assisted remedial reading. *Journal of Experimental Child Psychology, 77*, 197–235.

<Witt, J. C., & Elliott, S. N. (1982). The response cost lottery: A time efficient and effective classroom intervention. *Journal of School Psychology, 20*, 155–161.

*Witters, D. R., & Kent, G. W. (1972). Teaching without lecturing—evidence in the case for individualized instruction. *The Psychological Record, 22*, 169–175.

<Wolery, M., Bailey, D. B., & Sugai, G. M. (1988). *Effective teaching: Principles and procedures of applied behavior analysis with exceptional students.* Boston: Allyn & Bacon.

$Wortham, S. C. (1980). *Mastery learning in secondary schools: A first-year report.* San Antonio, TX. (ERIC Document Reproduction Service No. ED 194 453)

*Yeany, R. H., Dost, R. J., & Matthew, R. W. (1980). The effects of diagnostic-prescriptive instruction and locus of control on the achievement and attitudes of university students. *Journal of Research in Science Teaching, 17*, 537–545.

$Yildren, G. (1977). *The effects of level of cognitive achievement on selected learning criteria under mastery learning and normal classroom instruction.* Unpublished doctoral dissertation, University of Chicago.

REFERENCES FOR UTILIZING REPETITION EFFECTIVELY

#Anderson, L. M., Evertson, C. M., & Brophy, J. E. (1979). An experimental study of effective teaching in first grade reading groups. *The Elementary School Journal, l79*, 193–222.

&Ault, M. J., Wolery, M., Gast, D. L., Doyle, R. M., & Martin, C. R. (1990). Comparison of predictable and unpredictable trial sequences during small-group instruction. *Learning Disability Quarterly, 13*(1), 12–29.

Ausubel, D. P., & Youseff, M. (1965). The effect of space repetition on meaningful retention. *The Journal of General Psychology, 73*, 147–150.

&Ayllon, T., Layman, D., & Kandel, H. J. (1975). A behavioral educational alternative to drug control of hyperactive children. *Journal of Applied Behavior Analysis, 8*(2), 137–146.

&Barbetta, P. M., & Heward, W. L. (1993). Effects of active student response during error correction on the acquisition and maintenance of geography facts by elementary students with learning disabilities. *Journal of Behavioral Education, 3*, 217–233.

&Beals, V. L. (1985). The effects of large group instruction on the acquisition of specific learning disabled adolescents. *Dissertation Abstracts International, 45*(9-A), 2478.

&Bell, K. E., Young, K. R., Salzberg, C. L., & West, R. P. (1991). High school driver education using peer tutors, direction instruction, and precision teaching. *Journal of Applied Behavior Analysis, 24*(1), 45–51.

&Billingsley, F. F. (1977). The effects of self- and externally-imposed schedules of reinforcement on oral reading performance. *Journal of Learning Disabilities, 10*, 549–558.

&Blandford, B. J., & Lloyd, J. W. (1987). Effects of a self-instructional procedure on handwriting. *Journal of Learning Disabilities, 20*, 342–346.

&Blick, D. W., & Test, D. W. (1987). Effects of self-recording on high school students' on-task behavior. *Learning Disability Quarterly, 10*, 203–213.

&Boyer, A. W. (1991). Improving the expository paragraph writing of learning disabled elementary school students using small group strategies instruction and word processing. *Dissertation Abstracts International, 52*(1-A), 129–130.

+Bryant, D. P., Vaughn, S., Linan-Thompson, S., Ugel, N., Hamff, A., & Hougen, M. (2000). Reading outcomes for students with and without reading disabilities in general education middle-school content area classes. *Learning Disability Quarterly, 23*, 238–252.

&Bulgren, J. A., Hock, M. F., Schumaker, J. B., & Deshler, D. D. (1995). The effects of instruction in a paired associates strategy on the information mastery performance of students with learning disabilities. *Learning Disabilities Research & Practice, 10*(1), 22–37.

&Burkwist, B. J., Mabee, W. S., & McLaughlin, T. F. (1987). The effect of a daily report card system on inappropriate classroom verbalizations with a junior high school learning-disabled student. *Techniques, 3*, 265–272.

*Butler, A. (1954). Test-retest and split-half reliabilities of the Wechsler-Bellevue scales and subtests with mental defectives. *American Journal of Mental Deficiency, 59*, 80–84.

&Campbell, B. J., Brady, M. P., & Linehan, S. (1991). Effects of peer-mediated instruction on the acquisition and generalization of written capitalization skills. *Journal of Learning Disabilities, 24*, 6–14.

&Case, L. P., Harris, K. R., & Graham, S. (1992). Improving the mathematic problem-solving skills of students with learning disabilities: Self-regulated strategy development. *The Journal of Special Education, 26*(1), 1–19.

*Casey, M. L., Davidson, H. P., & Harter, P. I. (1928). Three studies on the effect of training in similar and identical material upon Stanford-Binet scores. *Twenty-seventh Yearbook of the National Society for the Study of Education, 1*, 431–439.

*Catron, D. W. (1978). Immediate test-retest changes in WAIS scores among college males. *Psychological Reports, 43*, 279–290.

*Catron, D. W., & Thompson, C. C. (1979). Test-retest gains and WAIS scores after four retest intervals. *Journal of Clinical Psychology, 35*, 352–357.

Chard, D. J., Vaughn, S., & Tyler, B. J. (2002). A synthesis of research on effective interventions for building reading fluency with elementary students with learning disabilities. *Journal of Learning Disabilities, 35*(5), 21–60.

&Chiang, B. (1986). Initial learning and transfer effects of microcomputer drills on LD students' multiplication skills. *Learning Disability Quarterly, 9*, 118–123.

&Chiang, B., Thorpe, H. W., & Darch, C. B. (1980). Effects of cross-age tutoring on word-recognition performance of learning disabled students. *Learning Disability Quarterly, 3*(4), 11–19.

&Cochrane, M., & Ballard, K. D. (1986). Teaching five special needs children in a regular primary classroom using a consultation-collaboration model. *The Exceptional Child, 33*(2), 91–102.

^Cohen, A. (1988). *An evaluation of the effectiveness of two methods for providing computer-assisted repeated reading training to reading disabled students.* Unpublished doctoral dissertation, Florida State University, Tallahassee.

#Coker, H., Lorentz, C. W., & Coker, J. (1980). *Teacher behavior in student outcomes in the Georgia study.* Paper presented at the annual meeting of the American Educational Research Association, Boston.

&Cole, K. B. (1993). Efficacy and generalization of instruction in sequential expository writing for students with learning disabilities. *Dissertation Abstracts International, 53*(7-A), 2326.

*Colver, R. M., & Spielberger, C. D. (1961). Further evidence of the practice effect on the Miller Analogies Test. *Journal of Applied Psychology, 50*, 126–127.

#Cook, L. K., & Meyer, R. E. (1983). Reading strategies training for meaningful learning from prose. In M. Presley & J. Levin (Eds.), *Cognitive strategies training and research.* New York: Springer-Verlag.

Cruickshank, D. R., Kennedy, J. J., Bush, A., & Myers, B. (1979). Clear teaching: What is it? *British Journal of Teacher Education, 5*(1), 27–32.

*Curr, W., & Gourlay, N. (1960). The effect of practice on performance and selected scholastic tests. *British Journal of Educational Psychology, 30*, 155–167.

&Cuvo, A. J., Ashley, K. M., Marso, K. J., Zhang, B. L., & Fry, T. A. (1995). Effect of response practice variables on learning spelling and sight vocabulary. *Journal of Applied Behavior Analysis, 28*, 155–173.

&^Daly, E. J., & Martens, B. K. (1994). A comparison of three interventions for increasing oral reading performance: Application of the instructional hierarchy. *Journal of Applied Behavior Analysis, 27*, 459–469.

&Danoff, B., Harris, K. R., & Graham, S. (1993). Incorporating strategy instruction with the writing process in the regular classroom: Effects on the writing of students with and without learning disabilities. *Journal of Reading Behavior, 25*, 295–322.

&Darch, C., & Carnine, D. (1986). Teaching content area material to learning disabled students. *Exceptional Children, 53*, 240–246.

&Darch, C., & Gersten, R. (1985). The effects of teacher presentation rate and praise on LD students' oral reading performance. *British Journal of Educational Psychology, 55*, 295–303.

&DiGangi, S. A., Maag, J. W., & Rutherford, R. B. (1991). Self-graphing of on-task behavior:

Enhancing the reactive effects of self-monitoring on on-task behavior and academic performance. *Learning Disability Quarterly, 14*, 221–230.

&DiVeta, S. K., & Speece, D. L. (1990). The effects of blending and spelling training on the decoding skills of young poor readers. *Journal of Learning Disabilities, 23*, 579–582.

&Dowis, C. L., & Schloss, P. (1992). The impact of mini-lessons on writing skills. *Remedial and Special Education, 13*(5), 34–42.

+Downhower, S. L. (1987). Effects of repeated reading on second-grade transitional readers' fluency and comprehension. *Reading Research Quarterly, 22*, 389–406 (see Note 9).

*Droege, R. C. (1966). Effects of practice on aptitude scores. *Journal of Applied Psychology, 50*, 306–310.

&DuPaul, G. J., & Henningson, P. N. (1993). Peer tutoring effects on the classroom performance of children with attention deficit hyperactivity disorder. *School Psychology Review, 22*(1), 134–143.

&Duvall, S. F., Delquadri, J. C., Elliott, M., & Hall, R. V. (1992). Parent-tutoring procedures: Experimental analysis and validation of generalization in oral reading across passages, settings, and time. *Journal of Behavioral Education, 2*, 281–303.

&Ellis, E. S., & Graves, A. W. (1990). Teaching rural students with learning disabilities: A paraphrasing strategy to increase comprehension of main ideas. *Rural Special Education Quarterly, 10*, 2–10.

*Evans, F. R. (1977). *The GRE-Q Coaching/Instruction Study*. Princeton, NJ: Graduate Record Examinations, Educational Testing Service. (ERIC Document Reproduction Service No. ED 163 088)

*Evans, F. R., & Pike, L. W. (1973). The effects of instruction for three mathematics item formats. *Journal of Educational Measurement, 10*, 257–272.

Evertson, C., Anderson, C., Anderson, L., & Brophy, J. (1980). Relationships between classroom behaviors and student outcomes in junior high mathematics and English classes. *American Educational Research Journal, 17*, 43–60.

#Evertson, C., Emmer, E., & Brophy, J. (1980). Predictors of effective teaching in junior high mathematics classrooms. *Journal for Research and Mathematics Education, 11*, 167–178.

&Fantasia, K. L. (1982). An investigation of formal analysis as an intervention to improve word problem computation for learning disabled children. *Dissertation Abstracts International, 42*(12-A), 5085.

+Faulkner, H. J., & Levy, B. A. (1999). Fluent and nonfluent forms of transfer in reading: Words and their message. *Psychonomic Bulletin and Review, 6*, 111–116.

#Fisher, C. W., Berliner, D. C., Filby, N. N., Marliave, R., Cahen, L. S., & Dishaw, M. M. (1980). Teaching behaviors, academic learning time, and student achievement: An overview. In C. Denham & A. Lieberman (Eds). *Time to learn* (pp. 7–32). Washington, DC: U.S. Government Printing Office.

*Frankel, E. (1960). Effects of growth, practice, and coaching on Scholastic Aptitude Test scores. *Personnel Guidance Journal, 33*, 713–719.

^Fuchs, D., Fuchs, L., Mathes, P., & Simmons, D. (1997). Peer-assisted learning strategies: Making classrooms more responsive to diversity. *American Educational Research Journal, 34*, 174–206.

^Gilbert, L., Williams, R., & McLaughlin, T. (1986). Use of assisted reading to increase correct reading rates and decrease error rates of students with learning disabilities. *Journal of Applied Behavior Analysis, 29*, 255–257.

*Goldsmith, R. P. (1980). The effects of training and test taking skills and test anxiety: Mexican American students' aptitude test performance. *Dissertation Abstracts International, 40,* 5790A (University Microfilms No. 80-09863)

#Good, T. L., & Grouws, D. A. (1979). The Missouri mathematics effectiveness project. *Journal of Educational Psychology, 71,* 355–362.

&Graham, S., MacArthur, C., Schwartz, S., & Page-Voth, V. (1992). Improving the compositions of students with learning disabilities: Using a strategy involving product and process goal setting. *Exceptional Children, 58,* 322–334.

*Greene, K. B. (1928). The influence of specialized training on tests of general intelligence. *Twenty-seventh Yearbook of the National Society for the Study of Education, 1,* 421–428.

&Hallahan, D. P., Lloyd, J., Kosiewicz, M. M., Kauffman, J. M., & Graves, A. W. (1979). Self-monitoring of attention as a treatment for a learning disabled boy's off-task behavior. *Learning Disability Quarterly, 2,* 24–32.

&Hallahan, D. P., Marshall, K. J., & Lloyd, J. W. (1981). Self-recording during group instruction: Effects on attention to task. *Learning Disability Quarterly, 4,* 407–413.

&Harper, J. A. (1986). A comparison of the effectiveness of microcomputer and workbook instruction on reading comprehension performance of high incidence handicapped students. *Dissertation Abstracts International, 46*(11A), 3318–3319.

&Harris, K. R. (1986). Self-monitoring of attentional behavior versus self-monitoring of productivity: Effects on on-task behavior and academic response rate among learning disabled children. *Journal of Applied Behavior Analysis, 19,* 417–423.

&Harris, K. R., & Graham, S. (1985). Improving learning disabled students' composition skills: Self-control strategy training. *Learning Disability Quarterly, 8,* 27–36.

&Harris, K. R., Graham, S., Reid, R., McElroy, K., & Hamby, R. S. (1994). Self-monitoring of performance: Replication and cross-task comparison studies. *Learning Disability Quarterly, 17,* 121–139.

&Hazel, J. S., Schumaker, J. B., Sherman, J. A., & Sheldon, J. (1982). Application of a group training program in social skills and problem solving to learning disabled and non–learning disabled youth. *Learning Disability Quarterly, 5,* 398–408.

*Heim, A. W., & Wallace, J. G. (1949). The effects of repeatedly retesting the same group on the same intelligence test: I. Normal adults. *Quarterly Journal of Experiment Experimental Psychology, 11, 151*–159.

+Herman, P. A. (1985). The effects of repeated readings on reading rate, speech pauses, and word recognition accuracy. *Reading Research Quarterly,* 20, 553–565.

Hines, C. V., Cruickshank, D. R., & Kennedy, J. J. (1985). Teacher clarity and its relationship to student achievement and satisfaction. *American Educational Research Journal, 22*(1), 87–99.

*Holloway, H. D. (1954). Effects of training on the SRA Primary Mental Abilities (Primary) and the WISC. *Child Development, 25,* 253–263.

+Homan, S. P., Klesius, J. P., & Hite, C. (1993). Effects of repeated readings and nonrepetitive strategies on students' fluency and comprehension. *Journal of Educational Research, 87,* 94–99.

&Hughes, C. A., & Schumaker, J. B. (1991). Test-taking strategy instruction for adolescents with learning disabilities. *Exceptionality, 2*(4), 205–221.

&Hutchinson, N. L. (1993). Effects of cognitive strategy instruction on algebra problem solving of adolescents with learning disabilities. *Learning Disability Quarterly, 16,* 34–63.

&Idol, L., & Croll, V. J. (1987). Story-mapping training as a means of improving reading comprehension. *Learning Disability Quarterly, 10,* 214–229.

&Idol-Maestas, L. (1981). Increasing the oral reading performance of a learning disabled adult. *Learning Disability Quarterly, 4,* 294–301.

*Jefferson, J. L. (1975). The effects of anxiety on the achievement of black graduate students taking standardized achievement tests. *Dissertation Abstracts International, 35,* 5121A. (University Microfilms No. 75-3105)

&Kitterman, J. R. (1984). Error verification and microcomputer mediation of a spelling task with learning disabled students. *Dissertation Abstracts International, 45*(2-A), 491–492.

*Klutch, M. I. (1976). The influence of test sophistication on standardized test scores. *Dissertation Abstracts International, 37,* 809A. (University Microfilms No. 75-10, 058)

&Kosiewicz, M. M., Hallahan, D. R., & Lloyd, J. (1981). The effects of an LD student's treatment choice on handwriting performance. *Learning Disability Quarterly, 4,* 281–286.

&Kosiewicz, M. M., Hallahan, D. R., Lloyd, J., & Graves, A. W. (1982). Effects of self-instruction and self-correction procedures on handwriting performance. *Learning Disability Quarterly, 5,* 71–78.

&Kraetsch, G. A. (1981). The effects of oral instructions and training on the expansion of written language. *Learning Disability Quarterly, 4,* 82–90.

*Kreit, L. H. (1968). The effects of test-taking practice on pupil test performance. *American Educational Research Journal, 5,* 616–625.

#Kulik, J. A., & Kulik C. C. (1979). College teaching. In P. L. Peterson & H. J. Wahlberg (Eds.), *Research on teaching: Concepts, findings, and implications* (pp. 70–93). Berkeley, CA: McCutchan.

Kulik, J. A., Kulik, C. C., & Bangert, R. L. (1984). Effects of practice on aptitude and achievement scores. *American Educational Research Journal, 21*(2), 434–447.

&Lahey, B. B., Busemeyer, M. K., Ohara, C., & Beggs, V. E. (1977). Treatment of severe perceptual-motor disorders in children diagnosed as learning disabled. *Behavior Modification, 1,* 123–140.

&Lalli, E. R., & Shapiro, E. S. (1990). The effects of self-monitoring and contingent reward on sight word acquisition. *Education and Treatment of Children, 13,* 129–141.

&Larson, K. A., & Gerber, M. M. (1987). Effects of social meta-cognitive training for enhancing overt behavior in learning disabled and low achieving delinquents. *Exceptional Children, 54,* 201–211.

&Lenz, B. K., Ehren, B. J., & Smiley, L. R. (1991). A goal attainment approach to improve completion of project-type assignments by adolescents with learning disabilities. *Learning Disabilities Research & Practice, 6,* 166–176.

+Levy, B. A., Abello, B., & Lysynchuk, L. (1997). Transfer from word training to reading in context: Gains in reading fluency and comprehension. *Learning Disability Quarterly, 20,* 173–188.

&Lloyd, J. W., Hallahan, D. R, Kosiewicz, M. M., & Kneedler, R. D. (1982). Reactive effects of self-assessment and self-recording on attention to task and academic productivity. *Learning Disability Quarterly, 5,* 216–227.

^Lovitt, T., & Hansen, C. (1976). The use of contingent skipping and drilling to improve oral reading and comprehension. *Journal of Learning Disabilities, 9,* 20–26.

&Maag, J. W., Reid, R., & DiGangi, S. A. (1993). Differential effects of self-monitoring attention, accuracy, and productivity. *Journal of Applied Behavior Analysis, 26,* 329–344.

*Macintosh, D. M. (1944). Effects of practice on intelligence test results. *British Journal of Educational Psychology, 14,* 44–45.

^Marston, D., Deno, S., Dongil, K., et al. (1995). Comparison of reading intervention approaches for students with mild disabilities. *Exceptional Children, 62,* 20–37.

&Martin, K. F., & Manno, C. (1995). Use of a check-off system to improve middle school students' story compositions. *Journal of Learning Disabilities, 28,* 139–149.

+^Mathes, P. G., & Fuchs, L. S. (1993). Peer-mediated reading instruction in special education resource rooms. *Learning Disabilities Research & Practice, 8,* 233–243.

&Mathews, R. M., & Fawcett, S. B. (1984). Building the capacities of job candidates through behavioral instruction. *Journal of Community Psychology, 12,* 123–129.

&McCurdy, B. L., Cundari, L., & Lentz, F. E. (1990). Enhancing instructional efficiency: An examination of time delay and the opportunity to observe instruction. *Education and Treatment of Children, 13,* 226–238.

&McIntyre, S. B., Test, D. W., Cooke, N. L., & Beattie, J. (1991). Using count-bys to increase multiplication facts fluency. *Learning Disability Quarterly, 14,* 82–88.

*McNamara, J. (1964). Zero error and practice effects in Moray House English Quotients. *British Journal of Educational Psychology, 34,* 315–320.

&McNaughton, D., Hughes, C., & Ofiesh, N. (1997). Proofreading for students with learning disabilities: Integrating computer and strategy use. *Learning Disabilities Research & Practice, 12*(1), 16–28.

*Melametsa, L. (1965). The influence of training on the level of test performance and the factor structure of intelligence tests. *Scandinavian Journal of Psychology, 6,* 19–25.

+Mercer, C. D., Campbell, K. U., Miller, M. D., Mercer, K. D., & Lane, H. B. (2000). Effects of a reading fluency intervention for middle schoolers with specific learning disabilities. *Learning Disabilities Research & Practice, 15,* 179–189.

*Merriman, C. (1927). Coaching for mental tests. *Educational Administration and Supervision, 13,* 59–64.

*Messick, S., & Jungeblut, A. (1981). Time and method in coaching SAT. *Psychological Bulletin, 89,* 191–216.

^Monda, L. (1989). *The effects of oral, silent, and listening repetitive reading on the fluency and comprehension of learning disabled students.* Unpublished doctoral dissertation, Florida State University, Tallahassee.

&Montague, M. (1992). The effects of cognitive and meta-cognitive strategy instruction on the mathematical problem solving of middle school students with learning disabilities. *Journal of Learning Disabilities, 25*(4), 230–248.

&Montague, M., & Bos, C. S. (1986). The effect of cognitive strategy training on verbal math problem solving performance of learning disabled adolescents. *Journal of Learning Disabilities, 19,* 26–33.

&Montague, M., & Leavell, A. G. (1994). Improving the narrative writing of students with learning disabilities. *Remedial and Special Education, 15*(1), 21–33.

^Moseley, D. (1993). Visual and linguistic determinants of reading fluency in dyslexics: A classroom study with talking computers. In S. F. Wright & R. Groner (Eds.), *Facets of dyslexia and its remediation* (pp. 567–584). London: Elsevier.

Nelson, T. O. (1977). Repetition and depth of processing. *Journal of Verbal Learning and Verbal Behavior, 16,* 151–171.

*Netley, C., Rachman, S., & Turner, R. K. (1965). The effect of practice on performance in reading attainment tests. *British Journal of Educational Psychology, 35*, 1–8.

&Newby, R. F., Caldwell, J., & Recht, D. R. (1989). Improving the reading comprehension of children with dysphonetic and dyseidetic dyslexia using story grammar. *Journal of Learning Disabilities, 22*, 373–380.

*Oakland, T. (1972). The effects of test-wiseness materials on standardized test performance of preschool disadvantaged children. *Journal of School Psychology, 10*, 355–360.

^O'Shea, L., Munson, S., & O'Shea, D. (1984). Error correction in oral reading: Evaluating the effectiveness of three procedures. *Education and Treatment of Children, 7*, 203–214.

+O'Shea, L. J., Sindelar, P. T., & O'Shea, D. J. (1985). The effects of repeated reading and attentional cues on reading fluency and comprehension. *Journal of Reading Behavior, 17*, 129–141.

+^O'Shea, L. J., Sindelar, P. T., & O'Shea, D. J. (1987). The effects of repeated reading and attentional cues on reading fluency and comprehension of learning disabled readers. *Learning Disabilities Research, 2*, 103–109.

#Palincsar, A. S. (1984). *Reciprocal teaching*. Paper presented at the annual meeting of the American Educational Research Association, New Orleans.

*Peel, E. A. (1951). A note on practice effects in intelligence tests. *British Journal of Educational Psychology, 69*, 122–125.

Péladeau, N., Forget, J., & Gagné, F. (2003). Effect of paced and unpaced practice on skill application and retention: How much is enough? *American Educational Research Journal, 40*(3), 769–801.

Peterson, H. A., Ellis, M., Toohill, N., & Kloess, P. (1935). Some measurements of the effects of reviews. *The Journal of Educational Psychology, 26*(2), 65–72.

Petros, T., & Hoving, K. (1980). The effects of review and young children's memory for prose. *Journal of Experimental Child Psychology, 30*, 33–43.

*Petty, N. E., & Harrell, E. H. (1977). Effects of program instruction related to motivation, anxiety, and test wiseness on group IQ test performance. *Journal of Educational Psychology, 69*, 630–635.

&Prater, M. A., Joy, R., Chilman, B., Temple, J., & Miller, S. R. (1991). Self-monitoring of on-task behavior by adolescents with learning disabilities. *Learning Disability Quarterly, 14*, 165–177.

*Quereshi, M. Y. (1968). Practice effects on the WISC subtest scores and IQ estimates. *Journal of Clinical Psychology, 24*, 79–85.

#Raphael, T. E. (1980). *The effect of metacognitive awareness training on students' question and answer behavior*. Doctoral dissertation, University of Illinois.

^Rashotte, C., & Torgesen, J. (1985). Repeated reading and reading fluency in learning disabled children. *Reading Research Quarterly, 20*, 180–188.

+Rasinski, T. (1990). Effects of repeated reading and listening-while-reading on reading fluency. *Journal of Educational Research, 83*, 147–150.

+Rasinski, T., Padak, N., Linek, W., & Sturtevant, E. (1994). Effects of fluency development on urban second-grade readers. *Journal of Educational Research, 87*, 158–165.

*Richardson, F., & Robinson, E. S. (1921). Effects of practice upon the scores and predictive value of the Alpha Intelligence Examination. *Journal of Experimental Psychology, 4*, 300–317.

&Rivera, D., & Smith, D. D. (1988). Using a demonstration strategy to teach midschool students with learning disabilities how to compute long division. *Journal of Learning Disabilities, 21,* 77–81.

&Roberts, M., & Smith, D. D. (1980). The relationship among correct and error oral reading rates and comprehension. *Learning Disability Quarterly, 3,* 54–64.

*Roberts, S. O., & Oppenheim, D. B. (1966). *The effects of specialized instruction upon test performance of high school students.* Princeton, NJ: Educational Testing Service. (ERIC Document Reproduction Service No. ED 053 158)

*Rodgers, A. G. (1936). The application of six group intelligence tests to the same children and the effects of practice. *British Journal of Educational Psychology, 6,* 291–305.

^Rose, T. (1984). The effects of two prepractice procedures on oral reading. *Journal of Learning Disabilities, 17,* 544–548.

^Rose, T., & Beattie, J. (1986). Relative effects of teacher-directed and taped previewing on oral reading. *Learning Disability Quarterly, 9,* 193–199.

&Rose, T. L., McEntire, E., & Dowdy, C. (1982). Effects of two error-correction procedures on oral reading. *Learning Disability Quarterly, 5*(2), 100–105.

&Rose, T. L., & Sherry, L. (1984). Relative effects of two previewing procedures on LD adolescents' oral reading performance. *Learning Disability Quarterly, 7,* 39–44.

&Rosenberg, M. S. (1986). Error-correction during oral reading: A comparison of three techniques. *Learning Disability Quarterly, 9,* 182–192.

&Rosenberg, M. S. (1989). The effects of daily homework assignments on the acquisition of basic skills by students with learning disabilities. *Journal of Learning Disabilities, 2,* 314–323.

Rosenshine, B. V. (1986). Synthesis of research on explicit teaching. *Educational Leadership, 43*(7), 60–69.

*Rutan, P. C. (1979). Test sophistication training: A program level intervention for the school psychologist. *Dissertation Abstracts International, 40,* 171A. (University Microfilms No. 79-14, 135)

&Salend, S. J., & Lamb, E. A. (1986). Effectiveness of a group-managed interdependent contingency system. *Learning Disability Quarterly, 9,* 268–273.

&Salend, S. J., & Meddaugh, D. (1985). Using a peer-mediated extinction procedure to decrease obscene language. *The Pointer, 30*(1), 8–11.

&Salend, S. J., Reeder, E., Katz, N., & Russell, T. (1992). The effects of a dependent group evaluation system. *Education and Treatment of Children, 15*(1), 32–42.

&Schiemek, N. (1983). Errorless discrimination training of digraphs with a learning disabled student. *School Psychology Review, 12,* 101–105.

&Schumaker, J. B., Deshler, D. D., Alley, G. R., Warner, M. M., Clark, F. L., & Nolan, S. (1982). Error monitoring: A learning strategy for improving adolescent academic performance. In M. W. Cruickshank & J. W. Lerner (Eds.), *Coming of age* (Vol. 3, pp. 170–183). Syracuse, NY: Syracuse University Press.

&Seabaugh, G. O., & Schumaker, J. B. (1994). The effects of self-regulation training on the academic productivity of secondary students with learning problems. *Journal of Behavioral Education, 4*(1), 109–133.

+Simmons, D. C., Fuchs, D., Fuchs, L. S., Hodge, J. P., & Mathes, P. G. (1994). Importance of instructional complexity and role reciprocity to classwide peer tutoring. *Learning Disabilities Research & Practice, 9,* 203–212.

+^Simmons, D. C., Fuchs, D., Fuchs, L. S., Mathes, P., & Hodge, J. P. (1995). Effects of explicit teaching and peer tutoring on the reading achievement of learning-disabled and low-performing students in regular classrooms. *The Elementary School Journal*, *95*, 387–408.

+^Sindelar, P. T., Monda, L. E., & O'Shea, L. J. (1990). Effects of repeated readings on instructional and mastery-level readers. *Journal of Educational Research, 83*, 220–226.

*Slaughter, B. A. (1976). An examination of the effects of teaching and practice in test-retest skills on student performance on a standardized achievement test. *Dissertation Abstracts International, 37*, 1505A. (University Microfilms No. 76-19, 931)

^Smith, D. (1979). The improvement of children's oral reading through the use of teacher modeling. *Journal of Learning Disabilities, 12,* 172–175.

*Smith, L., & Land, M. (1981). Low-inference verbal behaviors related to teacher clarity. *Journal of Classroom Interaction, 17,* 37–42.

#Soar, R. S. (1973). *Follow-Through Classroom Process Measurement and Pupil Growth (1970–1971). Final Report.* Gainesville: College of Education, University of Florida.

*Spielberger, C. D. (1959). Evidence of a practice effect on the Miller Analogies Tests. *Journal of Applied Psychology, 43,* 259–263.

#Spiro, R. J., & Meyers, A. (1984). Individual differences and underlying cognitive process. In P. D. Pearson, R. Barr, M. L. Camille, & P. Mosenthal (Eds.), *Handbook of reading research.* New York: Longman.

#Stallings, J., Corey, R., Fairweather, J., & Needles, M. (1977). *Early Childhood Education classroom evaluation.* Menlo Park, CA: SRI International.

#Stallings, J., Needles, M., & Staybrook, N. (1979). *The teaching of basic reading skills in secondary schools, Phase II and Phase III.* Menlo Park, CA: SRI International.

#Stallings, J. A., & Kaskowitz, D. (1974). *Follow-Through Classroom Observation.* Menlo Park, CA: SRI International.

*Steisel, I. M. (1951). The relation between a test and retest scores on the Wechsler-Bellevue Scale (Form 1) for selected college students. *Journal of Genetic Psychology, 79,* 155–162.

+Stoddard, K., Valcante, G., Sindelar, P. T., O'Shea, L., & Algozzine, B. (1993). Increasing reading rate and comprehension: The effects of repeated readings, sentence segmentation, and intonation training. *Reading Research and Instruction, 32,* 53–65.

^Stout, T. (1997). *An investigation of the effects of a repeated reading intervention on the fluency and comprehension of students with language-learning disabilities.* Unpublished doctoral dissertation, Georgia State University, Atlanta.

^Sutton, P. (1991). *Strategies to increase oral reading fluency of primary resource students.* Unpublished manuscript, Nova University.

^Swain, D., & Allinder, R. (1996). The effects of repeated reading on two types of CBM: Computer maze and oral reading with second-grade students with learning disabilities. *Diagnostique, 21,* 51–66.

&Swanson, H. L. (1985). Effects of cognitive-behavioral training on emotionally disturbed children's academic performance. *Cognitive Therapy and Research, 9,* 201–216.

&Swanson, H. L., Kozleski, E., & Stegink, P. (1987). Disabled readers' processing of prose: Do any processes change because of intervention? *Psychology in the Schools, 24,* 378–384.

&Swanson, H. L., & Scarpati, S. (1984). Self-instruction training to increase academic performance of educationally handicapped children. *Child & Family Behavior Therapy, 6*(4), 23–39.

&Swanson, L. (1981). Modification of comprehension deficits in learning disabled children. *Learning Disability Quarterly, 4*, 189–202.

Swanson, L., & Sachse-Lee, C. (2000). A meta-analysis of single-subject-design intervention research for students with LD. *Journal of Learning Disabilities, 33*(2), 114–136.

&Tansey, M. A. (1985). Brainwave signatures—An index reflective of the brain's functional neuroanatomy: Further findings on the effect of EEG sensorimotor rhythm biofeedback training on the neurologic precursors of learning disabilities. *International Journal of Psychophysiology, 3*(2), 85–99.

Therrien, W. J. (2004). Fluency and comprehension gains as a result of repeated reading: A meta-analysis. *Remedial and Special Education, 25*(4), 252–261.

&Thorpe, H. W., Lampe, S., Nash, R. T., & Chiang, B. (1981). The effects of the kinesthetic-tactile component of the VAKT procedure on secondary LD students' reading performance. *Psychology in the Schools, 18*, 334–340.

*Throne, F. M., Schulman, J. L., & Kaspar, J. C. (1962). Reliability and stability of the WISC for a group of mentally retarded boys. *American Journal of Mental Deficiency, 67*, 455–457.

*Tinney, R. E. (1969). The effect of training in test-taking skills on the reading test scores of fifth grade children of high and low socioeconomic levels. *Dissertation Abstracts International, 30*, 595A. (University Microfilms No. 69-11, 505)

#Tobias, S. (1982). When do instructional methods make a difference? *Educational Researcher, 11*, 4–10.

&Van Den Meiracker, M. (1986). Effectiveness of teacher-based versus computer-based instruction on reading comprehension of subtypes of learning disabled children. *Dissertation Abstracts International, 47*(9-A), 3398–3399.

+Vaughn, S., Chard, D. J., Bryant, D. P., Coleman, M., & Kouzekanani, K. (2000). Fluency and comprehension interventions for third-grade students. *Remedial and Special Education, 21*, 325–335.

*Vernon, P. E. (1954). Practice and coaching effects in intelligence tests. *Educational Forum, 18*, 269–280.

&Vivion, H. K. (1985). Using a modified cloze procedure to effect an improvement in reading comprehension in reading disabled children with good oral language. *Dissertation Abstracts International, 46*(3-A), 663.

&Wallace, G. W., & Bott, D. A. (1989). Statement-pie: A strategy to improve the paragraph writing skills of adolescents with learning disabilities. *Journal of Learning Disabilities, 22*, 541–545.

Watkins, M. J., & Kerkar, S. P. (1985). Recall of twice-presented item without recall of either presentation: Generic memory for events. *Journal of Memory and Language, 24*, 666–678.

&Weidler, S. D. (1986). The remediation of disabled readers' metacognitive strategies via cognitive self-instruction. *Dissertation Abstracts International, 46*(9-A), 2645–2646.

&^Weinstein, G., & Cooke, N. (1992). The effects of two repeated reading interventions on generalization of fluency. *Learning Disability Quarterly, 15*, 21–28.

&Whang, R. L., Fawcett, S. B., & Mathews, R. M. (1984). Teaching job-related social skills to learning disabled adolescents. *Analysis and Intervention in Developmental Disabilities, 4*(1), 29–38.

*Whitely, S. E., & Dawn, R. V. (1974). Effects of cognitive intervention on latent ability measured from analogy items. *Journal of Educational Psychology, 66*(5), 710–717.

*Wideman, S., & Wrigley, J. (1953). The comparative effects of coaching and practice on the results of verbal intelligence tests. *British Journal of Educational Psychology, 44*, 83–94.

&Wood, D. A., Rosenberg, M. S., & Carran, D. T. (1993). The effects of tape-recorded self-instruction cues on the mathematics performance of students with learning disabilities. *Journal of Learning Disabilities, 26*, 250–258.

+Young, A., Bowers, P. G., & MacKinnon, G. E. (1996). Effects of prosodic modeling and repeated reading on poor readers' fluency and comprehension. *Applied Psycholinguistics, 17*, 59–84.

&Zipprich, M. A. (1995). Teaching web making as a guided planning tool to improve student narrative writing. *Remedial and Special Education, 16*, 3–15.

REFERENCES FOR UTILIZING UNIFIERS

Abayomi, B. I. (1988). *The effects of concept mapping and cognitive style on science achievement.* Doctoral dissertation, Georgia State University. *Dissertation Abstracts International, 49*, 1420A.

#Alvermann, D. (1988). Effects of spontaneous and induced lookbacks on self-perceived high- and low-ability comprehenders. *Journal of Educational Research, 81*, 325–331.

#Alvermann, D., & Boothby, P. (1986). Children's transfer of graphic organizer instruction. *Reading Psychology: An International Quarterly, 7*, 87–100.

#Alvermann, D., & Swafford, J. (1989). Do content area strategies have a research base? *Journal of Reading, 32*, 388–394.

#Alvermann, D. E. (1981). The compensatory effect of graphic organizers on descriptive text. *Journal of Educational Research, 75*(1), 44–48.

#Alvermann, D. E. (1982). Restructuring text facilitates written recall of main ideas. *Journal of Reading, 25*(8), 754–758.

+Alvermann, D. E. (1991). The discussion web: A graphic aid for learning across the curriculum. *The Reading Teacher, 45*, 92–99.

#Alvermann, D. E., Boothby, P. R., & Wolfe, J. (1984). The effect of graphic organizer instruction on fourth graders' comprehension of text. *Journal of Social Studies Research, 8*(1), 13–20.

+Alvermann, D. E., Hynd, C. R., & Qian, G. (1995). Effects of interactive discussion and text type on learning counter-intuitive science concepts. *The Journal of Educational Research, 88*, 154.

=Amato, J. L., Bernard, R. M., D'Amico, M., & DeBellefeuille, B. (1989). Can instructional variables be combined effectively to enhance learning achievement? *Canadian Journal of Educational Communication, 18*(2), 85–109.

=Andre, M. E., & Anderson, T. H. (1979). The development and evaluation of a self-questioning study technique. *Reading Research Quarterly, 14*(4), 605–623.

=Armbruster, B. B., Anderson, T. H., & Ostertag, J. (1987). Does text structure/summarization instruction facilitate learning from expository text? *Reading Research Quarterly, 22*(3), 331–346.

=Atkinson, R. C., & Raugh, M. R. (1975). An application of the mnemonic keyword method to the acquisition of a Russian vocabulary. *Journal of Experimental Psychology: Human Learning and Memory, 104*(2), 126–133.

&Baker, C. E. (1992). *The effect of self-generated drawings on the ability of students with learning disabilities to solve mathematical word problems.* Unpublished doctoral dissertation, Texas Technology University, Lubbock.

Baker, S., Gersten, R., & Lee, D-S. (2002). A synthesis of empirical research on teaching mathematics to low-achieving students. *The Elementary School Journal, 103*(1), 51–92.

#Balajthy, E., & Weisberg, R. (1988, December). *Effects of transfer to real-world subject area materials from training in graphic organizers and summarizing on developmental college readers' comprehension of the compare/contrast text structure.* Paper presented at the annual meeting of the National Reading Conference, New Orleans, LA. (ERIC Document Reproduction Service No. ED 300 771)

#Balajthy, E., & Weisberg, R. (1990, December). *Effects of reading ability, prior knowledge, topic interest, and locus of control on at-risk college students' use of graphic organizers and summarizing.* Paper presented at the annual meeting of the National Reading Conference, Miami, FL. (ERIC Document Reproduction Service No. ED 325 838)

=Barnes, J. A., Ginther, D. W., & Conchran, S. W. (1989). Schema and purpose in reading comprehension and learning vocabulary from context. *Reading Research and Instruction, 28*(2), 16–28.

#Barron, R., & Schwartz, R. (1984). Graphic postorganizers: A spatial learning strategy. In C. D. Holley & D. F. Dansereau (Eds.), *Spatial learning strategies: Techniques, applications, and related issues* (pp. 275–289). San Diego, CA: Academic Press.

#=Barron, R., & Stone, V. (1974). The effect of student-constructed graphic post organizers upon learning vocabulary relationships. In P. Nacke (Ed.), *Interaction: Research in college adult reading* (pp. 172–176). Clemson, SC: National Reading Conference.

Basili, P. A. (1988). *Conceptual change strategies within cooperative groups of community college chemistry students: An experiment.* Doctoral dissertation, University of Maryland. *Dissertation Abstracts International, 49,* 1752A.

#=Bean, T. W., Singer, H., Sorter, J., & Frazee, C. (1986). The effects of metacognitive instruction in outlining and graphic organizer construction on students' comprehension in tenth-grade world history class. *Journal of Reading Behavior, 18,* 153–169.

&Bennett, K. K. (1981). *The effect of syntax and verbal mediation on learning disabled students' verbal mathematical problem scores.* Unpublished doctoral dissertation, Northern Arizona University, Flagstaff.

#Bernard, R. (1990). Effects of processing instructions on the usefulness of a graphic organizer and structural cueing in text. *Instructional Science, 19,* 207–217.

=Billingsley, B. S., & Wildman, T. M. (1988). The effects of prereading activities on the comprehension monitoring of learning disabled adolescents. *Learning Disablilities Research, 4*(1), 36–44.

*Blaha, B. A. (1979). *The effects of answering self-generated questions on reading.* Unpublished doctoral dissertation, Boston University School of Education.

Bodolus, J. E. (1986). *The use of concept mapping strategy to facilitate meaningful learning for ninth grade students in science.* Doctoral dissertation, Temple University. *Dissertation Abstracts International, 47,* 3387A.

#Boothby, P. R., & Alvermann, D. E. (1984). A classroom training study: The effects of graphic organizer instruction on fourth graders' comprehension. *Reading World, 23,* 325–339.

$&Bottge, B. A., & Hasselbring, T. S. (1993). A comparison of two approaches for teaching complex, authentic mathematics problems to adolescents in remedial math classes. *Exceptional Children, 59,* 556–566.

Bower, G. H., Clark, M. C., Lesgold, A. M., & Winzenz, D. (1969). Hierarchical retrieval schemes in recall of categorized word lists. *Journal of Verbal Learning and Verbal Behavior, 8,* 323–343.

%Boyle, J. R. (1996). The effects of a cognitive mapping strategy on the literal and inferential comprehension of students with mild disabilities. *Learning Disabilities Quarterly, 19,* 86–98.

*Brady, P. L. (1990). *Improving the reading comprehension of middle school students through reciprocal teaching and semantic mapping strategies.* Unpublished doctoral dissertation, University of Alaska.

=Bretzing, B. H., Kulhavy, R. W., & Caterino, L. C. (1987). Notetaking by junior high students. *Journal of Educational Research, 80*(6), 359–362.

=Brown, A. L., & Barclay, C. R. (1976). The effects of training specific mnemonics on the metamnemonic efficiency of retarded children. *Child Development, 47,* 71–80.

=Brown, A. L., Campione, J. C., & Barclay, C. R. (1979). Training self-checking routines for estimating test readiness: Generalization from list learning to prose recall. *Child Development, 50,* 501–512.

&Case, L. P., Harris, K. R., & Graham, S. (1992). Improving the mathematical problem-solving skills of students with learning disabilities: Self-regulated strategy development. *The Journal of Special Education, 26,* 1–19.

=Casey, M. B. (1990). A planning and problem-solving preschool model: The methodology of being a good learner. *Early Childhood Research Quarterly, 5,* 53–67.

&Cassel, J., & Reid, R. (1996). Use of self-regulated strategy intervention to improve word problem–solving skills of students with mild disabilities. *Journal of Behavioral Education, 6,* 153–172.

+Champagne, A. B., Gunstone, R. F., & Klopfer, L. E. (1983). Naive knowledge and science learning. *Research in Science and Technological Education, 1,* 175–183.

%Chan, L.K.S. (1991). Promoting strategy generalization through self-instructional training in students with reading disabilities. *Journal of Learning Disabilities, 24,* 427–433.

Cliburn, J. W., Jr. (1985). Concept maps to promote meaningful learning. *Journal of College Science Teaching, 19,* 212–217.

*Cohen, R. (1983). Students generate questions as an aid to reading comprehension. *Reading Teacher, 36,* 770–775.

Corkill, A. J., Bruning, R. H., & Glover, J. A. (1988). Advance organizers: Concrete versus abstract. *Journal of Educational Research, 82*(2), 76–81.

Corkill, A. J., Bruning, R. H., Glover, J. A., & Krug, D. (1988). Advance organizers: Retrieval context hypothesis. *Journal of Educational Psychology, 80*(3), 304–311.

=Danner, F. W., & Taylor, A. M. (1973). Integrated pictures and relational imagery training in children's learning. *Journal of Experimental Child Psychology, 16,* 47–54.

=Dansereau, D. F., McDonald, B. A., Collins, K. W., Garland, J., Holley, C. D., Diekhoff, G. M., & Evans, S. H. (1979). Evaluation of a learning strategy system. In H. O'Neil & C. Spielberger (Eds.), *Cognitive and affective learning strategies* (pp. 3–43). New York: Academic Press.

Darch, C., & Kameenui, E. J. (1987). Teaching LD students critical reading skills: A systematic replication. *Learning Disability Quarterly, 10,* 82–91.

#Darch, C. B., Carnine, D. W., & Kameenui, E. J. (1986). The role of graphic organizers and social structure in content area instruction. *Journal of Reading Behavior, 18*(4), 275–295.

*Davey, B., & McBride, S. (1986). Effects of question-generation on reading comprehension. *Journal of Educational Psychology, 78*, 256–262.

@De La Paz, S., & Graham, S. (1997). Effects of dictation and advanced planning instruction on the composing of students with writing and learning problems. *Journal of Educational Psychology, 89*(2), 203–222.

Dean, R. S., & Kulhavy, R. W. (1981). Influence of spatial organization in prose learning. *Journal of Educational Psychology, 73*(1), 57–64.

=Dendato, K. M., & Diener, D. (1986). Effectiveness of cognitive/relation therapy and study-skills training in reducing self-reported anxiety and improving the academic performance of test-anxious students. *Journal of Counseling Psychology, 33*(2), 131–135.

Denner, P. R. (1986, June). *Comparison of the effects of episodic organizers and traditional notetaking on story recall.* Paper submitted to the Faculty Research Committee of Idaho State University. (ERIC Document Reproduction Service No. ED 270 731)

*Dermody, M. (1988, February). *Metacognitive strategies for development of reading comprehension for younger children.* Paper presented at the annual meeting of the American Association of Colleges for Teacher Education. New Orleans, LA.

Dinnel, D., & Glover, J. A. (1985). Advance organizers: Encoding manipulations. *Journal of Educational Psychology, 77*(5), 514–521.

+Dole, J. A., Niederhauser, D. S., & Haynes, M. T. (1990, November). *Learning from science text: Students' reliance on prior knowledge for familiar and unfamiliar topics.* Paper presented at the annual meeting of the National Reading Conference, Miami, FL.

*Dreher, M. J., & Gambrell, L. B. (1985). Teaching children to use a self-questioning strategy for studying expository text. *Reading Improvement, 22*, 2–7.

+Driver, R., & Easley, F. (1978). Pupils and paradigms: A review of literature related to concept development in adolescent science students. *Studies in Science Education, 5*, 61–68.

Dunston, P. J., & Ridgeway, V. G. (1991). The effect of graphic organizers on learning and remembering information from connected discourse. *Forum for Reading, 22*(1), 15–23.

=Dwyer, C. A. (1986). The effect of varied rehearsal strategies in facilitating achievement of different educational objectives as measured by verbal and visual testing modes. *Journal of Experimental Education, 54*(2), 73–84.

@Englert, C. S., Garmon, A., Mariage, T., Rozendal, M., Tarrant, K., & Urba, J. (1995). The early literacy project: Connecting across the literacy curriculum. *Learning Disability Quarterly, 18*, 253–275.

%Englert, C. S., & Mariage, T. V. (1991). Making students partners in the comprehension process: Organizing the reading "POSSE." *Learning Disability Quarterly, 14*, 123–138.

=Englert, C. S., Raphael, T. E., Anderson, L. M., Anthony, H. M., & Stevens, D. D. (1991a). Making strategies and self-talk visible: Writing instruction in regular and special education classrooms. *American Educational Research Journal, 28*, 337–372.

@Englert, C. S., Raphael, T. E., Anderson, L. M., Anthony, H. M., & Stevens, D. D. (1991b).

Making writing strategies and self-talk visible: Cognitive strategy instruction in regular and special education classrooms. *American Educational Research Journal, 28,* 337–372.

=Feuerstein, R. (1979). Cognitive modifiability in retarded adolescents: Effects of Instrumental Enrichment. *American Journal of Mental Deficiency, 83*(6), 539–550.

=Feuerstein, R., Miller, R., Hoffman, M. B., Rand, Y., Mintzker, Y., & Jensen, M. R. (1981). Cognitive modifiablility in adolescence: Cognitive structure and the effects of intervention. *Journal of Special Education, 15*(20), 269–287.

Fisher, S. (1997). *Subject matter unifiers: Synthesis of a body of research.* Unpublished manuscript. Columbia: University of South Carolina.

@Fortner, V. L. (1986). Generalization of creative productive-thinking training to LD students' written expression. *Learning Disability Quarterly, 9*(4), 274–284.

=Gadzella, B. M., Goldston, J. T., & Zimmerman, M. L. (1977). Effectiveness of exposure to study techniques on college students' perceptions. *Journal of Educational Research, 71*(1), 26–30.

%Gajria, M., & Salvia, J. (1992). The effects of summarization instruction on text comprehension of students with learning disabilities. *Exceptional Children, 58,* 508–516.

Gersten, R., & Baker, S. (2001). Teaching expressive writing to students with learning disabilities: A meta-analysis. *The Elementary School Journal, 101*(3), 251–273.

Gersten, R., Fuchs, L. S., Williams, J. P., & Baker, S. (2001). Teaching reading comprehension strategies to students with learning disabilities: A review of research. *Review of Educational Research, 71*(2), 279–320.

Gillies, D. A. (1984). Effect of advance organizers on learning medical surgical nursing content by baccalaureate nursing students. *Research in Nursing and Health, 7,* 173–180.

&Gleason, M., Carnine, D., & Boriero, D. (1990). Improving CAI effectiveness with attention to instructional design in teaching story problems to mildly handicapped students. *Journal of Special Education Technology, 10,* 129–136.

+Good, R. (1991, April). *Constructivism's many faces.* Paper presented at the Thirteenth Conference on Curriculum Theory and Classroom Practice, Dayton, OH.

+Gordon, C. (1991, December). *A case study of conceptual change.* Paper presented at the annual meeting of the National Reading Conference, Palm Springs, CA.

%Graves, A. W. (1986). Effects of direct instruction and metacomprehension training on finding main ideas. *Learning Disabilities Research, 1,* 90–100.

=Greiner, J. M., & Karoly, P. (1976). Effects of self-control training on study activity and academic performance: An analysis of self-monitoring, self-reward, and systematic-planning components. *Journal of Counseling Psychology, 23*(6), 495–502.

#Griffin, C., Simmons, D., & Kameenui, E. (1991). Investigating the effectiveness of graphic organizer instruction on the comprehension and recall of science content by students with learning disabilities. *Reading, Writing, and Learning Disabilities, 7,* 355–376.

Griffin, C. C., & Tulbert, B. L. (1995). The effect of graphic organizers on students' comprehension and recall of expository text: A review of the research and implications for practice. *Reading & Writing Quarterly: Overcoming Learning Difficulties, 11,* 73–89.

Guri-Rosenbilt, S. (1989). Effects of a tree diagram on students' comprehension of main ideas in an expository text within multiple themes. *Reading Research Quarterly, 24*(2), 236–247.

Guzzetti, B. J. (2000). Learning counter-intuitive science concepts: What have we learned from over a decade of research? *Reading & Writing Quarterly, 16*, 89–96.

+Guzzetti, B. J., Hynd, C. R., Skeels, S. A., & Williams, W. O. (1995). Improving high school physics texts: Students speak out. *Journal of Reading, 36*, 656–663.

+Guzzetti, B. J., Snyder, T. E., Glass, G. V., & Gamas, W. S. (1993). Promoting conceptual change in science: Meta-analysis of instructional interventions from reading education and science education. *Reading Research Quarterly, 28*, 116–161.

+Guzzetti, B. J., Williams, W. O., Skeels, S. A., & Wu, S. M. (1997). Influence of text structure on learning counter-intuitive physics concepts. *Journal of Research in Science Teaching, 34*, 700–719.

=Haslam, W. L., & Brown, W. F. (1986). Effectiveness of study-skills instruction for high school sophomores. *Journal of Educational Psychology, 59*(4), 223–226.

Hattie, J., Biggs, J., & Purdie, N. (1996). Effects of learning skills interventions on student learning: A meta-analysis. *Review of Educational Research, 66*(2), 99–136.

#Hawk, P. P. (1986). Using graphic organizers to increase achievement in middle school life science. *Science Education, 70*(1), 81–87.

Heinze-Fry, J. A., & Novak, J. D. (1990). Concept mapping brings long-term movement toward meaningful learning. *Science Education, 74*, 461–472.

*Helfeldt, J. P., & Lalik, R. (1976). Reciprocal student-teacher questioning. *Reading Teacher, 33*, 283–287.

$Henderson, R. W., & Landesman, E. M. (1995). Effect of thematically integrated mathematics instruction on students of Mexican descent. *Journal of Educational Research, 88*, 290–300.

+Hewson, M. G., & Hewson, P. W. (1983). Effect of instruction using students' prior knowledge and conceptual change strategies on science education. *Journal of Research in Science Teaching, 20*, 731–743.

Horton, P. B., McConney, A. A., Gallo, M., Woods, A. L., Senn, G. J., & Hamil, D. (1993). An investigation of the effects of concept mapping as an instructional tool. *Science Education, 77*(1), 95–111.

#Horton, S., & Lovitt, T. (1989). Construction and implementation of graphic organizers for academically handicapped and regular secondary students. *Academic Therapy, 24*, 625–640.

#Horton, S., Lovitt, T., & Bergerud, D. (1990). The effectiveness of graphic organizers for three classifications of secondary students in content area classes. *Journal of Learning Disabilities, 23*, 12–22.

Huang, W. (1991). *Concept mapping and chemistry achievement, integrated science process skills, logical thinking abilities, and gender at teachers' colleges in Taiwan.* Unpublished doctoral dissertation, Florida Institute of Technology, Melbourne, FL.

&Huntington, D. J. (1994). *Instruction in concrete, semi-concrete, and abstract representation as an aid to the solution of relational problems by adolescents withlearning disabilities.* Unpublished doctoral dissertation, University of Georgia, Athens.

&Hutchinson, N. L. (1993). Effects of cognitive strategy instruction on algebra problem solving of adolescents with learning disabilities. *Learning Disability Quarterly, 16*, 34–63.

+Hynd, C. R., Alvermann, D. E., & Qian, G. (1994a). *Prospective teachers' comprehension and teaching of a complex science concept.* Reading Research Report No. 4. Athens: The University of Georgia, The National Reading Research Center.

+Hynd, C. R., & Guzzetti, B. J. (1998). When knowledge contradicts intuition: Conceptual change. In C. R. Hynd (Ed.), *Learning from text across conceptual domains*. Mahwah, NJ: Erlbaum.

+Hynd, C. R., Guzzetti, B. J., Fowler, P., & Williams, W. O. (in press). *Text in physics class: The contribution of reading to learning counter-intuitive physics principles*. Research Report. Athens: The University of Georgia, The National Reading Research Center.

+Hynd, C. R., McNish, M. M., Qian, G., Keith, M., & Lay, K. (1994). *Learning counterintuitive physics concepts: The effects of text and educational environment*. Reading Research Report No. 16. Athens, GA: National Reading Research Center.

+Hynd, C. R., McWhorter, Y., Phares, V., & Suttles, W. (1994). The role of instructional variables in conceptual change in high school physics topics. *Journal of Research in Science Teaching, 31*, 933–946.

@Jaben, T. H. (1983). The effects of creativity training on learning disabled students' creative written expression. *Journal of Learning Disabilities, 16*(5), 264–265.

@Jaben, T. H. (1987). Effects of training on learning disabled students' creative written expression. *Psychological Reports, 60*, 23–26.

Jegede, O. J., Alaiyemola, F. F., & Okebukola, P. A. (1989). *The effects of a metacognitive strategy on students' anxiety and achievement in biology*. (ERIC Document Reproduction Service No. ED 313 219)

&Jitendra, A., & Hoff, K. (1996). The effects of schema-based instruction on mathematical word-problem-solving performance of students with learning disabilities. *Journal of Learning Disabilities, 29*, 422–431.

=Judd, W., McCombs, B., & Dobrovolny, J. (1979). Time management as a learning strategy for individualized instruction. In H. O'Neil & C. Spielberger (Eds.), *Cognitive and affective learning strategies* (pp. 133–175). New York: Academic Press.

Karahalios, S. M., Tonjes, M. J., & Towner, J. C. (1979). Using advance organizers to improve comprehension of content text. *Journal of Reading, 22*, 706–708.

=Kiewra, K., & Benton, S. (1987). Effects of notetaking, the instructor's notes, and higher-order practice questions on factual and higher-order learning. *Journal of Instructional Psychology, 14*(4), 186–194.

*King, A. (1989). Effects of self-questioning training on college students' comprehension of lectures. *Contemporary Educational Psychology, 14*, 366–381.

*King, A. (1990). Improving Lecture Comprehension: Effects of a metacognitive strategy. *Applied Educational Psychology, 5*, 331–346

*King, A. (1992). Comparison of self-questioning, summarizing, and notetaking-review as strategies for learning from lectures. *American Educational Research Journal, 29*, 303–325.

=Klein, J. D., & Freitage, E. (1992). Training students to utilize self-motivational strategies. *Educational Technology, 32*(3), 44–48.

%Klingner, J. K., Vaughn, S., & Schumm, J. S. (1998). Collaborative strategic reading during social studies in heterogeneous fourth-grade classrooms. *Elementary School Journal, 99*, 3–22.

=Kratzing, M. (1992). *Learning management practice in the facilitation of learning*. Unpublished doctoral dissertation, University of Queensland, Australia.

*%Labercane, G., & Battle, J. (1987). Cognitive processing strategies, self-esteem, and reading comprehension of learning disabled students. *Journal of Special Education, 11*, 167–185.

=Lange, G., Guttentag, R., & Nida, R. (1990). Relationship between study organization, retrieval organization, and general and strategy-specific memory knowledge in young children. *Journal of Experimental and Child Psychology, 49,* 126–146.

Lawton, J. T., & Fowell, N. (1978). Effects of advance organizers on preschool children's learning of math concepts. *Journal of Experimental Education, 47,* 76–81.

&Lee, J. W. (1992). *The effectiveness of a novel direct instructional approach on math word problem solving skills of elementary students with learning disabilities.* Unpublished doctoral dissertation, Ohio State University, Columbus.

Lehman, J. D., Carter, C., & Kahle, J. B. (1985). Concept mapping, vee mapping, and achievement: Results of a field study with black high school students. *Journal of Research in Science Teaching, 22,* 663–673.

+Lipson, M. (1984). Some unexpected issues in prior knowledge and comprehension. *The Reading Teacher, 37,* 760–764.

=Lodico, M., Ghatala, E., Levin, J., Pressley, M., & Bell, J. (1983). The effects of strategy-monitoring training on children's selection of effective memory strategies. *Journal of Experimental Child Psychology, 35,* 263–277.

*Lonberger, R. B. (1988). *The effects of training in a self-generated learning strategy on the prose processing abilities of fourth and sixth graders.* Unpublished doctoral dissertation, State University of New York at Buffalo.

Loncaric, L. (1986). *The effects of a concept mapping strategy program upon the acquisition of social studies concepts.* Doctoral dissertation, University of Pittsburgh. *Dissertation Abstracts International, 47,* 2006A.

*Lysynchuk, L., Pressley, M., & Vye, G. (1990). Reciprocal instruction improves reading comprehension performance in poor grade school comprehenders. *Elementary School Journal, 40,* 471–484.

@MacArthur, C. A., Graham, S., Schwartz, S. S., & Schafer, W. D. (1995). Evaluation of a writing instruction model that integrated a process approach, strategy instruction, and word processing. *Learning Disability Quarterly, 18,* 278–291.

@MacArthur, C. A., Schwartz, S. S., & Graham, S. (1991). Effects of reciprocal peer revision strategy in special education classrooms. *Learning Disabilities Research, 6*(4), 201–210.

*MacGregor, S. K. (1988). Use of self-questioning with a computer-mediated text system and measures of reading performance. *Journal of Reading Behavior, 20,* 131–148.

%Malone, L. D., & Mastropieri, M. A. (1992). Reading comprehension instruction: Summarization and self-monitoring training for students with learning disabilities. *Exceptional Children, 58,* 270–279.

*Manzo, A. V. (1969). *Improving reading comprehension through reciprocal teaching.* Unpublished doctoral dissertation, Syracuse University.

+Maria, K. (1992, December). *The development of scientific concepts: A case study.* Paper presented at the annual meeting of the National Reading Conference, San Antonio, TX.

+Maria, K. (1993, August). *The development of earth concepts.* Paper presented at the Third International Seminar on Misconceptions in Science and Mathematics, Cornell University, Ithaca, NY.

+Maria, K. (1997). A case study of conceptual change in a young child. *Elementary School Journal, 98,* 43–64.

+Maria, K., & MacGinitie, W. (1987, December). Learning from texts that refute the reader's prior knowledge. *Reading Research and Instruction, 26,* 222–238.

&Marsh, L. G. (1996). The effects of using manipulatives in teaching math problem solving to students with learning disabilities. *Learning Disabilities Research & Practice, 11*, 58–65.

+Marshall, N. (1991, December). *The effects of social pressure and personal belief on overcoming science misconceptions*. Paper presented at the annual meeting of the National Reading Conference, Miami, FL.

+Marshall, N. (1992, December). *A case study of conceptual change in preservice elementary teachers*. Paper presented at the annual meeting of the National Reading Conference, San Antonio, TX.

=Martin, D. (1984). Cognitive modification for the hearing impaired adolescent: The promise. *Exceptional Children, 51*(3), 235–242.

Martin, D. J., & Lucy, E. C. (1992, March). *The effects of concept mapping on biology achievement of field dependent students*. Paper presented at the annual meeting of the National Association for Research in Science Teaching, Boston.

&Marzola, E. S. (1987). *An arithmetic verbal problem solving model for learning disabled students*. Unpublished doctoral dissertation, Columbia University, New York.

%Mastropieri, M. A., Scruggs, T. E., Hamilton, S. L., Wolfe, S., Whedon, C., & Canevaro, A. (1996). Promoting thinking skills of students with learning disabilities: Effects on recall and comprehension of expository prose. *Exceptionality, 6*, 1–11.

=McBride, S., & Dwyer, F. (1985). Organizational chunking and postquestions in facilitating student ability to profit from visualized instruction. *Journal of Experimental Education, 53*(3), 148–155.

%McCormick, S., & Cooper, J. O. (1991). Can SW3R facilitate secondary learning disabled students' literal comprehension of expository test? Three experiments. *Reading Psychology: An International Quarterly, 12*, 239–271.

=McKeachie, W., Pintrich, P., & Lin, Y. (1985). Teaching learning strategies. *Educational Psychologist, 20*(3), 153–160.

&Montague, M. (1992). The effects of cognitive and metacognitive strategy instruction on the mathematical problem solving of middle school students with learning disabilities. *Journal of Learning Disabilities, 25*, 230–248.

&Montague, M., Applegate, B., & Marquard, K. (1993). Cognitive strategy instruction and mathematical problem-solving performance of students with learning disabilities. *Learning Disabilities Research & Practice, 8*, 223–232.

&Montague, M., & Bos, C. S. (1986). The effect of cognitive strategy training on verbal math problem solving performance of learning disabled adolescents. *Journal of Learning Disabilities, 19*, 26–33.

#Moore, D., & Readence, J. (1980). A meta-analysis of the effect of graphic organizers on learning from text. In M. L. Kamil & A. J. Moe (Eds.), *Perspectives in reading research and instruction: Twenty-ninth yearbook of the National Reading Conference* (pp. 213–217). Washington, DC: National Reading Conference.

#Moore, D., & Readence, J. (1984). A quantitative and qualitative review of graphic organizer research. *Journal of Educational Research, 78*, 11–17.

&Moore, L. J., & Carnine, D. (1989). Evaluating curriculum design in the context of active teaching. *Remedial and Special Education, 10*, 28–37.

=Morgan, M. (1985). Self-monitoring of attained subgoals in private study. *Journal of Educational Psychology, 77*(6), 623–630.

=Narrol, H., Silverman, H., & Waksman, M. (1982). Developing cognitive potential in vocational high school students. *Journal of Educational Research, 76*(2), 107–112.

%Nelson, J. R., Smith, D. J., & Dodd, J. M. (1992). The effects of a summary skills strategy to students identified as learning disabled on their comprehension of science text. *Education and Treatment of Children, 15,* 228–243.

=Nist, S., Mealey, D., Simpson, M., & Kroc, R. (1990). Measuring the affective and cognitive growth of regularly admitted and developmental studies students using the "Learning and Study Strategies Inventory" (LASSI). *Reading Research and Instruction, 30*(1), 44–49.

=Nist, S., & Simpson, M. (1989). PLAE a validated study strategy. *Journal of Reading, 33*(3), 182–186.

&Noll, R. S. (1983). *Effects of verbal cueing and a visual representation on percent problem-solving performance of remedial adults.* Unpublished doctoral dissertation, Fordham University, New York.

*Nolte, R. Y., & Singer, H. (1985). Active comprehension: Teaching a process of reading comprehension and its effects on reading achievement. *The Reading Teacher, 39,* 24–31.

&Nuzum, M. (1983). *The effects of an instructional model based on the information processing paradigm on the arithmetic problem solving performance of four learning disabled students.* Unpublished doctoral dissertation, Columbia University, New York.

=Okebukola, P. A., & Jegede, O. (1988). Cognitive preferences and learning mode as determinants of meaningful learning through concept mapping. *Science Education, 72*(4), 489–500.

Okebukola, P. A., & Jegede, O. J. (1989). Students' anxiety towards and perception of difficulty of some biological concepts under the concept-mapping heuristic. *Research in Science and Technological Education, 7,* 85–92.

*Palincsar, A. S. (1987, April). *Collaborating for collaborative learning of text comprehension.* Paper presented at the annual meeting of the American Educational Research Association, Washington, DC.

*Palincsar, A. S., & Brown, A. L. (1984). Reciprocal teaching of comprehension-fostering and comprehension-monitoring activities. *Cognition and Instruction, 2,* 117–175.

Pankratius, W. J. (1987). *Building an organized knowledge base: Concept mapping and achievement in secondary school physics.* Doctoral dissertation, Georgia State University. *Dissertation Abstracts International, 49,* 474A.

+Pfundt, H., & Duit, R. (1991). *Students' alternative frameworks and science education: Bibliography.* Kiel, Germany: Institute for Science Education.

Prater, D. L., & Terry, C. A. (1988). Effects of mapping strategies on reading comprehension and writing performance. *Reading Psychology, 9,* 101–120.

=Purdie, N. (1989). *The effect of motivation training on approaches to studying and self-concept in female secondary students.* Unpublished master's thesis, University of Western Australia.

=Rand, Y., Mintzker, Y., Miller, R., et al. (1981). The Instrumental Enrichment Program: Immediate and long-term effects. In P. Mittler (Ed.), *Frontiers of knowledge in mental retardation* (Vol. 1, pp. 141–152). Baltimore: University Park Press.

=Rand, Y., Tannenbaum, A., & Feuerstein, R. (1979). Effects of Instrumental Enrichment on the psychoeducational development of low-functioning adolescents. *Journal of Educational Psychology, 71*(6), 751–763.

Relich, J., Debus, R., & Walker, R. (1986). The mediating role of attribution and self-efficacy variables for treatment effects on achievement outcomes. *Contemporary Educational Psychology, 11,* 195–216.

@Reynolds, C. J. (1986). *The effects of instruction in cognitive revision strategies on the writing skills of secondary learning disabled students.* Doctoral dissertation, Ohio State University, 1985. *Dissertation Abstracts International, 46*(9-A), 2662.

*Ritchie, P. (1985). The effects of instruction in main idea and question generation. *Reading Canada Lecture, 3*, 139–146.

Robinson, D. H., & Schraw, G. (1994). Computational efficiency through visual argument: Do graphic organizers communicate relations and text too effectively? *Contemporary Educational Psychology, 19*, 399–415.

Rosenshine, B., Meister, C., & Chapman, S. (1996). Teaching students to generate questions: A review of the intervention studies. *Review of Educational Research, 66*(2), 181–221.

@Sawyer, R. J., Graham, S., & Harris, K. R. (1992). Direct teaching, strategy instruction, and strategy instruction with explicit self-regulation: Effects on the composition skills and self-efficacy of students with learning disabilities. *Journal of Educational Psychology, 84*(3), 340–352.

Schmid, R. F., & Telaro, G. (1990). Concept mapping as an instructional strategy for high school biology. *Journal of Educational Research, 84*, 78–85.

%Schumaker, J., Deshler, D., Alley, G., Warner, M., & Denton, P. (1984). Multipass: A learning strategy for improving reading comprehension. *Learning Disability Quarterly, 5*, 295–304.

=Schunk, D., & Cox, P. (1986). Strategy training and attributional feedback with learning disabled students. *Journal of Educational Psychology, 78*(3), 201–209.

=Schunk, D., & Gunn, T. (1986). Self-efficacy and skill development: Influence of task strategies and attributions. *Journal of Educational Research, 79*(4), 238–244.

=Scruggs, T., & Mastropieri, M. (1986a). Acquisition and transfer of learning strategies by gifted and nongifted students. *Exceptional Children, 53*(1), 153–166.

=Scruggs, T., & Mastropieri, M. (1986b). Improving the test-taking skills of behaviorally disordered and learning disabled children. *Exceptional Children, 53*(1), 63–68.

=Scruggs, T., Mastropieri, M., Levin, J., et al. (1985). Increasing content-area learning: A comparison of mnemonic and visual-spatial direct instruction. *Learning Disabilities Research, 1*(1), 18–31.

Selinger, B. M. (1995). Summarizing text: Developmental students demonstrate a successful method. *Journal of Developmental Education, 19*(2), 14–19.

=Shayer, M., & Beasley, F. (1987). Does instrumental enrichment work? *British Educational Research Journal, 13*(2), 101–119.

&Shiah, R., Mastropieri, M. A., Scruggs, T. E., & Fulk, B.J.M. (1995). The effects of computer-assisted instruction on the mathematical problem solving of students with learning disabilities. *Exceptionality, 5*, 131–161.

*Short, E. J., & Ryan, E. B. (1984). Metacognitive differences between skilled and less-skilled readers: Remediating deficits through story grammar and attribution training. *Journal of Educational Psychology, 76*, 225–235.

=Simbo, F. (1988). The effects of notetaking approaches on student achievement in secondary school geography. *Journal of Educational Research, 81*(6), 377–381.

%Simmonds, E.P.M. (1992). The effects of teacher training and implementation of two methods of improving the comprehension skills of students with learning disabilities. *Learning Disabilities Research & Practice, 7*, 194–198.

#Simmons, D. C., Griffin, C. C., & Kameenui, E. J. (1988). Effects of teacher-constructed pre- and post-graphic organizer instruction on sixth-grade science students' comprehension and recall. *Journal of Educational Research, 82*(1), 15–21.

*Simpson, P. S. (1989). *The effects of direct training in active comprehension on reading achievement, self-concepts, and reading attitudes of at-risk sixth grade students.* Unpublished doctoral dissertation, Texas Tech University.

Slock, J. A., Snyder, I. S., & Sharp, W. L. (1980). Evaluation of the effectiveness of an advance organizer in a medical microbiology course. *Journal of Medical Education, 55*, 878–880.

&Smith, E. M. (1981). *The effect of teaching sixth graders with learning difficulties a strategy for solving verbal mathematical problems.* Unpublished doctoral dissertation, University of Kansas, Lawrence.

*Smith, N. J. (1977). *The effects of training teachers to teach students at different reading ability levels to formulate three types of questions on reading comprehension and question generation ability.* Unpublished doctoral dissertation, University of Georgia.

+Snyder, T. E. (1993). *Effects of cooperative and individual learning on student misconceptions in science.* Unpublished doctoral dissertation, Arizona State University, Tempe.

+Snyder, T. E., & Sullivan, H. (1995). Cooperative and individual learning and student misconceptions in science. *Contemporary Educational Psychology, 20*, 230–235.

Spaulding, D. T. (1989). *Concept mapping and achievement in high school biology and chemistry.* Doctoral dissertation, Florida Institute of Technology. *Dissertation Abstracts International, 50*, 1619A.

Stensvold, M. S., & Wilson, J. T. (1990). Concept maps as a heuristic for science curriculum development: Toward improvement in process and product. *Journal of Research in Science Teaching, 27*, 987–1000.

+Strike, K. A., & Posner, G. J. (1992). A revisionist theory of conceptual change. In R. A. Duschl & R. J. Hamilton (Eds.), *Philosophy of science: Cognitive psychology and educational theory and practice* (pp. 147–176). Albany: State University of New York Press.

#Swafford, J., & Alvermann, D. (1989). Postsecondary research base for content reading strategies. *Journal of Reading, 33*, 164–169.

=Swing, S., & Peterson, P. (1988). Elaborative and integrative thought processes in mathematics learning. *Journal of Educational Psychology, 80*(1), 54–66.

*Taylor, B. M., & Frye, B. J. (1992). Comprehension strategy instruction in the intermediate grades. *Reading Research and Instruction, 92*, 39–48.

&Tippins, C. H. (1987). *A training program for adolescent learning disabled students in the use of mathematical word problem solving strategies.* Unpublished doctoral dissertation, University of South Carolina, Columbia.

Titsworth, B. S., & Kiewra, K. A. (2004). Spoken organizational lecture cues and student notetaking as facilitators of student learning. *Contemporary Educational Psychology, 29*(4), 447–461.

Tompkins, R. S. (1991, April). *The use of a spatial learning strategy to enhance reading comprehension of secondary subject area text.* Paper presented at the Annual Indiana Reading Conference, Indianapolis, IN.

Troyer, S. J. (1994, April). *The effects of three instructional conditions in text structure on upper elementary students' reading comprehension and writing performance.* Paper presented at the annual meeting of the American Educational Research Association, New Orleans, LA. (ERIC Document Reproduction Service No. ED 373 315)

=Van Overwalle, F., & De Metsenaere, M. (1990). The effects of attribution-based intervention and study strategy training on academic achievement in college freshmen. *British Journal of Educational Psychology, 60,* 299–311.

&Walker, D. W., & Poteet, J. A. (1989). A comparison of two methods of teaching mathematics story problem-solving with learning disabled students. *National Forum of Special Education Journal, 1,* 44–51.

&Watanabe, A. K. (1991). *The effects of a mathematical word problem solving strategy on problem solving performance by middle school students with mild disabilities.* Unpublished doctoral dissertation, University of Florida, Gainesville.

*Weiner, C. J. (1978, March). *The effect of training in questioning and student question-generation on reading achievement.* Paper presented at the annual meeting of the American Educational Research Association, Toronto. (ERIC Document Reproduction Service No. ED 158 223)

=Weinstein, C., Underwood, V., Wicker, F., & Cubberly, W. (1979). Cognitive learning strategies: Verbal and imaginal elaboration. In H. O'Neil & C. Spielberger (Eds.), *Cognitive and affective learning strategies* (pp. 45–75). New York: Academic Press.

#Weisberg, R., & Balajthy, E. (1989, May). *Effects of topic familiarity and training in generative learning activities on poor readers' comprehension of comparison/contrast expository text structure: Transfer to real-world materials.* Paper presented at the annual meeting of the National Reading Conference, New Orleans, LA. (ERIC Document Reproduction Service No. ED 305 618)

#=Weisberg, R., & Balajthy, E. (1990). Development of disabled readers' metacomprehension ability through summarization training using expository text: Results of three studies. *Journal of Reading, Writing and Learning Disabilities International, 6,* 117–136.

@Welch, M. (1992). The PLEASE strategy: A meta-cognitive learning strategy for improving the paragraph writing of students with learning disabilities. *Learning Disability Quarterly, 15*(2), 119–128.

Willerman, M., & Mac Harg, R. A. (1991). The concept map as an advance organizer. *Journal of Research in Science Teaching, 28,* 705–711.

*Williamson, R. A. (1989). *The effect of reciprocal teaching on student performance gains in third grade basal reading instruction.* Unpublished doctoral dissertation, Texas A&M University.

&Wilson, C. L., & Sindelar, P. T. (1991). Direct instruction in math word problems: Students with learning disabilities. *Exceptional Children, 57,* 512–519.

=Wilson, N. (1986). Effects of a classroom guidance unit on sixth graders' examination performance. *Journal of Humanistic Education and Development, 25*(2), 70–79.

Wise, K. C. (1996). Strategies for teaching science: What works? *The Clearing House, 69*(6), 337–338.

Witzel, B. S., Mercer, C. D., & Miller, M. D. (2003). Teaching algebra to students with learning difficulties: An investigation of an explicit instruction model. *Learning Disabilities Research & Practice, 18*(2), 121–131.

*%Wong, B.Y.L., & Jones, W. (1982). Increasing metacomprehension in learning disabled and normally achieving students through self-questioning training. *Learning Disabilities Quarterly, 5*(3), 228–240.

%Wong, B.Y.L., & Wilson, M. (1984). Investigating awareness of and teaching passage organization in learning disabled children. *Journal of Learning Disabilities, 17*(8), 477–482.

$Woodward, J., & Baxter, J. (1997). The effects of an innovative approach to mathematics on academically low-achieving students in mainstreamed settings. *Exceptional Children, 63*(3), 373–388.

$Woodward, J., Baxter, J., & Robinson, R. (1999). Rules and reasons: Decimal instruction for academically low-achieving students. *Learning Disabilities Research & Practice, 14*, 15–24.

Yan, P. X., & Jitendra, A. K. (1999). The effects of instruction in solving mathematical word problems for students with learning problems: A meta-analysis. *Journal of Special Education, 32*(4), 207–238.

&Zawaiza, T.B.W., & Gerber, M. M. (1993). Effects of explicit instruction on community college students with learning disabilities. *Learning Disability Quarterly, 16*, 64–79.

REFERENCES FOR PROVIDING ONE-TO-ONE TUTORING

#Acalin, T. (1995). *A comparison of Reading Recovery to Project READ*. Unpublished doctoral dissertation, California State University, Fullerton.

+Adams, G., & Engelmann, S. (1996). *Research on Direct Instruction: 20 years beyond DISTAR*. Seattle, WA: Educational Achievement Systems.

^Allsop, D. (1997). Using classwide peer tutoring to teach beginning algebra problem-solving skills in heterogeneous classrooms. *Remedial and Special Education, 18*(6), 367–379.

+American Federation of Teachers. (1998). *Building on the best. Learning from what works: Seven promising reading and English language arts programs*. Washington, DC: American Federation of Teachers.

*Amerikaner, M., & Summerlin, M. L. (1982). Group counseling with learning disabled children: Effects of social skills and relaxation training on self-concept and classroom behavior. *Journal of Learning Disabilities, 15*, 340–343.

Anania, J. (1981). *The effects of quality of instruction on the cognitive and affective learning of students*. Unpublished doctoral dissertation, University of Chicago.

*Argulewicz, E. N. (1982). Effects of an instructional program designed to improve attending behaviors of learning disabled students. *Journal of Learning Disabilities, 15*, 23–27.

#Arnold, L., Barnebey, N., McManus, J., et al. (1977). Prevention by specific perceptual remediation for vulnerable first-graders. *Archives of General Psychiatry, 34*, 1279–1294.

*Ayres, A. J. (1972). Improving academic scores through sensory integration. *Journal of Learning Disabilities, 5*, 338–343.

^Baker, S., Gersten, R., & Keating, T. (2000). When less may be more: A 2-year longitudinal evaluation of a volunteer tutoring program requiring minimal training. *Reading Research Quarterly, 35*(4), 494–519.

Baker, S., Gersten, R., & Lee, D-S. (2002). A synthesis of empirical research on teaching mathematics to low-achieving students. *The Elementary School Journal, 103*(1), 51–92.

*Bakker, D. J., Bouma, A., & Gardien, C. J. (1990). Hemisphere-specific treatment of dyslexia subtypes: A field experiment. *Journal of Learning Disabilities, 23*, 433–438.

*Balcerzak, J. P. (1986). *The effects of an aptitude treatment interaction approach with intermediate aged learning disabled students based on emphasizing the individual's strength in simultaneous or sequential processing in the areas of mathematics, read-*

ing and self-concept. Doctoral dissertation, State University of New York, 1985. *Dissertation Abstracts International, 47*(3A), 630.

Barley, Z., Lauer, P. A., Arens, S. A., Apthorp, H. S., Englert, K. S., Snow, D., & Akiba, M. (2002). *Helping at-risk students meet standards: A synthesis of evidence-based classroom practices*. Aurora, CO: Mid-continent Research for Education and Learning.

*Bay, M., Stayer, J. R., Bryan, T., & Hale, J. B. (1992). Science instruction for the mildly handicapped: Direct instruction versus discovery teaching. *Journal of Research in Science Teaching, 29*, 555–570.

^Bell, K., Young, R., Blair, M., & Nelson, R. (1990). Facilitating mainstreaming of students with behavioral disorders using classwide peer tutoring. *School Psychology Review, 19*(4), 564–573.

*Belmont, I., & Birch, H. G. (1974). The effect of supplemental intervention on children with low reading-readiness scores. *Journal of Special Education, 8*, 81–89.

*Berninger, V. W., Lester, K., Sohlberg, M. M., & Mateer, C. (1991). Interventions based on the multiple connections model of reading for developmental dyslexia and acquired deep dyslexia. *Archives of Clinical Neuropsychology, 6*, 375–391.

+Block, J. H., Everson, S. T., & Guskey, T. R. (1995). *School improvement programs: A handbook for educational leaders*. New York: Scholastic.

Bloom, B. S. (1984, May). The search for methods of group instruction as effective as one-to-one tutoring. *Educational Leadership*, 4–17.

*Bos, C. S., & Anders, P. L. (1990). Effects of interactive vocabulary instruction on the vocabulary learning and reading comprehension of junior-high learning disabled students. *Learning Disability Quarterly, 13*, 31–42.

*%Bos, C. S., & Anders, P. L. (1992). Using interactive teaching and learning strategies to promote text comprehension and content learning for students with learning disabilities. *International Journal of Disability, Development and Education, 39*, 225–238.

*%Bos, C. S., Anders, P. L., Filip, D., & Jaffe, L. E. (1985). Semantic feature analysis and long-term learning. *National Reading Conference Yearbook, 34*, 42–47.

*%Bos, C. S., Anders, P. L., Filip, D., & Jaffe, L. E. (1989). The effects of an interactive instructional strategy for enhancing reading comprehension and content area learning for students with learning disabilities. *Journal of Learning Disabilities, 22*, 384–390.

-Bottge, B., & Hasselbring, T. S. (1993). A comparison of two approaches for teaching complex, authentic mathematics problems to adolescents in remedial math classes. *Exceptional Children, 59*, 556–566.

*Brailsford, A., Snail, F., & Das, J. P. (1984). Strategy training and reading comprehension. *Journal of Learning Disabilities, 17*, 287–293.

*Branwhite, A. B. (1983). Boosting reading skills by direct instruction. *British Journal of Educational Psychology, 53*, 291–298.

*%Brigham, F. J., Scruggs, T. E., & Mastropieri, M. A. (1992). Teacher enthusiasm in learning disabilities classrooms: Effects on learning and behavior. *Learning Disabilities Research & Practice, 7*, 68–73.

*Brown, I. S., & Felton, R. C. (1990). Effects of instruction on beginning reading skills in children at risk for reading disability. *Reading and Writing: An Interdisciplinary Journal, 2*, 223–241.

*%Brown, R. T., & Alford, N. (1984). Ameliorating attentional deficits and concomitant academic deficiencies in learning disabled children through cognitive training. *Journal of Learning Disabilities, 17*, 20–26.

!Bryant, D. P., Vaughn, S., Linan-Thompson, S., Ugel, N., Hamff, A., & Hougen, M. (2000). Reading outcomes for students with and without reading disabilities in general education middle-school content area classes. *Learning Disability Quarterly, 23*, 238–252.

Bryant, H. D., Edwards, J. P., & LeFiles, D. C. (1995, Fall). Early intervention and one-to-one mentoring help students succeed. *ERS Spectrum*, 3–6.

*Bryant, N. D., Drabin, I. R., & Gettinger, M. (1981). Effects of varying unit size on spelling achievement in learning disabled children. *Journal of Learning Disabilities, 14*, 200–203.

*Bryant, N. D., Fayne, H. R., & Gettinger, M. (1982). Applying the mastery learning model to sight word instruction for disabled readers. *Journal of Experimental Education, 50*, 116–121.

*Bryant, S. T. (1979). *Relative effectiveness of visual-auditory versus visual-auditory-kinesthetic-tactile procedures for teaching sight words and letter sounds to young, disabled readers.* Doctoral dissertation, Columbia University. *Dissertation Abstracts International, 40*(5A), 2588–2589.

*%Bulgren, J., Schumaker, J. B., & Deshler, D. D. (1988). Effectiveness of a concept teaching routine in enhancing the performance of LD students in secondary-level mainstream classes. *Learning Disability Quarterly, 11*(1), 3–17.

Burke, A. J. (1983). *Students' potential for learning contrasted under tutorial and group approaches to instruction.* Unpublished doctoral dissertation, University of Chicago.

#Butler, S. (1991). Reading program—Remedial, integrated and innovative. *Annals of Dyslexia, 41*, 119–127.

^Cardona, C., & Artiles, A. (1998, April). *Adapting classwide instruction for student diversity in math.* Paper presented at the Annual Convention of the Council for Exceptional Children, Minneapolis, MN

*Carte, E., Morrison, D., Sublett, J., Uemura, A., & Setrakian, W. (1984). Sensory integration therapy: A trial of a specific neurodevelopmental therapy for the remediation of learning disabilities. *Developmental and Behavioral Pediatrics, 5*, 189–194.

*Cartelli, L. M. (1978). Paradigmatic language training for learning disabled children. *Journal of Learning Disabilities, 11*, 54–59.

*Carter, B. G. (1985). *For the learning disabled: Semantic mapping or SQ3R?* Doctoral dissertation, University of Nevada–Reno, 1984. *Dissertation Abstracts International, 46*(3A), 674.

#Center, Y., Wheldall, K., Freeman, L., Outhred, L., & McNaught, M. (1995). An evaluation of Reading Recovery. *Reading Research Quarterly, 30*, 240–263.

*%Chan, L.K.S. (1991). Promoting strategy generalization through self-instructional training in students with reading disabilities. *Journal of Learning Disabilities, 24*, 427–433.

*%Chan, L.K.S., & Cole, P. G. (1986). The effects of comprehension monitoring training on the reading competence of learning disabled and regular class students. *Remedial and Special Education, 7*, 33–40.

*%Chan, L.K.S., Cole, P. G., & Morris, J. N. (1990). Effects of instruction in the use of a visual-imagery strategy on the reading-comprehension competence of disabled and average readers. *Learning Disability Quarterly, 13*, 2–11.

#Chapman, J., Tunmer, W., & Prochnow, J. (1998, April). *Reading recovery in relation to language factors, reading self-perceptions, classroom behavior difficulties and literacy achievement: A longitudinal study.* Paper presented at the annual meeting of the American Educational Research Association, San Diego, CA.

*%Chase, C. H., Schmitt, R. L., Russell, G., & Tallal, P. (1984). A new chemotherapeutic investigation: Piracetam effects on dyslexia. *Annals of Dyslexia, 34*, 29–43.

^Cobb, J. B. (1998). The social contexts of tutoring: Mentoring the older at-risk student. *Reading Horizons, 39*(1), 50–75.

^Cobb, J. B. (2001). The effects of an early intervention program with preservice teachers as tutors on the reading achievement of primary grade at risk children. *Reading Horizons, 41*(3), 155–173.

&Cochran, L, Feng, H., Cartledge, G., & Hamilton, S. (1993). The effects of cross-age tutoring on the academic achievement, social behaviors, and self-perceptions of low-achieving African-American males with behavioral disorders. *Behavioral Disorders, 18*(4), 292–302.

Cohen, P. A., Kulik, J. A., & Kulik, C-L. C. (1982). Educational outcomes of tutoring: A meta-analysis of findings. *American Educational Research Journal, 19*(2), 237–248.

*%Collins, M., & Carnine, D. (1988). Evaluating the field test revision process by comparing two versions of a reasoning skills CAI program. *Journal of Learning Disabilities, 21*, 375–379.

*Commeyras, M. (1992). *Dialogical-thinking reading lessons: Promoting critical thinking among "learning-disabled" students.* Doctoral dissertation, University of Illinois, 1991. *Dissertation Abstracts International, 52*(7A), 2480–2481.

#Compton, G. (1992). *The reading connection: A leadership initiative designed to change the delivery of educational services to at-risk children.* Unpublished doctoral dissertation, Western Michigan University, Kalamazoo.

*Cornelius, P. L., & Semmel, M. I. (1982). Effects of summer instruction on reading achievement regression of learning disabled students. *Journal of Learning Disabilities, 15*, 409–413.

*Cosden, M. A., & English, J. P. (1987). The effects of grouping, self esteem, and locus of control on microcomputer performance and help seeking by mildly handicapped students. *Journal of Educational Computing Research, 3*, 443–459.

%Darch, C., & Eaves, R.C. (1986). Visual displays to increase comprehension of high school learning-disabled students. *Journal of Special Education, 20*, 309–318.

*%Darch, C., & Gersten, R. (1986). Direction-setting activities in reading comprehension: A comparison of two approaches. *Learning Disability Quarterly, 9*, 235–243.

*Darch, C., & Kameenui, E. J. (1987). Teaching LD students critical reading skills: A systematic replication. *Learning Disability Quarterly, 10*, 82–90.

*Das, J. P., Mishra, R. K., & Pool, J. E. (1995). An experiment on cognitive remediation of word-reading difficulty. *Journal of Learning Disabilities, 28*, 66–79.

*%De La Paz, S. (1995). *An analysis of the effects of dictation and planning instruction on the writing of students with learning disabilities.* Unpublished doctoral dissertation, University of Maryland, College Park.

*De La Paz, S. (in press). Strategy instruction in planning: Teaching students with learning and writing disabilities to compose persuasive and expository essays. *Learning Disability Quarterly.*

*DeBoskey, D. (1982). *An investigation of the remediation of learning disabilities based on brain-related tasks as measured by the Halstead-Reitan neuropsychological test battery.* Doctoral dissertation, University of Tennessee. *Dissertation Abstracts International, 43*(6B), 2032.

*Deno, S. L., & Chiang, B. (1979). An experimental analysis of the nature of reversal errors in children with severe learning disabilities. *Learning Disability Quarterly, 2*, 40–50.

*%Dixon, M. E. (1984). *Questioning strategy instruction participation and reading comprehension of learning disabled students*. Doctoral dissertation, University of Arizona, 1983. *Dissertation Abstracts International, 44*(11-A), 3349.

#Dorval, B., Wallach, L., & Wallach, M. (1978). Field evaluation of a tutorial reading program emphasizing phoneme identification skills. *The Reading Teacher, 31*, 784–790.

!Downhower, S. L. (1987). Effects of repeated reading on second-grade transitional readers' fluency and comprehension. *Reading Research Quarterly, 22*, 389–406 (see Note 9).

^DuPaul, G., Ervin, R., Hook, C., & McGoey, K. (1998). Peer tutoring for children with Attention Deficit Hyperactivity Disorder: Effects on classroom behavior and academic performance. *Journal of Applied Behavior Analysis, 31*(4), 579–592.

Education Commission of the States. (1999). *Direct instruction*. Denver, CO: Education Commission of the States.

&Eiserman, W. D. (1986). *The effects of three types of tutoring on the attitudes of learning disabled students and their regular class peers*. Unpublished doctoral dissertation, Brigham Young University.

&Eiserman, W. D. (1988). Three types of peer tutoring: Effects on the attitudes of students with learning disabilities and their regular class peers. *Journal of Learning Disabilities, 21*, 249–252.

&Eiserman, W. D., & Osguthorpe, R. T. (1986). The effects of three types of tutoring on the attitudes of learning disabled students and their regular class peers. In R. T. Osguthorpe, W. D. Eiserman, L. Shisler, S. G. Whited, & T. W. Scruggs, *Handicapped children as tutors. Final report* (1985–86, pp. 65–96). Document submitted to the Office of Special Education and Rehabilitative Services, U.S. Department of Education, Washington, DC. (ERIC Document Reproduction Service No. ED 280 248)

Elbaum, B., Vaughn, S., Hughes, M., & Moody, S. W. (1999). Grouping practices and reading outcomes for students with disabilities. *Exceptional Children, 65*(3), 399–416.

Elbaum, B., Vaughn, S., Hughes, M. T., & Moody, S. W. (2000). How effective are one-to-one tutoring programs in reading for elementary students at risk for reading failure? A meta-analysis of the intervention research. *Journal of Educational Psychology, 92*(4), 605–619.

+Ellis, A. K., & Fouts, J. T. (1997). *Research on educational innovations* (2nd ed.). New York: Eye on Education.

*Ellis, E. S., Deshler, D. D., & Schumaker, J. B. (1989). Teaching adolescents with learning disabilities to generate and use task-specific strategies. *Journal of Learning Disabilities, 22*, 108–130.

*Englert, C. S., Hiebert, E. H., & Stewart, S. R. (1985). Spelling unfamiliar words by an analogy strategy. *Journal of Special Education, 19*, 291–306.

*&Englert, C. S., & Mariage, T. V. (1991). Making students partners in the comprehension process: Organizing the reading "POSSE." *Learning Disability Quarterly, 14*, 123–138.

*Englert, C. S., Raphael, T. E., & Anderson, L. M. (1992). Socially mediated instruction: Improving students' knowledge about talk and writing. *Elementary School Journal, 92*, 411–449.

*Englert, C. S., Raphael, T. E., Anderson, L. M., Anthony, H. M., & Stevens, D. D. (1991). Making strategies and self talk visible: Writing instruction in regular and special education classrooms. *American Educational Research Journal, 28*, 337–372.

&Epstein, L. (1975). *The effects of intra-class peer tutoring on the vocabulary development of "learning disabled" children.* Unpublished doctoral dissertation, Indiana University.

&Epstein, L. (1978). The effects of intraclass peer tutoring on the vocabulary development of learning disabled children. *Journal of Learning Disabilities, 11,* 518–521.

#Evans, T. (1996). *I can read deze books: A qualitative comparison of the Reading Recovery program and a small-group reading intervention.* Unpublished doctoral dissertation, Auburn University, Auburn, Alabama.

^Fantuzzo, J., Davis, G., & Ginsburg, M. (1995). Effects of parent involvement in isolation or in combination with peer tutoring on student self-concept and mathematics achievement. *Journal of Educational Psychology, 87*(2), 272–281.

^Fantuzzo, J., King, J., & Heller, L. (1992). Effects of reciprocal peer tutoring on mathematics and school adjustment: A component analysis. *Journal of Educational Psychology, 84*(3), 331–339.

^Fantuzzo, J., Polite, K., & Grayson, N. (1990). An evaluation of reciprocal peer tutoring across elementary school settings. *Journal of School Psychology, 28*(4), 309–323.

%Farmer, M. E., Klein, R., & Bryson, S. E. (1992). Computer-assisted reading: Effects of whole word feedback on fluency and comprehension in readers with severe disabilities. *Remedial and Special Education, 13,* 50–60.

!Faulkner, H. J., & Levy, B. A. (1999). Fluent and nonfluent forms of transfer in reading: Words and their message. *Psychonomic Bulletin and Review, 6,* 111–116.

*Fawcett, A. J., Nicolson, R. I., & Morris, S. (1993). Computer-based spelling remediation for dyslexic children. *Journal of Computer Assisted Learning, 9,* 171–183.

*%Fiedorowicz, C.A.M. (1986). Training of component reading skills. *Annals of Dyslexia, 36,* 318–334.

%Fiedorowicz, C.A.M., & Trites, R. L. (1987). *An evaluation of the effectiveness of computer-assisted component reading subskills training.* Toronto: Queen's Printer.

*Fletcher, C. M., & Prior, M. R. (1990). The rule learning behavior of reading disabled and normal children as a function of task characteristics and instruction. *Journal of Experimental Child Psychology, 50,* 39–58.

*Fortner, V. L. (1986). Generalization of creative productive-thinking training to LD students' written expression. *Learning Disability Quarterly, 9,* 274–284.

*%Foster, K. (1983). *The influence of computer-assisted instruction and workbook on the learning of multiplication facts by learning disabled and normal students.* Doctoral sissertation, Florida State University. *Dissertation Abstracts International, 42*(9-A), 3953.

&Friedman, J. (1990). *An evaluation of the relative sensitivity to student growth in reading and spelling of standardized achievement tests and curriculum-based measures.* Unpublished doctoral dissertation, Lehigh University.

&^Fuchs, D., Fuchs, L., Mathes, P., & Simmons, D. (1997). Peer-assisted learning strategies: Making classrooms more responsive to diversity. *American Educational Research Journal, 34*(1), 174–206.

^Fuchs, L., Fuchs, D., & Karns, K. (2001). Enhancing kindergarteners' mathematical development: Effects of peer-assisted learning strategies. *Elementary School Journal, 10*(5), 495–510.

^Fuchs, L., Fuchs, D., Phillips, N., Hamlett, C., & Karns, K. (1995). Acquistion and transfer effects of classwide peer-assisted learning strategies in mathematics for students with varying learning histories. *School Psychology Review, 24*(4), 604–620.

*^Fuchs, L. S., Fuchs, D., Hamlett, C. L., Phillips, N. B., & Bentz, J. (1994). Classwide curriculum-based measurement: Helping general educators meet the challenge of student diversity. *Exceptional Children, 60*, 518–537.

*%Gajria, M., & Salvia, J. (1992). The effects of summarization instruction on text comprehension of students with learning disabilities. *Exceptional Children, 58*, 508–516.

*Gelzheiser, L. M. (1984). Generalization from categorical memory tasks to prose by learning disabled adolescents. *Journal of Educational Psychology, 76*, 1128–1138.

+Gersten, R., & Keating. T. (1987). Long-term benefits from Direct Instruction. *Educational Leadership, 44*, 28–31.

+Gersten, R., Keating, T., & Becker, W. (1988). The continued impact of the Direct Instruction model: Longitudinal studies of follow through students. *Education and Treatment of Children, 11*(4), 318–327.

Gettinger, M., Bryant, N. D., & Fayne, H. R. (1982). Designing spelling instruction for learning disabled children: An emphasis on unit size, distributed practice, and training for transfer. *Journal of Special Education, 16*, 439–448.

^Ginsburg-Block, M., & Fantuzzo, J. (1997). Reciprocal peer tutoring: An analysis of "teacher" and "student" interactions as a function of training and experience. *School Psychology Quarterly, 12*(2), 134–149.

*Gittelman, R., & Feingold, I. (1983). Children with reading disorders—I. Efficacy of reading remediation. *Journal of Child Psychology and Psychiatry, 24*, 167–191.

*Glaman, G.M.V. (1975). *Use of ability measures to predict the most appropriate method or sequence of mathematics instruction for learning disabled junior high students.* Doctoral dissertation, University of Minnesota, 1974. *Dissertation Abstracts International, 35*(11A), 7154.

*Graham, S. (1990). The role of production factors in learning disabled students' compositions. *Journal of Educational Psychology, 82*, 781–791.

*%Graham, S., & Harris, K. R. (1989). Components analysis of cognitive strategy instruction: Effects on learning disabled students' compositions and self-efficacy. *Journal of Educational Psychology, 81*, 353–361.

*#%Graves, A. W. (1986). Effects of direct instruction and metacomprehension training on finding main ideas. *Learning Disabilities Research, 1*, 90–100.

*Graybill, D., Jamison, M., & Swerdlik, M. E. (1984). Remediation of impulsivity in learning disabled children by special education resource teachers using verbal self-instruction. *Psychology in the Schools, 21*, 252–254.

^Greenwood, C. (1991a). Classwide peer tutoring: Longitudinal effects on the reading, language, and mathematics achievement of at-risk students. *Reading, Writing, and Learning Disabilities, 7*(2), 105–123.

^Greenwood, C. (1991b). Longitudinal analysis of time, engagement, and achievement in at-risk versus non-risk students. *Exceptional Children, 57*(6), 521–535.

^Greenwood, C., Arreaga-Mayer, C., Utley, C., Gavin, K., & Terry, B. (2001). Classwide peer tutoring learning management system: Application with elementary-level English language learners. *Remedial and Special Education, 22*(1), 34–37.

^Greenwood, C., Delquadri, J., & Hall, R. (1999). Longitudinal effects of classwide peer tutoring. *Journal of Educational Psychology, 81*(3), 371–383.

^Greenwood, C., Dinwiddie, G., Bailey, V., Carta, J., Dorsey, D., Kohler, F. W., et al. (1987). Field replication of classwide peer tutoring. *Journal of Applied Behavior Analysis, 20*(2), 151–160.

^Greenwood, C., Terry, B., Utley, C., Montagna, D., & Walker, D. (1993). Achievement, placement, and services: Middle school benefits of classwide peer tutoring used at the elementary school. *School Psychology Review, 22*(3), 497–516.

*%Griffin, C. C., Simmons, D. C., & Kameenui, E. J. (1991). Investigating the effectiveness of graphic organizer instruction on the comprehension and recall of science content by students with learning disabilities. *Reading, Writing and Learning Disabilities, 7,* 355–376.

*%Guyer, B. P., & Sabatino, D. (1989). The effectiveness of a multisensory alphabetic phonetic approach with college students who are learning disabled. *Journal of Learning Disabilities, 22,* 430–434.

#Hagin, R., Silver, A., & Beecher, R. (1978). TEACH: Learning tasks for the prevention of learning disabilities. *Journal of Learning Disabilities, 11,* 54–57.

^Harris, R. E., Marchand-Martella, N., & Martella, R. C. (2000). Effects of a peer-delivered corrective reading program. *Journal of Behavioral Education, 10*(1), 21–36.

#Hedrick, D. (1996). *An administrative review of an early reading intervention.* Unpublished doctoral dissertation, University of North Carolina at Greensboro.

^Heller, L., & Fantuzzo, J. (1993). Reciprocal peer tutoring and parent partnership: Does parent involvement make a difference? *School Psychology Review, 22*(3), 517–534.

*Helper, M. M., Farber, E. D., & Feldgaier, S. (1982). Alternative thinking and classroom behavior of learning impaired children. *Psychological Reports, 50,* 415–420.

^Henderson, R., & Landesman, E. (1992). *Mathematics and middle school students of Mexican descent: The effects of thematically integrated instruction.* Research Report No. 5. Washington, DC: National Center for Research on Cultural Diversity and Second Language Learning, Center for Applied Linguistics.

=Henderson, R. W., & Landesman, E. M. (1995). Effect of thematically integrated mathematics instruction on students of Mexican descent. *Journal of Educational Research, 88,* 290–300.

!Herman, P. A. (1985). The effects of repeated readings on reading rate, speech pauses, and word recognition accuracy. *Reading Research Quarterly, 20,* 553–565.

*Hine, M. S., Goldman, S. R., & Cosden, M. A. (1990). Error monitoring by learning handicapped students engaged in collaborative microcomputer-based writing. *Journal of Special Education, 23,* 407–422.

*%Hollingsworth, M., & Woodward, J. (1993). Integrated learning: Explicit strategies and their role in problem-solving instruction for students with learning disabilities. *Exceptional Children, 59,* 444–455.

!Homan, S. P., Klesius, J. P., & Hite, C. (1993). Effects of repeated readings and nonrepetitive strategies on students' fluency and comprehension. *Journal of Educational Research, 87,* 94–99.

^Hooper, S., & Hannafin, M. (1988). *Cooperative learning at the computer: Ability based strategies for implementation.* Paper presented at the annual meeting of the Association for Educational Communications and Technology, New Orleans, LA. (ERIC Document Reproduction Service No. ED 295647)

*Howell, R., Sidorenko, E., & Jurica, J. (1987). The effects of computer use on the acquisition of multiplication facts by a student with learning disabilities. *Journal of Learning Disabilities, 20,* 336–341.

*Humphries, T. W., Wright, M., Snider, L., & McDougall, B. (1992). A comparison of the effectiveness of sensory integrative therapy and perceptual-motor training in treating children with learning disabilities. *Developmental and Behavioral Pediatrics, 13*, 31–40.

*Hurford, D. P. (1990). Training phonemic segmentation ability with a phonemic discrimination intervention in second- and third-grade children with reading disabilities. *Journal of Learning Disabilities, 23*, 564–569.

*Hurford, D. P., & Sanders, R. E. (1990). Assessment and remediation of a phonemic discrimination deficit in reading disabled second and fourth graders. *Journal of Experimental Child Psychology, 50*, 396–415.

%Hutchinson, N. L. (1993). Effects of cognitive strategy instruction on algebra problem solving of adolescents with learning disabilities. *Learning Disability Quarterly, 16*, 6–18.

*%Hutchinson, N. L., Freeman, J. G., Downey, K. H., & Kilbreath, L. (1992). Development and evaluation of an instructional module to promote career maturity for youth with learning disabilities. *Canadian Journal of Counseling, 26*, 290–299.

&Idol, L. (1987). Group story mapping: A comprehension strategy for both skilled and unskilled readers. *Journal of Learning Disabilities, 20*(4), 196–205.

Iversen, S., & Tunmer, W. (1993). Phonological processing skills and the Reading Recovery program. *Journal of Educational Psychology, 85*, 112–126.

*Jaben, T. H. (1983). The effects of creativity training on learning disabled students' creative written expression. *Journal of Learning Disabilities, 16*, 264–265.

*Jaben, T. H. (1985). Effect of instruction for creativity on learning disabled students' drawings. *Perceptual and Motor Skills, 61*, 895–898.

*Jaben, T. H. (1986). Impact of instruction on behavior disordered and learning disabled students' creative behavior. *Psychology in the Schools, 23*, 401–405.

*Jaben, T. H. (1987). Effects of training on learning disabled students' creative written expression. *Psychological Reports, 60*, 23–26.

*Jaben, T. H., Treffinger, D. J., Whelan, R. J., Hudson, F. G., Stainback, S. B., & Stainback, W. (1982). Impact of instruction on learning disabled students' creative thinking. *Psychology in the Schools, 19*, 371–373.

&^Jenkins, J. R., Jewell, M., Leicester, N., Jenkins, L., & Troutner, N. M. (1991). Development of a school building model for educating students with handicaps and at-risk students in general education classrooms. *Journal of Learning Disabilities, 24*(5), 311–320.

&Jenkins, J. R., Jewell, M., O'Connor, R. W., Jenkins, L. M., & Troutner, N. M. (1994). Accommodations for individual differences without classroom ability groups: An experiment in school reconstructuring. *Exceptional Children, 60*, 344–358.

^Johnson, J. (1987). *Adaptation of curriculum, instructional methods, and material component: Instructional aide program. Final evaluation report.* Columbus, OH: Columbus Public Schools.

*%Johnson, L., Graham, S., & Harris, K. R. (1998). *The effects of goal setting and self-instructions on learning a reading comprehension strategy: A study with students with learning disabilities.* Unpublished manuscript.

*%Jones, K. M., Torgesen, J. K., & Sexton, M. A. (1987). Using computer-guided practice to increase decoding fluency in learning disabled children: A study using the Hint and Hunt I program. *Journal of Learning Disabilities, 20*, 122–128.

^Juel, C. (1991). Cross-age tutoring between student athletes and at-risk children. *Reading Teacher, 45*(3), 178–186.

#Juel, C. (1996). What makes literacy tutoring effective? *Reading Research Quarterly, 31,* 268–289.

*%Kane, B. J., & Alley, G. R. (1980). A peer-tutored, instructional management program in computational mathematics for incarcerated learning-disabled juvenile delinquents. *Journal of Learning Disabilities, 13,* 148–151.

*Kendall, P. C., & Braswell, L. (1982). Cognitive-behavioral self-control therapy for children: A components analysis. *Journal of Consulting and Clinical Psychology, 50,* 672–689.

*%Kennedy, K. M., & Backman, J. (1993). Effectiveness of the Lindamood Auditory Discrimination In-Depth Program with students with learning disabilities. *Learning Disabilities Research & Practice, 8,* 253–259.

*%Kershner, J. R., Cummings, R. L., Clarke, K. A., Hadfield, A. J., & Kershner, B. A. (1990). Two-year evaluation of the Tomatis Listening Training Program with learning disabled children. *Learning Disability Quarterly, 13,* 43–53.

Kerstholt, M. T., Van Bon, W.H.J., & Schreuder, R. (1994). Training in phonemic segmentation: The effects of visual support. *Reading and Writing: An Interdisciplinary Journal, 6,* 361–385.

*Kim, Y. O. (1992). *The effect of teaching a test-taking strategy to high school students with learning disabilities.* Doctoral dissertation, University of West Virginia, 1991. *Dissertation Abstracts International, 53*(1A), 121.

*King-Sears, M. E., Mercer, C. D., & Sindelar, P. T. (1992). Toward independence with keyword mnemonics: A strategy for science vocabulary instruction. *Remedial and Special Education, 13,* 22–33.

^Klinger, J., & Vaughn, S. (2000). The helping behaviors of fifth graders while using collaborative strategic reading during ESL content classes. *TESOL Quarterly, 34*(1), 69–98.

*%Klingner, J. K., & Vaughn, S. (1996). Reciprocal teaching of reading comprehension strategies for students with learning disabilities who use English as a second language. *Elementary School Journal, 96,* 275–293.

#^Knapp, N. F., & Winsor, A. P. (1998). A reading apprenticeship for delayed primary readers. *Reading Research and Instruction, 38*(1), 13–29.

^Koheler, F., & Greenwood, C. (1990). Effects of collateral peer supportive behaviors within the classwide peer tutoring program. *Journal of Applied Behavior Analysis, 23*(3), 307–322.

+Kuder, J. (1990). Effectiveness of the DISTAR Reading Program for children with learning disabilities. *Journal of Learning Disabilities, 23*(1), 69–71.

*Kunka, A.S.K. (1984). *A modality-instruction interaction study of elementary learning disabled students using two types of electronic learning aids for math instruction.* Doctoral dissertation, University of Pittsburgh, 1983. *Dissertation Abstracts International, 45*(2A), 387.

#Lafave, C. (1995). *Impact of Reading Recovery on phonemic awareness.* Unpublished doctoral dissertation, University of Toledo, Toledo, Spain.

*Lenkowsky, R. S., Barwosky, E. I., Dayboch, M., Puccio, L., & Lenkowsky, B. E. (1987). Effects of bibliotherapy on the self-concept of learning disabled, emotionally handicapped adolescents in a classroom setting. *Psychological Reports, 61,* 483–488.

*%Leong, C. K., Simmons, D. R., & Izatt-Gambell, M. A. (1990). The effect of systematic training in elaboration on word meaning and prose comprehension in poor readers. *Annals of Dyslexia, 40,* 192–215.

*%Lerner, C. H. (1978). *The comparative effectiveness of a language experience approach and a basal-type approach to remedial reading instruction for severely disabled readers in a senior high school.* Doctoral dissertation, Temple University. *Dissertation Abstracts International, 39*(2-A), 779–780.

!Levy, B. A., Abello, B., & Lysynchuk, L. (1997). Transfer from word training to reading in context: Gains in reading fluency and comprehension. *Learning Disability Quarterly, 20,* 173–188.

*Lloyd, J., Cullinan, D., Hems, E. D., & Epstein, M. H. (1980). Direct instruction: Effects on oral and written language comprehension. *Learning Disability Quarterly, 3,* 70–76.

*Lorenz, L., & Vockell, E. (1979). Using the neurological impress method with learning disabled readers. *Journal of Learning Disabilities, 12,* 420–422.

*%Losh, M. A. (1991). *The effect of the strategies intervention model on the academic achievement of junior high learning-disabled students.* Doctoral dissertation, University of Nebraska. *Dissertation Abstracts International, 52*(3-A), 880.

*Lovett, M. W., Borden, S. L., DeLuca, T., Lacerenza, L., Benson, N. J., & Brackstone, D. (1994). Treating the core deficits of developmental dyslexia: Evidence of transfer of learning after phonologically- and strategy-based reading training programs. *Developmental Psychology, 30,* 805–822.

*Lovett, M. W., Ransby, M. J., & Barron, R. W. (1988). Treatment, subtype, and word type effects on dyslexic children's response to remediation. *Brain and Language, 34,* 328–349.

*Lovett, M. W., Ransby, M. J., Hardwick, N., Johns, M. S., & Donaldson, S. A. (1989). Can dyslexia be treated? Treatment-specific and generalized treatment effects in dyslexic children's response to remediation. *Brain and Language, 37,* 90–121.

*Lovett, M. W., & Steinbach, K. A. (in press). The effectiveness of remedial programs for reading disabled children of different ages: Is there decreased benefit for older children? *Learning Disability Quarterly.*

*Lovett, M. W., Warren-Chaplin, P. M., Ransby, M. J., & Borden, S. L. (1990). Training the word recognition skills of reading disabled children: Treatment and transfer effects. *Journal of Educational Psychology, 82,* 769–780.

+Lovitt, T., Rudsit, J., Jenkins, J., Pious, C., & Benedetti, D. (1986). Adapting science materials for regular and learning disabled seventh graders. *Remedial and Special Education, 7,* 31–39.

*Lucangeli, D., Galderisi, D., & Comoldi, C. (1995). Specific and general transfer effects following metamemory training. *Learning Disabilities Research & Practice, 10,* 11–21.

*Lundberg, I., & Olofsson, A. (1993). Can computer speech support reading comprehension? *Computers in Human Behavior, 9,* 283–293.

*MacArthur, C. A., & Haynes, J. B. (1995). Student assistant for learning from text (SALT): A hypermedia reading aid. *Journal of Learning Disabilities, 28,* 150–159.

*MacArthur, C. A., Haynes, J. B., Malouf, D. B., Harris, K., & Owings, M. (1990). Computer assisted instruction with learning disabled students: Achievement, engagement, and other factors that influence achievement. *Journal of Educational Computing Research, 6,* 311–328.

*%MacArthur, C. A., Schwartz, S. S., & Graham, S. (1991). Effects of a reciprocal peer revision strategy in special education classrooms. *Learning Disabilities Research, 6*(4), 201–210.

&Madden, N. A. (1986). *Reading instruction in the mainstream: A cooperative learning approach.* Report No. 5. Center for Research on Elementary and Middle Schools, Baltimore, MD. (ERIC Document Reproduction Service No. ED 297 261)

^Madrid, D., Terry, B., Greenwood, C., Whaley, M., & Webber, N. (1998). Active vs. passive peer tutoring: Teaching spelling to at-risk students. *Journal of Research and Development in Education, 31*(3), 236–244.

^Maheady, L., & Harper, G. F. (1987). A class-wide peer tutoring program to improve the spelling test performance of low-income, third and fourth-grade students. *Education and Treatment of Children, 10*(2), 120–133.

^Maheady, L., Sacca, M., & Harper, G. (1987). Classwide student tutoring teams: The effects of peer-mediated instruction on the academic performance of secondary mainstreamed students. *Journal of Special Education, 21*(3), 107–121.

^Maheady, L., Sacca, M., & Harper, G. (1988). Classwide peer tutoring with mildly handicapped high school students. *Exceptional Children, 55*(1), 52–59.

*Manning, B. H. (1984). Problem-solving instruction as an oral comprehension aid for reading disabled third graders. *Journal of Learning Disabilities, 17*, 457–461.

#^Mantzicopoulos, P., Morrison, D., Stone, E., & Setrakian, W. (1992). Use of the SEARCH/TEACH tutoring approach with middle-class students at risk for reading failure. *The Elementary School Journal, 92*(5), 573–586.

*Maron, L. R. (1993). *A comparison study of the effects of explicit versus implicit training of test-taking skills for learning-disabled fourth-grade students.* Doctoral dissertation, University of Wisconsin–Madison, 1992. *Dissertation Abstracts International, 53*(9B), 4613.

*Marsh, L. G., & Cooke, N. L. (1996). The effects of using manipulatives in teaching math problem solving to students with learning disabilities. *Learning Disabilities Research & Practice, 11,* 58–65.

^Mathes, P., & Babyak, A. (2001). The effects of peer-assisted literacy strategies for first-grade readers with and without additional mini-skills lessons. *Learning Disabilities Research & Practice, 16*(1), 28–44.

^Mathes, P., & Fuchs, L. (1994). The efficacy of peer tutoring in reading for students with mild disabilities: A best-evidence synthesis. *School Psychology Review, 23*(1), 59–71.

&Mathes, P. G. (1992). *Peer-mediated reading instruction in special education resource settings.* Unpublished doctoral dissertation, Vanderbilt University.

*&!Mathes, P. G., & Fuchs, L. S. (1993). Peer-mediated reading instruction in special education resource rooms. *Learning Disabilities Research & Practice, 8,* 233–243.

^Matz, K. A. (1989, October). *Strategic word attack: Acquired contextual strategies in young readers.* Paper presented at the annual meeting of the Northern Rocky Mountain Educational Research Association, Jackson, WY.

#^McCarthy, P., Newby, R. F., & Recht, D. R. (1995). Results of an early intervention program for first grade children at risk for reading disability. *Reading Research and Instruction, 34*(4), 273–294.

*%McCollum, P. S., & Anderson, R. P. (1974). Group counseling with reading-disabled children. *Journal of Counseling Psychology, 21*(2), 150–155.

#McGrady, D. (1984). *The effect of programmed tutoring upon the reading comprehension for fourth-grade students enrolled in a Chapter 1 reading program.* Paper presented at the annual meeting of the Association of Educational Communications and Technology, Dallas, TX. (ERIC Document Reproduction Service No. ED 243 430)

^Meier, J. D., & Invernizzi, M. (2001). Book buddies in the Bronx: Testing model for America Reads. *Journal of Education for Students Placed At Risk, 6*(4), 319–333.

!Mercer, C. D., Campbell, K. U., Miller, M. D., Mercer, K. D., & Lane, H. B. (2000). Effects of a reading fluency intervention for middle schoolers with specific learning disabilities. *Learning Disabilities Research & Practice, 15*, 179–189.

*%Meyer, L. A. (1982). The relative effects of word-analysis and word supply correction procedures with poor readers during word-attack training. *Reading Research Quarterly, 17*(4), 544–555.

+Meyer, L. A. (1984). Long-term academic effects of the Direct Instruction Project Follow Through. *Elementary School Journal, 84*, 380–394.

*Miller, S. P., & Mercer, C. D. (1993). Using data to learn about concrete-semiconcrete abstract instruction for students with math disabilities. *Learning Disabilities Research & Practice, 8*, 89–96.

*%Montague, M., Applegate, B., & Marquard, K. (1993). Cognitive strategy instruction and mathematical problem-solving performance of students with learning disabilities. *Learning Disabilities Research & Practice, 8*(4), 223–232.

&Moore, A. R. (1993). *Effects of strategy training and classwide peer tutoring on the reading comprehension of students with learning disabilities.* Unpublished doctoral dissertation, Indiana University.

*Moore, L., Carnine, D., Stepnoski, M., & Woodward, J. (1987). Research on the efficiency of low-cost networking. *Learning Disability Quarterly, 20*, 574–576.

*%Morgan, A. V. (1991). *A study of the effects of attribution retraining and cognitive self-instruction upon the academic and attentional skills, cognitive-behavioral trends of elementary-age children served in self-contained learning disability programs.* Doctoral dissertation, College of William and Mary, 1990. *Dissertation Abstracts International, 51*(8-B), 4035.

#Morris, D., Shaw, B., & Perney, J. (1990). Helping low readers in Grades 2 and 3: An after-school volunteer tutoring program. *The Elementary School Journal, 91*, 133–150.

^Morris, D., Tyner, B., & Perney, J. (2000). Early steps: Replicating the effects of a first-grade reading intervention program. *Journal of Educational Psychology, 92*(4), 681–693.

^Mortsweet, S., Utley, C., Walker, D., Dawson, H., Delquadri, J., Reddy, S., et al. (1999). Classwide peer tutoring: Teaching students with mild mental retardation in inclusive classrooms. *Exceptional Children, 65*(6), 524–536.

*Naylor, J. O., & Pumfrey, P. D. (1983). The alleviation of psycholinguistic deficits and some effects on the reading attainments of poor readers: A sequel. *Journal of Research in Reading, 6*, 129–153.

*Nelson, S. L. (1985). *Modifying impulsivity in learning disabled boys on matching, maze, and WISC-R performance scales.* Doctoral dissertation, University of Southern California, 1984. *Dissertation Abstracts International, 45*(7B), 2316–2317.

#Nielson, B. (1991). *Effects of parent and volunteer tutoring on reading achievement of third grade at-risk students.* Unpublished doctoral dissertation, Brigham Young University, Provo, UT.

*%O'Connor, P. D., Stuck, G. B., & Wyne, M. D. (1979). Effects of a short-term intervention resource-room program on task orientation and achievement. *Journal of Special Education, 13*(4), 375–385.

*%Olofsson, A. (1992). Synthetic speech and computer-aided reading for reading-disabled children. *Reading and Writing, 4*(2), 165–178.

*%Olsen, J. L., Wong, B.Y.L., & Marx, R. W. (1983). Linguistic and metacognitive aspects of normally achieving and learning disabled children's communication process. *Learning Disability Quarterly, 6*(3), 289–304.

*Olson, R. K., & Wise, B. W. (1992). Reading on the computer with orthographic and speech feedback. *Reading and Writing: An Interdisciplinary Journal, 4*, 107–144.

*Omizo, M. M., Cubberly, W. E., & Omizo, S. A. (1985). The effects of rational-emotive education groups on self-concept and locus of control among learning disabled children. *Exceptional Child, 32*, 13–19.

*Omizo, M. M., Lo, F. O., & Williams, R. E. (1986). Rational-emotive education, self-concept, and locus of control among learning-disabled students. *Journal of Humanistic Education, 25*, 58–69.

*Omizo, M. M., & Williams, R. E. (1982). Biofeedback-induced relaxation training as an alternative for the elementary school learning-disabled child. *Biofeedback and Self-Regulation, 7*, 139–148.

&Osguthorpe, R. T., Eiserman, W. D., Shisler, L., Top, B. L., & Scruggs, T. E. (1984a). Handicapped students tutoring younger nonhandicapped students in reading. In R. T. Osguthorpe, W. Eiserman, L. Shisler, B. L. Top, & T. E. Scruggs, *Handicapped children as tutors*. Final report (1983–1984, pp. 97–106). Document submitted to the Office of Special Education and Rehabilitative Services, U.S. Department of Education, Washington, DC. (ERIC Document Reproduction Service No. ED 255 018)

&Osguthorpe, R. T., Eiserman, W. D., Shisler, L., Top, B. L., & Scruggs, T. E. (1984b). Learning disabled and behaviorally disordered students as cross-age tutors. In R. T. Osguthorpe, W. Eiserman, L. Shisler, B. L. Top, & T. E. Scruggs, *Handicapped children as tutors*. Final report (1983–1984, pp. 136–154). Document submitted to the Office of Special Education and Rehabilitative Services, U.S. Department of Education, Washington, DC. (ERIC Document Reproduction Service No. ED 255 018)

!O'Shea, L. J., Sindelar, P. T., & O'Shea, D. J. (1985). The effects of repeated reading and attentional cues on reading fluency and comprehension. *Journal of Reading Behavior, 17*, 129–141.

!O'Shea, L. J., Sindelar, P. T., & O'Shea, D. J. (1987). The effects of repeated reading and attentional cues on reading fluency and comprehension of learning disabled readers. *Learning Disabilities Research, 2*, 103–109.

O'Sullivan, R. G., Puryear, P., & Oliver, D. (1994, April). *Evaluating the use of learning styles instruction to promote academic success among at-risk 9th graders.* Paper presented at the annual meeting of the American Educational Research Association, New Orleans, LA.

*Pany, D., & Jenkins, J. R. (1978). Learning word meanings: A comparison of instructional procedures. *Learning Disability Quarterly, 1*, 21–32.

*Pany, D., Jenkins, J. R., & Schreck, J. (1982). Vocabulary instruction: Effects on word knowledge and reading comprehension. *Learning Disability Quarterly, 5*, 202–215.

^Pigott, H., Fantuzzo, J., & Clement, P. (1986). The effects of reciprocal peer tutoring and group contingencies on the academic performance of elementary school children. *Journal of Applied Behavior Analysis, 19*(1), 93–98.

*Pihl, R. O., Parkes, M., Drake, H., & Vrana, F. (1980). The intervention of a modulator with learning disabled children. *Journal of Clinical Psychology, 36*, 972–976.

#Pinnell, G. (1988). *Success of children at risk in a program that combines writing and reading.* Washington, DC: U.S. Department of Education, Office of Educational Research and Improvement. (ERIC Document Reproduction Service No. ED 292 061)

#Pinnell, G., Lyons, C., DeFord, D., et al. (1994). Comparing instructional models for the literacy education of high-risk first graders. *Reading Research Quarterly, 29*, 9–39.

*Porinchak, P. M. (1984). *Computer-assisted instruction in secondary school reading: Interaction of cognitive and affective factors.* Doctoral dissertation, Hofstra University, 1983. *Dissertation Abstracts International, 45*(2A), 478.

^Pringle, B., Anderson, L., Rubenstein, M., & Russo, A. (1993). *Peer tutoring and mentoring services for disadvantaged secondary school students: An evaluation of the Secondary Schools Basic Skills Demonstration Assistance Program.* Washington, DC: ERIC.

*%Prior, M., Frye, S., & Fletcher, C. (1987). Remediation for subgroups of retarded readers using a modified oral spelling procedure. *Developmental Medicine and Child Neurology, 29*, 64–71.

#Ramaswami, S. (1994). *The differential impact of Reading Recovery on achievement of first graders in the Newark School District.* Newark, NJ: Newark Board of Education, Office of Planning, Evaluation and Testing. (ERIC Document Reproduction Service No. ED 374 180)

^Ramey, M. (1990). *Compensatory education sustained gains from Spring 1985 to Spring 1987* (Reports no. 90-4). Seattle, WA: Seattle Public Schools.

#^Ramey, M. (1991). *Compensatory education sustained gains from Spring 1988 to Spring 1990.* Seattle, WA: Seattle Public Schools. (ERIC Document Reproduction Service No. ED 338 774)

!Rasinski, T., Padak, N., Linek, W., & Sturtevant, E. (1994). Effects of fluency development on urban second-grade readers. *Journal of Educational Research, 87*, 158–165.

*Ratekin, N. (1979). Reading achievement of disabled learners. *Exceptional Children, 45*, 454–458.

*Reid, R., & Harris, K. R. (1993). Self-monitoring of attention versus self-monitoring of performance: Effects on attention and academic performance. *Exceptional Children, 60*, 29–40.

*%Reilly, J. P. (1991). *Effects of a cognitive-behavioral program designed to increase the reading comprehension skills of learning-disabled students.* Doctoral dissertation, College of William and Mary. *Dissertation Abstracts International, 52*(3-A), 865.

^Repman, J. (1993). Collaborative, computer-based learning: Cognitive and affective outcomes. *Journal of Educational Computing Research, 9*(2), 149–163.

*%Reynolds, C. J. (1986). *The effects of instruction in cognitive revision strategies on the writing skills of secondary learning disabled students.* Doctoral dissertation, Ohio State University, 1985. *Dissertation Abstracts International, 46*(9-A), 2662.

^Richardson, G. D., Abrams, G. J., Byer, J. L., & DeVaney, T. W. (2000, November). *UWA secondary education tutoring project for the West Alabama Learning Coalition.* Paper presented at the annual meeting of the Mid-South Educational Research Association, Bowling Green, KY.

^Riley, E. (2000). *The effect of metacognition and strategic training embedded in cooperative settings on mathematics performance of at-risk students.* Doctoral dissertation, Walden University. (UMI No. 9979207)

^Rimm-Kaufman, S. E., Kagan, J., & Byers, H. (1999). The effectiveness of adult volunteer tutoring on reading among "at risk" first grade children. *Reading Research and Instruction, 38*(2), 143–152.

*Ross, P. A., & Braden, J. P. (1991). The effects of token reinforcement versus cognitive behavior modification on learning-disabled students' math skills. *Psychology in the Schools, 28*, 247–256.

*%Rudel, R. G., & Helfgott, E. (1984). Effect of piracetam on verbal memory of dyslexic boys. *American Academy of Child Psychiatry, 23,* 695–699.

*Ruhl, K. L., Hughes, C. A., & Gajar, A. H. (1990). Efficacy of the pause procedure for enhancing learning disabled and nondisabled college students' long- and short-term recall of facts presented through lecture. *Learning Disability Quarterly, 13,* 55–64.

#Saginaw Public Schools, Department of Evaluation Services. (1992). *Compensatory education product evaluation: Reading Recovery Program 1991–92.* Saginaw: Author. (ERIC Document Reproduction Service No. ED 350 587).

*Sawyer, R. J., Graham, S., & Harris, K. R. (1992). Direct teaching, strategy instruction and strategy instruction with explicit self-regulation: Effects on the composition skills and self-efficacy of students with learning disabilities. *Journal of Educational Psychology, 84,* 340–352.

*Scanlon, D., Deshler, D. D., & Schumaker, J. B. (1996). Can a strategy be taught and learned in secondary inclusive classrooms? *Learning Disabilities Research & Practice, 11,* 41–57.

*Scheerer-Neumann, G. (1981). The utilization of intraword structure in poor readers: Experimental evidence and a training program. *Psychological Research, 43,* 155–178.

*Schulte, A. C., Osborne, S. S., & McKinney, J. D. (1991). Academic outcomes for students with learning disabilities in consultation and resource programs. *Exceptional Children, 57,* 162–172.

*%Schunk, D. H. (1985). Participation in goal-setting: Effects on self-efficacy and skills of learning-disabled children. *Journal of Special Education, 19,* 305–317.

*%Schunk, D. H., & Cox, P. D. (1986). Strategy training and attributional feedback with learning-disabled students. *Journal of Educational Psychology, 78,* 201–209.

*Scruggs, T. E., & Mastropieri, M. A. (1989). Mnemonic instruction of LD students: A field-based evaluation. *Learning Disability Quarterly, 12,* 119–125.

*Scruggs, T. E., & Mastropieri, M. A. (1992). Classroom applications of mnemonic instruction: Acquisition, maintenance, and generalization. *Exceptional Children, 58*(3), 219–229.

*Scruggs, T. E., Mastropieri, M. A., & Tolfa-Veit, D. (1986). The effects of coaching on the standardized test performance of learning disabled and behaviorally disordered students. *Remedial and Special Education, 7*(5), 37–41.

&Scruggs, T. E., & Osguthorpe, R. T. (1985, April). *Tutoring interventions within special education settings: A comparison of cross-age and peer tutoring.* Paper presented at the 63rd annual convention of The Council for Exceptional Children, Anaheim, CA. (ERIC Document Reproduction Service No. ED 258 419)

&Scruggs, T. E., & Osguthorpe, R. T. (1986). Tutoring interventions within special education settings: A comparison of cross-age and peer tutoring. *Psychology in the Schools, 23,* 187–193.

*Scruggs, T. E., & Tolfa, D. (1985). Improving the test-taking skills of learning-disabled students. *Perceptual and Motor Skills, 60,* 847–850.

*Sheare, J. B. (1978). The impact of resource programs upon the self-concept and peer acceptance of learning disabled children. *Psychology in the Schools, 15,* 406–412.

&Shisler, L., Top, B. L., & Osguthorpe, R. T. (1986). Behaviorally disordered students as reverse-role tutors: Increasing social acceptance and reading skills. *B.C. Journal of Special Education, 10,* 101–119.

&Shoulders, H.M.W. (1991). *The effects of rewards used on mildly handicapped students during peer teaching: Implications for instructional leadership.* Unpublished doctoral dissertation, University of Alabama, Tuscaloosa.

^Sideridis, G., Utley, C., Greenwood, C., Delquadri, J., Dawson, H., Palmer, P., et al. (1997). Classwide peer tutoring: Effects on the spelling performance and social interactions of students with mild disabilities and their typical peers in an integrated instructional setting. *Journal of Behavioral Education, 7*(4), 435–462.

*Simmonds, E.P.M. (1990). The effectiveness of two methods for teaching a constraint-seeking questioning strategy to students with learning disabilities. *Journal of Learning Disabilities, 23,* 229–232.

*Simmonds, E.P.M. (1992). The effects of teacher training and implementation of two methods for improving the comprehension skills of students with learning disabilities. *Learning Disabilities Research & Practice, 7,* 194–198.

&^!Simmons, D., Fuchs, D., Fuchs, L., Mathes, P., & Hodge, J. (1995). Effects of explicit teaching and peer tutoring on the reading achievement of learning-disabled and low-performing students in regular classrooms. *Elementary School Journal, 95*(5), 387–408.

^!Simmons, D. C., Fuchs, D., Fuchs, L. S., Hodge, J. P., & Mathes, P. G. (1994). Importance of instructional complexity and role reciprocity to classwide peer tutoring. *Learning Disabilities Research & Practice, 9,* 203–212.

*Simpson, S. B., Swanson, J. M., & Kunkel, K. (1992). The impact of an intensive multisensory reading program on a population of learning-disabled delinquents. *Annals of Dyslexia, 42,* 54–66.

*Sinatra, R. C., Stahl-Gemake, J., & Berg, D. N. (1984). Improving reading comprehension of disabled readers through semantic mapping. *The Reading Teacher, 38,* 22–29.

&Sindelar, P. T. (1977). *The ejects of hypothesis/test and fluency training, cross-aged tutoring and small-group instruction on reading skills.* Unpublished doctoral dissertation, University of Minnesota, Minneapolis.

&Sindelar, P. T. (1982). The effects of cross-age tutoring on the comprehension skills of remedial reading students. *The Journal of Special Education, 16,* 199–206.

*Sindelar, P. T., Honsaker, M. S., & Jenkins, J. R. (1982). Response cost and reinforcement contingencies of managing the behavior of distractible children in tutorial settings. *Learning Disability Quarterly, 5,* 3–13.

!Sindelar, P. T., Monda, L. E. , & O'Shea, L. J. (1990). Effects of repeated readings on instructional and mastery-level readers. *Journal of Educational Research, 83,* 220–226.

^Singhanayok, C., & Hooper, S. (1998). The effects of cooperative learning and learner control on students' achievement, option selections, and attitudes. *Educational Technology Research and Development, 46*(2), 17–33.

*%Smith, M. A. (1989). *The efficacy of mnemonics for teaching recognition of letter clusters to reading disabled students.* Doctoral dissertation, University of Oregon. *Dissertation Abstracts International, 50*(5-A), 1259–1260.

*Smith, P. L., & Friend, M. (1986). Training learning disabled adolescents in a strategy for using text structure to aid recall of instructional prose. *Learning Disabilities Research, 2,* 38–44.

*%Snider, V. E. (1989). Reading comprehension performance of adolescents with learning disabilities. *Learning Disability Quarterly, 12*(2), 87–96.

*Somerville, D. E., & Leach, D. J. (1988). Direct or indirect instruction? An evaluation of three types of intervention programs for assisting students with specific reading difficulties. *Educational Research, 30,* 46–53.

*Sowell, V., Parker, R., Poplin, M., & Larsen, S. (1979). The effects of psycholinguistic training on improving psycholinguistic skills. *Learning Disability Quarterly, 2,* 69–78.

&Stevens, R. J., Madden, N. A., Slavin, R. E., & Famish, A. M. (1987). Cooperative integrated reading and composition: Two field experiments. *Reading Research Quarterly, 22,* 433–454.

!Stoddard, K., Valcante, G., Sindelar, P. T., O'Shea, L., & Algozzine, B. (1993). Increasing reading rate and comprehension: The effects of repeated readings, sentence segmentation, and intonation training. *Reading Research and Instruction, 32,* 53–65.

*Straub, R. B., & Roberts, D. M. (1983). Effects of nonverbal-oriented social awareness training program on social interaction ability of learning disabled children. *Journal of Nonverbal Behavior, 7,* 195–201.

*%Sullivan, J. (1972). The effects of Kephart's perceptual motor training on a reading clinic sample. *Journal of Learning Disabilities, 5,* 545–551.

Swanson, H. L. (2001). Research on interventions for adolescents with learning disabilities: A meta-analysis of outcomes related to higher-order processing. *The Elementary School Journal, 101*(13), 331–349.

Swanson, H. L., & Hoskyn, M. (1998). Experimental intervention research on students with learning disabilities: A meta-analysis of treatment outcomes. *Review of Educational Research, 68*(3), 277–321.

*Swanson, H. L., & Trahan, M. F. (1992). Learning disabled readers' comprehension of computer mediated text: The influence of working memory, metacognition and attribution. *Learning Disabilities Research & Practice, 7,* 74–86.

^Taylor, B. M., Hanson, B. E., Justice-Swanson, K., & Watts, S. M. (1997). Helping struggling readers: Linking small-group intervention with cross-age tutoring. *The Reading Teacher, 51*(3), 196–209.

+Texas Center for Educational Research. (1997). *Reading programs for students in the lower elementary grades: What does the research say?* Austin, TX: TCER.

Therrien, W. J. (2004). Fluency and comprehension gains as a result of repeated reading: A meta-analysis. *Remedial and Special Education, 25*(4), 252–261.

*%Tollefson, N., Tracy, D. B., Johnsen, E. P., Farmer, A. W., & Buenning, M. (1984). Goal setting and personal responsibility training for LD adolescents. *Psychology in the Schools, 21,* 224–233.

^Tomlin, V. E. (1995). A mentor program for improving the academic attainment of black adolescent males. *Dissertation Abstracts International, 55*(9-A), 2728. (UMI No. 9502892)

&Top, B. L. (1984). *Handicapped children as tutors: The effects of cross-age, reverse-role tutoring on self-esteem and reading achievement.* Unpublished doctoral dissertation, Brigham Young University.

&Top, B. L., & Osguthorpe, R. T. (1985). The effects of reverse-role tutoring on reading achievement and self-concept. In R. T. Osguthorpe, W. Eiserman, L. Shisler, B. L. Top, & T. E. Scruggs, *Handicapped children as tutors.* Final report (1984–1985, pp. 18–43). Document submitted to the Office of Special Education and Rehabilitative Services, U.S. Department of Education, Washington, DC. (ERIC Document Reproduction Service No. ED 267 545)

&Top, B. L., & Osguthorpe, R. T. (1987). Reverse-role tutoring: The effects of handicapped students tutoring regular class students. *Elementary School Journal, 87,* 413–423.

#Torgesen, J., Wagner, R., Rashotte, C., Rose, E., Lindamood, P., Conway, T., & Garvan, C. (1998). *Preventing reading failure in young children with phonological processing disabilities: Group and individual responses to instruction.* Unpublished manuscript.

*Torgesen, J. K., Wagner, R. K., Rashotte, C. A., Alexander, A. W., & Conway, T. (1997). Preventive and remedial interventions for children with severe reading disabilities. *Learning Disabilities: A Multi-Disciplinary Journal, 8,* 51–61.

&Trapani, C. (1988, March–April). *Peer tutoring: Integrating academic and social skills remediation in the classroom.* Paper presented at the 66th annual convention of The Council for Exceptional Children, Washington, DC. (ERIC Document Reproduction Service No. ED 297 533)

*&%Trapani, C., & Gettinger, M. (1989). Effects of social skills training and cross-age tutoring on academic achievement and social behaviors of boys with learning disabilities. *Journal of Research and Development in Education, 23,* 1–9.

Trout, A. L., Epstein, M. H., Mikelson, W. T., Nelson, J. R., & Lewis, L. M. (2003). Effects of a reading intervention for kindergarten students at risk for emotional disturbance and reading deficits. *Behavioral Disorders, 28,* 313–326.

^Udupa, P. (1993). Concept mapping/cooperative learning as a technique to improve the learning of "at-risk" and nondisabled students. *Dissertation Abstracts International, 53*(8-A), 2757. (UMI No. 9239159)

#Vadasy, P., Jenkins, J., & Pool, D. (1998). *Effects of a first-grade tutoring program in phonological and early reading skills.* Unpublished manuscript.

#^Vadasy, P. F., Jenkins, J. R., Antil, L. R., Wayne, S. K., & O'Connor, R. E. (1997). The effectiveness of one-to-one tutoring by community tutors for at-risk beginning readers. *Learning Disability Quarterly, 20*(2), 126–139.

*VanDaal, V.H.P., & Reitsma, P. (1990). Effects of independent word practice with segmented and whole-word sound feedback in disabled readers. *Journal of Research in Reading, 13,* 133–148.

*VanDaal, V.H.P., & Reitsma, P. (1993). The use of speech feedback by normal and disabled readers in computer-based reading practice. *Reading and Writing: An Interdisciplinary Journal, 5,* 243–259.

*VanDaal, V.H.P., &VanDerLeij, D. (1992). Computer-based reading and spelling practice for children with learning disabilities. *Journal of Learning Disabilities, 25,* 186–195.

*VanReusen, A. K., & Bos, C. S. (1994). Facilitating student participation in individualized education programs through motivation strategy instruction. *Exceptional Children, 60,* 466–475.

*VanStrien, J. W., Stolk, B. D., & Zuiker, S. (1995). Hemisphere-specific treatment of dyslexia subtypes: Better reading with anxiety-laden words? *Journal of Learning Disabilities, 28,* 30–34.

!Vaughn, S., Chard, D. J., Bryant, D. P., Coleman, M., & Kouzekanani, K. (2000). Fluency and comprehension interventions for third-grade students. *Remedial and Special Education, 21,* 325–335.

*Vaughn, S., Schumm, J. S., & Gordon, J. (1993). Which motoric condition is most effective for teaching spelling to students with and without learning disabilities? *Journal of Learning Disabilities, 26,* 193–198.

*Wade, J., & Kass, C. E. (1987). Component deficit and academic remediation of learning disabilities. *Journal of Learning Disabilities, 20,* 441–447.

*Wade, J. F. (1979). *The effects of component deficit remediation and academic deficit remediation on improving reading achievement of learning disabled children.* Doctoral dissertation, University of Arizona. *Dissertation Abstracts International, 40*(3A), 1412.

#Wallach, M., & Wallach, L. (1976). *Teaching all children to read.* Chicago: University of Chicago Press.

*Wanat, P. E. (1983). Social skills: An awareness program with learning disabled adolescents. *Journal of Learning Disabilities, 16,* 35–38.

*Warner, J.M.R. (1973). *The effects of two treatment modes upon children diagnosed as having learning disabilities.* Doctoral dissertation, University of Illinois. *Dissertation Abstracts International, 34*(3A), 1142–1143.

*Waterman, D. E. (1974). *Remediation of word attack skills in slow readers by total body movement learning games.* Doctoral dissertation, University of Tulsa, 1973. *Dissertation Abstracts International, 34*(7A), 4049.

^Webb, N., & Farivar, S. (1994). Promoting helping behavior in cooperative small groups in middle school mathematics. *American Educational Research Journal, 31*(2), 369–395.

#Weeks, D. (1992). *A study of the implementation of Reading Recovery in Scarborough: 1990–1991.* Unpublished doctoral dissertation, University of Toronto.

*Welch, M. (1992). The PLEASE strategy: A meta-cognitive learning strategy for improving the paragraph writing of students with learning disabilities. *Learning Disability Quarterly, 15,* 119–128.

*%White, C. V., Pascarella, E. T., & Pflaum, S. W. (1981). Effects of training in sentence construction on the comprehension of learning-disabled children. *Journal of Educational Psychology, 71,* 697–704.

+White, W.A.T. (1988). A meta-analysis of the effects of Direct Instruction in special education. *Education and Treatment of Children, 11*(4), 364–374.

*Whitman, D. M. (1986). *The effects of computer-assisted instruction on mathematics achievement of mildly handicapped students.* Doctoral dissertation, University of South Carolina, 1985. *Dissertation Abstracts International, 46*(10A), 3000–3001.

*%Williams, J. P., Brown, L. G., Silverstein, A. K., & deCani, J. S. (1994). An instructional program in comprehension of narrative themes for adolescents with learning disabilities. *Learning Disability Quarterly, 17,* 205–221.

*Wilsher, C., Atkins, O., & Manfield, P. (1985). Effect of piracetam on dyslexics' reading ability. *Journal of Learning Disabilities, 18,* 19–25.

*Wilson, C., & Sindelar, P. T. (1991). Direct instruction in math word problems: Students with learning disabilities. *Exceptional Children, 57,* 512–519.

*Wise, B. W., Ring, J., Sessions, L., & Olson, R. K. (in press). Phonological awareness with and without articulation: A preliminary study. *Learning Disability Quarterly.*

*%Wong, B.Y.L., Butler, D. L., Ficzere, S. A., & Kuperis, S. (1996). Teaching low achievers and students with learning disabilities to plan, write, and revise opinion essays. *Journal of Learning Disabilities, 29,* 197–212.

*%Wong, B.Y.L., Butler, D. L., Ficzere, S. A., Kuperis, S., Corden, M., & Zelmer, J. (1994). Teaching problem learners revision skills and sensitivity to audience through two instructional modes: Student-teacher versus student-student interactive dialogues. *Learning Disabilities Research & Practice, 9,* 78–90.

*%Wong, B.Y.L., & Jones, W. (1982). Increasing metacomprehension in learning disabled and normally achieving students through self-questioning training. *Learning Disability Quarterly, 5,* 228–240.

=Woodward, J., & Baxter, J. (1997). The effects of an innovative approach to mathematics on academically low-achieving students in mainstreamed settings. *Exceptional Children, 63*(3), 373–388.

=Woodward, J., Baxter, J., & Robinson, R. (1999). Rules and reasons: Decimal instruction for academically low-achieving students. *Learning Disabilities Research & Practice, 14*, 15–24.

^Wright, J., Cavanaugh, R., Sainato, D., & Heward, W. (1995). Somos todos ayudantes y estudiantes: A demonstration of a classwide peer tutoring program in a modified Spanish class for secondary students identified as learning disabled or academically at-risk. *Education and Treatment of Children, 18*(1), 33–53.

^Yager, S., Johnson, D., & Johnson, R. (1985). Oral discussion, group-to-group individual transfer, and achievement in cooperative learning groups. *Journal of Educational Psychology, 77*(1), 60–66.

!Young, A., Bowers, P. G., & MacKinnon, G. E. (1996). Effects of prosodic modeling and repeated reading on poor readers' fluency and comprehension. *Applied Psycholinguistics, 17*, 59–84.

*Zieffle, T. H., & Romney, D. M. (1985). Comparison of self-instruction and relaxation training in reducing impulsive and inattentive behavior of learning disabled children on cognitive tasks. *Psychological Reports, 57*, 271–274.

^Zukowski, V. (1997). Teeter-totters and tandem bikes: A glimpse into the work of cross-age tutors. *Teaching and Change, 5*(1), 71–91.

REFERENCES FOR UTILIZING REMINDERS

*#@$Atkinson, R. C. (1975). Mnemotechnics in second language learning. *American Psychologist, 30*, 821–828.

&Atkinson, R. C., & Raugh, M. R. (1975). An application of the mnemonic keyword method to the acquisition of a Russian vocabulary. *Journal of Experimental Psychology: Human Learning and Memory, 104*, 120–123.

*Bellezza, F. S. (1996). A mnemonic based on arranging words on visual patterns. *Journal of Educational Psychology, 78*, 217–224.

&Berla, E., Persensky, F. F., & Senter, R. J. (1969). Learning time with a mnemonic system. *Psychonomic Science, 16*, 207–208.

*Berry, J. K. (1986). *Learning disabled children's use of mnemonic strategies for vocabulary learning.* Unpublished doctoral dissertation, University of Wisconsin, Madison.

@Beuring, T., & Kee, D. W. (1987). Elaborative propensities during adolescence: The relationships among memory and knowledge, strategy behavior, and memory performance. In M. A. McDaniel & M. Pressley (Eds.), *Imagery and related mnemonic processes* (pp. 257–273). New York: Springer-Verlag.

%Bissell, L. (1982). *Training with forced-choice cloze tasks.* Ann Arbor: University of Michigan.

+Blaha, B. A. (1979). *The effects of answering self-generated questions on reading.* Unpublished doctoral dissertation, Boston University School of Education.

@Bower, G. H. (1972). Mental imagery and associative learning. In L. Gregg (Ed.), *Cognition in learning and memory.* New York: Wiley.

&Bower, G. H., & Clark, M. C. (1969). Narrative stories as mediators for serial learning. *Psychonomic Science, 14*, 181–191.

&Bower, G. H., & Reitman, J. S. (1972). Mnemonic elaboration in multilist learning. *Journal of Verbal Learning and Verbal Behavior, 11*, 478–485.

!Boyle, J. R. (1996). The effects of a cognitive mapping strategy on the literal and inferential comprehension of students with mild disabilities. *Learning Disabilities Quarterly, 19*, 86–98.

+Brady, P. L. (1990). *Improving the reading comprehension of middle school students through reciprocal teaching and semantic mapping strategies.* Unpublished doctoral dissertation, University of Alaska.

@Bransford, J. D., Stein, B. S., Vye, N. J., Franks, J. J., Auble, P. M., Mezynski, K. J., & Perfetto, G. A. (1982). Differences in approaches to learning: An overview. *Journal of Experimental Psychology: General, 3*, 390–398.

&Bugelski, B. R. (1968). Images as mediator in one-trial paired-associate learning II: Self-timing in successive lists. *Journal of Experimental Psychology, 77*, 328–334.

&Bugelski, B. R. (1974). The image as mediators in one-trial paired-associate learning III: Sequential functions in serial lists. *Journal of Experimental Psychology, 103*, 298–303.

%Buikema, J., & Graves, M. (1993). Teaching students to use context clues to infer word meaning. *Journal of Reading, 36*(6), 450–457.

Carney, R. N., Levin, M. E., & Levin, J. R. (1993). Mnemonic strategies: Instructional techniques worth remembering. *Teaching Exceptional Children, 25*(4), 24–30.

#Carney, R. N., Levin, J. R., & Morrison, C. R. (1988). Mnemonic learning of artists and their paintings. *American Educational Research Journal, 25*, 107–125.

#Carney, R. N., Levin, J. R., Willis, D. L., & Smenner, A. D. (1992, August). *Mnemonic artwork learning: Remembering who painted what when.* Paper presented at the annual meeting of the American Psychological Association, Washington, DC.

%Carnine, D., Kameenui, E., & Coyle, G. (1984). Utilization of contextual information in determining the meaning of unfamiliar words. *Reading Research Quarterly, 19*(2), 188–204.

!Chan, L.K.S. (1991). Promoting strategy generalization through self-instructional training in students with reading disabilities. *Journal of Learning Disabilities, 24*, 427–433.

+Cohen, R. (1983). Students generate questions as an aid to reading comprehension. *Reading Teacher, 36*, 770–775.

%Cox, J. (1974). A comparison of two instructional methods utilizing the cloze procedure and a more traditional method for improving reading. *Dissertation Abstracts International, 35*(10). (University Microfilms No. AAC75-9580)

%Daalen-Kapteijns, M., Schouten-van Parreren, C., & De Glopper, K. (1997). *The training of a word learning strategy: results in process and product* (Rep. No. 463). Amsterdam: SCO-Kohmstamm Institute.

Darch, C., & Kameenui, E. J. (1987). Teaching LD students critical reading skills: A systematic replication. *Learning Disability Quarterly, 10*, 82–91.

+Davey, B., & McBride, S. (1986). Effects of question-generation on reading comprehension. *Journal of Educational Psychology, 78*, 256–262.

=De La Paz, S., & Graham, S. (1997). Effects of dictation and advanced planning instruction on the composing of students with writing and learning problems. *Journal of Educational Psychology, 89*(2), 203–222.

&Delprato, D. J., & Baker, E. J. (1974). Concreteness of peg words in two mnemonic systems. *Journal of Experimental Psychology, 102*, 520–522.

+Dermody, M. (1988, February). *Metacognitive strategies for development of reading com-*

prehension for younger children. Paper presented at the annual meeting of the American Association of Colleges for Teacher Education, New Orleans, LA.

+Dreher, M. J., & Gambrell, L. B. (1985). Teaching children to use a self-questioning strategy for studying expository text. *Reading Improvement, 22*, 2–7.

#Ehri, L. C., Deffner, N. D., & Wilce, L. S. (1984). Pictorial mnemonics for phonics. *Journal of Educational Psychology, 76*, 880–893.

=Englert, C. S., Garmon, A., Mariage, T., Rozendal, M., Tarrant, K., & Urba, J. (1995). The early literacy project: Connecting across the literacy curriculum. *Learning Disability Quarterly, 18*, 253–275.

!Englert, C. S., & Mariage, T. V. (1991). Making students partners in the comprehension process: Organizing the reading "POSSE." *Learning Disability Quarterly, 14*, 123–138.

=Englert, C. S., Raphael, T. E., Anderson, L. M., Anthony, H.M., & Stevens, D. D. (1991). Making writing strategies and self-talk visible: Cognitive strategy instruction in regular and special education classrooms. *American Educational Research Journal, 28*, 337–372.

@Epstein, W., Rock, I., & Zuckerman, C. B. (1960). Meaning and familiarity in associative learning. *Psychological Monographs, 74*(4, Whole No. 491).

=Fortner, V. L. (1986). Generalization of creative productive-thinking training to LD students' written expression. *Learning Disability Quarterly, 9*(4), 274–284.

Fukkink, R. G., & de Glopper, K. (1998). Effects of instruction in deriving word meaning from context: A meta-analysis. *Review of Educational Research, 68*(4), 450–469.

*Fulk, B. J., Mastropieri, M. A., & Scruggs, T. E. (1992). Mnemonic generalization training with learning disabled adolescents. *Learning Disability Quarterly, 7*, 2–10.

&Gamst, G., & Freund, J. S. (1978). Effects of subject-generated stories on recall. *Bulletin of the Psychonomic Society, 12*, 185–180.

!Gajria, M., & Salvia, J. (1992). The effects of summarization instruction on text comprehension of students with learning disabilities. *Exceptional Children, 58*, 508–516.

Gersten, R., & Baker, S. (2001). Teaching expressive writing to students with learning disabilities: A meta-analysis. *The Elementary School Journal, 101*(3), 251–273.

Gersten, R., Fuchs, L. S., Williams, J. P., & Baker, S. (2001). Teaching reading comprehension strategies to students with learning disabilities: A review of research. *Review of Educational Research, 71*(2), 279–320.

@Ghatala, E. S., Levin, J. R., Pressley, M., & Goodwin, D. (1986). A componential analysis of the effects of derived and supplied strategy-utility information on children's strategy selections. *Journal of Experimental Child Psychology, 41*, 76–92.

!Graves, A. W. (1986). Effects of direct instruction and metacomprehension training on finding main ideas. *Learning Disabilities Research, 1*, 90–100.

#$Graves, A. W., & Levin, J. R. (1989). Comparison of monitoring and mnemonic text-processing strategies in student-disabled students. *Learning Disability Quarterly, 12*, 232–236.

Griffith, D. (1979). *A review of the literature on memory enhancement: The potential and relevance of mnemotechnics for military training* (Technical Report No. 436). Fort Hood, TX: U.S. Army Research Unit for the Behavioral and Social Sciences.

&Griffith, D., & Actkinson, T. R. (1978a). *International road signs: Interpretability and training techniques* (Research Report 1202). Arlington, VA: U.S. Army Research Institute for the Behavioral and Social Sciences.

&Griffith, D., & Atkinson, T. R. (1978b). *Mnemonic enhancement in general technical ability* (ARI Technical Paper 336). Arlington, VA: U.S. Army Research Institute for the Behavioral and Social Sciences (NTIS No. AD-A061314).

%Guarino, E. (1960). *An investigation of the effectiveness of instruction designed to improve the reader's skill in using context clues to derive word meaning.* Syracuse, NY: Syracuse University [dissertation, UMI].

+Helfeldt, J. P., & Lalik, R. (1976). Reciprocal student-teacher questioning. *Reading Teacher, 33,* 283–287.

%Herman, P., & Weaver, C. (1988). *Contextual strategies for word meaning: Middle grade students look in and look around.* Paper presented at the National Reading Conference, Tucson, AZ.

#@Higbee, K. L., & Kunihira, S. (1985). Cross-cultural applications of the Yodai mnemonics in education. *Educational Psychologist, 20,* 57–64.

=Jaben, T. H. (1983). The effects of creativity training on learning disabled students' creative written expression. *Journal of Learning Disabilities, 16*(5), 264–265.

=Jaben, T. H. (1987). Effects of training on learning disabled students' creative written expression. *Psychological Reports, 60,* 23–26.

%Jenkins, J., Matlock, B., & Slocum, T. (1989). Two approaches to vocabulary instruction: The teaching of individual word meaning and practice in deriving word meaning from context. *Reading Research Quarterly, 24*(2), 215–235.

&Keppel, G., & Zavortink, B. (1969). Further test of the use of images as mediators. *Journal of Experimental Psychology, 82,* 190–192.

+King, A. (1989). Effects of self-questioning training on college students' comprehension of lectures. *Contemporary Educational Psychology, 14,* 366–381.

+King, A. (1990). Improving Lecture Comprehension: Effects of a metacognitive strategy. *Applied Educational Psychology, 5,* 331–346.

+King, A. (1992). Comparison of self-questioning, summarizing, and notetaking-review as strategies for learning from lectures. *American Educational Research Journal, 29,* 303–325.

!Klingner, J. K., Vaughn, S., & Schumm, J. S. (1998). Collaborative strategic reading during social studies in heterogeneous fourth-grade classrooms. *Elementary School Journal, 99,* 3–22.

%Kranzer, K. (1988). *A study of the effects of instruction on incidental word learning and on the ability to derive word meaning from context.* Newark: University of Delaware [dissertation, UMI].

@Kuhara-Kohma, K., & Hatang, G. (1985, April). *Dominion general strategy and domain-specific knowledge as determinants of paired associate learning performance.* Paper presented at the annual meeting of the American Educational Research Association, Chicago.

+!Labercane, G., & Battle, J. (1987). Cognitive processing strategies, self-esteem and reading comprehension of learning disabled students, *B.C. Journal of Special Education, 11,* 167–185.

Levin, J. (1988). Elaboration-based learning strategies: Powerful theory = powerful application. *Contemporary Educational Psychology, 13,* 191–205.

Levin, J. (1993). Mnemonic strategies and classroom learning: A twenty year report card. *The Elementary School Journal, 94*(2), 235–244.

@Levin, J. R. (1976). What have we learned about maximizing what children learn? In J. R. Levin & V. L. Allen (Eds.), *Cognitive learning in children: Theories and strategies* (pp. 105–134). New York: Academic Press.

*#@Levin, J. R. (1981). The mnemonic 80's: Keywords in the classroom. *Educational Psychologist, 16,* 65–82.

#@$Levin, J. R. (1985). Educational applications of mnemonic pictures: Possibilities beyond your wildest imagination. In A. A. Sheikh & K. S. Sheikh (Eds.), *Imagery in education: Imagery in educational process* (pp. 63–87). Farmingdale, NY: Baywood.

$Levin, J. R., Dretzke, B. J., McCormick, C. B., Scruggs, T. E., McGivern, J. E., & Mastropieri, M. A. (1983). Learning via mnemonic pictures: Analysis of the presidential process. *Educational Communication and Technology Journal, 31,* 161–173.

#Levin, J. R., Johnson, D. D., Pittelman, S. D., Hayes, B. L., Levin, K. M., Shirberg, L. K., & Toms-Bronoski, S. (1984). A comparison of semantic- and mnemonic-based vocabulary-learning strategies. *Reading Psychology, 5,* 1–15.

#Levin, J. R., Levin, M. E., Glassman, L. D., & Nordwall, M. B. (1992). Mnemonic vocabulary instruction: Additional effectiveness evidence. *Contemporary Educational Psychology, 17,* 156–174.

#Levin, J. R., McCormick, C. B., Miller, G. E., Barry, J. K., & Pressley, M. (1982). Mnemonic versus non-mnemonic vocabulary-learning strategies for children. *American Educational Research Journal, 19,* 121–136.

@Levin, J. R., & Pressley, M. (1981). Improving children's prose comprehension: Selected strategies that seem to succeed. In C. M. Santa & B. L. Hayes (Eds.), *Children's prose comprehension: Research and practice* (pp. 44–71). Newark, DE: International Reading Association.

$Levin, J. R., & Pressley, M. (1985). Mnemonic vocabulary instruction: What's fact, what's fiction. In R. F. Dillon (Ed.), *Individual cognitive differences in cognition* (Vol. 2, pp. 145–172). Orlando, FL: Academic Press.

*#$Levin, M. E., & Levin, J. R. (1990). Scientific mnemonomies: Methods for maximizing more than memory. *American Educational Research Journal, 27,* 301–321.

+Lonberger, R. B. (1988). *The effects of training in a self-generated learning strategy on the prose processing abilities of fourth and sixth graders.* Unpublished doctoral dissertation, State University of New York at Buffalo.

+Lysynchuk, L., Pressley, M., & Vye, G. (1990). Reciprocal instruction improves reading comprehension performance in poor grade school comprehenders. *Elementary School Journal, 40,* 471–484.

=MacArthur, C. A., Graham, S., Schwartz, S. S., & Schafer, W. D. (1995). Evaluation of a writing instruction model that integrated a process approach, strategy instruction, and word processing. *Learning Disability Quarterly, 18,* 278–291.

=MacArthur, C. A., Schwartz, S. S., & Graham, S. (1991). Effects of reciprocal peer revision strategy in special education classrooms. *Learning Disabilities Research, 6*(4), 201–210.

+MacGregor, S. K. (1988). Use of self-questioning with a computer-mediated text system and measures of reading performance. *Journal of Reading Behavior, 20,* 131–148.

#Machida, K., & Carlson, J. (1984). Effects of verbal mediational strategy on cognitive processes in mathematics learning. *Journal of Educational Psychology, 76,* 1382–1385.

!Malone, L. D., & Mastropieri, M. A. (1992). Reading comprehension instruction: Summarization and self-monitoring training for students with learning disabilities. *Exceptional Children, 58,* 270–279.

+Manzo, A. V. (1969). *Improving reading comprehension through reciprocal teaching.* Unpublished doctoral dissertation, Syracuse University.

@Marschark, M., Richman, C. L., Yuille, J. C., & Hunt, R. R. (1987). The role of imagery in memory: On shared and distinctive information. *Psychological Bulletin, 102,* 28–41.

@Martin, C. J., Cox, D. L., & Boersma, F. J. (1965). The role of associative strategies in the acquisition of paired-associate material: An alternative approach to meaningfulness. *Psychonomic Science, 3,* 463–464.

$Mastropieri, M. A. (1988). Use in the keyboard method. *TEACHING Exceptional Children, 20*(2), 4–8.

#$Mastropieri, M. A., & Scruggs, T. E. (1989). Constructing more meaningful relationships: Mnemonic instruction for special populations. *Educational Psychology Review, 1,* 83–111.

!Mastropieri, M. A., Scruggs, T. E., Hamilton, S. L., Wolfe, S., Whedon, C., & Canevaro, A. (1996). Promoting thinking skills of students with learning disabilities: Effects on recall and comprehension of expository prose. *Exceptionality, 6,* 1–11.

#Mastropieri, M. A., Scruggs, T. E., & Levin, J. R. (1987a). Learning-disabled students' memory for expository prose: Mnemonic versus nonmnemonic picture. *American Educational Research Journal, 24,* 505–519.

#$Mastropieri, M. A., Scruggs, T. E., & Levin, J. R. (1987b). Mnemonic instruction in special education. In M. A. McDaniel & M. Pressley (Eds.), *Imagery and related mnemonic processes: Theories, individual differences, and applications* (pp. 358–376). New York: Springer-Verlag.

#$Mastropieri, M. A., Scruggs, T. E., Levin, J. R., Gaffney, J. & McLoone, B. (1985). Mnemonic vocabulary instruction for learning disabled students. *Learning Disability Quarterly, 8,* 57–63.

#@$McCormick, C. B., & Levin, J. R. (1987). Mnemonic prose-learning strategies. In M. A. McDaniel & M. Pressley (Eds.), *Imagery and related mnemonic processes: Theories, individual differences, and applications* (pp. 392–406). New York: Springer-Verlag.

!McCormick, S., & Cooper, J. O. (1991). Can SW3R facilitate secondary learning disabled students' literal comprehension of expository test? Three experiments. *Reading Psychology: An International Quarterly, 12,* 239–271.

#McDaniel, M. A., & Pressley, M. (1989). Keyword and context instruction for new vocabulary meanings: Effects on text comprehension and memory. *Journal of Educational Psychology, 8,* 204–213.

#McGivern, J. E., & Levin, L. R. (1983). The keyword method of vocabulary learning: An interaction with vocabulary knowledge. *Contemporary Educational Psychology, 8,* 46–54.

Mevarech, Z. R., & Kramarski, B. (2003). The effects of metacognitive training versus worked-out examples on students' mathematical reasoning. *British Journal of Educational Psychology, 73,* 449–471.

@Milgram, N. A. (1967). Retention of remediation set in paired-associate learning of normal children and retardates. *Journal of Experimental Child Psychology, 5,* 341–349.

Morrison, C. R., & Levin, J. (1987). Degree of mnemonic support and students' acquisition of science facts. *Educational Communication and Technology Journal, 35,* 67–74.

&Murray, F. S. (1974). Effects of narrative stories on recall. *Bulletin of the Psychonomic Society, 100,* 6–8.

!Nelson, J. R., Smith, D. J., & Dodd, J. M. (1992). The effects of a summary skills strategy to students identified as learning disabled on their comprehension of science text. *Education and Treatment of Children, 15,* 228–243.

+Nolte, R. Y., & Singer, H. (1985). Active comprehension: Teaching a process of reading comprehension and its effects on reading achievement. *The Reading Teacher, 39,* 24–31.

@$O'Sullivan, J. T., & Pressley, M. (1984). Completeness of instruction and strategy transfer. *Journal of Experimental Child Psychology, 38,* 275–288.

#Ott, C. E., Butler, D. C., Blake, R. S., & Ball, J. P. (1973). The effect of interactive-image elaboration on the acquisition of foreign-language vocabulary. *Language Learning, 23,* 197–206.

+Palincsar, A. S. (1987, April). *Collaborating for collaborative learning of text comprehension.* Paper presented at the annual meeting of the American Educational Research Association, Washington, DC.

+Palincsar, A. S., & Brown, A.L. (1984). Reciprocal teaching of comprehension-fostering and comprehension-monitoring activities. *Cognition and Instruction, 2,* 117–175.

*Patton, G. W., D'Agaro, W. R., & Gaudette, M. D. (1991). The effect of subject-generated and experimenter-supplied code words on the phonetic mnemonic system. *Applied Cognitive Psychology, 5,* 135–148.

&Pavio, A. (1968). *Effects of imagery instructions and concreteness of memory pegs in a mnemonic system.* Proceedings of the 76th Annual Convention of the American Psychological Association (pp. 77–78).

@&Pavio, A. (1969). Mental imagery in associative learning and memory. *Psychological Review, 76,* 241–263.

&Perensky, J. J., & Senter, R. J. (1969). An experimental investigation of a mnemonic system in recall. *Psychological Record, 19,* 491–499.

#Peters, E. E., & Levin, J. R. (1986). Effects of the mnemonic imagery strategy on good and poor readers' prose recall. *Reading Research Quarterly, 21,* 179–192.

@Pressley, M. (1982). Elaboration and memory development. *Child Development, 53,* 296–309.

*@Pressley, M., Levin, J. R., & Delaney, H. G. (1982). The mnemonic keyword method. *Review of Educational Research, 52,* 61–91.

#Pressley, M., Levin, J. R., & McCormick, C. B. (1980). Young children's learning of foreign-language vocabulary: A sentence variation of the keyword method. *Contemporary Educational Psychology, 5,* 22–29.

$Pressley, M., Levin, J. R., & McDaniel, M. A. (1987). Remembering versus inferring what a word means: Mnemonic and contextual approaches. In M. G. McKeown & M. E. Curtis (Eds.), *The nature of vocabulary acquisition* (pp. 107–127). Hillsdale, NJ: Erlbaum.

*#@Pressley, M., Levin, J. R., & Miller, G. E. (1981). How does the keyword method affect comprehension and usage? *Reading Research Quarterly, 16,* 213–226.

@Pressley, M., McDaniel, M. A., Turnure, J. E., Wood, E., & Ahmad, M. (1987). Generation and precision of elaboration: Effects on intentional and incidental learning. *Journal of Experimental Psychology: Learning, Memory, and Cognition, 13,* 291–300.

@Pressley, M., Ross, K. A., Levin, J. R., & Ghatala, E. S. (1984). The role of strategy utility knowledge in children's decision-making. *Journal of Experimental Child Psychology, 38,* 491–504.

&Raugh, M. R., & Atkinson, R. C. (1974). *A mnemonic method for the acquisition of a second-language vocabulary.* Technical Report No. 224. Stanford, CA: Institute for Mathematical Studies in the Social Sciences, Stanford University.

&Raugh, M. R., & Atkinson, R. C. (1975). A mnemonic method for learning a second-language vocabulary. *Journal of Educational Psychology, 67,* 1–19.

=Reynolds, C. J. (1986). *The effects of instruction in cognitive revision strategies on the writing skills of secondary learning disabled students.* Doctoral dissertation, Ohio State University, 1985. *Dissertation Abstracts International, 46*(9-A), 2662.

+Ritchie, P. (1985). The effects of instruction in main idea and question generation. *Reading Canada Lecture, 3,* 139–146.

@Roberts, P. (1983). Memory strategy instruction with the elderly: What should memory training be the training of? In M. Pressley & J. R. Levin (Eds.), *Cognitive strategy research: Psychological foundations* (pp. 75–100). New York: Springer-Verlag.

&Robertson-Tchabo, E. A., Hausman, D. P., & Arenberg, D. (1976). A classical mnemonic for older learners: A trip that works! *Educational Gerontology, 1,* 215–216.

@Rohwer, W. D., Jr. (1973). Elaboration and learning in childhood and adolescence. In H. W. Reese (Ed.), *Advances in child development and behavior* (Vol. 8, pp. 1–57). New York: Academic Press.

@Rohwer, W. D., Jr., & Levin, J. R. (1968). Action, meaning, and stimulus selection in paired-associate learning. *Journal of Verbal Learning and Verbal Behavior, 7,* 137–141.

@Rohwer, W. D., Jr., & Thomas, J. W. (1987). The role of mnemonic strategies and study effectiveness. In M. A. McDaniel & M. Pressley (Eds.), *Imagery and related mnemonic processes: Theories, individual differences, and applications* (pp. 428–450). New York: Springer-Verlag.

@Rosenheck, M. B., Finch., M. E., & Levin, J. R. (1987, April). *Comparison of mnemonic and taxonomic science-learning strategies.* Paper presented at the annual meeting of the American Educational Research Association, Washington, DC.

#$Rosenheck, M. B., Levin, M. E., & Levin, J. R. (1989). Learning botany concepts mnemonically: Seeing the forest *and* the trees. *Journal of Educational Psychology, 81,* 196–203.

Rosenshine, B., Meister, C., & Chapman, S. (1996). Teaching students to generate questions: A review of the intervention studies. *Review of Educational Research, 66*(2), 181–221.

$Roth, K. J. (1989). Science education: It's not enough to "do" or "relate." *American Educator, 13*(4), 16–22, 46–48.

%Sampson, M., Valmont, W., & Allen, R. (1982). The effects of instructional cloze on the comprehension, vocabulary, and divergent production of third-grade students. *Reading Research Quarterly, 17*(3), 389–399.

=Sawyer, R. J., Graham, S., & Harris, K. R. (1992). Direct teaching, strategy instruction, and strategy instruction with explicit self-regulation: Effects on the composition skills and self-efficacy of students with learning disabilities. *Journal of Educational Psychology, 84*(3), 340–352.

!Schumaker, J., Deshler, D., Alley, G., Warner, M., & Denton, P. (1984). Multipass: A learning strategy for improving reading comprehension. *Learning Disability Quarterly, 5,* 295–304.

*Scruggs, T. E., & Mastropieri, M. A. (1992). Classroom applications of mnemonic instructions: Acquisition, maintenance, and generalization. *Exceptional Children, 58,* 219–229.

$Scruggs, T. E., Mastropieri, M. A., & Levin, J. R. (1985). Vocabulary acquisition by mentally retarded students under direct and mnemonic instruction. *American Journal of Mental Deficiency, 89,* 546–551.

@Scruggs, T. E., Mastropieri, M. A., & Levin, J. R. (1987). Implications of mnemonic strategy research for theories of learning disabilities. In H. L. Swanson (Ed.), *Memory and learning disabilities* (pp. 225–244). Greenwich, CT: JAI Press.

$Scruggs, T. E., Mastropieri, M. A., Levin, J. R., & Gaffney, J. (1985). Facilitating the acquisition of science facts in learning disabled students. *American Educational Research Journal, 22,* 575–586.

&Senter, R. J., & Hauser, G. K. (1968). An experimental study of a mnemonic system. *Psychonomic Science, 10,* 289–290.

+Short, E. J., & Ryan, E. B. (1984). Metacognitive differences between skilled and less-skilled readers: Remediating deficits through story grammar and attribution training. *Journal of Educational Psychology, 76,* 225–235.

#Shriberg, L. K., Levin, J. R., McCormick, C. B., & Pressley, M. (1982). Learning about "famous" people via the keyword method. *Journal of Educational Psychology, 74,* 238–247.

!Simmonds, E.P.M. (1992). The effects of teacher training and implementation of two methods of improving the comprehension skills of students with learning disabilities. *Learning Disabilities Research & Practice, 7,* 194–198.

+Simpson, P. S. (1989). *The effects of direct training in active comprehension on reading achievement, self-concepts, and reading attitudes of at-risk sixth grade students.* Unpublished doctoral dissertation, Texas Tech University.

+Smith, N. J. (1977). *The effects of training teachers to teach students at different reading ability levels to formulate three types of questions on reading comprehension and question generation ability.* Unpublished doctoral dissertation, University of Georgia.

&Smith, R. K., & Noble, C. E. (1965). Effects of a mnemonic technique applied to verbal learning and memory. *Perception and Motor Skills, 21,* 123–134.

@Stein, B. S., Littlefield, J., Branford, J. D., & Persampieri, M. (1984). Elaboration and knowledge acquisition. *Memory and Cognition, 12,* 522–529.

@Suzki-Slakter, N. (1988). Elaboration and metamemory during adolescence. *Contemporary Educational Psychology, 13,* 206–220.

!Swanson, H. L., Kozleski, E., & Steginik, P. (1987). Disabled readers' processing of prose: Do any processes change because of intervention? *Psychology in the Schools, 24,* 378–384.

*Sweeney, C. A., & Bellezza, F. S. (1982). Use of the keyword mnemonic in learning English vocabulary words. *Human Learning, 1,* 155–163.

@Taylor, A. M., & Turnure, J. E. (1979). Imagery and verbal elaboration with retarded children: Effects on learning and memory. In N. R. Ellis (Ed.), *Handbook of mental deficiency, psychological theory, and research* (pp. 659–697). Hillsdale, NJ: Erlbaum.

+Taylor, B. M., & Frye, B.J. (1992). Comprehension strategy instruction in the intermediate grades. *Reading Research and Instruction, 92,* 39–48.

@Thomas, J. W. (1988). Proficiency at academic studying. *Contemporary Educational Psychology, 13,* 265–275.

%Tomesen, M., & Aarnoutse, C. (1998). Effecten van een instructieprogramma voor het afleiden van woordbetekenissen [Effects of a training program in deriving word meanings]. *Pedogogische Studien, 75,* 1–16.

@Turnure, J. E. (1971). Types of verbal elaboration and the paired-associate performance of educable mentally retarded children. *American Journal of Mental Deficiency, 76*(3), 306–312.

#Velt, D. T., Scruggs, T. E., & Mastropieri, M. A. (1986). Extended mnemonic instruction with learning disabled students. *Journal of Educational Psychology, 78,* 300–308.

+Weiner, C. J. (1978, March). *The effect of training in questioning and student question-generation on reading achievement.* Paper presented at the annual meeting of the American Educational Research Association, Toronto. (ERIC Document Reproduction Service No. ED 158 223)

=Welch, M. (1992). The PLEASE strategy: A meta-cognitive learning strategy for improving the paragraph writing of students with learning disabilities. *Learning Disability Quarterly, 15*(2), 119–128.

&Willerman, B. S. (1977). *The effect of a keyword mnemonic on the recall of French vocabulary.* Unpublished doctoral dissertation, University of Texas at Austin.

+Williamson, R. A. (1989). *The effect of reciprocal teaching on student performance gains in third grade basal reading instruction.* Unpublished doctoral dissertation, Texas A&M University.

+!Wong, B.Y.L., & Jones, W. (1982). Increasing metacomprehension of learning disabled and normally achieving students through self-questioning training. *Learning Disabilities Quarterly, 5,* 228–240.

!Wong, B.Y.L., & Wilson, M. (1984). Investigating awareness of and teaching passage organization in learning disabled children. *Journal of Learning Disabilities, 17,* 477–482.

&Wood, G. (1967). Mnemonic systems and recall. *Journal of Educational Psychology Monographs, 58*(6, Part 2).

&Wortman, P. M., & Sparling, P. B. (1974). Acquisition and retention of mnemonic information in LTM. *Journal of Experimental Psychology, 102,* 22–26.

@Yussen, S. R., Matthews, S. R., & Hiebert, E. (1982). Metacognitive aspects of reading. In W. Otto & S. White (Eds.), *Reading expository material* (pp. 189–218). New York: Academic Press.

REFERENCES FOR UTILIZING TEAMWORK

$Allen, W., & Van Sickle, R. (1981) *Instructional effects of learning teams for low achieving students.* Unpublished manuscript, University of Georgia.

*Allen, W. H., & Van Sickle, R. L. (1984). Learning teams and low achievers. *Social Education, 48,* 60–64.

@Almack, J. C. (1930). Mental efficiency of consulting pairs. *Educational Research Bulletins, 9,* 2–3.

@Anderson, N. H. (1961). Group performance in an anagram task. *Journal of Social Psychology, 55,* 67–75.

@Armstrong, B., Johnson, D. W., & Balow, B. (in press). Cooperative growth goal structures as a means for integrating learning disabled with normal progress elementary pupils. *Contemporary Educational Psychology.*

@Barnlund, D. (1959). A comparative study of individual, majority, and group judgment. *Journal of Abnormal and Social Psychology, 58,* 55–60.

@Beach, L. (1974). Self-directed student groups and college learning. *Higher Education, 3,* 187–200.

@Beaman, A. L., Diener, A., Fraser, S. C., & Endresen, D. L. (1977). Effects of voluntary and semi-voluntary peer-monitoring programs on academic performance. *Journal of Educational Psychology, 69,* 109–114.

*Berg, K. F. (1993, April). *Structured cooperative learning and achievement in a high school mathematics class*. Paper presented at the annual meeting of the American Educational Research Association, Atlanta.

@Bodine, R. (1977, April). *The effects of cognitive style, task structure, and task setting on student outcomes: Cognitive and affective*. Paper presented at the annual meeting of the American Educational Research Association, New York.

#Bridgeman, D. (1977). *The influence of cooperative, interdependent learning on role taking and moral reasoning: A theoretical and empirical field study with fifth grade students*. Unpublished doctoral dissertation, University of California, Santa Cruz.

@Bruning, J., Sommer, D., & Jones, B. (1966). The motivational effects of cooperation and competition in the means-independent situation. *Journal of Social Psychology, 68,* 269–274.

*Chambers, B., & Abrami, P. C. (1991). The relationship between student team learning outcomes and achievement, casual attributions, and affect. *Journal of Educational Psychology, 83,* 140–146.

@Clifford, M. (1971). Motivational effects of competition and goal-setting in reward and non-reward conditions. *Journal of Experimental Education, 39,* 11–16.

@Clifford, M. (1972). Effects of competition as a motivational technique in the classroom. *American Educational Research Journal, 9,* 123–137.

@D'Antuono, M. (1979). *The implementation and results of peer interaction as a rehearsal technique*. Unpublished master's thesis, University of Maryland.

@DeCharms, R. (1957). Affiliation motivation and productivity in small groups. *Journal of Abnormal and Social Psychology, 55,* 222–226.

@Deutch, M. (1949). An experimental study of the effects of cooperation and competition upon group process. *Human Relations, 2,* 199–231.

#@DeVries, D., & Edwards, K. (1973). Student teams and learning games: Their effect on classroom process. *American Educational Research Journal, 10,* 307–318.

#DeVries, D., & Edwards, K. (1974a). *Expectancy theory and corporation-competition in the classroom*. Paper presented at the annual convention of the American Psychological Association, New Orleans.

#DeVries, D., & Edwards, K. (1974b). Student teams and learning games: Their effect on cross-race and cross-sex interaction. *Journal of Educational Psychology, 66,* 741–749.

+DeVries, D., Lucasse, P., & Shackman, S. (1979a, September). *Small group versus individualized instruction: A field test of their relative effectiveness*. Paper presented at the annual convention of the American Psychological Association, New York.

@DeVries, D., Lucasse, P. R., & Shackman, S. L. (1979b). *Small group vs. individualized instruction: A field test* (Report No. 217). Baltimore: Johns Hopkins University, Center for Social Organization of Schools.

*DeVries, D., Lucasse, P. R., & Shackman, S. L. (1980). *Small group vs. individualized instruction: A field test of relative effectiveness* (Report No. 293). Baltimore: Johns Hopkins University, Center for Social Organization of Schools.

*@DeVries, D., & Mescon, I. T. (1975). *Teams-Games-Tournaments: An effective task and reward structure in the elementary grades* (Report No. 189). Baltimore: Johns Hopkins University, Center for Social Organization of Schools.

*DeVries, D., Mescon, I. T., & Shackman, S. L. (1975a). *Teams-Games-Tournaments (TGT) effects on reading skills in the elementary grades* (Report No. 200). Baltimore: Johns Hopkins University, Center for Social Organization of Schools.

*@DeVries, D., Mescon, I. T., & Shackman, S. L. (1975b). *Teams-Games-Tournaments in the elementary classroom: A replication* (Report No. 190). Baltimore: Johns Hopkins University, Center for Social Organization of Schools.

*@DeVries, D., Mescon, I. T., & Shackman, S. L. (1976). *Student teams can improve basic skills: TGT applied to reading.* Paper presented at the annual meeting of the American Psychological Association, Washington, DC.

#DeVries, D., & Slavin, R. E. (1978). Teams-Games-Tournaments: A research review. *Journal of Research and Development in Education, 12*, 28–38.

*@+DeVries, D. L., Edwards, K. J., & Wells, E. H. (1974). *Teams-Games-Tournaments in instruction: Effects on academic achievement, student attitudes, cognitive beliefs, and classroom climate* (Report No. 173). Baltimore: Johns Hopkins University, Center for Social Organization of Schools.

*$+Edwards, K. J., & DeVries, D. L. (1972). *Learning games and student teams: Their effects on student attitudes and achievements* (Rep. No. 147). Baltimore: Johns Hopkins University, Center for Social Organization of Schools.

*@$+Edwards, K. J., & DeVries, D. L. (1974) *The effects of Teams-Games Tournaments and two structural variations on classroom process, student attitudes, and student achievement* (Rep. No. 172). Baltimore: Johns Hopkins University, Center for Social Organization of Schools.

*#@+$Edwards, K. J., DeVries, D., & Snyder, J. P. (1972). Games and teams: A winning combination. *Simulation and Games, 3*, 247–269.

*Fantuzzo, J. W., King, J. A., & Heller, L. R. (1992). Effects of reciprocal peer tutoring on mathematics and school adjustments: A component analysis. *Journal of Educational Psychology, 84*(3), 331–339.

@Faust, W. L. (1959). Group versus individual problem solving. *Journal of Abnormal and Social Psychology, 59*, 68–72.

*Frantz, L. J. (1979). *The effects of the student teams achievement approach in reading on peer attitudes.* Master's thesis, Old Dominion University, Norfolk, VA.

@Fraser, S. C., Beaman, A. L., Diener, E., & Kelem, R. T. (1977). Two, three, or four heads are better than one: Modification of college performance by peer monitoring. *Journal of Educational Psychology, 69*, 101–108.

@French, D., Brownele, C., Graziano, W., & Hartup, W. (1977). Effects of cooperative, competitive, and individualistic sets on performance in children's groups. *Journal of Experimental Child Psychology, 24*, 1–10.

@Garibadli, A. (1979). The affective contributions of cooperative and group goal structures. *Journal of Educational Psychology, 71*, 788–795.

@Goldman, M., Stockbauer, J., & McAuliffe, T. (1977). Intergroup and intragroup competition and cooperation. *Journal of Experimental Social Psychology, 13*, 81–88.

@Gordon, K. (1924). Group judgments in the field of lifted weights. *Journal of Experimental Psychology, 7*, 398–400.

@Graziano. W., French, D., Brownele, C., & Hartup, W. (1976). Peer interaction in same- and mixed-age triads in relation to chronological age and incentive condition. *Child Development, 47*, 707–714.

*Greenwood, C. R., Delquadri, J. C., & Hall, R. V. (1989). Longitudinal effects of classwide peer tutoring. *Journal of Educational Psychology, 81*, 371–383.

@Grunee, H. (1937). Maze learning in the collective situation. *Journal of Psychology, 13*, 437–443.

@Haines, D., & McKeachie, W. (1967). Cooperative versus competitive discussion methods in teaching introductory psychology. *Journal of Educational Psychology, 58,* 386–390.

$Hamblin, R. L., Hathaway, C., & Wodarski, J. S. (1971). Group contingencies, peer tutoring, and accelerating academic achievement. In E. Ramp & W. Hopkins (Eds.), *A new direction for education: Behavior analysis.* Lawrence: University of Kansas, Department of Human Development.

@Hammond, L., & Goldman, M. (1961). Competition and noncompetition and its relationship to individual and group productivity. *Sociometry, 24,* 46–60.

*Hawkins, J. D., Doueck, H. J., & Lishner, D. M. (1988). Changing teacher practices in mainstream classrooms to improve bonding and behavior of low achievers. *American Educational Research Journal, 25*(1), 31–50.

*Heller, L. R., & Fantuzzo, J. W. (in press). Reciprocal peer tutoring and parent partnership: Does parent involvement make a difference? *School Psychology Review.*

Henderson, R. W., & Landesman, E. M. (2001). Effects of thematically integrated mathematics instruction on students of Mexican descent. *The Journal of Educational Research, 88*(5), 290–300.

*$Hertz-Lazarowitz, R., Sapir, C., & Sharan, S. (1981). *Academic and social effects of two cooperative learning methods in desegregated classrooms.* Unpublished manuscript, Haifa University, Israel.

@Horner, M. S. (1974). Performance of men in noncompetitive and interpersonal competitive achievement-oriented situations. In J. Atkinson & J. Raynor (Eds.), *Motivation and achievement* (pp. 237–254). Washington, DC: Winston.

@Hovey, D., Gruber, H., & Terrell, G. (1963). Effects of self-directed study and course achievement, retention, and curiosity. *Journal of Educational Research, 56,* 346–351.

$Huber, G., Bogatzki, W., & Winter, M. (1981) *Cooperation: Condition and goal of teaching and learning in classrooms.* Unpublished manuscript, University of Tubingen, West Germany.

@Hudgins, B. Effects of group experience and individual problem solving. *Journal of Educational Psychology, 51,* 37–42.

*+Hulten, B. H., & DeVries, D. L. (1976). *Team competition and group practice: Effects on student achievement and attitudes* (Rep. No. 212). Baltimore: Johns Hopkins University, Center for Social Organization of Schools.

@Hulten, G. (1974, April). *Games and teams: An effective combination in the classroom.* Paper presented at the annual meeting of the American Educational Research Association, Chicago.

@$+Humphreys, B., Johnson, R., & Johnson, D. W. (1982). Effects of cooperative, competitive, and individualistic learning on students' achievement in science class. *Journal of Research in Science Teaching, 19,* 351–356.

+Humphreys, B., Johnson, R., & Johnson, D. W. (in press). Cooperation, competition, individualization, and the ninth grade science student. *Journal of Research on Science Teaching.*

@Hurlock, E. (1927). Use of group rivalry as an incentive. *Journal of Abnormal and Social Psychology, 22,* 278–290.

@Husband, R. (1940). Cooperation versus solitary problem solving. *Journal of Social Psychology, 11,* 405–409.

+Johnson, D. W., & Johnson, R. T. (1982). The effects of cooperative and individualistic instruction on handicapped and nonhandicapped students. *Journal of Social Psychology, 118,* 247–268.

#@$Johnson, D. W., Johnson, R. T., Johnson, J., & Anderson, D. (1976). The effects of cooperative vs. individualized instruction on student prosocial behavior, attitudes toward learning, and achievement. *Journal of Educational Psychology, 68*, 446–452.

*#@$Johnson, D. W., Johnson, R. T., & Scott, L. (1978). The effects of cooperative and individualized instruction on student attitudes and achievement. *Journal of Social Psychology, 104*, 207–216.

@Johnson, D. W., Johnson, R. T., & Skon, L. (1979). Student achievement on different types of tasks under cooperative, competitive, and individualistic conditions. *Contemporary Educational Psychology, 4*, 99–106.

Johnson, D. W., Muruyama, G., Johnson, R., Nelson, D., & Skon, L. (1981). Effects of cooperative, competitive, and individualistic goal structures on achievement: A meta-analysis. *Psychological Bulletin, 89*(1), 47–62.

@Johnson, D. W., Skon, L., & Johnson, R. T. (1980). The effects of cooperative, competitive, and individualistic goal structures on student achievement on different types of tasks. *American Educational Research Journal, 17*, 83–93.

*Johnson, L. (1985). *The effects of groups of four cooperative learning models on student problem-solving achievement in mathematics.* Doctoral dissertation, University of Houston.

*Johnson, L., & Waxman, H. C. (1985, March). *Evaluating the effects of the "groups of four" program.* Paper presented at the annual meeting of the American Educational Research Association, Chicago.

+Johnson, R., Johnson, D. W., DeWeerdt, N., Lyons, V., and Zaidman, B. (1983). Integrating severely adaptively handicapped seventh-grade students into constructive relationships with nonhandicapped peers in science class. *American Journal of Mental Deficiency, 87*(6), 611–618.

@Johnson, R. T., & Johnson, D. W. (1979). Type of task and student achievement and attitudes in interpersonal cooperation, competition, and individualization. *Journal of Social Psychology, 108*, 37–48.

Johnson, R. T., Johnson, D. W., Scott, L. E., & Romolae, B. A. (1985). Effects of single-sex and mixed-sex cooperative interaction on science achievement and attitudes and cross-handicap and cross-sex relationships. *Journal of Research in Science Teaching, 22*, 207–220.

*+Johnson, R. T., Johnson, D. W., & Stanne, M. B. (1985). Effects of cooperative, competitive, and individualistic goal structures on computer-assisted instruction. *Journal of Educational Psychology, 77*(6), 668–677.

+Johnson, R. T., Johnson, D. W., & Stanne, M. B. (1986). Comparison of computer assisted cooperative, competitive, and individualistic learning. *American Educational Research Journal, 23*, 381–391.

@Johnson, R. T., Johnson, D. W., & Tauer, M. (1979). Effects of cooperative, competitive, and individualistic goal structures on students' achievement and attitudes. *Journal of Psychology, 102*, 191–198.

@Jones, S., & Vroom, V. (1964). Division of labor and performance under cooperative-competitive conditions. *Journal of Abnormal Social Psychology, 68*, 313–320.

@Julian, J., & Perry, F. (1967). Cooperation contrasted with intra-group competition. *Sociometry, 30*, 79–90.

*Kagan, S., Zahn, G. L., Widaman, K. F., Schwarzwald, J., & Tyrell, G. (1985). Classroom structural bias: Impact of cooperative and competitive classroom structures on cooperative and competitive individuals and groups. In R. E. Slavin, S. Sharan, S. Kagan,

R. Hertz-Lazarowitz, C. Webb, & R. Schmuck (Eds.), *Learning to cooperate, cooperating to learn* (pp. 277–312). New York: Plenum.

@Kanekar, S., Libley, C., Engels, J., & John, G. (1978). Group performance as a function of group type, task condition, and scholastic level. *European Journal of Social Psychology, 8,* 439–451.

@Kelly, R., Rawson, R., & Terry, R. (1973). Interaction effects of achievement need and situational press on performance. *Journal of Social Psychology, 89,* 141–145.

*Kinney, J. H. (1989, May). *A study of the effects of a cooperative learning program on the achievement of ninth grade multi-cultural general biology classes.* Paper presented to the Alexandria City, Virginia School Board.

@Klugman, S. (1944). Cooperation versus individual efficiency in problem solving. *Journal of Educational Psychology, 35,* 91–100.

*Kosters, A. E. (1990). *The effects of cooperative learning in the traditional classroom on student achievement and attitude.* Unpublished doctoral dissertation, University of South Dakota.

*Lamberights, R., & Diepenbroek, J. W. (1992, July). *Implementation and the effects of an integrated direct and active instruction in a cooperative classroom setting.* Paper presented at the International Convention on Cooperative Learning, Utrecht, The Netherlands.

Lampe, J. R., Booze, G. E., & Tallent-Runnels, M. (2001). Effects of cooperative learning among Hispanic students in elementary social studies. *The Journal of Educational Research, 89*(3), 187–191.

@Laughlin, P. (1965). Selection strategies in concept attainment as a function of number of persons and stimulus display. *Journal of Experimental Psychology, 70,* 323–327.

@Laughlin, P. (1972). Selection versus reception concept-attainment paradigms for individuals and cooperative pairs. *Journal of Educational Psychology, 63,* 116–122.

@Laughlin, P., & Adamopoulos, J. (1980). Social combination processes and individual learning for six person cooperative groups on an intellective task. *Journal of Personality and Social Psychology, 38,* 941–947.

@Laughlin, P., & Bitz, D. (1975). Individual versus dyadic performance on a dysjunctive task as a function of initial ability level. *Journal of Personality and Social Psychology, 31,* 487–496.

@Laughlin, P., & Branch, L. (1972). Individual versus triadic performance on a complementary task as a function of initial ability level. *Organizational Behavior and Human Performance, 8,* 201–216.

@Laughlin, P., Branch, L., & Johnson, H. (1969). Individual versus triadic performance on a unidimensional complementary task as a function of initial ability level. *Journal of Personality and Social Psychology, 12,* 144–150.

@Laughlin, P., & Jaccard, J. (1975). Social facilitation and observational learning of individuals and cooperative pairs. *Journal of Personality and Social Psychology, 32,* 873–879.

@Laughlin, P., & Johnson, H. (1966). Group and individual performance on a complementary task as a function of initial ability level. *Journal of Personality and Social Psychology, 2,* 407–414.

@Laughlin, P., Kalowski, C., Metzler, M., Ostap, K., & Venclovas, S. (1968). Concept identification as a function of sensory modality, information, and number of persons. *Journal of Experimental Psychology, 77,* 335–340.

@Laughlin, P., Keer, N., Munch, M., & Haggerty, C. (1976). Social decision schemes of the same four-person groups on two different intellective tasks. *Journal of Personality and Social Psychology, 33*, 80–88.

@Laughlin, P., & McGlynn, R. (1967). Cooperative versus competitive concept attainment as a function of sex and stimulus display. *Journal of Personality and Social Psychology, 7*, 398–402.

@Laughlin, P., McGlynn, R., Anderson, J., & Jacobsen, E. (1968). Concept attainment by individuals versus cooperative pairs as a function of memory, sex, and concept rule. *Journal of Personality and Social Psychology, 8*, 410–417.

*Lazarowitz, R. (1991). Learning biology cooperatively: An Israeli junior high school study. *Cooperative Learning, 11*(3), 19–21.

+Lazarowitz, R., Baird, J. H., Hertz-Lazarowitz, R., & Jenkins, J. (1985). The effects of modified jigsaw on achievement, classroom social climate, and self-esteem in high-school science classes. In R. E. Slavin, S. Sharan, S. Kagan, R. Hertz-Lazarowitz, C. Webb, & R. Schmuck (Eds.), *Learning to cooperate, cooperating to learn* (231–253). New York: Plenum.

*Lazarowitz, R., & Karsenty, G. (1990). Cooperative learning and students' self-esteem in tenth grade biology classrooms. In S. Sharan (Ed.), *Cooperative learning, theory, and research* (pp. 123–149). New York: Praeger.

$Lew, M., & Bryant, R. (1981, April). *The use of cooperative groups to improve spelling achievement for all children in the regular classroom*. Paper presented at the Massachusetts Council for Exceptional Children, Boston.

#@$Lucker, G., Rosenfield, D., Sikes, J., & Aronson, E. (1976). Performance in the interdependent classroom: A field study. *American Educational Research Journal, 13*, 115–123.

$Madden, N. A., & Slavin, R. E. (1983a). Cooperative learning and social acceptance of mainstreamed academically handicapped students. *Journal of Special Education, 17*(2), 171–182.

*Madden, N. A., & Slavin, R. E. (1983b). Mainstreaming students with mild academic handicaps: Academic and social outcomes. *Review of Educational Research, 53*, 519–569.

@Maller, J. (1929). *Cooperation and competition: An experimental study of motivation.* New York: Teachers College, Columbia University.

*Martinez, L. J. (1990). *The effects of corporative learning on academic achievement and self-concept with bilingual third-grade students*. Unpublished doctoral dissertation, United States International University.

@Martino, L., & Johnson, D. W. (1979). Cooperative and individualistic experiences among disabled and normal children. *Journal of Social Psychology, 107*, 177–183.

*Mattingly, R. M., & Van Sickle, R. L. (1991). Cooperative learning and achievement in social studies: Jigsaw II. *Social Education, 55*(6), 392–395.

@McClintock, E., & Sonquist, J. (1976). Cooperative task-oriented groups in a college classroom: A field application. *Journal of Educational Psychology, 68*, 588–596.

@McCurdy, H., & Lambert, W. (1952). The efficiency of small human groups in the solution of problems requiring genuine cooperation. *Journal of Personality, 20*, 478–494.

@McGlynn, R. (1972). Four-person group concept attainment as a function of interaction format. *Journal of Social Psychology, 86*, 89–94.

*Mevarech, Z. R. (1985a, April). *Cooperative mastery learning strategies*. Paper presented at the annual meeting of the American Educational Research Association, Chicago.

*Mevarech, Z. R. (1985b). The effects of corporative learning strategies on mathematics achievement. *Journal of Educational Research, 78*, 372–377.

*Mevarech, Z. R. (1991). Learning mathematics in different mastery environments. *Journal of Educational Research, 84*(4), 225–231.

Mevarech, Z. R., & Kramarski, B. (1997). IMPROVE: A multidimensional method for teaching mathematics in heterogeneous classrooms. *American Educational Research Journal, 34*(2), 365–394.

Mevarech, Z. R., & Kramarski, B. (2003). The effects of metacognitive training versus worked-out examples on students' mathematical reasoning. *British Journal of Educational Psychology, 73*, 449–471.

@Michaels, J. (1978). Effects of differential rewarding and sex on math performance. *Journal of Educational Psychology, 70*, 565–573.

@Miller, F. (1971). Effects of small group instruction on achievement of technical information by ninth grade industrial arts students. *Dissertation Abstracts International, 32*, 5009A. (University Microfilms No. 72-10, 559)

@Nelson, L., & Madsen, M. C. (1969). Cooperation and competition in four-year-olds as a function of reward contingency and subculture. *Developmental Psychology, 1*, 340–344.

@Newcomb, A., Brady, J., & Hartup, W. (1979). Friendship and incentive condition as determinants of children's task-oriented social behavior. *Child Development, 50*, 878–881.

Newmann, F. M., & Thompson, J. A. (1987). *Effects of cooperative learning on achievement in secondary schools: A summary of research.* Unpublished manuscript, University of Wisconsin–Madison, School of Education, partially funded by National Center on Effective Secondary Schools.

@Nogami, G. (1976). Effects of group size, room size, or density? *Journal of Applied Social Psychology, 6*, 105–125.

@Nowicki, S., Duke, M., & Crouch, M. (1978). Sex differences in locus of control and performance under competitive and corporative conditions. *Journal of Educational Psychology, 70*, 482–486.

*+Okebukola, P. A. (1984). In search of a more effective interaction pattern in biology laboratories. *Journal of Biological Education, 18*(4), 305–308.

*+Okebukola, P. A. (1985). The relative effectiveness of cooperative and competitive interaction techniques in strengthening students' performance in science classes. *Science Education, 69*, 501–509.

*+Okebukola, P. A. (1986a). Impact of extended cooperative and competitive relationships on the performance of students in science. *Human Relations, 39*(7), 673–682.

*+Okebukola, P. A. (1986b). The influence of preferred learning styles on cooperative learning in science. *Science Education, 70*(5), 509–576.

+Okebukola, P. A. (1986c). The problem of large classes in science: An experiment in cooperative learning. *European Journal of Science Education, 8*(1), 73–77.

+Okebukola, P. A., & Ogunniyi, M. B. (1984). Cooperative, competitive, and individualistic science laboratory interaction patterns—effects on students' achievement and acquisition of practical skills. *Journal of Research in Science Teaching, 21*(9), 875–884.

@Okun, M., & Divesta, F. (1975). Cooperation and competition in coacting groups. *Journal of Personality and Social Psychology, 31*, 615–620.

@Olson, P., & Davis, J. (1964). Divisible tasks and pooling performance in groups. *Psychological Reports, 15*, 511–517.

*Peck, G. L. (1991). *The effects of corporative learning on the spelling achievement of intermediate elementary students.* Unpublished doctoral dissertation, Ball State University.

*Perrault, R. (1982). *An experimental comparison of cooperative learning to noncoopera-tive learning and their effects on cognitive achievement in junior high industrial arts laboratories.* Doctoral dissertation, University of Maryland.

@$Peterson, P. L., & Janicki, T. C. (1979). Individual characteristics and children's learn-ing in large-group and small-group approaches. *Journal of Educational Psychology, 71*, 677–687.

$Peterson, P. L., Janicki, T., & Swing, S. (1981). Ability x Treatment interaction effects on children's learning in large-group and small-group approaches. *American Educational Research Journal, 18*, 453–473.

*Phelps, J. D. (1990). *A study of the interrelationships between corporative team learning, learning preference, friendship patterns, gender, and achievement in middle school students.* Unpublished doctoral dissertation, Indiana University.

@Philip, A. (1940). Strangers and friends as competitors and cooperators. *Journal of Ge-netic Psychology, 57*, 249–258.

@Raven, B., & Eachus, H. (1963). Cooperation and competition in means-interdependent triads. *Journal of Abnormal and Social Psychology, 67*, 307–316.

+Rich, Y., Amir, Y., & Slavin, R. (1986). *Instructional strategies for improving children's cross-ethnic relations.* Institute for the Advancement of Social Integration in the Schools, Bar Ilan University, Israel.

@Richmond, B., & Weiner, G. (1973). Cooperation and competition among young children as a function of ethnic grouping, grade, sex, and reward condition. *Journal of Educa-tional Psychology, 64*, 329–334.

@Roberts, G. (1972). Effects of achievement motivation and social environment on perfor-mance of a motor task. *Journal of Motor Behavior, 4*, 37–46.

@$Robertson, L. (1982) *Integrated goal structuring in the elementary school: Cognitive growth in mathematics.* Unpublished doctoral dissertation, Rutgers University.

@Rorie, V. (1979). *The effects of cooperative versus competitive goal structure on student achievement among Afro-American students.* Unpublished Educational Specialist Thesis, University of Minnesota, Minneapolis.

@Rosenbaum, M., Groff, B., & Skowronski, J. (1980). Unpublished study cited in M. Rosenbaum, *Cooperation and competition.* In P. Paulus (Ed.), *Psychology of group influence.* Hillsdale, NJ: Erlbaum.

@Rosenbaum, M. E. (1980). Group productivity and process: Pure and mixed reward struc-ture and task interdependence. *Journal of Personality and Social Psychology, 39*, 626–642.

@Ryack, B. L. (1965). A comparison of individual and group learning of nonsense syl-lables. *Journal of Personality and Social Psychology, 2*, 296–299.

*Schaedel, B., Hertz-Lasarowitz, R., Walk, A., Lerner, M., Juberan, S., & Sarid, M. (in process). The Israeli CIRC (ALSASH): First year achievement in reading and compo-sition. *Helkat-Lashon* (Journal of Linguistic Education, in Hebrew).

@Scott, W., & Cherrington, D. (1974). Effects of competitive, cooperative, and individual-ized reinforcement contingencies. *Journal of Personality and Social Psychology, 30*, 748–759.

Sharan, S. (1980). Cooperative learning in small groups: Recent methods and effects on achievement, attitudes, and ethnic relations. *Review of Educational Research, 50*(2), 241–271.

$Sharan, S. (1984). *Cooperative learning in the classroom: Research in desegregated schools.* Hillsdale, NJ: Erlbaum.

$Sharan, S., Hertz-Lazarowitz, R., & Ackerman, Z. (1980). Academic achievement of elementary school children in small-group vs. whole class instruction. *Journal of Experimental Education, 48*, 125–129.

*+Sharan, S., Kussel, P., Hertz-Lazarowitz, R., Bejarano, Y., Raviv, S., & Sharan, Y. (1984). *Cooperative learning in the classroom: Research in desegregated schools.* Hillsdale, NJ: Erlbaum.

*Sharan, S., & Shachar, C. (1988). *Language and learning in the corporative classroom.* New York: Springer-Verlag.

@Shaw, M. (1958). A comparison of individuals and small groups in the rational solution of complex problems. *Journal of Personality, 26*, 155–169.

+Sherman, L. M., & Zimmerman, D. (1986, November). *Cooperative versus competitive reward-structured secondary science classroom achievement.* Paper presented to the national meeting of the School Science and Mathematics Association.

*Sherman, L. W. (1988). A comparative study of corporative and competitive achievement in two secondary biology classrooms: The group investigation model versus an individually competitive goal structure. *Journal of Research in Science Teaching, 26*(1), 35–64.

*+Sherman, L. W., & Thomas, M. (1986). Mathematics achievement in cooperative versus individualistic goal-structured high school classrooms. *Journal of Educational Research, 79*, 169–172.

*Sherman, L. W., & Zimmerman, D. (1986, November). *Cooperative versus competitive reward-structured secondary science classroom achievement.* Paper presented at the annual meeting of the School Science and Mathematics Association, Lexington, KY.

@Sims, V. (1928). The relative influence of two types of motivation on improvement. *Journal of Educational Psychology, 19*, 480–484.

@Skon, L., Johnson, D. W., & Johnson, R. (1981). Effects of cooperative, competitive, and individualistic learning situations on achievement and reasoning processes. *Journal of Educational Psychology, 73*(1), 83–92.

#Slavin, R. E. (1977a). Classroom reward structure: An analytical and practical review. *Review of Educational Research, 47*, 633–650.

@Slavin, R. E. (1977b). How student learning teams can integrate the desegregated classroom. *Integrated Education, 15*, 56–58.

$+Slavin, R. E. (1977c). *Student learning team techniques: Narrowing the achievement gap between the races* (Report No. 228). Baltimore: Johns Hopkins University, Center for Social Organization of Schools.

*@Slavin, R. E. (1977d). A student team approach to teaching adolescents with special emotional and behavioral needs. *Psychology in the Schools, 14*(1), 77–84.

@Slavin, R. E. (1978a). *Effects of biracial learning teams on cross-racial friendships and interaction* (Report No. 240). Baltimore: Johns Hopkins University, Center for Social Organization of Schools.

@Slavin, R. E. (1978b). *Effects of student teams and peer tutoring on academic achievement and time on-task* (Report No. 253). Baltimore: Johns Hopkins University, Center for Social Organization of Schools.

#+Slavin, R. E. (1978c). Student teams and achievement divisions. *Journal of Research and Development in Education, 12*, 39–49.

$+*@Slavin, R. E. (1978d). Student teams and comparison among equals: Effects on academic performance and student attitudes. *Journal of Educational Psychology, 70*, 532–538.

*$Slavin, R. E. (1979). Effects of biracial learning teams on cross-racial friendships. *Journal of Educational Psychology, 71*, 381–387.

*$Slavin, R. E. (1980). Effects of student teams and peer tutoring on academic achievement and time on-task. *Journal of Experimental Education, 48*, 252–257.

Slavin, R. E. (1995). *Cooperative learning* (2nd ed.). Boston: Allyn and Bacon.

Slavin, R. E. (1996). *Education for all*. Lisse, The Netherlands: Swets & Zeitlinger.

Slavin, R. E. (1997). When does cooperative learning increase student achievement? In E. Dubinsky, D. Mathews, & B. E. Reynolds, *Readings in Cooperative Learning for Undergraduate Mathematics* (pp. 71–84). Washington, DC: The Mathematical Association of America.

$*Slavin, R. E., & Karweit, N. (1981). Cognitive and affective outcomes of an intensive student team learning experience. *Journal of Experimental Education, 50*, 29–35.

$Slavin, R. E., & Karweit, N. (1982). *Student teams and mastery learning: An experiment in urban math 9 classes* (Report No. 320). Baltimore: Johns Hopkins University, Center for Social Organization of Schools.

*Slavin, R. E., & Karweit, N. L. (1984). Mastery learning and student teams: A factorial experiment in urban general mathematics classes. *American Educational Research Journal, 21*, 725–736.

*Slavin, R. E., & Karweit, N. L. (1985). Effects of whole-class, ability grouped, and individualized instruction on mathematics achievement. *American Educational Research Journal, 22*, 351–367.

$Slavin, R. E., Leavey, M., & Madden, N. A. (1983). *Combining student teams and individualized instruction in mathematics: An extended evaluation*. Paper presented at the Annual Convention of the American Educational Research Association, Montreal.

$*Slavin, R. E., Leavey, M., & Madden, N. A. (1984). Combining cooperative learning and individualized instruction: Effects on student mathematics achievement, attitudes, and behaviors. *Elementary School Journal, 84*(4), 408–422.

*Slavin, R. E., Madden, M. A., & Leavey, M. B. (1984). Effects of team assisted individualization on the mathematics achievement of academically handicapped students and nonhandicapped students. *Journal of Educational Psychology, 76*, 813–819.

*+$Slavin, R. E., & Oickle, E. (1981). Effects of cooperative learning on student achievement and race relations: Treatment by race interactions. *Sociology of Education, 54*, 174–180.

*Solomon, D., Watson, M. S., Delucchi, K. L., Schaps, E., & Battistich, V. (1988). Enhancing children's prosocial behavior in the classroom. *American Educational Research Journal, 25*, 527–554.

$Starr, R., & Schuerman, C. (1974). An experiment in small-group learning. *The American Biology Teacher, 36*(3), 173–175.

*Stevens, R. J., & Durkin, S. (1992). *Using student team reading and student team writing in middle schools: Two evaluations* (Report No. 36). Baltimore: Johns Hopkins University, Center for Research on Effective Schooling for Disadvantaged Students.

*Stevens, R. J., Madden, N. A., Slavin, R. E., & Farnish, A. M. (1987). Cooperative integrated reading and composition: Two field experiments. *Reading Research Quarterly, 22*, 433–454.

*Stevens, R. J., Slavin, R. E., & Farnish, A. M. (1991). The effects of cooperative learning and direct instruction in reading comprehension strategies on main idea identification. *Journal of Educational Psychology, 83*(1), 8–16.

*Stevens, R. J., Slavin, R. E., Farnish, A. M., & Madden, N. A. (1988, April). *Effects of* *cooperative learning and direct instruction in reading comprehension strategies on main idea identification.* Paper presented at the annual meeting of the American Educational Research Association, New Orleans.

Swanson, H. L. (2000). What instruction works for students with learning disabilities? Summarizing the results from a meta-analysis of intervention studies. In R. M. Gersten, E. P. Schiller, & S. Vaughn (Eds.), *Contemporary special education research: Syntheses of the knowledge base on critical instructional issues* (pp. 1–30). Mahwah, NJ: Erlbaum.

*Talmage, H., Pascarella, E. T., & Ford, S. (1984). The influence of cooperative learning strategies on teacher practices, student perceptions of the learning environment, and academic achievement. *American Educational Research Journal, 21,* 163–179.

*Tomblin, E. A., & Davis, B. R. (1985). *Technical report on the evaluation of the race/ human relations program: A study of cooperative learning environment strategies.* San Diego: San Diego Public Schools.

*Van Oudenhaven, J. P., Van Berkum, G., & Swen-Koopmans, T. (1987). Effects of cooperation and shared feedback on spelling achievement. *Journal of Educational Psychology, 79,* 92–94.

*Van Oudenhaven, J. P., Wiersma, B., & Van Yperen, N. (1987). Effects of cooperation and feedback by fellow pupils on spelling achievement. *European Journal of Psychology of Education, 2,* 83–91.

*Veder, P. H. (1985). *Cooperative learning: A study on process and effects of cooperation between primary school children.* The Hague, The Netherlands: Stichting voor Onderzoek van het Onderwijs.

$Webb, N., & Kenderski, C. (1984). Student interaction and learning in small groups and whole class settings. In P. Peterson, L. Cherry Wilkinson, & M. Hallinan (Eds.), *The social context on instruction: Group organization and group processes.* New York: Academic Press.

$Wheeler, R. (1977, September). *Predisposition toward cooperation and competition: Cooperative and competitive classroom effects.* Paper presented at the Annual Convention of the America Psychological Association, San Francisco.

$Wheeler, R., & Ryan, F. L. (1973). Effects of cooperative and competitive classroom environments on the attitudes and achievement of elementary school students engaged in social studies inquiry activities. *Journal of Educational Psychology, 65,* 402–407.

Whicker, K. M., Bol, L., & Nunnery, J. A. (2001). Cooperative Learning in the secondary mathematics classroom. *The Journal of Educational Research, 91*(1), 42–48.

$Ziegler, S. (1981). The effectiveness of cooperative learning teams for increasing cross-ethnic friendship: Additional evidence. *Human Organization, 40,* 264–268.

REFERENCES FOR REDUCING STUDENT/TEACHER RATIO BELOW 21 TO 1

&Abt Associates. (1997, April). *Prospects: Final report on student outcomes.* Cambridge, MA: Abt Associates. (Report prepared for U.S. Department of Education)

&Achilles, C. M. (1999). *Let's put kids first finally: Getting class size right.* Thousand Oaks, CA: Corwin Press.

Achilles, C. M. (2005). Class size and learning. In L. W. Hughes (Ed.), *Current issues in school leadership* (pp. 105–124). Mahwah, NJ: Erlbaum.

&Achilles, C. M., & Finn, J. D. (2000). Should class size be a cornerstone for educational policy? In M. C. Wang & J. D. Finn (Eds.), *How small classes help teachers do their best* (pp. 299–324). Philadelphia: Temple University Center for Research in Human Development in Education.

&Achilles, C. M., & Finn, J. D. (2002, December). The varieties of small classes and their outcomes. In J. D. Finn & M. C. Wang (Eds.), *Taking small classes one step further* (pp. 121–146). Philadelphia: Temple University Center for Research in Human Development in Education.

&Achilles, C. M., Finn, J. D., & Pate-Bain, H. (2002, February). Measuring class size: Let me count the ways. *Educational Leadership, 59*(5), 24–26.

&Achilles, C. M., Harman, P., & Egelson, P. (1995, Fall). Using research results on class size to improve pupil achievement outcomes. *Research in the School, 2*(2), 23–30.

&Achilles, C. M., Kise-Kling, K., Aust, A., & Owen, J. (1995, April). *A study of reduced class size in primary grades of a fully chapter-1 eligible school: Success starts small (SSS).* Paper presented at the annual meeting of the American Educational Research Association, San Francisco. (ERIC Document Reproduction Service No. ED 419 288)

&Achilles, C. M., & Price, W. J. (1999, January). Can your district afford smaller class sizes in grades K–3? *School Business Affairs, 65*(1), 5–10.

&Achilles, C. M., & Sharp, M. (1998, Fall). Solve your puzzles using class size and pupil-teacher ratio (PTR) differences. *Catalyst for Change, 28*(1), 5–10.

*Anderson, F. H., Bedford, F., Clark, V., & Schipper, J. (1963). A report of an experiment at Camelback High School. *The Mathematics Teacher, 56*, 155–159.

*Averill, L. A., & Mueller, A. D. (1925). Size of class and reading efficiency. *The Elementary School Journal, 25*, 682–691.

*#Balow, I. H. (1969). A longitudinal evaluation of reading achievement in small classes. *Elementary Education, 46*, 184–187.

*Bates, D. A. (1928). *The relation of the size of a class to the efficiency of teaching.* Unpublished master's thesis, University of Chicago.

*Bausell, R. B., Moody, W. B., & Walze, F. N. (1972). A factorial study of tutoring versus classroom instruction. *American Educational Research Journal, 9*, 591–598.

&Biddle, B. J., & Berliner, D. C. (2002). Small class size and its effects. *Educational Leadership, 59*(5), 12–23.

Blatchford, P., Bassett, P., Goldstein, H., & Martin, C. (2003). Are class size differences related to pupils' educational progress and classroom processes? Findings from the Institute of Education Class Size Study of Children Aged 5–7 Years. *British Educational Research Journal, 29*(5), 709–730.

Bloom, B. (1984). The 2 sigma problem: The search for methods of group instruction as effective as one-to-one tutoring. *Journal of Educational Research, 13*, 4–16.

&Bohrnstedt, G. W., Stecher, B. M., & Wiley, E. W. (2000). The California class size reduction evaluation: Lesson learned? In M. C. Wang & J. D. Finn (Eds.), *How small classes help teachers do their best* (pp. 201–226). Philadelphia: Temple University Center for Research in Human Development in Education.

&Boozer, M., & Rouse, C. (1995, May). *Intraschool variation in school size: Patterns and implications.* Princeton, NJ: Industrial Relations Section. (ERIC Document Reproduction Service No. ED 385–395)

&Borman, G. D., & D'Agostino, J. V. (1996, Winter). Title I and student achievement: A meta-analysis of federal evaluation results. *Educational Evaluation and Policy Analysis, 18*(4), 309–326.

*Bostrom, E. A. (1969). *The effect of class size on critical thinking skills.* Unpublished doctoral thesis, Arizona State University.

&Boyd-Zaharias, J., & Pate-Bain, H. (2000a, April). *The continuing impact of elementary small classes.* Paper presented at the annual meeting of the American Educational Research Association, New Orleans.

&Boyd-Zaharias, J., & Pate-Bain, H. (2000b). *Early and new findings from Tennessee's Project STAR* (pp. 65–98). Philadelphia: Temple University Center for Research in Human Development in Education.

*Boyer, P. A. (1914). Class size and school progress. *Psychological Clinic, 8,* 82–90.

*Breed, F. S., & McCarthy, G. D. (1916). Size of a class and efficiency of teaching. *School and Society, 4,* 965–971.

*Brown, A. E. (1932). The effectiveness of large classes at the college level: An experimental study involving the size variable and size-procedure variable. *University of Iowa Studies in Education, 7,* 1–66.

&Cahen, L. S., & Filby, N. (1979, March). The class size/achievement issue: New evidence and research plan. *Phi Delta Kappan, 492*–495, 538.

#Cahen, L. S., Filby, N., McCutchen, G., & Kyle, D. W. (1983). *Class size and instruction.* New York: Longman.

*Cammarosano, J. R., & Santopolo, F. A. (1958). Teaching efficiency and class size. *School and Society, 86,* 338–340.

#Carrington, A. T., Mounie, J. C., & Lovelace, D. W. (1982). The effects of class-load standards according to a weighted formula of relief among student achievement and attitude and teacher morale. In *Class Size Project 1980–81, Final Report* (pp. 1–8). Virginia Beach, VA Public Schools.

&Chase, C. I., Mueller, D. J., & Walden, J. D. (1986, December). *PRIME TIME: Its impact on instruction and achievement.* Final report. Indianapolis: Indiana Department of Education.

Christensen, J. J. (1960). The effects of varying class size in teaching procedures on certain levels of student learning.* Doctoral thesis, Wayne State University (60-2698).

*Clarke, S.C.T., & Richel, S. (1963). *The effect of class size and teacher qualifications on achievement.* Edmonton, Alberta: Alberta Teachers Association.

*Coleman, J. S., et al. (1966). *Equality of educational opportunity.* Washington, DC: U.S. Government Printing Office.

*Cook, J. J., & Blessing, K. R. (1970). *Class size in teacher aides as factors in the achievement of the educable mentally retarded.* Madison: Wisconsin Department of Public Instruction. (ERIC Document Reproduction Service No. ED 047 484)

*Cornman, O. P. (1909). Size of classes and school progress. *The Psychological Clinic, 3,* 206–212.

&Cortez, A. (2000, March). Why better isn't enough: A closer look at TAAS gaines. *IDRA Newsletter,* San Antonio, TX.

#Counelis, J. S. (1970). *First grade students in the Hunters Point Bayview SEED Project: A diagnostic review.* San Francisco University, CA. (ERIC Document Reproduction Service No. ED 052 905)

*Cram, B. M. (1968). *An investigation of the influence of class size upon academic attainment and student satisfaction.* Doctoral thesis, Arizona State University (68-14988).

&Darling-Hammond, L. (1998, January–February). Teachers and teaching: Testing policy hypothesis from a national commission report. *Educational Researcher, 27*(1), 5–15.

*Davis, C. O. (1923). The size of classes and the teaching load in the high schools accredited by the North Central Association. *School Review, 31*, 412–429.

*Davis E., & Goldizen, M. (1930). A study of class size in junior high school history. *The School Review, 38*, 360–367.

*Dawe, H. C. (1934). The influence of size of kindergarten group upon performance. *Child Development, 5*, 295–303.

*DeCecco, J. P. (1964). Class size and co-ordinated instruction. *British Journal of Instructional Psychology, 34*, 65–74.

#Dennis, B. D. (1986). *Effects of small class size (1:15) on the teaching/learning process in grade two*. Doctoral dissertation, Tennessee State University.

*Eash, M. J., & Bennett, C. M. (1964). The effects of class size on achievement and attitudes. *American Educational Research Journal, 1*, 229–239.

*Eastburn, L. A. (1937). Report of class size investigations in the Phoenix Union High School, 1933–34 to 1935–36. *Journal of Educational Research, 31*, 107–117.

*Edmonson, J. B., & Mulder, F. U. (1924). Size of class as a factor in university instruction. *Journal of Educational Research, 9*, 1–12.

%Educational Research Service. (1980, December). Class size research: A critique of recent meta-analyses. *Phi Delta Kappan, 70*, 239–241.

&Egelson, P., Harman, P., Hood, A., & Achilles, C. M. (2002). *How class size makes a difference*. Greensboro, NC: South East Regional Vision for Education (SERVE).

%Elliott, M. (1998). School finance and opportunities to learn: Does money well spent enhance students' achievement? *Sociology of Education, 71*, 223–245.

*Ellson, D. G., Barber, L., Engle, R. L., & Kampwerth, L. (1965). Programmed tutoring: A teaching aid and a research tool. *Reading Research Quarterly, 1*, 77–127.

*Ellson, D. G., Harris, P., & Barber, L. (1968). A field test of programmed and directed tutoring. *Reading Research Quarterly, 3*, 307–367.

&Evertson, C. M., & Golger, J. K. (1989, March). *Small class, large class: What do teachers do differently?* Paper presented at the annual meeting of the American Educational Research Association, San Francisco.

&Evertson, C. M., & Randolph, C. H. (1989, Fall). Teaching practices and class size: A new look at an old issue. *Peabody Journal of Education, 67*(1), 85–105.

&Fairfax County (VA) Schools. (1997, July). *Evaluation of the reduced-ratio program: Final report*. Fairfax, VA: Office of Program Evaluation, Fairfax County Schools.

*Feldhusen, J. F. (1963). The effects of small and large group instruction on learning of subject matter, attitudes, and interests. *Journal of Psychology, 55*, 357–362.

%Ferguson, R. F. (1991). Paying for public education: New evidence on how and why money matters. *Harvard Journal on Legislation, 28*, 465–498.

%Ferguson, R. F., & Ladd, H. F. (1996). How and why money matters: An analysis of Alabama schools. In H. F. Ladd (Ed.), *Holding schools accountable: Performance-based reform in education* (pp. 256–298). Washington, DC: Brookings Institution.

&#Filby, N., Cahen, L., McCutcheon, G., & Kyle, D. (1980). *What happens in small classes? A summary report of a field study*. San Francisco: Far West Laboratory for Educational Research and Development.

%Finn, J. D., & Achilles, C. M. (1990). Answers and questions about class size: A statewide experiment. *American Educational Research Journal, 27*(3), 557–577.

&Finn, J. D., & Achilles, C. M. (1999 Summer). Tennessee's class size study: Findings, implications, misconceptions. *Educational Evaluation and Policy Analysis, 21*(2), 97–107.

&%Finn, J. D., Gerber, S. B., Achilles, C. M., & Boyd-Zaharias, J. (2001). The enduring effects of small classes. *Teachers College Record, 103*(1), 145–183.

&Finn, J. D., Gerber, S. B., & Boyd-Zaharias, J. (2004, April). *Small classes in the early grades, academic achievement, and dropping out of school.* Paper presented at the annual meeting of the American Educational Research Association, San Diego, CA.

&Finn, J. D., Pannozzo, G. M., & Achilles, C. M. (2003, Fall). The "whys" of class size: Student behavior in small classes. *Review of Educational Research, 73*(3), 321–368.

*Flinker, I. (1972). Optimum class size: What is the magic number? *Clearing House, 8,* 471–473.

Flynn, D. L., Haas, A. E., & Al-Salam, N. A. (1976). An evaluation of the cost effectiveness of alternative compensatory reading programs. Vol. III: Cost-effectiveness analysis.* Bethesda, MD: RMC Research Corporation.

%Folger, J. (Ed.). (1989). Project STAR and class size policy. *Peabody Journal of Education, 67*(1) (Special Issue).

#Fox, D. (1967). *Expansion of More Effective Schools Program.* New York: Center for Urban Education.

*Frymier, J. R. (1964). The effect of class size upon reading achievement in first grade. *The Reading Teacher, 18,* 90–93.

*#Furno, O., & Collins, G. J. (1967). *Class size and pupil learning.* Baltimore City Public Schools. (ERIC Document Reproduction Service No. ED 025 003)

&Gerber, S. B., Finn, J. D., Achilles, C. M., & Boyd-Zaharias, J. (2001, Summer). Teacher aides and students' academic achievement. *Educational Evaluation and Policy Analysis, 23*(2), 123–143.

*Glass, G. V. (1970). *Data analysis of the 1968–69 Survey of Compensatory Education.* Boulder: Laboratory of Educational Research, University of Colorado.

&Glass, G. V. (1992). Class size. In M. C. Akin (Ed.), *Encyclopedia of Educational Research* (Vol. 1, 6th ed., pp. 164–166). New York: Macmillan Publishing Co.

&%Glass, G. V., Cahen, L. S., Smith, M. L., & Filby, N. N. (1982). *School class size: Research and policy.* Beverly Hills, CA: Sage Publications.

&Glass, G. V., & Smith, M. L. (1978). *Meta-analysis of research on the relationship of class size and achievement.* San Francisco: Far West Laboratory for Educational Research and Development.

%Glass, G. V., & Smith, M. L. (1979). Meta-analysis of research on class size and achievement. *Educational Evaluation and Policy Analysis, 1,* 2–16.

%Grissmer, D. (Ed.). (1999). Class size: Issues and new findings. *Educational Evaluation and Policy Analysis, 21*(2) (Special Issue).

&Haberman, M. (2000, November). Urban Schools: Day camps or custodial centers. *Phi Delta Kappan, 82*(3), 203–208.

*Haertter, L. D. (1928). An experiment of the efficiency of instruction in large and small classes in plane geometry. *Educational Administration and Supervision, 14,* 580–590.

&Haney, W. (2000, August 19). The myth of the Texas miracle in education. *Educational Policy Analysis Archives, 8*(41).

&Hanushek, E. A. (1998, February). *The evidence on class size.* Rochester, NY: The University of Rochester, W. Allen Wallis Institute.

&Hanushek, E. A. (1999, Summer). Some findings from an independent investigation of the Tennessee STAR experiment and from other investigations of class size effects. *Educational Evaluation and Policy Analysis, 21*(2), 143–163.

*Harland, C. L. (1915). Size of class as a factor in schoolroom efficiency. *Educational Administration and Supervision, 1*, 195–214.

*Haskell, S. (1964). Some observations on the effects of class size upon pupil achievement in geometrical drawing. *Journal of Educational Research, 58*, 27–30.

%Hedges, L. V., & Stock, W. (1983). The effects of class size: An examination of rival hypotheses. *American Educational Research Journal, 20*, 63–85.

*Holland, B. G. (1928). The effect of class size on scholastic acquirement in educational psychology. *School and Society, 27*, 668–670.

*Hoover, K. H., Baumann, V. H., & Shafer, S. M. (1970). The influence of class-size variations on cognitive and affective learning of college freshmen. *Journal of Experimental Education, 38*, 39–43.

*Horne, K. (1970). Optimum class size for intensive language instruction. *Modern Language Journal, 54*, 189–195.

*Husen, T. (1967). *International study of achievement in mathematics* (Vol. 2). Stockholm: Almquist & Wiskell.

%Hymon, S. (1997, July 7). A lesson in classroom size reduction: Administrators nationwide can learn from California's classroom size reduction plan and how districts implemented it. *School Planning & Management, 36*(7), 18–23, 26.

&Iannaccone, L. (1975). *Educational policy systems: A study guide for educational administrators*. Ft. Lauderdale, FL: Nova Southeastern University (esp. pp. 11–19).

#Indiana State Department of Pupil Instruction. (1983). *Project PRIMETIME: 1982–83 Report*. Bethesda, MD. (ERIC Document Reproduction Service No. ED 239 765)

*Jeffs, G. A., & Cram, B. M. (1968). *The influence of class size on academic attainment and student satisfaction*. Las Vegas: Edward W. Clark High School. (ERIC Document Reproduction Service No. ED 021 252)

*Johnson M., & Scriven, E. (1967). Class size and achievement gains in seventh and eighth grade English and mathematics. *The School Review, 75*, 300–310.

*Judd, C. H. (1929). Report of the consultative committee. *Bulletin: Department of Secondary School Principals, 25*, 49–61.

*Kirk, J. R. (1929). A study of class size, teaching efficiency, and student achievement. *Phi Delta Kappan, 12*, 59–61.

%Korostoff, M. (1998). Tackling California's class size reduction policy initiative: An up close and personal account of how teachers and learners responded. *International Journal of Educational Research, 29*, 797–807.

%Krueger, A. B. (1999). Experimental estimates of education production functions. *The Quarterly Journal of Economics, 114*(2), 497–532.

%Krueger, A. B. (2000). *Economic considerations and class size*. Princeton, NJ: Princeton University, Industrial Relations Section, Working Paper #447.

&Krueger, A. B., & Whitmore, D. M. (2000, March). *The effect of attending a small class in the early grades on college-test taking and middle school test results: Evidence from Project STAR*. Princeton, NJ: Princeton University Industrial Relations Section.

%Krueger, A. B., & Whitmore, D. M. (2001). The effect of attending a small class in the early grades on college-test taking and middle school test results: Evidence from Project STAR. *Economic Journal, 111*, 1–28.

&Lindbloom, D. H. (1970). *Class size as it affects instructional procedures and educational outcomes*. (ERIC Document Reproduction Service No. ED059 532)

*#Little, A., Mabey, C., & Russell, J. (1971). Do small classes help a pupil? *New Society, 18*, 769–771.

*Lundberg, L. D. (1947). Effects of smaller classes. *The Nation's Schools, 39*, 20–22.

*Macomber, F. G., & Siegel, L. (1957). A study in large group teaching procedures. *The Educational Record, 38*, 220–229.

*Martin, G. M. (1969). *The effect of class size on the development of several abilities involved in critical thinking.* Doctoral thesis, Temple University (71-10853).

*Mayeske, G. W., et al. (n.d.). *A study of our nation's schools.* Washington, DC: U.S. Office of Education.

%McGivern, J., Gilman, D., & Tillitski, C. (1989). A meta-analysis of the relation between class size and achievement. *The Elementary School Journal, 90*(1), 47–56.

*#Meredith, V. H., Johnson, L. M., & Garcia-Quintana, R. A. (1978). *South Carolina First Grade Pilot Project 1976–77: The effects of class size on reading and mathematics achievement.* Columbia: South Carolina Department of Education.

*Metzner, A. B., & Berry, C. (1926). Size of class for mentally retarded children. *Training School Bulletin, 23*, 241–251.

&Miles, K. H. (1995, Winter). Freeing resources for improving schools: A case study for teacher allocation in Boston public schools. *Educational Evaluation and Policy Analysis, 17*(4), 476–493.

*Miller, P. S. (1929). A quantitative investigation of the efficiency of instruction in high school physics. *Journal of Educational Research, 19*, 119–127.

&%Molnar, A., Smith, P., Zahorik, J., Palmer, A., Halbach, A., & Ehrle, K. (1999, Summer). Evaluating the SAGE program: A pilot program targeted pupil-teacher reduction in Wisconsin. *Educational Evaluation and Policy Analysis, 21*(2), 165–178.

&%Molnar, A., Smith, P., Zahorik, J., Palmer, A., Halbach, A., & Ehrle, K. (2000). Wisconsin's student achievement guarantee in education (SAGE) class size reduction program: Achievement effects, teaching, and classroom implications. In M. C. Wang & J. D. Finn (Eds.), *How small classes help teachers do their best* (pp. 227–278). Philadelphia: Temple University Center for Research in Human Development in Education.

*Moody, W. B., et al. (1973). The effect of class size on the learning of mathematics: A parametric study. *Journal of Research in Mathematics, 4*, 170–176.

*Moss, F. A., Loman, W., & Hunt, T. (1929). Impersonal measurement of teaching. *Educational Record, 10*(1), 40–50.

&%Mosteller, F. (1995). The Tennessee study of class size in the early school grades. *The Future of Children, 5*(2), 113–127.

&Mosteller, F., Light, R. J., & Sachs, J. A. (1986, Winter). Sustained inquiry in education: Lessons from skill grouping and class size. *Harvard Education Review, 66*(4), 797–828.

#Murnane, R. J. (1975). *The impact of school resources on the learning of inner-city children.* Cambridge, MA: Ballinger Publishing Company.

*Nachman, M., & Opochinsky, S. (1958). The effects of different teaching methods: A methodological study. *Journal on Educational Psychology, 49*, 245–249.

*Nelson, W. B. (1959). An experiment with class size in the teaching of elementary economics. *Educational Record, 40*, 330–341.

NICHD Early Child Care Research Network. (2004). Does class size in first grade relate to children's academic and social performance or observed classroom processes? *Developmental Psychology, 40*(5), 651–664.

%Nye, B., Hedges, L. V., & Konstantopoulos, S. (1999). The long-term effects of small classes: A five-year follow-up of the Tennessee Class Size Experiment. *Educational Evaluation and Policy Analysis, 21*, 127–142.

&Odden, S., & Archibald, S. (2001, August). Committing to class-size reduction and finding the resources to implement it: A case study of resource reallocation. *Education Policy Analysis Archives, 9*(30).

&Olson, M. N. (1971). Ways to achieve quality in school classrooms: Some definitive answers. *Phi Delta Kappan, 53*(1), 63–65.

*Perry, R. F. (1957). A teaching experiment in geography. *Journal of Geography, 56,* 133–135.

*Riviera, L.R.D. (1976). *The effects of increasing class size on achievement and the reactions of students and faculty toward this practice at the Catholic University of Puerto Rico.* Doctoral thesis, Lehigh University (77-10, 706).

*Robinson, J. S. (1963). *A study of the relationship of selected school and teacher characteristics to student performance on the BSCS Comprehensive Final Examination 1961–62.* Boulder, CO: BSCS.

*Rohrer, J. H. (1957). Larger and small sections and college classes. *The Journal of Higher Education, 28,* 275–279.

*Ronshausen, N. L. (1975). *The programmed math tutorial—Paraprofessionals provide one-to-one instruction in primary school mathematics.* Paper presented at the annual meeting of the American Educational Research Association, Washington, DC. (ERIC Document Reproduction Service No. ED 106 743)

*#Shapson, S. M., Wright, E. N., Eason, G., & Fitzgerald, J. (1980). An experimental study of the effects of class size. *American Educational Research Journal, 17,* 141–152.

*Shaver, J. P., & Nuhn, D. (1971). The effectiveness of tutoring under-achievers in reading and writing. *Journal of Educational Research, 65,* 107–112.

*Siegel, L., Macomber, F. G., & Adams, J. F. (1959). The effectiveness of large group instruction at the university level. *Harvard Educational Review, 29,* 216–226.

*Silver, A. B. (1970). *English department, large-small class study: English 50–60.* (ERIC Document Reproduction Service No. ED 041 586)

*Simmons, H. F. (1959). Achievement in intermediate algebra associated with class size at the University of Wichita. *College and University, 34,* 309–315.

#Sindelar, P. T., Rosenberg, M. S., Wilson, R. J., & Bursuck, W. D. (1984). The effects of class size and instructional method on the acquisition of mathematical concepts of fourth grade students. *Journal of Educational Research, 77,* 178–183.

*Smith, D. I. (1974). *Effects of class size on individualized instruction on the writing of high school juniors.* Doctoral thesis, Florida State University (74-25461).

*Smith, D. V. (1925). *Class size in high school English.* Minneapolis: University of Minnesota Press.

&Smith, M. L., & Glass, G. V. (1979). *Relationship of class-size to classroom processes, teacher satisfaction and pupil affect: A meta-analysis.* San Francisco: Far West Laboratory for Educational Research and Development.

Smith, P., Molnar, A., & Zahorik, J. (2003). Class-size reduction: A fresh look at the data. *Educational Leadership, 61*(1), 72–74.

*#Spitzer, H. F. (1954). Class size and pupil achievement in elementary schools. *Elementary School Journal, 55,* 82–86.

&Stasz, C., & Stecher, B. (2000, Winter). Teaching mathematics and language arts in reduced size and non-reduced size classrooms. *Educational Evaluation and Policy Analysis, 22*(4), 313–329.

&State of Texas. (1984). *General and special laws of the State of Texas. Sixty-Eighth Legislature June 4, 1884, to July, 1984.* Esp. Chapter 28, HB No.72.

&%Stecher, B., Bohrnstedt, G., Kirst, M., McRobbie, J., & Williams, T. (2001). Class-size reduction in California: A story of hope, promise, and unintended consequences. *Phi Delta Kappan, 82,* 670–674.

*Stevenson, P. R. (1925). *Class size in the elementary school.* Columbus: Ohio State University.

&Stewart, T. (1998, June 29). Reduced size classes. Data tables and narrative. Morganton, NC: Mimeo. (Updated 2000, 2003, Burke County Schools.)

*Summers, A. A., & Wolfe, B. L. (1975). *Equality of educational opportunity quantified: A production function approach.* Philadelphia: Department of Research, Federal Reserve Bank of Philadelphia.

#Taylor, D., & Fleming, M. (1972). *More Effective Schools Program, Disadvantaged Pupil Program Fund, 1971–72 Evaluation (Year 3).* Cleveland: Cleveland Public Schools Division of Research. (ERIC Document Reproduction Service No. ED 076 742)

&Tillitski, C. (1999, Fall). The longitudinal effect size of Prime Time, Indiana's state-sponsored reduced class size program. *Contemporary Education, 62*(1), 24–27.

*Tope, R. E., Groom, E., & Beeson, M. F. (1924). Size of class and school efficiency. *Journal of Educational Research, 9,* 126–132.

&U.S. Department of Education. (1999). *Digest of Education Statistics,* Office of Education Research and Improvement. Washington, DC: National Center for Educational Statistics.

*Verducci, F. (1969). Effects of class size upon the learning of a motor skill. *Research Quarterly, 40,* 391–395.

&Voelkl, K. (1995). *Identification with school.* Unpublished Ph.D. dissertation, State University of New York at Buffalo. (UMI No. 0538143)

#Wagner, E. (1981). *The effects of reduced class size upon the acquisition of reading skills in grade two.* Doctoral dissertation, University of Toledo.

*Wasson, W. H. (1929). *A controlled experiment in the size of classes.* Master's thesis, University of Chicago.

&Wayson, W. W., Mitchell, B., Pinnell, G. S., & Landis, D. (1988). *Up from excellence: The impact of the excellence movement on schools.* Bloomington, IN: The Phi Delta Kappa Educational Foundation.

*Weitzman, D. C. (1965). Effect of tutoring on performance and motivation ratings in secondary school students. *California Journal of Educational Research, 16,* 108–115.

%Wenglinsky, H. (1997). How money matters: The effect of school district spending on academic achievement. *Sociology of Education, 70,* 221–237.

*Wetzel, W. A. (1930). Teaching technique and size of class. *School Life, 15,* 181–182.

*Whitney, L., & Willey, G. S. (1932). Advantages of small classes. *School Executive's Magazine, 51,* 504–506.

#Whittington, E. H. (1985). *Effects of small class size (1:15) on the teaching/learning process in grade one.* Doctoral dissertation, Tennessee State University (105).

*Wilsgberg, M., Castiglione, L. V., & Schwartz, S. L. (1968). *A program to strengthen early childhood education in poverty areas schools.* New York: Educational Research Committee, Center for Urban Education. (ERIC Document Reproduction Service No. ED 034 003)

&Wong, K. K., & Meyers, S. J. (1998, Summer). Title I schoolwide programs: A synthesis of findings from recent evaluations. *Education Evaluation and Policy Analysis, 20*(2), 115–136.

*Woodson, M. S. (1968). Effect of class size as measured by an achievement test criterion. *IRA Research Bulletin, 8,* 1–6.

&Word, E., Johnston, J., Bain, H., Fulton, B., Zaharias, J., Lintz, N., Achilles, C. M., Folger, J., & Breda, C. (1990). *Student/teacher achievement ratio (STAR): Tennessee's K–3 class size study.* Final report and final report summary. Nashville: Tennessee State Department of Education.

Word, E. R., et al. (1990). *The State of Tennessee's Student/Teacher Achievement Ratio (STAR) Project: Technical Report.* Review of Literature (pp. 199–205). Nashville: Tennessee State University, Center of Excellence for Research in Basic Skills.

*Wright, E. N., et al. (1977). *Effects of class size in the junior grades.* Toronto: Ministry of Education.

%Zahorik, J. (1999). Reducing class size leads to individualized instruction. *Educational Leadership, 57*(1), 50–53.

REFERENCES FOR CLARIFYING COMMUNICATION

*Acland, H. (1976). Stability of teacher effectiveness: A replication. *Journal of Educational Research, 69,* 289–292.

*Adams, A., Carnine, D., & Gersten, R. (1982). Instructional strategies for studying content area texts in the intermediate grades. *Reading Research Quarterly, 18,* 27–55.

@Alexander, L., Frankiewicz, R., & Williams, R. (1979). Facilitation of learning and retention of oral instruction using advance and post organizers. *Journal of Educational Psychology, 71,* 701–707.

*Amarel, M. (1981, April). *Literacy: The personal dimension.* Paper presented at the annual meeting of the American Educational Research Association, Los Angeles.

*Anderson, L. M., Evertson, C. M., & Brophy, J. E. (1982). *Principles of small group instruction* (Occasional paper no. 32). East Lansing: Michigan State University, Institute for Research on Teaching.

*Anderson, L. M., Evertson, C. M., & Brophy, J. E. (1979). An experimental study of effective teaching in first-grade reading groups. *The Elementary School Journal, 79,* 193–222.

*Arehart, J. (1979). Student opportunity to learn related to student achievement of objectives in a probability unit. *Journal of Educational Research, 72,* 253–269.

@Ausubel, D. (1963). *The psychology of meaningful verbal learning.* New York: Grune and Stratton.

*Bennett, N. (1976). *Teaching styles and pupil progress.* London: Open Books.

*Bennett, N., Desforges, C., Cockburn, A., & Wilkinson, B. (1981). *The quality of pupil learning experiences: Interim report.* Lancaster, England: University of Lancaster, Centre for Educational Research and Development.

*Berliner, D. (1979). Tempus Educare. In P. Peterson and H. Wahlberg (Eds.), *Research on teaching: Concepts, findings, and implications* (pp. 120–135). Berkeley, CA: McCutchan.

*Blank, M. (1973). *Teaching learning in the preschool: A dialogue approach.* Columbus, OH: Charles Merrill.

*Borich, G., & Fenton, K. (Eds.). (1977). *The appraisal of teaching: Concepts and process.* Reading, MA: Addison-Wesley.

*Bossert, S. (1979). Task and social relationships in classrooms: *A study of classroom organization and its consequences.* New York: Cambridge University Press.

Brophy, J., & Good, T. (1986). Teacher behavior and student achievement. In M. C. Wittrock (Ed.), *Handbook of research on teaching* (3rd ed., pp. 328–375). New York: Macmillan.

*Bush, A., Kennedy, J., & Cruickshank, D. (1977). An empirical investigation of teacher clarity. *Journal of Teacher Education, 28,* 53–58.

Chesebro, J. L. (1999). *The effects of teacher clarity and immediacy on student learning, apprehension, and affect.* Unpublished doctoral dissertation, University of West Virginia.

*#Clark, C., Gage, N., Marx, R., Peterson, P., Staybrook, N., & Winne, P. (1979). A factorial experiment on teacher structuring, soliciting, and reacting. *Journal of Educational Psychology, 71,* 534–552.

Coker, H., Lorentz, C. W., & Coker, J. (1980). *Teacher behavior in student outcomes in the Georgia study.* Paper presented at the annual meeting of the American Educational Research Association, Boston.

Cook, L. K., & Meyer, R. E. (1983). Reading strategies training for meaningful learning from prose. In M. Presley & J. Levin (Eds.), *Cognitive strategies training and research.* New York: Springer-Verlag.

Cruickshank, D. (1976). Synthesis of selected recent research on teacher effects. *Journal of Teacher Education, 27*(1), 57–60.

@Cruickshank, D., & Kennedy, J. (1986). Teacher clarity. *Teaching & Teacher Education, 2*(1), 43–67.

*Cruickshank D. R., Kennedy, J. J., Bush, A., & Myers, B. (1979). Clear teaching: What is it? *British Journal of Teacher Education, 5*(1), 27–32.

#Demham, A., & Land, M. L. (1981). Research brief: Effect of teacher verbal fluency and clarity on student achievement. *The Technical Journal of Education, 8,* 227–229.

*Doyle, W. (1983). Academic work. *Review of Educational Research, 53,* 159–199.

*#Dunkin, M. J. (1978). Student characteristics, classroom processes, and student achievement. *Journal of Educational Psychology, 70,* 998–1009.

*#Dunkin, M. J., & Doenau, S. J. (1980). A replication study of unique and joint contributions to variance in student achievement. *Journal of Educational Psychology, 72,* 394–443.

*Eaton, J., Anderson, C., & Smith, E. (1984). Students' misconceptions interfere with science learning: Case studies of fifth-grade students. *Elementary School Journal, 84,* 365–379.

*Ebmier, H., & Good, T. (1979). The effects of instructing teachers about good teaching on mathematics achievement of fourth-grade students. *American Educational Research Journal, 16,* 1–16.

*Emmer, E., Evertson, C., & Anderson, L. (1980). Effective classroom management at the beginning of the school year. *Elementary School Journal, 80,* 219–231.

*Emmer, E., Evertson, C., & Brophy, J. (1979). Stability of teacher effects in junior high school classrooms. *American Educational Research Journal, 16,* 71–75.

*Evertson, C. (1979). *Student behavior, student achievement, and student attitudes: Descriptions of selected classrooms* (Report No. 4063). Austin: Research and Development Center for Teacher Education, University of Texas.

*Evertson, C., Anderson, C., Anderson, L., & Brophy, J. (1980). Relationships between classroom behaviors and student outcomes in junior high mathematics and English classes. *American Educational Research Journal, 17,* 43–60.

*Evertson, C., Anderson, L., & Brophy, J. (1978). *Texas Junior High School Study: Final report of process-outcome relationship* (Report No. 4061). Austin: Research and Development Center for Teacher Education, University of Texas.

*Evertson, C., & Emmer, E. (1982). Effective management at the beginning of the school year in junior high classes. *Journal of Educational Psychology, 74*, 485–498.

*Evertson, C., Emmer, E., & Brophy, J. (1980). Predictors of effective teaching in junior high mathematics classrooms. *Journal for Research in Mathematics Education, 11*, 167–178.

@Feldman, K. (1989). The association between student ratings of specific instructional dimensions and student achievement: Refining and extending the synthesis of data from multisection validity studies. *Research in Higher Education, 30*, 583–645.

*Fisher, C. W., Berliner, D. C., Filby, N. N., Marliave, R., Cahen, L. S., & Dishaw, M. M. (1980). Teaching behaviors, academic learning time, and student achievement: An overview. In C. Denham & A. Lieberman (Eds.), *Time to learn* (pp. 7–32). Washington, DC: U.S.Government Printing Office.

*Flanders, N. (1965). *Teacher influence, pupil attitudes, and achievement.* Washington, DC: U.S. Office of Education.

*Flanders, N. (1970). *Analyzing teacher behavior.* Reading, MA: Addison-Wesley.

*Fortune, J. (1967). *A study of the generality of presenting behaviors in teaching preschool children* (Final Report for U.S. Office of Education Project No. 6-8468). Memphis, TN: Memphis State University. (ERIC Document Reproduction Service No. ED 016 285)

*Gall, M., Ward, B., Berliner, D., Cahen, L., Winne, P., Elashoff, J., & Stanton, G. (1978). Effects of questioning techniques and recitation on student learning. *American Educational Research Journal, 15*, 175–199.

*Good, T. (1979). Teacher effectiveness in the elementary school: What we know about it now. *Journal of Teacher Education, 30*, 52–64.

*Good, T., Biddle, D., & Brophy, J. (1975). *Teachers make a difference.* New York: Holt, Rinehart & Winston.

*Good, T., & Brophy, J. (1984). *Looking in classrooms* (3rd ed.). New York: Harper & Row.

*Good, T., Ebmeier, H., & Beckerman, T. (1978). Teaching mathematics in high and low SES classrooms: An empirical comparison. *Journal of Teacher Education, 29*, 85–90.

*Good, T. L., & Grouws, D. A. (1977). Teaching effects: A process-product study in fourth-grade mathematics classrooms. *Journal of Teacher Education, 28*(3), 49–54.

*Good, T. L., & Grouws, D. A. (1979a). *Experimental Study of Mathematics Instruction in Elementary Schools* (Final Report, National Institute of Education Grant No. NIE-G-79-0103). Columbia: University of Missouri, Center for the Study of Social Behavior.

*Good, T. L., & Grouws, D. A. (1979b). The Missouri mathematics effectiveness project. *Journal of Educational Psychology, 71*, 355–362.

*Good, T. L., & Grouws, D. A. (1981). *Experimental research in secondary mathematics* (Final Report, National Institute of Education Grant No. NIE-G-79-0103). Columbia: University of Missouri, Center for the Study of Social Behavior.

*Good, T., Grouws, D., & Beckerman, T. (1978). Curriculum pacing: Some empirical data in mathematics. *Journal of Curriculum Studies, 10*, 75–81.

*Good, T., Grouws, D., & Ebmeier, M. (1983). *Active mathematics teaching.* New York: Longman.

*Hamilton, S. (1983). The social side of schooling: Ecological studies of classrooms and schools. *Elementary School Journal, 83*, 313–334.

*#Hiller, J., Fisher, G., & Kaess, W. (1969). A computer investigation of verbal characteristics of effective classroom lecturing. *American Educational Research Journal, 6*, 661–675.

#Hiller, J. H. (1968). *An experimental investigation of the effects of conceptual vagueness on speaking behavior*. Paper presented at the annual meeting of the American Educational Research Association, Chicago.

#Hiller, J. H. (1971). Verbal response indicators of conceptual vagueness. *American Educational Research Journal, 8*, 151–161.

#Hines, C. V., Cruickshank, D. R., & Kennedy, J. J. (1982). *Measures of teacher clarity and their relationships to student achievement and satisfaction*. Paper presented at the annual meeting of the American Educational Research Association, New York.

@Hines, C. V., Cruickshank, D. R., & Kennedy, J. J. (1985). Teacher clarity and its relationship to student achievement and satisfaction. *American Educational Research Journal, 22*(1), 87–99.

*Husen, T. (Ed.). (1967). *International study of achievement and mathematics* (Vol. 1). New York: John Wiley.

@Kallison, J., Jr. (1986). Effects of lesson organization on achievement. *American Educational Research Journal, 23*, 337–347.

@Kelley, D., & Gorham, J. (1988). Effects of immediacy on recall of information. *Communication Education, 37*, 198–207.

@Kiewra, K. (1985). Providing the instructor's notes: An effective addition to student notetaking. *Educational Psychologist, 20*, 33–39.

*Kulik, J. A., & Kulik, C. C. (1979). College teaching. In P. L. Peterson & H. J. Walberg (Eds.), *Research on teaching: Concepts, findings, and implications* (pp. 70–93). Berkeley, CA: McCutchan.

*#Land, M., & Smith, L. (1979). The effect of low inference teacher clarity inhibitors on student achievement. *Journal of Teacher Education, 31*, 55–57.

#Land, M., & Smith, L. (1981). College student ratings in teacher behavior: An experimental study. *Journal of Social Studies Research, 5*, 19–22.

*#@Land, M. L. (1979). Low-inference variables of teacher clarity effects on student concept learning. *Journal of Educational Psychology, 71*(6), 795–799.

#Land, M. L. (1980). Teacher clarity and cognitive level of questions: Effects on learning. *Journal of Experimental Education, 49*, 48–51.

#Land, M. L. (1981). Combined effects of two teacher clarity variables on student achievement. *Journal of Experimental Education, 50*, 14–17.

Land, M. L. (1985). Vagueness and clarity in the classroom. In T. Husen & T. Postlethwaite (Eds.), The *International Encyclopedia of Education Research and Studies* (Vol. 9, pp. 5405–5410). Oxford: Pergamon Press.

#Land, M. L., & Combs, A. (1981). *Teacher clarity, student instructional ratings, and student performance*. Paper presented at the annual meeting of the American Educational Research Association, Los Angeles.

#Land, M. L., & Smith, L. (1979). Effect of a teacher clarity variable on student achievement. *Journal of Educational Research, 73*, 19–22.

*Larrivee, B., & Algina, J. (1983, April). *Identification of teaching behaviors which predict success for mainstream students*. Paper presented at the annual meeting of the American Educational Research Association. Montreal. (ERIC Document Reproduction Service No. ED 232 362)

*MacKay, A. (1979). *Project Quest: Teaching strategies and pupil achievement* (Research Report No. 79-1-3). Edmonton: University of Alberta, Centre for Research in Teaching, Faculty of Education.

*Madike, F. (1980). Teacher classroom behaviors involved in micro-teaching and student achievement: A regression study. *Journal of Educational Psychology, 72*, 265–274.

@Mayer, R. (1979). Twenty years of research on advance organizers: Assimilation theory is still the best predictor of results. *Instructional Science, 8*, 133–167.

*McCaleb, J., & White, J. (1980). Critical dimensions in evaluating teacher clarity. *Journal of Classroom Interaction, 15*, 27–30.

*McConnell, J. (1977). *Relationship between selected teacher behaviors and attitudes/achievement of algebra classes.* Paper presented at the annual meeting of the American Educational Research Association. New York. (ERIC Document Reproduction Service No. ED 141 118)

*Medley, D. (1977). *Teacher competency and teacher effectiveness: A review of process-product research.* Washington, DC: American Association of Colleges for Teacher Education.

@Mehrabian, A. (1981). *Silent messages: Implicit communication of emotions and attitudes* (2nd ed.). Belmont, CA: Wadsworth.

*Mitzel, H. (1960). Teacher effectiveness. In C. Harris (Ed.), *Encyclopedia of educational research* (3rd ed., pp. 1481–1485). New York: Macmillan.

*Morsh, J., & Wilder, E. (1954). *Identifying the effective instructor: A review of the quantitative studies, 1900–1952* (Research Bulletin No. AFTRIC-TR-54-44). San Antonio, TX: USAF Personnel Training Research Center, Lackland Air Force Base.

@Murray, H. (1991). Effective teaching behaviors in the college classroom. In J. Smart (Ed.), *Higher education: Handbook of theory and research* (Vol. 7). New York: Agathon Press.

*Nuthall, G., & Church, J. (1973). Experimental studies of teaching behavior. In G. Chanan (Ed.), *Towards a science of teaching*. London: National Foundation for Educational Research.

*Palincsar, A. S. (1984). *Reciprocal teaching.* Paper presented at the annual meeting of the American Educational Research Association, New Orleans.

@Perry, R., Abrami, P., & Leventhal, L. (1979). Educational seduction: The effect of instructor expressiveness and lecture content on student ratings and achievement. *Journal of Educational Psychology, 71*, 109–116.

@Perry, R., & Penner, K. (1990). Enhancing academic achievement in college students through attributional retraining and instruction. *Journal of Educational Psychology, 82*, 262–271.

*Peterson, P., & Walberg, H. (Eds.). (1979). *Research on teaching: Concepts, findings, and implications.* Berkeley, CA: McCutchan.

*Ramp, E., & Rhine, W. (1981). Behavior analysis model. In W. Rhine (Ed.), *Making schools more effective: New directions from Follow Through* (pp. 155–197). New York: Academic Press.

*Raphael, T. E. (1980). *The effect of metacognitive awareness training on students' question and answer behavior.* Doctoral dissertation, University of Illinois.

*Redfield, D., & Rousseau, E. (1981). A meta-analysis of experimental research on teacher questioning behavior. *Review of Educational Research, 51*, 237–245.

*Romberg, T. (1983). A common curriculum for mathematics. In G. Fenstermacher & J. Goodlag (Eds.), *Individual differences and the common curriculum* (Eighty-second Yearbook of the National Society for the Study of Education, Part 1). Chicago: University of Chicago Press.

*Rosenshine, B. (1968). To explain: A review of research. *Educational Leadership, 26*, 275–280.

*Rosenshine, B. (1970a). Evaluation of instruction. *Review of Educational Research, 40*, 279–301.

*Rosenshine, B. (1970b). Experimental classroom studies of indirect teaching. *Classroom Interaction Newsletter, 5*(2), 7–11.

*#Rosenshine, B. (1971). *Teaching behaviors and student achievement*. London: National Foundation for Educational Research.

*Rosenshine, B. (1976). Classroom instruction. In N. L. Gage (Ed.), *The psychology of teaching methods* (Seventy-seventh Yearbook of the National Society for the Study of Education, pp. 335–371). Chicago: University of Chicago Press.

*Rosenshine, B. (1979). Content, time, and direct instruction. In P. Peterson & H. Walberg (Eds.), *Research on teaching: Concepts, findings, and implications* (pp. 28–56). Berkeley, CA: McCutchan.

*Rosenshine, B. (1983). Teaching functions in instructional programs. *Elementary School Journal, 83*, 335–351.

@Rosenshine, B. (1987). Explicit teaching. In D. C. Berliner & B. V. Rosenshine (Eds.), *Talks to teachers* (pp. 75–92). New York: Random House.

*Rosenshine, B., & Berliner, D. (1978). Academic engaged time. *British Journal of Teacher Education, 4*, 3–16.

*Rosenshine, B., & Furst, N. (1973). The use of direct observation to study teaching. In R.M.W. Travers (Ed.), *Second handbook of research on teaching* (pp. 37–74). Chicago: Rand McNally.

*Rosenshine, B., & Stevens, R. (1984). Classroom instruction in reading. In D. Pearson (Ed.), *Handbook of research on reading* (pp. 745–798). New York: Longman.

@Rosenshine, B., & Stevens, R. (1986). Teaching functions. In M. C. Wittrock (Ed.), *Handbook of research on teaching* (3rd ed., pp. 376–391). New York: Macmillan.

*Rowe, M. (1974). Wait-time and rewards as instructional variables, their influence on language, logic and fate control: Part I. Wait-time. *Journal of Research in Science Teaching, 11*, 81–94.

*Ryan, F. (1973). Differentiated effects of levels of questioning on student achievement. *Elementary School Journal, 41*, 63–67.

*Ryan, F. (1974). The effects on social studies achievement of multiple students responding to different levels of questioning. *Journal of Experimental Education, 42*, 71–75.

*Schuck, R. (1981). The impact of set induction on student achievement and retention. *Journal of Educational Research, 74*, 227–232.

@Smith, D. (1977). College classroom interactions and critical thinking. *Journal of Educational Psychology, 69*, 180–190.

*#Smith, L. (1977). Aspects of teacher discourse in student achievement in mathematics. *Journal for Research in Mathematics Education, 8*, 195–204.

*Smith, L. (1979). Task-oriented lessons and student achievement. *Journal of Educational Research, 73*, 16–19.

*@Smith, L., & Land, M. (1981). Low-inference verbal behaviors related to teacher clarity. *Journal of Classroom Interaction, 17*, 37–42.

*Smith, L., & Sanders, K. (1981). The effects on student achievement and student perception of varying structure and social studies content. *Journal of Educational Research, 74*, 333–336.

#Smith L. R., & Bramblett, G. H. (1981). The effect of teacher vagueness terms on student performance in high school biology. *Journal of Research in Science Teaching, 18,* 353–360.

*#@Smith, L. R., & Cotten, M. L. (1980). Effect of lesson vagueness and discontinuity on student achievement and attitudes. *Journal of Educational Psychology, 72*(5), 670–675.

#Smith, L. R., & Edmonds, E. M. (1978). Teacher vagueness and pupil participation in mathematics learning. *Journal of Research in Mathematics Education, 9,* 228–232.

#Smith, L. R., & Land, M. L. (1980). Student perception of teacher clarity in mathematics. *Journal of Research in Mathematics Education, 11,* 137–146.

*Soar, R. S. (1973). *Follow-Through Classroom Process Measurement and Pupil Growth (1970–1971) Final Report.* Gainesville: College of Education, University of Florida.

@Solomon, D. (1966). Teacher behavior dimensions, course characteristics, and student evaluations of teachers. *American Educational Research Journal, 3,* 35–47.

*Spiro, R. J., & Meyers, A. (1984). Individual differences and underlying cognitive process. In P. D. Pearson, R. Barr, M. L. Kamil, & P. Mosenthal (Eds.), *Handbook of reading research* (pp. 471–501). New York: Longman.

*Stallings, J. (1975). Implementation and child effects of teaching practices and Follow Through classrooms. *Monographs of the Society for Research in Child Development, 40* (7–8, Serial No. 163).

*Stallings, J., Corey, R., Fairweather, J., & Needles, M. (1977). *Early Childhood Education classroom evaluation.* Menlo Park, CA: SRI International.

*Stallings, J., Needles, M., & Staybrook, N. (1979). *The teaching of basic reading skills in secondary schools, Phase II and Phase III.* Menlo Park, CA: SRI International.

*Stallings, J. A., & Kaskowitz, D. (1974). *Follow-Through Classroom Observation.* Menlo Park, CA: SRI International.

Titsworth, B. S., & Kiewra, K. A. (2004). Spoken organizational lecture cues and student notetaking as facilitators of student learning. *Contemporary Educational Psychology, 29*(4), 447–461.

*Tobias, S. (1982). When do instructional methods make a difference? *Educational Researcher, 11,* 4–10.

*Tobin, K. (1980). The effect of an extended teacher wait-time on science achievement. *Journal of Research in Science Teaching, 17,* 469–475.

*Tobin, K., & Capie, W. (1982). Relationships between classroom process variables and middle-school science achievement. *Journal of Educational Psychology, 74,* 441–454.

*Winne, P. (1979). Experiments relating teachers' use of higher cognitive questions to student achievement. *Review of Educational Research, 49,* 13–50.

*Wright, C., & Nuthall, G. (1970). Relationships between teacher behaviors and pupil achievement in three experimental science lessons. *American Educational Research Journal, 7,* 477–491.

REFERENCES FOR UTILIZING QUESTION AND ANSWER INSTRUCTION

!Acland, H. (1976). Stability of teacher effectiveness: A replication. *Journal of Educational Research, 69,* 289–292.

*Amerikaner, M., & Summerlin, M. L. (1982). Group counseling with learning disabled children: Effects of social skills and relaxation training on self-concept and classroom behavior. *Journal of Learning Disabilities, 15,* 340–343.

!%Anderson, L. M., Evertson, C. M., & Brophy, J. E. (1979). An experimental study of effective teaching in first-grade reading groups. *The Elementary School Journal, 79,* 193–222.

!%Anderson, L. M., Evertson, C. M., & Brophy, J. E. (1982). *Principles of small group instruction* (Occasional paper no. 32). East Lansing: Michigan State University, Institute for Research on Teaching.

!Arehart, J. (1979). Student opportunity to learn related to student achievement of objectives in a probability unit. *Journal of Educational Research, 72,* 253–269.

*Argulewicz, E. N. (1982). Effects of an instructional program designed to improve attending behaviors of learning disabled students. *Journal of Learning Disabilities, 15,* 23–27.

%Arlin, M., & Webster, J. (1983). Time cost of mastery learning. *Journal of Educational Psychology, 75,* 187–195.

*Ayres, A. J. (1972). Improving academic scores through sensory integration. *Journal of Learning Disabilities, 5,* 338–343.

*Bakker, D. J., Bouma, A., & Gardien, C. J. (1990). Hemisphere-specific treatment of dyslexia subtypes: A field experiment. *Journal of Learning Disabilities, 23,* 433–438.

*Balcerzak, J. P. (1986). *The effects of an aptitude treatment interaction approach with intermediate aged learning disabled students based on emphasizing the individual's strength in simultaneous or sequential processing in the areas of mathematics, reading and self-concept.* Doctoral dissertation, State University of New York, 1985. *Dissertation Abstracts International, 47*(3A), 630.

*Bay, M., Stayer, J. R., Bryan, T., & Hale, J. B. (1992). Science instruction for the mildly handicapped: Direct instruction versus discovery teaching. *Journal of Research in Science Teaching, 29,* 555–570.

%Becker, W. C. (1977). Teaching reading and language to the disadvantaged—What we have learned from field research. *Harvard Educational Review, 47,* 518–543.

*Belmont, I., & Birch, H. G. (1974). The effect of supplemental intervention on children with low reading-readiness scores. *Journal of Special Education, 8,* 81–89.

!Berliner, D., Fisher, C., Filby, N., & Marliave, R. (1978). *Executive summary of Beginning Teacher Evaluation Study.* San Francisco: Far West Laboratory.

*Berninger, V. W., Lester, K., Sohlberg, M. M., & Mateer, C. (1991). Interventions based on the multiple connections model of reading for developmental dyslexia and acquired deep dyslexia. *Archives of Clinical Neuropsychology, 6,* 375–391.

*#Bos, C. S., & Anders, P. L. (1990). Effects of interactive vocabulary instruction on the vocabulary learning and reading comprehension of junior high learning-disabled students. *Learning Disability Quarterly, 13,* 31–42.

*#Bos, C. S., & Anders, P. L. (1992). Using interactive teaching and learning strategies to promote text comprehension and content learning for students with learning disabilities. *International Journal of Disability, Development and Education, 39,* 225–238.

*Bos, C. S., Anders, P. L., Filip, D., & Jaffe, L. E. (1985). Semantic feature analysis and long-term learning. *National Reading Conference Yearbook, 34,* 42–47.

*Bos, C. S., Anders, P. L., Filip, D., & Jaffe, L. E. (1989). The effects of an interactive instructional strategy for enhancing reading comprehension and content area learning for students with learning disabilities. *Journal of Learning Disabilities, 22,* 384–390.

*Brailsford, A., Snail, F., & Das, J. P. (1984). Strategy training and reading comprehension. *Journal of Learning Disabilities, 17*, 287–293.

*Branwhite, A. B. (1983). Boosting reading skills by direct instruction. *British Journal of Educational Psychology, 53*, 291–298.

*#Brigham, F. J., Scruggs, T. E., & Mastropieri, M. A. (1992). Teacher enthusiasm in learning disabilities classrooms: Effects on learning and behavior. *Learning Disabilities Research & Practice, 7*, 68–73.

!Brophy, J. (1973). Stability of teacher effectiveness. *American Educational Research Journal, 10*, 245–252.

!Brophy, J., & Evertson, C. (1974a). *Process-product correlations in a Texas Teacher Effectiveness Study: Final report* (Research Report 74-4). Austin: Research and Development Center for Teacher Education, University of Texas. (ERIC Document Reproduction Service No. ED 091 094)

!Brophy, J., & Evertson, C. (1974b). *The Texas Teacher Effectiveness Project: Presentation of non-linear relationships and summary discussion* (Research Report 74-6). Austin: Research and Development Center for Teacher Education, University of Texas. (ERIC Document Reproduction Service No. ED 099 345)

%!Brophy, J., & Evertson, C. (1976). *Learning from teaching: A developmental perspective*. Boston: Allyn and Bacon.

Brophy, J., & Good, T. (1986). Teacher behavior and student achievement. In M. C. Wittrock (Ed.), *Handbook of research on teaching* (3rd ed., pp. 328–375). New York: Macmillan.

*Brown, I. S., & Felton, R. C. (1990). Effects of instruction on beginning reading skills in children at risk for reading disability. *Reading and Writing: An Interdisciplinary Journal, 2*, 223–241.

*#Brown, R. T., & Alford, N. (1984). Ameliorating attention deficits and concomitant academic deficiencies in learning disabled children through cognitive training. *Journal of Learning Disabilities, 17*, 20–26.

*Bryant, N. D., Drabin, I. R., & Gettinger, M. (1981). Effects of varying unit size on spelling achievement in learning disabled children. *Journal of Learning Disabilities, 14*, 200–203.

*Bryant, N. D., Fayne, H. R., & Gettinger, M. (1982). Applying the mastery learning model to sight word instruction for disabled readers. *Journal of Experimental Education, 50*, 116–121.

*Bryant, S. T. (1979). *Relative effectiveness of visual-auditory versus visual-auditory-kinesthetic-tactile procedures for teaching sight words and letter sounds to young, disabled readers*. Doctoral dissertation, Columbia University. *Dissertation Abstracts International, 40*(5A), 2588–2589.

*#Bulgren, J., Schumaker, J. B., & Deshler, D. D. (1988). Effectiveness of a concept teaching routine in enhancing the performance of LD students in secondary-level mainstream classes. *Learning Disability Quarterly, 11*(1), 317.

*Carte, E., Morrison, D., Sublett, J., Uemura, A., & Setrakian, W. (1984). Sensory integration therapy: A trial of a specific neurodevelopmental therapy for the remediation of learning disabilities. *Developmental and Behavioral Pediatrics, 5*, 189–194.

*Cartelli, L. M. (1978). Paradigmatic language training for learning disabled children. *Journal of Learning Disabilities, 11*, 54–59.

*Carter, B. G. (1985). *For the learning disabled: Semantic mapping or SQ3R?* Doctoral dissertation, University of Nevada–Reno, 1984. *Dissertation Abstracts International, 46*(3A), 674.

*#Chan, L.K.S. (1991). Promoting strategy generalization through self-instructional training in students with reading disabilities. *Journal of Learning Disabilities, 24*, 427–433.

*#Chan, L.K.S., & Cole, P. O. (1986). The effects of comprehension monitoring training on the reading competence of learning disabled and regular class students. *Remedial and Special Education, 7*, 33–40.

*#Chan, L.K.S., Cole, P. O., & Morris, J. N. (1990). Effects of instruction in the use of a visual-imagery strategy on the reading-comprehension competence of disabled and average readers. *Learning Disability Quarterly, 13*, 2–11.

*#Chase, C. H., Schmitt, R. L., Russell, G., & Tallal, P. (1984). A new chemotherapeutic investigation: Piracetam effects on dyslexia. *Annals of Dyslexia, 34*, 29–43.

!Coker, H., Medley, D., & Soar, R. (1980). How valid are expert opinions about effective teaching? *Phi Delta Kappan, 62*, 131–134, 149.

*#Collins, M., & Carnine, D. (1988). Evaluating the field test revision process by comparing two versions of a reasoning skills CAI program. *Journal of Learning Disabilities, 21*, 375–379.

*Commeyras, M. (1992). *Dialogical-thinking reading lessons: Promoting critical thinking among "learning-disabled" students.* Doctoral dissertation, University of Illinois, 1991. *Dissertation Abstracts International, 52*(7A), 2480–2481.

*Cornelius, P. L., & Semmel, M. I. (1982). Effects of summer instruction on reading achievement regression of learning disabled students. *Journal of Learning Disabilities, 15*, 409–413.

*Cosden, M. A., & English, J. P. (1987). The effects of grouping, self esteem, and locus of control on microcomputer performance and help seeking by mildly handicapped students. *Journal of Educational Computing Research, 3*, 443–459.

!Crawford, J. (1983). A study of instructional processes in Title I classes: 1981–82. *Journal of Research and Evaluation of the Oklahoma City Public Schools, 13*(1).

*Darch, C., & Eaves, R. C. (1986). Visual displays to increase comprehension of high school learning-disabled students. *Journal of Special Education, 20*, 309–318.

*#Darch, C., & Gersten, R. (1986). Direction-setting activities in reading comprehension: A comparison of two approaches. *Learning Disability Quarterly, 9*, 235–243.

*Darch, C., & Kameenui, E. J. (1987). Teaching LD students critical reading skills: A systematic replication. *Learning Disability Quarterly, 10*, 82–90.

*Das, J. P., Mishra, R. K., & Pool, J. E. (1995). An experiment on cognitive remediation of word-reading difficulty. *Journal of Learning Disabilities, 28*, 66–79.

*#De La Paz, S. (1995). *An analysis of the effects of dictation and planning instruction on the writing of students with learning disabilities.* Unpublished doctoral dissertation, University of Maryland, College Park.

*De La Paz, S. (in press). Strategy instruction in planning: Teaching students with learning and writing disabilities to compose persuasive and expository essays. *Learning Disability Quarterly.*

*DeBoskey, D. S. (1982). *An investigation of the remediation of learning disabilities based on brain-related tasks as measured by the Halstead-Reitan neuropsychological test battery.* Doctoral dissertation, University of Tennessee. *Dissertation Abstracts International, 43*(6B), 2032.

*Deno, S. L., & Chiang, B. (1979). An experimental analysis of the nature of reversal errors in children with severe learning disabilities. *Learning Disability Quarterly, 2*, 40–50.

*#Dixon, M. E. (1984). *Questioning strategy instruction participation and reading com-*

prehension of learning disabled students. Doctoral dissertation, University of Arizona, 1983. *Dissertation Abstracts International, 44*(11-A), 3349.

!Dunkin, M. J. (1978). Student characteristics, classroom processes, and student achievement. *Journal of Educational Psychology, 70*, 998–1009.

!Ebmier, H., & Good, T. (1979). The effects of instructing teachers about good teaching on mathematics achievement of fourth-grade students. *American Educational Research Journal, 16*, 1–16.

*Ellis, E. S., Deshler, D. D., & Schumaker, J. B. (1989). Teaching adolescents with learning disabilities to generate and use task-specific strategies. *Journal of Learning Disabilities, 22*, 108–130.

!Emmer, E., Evertson, C., & Anderson, L. (1980). Effective classroom management at the beginning of the school year. *Elementary School Journal, 80*, 219–231.

!Emmer, E., Evertson, C., & Brophy, J. (1979). Stability of teacher effects in junior high school classrooms. *American Educational Research Journal, 16*, 71–75.

!%Emmer, E. T., Evertson, C., Sanford, J., & Clements, B. (1982). *Improving instruction management: An experimental study in junior high classrooms.* Austin: Research and Development Center for Teacher Education, University of Texas.

*Englert, C. S., Hiebert, E. H., & Stewart, S. R. (1985). Spelling unfamiliar words by an analogy strategy. *Journal of Special Education, 19*, 291–306.

*Englert, C. S., & Manage, T. V. (1991). Making students partners in the comprehension process: Organizing the reading "POSSE." *Learning Disability Quarterly, 14*, 123–138.

*Englert, C. S., Raphael, T. E., & Anderson, L. M. (1992). Socially mediated instruction: Improving students' knowledge about talk and writing. *Elementary School Journal, 92*, 411–449.

*Englert, C. S., Raphael, T. E., Anderson, L. M., Anthony, H. M., & Stevens, D. D. (1991). Making strategies and self talk visible: Writing instruction in regular and special education classrooms. *American Educational Research Journal, 28*, 337–372.

%Evertson, C. (1982). Differences in instructional activities in higher and lower achieving junior high English and mathematics classrooms. *Elementary School Journal, 82*, 329–351.

!%Evertson, C., Anderson, C., Anderson, L., & Brophy, J. (1980). Relationships between classroom behaviors and student outcomes in junior high mathematics and English classes. *American Educational Research Journal, 17*, 43–60.

!Evertson, C., Anderson, L., & Brophy, J. (1978). *Texas Junior High School Study—Final report of process-outcome relationship* (Report No. 4061). Austin: Research and Development Center for Teacher Education, University of Texas.

!Evertson, C., & Brophy, J. (1973). High-inference behavioral ratings as correlates of teacher effectiveness. *JSAS Catalog of Selected Documents in Psychology, 3*, 97.

!Evertson, C., & Brophy, J. (1974). *Texas Teacher Effectiveness Project: Questionnaire and interview data* (Research Report No. 74-5). Austin: Research and Development Center for Teacher Education, University of Texas.

!%Evertson, C., Emmer, E., & Brophy, J. (1980). Predictors of effective teaching in junior high mathematics classrooms. *Journal for Research in Mathematics Education, 11*, 167–178.

%Evertson, C. M., Emmer, E. T., Sanford, J. P., & Clements, B. S. (1983). Improving classroom management: An experiment in elementary classrooms. *Elementary School Journal, 84*, 174–188.

*#Farmer, M. E., Klein, R., & Bryson, S. E. (1992). Computer-assisted reading: Effects of whole word feedback on fluency and comprehension in readers with severe disabilities. *Remedial and Special Education, 13*, 50–60.

*Fawcett, A. J., Nicolson, R. I., & Morris, S. (1993). Computer-based spelling remediation for dyslexic children. *Journal of Computer Assisted Learning, 9*, 171–183.

*#Fiedorowicz, C.A.M. (1986). Training of component reading skills. *Annals of Dyslexia, 36*, 318–334.

*#Fiedorowicz, C.A.M., & Trites, R. L. (1987). *An evaluation of the effectiveness of computer-assisted component reading subskills training.* Toronto: Queen's Printer.

!%Fisher, C. W., Berliner, D. C., Filby, N. N., Marliave, R., Cahen, L. S., & Dishaw, M. M. (1980). Teaching behaviors, academic learning time, and student achievement: An overview. In C. Denham & A. Lieberman (Eds.), *Time to learn* (pp. 7–32). Washington, DC: U.S. Government Printing Office.

!%Fitzpatrick, K. A. (1981). *An investigation of secondary classroom material strategies for increasing student academic engaged time.* Doctoral dissertation, University of Illinois at Urbana–Champaign.

!%Fitzpatrick, K. A. (1982). *The effect of a secondary classroom management training program on teacher and student behavior.* Paper presented at the annual meeting of the American Educational Research Association, New York.

*Fletcher, C. M., & Prior, M. R. (1990). The rule learning behavior of reading disabled and normal children as a function of task characteristics and instruction. *Journal of Experimental Child Psychology, 50*, 39–58.

*Fortner, V. L. (1986). Generalization of creative productive-thinking training to LD students' written expression. *Learning Disability Quarterly, 9*, 274–284.

*#Foster, K. (1983). *The influence of computer-assisted instruction and workbook on the learning of multiplication facts by learning disabled and normal students.* Doctoral dissertation, Florida State University. *Dissertation Abstracts International, 42*(9-A), 3953.

*Fuchs, L. S., Fuchs, D., Hamlett, C. L., Phillips, N. B., & Bentz, J. (1994). Classwide curriculum-based measurement: Helping general educators meet the challenge of student diversity. *Exceptional Children, 60*, 518–537.

*#Gajria, M., & Salvia, J. (1992). The effects of summarization instruction on text comprehension of students with learning disabilities. *Exceptional Children, 58*, 508–516.

*Gelzheiser, L. M. (1984). Generalization from categorical memory tasks to prose by learning disabled adolescents. *Journal of Educational Psychology, 76*, 1128–1138.

*Gettinger, M., Bryant, N. D., & Fayne, H. R. (1982). Designing spelling instruction for learning disabled children: An emphasis on unit size, distributed practice, and training for transfer. *Journal of Special Education, 16*, 439–448.

*Gittelman, R., & Feingold, I. (1983). Children with reading disorders—I. Efficacy of reading remediation. *Journal of Child Psychology and Psychiatry, 24*, 167–191.

*Glaman, G.M.V. (1975). *Use of ability measures to predict the most appropriate method or sequence of mathematics instruction for learning disabled junior high students.* Doctoral dissertation, University of Minnesota, 1974. *Dissertation Abstracts International, 35*(11A), 7154.

!Good, T., Ebmeier, H., & Beckerman, T. (1978). Teaching mathematics in high and low SES classrooms: An empirical comparison. *Journal of Teacher Education, 29*, 85–90.

!Good, T., Grouws, D., & Beckerman, T. (1978). Curriculum pacing: Some empirical data in mathematics. *Journal of Curriculum Studies, 10*, 75–81.

!%Good, T., Grouws, D., & Ebmeier, M. (1983). *Active mathematics teaching.* New York: Longman.

!%Good, T. L., & Grouws, D. A. (1977). Teaching effects: A process-product study in fourth-grade mathematics classrooms. *Journal of Teacher Education, 28*(3), 49–54.

!Good, T. L., & Grouws, D. A. (1979a). *Experimental Study of Mathematics Instruction in Elementary Schools* (Final Report, National Institute of Education Grant No. NIE-G-79-0103). Columbia: University of Missouri, Center for the Study of Social Behavior.

!Good, T. L., & Grouws, D. A. (1979b). The Missouri mathematics effectiveness project. *Journal of Educational Psychology, 71,* 355–362.

!Good, T. L., & Grouws, D. A. (1981). *Experimental research in secondary mathematics* (Final Report, National Institute of Education Grant No. NIE-G-79-0103). Columbia: University of Missouri, Center for the Study of Social Behavior.

*Graham, S. (1990). The role of production factors in learning disabled students' compositions. *Journal of Educational Psychology, 82,* 781–791.

*#Graham, S., & Harris, K. R. (1989). Components analysis of cognitive strategy instruction: Effects on learning disabled students' compositions and self-efficacy. *Journal of Educational Psychology, 81,* 353–361.

*#Graves, A. W. (1986). Effects of direct instruction and metacomprehension training on finding main ideas. *Learning Disabilities Research, 1,* 90–100.

*Graybill, D., Jamison, M., & Swerdlik, M. E. (1984). Remediation of impulsivity in learning disabled children by special education resource teachers using verbal self-instruction. *Psychology in the Schools, 21,* 252–254.

*#Griffin, C. C., Simmons, D. C., & Kameenui, E. J. (1991). Investigating the effectiveness of graphic organizer instruction on the comprehension and recall of science content by students with learning disabilities. *Reading, Writing and Learning Disabilities, 7,* 355–376.

*#Guyer, B. P., & Sabatino, D. (1989). The effectiveness of a multisensory alphabetic phonetic approach with college students who are learning disabled. *Journal of Learning Disabilities, 22,* 430–434.

*Helper, M. M., Farber, E. D., & Feldgaier, S. (1982). Alternative thinking and classroom behavior of learning impaired children. *Psychological Reports, 50,* 415–420.

*Hine, M. S., Goldman, S. R., & Cosden, M. A. (1990). Error monitoring by learning handicapped students engaged in collaborative microcomputer-based writing. *Journal of Special Education, 23,* 407–422.

*#Hollingsworth, M., & Woodward, J. (1993). Integrated learning: Explicit strategies and their role in problem-solving instruction for students with learning disabilities. *Exceptional Children, 59,* 444–455.

*Howell, R., Sidorenko, E., & Jurica, J. (1987). The effects of computer use on the acquisition of multiplication facts by a student with learning disabilities. *Journal of Learning Disabilities, 20,* 336–341.

!Hughes, D. (1973). An experimental investigation of the effect of pupil responding and teacher reacting on pupil achievement. *American Educational Research Journal, 10,* 21–37.

*Humphries, T. W., Wright, M., Snider, L., & McDougall, B. (1992). A comparison of the effectiveness of sensory integrative therapy and perceptual-motor training in treating children with learning disabilities. *Developmental and Behavioral Pediatrics, 13,* 31–40.

*Hurford, D. P. (1990). Training phonemic segmentation ability with a phonemic discrimination intervention in second- and third-grade children with reading disabilities. *Journal of Learning Disabilities, 23*, 564–569.

*Hurford, D. P., & Sanders, R. E. (1990). Assessment and remediation of a phonemic discrimination deficit in reading disabled second and fourth graders. *Journal of Experimental Child Psychology, 50*, 396–415.

#Hutchinson, N. L. (1993). Effects of cognitive strategy instruction on algebra problem solving of adolescents with learning disabilities. *Learning Disability Quarterly, 16*, 6–18.

*#Hutchinson, N. L., Freeman, J. G., Downey, K. H., & Kilbreath, L. (1992). Development and evaluation of an instructional module to promote career maturity for youth with learning disabilities. *Canadian Journal of Counseling, 26*, 290–299.

*Jaben, T. H. (1983). The effects of creativity training on learning disabled students' creative written expression. *Journal of Learning Disabilities, 16*, 264–265.

*Jaben, T. H. (1985). Effect of instruction for creativity on learning disabled students' drawings. *Perceptual and Motor Skills, 61*, 895–898.

*Jaben, T. H. (1986). Impact of instruction on behavior disordered and learning disabled students' creative behavior. *Psychology in the Schools, 23*, 401–405.

*Jaben, T. H. (1987). Effects of training on learning disabled students' creative written expression. *Psychological Reports, 60*, 23–26.

*Jaben, T. H., Treffinger, D. J., Whelan, R. J., Hudson, F. G., Stainback, S. B., & Stainback, W. (1982). Impact of instruction on learning disabled students' creative thinking. *Psychology in the Schools, 19*, 371–373.

*#Johnson, L., Graham, S., & Harris, K. R. (1998). *The effects of goal setting and self-instructions on learning a reading comprehension strategy: A study with students with learning disabilities.* Unpublished manuscript.

*#Jones, K. M., Torgesen, J. K., & Sexton, M. A. (1987). Using computer-guided practice to increase decoding fluency in learning disabled children: A study using the Hint and Hunt I program. *Journal of Learning Disabilities, 20*, 122–128.

*#Kane, B. J., & Alley, G. R. (1980). A peer-tutored, instructional management program in computational mathematics for incarcerated learning-disabled juvenile delinquents. *Journal of Learning Disabilities, 13*, 148–151.

*Kendall, P. C., & Braswell, L. (1982). Cognitive-behavioral self-control therapy for children: A components analysis. *Journal of Consulting and Clinical Psychology, 50*, 672–689.

*#Kennedy, K. M., & Backman, J. (1993). Effectiveness of the Lindamood Auditory Discrimination In-Depth Program with students with learning disabilities. *Learning Disabilities Research & Practice, 8*, 253–259.

*#Kershner, J. R., Cummings, R. L., Clarke, K. A., Hadfield, A. J., & Kershner, B. A. (1990). Two-year evaluation of the Tomatis Listening Training Program with learning disabled children. *Learning Disability Quarterly, 13*, 43–53.

*Kerstholt, M. T., Van Bon, W.H.J., & Schreuder, R. (1994). Training in phonemic segmentation: The effects of visual support. *Reading and Writing: An Interdisciplinary Journal, 6*, 361–385.

*Kim, Y. O. (1992). *The effect of teaching a test-taking strategy to high school students with learning disabilities.* Doctoral dissertation, University of West Virginia, 1991. *Dissertation Abstracts International, 53*(1A), 121.

*#King-Sears, M. E., Mercer, C. D., & Sindelar, P. T. (1992). Toward independence with keyword mnemonics: A strategy for science vocabulary instruction. *Remedial and Special Education, 13*, 22–33.

*#Klingner, J. K., & Vaughn, S. (1996). Reciprocal teaching of reading comprehension strategies for students with learning disabilities who use English as a second language. *Elementary School Journal, 96*, 275–293.

!Kounin, J. (1970). *Discipline and group management in classrooms.* New York: Holt, Rinehart, & Winston.

*Kunka, A.S.K. (1984). *A modality-instruction interaction study of elementary learning disabled students using two types of electronic learning aids for math instruction.* Doctoral dissertation, University of Pittsburgh, 1983. *Dissertation Abstracts International, 45*(2A), 387.

!Larrivee, B., & Algina, J. (1983, April). *Identification of teaching behaviors which predict success from mainstream students.* Paper presented at the annual meeting of the American Educational Research Association. Montreal. (ERIC Document Reproduction Service No. ED 232 362)

*Lenkowsky, R. S., Barwosky, E. I., Dayboch, M., Puccio, L., & Lenkowsky, B. E. (1987). Effects of bibliotherapy on the self-concept of learning disabled, emotionally handicapped adolescents in a classroom setting. *Psychological Reports, 61*, 483–488.

*#Leong, C. K., Simmons, D. R., & Izatt-Gambell, M. A. (1990). The effect of systematic training in elaboration on word meaning and prose comprehension in poor readers. *Annals of Dyslexia, 40*, 192–215.

*#Lerner, C. H. (1978). *The comparative effectiveness of a language experience approach and a basal-type approach to remedial reading instruction for severely disabled readers in a senior high school.* Doctoral dissertation, Temple University. *Dissertation Abstracts International, 39*(2-A), 779–780.

*Lloyd, J., Cullinan, D., Hems, E. D., & Epstein, M. H. (1980). Direct instruction: Effects on oral and written language comprehension. *Learning Disability Quarterly, 3*, 70–76.

*Lorenz, L., & Vockell, E. (1979). Using the neurological impress method with learning disabled readers. *Journal of Learning Disabilities, 12*, 420–422.

*#Losh, M. A. (1991). *The effect of the strategies intervention model on the academic achievement of junior high learning-disabled students.* Doctoral dissertation, University of Nebraska. *Dissertation Abstracts International, 52*(3-A), 880.

*Lovett, M. W., Borden, S. L., DeLuca, T., Lacerenza, L., Benson, N. J., & Brackstone, D. (1994). Treating the core deficits of developmental dyslexia: Evidence of transfer of learning after phonologically- and strategy-based reading training programs. *Developmental Psychology, 30*, 805–822.

*Lovett, M. W., Ransby, M. J., & Barron, R. W. (1988). Treatment, subtype, and word type effects on dyslexic children's response to remediation. *Brain and Language, 34*, 328–349.

*Lovett, M. W., Ransby, M. J., Hardwick, N., Johns, M. S., & Donaldson, S. A. (1989). Can dyslexia be treated? Treatment-specific and generalized treatment effects in dyslexic children's response to remediation. *Brain and Language, 37*, 90–121.

*Lovett, M. W., & Steinbach, K. A. (in press). The effectiveness of remedial programs for reading disabled children of different ages: Is there decreased benefit for older children? *Learning Disability Quarterly.*

*Lovett, M. W., Warren-Chaplin, P. M., Ransby, M. J., & Borden, S. L. (1990). Training the word recognition skills of reading disabled children: Treatment and transfer effects. *Journal of Educational Psychology, 82,* 769–780.

*Lovitt, T., Rudsit, J., Jenkins, J., Pious, C., & Benedetti, D. (1986). Adapting science materials for regular and learning disabled seventh graders. *Remedial and Special Education, 7,* 31–39.

*Lucangeli, D., Galderisi, D., & Comoldi, C. (1995). Specific and general transfer effects following metamemory training. *Learning Disabilities Research & Practice, 10,* 11–21.

*Lundberg, I., & Olofsson, A. (1993). Can computer speech support reading comprehension? *Computers in Human Behavior, 9,* 283–293.

*MacArthur, C. A., & Haynes, J. B. (1995). Student assistant for learning from text (SALT): A hypermedia reading aid. *Journal of Learning Disabilities, 28,* 150–159.

*#MacArthur, C. A., Schwartz, S. S., & Graham, S. (1991). Effects of a reciprocal peer revision strategy in special education classrooms. *Learning Disabilities Research, 6*(4), 201–210.

*Manning, B. H. (1984). Problem-solving instruction as an oral comprehension aid for reading disabled third graders. *Journal of Learning Disabilities, 17,* 457–461.

*Maron, L. R. (1993). *A comparison study of the effects of explicit versus implicit training of test-taking skills for learning-disabled fourth-grade students.* Doctoral dissertation, University of Wisconsin–Madison, 1992. *Dissertation Abstracts International, 53*(9B), 4613.

*Marsh, L. G., & Cooke, N. L. (1996). The effects of using manipulatives in teaching math problem solving to students with learning disabilities. *Learning Disabilities Research & Practice, 11,* 58–65.

*Mathes, P. G., & Fuchs, L. S. (1993). Peer-mediated reading instruction in special education resource rooms. *Learning Disabilities Research & Practice, 8,* 233–243.

*#McCollum, P. S., & Anderson, R. P. (1974). Group counseling with reading-disabled children. *Journal of Counseling Psychology, 21*(2), 150–155.

!McConnell, J. (1977). *Relationship between selected teacher behaviors and attitudes/achievement of algebra classes.* Paper presented at the annual meeting of the American Educational Research Association. New York. (ERIC Document Reproduction Service No. ED 141 118)

!McDonald, F. (1976). Report on Phase II of the Beginning Teacher Evaluation Study. *Journal of Teacher Education, 27*(1), 39–42.

!McDonald, F. (1977). Research on teaching: Report on Phase II of the Beginning Teacher Evaluation Study. In G. Borich & K. Fenton (Eds.), *The appraisal of teaching: Concepts and process.* Reading, MA: Addison-Wesley.

!McDonald, F., & Elias, P. (1976). *Executive Summary Report: Beginning Teacher Evaluation Study, Phase II.* Princeton, NJ: Educational Testing Service.

*#Meyer, L. A. (1982). The relative effects of word-analysis and word supply correction procedures with poor readers during word-attack training. *Reading Research Quarterly, 17*(4), 544–555.

*Miller, S. P., & Mercer, C. D. (1993). Using data to learn about concrete-semiconcrete abstract instruction for students with math disabilities. *Learning Disabilities Research & Practice, 8,* 89–96.

*#Montague, M., Applegate, B., & Marquard, K. (1993). Cognitive strategy instruction and

mathematical problem-solving performance of students with learning disabilities. *Learning Disabilities Research & Practice, 8*(4), 223–232.

*Moore, L., Carnine, D., Stepnoski, M., & Woodward, J. (1987). Research on the efficiency of low-cost networking. *Learning Disability Quarterly, 20*, 574–576.

*#Morgan, A. V. (1991). *A study of the effects of attribution retraining and cognitive self-instruction upon the academic and attentional skills, cognitive-behavioral trends of elementary-age children served in self-contained learning disability programs.* Doctoral dissertation, College of William and Mary, 1990. *Dissertation Abstracts International, 51*(8-B), 4035.

*Naylor, J. O., & Pumfrey, P. D. (1983). The alleviation of psycholinguistic deficits and some effects on the reading attainments of poor readers: A sequel. *Journal of Research in Reading, 6*, 129–153.

*Nelson, S. L. (1985). *Modifying impulsivity in learning disabled boys on matching, maze, and WISC-R performance scales.* Doctoral dissertation, University of Southern California, 1984. *Dissertation Abstracts International, 45*(7B), 2316–2317.

!Nuthall, G., & Church, J. (1973). Experimental studies of teaching behavior. In G. Chanan (Ed.), *Towards a science of teaching.* London: National Foundation for Educational Research.

*#O'Connor, P. D., Stuck, G. B., & Wyne, M. D. (1979). Effects of a short-term intervention resource-room program on task orientation and achievement. *Journal of Special Education, 13*(4), 375–385.

*#Olofsson, A. (1992). Synthetic speech and computer-aided reading for reading-disabled children. *Reading and Writing, 4*(2), 165–178.

*#Olsen, J. L., Wong, B.Y.L., & Marx, R. W. (1983). Linguistic and metacognitive aspects of normally achieving and learning disabled children's communication process. *Learning Disability Quarterly, 6*(3), 289–304.

*Olson, R. K., & Wise, B. W. (1992). Reading on the computer with orthographic and speech feedback. *Reading and Writing: An Interdisciplinary Journal, 4*, 107–144.

*Omizo, M. M., Cubberly, W. E., & Omizo, S. A. (1985). The effects of rational-emotive education groups on self-concept and locus of control among learning disabled children. *Exceptional Child, 32*, 13–19.

*Omizo, M. M., Lo, F. O., & Williams, R. E. (1986). Rational-emotive education, self-concept, and locus of control among learning-disabled students. *Journal of Humanistic Education, 25*, 58–69.

*Omizo, M. M., & Williams, R. E. (1982). Biofeedback-induced relaxation training as an alternative for the elementary school learning-disabled child. *Biofeedback and Self-Regulation, 7*, 139–148.

*Pany, D., & Jenkins, J. R. (1978). Learning word meanings: A comparison of instructional procedures. *Learning Disability Quarterly, 1*, 21–32.

*Pany, D., Jenkins, J. R., & Schreck, J. (1982). Vocabulary instruction: Effects on word knowledge and reading comprehension. *Learning Disability Quarterly, 5*, 202–215.

*Pihl, R. O., Parkes, M., Drake, H., & Vrana, F. (1980). The intervention of a modulator with learning disabled children. *Journal of Clinical Psychology, 36*, 972–976.

*Porinchak, P. M. (1984). *Computer-assisted instruction in secondary school reading: Interaction of cognitive and affective factors.* Doctoral dissertation, Hofstra University, 1983. *Dissertation Abstracts International*, 45(2A), 478.

*#Prior, M., Frye, S., & Fletcher, C. (1987). Remediation for subgroups of retarded readers

using a modified oral spelling procedure. *Developmental Medicine and Child Neurology, 29,* 64–71.

*Ratekin, N. (1979). Reading achievement of disabled learners. *Exceptional Children, 45,* 454–458.

!%Reid, E. R. (1978–1982). *The Reader Newsletter.* Salt Lake City: Exemplary Center for Reading Instruction.

*Reid, R., & Harris, K. R. (1993). Self-monitoring of attention versus self-monitoring of performance: Effects on attention and academic performance. *Exceptional Children, 60,* 29–40.

*#Reilly, J. P. (1991). *Effects of a cognitive-behavioral program designed to increase the reading comprehension skills of learning-disabled students.* Doctoral dissertation, College of William and Mary. *Dissertation Abstracts International, 52*(3-A), 865.

*#Reynolds, C. J. (1986). *The effects of instruction in cognitive revision strategies on the writing skills of secondary learning disabled students.* Doctoral dissertation, Ohio State University, 1985. *Dissertation Abstracts International, 46*(9-A), 2662.

Rosenshine, B., & Stevens, R. (1986). Teaching functions. In M. C. Wittrock (Ed.), *Handbook of research on teaching* (3rd ed., pp. 376–391). New York: Macmillan.

*Ross, P. A., & Braden, J. P. (1991). The effects of token reinforcement versus cognitive behavior modification on learning-disabled students' math skills. *Psychology in the Schools, 28,* 247–256.

*#Rudel, R. G., & Helfgott, E. (1984). Effect of piracetam on verbal memory of dyslexic boys. *American Academy of Child Psychiatry, 23,* 695–699.

*Ruhl, K. L., Hughes, C. A., & Gajar, A. H. (1990). Efficacy of the pause procedure for enhancing learning disabled and nondisabled college students' long- and short-term recall of facts presented through lecture. *Learning Disability Quarterly, 13,* 55–64.

*Sawyer, R. J., Graham, S., & Harris, K. R. (1992). Direct teaching, strategy instruction and strategy instruction with explicit self-regulation: Effects on the composition skills and self-efficacy of students with learning disabilities. *Journal of Educational Psychology, 84,* 340–352.

*Scanlon, D., Deshler, D. D., & Schumaker, J. B. (1996). Can a strategy be taught and learned in secondary inclusive classrooms? *Learning Disabilities Research & Practice, 11,* 41–57.

*Scheerer-Neumann, G. (1981). The utilization of intraword structure in poor readers: Experimental evidence and a training program. *Psychological Research, 43,* 155–178.

!Schuck, R. (1981). The impact of set induction on student achievement and retention. *Journal of Educational Research, 74,* 227–232.

*Schulte, A. C., Osborne, S. S., & McKinney, J. D. (1991). Academic outcomes for students with learning disabilities in consultation and resource programs. *Exceptional Children, 57,* 162–172.

*#Schunk, D. H. (1985). Participation in goal-setting: Effects on self-efficacy and skills of learning-disabled children. *Journal of Special Education, 19,* 305–317.

*#Schunk, D. H., & Cox, P. D. (1986). Strategy training and attributional feedback with learning-disabled students. *Journal of Educational Psychology, 78,* 201–209.

*Scruggs, T. E., & Mastropieri, M. A. (1989). Mnemonic instruction of LD students: A field-based evaluation. *Learning Disability Quarterly, 12,* 119–125.

*Scruggs, T. E., & Mastropieri, M. A. (1992). Classroom applications of mnemonic instruction: Acquisition, maintenance, and generalization. *Exceptional Children, 58*(3), 219–229.

*Scruggs, T. E., Mastropieri, M. A., & Tolfa-Veit, D. (1986). The effects of coaching on the standardized test performance of learning disabled and behaviorally disordered students. *Remedial and Special Education, 7*(5), 37–41.

*Scruggs, T. E., & Tolfa, D. (1985). Improving the test-taking skills of learning-disabled students. *Perceptual and Motor Skills, 60,* 847–850.

*Sheare, J. B. (1978). The impact of resource programs upon the self-concept and peer acceptance of learning disabled children. *Psychology in the Schools, 15,* 406–412.

*Simmonds, E.P.M. (1990). The effectiveness of two methods for teaching a constraint-seeking questioning strategy to students with learning disabilities. *Journal of Learning Disabilities, 23,* 229–232.

*Simmonds, E.P.M. (1992). The effects of teacher training and implementation of two methods for improving the comprehension skills of students with learning disabilities. *Learning Disabilities Research & Practice, 7,* 194–198.

*Simpson, S. B., Swanson, J. M., & Kunkel, K. (1992). The impact of an intensive multisensory reading program on a population of learning-disabled delinquents. *Annals of Dyslexia, 42,* 54–66.

*Sinatra, R. C., Stahl-Gemake, J., & Berg, D. N. (1984). Improving reading comprehension of disabled readers through semantic mapping. *The Reading Teacher, 38,* 22–29.

*Sindelar, P. T., Honsaker, M. S., & Jenkins, J. R. (1982). Response cost and reinforcement contingencies of managing the behavior of distractible children in tutorial settings. *Learning Disability Quarterly, 5,* 3–13.

*#Smith, M. A. (1989). *The efficacy of mnemonics for teaching recognition of letter clusters to reading disabled students.* Doctoral dissertation, University of Oregon. *Dissertation Abstracts International, 50*(5-A), 1259–1260.

*Smith, P. L., & Friend, M. (1986). Training learning disabled adolescents in a strategy for using text structure to aid recall of instructional prose. *Learning Disabilities Research, 2,* 38–44.

*#Snider, V. E. (1989). Reading comprehension performance of adolescents with learning disabilities. *Learning Disability Quarterly, 12*(2), 87–96.

!Soar, R. S. (1966). *An integrative approach to classroom learning* (Report for NIMH Projects No. 5-R11 MH 01096 and R-11 MH 02045). Philadelphia: Temple University. (ERIC Document Reproduction Service No. ED 033 749)

!Soar, R. S. (1968). Optimal teacher-pupil interaction for pupil growth. *Educational Leadership, 26,* 275–280.

!Soar, R. S. (1973). *Follow-Through classroom process measurement and pupil growth (1970–1971) final report.* Gainesville: College of Education, University of Florida.

!Soar, R. S. (1977). An integration of findings from four studies of teacher effectiveness. In G. Borich & K. Fenton (Eds.), *The appraisal of teaching: Concepts and process.* Reading, MA: Addison-Wesley.

!Soar, R. S., & Soar, R. M. (1972). An empirical analysis of selected Follow Through Programs: An appraisal of a process approach to evaluation. In G. Borich & K. Fenton (Eds.).*The appraisal of teaching: Concepts and process.* Reading, MA: Addison-Wesley.

!Soar, R. S., & Soar, R. M. (1973). *Classroom behavior, pupil characteristics, and pupil growth for the school year and the summer.* Gainesville: University of Florida, Institute for Development of Human Resources.

!Soar, R. S., & Soar, R. M. (1978). *Setting variables, classroom interaction, and multiple pupil outcomes* (Final Report, Project No. 6-0432, Grant No. NIE-G-76-0100). Washington, DC: National Institute of Education.

!Soar, R. S., & Soar, R. M. (1979). Emotional climate and management. In P. Peterson & H. Walberg (Eds.), *Research on teaching: Concepts, findings, and implications.* Berkeley, CA: McCutchan.

!Solomon, D., & Kendall, A. (1979). *Children in classrooms: An investigation person-environment interaction.* New York: Praeger.

*Somerville, D. E., & Leach, D. J. (1988). Direct or indirect instruction? An evaluation of three types of intervention programs for assisting students with specific reading difficulties. *Educational Research, 30,* 46–53.

*Sowell, V., Parker, R., Poplin, M., & Larsen, S. (1979). The effects of psycholinguistic training on improving psycholinguistic skills. *Learning Disability Quarterly, 2,* 69–78.

!Stallings, J. (1980). Allocated academic learning time revisited, or beyond time on task. *Educational Researcher, 8*(11), 11–16.

!%Stallings, J., Corey, R., Fairweather, J., & Needles, M. (1977). *Early Childhood Education classroom evaluation.* Menlo Park, CA: SRI International.

!%Stallings, J., Needles, M., & Staybrook, N. (1979). *The teaching of basic reading skills in secondary schools, Phase II and Phase III.* Menlo Park, CA: SRI International.

!%Stallings, J. A., & Kaskowitz, D. (1974). *Follow-Through Classroom Observation.* Menlo Park, CA: SRI International.

*Straub, R. B., & Roberts, D. M. (1983). Effects of nonverbal-oriented social awareness training program on social interaction ability of learning disabled children. *Journal of Nonverbal Behavior, 7,* 195–201.

*#Sullivan, J. (1972). The effects of Kephart's perceptual motor training on a reading clinic sample. *Journal of Learning Disabilities, 5,* 545–551.

Swanson, H. L. (2001). Research on interventions for adolescents with learning disabilities: A meta-analysis of outcomes related to higher-order processing. *The Elementary School Journal, 101*(13), 331–349.

Swanson, H. L., & Hoskyn, M. (1998). Experimental intervention research on students with learning disabilities: A meta-analysis of treatment outcomes. *Review of Educational Research, 68*(3), 277–321.

*Swanson, H. L., & Trahan, M. F. (1992). Learning disabled readers' comprehension of computer mediated text: The influence of working memory, metacognition and attribution. *Learning Disabilities Research & Practice, 7,* 74–86.

!Tobin, K., & Caple, W. (1982). Relationships between classroom process variables and middle-school science achievement. *Journal of Educational Psychology, 74,* 441–454.

*#Tollefson, N., Tracy, D. B., Johnsen, E. P., Farmer, A. W., & Buenning, M. (1984). Goal setting and personal responsibility training for LD adolescents. *Psychology in the Schools, 21,* 224–233.

*Torgesen, J. K., Wagner, R. K., Rashotte, C. A., Alexander, A. W., & Conway, T. (1997). Preventive and remedial interventions for children with severe reading disabilities. *Learning Disabilities: A Multi-Disciplinary Journal, 8,* 51–61.

*#Trapani, C., & Gettinger, M. (1989). Effects of social skills training and cross-age tutoring on academic achievement and social behaviors of boys with learning disabilities. *Journal of Research and Development in Education, 23,* 1–9.

*VanDaal, V.H.P., & Reitsma, P. (1990). Effects of independent word practice with segmented and whole-word sound feedback in disabled readers. *Journal of Research in Reading, 13*, 133–148.

*VanDaal, V.H.P., & Reitsma, P. (1993). The use of speech feedback by normal and disabled readers in computer-based reading practice. *Reading and Writing: An Interdisciplinary Journal, 5*, 243–259.

*VanDaal, V.H.P., &VanDerLeij, D. (1992). Computer-based reading and spelling practice for children with learning disabilities. *Journal of Learning Disabilities, 25*, 186–195.

*VanReusen, A. K., & Bos, C. S. (1994). Facilitating student participation in individualized education programs through motivation strategy instruction. *Exceptional Children, 60*, 466–475.

*VanStrien, J. W., Stolk, B. D., & Zuiker, S. (1995). Hemisphere-specific treatment of dyslexia subtypes: Better reading with anxiety-laden words? *Journal of Learning Disabilities, 28*, 30–34.

*Vaughn, S., Schumm, J. S., & Gordon, J. (1993). Which motoric condition is most effective for teaching spelling to students with and without learning disabilities? *Journal of Learning Disabilities, 26*, 193–198.

*Wade, J., & Kass, C. E. (1987). Component deficit and academic remediation of learning disabilities. *Journal of Learning Disabilities, 20*, 441–447.

*Wade, J. F. (1979). *The effects of component deficit remediation and academic deficit remediation on improving reading achievement of learning disabled children.* Doctoral dissertation, University of Arizona. *Dissertation Abstracts International, 40*(3A), 1412.

*Wanat, P. E. (1983). Social skills: An awareness program with learning disabled adolescents. *Journal of Learning Disabilities, 16*, 35–38.

*Warner, J.M.R. (1973). *The effects of two treatment modes upon children diagnosed as having learning disabilities.* Doctoral dissertation, University of Illinois. *Dissertation Abstracts International, 34*(3A), 1142–1143.

*Waterman, D. E. (1974). *Remediation of word attack skills in slow readers by total body movement learning games.* Doctoral dissertation, University of Tulsa, 1973. *Dissertation Abstracts International, 34*(7A), 4049.

*Welch, M. (1992). The PLEASE strategy: A meta-cognitive learning strategy for improving the paragraph writing of students with learning disabilities. *Learning Disability Quarterly, 15*, 119–128.

*#White, C. V., Pascarella, E. T., & Pflaum, S. W. (1981). Effects of training in sentence construction on the comprehension of learning-disabled children. *Journal of Educational Psychology, 71*, 697–704.

*Whitman, D. M. (1986). *The effects of computer-assisted instruction on mathematics achievement of mildly handicapped students.* Doctoral dissertation, University of South Carolina, 1985. *Dissertation Abstracts International, 46*(10A), 3000–3001.

*#Williams, J. P., Brown, L. G., Silverstein, A. K., & deCani, J. S. (1994). An instructional program in comprehension of narrative themes for adolescents with learning disabilities. *Learning Disability Quarterly, 17*, 205–221.

*Wilsher, C., Atkins, O., & Manfield, P. (1985). Effect of piracetam on dyslexics' reading ability. *Journal of Learning Disabilities, 18*, 19–25.

*Wilson, C., & Sindelar, P. T. (1991). Direct instruction in math word problems: Students with learning disabilities. *Exceptional Children, 57*, 512–519.

*Wilson, C. L. (1989). *An analysis of a direct instruction procedure in teaching word prob-*

lem-solving to learning disabled students. Doctoral dissertation, Florida State University, 1988. *Dissertation Abstracts International, 50*(2A), 416.

*Wise, B. W., Ring, J., Sessions, L., & Olson, R. K. (in press). Phonological awareness with and without articulation: A preliminary study. *Learning Disability Quarterly.*

*#Wong, B.Y.L., Butler, D. L., Ficzere, S. A., & Kuperis, S. (1996). Teaching low achievers and students with learning disabilities to plan, write, and revise opinion essays. *Journal of Learning Disabilities, 29*, 197–212.

*#Wong, B.Y.L., Butler, D. L., Ficzere, S. A., Kuperis, S., Corden, M., & Zelmer, J. (1994). Teaching problem learners revision skills and sensitivity to audience through two instructional modes: Student-teacher versus student-student interactive dialogues. *Learning Disabilities Research & Practice, 9*, 78–90.

*#Wong, B.Y.L., & Jones, W. (1982). Increasing metacomprehension in learning disabled and normally achieving students through self-questioning training. *Learning Disability Quarterly, 5*, 228–240.

*Zieffle, T. H., & Romney, D. M. (1985). Comparison of self-instruction and relaxation training in reducing impulsive and inattentive behavior of learning disabled children on cognitive tasks. *Psychological Reports, 57*, 271–274.

REFERENCES FOR UTILIZING COMPUTERIZED INSTRUCTION

@Adams, C. (1986). Reading achievement of low socioeconomic seventh- and eighth-grade students with and without computer-assisted instruction. *Dissertation Abstracts International, 47*(11A), 3956.

%Anderson, R. C., Kulkavy, R. W., & Andre, T. (1971). Feedback procedures in programmed instruction. *Journal of Educational Psychology, 62*(2), 148–156.

%Anderson, R. C., Kulkavy, R. W., & Andre, T. (1972). Conditions under which feedback facilitates learning from programmed lessons. *Journal of Educational Psychology, 63*(3), 186–188.

%Armour-Thomas, E., White, M. A., & Boehm, A. (1987, April). *The motivational effects of types of feedback on children's learning concepts and retention of relational concepts.* Paper presented at the annual meeting of the American Educational Research Association, Washington, DC.

%Arnone, M. P., & Grabowski, B. L. (1992). Effects on children's achievement and curiosity in learner control over an interactive video lesson. *Educational Technology Research and Development, 40*(1), 15–27.

Azevedo, R., & Bernard, R. N. (1995). *The effects of computer-presented feedback on learning from computer-based instruction: A meta-analysis.* Paper presented at the annual meeting of the American Educational Research Association, San Francisco. (ERIC Document Reproduction Service No. ED 385235)

@Bailey, T. (1991). The effect of computer-assisted instruction in improving mathematics performance of low-achieving ninth-grade students (remediation). *Dissertation Abstracts International, 52*(11A), 3849.

*Baker, D. E. (1992). *The effect of self-generated drawings on the ability of students with learning disabilities to solve mathematical word problems.* Unpublished doctoral dissertation, Texas Technology University, Lubbock.

Barley, Z., Lauer, P. A., Arens, S. A., Apthrop, H. S., Englert, K. S., Snow, D., & Akiba, M. (2002). *Helping at-risk students meet standards: A synthesis of evidence-based classroom practices*. Aurora, CO: Mid-continent Research for Education and Learning.

*Bennett, K. K. (1981). *The effect of syntax and verbal mediation on learning disabled students' verbal mathematical problem scores*. Unpublished doctoral dissertation, Northern Arizona University, Flagstaff.

#Borton, W. M. (1988). The effects of computer managed mastery learning on mathematics test scores in the elementary school. *Journal of Computer-Based Instruction, 15*(3), 95–98.

*Bottge, B. A., & Hasselbring, T. S. (1993). A comparison of two approaches for teaching complex, authentic mathematics problems to adolescents in remedial math classes. *Exceptional Children, 59*, 556–566.

%Bumgarner, K. M. (1984). *Effects of informational feedback and social reinforcement on elementary students' achievement during CAI drill and practice on multiplication facts*. Unpublished doctoral dissertation, Seattle University.

*Case, L. P., Harris, K. R., & Graham, S. (1992). Improving the mathematical problem-solving skills of students with learning disabilities: Self-regulated strategy development. *The Journal of Special Education, 26*, 1–19.

*Cassel, J., & Reid, R. (1996). Use of self-regulated strategy intervention to improve word problem-solving skills of students with mild disabilities. *Journal of Behavioral Education, 6*, 153–172.

%Chanond, K. (1988, January). *The effects of feedback, correctness of response and response confidence on learner's retention in computer-assisted instruction*. Proceedings of selected research papers presented at the annual meetings of the Association for Educational Communications and Technology, New Orleans, LA.

#Childers, R. D. (1989). *Implementation of the writing to read instructional system in 13 rural elementary schools in southern West Virginia* (ED320744). Charleston, WV: Appalachia Educational Lab.

Christmann, E. P., & Badgett, J. L. (2003). A meta-analytic comparison of the effects of computer-assisted instruction on elementary students' academic achievement. *Information Technology in Childhood Education Annual, 1*, 91–104.

%Clariana, R. B., Ross, S. M., & Morrison, G. R. (1991). The effects of different feedback strategies using computer-administered multiple-choice questions as instruction. *Educational Technology Research & Development, 39*(2), 5–17.

#Collis, B. Ollila, L., & Ollila, K. (1990). Writing to read: An evaluation of a Canadian installation of a computer-supported initial language environment. *Journal of Educational Computing Research, 6*(4), 411–427.

@Dellario, T. (1987). The effects of computer-assisted instruction in basic skills courses on high-risk ninth-grade students. *Dissertation Abstracts International, 48*(04), 0892.

@Dungan, S. (1990). The relationship between computer-assisted instruction and the academic gains of selected elementary students in a rural school district. *Dissertation Abstracts International, 51*(10A), 3315.

%Elliot, B. A. (1986). *An investigation of the effects of computer feedback and interspersed questions on the text comprehension of poor readers*. Unpublished doctoral dissertation, Temple University.

@Emihovich, C., & Miller, G. (1988). Effects of Logo and CAI on black first graders' achievement, reflectivity, and self-esteem. *Elementary School Journal, 88*(5), 473–487.

#Ferrell, B. G. (1986). Evaluating the impact of CAL on mathematics learning: Computer immersion project. *Journal of Educational Computing Research, 2*(3), 327–336.

@Francis, M. (1990). *CCP: A diagnostic/prescriptive approach to remediation for "at-risk" students.* New Bedford, MA: New Bedford Public Schools, Career Development Center.

#Fraser, L. A. (1991). *Evaluation of chapter I take-home computer program* (ED337531). Atlanta: Georgia Public Schools, Department of Research and Evaluation.

%Gaynor, P. (1981). The effect of feedback delay on retention of computer-based mathematical material. *Journal of Computer-Based Instruction, 8*(2), 28–34.

%Gilman, D. A. (1969a). Comparison of several feedback methods for correcting errors by computer-assisted instruction. *Journal of Educational Psychology, 60*(6), 503–508.

%Gilman, D. A. (1969b). The effect of feedback on learner's certainty of response and attitude toward instruction in a computer-assisted instruction program for teaching science concepts. *Journal of Research in Science Teaching, 6,* 171–184.

#Gilman, D. A., & Brantley, T. (1988). *The effects of computer-assisted instruction on achievement, problem-solving skills, computer skills, and attitude* (ED302232). Terre Haute: Indiana State University, Professional School Services.

*Gleason, M., Carnine, D., & Boriero, D. (1990). Improving CAI effectiveness with attention to instructional design in teaching story problems to mildly handicapped students. *Journal of Special Education Technology, 10,* 129–136.

#Haines, J. G. (1988). *Using computers to enhance writing and reading instruction in the kindergarten classroom.* Doctoral dissertation, University of South Florida. *Dissertation Abstracts International, 49,* 2922-A.

#Hawley, D. E., Fletcher, J. D., & Piele, P. K. (1986). *Costs, effects, and utility of microcomputer-assisted instruction.* Eugene, OR: Center for Advanced Technology in Education. (ERIC Document Reproduction Service No. ED 284 531)

#Hess, R. D., & McGarvey, L. J. (1987). School relevant effects of educational uses of microcomputers in kindergarten classrooms and homes. *Journal of Educational Computing Research, 3*(3), 269–287.

#Hesser, L. A. (1988). *Effectiveness of computer-assisted instruction in developing music reading skills at the elementary level.* Doctoral dissertation, State University of New York at Albany. *Dissertation Abstracts international, 49,* 03-A.

%Hines, S. J., & Seidman, S. A. (1988, January). *The effects of selected CAI design strategies on achievement, and an exploration of other related factors.* Proceedings of selected research papers presented at the annual meeting of the Association for Educational Communications and Technology, New Orleans, LA.

#Hirsch, M. L. (1986). *The effect of computer assisted instruction in problem solving on the cognitive abilities of fifth grade students.* Doctoral dissertation, United States International University. *Dissertation Abstracts International, 47,* 04-A.

%Hodes, C. L. (1985). Relative effectiveness of corrective and noncorrective feedback in computer-assisted instruction on learning and achievement. *Journal of Educational Technology Systems, 13*(4), 249–254.

#Hoffman, J. T. (1984). *Reading achievement and attitude toward reading of elementary students receiving supplementary computer assisted instruction compared with students receiving supplementary traditional instruction.* Doctoral dissertation, Ball State University. *Dissertation Abstracts International, 45,* 07-A.

#Hopkins, J. F. (1989). *A comparison of two methods for teaching expository writing to fourth-grade students: computer-assisted language experience approach versus traditional textbook approach.* Doctoral dissertation, University of Oregon. *Dissertation Abstracts International, 51,* 397-A.

*Huntington, D. J. (1994). *Instruction in concrete, semi-concrete, and abstract representation as an aid to the solution of relational problems by adolescents with learning disabilities.* Unpublished doctoral dissertation, University of Georgia, Athens.

*Hutchinson, N. L. (1993). Effects of cognitive strategy instruction on algebra problem solving of adolescents with learning disabilities. *Learning Disability Quarterly, 16,* 34–63.

*Jitendra, A., & Hoff, K. (1996). The effects of schema-based instruction on mathematical word-problem-solving performance of students with learning disabilities. *Journal of Learning Disabilities, 29,* 422–431.

%Johansen, K. J., & Tennyson, R. D. (1983). Effect of adaptive advisement on perception in linear-controlled, computer-based instruction using a rule-learning task. *Educational Communication and Technology Journal, 31*(4), 226–236.

@Kestner, M. (1989). A comparative study involving the administration of computer-managed instruction in a remedial mathematics program. *Dissertation Abstracts International, 51*(03A), 0774.

@Kitabchi, G. (1987, November). *Evaluation of the Apple classroom of tomorrow.* Paper presented at the sixteenth annual meeting of the Mid-South Educational Research Association, Mobile, AL.

@Kochinski, V. (1986). The effects of CAI for remediation on the self-concepts, attitudes, and reading achievement of middle school readers (Chapter 1, affective). *Dissertation Abstracts International, 47*(06A), 2100.

@Koza, J. (1989). Comparison of the achievement of mathematics and reading levels and attitude toward learning of high risk secondary students through the use of computer aided instruction. *Dissertation Abstracts International, 51*(03A), 0687.

#Larter, S. (1987). *Writing with microcomputers in the elementary grades: Process, roles, attitudes, and products* (ED284261). Toronto: Ontario Department of Education.

#Leahy, P. E. (1991). *Results of multi-year formative evaluation for the "writing to read" program in a mid-size suburban school district.* Paper presented at the annual meeting of the American Educational Research Association, Chicago, IL.

*Lee, J. W. (1992). *The effectiveness of a novel direct instructional approach on word problem solving skills of elementary students with learning disabilities.* Unpublished doctoral dissertation, Ohio State University, Columbus.

@Ligas, M. (2002). Evaluation of Broward County Alliance of Quality Schools project. *Journal of Education for Students Placed at Risk, 7*(2), 117–139.

#Little, L. L. (1987). *Reinforcing reading readiness skills in kindergarten: A CAT tutorial versus teacher-directed instruction.* Doctoral dissertation, Northern Arizona University. *Dissertation Abstracts International, 48,* 2031-A.

#Liu, M., & Pederson, S. (1998). The effect of being hypermedia designers on elementary school students' motivation and learning of design knowledge. *Journal of Interactive Learning Research, 9*(2), 155–182.

#MacArthur, C. A., Haynes, J. B., Malouf, D., Harris, K., & Owings, M. (1990). Computer assisted instruction with learning disabled students: Achievement, engagement, and other factors that influence achievement. *Journal of Educational Computing Research, 6*(3), 311–328.

#MacGregor, S. K. (1988). Use of self-questioning with a computer-mediated text system and measures of reading performance. *Journal of Reading Behavior, 20*(2), 131–149.

#Manuel, S.L.Q. (1987). *The relationship between supplemental computer-assisted instruction and student achievement.* Doctoral dissertation, University of Nebraska, Lincoln. *Dissertation Abstracts International, 48,* 1643-A.

*Marsh, L. G. (1996). The effects of using manipulatives in teaching math problem solving to students with learning disabilities. *Learning Disabilities Research & Practice, 11,* 58–65.

*Marzola, E. S. (1987). *An arithmetic verbal problem solving model for learning disabled students.* Unpublished doctoral dissertation, Columbia University, New York.

#Mason, M. M. (1984). *A longitudinal study of the effects of computer assisted instruction on the mathematics achievement of the learning disabled and educable mentally retarded.* Doctoral dissertation, University of Iowa. *Dissertation Abstracts International, 48,* 2741-A.

#McClurg, P. A., & Kasakow, N. (1989). Wordprocessors, spelling checkers, and drill and practice programs: Effective tools for spelling instruction? *Journal of Educational Computing Research, 52*(2), 187–198.

#McCollister, T. S., Burts, D., Wright, V., & Hildreth, G. (1986). Effects of computer-assisted instruction and teacher-assisted instruction on arithmetic task achievement scores of kindergarten children. *Journal of Educational Research, 80*(2), 121–125.

#McCormack, S. K. (1985). *The effect of computer assisted instruction on letter-sound recognition and beginning reading skills for kindergarten students.* Doctoral dissertation, University of Colorado. *Dissertation Abstracts International, 47,* 839-A.

#Meyer, P. A. (1986). *A comparative analysis of the value of intrinsic motivation in computer software on the math achievement, attitudes, attendance, and depth-of-involvement of underachieving students.* Doctoral dissertation, College of William and Mary. *Dissertation Abstracts International, 47,* 1295-A.

@Mickens, M. (1991). Effects of supplementary computer-assisted instruction on Basic Algebra 1 and Basic Algebra 2 achievement levels of mathematics at-risk minority students. *Dissertation Abstracts International, 53*(03A), 0704.

#Miller, M. D., & McInerney, W. D. (1995). Effects of achievement of a home/school computer project. *Journal of Research of Computing in Education, 27*(2), 198–210.

*Montague, M. (1992). The effects of cognitive and metacognitive strategy instruction on the mathematical problem solving of middle school students with learning disabilities. *Journal of Learning Disabilities, 25,* 230–248.

*Montague, M., Applegate, B., & Marquard, K. (1993). Cognitive strategy instruction and mathematical problem-solving performance of students with learning disabilities. *Learning Disabilities Research & Practice, 8,* 223–232.

*Montague, M., & Bos, C. S. (1986). The effect of cognitive strategy training on verbal math problem solving performance of learning disabled adolescents. *Journal of Learning Disabilities, 19,* 26–33.

@Moore, B. (1988). Achievement in basic math skills for low performing students: A study of teachers' affect and CAI. *Journal of Experimental Education, 57*(1), 38–44.

*Moore, L. J., & Carnine, D. (1989). Evaluating curriculum design in the context of active teaching. *Remedial and Special Education, 10,* 28–37.

*Noll, R. S. (1983). *Effects of verbal cueing and a visual representation on percent problem-solving performance of remedial adults.* Unpublished doctoral dissertation, Fordham University, New York.

*Nuzum, M. (1983). *The effects of an instructional model based on the information pro-

cessing paradigm on the arithmetic problem solving performance of four learning disabled students. Unpublished doctoral dissertation, Columbia University, New York.

#Orabuchi, I. I. (1992). *Effects of using interactive CAI on primary grade students' higher-order thinking skills: Inferences, generalizations, and math problem solving.* Doctoral dissertation, Texas Women's University. *Dissertation Abstracts International, 53,* 3793-A.

#Phillips, J., & Soule, H. (1992, November). *A comparison of fourth graders' achievement: Classroom computers versus no computers.* Paper presented at the annual meeting of the Mid-South Educational Research Association, Knoxville, TN.

#Powell-Rahlfs, K. (1984). *Computer assisted and traditional instruction of multiplication facts with learning disabled elementary students.* Doctoral dissertation, Kansas State University. *Dissertation Abstracts International, 45,* 08-A.

@Ramey, M. (1991). *Compensatory education sustained gains from Spring 1988 to Spring 1990* (Report No. 91-1). Seattle, WA: Seattle Public Schools.

%Roper, W. J. (1977). Feedback in computer assisted instruction. *Programmed Learning and Educational Technology, 4*(1), 44–49.

%Schaffer, L. C., & Hannafin, M. J. (1986). The effects of progressive interactivity on learning from interactive video. *Educational Communication and Technology Journal, 34*(2), 89–96.

%Schloss, P. J., Wisniewski, L. A., & Cartwright, G. P. (1988). The differential effect of learner control and feedback in college students' performance on CAI modules. *Journal of Educational Computing Research, 4*(2), 141–150.

#Sexton, C. W. (1989). Effectiveness of DISTAR Reading 1 Program in developing first graders' language skills. *Journal of Educational Research, 82*(5), 289–293.

#Shanoski, L. A. (1986). *An analysis of the effectiveness of using microcomputer assisted mathematics instruction with primary and intermediate level students.* Doctoral dissertation, Indiana University of Pennsylvania. *Dissertation Abstracts International, 47,* 3653-A.

*Shiah, R., Mastropieri, M. A., Scruggs, T. E., & Fulk, B.J.M. (1995). The effects of computer-assisted instruction on the mathematical problem solving of students with learning disabilities. *Exceptionality, 5,* 131–161.

#Shutrump, G. S. (1993). *Demographic predictors of success in a CAL program among elementary students.* Doctoral dissertation, Florida Atlantic University. *Dissertation Abstracts International, 54,* 06-A.

@Sinkis, D. (1993). A comparison of Chapter One student achievement with and without computer-assisted instruction (Chapter One students, at risk). *Dissertation Abstracts International, 54*(2A), 0422.

*Smith, E. M. (1981). *The effect of teaching sixth graders with learning difficulties a strategy for solving verbal mathematical problems.* Unpublished doctoral dissertation, University of Kansas, Lawrence.

@Stegemann, J. (1986). The effect of computer-assisted instruction on motivation and achievement in fourth grade mathematics. *Dissertation Abstracts International, 47*(10A), 3705. (UMI No. 8703277)

#Suppes, P., & Morningstar, M. (1969). *Evaluation of three computer-assisted instruction programs.* Stanford, CA: Stanford University, Institute for Mathematical Studies in the Social Sciences (Technical Report No. 142).

@Swarm, C. (1991). *Computer-assisted mathematics prescription learning pull-out program in an elementary school.* (ERIC Document Reproduction Service No. ED 335 216)

@Tanner, D. (1987). *CAI and the high-risk student.* Fresno: California State University, School of Education and Human Development.

%Tennyson, R. D. (1980). Instructional control strategies and content structure as design variables in concept acquisition using computer-based instruction. *Journal of Educational Psychology, 72*(4), 525–532.

%Tennyson, R. D. (1981). Use of adaptive information for advisement in learning concepts and rules using computer-assisted instruction. *American Educational Research Journal, 18*(4), 425–438.

%Tennyson, R. D., & Buttrey, T. (1980). Advisement and management strategies as design variables in computer-assisted instruction. *Educational Communication and Technology Journal, 28*(3), 169–176.

*Tippins, C. H. (1987). *A training program for adolescent learning disabled students in the use of mathematical word problem solving strategies.* Unpublished doctoral dissertation, University of South Carolina, Columbia.

#Uhde, A. P. (1988). *The impact of the writing to read program on reading, spelling, and writing of kindergartners.* Doctoral dissertation, University of Georgia. *Dissertation Abstracts International, 50,* 2383-A.

#Underwood, J. (1996). Are integrated learning systems effective learning support tools? *Computers & Education, 26*(3), 33–40.

*Walker, D. W., & Poteet, J. A. (1989). A comparison of two methods of teaching mathematics story problem-solving with learning disabled students. *National Forum of Special Education Journal, 1,* 44–51.

#Ward, P. L. (1986). *A comparison of computer-assisted and traditional drill and practice on elementary students' vocabulary knowledge and attitude toward reading instruction.* Doctoral dissertation, University of Southern Mississippi. *Dissertation Abstracts International, 47,* 2977-A.

*Watanabe, A. K. (1991). *The effects of a mathematical word problem solving strategy on problem solving performance by middle school students with mild disabilities.* Unpublished doctoral dissertation, University of Florida, Gainesville.

#Watkins, M. W. (1986). Microcomputer-based math instruction with first-grade students. *Computers in Human Behavior, 2,* 71–75.

#Watkins, M. W., & Abram, S. (1985, April). Reading CAL with first grade students. *The Computing Teacher,* 43–45.

@Weller, L., Carpenter, S., & Holmes, C. (1998). Achievement gains of low-achieving students using computer-assisted vs. regular instruction. *Psychological Reports, 83*(3, Pt. 1), 834.

@Wepner, S. (1991, October). *The effects of a computerized reading program on "at-risk" secondary students.* Paper presented at the annual meeting of the College Reading Association, Crystal City, VA.

#Westbrook, J. (1987). *A comparison of four methods of study skills instruction for sixth and seventh grade students.* Doctoral dissertation, University of Alabama. *Dissertation Abstracts International, 48A,* 11.

@Willinsky, J., & Green, S. (1990). Desktop publishing in remedial language arts settings: Letting them eat cake. *Journal of Teaching Writing, 9*(2), 223–238.

*Wilson, C. L., & Sindelar, P. T. (1991). Direct instruction in math word problems: Students with learning disabilities. *Exceptional Children, 57*, 512–519.

Yan, P. X., & Jitendra, A. K. (1999). The effects of instruction in solving mathematical word problems for students with learning problems: A meta-analysis. *Journal of Special Education, 32*(4), 207–238.

*Zawaiza, T.B.W., & Gerber, M. M. (1993). Effects of explicit instruction on community college students with learning disabilities. *Learning Disability Quarterly, 16*, 64–79.

REFERENCES FOR UTILIZING DEMONSTRATIONS

Alfassi, M. (2004). Reading to learn: Effects of combined strategy instruction on high school students. *The Journal of Educational Research, 97*(4), 171–184.

&Amerikaner, M., & Summerlin, M. L. (1982). Group counseling with learning disabled children: Effects of social skills and relaxation training on self-concept and classroom behavior. *Journal of Learning Disabilities, 15*, 340–343.

&Argulewicz, E. N. (1982). Effects of an instructional program designed to improve attending behaviors of learning disabled students. *Journal of Learning Disabilities, 15*, 23–27.

*Armstrong, A. (1983). *Earth science instruction as a factor in enhancing the development of formal reasoning patterns with transitional subjects.* Doctoral dissertation, State University of New York at Albany. (University Microfilms No. 83-6819)

&Ayres, A. J. (1972). Improving academic scores through sensory integration. *Journal of Learning Disabilities, 5*, 338–343.

+Baer, D. M., Blount, R. L., Detrich, R., & Stokes, T. F. (1987). Using intermittent reinforcement to program maintenance of verbal/nonverbal correspondence. *Journal of Applied Behavior Analysis, 20*, 179–184.

&Bakker, D. J., Bouma, A., & Gardien, C. J. (1990). Hemisphere-specific treatment of dyslexia subtypes: A field experiment. *Journal of Learning Disabilities, 23*, 433–438.

&Balcerzak, J. P. (1986). *The effects of an aptitude treatment interaction approach with intermediate aged learning disabled students based on emphasizing the individual's strength in simultaneous or sequential processing in the areas of mathematics, reading and self-concept.* Doctoral dissertation, State University of New York, 1985. *Dissertation Abstracts International, 47*(3A), 630.

+Ballinger, C. (1993). *Annual report to the association on the status of year-round education.* (ERIC Document Reproduction Service No. ED 024 990)

Barley, Z., Lauer, P. A., Arens, S. A., Apthorp, H. S., Englert, K. S., Snow, D., & Akiba, M. (2002). Helping *at-risk students meet standards: A synthesis of evidence-based classroom practices.* Aurora, CO: Mid-continent Research for Education and Learning.

&Bay, M., Stayer, J. R., Bryan, T., & Hale, J. B. (1992). Science instruction for the mildly handicapped: Direct instruction versus discovery teaching. *Journal of Research in Science Teaching, 29*, 555–570.

&Belmont, I., & Birch, H. G. (1974). The effect of supplemental intervention on children with low reading-readiness scores. *Journal of Special Education, 8*, 81–89.

+Berkowitz, M. J., & Martens, B. K. (2001). Assessing teachers' and students' preferences for school-based reinforcement: Agreement across methods and different effort requirements. *Journal of Developmental and Physical Disabilities, 13*, 373–387.

&Berninger, V. W., Lester, K., Sohlberg, M. M., & Mateer, C. (1991). Interventions based on the multiple connections model of reading for developmental dyslexia and acquired deep dyslexia. *Archives of Clinical Neuropsychology, 6*, 375–391.

#Blaha, B. A. (1979). *The effects of answering self-generated questions on reading.* Unpublished doctoral dissertation, Boston University School of Education.

*Bluhm, W. (1979). The effects of science process skill instruction on preservice elementary teachers' knowledge of, ability to use, and ability to sequence science process skills. *Journal of Research in Science Teaching, 16*, 427–432.

&Bos, C. S., & Anders, P. L. (1990). Effects of interactive vocabulary instruction on the vocabulary learning and reading comprehension of junior-high learning disabled students. *Learning Disability Quarterly, 13*, 31–42.

&Bos, C. S., & Anders, P. L. (1992). Using interactive teaching and learning strategies to promote text comprehension and content learning for students with learning disabilities. *International Journal of Disability, Development and Education, 39*, 225–238.

&Bos, C. S., Anders, P. L., Filip, D., & Jaffe, L. E. (1985). Semantic feature analysis and long-term learning. *National Reading Conference Yearbook, 34*, 42–47.

&Bos, C. S., Anders, P. L., Filip, D., & Jaffe, L. E. (1989). The effects of an interactive instructional strategy for enhancing reading comprehension and content area learning for students with learning disabilities. *Journal of Learning Disabilities, 22*, 384–390.

@Bottge, B. (1999). Effects of contextualized math instruction on problem solving of average and below-average achieving students. *The Journal of Special Education, 33*(2), 81–92.

*Bowyer, J., Chen, B., & Thier, H. D. (1978). A free-choice environment: Learning without instruction. *Science Education, 62*, 95–107.

*Bowyer, J. B., & Linn, M. C. (1978). Effectiveness of the science curriculum improvement study in teaching scientific literacy. *Journal of Research in Science Teaching, 15*, 209–219.

#Brady, P. L. (1990). *Improving the reading comprehension of middle school students through reciprocal teaching and semantic mapping strategies.* Unpublished doctoral dissertation, University of Alaska.

&Brailsford, A., Snail, F., & Das, J. P. (1984). Strategy training and reading comprehension. *Journal of Learning Disabilities, 17*, 287–293.

&Branwhite, A. B. (1983). Boosting reading skills by direct instruction. *British Journal of Educational Psychology, 53*, 291–298.

*Bredderman, T. A. (1973). The effects of training on the development of the ability to control variables. *Journal of Research in Science Teaching, 10*, 189–200.

&Brigham, F. J., Scruggs, T. E., & Mastropieri, M. A. (1992). Teacher enthusiasm in learning disabilities classrooms: Effects on learning and behavior. *Learning Disabilities Research & Practice, 7*, 68–73.

@Brown, D. (1995). *Assisting eighth-grade at-risk students in successfully reading their textbooks through support strategies.* Unpublished practicum report, Nova Southeastern University, Florida.

&Brown, I. S., & Felton, R. C. (1990). Effects of instruction on beginning reading skills in children at risk for reading disability. *Reading and Writing: An Interdisciplinary Journal, 2*, 223–241.

@Brown, R., Pressley, M., Van Meter, P., & Schuder, T. (1995). *A quasi-experimental validation of transactional strategies instruction with previously low-achieving, second-*

grade readers. Reading Research Report No. 33. Universities of Georgia and Maryland, National Reading Research Center.

&Brown, R. T., & Alford, N. (1984). Ameliorating attentional deficits and concomitant academic deficiencies in learning disabled children through cognitive training. *Journal of Learning Disabilities, 17,* 20–26.

&Bryant, N. D., Drabin, I. R., & Gettinger, M. (1981). Effects of varying unit size on spelling achievement in learning disabled children. *Journal of Learning Disabilities, 14,* 200–203.

&Bryant, N. D., Fayne, H. R., & Gettinger, M. (1982). Applying the mastery learning model to sight word instruction for disabled readers. *Journal of Experimental Education, 50,* 116–121.

&Bryant, S. T. (1979). *Relative effectiveness of visual-auditory versus visual-auditory- kinesthetic-tactile procedures for teaching sight words and letter sounds to young, disabled readers.* Doctoral dissertation, Columbia University. *Dissertation Abstracts International, 40*(5A), 2588–2589.

&Bulgren, J., Schumaker, J. B., & Deshler, D. D. (1988). Effectiveness of a concept teaching routine in enhancing the performance of LD students in secondary-level mainstream classes. *Learning Disability Quarterly, 11,* 3–17.

Butler, F. M., Miller, S. P., Crehan, K. Babbitt, B., & Pierce, T. (2003). Fraction instruction for students with mathematics disabilities: Comparing two teaching sequences. *Learning Disabilities Research & Practice, 18*(2), 99-111.

@Cardelle-Elawar, M. (1990). Effects of feedback tailored to bilingual students' mathematics needs on verbal problem solving. *The Elementary School Journal, 91*(2), 165–170.

+Carnine, D. (1992). Expanding the notion of teachers' rights: Access to tools that work. *Journal of Applied Behavior Analysis, 24,* 13–19.

+Carr, E. G., & Durand, V. M. (1985). Reducing behavior problems through functional communication training. *Journal of Behavior Analysis, 18,* 111–126.

&Carte, E., Morrison, D., Sublett, J., Uemura, A., & Setrakian, W. (1984). Sensory integration therapy: A trial of a specific neurodevelopmental therapy for the remediation of learning disabilities. *Developmental and Behavioral Pediatrics, 5,* 189–194.

&Cartelli, L. M. (1978). Paradigmatic language training for learning disabled children. *Journal of Learning Disabilities, 11,* 54–59.

&Carter, B. G. (1985). *For the learning disabled: Semantic mapping or SQ3R?* Doctoral dissertation, University of Nevada–Reno, 1984. *Dissertation Abstracts International, 46*(3A), 674.

*Case, R. (1974). Structures and strictures: Some functional limitations on the course of cognitive growth. *Cognitive Psychology, 6,* 514–573.

*Case, R. (1977). *The process of stage transition in cognitive development.* Final Report to the Institute of Child Health and Development (Grant No. 1 RO 1 HD 09148-01). Berkeley: University of California.

*Case, R., & Fry, C. (1973). Evaluation of an attempt to teach scientific inquiry and criticism in a working class high school. *Journal of Research in Science Teaching, 10,* 135–142.

&Chan, L.K.S. (1991). Promoting strategy generalization through self-instructional training in students with reading disabilities. *Journal of Learning Disabilities, 24,* 427–433.

&Chan, L.K.S., & Cole, P. O. (1986). The effects of comprehension monitoring training on the reading competence of learning disabled and regular class students. *Remedial and Special Education, 7*, 33-40.

&Chan, L.K.S., Cole, P. O., & Morris, J. N. (1990). Effects of instruction in the use of a visual-imagery strategy on the reading-comprehension competence of disabled and average readers. *Learning Disability Quarterly, 13*, 2–11.

&Chase, C. H., Schmitt, R. L., Russell, O., & Tallal, P. (1984). A new chemotherapeutic investigation: Piracetam effects on dyslexia. *Annals of Dyslexia, 34*, 29–48.

#Cohen, R. (1983). Students generate questions as an aid to reading comprehension. *Reading Teacher, 36*, 770–775.

&Collins, M., & Carnine, D. (1988). Evaluating the field test revision process by comparing two versions of a reasoning skills CAI program. *Journal of Learning Disabilities, 21*, 375–379.

&Commeyras, M. (1992). *Dialogical-thinking reading lessons: Promoting critical thinking among "learning-disabled" students.* Doctoral dissertation, University of Illinois, 1991. *Dissertation Abstracts International, 52*(7A), 2480–2481.

+Cooper, B., Nye, B., Charlton, K., Lindsay, J., & Greathouse, S. (1996). The effects of summer vacation on achievement test scores: A narrative and meta-analytic review. *Review of Educational Research, 66*, 227–268.

&Cornelius, P. L., & Semmel, M. I. (1982). Effects of summer instruction on reading achievement regression of learning disabled students. *Journal of Learning Disabilities, 15*, 409–413.

&Cosden, M. A., & English, J. P. (1987). The effects of grouping, self esteem, and locus of control on microcomputer performance and help seeking by mildly handicapped students. *Journal of Educational Computing Research, 3*, 443–459.

*Crow, L. (1987, April). *The effects of teaching logical reasoning upon students' formal reasoning and science achievement.* Paper presented at the National Association for Research in Science Teaching Conference, Washington, DC.

+Daly, E. J., Lentz, F. E., & Boyer, J. (1996). The instructional hierarchy: A conceptual model for understanding the effective components of reading interventions. *School Psychology Quarterly, 11*, 369–386.

+Daly, E. J., Martens, B. K., Hamler, K., Dool, E. J., & Eckert, T. L. (1999). A brief experimental analysis for identifying instructional components needed to improve oral reading fluency. *Journal of Applied Behavior Analysis, 32*, 83–94.

*Danner, F. W., & Day, M. C. (1977). Eliciting formal operations. *Child Development, 48*, 1600–1606.

&Darch, C., & Gersten, R. (1986). Direction-setting activities in reading comprehension: A comparison of two approaches. *Learning Disability Quarterly, 9*(3), 235–243.

&Darch, C., & Kameenui, E. J. (1987). Teaching LD students critical reading skills: A systematic replication. *Learning Disability Quarterly, 10*, 82–90.

&Das, J. P., Mishra, R. K., & Pool, J. E. (1995). An experiment on cognitive remediation of word-reading difficulty. *Journal of Learning Disabilities, 28*, 66–79.

#Davey, B., & McBride, S. (1986). Effects of question-generation on reading comprehension. *Journal of Educational Psychology, 78*, 256–262.

*de Ribaupierre, A. (1975). *Mental space and formal operations.* Doctoral dissertation, University of Toronto.

&DeBoskey, D. S. (1982). *An investigation of the remediation of learning disabilities based on brain-related tasks as measured by the Halstead-Reitan neuropsychological test battery.* Doctoral dissertation, University of Tennessee. *Dissertation Abstracts International, 43*(6B), 2032.

&De La Paz, S. (1995). *An analysis of the effects of dictation and planning instruction on the writing of students with learning disabilities.* Unpublished doctoral dissertation, University of Maryland, College Park.

&De La Paz, S. (in press). Strategy instruction in planning: Teaching students with learning and writing disabilities to compose persuasive and expository essays. *Learning Disability Quarterly.*

&Deno, S. L., & Chiang, B. (1979). An experimental analysis of the nature of reversal errors in children with severe learning disabilities. *Learning Disability Quarterly, 2,* 40–50.

*Denson, D. (1986). *The relationship between cognitive styles, methods of instruction, knowledge and process skills of college chemistry students.* Doctoral dissertation, University of Southern Mississippi. (University Microfilms No. 87-05059)

#@Dermody, M. (1988, February). *Metacognitive strategies for development of reading comprehension for younger children.* Paper presented at the annual meeting of the American Association of Colleges for Teacher Education. New Orleans, LA.

@Dimino, J., Gersten, R., Carnine, D., & Blake, G. (1990). Story grammar: An approach for promoting at-risk secondary students' comprehension of literature. *The Elementary School Journal, 91*(1), 19–32.

&Dixon, M. E. (1984). *Questioning strategy instruction participation and reading comprehension of learning disabled students.* Doctoral dissertation, University of Arizona, 1983. *Dissertation Abstracts International, 44*(11A), 3349.

*Doty, L. (1985). *A study comparing the influence of inquiry and traditional science instruction methods on science achievement, attitudes toward science, and integrated process skills in ninth grade students and the relationship between sex, race, past performance in science, intelligence and achievement.* Doctoral dissertation, University of Southern Mississippi. (University Microfilms No. 86-00703)

#Dreher, M. J., & Gambrell, L. B. (1985). Teaching children to use a self-questioning strategy for studying expository text. *Reading Improvement, 22,* 2–7.

+DuPaul, G. J., & Henningson, P. N. (1993). Peer tutoring effects on the classroom performance of children with Attention Deficit Hyperactivity Disorder. *School Psychology Review, 22,* 134–143.

+Eisenberger, R., & Cameron, J. (1996). Detrimental effects of reward: Reality or myth? *American Psychologist, 51,* 1153–1166.

&Ellis, E. S., Deshler, D. D., & Schumaker, J. B. (1989). Teaching adolescents with learning disabilities to generate and use task-specific strategies. *Journal of Learning Disabilities, 22,* 108–130.

&Englert, C. S., Hiebert, E. H., & Stewart, S. R. (1985). Spelling unfamiliar words by an analogy strategy. *Journal of Special Education, 19,* 291–306.

@Englert, C. S., & Manage, T. V. (1991). Making students partners in the comprehension process: Organizing the reading "POSSE." *Learning Disability Quarterly, 14,* 123–138.

&Englert, C. S., Raphael, T. E., & Anderson, L. M. (1992). Socially mediated instruction: Improving students' knowledge about talk and writing. *Elementary School Journal, 92,* 411–449.

&Englert, C. S., Raphael, T. E., Anderson, L. M., Anthony, H. M., & Stevens, D. D. (1991). Making strategies and self-talk visible: Writing instruction in regular and special education classrooms. *American Educational Research Journal, 28*(2), 337–372.

+Erchul, W. P., & Martens, B. K. (2002). *School consultation: Conceptual and empirical bases of practice* (2nd ed.). New York: Plenum.

&Farmer, M. E., Klein, R., & Bryson, S. E. (1992). Computer-assisted reading: Effects of whole word feedback on fluency and comprehension in readers with severe disabilities. *Remedial and Special Education, 13*, 50–60.

&Fawcett, A. J., Nicolson, R. I., & Morris, S. (1993). Computer-based spelling remediation for dyslexic children. *Journal of Computer Assisted Learning, 9*, 171–183.

&Fiedorowicz, C.A.M. (1986). Training of component reading skills. *Annals of Dyslexia, 36*, 318–334.

&Fiedorowicz, C.A.M., & Trites, R. L. 1987). *An evaluation of the effectiveness of computer-assisted component reading subskills training.* Toronto: Queen's Printer.

&Fletcher, C. M., & Prior, M. R. (1990). The rule learning behavior of reading disabled and normal children as a function of task characteristics and instruction. *Journal of Experimental Child Psychology, 50*, 39–58.

&Fortner, V. L. (1986). Generalization of creative productive-thinking training to LD students' written expression. *Learning Disability Quarterly, 9*, 274–284.

&Foster, K. (1983). The influence of computer-assisted instruction and workbook on the learning of multiplication facts by learning disabled and normal students. Doctoral dissertation, Florida State University. *Dissertation Abstracts International, 42*(9A), 3953.

+Fuchs, L. S., & Fuchs, D. (1986). Effects of systematic formative evaluation on student achievement: A meta-analysis. *Exceptional Children, 53*, 199–208.

&Fuchs, L. S., Fuchs, D., Hamlett, C. L., Phillips, N. B., & Bentz, J. (1994). Classwide curriculum-based measurement: Helping general educators meet the challenge of student diversity. *Exceptional Children, 60*, 518–537.

&Gajria, M., & Salvia, J. (1992). The effects of summarization instruction on text comprehension of students with learning disabilities. *Exceptional Children, 58*, 508–516.

&Gelzheiser, L. M. (1984). Generalization from categorical memory tasks to prose by learning disabled adolescents. *Journal of Educational Psychology, 76*, 1128–1138.

&Gettinger, M., Bryant, N. D., & Fayne, H. R. (1982). Designing spelling instruction for learning disabled children: An emphasis on unit size, distributed practice, and training for transfer. *Journal of Special Education, 16*, 439–448.

+Gickling, E. E., & Armstrong, D. L. (1978). Levels of instructional difficulty as related to on-task behavior, task completion, and comprehension. *Journal of Learning Disabilities, 11*, 32–39.

&Gittelman, R., & Feingold, I. (1983). Children with reading disorders—Efficacy of reading remediation. *Journal of Child Psychology and Psychiatry, 24*, 167–191.

&Glaman, G.M.V. (1975). Use of ability measures to predict the most appropriate method or sequence of mathematics instruction for learning disabled junior high students. Doctoral dissertation, University of Minnesota, 1974. *Dissertation Abstracts International, 35*(11A), 7154.

&Graham, S. (1990). The role of production factors in learning disabled students' compositions. *Journal of Educational Psychology, 82*, 781–791.

&Graham, S., & Harris, K. R. (1989). Components analysis of cognitive strategy instruction: Effects on learning disabled students' compositions and self-efficacy. *Journal of Educational Psychology, 81*, 353–361.

&Graves, A. W. (1986). Effects of direct instruction and metacomprehension training on finding main ideas. *Learning Disabilities Research, 1*, 90–100.

&Graybill, D., Jamison, M., & Swerdlik, M. E. (1984). Remediation of impulsivity in learning disabled children by special education resource teachers using verbal self-instruction. *Psychology in the Schools, 21*, 252–254.

&Griffin, C. C., Simmons, D. C., & Kameenui, E. J. (1991). Investigating the effectiveness of graphic organizer instruction on the comprehension and recall of science content by students with learning disabilities. *Reading, Writing, and Learning Disabilities, 7*, 355–376.

@Guastello, E., Beasley, T., & Sinatra, R. (2000). Concept mapping effects on science content comprehension of low-achieving inner-city seventh graders. *Remedial and Special Education, 21*(6), 356–365.

&Guyer, B. P., & Sabatino, D. (1989). The effectiveness of a multisensory alphabetic phonetic approach with college students who are learning disabled. *Journal of Learning Disabilities, 22*, 430–434.

+Haring, N. G., Lovitt, T. C., Eaton, M. D., & Hansen, C. L. (1978). *The fourth R: Research in the classroom*. Columbus, OH: Merrill.

#Helfeldt, J. P., & Lalik, R. (1976). Reciprocal student-teacher questioning. *Reading Teacher, 33*, 283–287.

&Helper, M. M., Farber, E. D., & Feldgaier, S. (1982). Alternative thinking and classroom behavior of learning impaired children. *Psychological Reports, 50*, 415–420.

&Hine, M. S., Goldman, S. R., & Cosden, M. A. (1990). Error monitoring by learning handicapped students engaged in collaborative microcomputer-based writing. *Journal of Special Education, 23*, 407–422.

&Hollingsworth, M., & Woodward, J. (1993). Integrated learning: Explicit strategies and their role in problem-solving instruction for students with learning disabilities. *Exceptional Children, 59*, 444–455.

+Horner, R. H., Day, H. M., Sprague, J. R., O'Brien, M., & Heathfield, L. T. (1991). Interspersed requests: A nonaversive procedure for reducing aggression and self-injury during instruction. *Journal of Applied Behavior Analysis, 24*, 265–278.

*Howe, A., & Mierzwa, J. (1977). Promoting the development of logical thinking in the classroom. *Journal of Research in Science Teaching, 14*, 467–472.

&Howell, R., Sidorenko, E., & Jurica, J. (1987). The effects of computer use on the acquisition of multiplication facts by a student with learning disabilities. *Journal of Learning Disabilities, 20*, 336–341.

&Humphries, T. W., Wright, M., Snider, L., & McDougall, B. (1992). A comparison of the effectiveness of sensory integrative therapy and perceptual-motor training in treating children with learning disabilities. *Developmental and Behavioral Pediatrics, 13*, 31–40.

&Hurford, D. P. (1990). Training phonemic segmentation ability with a phonemic discrimination intervention in second- and third-grade children with reading disabilities. *Journal of Learning Disabilities, 23*, 564–569.

&Hurford, D. P., & Sanders, R. E. (1990). Assessment and remediation of a phonemic discrimination deficit in reading disabled second and fourth graders. *Journal of Experimental Child Psychology, 50*, 396–415.

&Hutchinson, N. L., Freeman, J. G., Downey, K. H., & Kilbreath, L. (1992). Development and evaluation of an instructional module to promote career maturity for youth with learning disabilities. *Canadian Journal of Counselling, 26*, 290–299.

&Jaben, T. H. (1983). The effects of creativity training on learning disabled students' creative written expression. *Journal of Learning Disabilities, 16*, 264–265.

&Jaben, T. H. (1985). Effect of instruction for creativity on learning disabled students' drawings. *Perceptual and Motor Skills, 61,* 895–898.

&Jaben, T. H. (1986). Impact of instruction on behavior disordered and learning disabled students' creative behavior. *Psychology in the Schools, 23,* 401–405.

&Jaben, T. H. (1987). Effects of training on learning disabled students' creative written expression. *Psychological Reports, 60,* 23–26.

&Jaben, T. H., Treffinger, D. J., Whelan, R. J., Hudson, F. G., Stainback, S. B., & Stainback, W. (1982). Impact of instruction on learning disabled students' creative thinking. *Psychology in the Schools, 19,* 371–373.

@Jakupcak, J., Rushton, R., Jakupcak, M., & Lundt, J. (1996). Inclusive education. *The Science Teacher, 63*(5), 40–43.

*Jaus, H. (1975). The effects of integrated science process skill instruction on changing teacher achievement and planning practices. *Journal of Research in Science Teaching, 12,* 439–447.

&Johnson, L., Graham, S., & Harris, K. R. (1998). *The effects of goal setting and self-instructions on learning a reading comprehension strategy: A study with students with learning disabilities.* Unpublished manuscript.

+Johnson, M. D., & Fawcett, S. B. (1994). Courteous service: Its assessment and modification in a human service organization. *Journal of Applied Behavior Analysis, 27,* 145–152.

&Jones, K. M., Torgesen, J. K., & Sexton, M. A. (1987). Using computer guided practice to increase decoding fluency in learning disabled children: A study using the Hint and Hunt I Program. *Journal of Learning Disabilities, 20,* 122–128.

&Kane, B. J., & Alley, G. R. (1980). Tutored, instructional management program in computational mathematics for incarcerated learning disabled juvenile delinquents. *Journal of Learning Disabilities, 13,* 148–151.

&Kendall, P. C., & Braswell, L. (1982). Cognitive-behavioral self-control therapy for children: A components analysis. *Journal of Consulting and Clinical Psychology, 50,* 672–689.

&Kennedy, K. M., & Backman, J. (1993). Effectiveness of the Lindamood Auditory Discrimination in Depth Program with students with learning disabilities. *Learning Disabilities Research & Practice, 8,* 253–259.

&Kershner, J. R., Cummings, R. L., Clarke, K. A., Hadfield, A. J., & Kershner, B. A. (1990). Two-year evaluation of the Tomatis Listening Training Program with learning disabled children. *Learning Disability Quarterly, 13,* 43–53.

&Kerstholt, M. T., Van Bon, W.H.J., & Schreuder, R. (1994). Training in phonemic segmentation: The effects of visual support. *Reading and Writing: An Interdisciplinary Journal, 6,* 361–385.

@Ketter, J., & Pool, J. (2001). Exploring the impact of a high-stakes direct writing assessment in two high school classrooms. *Research in the Teaching of English, 35,* 344–393.

&Kim, Y. O. (1992). *The effect of teaching a test-taking strategy to high school students with learning disabilities.* Doctoral dissertation, University of West Virginia, 1991. *Dissertation Abstracts International, 53*(1A), 121.

#King, A. (1989). Effects of self-questioning training on college students' comprehension of lectures. *Contemporary Educational Psychology, 14,* 366–381.

#King, A. (1990). Improving Lecture Comprehension: Effects of a metacognitive strategy. *Applied Educational Psychology, 5,* 331–346.

#King, A. (1992). Comparison of self-questioning, summarizing, and notetaking-review as strategies for learning from lectures. *American Educational Research Journal, 29,* 303–325.

&King-Sears, M. E., Mercer, C. D., & Sindelar, P. T. (1992). Toward independence with keyword mnemonics: A strategy for science vocabulary instruction. *Remedial and Special Education, 13,* 22–33.

*Klausmier, H. J., & Sipple, T. S. (1980). *Learning and teaching concepts: A strategy for testing applications of theory.* New York: Academic Press.

&Klingner, J. K., & Vaughn, S. (1996). Reciprocal teaching of reading comprehension strategies for students with learning disabilities who use English as a second language. *Elementary School Journal, 96,* 275–293.

*Kuhn, D., & Angelev, J. (1976). An experimental study of the development of formal operational thought. *Child Development, 47,* 697–706.

&Kunka, A.S.K. (1984). A modality-instruction interaction study of elementary learning disabled students using two types of electronic learning aids for math instruction. Doctoral dissertation, University of Pittsburgh, 1983. *Dissertation Abstracts International, 45*(2A), 387.

#Labercane, G., & Battle, J. (1987). Cognitive processing strategies, self-esteem, and reading comprehension of learning disabled students. *Journal of Special Education, 11,* 167–185.

*Lawson, A. E., Blake, A.J.D., & Nordland, F. H. (1975). Training effects and generalization of the ability to control variables in high school biology students. *Science Education, 59,* 387–396.

*Lawson, A. E., & Wollman, W. T. (1976). Encouraging the transition from concrete to formal cognitive functioning—An experiment. *Journal of Research in Science Teaching, 13,* 413–430.

*Leising, R. (1986). *Investigation of the relationship between personability type and selected teaching strategies in developing students' science process ability, logical thinking ability and science achievement.* Doctoral dissertation, University of Michigan. (University Microfilms No. 86-12572)

&Lenkowsky, R. S., Barwosky, E. I., Dayboch, M., Puccio, L., & Lenkowsky, B. E. (1987). Effects of bibliotherapy on the self-concept of learning disabled, emotionally handicapped adolescents in a classroom setting. *Psychological Reports, 61,* 483–488.

*Leonard, W. (1976). *An experimental comparison of two instructional methods for high school laboratory investigations.* Doctoral dissertation, University of California, Berkeley. (University Microfilms No. 77-15756)

&Leong, C. K., Simmons, D. R., & Izatt-Gambell, M. A. (1990). The effect of systematic training in elaboration on word meaning and prose comprehension in poor readers. *Annals of Dyslexia, 40,* 192–215.

&Lerner, C. H. (1978). *The comparative effectiveness of a language experience approach and a basal-type approach to remedial reading instruction for severely disabled readers in a senior high school.* Doctoral dissertation, Temple University. *Dissertation Abstracts International, 39*(2A), 779–780.

*Lewis, N. (1986). *A study of the effects of concrete experiences on the problem-solving ability of tenth-grade students.* Doctoral dissertation, University of Southern Mississippi. (University Microfilms No. 86-26454)

*Linn, M. C. (1978). Influence of cognitive style and training on tasks requiring the separation of variables schema. *Child Development, 49,* 874–877.

*Linn, M. C. (1980a). Free-choice experiences: How do they help children learn? *Science Education, 64,* 237–248.

*Linn, M. C. (1980b). Teaching students to control variables: Some investigations using free choice experiences. In S. Modgil & C. Modgil (Eds.), *Toward a theory of psychological development within a Piagetian framework* (pp. 673–697). London: National Foundation for Educational Research.

*Linn, M. C., Chen, B., & Thier, H. D. (1976). Personalization in science: Preliminary investigation at the middle school level. *Instructional Science, 5,* 227–252.

*Linn, M. C., Chen, B., & Thier, H. D. (1977). Teaching children to control variables: Investigation of a free-choice environment. *Journal of Research in Science Teaching, 14,* 249–255.

*Linn, M. C., & Thier, H. D. (1975). The effect of experimental science on development of logical thinking in children. *Journal of Research in Science Teaching, 12,* 49–62.

&Lloyd, J., Cullinan, D., Hems, E. D., & Epstein, M. H. (1980). Direct instruction: Effects on oral and written language comprehension. *Learning Disability Quarterly, 3,* 70–76.

#Lonberger, R. B. (1988). *The effects of training in a self-generated learning strategy on the prose processing abilities of fourth and sixth graders.* Unpublished doctoral dissertation, State University of New York at Buffalo.

&Lorenz, L., & Vockell, E. (1979). Using the neurological impress method with learning disabled readers. *Journal of Learning Disabilities, 12,* 420–422.

&Losh, M. A. (1991). The effect of the strategies intervention model on the academic achievement of junior high learning-disabled students. Doctoral dissertation, University of Nebraska. *Dissertation Abstracts International, 52*(3A), 880.

&Lovett, M. W., Borden, S. L., DeLuca, T., Lacerenza, L., Benson, N. J., & Brackstone, D. (1994). Treating the core deficits of developmental dyslexia: Evidence of transfer of learning after phonologically- and strategy-based reading training programs. *Developmental Psychology, 30,* 805–822.

&Lovett, M. W., Ransby, M. J., & Barron, R. W. (1988). Treatment, subtype, and word type effects on dyslexic children's response to remediation. *Brain and Language, 34,* 328–349.

&Lovett, M. W., Ransby, M. J., Hardwick, N., Johns, M. S., & Donaldson, S. A. (1989). Can dyslexia be treated? Treatment-specific and generalized treatment effects in dyslexic children's response to remediation. *Brain and Language, 37,* 90–121.

&Lovett, M. W., & Steinbach, K. A. (in press). The effectiveness of remedial programs for reading disabled children of different ages: Is there decreased benefit for older children? *Learning Disability Quarterly.*

&Lovett, M. W., Warren-Chaplin, P. M., Ransby, M. J., & Borden, S. L. (1990). Training the word recognition skills of reading disabled children: Treatment and transfer effects. *Journal of Educational Psychology, 82,* 769–780.

&Lovitt, T., Rudsit, J., Jenkins, J., Pious, C., & Benedetti, D. (1986). Adapting science materials for regular and learning disabled seventh graders. *Remedial and Special Education, 7,* 31–39.

+Lovitt, T. C., & Esveldt, K. A. (1970). The relative effects on math performance of single-versus multiple-ratio schedules: A case study. *Journal of Applied Behavior Analysis, 3,* 261–270.

&Lucangeli, D., Galderisi, D., & Comoldi, C. (1995). Specific and general transfer effects following metamemory training. *Learning Disabilities Research & Practice, 10,* 11–21.

&Lundberg, I., & Olofsson, A. (1993). Can computer speech support reading comprehension? *Computers in Human Behavior, 9*, 283–293.

#Lysynchuk, L., Pressley, M., & Vye, G. (1990). Reciprocal instruction improves reading comprehension performance in poor grade school comprehenders. *Elementary School Journal, 40*, 471–484.

&MacArthur, C. A., & Haynes, J. B. (1995). Student assistant for learning from text (SALT): A hypermedia reading aid. *Journal of Learning Disabilities, 28*, 150–159.

&MacArthur, C. A., Haynes, J. B., Malouf, D. B., Harris, K., & Owings, M. (1990). Computer assisted instruction with learning disabled students: Achievement, engagement, and other factors that influence achievement. *Journal of Educational Computing Research, 6*, 311–328.

&MacArthur, C. A., Schwartz, S. S., & Graham, S. (1991). Effects of a reciprocal peer revision strategy in special education classrooms. *Learning Disabilities Research, 6*, 201–210.

#MacGregor, S. K. (1988). Use of self-questioning with a computer-mediated text system and measures of reading performance. *Journal of Reading Behavior, 20*, 131–148.

&Manning, B. H. (1984). Problem-solving instruction as an oral comprehension aid for reading disabled third graders. *Journal of Learning Disabilities, 17*, 457–461.

#Manzo, A. V. (1969). *Improving reading comprehension through reciprocal teaching.* Unpublished doctoral dissertation, Syracuse University.

&Maron, L. R. (1993). A comparison study of the effects of explicit versus implicit training of test-taking skills for learning-disabled fourth-grade students. Doctoral dissertation, University of Wisconsin–Madison, 1992. *Dissertation Abstracts International, 53*(9B), 4613.

&Marsh, L. G., & Cooke, N. L. (1996). The effects of using manipulatives in teaching math problem solving to students with learning disabilities. *Learning Disabilities Research & Practice, 11*, 58–65.

+Martens, B. K., Ardoin, S. P., Hilt, A., Lannie, A. L., Panahon, C. J., & Wolfe, L. (2002). Sensitivity of children's behavior to probabilistic reward: Effects of a decreasing-ratio lottery system on math performance. *Journal of Applied Behavior Analysis, 35*, 403–406.

+Martens, B. K., & Daly, E. J. (1999). Discovering the alphabetic principle: A lost opportunity for educational reform. *Journal of Behavioral Education, 9*, 33–41.

+Martens, B. K., Hilt, A. M., Needham, L. R., Sutterer, J. R., Panahon, C. J., & Lannie, A. L. (2003). Carryover effects of free reinforcement on children's work completion. *Behavior Modification, 27*, 560–577.

Martens, B. K., & Witt, J. C. (2004). Competence, persistence, and success: The positive psychology of behavioral skill instruction. *Psychology in the Schools, 41*(1), 19–30.

&Mathes, P. G., & Fuchs, L. S. (1993). Peer-mediated reading instruction in special education resource rooms. *Learning Disabilities Research & Practice, 8*, 233–243.

*Mazzei, S. L., Fogli-Muciaccia, M. T., & Picciarelli, V. (1986). Effect of a Piagetian mini-laboratory on the acquisition of typical formal operational schemata. *European Journal of Science Education, 8*, 87–93.

&McCollum, P. S., & Anderson, R. P. (1974). Group counseling with reading disabled children. *Journal of Counseling Psychology, 21*, 150–155.

+McCurdy, M., Skinner, C. H., Grantham, K., Watson, T. S., & Hindman, P. M. (2001). Increasing on-task behavior in an elementary student during mathematics seatwork by interspersing additional brief problems. *School Psychology Review, 30*, 23–32.

+McDowell, C., & Keenan, M. (2001). Developing fluency and endurance in a child diagnosed with attention deficit hyperactivity disorder. *Journal of Applied Behavior Analysis, 34,* 345–348.

+McGinnis, J. C., Friman, P. C., & Carlyon, W. D. (1999). The effect of token rewards on "intrinsic" motivation for doing math. *Journal of Applied Behavior Analysis, 32,* 375–379.

*McKinnon, J., & Renner, J. (1971). Are colleges concerned with intellectual development? *American Journal of Physics, 39,* 1047–1052.

@McLain, K. (1991, November). *Effects of two comprehension monitoring strategies on the metacognitive awareness and reading achievement of third and fifth grade students.* Paper presented at the annual meeting of the National Reading Conference, Miami, FL.

&Meyer, L. A. (1982). The relative effects of word-analysis and word-supply correction procedures with poor readers during word-attack training. *Reading Research Quarterly, 17,* 544–555.

+Miller, D. L., & Kelley, M. L. (1994). The use of goal setting and contingency contracting for improving children's homework performance. *Journal of Applied Behavior Analysis, 27,* 73–84.

&Miller, S. P., & Mercer, C. D. (1993). Using data to learn about concrete-semiconcrete abstract instruction for students with math disabilities. *Learning Disabilities Research & Practice, 8,* 89–96.

&Montague, M., Applegate, B., & Marquard, K. (1993). Cognitive strategy instruction and mathematical problem-solving performance of students with learning disabilities. *Learning Disabilities Research & Practice, 8,* 223–232.

&Moore, L., Carnine, D., Stepnoski, M., & Woodward, J. (1987). Research on the efficiency of low-cost networking. *Learning Disability Quarterly, 20,* 574–576.

&Morgan, A. V. (1991). *A study of the effects of attribution retraining and cognitive self-instruction upon the academic and attentional skills, and cognitive-behavioral trends of elementary-age children served in self-contained learning disabilities programs.* Doctoral dissertation, College of William and Mary, 1990. *Dissertation Abstracts International, 51*(8B), 4035.

&Naylor, J. O., & Pumfrey, P. D. (1983). The alleviation of psycholinguistic deficits and some effects on the reading attainments of poor readers: A sequel. *Journal of Research in Reading, 6,* 129–153.

+Neef, N. A., & Lutz, M. N. (2001). Assessment of variables affecting choice and application to classroom interventions. *School Psychology Quarterly, 16,* 239–252.

+Neef, N. A., Shade, D., & Miller, M. S. (1994). Assessing influential dimensions of reinforcers on choice in students with serious emotional disturbance. *Journal of Applied Behavior Analysis, 27,* 575–583.

&Nelson, S. L. (1985). *Modifying impulsivity in learning disabled boys on matching, maze, and WISC-R performance scales.* Doctoral dissertation, University of Southern California, 1984. *Dissertation Abstracts International, 45*(7B), 2316–2317.

#Nolte, R. Y., & Singer, H. (1985). Active comprehension: Teaching a process of reading comprehension and its effects on reading achievement. *The Reading Teacher, 39,* 24–31.

+Northup, J., George, T., Jones, K., Broussard, C., & Vollmer, T. R. (1996). A comparison of reinforcer assessment methods: The utility of verbal and pictorial choice procedures. *Journal of Applied Behavior Analysis, 29,* 201–212.

&O'Connor, P. D., Stuck, O. B., & Wyne, M. D. (1979). Effects of a short-term intervention resource-room program on task orientation and achievement. *Journal of Special Education, 13*, 375–385.

&Olofsson, A. (1992). Synthetic speech and computer aided reading for reading disabled children. *Reading & Writing, 4*, 165–178.

&Olsen, J. L., Wong, B.Y.L., & Marx, R. W. (1983). Linguistic and metacognitive aspects of normally achieving and learning disabled children's communication process. *Learning Disability Quarterly, 6*, 289–304.

&Olson, R. K., & Wise, B. W. (1992). Reading on the computer with orthographic and speech feedback. *Reading and Writing: An Interdisciplinary Journal, 4*, 107–144.

@O'Malley, J., Chamot, A., Stewner-Manzanares, G., Russo, R., & Kupper, L. (1985). Learning strategy applications with students of English as a second language. *TESOL Quarterly, 19*(3), 557–584.

&Omizo, M. M., Cubberly, W. E., & Omizo, S. A. (1985). The effects of rational-emotive education groups on self-concept and locus of control among learning disabled children. *Exceptional Child, 32*, 13–19.

&Omizo, M. M., Lo, F. O., & Williams, R. E. (1986). Rational-emotive education, self-concept, and locus of control among learning-disabled students. *Journal of Humanistic Education, 25*, 58–69.

&Omizo, M. M., & Williams, R. E. (1982). Biofeedback-induced relaxation training as an alternative for the elementary school learning-disabled child. *Biofeedback and Self-Regulation, 7*, 139–148.

*O'Sullivan, K. (1985). *A study of the effects of cooperative biological research experiences on high school teachers, students and university scientists.* Doctoral dissertation, University of Texas at Austin. (University Microfilms No. 86-09409)

*Padilla, M. J., Okey, J. R., & Garrard, K. (1984). The effects of instruction on integrated science process skill achievement. *Journal of Research in Science Teaching, 21*, 277–287.

#Palincsar, A. S. (1987, April). *Collaborating for collaborative learning of text comprehension.* Paper presented at the annual meeting of the American Educational Research Association, Washington, DC.

#Palincsar, A. S., & Brown, A. L. (1984). Reciprocal teaching of comprehension-fostering and comprehension-monitoring activities. *Cognition and Instruction, 2*, 117–175.

&Pany, D., & Jenkins, J. R. (1978). Learning word meanings: A comparison of instructional procedures. *Learning Disability Quarterly, 1*, 21–32.

&Pany, D., Jenkins, J. R., & Schreck, J. (1982). Vocabulary instruction: Effects on word knowledge and reading comprehension. *Learning Disability Quarterly, 5*, 202–215.

+Patterson, G. R., Reid, J. B., & Dishion, T. J. (1992). *Antisocial boys.* Eugene, OR: Castalia Publishing.

*Pendarvis, M. (1986). *The impact of integrated process skills training on in-service junior high school science teachers' integrated process skills abilities, teaching anxieties, and classroom performance.* Doctoral dissertation, University of Southern Mississippi. (University Microfilms No. 87-05091)

*Peterson, K. (1977). *An experimental evaluation of a science inquiry training program for high school students.* Doctoral dissertation, University of California, Berkeley. (University Microfilms No. 77-4568)

&Pihl, R. O., Parkes, M., Drake, H., & Vrana, F. (1980). The intervention of a modulator with learning disabled children. *Journal of Clinical Psychology, 36*, 972–976.

&Porinchak, P. M. (1984). *Computer-assisted instruction in secondary school reading: Interaction of cognitive and affective factors.* Doctoral dissertation, Hofstra University, 1983. *Dissertation Abstracts International, 45*(2A), 478.

&Prior, M., Frye, S., & Fletcher, C. (1987). Remediation for subgroups of retarded readers using a modified oral spelling procedure. *Developmental Medicine and Child Neurology, 29,* 64–71.

*Purser, R. K., & Renner, J. W. (1983). Results of two tenth-grade biology teaching procedures. *Science Education, 67,* 85–98.

&Ratekin, N. (1979). Reading achievement of disabled learners. *Exceptional Children, 45,* 454–458.

&Reid, R., & Harris, K. R. (1993). Self-monitoring of attention versus self-monitoring of performance: Effects on attention and academic performance. *Exceptional Children, 60,* 29–40.

&Reilly, J. P. (1991). *Effects of a cognitive-behavioral program designed to increase the reading comprehension skills of learning-disabled students.* Doctoral dissertation, College of William and Mary. *Dissertation Abstracts International, 52*(3A), 865.

&Reynolds, C. J. (1986). *The effects of instruction in cognitive revision strategies on the writing skills of secondary learning disabled students.* Doctoral dissertation, Ohio State University, 1985. *Dissertation Abstracts International, 46*(9A), 2662.

+Rhymer, K. N., Henington, C., Skinner, C. H., & Looby, E. J. (1999). The effects of explicit timing on mathematics performance in Caucasian and African American second-grade students. *School Psychology Quarterly, 14,* 397–407.

#Ritchie, P. (1985). The effects of instruction in main idea and question generation. *Reading Canada Lecture, 3,* 139–146.

*Rivers, R. H., & Vockell, E. (1987). Computer simulations to stimulate scientific problem solving. *Journal of Research in Science Teaching, 24,* 403–415.

Rosenshine, B., Meister, C., & Chapman, S. (1996). Teaching students to generate questions: A review of the intervention studies. *Review of Educational Research, 66*(2), 181–221.

*Ross, J. A. (1986). Cows moo softly: Acquiring and retrieving a formal operations schema. *European Journal of Science Education, 8,* 389–397.

Ross, J. A. (1988a). Controlling variables: A meta-analysis of training studies. *Review of Educational Research, 58*(4), 405–437.

*Ross, J. A. (1988b). Improving social-environmental problem solving through cooperative learning. *American Educational Research Journal, 25,* 573–591.

*Ross, J. A. (in press). Learning to control variables: Main effects and aptitude treatment interactions of two rule governed approaches to instruction. *Journal of Research in Science Teaching.*

*Ross, J. A., & Maynes, F. J. (1983a). Development of a test of experimental problem-solving skills. *Journal of Research in Science Teaching, 20,* 63–75.

*Ross, J. A., & Maynes, F. J. (1983b). Experimental problem solving: An instructional improvement field experiment. *Journal of Research in Science Teaching, 20,* 543–556.

&Ross, P. A., & Braden, J. P. (1991). The effects of token reinforcement versus cognitive behavior modification on learning-disabled students' math skills. *Psychology in the Schools, 28,* 247–256.

*Rowell, J. A., & Dawson, C. J. (1984). Controlling variables: Testing a programme for teaching a general solution strategy. *Research in Science & Technological Education, 2,* 37–46.

*Rowell, J. A., & Dawson, C. J. (1985). Equilibration, conflict and instruction: A new class-oriented perspective. *European Journal of Science Education, 7*, 331–344.

&Rudel, R. O., & Helfgott, E. (1984). Effect of piracetam on verbal memory of dyslexic boys. *American Academy of Child Psychiatry, 23*, 695–699.

&Ruhl, K. L., Hughes, C. A., & Gajar, A. H. (1990). Efficacy of the pause procedure for enhancing learning disabled and nondisabled college students' long- and short-term recall of facts presented through lecture. *Learning Disability Quarterly, 13*, 55–64.

*Saunders, W., & Shepardson, D. (1984, April). *A comparison of concrete and formal science instruction upon science achievement and reasoning ability of sixth grade students*. Paper presented at the Annual National Association for Research and Science Teaching (NARST) Conference, New Orleans, LA.

&Sawyer, R. J., Graham, S., & Harris, K. R. (1992). Direct teaching, strategy instruction and strategy instruction with explicit self-regulation: Effects on the composition skills and self-efficacy of students with learning disabilities. *Journal of Educational Psychology, 84*, 340–352.

&Scanlon, D., Deshler, D. D., & Schumaker, J. B. (1996). Can a strategy be taught and learned in secondary inclusive classrooms? *Learning Disabilities Research & Practice, 11*, 41–57.

*Scardamalia, M. (1977). *The interaction of perceptual and quantitative load factors in the control of variables*. Doctoral dissertation, York University.

&Scheerer-Neumann, G. (1981). The utilization of intraword structure in poor readers: Experimental evidence and a training program. *Psychological Research, 43*, 155–178.

*Schneider, L. S., & Renner, J. W. (1980). Concrete and formal teaching. *Journal of Research in Science Teaching, 17*, 503–517.

&Schulte, A. C., Osborne, S. S., & McKinney, J. D. (1991). Academic outcomes for students with learning disabilities in consultation and resource programs. *Exceptional Children, 57*, 162–172.

&Schunk, D. H. (1985). Participation in goal setting: Effects on self-efficacy and skills of learning-disabled children. *Journal of Special Education, 19*, 305–317.

&Schunk, D. H., & Cox, P. D. (1986). Strategy training and attributional feedback with learning disabled students. *Journal of Educational Psychology, 78*, 201–209.

&Scruggs, T. E., & Mastropieri, M. A. (1989). Mnemonic instruction of LD students: A field-based evaluation. *Learning Disability Quarterly, 12*, 119–125.

&Scruggs, T. E., & Mastropieri, M. A. (1992). Classroom applications of mnemonic instruction: Acquisition, maintenance, and generalization. *Exceptional Children, 58*(3), 219–229.

&Scruggs, T. E., Mastropieri, M. A., & Tolfa-Veit, D. (1986). The effects of coaching on the standardized test performance of learning disabled and behaviorally disordered students. *Remedial and Special Education, 7*(5), 37–41.

&Scruggs, T. E., & Tolfa, D. (1985). Improving the test-taking skills of learning-disabled students. *Perceptual and Motor Skills, 60*, 847–850.

*Shaw, T. (1983). The effect of process-oriented science curriculum upon problem-solving ability. *Science Education, 67*, 615–623.

&Sheare, J. B. (1978). The impact of resource programs upon the self-concept and peer acceptance of learning disabled children. *Psychology in the Schools, 15*, 406–412.

*Sheehan, D. (1970). *The effectiveness of concrete and formal instructional procedures with concrete-operational and formal-operational students*. Doctoral dissertation, State University of New York at Albany. (University Microfilms No. 70-25479)

+Shinn, M. R. (1989). *Curriculum-based measurement: Assessing special children.* New York: Guilford.

#Short, E. J., & Ryan, E. B. (1984). Metacognitive differences between skilled and less-skilled readers: Remediating deficits through story grammar and attribution training. *Journal of Educational Psychology, 76,* 225–235.

*Siegler, R. S., Liebert, D. E., & Liebert, R. M. (1973). Inhelder and Piaget's pendulum problem: Teaching preadolescents to act as scientists. *Developmental Psychology, 9,* 97–101.

&Simmonds, E.P.M. (1990). The effectiveness of two methods for teaching a constraint-seeking questioning strategy to students with learning disabilities. *Journal of Learning Disabilities, 23,* 229–232.

&Simmonds, E.P.M. (1992). The effects of teacher training and implementation of two methods for improving the comprehension skills of students with learning disabilities. *Learning Disabilities Research & Practice, 7,* 194–198.

+Simonton, D. K. (2000). Creativity: Cognitive, personal, developmental, and social aspects. *American Psychologist, 55,* 151–158.

#Simpson, P. S. (1989). *The effects of direct training in active comprehension on reading achievement, self-concepts, and reading attitudes of at-risk sixth grade students.* Unpublished doctoral dissertation, Texas Tech University.

&Simpson, S. B., Swanson, J. M., & Kunkel, K. (1992). The impact of an intensive multisensory reading program on a population of learning-disabled delinquents. *Annals of Dyslexia, 42,* 54–66.

&Sinatra, R. C., Stahl-Gemake, J., & Berg, D. N. (1984). Improving reading comprehension of disabled readers through semantic mapping. *The Reading Teacher, 38,* 22–29.

&Sindelar, P. T., Honsaker, M. S., & Jenkins, J. R. (1982). Response cost and reinforcement contingencies of managing the behavior of distractible children in tutorial settings. *Learning Disability Quarterly, 5,* 3–13.

+Skinner, C. H. (2002). An empirical analysis of interspersal research: Evidence, implications, and applications of the discrete task completion hypothesis. *Journal of School Psychology, 40,* 347–368.

+Skinner, C. H., Fletcher, P. A., & Henington, C. (1996). Increasing learning trial rates by increasing student response rates: A summary of research. *School Psychology Quarterly, 11,* 313–325.

Smeltzer, L. R., & Watson, K. W. (1985). A test of instructional strategies for listening improvement in a simulated business setting. *The Journal of Business Communication, 22*(4), 33–42.

&Smith, M. A. (1989). *The efficacy of mnemonics for teaching recognition of letter clusters to reading disabled students.* Doctoral dissertation, University of Oregon. *Dissertation Abstracts International, 50*(5A), 1259–1260.

#Smith, N. J. (1977). *The effects of training teachers to teach students at different reading ability levels to formulate three types of questions on reading comprehension and question generation ability.* Unpublished doctoral dissertation, University of Georgia.

&Smith, P. L., & Friend, M. (1986). Training learning disabled adolescents in a strategy for using text structure to aid recall of instructional prose. *Learning Disabilities Research, 2,* 38–44.

*Sneider, C., Kurlich, K., Pulos, S., & Friedman, A. (1984). Learning to control variables with model rockets: A neo-Piagetian study of learning in field settings. *Science Education, 68,* 463–484.

&Snider, V. E. (1989). Reading comprehension performance of adolescents with learning disabilities. *Learning Disability Quarterly, 12,* 87–96.

&Somerville, D. E., & Leach, D. J. (1988). Direct or indirect instruction? An evaluation of three types of intervention programs for assisting students with specific reading difficulties. *Educational Research, 30,* 46–53.

&Sowell, V., Parker, R., Poplin, M., & Larsen, S. (1979). The effects of psycholinguistic training on improving psycholinguistic skills. *Learning Disability Quarterly, 2,* 69–78.

@Spiegel, D., Jackson, F., Graham, M., & Ware, W. (1990, November). *The effects of four study strategies on main idea and detail comprehension of sixth grade students.* Paper presented at the annual meeting of the National Reading Conference, Miami, FL.

+Stahl, S. A., & Kuhn, M. R. (1995). Does whole language or instruction matched to learning styles help children learn to read? *School Psychology Review, 24,* 393–404.

*Stallings, E. S., & Snyder, W. R. (1977). The comparison of the inquiry behavior of ISCS and non-ISCS science students as measured by the TAB Science Test. *Journal of Research in Science Teaching, 14,* 39–44.

*Stone, C. A., & Day, M. C. (1978). Levels of availability of a formal operational strategy. *Child Development, 49,* 1054–1065.

&Straub, R. B., & Roberts, D. M. (1983). Effects of nonverbal-oriented social awareness training program on social interaction ability of learning disabled children. *Journal of Nonverbal Behavior, 7,* 195–201.

*Strawitz, B. M. (1984a). Cognitive style and the acquisition and transfer of the ability to control variables. *Journal of Research in Science Teaching, 21,* 133–141.

*Strawitz, B. M. (1984b). Cognitive style and the effects of two instructional treatments on the acquisition and transfer of the ability to control variables: A longitudinal study. *Journal of Research in Science Teaching, 21,* 833–841.

*Strawitz, B. M. (1987, April). *The learning of process skills from programmed instruction. Effects of review.* Paper presented at the National Association for Research in Science Teaching Conference, Washington, DC.

*Strawitz, B. M., & Malone, M. (1987). Preservice teachers' acquisition and retention of integrated science process skills: A comparison of teacher-directed and self-instructional strategies. *Journal of Research in Science Teaching, 24,* 53–60.

&Sullivan, J. (1972). The effects of Kephart's perceptual motor-training on a reading clinic sample. *Journal of Learning Disabilities, 5,* 545–551.

Swanson, H. L., & Hoskyn, M. (1998). Experimental intervention research on students with learning disabilities: A meta-analysis of treatment outcomes. *Review of Educational Research, 68*(3), 277–321.

&Swanson, H. L., & Trahan, M. F. (1992). Learning disabled readers' comprehension of computer mediated text: The influence of working memory, metacognition and attribution. *Learning Disabilities Research & Practice, 7,* 74–86.

#Taylor, B. M., & Frye, B. J. (1992). Comprehension strategy instruction in the intermediate grades. *Reading Research and Instruction, 92,* 39–48.

*Thomas, W. E., & Grouws, D. A. (1984). Inducing cognitive growth in concrete-operational college students. *School Science and Mathematics, 84,* 233–243.

*Tobin, K. (1980). *The effects of variations in teacher wait-time and questioning quality on integrated science process achievement for middle school students of differing formal reasoning ability and locus of control.* Doctoral dissertation, University of Georgia. (University Microfilms No. 80-23182)

&Tollefson, N., Tracy, D. B., Johnsen, E. P., Farmer, A. W., & Buenning, M. (1984). Goal setting and personal responsibility training for LD adolescents. *Psychology in the Schools, 21,* 224–233.

*Tomlinson-Keasey, C. (1972). Formal operations in females from eleven to fifty-four years of age. *Developmental Psychology, 6,* 364.

&Torgesen, J. K., Wagner, R. K., Rashotte, C. A., Alexander, A. W., & Conway, T. (1997). Preventive and remedial interventions for children with severe reading disabilities. *Learning Disabilities: A Multi-Disciplinary Journal, 8,* 51–61.

&Trapani, C., & Gettinger, M. (1989). Effects of social skills training and cross-age tutoring on academic achievement and social behaviors of boys with learning disabilities. *Journal of Research and Development in Education, 23,* 1–9.

&VanDaal, V.H.P., & Reitsma, P. (1990). Effects of independent word practice with segmented and whole-word sound feedback in disabled readers. *Journal of Research in Reading, 13,* 133–148.

&VanDaal, V.H.P., & Reitsma, P. (1993). The use of speech feedback by normal and disabled readers in computer-based reading practice. *Reading and Writing: An Interdisciplinary Journal, 5,* 243–259.

&VanDaal, V.H.P., & VanDerLeij, D. (1992). Computer-based reading and spelling practice for children with learning disabilities. *Journal of Learning Disabilities, 25,* 186–195.

&VanReusen, A. K., & Bos, C. S. (1994). Facilitating student participation in individualized education programs through motivation strategy instruction. *Exceptional Children, 60,* 466–475.

&VanStrien, J. W., Stolk, B. D., & Zuiker, S. (1995). Hemisphere-specific treatment of dyslexia subtypes: Better reading with anxiety-laden words? *Journal of Learning Disabilities, 28,* 30–34.

&Vaughn, S., Schumm, J. S., & Gordon, J. (1993). Which motoric condition is most effective for teaching spelling to students with and without learning disabilities? *Journal of Learning Disabilities, 26,* 193–198.

*Vockell, E., & Rivers, R. (1984). *Computer simulations to stimulate scientific problem solving.* Final report to the National Science Foundation. Hammond, IN: Purdue University, Calumet.

+Vollmer, T. R., Ringdahl, J. E., Roane, H. S., & Marcus, B. (1997). Negative side effects of noncontingent reinforcement. *Journal of Applied Behavior Analysis, 30,* 161–164.

&Wade, J., & Kass, C. E. (1987). Component deficit and academic remediation of learning disabilities. *Journal of Learning Disabilities, 20,* 441–447.

&Wade, J. F. (1979). *The effects of component deficit remediation and academic deficit remediation on improving reading achievement of learning disabled children.* Doctoral dissertation, University of Arizona. *Dissertation Abstracts International, 40*(3A), 1412.

*Walkosz, M., & Yeany, R. (1984, April). *Effects of lab instruction emphasizing process skills on achievement of college students having different cognitive development levels.* Paper presented at the Annual NARST Conference, New Orleans, LA. (ED 244 805)

&Wanat, P. E. (1983). Social skills: An awareness program with learning disabled adolescents. *Journal of Learning Disabilities, 16,* 35–38.

&Warner, J.M.R. (1973). *The effects of two treatment modes upon children diagnosed as having learning disabilities.* Doctoral dissertation, University of Illinois. *Dissertation Abstracts International, 34*(3A), 1142–1143.

&Waterman, D. E. (1974). *Remediation of word attack skills in slow readers by total body movement learning games*. Doctoral dissertation, University of Tulsa, 1973. *Dissertation Abstracts International, 34*(7A), 4049.

@Waxman, H., de Felix, J., Martinez, A., Knight, S., & Padron, Y. (1994). Effects of implementing classroom instructional models on English language learners' cognitive and affective outcomes. *Bilingual Research Journal, 18*(3/4), 1–22.

+Weeks, M., & Gaylord-Ross, R. (1981). Task difficulty and aberrant behavior in severely handicapped students. *Journal of Applied Behavior Analysis, 14*, 19–36.

#Weiner, C. J. (1978, March). *The effect of training in questioning and student question-generation on reading achievement*. Paper presented at the annual meeting of the American Educational Research Association, Toronto. (ERIC Document Reproduction Service No. ED 158 223)

&Welch, M. (1992). The PLEASE strategy: A meta-cognitive learning strategy for improving the paragraph writing of students with learning disabilities. *Learning Disability Quarterly, 15*, 119–128.

&White, C. V., Pascarella, E. T., & Pflaum, S. W. (1981). Effects of training in sentence construction on the comprehension of learning disabled children. *Journal of Educational Psychology, 71*, 697–704.

&Whitman, D. M. (1986). *The effects of computer-assisted instruction on mathematics achievement of mildly handicapped students*. Doctoral dissertation, University of South Carolina, 1985. *Dissertation Abstracts International, 46*(10A), 3000–3001.

&Williams, J. P., Brown, L. O., Silverstein, A. K., & deCani, J. S. (1994). An instructional program in comprehension of narrative themes for adolescents with learning disabilities. *Learning Disability Quarterly, 17*, 205–221.

#Williamson, R. A. (1989). *The effect of reciprocal teaching on student performance gains in third grade basal reading instruction*. Unpublished doctoral dissertation, Texas A&M University.

&Wilsher, C., Atkins, O., & Manfield, P. (1985). Effect of piracetam on dyslexics' reading ability. *Journal of Learning Disabilities, 18*, 19–25.

*Wilson, A. (1987). Teaching formal thought for improved chemistry achievement. *International Journal of Science Education, 9*, 197–202.

&Wilson, C., & Sindelar, P. T. (1991). Direct instruction in math word problems: Students with learning disabilities. *Exceptional Children, 57*, 512–519.

&Wilson, C. L. (1989). *An analysis of a direct instruction procedure in teaching word problem-solving to learning disabled students*. Doctoral dissertation, Florida State University, 1988. *Dissertation Abstracts International, 50*(2A), 416.

&Wise, B. W., Ring, J., Sessions, L., & Olson, R. K. (in press). Phonological awareness with and without articulation: A preliminary study. *Learning Disability Quarterly*.

Wise, K. C. (1996). Strategies for teaching science: What works? *The Clearing House, 69*(6), 337–338.

+Witt, J. C., & Elliott, S. N. (1982). The response cost lottery: A time efficient and effective classroom intervention. *Journal of School Psychology, 20*, 155–161.

Witzel, B. S., Mercer, C. D., & Miller, M. D. (2003). Teaching algebra to students with learning difficulties: An investigation of an explicit instruction model. *Learning Disabilities Research & Practice, 18*(2), 121–131.

+Wolery, M., Bailey, D. B., & Sugai, G. M. (1988). *Effective teaching: Principles and procedures of applied behavior analysis with exceptional students*. Boston: Allyn & Bacon.

*Wollman, W. T., & Chen, B. (1982). Effects of structured social interaction on learning to control variables: A classroom training study. *Science Education, 66,* 717–730.

@&Wong, B., Butler, D., Ficzere, S., & Kuperis, S. (1996). Teaching low achievers and students with learning disabilities to plan, write, and revise opinion essays. *Journal of Learning Disabilities, 29*(2), 197–212.

&Wong, B.Y.L., Butler, D. L., Ficzere, S. A., Kuperis, S., Corden, M., & Zelmer, J. (1994). Teaching problem learners revision skills and sensitivity to audience through two in-structional modes: Student-teacher versus student-student interactive dialogues. *Learning Disabilities Research & Practice, 9,* 78–90.

#&Wong, B.Y.L., & Jones, W. (1982). Increasing metacomprehension in learning disabled and normally achieving students through self-questioning training. *Learning Disability Quarterly, 5,* 228–239.

&Zieffle, T. H., & Romney, D. M. (1985). Comparison of self-instruction and relaxation training in reducing impulsive and inattentive behavior of learning disabled children on cognitive tasks. *Psychological Reports, 57,* 271–274.

Index of Researchers

Subject Index

Note: An effort has been made to provide a complete index by subject of the plain-English terminology used in this handbook. Additionally, we have attempted, as completely as possible, to cross-reference the terminology used in the handbook with corresponding professional terminology used by educational psychologists and educators.

About the Authors

MYLES I. FRIEDMAN, Ph.D., Distinguished Professor Emeritus of Education at the University of South Carolina and CEO of the Institute for Evidence-Based Decision-Making in Education, has earned master's and doctorate degrees in Educational Psychology from the University of Chicago. He is sole or senior author of eleven professional books including *Teaching Reading and Thinking Skills, Improving Teacher Education, Teaching Higher Order Thinking Skills to Gifted Students, Taking Control: Vitalizing Education, Ensuring Student Success, Handbook on Effective Instructional Strategies*, and *Educators' Handbook on Effective Testing*. He has spent more than 30 years conducting and applying research to improve education and founded the doctoral program in educational research at the University of South Carolina.

DIANE H. HARWELL, Ph.D., has an earned educational specialist degree and doctorate in Educational Administration from the University of South Carolina and bachelor's and master's degrees in English. She presently serves as Clinical Associate Professor in the Department of Educational Leadership and Policies, University of South Carolina. During her 40 years in education, she has also served as teacher, assistant principal, district consultant for curriculum and instruction, and coordinator of school improvement, professional development, and leadership training at the South Carolina Department of Education. She serves as a consultant to help schools improve their instructional programs and help teachers enhance their teaching skills.

KATHERINE C. SCHNEPEL, Ph.D., is a self-employed consultant on instruction and educational research. She has earned master's and doctoral degrees in Educational Research with an emphasis on instruction and a bachelor's degree in Psychology. She has served as an adjunct professor in the Departments of Educational Psychology and Educational Leadership and Policies at the University of South

Carolina. She has made presentations on effective instruction and has been engaged in the evaluation of instructional programs. She is the author of the "Instructional Prescription Testing" section of the *Educators' Handbook on Effective Testing*. She has been involved in numerous evaluations of instructional programs throughout the Southeast. Her primary role in these evaluations was conducting classroom observations and interviewing of teachers and administrators.